The Blackwell Encyclopedia of Sociology

Volume VII

N–P

Edited by

George Ritzer

Blackwell
Publishing

© 2007 by Blackwell Publishing Ltd

BLACKWELL PUBLISHING
350 Main Street, Malden, MA 02148-5020, USA
9600 Garsington Road, Oxford OX4 2DQ, UK
550 Swanston Street, Carlton, Victoria 3053, Australia

The right of George Ritzer to be identified as the Author of the Editorial Material in this Work has been asserted in accordance with the UK Copyright, Designs, and Patents Act 1988.

First published 2007 by Blackwell Publishing Ltd

1   2007

Library of Congress Cataloging-in-Publication Data

Blackwell encyclopedia of sociology, the / edited by George Ritzer.
     p. cm.
Includes bibliographical references and index.
ISBN 1-4051-2433-4 (hardback : alk. paper) 1. Sociology—Encyclopedias. I. Ritzer, George.

HM425.B53 2007
301.03—dc22

                                                    2006004167

ISBN-13: 978-1-4051-2433-1 (hardback : alk. paper)

A catalogue record for this title is available from the British Library.

Set in 9.5/11pt Ehrhardt
by Spi Publisher Services, Pondicherry, India
Printed in Singapore
by COS Printers Pte Ltd

The publisher's policy is to use permanent paper from mills that operate a sustainable forestry policy, and which has been manufactured from pulp processed using acid-free and elementary chlorine-free practices. Furthermore, the publisher ensures that the text paper and cover board used have met acceptable environmental accreditation standards.

For further information on
Blackwell Publishing, visit our website:
www.blackwellpublishing.com

Contents

narrative

Sam Binkley

A sociological interest in narrative has followed upon what is termed the post-positive interpretive turn. With challenges to the presumed detachment and objectivity of social inquiry, skepticism about structural causality and quantification as shibboleths of sociological explanation, and with increasing demands for the foregrounding of the unique experiences and perspectives of actors themselves in accounts of social phenomena, the study of narrative has emerged as a key methodological and interpretive focus (Maines 1993). The "narrative turn" in sociological research has many precedents in the interpretive and qualititative traditions that preceded the institutionalization of sociology as a positive science in the the post-World War II period. Thomas and Znaniecki's study *The Polish Peasant in Europe and America* and other classics of the Chicago School were celebrated works of interpretive research which highlighted the importance of narrative, though this tradition was largely marginalized with post-war American sociology's embrace of quantitative research and other positivistic methodologies.

A return to narrative in sociology began in the 1980s with such works as Mitchel's *On Narrative* (1981) and Plummer's *Documents of Life* (2001), which variously asserted the value of biographical and historical narrative from a range of interdisciplinary perspectives. Two decades later, reflections on narrative have provided openings for feminist and postmodernist engagements with the sociological tradition, primarily through the study of biographical life history.

Indeed, narrative has entered the sociological lexicon in at least two distinct ways. First, narratives situate the self-understandings and group affiliations of actors in the experienced time of action itself. Narratives explain actions through the specific linguistic conventions used by actors to make sense of, or tell stories about, their own choices and behaviors. Narrative explanations highlight the cultural frameworks surrounding behavior, while playing down various structural causal factors. Second, narrative is applied to the products of sociological researchers themselves, who (following Clifford Geertz's assertion that all research accounts are equally the "fictions" of their authors' creations) conceive of their own sociological studies in terms of their implicit rhetorical and narrative structures (Geertz 1973). Recent interest in the reflexivity of sociological inquiry as a textual rather than merely technical accomplishment has inspired ethnographic departures in the direction of "auto-ethnography," studies of human experience which interrogate the narrative and discursive conventions of their own construction (Clough 1998).

Moreover, studies of narratives have become useful in the study of identity formation in the context of contemporary society. Anthony Giddens (1991) has described identity as a fundamentally narrative production, a "reflexive project of the self" in which the retrospective storying of one's experiences defines the core of a durable sense of self. For many authors, such narrative identity is difficult to achieve under conditions of accelerated cultural and social change, temporal fragmentation, and generational discontinuity. Postmodern theorists, while welcoming of narrative methodologies for their power to dislodge the univocal authority of positivistic scientific inquiry, are at the same time doubtful that contemporary conditions can produce stable social and personal narratives to the extent once possible.

SEE ALSO: Biography; Ethnography; Identity Theory; Journaling, Reflexive; Life History; Reflexivity; Self

REFERENCES AND SUGGESTED READINGS

Clough, P. (1998) *The End(s) of Ethnography*. Peter Lang, New York.

Denzin, N. (1989) *Interpretive Biography*. Sage, New York.

Geertz, C. (1973) *The Interpretation of Cultures*. Basic Books, New York.

Giddens, A. (1991) *Modernity and Self-Identity*. Stanford University Press, Stanford.

Maines, D. R. (1993) Narrative's Moment and Sociology's Phenomena: Toward a Narrative Sociology. *Sociological Quarterly* 34(1): 17–37.

Mitchell, W. J. T. (1981) *On Narrative*. University of Chicago Press, Chicago.

Plummer, K. (2001) *Documents of Life 2*. Sage, London.

Ricoeur, P. (1984) *Time and Narrative*. University of Chicago Press, Chicago.

nation–state

Walker Connor

The term nation-state was originally intended to describe a political unit (a state) whose borders coincided or roughly coincided with the territorial distribution of a nation, the latter in its pristine sense of a human grouping who share a conviction of being ancestrally related. The word nation derives from the Latin verb *nasci* (meaning to be born) and its noun form, *natio* (connoting breed or race). The very coining of the hyphenate, nation-state, illustrated an appreciation of the essential difference between its two components, but careless terminology has subsequently tended to obscure the difference. Today, nation is often used as a substitute for a state (as in "the United Nations") or as a synonym for the population of a state without regard to its ethnonational composition (e.g., "the British nation"). With the distinction between nation and state thus blurred, the term nation-state has lost much of its original value as a means of distinguishing among types of states. Although only some 10 percent of all states are sufficiently ethnically homogeneous to merit being described as nation-states, it has become an increasingly common practice to refer to all states as nation-states.

The confusing of nation with state would not be so troublesome were all states nation-states. In such cases, loyalty to nation (nationalism) and loyalty to the state (patriotism) reinforce one another in a seamless manner. The state is perceived as the political extension or expression of the nation, and appeals to the one trigger the same associations and emotions as do appeals to the other. The same blurring of the two loyalties is common in the case of a *staatvolk*, a nation which is sufficiently preeminent – politically, culturally, and usually numerically – that its members also popularly perceive the state in monopolistic terms as the state of our nation, even though other nations are present. (Examples include the Han Chinese, the Russians, and, at least prior to the very late twentieth century, the English.)

For people with their own nation-state and for *staatvolk*, then, nationalism and civic loyalty coincide and reinforce. But the overwhelming number of nations neither have their own state nor constitute a *staatvolk*. For them, civic and national loyalty do not coincide and may well conflict. And, as substantiated by the commonness of secessionist movements waged under the banner of national self-determination, when the two loyalties are perceived as being in irreconcilable conflict, nationalism has customarily proven the more powerful of the two loyalties.

The nation-state therefore best lends itself to the concentration of authority because it is the simultaneous focus of two powerful loyalties (nationalism and patriotism) on the part of all major segments of the population. The fanatical devotion that the ruling regime of such a state can muster was demonstrated during World War II by the willingness of the German and Japanese people to make any sacrifice, including a willingness to continue, with great loss of life, to pursue a war after they were aware that it was unwinnable. Such devotion, when observed in a war of national liberation, can be attributed to nationalism, but the German and Japanese leadership were able to elicit such fidelity in an imperialistic war to create multinational empires because the state and its goals had blended with the nation and its interests in a homogeneous mix. *Raison d'état* and *raison de la nation* were one. And thus for a Japanese kamikaze pilot or a banzai-charge (a mass death charge) participant to be asked whether he was about to die for Nippon or for the Nipponese people or for the emperor (who was regularly extolled as the "father" of the nation) would be an incomprehensible query since the three blurred into an inseparable whole. Similarly, Hitler, who in *Mein Kampf* had noted that "We as Aryans are therefore able to imagine a State only to be the living organism of a nationality" (Hitler 1940), could variously make his appeals to the German people in the name of state (Deutsches Reich), nation (Volksdeutsch), or homeland (Deutschland) because all triggered the same emotional associations.

In recognition of the unparalleled advantage that the nation-state enjoys over other forms of states for mobilizing the entire population under its jurisdiction, governments have adopted policies aimed at increasing national homogeneity. Although, in a very few cases, governments have permitted – in still rarer cases, even encouraged – a homeland-dwelling minority to secede, determination to maintain the territorial integrity of the state customarily places secession beyond governmental contemplation. More commonly, governments have pursued homogenization through what is currently called "ethnic cleansing." Genocide, expulsion, and population transfers, employed separately or in combination, are the usual means of achievement. Far more commonly, however, governments of heterogeneous states accept the current inhabitants of the state as a given and pursue homogenization through assimilationist programs. Such programs vary considerably in scope, complexity, intensity, ingenuity, degree of coerciveness/persuasion, envisaged timetable, and fervidity of the implementors. But programmed assimilation does not have an impressive record, as we are reminded by the history of the Soviet Union wherein national consciousness and resentment grew among non-Russian peoples despite 70 years of comprehensive and sophisticated governmental efforts to solve what was officially termed "the national question." As a result of such failures,

an increasing number of governments have elected to shun the nation-state model in favor of programs seeking to peacefully accommodate national diversity through the granting of greater cultural and political autonomy to minority nations.

SEE ALSO: Assimilation; Ethnic Cleansing; Ethnonationalism; Genocide; Multiculturalism; Nation-State and Nationalism; Nationalism; State

REFERENCES AND SUGGESTED READINGS

Cook, H. & Cook, T. (Eds.) (1992) *Japan at War: An Oral History*. New Press, New York.

Connor, W. (1994) *Ethnonationalism: The Quest for Understanding*. Princeton University Press, Princeton.

Guibernau, M. (2004) Anthony D. Smith on Nations and National Identity: A Critical Assessment. *Nations and Nationalism* 10: 125–41.

Hitler, A. (1940) *Mein Kampf*. Reynal & Hitchcock, New York.

Tilly, C. (Ed.) (1975) *The Formation of National States in Western Europe*. Princeton University Press, Princeton.

nation-state and nationalism

Lloyd Cox

Nationalism can be defined in a broad and a narrow sense. In its broadest sense it refers to the sum of those beliefs, idioms, and practices oriented to a territorially delineated "nation," and embodied in the political demands of a people who collectively identify with a nation. This may or may not entail the existence of or demand for a separate national state, or be realized in a self-conscious nationalist movement, though historically this is often the eventual outcome of national identification. In its narrower meaning, nationalism refers to a political ideology or doctrine whose object is an existing or envisaged nation-state wherein cultural and political boundaries coincide.

Both of these meanings presuppose the nation, which analytically, though not necessarily historically, precedes that of nationalism. The origins of the term nation and its non-English, Western European equivalents can be located in the Latin term *natio* – "something born" (similar in meaning to the Greek *ta ethne* and the Hebrew *amamim*). This label was once reserved for "foreigners," and originally had a derogatory meaning. In medieval Western Europe it came to be applied to groups of students at some universities who were united by their place of origin. The word gradually lost its derogatory connotation and also came to refer to a "community of opinion and purpose." It then underwent successive changes in meaning, until in sixteenth-century England the nation became synonymous with the collective noun "the people" (Greenfeld 1992: 3–9). While it is debatable whether or not this launched the modern era of nationalism, as Greenfeld claims, it certainly represented a watershed in the development of a specifically modern vocabulary of "nation-ness." But this vocabulary has always been ambiguous. It has been ambiguous because of the sociological diversity of nations' concrete instantiations, the political capital at stake in determining who and what should count as a nation, and because of a bifurcation between definitions of the nation based on political criteria and those based on cultural criteria; a cleavage rooted in differences between Enlightenment and Romanticist accounts of nationality.

Friedrich Meinecke (1970 [1907]) famously elaborated this distinction between the *Staatsnation* and the *Kulturnation*. The former refers to a political and territorial conception of nationality, whereby the nation either forms on the basis of a voluntary association of individuals within a given territory, claiming citizenship rights and self-determination in the form of their own state, or forms around a preexisting state. The latter refers to a prepolitical cultural entity, where a spirit of solidarity and community derives from commonalities of custom, language, heritage, and collective memory.

While this ideal-typical distinction is valid for some purposes, too often it has had the misfortune to be linked with ethnocentric accounts that equate civic conceptions of the nation with the West and all that is progressive and enlightened, and cultural conceptions with the East and all that is primordial, archaic, and backward-looking. In reality, there is no firewall between *Staatsnation* and *Kulturnation*, as political and cultural elements can be identified in *all* expressions of nationalism, even though they vary with time and circumstance and are constantly contested. It is the conjoining of culture and politics, rather than their separation, which gives the national principle its specificity.

HISTORICAL CONTEXT

The conjoining of culture and politics in the form of the modern national state occurred over the course of several centuries of early modern European history, between roughly the beginnings of the sixteenth and nineteenth centuries. While "modernists," "ethnosymbolists," and "primordialists" disagree on periodization (and much more besides, as discussed below), there is some convergence of opinion in respect of developments widely viewed as crucial in the growth of a *modern national field* of political orientation and action. These developments include the growth of powerful centralized states and the formation of a multipolar interstate system premised on exclusive, clearly demarcated territorial jurisdiction. In addition, the consolidation of written vernacular languages by commercial printing, the spread of Protestantism, and the decline of Latin facilitated the crystallization of more uniform, large-scale domains of communication and cultural intercourse. This was coupled with the growth of capitalism, which encouraged the emergence of relatively unified fields of exchange and administration, as well as driving highly uneven economic development that was a potential source of nationalist conflict. Finally, the birth of an individualized public sphere, with its associated extension of disembodied, abstract social relations on the one hand, and the ideals of democracy and civic equality on the other, was central to the formation of national consciousness (see the entries in Hutchinson & Smith 2000 for extensive coverage of the relationship between these developments and nationalism). All of this contributed to a gradually sharpening national frame of reference which, in Western Europe at least, had condensed into a recognizably nationalist politics by the eighteenth century.

The American and French Revolutions and their aftermaths provided a further impetus to nationalism. The declaration of independence by Britain's 13 American colonies marked an early experiment in anti-colonial nationalism, though it was not at first articulated in nationalist terms. The anti-colonial rhetoric and practice of the American rebels would be emulated in future anti-colonial struggles, not least those waged in Ireland in the 1790s and by their South American counterparts in the early decades of the nineteenth century. In fact, the fracturing of Spain's American Empire into 18 separate states represents the first major wave of secessionist nationalism, which in turn provided a model for other nationalist movements to emulate.

The French Revolution also made a profound contribution to this new nationalist political language and practice upon which aspiring "nations" could draw inspiration. Its founding document, the *Declaration of the Rights of Man*, asserts that the "principle of all sovereignty resides in the nation," and that political authority is derived from the "general will" of the nation conceived as the entire people, composed of citizens with equal rights before the law. Ironically, this vision was disseminated through Europe on the points of Napoleon's bayonets, sharpening national sentiments in territories that were occupied.

In the aftermath of the Napoleonic Wars, the quickening tempo of uneven economic and industrial development was a key stimulus to the nationalizing of politics in Europe and, from the latter part of the nineteenth century, parts of the Middle East, Asia, and Africa. Many commentators have noted how economic underdevelopment has frequently become a source of nationalist umbrage, and has intensified nationalism amongst late industrializers. States that were not in the vanguard of industrialization were subject to the economic, political, and military disadvantages of their positions within a hierarchy of industrializing states. This was responded to with economic protectionism, heightened political particularism, and a sharpened consciousness and promotion of cultural distinctiveness in the second half of the nineteenth century, encouraged by mass education, conscript armies, and colonial adventures. The unification of Italy from 1860, Germany in 1870, and the Meiji Restoration in Japan in 1868 represent the most well-known examples of nationalist projects initiated from above and energized by uneven industrial development.

But nationalism was by no means limited to these cases. Uneven industrial development, combined with internal repression by culturally distinct elites, led to a proliferation of national claims in the Ottoman and Habsburg Empires from the middle of the nineteenth century. Serbia, Romania, and Bulgaria followed the precedent set by Greece in 1830, and achieved independence from the Ottoman Turks on the basis of ethnoreligious claims to nationhood, thus accelerating the "Balkanization" of the Balkans (Hobsbawm 1990). Similarly, the nationalities question, as it was then termed, was the preeminent political issue throughout the Habsburg Empire, being reflected in numerous demands for autonomy or secession, in addition to mass nationalist mobilizations and outright nationalist revolts. These challenges to imperial power were usually met with brutal repression, thus fueling nationalist grievances which in turn prompted more repression and a downward spiral of political violence – a dynamic common in many subsequent nationalist conflicts.

EARLY APPROACHES TO UNDERSTANDING NATIONALISM

It was against this historical background that socialist, conservative, and liberal thinkers began to grapple more seriously with national phenomena in the second half of the nineteenth century. As implied above, the language of nation had infused politics and scholarship much earlier than this, being evident, for example, in the sixteenth-century works of Machiavelli and Shakespeare, and numerous works of political philosophy in the following two centuries (Diderot, Hegel, Kant, Rousseau, Voltaire, Paine, Herder, and Fichte). Yet none of these strands of thought dealt systematically with nationalism and the nation as phenomena whose sociological roots could or should be explained. This changed in the decades after the "springtime of peoples" revolutions in 1848.

Despite the frequently noted judgment that nationalism "represents Marxism's great historical failure" (Nairn 1975: 3), Marx and Engels were amongst the first of a new wave of mid-nineteenth-century thinkers to register the political significance of what they termed the "national question." Their legacy is a contradictory one. On the one hand, they resurrected the Hegelian distinction between "historic" and "non-historic" nations, in the context of revolution and counterrevolution in Europe in 1848. In spite of its invocation of history, this distinction was ahistoric. It represented a crude dualism that was burdened with evolutionary assumptions and dubious judgments about the "non-viability" of particular nations, many of which would go on to achieve independence in the aftermath of World War I. On the other hand, they adopted a position that was more accommodating of the nationalism of the oppressed. This was most clearly expressed in their changed attitude to Irish and Polish nationalism from the 1860s. They not only supported the rights of Poland and Ireland to self-determination, they also positively encouraged the exercise of those rights, as summed up in Engels's stricture that the Poles and Irish had a "duty to be nationalistic before they become internationalistic." This was part of a realization that colonialism could just as well retard capitalist development as promote it, and that national oppression was an impediment to class consciousness and solidarity in oppressed and oppressor nations alike. As Marx famously stated, a nation that oppresses another "forges its own chains."

But socialists were not the only thinkers to become interested in nationalism in the second half of the nineteenth century. In 1864, the militaristic conservative Heinrich von Treitschke echoed the liberal John Stuart Mill in identifying nationality as the legitimate basis of state power. In 1882, and in explicit opposition to Treitschke, the liberal French historian Ernest Renan confronted head on the question *Qu'est-ce que c'est qu'une nation?* His memorable answer was that it is "an everyday plebiscite," a "perpetual affirmation of life," based on shared remembrances of the past, and a collective consent to live together in the present. It is the collective memory as embodied and reproduced in myth, especially of past sacrifices by national "ancestors," which is "the essential condition of being a nation" (Renan in Hutchinson & Smith 1994: 17–18).

Curiously, a specifically sociological perspective on nations and nationalism has its roots in the works of Durkheim and Weber, even though neither wrote a great deal on the subject. With respect to Durkheim, the key text is *The Elementary Forms of Religious Life* (1915). Here Durkheim argued that any human community, small or large, must periodically regenerate itself through the public reaffirmation of shared beliefs and values. It does so through collective rituals and rites, which take on a sacred, transcendent character, irrespective of the content of the beliefs expressed. Consequently, in all relevant respects Christian or Jewish rituals are no different from "a reunion of citizens commemorating the promulgation of a new moral or legal system or some great event in the national life" (1915: 427). Here nationalism is presented as a functional equivalent to religion: a meaning-bestowing and cohesion-enhancing phenomenon in a world where anomie grows and mechanical solidarity has been effaced, but where organic solidarity alone is unable to perform all of the morally integrative functions necessary for ordered social life.

The situating of nations, nationalism, and the related concept of ethnic group within the broader problematic of modernity is also characteristic of Max Weber's work. While in Weber's view nations and states existed under premodern conditions, it is only in modern Europe that they became conjoined in the nation-state. Nationalism is bound up with this conjoining. He suggests that national identity is derived from diverse sources, which can include religion, race, ethnicity, customs, language, and political memories. While these "objective factors" might contribute to the formation of national sentiment, they do not necessarily do so. For a nation to actually emerge depends on a given population believing that they are a nation, and expressing this belief in the formation of, or demand for, their own state. In other words, in addition to objective factors facilitating nation formation, there is also an important subjective element. The form that this subjective element takes is strongly influenced by the objective features of a given nation, which are imbibed with value and invoked as markers of cultural distinctiveness. Hence, "the 'nation' is usually anchored in the superiority, or at least the irreplaceability, of the culture values that are to be preserved and developed only through the cultivation of the peculiarity of the group" (Weber in Gerth & Mills 1949: 176). But for these culture values to have a specifically national expression, they must be oriented to a state.

CONTEMPORARY APPROACHES TO UNDERSTANDING NATIONALISM

In the decades following the death of Durkheim and Weber, in 1917 and 1920 respectively, the reality of intensified nationalism was not reflected in an equally vigorous sociology of nationalism; certainly not in the English-speaking world. The nationalistic cataclysm of World War I had ended with the dismemberment of the multinational Habsburg and Ottoman Empires along national lines. This paralleled the proclamation of the universality of the principle of national self-determination by the liberal Woodrow Wilson and the communist Vladimir Lenin. It was followed by the new, supposedly internationalist Soviet state embracing the nationalistic doctrine of "socialism in one country," and by the growth of European fascism and Japanese militarism with their virulent nationalist ethos married to a grand imperial vision. The Great Depression only served to magnify these nationalistic tendencies, with a beggar-thy-neighbor economic nationalism marking most liberal democratic governments' trade policies in the 1930s. At the same time, anti-colonial national liberation struggles – led by such nationalist icons as Gandhi, Nehru, Ho Chi Minh, Sukarno, and Kenyatta – were gaining momentum in many parts of Asia and Africa, which would be realized in the independence of dozens of new states in the two decades after the end of World War II. Most if not all of these were formed on the administrative space of the previous colonial regime, with little or no regard for cultural, linguistic, and political differentiation within that space. This laid the foundations for much of the nationalist contention that punctuated the rest of the century. The most recent proliferation of subnational challenges to failed or failing states in Africa, Asia, and Oceania in the 1990s, along with the breakup of the Soviet Empire and Yugoslavia and the growth of far right nationalist populism in western countries, marked the zenith of this contention.

All of this bespeaks a reality in which nationalism was central to twentieth-century social and political life. But this centrality was in an inverse proportion to the importance accorded to the study of nationalism in sociology, where it remained marginal until the 1980s. Why was this? There were two main reasons. On the one hand, mainstream sociology was itself premised on a pervasive methodological nationalism, which assumed that the discipline's object of investigation was a bounded "society" that was congruent with a nation-state. This elision and reification had the effect of diverting attention away from the historically contingent, socially constructed foundations of nations and nationalism. On the other hand, the intellectual division of labor that was cemented in the middle decades of the century institutionalized the view that the proper focus of sociology was the industrialized West. Given that the most prominent sites of nationalist contention after World War II were in less developed zones – the preserve of anthropologists and political scientists – it is understandable, if not excusable, that nationalism was neglected by sociologists. But this changed in the 1980s, after the publication of Benedict Anderson's *Imagined Communities* and Ernst Gellner's *Nations and Nationalism*. Irrespective of the veracity of the substantive claims advanced in these texts, their enduring significance is to have stimulated two key debates. These are, namely, a debate about the "nature of nations" and a debate about the origins of nations, nationality, and nationalism, and their relationship to modernity.

THE "NATURE OF NATIONS"

In terms of the first debate on the nature of nations, five main approaches can be identified. These are not mutually exclusive, but can be distinguished by their characteristic emphases.

While they all transcend nationalist images of the nation – in that they accept that nations ought not be naturalized by defining them exclusively with reference to some objective, national substance, but must embody a degree of historical contingency and subjective, national self-definition on the part of a given population – some are closer to that image than others.

In the first approach, for example, nations are conceptualized in terms of a number of essential features. These usually include attributes such as a common language, a shared culture, a contiguous territory, a common stock of memories and shared sense of belonging, which become the bases for the veneration of or the placing of demands on an existing state, or the striving for a new state. In this view, nations are treated as real, tangible, and enduring entities, which have the continuity of subjects and which embody the distinctive character, culture, and political aspirations of a clearly delineated people. Here nations are a source rather than an expression of nationalism.

The second approach rejects this "objectivist" view, arguing instead that nations can only be conceived with reference to people's subjective states, as it is these that ultimately underlie all instances of the nation. Here a nation exists "when a significant number of people in a community consider themselves to form a nation, or behave as if they formed one" (Seton-Watson 1977: 5). In Walker Connor's similar formulation, the nation is in essence "a psychological bond that joins a people and differentiates it, in the subconscious conviction of its members, from all other people in a most vital way" (1994: 92).

A third approach eschews what it views as the naturalizing myths of nationhood, insisting that nations are invented categories rather than real collectivities. In Ernst Gellner's (1983: 55) frequently cited argument, nations are invented by nationalism rather than being the latter's source. They are invented in order to fulfill some functional needs generated by the structural transformations wrought by industrialization. This is a view that informs all of those positions that emphasize the "invention of tradition" in the constitution of national phenomena, as well as Marxist-inspired analyses that view the nation as a socially constructed entity that serves the structural requirements of the capitalist economy and the ideological interests of the bourgeoisie.

In the fourth approach identified here, nations are viewed as "imagined communities," though they are no less real for being imagined. This was of course the definition popularized by Benedict Anderson (1991 [1983]), for whom nations are imagined because their individual members envisage a common bond, "a deep horizontal comradeship," despite never knowing, meeting, or hearing of the vast majority of their co-nationals. In the mind of each lives an image of their national communion, Anderson suggests.

Finally, in more recent writings, nations are conceived of as *symbolic frames* (Delanty & O'Mahony 2002) or *discursive formations* (Calhoun 1997), defined not so much by any identifiable empirical property as by the claims made in evoking and promoting nations. Here nations are constituted "by the way of talking and thinking and acting that relies on these sorts of claims to produce collective identity" (Calhoun 1997: 5). The precise content of the claims will differ from case to case, but they share a "pattern of family resemblance," which allows us to identify them as features of the "rhetoric of nations" rather than as essential features of some empirically verifiable entity.

All of these positions on the nature of nations and nationalism have been critiqued. Drawing upon the fifth approach, it has been suggested that the first concedes too much to nationalist mythologizing, in that it reifies nations, treating them as real, tangible, and enduring entities rather than as discursive formations and cognitive frames that arise in particular political and cultural fields. Categories of nationalist practice are thereby adopted as categories of analysis, which risks reproducing in scholarship the naturalizing myths that sustain nationalism (Brubaker 1996: 15–16).

The second approach is open to the general charge of idealism or psychological reductionism. That is, people's ideas are taken to determine their reality, without due regard to the institutional and power configurations in which those ideas are embedded. While it is of course mistaken to think that people's ideas, collectively and individually, are irrelevant in the determination of group formation and societal interactions, those ideas must, it is said, be located within the broader structures of constraint and enablement provided by their social circumstances. Furthermore, defining the nation exclusively with reference to psychological states is viewed by many as severing the necessary connection between social identity formation and group formation. Michael Hechter (2000: 97) has persuasively made the point that social identities are parasitic on group formation, rather than being their basis. Posed differently, to have a social identity is to identify with a particular group. Therefore, national identity presupposes the existence of national groupings.

The third approach still has a good deal of influence in the literature, but has been subject to sustained criticism in recent years. Its main drawback is said to be its inability to explain how and why what is essentially a "fiction" has been so successful in firing people's imaginations and actuating their behavior. Starkly positing that nationalism invents nations where they do not exist underestimates the degree to which pre-national cultural communities may contribute to the formation of national ones. While we should avoid conflating premodern cultural identities with specifically *national* identities, there is certainly a need to acknowledge demonstrable cultural continuities that provide fertile grounds upon which nationalists can promote and mobilize "their" nation. Part of the problem is that this third approach wrongly counterposes national communities to *real* communities, which belies a very impoverished conception of the real. Benedict Anderson drew out this problem when he rebuked Gellner for assimilating "'invention' to 'fabrication' and 'falsity,' rather than to 'imagining' and 'creation'" (1991: 6).

Despite its continuing popularity, the imagined communities approach to nations and nationalism has not been without its detractors. Anderson's emphasis on imagination has been criticized for dissolving the nation into a chimera that is no more than the sum of its cultural representations. For Anthony Smith, this unduly emphasizes the idea of the nation as a narrative that can be deconstructed. As a result, "causal explanations of the character and spread of a specific type of community and movement tend to be overshadowed or relegated" (1998: 138). The imagined communities approach has also been criticized for neglecting the ideological power of nationalism,

in the sense of underestimating the strategic and self-conscious political uses to which nationalism is put by various social groups pursuing their sectional interests under the guise of the national interest. While it is laudable to accentuate the expressive basis of the nation as Anderson does, this should not be at the expense of its instrumental dimensions or its contested character. Finally, Anderson has also been taken to task for projecting onto the rest of the world models of the nationally imagined community that developed in Europe and the Americas and which then allegedly became modular. This relegates nationalism and nationalist agency in the colonial and postcolonial world to pale imitations of their western forebears.

The final approach to the conceptualization of nations and nationalism is vulnerable to many of the criticisms made of the second and fourth approaches. In addition, it has been suggested that it tends to reduce nations to their symbolic and discursive dimensions. It thereby neglects the institutional reality of the social allegiances, networks of interaction, bonds of belonging, and reciprocal obligation that constitute the sociological foundations of any nation. Consequently, while we might agree that nations *do* function as "symbolic frames," "discursive formations," and "categories of practice," this should not preclude us from recognizing them as "real" communities, even if these are socially constructed, partly invented, and cannot be observed directly.

NATIONALISM AND MODERNITY

The debate about the nature of nations is closely bound up with a broader debate about the origins of nations and nationalism, and about their relationship to modernity. This debate can be most simply characterized as one between "modernists" on the one hand, and "ethnosymbolists" on the other (with earlier "primordialist" perspectives having been widely discredited, and hence not necessary to this discussion).

Despite many substantive differences, what all modernists share is a view that the origins of nations and nationalism are to be located in the transformations wrought by modernity. Here the development of the modern centralized state and the interstate system and the subsequent emergence of democracy and capitalism are viewed as key determinants in the growth of a national field of political action and orientation. Within this general modernist frame, we can identify accounts that emphasize the socioeconomic foundations of nationalism as against those that emphasize its political bases, and those that are functionalist in tone as opposed to those that offer causal explanations.

Modernist accounts emphasizing the socioeconomic foundations of nations and nationalism have typically, but not exclusively, been articulated by those influenced by Marxism. Here modernity is largely coterminous with capitalism. Nations and nationalism are viewed both as ideologically biased, reintegrative responses to the community-dissolving effects of capitalism and as byproducts of uneven capitalist development at the level of the world-system. Either way, nations and nationalism are seen to serve the structural requirements of capitalism and the ideological interests of the bourgeoisie, by obscuring the class bases of power and privilege upon which all states are founded.

But socioeconomic and functionalist accounts of national phenomena have not been limited to Marxists. The most influential non-Marxist account in this genre is that of Ernst Gellner (1983). For Gellner, it is not capitalism but industrialism that demands and begets nationalism – defined as the principle of political legitimacy demanding that ethnic and political boundaries coincide. This principle was necessarily absent in pre-agrarian and agrarian societies, Gellner contends, but became an imperative with the transition to industrial society and its characteristic fusion of a polity with a "high culture." He argues that the extensive division of labor in industrialized societies necessitates and engenders a high degree of social mobility. This in turn demands a universal, standardized education system, staffed by specialists, so that people can adequately fulfill plural roles as well as communicate with the anonymous persons with whom these roles will bring them into contact. As a result, the state's monopoly over legitimate education is now more important than its monopoly over legitimate violence, and provides the main key to understanding the roots of nationalism. It is the main clue to understanding why state and

culture *must* be linked. The modern state's attempts to homogenize its population through a standardized education system expresses the objective needs of a social order based on industrialization, a complex division of labor, and social mobility. It is not so much that nationalism imposes homogeneity, but that the objective need for homogeneity under modern conditions is reflected in nationalism (Gellner 1983: 39, 46).

These views have been criticized for their functionalism, for their unwarranted linking of nationalism to industrialism and capitalism, and for their reduction of politics to economics. The functionalist explanation of nationalism, for instance, is viewed as wrongly positing consequences as causes, which obscures the causal mechanisms connecting the alleged societal need (the need for effective communication, cultural homogeneity, and ideological cohesion) to the phenomenon that is said to meet that need (in this case, nationalism). In addition, many thinkers have rightly pointed out that nationalism has often been present where industrialism and capitalism are absent, thus undermining the case for their necessary connection. Finally, socioeconomic accounts have been criticized for their mishandling of politics: in Gellner's case, for his insensitivity to the impact of different political and constitutional structures on nationalism; in the Marxist case, for its reduction of politics to economics, even if in the last instance. Such criticisms inform modernist positions that emphasize the centrality of politics.

Michael Mann (1993) and John Breuilly (1993) have been amongst the most influential modernist thinkers offering non-functionalist and essentially political accounts of the rise of nations. While both concede that national sentiments existed as early as the sixteenth century, these were not sufficient to constitute either nations or nationalism. They were at best expressions of a "proto-nationalism," which was not yet liberated from dynastic and religious principles of political legitimacy. This liberation would have to wait until the latter part of the eighteenth century whereupon centralized states, and political oppositions to those states, increasingly articulated a nationalistic rhetoric centered upon the sovereignty of the "people" understood as a nation. This in turn generated new forms of participation within and loyalty to the state, and connected culture and politics in novel ways. Thus the rise of the nation and nationalism, for both Mann and Breuilly, was very much bound up with the struggle toward representative government and citizenship.

These modernist positions, in both their socioeconomic and political guises, have been subject to increasing challenges in recent years by what Anthony Smith (2001) has labeled as ethnosymbolic accounts of the origins of nations. These take modernists to task for mythologizing the modernity of nations, for failing to discern the continuities between "modern" nations and premodern cultural collectivities, and for neglecting the centrality of myth and symbolism in the constitution of national identity.

By contrast, ethnosymbolists argue that nations and national identity have premodern cultural roots, and that it is the longevity and depth of these roots that help explain the emotional appeal and enduring power of national sentiment. In the trailblazing account *Nations Before Nationalism* (1982), for example, John Armstrong focuses on the persistence of group identities within the civilizational zones centered upon the Judaic-Christian and Islamic religions. He suggests that these religions were particularly well suited to penetrating the masses of a population because of their commitment to proselytizing and their tendency to fracture along sectarian lines. Both attributes necessitated forms of communication that were accessible to non-elite groups. This stimulated the use of vernacular languages, which in turn served as symbolic boundary markers of group identity and encouraged the persistence of large-scale collective identities. Of these, Armstrong views the Jews beginning from around 1000 BCE, and the Armenians from around 400 CE, as constituting the first premodern nations. While the cultural content of what it means to be Jewish or Armenian has changed dramatically since then, the symbolic boundary distinguishing insiders from outsiders has remained intact, thus preserving the continuity of Jewish and Armenian national identity.

Not all ethnosymbolists, however, are prepared to countenance the existence of nations in antiquity or even, for that matter, in medieval Europe. Anthony Smith's voluminous works, for example, generally suggest that this view mistakenly conflates ethnicity with nationality and overstates the importance of boundary maintenance in the constitution of nations. Yet at the same time he also takes issue with modernists, who are said to neglect the continuities between modern and premodern collective identities. Most important here are premodern *"ethnies"* – "a named population with common myths and shared historical memories, elements of shared culture, a link with a historical territory, and some measure of solidarity, at least among the elites" (1995: 57). These constituted the "ethnic cores" around which many modern nations formed, which Smith claims helps explain the emotional depth and appeal of nationalism. In this way, Smith can argue for a relative degree of continuity between modern and premodern collective identities, without conflating group identities whose differences are too great to be subsumed under the single concept of the nation.

While Smith's position has the virtue of avoiding some of the more inflated claims of the modernist and ethnosymbolist perspectives, his main theses are not without difficulties. In particular, it is not at all clear why relatively ancient ethnic sentiments should have a more powerful emotional appeal than more recent ones. Even where Smith's thesis seems to be on firmer ground – in the first states of Europe – it can be challenged for essentializing ethnic sentiment. Many have argued that shared ethnicity in centralizing states such as France and England was a product rather than a cause of what he calls nation-ness. Similarly, many "instrumentalists" have argued that ethnic groups and ethnicity more generally are the creation of modern elites who draw very selectively on the cultural materials of groups that they claim to represent, as a way of advancing their own sectional interests. Finally, the ethnosymbolist position of Smith and others has been criticized for failing to specify the mechanisms that link old *ethnies* and new nations. Part of the problem here is the failure to distinguish between culture and identity, and the misplaced tendency to assume that a demonstration of continuity in the former is enough to prove continuity in the latter (Delanty & O'Mahony 2002: 84–5). Identity is not simply derivative of some preexisting cultural substrate, but can be a conscious project that can be created and recreated.

NATIONALISM TODAY

It is a curiosity of contemporary intellectual history that the "global turn" in sociology has coincided with a sharp increase in substantive and theoretical work on nationalism. The proliferation of books, journals, articles, and symposia on nationalism and national identity has vastly expanded our knowledge of and conceptual tools for analyzing these phenomena. This reflects not so much Hegel's wise owl of Minerva flying at dusk (i.e., our understanding increasing in the period of nationalism's dénouement) as the contemporary efflorescence of nationalism itself, despite what some had supposed about the universalizing and homogenizing thrust of intensified globalization. Far from dissipating nationalist convictions, increased global interdependencies seem to have enhanced national particularism, as evidenced in nationalist conflicts from the states of the former Yugoslavia and Soviet Union to the failed and failing states of Africa. The mechanisms connecting these contradictory tendencies are still imperfectly understood, as is the continuing emotional power of national identity and its relationship to contemporary religious forms. These are but some of the areas demanding the attention of nationalism scholars. Unfortunately, if the opening years of this century are anything to go by, it seems that their analytical skills and insights will be in heavy demand in the years ahead.

SEE ALSO: Capitalism; Citizenship; Democracy; Empire; Gellner, Ernst; Global Politics; Imagined Communities; Modernity; Nation-State; Nationalism; Postnationalism; State

REFERENCES AND SUGGESTED READINGS

Anderson, B. (1991 [1983]) *Imagined Communities: Reflections on the Origin and Spread of Nationalism*, rev. edn. Verso, London.

Armstrong, J. A. (1982) *Nations Before Nationalism*. University of North Carolina Press, Chapel Hill.

Breuilly, J. (1993) *Nationalism and the State*, 2nd edn. Manchester University Press, Manchester.

Brubaker, R. (1996) *Nationalism Reframed: Nationhood and the National Question in the New Europe*. Cambridge University Press, Cambridge.

Calhoun, C. (1997) *Nationalism*. Open University Press, Buckingham.

Connor, W. (1994) *Ethnonationalism: The Quest for Understanding*. Princeton University Press, Princeton.

Delanty, G. & O'Mahony (2002) *Nationalism and Social Theory: Modernity and the Recalcitrance of the Nation*. Sage, London.

Durkheim, É. (1915) *The Elementary Forms of Religious Life*. George Allen & Unwin, London.

Gellner, E. (1983) *Nations and Nationalism*. Blackwell, Oxford.

Gerth, H. H. & Mills, C. W. (Eds.) (1949) *From Max Weber: Essays in Sociology*. Routledge & Kegan Paul, London.

Greenfeld, L. (1992) *Nationalism: Five Roads to Modernity*. Harvard University Press, Cambridge, MA.

Hechter, M. (2000) *Containing Nationalism*. Oxford University Press, Oxford.

Hobsbawm, E. (1990) *Nations and Nationalism Since 1780: Programme, Myth, Reality*. Cambridge University Press, Cambridge.

Hutchinson, J. & Smith, A. D. (Eds.) (1994) *Nationalism*. Oxford University Press, Oxford.

Hutchinson, J. & Smith, A. D. (Eds.) (2000) *Nationalism: Critical Concepts in Political Science*, Vol. 2. Routledge, London.

Mann, M. (1993) The Sources of Social Power. Vol. 2: *The Rise of Classes and Nation-States, 1760–1914*. Cambridge University Press, Cambridge.

Meinecke, F. (1970 [1907]) *Cosmopolitanism and the National State*. Trans. R. B. Kimber. Princeton University Press, Princeton.

Nairn, T. (1975) The Modern Janus. *New Left Review* 94: 3–29.

Seton-Watson, H. (1977) *Nations and States: An Enquiry into the Origins of Nations and the Politics of Nationalism*. Methuen, London.

Smith, A. (1995) *Nations and Nationalism in a Global Era*. Polity Press, Cambridge.

Smith, A. (1998) *Nationalism and Modernism*. Routledge, London.

Smith, A. (2001) Nations and History. In: Guibernau, M. & Hutchinson, J. (Eds.), *Understanding Nationalism*. Polity Press, Cambridge.

nationalism

Athena S. Leoussi

Nationalism is a complex social phenomenon with the nation as its object. Rooted in the Latin *natio*, denoting community of birth, the term *nationalismus* seems to have been coined by Johann Gottfried Herder as a part of his Romantic celebration of cultural diversity. Nevertheless, modern nationalism has its ideological roots in both the Enlightenment and the Romantic reaction to it. Definitions of "nationalism" as, indeed, of the "nation" vary in the social sciences: first, according to the particular aspect of "nationalism" that they emphasize as essential to its nature. From this perspective, definitions can be divided mainly between political and cultural variables. Some scholars, like Hans Kohn, Carlton J. H. Hayes, John Plamenatz, Hugh Seton-Watson, and A. D. Smith, have favored either typological or more inclusive definitions. Second, definitions vary according to the dating of nationalism, either before or during the French Revolution. This dating divides them into premodernist and modernist theories. Variations can also be found in explanations of nationalism, i.e., in the motivations and circumstances behind the rise of nationalist demands. Apart from the lack of consensus regarding the nature of nationalism, there is the further difficulty of distinguishing between the ideological and the analytical approaches to the phenomenon.

Political definitions of nationalism present it as a primarily political doctrine and movement, centered on the state. According to these definitions, nationalism is the demand that the ruler and the ruled should be the same, either culturally or politically.

The cultural convergence of ruler and ruled may involve the following.

(1)   The acquisition or maintenance of a nation-state. This implies either the defense of the political independence of cultural communities called nations which already possess a state and are faced with an external threat, or the acquisition of statehood for nations living in multinational states and dominated or persecuted by other and more powerful nations who control the state. A nationalist movement may thus consist of resistance to foreign rule or pursuit of national self-government (self-determination) to ensure the physical and cultural survival of the nation. This kind of political nationalism considers the nation-state, the principle of

"one nation one state, one state one nation," as the ideal form of human political organization. This makes nationalism an independence movement, and, to some extent, a liberal movement.

The chief representative as well as critic of this vision of statehood is Elie Kedourie. For Kedourie (1960), nationalism is a type of *doctrine* of self-government taken from German Enlightenment and Romantic philosophy, and especially from Kant, Herder, and Fichte.

(2)   State-led cultural homogenization of the people of a state. In this case, the state assumes a new role: a cultural role. The state now becomes the protector of a culture and the educator of a people. It "builds" the nation. State-led cultural homogenization or, as we should say, nationalization, may involve: first, the creation of state-sponsored schools whose attendance is compulsory for all; second, standardization of some preexisting cultural elements, and especially language, by state-sponsored, national academies which guide the educational institutions of the state. The standardization of language was first introduced in Europe by Louis XIV in France with the founding of the French Academy in 1635, but its users were a small educated elite. State-led cultural homogenization can have positive implications, such as the *incorporation* of the periphery, the mass of a population, into the center as part of the whole, as equals. This, according to Eugene Weber's famous phrase, turns "peasants into Frenchmen." The process also leads to the creation of a common culture in all spheres of life and across classes through the mixture of folk, peripheral cultural motifs with "high" elite and modern cultural orientations. This helps the creation of unanimity: the sharing of common ideas and purposes. The demand for homogeneity can have *negative* implications: first, conflict over the nature of the national culture; second, forced solidarity on the basis of cultural similarity; third, ethnic cleansing of cultural minorities; fourth, forced assimilation of

minorities; fifth, the loss of personal freedom through state coercion to conform.

Among the scholars who have described nationalism as a state-led homogenizing enterprise, Ernst Gellner is probably the most subtle. For Gellner (1983), the cultural homogenization of the people of a state is specifically associated with the modern state, and is distinct from earlier policies of, say, forced religious homogenization. Modern state-led nationalization of populations is unique in its aim, means, and content. The aim is economic growth and general prosperity. The means is education of the whole population into modern scientific reasoning and knowledge. This is done through socialization in state schools and universities. It is this state-sponsored scientific culture that constitutes the modern "high culture." Its vehicle is a standardized version of a native, vernacular mode of speech, which becomes the official, national language. And it is this native language that particularizes what is otherwise a potentially universal civilization. Gellner has stressed the importance of both education and literacy, and especially literacy in one's own language for gaining access to the benefits of modern civilization. This economically oriented civilization consists, first, in the application of science to technology for industrial production; and second, in the manipulation of information through literacy and the expanding communication technologies which constitutes "work" in modern societies.

The political convergence between ruler and ruled involves political homogenization: the equal participation, through representation, of all the people of a state in the political process. It involves the abolition of the distinction between ruler and ruled through citizenship rights for the "demos." Nationalism demands "power for the people," with, or without, cultural qualifications for being or becoming a citizen. Scholars who have defined nationalism as a primarily democratic movement for creating territorially defined communities of citizens include Ernest Renan and Dominique Schnapper (1998).

Cultural definitions of nationalism emphasize the cultural and specifically traditionalist aspects of national project. They describe nationalism as a movement which advocates the revival of the traditional culture and especially the "golden age" of the community into which one is born, the ethnic community. As such, nationalism is an educational movement directed to inner reform. It provides the individual and the group with collective identity: a sense of origins and a set of values found in the community of birth. Nationalism advocates and defends individual (and collective) identification with one's own ethnic origins, physical type, language, territory, history, myths, symbols, and traditions; in short, with the way of life of one's parents and ancestors. The maintenance and revival of these cultural resources considered to be, according to Max Weber, "irreplaceable culture values" constitute this form of nationalism.

These values may be part of a low (folk) or high (elite) culture, or, indeed, a world civilization. This conception of nationalism emphasizes the role of intellectuals, poets, musicians, and artists in the affirmation, articulation, and regeneration of the ethnic culture. Such a cultural understanding of nationalism minimizes the importance of independent statehood in nationalist movements. In fact, it presents the acquisition of statehood as just one of many possible ways in which a community can satisfy its primarily expressive need: to live out its culture, or *Weltanschauung*. And, indeed, nationalism, thus defined, can emerge among members of a cultural community or nation which already possesses a state. Scholars associated with this account of nationalism include Herder and John Hutchinson.

Both political and cultural definitions of nationalism recognize the community-forming role of the nationalist demand for either statehood or cultural renewal. They recognize nationalism as a principle, on the one hand, of social selection, and, on the other, of unity and solidarity. Thus, nationalism offers criteria for *commensality, connubium, commercium,* and political loyalty: cultural affinity and/or shared freedoms. As such, it is a particularist principle of human association. It advocates association and obligation, *either* to the state and fellow citizens who guarantee with the force of law one's freedoms and way of life, *or* to the cultural community of birth (ethnocultural community), which it presents as an extended family.

Some scholars, and above all Isaiah Berlin, as well as Gellner and Liah Greenfeld, have perceived the desire for *status* or prestige in nationalist movements. Berlin (1998) has specifically defined nationalism as a movement for *Annerkenung*: for raising one's bent back from humiliation. Nationalism demands the recognition of the value of one's own cultural community and, by extension, of one's own collective self as at least equal to all other cultures and communities. This recognition can be achieved, first, through the acknowledgment of the sovereignty of a cultural community in its own homeland or through the reaffirmation of its hitherto suppressed culture. Similarly, Greenfeld (1992) has argued that *ressentiment* toward a repressive dominant culture is the principal cause of nationalism.

Political or state-centered definitions of nationalism typically present it as a modern phenomenon, associated with the specificities of the modern state, whereas cultural definitions emphasize the cultural and social continuities of modern nations with premodern societies. More inclusive definitions of nationalism emphasize the complexity and mutability of movements on behalf of the nation. This also applies to typological definitions. Anthony D. Smith's definition of nationalism is probably the most inclusive. It describes it as an ideological movement for attaining and maintaining, first, political and economic autonomy (or independence) and citizenship rights; second, ethnocultural identity; and third, social unity, on behalf of a population which is deemed by some of its members to constitute a nation.

Two typologies of nationalism have been particularly influential since World War II. Those of Hans Kohn and Carlton J. H. Hayes recognize the existence of different kinds of nationalism and reconcile the division between political and cultural theorists. Kohn (1961 [1944]) distinguished between "West" and "East" (of the Rhine) European nationalisms. Kohn's two types of nationalism are now usually referred to as "civic" and "ethnic" nationalisms and are applicable outside European societies, to Asia and Africa, where they have been diffused. Civic nationalisms of the West European type are inspired by the political, democratic, rational, and classical values of the Enlightenment and the French Revolution:

liberté, égalité, fraternité. Ethnic nationalisms of the East European type are inspired by the traditionalism, mysticism, historicism, and folklorism of Romanticism. Hayes (1960) distinguished between "political" and "cultural" nationalisms. Political nationalism is when a cultural group or "nationality" strives for a state of its own; cultural nationalism is when a nationality cherishes and extols its common language and traditions without political ends.

Different *explanations* have been proposed for nationalism in its various manifestations. As with disputes over the definition of the phenomenon, disputes over its causes can be broadly divided into modernist and premodernist.

Modernist explanations can be either structural functionalist or instrumentalist. The former claim that the structures of modernity require nationalism. Instrumentalist explanations affirm the existence of ulterior motives in the minds of the leaders of nationalist movements. They particularly challenge the cultural pronouncements on behalf of the nation as pretexts masking essentially political and economic ends. The modern conditions which require or make use of nationalism can be political, economic, or cultural.

(1) *Political*: For scholars like Charles Tilly (1975) and John Breuilly (1982), the modern centralist, sovereign, and militarist state requires linguistic-cultural homogeneity for staffing its vast bureaucratic administrative machine and for organizing a rational and scientific army led by professionally trained personnel. For Paul R. Brass (1991), in modern mass democracies, elites manipulate the masses for support in their competition with other elites for gaining positions of power. The "masses" tend to support those who advocate emotionally powerful ideas of common descent and cultural values and especially religion. These "nationalist" elites mask their real motive: the quest for power.

(2) *Economic*: According to Gellner (1983), modern industrial society bent on economic growth requires nationalism, in the sense of a homogeneously literate and scientifically educated workforce which can be easily deployed throughout its

borders without encountering problems of communication and manipulation of information. For the manipulation of matter is now undertaken by machines operating to human instructions. The great scientists, inventors, and entrepreneurs of the Industrial Revolution did not know what they were doing: they were creating the conditions essential for nationalism – cultural homogeneity. Thus, for Gellner, nationalism is a movement for prosperity through sociocultural modernization and homogenization. It pursues not the old culture, but the new, scientific culture made available in one's own language. Consequently, loyalties become national because language determines one's employability. Another economic reason for nationalism is provided by Eric Hobsbawm. Hobsbawm (1990; Hobsbawm & Ranger 1983) maintains that the new bourgeois capitalist society, which is effectively divided by competing class interests and which requires exploitation for the accumulation of profit, also requires the solidarity of the workers with the capitalist owners of the means of production. To this end, bourgeois intellectuals invent and propagate the *ideology* of a common ethnocultural identity and a shared past between the two classes. On this basis, they claim national solidarity: the cooperation and sympathy existing among kin members, i.e., members of the same family. Thus national identity and national solidarity are inventions: false consciousness for exploitation as against the reality of class identity and solidarity.

(3) *Cultural*: According to Kedourie (1960), the experience of uprooting, dislocation, and loss of a sense of community caused by modernity's urbanization and triumph of cold, scientific reason lies at the root of nationalism. Nationalism is a doctrine developed by alienated intellectuals, a form of neotribalism. It is a way of coping with modernity, first, through a return to the warm community of birth, the village of premodern times for which statehood is claimed; and second, through the uncritical absorption in the certainties of traditional culture. Nationalism represents the ethnic culture and community as the natural and authentic conditions of human existence.

In another variant of this approach, Benedict Anderson (1983) has proposed a relatively *longue durée* of modernization and national development. Initially, religious and economic conditions, and especially Protestantism and print capitalism, require linguistic homogeneity and literacy in the vernacular: partly for religious reasons concerning direct access to the word of God; and partly for economic reasons of profit – the more there are people who can read books, the greater the profit from the sale of books. At a later stage, with secularization, the community of faith is replaced by the community of language as a new "imagined community" made possible through communication via newspapers and the novel.

Anti-modernist explanations are of four main types: sociobiological, primordial, perennialist, and ethnosymbolist.

(1) *Sociobiologists* like Pierre L. van den Berghe (1987) claim that nationalism as a social movement demanding solidarity among culturally similar persons is biologically determined. Nationalism is the rationalization or realization of the biological impulse toward kin selection. Kin selection ensures the survival or reproduction, through mating with genetically similar individuals, of one's own genes. Nationalism is conscious Darwinism.

(2) *Primordialists* like Edward Shils (1957) and Steven Grosby (1994) see the origins of nationalism in the facts of birth in a particular community and territory. Human beings are naturally attached to the primary, life-giving forces of family and territory. Human beings tend to perceive these ethnic attachments as given, vital, and overriding social bonds. Unlike sociobiologists, primordialists view nationalism as a sentiment of affection, obligation, and sympathy toward the sources of human life: the family and the land, and the persons associated with them through cultural similarity and place of residence. Similarly, Walker Connor (1994) has emphasized the emotional basis

of nationalism, which he calls ethnonationalism: the powerful bond felt toward, if not actual, presumed kinsmen and co-ethnics.

(3) *Perennialists* like John A. Armstrong (1982) see nations as premodern ethnocultural social formations shaped over a *longue durée* by an accumulation of collective experiences, myths, and symbols and by encounters with other nations. Nationalism, however, as an often fanatical and aggressive ideology, disseminated by elites to mobilize nations against one another, is modern. Nationalist elites scan the fund of popular beliefs and symbols to mobilize their constituency for status, territorial as well as material interests.

(4) *Ethnosymbolists* like Anthony D. Smith (1986) and John Hutchinson (1987) are neither modernist nor anti-modernist but can be described as "qualified modernist." These theorists explain modern nationalism, first, in its own terms: as a new doctrine or ideology which advocates the pursuit of its declared ends for their own sake; and second, as a response to the socially and morally disruptive impact of modernity. Triggered by modernity's triple revolution of universalistic democratic politics, secularizing scientific culture, and the prosperity of industrial-capitalist economy, nationalism is not a conservative, neotraditionalist rejection of modernity. Rather, it is a way of facilitating the transition to its advantages and compensating for its disadvantages. First, by selectively reviving and emphasizing those experiences from the community's own past which have affinities with modernity and especially its openness to change, innovation, and exchange with other cultures, thereby legitimizing change from within. And, second, by remoralizing the community, disoriented by modernity's anomie. The ethnic culture provides a repertoire of models and symbols of human association and belonging, including religious principles and ethnocultural bonds, and stabilizes modern personalities confronted with the dilemmas of the age of reason. Consequently, for these theorists, nationalism combines the old with the new and its success is given as evidence of the persistence of the past, the flexibility rather than fixity of cultural identities, and the human need for continuity with the past as against the modernist belief that humankind can be and was recreated *ex nihilo* in 1789.

The collapse of international communism in the former Soviet bloc, beginning with the fall of the Berlin Wall in 1989, and the "ever closer" unification of the member states of the European Union since the Maastricht Treaty of 1992, have given rise to two apparently contradictory tendencies: the revival of nationalism and the reduction of the salience of personal identification with the national state. The latter tendency has been reinforced by an expansion of multicultural policies on a world scale, underpinned by the United Nations Universal Declaration of Human Rights. Both trends, notwithstanding the forces of globalization, converge on the importance of ethnocultural tradition and community in the twenty-first century.

SEE ALSO: Collective Identity; Ethnic Groups; Ethnonationalism; Gellner, Ernst; Imagined Communities; Nation-State; Nation-State and Nationalism; Nationalism and Sport; Postnationalism

REFERENCES AND SUGGESTED READINGS

Anderson, B. (1983) *Imagined Communities.* New Verso, London.

Armstrong, J. A. (1982) *Nations Before Nationalism.* University of North Carolina Press, Chapel Hill.

Berlin, I. (1998) *The Proper Study of Mankind.* Farrar, Straus, & Giroux, New York.

Brass, P. R. (1991) *Ethnicity and Nationalism: Theory and Comparison.* Sage, London.

Breuilly, J. (1982) *Nationalism and the State.* Manchester University Press, Manchester.

Connor, W. (1994) *Ethnonationalism: The Quest for Understanding.* Princeton University Press, Princeton.

Gellner, E. (1983) *Nations and Nationalism.* Blackwell, Oxford.

Greenfeld, L. (1992) *Nationalism: Five Roads to Modernity.* Harvard University Press, Cambridge, MA.

Grosby, S. (1994) The Verdict of History: The Inexpungeable Ties of Primordiality. *Ethnic and Racial Studies* 17: 164–71.

Hayes, C. J. H. (1960) *Nationalism: A Religion.* Macmillan, New York.

Hobsbawm, E. (1990) *Nations and Nationalism since 1780: Programme, Myth, Reality.* Cambridge University Press, Cambridge.

Hobsbawm, E. & Ranger, T. (Eds.) (1983) *The Invention of Tradition.* Cambridge University Press, Cambridge.

Hutchinson, J. (1987) *The Dynamics of Cultural Nationalism.* Allen & Unwin, London.

Kedouric, E. (1960) *Nationalism.* Hutchinson, London.

Kohn, H. (1961 [1944]) *The Idea of Nationalism.* Collier-Macmillan, New York.

Schnapper, D. (1998) *Community of Citizens.* Transaction, New Brunswick.

Shils, E. (1957) Primordial, Personal, Sacred and Civil Ties. *British Journal of Sociology* 8: 130–45.

Smith, A. D. (1986) *The Ethnic Origins of Nations.* Blackwell, Oxford.

Tilly, C. (Ed.) (1975) *The Formation of National States in Western Europe.* Princeton University Press, Princeton.

Van den Berghe, P. L. (1987) *The Ethnic Phenomenon.* Praeger, New York.

nationalism and sport

Alan Bairner

The existence of a close relationship between sport and nationalism is widely accepted. This relationship manifests itself in the concept of national sports, in the enduring popularity of international competitions, events, and contests, and in the myriad ways in which politicians and politically motivated groups have sought to harness sport to national causes. On the other hand, questions are increasingly being asked not only about the future of the relationship between nationalism and sport, but also about the fate of the nation itself. The argument is perfectly straightforward, even though it is commonly expressed in far from accessible language. Put simply, it is asserted that economic, political, cultural, and ideological trends, supported by a pervasive and all-powerful global media industry, must inevitably destroy the distinctiveness upon which nations, nationalism, and national identities depend for their very existence.

Specifically in relation to sport, it is claimed that the global exchange of sporting bodies makes it increasingly difficult for the nation-state to be represented by conventional corporeal symbols. As a consequence of this and other far-reaching developments, it is believed by some that we may be at the earliest stages of the development of a transnational or global culture, of which sport is a part. Yet, sport also provides considerable evidence of cultural exchange that is undoubtedly at odds with the vision of a process of homogenization that is often encapsulated in the concept of Americanization. Furthermore, in any debate of this type it is dangerously misleading to equate the nation with the nation-state. Indeed, it can be claimed that the forces associated with the idea of globalization have actually created political and cultural space in which nations and nationalities that have historically been submerged within nation-states have been reawakened and infused with new vitality.

One need go no further than the United Kingdom in order to clarify the distinction between nation and nation-state. "Britain" is in itself a nationless entity. Nowhere is this demonstrated more publicly than in the world of international sport. With a single Olympics squad, four "national" soccer teams and three "national" rugby teams together with Northern Ireland's part share in the Irish team, the UK's sporting landscape is testimony to the complex relationship between nations and nation-states. Thus, when we refer to the prestige that nations can derive from sport, it is important to think in terms not only of internationally recognized states whose politicians seize upon sporting success for ideological and propagandist reasons, but also of submerged nations (Scotland, Wales, Québec, the Basque nation, Catalonia, and so on) for which sport has commonly been one of the most effective vehicles for cultural resistance by both cultural and political nationalists. For them, sport provides athletes and fans with opportunities to celebrate a national identity that is different from, and in some cases opposed to, their ascribed nationality. The two forms of engagement need not be mutually exclusive. It is possible to support both British teams and Scottish ones or to represent Wales and also the United Kingdom. It can be argued, though, that national identity takes priority in the minds of sports fans. Nationality, however, is likely to be what matters to athletes since this alone guarantees the right to compete on behalf of nation-states, which, unlike many nations, may be represented in international sport just as they are at the United Nations itself. It is worth noting, of course, that nationality rules have become increasingly flexible in sport as a response to labor migration.

The desire, particularly on the part of fans, to express their national identity in the realm of sport is clearly linked to nationalism in the broadest sense or, at the very least, to patriotism. Former Member of Parliament Jim Sillars dismissed the attitude of his fellow Scots toward national sporting representatives as "ninety-minute patriotism." For example, Irish support for national representatives in global sporting activities such as track and field, rugby union, and soccer is in most cases patriotic and, by implication, relatively politically shallow. The relationship between Gaelic games and Irish nationalism is, on the other hand, much more profound. In general, however, attempts to distinguish the passions aroused by international sport from "real" nationalism miss the point. It is undeniable that expressions of solidarity for players and teams that represent one's nation are closely linked to cultural nationalism. Whether or not they are also bound up with political nationalism is a different question, the answer to which necessarily varies from one individual to the next. For many people, even ones whose national identity is associated with a submerged nation, cultural nationalism is enough. They may well feel that they could not become any more Scottish or Welsh or Catalan than they already are with the formation of a nation-state that would correspond to their sense of national identity. For others, though, cultural nationalism is nothing more than the emotional embellishment of a strongly held political ideology that will settle for nothing less than national sovereignty.

For most sportsmen and women, even in an era when money is a major incentive for sporting success, representing the nation remains important. It is not inconceivable that they might represent more than one nation, with neither ethnic origin nor even well-established civic connections being necessary for a move

from one to another. However, for the overwhelming majority of athletes engaged in international sport, the matter is still relatively clear-cut. For fans, things are arguably even simpler. In the modern era, following one's "proxy warriors" into international competition is one of the easiest and most passionate ways of underlining one's sense of national identity, one's nationality, or both. Needless to say, not everyone wishes to celebrate their national affiliation in this way, in most instances for the simple reason that they are not interested in sport, the nation, or the relationship between the two. But just as for most active participants, for the majority of sports fans the choice is relatively straightforward. This is not to deny that in certain circumstances athletes and fans alike may well understand their nations in different ways. Furthermore, it is not only sporting individuals who demonstrate the contested character of most, if not all, nations. Sports themselves also do so to the extent that they become "national" in the popular imagination for a variety of reasons.

National sports take different forms and, in so doing, they provide us with insights into the character of particular nations. Indeed, the concept of the "national" sport not only provides insights into the relationship between the various terms listed above that are associated with the nation, but also helps us to understand how it is that nations resist globalization even in a global era. Some "national" sports are peculiar to specific nations. Their "national" status is ring-fenced by their exclusivity – echoes here of ethnic nationalism. National sports and games of this type are in some sense linked to the essence of the nations in question, even though their actual origins may be prenational or at least prior to the emergence of nation-states. They represent "the nation" symbolically despite the fact that they may well have demonstrably failed to capture the interest of most of the people who constitute the civic nation and/or the nation-state.

It should be noted that those activities that are most likely to be ring-fenced because of their specific cultural resonance do not always find favor with members of particular nations' cosmopolitan elites, who may well believe that the nation is better represented by sports that are both modern and transnational. Certainly, the *corrida de toros*, the classic form of the bullfight, is not universally popular throughout Spain, nor does it even take place at all in some Spanish regions. In terms of popularity, the "national sport" of Spain is almost unarguably association football (soccer). Yet, at least as much as taurine activities, the game helps us to appreciate the extent to which Spain is at best a divided nation and, at worst, not a nation at all – merely a nation-state.

In Ireland, whilst hurling may well be the sport of choice in the eyes of Bord Failte or the executives responsible for selling a variety of Irish products, including stout and whiskey, the sport's popularity varies considerably from one county, and even one parish, to another. Gaelic football is more uniform in terms of the support that it receives throughout the 32 counties. Yet there are isolated pockets where it loses out to hurling. Furthermore, the right of any Gaelic game to be assigned "national status" is considerably weakened not only because some Irish nationalists opt for other sports, such as rugby union and soccer, but also because the overwhelming majority of the Protestant community in the north of Ireland have resolutely turned their backs on the whole Gaelic games tradition. It might seem easy to dismiss this difficulty by simply taking these people at their word and accepting that, since they do not consider themselves to be truly Irish, their sporting preferences need have no impact on what does or does not constitute an Irish national sport. But this would be to ignore the basic precepts of Irish republican ideology that has consistently sought to embrace not only Catholics but Protestants and dissenters as well.

Games such as rugby union and soccer have some claim on the right to be called "national" in the Irish context. Despite their British origins, they are played throughout the island. Moreover, although rugby tends to be played by Protestants rather than Catholics in Northern Ireland, both football codes enjoy considerable supports from both traditions on the island as a whole. They offer Irish sportsmen the opportunity to represent the nation at the international level. Indeed, rugby, unlike soccer, allows northern unionists the chance to acknowledge their sporting Irishness whilst retaining a political allegiance to the union of the United Kingdom and Northern Ireland. It should be noted, however, that regardless of any claims that either sport may have to be recognized as "national," neither has escaped the influence of globalization. The two Irish "national" soccer teams have both fielded players whose ethnic "right" to belong has been relatively weak. The same thing has happened in rugby union, which in recent years has witnessed a flood of antipodean coaches and players, some of whom have qualified to play for Ireland despite having accents that conjure up images of Dunedin or Durban, not Dublin or Dungannon.

Gaelic games have been less affected by the movement of people that is commonly linked to globalization, except in the sense that Irish migrants have taken their traditional activities to other parts of the world, most notably North America. This is not to deny that changes taking place beyond the shores of Ireland have had an impact on the Gaelic Athletic Association (GAA). Nevertheless, the factors that have been most influential are best understood in terms of modernization and capitalism as opposed to the more specific category of globalization. Gaelic games have been relatively unscathed by the latter. As a result, the GAA offers rich insights into the processes whereby the nation has been able to resist the global in sport as in much else.

There are some grounds for believing that the link between nationalism and sport is becoming weaker and that the very existence of international competition is threatened by the twin forces of globalization and consumer capitalism. For the time being, however, the relationship between sports and nations remains strong, although this relationship manifests itself in many ways.

SEE ALSO: Globalization, Sport and; Identity, Sport and; Nationalism; Olympics; Politics and Sport; Sport and Culture

REFERENCES AND SUGGESTED READINGS

Allison, L. (2000) Sport and Nationalism. In: Coakley, J. & Dunning, E. (Eds.), *Handbook of Sports Studies*. Sage, London, pp. 344–5.

Bairner, A. (2001) *Sport, Nationalism, and Globalization: European and North American Perspectives*. SUNY Press, Albany.

Ball, P. (2001) *Morbo: The Story of Spanish Football.* When Saturday Comes Books, London.

Billig, M. (1995) *Banal Nationalism.* Sage, London.

Cronin, M. (1999) *Sport and Nationalism in Ireland: Gaelic Games, Soccer, and Irish Identity since 1884.* Four Courts Press, Dublin.

Douglass, C. B. (1997) *Bulls, Bullfighting, and Spanish Identities.* University of Arizona Press, Tucson.

Hoberman, J. (1984) *Sport and Political Ideology.* Heinemann, London.

Miller, T., Lawrence, G., McKay, J., & Rowe, D. (2001) *Globalization and Sport.* Sage, London.

Nairn, T. (2002) *Pariah: Misfortunes of the British Kingdom.* Verso, London.

Rowe, D. (2003) Sport and the Repudiation of the Global. *International Review for the Sociology of Sport* 38(3): 281–93.

Smith, A. D. (1995) *Nations and Nationalism in a Global Era.* Polity Press, Cambridge.

naturalistic inquiry

Yvonna S. Lincoln

Naturalistic inquiry is a label given to certain forms of phenomenological inquiry, including some qualitative research, much interpretive research, and many other forms of non-experimental and non-positivist inquiry, which relies heavily on the assumption that sensemaking or meaning-making activities constitute forms of reality[ies] as meaningful, or more meaningful, to study than physical realities when dealing with human research. While positivist and experimental forms of inquiry rely heavily on factors which can be weighed, measured, assessed, or otherwise quantified, naturalistic inquiry – or constructivist inquiry, as it is more accurately labeled today – balances the inquiry focus by moving beyond tangible or measurable variables to focus on the *social constructions* of research participants. Social constructions are those products of the meaning making, sensemaking (Weick 1995) mental activities that human beings engage in as a consequence of interaction with other human beings.

Social constructions are critical simply because they determine how individuals (and groups) will respond to interactions, situations, events, and the other phenomena that swirl by them. It is not the situation, event, or interaction which determines an individual's response, but rather the social location, standpoint, gender, age, social class, attitudes, values, beliefs, and other attributes of his standpoint that frame the meaning-making possibilities for that individual. In short, the world of physical and social phenomena is not received directly by individuals (or groups), but rather is mediated by unmeasured and theoretically unmeasurable characteristics the individuals carry with themselves as a part of their own identity, heritage, and personality structure. The ability to know, to comprehend, and to construct meaning from individual and group identities is termed standpoint epistemology.

Naturalistic (or constructivist) inquiry is characterized by an ontology, epistemology, methodology, and axiology/aesthetics which differ considerably from conventional (or positivistic or experimental) models of research. Taken together, the postures on reality (ontology), ways of coming to know (epistemology), means of knowing (methodology), and values and aesthetics (axiology) form a *metaphysics*, a paradigm (model) which is philosophically integrated and mutually reinforcing within itself. When naturalistic, constructivist, or interpretivist inquirers speak of a paradigm for their research, it is to this internally coherent, mutually reinforcing and integrated philosophical system that they are speaking. The paradigm itself suggests certain methods are more useful, frequently, than others, but paradigm does not refer to the methods themselves (e.g., qualitative); as a result, it is likely a misnomer to speak of some *qualitative paradigm*. As constructivists deploy the term paradigm, it is incorrect to speak of a qualitative paradigm, since constructivists can and do frequently employ quantitative methods in their work, particularly in creating thick descriptions of phenomena under investigation (Guba & Lincoln 1981, 1989, 1994; Lincoln & Guba 1985, 2000). Those inquirers who are persuaded that constructivist inquiry utilizes solely qualitative methods sometimes argue for an expanded repertoire, to include quantitative methods, and consequently advocate for *mixed-methods research*. All research, however, holds the possibility for mixing of methods, and naturalistic, constructivist, and interpretivist inquiry is no exception, as Lincoln and Guba (1985, 2000) and Guba and Lincoln (1981, 1989, 1994) have made clear from 1981 onward.

METAPHYSICS AND THE PARADIGM

The ontological position for naturalistic inquiry holds that reality is not merely physical, although physical realities (those factors which can be weighed, measured, parceled, or subdivided) are often important, but is also those entities known as social constructions. Constructions are the mental and sensemaking processes and products which humans engage as they make sense of, and organize, the physical realities, sensory data, situations, contexts, experiences, attitudes, values, beliefs, expectations, and the like which swirl around them. Inasmuch as humans act on their own (and others') constructions, constructions acquire an ontological status equivalent to, if not exceeding, physical or tangible realities. Unlike "measurable" physical realities, constructions cannot be dealt with adequately, that is, in a scientific sense, by parsing or fragmenting them into smaller units, or variables; they can only be dealt with holistically, as an integrated set of meaning instances. Further, they are not reducible to a single, "true" picture of some reality, but rather exist as individual and group idiographic portraits of some sensemaking activity. In other words, they are not singular, but rather multiple, existing in as many forms and instances as the individuals from whom they have been sought.

Epistemological questions likewise diverge significantly from those of conventional inquiry. The first and foremost question epistemology raises is: What is the nature of the relationship between the inquirer and the inquired? The second question epistemology raises is: What shall we agree is a truth statement? What is truth, within the paradigm? The third epistemological question is: What would be the nature of causality, if we are to include causal statements? The fourth and final epistemological question is: How shall we come to know what we are inquiring about (the methodological question)?

The major issue, currently under serious discussion, is the nature of the relationship between the inquirer and her respondents. There are a variety of serious proposals abroad, from feminists, poststructuralists, postmodernists, race and ethnic studies scholars, queer theorists, and others. Each varies from the other, some in serious ways. The naturalistic or constructivist's answer to this question is that the relationship is far more subjective, in that the relationship often "creates" the data proffered for research purposes, but that researcher and researched exchange roles several times between teacher and learner, between researcher and researched, as the researcher teaches the respondent what she is interested in, and the respondent then assumes the role of teacher, teaching the researcher about his or her lived experience. Respondents are not objectified, but rather are accorded respect as agents with dignity, rights of refusal, full locus of control, and self-agency. Deception is disavowed, and often researchers share themselves and their own lives as a part of the research relationship.

Truth statements are considered not only "factual" data (e.g., number of children enroled in a school district, number of patients administered flu shots in a single clinic), but also the many constructions around the phenomenon of interest. Both physical and sensemaking data are given equal weight, with social constructions being accorded status as wholly meaningful and indeed critical scientific data. Thus, there is a rebalancing between physical and mental data, with meaning-making constructions accorded heavy weight in terms of their ability to bring about, affect, effect, or influence human behavior and values.

Causality is a particular issue with naturalistic inquiry. Conventional models of causality assume a unidirectional and linear relationship between cause and effect. Constructivist inquiry assumes a multidirectional field of influence, often termed "mutual causality" to indicate the difficulty in sorting cause and effect. Feedback, feed forward, and feed through all become important concepts, as "causes," or mutual shaper and shaping forces, move through situations and contexts. Thus, naturalistic inquirers speak little of cause and effect, but rather speak of "webs of influence," "plausible inferences," and "mutual shaping."

Methodological issues, as a part of epistemology, have come to the fore, and indeed, some researchers term interpretive inquiry "qualitative paradigms," a term which we believe to be a misnomer (since practitioners from many paradigms can and do utilize qualitative research). The reason, however, that naturalistic, constructivist, and interpretivist research has come to be called the qualitative paradigm is because, in the collection of social constructions, qualitative methods turn out to be the best adapted to the task of probing the constructions of respondents, requesting clarifications and examples, and exploring the deeper values which undergird those constructions.

The final paradigmatic concern is axiology, or the place of values in naturalistic and/or constructivist values. Like related paradigms, such as critical theory, and unlike conventional inquiry, where objectivity is the presumed stance of the researcher, values are openly acknowledged as a part of the inquiry effort. Bias is attended to by explicating, as fully as possible, the values of the inquirer, and the values which inhere in the research context. Naturalistic inquirers believe values to be a part of any human project, including scientific research, and prefer to deal with values as a part of the systematic and disciplined inquiry effort, rather than attempt to obscure the role of values by claiming a philosophically impossible value neutrality (Hesse 1980) or unattainable objectivity (Bullock & Trombley 1999). Researchers have a variety of means to explore their own values and the manner in which their values impinge on a particular inquiry, and research more broadly, but whatever systematic strategies are chosen, value exploration is always a part of any inquiry project.

Naturalistic inquiry offered the first organized effort to attempt to codify an alternative to conventional and experimental inquiry in terms of an overarching paradigm. In subsequent years, thoughtful inquirers have both criticized and enlarged the considerations of method and epistemology around a variety of alternatives, and today, naturalistic inquiry is one among several paradigms, and one among many theoretical lenses (e.g., feminist theory, critical race theory, queer theory) which can be adopted to explore social issues and problems.

SEE ALSO: Epistemology; Interviewing, Structured, Unstructured, and Postmodern; Journaling, Reflexive; Methods, Mixed; Paradigms; Phenomenology

REFERENCES AND SUGGESTED READINGS

Bullock, A. & Trombley, S. (Eds.) (1999) *The Norton Dictionary of Modern Thought.* W. W. Norton, New York.

Guba, E. G. & Lincoln, Y. S. (1981) *Effective Evaluation.* Jossey-Bass, San Francisco.

Guba, E. G. & Lincoln, Y. S. (1989) *Fourth Generation Evaluation.* Sage, Thousand Oaks, CA.

Guba, E. G. & Lincoln, Y. S. (1994) Competing Paradigms in Qualitative Research. In: Denzin, N. K. & Lincoln, Y. S. (Eds.), *Handbook of Qualitative Research.* Sage, Thousand Oaks, CA, pp. 105–17.

Hesse, M. (1980) *Revolutions and Reconstructions in the Philosophy of Science.* Indiana University Press, Bloomington.

Lincoln, Y. S. & Guba, E. G. (1985) *Naturalistic Inquiry.* Sage, Thousand Oaks, CA.

Lincoln, Y. S. & Guba, E. G. (2000) Paradigmatic Controversies, Contradictions and Emerging Confluences. In: Denzin, N. K. & Lincoln, Y. S. (Eds.), *Handbook of Qualitative Research,* 2nd edn. Sage, Thousand Oaks, CA, pp. 163–88.

Weick, K. E. (1995) *Sensemaking in Organizations.* Sage, Thousand Oaks, CA.

nature

Adrian Franklin

The sociological analysis of nature as it is used in the modern West (by specific cultures and space(s)) is fraught with definitional problems, notably the seemingly very different and overlapping senses of the word nature. "Nature," says Williams (1983: 219), "is perhaps the most complex word in the language." However, on the same page, he is able to show that it is usually not difficult to distinguish its varied meanings: "indeed it is often habitual and in effect not noticed in reading." Three meanings can be distinguished: (1) nature as an essential quality of something; (2) nature as a force at large in the world; and (3) nature as the world itself including objects, humans, and nonhuman organisms.

Williams says that the meanings are variable across (2) and (3) but that the area of reference is broadly clear; that these senses relate to each other in an important historical developmental sequence and that all three senses are still common and actively used. The first sense is a specific singular and was in use in the thirteenth century. The second and third senses are abstract singulars, the former deriving from the fourteenth century and the latter from the seventeenth century, though they overlapped in the sixteenth century. Williams relates this linguistic transformation to changes in religious and scientific thought where sense (1) derived from a more plural pantheistic worldview of gods and forces, and where sense (2) derived from a more omnipotent singular directing force as a universal power, while sense (3) emerged later to describe the unity of the material world so ordered. The seeming diversity of the material world is therefore made to have a commonality in post-Enlightenment thinking, although the source of the singularity of nature changed from a creating, omnipotent God via singular personifications such as "mother nature" to the playing out of natural laws, the laws governing all things in the universe, where nature was personified as a constitutional lawyer, and later, after Darwin, as a selective breeder (Williams 1972: 152).

While Williams was able to tease out fascinating social constructions of nature, it was not equally true that sociology took much notice of nature until very recently. Nature and society were opposing poles in the "Great Divide" between the sciences and the humanities. While all along scholars have upheld connection over separation, the nature of disciplinary cultures has meant that very little connectivity actually took place. It is partly an artifact of sociology's success in making a case for its specialist field. When Durkheim argued for social facts as a separable class of reality, it became possible for the new discipline of sociology to bracket out nature, leaving it to the mercies of the natural sciences. The irony is that social anthropology, a fertile site of sociological theory, focused specifically on the connections between nature and culture. In the work of Durkheim, Lévi-Strauss, Evans Pritchard, Mary Douglas, and Tim Ingold, we can chart a history of at least 100 years of scholarship and development – yet

very little crossed into mainstream sociology (Franklin 2002).

One reason for this is that by the time sociology emerged, western humanity was increasingly urbanized and the city was clearly taken to be outside and opposed to the natural world. This separation of civic society from the countryside, its agricultural hinterland, and from wild nature, its opposed other, enabled sociologists to imagine a province comprised purely of the social and cultural. In essays such as "The Metropolis and Mental Life," Simmel was thus able to describe the specificities of a big city culture, as a self-contained sociality (Frisby & Featherstone 1997). Moreover, this essay shows how the city produced a new kind of person from the small town or rural village, with a different psychological makeup, emotional content, and intellectual capacities born of a different environment of stimulations. Because the city was not governed or anchored in nature, natural rhythms, or cycles, it was cut loose to develop in new ways. Sociology is almost exclusively urban in location and has been able to ignore the nature of the countryside or wilderness as an irrelevant variable.

Macnaghten and Urry suggest that the work of Dunlap and Catton (1979, 1994) was the only exception to this trend. Their work was predicated on an interdisciplinary approach to "environmental" problems, and as Macnaghten and Urry (1998: 5–6) point out, they played second fiddle to the more obviously significant and dominant scientific disciplines. The environment was a problematized nature, the problem being caused largely by people. While the environmental problem was to be defined, monitored, and fixed by science, sociologists could do their bit by explaining the social dimensions and causes of environmental harm and its impacts and suggesting the means by which a social solution could be arrived at. By these collaborations, sociologists found themselves working according to an agenda set by science in which they were able to develop only a partial and instrumental sociology of nature.

The call for a sociology of nature can be dated in one way to 1995, when two influential articles were published. Murphy's plea for "a sociology where nature mattered" argued that the immanent and irrefutable environmental and ecological crisis could not be ignored any longer by sociology; that the environmental and ecological movement required collaboration with sociology because the environmental crisis was composed of two challenges: to produce the right scientific diagnoses and responses to questions of sustainability and the right social responses that would be consistent with those. More broadly, and in the medium term, he asked how we were to change society in order to live *with* nature. How could two separate systems be restored to equilibrium? This was a noble initiative, even if it did disregard the entire work of the sociology of science – both the sociology of scientific knowledge and its opponents in science and technology studies (STS) – and especially STS's justifiably skeptical position on the ontological separability of nature from humanity. Those writing from the STS position argue that it is pointless to shift our allegiance and identity from the human to the natural realm. Rather, we should concentrate our energies on how to bring about good associations between humans and non-humans (see especially Braun & Castree 1998: 171).

In common with realist demands for more sociological participation in environmental issues and theory, Murphy preserved the ontologically separable status of society and nature and wished only to understand (and change) the exchanges between them. Critical realist thinkers (e.g., Dickens 1996) theorized a dialectical relationship between humanity and nature such that both have agency conceived very abstractly as "causal powers." These were conceived as inherent in natural and social objects. Such objects were not constituted by and through their ongoing relations with heterogeneous others, an ontology preferred by Donna Haraway, Bruno Latour, and John Law. Rather, since their existence was a given and relatively enduring condition, their causal powers remained fixed aspects of their scientific makeup. This is why those critical realists who have contributed to environmental debates tend to adopt a restorative approach; that the natural world has a proper shape and content that humanity has disturbed and imbalanced. Environmentalists should therefore seek to restore or repair nature and find ways of mirroring nature's proper balance with sustainable and socially just human footprints on the world

(Peter Dickens's book of 1996, for example, was titled *Reconstructing Nature*).

In this was preserved both the separable and separated objects of nature and society in a dutiful Enlightenment manner, preserving too the distinct and separate domains of science and sociology. It is for these reasons that sociology was called upon to play a supporting role; to find ways of sustaining a world that only science could properly diagnose and prescribe. And it was for these reasons that critical realism concentrates predominantly on the social side of the equation, the side of the Great Divide that, according to its adherents, is the source of change and the source of salvation. In this way, like political ecology itself, critical realism has remained predominantly interested in issues of social justice, health, ethics, Marxism, and capitalism (see, e.g., Dickens 2001).

Macnaghten and Urry's 1995 paper, on the other hand, was warranted by the considerable social content already manifest in environmental agendas and ontologies, and this became of interest to those working in many established fields of sociology: social movements; social justice; leisure and tourism; feminism; science and technology studies; neo-Durkheimian studies. This paper, together with their book *Contested Natures* (1998), spawned one of the most healthy and vital domains of sociology of the past 10 years, sensibly avoiding or bypassing the squabble between social constructivism and critical realism.

Macnaghten and Urry were aware of poststructural currents that were rapidly undermining the nature–culture binary and they tried to account for the contested, culturally specific biopolitics of environment by looking at nature and society as a conjoined human lived experience. Usefully, they forged a synthesis between the sociology of the body and sensual engagements with the world and Heidegger's notion of *dwelling* via the work of anthropologist Tim Ingold (1993, 1995). The result was an inspiring sketch of the multiple ways in which modern Europeans were embedded in their natural world, the way nature was inscribed on modern sensibilities and bodies, but also the way in which nature and humanity were a mutual unfolding or becoming where neither forms a controlling or prior center. This had a radically different feel to the purist boundaries of critical realism and it offered a valuable perspective to environmental organizations that were just beginning to feel the chill away from the zeitgeist. Clearly, environmental organizations could not rely on the power of argument alone and they needed to acknowledge that environmental support had personal, lived, embodied, and local dimensions; that global crises had to be felt as well as related.

Since these debates, nature or the non-human has become far more significant in a range of sociological work. In particular, discussions have moved away from a primary focus on the environment to embrace such things as the relation between biology and society, biopolitics, and "life itself" (Rose 2005); the implications of dissolving the nature–culture difference (e.g., Haraway 2003); the fluid and commodified nature of "life itself" in post-genomic society (Franklin 2001); and new ontological understandings of relations between humans and non-humans (Michael 2000). The sociology of nature is one of the most exciting leading edges of sociology.

SEE ALSO: Actor-Network Theory; Actor-Network Theory, Actants; Animal Rights Movements; Culture, Nature and; Ecofeminism; Ecological Problems; Ecological View of History; Ecology; Ecology and Economy; Environmental Movements; Globalization, Culture and; Human–Non-Human Interaction; Posthumanism; Society and Biology

REFERENCES AND SUGGESTED READINGS

Braun, B. & Castree, N. (1998) *Remaking Reality: Nature at the Millennium*. Routledge, London.

Dickens, P. (1992) *Society and Nature: Towards a Green Social Theory*. Harvester Wheatsheaf, Hemel Hempstead.

Dickens, P. (1996) *Reconstructing Nature: Alienation, Emancipation, and the Division of Labour*. Routledge, London.

Dickens, P. (2001) Linking the Social and Natural Sciences: Is Capital Modifying Human Biology in its Own Image? *Sociology* 35(1): 93–110.

Dunlap, R. & Catton, W. (1979) Environmental Sociology. *Annual Review of Sociology* 5: 243–73.

Dunlap, R. & Catton, W. (1994) Struggling with Human Exceptionalism: The Rise, Decline, and Revitalization of Environmental Sociology. *American Sociologist* 25: 5–30.

Franklin, A. S. (2002) *Nature and Social Theory*. Sage, London.

Franklin, S. (2001) Are We Post-Genomic? Online. www.comp.lancs.ac.uk/sociology/soc047sf.html.

Frisby, D. & Featherstone, M. (1997) *Simmel on Culture*. Sage, London.

Haraway, D. (2003) *The Companion Species Manifesto*. Prickly Paradigm Press, Chicago.

Ingold, T. (1993) The Temporality of the Landscape. *World Archaeology* 25(2): 152–74.

Ingold, T. (1995) Building, Dwelling, Living. In: Strathern, M. (Ed.), *Transformations in Anthropological Knowledge*. Routledge, London.

Macnaghten, P. & Urry, J. (1995) Towards a Sociology of Nature. *Sociology* 29(2): 124–37.

Macnaghten, P. & Urry, J. (1998) *Contested Natures*. Sage, London.

Michael, M. (2000) *Reconnecting Culture, Technology, and Nature: From Society to Heterogeneity*. Routledge, London.

Murphy, R. (1995) Sociology as if Nature Did Not Matter: An Ecological Critique. *British Journal of Sociology* 46(4): 688–707.

Rose, N. (2005) *The Politics of Life Itself*. Princeton University Press, Princeton.

Williams, R. (1972) Ideas of Nature. In: Benthall, J. (Ed.), *Ecology: The Shaping Enquiry*. Longman, London.

Williams, R. (1973) *The City and the Country*. Chatto & Windus, London.

Williams, R. (1983) *Keywords*. Fontana, London.

negative case analysis

Lonnie Athens

Negative case analysis boils down to using a small set of powerful heuristic principles to generate scientific hypotheses that enjoy strong empirical support from the intensive study of a small sample of cases. Over the years, negative case analysis also has been referred to as analytic induction or the limited case study method. Regardless of the name, the researchers who use this method deliberately search for empirical cases that contradict a scientific law or a working hypothesis with the goal of improving the hypothesis or law as well as the underlying conception of the problem to which the law or hypothesis applies. Thus, researchers who use this method do not eschew the discovery of a negative case. On the contrary, they would welcome such a discovery because it not only gives them the opportunity to overturn an established scientific law, but it also gives them a chance to invent an alternative hypothesis that could potentially become a pathbreaking scientific discovery (Becker 1998: 194–212).

Although seldom recognized, negative case analysis actually has been applied for two different but related purposes. One purpose is to chronicle the development of scientific knowledge about a particular problem. According to Mead (1917), scientific advance takes place over a process which, for expository purposes, can be divided into three distinct stages. During the first stage, *refutation*, researchers detect what Mead calls an "anomaly," a negative case that, at the moment, appears only to them to contradict an established scientific law, which for him simply represents a long and widely accepted hypothesis. According to Mead, the detection of negative cases is "the growing point of science." During *invention*, the second stage, researchers mull over the precise nature of the anomaly or negative case discovered earlier until they can finally devise an alternative hypothesis that, at this early point, they alone believe can account for the negative case. With the inception of this new hypothesis, the anomaly becomes transformed into what Mead called an "instance," a case that affirms rather than disconfirms a hypothesis or scientific law. During the third stage, *endorsement*, the larger scientific community must give its stamp of approval to this alternative hypothesis, which raises its status from lowly working hypothesis to acknowledged scientific law.

Although enlightening, Mead's use of negative case analysis to explain the evolution of scientific knowledge suffers from some obvious flaws. The most important one is overlooking the impact of scientific cliques on how long it takes for the scientific community as a whole to accept new hypotheses as legitimate scientific laws. Depending on these cliques' perceived interests and power, they can create or remove obstacles toward achieving the ultimate acceptance of new scientific laws. Another obvious flaw is that in some scientific fields, such as sociology, there are relatively few well-established laws, yet many different hypotheses vying to become one. Despite the disregard for the influence of scientific cliques and the relative absence of scientific laws in some fields, Mead's use

of negative case analysis to chronicle the evolution of scientific knowledge retains a certain charm.

The second and more important purpose for which negative analysis has been applied is as a general research method that can be effectively used in any science, sociology included. In the *Method of Sociology*, originally published in 1934, Florian Znaniecki argued that what he called "analytic induction," rather than "enumerative induction" had to be used in sociology if it was to advance as an empirical science. According to Znaniecki, analytical induction is superior to the enumerative form, which, according to him, reaches its highest expression in statistical tests because only analytic induction can satisfy the requirement that "all S are P." Unfortunately, he did not always define "S" and "P" in a consistent manner. When Znaniecki defined "S" as the hypothesis and "P" as the problem under study, he meant by this phrase that a hypothesis must explain all the cases falling under a researcher's definition of the problem, rather than only a significant portion of these cases. Restated in more contemporary terms, Znaniecki means that a hypothesis must be able to account for 100 percent of the variation in the cases that he studied. Thus, negative case analysis can aptly be described as a method for developing "universal" or, more precisely, invariant hypotheses.

In Znaniecki's opinion, analytic induction is not only superior to enumerative induction, but it also makes the use of enumerative induction a superfluous research exercise. However, one can recognize the superiority of analytic over enumerative induction without completely dismissing the need for using the latter. In fact, it could be forcibly argued that they can be used effectively in conjunction with one another (Turner 1953). On the one hand, the statistical findings that researchers produce through enumerative induction can be used to help identify the crude outlines of the underlying causal process that produces a problem. On the other hand, the causal processes that researchers pinpoint by their use of analytic induction can be used to help explain the statistical findings grossly associated with the problem, a point that Sutherland (1942) demonstrated in the development of his famous theory of differential association. Thomas (1967: 244) sublimely describes the reciprocal relationship between these two forms of induction in his often-repeated remark that "taken in themselves statistics are nothing more than the symptoms of unknown causal processes." Thus, regarding Znaniecki's contention that analytic induction renders statistical analyses gratuitous, time has shown that he was dead wrong (Turner 1953).

Using negative case analysis, researchers develop invariant hypotheses by performing the following four steps. First, on the basis of their first-hand knowledge, scouring of previous research, especially extant theories, or preferably both, researchers must develop a working definition of the problem chosen for study and a provisional hypothesis to explain it. In developing the initial and all subsequent hypotheses, the researcher must identify by successive approximation the "causal process" and, thereby, both the necessary and sufficient stages for the problem under study to appear. By "necessary" and "sufficient," it is meant that the problem under study only occurs after all the stages identified by the researcher have occurred, so that if even one of these stages fails to occur, then the problem will also fail to occur. Moreover, the researcher must not only identify provisionally the necessary and sufficient stages involved in this process, but also the specific order in which they must unfold.

Second, the researcher must examine a few empirical cases that fall under their provisional definition to determine whether their working hypothesis can explain these cases. If any of the cases examined contradict this working hypothesis, then researchers have one of two options. They can either (1) alter their hypothesis so that it can account for the negative case, or else (2) modify their provisional definition of the problem under study to exclude the negative case from their study's purview. It must be underscored here, however, that researchers should never eliminate a negative case from the problem under study merely for the purpose of excluding it, but only if its elimination will improve their conception of the problem. Thus, before deciding to eliminate a negative case from the scope of their study, researchers must be always certain that their problem was, in fact, earlier misconceived.

Third, if researchers develop a hypothesis that can account for all the cases examined so far that fall under their current definition of the problem, then they must deliberately search for empirical cases that negate their latest hypothesis, for the purpose of further perfecting either this new hypothesis or the definition of the problem to which it applies. If new negative cases are uncovered from this search, then researchers must once again revise either their working hypothesis or their definition of the problem, a process that one can expect to repeat many times during the course of a study. The need for researchers to revise their hypotheses or their definition of the problem should not be construed as a bad sign, but as a positive indication that they are learning something from their study of actual cases and, thereby, their contact with the empirical world.

Fourth, if researchers feel confident that they have reached a final definitive hypothesis after having studied a number of different cases, then they must restart their search for negative cases. This time, however, they would not deliberately look for negative cases that fall inside their present definition of the problem. Instead, they would intentionally look for negative cases that fall outside their present definition of the problem. If their latest hypothesis does not apply to these exogenous cases, then the researchers can be reasonably assured that their final definitive hypothesis has been empirically confirmed. Although this is the last step in the method that researchers must carry out, it is no less important than the earlier ones.

Only rarely have sociologists used negative case analysis as it is described in these steps. In fact, there exists probably no more than a handful of published sociological studies that utilize negative case analysis in this rigorous form (Becker 1998: 194–6), and most of these have been conducted in the subfield of criminology, which often requires methods that can be applied to small samples (Cressey 1953; Becker 1963: 41–78; Lindesmith 1968). At least two good reasons may be surmised for sociologists' apparent hesitancy to adopt this method for their studies. Even when compared against other qualitative methods of analysis, there are relatively few methodological guidelines for using negative case analysis, an important shortcoming that critics have missed. This general lack of rules of thumb forces researchers who use this method to rely on their own devices, which may prove unnerving, especially to those just starting their careers.

No doubt, sociologists also may be apprehensive that negative case analysis may not be well received in the sociological community because of the criticisms that it has drawn. Among other things, critics (Robinson 1951; Turner 1953; Denzin 1989: 166–9) have charged that in its strictest form this method (1) generates quasi-tautologies rather than logically sound theories; (2) identifies only the necessary causes, instead of both the necessary and sufficient causes; (3) isolates factors associated with but not necessarily the essences of the problem under study; and (4) demands a large investment of time and energy on the part of the researcher with no guarantee of a significant research payoff.

All these criticisms of negative case analysis, except for the last one, however, can be largely discounted on two grounds. Despite claims to the contrary (Turner 1953), some of the early critics of negative case analysis have confused weaknesses in particular research applications of the method or statements of its operating principles with inherent defects in its underlying logic. Also, critics have either intentionally or inadvertently given the false impression that some of these weaknesses are unique to negative case analysis when, in fact, they can be equally applied to statistical methods of analysis. If these criticisms are placed in proper perspective, then it may be concluded that negative case analysis remains a relatively powerful although admittedly underdeveloped logical procedure. As for the perennial problem in sociology of the divorce between our theories and the empirical world to which they refer, no better palliative now exists than negative case analysis (Blumer 1969: 21–47).

Nevertheless, researchers will be unable to exploit its full potential until more methodological guidelines for discovering negative cases and inventing new hypotheses or definitions of the problem under study to accommodate them become developed. To help systematize the process whereby these new hypotheses and definitions are devised, Becker (1998) argues that researchers can construct what Ragan

(1994) aptly labels a truth table – a table where the columns represent the conditions or stages in a process that are either absent or present and rows represent each case studied. By constructing truth tables, researchers can record whether a particular condition or stage takes place and the time order in which that stage or condition occurs in the cases subsumed under their varying conceptions of the problem under study. Although the use of truth tables would represent a significant methodological advance as far as the use of negative case analysis is concerned, other rules of thumb also need to be developed. In the meantime, sociologists who possess both real ingenuity and great confidence in their ability to solve empirical puzzles should not let these criticisms dissuade them from using negative case analysis, especially if they have a burning desire to conduct a study that challenges the prevailing wisdom in their field.

Finally, the relationship between the two different uses for negative case analysis needs to be pointed out. On the one hand, if researchers successfully use negative case analysis as a general research method, then they can potentially discover new laws that could revolutionize their scientific fields. On the other hand, if researchers use negative case analysis only for unraveling the evolution of scientific knowledge, then they can use the former discoveries as they chronicle the development of that particular scientific field's development. Thus, ultimately, the use of negative case analysis as a specific method for understanding the accumulation of scientific knowledge depends on its success as a general research method for conducting scientific studies.

SEE ALSO: Analytic Induction; Sampling, Qualitative (Purposive); Scientific Revolution

REFERENCES AND SUGGESTED READINGS

Becker, H. (1963) *Outsiders*. Free Press, New York.
Becker, H. (1998) *Tricks of the Trade*. University of Chicago Press, Chicago.
Blumer, H. (1969) *Symbolic Interactionism: Perspective and Method*. Prentice-Hall, Englewood Cliffs, NJ.

Cressey, D. (1953) *Other People's Money*. Free Press, New York.

Denzin, N. K. (1989) *The Research Act*. Prentice-Hall, Englewood Cliffs, NJ.

Lindesmith, A. (1968) *Addiction and Opiates*. Aldine, Chicago.

Mead, G. H. (1917) Scientific Method and the Individual Thinker. In: Dewey, J. (Ed.), *Creative Intelligence: Essays in the Pragmatic Attitude*. Holt, Rinehart, & Winston, New York, pp. 176–277.

Ragan, C. (1994) *Constructing Social Research*. Pine Forge Press, Thousand Oaks, CA.

Robinson, W. S. (1951) The Logical Structure of Analytic Induction. *American Sociological Review* 16: 812–18.

Sutherland, E. (1942) The Development of the Theory. In: Schuessler, K. (Ed.), *Edwin H. Sutherland: On Analyzing Crime*. University of Chicago Press, Chicago, pp. 13–29.

Thomas, W. I. (1967 [1923]) *The Unadjusted Girl*. Harper & Row, New York.

Turner, R. (1953) The Quest for Universals in Sociological Research. *American Sociological Review* 18: 604–11.

Znaniecki, F. (1934) *The Method of Sociology*. Farrar & Rinehart, New York.

nenko chingin

Ross Mouer

Nenko chingin was a central concept in discussions of Japanese-style management in the 1960s, 1970s, and 1980s. A shorthand for *nenko joretsu chingin seido* (literally, "age-merit ordered wage system"), the term has commonly been rendered in English as the seniority wage system. It continues to be used to describe a variety of payment schemes which link age and merit to the wages received by Japanese employees in many established firms. Although the term is readily recognized by most employees in Japan, it is the first component of the term, *nenko* (meaning age and merit), that allows for interpretation and ultimately clouds debates about the importance of seniority in determining wages in Japanese firms. The first character of the Chinese compound for *nenko* is *nen*, which is read alternatively as *toshi* and means year or age. The second character means merit.

Nenko-based wage systems were adopted for tenured administrative staff and managers in many of Japan's large pre-war firms. There has been debate on the origins of that approach to remunerating tenure. Some have emphasized its importance as an effective strategy in firms wishing to retain skilled labor that is in short supply in order to protect their investment in training staff in new technologies and in the organization's administrative procedures. Others, including Hazama (1971), have come to emphasize the extent to which the system was an outgrowth of a peculiarly Japanese approach to paternalistic management, although such explanations are pressed to explain variations in its application. Still others, such as Kaneko (1980), have pointed to the practice of Japan's more successful commercial establishments which through a practice known as *norenwake* rewarded employees by giving them franchise rights (and hence the opportunity to increase their income) as they moved through the latter half of their work careers. Kaneko also noted that Japan's wartime government sought to implement an age-based system in certain critical industries in order to stop the rampant job-shifting which accompanied inflationary conditions during the early 1940s. Nevertheless, age-based and seniority-based wage systems were in place for only a small minority of Japan's labor force at the end of the war in 1945.

It was in the immediate post-war years that the *nenko* system became fully institutionalized. At a time when Japanese were experiencing great poverty, high unemployment, and continuing inflation, left-wing unions sought to take over the running of enterprises and pushed for a new social contract with management at a time when many managers were still tainted by their association with Japan's wartime effort. The resultant struggle culminated in a long strike in the electric power industry and in the union winning its demands for an age-based wage system. Known as the *Densan-gata* [electric power industry] scheme, that approach was soon adopted in a wide range of firms. At a time when many were living at a subsistence level, it was based on a notion of life-cycle needs similar to those associated with the paternalism that characterized the way many of Japan's large pre-war firms managed their elite employees. Unions sought to have this tenure-linked system in place for all regular employees. Many unionists believed it was a transparent, fair system that remunerated all workers/employees according to their life-cycle needs and removed the discretion of management to discriminate among employees according to nebulous and/or non-transparent criteria simply to increase their profits at the expense of the working class. Employers saw it as a system that would secure the cooperation and support of all employees at that particular juncture in history.

The implementation of the *Densan-gata* wage system meant a considerable loss of managerial prerogative in the setting of wage rates. It limited the discretion of firms to adjust wage rates as a means of regulating their supply of labor and/or disciplining their employees. Although the system worked for management in securing a certain class of skilled employees, much of Japan's industrial relations over the quarter century following the war revolved around *nenko*-based wages and management's attempts to rationalize the use of labor by tying wages to other criteria. In combating militant left-wing industrial unionism over that period a major aim of management was to limit the weight given to age in the setting of wage rates and the accompanying guarantees of long-term employment. It initially sought to alter the *nen* component by replacing age with notions of seniority. The other longer-term strategy was to alter the *ko* component, and over time it evolved to incorporate level of education attained, skill levels, job categories, and various aspects of performance.

In the late 1970s debate came to focus on the extent to which the *nenko* wage system was unique to Japan. Those seeing it as unique tended to link it to the practice of long-term employment, arguing that the two were underpinned by a unique set of Japanese values which emphasized group loyalty and vertical interpersonal relationships. Those skeptical of such arguments pointed to the widespread research of Becker and others (see Blaug 1968) studying the economics of education. That scholarship revealed how similar age–wage earnings profiles differentiated by level of education could be found in most industrialized societies. Koike (1989) argued against notions of cultural difference setting each worker's values concerning work, accepting that the

choices of Japanese workers with regard to work and their firm were influenced markedly by the more universally valid rationality associated with calculated returns to an individual's or a family's investment in education. He documented how institutional arrangements in Japan might account for different behavioral outcomes even though workers were guided by a universal set of values. He argued that Japanese firms had elected to hire a small number of outstanding high school graduates and then invest corporate funds in their careers as highly skilled blue-collar workers. According to Koike, firms sought to protect their investment in human capital by placing those individuals on age-earnings curves similar to those normally generally associated only with more educated and skilled employees in most other societies. For Koike, this was the critical difference in Japan that bound that category of employee to the firm. It explained how rational workers would make market-conforming decisions to work long hours of overtime and to make a serious commitment to quality control schemes and other procedures that contributed to the overall success of their firms. In the 1980s Koike continued to develop his research around theories of skill formation and internal labor markets that emphasized the effect of specific organizational techniques he characterized as Japanese-style management.

While Koike's propositions about *nenko* came to be widely accepted, debate on the overall significance of *nenko* in determining wages continued into the 1990s. Scholars had noted for some time that the *nenko* criteria were most heavily weighted in remunerating regular (male) employees in Japan's large unionized firms. Although they noted that the majority of Japan's employees worked for firms with fewer than 100 employees and that many employees were employed on a casual basis even in large firms, others continued to emphasize the importance of seniority and the *nenko* criteria as social ideals. In the final analysis, arguments about *nenko* have been hard to resolve for several reasons. As Matsushige and Ohashi (1993) concluded in their study of wage setting in an iron and steel plant, the remuneration system in most Japanese firms is so complex that even employees have difficulty assessing how their fellow employees are rewarded in any precise manner. Given a work culture that discourages individuals from openly discussing their incomes with workmates, many employees seem to be uncertain as to how their wages are ultimately calculated, although most know that *nenko*, performance assessments, overtime, and bonuses all contribute to their annual earnings.

To some extent the concern with *nenko* receded in the late 1990s. The salaried university graduate with long-term career prospects in the internal labor market of a large firm is no longer a universally held ideal for Japanese males entering the labor force. The economic slow-down and recession of the 1990s saw many firms implement redundancy packages, and the long-term employment guarantees associated with the *nenko* wage system were undermined. Immigration and the spread of a new work culture among Japan's youth have also contributed to the multiculturalization of the Japanese labor force. Today, casualized forms of employment have become more common for young men, and career-linked seniority is less critical to economic survival in a more affluent Japan than was the case immediately after the war. While *nenko* has a universal validity in terms of the more general theories associated with the economics of education, it must be seen as only one factor shaping choices at work among members of Japan's increasingly diversified labor force. Mouer and Kawanishi (2004) discussed how growing income inequality in Japan needs to be understood not only in terms of firm-based remuneration schemes, but also in terms of policy choices at the national level that shape the overall distribution of rewards which flow from active involvement in the Japanese labor force.

SEE ALSO: Aging and the Life Course, Theories of; Educational and Occupational Attainment; Income Inequality and Income Mobility; Japanese-Style Management; *Nihonjinron*; *Shushin Koyo*

REFERENCES AND SUGGESTED READINGS

Blaug, M. (Ed.) (1968) *Economics of Education*, Vol. 1: *Selected Readings*. Penguin, London.

Hazama, H. (1971) *Nihonteki Keiei: Shudanshugi no Kozai* (Japanese-Style Management: The Merits and Demerits of Japan's Strong Group-Oriented Ethos). Nihon Keizai Shinbunsha, Tokyo.

Kaneko, Y. (1980) The Future of the Fixed-Age Retirement System. In: Shunsaku, N. (Ed.) & Mouer, R. (Trans.), *The Labor Market in Japan: Selected Readings*. Tokyo University Press, Tokyo, pp. 104–23.

Koike, K. (1989) Some Conditions for QC Circles: Long-Term Perspectives in the Behaviour of Individuals. In: Sugimoto, Y. & Mouer, R. (Eds.), *Constructs for Understanding Japan*. Kegan Paul International, London, pp. 94–129.

Matsushige, H. & Ohashi, I. (1993) *Seniority Wage, Promotion and Assessment in a Japanese Iron and Steel Company*. Working Papers in Japanese Studies no. 4. Japanese Studies Centre, Melbourne.

Mouer, R. & Kawanishi, H. (2004) *A Sociology of Work in Japan*. Cambridge University Press, Cambridge.

neoconservatism

Andrew Gamble

Neoconservatism is a particular variant of American conservatism. The label was first applied in the 1970s to a group of dissident liberal intellectuals around particular journals such as the *Public Interest* and *Commentary*. They included Irving Kristol, Norman Podhoretz, Daniel Bell, and Seymour Martin Lipset. Unlike the term neoliberal, the neoconservatives adopted the label with enthusiasm, describing it as a persuasion rather than as a faction. As an important if small intellectual elite, they became a component of the growing conservative movement in America through the 1980s and 1990s. Some neoconservatives were influential in the Reagan administration, but they appeared to be in decline in the 1990s. Nevertheless, several neoconservatives were appointed to significant posts in the George W. Bush administration, and speculation on the influence of neoconservatism on the policies of the administration after 9/11, particularly the war against Iraq, mounted.

Most of the neocons did not start off as conservatives. They came from a range of ideological backgrounds, including various kinds of liberalism as well as Trotskyism. The formative experience which made them neo-cons was their reaction to the events of the 1960s, in particular the student movement, the anti-war movement, and the counterculture with its strident denunciations of traditional culture. They criticized the cultural nihilism of the counterculture as well as the conse-quences of big government, in particular the expansionary welfare programs of the Great Society under Lyndon Johnson. They rejected defeatism about America, particularly in the aftermath of the Vietnam War, and celebrated the virtues of the American republic and the need to defend it as a unique regime. Many neocons were against the policies of détente with the Soviet Union pursued first by Nixon, then by Carter, favoring a more robust foreign policy of the kind pursued by Israel. From the beginning, Israel as a democratic nation that deserved to be defended against its enemies figured as a major presence in the neocon ima-gination.

Neoconservatism is hard to distill into a sin-gle doctrine because neoconservatives tend to be highly individual and idiosyncratic and frequently disagree with one another. Never-theless, some broad themes do emerge. As a political doctrine, neoconservatism has an acute sense of the political and stresses the primacy of politics. This is in sharp contrast to neoliberal-ism, which presents itself as an anti-political doctrine, seeking to minimize the role of poli-tics as much as possible. Neoconservatism could hardly be more different in this respect. Its instincts belong to the classical republican tradition, with its concern for the virtues and institutions that will sustain a public realm and maintain the security of a political regime. The economy, though important, is a secondary concern to the well-being of the political com-munity. This allows neocons to celebrate the public and public service in a manner that neoliberals always find difficult. Neocons do not hate the state; instead they have high ambi-tions for it, and high standards. The values that are uppermost for them are leadership, secur-ity, and strength.

A notable influence on several of the neocons was Leo Strauss, the political philosopher who taught at the University of Chicago until his death in 1973, though his importance is often exaggerated. Strauss himself was not a neocon and wrote little directly on contemporary poli-tics, and only a handful of those who became neocons actually studied under him. Many myths have developed about his influence. What he did provide was a reevaluation of politics in the classical world, of the importance of the education of elites, of the codes and values by which they operated for sustaining particular conceptions of politics and the poli-tical regime itself, of the weaknesses of democ-racy and the dangers of tyranny. It is the importance of a positive conception of politics that Strauss bequeathed to the neocons, rather than any substantive political program.

One implication of the neocon outlook is wariness toward democracy. But whereas neo-liberals reject democracy because of the dangers of popular sovereignty legitimating an exten-sion of state powers, neocons are much more concerned that democracy may breed a cultural atmosphere which leads to a weak government that is supine in relation to external threats and security, defeatist, prone to appeasement, slow to arouse, self-indulgent, decadent, shallow, and ruled by fashion and passion rather than by reason. Democracy tends to undermine tra-ditional elites and promotes celebrity rather than leadership, and in so doing removes one of the most important supports for a public realm and an independent politics.

As an economic doctrine neoconservatism adopts in practice many neoliberal prescrip-tions. It shares in particular the critique of the welfare state, attacking the programs of the Great Society for creating an underclass and a permanent category of poor people dependent on welfare. According to the neocons, the Great Society enfeebled American society while at the same time creating a new class to run it – the public sector workers, lawyers, social workers, administrators, and academics. These formed a new elite, but their values are seen by neocons as inimical to the traditional values of the elites that formed the American republic. The argument is not one about big government as such. Neocons do not favor a minimal state on a point of prin-ciple; if the purposes are right ones, it is legit-imate to expand the state. Neoconservatives are scornful about the neoliberal concern with balanced budgets and neoliberal worries about deficits under Reagan and George W. Bush. For neoconservatives, such deficits are justified given the security threat faced by the nation. Politics trumps economics every time.

As a cultural doctrine, neoconservatism has strong affinities with traditional conservatism. Neoconservatives oppose cultural nihilism, regarding it as a serious internal threat to the survival of the nation and the state. They tend as a consequence to be moral fundamentalists, believing in the traditional values that have defined Americans as a community, with their clear lines of good and evil. This acceptance of the Christian basis of the republic is a vital point of principle for neocons, and anything that tends to undermine it has to be opposed. It is also the basis for their aggressive stance on security. Evil must not only be denounced, it must be confronted, and the republic keeps itself pure and renews itself by distinguishing clearly between its friends and its enemies and by challenging and defeating the latter. The neoliberal utopia of a politics-free world strikes neoconservatives as complacent, inert, and mediocre. Only challenge and struggle can bring out the highest human qualities.

Neocons are not shy in pointing to dangers threatening the republic. For them the nation is always in danger, requiring the right kind of leadership to guide it. The cultural and moral crisis of the 1960s, the new cold war of the 1970s and 1980s, and the security crisis after 9/11 led neocons to call for the formation of a new American leadership which could restore the founding values of the republic. The collapse of the Soviet Union in 1990 led to a period in which the neocon vision seemed to be irrelevant, and neocon warnings were increasingly disregarded. With the disappearance of the regime that had been the main enemy of the United States since 1945, there was a vacuum in American policy and cosmopolitan dreams of a world of peace and harmony and steady, unspectacular economic and social progress flourished. This vision was even articulated by a leading neoconservative, Francis Fukuyama, when he declared, following Hegel, that history had ended.

The end of history, however, did not fit the pessimistic neocon view of the world. Neoconservative concerns were reflected more sharply by Samuel Huntington with his warnings of a possible clash of civilizations. Huntington argued that the West, and in particular the leader of the West, the United States, had to be ready to defend its own heritage and values against challenge if conflict were to be avoided. The West could not afford to be defensive in relation to other civilizations, or to accept dilution of western values or any kind of multiculturalism. Americans needed to be clear of their own identity and how it could be preserved and strengthened.

The concern with identity and how to prevent its loss permeated neoconservative thinking, and also shaped discussion of the security doctrine the United States should develop in the new global order where it was overwhelmingly the dominant superpower. *The Project for the New American Century*, published at the end of the Clinton presidency, argued for a doctrine of US primacy, putting US interests first in the determination of its foreign policy, disregarding when necessary international opinion, especially as represented by the United Nations, and being prepared to intervene diplomatically, economically, and militarily whenever American interests were threatened. The novelty of the doctrine was that it suggested that it was no longer in America's interests, as it had been for much of the Cold War, to give support to authoritarian regimes and military dictatorships so long as they were pro-American. Instead, the neocons now argued that the United States should seek wherever possible to encourage the development of pro-western democracies, removing by force those regimes which tyrannized their people.

This doctrine was a long way from traditional American conservative foreign policy, with its strong isolationist emphasis and its desire to keep the United States free of foreign entanglements. To some critics it sounded like a reworking of the universalist liberalism of Woodrow Wilson, with its ambition to remold the whole world in the image of America, bringing with it the benefits of democracy and liberty. But where the neocons differ from Wilson is in their realist doctrine about international relations. They have no illusions about the nature of the world, they merely think that America is likely to be safer if it acts preemptively to remove "rogue" regimes and "failed states" and obliges the whole world to adopt democracy. Leaving things as they are is not an option.

This vision of the world was only one strand inside the George W. Bush administration after 2000, and not at first the most influential one. Isolationist and traditional conservative tendencies were uppermost. September 11, 2001, changed the balance of forces within the administration and allowed a coalition to be forged between neoconservatives like Paul Wolfowitz and Elliott Abrams and nationalist conservatives like Donald Rumsfeld, Dick Cheney, and Condoleezza Rice, isolating other voices such as Colin Powell. What the neoconservatives both inside and outside the administration provided was a clear new doctrine for the conduct of American foreign policy in a world in which America could seemingly be attacked at its heart by a new enemy. The sliding together in the new discourse of the terrorist network of al-Qaida with states accused of supporting terrorism or producing weapons of mass destruction – the axis of evil – provided a new set of enemies, and with it a new way of defining friends. The attacks on Afghanistan and on Iraq at first rallied international support to the United States and then shattered it, dividing the US from many of its allies in Europe. From a traditional post-war American foreign policy perspective this looked foolhardy, but from a neocon perspective it was exactly what was needed to sharpen American will and purpose, freeing itself from false friends and entanglements and providing clarity to the exercise of American power.

Neoconservatism is an unsettling and dynamic doctrine, which shares much in common with other doctrines of political will and power such as those of Carl Schmitt. It puts supreme importance on leadership and identity, and therefore on the public realm as the place where these must find expression. Not any leadership will do, however. It must be leadership of the right kind that is true to the historical experience of the nation and its traditional values. It is very hard to organize such leadership in a democracy, but not impossible. Neoconservatives are rarely satisfied with what they have achieved, but for them politics is fundamentally a constant struggle for good to triumph over evil, and the battle is never finally won.

SEE ALSO: Conservatism; Democracy; Neoliberalism; Political Leadership

REFERENCES AND SUGGESTED READINGS

Drury, S. (1997) *Leo Strauss and the American Right*. St. Martin's Press, New York.

Halfer, S. & Clarke, J. (2004) *America Alone: The Neoconservatives and the Global Order*. Cambridge University Press, Cambridge.

Kristol, I. (1983) *Reflections of a Neoconservative*. Basic Books, New York.

Steinfels, P. (1980) *The Neoconservatives: The Men Who Are Changing America*. Simon & Schuster, New York.

Stelzer, I. (Ed.) (2004) *Neoconservatism*. Atlantic Books, London.

neoliberalism

Andrew Gamble

Neoliberalism as a distinctive strand of liberal ideology first appeared in the 1940s, but its period of major influence is usually dated from the 1970s. The label is disliked by neoliberals themselves, who generally prefer to be known as classical liberals, libertarians, social market liberals, or simply liberals. Neoliberalism is not a uniform doctrine and has many internal tensions, not least between a *laissez-faire* strand which believes that the best policy is to allow markets to operate with as few impediments as possible, and a social market strand which believes that for the free market to reach its full potential the state has to be active in creating and sustaining the institutions which make that possible.

The first people to call themselves neoliberals were German liberals such as Alexander Rüstow, who first used the term in the 1930s to describe new currents of liberal thought that were hostile to the forms of statism and collectivism which had been so dominant in the first half of the twentieth century, and sought a new form of political economy that would give priority to market rather than bureaucratic or hierarchical means of ordering the economy, within a framework of law. The German neo-liberals sought to revive liberal principles after the devastating impact of Nazi totalitarianism on German society and politics, by calling for a return to the rule of law, a competitive market economy, private property rights, and an ethic of personal responsibility, while also allowing the state to be active in guaranteeing a social minimum. These ideas crystallized in the conception of the social market economy, which provided the intellectual underpinnings of the post-war German economic recovery under Ludwig Erhard.

The German neoliberals became part of a wider movement of western liberals after 1945 seeking to reverse the long retreat of liberalism in the face of collectivist ideologies and reasserting what they saw as the basic principles of liberalism – the rule of law, the minimal state, individual liberty – against all forms of collectivism, including many versions of liberalism, such as New Liberalism and Keynesianism, which had sanctioned an expanding state to provide welfare programs, full employment, and economic prosperity. Under the guidance of F. A. Hayek, the Mont Pelerin society was launched in Switzerland in 1947. It included prominent liberals such as Ludwig von Mises, Milton Friedman, Max Hartwell, Lionel Robbins, and Karl Popper.

The classic statement of neoliberal principles was Hayek's *The Constitution of Liberty*, published in 1960. This set out the political institutions and rules necessary for a liberal order, drawing on the classical liberal tradition, in particular the critical rationalism of Adam Smith. Hayek was keen to distinguish true liberalism from false liberalism, and to recapture the term liberal from its contamination by collectivist ideas. His efforts were heavily criticized as a return to the discredited *laissez-faire* liberalism of the nineteenth century. Many thought that the basics for such a creed had disappeared and could not be resurrected. The bureaucratic organization needed to coordinate the economy made a return to the minimal state impractical.

Neoliberal ideas began to gain ground, however, through the 1960s and 1970s. The adoption of basic neoliberal precepts by the international agencies such as the IMF for containing the problems of stagflation was key. The translation of these ideas into the dominant ideological common sense in several key western states, notably the United States, Britain, and Australia, followed. Reasons for the rise of neoliberalism to such prominence and the discrediting of Keynesianism included the economic difficulties faced by the western economy from the late 1960s onwards, with the erosion of the exceptional conditions for economic growth that had existed in the early 1950s, the acceleration of inflation and growth of unemployment, and the resultant fiscal crisis of the western welfare states. These problems were exacerbated by the collapse of the post-war monetary system in 1971, the floating of the dollar, and a series of financial shocks, most notably the quadrupling of oil prices by OPEC in 1973. The need for a new set of guiding principles to manage the global economy was supplied by neoliberalism, initially in the ideas of monetarism put forward by economists such as Milton Friedman to tackle inflation, but soon widened into a more general neoliberal political economy for removing the wider institutional causes of inflation, which included trade union power, welfare states, taxation, regulation, and barriers to competition.

Neoliberalism revived many (although not all) of the basic principles of classical liberalism, but expressed them in novel ways. The result has been a distinctive new form of liberalism which has attracted many intellectual adherents and has had a lasting influence on public policy. As an economic doctrine, the core of neoliberalism has been an attempt to revive the case for reducing the role of government in the management of the economy as much as possible, giving primacy to markets and the free play of competition. It is axiomatic in neoliberalism that government solutions are inferior to market solutions because they are less efficient in economic terms and they harm individual liberty. The solution to every public policy problem is to take responsibility away from government and allow markets to function freely. Typical neoliberal policy prescriptions are therefore for deregulation of economic activity, privatization of assets owned by the state, and reduction of welfare spending except for the provision of a safety net for the very poorest. This, combined with a more general withdrawal of the state from involvement in many other areas of social and economic life, gives scope for large cuts in taxation and the share of state spending in national income.

The role of the state in the neoliberal program is not a passive one. It has to be both active and forceful. The free economy requires a strong state in order to function properly. The state should not intervene directly in the workings of the market; instead, its task is to guarantee the basic institutional requirements of a liberal market order. These include the minimal state functions of external defense and internal order, the rule of law, sound money, and the enforcement of property rights. Without these requirements individuals do not have the confidence or the incentive to produce and exchange freely. The market order is a natural spontaneous growth, but it is also very fragile and easily damaged by state intervention and state control, or by private monopolies which prevent free exchange. The state has to reform its own practices so as to minimize their harmful effects on the economy; at the same time it needs to remove all other obstacles to the free working of the economy. These may include restrictive practices of all kinds, by companies, trade unions, professions, and public bodies. The role of the state is to be the champion and defender of the free market, by enabling the institutions it requires and empowering its agents.

As a political doctrine neoliberalism sees the state as a necessary evil, which has vital functions to perform in respect of the market order, but which has always to be watched. Neoliberals are suspicious of the state and of the motives of politicians and civil servants and are therefore always seeking additional checks and balances. They take the classical liberal principle that government should be of laws rather than of men in arguing for a return to a strict *Rechtstaat*, in which government is by general rules and the amount of discretion allowed to the individual public official is reduced to the minimum. The constitutionalist wing of neoliberalism associated with James Buchanan and the Virginia School has argued for amendments to be inserted into the US Constitution to curb big government, obliging the federal government, for example, to maintain a balanced budget as a matter of law.

Similar tendencies are at work in respect of neoliberal ideas about democracy. Although neoliberals favor democracy as the least worst form of government, they are also extremely wary of it, since the doctrine of popular sovereignty and the idea of the sovereign nation in the modern era have legitimated the expansion of the state and infringements of the market order under governments of both left and right. For neoliberals, democracy is therefore at best an imperfect mechanism for government, and certainly does not represent a higher value than individual liberty. Neoliberals prefer authoritarian regimes that respect basic economic freedoms to democratic regimes that do not. This was the justification that Hayek and Friedman gave in supporting the Pinochet regime in Chile. Civil and political liberties are important, but less important than the liberties that are at the heart of the market order. Neoliberals have sometimes proposed ways in which democracy might be reformed, which involve restrictions on the right to vote and restrictions on the powers of elected governments. This means placing basic principles of the market order in a category where they are beyond the reach of the elected government of the day.

As a cultural doctrine neoliberalism is less distinct. Many of its critics argue that neoliberalism concentrates too heavily on economic liberty, neglecting other forms of liberty with which classical liberals were equally concerned, as well as the values of autonomy and self-development. The situation is also confused because of the rise alongside neoliberalism of libertarianism, which shares many neoliberal assumptions but extends them much further. Neoliberals are not ultimately libertarians, since one of their core beliefs is that there has to be a state, however regrettable. A minimal state is required for a market order to exist. But what are the cultural conditions for a market order? The libertarian wing of neoliberalism argues for personal freedom to be extended to all areas of social life, with the state withdrawing from the regulation of sexual behavior, drugs, alcohol, and gambling, as well as removing controls on immigration. The communitarian and conservative wings of neoliberalism which Hayek increasingly articulated in his later writings argue strongly against permissiveness, believing instead in the necessity of morals, nations, and languages as spontaneous orders which have grown up with market orders and which provide an essential underpinning for them. This provides one of the bridges between neoliberalism and neoconservatism.

From being a heresy, neoliberalism became an orthodoxy in the 1980s and 1990s, and many of its favorite nostrums were crystallized in the Washington consensus, a set of assumptions and prescriptions about the world and how it should be governed that was widely shared in the Washington policy community. Neoliberalism became the policy prescription of globalization, setting out the conditions which countries had to meet in order to integrate fully into the global economy and be in good standing with the financial markets. To its critics neoliberalism had become a form of market fundamentalism, which advocated the breaking down of obstacles to the commodification of social life and the penetration of market forces into all areas of economy, society, and politics.

With the collapse of the Soviet Union neoliberalism was triumphant, and its message that there was no alternative to markets and private property in coordinating modern, complex, large-scale economies appeared unchallenged. The absence of alternatives to neoliberal ideas forced all governments to become in some sense neoliberal, since they were obliged to operate within a set of structures in the global economy that reflected, however imperfectly, neoliberal principles of global order. This new order proved able to accommodate a wide variety of different regimes, many of them social democratic in their orientation, reflecting the two faces of neoliberalism, the *laissez-faire* and social market strands. However, it also came under challenge as a result of some of its own internal tensions, between its urge to shrink the state as much as possible and its need for an active state to ensure the democratic legitimacy of the market order, and also from the rise of neoconservatism, which challenged some key elements of neoliberal political economy, in particular its hostility to government and the public realm and its adherence to strict rules such as sound finance as priorities above all other political objectives.

SEE ALSO: Conservatism; Democracy; Liberalism; Markets; Neoconservatism

REFERENCES AND SUGGESTED READINGS

Cockett, R. (1994) *Thinking the Unthinkable: Think-tanks and the Economic Counter-Revolution*. HarperCollins, London.

Gamble, A. (1996) *Hayek: The Iron Cage of Liberty*. Polity Press, Cambridge.

Harvey, D. (2005) *A Brief History of Neoliberalism*. Oxford University Press, New York.

Hayek, F. A. (1960) *The Constitution of Liberty*. Routledge, London.

Robison, R. (Ed.) (2006) *The Neoliberal Revolution: Forging the Market State*. Palgrave Macmillan, London.

neo-Marxism

Alberto Toscano

Neo-Marxism is a wide-ranging term referring to the critical renaissance of Marxist theory in the post-war period, most often used to denote work in radical political economy which tried to combine the revolutionary aspirations and orienting concepts of Marxism with some of the tools provided by non-Marxist economics, especially the work of Keynes. Though the label "neo-Marxist" is sometimes applied to figures (e.g., the members of the Frankfurt School) who combined a fidelity to Marx's critical and political aims with a sense of the limitations of Marxism in the face of phenomena like fascism or mass culture, it seems to have been first introduced to describe thinkers – such as Joan Robinson, Paul A. Baran, and Paul M. Sweezy – who sought to renew the critique of political economy in a situation marked by the rise of global corporations, anti-colonial struggles for national liberation, and the politics of American imperialism.

Whereas, following the distinction proposed by Perry Anderson, the post-World War I Marxist concern with the cultural sphere and political subjectivity can be put under the aegis of "western Marxism" (as opposed to "classical Marxism"), neo-Marxism is a useful designation for the attempt, during and after World War II, to reflect on the pertinence of Marxist categories for an understanding of the changed conditions of capital accumulation and the political realities that accompanied them. Having intersected the Frankfurt School (Baran was present at the Institute for Social Research in 1930), and later influencing some of its erstwhile members (*Monopoly Capital* was a considerable reference for Marcuse's *One-Dimensional Man*), neo-Marxists shared with them a conviction regarding the increasingly prominent role of the state within the capitalist system. Hence the influential use of the expression "state monopoly capitalism" to designate a situation where the state itself becomes a "collective capitalist" rather than the mere enforcer of the capitalist system of social relations.

The experience of Roosevelt's New Deal, as well as those of the Marshall Plan and the rise of what Eisenhower would dub the "military-industrial complex," persuaded the likes of Baran and Sweezy that the orthodox Marxist understanding of crisis and development within capitalism was insufficient to grasp post-war realities. Thus, they tended to give short shrift to the labor theory of value and to regard the tendency of the rate of profit to fall as an inadequate tool in light of the long boom of an American-led capitalist system after 1945. Furthermore, following Keynes, they replaced the notion of surplus value with a far broader one of "economic surplus." Most significantly, though returning to Lenin's discussion of the link between monopolies and imperialism, neo-Marxists broke with classical Marxism by radically downplaying the importance of price competition between corporations, arguing that their profits were generated instead by competition in other spheres (advertising, marketing, finance).

With regard to their understanding of imperialism, Baran and Sweezy saw monopoly capital as a system unable to absorb surplus either in terms of effective demand or through productive investments. Moreover, they conceived of monopoly capitalism as fundamentally irrational, insofar as it subordinated all dimensions of social existence (from sexuality to art, body posture to religion) to the calculated, "rationalized" attempt to realize economic surplus. Even the capitalist rationality of quid pro quo breaks down: "Human and material resources remain idle because there is in the market no *quid* to exchange against the

quo of their potential output" (Baran & Sweezy 1966: 325).

The anti-imperialist bent of neo-Marxism, and specifically Baran's notion that monopoly capitalism led to the "development of underdevelopment" in peripheral settings, was a significant component in the formulation of dependency theory and the work of figures such as André Gunder Frank and Samir Amin. Its political influence on debates about socialism and national liberation in Cuba, Latin America, and elsewhere, especially through the journal the *Monthly Review*, was massive.

In Anglo-American sociology, this renewed emphasis, from the standpoint of political economy, on questions of exploitation and imperialism in the new, "affluent" society influenced a host of research programs that have often been described as neo-Marxist. Thus, in the work of Willis, or Bowles and Gintis, we encounter a neo-Marxist sociology of education that seeks to analyze the reproduction of capitalist socioeconomic structures through curricula, as well as the forms of resistance and conflict that accompany these processes. In works by Braverman and Burawoy, the labor process and its ideological reproduction are subjected to neo-Marxist scrutiny. In the domain of class analysis, the work of Erik Olin Wright has sought to combine a Marxist analysis of class exploitation with a Weberian analysis of status and domination, crystallized in the notion of "contradictory class locations." Spurred by the work of Nicos Poulantzas, Bob Jessop and others synthesized a neo-Marxist analysis of the capitalist state, questioning any univocal correspondence between the form of the state and its economic function, and seeking to delve into the class relations and class fractions that traverse the state itself. In the field of political economy, the neo-Marxist label has also been applied to the French Regulation School – with its emphasis on the social and governmental "modes of regulation" that contingently govern the reproduction of "regimes of accumulation" – as well as to more orthodox Marxists seeking to analyze the transformations of "late capitalism" (Ernest Mandel).

Despite the absence of any single, coherent program or statement of its departures from classical Marxism, neo-Marxism is best periodized and comprehended as an intellectual sensibility which tried to amalgamate a fidelity to certain guiding ideas of classical Marxism (economic exploitation, class struggle, the horizon of social emancipation) with an attention to the transformed conditions under which capitalist social relations were being reproduced in the post-war period. This entailed attending to the specificity and relative autonomy of the contemporary capitalist state, as well as to the political and economic consequences of militarism, imperialism, and the rise of the corporation as a social force. Many neo-Marxist authors felt compelled to inject non-Marxist ideas (from the likes of Keynes or Weber) into Marxism to cope with unprecedented transformations within capitalist society – whence the eclecticism that critics have often accused in their work. Politically, neo-Marxist ideas on power, the state, and political subjectivities beyond the traditional working class fed into the development of the new left in the 1960s and 1970s.

In the past 20 years or so, many neo-Marxist writers have abandoned any residual commitment to Marxism proper, though some, like Wright, remain wedded to foundational Marxist concepts. The work of neo-Marxists has also been profitably and critically integrated by authors happy to remain within the classical Marxist or historical materialist camp.

SEE ALSO: Class; Critical Theory/Frankfurt School; Dependency and World-Systems Theories; Imperialism; Marx, Karl; Marxism; Marxism and Sociology; New Left; Regulation Theory; Weber, Max

REFERENCES AND SUGGESTED READINGS

Anderson, P. (1983) *In the Tracks of Historical Materialism*. Verso, London.

Baran, P. A. & Sweezy, P. M. (1966) *Monopoly Capital: An Essay on the American Economic and Social Order*. Penguin, London.

Bowles, S. & Gintis, H. (1976) *Schooling in Capitalist America: Educational Reform and the Contradictions of Economic Life*. Routledge, London.

Brewer, A. (1980) *Marxist Theories of Imperialism: A Critical Survey*. Routledge, London.

Clarke, S. (1978) Capital, Fractions of Capital, and the State: "Neo-Marxist" Analysis of the South African State. *Capital and Class* 5: 32–77.

Cleaver, H. (2000) *Reading Capital Politically*, 2nd edn. AK Press, London.

Jessop, B. (1991) *State Theory: Putting the Capitalist State in its Place*. Penn State University Press, Pennsylvania.

Wright, E. O. (1990) *The Debate on Classes*. Verso, London.

network society

Stuart Allan

Social theorist Manuel Castells coined the phrase the "network society" as a form of analytical shorthand to characterize the global forces transforming collective action and institutions from one national context to the next. The network society is the social structure of the Information Age, being organized around relationships of production/consumption, power, and experience. Its prevailing logic, while constantly challenged by conflicts, nevertheless gives shape to the pervasive infrastructure of cultural life in most societies – albeit with unpredictable outcomes.

Castells's (1996, 1997, 1998) major work, the three-volume *The Information Age: Economy, Society, and Culture* spanning some 1,500 pages, provides a dazzling array of insights into how "informational capitalism" operates. In essence, he argues that this distinctive form of capitalism – with its globalizing reach and flexible adaptability to change – is recasting the imperatives of time, space, and distance around the globe. In tracing the origins of its organizing principles to the early 1970s, Castells maintains that the historical coincidence of three processes became evident at that time: the information technology revolution; the economic crises of both capitalism and statism (and their subsequent restructuring); and the "blooming" of cultural social movements. By examining the interaction between these interdependent processes, together with the responses they engender, he discerns the emergence of the network society as a new dominant social structure (see also Castells 2000, 2001).

From this perspective, the familiar notion of an "information society" can be safely discarded. In its place, Castells seeks to elaborate a grounded theory of information technology-powered networks. The distinguishing feature of the network society, he believes, is its dialectical interaction between modes of production (goods and services are created in specific social relationships) and those of development (especially technological innovation). This interaction is neither linear nor mechanical in the manner in which it operates. Nor, crucially, is it contained within the authority of the nation-state. Rather, the network society is indicative of a new power system, where the once sovereign nation-state's very legitimacy is tested by factors largely beyond its control.

Castells's approach has been heralded for being suggestive of fresh ways to investigate the geometry of power unfolding around us. We are poised at the cusp of a technological revolution, he explains, one centered around microelectronics-based information/communication technologies and related sciences (such as genetic engineering and nanotechnology). Knowledge generation, together with information processing, are at the heart of this dramatic transformation. Evolving in conjunction with this emergent "ecosocial system," he contends, is a new informational/global economy, as well as a new culture of real virtuality.

Turning first to the dynamics of this new economy, Castells describes how the international division of labor is changing, and in so doing becoming increasingly reliant on informational-based production and competition. This informational economy is global and networked, that is, it is marked by its interdependence, its asymmetry, and its dissolution of the familiar features of historical and economic geography. Capitalism is rapidly acquiring an enhanced flexibility mainly due to the decisive role played by these emergent "tools for networking, distant communication, storing/processing of information, coordinated individualization of work, and [the] simultaneous concentration and decentralization of decision-making" (1998: 368). This "new brand of capitalism," with its new rules for investment, accumulation, and reward, is encompassing almost the entire planet (North Korea, he notes, being the one exception) for the first time in human history.

Against this backdrop, Castells discerns the culture of real virtuality. In his words, it is "a system in which reality itself (that is, people's material/symbolic existence) is fully immersed in a virtual image setting, in the world of make believe, in which symbols are not just metaphors, but comprise the actual experience" (1998: 381). To clarify, this culture is real, but also virtual in that it is constructed primarily through electronically based processes of communication. This virtuality is, in effect, a "fundamental reality" where questions of identity are made meaningful. That is, in Castells's view, it is "the material basis on which we live our existence, construct our system of representation, practice our work, link up with other people, retrieve information, form our opinions, act in politics, and nurture our dreams" (2001: 203). Efforts to explicate the lived materiality of this culture at the level of experience thus need to recognize that all domains of social life are implicated ever more deeply in the time-spaces of networked communication.

More specifically, two emergent forms of time and space, namely, "timeless time" and "the space of flows," characterize the network society. While both coexist with prior forms of time and space, their inflection in the new social structure pinpoints their significance. Timeless time, defined in contrast with the rhythm of biological time and the tick of clock time, represents the way new information/communication technologies are exploited to "annihilate time." That is, time is both compressed (e.g., split-second global financial transactions) and desequenced (e.g., in the blurring of past, present, and future by electronic hypertext). The space of flows refers to the ways in which social practices can be organized without geographical contiguity. Citing examples such as financial markets, transnational production, media systems, even social movements, Castells shows how they revolve around relationships connecting people and places (often in real time) that are otherwise being processed within distant, decentered networks. These relationships entail a territorial dimension, but are not conditioned by it in the same way that the space of places (where meaning, function, and locality are closely related) tend to be negotiated.

In documenting the contours of the network society, then, this approach underscores the ways in which information has become the "privileged political weapon" in the age of the Internet. The displacement of human values by commercial ones is rendered especially sharp where the uneven structures of the digital divide are concerned. As Castells points out, to be "disconnected, or superficially connected, to the Internet is tantamount to marginalization in the global, networked system" (2001: 269). Precisely how the dynamics of differential access unfold in different social contexts is largely a matter of possessing the capacity – or not – to adapt to the speed and uncertainty of change. "The differentiation between Internet-haves and have-nots," he observes, "adds a fundamental cleavage to existing sources of inequality and social exclusion in a complex interaction that appears to increase the gap between the promise of the Information Age and its bleak reality for many people around the world" (2001: 247).

These and related issues highlight several of the reasons why the "network society" concept continues to figure so prominently in sociological research and debate. Castells's conceptual elucidation of its myriad features using empirical, cross-cultural modes of investigation constitutes a major contribution.

SEE ALSO: Capitalism; Global Economy; Globalization, Culture and; Information Society; Information Technology; Internet; Media and Globalization; Media, Network(s) and; Networks; Spatial Relationships; Time

REFERENCES AND SUGGESTED READINGS

Castells, M. (1996) *The Rise of the Network Society.* Blackwell, Oxford.
Castells, M. (1997) *The Power of Identity.* Blackwell, Oxford.
Castells, M. (1998) *End of Millennium.* Blackwell, Oxford.
Castells, M. (2000) Materials for an Exploratory Theory of the Network Society. *British Journal of Sociology* 51(1): 5–24.
Castells, M. (2001) *The Internet Galaxy.* Oxford University Press, Oxford.

networks

James J. Chriss

The concept of social networks finds its beginnings in the work of Georg Simmel. Simmel argued that a pure or formal sociology ought to take as its special focus the study of societal forms. Employing a geometric analogy, Simmel suggested that social forms can be identified and defined, thereby allowing the sociologist to group together a myriad of substantive phenomena under the broader or more abstract formal categories.

But instead of geometric sides and angles, the essential elements comprising the forms for sociological analysis are simply human social interaction (or what Simmel called "sociation"). As Simmel (1950: 22) explained, the societal forms "are conceived as constituting society (and societies) out of the mere sum of living men. The study of this second area may be called 'pure sociology,' which abstracts the mere element of sociation." Building on Simmel and certainly going beyond him, the social networks approach is a type of structural sociology which emphasizes the relationships between social units (see Blau 1994: 3–8). It was not until the 1930s that an explicit networks research agenda appeared, first in the guise of Jacob Moreno's sociometric studies (see, e.g., Moreno 1941) and later, for example, in Elizabeth Bott's (1957) study of the network characteristics of the family.

The social units of network analysis can be persons, small groups, organizations, and even larger entities. A good illustration of network analysis couched at the macro level is Alderson and Beckfield's (2004) study of power and position in the world city or global system. This research verifies that certain "world cities" such as Tokyo, New York, and Paris are more powerful and prestigious within the global city system because of their high degree of centrality (for more on this concept, see below) relative to other cities.

A convention of network theory is to use the term node to refer to a position, that is, a network location occupied by an actor (whether an individual, group, or organization). Actors in this sense are "decision-making entities" that occupy positions (nodes) linked by relations (or ties) (Markovsky et al. 1988). Owing largely to the work of Linton Freeman (1979), one of the more important network concepts is centrality, namely, the extent to which an actor is centrally located within a network. Degree centrality is the number of direct links with other actors. Betweenness centrality is the extent to which an actor mediates, or falls between, any other two actors on the shortest path between those actors (Brass 1995). In whichever guise it appears, the issue of centrality is of abiding concern to network theorists. Actors in central network positions have greater access to, and potential control over, relevant resources. Actors who are able to control relevant resources are able to acquire power, largely by increasing others' dependence on them (Krackhardt & Brass 1994: 210).

Although much early network research had indeed found support for the idea that nodes centrally located in networks tend to hold more power relative to other nodes, later generations of researchers, who have introduced more complexity into their research designs with the introduction of elements of exchange theory (e.g., the research tradition of network exchange theory innovated by David Willer), have been more apt to view the association between power and centrality as a hypothesis requiring empirical confirmation (see Mizruchi & Potts 1998).

How centrality is related to power has much to do with the starting assumptions researchers make about the nature of networks. In network theory, one of the preferred research strategies is small group experimental research. An example of this kind of small group experimental design is the network exchange model of identity developed by Peter J. Burke (1997). Burke seeks to augment the general finding from network theory that power is associated with one's position in network structures (again, those with higher centrality tend to be more powerful in exchange relations), by examining more closely the processes at work in exchange networks. In other words, Burke seeks to answer the question: "What are actors trying to accomplish from the positions they occupy in particular networks?" Although network location is indeed important, perhaps just as important in determining what actors are attempting to accomplish is the way identity processes operate to structure exchanges.

Burke placed research subjects into simulated exchange situations, taking them through 40 rounds of exchange to determine how a preestablished pool of points (in this case, 24) would be distributed upon completion of the rounds of exchange. What Burke discovered was that, by introducing identity (by way of the assumptions concerning actors' participation reference standards) into the network exchange design, long-term stability was reached only after actors made the decision to break off into smaller subnetworks. Since the highest-level identity standard is to participate in exchange 100 percent of the time, actors found that subnetworking helped them achieve close to the 100 percent participation reference standard. In networks consisting of odd numbers of nodes – such as the five-node kite structure – actors who exchanged did so in adjacent dyads, which meant one node was always excluded. The excluded persons would always offer slightly more (13 points), then upon reentry into the exchange relationship would settle back on the 12/12 point of stability characteristic of the dyadic exchanges. This also appears to be a living, breathing example of the way equity considerations structure such activities.

Burke's study of how identity processes affect exchange relations is consistent with the concept of negotiated exchange, the latter of which is illustrated in a study conducted by Lovaglia et al. (1995). These authors set up experiments in which profit expectations of the subjects were taken into account. Two factors that have been found to affect profit expectations, and hence the actual forms of exchange and negotiation taking place between actors in various network configurations, are degree centrality and the likelihood of a person completing exchanges with another. Actors who perceive themselves to be central as a result of many direct ties to others are more likely to expect that they will do well in exchanges as a result of their central position, and this expectation of profit affects negotiation strategy; for example, they are more likely to resist an offer that appears to be lower than what they could reasonably expect given their location and history of negotiations. This illustrates a general trend within network studies, namely, the move toward a more dynamic model of exchange that takes into account the history of ongoing negotiations, rather than relying on initial offers as in the case of earlier experimental studies.

As Simmel (1950) noted long ago, triads are stable to the extent that they are transitive, meaning that feelings and relations among the members of the group are balanced or consistent (Caplow 1968). However, if for example one member of the triad begins accumulating resources far above the level of the other two members, we now have an intransitive triad in which the ties between members are qualitatively unequal, as in Granovetter's (1973) "forbidden triad." Intransitive triads are unstable and therefore susceptible to coalition formation, a situation in which the two weaker or oppressed members of the triad combine their resources to oppose the stronger member. Indeed, coalition formation is one method by which weak or exploited members of coalitions seek to reduce power differences.

Bonacich and Applebaum's (2000) research on the basic structure of the garment industry in Los Angeles is a useful illustration of coalition formation within networks. These authors discovered that manufacturers try to ensure that the various contractors they work with are not known to one another. By doing this, manufacturers hope to strengthen their bargaining position with contractors because they can always claim that some unknown contractor has tendered a better offer. This prevents concerted action, that is, coalition formation, on the part of contractors to nullify or reduce the advantageous position manufacturers enjoy. Bonacich and Applebaum (2000) go on to report that manufacturers ensure their edge by proclaiming their contractor lists are "trade secrets," a position backed and enforced by federal trade law.

Perhaps the single most influential contribution to network analysis is Mark Granovetter's (1973) conceptual distinction between weak and strong ties. According to Granovetter, strong ties exist between persons who know one another very well (e.g., family members and close friends). Weak ties, on the other hand, exist between loosely associated nodes, that is, between persons who are merely acquaintances. Persons who are loosely associated may act as a

bridge between clumps of densely tied friendship networks. These dense networks of strong ties would have no connections with other networks were it not for the occasional node weakly tied between them. Hence, in an ironic twist, Granovetter illustrates the strength of weak ties. Weak ties have a special role in a person's opportunity for mobility. Individuals with few or no weak ties will be deprived of information from distant parts of the network, and by the same token, being caught up in strong-tie networks, they will receive only news and views of their close friends. The lack of interaction with diverse individuals situated beyond a person's local, dense network means that the person will be less likely to hear about potential job openings, and hence, mobility is restricted (Granovetter 1983).

The advantages of weak ties, whereby an actor acts as a bridge between two densely tied networks or subnetworks, has also been explored by Ronald Burt. Burt's (1992) concept of structural holes is almost as well known as Granovetter's weak tie/strong tie distinction. Whereas the great majority of network analysis is concerned with the nature and strength of ties between nodes, structural holes turn analytical attention toward the absence of ties. Because nodes in densely clustered networks tend to receive redundant information, some actors may seek to invest in connections to diverse others in order to receive novel or non-redundant information. These nodes must be disconnected from other nodes in order to ensure information is non-redundant. It is these disconnections between diverse others that are structural holes. For example, expertise in a particular field (such as the position of journal editor) allows gatekeepers to monopolize information and maintain structural holes (Corra & Willer 2002). Similarly, ideas which are endorsed by more distant contacts (such as external reviewers) are more likely to be considered good or important than those endorsed by friends or other close acquaintances (Burt 2004).

SEE ALSO: Economy, Networks and; Exchange Network Theory; Power, Theories of; Simmel, Georg; Social Exchange Theory; Social Movements, Networks and; Social Network Analysis; Social Network Theory; Weak Ties (Strength of)

REFERENCES AND SUGGESTED
READINGS

Alderson, A. S. & Beckfield, J. (2004) Power and
Position in the World City System. *American Journal of Sociology* 109(4): 811–51.

Blau, P. M. (1994) *Structural Contexts of Opportunity*.
University of Chicago Press, Chicago.

Bonacich, E. & Applebaum, R. (2000) *Behind the
Label: Inequality in the Los Angeles Apparel Industry*. University of California Press, Berkeley.

Bott, E. (1957) *Family and Social Network: Roles,
Norms, and External Relationships in Ordinary
Urban Families*. Tavistock, London.

Brass, D. J. (1995) A Social Network Perspective on
Human Resources Management. In: Ferris, G. R.
(Ed.), *Research in Personnel and Human Resources
Management*, Vol. 13. JAI Press, Stamford, CT,
pp. 9–79.

Burke, P. J. (1997) An Identity Model for Network
Exchange. *American Sociological Review* 62: 134–50.

Burt, R. S. (1992) *Structural Holes*. Harvard University Press, Cambridge, MA.

Burt, R. S. (2004) Structural Holes and Good Ideas.
American Journal of Sociology 110(2): 349–99.

Caplow, T. (1968) *Two Against One: Coalitions in
Triads*. Prentice-Hall, Englewood Cliffs, NJ.

Corra, M. & Willer, D. (2002) The Gatekeeper.
Sociological Theory 20(2): 180–207.

Freeman, L. C. (1979) Centrality in Social Networks
I: The Conceptual Clarification. *Social Networks* 1:
215–39.

Granovetter, M. S. (1973) The Strength of Weak
Ties. *American Journal of Sociology* 78(6): 1360–80.

Granovetter, M. S. (1983) The Strength of Weak
Ties: A Network Theory Revisited. *Sociological
Theory* 1: 201–33.

Krackhardt, D. & Brass, D. J. (1994) Intraorganizational Networks: The Micro Side. In: Wasserman,
S. & Galaskiewicz, J. (Eds.), *Advances in Social
Network Analysis: Research in the Social and Behavioral Sciences*. Sage, Thousand Oaks, CA,
pp. 207–29.

Lovaglia, M. J., Skvoretz, J., Willer, D., & Markovsky, B. (1995) Negotiated Exchanges in Social
Networks. *Social Forces* 74: 123–55.

Markovsky, B., Willer, D., & Patton, T. (1988)
Power Relations in Exchange Networks. *American
Sociological Review* 53: 220–36.

Mizruchi, M. S. & Potts, B. B. (1998) Centrality and
Power Revisited: Actor Success in Group Decision Making. *Social Networks* 20: 353–87.

Moreno, J. L. (1941) *Foundations of Sociometry*. Beacon House, New York.

Simmel, G. (1950) *The Sociology of Georg Simmel*.
Trans. and Ed. K. H. Wolff. Free Press, New York.

neurosociology

David D. Franks

Neurosociology is an inquiry into the social
dimensions of functioning brains and the fusion
of brain functioning with minded behavior and
self processes. Neurosociology puts individualistic tabula rasa theories of knowledge to rest.
The environment may trigger responses, but
the brain selects, interprets, edits, and changes
the very quality of incoming information to
fit its own requirements and limitations. Much
of this "revisionism" is produced by its robust
cognitive and emotional capacities. The "living
content" of these capacities (meanings) are
supplied by culture and human talk. Working brains develop only in interaction with other
brains and the cultural content they produce
(Brothers 1997). This makes experience more
of a projection than a recording. Thus, the
largely interpretive and culture-dependent nature of selfhood, memory, and even sensed perception opens the door to neurosociology. It
studies the effect of culture and learning environments on brain processes and neuronal structure, as well as the effect of brain processes in
creating emergent social structures.

In 1972 TenHouten was a co-author of the
first publication using the term neurosociology. The next year, TenHouten co-authored
the first sociological inquiry into scientific
and synthetic modes of thought based on the
different capacities of the brain's hemispheres.
In the late 1980s and early 1990s TenHouten
was editor of the Social Neuroscience Bulletin
and has continually contributed to what he has
referred to as neurosociology since that date.
The first collection of works in neurosociology, edited by Franks and Smith, was published
in 1999.

Some exemplar findings from that volume
are as follows. Culture "works down" to effect
neuronal structure. Ecological demands on various cultures differentially select certain brain
capacities as valuable for that society. Since
different parts of the brain have different capacities, certain neurological systems are used and
developed more than others depending on the
society. TenHouten has found that Australian

Aborigines utilize the gestalt-synthetic capabilities of the right brain more than westerners, who make relatively more use of the logical-analytic left brain capacities. This leads, for example, to extraordinary aboriginal skills in tracking and route-finding valuable in their desert culture. It also means that time is experienced cyclically rather than in western linearity. When the experience of time differs fundamentally, so do many other aspects of existence.

In contrast, brain structures also "work up" to influence structure. Smith et al. have investigated the way brain processes that help control anxiety create emergent qualities in family organization. Neurosociology has also drawn on the predominantly emotional makeup of the human brain to challenge the model of affect-free rationality assumed by rational decision-making theorists. Highly intelligent persons injured in the ventromedial prefrontal cortexes can think of an emotion but cannot feel it. Having no felt preferences, decision-making is limited and learning is impaired (Damasio 1994). Not able to care about people or their own futures, patients lack the social skills and impulse control necessary for social interaction and business judgments. Turner (2000) has investigated the biological embeddedness of social interaction and the subliminal emotional cues communicated to others in face-to-face encounters. He has also offered an evolutionary theory of the brain which explains why humans frequently chafe at social constraint; this perspective suggests corrections to sociology's "oversocialized conception of man."

Gregory has investigated subliminal voice accommodation and how social status signals embedded in the human soundwaves communicate dominance and subordination to audiences. Such an analysis was effective in predicting the outcome of the 1992 presidential and vice presidential debates between Clinton and Dole as well as Gore and Kemp. Tredway et al. have reanalyzed Spitz's findings that lack of emotional support caused major physiological, social, and psychological dysfunctions in infants to the point of breakdown in their immune systems and death. The identification of these brain processes is critical for effective intervention and social policy decisions.

TOPICS OF MUTUAL INTEREST BETWEEN NEUROSCIENCE AND SOCIOLOGY

Despite the vast differences in methods and paradigms, current social psychology and neuroscience have agreed on several important topics as critical for understanding human behavior. Research using highly technical imaging techniques as well as patient brain injuries is in strong contrast to methods of sociology. However, a very strong argument for validity is made possible when convergence occurs regardless of differences in method and conceptual frameworks.

In both fields the linguistically generated self, once seen as a notion of dubious value to science, has risen to a key concept in understanding human behavior. These convergences include the importance of an "agentive" view of the self regardless of its fictional nature, and the crucial nature of role-taking (or mind reading) in establishing a normally functioning brain (see Brothers 1997 on the lack of this ability in autism). Convergence is especially interesting on the importance of viewing self as a process enabling the flexible control of behavior and the self-conscious monitoring and control of impulses (see LeDoux et al. 2003).

Following from the image of the brain as a "projective" editor of experience, both fields converge on some form of constructionism (Franks 2003). Findings leading to this conclusion are as follows. (1) The brain manufactures patterns even where there are none. (2) Our brains are not perfect. Recently evolved brain mechanisms must be built on and constrained by preexisting structures. (3) The brain must heavily edit and simplify perceptual information for it to be processed as meaningful. (4) The brain has a tendency to capture and remember only "the gist" of things. (5) The number of human senses is totally inadequate to apprehend "what is out there." (6) The boundaries of human reason are limited to concepts arising from contact experience with the physical world and the metaphors they allow. The possibility of generating determinate knowledge transcending the peculiar nature of the human body and brain becomes highly questionable in light of current neuroscience.

Another long-recognized convergence is the continued neuroscience finding concerning the critical function that language plays in the construction of human thought and the normal functioning of the brain. As early as 1969, Lindesmith and Strauss noted the sociological importance of work on aphasia by Head in 1926, Goldstein in 1948, and Luria in 1966. Both fields are interested in the way language permeates human thought when seen as inner dialogue.

DIVERGENCES AND APPARENT DIVERGENCES

Many sociologists still see any biological framework as reductionistic and antithetical to sociocultural explanations. Certainly, the charge is not accurate among most of the leading neuroscientists writing to audiences beyond neuroscience. In 1965 the Nobel Prize winner Roger Sperry wrote that thought itself was an emergent from the parts of the brain's neuronal communication process. He argued that self-conscious thought in the dominant left hemisphere of the brain exerted causal, top-down control over the more specific modular parts of the non-verbal right brain. This put mind back into positivistic neuroscience and, as Sperry and his influential students knew, where there is mind there is society. Michael Gazzaniga, Sperry's student, built on his non-reductionist approach in his seminal split-brain research so commonly accepted in neuroscience and also so important to neurosociology (see Franks & Smith 1999; TenHouten 1999).

Importance of the Unconscious

Some sociologists may be uncomfortable with the neuroscience emphasis on the unconscious because they associate it with the more fanciful early notions of Sigmund Freud. The unconscious of neuroscience is derived from very different methods of investigation and has little resemblance to such ideas. For example, Lakoff and Johnson (in Franks & Smith 1999) state that at least 95 percent of cognitive functioning is outside of awareness, and Gazzaniga (1998) insists on 97 percent. For a three-pound brain that consists of between ten to one hundred

billion neurons, one hundred trillion synaptic connections, and nine times as many gial cells, however, the remaining 3 percent of conscious deliberation is more than significant for sociologists. It includes the processes of self-awareness, role-taking, and the agentive self as well as the social control making society possible. None of this challenges theories of self-awareness. One smells, tastes, and sees with no knowledge of the brain mechanisms involved. In this context, thinking, feeling, and self-monitoring are accomplished with equal unawareness of the brain dynamics making this possible.

A second issue relating to the importance of unconscious processes is the fact that most of what humans become aware of doing actually begins one-quarter of a second before it becomes conscious (see Gazzaniga 1998). However, this finding is not that different from G. H. Mead's insight concerning the four stages of the act: "Stimuli are means," he wrote to Dewey, "[t]endency is the real thing." Here, impulse and tendency overlap significantly. Perception, manipulation, and consummation as other stages of the act subserve these impulses, most of which come too fast for conscious recognition. For example, we selectively perceive those stimuli that support or block manipulations gratifying our impulses. Current neurological evidence for this comes from many sources, but perhaps findings from split-brain research have been most dramatic on this general point.

When the two brain halves have been severed from each other (in order to control epilepsy), researchers can communicate orders to the mute right brain without the patient's conscious left brain knowing what the orders were. This is because the usual electrical and chemical communication between the hemispheres no longer exists. When the patients act according to the researchers' orders, their linguistic and cognitively oriented left brain immediately produces what amounts to an ad hoc rationalization or motive statement for the action. The only ones fooled about the source of the behavior are the patients, whose totally contrived explanations come too fast to notice the effort involved in creating their own reasons. There is ample evidence that normals also generally act first and rationalize later. Once again, impulse (much of which can be below awareness) is the beginning of the act, as G. H. Mead suggested. Gazzaniga explicitly views these rationalizations as sociological "accounts" with their concern for culpability in the eyes of others. This produces impressive convergence on the importance of accounts as well as very strong supporting evidence for them.

The modular makeup of the brain also gives insight into the sources of impulses that the self must monitor. The brain is comprised of separate modules, each with their own tendencies for memories, moods, actions, and other responses. The modules of the right brain deal with special perception such as face recognition, tactile information, and special orientation. The right brain, lacking ability or interest in cognitive interpretations, is accurate, precise, and literalistic. Its modules have no deductive capacity. In contrast, the left brain is interpretive to the extent of rendering things meaningful even when they are not. Guided by cognitions mainly generated and organized by language and social learning, it allows predictions, deductive powers, and flexibility at the cost of guaranteed accuracy. Nonetheless, the left brain provides executive power and goal direction to the brain's impulsive cross-purposes and it must struggle to make the unity necessary for sanity out of the "modular army of idiots," as they are called by Dennett. The left brain is called the "interpreter" because of this integrative, executive character. The sense of unity and control it supplies, being the result of its own prioritizing and editing, is by necessity fictional. There is no real way to make sense of the various contradictory modular impulses. But this fiction is essential for effective action and must be seen as important in its own right. It becomes who we are. Patients traumatized in the medial prefrontal cortex (where self-related processes come together) lose the sense of ownership of their bodies. Since unity demands continuity, the self becomes a narrator taking its content from memory and being the owner of its story. Memory, however, is a notoriously inaccurate, self-enhancing process always recreated in the present rather than reproducing actual past events. Emotionally experienced events are those most often remembered. The necessary sense of unity and continuity of the self is built on shifting sands. The question is not so much "from whence comes insanity?" as "from whence comes sanity?"

The most significant finding about the unconscious for social psychology is the ubiquity of implicit social learning. The emotional amygdala, in the primitive part of the brain, functions to give lightning-fast assessments of the self-relevance of oncoming stimuli. Without cognitive contributions, it enables quick responses to danger but is often very wrong. Banaji (2003) has used this fast, unmonitored response to measure prejudice, asking respondents to answer questions so quickly that self-monitoring cannot come into play. She found that black, white, and Asian unmonitored responses overwhelmingly showed a preference for their own kind regardless of one's self-conscious convictions otherwise. Banaji's research has been broadened to measure a host of unconscious group preferences like class standings, ethnicities, and places of residence. Here too, people implicitly prefer the company of others seen as similar to themselves. Therefore, much prejudice and ethnocentrism is learned implicitly and not under cognitive control. Prejudiced persons are frequently the last to know. This not only contributes to our understandings of race relations, but also directs attention to the importance of human impulses and unconscious selfhood.

The self and its monitoring functions are nonetheless real in terms of interactional consequences and the authentic determination to control certain impulses. Another possible divergence has to do with the importance of unconscious emotions and how they (1) determine the agenda for thought; (2) select what is salient to one's thinking; and (3) become the terms in which one sees the world. Being the lens through which the world is experienced, emotions can be the last to be noticed. For example, insofar as beliefs are ideas held with the emotion of conviction, persons evaluate evidence only insofar as it maintains the belief. Thus, political and religious arguments between equally intelligent people have little to do with reasoned opinion, because the opinion guides the reason. They usually lead nowhere.

In contrast to purely constructionist views of emotions seen as linguistic products through and through, neuroscience has generated other evidence that non-verbal, unconscious emotion is a prime driver of minded behavior. The neural pathways between cognition in the prefrontal cortex and emotional systems in the so-called limbic system influence each other because they run both ways. Nonetheless, the connections running from emotional systems to the cognitive ones are far greater. Emotion fixes us in the world and cognition allows flexibility, but as with the impulses produced in split-brain research, emotionally driven impulses are prior to cognitive considerations. Once again, by the time an event becomes conscious, the brain's emotional systems "shower the neocortex with emotional messages that condition its perception" (Massy 2002). Every phenomenological event has a neurological substratum. Each is as real as the other.

SEE ALSO: Biosociological Theories; Emotion: Social Psychological Aspects; Mead, George Herbert; Reflexivity; Role-Taking; Self; Social Cognition; Symbolic Interaction

REFERENCES AND SUGGESTED READINGS

Banaji, M. R. (2003) *Mind Bugs: The Psychology of Ordinary Prejudice*. Mind Science Institute, San Antonio, TX.
Brothers, L. (1997) *Friday's Footprint: How Society Shapes the Human Mind*. Oxford University Press, New York.
Damasio, A. (1994) *Descartes' Error: Emotion, Reason, and the Human Brain*. Avon Books, New York.
Franks, D. (2003) Mutual Interests, Different Lenses: Current Neuroscience and Symbolic Interaction. *Symbolic Interaction* 26: 613–30.
Franks, D. & Smith, T. (Eds.) (1999) Mind, Brain, and Society: Towards a Neurosociology of Emotion. Vol. 5: Social Perspectives on Emotions. Elsevier Sciences, Amsterdam.
Gazzaniga, J. (1969) *The Social Brain: Discovering the Networks of the Mind*. Basic Books, New York.
Gazzaniga, J. (1998) *The Mind's Past*. University of California Press, Berkeley.
LeDoux, J. (1996) *The Emotional Brain: The Mysterious Underpinnings of Emotional Life*. Simon & Schuster, New York.
LeDoux, J., Debiec, J., & Moss, H. (Eds.) (2003) *The Self from Soul to Brain: Annals of the New York Academy of Sciences*, Vol. 1001. New York Academy of Sciences, New York.
Massy, D. S. (2002) A Brief History of Human Society: The Origin and Role of Emotion in Social Life. *American Sociological Review* 67(1): 1–29.
TenHouten, W. (1999) Explorations in Neurosociological Theory: From the Spectrum of Affect to Time Consciousness. In: Franks, D. & Smith, T. (Eds.), Mind, Brain, and Society: Towards a Neurosociology of Emotion. Vol. 5: Social Perspectives on Emotions. Elsevier Sciences, Amsterdam, pp. 41–80.
Turner, J. (1999) The Neurology of Emotion: Implications for Sociological Theories of Interpersonal Behavior. In: Franks, D. & Smith, T. (Eds.), Mind, Brain, and Society: Towards a Neurosociology of Emotion. Vol. 5: Social Perspectives on Emotions. Elsevier Sciences, Amsterdam, pp. 81–108.
Turner, J. (2000) *On the Origins of Human Emotions: A Sociological Inquiry into the Evolution of Human Affect*. Stanford University Press, Stanford.

New Age

Massimo Introvigne

Although "New Age" is now a household term throughout the world, its precise definition remains elusive. Sociologists have insisted that, although it is often referred to as the "New Age movement," it is not really a social movement but a network. Disparate "alternative" groups started networking together in the 1960s and met in common festivals, meetings, and conferences under the general label of "New Age," and the common concept that a new, better era was coming. The Findhorn community in Scotland and the Esalen Institute in Big Sur, California, both established in 1962, are regarded by many as the beginning of the international network, although "New Age" became internationally well known only in the 1970s. The network emphasized its "alternative" nature, seeking at the same time forms of spirituality different from western mainline Christianity, healing techniques alternative to mainline medicine and psychology, and a style of political participation different from traditional parties and organizations. New Age was largely a coming together of preexisting networks, from

those focused on eastern or metaphysical spirituality to those interested in non-mainstream
medicine or "deep" ecology. In this sense, some
sociologists defined New Age as a network of
networks, or metanetwork.

The roots of this metanetwork lie in different
traditions. It may be suggested that the international network of New Age really included
two rather different conflicting wings. The first
had its roots in the occult subculture, and was
influenced by both the western esoteric tradition and eastern religions. Influenced by the
Theosophical Society and by the movement of
Alice Bailey (1880–1949), who first used the
term "New Age" in its contemporary meaning
in the 1920s, this esoteric tradition also included
a form of progressive or optimistic millennialism (Wessinger 1988) inspired by Annie Besant
(1847–1933). This wing of New Age focused on
the coming of a global renewal and of an "Age
of Aquarius," an astrological concept originating with French esoteric author Paul Le Cour
(1871–1954) and supposedly connected with a
forthcoming golden age.

On the other hand, New Age included a
second wing which was influenced by the tradition of a much more individually oriented
spirituality, including the nineteenth- and early
twentieth-century New Thought and positive
thinking (Melton et al. 1991: 346). Neither of
these traditions, unlike those influential on the
New Age's first wing, were millenarian, nor did
they focus on a future global renewal of the
society. Rather, they focused on the individual.
Occasionally, seminars and groups centered on
the promise of individual happiness were criticized within the New Age as spiritually selfish,
or as a form of narcissism. On the other hand,
British sociologist Paul Heelas (1996) indicated
that individualistic "seminar religion" was
always part and parcel of the New Age.

While in the 1970s and 1980s the utopian first
wing dominated the New Age, by the 1990s
several leading New Age spokespersons were
discussing a "crisis" of the network, which eventually led to the emergence of a "second" New
Age (occasionally referred to in some continental
European countries, but never in the United
States, as "Next Age") much more focused
on the aims and techniques of the individualistic second wing. A significant event spelling
out the New Age crisis was the publication

in 1991 of *Reimagination of the World*, by David
Spangler, possibly the most authoritative spokes-
person for the New Age movement internationally, and William Irwin Thompson (Spangler &
Thompson 1991). The book presented lectures given by Spangler and Thompson at two
1988–9 seminars, where they concluded that
New Age had been "degraded" by commercialism and was in a state of deep crisis. When this
crisis was examined by social scientists, they did
not mention commercialism as the only (or even
the most important) cause. Melton (1998a)
argued, for instance, that, in the United States
at least, there were empirically verifiable indicators of New Age's impending crisis, including
the bankruptcy of several New Age bookstores,
publishing houses, and magazines, and the fall
in the price of crystals, a crucial commodity in
the New Age market. Melton acknowledged
that commercialism was deeply resented by a
number of New Agers. However, he also mentioned that the utopian, millenarian expectation
of a golden age had failed the empirical test.

Sociological theories on millennial thought
have proposed a distinction between "catastrophic" and "progressive" millennialism
(Wessinger 2000). While catastrophic millennialism can usually claim that at least some small
catastrophe has confirmed its doomsday predictions, progressive millennialism is more exposed
to empirical disconfirmation. When a prophecy
about an apocalyptic event fails, it is easier to
claim that wars, epidemics, and other catastrophic events have at any rate occurred somewhere in the world. But, when a "progressive"
millennial group such as the New Age
announces a golden age, and fails to deliver,
crisis is inevitable. When its promised golden
age failed to materialize, New Age first resorted
to messages channeled by supernatural
"entities." It claimed that these entities were
in a position to know better, and perhaps a
new, golden age was in fact emerging on Planet
Earth. Human eyes were not capable of seeing it,
but superhuman channeled Masters had other
and safer ways of knowing. Ultimately, however, the idea that a "New Age" of general
happiness was in fact manifesting itself, notwithstanding any evidence to the contrary,
could not be sustained. Empirical disconfirmation prevailed over prophetic utterances. The
New Age crisis was, thus, neither purely a

byproduct of excessive commercialism nor an invention of scholars, as some irate New Agers claimed. Ultimately, New Age went the same way as many other forms of progressive millennialism had gone before it.

In the face of the crisis, a number of New Agers simply abandoned the movement, but there is no evidence that this was the prevailing response. The two main tenets of "classic" New Age were, firstly, that a golden age of higher consciousness was manifesting itself on Planet Earth; and secondly, that it was possible to cooperate with this happy manifestation without the need of a dogmatic creed or formal structures. When crisis struck, one possible reaction was to claim that the utopian aim of the New Age was still achievable, but that the flexible network was not the most appropriate tool. Rather, organized, hierarchical movements with a strong and clearly identified leadership were needed. "Classic" New Age was not a new religious movement. It did not, for instance, recognize, and indeed often scorned, leaders authorized by definition to declare a creed. Post-New Age movements entrust precisely their authoritative leaders with the task of "saving" New Age from its crisis. While J. Z. Knight started her career as the quintessential New Age channeler, she later established what she calls an American Gnostic school in Yelms (Washington). There, nobody questions her right (or, rather, the right of Ramtha, the ancient spirit she channels) to define a creed or a doctrine. The New Age audience of J. Z. Knight, the channeler, thus became Ramtha's School of Ancient Wisdom, a post-New Age new religious movement (Melton 1998b). Older movements, marginalized in "classic" New Age because they operated within closed (rather than open) structures with a precise creed and an authoritative leader, saw themselves revitalized in the wake of the New Age crisis. In Italy a number of former New Agers joined Damanhur, a community of some 400 members near Turin which calls itself "Aquarian" but, at the same time, makes clear creedal statements (see Berzano 1997) and affirms the authority of the founder-leader, Oberto Airaudi, to define or change doctrine. Joining a post-New Age new religious movement is not, however, the only possible solution to the New Age crisis for those unwilling to simply abandon it. A larger number of New Agers seem more interested in redefining New Age itself.

That redefinition involved New Age's passage from the third to the first person. While New Age had been described as a "sacralization of the Self" (Heelas 1996), the "second New Age" is rather a "sacralization of myself." Classic, utopian New Age argued that Planet Earth, as a whole, was heading toward a new age of collective higher consciousness and happiness. The neo-New Age recognizes that a golden age may never happen collectively, in and for the whole planet. What remains possible, however, is that an enlightened minority will enter into its personal New Age through certain exercises and techniques. Whilst such techniques are not substantially different from those advocated by classic New Agers, the "second" New Age is conceived as private while the first was public and collective. The new trend confines itself to nothing more than a promise of individual happiness. The network itself becomes less important and organized, and most remain in contact with this neo-New Age by simply reading books or renting videos. Whether or not individual well-being achieved by a significant number of individuals will also cause Planet Earth to heal is a vague, secondary possibility, and is no longer regarded as crucial. To this, a mythological self-reinterpretation of New Age history is added, whereby it is claimed that the original network was never really millenarian or utopian, that the idea of a future Aquarian Age was merely a poetic metaphor, and that individual self-transformation was always the movement's primary aim.

"When prophecy fails," it has been argued, catastrophic millennialism may nonetheless prosper through processes of cognitive dissonance (Festinger et al. 1956). The evolution of the New Age indicates that the process may indeed be different in catastrophic and progressive millennialism. When the optimistic prophecy of progressive millennialism fails, one possibility is privatization. The prophecy, it could be argued, may still come true for a selected group of individuals, although it will probably *not* come true for society, or Planet Earth, as a whole. When progressive millennial utopia fails, private utopias restricted to personal life may develop through privatization processes.

Whether there are really two different New Ages, the first and the second, or whether the New Age is one and differences should not be overemphasized, depends on how New Age is reconstructed. If one assumes, as Hanegraaff (1996) does, that utopianism was or is not crucial for New Age, it could be argued that no New Age crisis has ever taken place, and that the movement in the 2000s remains essentially the same phenomenon as existed in the 1980s. Definitions are, of course, result-oriented tools, and no definition of New Age is any more "true" than another. It may be argued, however, that definitions (or descriptions) of New Age, in which the utopia of a forthcoming golden age was crucial, were widespread within the community of New Agers themselves. In this respect, the non-utopian "second" New Age is a phenomenon which exhibits important differences from the original network.

SEE ALSO: Millenarianism; New Religious Movements; Utopia

REFERENCES AND SUGGESTED READINGS

Berzano, L. (1997) *Damanhur: Popolo e comunità (Damanhur: People and Community)*. Elledici, Leumann, Turin.

Festinger, L., Riecken, H. W., & Schachter, S. (1956) *When Prophecy Fails*. University of Minnesota Press, Minneapolis.

Hanegraaff, W. J. (1996) *New Age Religion and Western Culture: Esotericism in the Mirror of Secular Thought*. Brill, Leiden.

Heelas, P. (1996) *The New Age Movement: The Celebration of the Self and the Sacralization of Modernity*. Blackwell, Oxford.

Introvigne, M. (2000) *New Age and Next Age*. Piemme, Casale Monferrato, Alessandria.

Melton, J. G. (1998a) The Future of the New Age Movement. In: Barker, E. & Warburg, M. (Eds.), *New Religions and New Religiosity*. Aarhus University Press, Aarhus and London, pp. 133–49.

Melton, J. G. (1998b) *Finding Enlightenment: Ramtha's School of Ancient Wisdom*. Beyond Words Publishing, Hillsboro, OR.

Melton, J. G., Clark, J., & Kelly, A. A. (1991) *New Age Almanac*. Visible Ink Press, Detroit.

Spangler, D. & Thompson, W. I. (1991) *Reimagination of the World: A Critic of the New Age, Science, and Popular Culture*. Bear & Company, Santa Fe.

Wessinger, C. (1988) *Annie Besant and Progressive Messianism (1847–1933)*. Edwin Mellen, Lewiston, NY.

Wessinger, C. (2000) *How the Millennium Comes Violently: From Jonestown to Heaven's Gate*. Seven Bridges Press, New York and London.

new left

Richard Flacks

Although the phrase "new left" was used as a shorthand for a variety of social movement phenomena of the 1960s, it refers specifically to a project in Britain and the US aimed at renovating the discourses and practices of the established lefts in both societies.

The term "new left" came into use in the late 1950s, when it was adopted by British intellectuals who came together after the Khrushchev revelations about Stalin, the Soviet invasion of Hungary, and the British invasion of Suez. Politically, this group shared a rejection of both Stalinism and the rightward drift of social democracy and a determination to oppose the political framework defined by the Cold War. As intellectuals, they sought new directions for critical social theory, questioning economistic versions of Marxian class analysis in favor of an emphasis on culture and consciousness as frameworks of both domination and resistance. The group included many who would become seminal in historical and cultural analysis: E. P. Thompson, Stuart Hall, and Raymond Williams. The journal *New Left Review*, founded in 1960, gave international visibility to this intellectual/political project and to its label, and became the primary English-language periodical for articulation and dissemination of new critical theory.

The main figures in the British new left were not primarily sociologists as such, but their work was both deeply sociological and became deeply influential in sociology, especially for those in the generation of the 1960s and 1970s. But a similar US-based intellectual/political dynamic paralleled the British formation, and, though influenced by it, had its own indigenous roots. Restlessness among American socialists and other radicals with ideological and theoretical foundations originating in Europe was emerging in the late nineteenth and early twentieth centuries. Historian Christopher Lasch identified what he called a "new radicalism" in the political practice and thought of such early twentieth-century intellectuals as Jane Addams, Walter Lippman, and Randolph Bourne, who shared a sense that cultural and educational change was fundamental to the fulfillment of visions of radical democracy. One can see in the thought and action of John Dewey a restless quest, over several decades, for a radical political formation that would be grounded in American experience and language.

The organizational experiments of A. J. Muste to create a revolutionary framework rooted in Ghandian and Thoreauvian pacifism resulted in formations, including the Congress On Racial Equality (CORE) and the Committee for Non-Violent Action, which, by the 1960s, transformed American protest strategies and tactics as well as the ideological premises of many American radicals. His journal, *Liberation*, joined several other newly created publications in the 1950s that, each in its own way, tried to chart a new direction for American radical analysis and politics. *Dissent*, co-edited by sociologist Lewis Coser, represented a home, during the McCarthy era, for radical critique of American society, while maintaining a staunch anti-communist perspective. *Monthly Review*, although continuing an "old left" posture of support for the Soviet and Chinese revolutions, sought to define a type of Marxian political economy that would be relevant to the analysis of the US as the global center of capitalism, and challenged orthodox Communist Party strategies from the left.

By the late 1950s, efforts to define a radical critique and to articulate alternative social possibilities were being advanced by several public intellectuals who commanded large audiences. Paul Goodman used a fusion of anarchism, pragmatism, and social psychology to revive utopian imagination and sharpen critical awareness. Erich Fromm popularized ideas derived from Frankfurt School fusions of Marx and Freud in a number of bestselling books. The most explicit exponent of the need and possibility for an American new left was sociologist C. Wright Mills. Mills's intellectual

development was itself a synthesis of many of the strands of critical theory and radical tradition that became the defining features of the new left project. He was schooled in the pragmatism of Mead and Dewey and in the critical theory of Frankfurt School and other European Marxists. His social worlds spanned both the academy and the circles of labor and socialist intellectuals. In the space of some seven years, Mills wrote a series of books and articles that contributed much to setting the agenda of what became the new left formation in the US. These included the *Power Elite* (an effort to rework radical analysis of power relations), a reader on Marxism with his own theoretical annotations, *The Sociological Imagination* (a scathing critique of academic sociology combined with a stirring program for its renovation), pamphleteering analysis and denunciation of the Cold War and its politics, and a "Letter to the New Left" enunciating a hope for new sources of radical political agency.

Alongside these fresh intellectual fusions and visions came, as the 1950s turned into the 1960s, an outburst of unexpected grassroots social movement. The prevailing understanding of post-war America, as depicted by many academic and independent writers, emphasized its political quiescence, conformity, and conservatism. The rise of mass protest by African Americans in the South, and the simultaneous emergence of a movement against the nuclear arms race in Britain and the US, challenged that understanding. On the other hand, these movements provided a popular validation and further inspiration for new left social criticism of established structures of power and opportunity. Moreover, the social sources of the new protest challenged orthodox Marxian class analysis, as well as functionalist social systems analysis.

Emerging civil rights and peace movements appealed strongly to significant fractions of the American student body. The first wave of youthful activism was the mass non-violent actions, including sit-ins and freedom rides, of mostly black students in the South, beginning in 1960. White and black students on a number of Northern campuses engaged in sympathy protests in support of the Southern sit-ins; these actions sparked a strong moral/political turn in the intellectual subcultures of university towns after years of self-conscious disaffiliation.

A number of new journals, some modeled on *New Left Review*, were suddenly coming out of these towns (these included *Studies on the Left* in Madison, *New University Thought* in Chicago, and *Root and Branch* in Berkeley). Their shared theme: the new potential for a resurgent left, and the need to ground that left on new terms. There was, as well, a considerable emphasis on the failures of higher education and academic research to provide critical resources for the search for social alternatives.

A major breakthrough in the development of the new left was the founding meeting of a new national student organization: Students for a Democratic Society (SDS). The organization had its roots in the "old left" tradition: it grew out of the Student League for Industrial Democracy (SLID), which itself had begun as the Intercollegiate Socialist Society in 1905. The League for Industrial Democracy was founded by a number of prominent intellectuals and labor leaders (John Dewey was an early president), and SLID had been an important campus organization in the activist 1930s. A small group of students, led by Al Haber, persuaded the LID board to turn the moribund SLID over to them in hopes of creating a new organizational format for the emerging student activism of the early 1960s. With this ambition and a small budget, Haber was able to recruit a number of local leaders of the campus activism to the project. Among these, Tom Hayden, editor of the University of Michigan *Daily*, was perhaps the most ambitious to create a new radical intellectual as well as organizational synthesis. Hayden, a voracious reader and stylish writer, strongly identified with the British new left. In addition to reading their work, he, like other early 1960s activists, was affected by Camus's critique of revolutionary strategies based on power and violence. He was impressed with Mills's work, his social analysis, and his presentational style. He could see, in all of these, sources for crafting a morally grounded political manifesto for a new generation of the left. He persuaded the SDS initiators that their organizational founding should focus on just such a project. He brought a draft of the manifesto to the founding meeting at Port Huron, Michigan in 1962; the several dozen assembled there spent some days debating its substance. Out of this deliberation came the *Port Huron Statement*, which is generally regarded as the seminal document of the American new left.

In addition to the Northern white activists who came to Port Huron, there were several leaders of the Student Non-Violent Coordinating Committee (SNCC). Their own visions of direct democracy and beloved community were part of what inspired the themes and language of the final document. The SNCC critique of top-down leadership and hierarchical organization, and the radical populism it expressed ("let the people decide" was a slogan), had many religious, cultural, and generational sources. But a particularly strong influence was Ella Baker, a seasoned veteran of the Civil Rights Movement who strongly articulated, to her SNCC protégés, an organizing vision that converged with the spirit of "participatory democracy."

That phrase captures the central idea of the *Port Huron Statement*. A young pragmatist philosopher (and teacher of Hayden and other SDS founders) at Michigan, Arnold Kaufman, coined the term, but it was the *Port Huron Statement* that gave it currency. The phrase itself condenses much of what the new left project was about: it was a neologism designed to displace "socialism" in defining left vision and program; it tried to situate the left squarely in the American democratic tradition; it was, however, a *radicalization* of that tradition because it extended democracy's meaning beyond the conventionally political and electoral. "Participatory democracy" establishes a critical standard for evaluating all institutional arrangements: the family, the school, the church, the prison, the workplace – as well as the state (and by so doing connects to the culturally based social critiques identified with John Dewey, as well as with a multiplicity of anarchist thought streams). Indeed, the phrase quickly became identified with efforts to create new forms of *internal* organization within the new social movements of the 1960s, replacing "party" style structures with forms of direct democracy, consensus decision-making, and decentered leadership.

There were a number of other "new" ideas expressed by the *Port Huron Statement*. The manifesto explicitly rejects the Cold War as a framework for thought and action, condemning the communism of the Soviet bloc and the communist parties as profoundly anti-democratic, but also criticizing anti-communism as a major barrier to articulate social criticism and collective action. Its anti-anti-communism greatly distressed most "adult" leaders of the old "democratic left" (although it was prescient about how the left in both Europe and the US would be reconstituted in the decade to follow).

Equally prescient was the statement's argument that a new left must have an important base in the university. The university, it declares, is now a crucial social institution; the knowledge it creates and distributes is critical for social change; its inhabitants, especially the students, may be ready for active mobilization. But academia as currently constituted needs reform: it must be a space where scholars and students can connect both to the world of ideas and to the public sphere (especially the social movements).

Thus, in its formal beginning, the American new left was an effort to: (1) define a post-Marxian radical democratic ideological foundation for radicalism; (2) foster new strategies, organizational forms, and tactics of grassroots collective action; (3) legitimize the role of the "public intellectual" within the university; and (4) sustain ongoing internal critique of radical activism itself in terms of a radical, participatory democratic standard.

SDS, by 1965, had become a mass student organization, because of its early leadership of protest against the Vietnam War. As it quickly grew, and because of its participatory democratic insistence on decentralized, rotating leadership, its founding generation soon gave way to a much more politically diverse set of leaders, and the Port Huron definition of the new left no longer characterized the organization. The founding generation, after fitful effort, failed to establish an "adult" organization; as a result, no new left organizational structure capable of national leadership came into being. Instead, new left discourse continued to be carried on in a variety of journals and periodicals on both sides of the Atlantic.

At the same time, parallel new lefts were being formed, largely by the rising generations of radical activists and intellectuals in various European countries as the spirit of the student movement spread. The German new left was a particularly important political and intellectual formation. The German social theorist Jürgen Habermas began an ambitious effort to reinterpret and resynthesize Marxism, psychoanalysis, and pragmatism to create a critical theory appropriate to late capitalism. He and other European theorists took serious note of the new left and the emergence of "new" social movements as signs of a new stage of social development.

Meanwhile, in Latin America, the Cuban revolution had spawned a wide range of revolutionary groupings which, like those headed by Castro and Guevara, challenged orthodox Leninist revolutionary theory and practice. American new leftists perceived these developments, as well as the struggle of the NLF in Vietnam, as somehow akin to their own struggle against institutional power and efforts to empower the disenfranchised. The obvious contradictions between non-violent and armed revolution and between an "American" and "third world" left orientation contributed to growing internal conflict in SDS and other new left groupings.

As the years went on, the self-consciously post-Marxian and radical character of the early new left discourse gave way to a variety of diverse and contradictory orientations. On the one hand, there were those who identified with Maoist and other third world revolutionary perspectives. In opposition to that tendency, there was a revival of Marxian political economy ("neo-Marxism"), a variety of socialist feminist perspectives, a revival of left-wing social democratic programs (in the US often called "economic democracy"), and, as the strength of the electoral right grew in both countries, a return to electorally oriented national and local politics.

Although the specific new left projects of the early 1960s were not sustained, important elements or traces of their perspectives were incorporated into social theory, analysis, and movement. Among these:

• A continuing demand for forms of participatory democratic decision-making. This can be seen in the global emergence of community-based movements seeking local voice or control over development; in the spread of environmentalist consciousness, questioning market- or technology-based planning; in mass street mobilizations challenging authoritarian regimes in many countries; in the World Social Forum and related manifestations challenging established global trade and economic structures; in the rise of the Green Party in several European countries whose program tried to embody these values.

- Decentralized forms of social movement mobilization and decision-making based on affinity groups, loose coalitional networks, Internet-based communication, and so on.
- Emphasis on "cultural" and social psychological rather than "economistic" frameworks for analysis of political consciousness and for framing political perspectives; use of "race," "gender," and other non-class frameworks for interpreting collective identity and conflict.
- Continuing efforts to legitimize and promote "public" social science (as opposed to strictly "academic" or "policy" bases of legitimation). As the *Port Huron Statement* argued, and as some sociologists since have tried to practice, the fulfillment of the new left project depends on processes of interaction between the intellectual worlds of universities and of social movements in hope of generating knowledge of democratic use.

SEE ALSO: Anti-War and Peace Movements; Civil Rights Movement; Critical Theory/ Frankfurt School; Democracy and Organizations; Fromm, Erich; Marx, Karl; Marxism and Sociology; Mills, C. Wright; New Left Realism; New Social Movement Theory; Socialism

REFERENCES AND SUGGESTED READINGS

Breines, W. (1989) *Community and Organization in the New Left: 1962–1968.* Rutgers University Press, New Brunswick, NJ.
Dworkin, D. (1997) *Cultural Marxism in Post-War Britain: History, the New Left, and the Origins of Cultural Studies.* Duke University Press, Raleigh.
Flacks, R. (1988) *Making History: The American Left and the American Mind.* Columbia University Press, New York.
Isserman, M. (1987) *If I Had a Hammer: The Death of the Old Left and the Birth of the New.* Basic Books, New York.
Jamison, A. & Eyerman, R. (1994) *Seeds of the Sixties.* University of California Press, Berkeley.
Mattson, K. (2002) *Intellectuals in Action: The Origins of the New Left and Radical Liberalism, 1945–1970.* Pennsylvania State University Press, University Park.
Miller, J. (1994) *Democracy is in the Streets: From Port Huron to the Streets of Chicago.* Harvard University Press, Cambridge, MA.
Mills, C. W. (1963) *Power, Politics, and People.* Oxford University Press, New York.
Ransby, B. (2003) *Ella Baker and the Black Freedom Movement: A Radical Democratic Vision.* University of North Carolina Press, Chapel Hill.

new left realism

Walter S. DeKeseredy

Left realism is "[o]ne of the most important critical criminologies in the world" (Schwartz & Hatty 2003: xii). Although there are variations in this school of thought, all versions begin with the assertion that inner-city crime is a major problem for socially and economically disenfranchised people, regardless of their sex or ethnic/cultural background. Further, left realists contend that chronic urban poverty and an exclusionary labor market are major symptoms of contemporary capitalism, which in turn spawn crimes committed in public housing complexes and other poor areas. However, for left realists, it is not sheer poverty and the absence of prized material possessions (e.g., cars, high-definition television sets) that motivate socially and economically marginalized people to prey on each other. Rather, it is a "lethal combination" of relative deprivation and market individualism (Young 1999). Thus, as left realists remind us, it is not absolute poverty, but poverty experienced as unfair (relative deprivation when compared to someone else) that breeds discontent. The form of capitalism that is predominant in North America, individualism, takes such discontent to the extremes, where in the most exaggerated situations one finds the urban poor living in a "universe where human beings live side by side but not as human beings" (Hobsbawm 1994: 341). Crime, then, is an individualistic solution to experiences of injustice (Young 1997).

Left realists also argue that people who lack legitimate means of solving the problem of relative deprivation may come into contact with other frustrated disenfranchised people and form subcultures, which, in turn, encourage and legitimate criminal behaviors (Lea & Young 1984). For example, receiving respect from peers is highly valued among ghetto adolescents who are denied status in mainstream, middle-class society. However, respect and status are often granted by inner-city subcultures when one is willing to be violent, such as using a gun.

Although left realists devote considerable attention to theorizing about crime and its control, they also offer may different progressive crime control and prevention policies. Still, all left realists have two things in common. First, while they would all like to see a major transformation from a society based on class, race/ethnic, and gender inequality to one that is truly equitable and democratic, they realize that this will not happen in the immediate future. This view is well founded, given that there is massive public support for neoconservative governments and their economic and social policies, such as government cuts to health care and unemployment insurance. So, left realists seek short-term gains while remaining committed to long-term change. This is why they propose practical initiatives that can be implemented immediately and that "chip away" at patriarchal capitalism. Examples of such policies are higher minimum wage, job creation and training programs, and housing assistance.

Second, all left realists are sharply opposed to policies heavily informed by what Jock Young (1998) defines as "establishment criminology." Establishment criminologists see crime as a property of the individual rather than of broader social, cultural, economic, and political forces. Moreover, they call for policies such as bringing back chain gangs, longer prison sentences, and using other draconian means to prevent and reduce crime. This is not to say, however, that left realists are opposed to criminal justice reform. For example, British left realists call for strategies such as democratic control of policing and community participation in crime prevention and policy development.

Left realism was born in the 1980s and was primarily a response by North American and British scholars to their respective governments' "law and order" programs with progressive analyses that accepted as legitimate poor urban communities' fear of crime (DeKeseredy & Schwartz 1991). In doing so, they answered the late Ian Taylor's (1981: xxi) famed call for the "reconstruction of socialist crime politics" by proposing practical crime control strategies. These methods, some of which were briefly described above, were meant as important alternatives not only to the programs of liberals and conservatives, but also to those programs implicit in the analyses of the so-called "left idealists" who have a tendency to idealize oppressed socioeconomic groups and to overlook antisocial behavior within them.

Despite their common ground, however, there are important differences between British, Canadian, and US left realists, rooted in very distinct political agendas. For example, there has been a more receptive audience, at least at the local level, for socialist suggestions in Great Britain and Canada. The marginalization of US socialist scholars, when combined with a limited discussion of concrete recommendations for change on the local level, has meant that they have had less impact on social policy than British and Canadian left realists.

US left realists also do little, if any, empirical work, while their Canadian and British counterparts rely heavily on local victimization surveys to elicit rich data that can be used to challenge erroneous right-wing interpretations of both street crime and male-to-female violence in intimate relationships, and ineffective means of curbing these problems (e.g., imprisonment). Consider, too, that left realist surveys typically uncover much higher rates of woman abuse, racial harassment, and other crimes committed by and against socially and economically excluded people than those uncovered by major government studies like the National Crime Victimization Survey.

Left realism has undergone some major changes since its inception in the 1980s. For example, left realists were heavily criticized for ignoring crimes of the powerful, such as corporate crime. In response to this major concern, some left realists conducted local surveys on workplace hazards, unlawful trading practices, the victimization of housing tenants, and corporate violence against Punjabi farm workers. Note, too, that left realists now devote more theoretical, empirical, and political attention to the ways in which broader structural changes that have occurred in capitalist countries since the 1970s (e.g., deindustrialization, the North American Free Trade Agreement) contribute to woman abuse and other harms in poor urban communities (see Young 1999; DeKeseredy & Schwartz 2002; DeKeseredy et al. 2003).

Despite effectively addressing some major criticisms raised by a myriad of conservative and progressive scholars, left realists still continue to ignore women's experiences of crime as suspects, offenders, defendants, and inmates. To date, left realists have not attempted to theorize about both why women's offenses are distinct from men's and the sexist nature of the criminal justice system. Further, thus far there has been no attempt to develop and/or test a left realist theory of corporate crime. In its current form, left realist theory cannot explain crimes committed by corporations like Enron because it mainly focuses on how broader economic, social, cultural, and political forces influence interpersonal relations between economically and socially excluded individuals (Pearce & Tombs 1992; DeKeseredy 2003).

There are several other criticisms of left realism and because they are well documented elsewhere, they will not be repeated here. Many more new ones are likely to emerge too, given that left realists are constantly modifying their theoretical, empirical, and policy contributions in accordance with rapid social, economic, political, and cultural changes now occurring in societies such as Canada, the US, and the UK. For example, several North American left realists have developed integrated theories to explain separation/divorce, woman abuse in public housing, and woman abuse in cohabitation. Moreover, some left realists are becoming much more involved in qualitative research on issues related to inequality, crime, and social control.

SEE ALSO: Crime; Crime, Radical Marxist Theories of; Criminology; Deviance; Deviance, Crime and; Theory; Urban Crime and Violence; Urbanization

REFERENCES AND SUGGESTED READINGS

DeKeseredy, W. S. (2003) Left Realism on Inner-City Crime. In: Schwartz, M. D. & Hatty, S. E. (Eds.), *Controversies in Critical Criminology*. Anderson, Cincinnati, pp. 29–42.

DeKeseredy, W. S. & Schwartz, M. D. (1991) British and US Left Realism: A Critical Comparison. *International Journal of Offender Therapy and Comparative Criminology* 35(3): 248–61.

DeKeseredy, W. S. & Schwartz, M. D. (2002) Theorizing Public Housing Woman Abuse as a Function of Economic Exclusion and Male Peer Support. *Women's Health and Urban Life* 1(2): 26–45.

DeKeseredy, W. S., Alvi, S., Schwartz, M. D., & Tomaszewski, E. A. (2003) *Under Siege: Poverty and Crime in a Public Housing Community*. Lexington, Lanham, MD.

Hobsbawm, E. (1994) *The Age of Extremes*. Vintage, New York.

Lea, J. & Young, J. (1984) *What Is To Be Done About Law and Order?* Penguin, New York.

Pearce, F. & Tombs, S. (1992) Realism and Corporate Crime. In: Matthews, R. & Young, J. (Eds.), *Realist Criminology*. Sage, London, pp. 70–101.

Schwartz, M. D. & Hatty, S. E. (2003) Introduction. In: Schwartz, M. D. & Hatty, S. E. (Eds.), *Controversies in Critical Criminology*. Anderson, Cincinnati, pp. ix–xvii.

Taylor, I. (1981) *Law and Order: Arguments for Socialism*. Macmillan, London.

Young, J. (1997) Left Realism: The Basics. In: Maclean, B. D. & Milovanovic, D. (Eds.), *Thinking Critically About Crime*. Collective Press, Vancouver, pp. 28–36.

Young, J. (1998) Left Realist Criminology: Radical in its Analysis, Realist in its Policy. Paper presented at the annual meetings of the American Society of Criminology, San Diego.

Young, J. (1999) *The Exclusive Society*. Sage, London.

new middle classes in Asia

Abdul Rahman Embong

Asia is the world's largest continent with great complexity, diversity, and different levels of economic development. Such characteristics make it difficult to describe the continent – and by extension its new middle class – in any general way. Necessary as they may be, we should thus be careful when making generalizations about the Asian middle class lest we unwittingly gloss over its heterogeneity across regions.

It may be recalled that while the past two centuries have respectively been hailed as "the European century" and "the American century," the twenty-first century has been hailed as "the Asian century." This generalization – undoubtedly problematic – does, however, draw attention to one striking fact that the economies of a sizable part of Asia, namely, East and Southeast Asia, have recorded impressive growth rates and undergone deep-rooted transformation since the 1970s. Thanks to such growth and newfound prosperity, Asia today has produced the world's largest middle class, estimated to be between 800 million to 1 billion, thus making Asia "the biggest market for almost everything."

THE MIDDLE CLASS IN EAST AND SOUTHEAST ASIA

In the several decades before the 1997–8 Asian crisis, the East and Southeast Asian rapid economic growth was regarded as a "miracle." Being late industrializers, the respective states in the region played a strong developmental role, attracting foreign investment and stimulating export-oriented industrialization as well as urbanization and modernization, leading to the growth of a burgeoning new middle class. With their proportion in the workforce of these countries ranging from about 15 percent to over 40 percent and still growing, members of this class have come to occupy important positions as managers, administrators, professionals, and technical workers in both the public and private sectors, including in many transnational firms.

The rise of the middle class or the "new rich" in Asia has been described as a "revolution," with some writers suggesting that the twentieth century is "the age of the middle class." Many studies have been undertaken to analyze this new phenomenon, with some using an eclectic approach of a convergence between the Marxist and the Weberian perspectives. Worthy of note are two major research projects undertaken since the early 1990s – the East and Southeast

Asian Middle Class Project based in Academia Sinica, Taipei, coordinated by Professor Michael Hsiao, and the Murdoch Middle Class Project coordinated by Professor Robison.

What are some of the salient characteristics of the Asian middle class based on these studies? First, the middle class is heterogeneous, with fairly clear internal differentiation, making it more appropriate to use the term in the plural, "middle class*es*." They can be divided into three categories – the *new* middle class (managers, administrators, and professionals), the *old* middle class (small employers and shopkeepers or the petite bourgeoisie), and the *marginal* middle class (routine non-manual employees). Unlike in the West, the rise of the new middle class in this region has not led to the decline of the old as well as the marginal middle classes. Instead, rapid economic growth has also spurred the growth and expansion of the latter.

Second, the Asian new middle class is a *first-generation* middle class. The majority of its members came from non-middle-class backgrounds such as farmers and agricultural workers (e.g., in South Korea, Taiwan, and Malaysia) and working-class or self-employed worker families (e.g., in Hong Kong and Singapore). Born mainly after World War II and originating mostly from such humble backgrounds, many of them experienced poverty and hardship during their childhood years. Their upward mobility was made possible by opportunities for higher education as well as the availability of middle-class occupations.

Third, being the beneficiary of the rapid capitalist development, the middle class is relatively affluent, enabling its members to enjoy a different lifestyle from that of their parents. They lead a life of conspicuous consumption, owning property such as modern urban houses, cars, and other expensive items including household items, patronizing shopping complexes and hotels, becoming members of exclusive clubs, as well as engaging in foreign travel and tourism. However, being a class that has just "arrived," they also have a fear of falling and are very concerned about middle-class reproduction to ensure their children remain in the same class. Their families are mainly nuclear, but they attempt to maintain or recreate the old extended kinship network with their family of origin under new urban conditions.

Fourth, the middle class is also regarded as an "ascending class" and a modernization force providing indispensable professional services to society. Often associated with the proliferation of NGOs, the middle class is an ascending political force that attempts to define the society's sociopolitical agendas such as the advancement of democracy, human rights, gender issues, environmentalism, consumer rights, and so on, thus imprinting its own stamp on its country's trajectory.

THE MIDDLE CLASS IN JAPAN AND CHINA

Special mention must be made of the middle class in Japan and China, which followed different paths than the countries mentioned above. Japan had no colonial experience and is the first Asian country to join the ranks of the developed nations. Emerging from the ashes of the war in 1945, it undertook rapid economic reconstruction under American supervision until 1950. Although the Japanese middle class was already visible, what is more important is the new generation of the Japanese middle class that emerged out of the post-war reconstruction and the subsequent Japanese economic boom when the ambitious 10-year Income Doubling Plan was announced in 1960. The class consists of white-collar employees, clerks, shopkeepers, and others regardless of the line of business they are in. The improved living standards due to high economic growth particularly helped make achieving middle-class status a symbolic goal of affluence. As in other industrialized countries, the proportion of the workforce occupied by white-collar workers grew rapidly. The increased number of white-collar workers not only reflected higher social mobility, promoting the formation of a new middle class, but also contributed to the creation of a "mass society." In fact, from the 1960s onwards, Japanese middle-class men holding white-collar jobs in companies and who became known as *sararimen* ("salary men") represent a social status symbolizing economic success and comfort, and their lifestyle came to be regarded as "ideal" among many Japanese.

The middle class in Japan is a class position defined subjectively by members of the middle class themselves, i.e., in terms of their consumption made possible, and in fact spurred, by the economic prosperity and the increased purchasing power of the employees. According to surveys conducted under the auspices of the Japanese Prime Minister's Office, while 76.2 percent of Japanese identified themselves as "belonging to the middle class" in 1960, the figure rose sharply to 90.0 percent three decades later. By the early 1990s, the proportion of the Japanese people who identified themselves as upper class and lower class were made up only of very small proportions, 1.2 percent and 5.6 percent, respectively. More than half of the Japanese (57.0 percent) ranked themselves as being "in the middle of the middle class." This shows that the overwhelming majority of the Japanese regarded themselves as having "arrived," i.e., enjoying the middle-class standard of living and social status.

The situation is different in China, the world's largest nation with a population of 1.2 billion. China has a checkered history of colonial intrusion, revolutionary wars, and the adoption of socialism and centralized planning since 1949 until it opened up and adopted the market economy after 1978. As China has been focused on social leveling and the elimination of classes under the guidance of the Communist Party's Marxist ideology, one would not expect a middle class to grow under such a system. However, with the introduction of the market economy and the resulting new prosperity, unprecedented social transformation has taken place, and new social formations, namely the middle class, are emerging. To date, not many studies have been conducted on the Chinese middle class, and most of the writings have been rather anecdotal. Nevertheless, some market analysts estimate the size of the middle class as already huge, i.e., some 150 million persons or about 12.5 percent of the Chinese population, comprising particularly those living in major coastal cities. By 2010, this class is expected to constitute about two-fifths or 40 percent of the population.

If we take consumption as a proxy, we will have an idea of the emergence of this new class. Following China's open door policy in the late 1970s, China's economy has been growing at 10 percent per annum since 1980, and the growth rate is still sustained today. China's industrialization has made impressive records, with the industrial sector's contribution to the gross national product (GDP) increasing from 42 percent in 1990 to 51 percent in 2000. The Chinese "consumption ladder," as some scholars call it, has continued to rise with China's rapid development and increased prosperity. This is manifested socially in changing patterns of ownership of household items. For example, prior to the economic reform when most of the family income was spent on basic necessities such as food and clothing, the most popular household goods were the "four big items" – sewing machines, watches, bicycles, and radios. In the 1980s, the old "four big items" had been replaced by the new "six big items" – color televisions, refrigerators, cameras, electric fans, washing machines, and tape recorders. By the 1990s the luxury items consisted of video-recorders, hi-fi systems, and air conditioners, while by the 2000s other luxury items have been added, namely cars and condominiums.

Other important indicators of the changing lifestyle of China's middle class are its members' craze for shopping as well as their participation in overseas travel and tourism. However, a new indicator of affluence is the increasing number of golf players and enthusiasts, together with the emergence of golf clubs patronized by the "new rich."

While the new middle class in Asia advocates modernization, the latter should not be equated with westernization. Members of the Asian middle class are in search of themselves and their identity. In this regard, we see the revival of traditional ethnic cultures with new elements of universality, and all these are spearheaded by the middle class. Some scholars are observing that a new artistic style is emerging, drawing on both Asian and western cultures but with an emphasis on the East. Thus, while Asia may be bombarded by western, namely American, middle-class values, members of the Asian middle class are also turning to their sociocultural roots. All these will mean the assertion of certain distinct features of the Asian middle class that differentiate it from its western counterpart.

SEE ALSO: Civil Society; Class; Consumption; Developmental State; Marx, Karl; Modernization; Salary Men; Social Change, Southeast Asia; Urbanization; Weber, Max

REFERENCES AND SUGGESTED READINGS

Beng-Huat, C. (Ed.) (2000) *Consumption in Asia: Lifestyles and Identities*. Routledge, New York.

Embong, A. R. (Ed.) (2001) *Southeast Asian Middle Classes: Prospects for Social Change and Democratization*. Penerbit Universiti Kebangsaan Malaysia, Bangi.

Embong, A. R. (2002) *State-Led Modernization and the New Middle Class in Malaysia*. Palgrave Macmillan, Houndmills.

Fujimura, M. (2000) The Welfare State, the Middle Class, and the Welfare Society. *Review of Population and Social Policy* 9: 1–23.

Goldthorpe, J. (1982) Service Class. In: Giddens, A. & McKenzie, G. (Eds.), *Social Class and the Division of Labour*. Cambridge University Press, Cambridge.

Hsiao, H. M. (Ed.) (1993) *Discovery of the Middle Classes in East Asia*. Academia Sinica, Taipei.

Hsiao, H. M. (Ed.) (1999) *East Asian Middle Classes in Comparative Perspective*. Academia Sinica, Taipei.

Hsiao, H. M. (Ed.) (2001) *Exploration of the Middle Classes in Southeast Asia*. Academia Sinica, Taipei.

Imada, T. (1999) The Japanese Middle Class and Politics After World War II. In: Hsiao, H. M. (Ed.), *East Asian Middle Classes in Comparative Perspective*. Academia Sinica, Taipei.

Marshall, G. (1997) *Repositioning Class: Social Inequality in Industrial Societies*. Sage, London.

Robison, R. & Goodman, D. S. G. (Eds.) (1996) *The New Rich in Asia: Mobile Phones, McDonald's, and Middle-Class Revolution*. New York, Routledge.

new religious movements

Eileen Barker

The term new religious movement has been employed to refer to a number of distinguishable but overlapping phenomena, not all of which are unambiguously new and not all of which are, by at least some criteria, religious. There have, of course, always been new religions – Zoroastrianism, Buddhism, Christianity, and Islam all started off as such. With the hindsight of history, it is possible to recognize periods that have been particularly prone to the growth of new religions. Examples would be the 1530s in Northern and Central Europe; England between 1620 and 1650 and again at the turn of the nineteenth century; the Great Awakening of the late 1730s followed by the Second Great Awakening of 1820–60 in the United States; and a "Rush Hour of the Gods," to borrow Neill McFarland's (1967) term, arrived in Japan when the new religions that had been suppressed during World War II became liberated in the mid-1940s; then, roughly 30 years later, they were joined by what are now referred to as the Japanese new new religions (Shimazono 2004).

TERMINOLOGICAL PROBLEMS

The fact that no social phenomenon is ever completely new and that none is ever completely unchanging can make the term "new" problematic. But around the late 1960s the term "new religious movement" (NRM) started to be used to describe a special subject of study within the scholarly community of North America and Western Europe. It referred to two types of "new" religions: first, as in *The New Religions* (1970) by Jacob Needleman, it covered various forms of eastern spirituality that were new to most westerners. These new arrivals, which had frequently been in existence for hundreds or even thousands of years in their countries of origin, did not change much in their traditional beliefs and practices insofar as they were restricted to immigrants from those countries. Some, however, adopted new characteristics when they were embraced by westerners, making it possible to argue that they had become new movements in the more common, second sense, which referred to the motley assortment of groups that had been founded since World War II and were being identified as "cults" or "sects" in the popular media. These NRMs were new in the sense that they consisted predominantly of first-generation converts, and their founding leaders were still alive.

Another terminological difficulty arose when many of those movements resisted being called a religion – the Brahma Kumaris, for example, prefer to be seen as a spiritual or educational movement. On the other hand, the Church of Scientology, although called a new religion by its founder, L. Ron Hubbard, has had to fight in courts around the world to be recognized as

a religion in order to obtain such secular benefits as tax exemption.

Most NRMs would fit into the sociological category of either sect or cult, but scholars came to favor the term NRM in order to avoid the pejorative overtones associated in the public mind with these labels. This has, however, led to "NRM" being associated in the rhetoric of the movements' opponents with what they consider to be not a neutral but a "cult apologist" position. This politicizing of the term, the confusions caused by the fact that many of the movements had (or now have) been in existence for some time, and the ambiguities associated with the label "religious" have led to attempts to find other terms, such as alternative religions, minority faiths, or spiritual communities. But none of these had successfully replaced "new religious movement" by the beginning of the third millennium.

CHARACTERISTICS OF NRMS

The enormous diversity within the current wave of new religions cannot be overemphasized. Whilst nineteenth-century sects such as the Jehovah's Witnesses, Mormons, and Seventh-Day Adventists certainly differ from one another, they do share some sort of relationship to the Judeo-Christian tradition. The new religions come, however, from a far wider range of traditions – not only Buddhist, Hindu, Muslim, Shinto, paganism, and various combinations of these, but also from other sources such as science fiction, psychoanalytic theories, and political ideologies.

There are those, particularly historians of religion such as J. Gordon Melton (2004), who have argued that NRMs have more in common with the traditions from which they emerged than with each other, and certainly it would be difficult to understand Krishna Consciousness without knowing something of the Hindu tradition, The Family without a knowledge of Christianity, or Soka Gakkai without knowing about Buddhism in general and the Nichiren tradition in particular. That said, however, it is also the case that there are certain characteristics which the movements might be expected to share insofar as they are new and religious.

Firstly, almost by definition, NRMs have a membership of converts, and converts to any religion are notoriously more committed and enthusiastic than those born into their religion. Secondly, founding leaders are frequently accorded a charismatic authority by their followers. This means they are accorded the right to have a direct say over more aspects of their followers' lives than, say, the pope, or even an ayatollah, and are unlikely to be held accountable to anyone, except perhaps the God(s) to whom they alone may have a direct hotline. Furthermore, being unbounded by rules or traditions, they are likely to be unpredictable, changing revelations and instructions at a moment's notice.

Thirdly, NRMs tend to appeal to an atypical representation of the population. Those that appeared in the West in the second half of the twentieth century were, for example, disproportionately young Caucasian adults from the better-educated middle classes, although there were NRMs that attracted converts with different demographic profiles, such as the young black males who joined the Rastafarians or the Nation of Islam.

A fourth, but by no means universal, characteristic of new religions is that they frequently operate with a dichotomous mindset. Their belief system is seen as unquestionably True and Godly, and that of others as false and possibly satanic; their morals are good, others are bad. The primary defining identity is membership – one is either a Jesus Christian or one is not; and, to protect a vulnerable membership that has embraced beliefs and practices alien to those of their relatives and friends, NRMs throughout history have frequently encouraged their members to sever close contact with non-members (Luke 14:26). Clear boundaries are, thus, drawn between "true" and "false"; "good" and "bad"; "them" and "us"; and "before" and "after" (conversion).

Fifthly, NRMs have been greeted with suspicion, fear, and even hatred by those to whom they pose an alternative. The early Christians were fed to the lions, the Cathars were burned at the stake, the Baha'i continue to be persecuted in Iran and the Ahmiddya in Pakistan. At the turn of the third millennium, the People's Republic of China have imprisoned tens of thousands of Falun Gong practitioners for "reeducation" on the grounds that they are considered a threat to individuals and the state; Jehovah's Witnesses have been physically attacked in Georgia, and "liquidated" by a Moscow court. Parents have paid tens of thousands of dollars to have their (adult) children kidnapped from NRMs and involuntarily imprisoned until either they escaped or promised to renounce their faith. This practice of deprogramming, although not entirely abandoned, is now rare in North America and Western Europe, but it continues in Japan and elsewhere. A number of countries have amended their constitutions or passed laws that distinguish (crudely or subtly) between new and more traditional religions, denying the former privileges or rights accorded to the latter (Richardson 2004). The European Court of Human Rights has accepted a number of cases from NRMs objecting to such practices, and the Organization for Security and Cooperation in Europe (OSCE) has issued numerous statements criticizing the treatment meted out to minority religions.

A sixth characteristic of NRMs, and one that has been surprisingly often ignored, is that they are likely to change more fundamentally and rapidly than older religions. This is obvious merely from a demographic perspective. Converts, who had enjoyed the freedoms of youth, find themselves with the responsibilities of parenthood and dealing with children who, unlike dissident converts, cannot be expelled. Paying the rent or coping with aging and ill health can become more pressing challenges than saving the world. Charismatic leaders die; the organization becomes increasingly bureaucratized and governed by rules and traditions, and, thus, more accountable and predictable. Unfulfilled prophecies may result in a relaxation of theological fervor and contribute to accommodation to the host society. NRMs that were at such pains to explain how different they were from the rest of the world might start to insist that they are basically just like anyone else. Non-members can become more familiar with at least some NRMs and lose some of their fear as the movements merge into the ever-growing diversity of religions, cultures, and moralities of an increasingly globalizing world.

Furthermore, economic, political, and social changes in the outside world can introduce radical changes within the "cult scene." With the collapse of the Berlin Wall in 1989, hundreds of

NRMs swept into Eastern Europe, initially enjoying the freedom that was celebrated throughout the region, but gradually being repressed and controlled, particularly with the traditional churches objecting to foreign organizations "stealing their flock" (Borowik & Babinski 1997). Another significant change has been the arrival of the Internet, facilitating the rapid exchange of information both for the benefit and to the detriment of NRMs (Hadden & Cowan 2000).

While the earlier Christian sects were classified in *Religious Sects* (1970) by Bryan Wilson according to the actions that they believed necessary to achieve salvation, no such satisfactory typology has been developed for the more disparate NRMs. Possibly the most useful distinction is that elaborated in *The Elementary Forms of the New Religious Life* (1984) by Roy Wallis between world-rejecting, world-affirming, and world-accommodating movements. World-rejecting movements (such as the Children of God in its early days) typically entertain some kind of millennial expectation that the world will undergo radical change. World-affirming groups (such as Scientology) claim to help the individual to cope with and/or succeed in society with its current values. World-accommodating movements (to which Wallis assigns the Aetherius Society, Subud, and Charismatic Renewal) are fairly content with, or indifferent to, the world as it is.

Some have argued that the movements are a reflection of society, others that they arise in reaction to it; both accounts have some truth in them. It has often been observed that the more fundamentalist NRMs arose as a reaction to modernization and secularism. Bryan Wilson (1990; Wilson & Dobbelaere 1994) has argued that NRMs such as Scientology and Soka Gakkai reflect the preoccupations of a modern, secularized society in which individuals exhibit a greater concern for self-development and psychic well-being than for otherworldly salvation. As society moved from a production-oriented economy (with the work ethic playing a central role) to a consumer economy, the image of a personal God was replaced by the idea of an impersonal force or spirit, and rewards became increasingly sought in this life, in this world – or, via reincarnation, in the next life, but still in this world.

COUNTING NRMS AND THEIR MEMBERS

No one knows exactly how many NRMs there are. The uncertainty lies partly in the definition, and partly in deciding where to draw boundaries. Are the hundreds of New Age groups all to be individually listed or should they be counted in clusters? There are, moreover, undoubtedly NRMs about which few but their members have ever heard. It is, however, probable that there are around 2,000 identifiable NRMs in Europe and North America, with a roughly similar number in Asia and possibly (depending again on what is included by the definition) several thousand more in Africa and elsewhere.

But while the number of NRMs is large, the number of members is usually relatively small. Again, it is difficult to estimate precise figures for most movements. Both NRMs and their opponents tend to exaggerate membership statistics, but further confusion arises because, just as with older religions, there are several ways of counting: there are core members who, like priests, nuns, or missionaries, devote their entire lives to the movements; but there are also congregational members, others who participate on special occasions only, and yet others who are sympathizers, but might be included as members, even though they could belong to another religion. In fact, although core members of world-rejecting movements tend to have an exclusive relationship with their particular movement, those who associate with world-affirming groups may be quite promiscuous in their allegiances at a more peripheral level, practicing transcendental meditation, partaking in a number of complementary medicines, attending an assortment of encounter groups, communicating with the angelic realm, and dropping into a Krishna restaurant for a vegetarian meal.

Another difficulty is a high turnover rate, with joiners being counted more assiduously than leavers. Many people have joined an NRM for a short period of time, but then decided that it was not for them after all, and have left. This fact, which has been demonstrated by a large number of scholarly studies of a variety of movements, causes embarrassment for both the NRMs and their opponents, the latter being eager to explain membership of

NRMs in terms of brainwashing or mind control – especially when they have had an interest in the illegal practice of involuntary deprogramming. However, while it is true that many NRMs, at least in their early days, have, like evangelical Christians, put considerable pressure on potential converts, this tends not to be all that effective. A study of the Unification Church in the late 1970s, when accusations of brainwashing were at their height, discovered that over 90 percent of those who became sufficiently interested in the movement to attend a residential workshop decided not to join, and the majority of those who did join left within two years (Barker 1984). Indeed, many NRMs fail to survive much beyond two or three generations.

RESPONSES TO NRMS

Different individuals, groups, and societies have responded to the contemporary NRMs in a variety of ways. Some individuals have become involved in active opposition – particularly the parents of young converts who have given up promising careers and cut themselves off from family and former friends. Not that all parents have been upset – there are those who have welcomed their children's new-found faith, and more who, while not exactly overjoyed, have become resigned to the situation. At least part of the variation is likely to be traceable to previous relationships, and part to the extent to which an NRM demands exclusive commitment from its members.

Since the 1970s there has been a mushrooming of groups formed by parents and others opposed to specific NRMs or the movements in general. These began to network and came to be generically referred to as the anti-cult movement. As with the NRMs, these groups and their members can differ quite radically from one another, but generally speaking they have been primarily concerned about the actual and potential harm that NRMs might cause, and have tended to select only negative actions in their depiction of what they frequently refer to as "destructive cults." There are also a number of frequently overlapping groups, referred to as the countercult movement, concerned

more with the "wrong theology" than the "bad actions" of NRMs. Another type of "cult-watching" group that has arisen is the research-oriented group. These adopt the methods of the social sciences in trying to be as objective and balanced as possible in their analyses of NRMs, using, for example, the comparative method to discover whether a particular action (such as suicide or child abuse) might be found at the same or even a higher rate among members of traditional religions as it is amongst NRMs, although the action has become far more visible when reported in the media as a "cult activity" (the religious affiliation of members of mainstream religions rarely being reported in accounts of their crimes). Fourthly, there are what have been referred to as cult-apologist groups, which are often closely associated with the NRMs themselves. These form a mirror image of anti-cult groups insofar as they select only positive aspects of NRMs and highlight the negative features of the anti-cultists.

Official responses to the NRMs have varied, from their being completely outlawed in some Islamic countries to their being treated in the same way as any other religion in countries such as the Netherlands or the US, although actual practices have not always been as even-handed as the law would seem to demand. Several countries require religions to register in order to become recognized legal entities, and sometimes there are two or more levels at which registration may occur, with special privileges for, say, established, state, or traditional religions. Sometimes criteria for registration require having been active in the country for a certain number of years, or having a minimum number of members, both of which can militate against NRMs. Several governments have commissioned official reports about the movements. Some, such as the Dutch and Swedish reports, concluded that the law as it stood was adequate to deal with any antisocial behavior in which NRMs might indulge; other reports have recommended strong action being taken against the movements; and the French and Belgian reports included lists of "sects" (including the Quakers and the YWCA) which, although not officially adopted by the respective governments, have unofficially "given permission" to people to treat religions on the list in a discriminatory fashion.

SEE ALSO Charisma; Charismatic Movement; Fundamentalism; Globalization, Religion and; Millenarianism; New Age; Religious Cults; Satanism; Scientology; Sect

REFERENCES AND SUGGESTED READINGS

Barker, E. (1984) *The Making of a Moonie: Brainwashing or Choice?* Blackwell, Oxford.

Barker, E. (1989) *New Religious Movements: A Practical Introduction.* HMSO, London.

Borowik, I. & Babinski, G. (Eds.) (1997) *New Religious Phenomena in Central and Eastern Europe.* Nomos, Krakow.

Bromley, D. G. & Melton, J. G. (Eds.) (2002) *Cults, Religion, and Violence.* Cambridge University Press, Cambridge.

Dawson, L. L. (Ed.) (2003) *Cults and New Religious Movements.* Blackwell, Oxford.

Hadden, J. K. & Cowan, D. E. (Eds.) (2000) *Religion on the Internet.* JAI Press, Amsterdam.

McFarland, H. N. (1967) *Rush Hour of the Gods.* Macmillan, New York.

Melton, J. G. (1992) *Encyclopedic Handbook of Cults in America.* Garland, New York.

Melton, J. G. (2004) Perspective: Toward a Definition of "New Religion." *Nova Religio* 8: 73–87.

Richardson, J. T. (Ed.) (2004) *Regulating Religion: Case Studies from Around the Globe.* Kluwer, Dordrecht.

Shimazono, S. (2004) *From Salvation to Spirituality: Popular Religious Movements in Modern Japan.* TransPacific, Melbourne.

Wilson, B. (1990) *The Social Dimensions of Sectarianism: Sects and New Religious Movements in Contemporary Society.* Clarendon, Oxford.

Wilson, B. & Dobbelaere, K. (1994) *A Time to Chant: The Soka Gakkai Buddhists in Britain.* Clarendon, Oxford.

new reproductive technologies

Karen Throsby

The new reproductive technologies constitute a broad constellation of technologies aimed at facilitating, preventing, or otherwise intervening in the process of reproduction. This includes, for example, contraception, abortion, antenatal testing, birth technologies, and conceptive technologies. These interventions focus predominantly, although not exclusively, on the female body and, with some notable exceptions (e.g., a privately arranged and implemented donor insemination), operate within the medical domain. The description of these technologies as "new" is contested, particularly by some feminists who have argued that they are simply part of a long history of attempts to control women's bodies (Klein 1987). However, others have highlighted the extent to which the new reproductive technologies are both produced by, and productive of, contemporary biomedicine, and that women are not simply passive recipients or victims of those technologies but are actively involved in their production (Saetnan et al. 2000).

The new reproductive technologies constitute a highly controversial and contested site. One of the key areas of debate is in relation to the disputed "life" status of embryos and fetuses. These debates lie at the heart of attempts to draw ethical, moral, and legal boundaries around the conditions under which women are allowed to terminate pregnancies. Imaging and antenatal testing technologies are central to these debates, making the fetus visible during pregnancy and leading to the production of images that have been readily taken up by the "pro-life" movement as demonstrative of its "life" status. However, many feminists have highlighted the ways in which particularly ultrasound imaging focuses only the fetus, to the exclusion of the broader context of that image – the body of the pregnant woman. The title of Rayna Rapp's book *Testing Women, Testing the Foetus: The Social Impact of Amniocentesis in America* (1999) challenges this technological separation of woman and fetus, and in the book she highlights the ways in which antenatal testing offers significant possibilities for women to terminate pregnancies affected by serious disabilities, but also confronts them with difficult choices and dilemmas. More recently, not only fetuses in the uterus but also embryos created outside of the body, for example in in vitro fertilization (IVF) treatment, have become a focus for these debates, particularly in relation to the destruction of embryos not needed for further treatment, or the use of embryos for research (Williams et al. 2003).

Another feature of the new reproductive technologies is their role in the production of novel, and often controversial, family structures, redefining relationships and kinship categories (e.g., Edwards et al. 1999). In addition to the longstanding use of donor insemination techniques by single and lesbian women to facilitate reproduction outside of the heterosexual nuclear family structure, IVF techniques and the ability to cryo-preserve gametes and embryos have led to the fragmentation of the conventional categories of reproduction. Social, genetic, and gestational parenthood can become separated out in surrogacy and donor gamete arrangements, and conventional kinship categories are confounded by intergenerational and intrafamilial surrogacies. These novel family structures are controversial, and are often reported in the media as indicative of a potential breakdown of "family values" and the "natural" reproductive order. However, the new reproductive technologies also offer new family-building possibilities for those for whom reproduction within the normatively prescribed boundaries of the heterosexual nuclear family is either undesirable or impossible.

These very high-profile and extraordinary cases tap into widely held concerns about the extent to which the new reproductive technologies might go "too far." These fears are encapsulated in the increasingly ubiquitous figure of the "designer baby" (e.g., Gosden 1999) – a shorthand referent which bundles together a wide range of present and (imagined) future technologies of embryo selection, design, and cloning which are seen as fundamentally challenging what it means to be human. However, while these present and imagined future cases are undoubtedly significant in sociological terms, they are also not representative of the more mundane, everyday experience of the new reproductive technologies. In particular, the technologies themselves are inaccessible to many people, either through religious, social, or cultural proscription, or because of the prohibitive costs. This is true not only for the more "high-tech" technologies such as IVF, but also for contraception, abortion, and antenatal and birth technologies. Conversely, while women in many countries have fought high-profile struggles for the right to have an abortion, other women have found themselves struggling for the right *not* to use particular technologies. For example, some women are coerced into unwanted abortions as a result of strict population control policies or socially held preferences for children of a particular sex; others have been subject to coercive sterilization programs, or to fertility-damaging and harmful contraceptives. Race and class are therefore crucial dimensions to people's experiences of the new reproductive technologies, both within national contexts and internationally. This international dimension is becoming increasingly important with the growing global trade in gametes, embryos, and stem cells, raising important questions about the power relations between donors and purchasers.

SEE ALSO: Abortion as a Social Problem; Body and Society; Cloning; Family Planning, Abortion, and Reproductive Health; Genetic Engineering as a Social Problem; Infertility; Pro-Choice and Pro-Life Movements; Women's Health

REFERENCES AND SUGGESTED READINGS

Edwards, J., Franklin, S., Hirsch, E., Price, F., & Strathern, M. (1999) *Technologies of Procreation: Kinship in the Age of Assisted Conception*, 2nd edn. Routledge, London.
Gosden, R. (1999) *Designer Babies: The Brave New World of Reproductive Technology*. Phoenix, London.
Klein, R. D. (1987). What's "New" About the "New" Reproductive Technologies. In: Corea, G., Klein, R. D., Hanmer, J. et al. (Eds.), *Man-Made Women: How New Reproductive Technologies Affect Women*. Indiana University Press, Bloomington, pp. 64–73.
Saetnan, A. R., Oudshoorn, N., & Kirejczyk, M. (Eds.) (2000) *Bodies of Technology: Women's Involvement with Reproductive Medicine*. Ohio State University Press, Columbus.
Williams, C., Kitzinger, J., & Henderson, L. (2003) Envisaging the Embryo in Stem Cell Research: Rhetorical Strategies and Media Reporting of the Ethical Debates. *Sociology of Health and Illness* 25 (7): 793–814.

new social movement theory

Steven M. Buechler

New social movement theory (NSMT) emerged in the 1980s in Europe to analyze new types of social movements that appeared from the 1960s onward. These movements were seen as "new" in contrast to the "old" working-class movement identified by Marxist theory as the major challenger to capitalist society. By contrast, new social movements are organized around race, ethnicity, youth, sexuality, countercultures, environmentalism, pacifism, human rights, and the like. NSMT is a distinct approach to the study of social movements, albeit with significant internal variations (Cohen 1985; Klandermans 1991; Larana et al. 1994).

The distinctiveness of NSMT became evident when it was transplanted into US sociology where it contrasted sharply with resource mobilization theory and shared some affinities with social constructionism. Both NSMT and social constructionism signified a cultural turn in social movement theory. NSMT emphasized culture as both the arena and the means of protest. As an arena, this meant a shift from conventional instrumental struggle in the political sphere to contests over meanings, symbols, and identities in the cultural sphere. As a means, this meant that activists were less concerned with accumulating material resources and more interested in promoting expressive, identity-oriented actions whose very form challenged the instrumental rationality of political elites. New social movements and theories about them thereby decentered politics as the central site of struggle and shifted attention to culture and civil society instead (Melucci 1996).

A second aspect of NSMT most clearly reflected its European heritage; this was the tendency to analyze new social movements as a historically specific response to new social formations. These theorists were as interested in the changing contours of the larger society as they were with the new movements that responded to them; the emphasis on "newness" was as much about changes in social order as it

was about new protest forms. Thus, just as Marxists argued that the "old" labor movement was a logical response to industrial capitalism, new social movement theorists argued that new movements were equally logical responses to a new social formation identified as postindustrial, information-based, postmodern, or advanced capitalist society. This insistence on examining the links between changes in social structure and social activism was the most distinctive aspect of NSMT (Buechler 2000).

What resonated in the US context was NSMT's emphasis on collective identity, which has been widely adopted by mainstream US social movement theory. Again, a contrast with the "old" labor movement is helpful. Marxists often wrote as if an "objective" class-based identity was unproblematic and the only challenge was to cultivate a corresponding "subjective" class consciousness. For NSMT, no group identity is objectively more central than any other, and every collective identity must be socially constructed before collective action is possible. The "old" issue of cultivating class consciousness has been replaced with the "new" one of constructing collective identity itself. This issue has moved to center stage precisely because recent social transformations have replaced stable identities rooted in neighborhoods, churches, and unions with transient and multiple identities refracted through the lenses of mass culture. In this new social formation, the social construction of a symbolically meaningful collective identity is a major accomplishment of new social movements and a prerequisite for other movement objectives (Melucci 1996).

These premises about cultural politics, social formations, and collective identity are the core of NSMT; additional themes appear in most versions of the theory. One concerns the diffuse social base of new social movements. In contrast to the working-class base of old social movements, new social movements are more often identified as broadly middle class or specifically new middle class, drawing on knowledge-based professions for their base (Kriesi 1989). Alternatively, new social movements may be rooted in other social identities that cross-cut class categories, such as race, ethnicity, generation, gender, or sexuality. Finally, some new social movements defy classification by standard group identities because they revolve around a common ideology or worldview such as environmentalism or pacifism.

The types of values that underlie these movements are another theme in much NSMT work. If the old social movement was rooted in materialist values, new social movements are seen as rooted in postmaterialist values (Inglehart 1990). Hence, the concern is less with redistributive struggles and quantity of life as it is with quality-of-life issues that are especially salient for middle-class constituencies who can presume some level of material comfort. Other postmaterialist values are reflected in campaigns that seek self-determination and autonomy from intrusive social controls. Rather than seeking to "get more," such struggles strive to "get free" from forces that control, colonize, or commodify life in late modern society (Habermas 1987).

Another theme in much NSMT is the politicization of everyday life. Again, this is a feature not just of movements but also of new social formations whose increasingly intrusive forms of power saturate everyday existence and thereby create new terrains of struggle. As a result, new social movement activists do not make sharp distinctions between their politics and their lives; they see politics as embedded in and flowing out of private life. The 1960s slogan that "the personal is political" reflects this politicization of everyday life that typifies many new social movements (Larana et al. 1994).

A final theme in NSMT concerns organizational form. Whereas both Marxism-Leninism and resource mobilization privilege large, centralized, bureaucratic, and hierarchical structures, new social movements favor decentralized, nonhierarchical, participatory processes. Although centralized organization may be more likely to succeed, new social movement activists reject it on multiple grounds. First, centralized organization creates problems of oligarchy and power differences within the movement. Second, the values of activists often lead them to favor egalitarian participation over instrumental success. Such movements prefer "prefigurative politics" whereby the movement's egalitarian organizational form foreshadows the larger social changes it seeks. If the old organizational image was a centralized army ready to do battle, the new image is diffuse, submerged, intersecting

cultural networks where membership and participation are valued over discipline and success. Such forms may not be the most strategically effective, but they can be powerful mechanisms for creating and sustaining member loyalty and commitment (Melucci 1996).

These themes distinguish NSMT from both classical Marxism and resource mobilization with their emphases on political contention, material resources, formal organization, and instrumental success. They also suggest some common concerns between NSMT and collective behavior or social constructionist approaches with their emphases on symbolic meaning, grievance articulation, fluid processes, and malleable identities. Having described NSMT, it is also important to acknowledge some internal variations in this paradigm as it emerged in European sociology.

Four founders of this perspective help illustrate its common as well as variable features. For Manuel Castells (1983), it is capitalist development that has transformed urban space and provoked new urban movements demanding non-commodified forms of collective consumption, emphasizing community identity and culture, and seeking political self-management and autonomy. For Alain Touraine (1981), it is post-industrial society that has made possible the increasing self-production of society, but control of this capacity is the object of a new class struggle between state managers and technocrats on the one hand, and consumers and clients on the other. For Jürgen Habermas (1987), it is advanced capitalism's imperatives of money, power, and instrumental rationality that threaten to colonize the everyday life world and have provoked new constituencies to mobilize and articulate a communicative rationality in defense of a beleaguered life world. For Alberto Melucci (1996), it is postmodern forms of social control, conformity pressures, and information processing that have provoked new social movements to develop personal, spiritual, and expressive forms of protest that create new collective identities while rejecting the instrumental rationality of the dominant social order. These examples illustrate different emphases within NSMT while also underscoring common efforts to link changes in social formations with new social movements.

Much of the variation within NSMT may be captured in an ideal-typical contrast between "political" and "cultural" versions of the theory. The political version of NSMT is a neo-Marxist approach that identifies advanced capitalism as the dominant social formation that provokes new social movements. This variant sees power as systemic and centralized, is macro-oriented and state-centered, and envisions a politics that retains an instrumental orientation while also building alliances between traditional class actors and new social movements. The cultural version of NSMT is a post-Marxist approach that identifies a post-industrial or postmodern information society as the dominant social formation provoking new social movements. This variant sees power as diffuse and decentralized, is meso- and micro-oriented with a focus on civil society, and envisions a politics that is culturally driven and privileges new social movements over class actors. The political version still sees merit in instrumental struggles and views culturally oriented groups as a potentially apolitical diversion from such struggles. Conversely, the cultural version sees conventional tactics and struggles as a trap that coopts political movements, and instead portrays culturally subversive actions as posing the most fundamental challenges (Buechler 2000).

Despite these variations, NSMT was seen as a unified perspective alongside resource mobilization and social constructionism within US social movement theory. The most common criticism of NSMT concerned its apparent claim of a sharp disjuncture between old labor movements with one set of characteristics and new cultural movements with another. The most incisive critiques reexamined the history of labor movements and argued that many of the supposedly distinctive features of new social movements were crucial to the mobilization of this "old" movement, including an expressive politics of cultural symbols and ongoing efforts to establish a collective identity. The role of "new" social movement characteristics in the "old" labor movement poses serious questions for some NSMT claims.

The more interesting story about the reception of NSMT in US sociology is one of selective cooptation. The grand theorizing behind European versions of NSMT was simply too foreign to take root in the pragmatic, middle-range, and frequently positivist soil of US sociology. Thus, as it entered US sociology, NSMT was stripped of its most sweeping and distinctive claims about the connections between social formations and types of movements. Instead, the paradigm was reduced in elementarist fashion to new dimensions or factors that needed to be considered alongside more familiar ones. It is ironic that once NSMT was distorted in this fashion, the decontextualized concept of collective identity became very popular in mainstream research as well as attempts to synthesize different traditions by combining notions of mobilizing structures and framing processes with that of collective identity. For these reasons, the story of NSMT remains entangled with larger differences in theoretical style between European and US sociology (Buechler 2000).

SEE ALSO: Anti-War and Peace Movements; Civil Rights Movement; Collective Identity; Culture, Social Movements and; Environmental Movements; Framing and Social Movements; Global Justice as a Social Movement; Identity Politics/Relational Politics; Personal is Political; Resource Mobilization Theory; Social Movements; Student Movements; Women's Movements

REFERENCES AND SUGGESTED READINGS

Buechler, S. (2000) *Social Movements in Advanced Capitalism*. Oxford University Press, New York.

Castells, M. (1983) *The City and the Grassroots*. University of California Press, Berkeley.

Cohen, J. (1985) "Strategy or Identity"? New Theoretical Paradigms and Contemporary Social Movements. *Social Research* 52: 663–716.

Habermas, J. (1987) *The Theory of Communicative Action*, Vol. 2. Beacon, Boston.

Inglehart, R. (1990) Values, Ideology, and Cognitive Mobilization in New Social Movements. In: Dalton, R. & Kuechler, M. (Eds.), *Challenging the Political Order*. Oxford University Press, New York, pp. 43–66.

Klandermans, B. (1991) New Social Movements and Resource Mobilization: The European and American Approaches Revisited. In: Rucht, D. (Ed.), *Research on Social Movements*. Westview, Boulder, CO.

Kriesi, H. (1989) New Social Movements and the New Class in the Netherlands. *American Journal of Sociology* 94: 1078–116.

Larana, E., Johnston, H., & Gusfield, J. (Eds.) (1994) *New Social Movements: From Ideology to Identity.* Temple University Press, Philadelphia.

Melucci, A. (1996) *Challenging Codes.* Cambridge University Press, Cambridge.

Touraine, A. (1981) *The Voice and the Eye.* Cambridge University Press, New York.

new urbanism

Elyshia Aseltine

New urbanism is a philosophical and spatial-use approach to architectural and city planning that emphasizes creating high-density, self-contained communities that meet both the spatial and social needs of neighborhood residents. The ideal new urbanism community is compact, multi or mixed use, diverse in terms of race, ethnicity, income, and age, and pedestrian and public transportation friendly. New urbanist ideals have been used in both revitalization efforts of existing neighborhoods as well as in the creation of new communities, such as Celebration, Florida, Kentlands, Maryland and Laguna, California. New urbanism gained popularity as a planning approach in the 1980s as a criticism of mid-nineteenth century development patterns of suburban sprawl and disinvestment in central cities. Despite the recent increase in support of new urbanist ideals, new urbanism is not considered a new approach to community planning; instead, its proponents espouse a return to a more "traditional urbanism" (i.e., compact, close-knit communities that developed naturally until the twentieth century). For advocates of new urbanism, current zoning regulations and subdivision laws are creating communities that are environmentally, physically, and socially destructive. New urbanism supporters suggest that suburban sprawl and central city disinvestment lead to increasing racial and economic segregation, overuse and destruction of environmental resources and habitats, threats to distinct local cultures of place, and limited access of the poor to decent,

affordable housing, as well as adequate services and employment opportunities. Advocates propose the principles of new urbanism as a means of revitalizing declining urban areas, promoting local culture, preserving limited natural resources, assisting in addressing social inequalities, and creating spaces more conducive to challenging social problems, such as crime. While the link between the spatial organization of a community and its social health is not new to urban planning overall, new urbanism is unique in that it makes this connection explicit in its planning strategies (Congress for the New Urbanism 2000). Given its broad depth of concerns, new urbanism has piqued the interests of individuals and groups concerned with environmental protection, historical preservation, smart growth, transportation, and social justice.

Despite new urbanism's popularity, there has been little concrete investigation and documentation of how effectively new urbanism developments meet the spatial and social goals espoused by new urbanism proponents. Critics of new urbanism as a planning approach argue that "New Urbanism is much too malleable to provide meaningful regulation of inner-city renewal efforts ... Extremely broad and conflicting sets of agendas can be accommodated under principals of New Urbanism [i.e. diversity, pedestrian orientation, accessible public spaces and community institutions, and celebration of unique local elements], rendering its design guidelines so elastic as to be ineffective" (Elliot et al. 2004). Critics of the resulting neighborhoods of new urbanism projects argue that these communities are predominantly high-income, ethnically homogeneous communities that fail to demonstrate achievement of the social goals outlined by new urbanism (Bohl 2000). Despite criticism, most agree that new urbanism has "rekindled the longstanding debate over the relationship between environment and behavior" (Bohl 2000). In the future, expect to see an increase in research that scrutinizes the connection between place and social health, that examines the effectiveness of new urbanism endeavors in meeting its social goals, and that explores the policy and financing barriers and limitations to new urbanism projects.

SEE ALSO: Built Environment; City; City Planning/Urban Design; Suburbs; Urban;

Urban Renewal and Redevelopment; Urbanism/Urban Culture; Urbanization

REFERENCES AND SUGGESTED READINGS

Bohl, C. (2000) New Urbanism and the City: Potential Applications and Implications for Distressed Inner-City Neighborhoods. *Housing Policy Debate* 11: 751–801.

Calthorpe, P. (1993) *The Next American Metropolis: Ecology, Community and the American Dream*. Princeton Architectural Press, New York.

Congress for the New Urbanism (2000) *Charter of the New Urbanism*. McGraw Hill, New York.

Elliot, J., Gotham, K., & Milligan, M. (2004) Framing the Urban: Struggles over HOPE VI and New Urbanism in a Historic City. *City and Community* 3: 373–94.

Katz, P. (1994) *The New Urbanism*. McGraw Hill, New York.

Talen, E. (2002) The Social Goals of New Urbanism. *Housing Policy Debate* 13: 165–88.

NGO/INGO

Leslie Sklair

Non-governmental organizations (NGOs) and international non-governmental organizations (INGOs) are umbrella terms that refer to organizations not directly controlled by the state or governments, mostly concerned with human rights of various kinds (including civic and political, economic and social, and environmental rights), professional and occupational interests, and various other enthusiasms. They range from very large organizations with considerable budgets and international recognition, through national organizations with a strictly domestic agenda, to small, locally funded neighborhood groups. Many are connected and overlap with social and political movements. However, the existence of many domestically and internationally powerful QUANGOs (quasi-NGOs) and GONGOs (government-organized NGOs) suggests that, in practice, "non-governmental" is not as straightforward as it at first appears. The close involvement of many NGOs/INGOs with governments, intergovernmental bodies (notably the UN and the World Bank), and transnational corporations and other organs of big business is a constant source of controversy.

The most influential human rights INGO is Amnesty International, with around a million members in more than 160 countries and national sections in over 50 countries. Its budget of around US$25 million is raised from individual subscriptions and funding from private foundations. It does not accept money from governments, although most NGOs/INGOs do. The AI website is heavily used and the AI link with the UN Commission on Human Rights is particularly useful for studying the contradictions inherent for genuinely non-governmental INGOs forced to work with governments and intergovernmental agencies. Despite the work they do, many human rights INGOs have become rather elitist organizations and this has created difficulties for those they are dedicated to serve. The same can be said for the major environmental INGOS, notably Greenpeace and Friends of the Earth. The mainstream view of NGOs/INGOs is that their growth has paralleled the growth of global civil society (indeed, for many scholars in the field, this is a tautology). The success of the largest of them has led to the creation of a new class of activist-lobbyists, who command respect if not affection from governments and big business for their expertise (particularly their use of the media to highlight abuses of human rights and environmental justice). As a result, some prominent NGO/INGO leaders have taken up lucrative job offers in the state apparatus or in big business. This has led to splits between the large, powerful NGOs/INGOs and some of their smaller, more radical, anti-establishment counterparts, who came together in the meetings of the World Social Forum first in Porto Alegre, Brazil in 2001, and all over the world since then.

SEE ALSO Civil Society; Global Justice as a Social Movement; Human Rights; Organizations, Voluntary; Social Movements; Transnational Movements

REFERENCES AND SUGGESTED READINGS

Fisher, W. & Ponniah, T. (eds.) (2003) *Another World is Possible: Popular Alternatives to Globalization at the World Social Forum*. Zed Books, London.

Rajagopal, B. (2003) *International Law from Below: Development, Social Movements and Third World Resistance.* Cambridge University Press, Cambridge.

Sklair, L. (2002) *Globalization: Capitalism and Its Alternatives.* Oxford University Press, Oxford.

Nietzsche, Friedrich (1844–1900)

Robert J. Antonio

When Nietzsche was only 25 years old he was granted a doctoral degree from the University of Leipzig without completing a dissertation, and was appointed to a position in classical philology at the University of Basel. From the start, his philosophical writing was brilliant, unorthodox, and controversial. He dispensed with the formalities of academic writing and systemic philosophizing. Arthur Schopenhauer's philosophy and Richard Wagner's music exerted influence on young Nietzsche's thinking. Brief service as a medic in the Franco-Prussian war and the experience of wartime devastation led him to criticize the modern state and view patriotic fervor as the bane of all genuine culture. After 10 years of teaching, poor health forced him to leave his academic position. He wrote his major philosophical works in relative obscurity, but his fame grew meteorically shortly after madness ended his writing in 1889. He had enormous literary and cultural impact and influenced many of the twentieth century's most important philosophers and social theorists.

However, Nietzsche's impacts are not easy to trace because they have been multifarious and diffuse. Relatively few social theorists directly engage his texts or quote extensively from them. Rather, many Nietzsche-influenced thinkers just mention his ideas or name him in poignant passages at key junctures, draw on Nietzschean themes that have been incorporated into the cultural atmospherics, or declare simply that he had a major impact on their thinking. Carl Jung spoke compellingly of his trepidation about reading Nietzsche – a journey of discovery to the world's "other pole" that can take away the ground from under one's feet, he feared. Although rejecting Nietzsche, Jung declared that engaging and being deeply disturbed by the philosopher, who he thought went "over the brink of the world," was a "tremendous experience" that left a deep imprint. Many other thinkers of Jung's generation spoke similarly of being moved by Nietzsche, albeit with diverse results. Max Weber said that "after Nietzsche" only a "few big children" believe that science could save us from ethical decision or give meaning to life. He purportedly declared that Nietzsche, along with Marx, changed profoundly social theory's discursive field and that all serious social theorists must address the two thinkers, at least indirectly. Nietzsche's shadow can be seen at important points in Weber's work. However, even obvious Nietzschean themes are often missed by readers who have not engaged with Nietzsche.

Intellectual historians and philosophers often have argued that Nietzsche contributed substantially to and became emblematic of growing doubts about Enlightenment rationality and about related ideas of social progress and modern political ideology, which deepened along with intensification of modern industrial society's problems and increased application of its scientific and technological powers in the service of mass regimentation, indoctrination, and warfare. Nietzsche's trenchant criticism of modernity has been attractive to thinkers with diverse points of view, and his aphoristic, fragmented texts have been interpreted in divergent ways and fused with contradictory approaches. In moments of perceived crisis, Nietzschean discourses explode on the scene, amplifying wider public sensibilities that liberal, left, and conservative politics are exhausted. At the end of World War I's mass blood-letting, Thomas Mann's declaration that he saw "Nietzsche, only Nietzsche" and Randolph Bourne's assertion that Nietzsche was *the* needed tonic to counter "optimism-haunted philosophies" gave voice to growing alienation from the political and cultural circles who supported uncritically and even celebrated entry into the war and opposed wartime dissent. Also addressing the war-related malaise, Weber expressed fears, in his famous "politics as a vocation" speech, that impatience with liberal democratic politics was opening the door to extremist demagogues.

He warned prophetically that antiliberal currents were creating conditions for the rise of authoritarian leaders and true-believer followers who would impose, within a decade, a "period of reaction" and "polar night of icy darkness and hardness." Weber did not mention Nietzsche in this speech, but its main theme converged with the philosopher's warnings about the likely apocalyptic consequences of the new forms of political fanaticism. In the late 1980s, neoconservative Alan Bloom attacked "Nietzschean" postmodern, poststructuralist, and multicultural theorists. He charged that Nietzsche had replaced Marx as the totemic theorist of the cultural left and that they fueled destructive relativism, which diluted culture, empowered "politically correct" know-nothings, weakened moral discipline, and paved the way for protofascist currents. However, Bloom himself deployed Nietzschean themes against the cultural left "Nietzscheans." Other prominent neoconservative, paleoconservative, and New Right theorists also borrowed from Nietzsche, or claimed to be inspired by his ideas.

Just before the onset of debilitating madness, Nietzsche declared that one day he would be linked to "a crisis without equal on earth." The iconic photographs of Hitler being greeted by Nietzsche's sister at the door of her deceased brother's archive and pondering intently the philosopher's bust provide evidence that the prophecy came true in a way that this self-identified "antipolitical" thinker would have detested. Hitler and Mussolini both claimed to follow in his tracks. Yet Nietzsche's imprint also is easily visible in major left critiques of fascism, Stalinism, and corporate capitalism, such as Adorno and Horkheimer's *Dialectic of Enlightenment* and Marcuse's *Eros and Civilization*. Karl Löwith (1986: 83) declared that Nietzsche was "precursor of the German present, and at the same time its sharpest negation – 'National Socialist' and 'Cultural Bolshevik'." Nietzsche's vehement attacks on mediocrity and clarion call for entirely new types of leaders, who are "beyond good and evil" and who have the ability to create a fundamentally new cultural order, transcending "decadent" western civilization, have inspired counterculture dropouts, quasi-religious aesthetes, and political extremists, as well as serious artists, intellectuals, and radicals with high aspirations. He

also influenced theorists who support cultural openness, diversity, and tolerance against chauvinism, hubris, and cruelty. Still, most Nietzscheans have warned about cultural decline, disintegration, crisis, and consequent political exhaustion. Today, Nietzscheans on the left and on the right pose parallel "end of modernity" and "end of alternatives" scenarios, chronicling the collapse of post-World War II modernization theories and their optimistic hopes for social progress.

Nietzsche posed a radical subversive challenge to the presuppositions of canonical views of western modernity as a progressive transcendence of tradition and mythology. Like many other western philosophers and social theorists, Nietzsche traced the roots of modernity to classical Greek antiquity. Stressing emphatically culture's formative powers, he argued that an "order of rank" (i.e., an enduring value system and worldview) gives shape to civilizations, which can last for millennia. Nietzsche declared that he wanted to replace "sociology" with a "theory of the forms of domination" and the concept of "society" with (his chief interest) the "culture complex." He held that civilizational culture complexes' long-lasting values and ideas take on different forms under divergent historical circumstances, which they also paradoxically shape. He held that "ascetic priests" or ingenious philosophical elites fashion civilization's normative and ideational foundations; they frame mythologies that cultivate self-control and self-discipline among the vast majority, a mass of mediocre people, and that forge them into a compliant "herd" or society. "Slave moralities" force the herd to act in socially acceptable ways, stem their potentially disruptive biological drives, and redirect their consequent frustration into "imaginary revenge" inward against the self (i.e., guilt) and outward against cultural enemies (i.e., hatred of noncompliant, different, and exceptional people). Promising salvation for the obedient, slave moralities create social order and provide meaning to human suffering by establishing blame and punishing outliers. Nietzsche claimed that healthy, uninhibited, superior individuals are prime targets of the herd's rancorous social psychology or "ressentiment" and consequent hostile inclinations. But he argued that the strongest, cleverest people of this "noble" stratum of "sovereign individuals" resist the herd's machinations, stand above slave morality, and will give rise to *Übermenschen*, who will fashion a new postmodern civilization. Considering Herbert Spencer to be a "decadent," Nietzsche contended that his utilitarian "shopkeeper's philosophy" and Social Darwinism put mediocrity on a pedestal and celebrated the victory of ascetic priests and their herd of weaklings over the strong and noble as evolutionary progress. Nietzsche's elitist individualism animated his "antisociological" critique of mass political leaders, obedient masses, and modern society. In *Civilization and Its Discontents* Freud drew in part from Nietzsche's argument that cultural elites forge individuals into a society by acculturating them to values that repress their impulses, shape them into conformist social beings, and thus "make them sick."

In contrast to Eurocentric theories, however, Nietzsche portrayed the "rise" of the West to be a history of cultural decline rather than cultural progress. Seeing western civilization's "subjectified culture" as the prototype slave morality, Nietzsche argued that Christianity fused Judaic prophetic religion with Socrates' Hellenic break with pre-Socratic antiquity's naturalistic, aesthetic culture. Nietzsche charged that Christianity's brutal vision of the crucifixion, repressive approach to sexuality, threat of eternal damnation, and extreme violence against heretics and infidels gave rise to generations of inward, guilt-ridden, timid, "decadent" masses who comply readily with authority or the "good"and, on command, smash cultural foes, or "evil." He held that Christian cultural roots have been refashioned into secular forms (e.g., socialism, feminism, liberalism, democracy), which employ more multifaceted, comprehensive, and rationalized mechanisms of cultural control, but preserve Christianity's binary frameworks of good versus evil and friend versus foe. He charged that sociology sanctifies "decaying forms of society" by treating western modernity's secular cultural control system (i.e., decadent values, tireless work, repressed drives, and strategically managed, artificial, conformist selves) as progress. Attacking the Protestant work ethic and "industrial culture," he condemned the need for workers to submit to "vulgar," "bloodsucking" employers and to a dreary life of "work without pleasure." Nietzsche

denounced the vast cultural damages of capitalist rationalization; he contended that its philistine instrumentalization and homogenization erode genuine belief and character and produce confused, indiscriminate selves who embrace enthusiastically deranged, fanatic, ersatz versions of ascetic priests and unleash repressed impulses in socially disintegrative ways. He portrayed later modernity to be on the absolute brink of total cultural meltdown. Nietzsche held that European "nationalism" and "race hatred" ("scabies of the heart and blood poisoning") and, especially, German nationalist, anti-Semitic impulses demolished cultural creativity and was a harbinger of a frightening new mass politics that would carry authoritarian regimentation and viciousness toward outsiders to unimaginable heights and put an ultra-violent end to the most decadent, final phase of western civilization.

Although mostly indirect and often unrecognized, Nietzsche's contribution to sociology and modern social theory is multifaceted and basic. His critique of Enlightenment rationality and arguments about the limits of modern science have contributed, especially through Weber's appropriation, to discourse about the relation of facts and values, the role of science in modernity's disenchanted public spheres, and the problem of meaning in post-traditional cultures. Nietzsche's stress on the importance of aesthetic, emotional, bodily sensibilities as a source of value and pivotal element in interpersonal relations counters overly rational, cognitive, conformist theories of socialization. His perspectivist critique of absolutist truth-claims and a connection of knowledge and value creation to situated cultural interests and, especially, his "genealogy of morals" contributed to the rise of the sociology of knowledge, critical theories, and standpoint theories. His views about the primacy of culture and crucial role of cultural reproduction in the formation and perpetuation of enduring civilizations anticipated the rise of cultural sociology and comparative civilizational studies. Nietzsche's argument about western "decadence" influenced later twentieth-century critiques of "Eurocentrism" and "declinist" cultural theories.

However, Nietzsche's argument about the entwinement of morality and power is likely his most important contribution to social theory;

it provokes fundamental questioning of the taken-for-granted identity of the moral with the good. This core, ironically sociological facet of his antisociology has stimulated theorists such as Weber, Mannheim, Heidegger, Arendt, Strauss, Adorno, and Foucault to ponder the normative presuppositions of modern social theory and social science and the overall normative directions of modern culture and politics. Nietzsche held that moral claims often call for unreflective obedience and put halos around manipulation and violence. His self-identified "immoralism" calls on social theorists to reflect critically on normatively guided actions and expose their hidden intentions and divergent, often unintended, sociological and political consequences. Nietzsche understood that determination of culpability and aversion to imprudent moral responses and unfair, inhumane, immoral consequences require deliberate, critical reflection on the problematic relation of values and norms to particular conditions of specific situations. Thus, Nietzsche held that unquestioned obedience to morality obliterates ethical reflexivity. He also questioned modern social theorists' tendency to endorse too readily internalized values and norms as the prime source of healthy individuality and of the good society. Deconstructing conventional morality's good-versus-evil and friend-versus-foe binaries, Nietzsche saw hasty moral rhetoric as producing prejudicial snap judgments, which justify narrow mindedness, exclusion, or violence. He warned that the social costs of these moralizing tendencies can be enormous when they are manifested by persuasive demagogic leaders, who control the means of mass violence and aim to justify the use of force against cultural enemies.

Nietzsche argued that the leaders of nations at war would block critical opposition by identifying the enemy and their alleged collaborators with evil and draping the mass violence with the cloak of morality (e.g., "following God's will," "defending the homeland," "creating democracy," "liberating the people," and "patriotism"). He also held that the herd would follow their lead. What Nietzsche feared came true; the twentieth century was marked by fanatical politics, fundamentalism, ethnic and religious struggles, bloodbaths, and genocide. Its mass warfare killed and maimed tens of millions of people, including enormous numbers of innocent noncombatants. Even "small wars" have had huge "collateral damage." The Vietnam War alone incurred an estimated 2–4 million civilian casualties. Assuming that "stopping communism" and "fulfilling national obligations" were worth the extraordinary bloodshed and destruction, some pundits still assert that the US quit Vietnam prematurely. Nietzsche urged people to slow down their moral impulses and to think them over from multiple perspectives. In the wake of globalization and the events of 9/11, resurgent fundamentalism and the rampant political invocation of the good-versus-evil and friend-versus-foe binaries make Nietzsche a most timely twenty-first century theorist. Nietzsche's method of exposing the linkage of morality and power also has powerful ethical force and stimulates provocative sociological questions when it is deployed to interrogate the role of morality in more taken-for-granted and private social and cultural spaces, including one's own scientific, political, and (even) caring and loving beliefs and practices. As Foucault's Nietzsche-inspired inquiries demonstrate, the exercise of power through moral attributions and related complexes of knowledge and culture stretches from the microscopic to the macroscopic level and suffuse modern culture. However, Nietzsche's popularity has itself derived in part from his own intense moralizing and gnostic tones. Thinkers such as Mann and Bourne embraced him because they were taken by his inspiring, ethically driven deconstructive jabs at modernity's fusion of morality, cultural control, and violence, which made problematic what all too many rationally argued, "moderate" approaches have left unquestioned. Foucault and his followers alike have been attracted by the same powerful ethical impulses.

Nietzsche held that we are valuing beings who cannot live well without the normative ends provided by and which animate a cultural order of rank. He attributed the west's worst pathologies to its "nihilism." In his view, Christian-rooted morality has lost vitality, is detached from genuine "life," and does not give people adequate direction. However, he also held that late modernity contained seeds of *Übermenschen*, who will arrive "the day after tomorrow" and create a new culture complex that valorizes bodily needs, cultivates more uninhibited, spontaneous living, balances rational control with aesthetic freedom, and, ultimately, expunges *ressentiment*. Nietzsche employed the term "good European" to praise the emergent hybrid peoples that he saw arising in the contradictory interstices of late modernity's urbanization and deterritorialized cosmopolitan culture. He argued that exposure to divergent values and ways of life provided the vital cultural resources that allow people to see from multiple perspectives and share attitudes, aesthetic experiences, and emotions with outsiders. George Herbert Mead and John Dewey later framed a parallel cultural theory based on a more elaborate social psychology. Nietzsche thought that cultural diversity would cultivate new capacities for pleasure, imagination, and vision. He held that this multiplicity would produce beings capable of forging a postmodern civilization that would recover the vigor of the pre-Socratic world's "tragic culture" and preclude a return to insular tradition. Nietzsche called for a reinvigorated culture complex, anchored in aesthetic pleasure and creativity, to replace the gray on gray, bourgeois economic imperative and workaday life.

However, Nietzsche's virulent antiliberalism, apocalyptic tone, and failure to clarify the institutional structure of his hoped-for postmodern civilization left his vision politically ambiguous and opened it to conflictive appropriations. Moreover, his castigation of weakness and affirmative references to warlike, masculinist qualities resonated with the far right. Later twentieth-century protofascists reinvoked his name in calls for a remilitarized, hierarchical culture and in bitter opposition to social democrats, feminists, lesbians and gays, immigrants, and other "outsiders." Clear traces of right-wing Nietzscheanism were also visible in major neoconservative critiques of social liberalism, multiculturalism, and anti-militarism. Yet Nietzschean threads were also prominent in many opposing postmodern, postcolonial, and neopragmatist theories. Left-leaning globalization, human rights, immigration, and citizenship studies discourses also were framed in a climate influenced by neo-Nietzschean countercurrents. Marcuse's impassioned argument about opposing "the body against the machine"invoked Nietzsche in a call for cultural revolt against post-World War II capitalism's workaday life, consumer culture, military-industrial complex, and "society without opposition." Today's anti-globalization actions, critiques of neoliberalism, and post-9/11 risks of terror, war, and environmental catastrophe provide fertile cultural and political grounds for similar Nietzsche appropriations.

SEE ALSO: Critical Theory/Frankfurt School; Foucault, Michel; Knowledge, Sociology of; Marx, Karl; Weber, Max

REFERENCES AND SUGGESTED READINGS

Antonio, R. J. (1995) Nietzsche's Antisociology: Subjectified Culture and the End of History. *American Journal of Sociology* 101: 1–43

Aschheim, S. E. (1992) *The Nietzsche Legacy in Germany 1890–1990*. University of California Press, Berkeley.

Gilman, S. L. (Ed.) (1987) *Conversations With Nietzsche: A Life in the World of His Contemporaries*. Trans. D. J. Parent. Oxford University Press, New York.

Kaufmann, W. (1974) *Nietzsche: Philosopher, Psychologist, Antichrist*. Princeton University Press, Princeton.

Löwith, K. (1986 [1933]) *My Life in Germany Before and After 1933: A Report*. Trans. E. King. University of Illinois Press, Urbana.

Nietzsche, F. (1966 [1886]) *Beyond Good and Evil: Prelude to a Philosophy of the Future*. Trans. W. Kaufmann. Vintage Books, New York.

Nietzsche, F. (1969 [1887–8]) *On the Genealogy of Morals*. Trans. W. Kaufmann & R. J.Hollingdale; *Ecce Homo*. Trans. W. Kaufmann. Vintage Books, New York.

Nietzsche, F. (1969 [1883–5]) *Thus Spoke Zarathustra*. Trans. R. J. Hollingdale. Penguin, London.

Nietzsche, F. (1974 [1882]) *The Gay Science: With a Prelude in Rhymes and an Appendix of Songs*. Trans. W. Kauffmann. Vintage Books, New York.

Safranski, R. (2002) *Nietzsche: A Philosophical Biography*. Trans. S. Frisch. W. W. Norton, New York.

nihonjinron

Kosaku Yoshino

The Japanese term *nihonjinron* refers to discourses on the distinctiveness of the society, culture, and national character of the Japanese. As such, *nihonjinron* have manifested themselves periodically from the Meiji era (1868–1911) to the present, while continually undergoing changes in form. In its narrower and most recent sense, the term refers to the vogue of such discourses during the 1970s and the early 1980s, when a very large quantity of works on the unique qualities of the Japanese inundated bookstores – the so-called *nihonjinron* boom. In the aftermath, a period of critical reaction to the *nihonjinron* set in, and this in turn has had a large impact on the ways in which Japanese society and culture are discussed today.

For the most part, the *nihonjinron* were not written as rigorous, objective studies of Japanese society, culture, and national character, but rather as works of popular sociology intended to be received favorably by wider sections of the population. The works reflect the concerns of the particular historical period in which they were written, concerns with the social, cultural, and economic conditions of the times, as well as the prevailing international relations. Characteristics of the Japanese chosen for discussion as well as the tone of discussion vary according to each historical epoch.

For example, works written in the 1950s mainly took on a self-critical tone and dealt with the feudalistic aspects of Japanese society as causes of ultra-nationalism and militarism that led Japan into World War II. During that introspective period, Japanese intellectuals produced a series of works on some distinctive features of Japanese society and depicted them as feudalistic obstacles to the democratization of Japan. Among such works were sociologist Kawashima's *The Familial Structure of Japanese Society* (1950), anthropological geographer Iizuka's *The Mental Climate of the Japanese* (1952), and social psychologist Minami's *The Psychology of the Japanese People* (1953).

In contrast to this, the *nihonjinron* that flourished in the 1970s and the early 1980s sought a more positive reevaluation of Japaneseness. The literature portrayed the distinctive features of the society and culture of Japan taking the West as the main standard of comparison. The *nihonjinron* of this period featured a wide range of participants including, in addition to academics, cultural elites with diverse backgrounds such as business elites.

IMAGES OF JAPANESE SOCIETY AND CULTURE

The *nihonjinron* of the 1970s and the early 1980s focused on and consolidated certain images of Japanese society, culture, and national character. These may be summarized in terms of the following propositions and assumptions.

First, Japanese society is characterized in the *nihonjinron* by groupism or "interpersonalism" (*kanjinshugi*), vertical stratification (intracompany solidarity), and dependence, as opposed to western society which is characterized by individualism, horizontal stratification (class solidarity), and independence. Among the many books written on Japanese group orientation, Nakane's *Japanese Society* (1970) and Doi's *The Anatomy of Dependence* (1973) are two of the most prominent. Social anthropologist Nakane employed the key concept "vertical society" in an attempt to identify peculiarly Japanese forms of social organization and interactions. The Japanese are described as a group-oriented people preferring to act hierarchically within the framework of a group, typically, a company. Psychiatrist Doi identified the attitude of passive dependence (*amae*) as being prolonged into adulthood in Japanese society. *Amae* is considered to occur typically as a quasi-parent–child relationship in companies and political factions, where a person in a subordinate social position assumes the role of a child toward his superior who plays the role of a parent. The notion of group orientation was often discussed in the context of business organization, management practices, and industrial relations.

Generally, the concept of groupism is contrasted with that of individualism. Some argue, however, that groupism does not accurately conceptualize Japanese patterns of behavior and thought, as it tends to imply group members' immersion into and loyalty to the organization. Hence, sociologist Hamaguchi proposed the notion of *kanjinshugi* (literally, "interpersonalism," or in his own translation, "contextualism"), which is characterized by mutual dependence, mutual trust, and human relation in itself. It is maintained that this better describes what it really feels like to be part of the group for the Japanese in their everyday life.

The second major proposition of the *nihonjin-ron* concerns the patterns of interpersonal communication of the Japanese. Again, in contrast with the communication style of the West, which is said to value verbal skills and logical presentation, the non-verbal and supralogical Japanese style of communication was stressed. Essential interpersonal communication among the Japanese is supposed to be performed non-verbally, non-logically, and empathetically. Supposedly Japanese characteristics such as "belly talk" (*haragei*) and empathetic understanding (*ishin-denshin*) were often discussed in this connection.

Thirdly, the *nihonjinron* emphasized and assumed the homogeneity and uniformity of Japanese society. Here again, the contrast is with the multi-ethnic and multiracial composition of the West, in particular the society of the US, with the racial and ethnic homogeneity of Japan underscored.

Fourth, social and cultural traits such as groupism, "interpersonalism," non-verbalism, and supralogicalism are usually explained in terms of historical formation deriving from climatic conditions and modes of production, that is, rice cultivation, which required solidarity and mutual dependence in a village community. In this instance the contrast is with what are taken to be western historical modes of production such as pastoralism and nomadism, which are conducive to individualism (e.g., Aida 1972).

The above themes are interrelated. The Japanese patterns of interpersonal communication, which discourage logical and verbal confrontation, are strongly related to the high value placed on consensus and harmony in interpersonal relations, while non-verbal, empathetic, and supralogical communication is assumed to be a product of homogeneous society. This leads to an assumption that the Japanese patterns of behavior and communication are so unique that they can only be understood by persons born Japanese.

NATIONAL IDENTITY AND NATIONALISM

Although one may be inclined to think that *nihonjinron*-type discourse is peculiar to Japan,

intellectual curiosity about the perceived unique traits of one's own nation has been widely observed in various periods of history and in many parts of the world. In fact, exploration and articulation of ideas of national distinctiveness are an essential part of cultural nationalism. *Nihonjinron* should be regarded as one variation of the more general phenomenon of discourses on national distinctiveness. This enables comparison with other national cases as well as theoretical understanding of national identity and cultural nationalism.

If cultural nationalism is the project of creating, preserving, and strengthening a people's cultural identity when such identity is felt to be lacking, inadequate, or threatened, it is understandable that intellectuals should play a prominent role in systematizing ideas of national distinctiveness. In fact, the history of modernity saw an evolution of a systematic comparison of the characters of different peoples – whether in terms of a holistic construct such as *Volksgeist* or by reference to institutions as key elements in creating a sense of national identity.

If *nihonjinron* gives the impression of being an extreme case of such a phenomenon, it is partly because Japanese intellectuals' ideas of Japanese uniqueness have been highly holistic. Their primary concern is, on the assumption of Japanese society as a homogeneous and holistic entity, to explore and describe the cultural ethos or collective spirit or, to be more exact, the characteristic mode of behaving and thinking of the Japanese that underlies objectified institutions and practices.

CRITICISMS OF THE *NIHONJINRON*

In the 1980s criticisms of the *nihonjinron* began to be expressed by scholars concerned about the large influence of these types of writings. In turn, discourses critical of the *nihonjinron* came to form their own genre in intellectual debates in and out of Japan. Sugimoto and Mouer's *Are the Japanese Very Japanese?*, published in 1982, pioneered a critique of the *nihonjinron*. Befu was also one of the earliest critics, notably in *The Discourse on Japanese Culture as an Ideology* (1987). Another noteworthy effort in this vein was Dale's The *Myth of Japanese Uniqueness*

(1986), which leveled criticism at a wide range of *nihonjinron*-type materials, both contemporary and historical.

Criticisms took many forms. There was, first of all, a methodological criticism. Writers of the *nihonjinron*, it was pointed out, based their conclusions on personal experiences and everyday anecdotes, picking and choosing evidence in an arbitrary manner that supported their arguments, and thus their conclusions lack a sound methodological basis and any scholarly value. As to why the writers employed such a self-serving method of amassing examples to back their theories, one answer is to be found in their ideological orientations.

Second, the *nihonjinron* was criticized as constituting a conservative ideology well in tune with the interests of the ruling elite in society. It is true that there was, as discussed earlier, a strong tendency to expound on the virtues of village communal culture, rice cultivation culture, and so on, and this tended to affirm and support the group solidarity ethos of Japanese corporations. Rather than class solidarity, the *nihonjinron* theories can be used to buttress intracompany solidarity and group harmony, and it is this conservative ideological bent that was criticized. A third type of criticism leveled at the *nihonjinron* was that it was a nationalist ideology that extolled the superiority of Japanese culture by explaining Japan's post-war economic growth and success by reference to Japan's supposedly unique group harmony and communal style of interpersonal communication. A fourth line of criticism voiced in many quarters was that the *nihonjinron* overemphasized the cultural and social homogeneity of the Japanese, to the serious neglect of diversity existing within the society.

In response to such criticisms, there began to appear in the 1990s a new type of discourse that endeavored to take into account Japan's internal diversity as well as similarities between Japan and other societies. For example, Amino's *Perspectives on Discourses on Japan* (1990) and Oguma's *A Genealogy of "Japanese" Self-Images* (2002) are representative of this trend. It is fair to say that an approach that favors demythologizing of Japan's homogeneity has become the norm in studies of Japanese society.

CONSUMERS OF THE *NIHONJINRON*

Nihonjinron-critical literature also sought to provide explanations about why discussions of Japanese distinctiveness became such a significant social phenomenon. It was commonly argued that readers were attracted to the *nihonjinron* because they offered a salvation from an identity crisis derived from the westernization of Japanese culture, or that such works promoted feelings of cultural superiority by way of their explanations of Japanese economic success as the result of unique cultural traits.

Such assertions prompt the following sociological questions to be raised: who, in fact, read the *nihonjinron*, and in what manner? What types of social groups for what reasons responded actively to and consumed these writings? These issues are addressed in Yoshino's *Cultural Nationalism in Contemporary Japan* (1992), which analyzed the social process of the consumption (acceptance) of the *nihonjinron*. Unlike cultural, business, and other elites, who concerned themselves with abstract notions such as threatened identity and culturalist rationalization of economic strength, consumers of the *nihonjinron* tended to be attracted to what they felt to be practical benefits in their immediate personal environments such as in understanding and dealing successfully with problems of the workplace.

Several types of concrete concerns became apparent. For example, as the *nihonjinron* often concerned themselves with peculiarly Japanese social characteristics of business management and company organizations, they exercised an especially strong appeal to the likes of businessmen in companies. Furthermore, the *nihonjinron* appealed to people with an interest in intercultural communication. Such people tended to feel that true international understanding required not just knowledge of English, the international language, but also a firm grasp of cultural differences between Japan and non-Japanese (European and North American) societies. The *nihonjinron*, with their characteristic style of comparisons and contrasts between Japanese and western cultures, provided them with fertile ground to explore and understand problems of intercultural communication.

GLOBALIZATION AND CULTURAL DIFFERENCES

Nihonjinron as the activity of intellectuals and cultural elites had its heyday in the 1970s and the early 1980s and then became subject to criticism. This is not to say, however, that *nihonjinron* lost their importance in the time that followed. On the contrary, *nihonjinron* discourses in various guises underwent a process of reproduction and were diffused to broader segments of the population. To take one example, *nihonjinron* themes have been reproduced in the foreign language education industry. Mastery of foreign language skills is a requisite qualification for employment in a globalizing world; so too is knowledge of cultural differences. Reproduction of *nihonjinron* discourses is typically seen in the private English-language teaching (ELT) industry, where these types of discourses about Japanese society and national character find their way into the classroom as part of the project of improving intercultural communication. This is not limited to ELT. In foreign language training in general, we often see two cultures, one represented by the mother tongue and the other by the foreign language, being compared and contrasted as part of language instruction. Also, in the case of Japanese language teaching for non-Japanese, comparative cultural discussion is often added to the teaching content. Students of Japanese do not merely receive instruction in Japanese grammar and vocabulary, but often the teacher will feel compelled to proffer *nihonjinron*-type insights to students and will use *nihonjinron* writings as study materials. Indeed, in more advanced Japanese classes the trend is to use quite a lot of *nihonjinron* writings as study materials. Thus, classic stereotypical images of the Japanese propagated by the *nihonjinron* continue to be reproduced and consumed in the realm of language teaching.

The thematic importance of *nihonjinron* can be said to be actually gaining weight. Ideas of national distinctiveness and cultural differences, while ever shifting in shape, continue to be reproduced in new and different settings. Indeed, it may be said that discourses on cultural differences are flourishing more than ever in the age of globalization.

SEE ALSO: Japanese-Style Management; *Minzoku*; Nationalism; *Seken*; *Tatemae/Honne*

REFERENCES AND SUGGESTED READINGS

Aida, Y. (1972) *Nihonjin no Ishiki Kozo (The Structure of Japanese Consciousness)*. Kodansha, Tokyo.

Amino, Y. (1990) *Nihonron no Shiza: Retto no Shakai to Kokka (Perspectives on Discourses on Japan: Society and State of the Archipelago)*. Shogakkan, Tokyo.

Befu, H. (1987) *Ideorogii to shiteno Nihonbunkaron (The Discourse on Japanese Culture as an Ideology)*. Shiso no Kagaku Sha, Tokyo.

Befu, H. (2001) *Hegemony of Homogeneity: An Anthropological Analysis of Nihonjinron*. Melbourne: TransPacific Press.

Dale, P. (1986) *The Myth of Japanese Uniqueness*. Croom Helm, London.

Doi, T. (1973) *The Anatomy of Dependence*. Trans. J. Bestor. Kodansha International, Tokyo.

Hamaguchi, E. (1982) *Kanjinshugi no Shakai Nihon (Japan: The Interpersonalistic Society)*. Toyo Keizai Shinposha, Tokyo.

Iizuka, K. (1952) *Nihon no Seishin-teki Fudo (The Mental Climate of the Japanese)*. Hyoronsha, Tokyo.

Kawashima, T. (1950) *Nihon Shakai no Kazoku-teki Kosei (The Familial Structure of Japanese Society)*. Nihon Hyoronsha, Tokyo.

Minami, H. (1971 [1953]) *The Psychology of the Japanese People*. Trans. A. R. Ikuma. University of Tokyo Press, Tokyo.

Mouer, R. & Sugimoto, Y. (1986) *Images of Japanese Society*. Kegan Paul International, London.

Nakane, C. (1970) *Japanese Society*. University of California Press, Berkeley.

Oguma, E. (2002) *A Genealogy of "Japanese" Self-Images*. Trans. D. Askew. TransPacific Press, Melbourne.

Sugimoto, Y. & Mouer, R. (1982) *Nihnojin wa Nihonteki ka? (Are the Japanese Very Japanese?)*. Toyo Keizai Shimpo Sha, Tokyo.

Yoshino, K. (1992) *Cultural Nationalism in Contemporary Japan: A Sociological Enquiry*. Routledge, London and New York.

Yoshino, K. (1999) *Consuming Ethnicity and Nationalism: Asian Experiences*. Curzon Press, London.

Nobel Prizes and the scientific elite

Steve Fuller

The elite basis of scientific knowledge is traceable to the Greeks. Plato treated knowledge as a principle of social stratification that is distributed as talents across the population. Accordingly, education is about discovering the social role or function for which one has been biologically endowed. In a highly differentiated society, all such roles are "elite" in that a select few can play them well. The distinctiveness of science for Plato is that its form of knowledge makes one, at least in principle, fit to rule society as a whole. It is worth contrasting Aristotle's somewhat different view of the situation. He shared Plato's views about genetically based individual differences but treated the capacity to rule as a general talent common to those whose families have a proven track record of estate management. For Aristotle, science was "elite" in the sense of a leisure activity that such people should undertake, much like sports, once they have attended to matters of the estate.

Both Plato's and Aristotle's perspectives on the elite nature of science underwent significant change in the modern period, especially as science metamorphosed from a specialized mental discipline to the basis of technological innovation and society's infrastructure. Yet, relatively pure versions of these classical views have persisted. On the one hand, Platonism survives in the idea of an "internal history of science," whereby science proceeds according to a trajectory defined by a self-selecting class of scientists. Once sufficiently matured, the knowledge of this class is then applicable to society at large, with varying degrees of consent from those to whom it is applied. This idea was enshrined by Cold War theorists of science like James Bryant Conant and Thomas Kuhn. On the other hand, Aristotelianism survives in the neoliberal political economist Charles Murray, who has questioned the increasing relevance of science, and academic knowledge more generally, to job training across all sectors of society. According to Murray, this only ends up dissipating and corrupting science, while providing a

false sense of competence to the intellectually deficient.

The monotheistic idea that humans are created in the image and likeness of God reoriented the Greek elitist heritage by implying that science is not the knowledge of an elite but the elite part of universally available knowledge. As this idea was secularized, scientists justified their elite status as merely temporary, portraying themselves as the vanguard of overall social progress. The expectation, then, was that scientific knowledge would ultimately "rationalize" all of society. Early scientific societies in the seventeenth and eighteenth centuries argued this way in return for political protection and legal autonomy. The image has remained persuasive as scientific societies and state power fed off each other: the intensification of scientific effort required more full-time workers in the field. States realized that these scientific recruits could also function as civil servants. By the late nineteenth century, the image of scientists as salaried professionals requiring specialized, yet non-esoteric, training began to receive widespread acceptance. Indeed, as opposed to the class snobbery that persisted in the humanities, a career in science came to be seen as a means for upward social mobility.

However, this anti-elitist tendency was undermined in the twentieth century from two directions, one subtle and infrastructural, the other more public and symbolic. The former involved the so-called peer review process by which scientific research has been evaluated since the seventeenth century. Originally, peer review enabled science to function as an egalitarian community, in which any scientist (at least in a given specialty) was literally eligible to evaluate the work of any other scientist. But as the ranks of scientists swelled, and perceptions about their merit became more discriminating, peer review itself became elitist: relatively few pass judgment on the increasingly many.

This tendency has been exacerbated by the extension of peer review's purview from publication to funding issues – not just whose research is meritorious, but who is fit to do research in the first place. Robert Merton has called this the principle of cumulative advantage, popularly known as the Matthew effect. Scientists whose work is cited more tend to publish more, which usually implies greater access to resources (including time), which in turn reflects the scientist's institutional location, itself a product of job market considerations, which are themselves biased toward the scientist's academic pedigree. While Merton hailed these nested constraints as evidence of science's own version of the "invisible hand," it equally looks like a return to the hereditary transmission of status, albeit not along strictly biological lines.

The second elitist revival in twentieth-century science has come from the institution of the Nobel Prizes, awarded annually since 1901, from an endowment provided in the will of the inventor of dynamite, Alfred Nobel. Against the ongoing professionalization of science, the idea of prizes for scientific achievement recalled an older amateur ethic, whereby clever people from various walks of life competed to solve practically inspired problems by scientific means. In fact, the main difficulty in implementing Nobel's wishes was his desire to reward the latest and most beneficial achievements, yet as defined in terms of scientific disciplines (physics, chemistry, physiology, and medicine) which are naturally organized along a longer temporal and deeper theoretical horizon. This tension has been historically resolved by a tendency to award Prizes for empirical, but rarely theoretical, work of clear academic significance. And given that the Nobel Prizes were conceived before biology became institutionalized as an academic discipline, no prize has ever been given for work specifically related to the neo-Darwinian synthesis that theoretically unifies the field.

The sociological impact of the Nobel Prizes on scientific enterprise has been complex. The large purse associated with each prize (about $1.5 million) has made scientists more focused, competitive, and proprietary as they try to second-guess the inclinations of the Sweden-based award committees. However, since these committees operate by consensus, controversy arises more over who should be included in an award (up to three people allowed) than the achievement recognized in the award. At the same time as the prizes have lived up to Nobel's desire for the internationalization of science, they have also enabled certain countries, notably the United States, to serve as magnets for

researchers with Nobelist ambitions. Finally, the Nobel Prizes have inspired comparably funded prizes in other disciplines. Together they have provided significant public relations for science as a whole, while reinforcing the difference between its elite and rank-and-file practitioners.

SEE ALSO: Expertise, "Scientification," and the Authority of Science; Matthew Effect; Merton, Robert K.; Peer Review and Quality Control in Science; Speaking Truth to Power: Science and Policy

REFERENCES AND SUGGESTED READINGS

Crawford, E. (1992) *Nationalism and Internationalism in Science.* Cambridge University Press, Cambridge.

Feldman, B. (2000) *The Nobel Prize.* Arcade, New York.

Fuller, S. (2002) *Knowledge Management Foundations.* Butterworth-Heinemann, Woburn.

Harrgitai, I. (2002) *The Road to Stockholm.* Oxford University Press, Oxford.

Merton, R. K. (1973) *The Sociology of Science.* University of Chicago Press, Chicago.

Zuckerman, H. (1977) *Scientific Elite.* Free Press, New York.

non-resident parents

Bruce Smyth

Family life has undergone dramatic change in recent decades, especially in relation to family structure. Marked increases in union dissolution and nonmarital childbearing have resulted in a growing number of children living apart from one of their parents. Most non-resident parents are fathers but with resident fathers becoming one of the fastest-rising family forms in many western countries, non-resident mothers too are increasing in number.

Throughout history, fathers have been absent from their children's lives for many reasons: for work, to fight wars, or through incarceration. But more recently, the transition to non-resident parenthood typically occurs in one of three ways: nonmarital childbearing where parents never live together; the breakdown of the relationships of unmarried cohabiting parents; or marital dissolution between parents. Non-resident parenthood has become a common transition in the life course of many parents, even though most parents, of course, never anticipate such a transition.

Up until recently, not a great deal has been known about non-resident fathers. Even less remains known about non-resident mothers. While concern for children's well-being has catalyzed research efforts, researching non-resident parents is no easy task. Non-resident parents are hard to identify, locate, and recruit for research. They can be geographically mobile, and can have tenuous living arrangements as boarders, housemates, or as those not legally related to other people in a household. As such, they can slip through surveys that make use of traditional household rosters to identify target respondents. Non-resident parents have been found to underreport their parental status – some may be reluctant to declare it; some fathers may not know this status. The relatively small proportion of non-resident mothers, in particular, means that even in large national surveys there are often insufficient numbers of them to explore meaningfully and reliably.

Non-resident parents have attracted much negative attention in recent years – stigmatized as *deadbeat dads* or as *bad moms* – and so their reluctance to participate in research is perhaps not surprising. This negative attention is beginning to give way to emerging evidence that many non-resident parents want to play an active role in their children's lives but struggle to do so in the face of numerous emotional and practical obstacles. Emotional issues include: dealing with the loss of daily interactions with children and familiar family activities; the pain of brief, superficial contact "visits" with children; role ambiguity; a sense of inadequacy and rejection; and feeling disenfranchised and disconnected (Am I a "real" parent?). Practical difficulties include: fewer financial resources in the aftermath of parental separation (particularly in light of rigorous child support enforcement regimes); finding adequate housing that can provide a home or home-like space for caring for children; and maintaining a connection with children in the face of parental conflict,

physical distance, new family responsibilities, and children's peer, school, and extracurricular activities. These challenges, individually and in combination, lead many non-resident parents to believe that they cannot maintain much more than a superficial relationship with their children. In particular, the time-limited nature of contact means that non-resident parents often feel under pressure to engage in recreational and social activities with children (giving rise to the phrase *Disneyland Dads/Disneyland Moms*).

It is noteworthy that a sizable proportion of non-resident parents (especially fathers) do not appear to be able to overcome the above challenges, and as a consequence have little or no contact with their children (estimates vary in time and place from 20 to 50 percent of separated/divorced parents). Father absence has enormous implications for children's well-being, and has been shown to be associated with a plethora of social ills for children (from poor academic achievement to youth suicide), spurring a flurry of concerned social commentary in recent years. However, there is compelling evidence that parental conflict and the economic fallout from parental separation drives·many of the negative consequences of divorce for children – not parental absence per se.

Much of the research into non-resident parenting has focused on two domains of critical importance to children's well-being: *parent–child contact* and *child support*.

Most studies of parent–child contact have taken a quantitative tack, measuring the frequency and/or overall amount of face-to-face contact between non-resident parents and their children. There is mounting evidence, however, that the nature and quality of the interaction are more important than how often contact occurs. In particular, *authoritative parenting* (encompassing warmth and involvement, the encouragement of psychological autonomy, and monitoring and boundary setting) has been shown to be an important dimension of relationship quality. In pursuit of a better understanding of what non-resident parents do when they are with their children, research is moving away from the use of simple measures of contact frequency toward approaches that aim to recognize and describe the multiple qualitative and quantitative differences in the ways that non-resident parents can share the care of children.

In the meantime, there is much to suggest that family dynamics in tandem with demographic factors temper the form that contact takes. These factors largely reduce to the three Rs – repartnering, relocation (i.e., physical distance), and residual bad feelings (particularly conflict) between parents. To this list may be added three other Rs – relative economic disadvantage, "rotten behavior" by a parent (including abuse, domestic violence, or obstruction of contact), and regard for parents' work patterns, and children's age, developmental stage, individual temperament, resilience, experience, and wishes. Not surprisingly, higher levels and qualitatively richer types of contact appear to be associated with lower levels of interparental conflict, lower rates of repartnering, less physical distance between parents' households, and higher levels of financial resources.

The above factors also appear to influence or mediate the close but complex links between contact and child support. Parent–child contact and child support often go hand in hand (the so-called *access–maintenance nexus*). Non-resident parents who pay child support also tend to spend time with their children; those who do not see their children tend not to pay child support. Seltzer et al. (1989) have proposed three broad causal explanations for this seeing–paying relation: common demographic causes, unobserved psychosocial factors, and more direct causal relationships between contact and child support themselves.

Common demographic factors constrain or enhance the resources necessary for contact and the payment of child support. For example, the presence of new children in the non-resident parent's household places constraints on time and money and this is likely to reduce the frequency of contact and the amount of child support paid to children of a previous union. *Unobserved psychosocial factors* can also influence the co-occurrence of contact and child support. For example, non-resident parents' commitment to their children and the desire for a close emotional bond might result in the payment of child support and regular parent–child contact. Finally, contact and child support can themselves be *causally related*. For example, parent–child contact can foster a context in which non-resident parents stay in touch with children's material needs, and the costs of these

needs. They might thus be more inclined to provide financial support than parents who do not see their children. Where conflict exists between parents, the causal links between contact and child support can be quite explicit: both activities can become power-play activities whereby children become "pawns" in a power struggle between parents in which the pieces traded are contact and child support: money from the non-resident parent is traded for contact with children ("I-pay-so-I-see"), or vice versa ("You-don't-pay-so-you-don't-see").

These three causal explanations are not mutually exclusive. Indeed, a combination of these processes is likely to define the particular seeing–paying relation (such as where parents' commitment to raising their children influences their decision to live near one another). These processes are also likely to alter over time as parents' circumstances change and as children grow older. Changing relational, economic, and life circumstances can trigger sudden shifts in parenting arrangements (and vice versa). For example, informal parenting arrangements around contact and financial support might become highly structured as a result of one parent repartnering and moving some distance from the children's other parent. The contact–child support nexus, and the dynamics around it, can thus be quite complex and fluid.

Complexities aside, a solid body of data indicates that the payment of child support by non-resident parents improves children's well-being on many levels, and significant gains have generally been made in the collection rate and amount of child support paid for children since enforcement regimes were introduced in recent decades – although some schemes have been more successful than others.

Child support nonetheless continues to act as a "lightning rod" for much pent-up anger, grief, and disappointment by non-resident parents surrounding relationship breakdown and the loss of everyday family life. Not surprisingly, non-resident parents and resident parents differ markedly in their criticisms of legally mandated collection regimes. The most common complaint by parents who pay child support (mostly non-resident fathers – especially those who have new families to support) is that they are paying too much. By contrast, the most common complaint by resident parents eligible for child support (mostly mothers) is that payments do not occur, debts are not pursued, or that the child support system can be manipulated in order to minimize or avoid child support obligations altogether. In recent years, these different perceptions have been given voice through the emergence of a number of grassroots fathers' or mothers' pressure groups that seek to shape policy reform. Gender politics loom large in relation to contact and child support issues.

Gender differences also pervade non-resident parenting itself. While non-resident mothers report experiencing many of the same pressures and feelings as non-resident fathers, they typically carry the additional burden of greater economic vulnerability. Women are generally more vulnerable financially across the life course than men; marital disruption often exposes this vulnerability. Non-resident mothers are generally poorer than non-resident fathers, and a lack of economic resources in the first place is one of the most common reasons that mothers voluntarily give up the full-time care of their children. Many non-resident mothers believe that their children's father is in a better position financially to raise their children. Related to their often weaker economic circumstances, non-resident mothers are less likely to pay child support than non-resident fathers (but still provide in-kind contributions such as clothing, toys, and outings).

Social attitudes toward non-resident mothers are also more likely to be negative than toward non-resident fathers. This is because society expects women to be the nurturers and carers of children. Traditional gender role expectations place greater pressure on non-resident mothers than on non-resident fathers to stay in touch with children. The empirical data (albeit piecemeal) suggest that this is indeed the case. Non-resident mothers are more likely than non-resident fathers to see their children, and to do so more often and in qualitatively richer ways (such as through overnight stays or extended contact). Non-resident mothers may also be more inclined than non-resident fathers to use other forms of communication (such as telephone and letters) to maintain a connection with their children in the absence of daily face-to-face contact. Moreover, there may be greater intimacy between non-resident mothers and

their children and a higher level of involvement than is the case for non-resident fathers, as evidenced by the discussion of feelings, talking about daily problems and concerns, and more open communication generally. These apparent qualitative differences between non-resident mothers' and non-resident fathers' relationships with their children probably mimic pre-separation gender-differentiated parenting roles.

Regardless of gender, one of the fundamental challenges for all non-resident parents is to learn new ways of contributing to their children and staying involved in their lives while living elsewhere. A broad array of policies, interventions, and research continues to be developed to support non-resident parents in this crucial endeavor.

SEE ALSO: Child Custody and Child Support; Children and Divorce; Divorce; Family Demography; Family Structure; Life Course and Family; Lone-Parent Families; Stepfamilies; Stepfathering; Stepmothering

REFERENCES AND SUGGESTED READINGS

Amato, P. R. & Gilbreth, J. G. (1999) Nonresident Fathers and Children's Well-Being: A Meta-Analysis. *Journal of Marriage and the Family* 61: 557–73.

Arditti, J. A. (1995) Noncustodial Parents: Emergent Issues of Diversity and Process. *Marriage and Family Review* 20: 283–304.

Bradshaw, J., Stimson, C., Skinner, C., & Williams, J. (1999) *Absent Fathers?* Routledge, London.

Braver, S. & O'Connell, D. (1998) *Divorced Dads: Shattering the Myths.* Tarcher/Putnam, New York.

Depner, C. E. & Bray, J. H. (Eds.) (1993) *Nonresidential Parenting: New Vistas in Family Living.* Sage, Newbury Park, CA.

Herrerías, C. (1995) Noncustodial Mothers following Divorce. *Marriage and Family Review* 20: 233–55.

Nord, C. W. & Zill, N. (1997) Non-Custodial Parents' Participation in their Children's Lives. *Child Support Report* 19: 1–2.

Seltzer, J. A. & Bianchi, S. M. (1988) Children's Contact with Absent Parents. *Journal of Marriage and the Family* 50: 663–77.

Seltzer, J. A., Schaeffer, N. C., & Charng, H. (1989) Family Ties after Divorce: The Relationship between Visiting and Paying Child Support. *Journal of Marriage and the Family* 51: 1013–32.

Smyth, B. (Ed.) (2004) *Parent–Child Contact and Post-Separation Parenting Arrangements.* Australian Institute of Family Studies, Melbourne.

Stewart, S. D. (1999a) Disneyland Dads, Disneyland Moms? How Nonresidential Parents Spend Time with Absent Children. *Journal of Family Issues* 20: 539–56.

Stewart, S. D. (1999b) Nonresident Mothers' and Fathers' Social Contact with Children. *Journal of Marriage and the Family* 61: 894–907.

norm of reciprocity

James J. Chriss

According to Lester Ward (1883, 1: 464–8), human society has passed through three stages of development, with a fourth stage not yet realized. In the first stage (the autarchic), human beings were savage and solitary creatures. With their higher mental powers in comparison to the lower animals, human beings gained mastery over most other creatures, yet what they required most was protection from their own kind.

Even so, their relative security against external threats (save those of other tribes) meant that at some point human populations began to multiply. In this second, or anarchic, stage, human beings were forced into closer contact with greater numbers of others, but since they were ill adapted to association and social conditions – conditions in which ethics and virtues had not yet arisen – selfish passion continued to hold sway.

As headships emerged to rule over human populations along tribal and communal lines, rules were created to regulate important forms of human association, including most importantly sexual relations. This establishment of the first rudimentary elements of government represents the third or politarchic stage. As population growth continued and as more tribes came into contact, the ancient pattern of conflicts fueled by ingroup/outgroup hostilities – ethnocentrism in Sumner's later terminology – gave way to cooperation and the enlargement of the spheres of social organization.

To keep the peace, otherwise warring tribes offered things of value to one another, thereby giving rise to the "gift" or the norm of reciprocity more generally. One of the great inventions of this third, politarchic, stage of societal development, for example, was the rule of exogamy and the creation of a dowry system within the marriage institution. This created obligations between families as they exchanged daughters (or other valued items) for sons in marriage, thereby reducing conflict and expanding the notion of the "we" beyond the isolated kinship group.

The fourth stage of the development of human society, the so-called pantarchic, is not yet realized. According to Ward, government, which became necessary as population growth pushed disparate groups of humans into conflictual relations, will eventually disappear as the ideas of reciprocity, altruism, and social support spread out beyond the level of the tribe or community or nation, eventually uniting all elements of the world community into one global solidarity that will render the idea of the nation obsolete. (We will see this idea of a one world order resurface in the later writings of George H. Mead, to be discussed shortly.)

To summarize, human beings evolved from brutish and solitary (the original state of nature envisioned by Hobbes) to sympathetic, social, and oriented toward the provision of mutual aid beginning in the third or politarchic stage. Echoing Ward but also borrowing the notion of sympathy from Adam Smith, Franklin Giddings (1896) made the "consciousness of kind" the foundation of organized, stable human society. About the same time Ferdinand Tönnies in Germany argued that human society is held together only to the degree that its members mutually or reciprocally influence one another. Somewhat later, fellow German Georg Simmel had arrived at the same position, stating that the reciprocal influences persons exerted on one another were the basis of sociation and the social order more broadly (Thon 1897).

Sympathy or "fellow feeling," which first came into view during the third stage of the development of human society, is the basis of the norm of reciprocity. According to Gouldner (1960) and Uehara (1995), the norm of reciprocity consists of three interrelated moral ideals: (1) people should help those who have helped them; (2) people should not injure those who have helped them; and (3) people should avoid overbenefiting from (i.e., should not take advantage of) those who have helped them.

Explicit statements concerning the nature of reciprocity began appearing during the 1920s. For example, in his 1922 book *Argonauts of the Western Pacific*, Bronislaw Malinowski discovered that inhabitants of these islands had created a circular system of exchange whereby local cultural artifacts – shell armlets and shell bracelets – traveled in different but predictable directions between the various groups. Although the exchanges had little or no economic value, they did help to maintain social solidarities.

Generalizing from the studies of Malinowski and others, Marcel Mauss argued in his 1925 book *The Gift* that human social relations are stabilized with the rise of the archaic form of exchange appearing in the politarchic stage. The "gift" is a special form of exchange based on three unwritten laws, namely, the obligation to give, the obligation to receive, and the obligation to repay (Burke 1992: 70). Several decades later Claude Lévi-Strauss published his *Elementary Structures of Kinship*, wherein he argued that such things as the incest taboo, rules of exogamy, wife buying, and even marriage through capture were all examples of the law of reciprocity. Even further, this law of reciprocity, which places under its rubric a number of seemingly disparate acts taking place within the marriage institution, is itself generated by a still more fundamental phenomenon, namely, the structure and functioning of the human brain. In tracing the form and function of society to mental constraints, Lévi-Strauss developed a form of structuralism which repudiated the naïve realism characteristic of positivism and naturalism.

Whereas Ward speaks of master transitions in the development of human society paralleling the upgrading of the intellect and the rational faculty – that is, from egoistic passion and hedonism to thoughtful contemplation of others – George H. Mead focuses on the acquisition of language as the foundation upon which sympathy and reciprocity were built. Mead's theory of the social self is in essence an effort to explain the social nature of ethical conduct in other than behavioristic or individualistic terms. For Mead, communication – which is the major tool

through which cooperation and shared social worlds are forged – does not arise out of competition ("survival of the fittest") nor in imitation (Tarde), but in constructive cooperation. Rather than a prudent strategy for individual survival or dominance, sociability was actually present with the appearance of language. And rather than the lower-level conversation of gestures in which animals engage, human desires are laden with emotions, and the significant symbols which arise in human communication externalize these otherwise private or internal plans of action. According to Mead's theory of self, it is through the response of others that we become aware of our own attitudes and selves. Importantly, we cannot know ourselves without first being involved in symbolic communication with others. In contrast to Ward and others, then, this implies that sociability is already implicated in human communication.

For Mead, self's knowledge of the other's role is the basis of human cooperation and the starting point of ethical reciprocity. Role-taking is not only something that occurs naturally in the human condition, it also provides a means by which human beings are able to cooperate and ideally realize the democratic ideals of the just and good life. For example, the notion of "rights" makes sense only to the extent that self-consciousness arises as we take on the attitude of others, that is, as we assume the attitude of assent of all members of the community (the "generalized other"). Like Ward before him, Mead held out hope that this generalized other would expand outward from communities to nation-states and eventually to the global level. As Mead (1932: 195) stated, "The World Court and the League of Nations are other such social objects that sketch out common plans of action if there are national selves that can realize themselves in the collaborating attitudes of others."

Even given their seeming differences, Ward and Mead are not as divergent on the issue of sociability and reciprocity as it would initially appear. This is because both theorists' views on human cooperation and sociality – and thus reciprocity – are close to the sympathy theories of society beginning with Aristotle, but which were developed most fully in the modern era beginning with Adam Smith's *The Theory of Moral Sentiments*. For example, Ward's (1883) emphasis on feelings is a type of sympathy theory, to the extent that he emphasizes not merely the innate, physiological side of feelings, but more importantly, the cognitive and subjectivist side. For Ward, sympathy makes possible altruism and, hence, all humanitarian advances in society. As Ellwood (1912: 318) notes, "The sympathetic feelings are, then, according to Ward, the essentially progressive forces in human social life."

We see, then, how Smith's theory of moral sentiments cut two divergent paths into modern social science, one running through the naturalism and positivism of Ward, Giddings, and other early American sociologists, the other through Mead and modern social psychology (see Park 1904). Sympathy, although rarely explicitly invoked in the anthropological literature discussed above, also lies behind the conceptualization of reciprocity as a universal feature of human social order.

SEE ALSO: Generalized Other; Gift; Gift Relations; Mead, George Herbert; Norms; Role-Taking; Self; Structuralism; Ward, Lester Frank

REFERENCES AND SUGGESTED READINGS

Burke, P. (1992) *History and Social Theory*. Cornell University Press, Ithaca, NY.
Ellwood, C. A. (1912) *Sociology in its Psychological Aspects*. Appleton, New York.
Giddings, F. H. (1896) *The Principles of Sociology*. Macmillan, New York.
Gouldner, A. W. (1960) The Norm of Reciprocity: A Preliminary Statement. *American Sociological Review* 25(2): 161–78.
Mead, G. H. (1932) *The Philosophy of the Present*. Ed. A. E. Murphy. Open Court, Chicago.
Park, R. E. (1904) *Masse und Publikum: Eine methodologische und soziologische Untersuchung*. Lack & Grunau, Bern.
Thon, O. (1897) The Present Status of Sociology in Germany, II. *American Journal of Sociology* 2 (5): 718–36.
Uehara, E. S. (1995) Reciprocity Reconsidered: Gouldner's "Moral Norm of Reciprocity" and Social Support. *Journal of Social and Personal Relationships* 12(4): 483–502.
Ward, L. F. (1883) *Dynamic Sociology*, 2 vols. Appleton, New York.

norms

Steven P. Dandaneau

Norms are informal rules that guide social interaction. They are, as Cristina Bicchieri (2006) calls them, "the rules we live by." As such, norms constitute a critical component in the makeup of human cultures and therefore play a highly significant role in determining what it means to be human. When codified, norms are rendered laws or other types of institutionalized regulatory strictures. When conceived without moral consequence, the term can also refer to mere behavioral regularities, even though adherence or lack thereof to these can and often does result in significant consequences (e.g., it would be highly unusual as well as probably harmful to name an American child Adolf Osama or, depending on one's constructed gender, Sue). Variously defined even by sociologists themselves, there is perhaps no other sociological concept more regularly and widely deployed in everyday talk, nor one about which more has been written and discussed. It is therefore not surprising that a concept as equally vague as it is elemental to the sociological enterprise is also one that is the subject of continuous theoretical debate.

Typically considered the founder of modern sociology, Émile Durkheim famously theorized society as both a system of integration involving social bonds and institutions and, even more importantly, as a normative order sui generis. While the former manifestation of society is highlighted in the title of his *The Division of Labor in Society* (1893), the latter is more clearly at stake in his last great book, *The Elementary Forms of Religious Life* (1912). For Durkheim, society was said to function to produce varying degrees of cohesiveness and regulation within groups, the former an attribute of the type and quality of reciprocal social bonds produced by a given division of labor, the latter the outcome of external repressive forces exerted by a moral fabric that is greater than, objective to, and constraining of individuals. The threads composing this fabric are norms. ·

In this view, the existence of norms is empirically given in the non-random patterns of behavior common in one and another social situation. Though invisible, norms nonetheless exert considerable force, as actors consult them in order to anticipate how they are expected and not expected to act in a given situation. Norms also, therefore, guide the distribution of sanctions, both positive (rewards) and negative (punishments). Conformity to expected behavior typically meets with approval (e.g., standing quietly on the elevator nets the actor a reputation as trustworthy), whereas deviation from expected behavior is likely to meet with informal punishment (e.g., facing the back of the elevator while singing the National Anthem quietly to oneself leads others to deem the actor odd and untrustworthy, with negative consequences following the actor into future interactions). Indeed, in Durkheim's estimation, the success or failure of a given normative order to regulate such simple, everyday behavior is tantamount to the success or failure of society to reproduce itself as a coherent totality. Durkheim thus imagined that society as such – as an essentially normative or what he called *moral* phenomenon – separated human action, or at least the great part of it, from mere animal behavior. In a word, norms make humans.

Norms can also, however, undo humans. In *Suicide* (1897), Durkheim addressed what he regarded as the twin threats undermining modern society's ability to maintain itself as a stable going concern. In terms of social integration, he warned against excessive individualism, while in terms of normative regulation, he saw in modernity a tendency toward "anomie," the fragmentation and weakening of social norms to the point where resultant aggregate social behavior exhibited a pathological level of confusion and unchecked expression of raw animal emotion. In an attempt to provide empirical evidence of society's integrating and regulating functions, *Suicide* presented data that seemed to correlate with Durkheim's basic sense that humans thrived only in the context of socially integrated and morally regulated groups. In groups with evidently less integration and fewer regulating norms (e.g., Protestants versus Roman Catholics and Jewish groups or married couples with children versus individuals who were not married and were without children), rates of suicide tended to be elevated. In other words, in the absence of sufficient bonds (emotional

attachments, mutual obligations, shared lives, etc.) and coherent and constraining norms (informal yet clear rules that define the meaning of success/failure, good/bad, progress/regress, etc.), a truly human existence threatens to decay into premoral forms. At the extreme, a human life worth living becomes so remote, the actuality of daily social existence so intolerably isolating and vacuous, as to lead to self-destruction. Durkheim feared that anomie would characterize the social situations faced by a growing scatter-plot of individuals in *les temps modernes*.

But not only under conditions of modernity. A classic empirical description of a decaying normative order is found in anthropologist Colin Turnbull's famous *The Mountain People* (1972). The Ik, a hunter-gatherer people of Uganda, once exhibited an unsurprising humanity that entailed considerable attention to mutually beneficial integration and reciprocity. But the Ik society that is the subject of Turnbull's fieldwork was one that was decimated to the point of starvation, and in this situation the Ik turned against one another in favor of extreme individualism. Instead of regular adherence to norms understood to benefit all, the Ik were reduced to aggressively avoiding norms that, if accepted and acted upon, would only thrust them, at least individually, into further peril. Turnbull illustrates their normative condition with an anecdote: having provided his informant medicine for the informant's ailing spouse, Turnbull learns from another that his informant is selling the medicine for profit and that the wife is several weeks dead and secretly buried so as to avoid Turnbull's detection. When Turnbull then confronts his informant with his knowledge of his informant's deceit and callousness, his informant is unembarrassed, much less ashamed. Instead, and to Turnbull's chagrin, he simply changes the subject of conversation. This raises the question as to whether norms that are ignored in practice and largely unfelt as an internal guide can be said to truly exist.

Another example of the use and abuse of norms is given in Stanley Milgram's famous study, *Obedience to Authority* (1969). In this case, and in contrast to the Ik's *avoidance* of norms, western scientists in New Haven, Connecticut, *imposed* norms upon unsuspecting research participants. In order to test the degree of authority that norms might hold over everyday people in western society, Milgram and his colleagues concocted a faux learning experiment in which research participants were compelled to administer electric shocks to hidden "learners" (people who were actually working for Milgram). These shocks were given in increasing voltages to the point of causing apparent discomfort, pain, severe harm, and in some cases even the learner's apparent death. Although complicated by numerous intervening variables, Milgram found that as many as two-thirds of the participants followed the faux rules of behavior that defined his experimental situation. Often begrudgingly but nonetheless voluntarily, the majority of research participants substituted new and morally dubious rules of conduct for those, such as Thou Shall Not Kill, they had presumably spent a lifetime internalizing as their own. Many, however, rejected Milgram's authoritative definition of the situation. Their prior socialization provided them with sufficient strength to resist his concocted external constraints. That Milgram and his colleagues felt their experimental design and its predictable negative consequences for hundreds of everyday citizens normative, that is, conforming to prevailing rules for how research should and should not be conducted, is itself a fact that sparked controversy and that remains a touchstone for continued debate on research ethics.

An instructive history of norms is given in Lennard J. Davis's *Enforcing Normalcy: Disability, Deafness, and the Body* (1995). In a style of theory reminiscent of George Canguilhem and Michel Foucault, Davis argues that it was not until 1840 and concurrent with the strengthening of the western eugenics movement that the notion of "normal" came to be associated with adherence to a common standard as defined statistically or by other rational means. Here, norm is rendered in the sense of a bell curve, where distance from a calculated equilibrium constitutes a measurable level of deviation. When such types of conceptualization are applied to human beings, diverse in all manner of ways as they actually are, the result is a type of forcing of empirically square pegs into conceptually round holes. Davis is especially keen to demonstrate the historical construction of otherwise taken-for-granted assumptions about what is and is not "normal," as he does, for example, with

respect to the invention of deafness. He is also wont to stress the profoundly harmful consequences such supposedly rational, scientific norm-making has wrought on persons deemed deviant due to so-called defective, broken, and flawed bodies.

Yet, even social Darwinists have made important contributions to the study of norms. In his famous *Folkways: A Study of the Sociological Implications of Usages, Manners, Customs, Mores, and Morals* (1906), the early American sociologist William Graham Sumner usefully distinguished between mores (pronounced more-ays), which are norms whose violation meets with the utmost severe sanctions, and folkways, which are norms with no discernible negative sanctions at all. Dining on human flesh violates mores against cannibalism, whereas whether one so dines with a table or a salad fork, an example of a folkway, will add nothing to the moral reprobation caused by the former. While mores vary from society to society and across historical periods, cannibalism, bestiality, and incest, not to mention combinations of the three, are among those acts most regularly proscribed at the level of mores. The violation of mores typically produces immediate and widespread revulsion as well as sure and swift humiliation, severe punishment, perhaps torture, and, just as often, capital punishment.

Folkways, on the other hand, are as common as every myriad pattern of regular behavior, from the sequence by which one puts on socks and shoes (both socks first, then both shoes, or one sock and one shoe followed by the second sock and second shoe, assuming two feet and the presence of shoes), to the rules governing a professor's behavior at the front of a lecture hall (stand behind a lectern or pace back and forth, maintain distance from the students or enter *their* space by patrolling the aisles and stairs while lecturing, clear throat before first speaking or deploy another method of opening the interaction). Mores are norms that are so taken for granted as to be thought basic to nature, human and otherwise, hence the fear and violence associated typically with reactions to their violation. Folkways, for their part, are norms that regulate superficial and largely inconsequential behavior, hence the mild amusement and titillation, if not outright indifference, that typically greet their violation. Shame and guilt can follow even the thought of violating mores, whereas folkways tend to loiter in our minds only when called to our attention by "did-you-ever-notice?" comedians.

The state of norms in postmodernity remains contested terrain for contemporary sociology. Rational choice theorists, for example, have looked to norms as potential explanation for otherwise seemingly irrational individual behavior. As Hechter and Opp (2001) argue, basic phenomena such as cooperation and collective action, not to mention social order itself, are difficult to explain using only "rational egoistic behavioral assumptions" of the sort typical of rational choice theory. In Bicchieri's (2006) noted account, the power of norms to constrain behavior is tested primarily using game theory simulations, such as Ultimatum, Dictator, Trust, and Social Dilemma.

Thus, on the one side there is speculation as to whether certain fundamental norms are inherent and universal in human sociation. Alvin Gouldner (1960) once famously argued that "the norm of reciprocity," like the incest taboo, was very probably a cultural universal, which meant that guidelines were everywhere and always in some manner in effect that encouraged actors to help, and not harm, those who have helped them. This comes very close to positing a Golden Rule, although sociologically. On the other hand, there is attention to the power of actors to suppress, reject, alter, fabricate, or create spontaneously norms of one or another type and consequence, even with respect to those previously deemed sacred and connected to emotionally entrenched values. For Bicchieri (2006), norms can even "endogenously emerge" as a result of nothing more than the interaction among actors sharing prior dispositions.

Alan Wolfe's (1989, 1998) influential sociology seeks to merge these two tendencies in a coherent analysis of contemporary norms. Drawing, for example, on Émile Durkheim and William James, Wolfe (2001) argues that the current century will be "the century of moral freedom," which is to say, that individuals will increasingly choose their own norms from the plurality of normative systems characteristic of postmodern society, thus setting for themselves their own course toward the true, right, and good. While this proposition may seem out of sync with Durkheim's concern about anomie, Wolfe is keen to emphasize individuals' capacity for moral discernment and decision, which is not at all inconsistent with Durkheim's (1973 [1898]) own advocacy for a type of moral individualism. Likewise, Jamesian attention to the "varieties of moral experience" is not inconsistent with cohesion in a pluralistic society that values its own pluralism.

SEE ALSO: Deviance, Theories of; Durkheim, Émile; Gift; Gift Relationships; Milgram, Stanley (Experiments); Norm of Reciprocity; Scientific Norms/Counternorms

REFERENCES AND SUGGESTED READINGS

Bicchieri, C. (2006) *The Grammar of Society: The Nature and Dynamics of Social Norms*. Cambridge University Press, Cambridge.

Davis, L. J. (1995) *Enforcing Normalcy: Disability, Deafness, and the Body*. Verso, London.

Durkheim, É. (1951 [1897]) *Suicide*. Free Press, New York.

Durkheim, É. (1973 [1898]) Individualism and the Intellectuals. In: Bellah, R. N. (Ed.), *Émile Durkheim on Morality and Society*. University of Chicago Press, Chicago, pp. 43–60.

Durkheim, É. (1984 [1893]) *The Division of Labor in Society*. Free Press, New York.

Durkheim, É. (1995 [1912]) *The Elementary Forms of Religious Life*. Free Press, New York.

Gouldner, A. (1960) The Norm of Reciprocity. *American Sociological Review* 25(2): 161–78.

Hechter, M. & Opp, K.-D. (Eds.) (2001) *Social Norms*. Russell Sage Foundation, New York.

Komter, A. E. (Ed.) (1996) *The Gift: An Interdisciplinary Perspective*. Amsterdam University Press, Amsterdam.

Milgram, S. (1969) *Obedience to Authority*. Harper & Row, New York.

Sumner, W. G. (1940 [1906]) *Folkways: A Study of the Sociological Implications of Usages, Manners, Customs, Mores, and Morals*. Ginn, Boston.

Turnbull, C. (1972) *The Mountain People*. Simon & Schuster, New York.

Wolfe, A. (1989) *Whose Keeper? Social Science and Moral Obligation*. University of California Press, Berkeley.

Wolfe, A. (1998) *One Nation, After All?* Viking, New York.

Wolfe, A. (2001) *Moral Freedom*. W. W. Norton, New York.

Nozick, Robert (1938–2002)

Stephen Hunt

Robert Nozick, a noted Harvard philosopher, emerged as something of an icon for the libertarian right from the 1970s. Perhaps his most renowned work, *Anarchy, State, and Utopia* (1974), marked a powerful philosophical challenge to the most widely held political social stances of liberals, socialists, and conservatives. In this volume, Nozick advances a sophisticated defense of the rights of the individual in relation to the state. He argues that the legitimacy of the state is only justified when it is severely limited to the narrow function of protecting the citizen against force, theft, and fraud, and the enforcement of contracts. Any more extensive activities by the state, Nozick insists, will inevitably violate individual rights.

By offering critiques of John Locke's justification of the governance of citizens founded on the state of nature, as well as what he views as the flawed thesis of John Rawls, Nozick develops a new theory of "distributive justice" and, in doing so, attempts to integrate a system of ethics, legal philosophy, and economic theory. In this regard, Nozick brings his own distinctive model of a utopia which he sees as equivalent to the minimal state. Such a state, Nozick insists, ideally treats its individuals as inviolate individuals, who may not be used in specific ways by others as a means, tool, instrument, or resource. Hence, the state should treat the individual as having perfect rights and with the dignity that this constitutes. It follows that freedom to choose one's life preferences and realize personal ends comes merely through the voluntary cooperation of other individuals with the same rights and dignity.

Continuing his search for the connection between philosophy and ordinary experience, a key concern of Nozick's work, as evident in his volume *The Nature of Rationality* (1991), was to demonstrate how the rationalities of decision and belief function at the everyday level and underscore efforts of productivity and peaceful coexistence with others. This allows Nozick to move beyond the confines of political philosophy to address a range of ethical and social problems, as well as embarking upon a search for the connections between philosophy and "ordinary" experience that constitutes humanity's "specialness."

In Nozick's view, misconceptions of rationality have resulted in many intractable philosophical problems. For example, the Kantian attempt to make principled behavior the sole ultimate standard of conduct extends rationality beyond its bounds. While acknowledging the limits of instrumental rationality, Nozick proposes a new rule of rational decision: "maximizing decision-value," which is a weighted sum of causal, evidential, and symbolic utility. Nozick thus advances what he views as a new evolutionary account that explains how some factual connections are instilled in social actors as seemingly self-evident. This leads Nozick to advocate a theory of rational belief that includes both the intellectual credibility of the belief and practical consequences of believing it.

SEE ALSO: Anarchism; Economic Sociology: Classical Political Economic Perspectives; Economy, Culture and; Neoliberalism; Political Economy; Rawls, John; Utopia

REFERENCES AND SUGGESTED READINGS

Nozick, R. (1974) *Anarchy, State, and Utopia.* Oxford, Blackwell.

Nozick, R. (1981) *Philosophical Explanations.* Oxford, Oxford University Press.

objectivity

Thomas A. Schwandt

In everyday life we worry about objectivity. We hear things like: "that judge wasn't very objective"; "he is speaking from his own prejudices"; "that was a very biased comment," and so on. If we analyze these ways of speaking, we realize several different uses of the term *objectivity*. It can refer to *a property or quality of a claim*: a claim or statement is objective if it is supported with reasons and evidence (or warrantable, supportable), and it is subjective if it is not so supported and only an expression of individual taste or preference. Objectivity can also refer to *a characteristic of a person*: the objective person is unbiased, unprejudiced, and evinces respect for the importance of evidence and argument. Finally, *an aspect or characteristic of a process* or means by which a claim is warranted can be called objective. Hence, some argue that the enterprise of science is objective because the claims of scientists are subject to public scrutiny and intersubjective criticism.

In the literatures on social science methodology and philosophy there are several interrelated but distinct senses of this term:

1 An absolute or ontological sense reflecting a belief in metaphysical realism. Thus, objectivity here refers to the idea of objectively perceiving an independently existing reality.
2 A disciplinary or critically intersubjective sense that associates objectivity with a particular aspect of the process of inquiry, specifically, the ability to reach consensus within some specialized disciplinary community through dialogue, debate, and reasoned argument.

3 A mechanical sense in which objectivity connotes following the rules or procedures because these are a check on subjectivity and restrain idiosyncrasy and personal judgment.
4 A moral-political sense in which to be objective means to be fair and impartial, and to avoid the kinds of self-interest or prejudice that distort judgment.

Objectivity has also been associated (for better or worse) with three other important notions in social science methodology: value neutrality, objectivism, and objectification. Value neutrality is an ideology that holds that politics and values should be external to the practice of scientific inquiry. Scientists ought to maintain a certain distance or detachment from social and political values; objectivity in science demands such neutrality. Objectivism is a term that designates a complex set of interlocking beliefs about the nature of knowledge (foundationalist epistemology), the nature of reality (metaphysical realism), the manner in which that reality can be known and knowledge claims justified (logical positivist or representationalist epistemology), the role of the scientist (an axiology of disinterest), and the Enlightenment belief in the unquestioned power (and authority) of science to shape society. Objectification is a belief in a particular metaphysical and epistemological relation of subject to object often characterized by the ideas of disengagement from and yet an attempt to control the object of knowledge. For example, Bourdieu (1990: 52) defines objectivism as the "theoretical relation" to the world. In that relation, the social world is "a spectacle offered to an observer who takes up a 'point of view' on the action and who ... proceeds as if it were intended solely for knowledge." For Bourdieu, the important contrast is between the theoretical relation to the world with its attendant attitude of objectification and a practical relation to the world.

When the notion of objectivity is criticized in social science it is important to fully understand just which of these meanings of objectivity are the object of the critique. One can endorse objectivity in the sense that one expects others not to always speak from self-interest and to offer warrants for their claims, and yet reject ideas such as disengagement, purely objective perception of reality, and value neutrality. Some who are critical of objectivity are probably expressing disdain for metaphysical realism – the belief in an ability to know things as they really are. Other kinds of criticisms are aimed at objectivity as disengagement – a stance or posture from which an inquirer allegedly can view social life unencumbered by prejudices and personal characteristics. Still other kinds of criticisms, specifically those raised in feminist epistemologies, are often simultaneously political and epistemological; for example, putatively objective science has a sexist bias; a concern with scientific objectivity has imposed a hierarchical and controlling relationship on the researcher–researched pair; holding to objectivity as a regulative ideal has meant excluding personal, subjective knowledge from consideration as legitimate knowledge.

SEE ALSO: Epistemology; Realism and Relativism: Truth and Objectivity; Strong Objectivity; Subjectivity

REFERENCES AND SUGGESTED READINGS

Bernstein, R. J. (1983) *Beyond Objectivism and Relativism: Science, Hermeneutics, and Praxis*. University of Pennsylvania Press, Philadelphia.
Bourdieu, P. (1990) *Logic of Practice*. Stanford University Press, Stanford.
Fay, B. (1996) *Contemporary Philosophy of Social Science*. Blackwell, Oxford.
Harding, S. (1991) *Whose Science? Whose Knowledge?* Cornell University Press, Ithaca, NY.
Megill, A. (Ed.) (1994) *Rethinking Objectivity*. Duke University Press, Durham, NC.
Natter, W., Schatzki, T. R., & Jones, J. P., III (Eds.) (1995) *Objectivity and the Other*. Guilford Press, New York.
Porter, T. M. (1995) *Trust in Numbers: The Pursuit of Objectivity in Science and Public Life*. Princeton University Press, Princeton.
Proctor, R. N. (1991) *Value-Free Science? Purity and Power in Modern Knowledge*. Harvard University Press, Cambridge, MA.
Rescher, N. (1997) *Objectivity: The Obligations of Impersonal Reason*. Notre Dame University Press, Notre Dame, IN.

observation, participant and non-participant

Martyn Hammersley

As a method of inquiry, observation is an alternative or complement to the use of interview, documentary, or questionnaire data. It is usually conceived as taking place in "natural" rather than experimental situations, even though experiments necessarily rely on observation by the experimenter. At a minimum, observation involves a researcher watching and listening to actions and events within some context over some period of time, and making a record of what has been witnessed.

The distinction between participant and non-participant observation draws attention to the fact that the role of an observer can vary a good deal. He or she may play a participant role in the setting or the events being observed, albeit perhaps a marginal one, or may play no such role. The primary concern motivating this distinction is reactivity, in other words, the extent to which and ways in which the behavior of the people being studied is shaped both by the fact of being researched in a given way (procedural reactivity) and by the particular characteristics of the researcher (personal reactivity). Reactivity is widely regarded as a potential source of error: it may render inferences from observational data about what happens on other occasions and in other contexts false; indeed, it may be concluded that reactive data can only tell us how people behave when they are being researched.

While useful for some purposes, the distinction between participant and non-participant observation is not entirely clear in its meaning, and can be misleading. This is because it refers not to a dichotomy but to a multidimensional space that can properly be made sense of only by more subtle distinctions. The following *dimensions* are involved:

1 The extent to which and ways in which the people being studied are aware that they are being observed. Two types of covert observational strategy are possible: the researcher may observe from a position that is not visible to participants, for example by means of hidden cameras or via a one-way mirror; or the researcher may do the research by covertly playing a participant role within the setting. Of course, if the people concerned know that they are being researched, even without being able to see the researcher, there is an important residual sense in which he or she nevertheless has a presence: some identity and purposes will be ascribed, and this may affect how people behave. Where the people being studied are completely unaware of being researched, procedural reactivity will be absent, though personal reactivity will still occur in the case of covert participation. Where research is overt there will usually be both kinds of reactivity, but their level and direction can vary significantly. It is important to remember that overt/covert is not a dichotomy: some of the people being studied may know about the research while others do not; and there may also be variation in how much, and what, particular people know.

2 Where the researcher takes on some role in a setting, there may be variation in how central that role is to the events being observed – in other words, in how consequential the ethnographer's actions are for what happens in the setting. It is important to remember the complexities of role-taking. Even where the formal role is that of visiting researcher, the observer may well engage in informal conversation with participants and this will give information about him or her as a person. Furthermore, refusing to engage will almost certainly stimulate speculation about who the researcher is and about the underlying purpose. Indeed, it is not uncommon for characteristics and purposes that go beyond, or even conflict with, the researcher role to be ascribed: the observer may be seen as a spy, as a potential friend or target, and so on. Thus, even where a relatively marginal role is adopted, both procedural and personal reactivity may be involved. Where the researcher adopts one of the established participant roles in the field, rather than that of visitor, the effects of procedural reactivity may be lower. However, much depends upon the nature of that role, since to some degree what people say and do in front of the observer will be shaped by their perceptions of his or her role, and these may vary across different categories of participant. The researcher's personal and social characteristics (gender, age, social class, ethnicity, knowledge or skills, and so on) may have implications for what participant role it is possible to take on, as well as for how people respond. Furthermore, participants may seek to alter the role that the researcher plays: requests for help may be made, invitations to participate in particular activities offered, or threats made to dissuade certain lines of action. As a result, the nature of the role may change over time, by no means entirely under the control of the observer.

3 A final dimension sometimes implied in the distinction between participant and non-participant observation concerns the degree to which the observation is structured: whether or not it involves the assignment of events to pre-identified categories (see Foster 1996). In structured observation the focus is usually on counting or measuring the frequency of particular types of act. By contrast, in much qualitative research observation is relatively unstructured, in that it is not governed by any pre-established set of categories. Of course, it *will* be guided by initial research problems, ideas about the setting and the people who live or work there, and so on. However, there is often an attempt to minimize the effect of these initial assumptions, so as to be open to surprise, to noticing things that are puzzling, without being overly concerned, initially, about whether or not they are relevant to the research topic. Unstructured observation may rely on recording of fieldnotes, often complemented, or even largely replaced, by audio- or video-recording. Fieldnotes are usually jotted down during the course of observation and written up as soon as

possible afterwards, employing relatively concrete language and aiming at verbatim accounts of what was said (see Emerson et al. 1995). There may also be use of photography and other sources of visual data. The structured–unstructured dimension obviously has direct implications for the nature of the data collected (qualitative or quantitative), but it may also affect the level of reactivity. It may be hard for someone carrying out structured observation to blend into the scene in the way in which many participant observers seek to do. Equally important, audio-recording, and especially video-recording, may generate reactivity.

Whether reactivity is a problem, how serious a problem it is, and how it can best be dealt with, are issues about which there are currently discrepant views among researchers. Some argue that, in order to minimize reactivity, the people and situations studied must all be dealt with in the same way, so that the stimulus presented is similar for all. Other commentators point out that standardization of the research approach does not standardize reactivity, because people do not respond to stimuli in fixed ways but on the basis of diverse cultural orientations. For this reason, it may be argued that reactivity can best be minimized through the researcher adapting differently to different situations, in order to fit in with them and thereby minimize disturbance. Moreover, staying a long time in a setting may allow patterns of behavior to revert to their usual forms. A third argument is that reactivity is unavoidable but that this does not prevent sound conclusions being drawn from the data. It is argued that, by reflecting on what people are saying and doing, the effects of reactivity should be detectable. Furthermore, we may be able to draw parallels between how people respond to being researched and how they respond to outsiders of particular kinds. A related argument is that the sheer fact of reactivity is not, in itself, a source of error. What matters is whether or not the reactive effects are relevant to the focus of inquiry, and sometimes they will not be. Finally, it may be pointed out that any concern with reactivity is premised on a commitment to producing knowledge about phenomena that are assumed to be independent of the research process. For any researcher who

abandons that commitment, and some claim to do this, reactivity is no longer a problem. Overall, then, there is not much agreement at the present time about how significant a threat to validity reactivity is, what form the threat takes, and how it can be or whether it needs to be dealt with.

As these differences in view about the significance of reactivity indicate, we need to take account not only of internal variation in the character of observation, but also of the broader kinds of inquiry within which it is employed. Participant observation is closely associated with ethnography, where it is often given a central but by no means an exclusive role, being combined with the use of both informal and more formal interviews, documents, and even official statistics or questionnaires. Observation of more structured kinds often forms part of research projects that are closer in character to large-scale surveys and rely primarily on quantitative analysis, though this is not necessarily the case (McCall 1984; Croll 1986). And conversation and discourse analysis rely heavily, and sometimes exclusively, on audio- or video-recordings, with the analyst often not having been present to observe events in person. There is potential disagreement about whether this amounts to observation, as there is also in the case of Internet data.

Reactivity is not the only methodological issue relevant to observational research. Others include: problems in gaining access, the personal qualities required for participant observation, sampling, variation in the types of data produced, and ethical issues. The remainder of the discussion will focus on these.

The problem of access takes on different forms depending on the nature of the observational role. Where the research is overt, entry to sites will usually have to be negotiated, perhaps through gatekeepers, and access to the kinds of data required will also need continually to be secured, as well as agreement reached about what roles can and cannot be taken by the observer in the field. Where the research is covert, access may not need to be negotiated, but the researcher must still find some way of getting into a position to be able to observe the situations and people of interest. In both forms of research the personal and social characteristics of the researcher may play an important role in easing access or making it difficult, depending on the nature of the people being studied; though no characteristics should be regarded as inevitable barriers or automatic entry tickets.

There are some general personal qualities that are required for participant observation. These include at least a minimum ability to converse with people, to hang around with them without looking too uncomfortable, and to avoid dominating situations. Also required is a capacity for toleration both of people and of ambiguity and uncertainty, and a preparedness to allow one's preconceptions to be undermined. Some boldness may also be required to get behind official appearances and fronts, and the disguises that people use to protect their interests. Above all, there must be a commitment to inquiry, to understanding other people's lives, over and above any attachment to particular ethical, religious, or political principles. Some of these qualities are less necessary for structured observation, but training and practice may be required to facilitate effective use of observational schedules or instruments: learning how to recognize relevant types of actions and events, how to record these speedily and clearly, and so on.

There are sampling issues involved in observation, as with other research methods. These include: what situations to observe, at what times, and on whom or what to focus one's attention within the scene. There can be various strategies here: concentrating on a particular place and the behavior that occurs there over lengthy periods of time; comparing what goes on in several locations of the same or contrasting kinds; concentrating on a particular type of event or series of events; or shadowing, going along with, a particular person playing a particular role as he or she moves through various contexts over the course of time. These strategies will tend to provide different kinds of information: about temporal patterns in particular locales, significant similarities and differences across settings, or variations in orientation on the part of the same person across contexts. Also relevant here are questions about how long observation periods need to be in order to capture what is important. Besides these concerns, sampling of what to observe and when may also be governed by emerging theoretical ideas, in the manner of grounded theorizing. With

structured observation, time sampling may also be necessary within periods of observation, where the actions or events being identified are very frequent.

We have already noted that the character of observational data can vary according to whether it is structured or unstructured. In some respects, this is a matter of degree, since many modes of structured observation include room for nonstructured description, in much the same way that questionnaires sometimes include free response items. Furthermore, there are different kinds of structured observation, varying not just in the specific categories used but also in the kind of time sampling employed (Croll 1986). Unstructured observation also varies in how the data are recorded: fieldnotes, audio- and video-recording transcriptions, or some combination of these. There is further variation within each of these categories, concerning the form and style of fieldnote writing or the nature of the transcription system employed. In the case of participant observation, data may also be derived from the experience of participation. There are different attitudes toward this source of data and their significance. Some emphasize that participation can provide first-hand experience that may enhance the researcher's understanding of how people feel and why they behave in the ways that they do. A few commentators even recommend a period of immersion in the field in which the role of researcher is abandoned. Others point to the dangers of "going native," emphasizing the need to maintain a marginal position so as to retain the analytic distance required to see the familiar as strange. Of course, in some contexts, participation may be essential in order to learn the culture, and/or the language, of the people being studied. And keeping a journal in which personal responses and feelings are recorded is common practice among participant observers.

The particular role taken on by an observer has consequences not only for reactivity but also for the kinds of data that will be available and the likely sources of error involved. If the research is covert, certain sources of data may not be available, formal interviews are probably ruled out, access to some parts of a setting may be barred that would have been accessible to an open researcher (though the reverse may also be true), and there may be implications for how (and how easily) the data can be recorded (this, in turn, having implications for their accuracy). Some participant roles will allow note-taking at the time, and perhaps even the use of recording devices, while others will not. Similarly, taking on particular roles in the field will open up some sources of information, and perhaps close down others; for example, there will usually be restrictions on who will tell what to whom. Playing a particular role may enable one to be accepted on equal terms by people in that role, but undermine the possibility of building rapport with other groups. Some researchers switch roles in the course of the fieldwork to try to get over this problem. These issues are sometimes conceptualized in terms of how far the researcher succeeds in becoming a member of the group being observed. However, membership is a complex matter, permitting various degrees and kinds, and very often multiple groupings operate within a setting (Adler & Adler 1987).

There are ethical issues to do with covert research, about which there has been considerable debate over the years (Bulmer 1982), as well as issues to do with personal safety. However, there are also important ethical problems involved in overt research. While covert research is often rejected because it entails deceit, potential invasion of privacy, etc., these issues are by no means absent where observation is overt; arising partly from the fact that, as we have seen, the distinction is a matter of degree. There are thorny issues about what counts as informed consent, given that people may understand what they are told in different ways, forget they are being researched, or feel that they cannot refuse to be observed for one reason or another. In addition, there are ethical issues surrounding any participant role that an observer adopts in the field, for example to do with the use of information gained under one role for the purposes of the other. Finally, building rapport means building trust and thereby establishing implicit contracts with people. As a result, they may come to see the researcher as a friend and therefore be hurt and upset when he or she behaves in ways that are necessary for the inquiry but that they regard as failing to honor the duties of friendship.

Observation is an important method of data collection that has been widely used by sociologists. It can take a variety of forms, and a wide range of considerations needs to be taken into account when it is used. The significance of these will vary depending upon both the researcher and the nature of the people and places being studied: some quite different issues would arise, for example, in studying accountants, motorcycle gangs, or kindergarten children. Furthermore, what is possible, and to some extent what is ethical, will vary considerably according to the society and local community in which the research is carried out.

SEE ALSO: Ethics, Fieldwork; Ethnography; Grounded Theory; Role-Taking; Validity, Qualitative

REFERENCES AND SUGGESTED READINGS

Adler, P. A. & Adler, P. (1987) *Membership Roles in Field Research*. Sage, Newbury Park, CA.

Bulmer, M. (1982) *Social Research Ethics: An Examination of the Merits of Covert Participant Observation*. Macmillan, London.

Croll, P. (1986) *Systematic Classroom Observation*. Falmer, London.

Emerson, R. M., Fretz, R. I., & Shaw, L. I. (1995) *Writing Ethnographic Fieldnotes*. University of Chicago Press, Chicago.

Foster, P. (1996) *Observing Schools: A Methodological Guide*. Paul Chapman, London.

McCall, G. J. (1984) Systematic Field Observation. *Annual Review of Sociology* 10: 263–82.

McCall, G. J. & Simmons, J. L. (Eds.) (1969) *Issues in Participant Observation*. Addison-Wesley, Reading, MA.

occupational mobility

Donald J. Treiman

Occupational mobility refers to changes in the kind of work people do across generations (*inter*generational mobility) or over the course of people's lives (*intra*generational or career mobility). This entry focuses on intergenerational mobility, a topic that has given rise to a large and truly international research literature despite difficult conceptual and measurement issues.

In its simplest form, research on intergenerational occupational mobility involves analysis of a single two-variable table, in which the occupations of men (almost all of the research to date has been restricted to men) are crosstabulated by the occupations of their fathers when the men were young (e.g., at age 14). In early research, the focus was simply on the degree of association in such tables – the extent to which the occupations of sons could be predicted from the occupations of their fathers – which was taken as an indicator of the degree of societal "openness." The idea was that societies in which men "follow their father's footsteps" can be thought of as more rigid and less open to achievement based on individual merit than societies in which the occupations of men are largely independent of those of their fathers. Later research began to be concerned about the *pattern* as well as the *amount* of mobility.

Almost from the outset, such research has been comparative, asking either whether the extent of mobility has changed over time or whether it varies across societies, or both. One reason for this is that it is hard to assess in absolute terms how open a society is; that is, whether any measured amount of openness is large or small.

MEASUREMENT ISSUES

To study occupational mobility it is first necessary to define what occupations are. There are many ways to aggregate the specific jobs people do into categories. One way is to classify jobs on the basis of similarity in the kinds of tasks performed – driving a bus, installing or repairing plumbing, teaching high school students, etc. Such aggregations produce *occupational* classifications (as distinct from *industrial* classifications, which aggregate jobs on the basis of the kind of enterprise within which they are performed, or *employment status* classifications, which distinguish self-employed, salaried, and other kinds of workers). Jobs may be aggregated into occupational classifications at successively higher levels. For example, the *Dictionary of*

Occupational Titles distinguishes about 12,000 occupations; the US Census detailed occupational classification distinguishes about 500 occupations; and many occupational mobility tables distinguish no more than a handful of occupational categories (often fewer than ten). The level of aggregation is very substantial, since in 2000 there were about 130 million employed people in the US, each holding a distinct job (or sometimes more than one job).

A variety of principles have been used to aggregate specific occupations (e.g., carpenter) into a small number of categories. However, most such classifications group occupations on the basis of some combination of the degree of skill entailed, the amount of responsibility exercised, the extent to which people in particular occupations supervise or are supervised by others, and the terms of employment and conditions under which the work is performed. A conventional set of distinctions is between professional, managerial, clerical, sales, manual, service, and agricultural occupations, with manual occupations often subdivided on the basis of skill, into skilled, semi-skilled, and unskilled categories, and agricultural occupations often subdivided into farm owners and managers and agricultural laborers. An overarching distinction is often made between "non-manual occupations" (the first four categories) and "manual" occupations (the remaining categories), on the ground that nonmanual work usually involves working with symbols rather than objects, is often paid a salary (fixed income per week or month) rather than a wage (payment per hour of work performed), and usually entails greater job security. Of course, there are many exceptions to these generalizations.

An important development in the study of occupational mobility has been the construction of scales of occupational status. It has been shown that the relative prestige of occupations is more or less invariant over time and across societies, and also that the prestige of occupations mainly reflects the knowledge and skill required and the income and other rewards attached to each occupation. These results have given rise to scales that measure the relative prestige or the relative socioeconomic status of occupations, which in turn make it possible to study occupational mobility, or occupational status attainment, with multivariate methods.

AMOUNT AND PATTERN OF MOBILITY

At the descriptive level, it is evident that, at least in modern industrial societies, the dominant pattern is one of occupational mobility rather than occupational inheritance. Most men do different work from their fathers. Specifically, in industrial societies about 90 percent of men hold jobs in different 3-digit census occupational categories (e.g., "truck drivers," "accountants and auditors," "electricians") from the jobs held by their fathers when they were growing up. Moreover, most men do not even work in the same general occupational "class" (or census major occupational group) as their fathers; even when highly aggregated (e.g., 6-category) occupational classifications are considered, typically about 70 percent of men end up in different categories from their fathers. Farmers' sons become factory workers; factory workers' sons become salesmen; the sons of manual workers become professionals; the sons of managers or professionals become manual workers or low-level clerical workers; and so on.

To a considerable extent, intergenerational occupational mobility reflects the striking shift in the distribution of the labor force in industrialized nations over the past 150 years and a corresponding, but much compressed and still ongoing, shift in developing nations – from agriculture to manual work to nonmanual work. Between 1900 and 2000 in the US, the percentage of the labor force doing agricultural work declined from 38 percent to 1 percent, while the percentage doing nonmanual work increased from 18 percent to 60 percent. This pattern of change can be found in most industrialized nations. Such shifts over time have induced considerable mobility between generations; clearly, if 25 percent of fathers and 10 percent of sons do agricultural work, most sons of agricultural workers must be occupationally mobile relative to their fathers. This observation has led researchers to distinguish between "structural" mobility (that caused by the shift in the distribution of jobs across occupations) and "exchange" or "relative" mobility (mobility other than that caused by structural shifts) and to develop new statistical methods (log linear and log multiplicative models) to appropriately distinguish between the two. Much of the interest of students of occupational mobility has been in the "relative" mobility chances of those from different social origins: for example, the relative odds that the son of a laborer and the son of a professional will become a professional.

Several generalizations have emerged from such research. The *pattern* of mobility – the relative chances of moving between particular occupational categories – is more or less invariant across industrial societies. The pattern of mobility is also more or less invariant over time in stable societies such as the US and Great Britain, but can change substantially as a consequence of abrupt social change (e.g., the establishment of communist governments usually resulted in the abolition of independent farming and a very substantial reduction in the proportion of small shop keepers). Relative mobility chances generally follow a status gradient. That is, mobility is greater between categories that are similar in socioeconomic status or prestige than between categories that are dissimilar. Despite considerable intergenerational mobility, there remains a substantial amount of "occupational class" inheritance. That is, men are disproportionately likely to do jobs that are in the same general category as their fathers' jobs – the sons of professionals are disproportionately likely to become professionals; the sons of managers to become managers; and so on. The *amount* of mobility has been increasing over time. There is considerable variability in the amount of mobility in different nations, but there is as yet no consensus regarding the determinants of cross-national variations.

OCCUPATIONAL STATUS ATTAINMENT

A second, distinct strand of research on intergenerational mobility has been the study of occupational status attainment. The development of occupational status scales accompanied a shift in focus on the part of some researchers from the study of two-variable occupational mobility tables to the study of the determinants of occupational status, where fathers' occupational status was only one of several factors affecting occupational outcomes. The new conception was that parental status (father's occupation, father's and mother's education, etc.)

affects educational attainment and that parental status and educational attainment affect occupational status attainment. Each of these factors can be measured in a quantitative way, which meant that it was possible to determine the relative importance of various "paths" linking occupational status across generations. Most of the early research in this tradition was also confined to men, though gender has more often been a focus of more recent research.

The main result of this research has been the demonstration that education is both the principal engine of intergenerational mobility and the main vehicle of intergenerational status transmission. The extent of intergenerational occupational status transmission – the propensity for those from high-status families to acquire high-status positions themselves – is generally quite modest in industrial societies. The principal way that intergenerational status transmission occurs is through education. Those from high-status families tend to do better and hence go further in school; and those with the best education win out in the competition for the highest status jobs. In this way, education is the main vehicle of intergenerational status transmission. But education itself is only moderately affected by social origins. In industrial societies education tends to be available at no or low cost, which provides an opportunity for the bright and well-motivated children of disadvantage to further their schooling and hence achieve high-status occupational positions. At the same time, since many positions now require educational credentials, even those from high-status families who do not do well in school are precluded from many high-status occupational opportunities.

One advantage of the status attainment approach, and the accompanying statistical technology (structural equation modeling, originally known as path analysis), is that it is easy to introduce additional factors into the attainment process. This has led to an increasingly elaborate and sophisticated understanding of how the status attainment process works. Much of the elaboration has focused on the link between social origins and educational attainment, with attention to social psychological factors, peer influences, the role of family cultural capital, and school curriculum tracking and other school effects. Some research has focused specifically on the link between schooling and work and

how that linkage varies across countries depending on characteristics of schools (whether there is a single system or separate academic and vocational systems and, in dual-track systems, how early the choice must be made between them) and how labor markets are organized.

A promising new development in comparative research on occupational status attainment is the use of multilevel modeling methods. The strategy is to combine data from sample surveys conducted at different points in time and for different nations into a single large data set and then to reorganize the data to represent social "contexts," defined by dividing the data from each nation into five-year birth cohorts. For example, if complete data were available for 50 nations covering the entire twentieth century, it would be possible to define 1,000 (= 50*20) contexts. Of course, complete data are not available, since for many nations national sample surveys began to be conducted only recently, but nonetheless the method typically yields several hundred contexts. The process of status attainment is then studied within each context and, in a second step, variations in the process are linked to variations in the characteristics of the social context (e.g., the level of economic development, the availability of free education, whether the political system is communist or capitalist, and so on). While most of the work to date has been concerned with educational attainment, this is a promising approach to the comparative study of occupational status attainment as well.

SEE ALSO: Educational Inequality; Educational and Occupational Attainment; Intergenerational Mobility: Core Model of Social Fluidity; Intergenerational Mobility: Methods of Analysis; Mobility, Horizontal and Vertical; Mobility, Intergenerational and Intragenerational; Occupational Segregation; Occupations, Scaling of; Stratification Systems: Openness; Transition from School to Work

REFERENCES AND SUGGESTED READINGS

Blau, P. M. & Duncan, O. D. (1967) *The American Occupational Structure*. Wiley, New York.

DiPrete, T. A. & Forrestal, J. D. (1994) Multilevel Models: Methods and Substance. *Annual Review of Sociology* 20: 331–57.

Erikson, R. & Goldthorpe, J. H. (1992) *The Constant Flux: A Study of Class Mobility in Industrial Societies*. Clarendon Press, Oxford.

Ganzeboom, H. B. G. & Treiman, D. J. (1996) Internationally Comparable Measures of Occupational Status for the 1988 International Standard Classification of Occupations. *Social Science Research* 25: 201–39.

Ganzeboom, H. B. G., Luijkx, R., & Treiman, D. J. (1989) Intergenerational Class Mobility in Comparative Perspective. *Research in Social Stratification and Mobility* 8: 3–84.

Hauser, R. M. and Warren, J. R. (1997) Socioeconomic Indexes for Occupations: A Review, Update, and Critique. In: Raftery, A. E. (Ed.), *Sociological Methodology 1997*. American Sociological Association, Washington, DC, pp. 177–298.

Hout, M. & Hauser, R. M. (1992) Symmetry and Hierarchy in Social Mobility: A Methodological Analysis of the CASMIN Model of Class Mobility. *European Sociological Review* 8: 239–66.

Shavit, Y. & Müller, W. (1998) *From School to Work: A Comparative Study of Educational Qualifications and Occupational Destinations*. Clarendon Press, Oxford.

Treiman, D. J. (1977) *Occupational Prestige in Comparative Perspective*. Academic Press, New York.

Treiman, D. J. & Yip, K. B. (1989) Educational and Occupational Achievement in 21 Countries. In: Kohn, M. L. (Ed.), *Cross-National Research in Sociology*. ASA Presidential Series. Sage, Beverly Hills, CA.

occupational segregation

Kim Weeden

Occupational segregation refers to the differential distribution of groups defined by ascribed characteristics (e.g., sex, race/ethnicity) across occupations. The *level* of segregation indicates the strength of the association between group membership and occupations. Levels vary on a continuum bracketed by perfect segregation and perfect integration. Perfect segregation occurs where occupation and group membership correspond perfectly, such that no occupations are populated by more than one group. Perfect integration occurs if there is no association between occupation and group membership, where this typically means that each group holds the same proportion of positions in each occupation as it holds in the labor force.

The *pattern* of segregation refers to the precise configuration of a group's over- or underrepresentation in particular occupations. Patterns can vary independently from levels. For example, the segregation level may remain stable even if a particular occupation switches from male overrepresentation to (equivalent) female overrepresentation. Conversely, levels may decline without altering the underlying pattern if all occupations shift from being highly segregated to only moderately so.

Interest in occupational segregation stems from two sources. Segregation is a known precursor to inequalities in pay, autonomy, promotions, working conditions, prestige, and even lifestyles. Recent evidence suggests, for example, that the gender gap in wages is driven more by segregation across jobs than by pay discrimination within jobs. At the same time, segregation is an outcome of interest in its own right, for it is a fundamental indicator of the extent to which a society is characterized by ascriptive inequality. Segregation scholars have focused on three tasks, each of which is elaborated below: describing how segregation varies across time and space; understanding its sources; and accounting for trends and cross-national variations or similarities.

Descriptive research shows that segregation is extensive, characterizes all known societies, and is remarkably persistent over time. In the United States, blacks are over- or underrepresented in the average occupation by a factor of 2.1, and nearly 21 percent would need to change occupations in order to reach perfect integration with whites. Sex segregation is yet more extreme: men are over- or underrepresented in the average occupation by a factor of 5.5, and 51 percent would need to change occupations for full integration (author's calculations, 2000 Census PUMS). In terms of the pattern of segregation, men are disproportionately found in managerial, craft, and farming occupations and women in clerical and service occupations.

Conventional wisdom holds that levels of race and sex segregation were relatively stable in the United States until the 1970s. Since 1970, integration by both race and sex has been appreciable, but slower than one might expect given the rapid diffusion of egalitarian views, the decline in (and criminalization of) overt employment discrimination, and the shrinking gap in college attainment. Evidence on patterns of sex segregation indicates that integration has also been uneven: some formerly male-dominated occupations (e.g., accountants) have integrated while others remain female-dominated (e.g., nurses), and yet others have tipped past full integration to become female-dominated (e.g., court reporters). Such "feminization" is often accompanied by a decline in the occupation's skills, position on promotion ladders, and wages, although it is unclear whether this "downgrading" is a cause or consequence of feminization. We know far less about changing patterns of race segregation, but it is plausible that racial integration has also been more pronounced in some occupations than others.

Race and sex segregation also vary across space. Some of the highest levels of sex segregation, for example, are found in countries known for gender-egalitarian ideologies (e.g., Sweden), while the lowest levels are in countries with more traditional ideologies (e.g., Japan). Similarly, although the general pattern of sex segregation across major occupational groups that obtains in the United States characterizes most advanced industrial countries, the sex-type of particular occupations can vary substantially across countries. Physicians, for example, are disproportionately male in the United States, but not in post-socialist Eastern Europe. Analogous cross-national comparisons of racial segregation are lacking, but comparisons across local labor markets in the US show segregation increases with the size of the black population.

Efforts to understand the sources of segregation are typically categorized into supply-side accounts, which emphasize the investment decisions and choices of workers, and demand-side accounts, which focus on the hiring and promotion decisions of employers. The line between supply- and demand-side forces is blurred, though, whenever workers' choices reflect demand-side constraints. Moreover, segregation may be jointly determined by workers' and employers' decisions.

Supply-side forces include socialization, stereotypes about competence, and income-maximizing decisions. Socialization refers to the lifelong processes through which people internalize attitudes, skills, beliefs, and knowledge. If the content of socialization differs across groups, it will generate group-specific occupational preferences, or "tastes" for types of work, and occupational expectations, or "realistic" judgments about occupations where success is likely. If such judgments are affected by existing patterns of segregation and discrimination, socialization is no longer a purely supply-side process.

Even absent differential socialization, group-linked stereotypes about competence ("status beliefs") can generate differences in workers' behaviors and preferences. Cecilia Ridgeway (1997), for example, has argued that in mixed-sex, task-oriented settings (e.g., work, school) where direct evidence of competence is lacking, men and women alike typically assume that men are more competent at all but the most "feminine" tasks. As a result, male group members are more influential, obtain higher evaluations (from self and others), and emerge as leaders. While the theory has obvious promise for explaining the dearth of women (and racial minorities) in management, it may also help explain why young women who are skilled at math and science are reluctant to pursue related careers.

A third supply-side account argues that segregation stems from workers' rational decisions to maximize lifetime or household earnings. Workers who expect intermittent participation in the paid labor force (e.g., to raise children) will choose occupations in which wages depreciate least during unemployment. Workers who expect that their energies will be spread across paid and unpaid labor will choose low-effort occupations that entail little overtime or travel. And, whether because of gender discrimination in the labor market or women's lower pre-market investments in training, household earnings can be maximized if women specialize in unpaid labor.

Demand-side explanations emphasize the organizational hiring and promotion practices that create segregation, some of which are overtly discriminatory. Pure discrimination occurs when employers, customers, or co-workers simply prefer to hire, purchase from, or work with members of a favored group. Employers hire members of the disfavored group only at wages low enough to compensate for the disutility of hiring them, losing customers, or angering co-workers. Statistical discrimination occurs when employers avoid hiring one group because (1) they believe that, on average, members of the group are less productive *and* (2) no other cost-effective screens for productivity are available. Unlike pure discrimination, statistical discrimination is therefore economically rational. Radical scholars note that discrimination may also be "rational" in that it perpetuates capitalism (by dividing workers and providing a pool of cheap labor), patriarchy (by ensuring women's dependency), and racism (by solidifying and legitimating whites' economic advantages).

Other demand-side accounts emphasize that organizational hiring and promotion practices need not be overtly discriminatory to generate segregation (see Reskin et al. 1999). For example, employers who recruit through their employees' social networks will tend to hire workers who are the same sex or race as existing employees. Likewise, seniority-based promotion systems and formalized job ladders in which upper-level positions are filled exclusively from "port-of-entry" jobs that are male-dominated, limit women's access to upper-level positions. In both cases, disadvantages are embedded in formally gender- or race-neutral rules.

Efforts to understand cross-national variations and historical trends in segregation borrow heavily from these theories. To account for sex segregation's stability over time and space, for example, scholars emphasize the pervasiveness of sex-typed socialization, role divisions within the family, biological differences between men and women, gendered job information networks, and systems of patriarchy. To account for the gradual decline of segregation levels since the 1970s, scholars emphasize the egalitarian pressures that eroded discriminatory tastes among employers, loosened gender-specific socialization, equalized occupational aspirations and human capital accumulation, shifted the focus of labor markets from the family to the individual, promoted equal rights legislation, and led to the diffusion of bureaucratic organizational forms.

These theories speak to variability (or stability) in the level of segregation more than its pattern. They are accordingly at odds with the empirical evidence, which suggests that egalitarian pressures do not affect all occupations equally nor necessarily even reduce segregation, as the case of Sweden illustrates. To begin to reconcile theories with evidence, some scholars distinguish between *vertical segregation*, which occurs when one group holds a disproportionate share of the occupations with high pay, prestige, and promotion prospects, and *horizontal segregation*, which occurs when groups hold "separate but equal" occupations. Vertical segregation is incompatible with contemporary forms of egalitarianism, and hence should decline over time. Horizontal segregation, by contrast, is compatible both with liberal egalitarianism and with essentialist ideologies that characterize group-linked skills and preferences as "natural."

The theoretical literature on segregation is thus reasonably rich. The methodological literature has, until recently, struggled to keep pace. Early methodological efforts focused on quantifying the level of segregation, but not its pattern. This work yielded the important observation that the more fine-grained the labor market structure, the more segregation one observes: segregation is greater across detailed occupations (e.g., physician) than major occupational groups (e.g., professional), and greater across jobs (e.g., Associate General Counsel at IBM) than occupations (e.g., lawyer). In light of this, standard practice is to disaggregate as much as possible while retaining comparable categories across the contexts (e.g., nations, time). Even so, scholars typically must assume that trends or cross-national variations in segregation are parallel at different levels of aggregation.

The early quantitative literature also became mired in debates over which summary index is most appropriate for measuring segregation levels. Two indices are most often used: the index of dissimilarity (D), which is the percentage of one group who would need to change occupations in order to bring about full integration, and a size-standardized variant (D_s), which adjusts D to compensate for its sensitivity to historical or cross-national variations in the relative size of occupations. D_s is sensitive to variations in the gender or racial composition of the labor force.

More recently, Maria Charles and David Grusky (e.g., 2004) argued that if the goal of segregation research is to reveal contextual variations in the strength of the underlying association between occupation and group membership, scholars should use an index that is unaffected by the occupational structure or the composition of the labor force. They define an index, based on odds ratios, that meets both criteria. Their core, and often overlooked, methodological critique, though, is that all indices implicitly assume that the pattern of segregation is either constant or uninteresting. They instead offer a log-linear modeling approach that allows scholars to (1) evaluate whether variation in segregation is in fact merely a matter of degree; (2) assess whether cross-national or historical similarities in the pattern of segregation hold at all levels of aggregation; (3) formally test whether groups are segregated vertically, horizontally, or both; and (4) evaluate explanatory models of segregation.

Many descriptive, theoretical, and methodological challenges still face segregation researchers. First, the obsession with occupational segregation has led scholars to ignore all other market structures (e.g., industries) or treat them as contexts across which occupational segregation varies. This strategy fails to appreciate that what appears to be occupational segregation may reflect the unequal distribution of occupations across other labor market structures that are themselves segregated. Substantively, such "unidimensional" thinking fails to do justice to theories of inequality that recognize the complex interplay between labor market structures.

Similarly, the race and sex segregation literatures have developed largely independently of each other. The few scholars who are interested in both typically analyze sex segregation by racial group, race segregation by sex, or the segregation of jointly defined groups (e.g., white women). This line of research, while undeniably influential, is hampered by the inability of conventional methodologies (but not log-linear methods) to gracefully incorporate multiple race categories and to tease apart "net" patterns and levels of segregation. More generally, the separation of the segregation literatures on race and sex has led to a superficial treatment of interdependencies in systems of racial and gender-based inequalities. Finally, there is still much room to elaborate and evaluate causal theories of patterns of segregation and how they vary across time and space.

SEE ALSO: Affirmative Action (Race and Ethnic Quotas); Divisions of Household Labor; Gender, Work, and Family; Inequality/Stratification, Gender; International Gender Division of Labor; Intersectionality; Occupations, Scaling of; Sex-Based Wage Gap and Comparable Worth; Socialization, Gender; Stratification, Gender and; Stratification, Race/Ethnicity and

REFERENCES AND SUGGESTED READINGS

Charles, M. & Grusky, D. B. (2004) *Occupational Ghettos: The Worldwide Segregation of Women and Men*. Stanford University Press, Stanford.

Correll, S. (2001) Gender and the Career Choice Process: The Role of Biased Self-Assessments. *American Journal of Sociology* 106: 1691–1730.

Jacobs, J. (1989) *Revolving Doors: Sex Segregation and Women's Careers*. Stanford University Press, Stanford.

Petersen, T. & Morgan, L. A. (1995) Separate and Unequal: Occupation-Establishment Sex Segregation and the Gender Wage Gap. *American Journal of Sociology* 101: 329–65.

Reskin, B. & Roos, P. (1990) *Job Queues, Gender Queues: Explaining Women's Inroads into Male Occupations*. Temple University Press, Philadelphia.

Reskin, B., McBrier, D. B., & Kmec, J. (1999) The Determinants and Consequences of Workplace Sex and Race Composition. *Annual Review of Sociology* 25: 335–61.

Ridgeway, C. (1997) Interaction and the Conservation of Gender Inequality: Considering Employment. *American Sociological Review* 62: 218–35.

Weeden, K. (1998) Revisiting Occupational Sex Segregation in the United States, 1910–1990: Results from a Log-Linear Approach. *Demography* 35: 475–87.

occupations

Steven Rytina

Occupation refers to the kind of work usually done for a living. Type of work provides one of the best single indicators of the overall life situation of workers. This rests on a thesis that is powerful (but varies in validity) − type of work is a key cause and consequence of relative position with respect to stable inequalities or social stratification.

Occupation is one of the most complex indicators in social science. There are many ways of classifying work into types. An initial issue is what counts as occupation and what does not.

Many authors, and most government statistical agencies, restrict occupation to work performed for pay outside the home. Unpaid domestic or household labor is thus commonly excluded. Agricultural labor by kin for kin, including that by children, is also not counted. These excluded possibilities lack traits that equate "usual occupation" with work divided into distinct kinds, including task specialization, contractual regulation, and barriers to entry like required formal training, licensing, or previous experience.

These traits help delimit the ever-finer divisions of work that emerge wherever rural, agricultural economies were displaced by urban and industrial alternatives. Unspecialized work gave way to specialized, potentially lifelong vocations that became a key determinant of mode and level of living. (Living levels for dependent household members also turn on occupations, but complications arise when no one is gainfully employed or more than one member is.) Government concern for distribution over vocations is almost as old as urbanism – in 305 BCE, the Roman emperor Diocletian decreed that all sons would follow the trade of their fathers, apparently without much success. Modern occupational tabulations date from the early industrial era when the term statistics retained its older meaning of measures created for purposes of state (Desrosières 1998).

From the outset, designers of codes took occupation as a potential master status, "the best single criterion of a man's social and economic status" encompassing "the kind of associates he will have," "the kind of food he will eat," and "the cultural level of his family" (Alba Edwards, in charge of occupational statistics for the US Census Bureau 1920–40, quoted in Conk 1980: 26). Reliable, and often large, differences between occupations indeed run the gamut from leisure pursuits (Bourdieu 1984) to death rates (Johnson et al. 1999).

Such empirical potency is achieved in spite of uneven foundations. Since a principal goal was to code census responses to questions about the work usually performed, designers incorporated folk distinctions among well-known trades, such as carpentry, that were skilled (or thought to be so). New industries, based on novelties like chemicals or electricity, were added by analogy, not without expressed doubt that such work required much in the way of distinguishing skills. Categories were added for jobs titled to reflect educational specialties that grew apace as science and engineering played ever larger roles in the economy. Sound reasons mingled with guesses and hunches – the paucity of specific information about specific jobs and industries is often cited in accounts of code design. This uncertainty is reflected in residual categories, such as Machine Operatives, Not Elsewhere Classified, that are left open as catch-alls for cases that do not fit elsewhere.

This state of affairs resists easy summary. Codes are compromises – dictionaries of occupation titles distinguish upwards of 10,000 occupations while data collectors distinguish several hundred, at most. Any coding effort achieves no more than partial separation by exclusion – code assignments record unambiguous disqualification from most possibilities, even while final assignments can be uncertain over some short-list and much variety remains among jobs collected in specific categories. The end result is simultaneously potent and incomplete. Empirical summaries fall into the fuzzy mid-range where half-empty meets half-full. Typically, somewhere between one- to two-thirds of variation in concomitants like education or earnings are between occupational categories, entailing ample residual variation among individuals who share occupational categories.

This pattern of robust but imperfect connection to diverse forms of inequality raises challenging issues. Since codes are, at best, fallible overlays riddled with uncertainty, why do they work – why do categories of jobs exhibit homogeneity on just about any criterion of social rank? Another issue is the stability implicit in taking occupation as an indicator of individual social standing, as rank that persists over time and even across changes of job.

Homogeneity and contrast are generally seen as fostered by labor markets. Market logic forces buyers and sellers toward agreement on categories defining interchangeable substitutes, segregating non-substitutes into separate categories.

The disruption inherent in adding replacements to work teams shapes categories. Technical demands motivate screening replacements for training that will reduce transition strains. Where that training takes more time, to the exclusion of alternatives, barriers arise against substitution, reserving collections of jobs to ever-narrower pools of persons that undergo specific preliminary sequences. Persons holding jobs acquire stakes in jobs defined as open to them, sometimes in tension with the interests of employers and holders of other jobs. Stakeholding potentially induces collective actors formed around joint interests, including limiting competition by imposing criteria of gender, ethnicity, or training beyond what is needed to do the job.

Conversely, where neither technical intricacies nor worker organization raise barriers to replacement, there are limited bases for securing advantages or for cementing lifetime attachments. In this sense, degree of occupational articulation is a facet of stratification, with clarity of occupation weaker where advantage is lesser.

Coded finely or coarsely, type of work thus provides a rough-cut of similarity with respect to key components of bargaining power between jobholders and those with an interest in keeping a job filled (usually employers). Employees gain relative power when reliability in coming to work is more crucial, when team outcomes are more dependent on individual contribution, and when replacements are scarce relative to demand and thus expensive. As a rough but reasonably accurate summary, levels of formal education summarize relative scarcity and hence rank.

One tradition has taken relative rank as an externally fixed, hence rigid, framework within which attributes of individuals "cause" relative placements. Blau and Duncan (1967) termed this scaffolding. The referent was flexible – occupation referred to 400-plus detailed occupations arranged along a dimension by Duncan's socioeconomic index (commonly called SEI) and to a 17-fold category scheme generated by imposing industry subdivisions onto a tenfold scheme traceable to Alba Edwards.

This shifting referent of occupation reveals a central difficulty – occupation must be mapped into one of several forms that are more methodologically tractable before empirical application is possible. Sometimes heated controversies have emerged among proponents of, for example, class schemes drawing on relatively few categories and schemes for supplying numerical ranks to detailed categories.

Another stance takes entry requirements and relative rewards of occupations as outcomes shaped by collective action and contest. Abbott (1988) showed how professions competed in carving out domains of expertise. The most successful groupings further got schooling and/or licensing requirements established in law, thereby limiting numbers and raising rewards. Parkin (1979) grouped such processes with comparable attempts at exclusion by wage-workers that also aimed to control or restrict labor supply to enhance the advantages of those inside relevant boundaries. Such arguments emphasize that occupations are created when interested parties draw lines around jobs and enforce restrictions over entry.

What counts as qualification is subject to change. Conk (1980) reports late nineteenth-century manuals for employers that stereotyped ethnic groups as distinctively suited or unsuited for long lists of specific occupations. In practice, occupational specialization by ethnic origin was extremely marked during the high tide of European immigration. This gradually faded as generations succeeded, except for those of African descent (Lieberson 1980). Occupational segregation by gender is extremely marked and the changes have been compared to queues where the "lesser" gender only takes over the least desirable or tail-end of available jobs (Reskin & Roos 1990). Tilly (1998) has even argued that occupational categories are not so much causes as empty containers that organization designers assign to contrasting genders, ethnic backgrounds, or other bases to stabilize and legitimate unequal work relations and unequal outcomes. Occupations thus remain central to understanding how stable differences are marked and managed, even as debate persists over how and why work specialization channels inequalities.

SEE ALSO: Division of Labor; Labor Markets; Labor Movement; Labor Process; Mobility, Horizontal and Vertical; Mobility, Intergenerational and Intragenerational; Mobility, Measuring the Effects of; Occupational

Mobility; Occupational Segregation; Occupations, Scaling of; Professions; Stratification and Inequality, Theories of

REFERENCES AND SUGGESTED READINGS

Abbott, A. (1988) *The System of the Professions: An Essay on the Division of Expert Labor*. University of Chicago Press, Chicago.

Blau, P. M. & Duncan, O. D. (1967) *The American Occupational Structure*. Academic Press, New York.

Bourdieu, P. (1984) *Distinction: A Social Critique of the Judgment of Taste*. Harvard University Press, Cambridge, MA.

Conk, M. A. (1980) *The United States Census and the New Jersey Urban Occupational Structure, 1870–1940*. UMI Research Press, Ann Arbor, MI.

Desrosières, A. (1998) *The Politics of Large Numbers: A History of Statistical Reasoning*. Harvard University Press, Cambridge, MA.

Johnson, N. J., Sorlie, P. D., & Backlund, E. (1999) The Impact of Specific Occupation on Mortality in the US National Longitudinal Mortality Study. *Demography* 36(3): 355–67.

Lieberson, S. (1980) *A Piece of the Pie*. University of California Press, Berkeley.

Parkin, F. (1979) *Marxism and Class Theory*. Columbia University Press, New York.

Reskin, B. F. & Roos, P. A. (1990) *Job Queues, Gender Queues: Explaining Women's Inroads into Male Occupations*. Temple University Press, Philadelphia.

Tilly, C. (1998) *Durable Inequality*. University of California Press, Berkeley.

occupations, scaling of

Wout Ultee

In their empirical research on societal stratification, sociologists in national sample surveys often ask people about their present occupation, first occupation, the occupation of their father and of their mother, and the occupation of their spouse and their siblings. The occupational titles obtained in this way nowadays are coded according to the International Standard Classification of Occupations (ISCO) issued by the International Labor Office, or the equivalent of this classification used by official national bureaus of statistics. The 1988 ISCO reduces occupational titles to 10 major groups, 28 submajor groups, 116 minor groups, and 390 unit groups. Major groups are given one digit, unit groups four digits. Since these groups are no more than nominal ones and not attuned to questions in sociology about societal phenomena like downward mobility and "marrying up," sociologists have developed scales that rank occupations from higher to lower.

One way to do so is to have a representative sample of persons rate occupational titles for the standing accorded to them by society at large, with the percent rating an occupation in the highest category giving the value for this occupation on the occupational prestige scale. It turns out that there is much agreement about this among respondents of different backgrounds (if they differed strongly, the scores for all occupational titles would be about average, which they are not). Also, as Treiman (1977) showed, occupational prestige ladders for various countries closely resemble one another. It should be added that Haller and Bills (1979) found that a prestige ladder for a social-democratic country (or a communist country) resembles that for a conservative country less than do the scales for two social-democratic countries (or two communist countries, or two conservative ones). So, assume that sociologists have a sample of respondents from a country's population who rate a sufficiently high number of occupational titles according to social standing. Also, assume that these sociologists selected these titles in line with existing nominal occupational classifications. Finally, assume that these sociologists know the title of the present occupation of a sample of persons and the occupational title for their parental home. If these three assumptions hold, then sociologists avail themselves of a criterion with which to measure the extent to which the inhabitants of a country are upwardly or downwardly mobile, and similar phenomena.

Given the unwieldy number of occupational titles to be rated by respondents, scores for titles not rated have been obtained by another procedure. If it is known from censuses or labor force surveys what are the average income and the average education of persons with a four-digit ISCO score, it is possible to estimate a mathematical equation which predicts the observed prestige for rated titles, from the average level of education and the average income of the persons with this occupational title. Given this equation, it is possible to predict a prestige score for non-rated occupational titles with known average income and education of the holders of this occupation. The first example of this exercise was performed by Duncan (1961) on US data for the 1960s. This scale was used in the first big study of inter- and intragenerational occupational mobility in the US, conducted by Blau and Duncan (1967).

Occupations also have been scaled by way of tables in which detailed occupational titles for husbands and wives and for pairs of good friends are cross-classified. A computer program orders the titles in such a way that the best fit is obtained by placing frequent combinations close to one another and infrequent combinations further away from one another. It is possible that these statistical exercises yield more than one dimension along which occupations can be ranked, leading to the question of how to interpret these dimensions. One refers to general standing, another sometimes seems to pertain to close proximity in the working place (e.g., surgeons and nurses). It is clear that there are special difficulties in using the occupational scales so obtained when studying changes in who marries whom.

Finally, there are schemas which reduce occupational titles to a small number of categories that are not fully ordered in a hierarchical way. A prime example is the often used class-schema originally developed by John Goldthorpe for the UK and later amended for country comparisons with respect to father–son mobility by Goldthorpe together with Robert Erikson. This scale has a clear bottom and a clear top, but leaves various categories below the top and above the bottom unordered. This is because the schema is not supposed to capture occupational prestige – according to some theories a more tangential phenomenon of societal stratification – but the nature of work relations, an aspect of stratification held to be more fundamental to the outcome of various societal processes like unemployment and educational inequality.

SEE ALSO: Class; Connubium (Who Marries Whom?); Occupational Segregation; Occupations; Regression and Regression Analysis; Status

REFERENCES AND SUGGESTED READINGS

Blau, P. M. & Duncan, O. D. (1967) *The American Occupational Structure*. Wiley, New York.

Duncan, O. D. (1961) A Socio-Economic Index For All Occupations. In: Reiss, A. J. et al. (Eds.), *Occupations and Social Status*. Free Press, New York, pp. 109–36.

Erikson, R. & Goldthorpe, J. H. (1992) *The Constant Flux*. Oxford University Press, Oxford.

Haller, A. O. & Bills, D. B. (1979) Occupational Prestige Hierarchies: Theory and Evidence. *Contemporary Sociology* 8: 721–34.

Haug, M. R. (1987) Measurement in Social Stratification. *Annual Review of Sociology* 3: 51–77.

International Labor Office (1990) *International Standard Classification of Occupations – ISCO-88*. International Labor Office, Geneva.

Stewart, A., Prandy, K., & Blackburn, R. M. (1973) Measuring the Class Structure. *Nature* 245: 415–17.

Treiman, D. (1977) *Occupational Prestige in Comparative Perspective*. Academic Press, New York.

office ladies

Tomoko Kurihara

"Office lady" (*ofisu red*), or in its shortened form OL (*ō eru*), is a term commonly used in Japan to describe female workers who are employed in submanagerial positions in white-collar workplaces. In its popular usage, the term OL lacks specificity and usually refers to women who work in any office environment, in a firm of any size, and in any sector or occupation, whereas the scholarly work on OLs has tended to focus on women working in large companies employing over 1,000 people. Typically, OL refers to young unmarried women in their twenties and thirties, but its usage is flexible and may refer to the full range of marital statuses, including married individuals with or without children, and older, either single or widowed working women. The term OL was coined by the media in the 1960s to represent the greater numbers of women who had entered the labor market following the structural changes in the post-war economy, mainly in the expansion of the service, wholesale, and retail industries. The emergence of the term appeared to mark the empowerment of women in society, suggesting that women were able to form an identity primarily based on their role as workers. In spite of this, for much of the twentieth century the image of the independent working woman in Japan was limited to her main role as a powerful consumer of high fashion and overseas travel. For this reason, in parallel to the feminist critiques of patriarchy and workplace employment practices, it seems that the term OL has acquired somewhat pejorative connotations, as keeping women on the periphery of economy, workplace, and society. From the late 1990s onwards, the term "career woman" has become a respectful self-reference preferred among the new generation of OLs. Indeed, postmodernization and the expansion of knowledge-intensive occupations have allowed a greater proportion of female workers to take up jobs in specialist clerical, professional, and managerial positions in the fields of banking, finance and retail distribution, and information technology.

Although individual OLs' specific experience of work will vary depending on the size and location of the firm, industry, occupation, age, and personal political views, OLs can, nonetheless, be viewed as a Durkheimian category insofar as the group shares common experiences and a collective representation. Upon graduating from four-year university courses and two-year junior college courses, OLs are recruited by large companies to fill full-time positions. Following the career tracking system (*kōsu-betsu-koyō-seido*) introduced by the Equal Employment Opportunity Law (EEOL) (1986), large companies divide new recruits into clerical (*ippan-shoku*) and managerial/career tracks (*sōgō-shoku*). The clerical track is characterized by less complex and more manual jobs, lower pay, fewer job rotations and only limited transfers, and promotion limited to lower-level or local management positions. In contrast, jobs in the career or managerial track are seen to require complex judgments such as business negotiations, personnel management, designing

or developing products, and planning company policies or strategies. Further, there is no limit to promotion and the individual is subject to job rotations and transfers. The majority of women are channeled into the clerical track, and where only a select few successfully make the career track, male graduates are automatically assigned to career track positions.

In fact, the EEOL introduced official status differences among women, while it did not necessarily put women on an equal footing to their male counterparts in the company. In *Women and Japanese Management: Discrimination and Reform* (1992), Lam explains that the career tracking system was designed to prohibit employers from engaging in unlawful discriminatory practice in the hiring, retirement age, resignation, and dismissal of women, as well as in the provision of basic training and fringe benefits. In spite of this legislation, companies are given considerable leeway to practice discrimination in order to preserve the core management system. Moreover, the tracking system complicated the relationships between women. Educational background remained the principal structural barrier to promotion for women with fewer years of education, even though they might have outperformed women with higher educational qualifications, evaluated in terms of length of service and amount of responsibility handled on the job. This further complicated social relations between women already compounded by factors of age, tenure, and status. Also, the women in the career track face complications in their social relations with male colleagues who confine them to supporting roles on account of an inability to surrender their traditional gender role expectations.

On the whole, then, OLs' wages, employment status, occupational roles, and promotional chances remain low in relation to their male colleagues. Moreover, OLs tend to encounter the problem of status ambiguity (see Lebra 1981). This is because OLs hired by large companies have been educated at Japan's most prestigious universities and colleges, and in working for large corporations such women are among the economic elite or new middle class. As a status group, the qualities of the economic elite are defined by achievement (not ascribed characteristics), power (not prestige), and class of wealth (as opposed to "status of honor").

Female workers who enter this status group find, nevertheless, that ascribed characteristics, mainly sex, when combined with sociocultural norms expected of women's lives, produce status differences between men and women in the office. Thus, formal structural inequalities in wage and promotion give women, including those on the career track, low status in comparison to men, producing the effect of status ambiguity.

In the academic literature, the position, status, and identity of OLs have been an important means by which the perpetuation of gender inequality in Japanese society and workplaces has been explained. Even predating the literature on OLs, however, there has been a tradition of representing female workers in the Japanese labor market as oppressed victims of patriarchal society. Historical accounts of the role of women in the development of industry in modern Japan have thoroughly documented the structural basis which precipitates this reality (see Bernstein 1991; Hunter 1993). Other macro-level studies of female workers have provided insightful critiques that explain women's peripheral status in the workplace in terms of their exclusion from the benefits of internal labor markets, specifically the lifetime employment system (see Rohlen 1974; Brinton 1993; Osawa Machiko 1993; Osawa Mari 1996). Also within this paradigm (labeled the gendered organizations framework), ethnographies of female office workers have accounted for the low status of women by showing how organizations are structured in terms of a dichotomy between masculine and feminine roles (see Lo 1990; Saso 1990). Ethnographies under this framework also include Dorrine K. Kondo's *Crafting Selves: Power, Gender, and Discourses of Identity in a Japanese Workplace* (1990), Yuko Ogasawara's *Office Ladies and Salaried Men: Power, Gender, and Work in Japanese Companies* (1998), and Tomoko Kurihara's *Japanese Corporate Transition in Time and Space: An Ethnography of Community, Status Politics, and the Introduction of ICTs* (2006). These authors apply a deconstructionist framework to analyze the process of gendering at the level of discourse, individual identity, and interaction, and place importance on the meaning women give to their own work. Such studies maintain the significance of the historical and culturally specific conditions under which gendering in white-collar organizations occurs, yet they allow room to account for improvement in gender relations within work environments and the social sphere.

Although status ambiguity and gender inequality persist, the conditions in workplaces appear to be improving, albeit slowly, and this was particularly clear in the late 1990s. The EEOL (1986) was revised in 1997. The modifications that came into effect in April 1999 took account of a number of social trends: the increases in the total number of female recruits; the prolonged length of women's service in the workplace; the expansion in the type of jobs to which women applied; changing awareness among the general public regarding women's work; and changes to the way companies tackled human resource issues with regard to the equal treatment of female workers. Notably, the most significant shift of recent times is in relation to women's attitudes toward balancing their careers with domestic responsibility, and their wish to continue working in jobs which are equal to or better than the position held before childbirth. Furthermore, addressing a highly problematic domain, a directive on the prevention of sexual harassment in the workplace was issued. However, a clear definition of sexual harassment is still lacking, and judicial policy on the subject largely seems to consist of an empty formality, designed only to raise awareness of sexual harassment in Japanese workplaces in alignment with western standards. The restrictions on overtime and late-night work by women (including those engaged in child or family care) have also been lifted, a change that is expected to increase the promotional prospects of women. Moreover, the Japanese government is now playing a more active role in its attempts to enforce the law. The Ministry of Labor has agreed to provide the necessary administrative guidance to companies in the form of advice, instructions, and recommendations. Provisions are being made for a consultation and arbitration service to enterprise owners, voluntary in-house resolution of complaints, assistance for dispute settlements through the Director of Prefectural Women's and Young Workers' Office, and relief from disputes through mediation by the Equal Opportunity Mediation Commission. As a further means of reinforcing this new standard, the government is regulating companies known to be exercising discriminatory practices through threat of public exposure (*kigyōmei-kōhyō-seido*). But the extent of the success of this measure is questionable given the influence of large companies on political matters. It seems clear that the EEOL cannot be enforced effectively in companies if the wider social context is not supportive of working women, yet it is necessary to account for and improve the working conditions of men if gender equality is to be achieved (see Ueno 1995).

SEE ALSO: Discrimination; Gender Ideology and Gender Role Ideology; Gendered Organizations/Institutions; Japanese-Style Management; Salary Men; *Shushin Koyo*

REFERENCES AND SUGGESTED READINGS

Bernstein, G. L. (1991) Introduction. In: Bernstein, G. L. (Ed.), *Recreating Japanese Women, 1600–1945*. University of California Press, Berkeley, pp. 3–30.
Brinton, M. C. (1993) *Women and the Japanese Economic Miracle: Gender and Work in Postwar Japan*. University of California Press, Berkeley.
Hunter, J. (1993) Introduction. In: Hunter, J. (Ed.), *Japanese Women Working*. Routledge, London, pp. 1–15.
Lebra, T. S. (1981) Japanese Women in Male Dominant Careers: Cultural Barriers and Accommodations for Sex-Role Transcendence. *Ethnology* 20: 291–306.
Lo, J. (1990) *Office Ladies, Factory Women: Life and Work at a Japanese Company*. M. E. Sharpe, Armonk, NY.
Osawa, Machiko (1993) *Keizai Henka to Joshi Rōdō: Nichibei to hikaku kenkyū (Economic Change and Female Labor: A US–Japan Comparison)*. Nihon Keizai Hyōronsha, Tokyo.
Osawa, Mari (1996) Will the Japanese Style System Change? Employment, Gender, and Welfare State. Trans. R. LeBlanc. *Journal of Pacific Asia* 3: 69–94.
Rohlen, T. P. (1974) *For Harmony and Strength: Japanese White-Collar Organization in Anthropological Perspective*. University of California Press, Berkeley.
Saso, M. (1990) *Women in the Japanese Workplace*. Hilary Shipman, London.
Ueno, C. (1995) Introduction to "The Oppression of a Corporate Centred Society: Amidst an 'Insular Society' of the Corporation." In: Inoue, T. et al. (Eds.), *Feminism in Japan: Studies of Masculinity*. Iwanami Shoten, Tokyo, p. 216.

older adults, economic well-being of

Stephen Crystal

In the contemporary world, and especially in the developed countries with their aging populations, providing for the economic needs of the elderly has become a central and increasingly controversial social problem. Expenditures aimed at meeting these needs – directly through income benefits such as those provided by Social Security in the US, and indirectly through tax expenditures and in-kind programs such as health benefits – constitute a dominant share of public spending in the developed countries, and will increase further as the large post-World War II birth cohort reaches old age and the proportion of retirees to workers increases. While economists have been more prominent than sociologists in the literature on the size and distribution of the elderly's economic resources, these issues pose fundamental sociological questions, and sociological perspectives are vital in understanding the processes that shape these outcomes. Work in the neoclassical economic tradition, for example, has often begun with the assumption that consumers are rational, well-informed utility maximizers who actively organize their economic affairs and choices so as to optimally distribute consumption over the life course (Modigliani 1988). (Under some versions of economic life cycle theory, utility maximizing would be predicted to result in spending one's last dollar on the last day of one's life). As sociologists might suspect, such models tend not to do well in predicting actual patterns of accumulation and spending down of savings over the life course.

Sociological perspectives are particularly important in understanding economic inequality in late life and the processes that generate or moderate them, as part of a more general analysis of social stratification and status attainment processes and of the distributional consequences of public policies. From a sociological perspective, the pattern of late-life economic outcomes can be seen as the result of influences and interactions over the life course among individual life events (e.g., educational attainment, health changes, labor-force participation); social-structural and cultural influences (e.g., family structures, gender role expectations); and formal systems and public policies (e.g., structure and rules of public and private retirement income systems, health care financing, disability benefit systems) (Crystal & Shea 2003). Thus, longitudinal analyses of data from panel surveys – such as the Health and Retirement Study, Panel Study of Income Dynamics, National Longitudinal Surveys, and others – are key to understanding the dynamics of late-life economic well-being (Crystal & Waehrer 1996; Juster & Smith 1997). As sociologists, particularly demographers, have noted, these longitudinal processes can be viewed from an age, cohort, or period perspective. While aging processes bear similarities across cohorts, each birth cohort can also be seen as experiencing a unique historical experience as it encounters changing social and economic circumstances at particular ages. With respect to the net impact of life course events and social policies on late-life income outcomes as compared with those earlier in the life course, conceptual models that have been proposed include leveling (Fuchs 1984); status maintenance (Henretta & Campbell 1976); and cumulative advantage and disadvantage (Crystal & Shea 1990).

In the years following World War II, growth in the US economy created new economic opportunities and income growth for the working-age population, but incomes of the elderly lagged behind. In 1959, for example, 35 percent of persons over 65 had incomes below the poverty line; elderly persons were often, of necessity, financially dependent on adult children; and political pressures to address the unmet income and health care needs of older people began to increase. Substantial improvement in elderly poverty rates in the following years, largely as a result of increases in Social Security benefits, represented a social policy success story, particularly in contrast to the lack of sustained improvement in child poverty rates despite the War on Poverty. By the mid-1970s the elderly poverty rate had fallen to 15 percent, lower than the 17 percent rate for children. And by 2002 the elderly poverty rate had further dropped to 10.4 percent, slightly lower than the rate for persons 18–64, while the child poverty rate was again at 17 percent (Federal Interagency Forum 2004).

The elderly also compare favorably to the non-elderly on overall average levels of income and assets. Taking account of household size, the economic value of assets as well as income, and the known underreporting of non-salary income such as pensions, interest, and dividends, Crystal and Shea (1990) estimated that by the mid-1980s, mean income of persons over 65 was higher than at any other age except for ages 55 to 64. Mean income of the elderly has continued to compare favorably to that of non-elderly adults, while mean assets have steadily improved as a result of appreciation in stocks, real estate, and other investments. In 2001, mean asset holdings for elderly-headed households were estimated at $180,000, a 50 percent increase from the 1994 level, based on Panel Survey of Income Dynamics data (Federal Interagency Forum 2004).

However, closer examination of the elderly's income and wealth patterns suggests that important issues of adequacy and equity remain. Income distribution among the US elderly is highly skewed. It has been estimated that the least well-off 40 percent of the elderly in 1997 shared 13 percent of the elderly's income, while the best-off 20 percent shared 52 percent, a higher rate of income concentration than prevails at younger ages (Rubin et al. 2000). These estimates probably underestimate income concentration among the elderly, as they do not adjust for underreporting of pension income and investment interest, which predominate among higher-income elderly, and are less completely reported than Social Security income, which predominates in lower-income quintiles. Disparities by race, marital status, and health status among the elderly are large for income and especially large for wealth (Wolff 2003). For example, in 2001, mean wealth for elderly-headed African American households was only one-fifth that of their white counterparts, and the gap was even greater (more than six to one) for households with an elderly head with less than high school education, as compared with those with a college education (Federal Interagency Forum 2004). Early advantages and disadvantages strongly foreshadow late-life disparities in economic outcomes. For example, years of schooling attained in early life predict post-retirement age income even more strongly than income at earlier ages (Crystal et al. 1992). High out-of-pocket expenditures resulting from gaps in Medicare coverage disproportionately erode the economic resources of lower-income elderly (Crystal et al. 2000). Despite the relatively low proportion below the official poverty line, many elderly are clustered in the near-poor income range; for these elderly, the relatively high mean income of the overall elderly population, driven largely by high incomes among those in the upper quintile, provides little comfort.

In projecting the likely pattern of outcomes for the large baby boom cohort, it is important to distinguish between means and distributional outcomes. Despite much publicity about problematic prospects for the economic future of the baby boomers, comparisons of income trajectories of baby boomers compared to those of pre-boomer cohorts suggest that their average prospects *as a group* are more favorable than those of preceding cohorts (Johnson & Crystal 2003). However, outcomes for disadvantaged subgroups – such as racial-ethnic minorities, those with limited formal education, and those with serious chronic health problems – are more questionable.

It is reasonable to project continued high, if not exacerbated, levels of economic inequality for future cohorts of elderly in the US, continuing existing patterns. Longitudinal studies across multiple cohorts have demonstrated that income inequality in the US increases within cohorts as they age (Crystal & Waehrer 1996). Cross-national studies also show that late-life economic inequality is substantially higher in the US than in nearly all other developed countries, due largely to the smaller proportion of the elderly's overall income that is accounted for by public retirement benefits (Social Security) and the relatively low level of minimum benefits (O'Rand & Henretta 1999; Disney & Whitehouse 2003). Nevertheless, the Social Security program in the US does have a leveling influence that reduces what would otherwise be even higher levels of late-life inequality. The importance of the program in its current form to lower and moderate income elderly is suggested by the estimate that Social Security in 2002 accounted for 83 percent of the income of those elderly in the lower 40 percent of the income distribution, and 67 percent for those in the middle fifth. In contrast, Social Security accounts for less than 20 percent of income for those in the highest income quintile (Federal Interagency Forum 2004).

In the US, proposals put forward by President George W. Bush in 2005 suggested the erosion of what had been a long period of relative consensus on the basic structure of the Social Security system. Critics of these proposals suggested that the redistributional features of the existing system would be difficult to retain if Social Security revenues were diverted, as proposed, into individual, private retirement accounts. Regardless of the short-term outcome of the Social Security debates of the mid-2000s in the US – and of public policy debates taking place worldwide as public pension systems come under financial pressure – financing the economic needs of the elderly is likely to become an increasingly contentious issue in all the developed countries in coming years. Social insurance systems that provide retirement pensions will continue to play a central role in buffering high levels of inequality that are produced by processes of cumulative advantage and disadvantage over the life course. However, the level of national resources devoted to these systems is likely to be a central issue in public policy debates, along with the design choices that determine who pays, who benefits, and how much. Thoughtful and rigorous sociological analyses will be much needed to clarify the potential impact of alternative public policy choices, and to link these considerations to a broader understanding of processes of social stratification and life course dynamics.

SEE ALSO: Age, Period, and Cohort Effects; Aging, Demography of; Aging, Longitudinal Studies; Aging and Social Policy; Aging and Work Performance; Gender, Aging and; Income Inequality and Income Mobility

REFERENCES AND SUGGESTED READINGS

Crystal, S. & Shea, D. (1990) Cumulative Advantage, Cumulative Disadvantage, and Inequality Among Elderly People. *Gerontologist* 30(4): 437–43.

Crystal, S. & Shea, D. (2003) Cumulative Advantage, Public Policy, and Late-Life Inequality. In: Crystal, S. & Shea, D. (Eds.), *Economic Outcomes in Later Life: Public Policy, Health, and Cumulative Advantage* (2002 volume of the Annual Review of Gerontology and Geriatrics). Springer, New York, pp. 1–13.

Crystal, S. & Waehrer, K. (1996) Later-Life Economic Inequality in Longitudinal Perspective. *Journal of Gerontology: Social Sciences* 51B(6): S307–18.

Crystal, S., Shea, D., & Krishnaswami, S. (1992) Educational Attainment, Occupational History, and Stratification: Determinants of Later-Life Economic Resources. *Journal of Gerontology: Social Sciences* 47(5): S213–21.

Crystal, S., Harman, J., Sambamoorthi, U., Johnson, R., & Kumar, R. (2000) Out of Pocket Health Care Costs among Older Americans. *Journal of Gerontology: Social Sciences* 55B(1): S51–62.

Disney, R., & Whitehouse, E. (2003) The Economic Well-Being of Older People in International Perspective: A Critical Review. In: Crystal, S. & Shea, D. (Eds.), *Economic Outcomes in Later Life: Public Policy, Health, and Cumulative Advantage.* Springer, New York, pp. 59–94.

Federal Interagency Forum on Aging-Related Statistics (2004). *Older Americans 2004: Key Indicators of Well-Being.* Government Printing Office, Washington, DC.

Fuchs, V. R. (1984) "Though much is taken": Reflections on Aging, Health, and Medical Care. *Milbank Memorial Fund Quarterly: Health and Society* 62: 143–66.

Henretta, J. & Campbell, R. (1976) Status Attainment and Status Maintenance: A Study of Stratification in Old Age. *American Sociological Review* 41: 981–92.

Johnson, R. W. & Crystal, S. (2003) The Economic Future of the Baby Boom Generation. In: Crystal, S. & Shea, D. (Eds.), *Economic Outcomes in Later Life: Public Policy, Health, and Cumulative Advantage.* Springer, New York, pp. 229–55.

Juster, F. T. & Smith, J. P. (1997) Improving the Quality of Economic Data: Lessons from HRS and AHEAD. *Journal of the American Statistical Association* 92: 1268–78.

Modigliani, F. (1988) The Role of Intergenerational Transfers and Life Cycle Saving in the Accumulation of Wealth. *Journal of Economic Perspectives* 2(2): 15–40.

O'Rand, A. M. & Henretta, J. C. (1999) *Age and Inequality: Diverse Pathways Through Later Life.* Westview Press, Boulder.

Rubin, R. M., White-Means, S. I., & Daniel, L. M. (2000) Income Distribution of Older Americans. *Monthly Labor Review* (November): 19–30.

Wolff, E. N. (2003) Income, Wealth, and Late-Life Inequality in the United States. In: Crystal, S. & Shea, D. (Eds.), *Economic Outcomes in Later Life: Public Policy, Health, and Cumulative Advantage.* Springer, New York, pp. 31–58.

oligarchy and organization

Dieter Rucht

In the classical Greek period, oligarchy (literally, the rule by a few) usually had a negative connotation. In Aristotle's typology of political systems, oligarchy refers to a rule that mainly serves the interests of the rich at the expense of the large majority of the community. By contrast, aristocracy, though also being a rule by a small minority, was understood as a government of "the best" in service of the public good. In common language from the Roman Empire to the Middle Ages to the present, oligarchy denotes a political regime in which the power is concentrated in the hands of a small group, regardless of whether this power is based on wealth (usually referred to as a plutocratic system), weapons, or other sources of influence and control. In line with Aristotle's understanding, many political theorists and sociologists use the term oligarchy in a pejorative sense, denoting a degenerate rule to the disadvantage of the political community at large.

Other theorists consider oligarchy to be inevitable, at least in large and complex societies. Because human beings, by nature and/or due to opportunities, differ in their capacities to accumulate resources, power always will be distributed unevenly. Therefore, oligarchy is not the exception but the rule, regardless of whether the political system is called a democracy, an aristocracy, or something else. In this view, oligarchy is not per se negative for society at large, provided that elites do not exclusively recruit from their own milieus and/or that they can be replaced by other elites on the basis of democratic elections.

In modern social sciences, Robert Michels is widely considered as *the* theorist of oligarchy. Michels's empirical reference point was the German Social Democratic Party (SPD), which had its roots in the socialist labor movement. According to Michels's seminal work *Political Parties* (1911), the SPD, rather than pursuing the initial goals of the socialist labor movement, became preoccupied with maintaining and enlarging its own organization. Leadership became separated from the rank and file, and the apparatus of the party developed an interest in itself.

To Michels, the SPD was merely a paradigmatic case of a more general development that can be observed wherever large groups come into existence. Oligarchy is a universal pattern inherent to any complex society, including democratic states and even libertarian organizations. "By a universally applicable social law, every organ of the collectivity, brought into existence through the need for the division of labor, creates for itself, as soon as it becomes consolidated, interests peculiar to itself" (Michels 2001 [1911]: 233). Consolidation implies organization which, in turn, implies oligarchy according to the famous dictum: "Whoever says organization, says oligarchy." Organization "gives birth to the dominion of the elected over the electors, of the mandataries over the mandators, of the delegates over the delegators" (p. 241). Michels sees the underlying reason for organization, and hence the "historic necessity of oligarchy" (p. 240), in the political indifference of the majority and the necessity of leadership. He registers a tension between the fact of oligarchy and the ideals of democracy (p. 241). Even though oligarchy is declared as inevitable, Michels believes that it can, and indeed should, be limited. He therefore advocates a "social education" that teaches people, in their search for democracy, about the necessity of fighting oligarchy (Michels 1987 [1908]: 172; Michels 2001 [1911]: 244). At the end of his book, Michels compares the democratic tendencies in history at large with a sequence of waves that carry despair but also hope. Democracy, after

some time, degenerates to a structure from which it initially sets itself apart. Yet this very process of degeneration also creates new forces that oppose oligarchy, become part of the ruling class, and thereby initiate a new oligarchic cycle that is doomed to further contestation. While deploring oligarchy on the basis of his socialist and democratic stance in *Political Parties*, Michels gradually changed his views, moving to the political right and joining the fascist party in Italy in 1923.

Michels's "iron law of oligarchy" is widely cited and continues to be debated in the social sciences, particularly since we now live in a "society of organizations," as Perrow (1991) has put it. Taken as an empirical "tendency" rather than a "law" (Michels uses both terms in his writings), most social scientists would agree with his observations. For example, few would deny that economic corporations and state administrations are based on the rule of the many by the few, lead to concentration of power, and hence can be called oligarchic. In these cases, oligarchy, along with hierarchy, may be taken as almost "natural." However, oligarchy is a pertinent problem for all those who strongly value democracy and equality, and who believe that these principles can and should be realized in at least some parts of society, for example in political systems, political parties, public interest groups, or social movements. To these critics, oligarchy is an evil that should be kept to a minimum if not abolished altogether.

In the scholarly world, problems of organization and oligarchy have probably been most intensively discussed in social movement research. According to one tradition which was strongly influenced by the mass psychology that flourished in Europe around the turn of the twentieth century, social movements were seen as unorganized crowds that are affected and driven by emotions. Following this line of thinking (which also influenced Michels), quite a number of scholars have argued that social movements start out as energetic and largely informal enterprises, but lose their social movement character as they become professionalized and institutionalized. Often, such a structural change is seen as necessarily accompanied by a trend toward deradicalization. These ideas have also inspired various life cycle models of social movements that typically end with a stage of institutionalization or even bureaucratization. Movement and institution are thus mutually exclusive, as Alberoni (1984 [1977]) and others have argued.

Another tradition in social movement literature recognizes the reality of and need for organization – though not necessarily oligarchy – in social movements. This way of thinking was particularly salient among European political leaders and analysts who were close to either leftist or rightist ideas. With regard to the labor movement, for example, the main issue was not about the need for organization, but rather the specific form it should take. Following the Leninist concept of the avant-garde, one ideological current within the communist left emphasized the need for strong leadership and firm organization. Another current, represented by German communist Rosa Luxemburg, favored a more decentralized and democratic organization of the left. A small minority of anarchists went even further, distrusting all forms of formal organization because they saw them as sources of unacceptable power.

With the rise of the new left in the 1960s and the subsequent wave of new social movements in many countries of the western world and beyond, much emphasis was given to the principles of participatory democracy and the building of networks rather than firm organizations. These groups were convinced that oligarchy could be mitigated, if not avoided completely, by insisting on decentralization, subsidiarity, rotation of tasks and responsibilities, imperative mandates of delegates, and consensus as a precondition for taking action. Scholars sympathizing with such values also tend to see oligarchy as evitable (Breines 1982). This preference for informal networks is to be found as well in the more recent wave of global justice movements. In practice, however, a diversified movement infrastructure has emerged, ranging from largely informal and decentralized networks of grassroots groups (e.g., Peoples' Global Action) to loose alliances or umbrella groups of fairly democratic associations based on formal individual membership (e.g., Friends of the Earth) to more hierarchically structured transnational organizations (such as Amnesty International, Greenpeace, or Transparency International). While oligarchy is an ongoing concern and

a matter of intense debate for these groups, right-wing movements usually embrace strong, hierarchical organizations. The organizational ideal of right-extremists may even go beyond oligarchic principles insofar as they long for a single leader at the top of the organizational pyramid rather than an oligarchic clique.

Few studies have been undertaken to empirically examine the process of organization building as a path leading to potential or actual oligarchization. One of the exceptions is Lipset et al.'s *Union Democracy* (1956), in which the authors suggest that oligarchy can be avoided even in large organizations, though only under certain conditions and to a limited extent. The debate on oligarchy has become more differentiated in light of empirical, and often inconclusive, findings in social movement studies during the last few decades (Clemens & Minkoff 2005). The so-called resource mobilization approach has emphasized the need of social movements to rely on organization and has promoted the use of terms analogous to economic phenomena, such as "social movement industry" and "social movement entrepreneur." Key representatives of this approach have also pointed to a trend toward professionalization in American social movements (McCarthy & Zald 1973), though they only casually engage in the debate on oligarchy and life cycles of social movements. Comparative research seems to indicate that the degree of formalization and oligarchization varies considerably across movements and across countries, suggesting that the overriding theme and ideology of a movement, along with its political and sociocultural environment, may have an impact on its organizational form. For example, a movement for democratization is more likely to resist oligarchic tendencies within its own ranks than, say, a farmers' movement demanding more state subsidies. The fact that external factors also influence the propensity to institutionalization (and, ultimately, oligarchy) is exemplified by the higher degree of structuration of the women's movement in the US compared to most European countries. Still, the empirical basis in social movement research is too weak to draw strong conclusions. Most studies on social movements cover a time span too short to make a grounded statement on whether or not oligarchy necessarily emerges and which factors might account for this. In addition, the concept of oligarchy, to the extent that it implies goal displacement and bureaucratic conservatism, cannot account for radical organizations that are dominated by a ruling elite (Leach 2005). Furthermore, as Freeman (1982 [1970] has argued, formal structures have the advantage of making power visible, while informal power structure may lead to a "tyranny of structurelessness."

Based on his study of various movement groups and their protest activities in Germany, Rucht (1999) finds that groups tend to become more formalized and centralized over time. However, contrary to what Michels assumed, the results are inconsistent on the question of whether or not movement groups also become more moderate over time. Hence Rucht (1999: 166) concludes that "there is no such thing as an 'iron law' at work" leading to deradicalization.

In the field of organizational studies and the sociology of organizations, explicit references to oligarchy are rare. It appears that basic elements of Michels's concept of oligarchy are too crude (e.g., the separation between leaders and followers), unclear, or largely inapplicable to many organizations (e.g., the tendency to be compromised). Greater emphasis is generally placed instead on concepts *related* to oligarchy, such as formal and informal power, functional differentiation, division of labor, hierarchy, styles of leadership, authority, governance, and control. In surveying the broad development in this field during the past decades, it seems that there is a shift of emphasis from the formal to the informal, from high to low hierarchies, from binding orders to directives, from organizational structure to organizational culture, and from organizations to networks (Castells 1996). To borrow an analogy from the computer world, this development reflects a shift from the "hardware" of organizations to their "software."

Although there is to date little mutual attention or recognition between organizational studies on the one hand and social movement studies on the other hand (for an exception, see Davis et al. 2005), a convergence of interests and paradigms seems to occur. For example, striking similarities can be found on the conceptual level between the work of the French school of organizational studies, represented by Crozier and Friedberg (1980), and the resource mobilization school in social movement studies, as represented by McCarthy and Zald (1977).

Both in the world of economic, political, and administrative actors and among their scholarly observers, the relationship between organization and oligarchy remains a contested issue. While, with very few exceptions, nobody would deny the need for organization of and within complex societies, there remain strikingly different views on *how* social entities can and should be organized. Of course, such views depend on the kind of organization in question, its aims and its contexts. A transnational capitalist corporation, for example, rests on different principles and needs than a charity association devoted to humanitarian aid. In spite of these differences, there is, on a prescriptive level, a major dividing line between those who favor "strong," hierarchical organizations that concentrate power in the hands of a few and those who favor a decentralized and participatory structure in which the organizational subunits and individuals enjoy a high degree of autonomy. These two poles also serve as points of reference and mark tensions within many organizations. While it appears that the actual leeway for decentralization and autonomy is very small in capitalist enterprises and all kinds of state administrations, there is considerable room for maneuver in most civic associations, and even more in social movements, as variation between such groups demonstrates. In some of these, a marked oligarchy not only exists but is also even perceived as a strength. For example, leading representatives of Greenpeace have argued that participatory democratic principles would undermine the organization's ability to deal quickly, professionally, and effectively with mass media.

To other groups, oligarchy (often associated with inequality, hierarchy, bureaucracy, centralization, etc.) is a threat that constantly requires not only attention but also active countermeasures. While very few large civic associations and networks would claim for themselves to be completely free of oligarchy, most civic associations accept concentration of power within certain limits. To the extent that they believe in the value of democracy not just as a formal principle of government but as a way of life, they continue to struggle with and against the trend toward oligarchy in many spheres and at all levels, from the local to the global. Accordingly, these groups are marked by sometimes heated internal debates about reconciling the "logic of membership" with the "logic of influence" (Schmitter & Streeck 1981). Put another way, they seek to find a balance between a group structure offering room for self-realization, respect, and reciprocity on the one hand, and, on the other, a framework guaranteeing a certain degree of unity and allowing for effective decision-making and outward-directed strategic action. The theoretical assumption is that an oligarchic structure enhances the capacity for strategic intervention but at the same time may undermine the members' commitment to the group or organization. Particularly in the absence of charismatic or at least widely accepted leadership, members lose motivation, become frustrated, and may therefore choose to quit the group.

Similar problems also arise at the level of nation-states. While in this case "exit," to use Hirschman's (1970) typology, is not an option for most citizens, oligarchic structures within a nominally democratic framework are problematic for other reasons. Oligarchy is likely to either foster a disenchanted and increasingly passive citizenry or stimulate "voice," i.e., protest movements that challenge the incumbent oligarchic powerholders. Whether this leads to a mere "circulation of elites" (Pareto 1935) and thus to the perpetuation of oligarchic structures or toward a "strong democracy" (Barber 1984) is an open empirical matter.

SEE ALSO: Authority and Legitimacy; Bureaucracy and Public Sector Governmentality; Democracy; Democracy and Organizations; Global Justice as a Social Movement; Globalization and Global Justice; Leadership; Luxemburg, Rosa; Michels Robert; New Left; Political Leadership; Political Parties; Resource Mobilization Theory; Social Movements; Social Movements, Leadership in; Social Movements, Participatory Democracy in

REFERENCES AND SUGGESTED READINGS

Alberoni, F. (1984 [1977]) *Movement and Institution*. Columbia University Press, New York.

Barber, B. R. (1984) *Strong Democracy*. University of California Press, Berkeley.

Breines, W. (1982) *The Great Refusal: Community and Organization in the New Left, 1962–1968*. Praeger, New York.

Castells, M. (1996) *The Rise of the Network Society*. Blackwell, Malden, MA.

Clemens, E. S. & Minkoff, D. C. (2005) Beyond the Iron Law: Rethinking the Place of Organizations in Social Movement Research. In: Snow, D. A., Soule, S. A., & Kriesi, H. (Eds.), *The Blackwell Companion to Social Movements*. Blackwell, Malden, MA, pp. 155–70.

Crozier, M. & Friedberg, E. (1980) *Actors and Systems*. University Press of Chicago, Chicago.

Davis, G. F., McAdam, D., Scott, W. R., & Zald, M. N. (Eds.) (2005) *Social Movements and Organization Theory*. Cambridge University Press, Cambridge.

Freeman, J. (1982 [1970]) *The Tyranny of Structurelessness*. Dark Star, London.

Hirschman, A. O. (1970) *Exit, Voice, and Loyalty*. Harvard University Press, Cambridge, MA.

Leach, D. (2005) The Iron Law of What Again? Conceptualizing Oligarchy Across Organizational Forms. *Sociological Theory* 23(3): 312–37.

Lipset, S. M., Trow, M., & Coleman, J. (1956) *Union Democracy*. Free Press, Glencoe, IL.

McCarthy, J. D. & Zald, M. N. (1973) *The Trend of Social Movements in America: Professionalization and Resource Mobilization*. General Learning Press, Morriston, NJ.

McCarthy, J. D. & Zald, M. N. (1977) Resource Mobilization and Social Movements: A Partial Theory. *American Journal of Sociology* 82(6): 1212–41.

Michels, R. (1987 [1908]) Die oligarchischen Tendenzen der Gesellschaft. In: *Robert Michels, Masse, Führer, Intellektuelle. Politisch-soziologische Aufsätze 1906–1933*. Campus, Frankfurt/M.

Michels, R. (2001 [1911]) *Political Parties: A Sociological Study of the Oligarchical Tendencies of Modern Democracies*. Trans. E. and C. Paul. Batoche Books, Kitchener, Ontario.

Pareto, V. (1935) *The Mind and Society*. Ed. A. Livingston. Trans. A. Bongiomo. Harcourt, Brace, New York.

Perrow, C. (1991) A Society of Organizations. *Theory and Society* 20: 725–62.

Rucht, D. (1999) Linking Organization and Mobilization. *Michels's Iron Law of Oligarchy Reconsidered*. Mobilization 4(2): 151–69.

Schmitter, P. C. & Streeck, W. (1981) The Organization of Business Interests: A Research Design to Study the Associative Action of Business in the Advanced Industrial Societies of Western Europe. Discussion Paper. Wissenschaftszentrum, Berlin.

Streeck, W. (1994) Staat und Verbände: Neue Fragen. Neue Antworten? In: Streeck, W. (Ed.), *Staat und Verbände*. Sonderheft 25 der Politischen Vierteljahresschrift. Opladen, pp. 7–34.

Olympics

Jeffrey O. Segrave

The Olympics comprise both the athletic and cultural dimensions of the modern International Olympic Movement. The brainchild of the widely acknowledged founder of the modern Olympics, Pierre de Coubertin, the modern International Olympic Movement was voted into being on June 23, 1894 at the International Congress in Paris. A total of 79 delegates representing 49 sports associations from 12 countries unanimously voted for the restoration of the Olympic Games and for the creation of a permanent International Olympic Committee (IOC). With unquestionable powers as guide, guardian, and arbiter, the IOC remains the umbrella organization and ultimate authority in the conduct of the games.

The first modern Olympic Games were held in 1896 in Athens, and with the exception of the war years (1916, 1940, 1944) and the interim games of 1906, the games have been held quadrennially ever since. The first winter games were held in 1924 in Chamonix. Beginning in 1994, the winter and summer adopted alternating quadrennial calendars. Both summer and winter games have remained ambulatory throughout their history.

The fine arts competition, the Pentathlon of the Muses, was first held in conjunction with the 1912 Stockholm games, with awards in architecture, dramatic art, choreography, decoration, literature, music, painting, and sculpture. In 1948 the arts competitions were replaced with cultural festivals, gymnastic and dance demonstrations, art exhibits, and theater and music performances. After the 1968 Mexico City games, the IOC amended the rules and regulations and the cultural Olympiad was subsequently limited to national rather than international exhibitions and performances.

As the chief architect of the modern Olympic Movement, Coubertin revived the ancient games as an expression of his profound belief in the enduring educational values inherent in competitive sport, what he called *la pédagogie sportive*. Committed to the ideal of sport as a social and moral endeavor, Coubertin conceived of the Olympic Movement as a broad-based humanitarian project, and he enlisted the services of the games in the pursuit of international harmony, peace, and goodwill. To this day, the ideology of the Olympics, Olympism, broadly construed, connotes education, international understanding, equal opportunity, fair and equal competition, cultural expression, the independence of sport, and excellence.

The modern games have evolved from a *fin-de-siècle* curiosity of the late nineteenth century into an early twenty-first-century spectacle of truly global magnitude. In 1896, 245 male athletes from 14 countries competed in 43 events. More than 10,500 male and female athletes from 102 countries competed in 300 events in the 2004 Athens games. While the first IOC comprised 15 male members from three continents, the current IOC is comprised of 122 members, including 12 women, representing five continents. Over 20 commissions study relevant issues and make recommendations to the Executive Committee of the IOC. Once a fledgling athletic event, the Olympic Games of today attract the attention of a massive worldwide audience and are organized and administered on the basis of multibillion-dollar budgets. The 2004 Athens games cost an estimated $10–$12 billion and the organizing committee spent an additional $1.2 billion on security measures.

One of the most spectacular and successful expressions of modern international sport, the Olympics are in fact a derivative of an ancient Greek project that located competitive athletics at the heart of Hellenic culture. First held in 776 BCE at Olympia, the games remained a significant feature of the ancient Greek calendar until their abolition in 393 CE by the Holy Roman Emperor, Theodosius I. One of a series of Pan-Hellenic games, the games at Olympia were the oldest, most prestigious, and most famous of all the sporting festivals of antiquity. Although the precise origins of the games remain shrouded in prehistory, the Olympics began as religious ceremonies and developed into cultural celebrations whose influence was felt throughout the ancient Greek world. A classic expression of the Greek love of athletics, the games also promoted unity and solidarity among the various city-states. Held every four years in conjunction with the worship of Olympian Zeus, the Olympic Games glorified the quest for excellence and perfection that became the hallmark of ancient Greek culture. Increasingly trained by professionals, sponsored by city-states, and awarded lavish prizes and privileges at home, Olympic athletes attained heroic status and were immortalized in history and verse. Despite the cultural preeminence of the games, the truly refined notion of Hellenic athleticism gradually declined. Buffeted and compromised by civil war, military conquest, and Christian asceticism, the last of the ancient Olympic Games was held in 392 CE. Although various forms of Olympics were held sporadically throughout medieval, Enlightenment, and modern times and reference to the ancient games survived in the professional records of historians, travelers, archaeologists, cartographers, and palaeographists, and in the works of educational theorists, philosophers, and artists, only Coubertin's modern creation has attained significant institutionalized permanence.

Notwithstanding early works on the history of the ancient and modern Olympics, accounts by those most closely connected with the modern Olympics, including Coubertin's own memoirs, as well as journalistic reports and official records, it was not until the 1970s that the Olympics began to attract serious and sustained scholarly interest. Once disorganized, nationally segregated, and often marginalized with their own disciplines, social scientists, including sociologists, social psychologists, political scientists, social historians, anthropologists, and critical theorists have increasingly established a credible, legitimate, and coherent body of Olympic scholarship.

Sociologies of the Olympics have been derived from descriptive analyses, studies of the Olympics as a formal organization, analyses of the relationship between the Olympics and various regulative and expressive cultural institutions, most especially the national state, and studies of the Olympics as a cultural system. More recent studies have analyzed the games within the context of postcolonialism, feminist theory, and postmodernism. Postmodernist analyses of the games, for example, locate the Olympics at the heart of the media culture and within the context of the cultural logic of late capitalism. As a result the games are characterized as a powerful amalgam of corporate and classical mythology whose semiotic and spectatorial power is diverse, fungible, and endlessly productive on a global and local basis. One of the most prominent sociological genres in the recent study of the Olympics derives from the definition of the games as "mega-events," large-scale cultural events that have dramatic character, mass popular appeal, and global significance. Studies analyze the ways in which the Olympics as mega-events contribute to the meaning and development of public culture, cultural citizenship, and cultural inclusion/exclusion in modern societies. Mega-event sociology adopts a multiperspectival approach and calls for a combination of dramatological (ethnography, textualism, cultural functionalism) and contextual (economic functionalism, political instrumentalism, critical functionalism) approaches.

Social psychological analyses of the Olympics have been derived from two main perspectives: first, those that have sought to investigate how the human mind and body respond to the demands of high-level Olympic sport; and, second, those that have sought to plumb the depths of human athletic potential and to determine how to adapt the athlete's body and mind to the ever-increasing demands of Olympic sport. The latter technocratic perspective has invariably been adopted by those seeking to produce record-breaking performances and has been contextualized within the framework of a nationalized and technologized performance-enhancing drug culture.

Notwithstanding claims of a categorical distinction between politics and sport, early Olympic political science employed largely descriptive methods grounded in rational choice theory, formal modeling, and quantitative methods as the preferred approach to understanding the role and scope of the Olympic Games within the panoply of national and international politics, especially with regard to co-optation of the Olympic Games in the service, and as a reflection, of particularized nation-state objectives. This hegemonic approach has more recently been challenged by Olympic political scientists, who have argued that reliance on deductive theory and quantitative methods has caused neglect to the historical and contextual processes that shape particular political institutions, practices, cultures, ideologies, and identities. As a result, qualitative methods of inquiry, including interpretive textual analyses, ethnographic fieldwork, media analysis, in-depth interviews, and case studies, have augmented traditional methodologies as ways of identifying the institutional, historical, and cultural factors that constitute the Olympic Movement both as a political phenomenon in itself and as a dimension of international diplomacy, nation building, and cosmopolitanism.

While traditional Olympic histories and biographies abound, recent Olympic history has sought to place the games within the panoply of social history and has typically adopted a postmodern historiography that is both self-reflective and cognizant of the philosophical and ideological ingredients in geographical and historical representation. As a result, social histories recognize the Olympics as a response to the human need for identity and agency, as negotiated and invented tradition, and as a significant component of "the life world" (interpersonal structures of meaning and experience relating to self, others, embodiment, time, and space) (Roche 2000).

Olympic anthropology emerged in the context of semiotic and structural anthropologies, of cultural performance theories born from a renewed interest in myth, symbol, and ritual, and of culturalist approaches to national and international phenomena. Carried out in a post-Cold War world of increasingly significant transnational identities, the most recent Olympic anthropology reflects and employs postmodern concerns with familiar issues such as the production of national identity on international occasions, traditional compared to modern forms of each, and the recruitment and fate of individual actors in such mass-mediated public dramas as the Olympics (MacAloon 1999).

Olympic critical theories include a Marxist critique of the games as a repressive social practice that mirrors the dominant values of capitalism and bourgeois imperialism, Gramscian accounts in which the games are viewed as a significant site at which the dominant ideology is constructed and dominant interests served, and feminist and postcolonial critiques which

have respectively depicted the games as models of masculinism and westernization (Americanization, creolization). Most recent critical accounts view the games as globalized events in which social activist, minority, and specialized local interests are summarily dismissed in the face of a nationalistic entertainment juggernaut that serves the interests of the corporate, political Olympic establishment and in which the values of democracy and social justice are threatened (Lenskyj 2002).

As the focus of a broad range of sociohistorical explorations and theorizations, future sociologies of the Olympics will need to consider a wide variety of interlocking issues including the recognition that politics, ideology, and culture are intertwined discursive formulations, the understanding that the international and the domestic are simultaneously mutually constituting phenomena, the personal and interpersonal meanings attributable to mega-events such as the Olympics, the main elements of the Olympics that contribute to the production of a world society (including global governance, global citizenship, economic and cultural globalization, global structuration, mesosocial processes), and the notion of the Olympic Games as "makers of history."

SEE ALSO: Globalization, Sport and; Nationalism and Sport; Sport and Culture; Sport and the State

REFERENCES AND SUGGESTED READINGS

Dyreson, M. (1998) *Making the American Team: Sport, Culture, and the Olympic Experience.* University of Illinois Press, Urbana.

Gerlach, L. R. (Ed.) (2004) *The Winter Olympics: From Chamonix to Salt Lake City.* University of Utah Press, Salt Lake City.

Hoberman, J. (1992) *Mortal Engines: The Science of Performance and the Dehumanization of Sport.* Macmillan, New York.

Klausen, A. M. (Ed.) (1999) *Olympic Games as Performative and Public Event: The Case of the XVII Winter Olympic Games in Norway.* Berghahn Books, New York.

Lenskyj, H. (2002) *The Best Olympics Ever: Social Impacts of Sydney 2000.* State University of New York Press, Albany.

MacAloon, J. J. (1981) *This Great Symbol: Pierre de Coubertin and the Origins of the Modern Olympic Games*. University of Chicago Press, Chicago.

MacAloon, J. J. (1999) Anthropology at the Olympic Games: An Overview. In: Klausen, A. M. (Ed.), *Olympic Games as Performative and Public Event: The Case of the XVII Winter Olympic Games in Norway*. Berghahn Books, New York, pp. 9–26.

Perrottet, T. (2004) *The Naked Olympics: The True Story of the Ancient Games*. Random House, New York.

Roche, M. (2000) *Mega-Events and Modernity: Olympics and Expos in the Growth of Global Culture*. Routledge, New York.

Schaffer, K. & Smith, S. (Eds.) (2000) *The Olympics at the Millennium: Power, Politics, and the Games*. Rutgers University Press, New Brunswick, NJ.

Tomlinson, A. & Whannel, G. (Eds.) (1984) *Five Ring Circus: Money, Power, and Politics at the Olympic Games*. Pluto Press, London.

one drop rule

Anthony Lemelle

The one drop rule was a social construction that emerged discursively in US history. The language was first used by the government in the Fourteenth Census in 1920 when the color line was redefined by the Census Bureau. Instead of using the category "mulattoes," the Bureau adopted the one drop rule. According to it, "the term 'white' as used in the census report refers to persons understood to be pure-blooded whites. A person of mixed blood is classified according to the nonwhite racial strain." Thus, "a person of mixed white ... and Negro ... is classified as ... a Negro ... regardless of the amount of white blood" (Bureau of the Census 1923). By 1924 the term one drop rule was also being used in state legislation. For example, in 1924, a Virginia Act for "Preservation of Racial Integrity" defined a white person as someone with "no trace whatsoever of any blood other than Caucasian" (Hickman 1967). And the Virginia legislature in 1930 defined as colored anyone "in whom there is ascertainable any negro blood" (Hickman 1967).

The one drop rule became pervasive and courts ruled on it as a principle of law, particularly in the confiscation of property, or in such codified exclusions as denying legal redress to persons of color. The history of the one drop rule is marked by two major interventions by the powerful in jurisprudential thinking: (1) it was necessary to transform the way blacks were socially identified from skin color to blood content; (2) it was necessary to change the rule of descent from father to child to from mother to child. Accomplishing these two adjustments in the social order allowed white males to benefit from the eventual enactment of the one drop rule. White males benefited most from the mulatto practice leading to the enactment of the rule because it protected them from any responsibility for supporting their children by black women slaves. In fact, the children became property and the slaveholders could count them as capital value.

Therefore, the birth of mulattoes provided an economic advantage to both the father, because he did not have to care for his black children, and the mother's slaveholder, because he acquired another slave with a birth to a mulatto. And of course, this whole system encouraged the psychological and physical degradation of the mulatta, not to mention the degradation that was afforded her children for their "condition." Initially the practice and jurisprudence of determining blackness was a matter of observation and not blood content. The goal of creating the mulatto category and the rise of miscegenation law was, as noted black historian Carter G. Woodson remarked, "to debase to a still lower status the offspring of blacks" and to finally leave women of color without protection against white males (Woodson 1925: xv).

In her distinguished study of blacks and the law, Helen Catterall observes that by 1667 in Virginia, "baptism ceased to be the test of freedom and color became the 'sign' of slavery: black or graduated shades thereof. A negro was presumed to be a slave" (Catterall 1968: 57). By the founding of the US, the father of American psychiatry, Dr. Benjamin Rush, had discovered a "cure" for blackness. His therapy was totally concerned with changing the "awful" skin color of blacks through methods like bloodletting and purging through enemas. To Rush, the problem of skin color was in part a problem of blood. He argued that non-white skin color was one form of leprosy and the bacterium had obviously contaminated the blood: "Depletion, whether by bleeding, purging, or abstinence, has been often observed to lessen the black color of negroes" (Rush 1799: 295).

The end of the eighteenth century brought a new discourse that focused on blood and genealogy to explain blackness and this influenced the rise of the eventual one drop rule. For example, in 1785, Virginia legally defined a Negro as an individual with a black parent or grandparent (Davis 1991). Prior to 1785, a mulatto could own up to one-half "African blood." With the 1785 law's enactment, anyone having one-quarter or more of African blood would be considered a Negro and presumed to be a slave.

A statute passed by the Virginia legislature in 1662, 43 years after the first Africans arrived, shows the early importance of drawing broad boundaries around the Negro race. Undoubtedly in recognition of the fact that most interracial fornication occurred between white men and black women, the law provided: "children got by an Englishman upon a negro woman ... shall be held bond or free only according to the condition of the mother" (Finkelman 1986: 16). This was a major change in traditional English common law, which held that children follow patriarchal descent (Higginbotham 1978: 44, 194).

This precedence in law had widespread influence in the demarcation of blackness. It provided that children born of a black mother and white father would follow the common law applicable to farm animals (Higginbotham 1978). The law was very explicit about this in its tradition; animals belonged to the owner of the mother of the offspring. In fact, the imagery may have deeper expression in language since the root of the word mulatto derives from the Spanish *mulatto*, the diminutive of *mulo*, which means a mule. Here then, through law, we find a key element in the construction of the tradition of the so-called black matriarchy.

The function of the one drop rule was the subjugation of those who came to be defined as black. It increased the number of individuals who would be placed in that category. It developed over a long history of customs, folkways, mores, norms, and juridical developments. Its discursive development was linked to debates about skin color and rights associated with inheritance. But use of the concept of race functioned to subjugate those who fell under its

categorization. This led W. E. B. Du Bois (1986 [1897]) to opine that race "is a vast family of human beings, generally of common blood and language, always of common history, traditions and impulses, who are both voluntarily and involuntarily striving together for the accomplishment of certain more or less vividly conceived ideals of life." However, as English professor Teresa Zackodnik points out, "For Du Bois, blood becomes a metaphor for political commitment, not the carrier of inherent racial traits; racial groups are not natural formations along heritable blood lines but a group of individuals sharing certain loyalties and a degree of common experience while pursuing shared economic, political, and philosophical goals" (2004: 28).

SEE ALSO: Biracialism; Color Line; Double Consciousness; Interracial Unions; Race and the Criminal Justice System; Race (Racism); Racialized Gender; Slavery; Whiteness

REFERENCES AND SUGGESTED READINGS

Bureau of the Census (1923) *Fourteenth Census of the United States: 1920.* US Department of Commerce, Washington, DC.

Catterall, H. T. (Ed.) (1968) *Judicial Cases Concerning American Slavery and the Negro.* Vol. 1. Irish University Press, Shannon.

Davis, F. J. (1991) *Who is Black? One Nation's Definition.* Pennsylvania State University Press, University Park.

Du Bois, W. E. B. (1986 [1897]) The Conservation of Races. In: Huggins, N. (Ed.), *W. E. B. Du Bois: Writings.* Library of America, New York, pp. 815–26.

Finkelman, P. (1986) *The Law of Freedom and Bondage: A Casebook.* Oceana Publications, New York.

Hickman, C. B. (1967) The Devil and the One Drop Rule: Racial Categories, African Americans, and the US Census. *Michigan Law Review* 95(5): 1166–266.

Higginbotham, A. L. (1978) *In the Matter of Color, Race, and the American Legal Process: The Colonial Period.* Oxford University Press, New York.

Rush, B. (1799) Observations Intended to Favour a Supposition that the Black Color (as it is called) of the Negroes is Derived from the Leprosy. *Transactions of the American Philosophical Society* 4: 289–97.

Woodson, C. G. (1925) *Free Negro Heads of Families in the United States in 1830*. Association for the Study of Negro Life and History, Washington, DC.

Zackodnik, T. C. (2004) *The Mulatta and the Politics of Race*. University Press of Mississippi, Jackson.

operations management

John Edwards

Operations management is a discipline that is seen by some as caught between the pragmatic and the theoretical. In common with its cognate disciplines such as operational/operations research and information systems – and indeed systems thinking more generally – there is often an uneasy tension between the need to be able to carry out research that leads to generalizable findings and the desire for actions that make an impact in specific cases.

With a field that is practice-based, and thus constantly evolving, such as operations management (OM), too precise an attempt at definition can be unhelpful. The definition used here will thus be the one implied from the Academy of Management's Operations Management Division: "the management of the transformation processes that create products or services" (aom2.pace.edu/om/, accessed January 24, 2005). Since every organization offers some kind of product and/or service, it may be seen that the scope of OM is, quite literally, the management of these transformation processes in all organizations. An authoritative and readily accessible source of definitions for the field of operations management is Hill's *Encyclopedia of OM Terms* (www.poms.org/POMSWebsite/EducationResources/omencyclopedia.pdf, accessed January 24, 2005).

It is difficult, if not impossible, to establish a precise starting point for the field of operations management. OM problems have been investigated for centuries, if not millennia. Some trace the discipline of OM back to F. W. Taylor's "scientific management" in the early twentieth century, or indeed the development of interchangeable parts by Eli Whitney at the beginning of the nineteenth century. As a discipline, however, OM emerged somewhere between the 1940s, when it was certainly being widely pursued, and the 1960s, when the term operations management began to come into widespread use.

The definition above is a very modern one: modern in the sense of "up to date" rather than that of modernist thinking. Two aspects of the definition are significantly different from what might have been seen in a 1970s definition: the inclusion of services and the emphasis upon processes.

The phrase "products or services" in the definition signals probably the most significant change in the field of OM over its history. As indicated above, management of operations as a field of interest was originally identified and then studied in the context of manufacturing industry. As a consequence, OM originally concentrated on manufacturing management, and was generally described either by the latter label or more frequently by the term production management. As the global economy, especially in the industrialized western countries, has come to place an increasing emphasis on service industries, so the importance of studying the management of their operations has correspondingly increased. There has therefore been a fundamental shift in the scope of the field, from a concentration on manufacturing only, to encompass service industries in addition, and indeed to embrace other sectors such as the delivery of health care, which might not always be seen to fall within the "service industry" definition.

This shift has also led to concomitant changes, not always universally agreed, in the terminology of the field. As an illustration, the British Production and Inventory Control Society (BPICS) was founded in the 1960s as the result of the establishment of chapters of the American Production and Inventory Control Society (APICS) in Britain. In 1996, BPICS members voted to change the name of the society to the Institute of Operations Management.

The "manufacturing or service" issue continues to affect the field, particularly in debates as to whether the field should be called production and operations management, or operations and production management, or whether or not operations management includes production management. The assumption here is that operations management includes production management.

The second major shift encapsulated in the earlier definition stems from the use of the phrase "transformation processes." OM in the 1960s tended to adopt a functionalist view of the organization. This would be consistent with the pragmatic focus, as most manufacturing companies at that time were structured on the basis of functional hierarchies. Later developments such as total quality management (TQM) and business process reengineering (BPR) fostered a process view of organizations. The principal difference is that the process view looks first at what organizations do rather than how they are structured. This process view has now become part of mainstream thought, not only in OM but also in management more widely, with the processes variously described as business processes, transformation processes, or realization processes, the latter being the term used in the 2001 version of the ISO9000 standard for quality management systems.

CONCEPTUAL FRAMEWORKS

The pragmatic nature of the OM field gives free rein in terms of both frameworks and methodologies. To quote from the website of the Production and Operations Management Society (POMS), "the Society's approach to Production and Operations Management is problem-centered; it does not rely on particular methodologies" (www.poms.org/POMSWebsite/About.html#History, accessed January 24, 2005). Note that the term "methodologies" as used in the POMS definition appears also to cover theoretical frameworks. As will be seen in this section, there is an interesting tendency for many of the frameworks to have a geographical association. Pilkington and Liston-Heyes (1999) considered whether indeed OM was a discipline at all. They concluded that it was, but that there were significant differences between thinking in different parts of the world.

Given its origins in manufacturing, it is not surprising that one major strand of thinking in OM has always followed a strongly positivist tendency derived from its roots in industrial engineering and engineering management.

Here the paradigm is that of "hard" operations research, management science or systems engineering – a single, agreed objective (at worst, multiple agreed objectives), a well-defined system, and non-controversial implementation. The challenge in any study is therefore to understand the difficulties and then design an appropriate "solution."

The pragmatic nature of the field also means that academic OM has found very fertile ground in surveys of practice, generally also from a positivist, hypothesis-testing standpoint. Most of the professional societies in OM embrace both academic and practitioner membership, providing academics with useful networks for identifying survey populations and samples.

Independently of the broadening of the scope to embrace service industries, the realization was developing that these approaches were not appropriate for all OM problems. Three of these will be mentioned here: all began during the 1960s, interestingly in different geographical locations – the UK, Scandinavia, and Japan, respectively.

Although it is not now generally associated with an OM label, the OM problems of the petrochemical company ICI were the main stimulus leading to the development by Peter Checkland of his soft systems methodology (Checkland 1999) from the late 1960s onwards. Beginning at about the same time, there came to be a wider appreciation of humanistic, people-centered approaches to OM, stemming originally from Scandinavian countries. Here the concerns were again driven by manufacturing, but mainly from the issues of implementation. Swedish companies such as Volvo and Saab were seen as pioneering these approaches – for example in the use of assembly teams rather than a production line specialization approach.

Meanwhile, there was another parallel development, mainly applied in Japan, with an emphasis on participation in the problem identification and solution design activities. This had begun earlier, but came into prominence more gradually. This school of thought was combined with American influences in quality control approaches (Juran 1964) to lead to the development of TQM, as mentioned above, and also led to other areas of progress such as Toyota's production system (Swamidass 1991).

CURRENT EMPHASES

All of the frameworks mentioned above are still alive and well in current OM. Hard, positivist, single-objective approaches, softer, phenomenological approaches, and humanistic, participative approaches may all be found. Volvo even continues to feature in teamworking articles after some 40 years (Van Hootegem et al. 2004)!

Both quantitative and qualitative approaches are common in current OM, often even within the same project or case study. Naturally, the positivist approaches lend themselves to quantitative measurements. However, any published work focusing on practical considerations is likely to give explicit consideration to human aspects of implementation. An analysis of a case in terms of "people, processes, and technology" is a structure commonly found.

Nevertheless, this consideration of "softer" aspects does not usually go as far as acknowledging the problem as complex in the way that Checkland sees it, let alone further criticisms of "soft" approaches relating to issues such as power and coercion. Systems approaches in OM, as elsewhere, received a boost from the popularity of the book by Senge (1990) and its advocacy of system dynamics, but many who draw on Senge's work seem to take a much more positivist approach than those using other systems theories.

It remains the case that "outsider" views of OM often perceive only the quantitative side, for example: "in general, operations management uses a quantitative or mathematical approach" (Williams et al. 2004: 26).

The pragmatic nature of OM means that there can be very strong emphases on certain areas for a period, which then fade away, either partially or completely. The latter topics can be fairly categorized as "fads." Other topics, by contrast, have maintained their importance since OM began, and are likely to continue to do so in the future. Only one example of an article relevant to each area is given here.

At the time of writing, the main "new" areas that are at their peak are e-business (Olson & Boyer 2005) and supply chain management, together with knowledge management, although the latter is generally seen as not specifically an OM concern, and therefore somewhat peripheral to the main literature. Areas possibly just past their peak but still finding their longer-term levels include lean manufacturing, agile manufacturing (Guisinger & Ghorashi 2004) and "just in time" (JIT) approaches. More permanent areas include operations strategy (Aranda 2003), systems design (Johansson & Johansson 2004), quality (Sanchez-Rodriguez & Martinez-Lorente 2004), logistics (van Hoek 2002), teamworking (Van Hootegem et al. 2004), performance measurement (Melnyk et al. 2004), and project management (Zwikael & Globerson 2004). Naturally these permanent areas have evolved over time and have been influenced by management thought in other areas, for example in the way that performance measurement in OM has been influenced by "balanced scorecard" approaches.

A further topic which is at present of concern in several different areas within OM is trust. This can take several forms, including: trust between organizations in a supply chain or an alliance; customer trust in online businesses; and trust between team members (Adler 2003).

METHODOLOGICAL ISSUES AND PROBLEMS

The appropriate relationship between theory and practice for such a practice-driven field continues to be a subject for debate within OM. See, for example, the paper by Slack et al. (2004), Slack being the lead author of one of the foremost UK textbooks on OM. Epistemology, however, is rarely explicitly discussed in the OM literature. A literature search carried out on Web of Science in late 2004, for the phrases "operations management" and "epistemology," yielded no hits at all.

The most preferred approaches for articles currently appearing in journals tend to be either detailed single case studies or large-scale surveys. The former show an increasing proportion of interpretive approaches, while the latter continue to be mainly positivist. A significant difficulty is emerging for the latter in the form of "survey overload." A recent call for papers for a special issue of the *Journal of Operations Management* observed: "Unfortunately, there is considerable anecdotal evidence that practitioner willingness to participate in survey research is declining." Although this problem is by no means unique to OM studies, there may be some data sources highly relevant to OM that can be used as alternatives, or for triangulation, for example the increasing number of performance indicators that must be reported publicly, or web-based customer rating and self-reporting sites.

Partly because of the increase in interpretive approaches, the status of action research is still seen as a current issue in OM (Coughlan & Coghlan 2002), even though Checkland identified the inadequacy of hard systems action research approaches as one of the drivers behind the development of his soft systems methodology. The two main positions are those from the positivist viewpoint who would not see action research as presenting a sufficiently generalizable result, and those who acknowledge that action research has a different epistemology. Coughlan and Coghlan (2002) advocate action research for "its ability to address the operational realities experienced by practising managers while simultaneously contributing to knowledge," but there is perhaps a third position apparent in the literature. This accepts the difference in epistemology and the theoretical benefits, but questions whether many real projects labeled as "action research" actually do contribute to knowledge, as opposed to carrying out what is effectively consultancy for the organization concerned.

FUTURE DIRECTIONS

The two major current areas identified above (e-business and supply chain management) point the way to future developments, especially when combined with the continuing theme of teamworking, in a world where those teams are increasingly likely to be virtual. More pervasive and more rapid communications change not only working practices, but also the way in which organizations are structured, and perhaps even conceived. The image of the fixed organization with clearly identifiable boundaries may have to give way to one of a fluid coalition formed for a specific purpose and dissolved when that purpose has been achieved. The transformation processes of such an organization are likely to draw in the organization's

customers and suppliers much more closely. If recent developments such as the explosion in use of the Internet and World Wide Web may be characterized as "e-everything," then the next trend that is already visible can be called "m-everything," with the m standing for "mobile." The cell phone has already revolutionized communication for business people, teenagers, and soccer hooligans alike. Developments such as radio frequency identification (RFID) tags, at present being pioneered by organizations such as Wal-Mart in the US, seem likely to continue these trends further. The likelihood is that there will be increasing convergence between the disciplines (if such they are) of operations management and information systems, as these systems become more and more central to carrying out transformation processes – operations – in all kinds of organizations. Yet as the technology leads to convergence and integration, so the increasing fluidity and virtuality of operations will surely lead to more difficulty in identifying stakeholders and objectives. The tension between "hard" and "soft" approaches is thus likely to continue.

SEE ALSO: Action Research; Fordism/Post-Fordism; Knowledge Management; Supply Chains; Taylorism

REFERENCES AND SUGGESTED READINGS

Adler, T. R. (2003) Member Trust in Teams: A Synthesized Analysis of Contract Negotiation in Outsourcing IT Work. *Journal of Computer Information Systems* 44(2): 6–16.

Aranda, D. A. (2003) Service Operations Strategy, Flexibility, and Performance in Engineering Consulting Firms. *International Journal of Operations and Production Management* 23(11/12): 1401–21.

Checkland, P. (1999) *Systems Thinking, Systems Practice*. Wiley, Chichester.

Coughlan, P. & Coghlan, D. (2002) Action Research for Operations Management. *International Journal of Operations and Production Management* 22(2): 220–40.

Guisinger, A. & Ghorashi, B. (2004) Agile Manufacturing Practices in the Specialty Chemical Industry: An Overview of the Trends and Results of a Specific Case Study. *International Journal of Operations and Production Management* 24(5/6): 625–35.

Johansson, E. & Johansson, M. I. (2004) The Information Gap Between Design Engineering and Materials Supply Systems Design. *International Journal of Production Research* 42(17): 3787–801.

Juran, J. (1964) *Breakthrough Management*. Macmillan, London.

Melnyk, S. A., Stewart, D. M., & Swink, M. (2004) Metrics and Performance Measurement in Operations Management: Dealing With the Metrics Maze. *Journal of Operations Management* 22(3): 209–17.

Olson, J. R. & Boyer, K. K. (2005) Internet Ticketing in a Not-For-Profit, Service Organization: Building Customer Loyalty. *International Journal of Operations and Production Management* 25(1): 74–92.

Pilkington, A. & Liston-Heyes, C. (1999) Is Production and Operations Management a Discipline? A Citation/Co-Citation Study. *International Journal of Operations and Production Management* 19(1): 7–20.

Sanchez-Rodriguez, C. & Martinez-Lorente, A. R. (2004) Quality Management Practices in the Purchasing Function: An Empirical Study. *International Journal of Operations and Production Management* 24(7): 666–87.

Senge, P. M. (1990) *The Fifth Discipline, The Art and Practice of the Learning Organization*. Doubleday, New York.

Slack, N., Lewis, M., & Bates, H. (2004) The Two Worlds of Operations Management Research and Practice: Can They Meet, Should They Meet? *International Journal of Operations and Production Management* 24(3/4): 372–87.

Swamidass, P. M. (1991) Empirical Science: New Frontier in Operations Management Research. *Academy of Management Review* 16(4): 793–814.

Van Hoek, R. I. (2002) Using Information Technology to Leverage Transport and Logistics Service Operations in the Supply Chain: An Empirical Assessment of the Interrelation Between Technology and Operations Management. *International Journal of Technology Management* 23(1/3): 207–22.

Van Hootegem, G., Huys, R., & Delarue, A. (2004) The Sustainability of Teamwork Under Changing Circumstances. *International Journal of Operations and Production Management* 24(8): 773–86.

Williams, C., Kondra, A. Z., & Vibert, C. (2004) *Management*. Thomson Nelson, Scarborough, ON, Canada.

Zwikael, O. & Globerson, S. (2004) Evaluating the Quality of Project Planning: A Model and Field Results. *International Journal of Production Research* 42(8): 1545–56.

opportunities for learning

Adam Gamoran

Central to the sociology of education are questions about how schools operate to produce learning. Sociological models of schooling recognize that school systems are complex organizations, with a technical core consisting of classrooms in which teaching and learning – the core technology of schooling – take place. The concept of opportunities for learning provides a key to answering questions about how schools and classrooms can produce higher rates of learning (educational productivity), and about why some students learn more than others (educational inequality).

The notion is a simple one: students are more likely to learn what they have been taught, and stand less chance of learning what they have not been taught. More generally, the concept of opportunities for learning refers to the content and quantity of curricular materials, activities, and assignments that students encounter in their classrooms; that is, the *manifest curriculum*, as opposed to the *hidden curriculum*. Analysts frequently refer to three dimensions of the manifest curriculum: the *intended curriculum*, which the state or district may set forth, the *enacted curriculum*, which teachers cover in classrooms, and the *achieved curriculum*, what students actually learn (e.g., Smithson & Porter 2004). Opportunities for learning are reflected in the enacted curriculum.

BACKGROUND TO RESEARCH ON OPPORTUNITIES FOR LEARNING

An early use of the concept appeared in Carroll's (1963) "model for school learning." For Carroll, "opportunity to learn" referred to the time available for learning which, when combined with the quality of instruction and student effort and ability, would have a major influence on student performance. Recent writers use the term more broadly to refer not only to time, but also to instructional content and pedagogy. While a few studies followed up directly on Carroll's model, two subsequent literatures served as major stimuli to research on opportunities for learning: studies of tracking and ability grouping, and international comparative research on educational achievement.

Opportunities for Learning in Research on Tracking

In response to the Coleman Report's findings that student achievement varied far more within schools than among schools (Coleman et al. 1966), sociologists began to explore aspects of schools that contributed to within-school achievement inequality. Chief among these was the practice of dividing students for instruction according to their purported interests and abilities into separate groups or tracks. Students assigned to higher-status positions learned more, and students in lower-status positions learned less over time, even after taking account of differences among students before they were assigned to their tracks. Why did this occur? Researchers have pointed to differentiated opportunities for learning as a major explanation for growing inequality of achievement among students placed in different groups and tracks (Barr & Dreeben 1983; Rowan & Miracle 1983; Gamoran et al.1995, 1997; Applebee et al. 2003). Teachers in high-track groups and classes tend to cover richer material at a faster pace, while teachers in low-track classes commonly introduce a more fragmented, slower-paced curriculum. In the US and internationally, learning opportunities are embedded in curricular divisions and course sequences (Oakes et al. 1992).

Partly due to their association with tracking, opportunities for learning tend to be differentially available to students from different racial, ethnic, and economic groups (Oakes et al. 1992). When students are divided for instruction on the basis of prior achievement, they are also separated by social background, which tends to be correlated with achievement. Consequently, when opportunities for learning differ across tracks, they differ for students from varied backgrounds. Learning opportunities may also vary from one school to the next, for example when schools with small numbers of high-achieving students fail to offer advanced courses such as

middle school algebra or high school physics, calculus, or AP English. This practice also works to the disadvantage of students from minority and low-income backgrounds, who are overrepresented in such schools. Schools with predominantly working-class populations may also offer less challenging elementary curricula than schools with middle-class populations. These school-level patterns may be mitigated by a countervailing tendency: even schools with many low-achieving students tend to have *some* high-level classes, and students from disadvantaged backgrounds have relatively *greater* access to these classes in such schools, apparently due to the lower levels of competition for enrollment. Overall, however, unequal access to valued opportunities for learning is an important dimension of educational inequality for students from varied racial, ethnic, and socioeconomic groups.

Learning opportunities have also played a prominent role in gender inequality, specifically in the gaps between boys and girls in mathematics and science achievement. US-based research in the 1980s showed that test score differences among secondary school boys and girls were substantially attributable to differences in mathematics and science course taking (Pallas & Alexander 1983). More recently, gender gaps in both achievement and course taking are smaller, with girls enrolled at equal or higher rates in most advanced courses, and boys' advantage now limited to physics and calculus (US Department of Education 1999). Similar patterns are emerging in other nations (e.g., Croxford 1994).

International Comparisons of Educational Achievement

Another major motivation for research on opportunities for learning has come from research on international comparisons of educational achievement, primarily in the areas of mathematics and science (Floden 2003). Dating at least back to the First International Mathematics Study (Husen 1967), researchers and policymakers have been interested not only in how nations compare in the performance of their students, but also in what some reasons might be for cross-national variation. Differences in opportunities for learning were seen as a prominent possibility, so researchers asked teachers to indicate what proportion of their students had the opportunity to learn each item on the international test. The original purpose of the question was to check whether the common international test was equally appropriate for each country, but the question took on more policy relevance by the time of the Second International Mathematics Study (McKnight et al. 1987), when it was refined to focus on whether the topic reflected by the test item had been covered *in that year*. Even more specific questions were posed to teachers about classroom coverage and other potential sources of opportunities for students to learn content in science as well as in mathematics for the Third International Mathematics and Science Study and its successors, which have been renamed the Trends in Mathematics and Science Study (TIMSS). Generally, countries in which achievement levels are higher also provide more opportunities for students to learn tested content (Floden 2003), leading to speculation that differences *within* countries may also be attributable to differences in students' opportunities for learning (Schmidt et al. 1999). From this literature, the concept of opportunities for learning has emerged as a major policy variable, potentially manipulable as a force to improve achievement levels and reduce inequality.

MEASURING OPPORTUNITIES FOR LEARNING

A major challenge to testing hypotheses about the impact of opportunities for learning on student achievement within countries – and to using opportunities for learning as a policy instrument – is the difficulty of developing powerful measures. While aggregate associations between tested content and average performance are high, the associations are more modest at the individual level within countries (Floden 2003). Moreover, the international studies' approach to measuring "opportunity to learn" focuses exclusively on content topics, whereas the general concept is broader, particularly in its policy use. While early studies in the US focused on time as the indicator of opportunity, more recent concerns emphasize additional elements including time allocated to

specific activities, salience of content areas, cognitive demands in tasks for students, teacher–student interaction in classrooms, the use of homework assignments, and other aspects of teachers' instructional strategies.

In first grade reading, Barr and Dreeben (1983) discovered that a count of the number of new words and phonics to which students were introduced, along with the time spent on these activities, was highly predictive of students' learning over the course of first grade: the more students were taught, the more they learned. Gamoran showed that these measures of opportunity accounted for all of the effects of ability grouping on first grade reading achievement. Rowan and Miracle (1983) similarly demonstrated that one could predict third grade reading achievement by counting the number of stories to which students were exposed in their reading materials. However, as students progress through the grade levels, it becomes increasingly difficult to measure opportunities for learning by simply counting the curricular units to which students have been exposed. Nystrand responded to this challenge by using classroom observations to assess learning opportunities embedded in teacher–student interaction, focusing particularly on whether classroom instruction is "dialogic," involving authentic exchanges of information between teachers and students and among students, instead of recitation of facts and ideas predetermined by teachers. While dialogic instruction predicts learning in English and social studies, and partially accounts for the effects of ability grouping in English (Gamoran et al. 1995; Applebee et al. 2003), it is not as powerful a predictor as curricular units in the early elementary years, and it lacks the content focus of those measures. Observational measures of learning opportunities have the advantage of being objectively rated across a wide range of classrooms, but the high cost of sending observers to classrooms may limit the scale to which this approach can be applied.

Other approaches to measuring opportunities for learning have adopted much more fine-grained perspectives. Porter (2002) has used questionnaires to ask mathematics teachers to report their instruction on a grid of 93 mathematics topics (e.g., place value, functions) by six cognitive demands (memorize facts, understand concepts, perform procedures, collect/interpret data, solve word problems, and solve novel problems). The resulting grid can then be mapped onto an assessment to indicate the degree of alignment between instruction and assessment. Similar schemes have been developed for science (Smithson & Porter 2004), and work is underway on a comparable approach to assessing opportunity in literacy. Gamoran et al. (1997) found that Porter's approach to measuring opportunities predicted learning gains in mathematics, and explained most of the variation between different types of ninth grade mathematics classes (e.g., general math, algebra). Floden (2003) has noted two limitations of the approach: first, completing the survey is demanding and time-consuming for teachers; and second, if opportunity is measured according to the alignment between instruction and assessment, that may only be useful information if the assessment is inherently meaningful. Current work by Smithson and Porter (2004) has extended the approach to develop the *Survey of Enacted Curriculum*, a tool for assessing the degree of alignment between state, district, or professional standards, instruction, and assessment. This development provides a way to ensure that the opportunities measured with the teacher survey are indeed meaningful, insofar as they are represented in external standards.

Recent US national surveys have included questionnaires for teachers about their instructional strategies and emphases, and these items have been used as measures of learning opportunities to predict student achievement. National surveys are much less detailed than Porter's (2002) fine-grained approach, and one may question whether they have sufficient reliability to serve as adequate measures of opportunity. Burstein et al. (1995) argued that mismatches between measures obtained from year-end questionnaires and those from ongoing teacher logs indicated that questionnaire measures tended to be unreliable, although the authors found that questions about time spent in particular activities could be addressed more reliably than questions about general emphases on instructional topics or goals. Mayer (1999) also questioned the reliability of teacher survey measures, but he acknowledged that scales constructed from such measures may have sufficient reliability to be useful. Reviewing

progress in the development of opportunity to learn measures, Floden (2003) commented that just as achievement tests have been developed over several iterations, with more reliable items replacing less reliable ones over time, survey measures of opportunity to learn may also improve with experience.

New international comparative work has also focused on differences in the cognitive demands of instruction and assessment (Klieme & Baumert 2001). This research has identified distinct national profiles of learning outcomes, which are interpreted as reflecting different opportunities for learning present in instructional approaches that vary internationally.

OPPORTUNITIES FOR LEARNING IN AN ERA OF ACCOUNTABILITY: A US EXAMPLE

Opportunities for learning have been examined in many national contexts, with a common focus on the differentiation of opportunities to students of varied backgrounds and destinations (Oakes et al. 1992). The US provides an example of how this research may enter the policy realm.

Issues of opportunities for learning have taken on new salience in the US in light of recent changes in federal education policy. The No Child Left Behind Act of 2001 (NCLB) requires states to set standards for student performance, to assess students according to these standards, and to hold schools accountable for achieving standards. Schools must meet standards not only for the performance of their students on average, but also for a variety of sociodemographic subgroups, including those who – in part due to limited learning opportunities – have traditionally underperformed. If schools are to be held accountable for the performance of *all* students, the goal of creating more equitable opportunities for learning gains increasing prominence. Moreover, if schools are applying sanctions to *students* who fail to meet standards, as is occurring in many districts, questions of fairness may arise if students are being held accountable for learning yet lack the relevant learning opportunities.

As the US standards movement developed from *A Nation at Risk* in the early 1980s through *Goals 2000* during the 1990s, efforts to balance the federal role with states' rights and the tradition of local control over education included plans to allow states to set content standards for opportunities for learning, overseen by a federal agency that would certify the quality of state standards. This plan was soon abandoned in the face of two major objections. First, states were unwilling to subject their standards to federal oversight, on grounds of both local autonomy and the cost of enforcement. Second, scholars and policymakers alike questioned the strategy of monitoring *input* standards, when *output* standards (i.e., student achievement) were the ultimate goal. After all, even the best measures of opportunities for learning exhibit substantial slippage from opportunities to performance, as has long been recognized in the distinction between the enacted and the achieved curriculum. As Porter (1994: 431–2) noted, "opportunity to learn does not translate directly into student achievement. Schools must provide a quality educational experience, and students must apply themselves."

The most recent federal legislation, NCLB, does not attempt to legislate opportunities for learning directly. Instead, NCLB's approach to improving learning opportunities is to call for "highly qualified teachers" in every classroom. In particular, NCLB emphasizes subject matter expertise, on the theory that teachers with greater subject matter expertise will provide more rigorous, content-focused instruction that will enable students to reach achievement standards. On the one hand, it is hard to argue against teachers having greater subject matter knowledge. On the other hand, only a modest research base supports teacher content knowledge as a lever for change in student achievement. Consequently, the impact of increasing access to "highly qualified teachers" cannot be predicted at this time. The importance of high-quality opportunities for learning is also reflected in NCLB's demand for instructional practices that reflect scientific evidence of their effectiveness. Whether such practices can be identified and implemented on a mass scale also remains to be seen.

Sociologists have long recognized that the contribution of schools and schooling to variation in learning among individual students is modest, compared to the importance of family background (Coleman et al. 1966). Schools produce learning, but variation from one school to another is relatively small compared to the wider variation within schools. Among the elements of schooling that do matter for how much learning schools produce – and why some students learn more than others – opportunities for learning are perhaps the most powerful predictor that has yet been detected. Despite the challenges of measuring opportunities, a variety of viable schemes has been developed, and ongoing research in this area will likely lead to further improvement. Opportunities for learning thus offer potential leverage for policy intervention.

SEE ALSO: Coleman, James; Cultural Capital; Education; Educational Inequality; Globalization, Education and; Hidden Curriculum; Math, Science, and Technology Education; Stratification and Inequality, Theories of; Teaching and Gender; Tracking

REFERENCES AND SUGGESTED READINGS

Applebee, A. N., Langer, J., Nystrand, M., & Gamoran, A. (2003) Discussion-Based Approaches to Developing Understanding: Classroom Instruction and Student Performance in Middle and High School English. *American Educational Research Journal* 40: 685–730.

Barr, R. & Dreeben, R. (1983) *How Schools Work*. University of Chicago Press, Chicago.

Burstein, L., McDonnell, L. M., Van Winkle, J., Ormseth, T., Mirocha, J., & Guitton, G. (1995) *Validating National Curriculum Indicators*. RAND, Santa Monica, CA.

Carroll, J. (1963) A Model for School Learning. *Teachers College Record* 64: 723–33.

Coleman, J. S., Campbell, E. Q., Hobson, C. F., McPartland, J. M., Mood, A. M., Weinfeld, F. D., & York, R. L. (1966) *Equality of Educational Opportunity*. US Department of Education, Washington, DC.

Croxford, L. (1994) Equal Opportunities in the Secondary School Curriculum in Scotland, 1971–1991. *British Educational Research Journal* 20: 371–91.

Floden, R. E. (2003) The Measurement of Opportunity to Learn. In: Porter, A. C. & Gamoran, A. (Eds.), *Methodological Advances in Cross-National Surveys of Educational Achievement*. National Academy Press, Washington, DC, pp. 231–66.

Gamoran, A., Nystrand, M., Berends, M., & LePore, P. C. (1995) An Organizational Analysis of the Effects of Ability Grouping. *American Educational Research Journal* 32: 687–715.

Gamoran, A., Porter, A. C., Smithson, J., & White, P. A. (1997) Upgrading High School Mathematics Instruction: Improving Learning Opportunities for Low-Income, Low-Achieving Youth. *Educational Evaluation and Policy Analysis* 19: 325–38.

Husen, T. (Ed.) (1967) *International Study of Achievement in Mathematics: A Comparison of Twelve Countries*. Wiley, New York.

Klieme, E. & Baumert, J. (2001) Identifying National Cultures of Mathematics Education: Analysis of Cognitive Demands and Differential Item Functioning in TIMSS. *European Journal of Psychology of Education* 16: 385–402.

McKnight, C. C., Crosswhite, F. J., Dossey, J. A., Kifer, E., Swafford, J. O., Travers, K. J., & Cooney, T. J. (1987) *The Underachieving Curriculum*. Stipes, Champaign, IL.

Mayer, D. P. (1999) Measuring Instructional Practice: Can Policymakers Trust Survey Data? *Educational Evaluation and Policy Analysis* 21: 29–45.

Oakes, J., Gamoran, A., & Page, R. N. (1992) Curriculum Differentiation: Opportunities, Outcomes, and Meanings. In: Jackson, P. W. (Ed.), *Handbook of Research on Curriculum*. Macmillan, New York, pp. 570–608.

Pallas, A. & Alexander, K. L. (1983) Sex Differences in Quantitative SAT Performance: New Evidence on the Differential Coursework Hypothesis. *American Educational Research Journal* 20: 165–82.

Porter, A. C. (1994) National Standards and School Improvement in the 1990s: Issues and Promise. *American Journal of Education* 102: 421–49.

Porter, A. C. (2002) Measuring the Content of Instruction: Uses in Research and Practice. *Educational Researcher* 31(7): 3–14.

Rowan, B. & Miracle, A. W., Jr. (1983). Systems of Ability Grouping and the Stratification of Achievement in Elementary Schools. *Sociology of Education* 56: 133–44.

Schmidt, W. H., McKnight, C. C., Cogan, L. S., Jakwerth, P. M., & Houang, R. T. (1999) *Facing the Consequences: Using TIMSS for a Closer Look at US Mathematics and Science Education*. Kluwer Academic Press, Boston.

Smithson, J. & Porter, A. C. (2004) From Policy to Practice: The Evolution of One Approach to Describing and Using Curriculum Data. In: Wilson, M. (Ed.), *Towards Coherence Between Classroom Assessment and Accountability. One Hundred and Third Yearbook of the National Society for the Study of Education, Part II*. National Society for the Study of Education, Chicago, pp. 105–31.

US Department of Education (1999) *The Digest of Educational Statistics, 1999*. US Department of Education, Washington, DC.

oral sex

Bruce Curtis

Oral sex is broadly defined as oral-genital stimulation. Cunnilingus refers to oral-vaginal stimulation, fellatio to oral-penile stimulation, and analingus to anal-lingual stimulation. Across the sweep of sexual practices in human societies both historically and cross-culturally, oral sex figures in an extremely wide variety of forms, themselves valued in very different ways. The focus here is on oral sex within heterosexual relations, but oral sex plays an important part in homosexual relations. In some historical configurations of sexual practices in South Asia, for instance, the tasting of another man's semen was thought to stimulate the desire for heterosexual intercourse. In another configuration, fellatio was seen as a substitute for heterosexual intercourse, something to be received from a eunuch, but certainly not by a man from his wife. In the West, oral sex was often subject to legal prohibitions against "sodomy," both hetero- and homosexual, and in some states in the US it remains a criminal offense.

The location of oral sex in typical sequences of sexual practice has been immensely variable. Public attention has been focused recently on the shifting place of oral sex in the repertoire of western heterosexual practices. In Victorian erotic literature, cunnilingus or "gamahuching" was presented as both a pleasurable and a contraceptive practice. Authors of English-language sex advice and marriage manuals from the early 1900s to the 1940s gradually came to endorse what they called "the genital kiss," initially referring not to fellatio but rather to cunnilingus. This endorsement of cunnilingus stemmed from the commonly held belief that women were far slower to arouse sexually, if they were capable of sexual pleasure at all, than were their husbands. Husbands were counseled to prepare their wives for intercourse by carefully graduated caresses, which could include oral-genital contact to encourage lubrication and receptivity.

Before the end of World War I, there was a noticeable absence of discussion of sexual relations except as necessary elements in reproduction. For reasons which remain unclear, marriage and advice manuals in the period from about 1920 witnessed both a "discovery" of women's sexual pleasure and the invention of sexual foreplay. It is tempting to relate these changes to transformations wrought by women's wartime employment, the relaxation of moral codes in the wake of the war, and the ongoing decline in most western countries in both fertility and infant mortality rates. In any case, advice manuals began to emphasize the importance of female orgasm in the marital sexual relation and to stress the exchange of mutually enjoyable preliminary caresses before intercourse. Heightened emphasis was placed on the acceptability and importance of cunnilingus. It was only sometime after the discovery of women's sexual pleasure and the invention of foreplay that fellatio began to be spoken of approvingly as a marital sexual practice. Women were increasingly portrayed as active participants in foreplay and intercourse, able to give as well as to receive caresses, including fellatio. Still, authors were initially very hesitant about recommending that women engage in the practice and urged caution on them. On the one hand, fellatio had a reputation as a homosexual practice and wives were warned that they risked unmanning their husbands through the assertive pursuit of the practice. On the other hand, sexual pleasure was still primarily seen as an adjunct to reproduction, and it was feared that fellatio leading to orgasm might lead couples to neglect their social obligations to produce children.

The post-war period witnessed an enormously significant change in the evidence made available by a new wave of sexology studies. The Kinsey (1948, 1953) and Masters and Johnson (1966) studies quickly reached a much wider audience which had a thirst for sexual knowledge that was a product of the ongoing sexual responsibilization of adults for the success of their sexual relations, and these studies further legitimized the public discussion of sex. It was into this milieu that the double ideological thrusts of these studies were projected. First, from Kinsey came the emphasis on human sexual variability, which fractured the paradigm that had normalized a single model of heterosexual marital sex outside of which all else was deviant. From Masters and Johnson came the highlighting of an essential similarity in the

sexual responses of males and females; their "human response cycle" eroded the longstanding preoccupation with the differences between the sexes. These studies accentuated the theme that the pursuit of sexual pleasure was important in securing marital stability. From the 1960s oral sex came to be regarded as an act of considerable intimacy which typically followed marriage and intercourse for most heterosexual couples. Alex Comfort epitomized this view through his analogy between the sexual and the culinary arts. Sex, like a good meal, consisted of a number of courses; and one of these would frequently involve mutual oral sex.

The coming of age of the post-war baby boom generation coincided with the diffusion of reliable oral contraceptives for women, effective treatments of most sexually transmitted diseases, sustained economic growth, the relaxation of sexual mores, and the elimination by many governments of attempts at regulating non-heterosexual marital practices. Popular sex manuals, such as the various versions of Comfort's agreeably illustrated *The Joy of Sex*, provided technical advice and active encouragement for a broad range of mutually accepted hetero- and homosexual practices, including all forms of oral sex. Fellatio was publicized and perhaps popularized as well by widely distributed early pornographic films such as *Deep Throat*. By the 1990s, there was a considerable English-language market for specialized oral sex instruction manuals. The practice was something every sexually competent person was expected to master. While there are important national and regional variations in the popularity and prevalence of various sexual practices, oral sex has become commonplace in the sexual repertoire of adults and adolescents. These changes are signaled in shifts in the language used to refer to sexual practices and relations. The "petting," "making out," or "snogging" of an earlier period are displaced by "hooking up," which in North America is understood by adolescents to refer to oral sex, especially fellatio. Some adults point to a worrisome fellatio "epidemic," in which teens and at times preteen girls give older, higher-status boys unreciprocated "blowjobs" to achieve standing with their peers. Adolescent boys seem less interested in performing cunnilingus. Medical professionals express concern that adolescents believe unprotected oral sex to be "safe sex," while in fact the practice may be a transmission vector for disease. Still, in a context of campaigns against HIV/AIDs which privilege condom use as a means of "safe sex," oral sex can easily be redefined as "not having sex." Fellatio has been redefined for a majority of the post-AIDS generation as casual "outercourse," in contrast to vaginal-penile intercourse, and as a practice compatible with notions both of sexual "abstinence" and "safe sex."

SEE ALSO: Age, Period, and Cohort Effects; Body and Sexuality; Femininities/Masculinities; Intimacy; Masturbation; Pornography and Erotica; Sexuality; Sexuality and the Law; Sexuality, Masculinity and

REFERENCES AND SUGGESTED READINGS

Gagnon, J. H. & Simon, W. (1987) The Sexual Scripting of Oral Genital Contacts. *Archives of Sexual Behavior* 16(1): 1–37.

Herold, E. S. & Way, L. (1983) Oral-Genital Sexual Behavior in a Sample of University Females. *Journal of Sex Research* 19: 327–38.

Laumann, E. O., Gagnon, J. H., Michael, R. T., & Michaels, S. (1994) *The Social Organization of Sexuality: Sexual Practices in the United States.* University of Chicago Press, Chicago.

Newcomer, S. F. & Ruddy, J. (1985) Oral Sex in an Adolescent Population. *Archive of Sexual Behavior* 14: 41–6.

Sanders, S. A. & Reinisch, J. M. (1999) Would You Say You "Had Sex" If. . .? *Journal of the American Medical Association* 281(3): 275–7.

orality

Martin M. Jacobsen

Orality describes cultures or populations whose worldviews, rhetorical principles, and mental constructs develop in the absence of widespread, systematic, and habitual literacy and also refers to the coexistent or residual presence of orality in habitually literate cultures. Thus, it is necessary to distinguish between primary orality and secondary orality. Primary orality

(and thus primary oral cultures) describes cultures that privilege the spoken word as the only means of social and interpersonal communication, often lacking even a basic orthography. Secondary orality describes the presence of oral and/or pseudo-oral elements in habitually literate cultures. Each of these will be discussed in more detail.

Much early work on orality is grounded in the literary concept of the "oral tradition," a literary term used to postulate the state of important western narratives prior to their being written down. Most of the discussion focused on elements in the written versions that reflected the rhetorical aspects of spoken discourse, for instance, the use of stock phrases. Later work by psychologists, sociologists, anthropologists, folklorists, and other social scientists drew on data and observation drawn from actual populations participating in an oral life world in the Balkans, the former Soviet Union, Australia, Africa, and other places. These studies confirmed much of the speculative work of earlier theorists but also exposed gaps in the literary analysis. Together, these approaches codify orality.

The most influential figure in the study of orality is Walter J. Ong, whose landmark book *Orality and Literacy* (1982) popularized the concept of orality across many disciplines. Ong draws together the literary and social scientific sources concerned with orality to that point in time in a remarkably brief but comprehensive way and then discusses how literacy emerged from orality. The concept of primary and secondary orality delineated in his work will underlie those definitions here.

Intellectual, psychological, cultural, and linguistic paradigms in primary oral cultures differ significantly from those of a habitually literate society. Ong's inventory of characteristics for a primary oral culture abstracts the nature of such a culture, linguistically, rhetorically, intellectually, and socially. Linguistically, the grammar of primary orality tends toward parataxis, which Ong calls "additive rather than subordinative" (1982: 37–8), repetition or the "redundant" inclusion of what was just said (pp. 39–40), and aggregation or the use of clichés and other stock phrases (pp. 38–9).

Rhetorical practices are immediate, concrete, and communal. It may seem difficult to reconcile

Ong's assertion that primary oral cultures are "agonistically toned" (pp. 43–5) with the argument that rhetorical practices are communal. The point is, however, that the agonistic nature of face-to-face confrontation requires the participants to actually be face to face. In a literate culture, challenges and claims are often made in writing (or by telephone). The idea of confrontation is lessened by the fact that the writer is not there to question and the recipient is not immediately able to respond. Perhaps less peculiar is Ong's claim that primary orality is "empathetic and participatory" (pp. 45–6), meaning that a person cannot participate if absent and does not know the story unless able to see the storyteller. In such a context even the act of confrontation is the hallmark of a communal system, in that such an agonistic tone requires the co-presence of foes.

Intellectually, Ong argues that primary oral culture observes a number of guiding principles that seem out of place in a habitually literate society. The absence of writing affects the importance of memory to the culture. The primary oral culture tends to be "homeostatic" (pp. 46–9): constantly purging memories so that intellectual space can remain available for use in the here and now. Thus, words seldom have layers of meaning because they are not objects stored in dictionaries where they can be retrieved, revived, or expanded upon. Homeostasis is a natural fit, then, with the more "traditionalist" (pp. 41–2) lifestyle of the primary oral culture. Learning new ideas in a literate culture is not threatening because the old ideas are only a few pages away at any moment, much like the words in the dictionary. In a primary oral culture, traditional beliefs and practices sustain and are sustained by a citizenry that finds experimentation risky. Even the most basic lifestyle requires considerable mental activity, and knowing what one knows provides comfort and stability. Clearly, the traditionalist approach is concomitant with Ong's theory that primary orality is "situational rather than abstract" (pp. 49–57), meaning that ideas are interpreted as living things needed to encounter daily challenges rather than objects stored and available for use through a recall process. Every situation presents as a total experience (like the action in an oral epic – foregrounded and completely delineated). Thus, in Ong's view,

primary oral cultures do not need advanced mathematical or logical systems, elaborate and refined definitions, or even a well-delineated concept of themselves. Rather, as Ong states, the lifestyle in a primary oral culture is "close to the human lifeworld" (pp. 42–3); that is, the members of such a community are little concerned with anything outside their physical ability to perceive. Their lives are immediate – concerned with what happens here and now. Habitually literate cultures, especially post-industrial societies of the first world, live highly mediated lives and are concerned with abstractions such as past and future, so consumed by signs that an authentic experience may pass unnoticed, or worse, need to be put into some series of signs before existing at all. Primary oral cultures live in the moment and space that they inhabit.

Ong accounts for the presence of orality in habitually literate cultures with the term secondary orality. Secondary orality describes the way in which traditionally oral situations in literate cultures mimic orality but are based on textual practices. For instance, oral events that are recorded, televised, conducted by telephone, or otherwise mediated by technology render the spoken word into a transmitted text. Even the act of recitation is secondarily oral because of its basis in a written text that is then memorized word for word (a concept somewhat foreign to primary oral culture because there are no texts to memorize). Further, much of the orality disseminated through technological means derives from written foundations such as scripts. In fact, one theorist (Killingsworth 1993) argues that literate cultures have reached the point of secondary literacy, which encodes secondary orality in written form or perhaps even lessens the need for writing because so many avenues of technologically assisted orality exist. For example, the notion and practice of "voicemail" exhibits the developing nature of both secondary orality and secondary literacy.

Some theorists argue that comparing orality to literacy, or, in effect, seeing the former through the latter, reflects the bias of the literate perspective and derogates primary oral culture. This bias is shown through the use of a term such as "preliterate," implying that literacy is the touchstone rather than seeing literacy as an encoding of the spoken word and a symbolic expression of the oral foundation of human language. "Oral literature" suggests that the cultural space occupied by narrative in primary oral culture must be validated by being named literature, even though the very word literature denies the nature and importance of narrative in oral societies. Moreover, the concept of illiteracy is sometimes confused with primary orality, even though they are completely unrelated because illiteracy can only exist in cultures with widespread, systematic, and habitual literacy. This false comparison further disparages primary oral cultures by suggesting they could write and decide not to learn. A primary oral culture has no writing system to learn.

While comparing orality to literacy may very well diminish or derogate primary orality, literate cultures are as bound by their need to make the comparison as oral systems are by their inability to do so. It is difficult to escape the irony of our learning about orality through books, articles, transcripts, and other written means or through recordings of oral systems. These render the oral act the theorist hopes to capture secondarily oral because the oral event is trapped in a textual form and elaborated as a text, usually accompanied by other texts that explain, refine, or contextualize it. What Ong calls the "evanescent" (p. 32) nature of sound – that it disappears as soon as it is produced – becomes permanent, therefore changing its nature. This is similar to the idea that "saving" a language means "giving it an alphabet" and "writing it down," which changes the nature of that language.

The current research trends regarding orality are puzzling. Scholars continue to examine classical texts for evidence of the oral tradition that preceded their written analogues. Literary theorists are examining the way orality is elaborated in written literary texts of virtually every period and genre, both in the West and beyond. Both of these enterprises are in many ways an examination of secondary orality. There is also some interest in orality among African, Native American, and other tribal or postcolonial peoples; however, even some of this work is being done by examining evidence of orality in texts, rather than by listening to the primary oral cultures. Attempts to codify and standardize contact languages such as pidgins and creoles offer an interesting interstitial domain between

orality and the advent of literacy; however, little attention has been given to this area.

Areas of possible interest for researchers interested in orality include the nature of the "home" language spoken by many in bilingual situations, where the person's written language is a second language and the home language is a first language and is often used in a primary oral situation, something of a reverse of the contact language issue. Anthropologists and others study primary oral cultures for a variety of linguistic (often sociolinguistic) reasons. However, interest in primary orality remains limited or perhaps assumed as a characteristic of the culture but not considered interesting as a focus of study. Further, some may see the question of orality and literacy as too prejudicial to oral communities to approach. Much of the theory elaborated here borders on the concept of linguistic relativity (if not linguistic determinism) based on the mode of expression rather than grammatical structures. This may spark a backlash among theorists who suspect the pejorative and hegemonic potential of the linguistic relativity hypothesis may serve to demean primary oral culture.

Finally, the immediacy of communication in every form facilitated by the Internet has led to inevitable comparisons to the immediacy of orality. While some work has been done in this area, no definitive or perhaps even adequately critical examination has emerged, perhaps because scholars have focused more attention on the way in which computer-mediated communication influences textuality. The relationship between orality, literacy, and computer-mediated discourse has received some critical analysis and stands as another potential area of interest.

SEE ALSO: Discourse; Globalization, Education and; Literacy/Illiteracy; Mass Culture and Mass Society; Mass Media and Socialization; Media; Media and Globalization; Media Literacy

REFERENCES AND SUGGESTED READINGS

Havelock, E. A. (1986) *The Muse Learns to Write: Reflections on Orality and Literacy from Antiquity to the Present.* Yale University Press, New Haven.

Jacobsen, M. M. (2002) *Transformations of Literacy in Computer-Mediated Communication: Orality, Literacy, Cyberdiscursivity*. Edwin Mellen, Lewiston, NY.

Killingsworth, M. J. (1993) Product and Process, Literacy and Orality: An Essay on Composition and Culture. *College Composition and Communication* 44(1): 26–39.

Ong, W. J. (1982) *Orality and Literacy: The Technologizing of the Word*. Routledge, London.

Welch, K. E. (1999) *Electric Rhetoric: Classical Rhetoric, Oralism, and a New Literacy*. MIT Press, Cambridge, MA.

organization theory

Royston Greenwood

Organization theory is concerned with organizations, the relationship between organizations and their environment, the effects of those relationships upon intra-organizational functioning, and how organizations affect the distribution of privilege within society. A central concept is *organizational form*. The ability of societies to respond to social and economic problems depends upon the availability of diverse forms. Organization theorists are thus interested in the range of organizational forms, their capabilities and consequences, in how new organizational forms arise and become established, and in who controls them for what purposes.

Although the origins of organization theory reside in the early twentieth century, especially in the contributions of scientific management, classical management theory, and Weberian analysis of bureaucracy, organization theory as a discipline is better traced to the late 1950s and early 1960s. The discipline contains multiple theoretical perspectives that provide a rich array of approaches and insights. Two foundational perspectives are *structural contingency theory* and the *behavioral theory of the firm*. The former focuses upon the alignment of organization form and environmental context, answering which forms are effective in which contexts. The latter focuses upon how alignment and adaptation might happen.

Prior to the 1960s, "bureaucracy" was regarded as the most efficient organizational form because it imbued organizations with technical rationality. Beginning in the late 1950s, a series of studies showed that the relevance of the Weberian model was "contingent" upon the degree of task uncertainty, complexity, and organizational size. Burns and Stalker (1961), for example, found the bureaucratic form effective only in stable and predictable environments. In unpredictable contexts, loosely structured "organic" forms are more successful. Chandler (1962) traced how diversification strategies affect the appropriateness of particular structural arrangements by increasing decision-making complexity. Pugh et al. (1968) measured organizational structures and produced a taxonomy of forms associated with (caused by) contingencies of size, age, technology, and uncertainty.

The term structural contingency theory thus defines organizational form as dependent upon situational contingencies. Researchers in this tradition seek to identify differences in organizational forms and to understand which forms are appropriate for which circumstances. Noticeably, the focus of contingency analysis is the individual organization, the dependent variable is organizational structure (form), the determining variables (size, environment, strategy) are economic (technical) in nature, and a diversity of organizational forms is anticipated. Further, the imagery is rationalistic with organizations portrayed as mechanically adjusting to technical exigencies in pursuit of economic goals. Missing is any recognition that organizations have difficulties either identifying which contingencies are important or in selecting appropriate responses. Nor is there recognition that changing structures to achieve fit might be problematic.

Structural contingency theory dominated thinking about organizations well into the 1970s and developed in two directions: strategic choice theory and configuration theory. *Strategic choice theory* challenges the idea that organizations are determined by their contingencies and that executives have minimal discretion in selecting organizational forms. Decision-makers occasionally have the power to manipulate their environments (a thesis elaborated as resource dependency theory, discussed below).

Moreover, perceptions are an intervening link between contingencies and organizational actions (see sensemaking theory, below). *Configuration theory* emphasizes that strategies, structures, and processes are underpinned and given coherence by resilient core values, making change difficult to achieve. Further, organizational forms are not free-floating assemblages of structures and processes easily discarded or rearranged; they are tightly aligned patterns of dynamic routines that work *against* change.

A second foundational perspective is the behavioral theory of the firm. Cyert and March (1963) explored how individuals use simplifying decision rules to model and cope with complexity. Decision-making is thus "boundedly rational." Bounded rationality acknowledges the intendedly rational behavior of organizational actors, whilst recognizing cognitive limitations and the high costs of information search. Unlike structural contingency theorists, who sought to understand which organizational forms matched contingent situations, Cyert and March (1963) sought to understand how organizations adapt to their environments. The image is of organizations as intendedly adaptive systems struggling to cope with complex and ambiguous information. Further, organizations are composed of participants with different preferences, leading to contested goals. Portrayed in this manner, the key managerial challenges are computational (how to handle uncertainty) and political (how to secure cooperation).

Central to the theory is the idea of learning achieved through organizational routines. Subsequent research has drawn an important distinction between routines that enable learning within a prevailing set of parameters (single-loop learning) and double-loop learning, where the organization breaks from existing assumptions. Unlike structural contingency theory, which assumes that adaptation to changing circumstances is non-problematic, research in the behavioral tradition shows that most organizational learning is essentially conservative.

Structural contingency theory and the behavioral theory of the firm share the idea that there is an environment "out there," to which organizations respond. Weick (1995) shifted this emphasis, offering a *sensemaking theory* of how organizations relate to their contexts. This theory denies that contexts are detached from organizations. The shift is from seeing the problem as one of information processing to one of understanding how managers socially construct their world. Managers build "mental models" that shape how they think about their industry and understand possible courses of action. How such mental models develop, how they shape behavior, how they constitute organizational routines, and how they can change, remain important questions. Weick also introduced the idea that organizations *enact* their contexts. That is, sensemaking concurrently involves reflection (often retrospective) and action to "test out" tentative and incomplete understandings. But actions shape contexts, bringing them into being, thus "confirming" emergent mental models. Weick's thesis anticipates Giddens's notion of structuration, albeit at the level of the organization.

A fundamentally different theory addresses a logically prior question: why do organizations exist at all? *Transaction cost theory* (Williamson 1981) points to market failures as the reason for organizations. The theory assumes that the motivation of managers is to maximize profits and that their efforts are constricted by uncertainty (e.g., the inability to draft contracts that fully anticipate future circumstances) and opportunities for opportunistic behavior (e.g., where a party to an exchange invests in an asset that cannot easily be used elsewhere and thus becomes dependent upon its users). Unanticipated disagreements and investments in specific assets are managed by incorporating activities into an organization, using hierarchy rather than markets as the governance mechanism. Transaction cost theory resonates with recent interest in the disaggregation of vertically integrated firms.

Structural contingency theory and the behavioral theory of the firm assume that organizations adapt to their contexts. *Resource dependence (R/D) theory* (Pfeffer & Salancik 1978) takes a different stance, proposing that organizations seek to control their environments by not becoming overdependent on other organizations for resources necessary for organizational survival, whilst creating and exploiting situations where organizations are dependent upon them. Resources are both material (e.g., finance, labor, supplies) and symbolic (e.g., social approval). Building alliances, engaging in joint ventures, and using interlocking board directorates are examples of how organizations seek to manage their resource dependencies.

The central insight of resource dependence is that the relationship between context and organization is not unidirectional but reciprocal. However, although organizations can act individually or collectively (e.g., through associations or the professions), only modest attention has been given to how organizations act collectively, possibly missing the more dramatic instances of how organizations shape societal institutions and public policies. A second contribution of the theory is its explanation of why some groups have power within organizations. Power resides with those subunits best able to handle critical external dependencies.

The above theories provide insights into how organizations understand, enact, and respond to their "environments." The environment is understood as an economic context, comprising consumers, competitors, suppliers, and, to a lesser extent, regulators who set the rules of the marketplace. Organizations are portrayed as social systems responding to contextual factors in pursuit of collective ends. *Neo-institutional theory* expands the meaning of environment and questions the functionalist tone of earlier theories. Meyer and Rowan (1977) observed that within any given industry, organizations use similar organizational forms because social conventions prescribe socially acceptable ways of doing things. Organizations conform because doing so provides social legitimacy and enhances survival prospects. Neo-institutional theory thus advises that organizations are not simply production systems but social and cultural systems embedded within an "institutional" context, comprising the state, professions, interest groups, and public opinion. Importantly, institutionalized prescriptions are enduring and often taken for granted. One consequence is that organizations founded in the same era tend to adopt and retain organizational forms fashionable in their early years. This idea of "organizational imprinting" contradicts the logic of structural contingency theory. Importantly, neo-institutional theory implies that organizational forms, patterns of control, and distributions of benefits are not derived from immutable laws of "markets" but are outcomes of socially constructed, institutionalized conventions and beliefs. Market structures are institutionally

defined and thus institutions frame and legitimate outcomes of those structures.

During the 1980s and early 1990s, considerable effort was applied to confirming the effects of institutional processes, especially patterns of diffusion. Less attention was given to coercive processes (associated with the state) or normative processes (associated with the professions), reflecting a neglect of important power structures. The late 1990s heralded a shift in emphasis in favor of understanding institutional change and the emergence of new organizational forms. Current research acknowledges the importance of motivated agency ("institutional entrepreneurship"), correcting the previous imagery of institutional determinism. Further, it is more openly examining how institutional structures embed patterns of privilege and power and suppress and/or disadvantage certain interests.

Typically, institutional research describes *field-level* processes, contrary to previous theories that focused upon individual organizations. Fields consist not only of organizations using similar organizational forms to deliver a given set of services or goods, but also suppliers of resources, consumers, and regulatory agencies. Field-level analysis draws attention to processes of structuration. That is, organizations are constrained by institutional prescriptions, but, in acting out those prescriptions, reproduce and translate them, sometimes imperfectly. The imagery, then, is of organizations responding to institutionalized expectations and, in so doing, amplifying, elaborating, and modifying them. New organizational forms can thus arise by accidents of translation or deliberate insurgence as disadvantaged interests seek change.

Population ecology appeared at the same time as neo-institutional theory and rapidly developed into one of the most rigorous approaches within organization theory (Hannan & Freeman 1977). It is concerned with the variety of organizational forms and regards organizational survival as the product of fit between organizational forms and, primarily, market forces. The theory is distinctive in two ways. First, ecological theories are interested in why organizational forms per se (not individual organizations) become established and survive or decline. A core idea is that forms best aligned to given contextual locations flourish. Less well-aligned forms disappear. Second, changes in context pose survival challenges because managers are unable to change organizations quickly enough. Movement between organizational forms is thus highly problematic. Instead, organizations using a particular form cease to exist as environmental shifts render the form inappropriate. By highlighting the difficulties of achieving change, ecologists are at the opposite extreme to structural contingency theory and distant from resource dependence. Nevertheless, ecological theories echo the basic assumption of those theories, that organizational forms survive to the extent that they match the exigencies of the economic context.

Ecological theory emphasizes that the ability of organizations to achieve radical change is low. Nevertheless, some organizations exhibit adaptive behavior. Hence, recent research seeks to understand how environmental factors interact with organizational forms, affecting the rates at which existing forms prosper and new forms arise, and the rates at which existing forms mutate. *Evolutionary theory* emphasizes three things: classification of organizational forms to identify their defining features; attention to the mechanisms by which organizational forms are "isolated" and retain their distinctiveness; and the interactions between organizations and their environments that enable them to explore new forms of adaptation. In other words, evolutionary theory portrays organizational alignment and adaptation as the balance or imbalance between genealogical processes that reproduce existing practices whilst allowing for organizational learning and ecological processes that shape survival rates. The implicit assumption is that efficiency considerations drive selection of organizational forms.

The shift in level of analysis displayed by institutional and ecological theories, from organizations to organizational fields and populations, is also found in *network theory*. The study of networks flourished in the 1990s, partly arising from the desire to understand the success of geographical locations such as Silicon Valley and the Japanese *keiretsu*. Three distinct streams of research can be identified. One approach focuses upon the topography of links ("ties") connecting organizations. In this approach the network is a structure of resource opportunities which organizations differentially access by their connections and positions within the network (e.g., Burt 1992). This way of looking at networks has a clear affinity with resource dependence theory. A second approach, closer to institutional theory, sees organizations not as taking advantage of a network but as being shaped by it. Research in this tradition explores how ideas and practices disseminate through networks resulting in convergence around a limited range of organizational forms. A third approach conceptualizes networks as embedded relationships. These studies focus upon how networks are constructed and the consequences of networks, such as their ability to innovate.

The difference between networks as relationships and networks as opportunities is significant. Those who regard networks as structures of opportunities see benefits arising from the diversity and pattern of an organization's ties. The relational approach, in contrast, sees benefits arising from social norms that enable coordination and cooperation between organizations by removing the fear of opportunism in economic exchanges. An organization's advantage is thus a function of the normative strength of the network in which it is embedded. This distinction is important because it redefines the concept of organizational form. That is, although interest in networks began by depicting networks as context and thus as a determinant of organizational form, recent research treats networks as organizational forms in their own right.

The dominant theme reflected in the above theories is understanding the relationship between organizations and their contexts. Central questions concern the reasons for diversity in organizational forms, the extent to which organizations are contextually determined (whether by economic and/or institutional forces), whether and to what extent organizations are capable of adaptation, and, if so, how that occurs. These themes resonate within structural contingency theory, the behavioral theory of the firm, institutional theory, resource dependence, ecological and evolutionary theories. Missing from these accounts is systematic attention to issues of power and consequences. Insofar as consequences are considered, it is in terms of efficiency, innovative capability, or the speed of decision-making. There is an implicit assumption that organizations are instruments of collective effort whose consequences are beneficial. *Critical theory* takes a fundamentally different and more radical stance.

Critical theory asks, who controls organizations and for whom? The theory has several disparate strands but its focus upon power and distributive outcomes is a longstanding theme in organization theory (Clegg & Dunkerley 1980). The theory proposes that organizations be regarded as instruments of political exploitation with distributive consequences. Perrow (2002), for example, sees the large modern corporation not as a response to functional pressures but as the means by which elite interests preserve and enhance positions of privilege. Critical theory, in this form, is inspired by Karl Marx, not, as are most organization theories, by Max Weber. As such, the theory reinterprets much organization theory. For example, it sees networks as mechanisms by which class interests are nurtured and sustained. It treats taken-for-granted institutional prescriptions not as processes for coping with ambiguity but as hegemonies of ideas serving particular interests. Similarly, it regards organizational forms not as responses to economic requirements but as socially constructed means of generating resources and opportunities and for sustaining their (unequal) distribution. Critical theorists thus question whether organizational forms are a "natural" response to contextual exigencies; instead, they portray organizational forms as expressions of power. A more modest version of critical theory points not to the hidden hand of elite, class interests but to the unequal distribution of benefits within organizations and the marginalization of certain interests (e.g., those of women, lower-level employees, ethnic minorities).

The range of perspectives within organization theory continues to grow. For some, the result is confusion rather than coherence, even though attempts are being made to combine or compare perspectives. Others criticize the relative solitudes of North American and non-North American scholarship. There is, thus, no organization theory per se, but a fertile array of complementary, competing, and enlightening insights into one of the most significant societal constructs: the modern organization.

SEE ALSO: Bureaucracy and Public Sector Governmentality; Critical Theory/Frankfurt School; Institutional Theory, New; Management Theory; Networks; Organizational Contingencies; Organizational Learning; Organizations as Social Structures; Organizations and the Theory of the Firm; Organizations as Total Institutions; Power, Theories of; Strategic Management (Organizations); Weber, Max

REFERENCES AND SUGGESTED READINGS

Aldrich, H. (1999) *Organizations Evolving*. Sage, Thousand Oaks, CA.

Burns, T. & Stalker, G. M. (1961) *The Management of Innovation*. Tavistock, London.

Burt, R. S. (1992) *Structural Holes: The Social Structure of Competition*. Harvard University Press, Cambridge, MA.

Chandler, A. D. (1962) *Strategy and Structure: Chapters in the History of the Industrial Enterprises*. MIT Press, Cambridge, MA.

Clegg, S. R. & Dunkerley, D. (1980) *Organization, Class, and Control*. Routledge & Kegan Paul, London.

Cyert, R. M. & March, J. G. (1963) *A Behavioral Theory of the Firm*. Prentice-Hall, Englewood Cliffs, NJ.

Hannan, M. T. & Freeman, J. (1977) The Population Ecology of Organizations. *American Journal of Sociology* 82(5): 929–64.

Meyer, J. W. & Rowan, B. (1977) Institutionalized Organizations: Formal Structure as Myth and Ceremony. *American Journal of Sociology* 83(2): 440–63.

Perrow, C. (2002) *Organizing America*. Princeton University Press, Princeton.

Pfeffer, J. (1997) *New Directions for Organization Theory: Problems and Prospects*. Oxford University Press, New York.

Pfeffer, J. & Salancik, G. R. (1978) *The External Control of Organizations*. Harper & Row, New York.

Pugh, D. S., Hickson, D. J., Hinings, C. R., & Turner, C. (1968) The Context of Organizational Structures. *Administrative Science Quarterly* 14: 91–114.

Scott, W. R. (2003) *Organizations: Rational, Natural, and Open Systems*. Prentice-Hall, Upper Saddle River, NJ.

Weick, K. E. (1995) *Sensemaking in Organizations*. Sage, Thousand Oaks, CA.

Williamson, O. E. (1981) The Economics of Organization: The Transaction Cost Approach. *American Journal of Sociology* 87(3): 548–77.

organizational careers

Catherine Paradeise

Everett Hughes (1958), the leader of the so-called Second School of Chicago, noticed that life in any society is ordered partly according to individual choices, and this order is partly institutionalized. Over time, individual choices in partly institutionalized environments build social careers. In that sense everyone experiments with a social career, even though this remains to a certain extent unconscious and unseen. A career has a subjective facet, moving with the career itself. It is the way in which someone sees her life as a whole and interprets the meaning of the various attributes, actions, and occurrences that happen through life. It also has an objective facet, consisting of a series of social statuses. In modern societies, social order largely derives from interaction between persons and their work. An individual career has been first objectively described as a sequence of jobs, orderly or otherwise, that originates from early socialization and education and has consequences for status. Socialization generates capabilities, social capital, and aspirations that qualify one for a work career. In industrial societies, prestige, power, and wealth in society at large are in turn strongly shaped by work careers.

Careers develop inside, outside, or between organizations. The number and size of bureaucratic organizations have increased with the rise of modern society. During the twentieth century, large private and public organizations shaped orderly career patterns by developing internal labor markets. Organizational careers developed at the point between individual capabilities and aspirations and occupational routes built into organizations. At the end of the century, downsizing and flexibilization of firms led to changes in the role of organizations in the building of individual work career paths.

FROM ORGANIZATIONAL CAREERS...

A number of social science disciplines focus on the various perspectives opened up by the dual nature of careers.

Psychology stresses the subjective facet of careers. It centers on "people looking for jobs." In *Careers in Organizations*, Hall (1976) defines career as the individually perceived sequence of attitudes and behaviors associated with work-related experiences and activities over the span of a person's life. Early studies on organizational careers started in the 1950s in the Department of Education, Psychology, and Philosophy of the University of Columbia. Scholars such as Roe (1956) and Super (1957) developed an interest in personal mobility behavior in organizations. Psychology understands career as a subjective personal history relating individual vocational interests, internalized career images, rational choice of an occupation, and actual work experience. It embraces topics regarding the process of career choice, the passage through career stages, and the attributes of career effectiveness (psychological success, performance, adaptability, identity). It explores questions such as career motivation, loyalties, and commitment within organizational settings.

Administrative science and institutional economics look at the other side of the coin, jobs looking for persons. They describe career structures as regulated administrative processes of workforce allocation into positions, with the purpose of inducing performance. They scrutinize the building of career patterns by organizations through recruitment, promotion, demotion, and succession rules. They treat rules as a set of incentives to employees. The function of rules is to regulate an adequate provision of organizational capabilities in relation to scarcity and quality of the labor force. The open market can provide an unskilled labor force that does not require investment in costly specific training and does not ensure upward mobility. On the other hand, skilled labor is costly, usually combining formal training and learning by experience, and may be scarce. As first noticed by Weber in *Economy and Society* (1921), one way to solve the problem of adequate provision of a qualified workforce is by "mutual appropriation" of employees and employers within organizations. Mutual appropriation (or labor market closure) is based on mutual benefit. It favors loyalty rather than exit or voice. Employers exchange incentives such as differentials in salaries, marginal benefits, and the promise of upward intraorganizational mobility for their employees' faithfulness and dedication. Psychologists analyze such an exchange as a relational contract (Rousseau 1995). Institutional economists conceptualize the frame for orderly intraorganizational careers as internal labor markets, defined as "administrative units, such as a manufacturing plant, within which the pricing and allocation of labor is governed by a set of administrative rules and procedures" (Doeringer & Piore 1971).

It took some time for sociology to overcome the limitations built into the Weberian ideal type of bureaucratic career. This concept was extensively used in sociological research during the 1950s to analyze topics such as the patterns of industrial bureaucracy, social mobility in industrial society, and bounded rationality in organizations. Wilensky (1961) insisted that to be precise, the concept of career should be restricted to individual progression within an organization. Yet another trend led to approaching careers as interaction processes between individuals and organizations (or occupations), sustained by continuous socialization and adjustment experienced by mobile individuals.

Miller and Form's *Industrial Society* (1951) stressed career as a socialization process, adjusting individuals to their social and occupational environment. Hughes (1958) and his students exploited a similar vein later on in Chicago, aiming to relate the objective and subjective facets of career. Following the life history methods developed by Thomas and Znaniecki to study *The Polish Peasant* (1918), they concentrated on producing extensive empirical monographs on all kinds of occupations, from the most prestigious, such as medical doctors, to the most modest or marginal, like nurses, schoolteachers, or jazz musicians. When studying an individual's career, they not only addressed socialization at the early stage of the working life, they also explored roles and status building at each stage of the career as a continuous reconstruction of the meaning of work. They showed that career development went along with discovering new work contents and possibly leaving one's central occupational activity to fill higher managerial positions. While labor markets are not all socially organized to the same extent, they each follow rules and conventions that are neither fully conscious nor formally set. When studying occupational

(rather than organizational or professional) careers, the Chicago sociologists aimed to discover these norms even when not expressed in bureaucratic terms. Taking socialization processes and occupational norms together, they stressed the interdependency of careers and the social worlds in which they are embedded. Careers are shaped by (and shape) these worlds' conventions. Formal and informal rules and conventions are critical for social order in modern societies because they relate two time scales. They link institutional patterns developed at the generally stable time scale of society to conscious and unconscious choices in the short time scale of the life of a human career. Careers express the dialectics between generality and uniqueness in social life.

Most pioneer works on careers also paid attention to organizations, as they appeared as the settings in which most careers develop (Glaser 1968). In the 1970s, organizational behaviorists at the Leadership Center of the MIT Sloan School of Management planned to elaborate "organizational careers" as a specific field. This interdisciplinary concept integrating both the individual and organizational side of careers would deal with the subjective and objective aspects of all stages in the work life, whatever the social status or the type of organization. It would help in building optimal careers for individuals and aid organizations by matching individual characteristics and organizational environment. This perspective is based on a functionalist psychological trait factor theory. Individuals are supposed to possess objective personality traits whose measurement could favor their adaptability to given environments (Van Maanen 1977; Shein 1978). Organization theory continues exploring the dual nature of careers, for instance building integrated models predicting actual mobility patterns by accounting for individual-level and organizational-level variables and their interaction (Vardi 1980).

Wilensky's (1961) criticisms of the Chicago concept of career exhibit the path favored by organizational career theory in the 1970s and 1980s. It focused research on particular white-collar managerial, technical, and professional careers. Careers are identified with upward intraorganizational mobility, where the notion of "orderly career" makes sense. It neglects considering people who, for whatever reason, do not experiment with orderly careers and total dedication to their organizational work. Explanatory variables basically link career differentiation to organizational factors. This approach pays no attention to the embeddedness of work careers in a variety of concrete social worlds. The latter are conceptually reduced to an all-embracing environment. For instance, research on female careers remained rare until the 1990s. Women at work were paid no real attention for what they were (for instance, a major source of administrative labor force in firms) or in relation to the career tracks they were (not) offered. Women were mostly considered through the lenses of their conflicting roles as wife, mother, and employee and the implied ways of solving the dilemmas (Crouter 1984; Silberstein 1992).

...TO BOUNDARYLESS CAREERS

The interest in organizational careers theory arose with human resource problems specific to the "new industrial state" analyzed by Galbraith in his 1971 book of that title. Performance was based on the management of the internal labor market in large, stable, multidivisional firms. Employees weigh up intraorganization career opportunities according to the current and likely forthcoming value of incentives they offer. Human resource management thus builds a winner–winner game involving individuals and organizations. Organizational careers offer a life goal to individuals looking for identity, security, and increasing rewards through work. Organizations are protected from qualitative and quantitative manpower shortages by pooling faithful, trustworthy, and competent human resources to fill vacancy chains within their boundaries.

As described by Arthur (1994), the concept of boundaryless careers reciprocally refers to a new principle of management based on individualization of rewards and flexibility of jobs. By associating corporate restructuring and downsizing with subcontracting of expertise outside the core competencies of firms, human resource management opens the way to decreased job security within organizations. Organizations lose interest in managing career tracks, because they have lost the structural stability and job content continuity that made this a solution to human

resource management (Peiperl et al. 2002). The focus of research on intraorganizational issues raised by managerial, professional, and hierarchical careers minimized the gap between subjective and objective career views. The divergence between individual and organizational orientations reopens this gap. Individuals now have to take care of what the organizations had previously secured: their continuous marketability on the objective side of their career and the meaning of work on the subjective side.

The theory of boundaryless careers relates to the transition from industrial to professional rationality in organizations. In *The Rise and Fall of Strategic Planning* (1994), Mintzberg argues that lower-status internal labor markets characterizing "machine bureaucracies" shrink and leave the field to flexible neo-Taylorist organizations. When they do not outsource the labor force to the external labor market, they offer new forms of stabilization based on internal flexibility, experience-built capabilities, and highly horizontal intrafirm mobility contrasting with former upward routes. "Professional bureaucracies" decline in favor of new "adhocratic organizations." Instead of allocating standardized certified skills to tasks by way of rigid organizational norms, adhocratic organizations aim at adjusting technically specific skills to given short-term projects requiring cooperation between rapidly evolving capabilities, largely built by experience outside formal training. Valuable people become those who can work with different persons in various places (Gadrey & Faiz 2002).

Most career research assumed in the 1980s and early 1990s that "organizations cause careers." If organizational careers are no longer feasible, individuals must find new routes to marketability and work meaning. Careers become non-foreseeable, non-linear, non-hierarchical. A new research agenda is needed to deal with the "crisis of careers" by turning the problem the other way round. Careers impact organizations as much as the reverse. It is of little theoretical interest to consider career as a sequence of positions. What makes sense is that employment is a vehicle for individuals to accumulate both explicit and tacit knowledge. For organizations, it offers an opportunity to develop capability, cooperation, and competition (Hall et al. 1996).

In that sense, "careers cause organizations." The more specialized the skills, the more sticky the knowledge, the more critical the recruitment of the right person at the right time and place.

Independent careers, like professions or traditional skilled manual work dedicated to personal services, develop outside organizational boundaries. The external market regulates a large proportion of low-skill jobs. Skilled jobs, on the contrary, come to be largely embedded in internal, intraorganizational labor markets. Career tracks afford personal security and promotion by withdrawing employees from the market. Increasing job complexity, skill requirements, and rapidity of knowledge obsolescence in quality-based performance now lead to a stress on achievement through horizontal interorganizational mobility rather than intraorganizational advancement. Hierarchical ladders are broken (Osterman 1996). Work identities are withdrawn from organizations. The value of highly skilled occupations is defined by external occupational markets of qualities, where individuals compete by networking and building reputation (Granovetter 1973). New, highly skilled occupational markets bring back uncertainty. Bennett proclaimed *The Death of the Organization Man* (1990). Salaried employees leave the organization to become freelance "portfolio workers" with "portable" skills that are hired for short-term jobs (Cohen & Mallon 1999). Continuous acquisition of knowhow maintains skills. Embeddedness in occupational networks maintains reputation. Taken together, they preserve employability. Individuals build their own careers by self-organizing weak environments. From bounded to boundaryless careers, the psychological contract that founds the exchange between employers and employees moves from relational to transactional. Stress becomes an ever more important new occupational pathology, as the new "occupational man" has, so to speak, to "carry society on his shoulders."

THEORY AND THE REAL WORLD

Yet, how well does this theorization grasp the real world? Low-skilled labor markets have profoundly changed through extensive externalization, while high-skilled careers have diversified. At the other end of the status spectrum, labor markets diversify. New occupational labor markets develop in high-skill jobs where careers may look like an odyssey. Individual occupational history is no longer built according to a standard upward organizational pattern but can be described as the complex outcome resulting from the interaction between changes in job supply and changes in individual self-image and life sense-making (Dany et al. 2003). The situation in a way resembles professional labor markets with a low level of institutionalization. Individuals may develop positive identities and rewarding careers without being submitted to the iron rule of upward mobility in organizations. In that sense, interfirm mobility as well as career reorientation could be considered as achievements rather than being stigmatized as sterile instability. This opens the way for an understanding of specific social or gender group behaviors at work.

Many authors are cautious about the subjectivist and postmodernist myth of free actors in boundaryless careers (Dany et al. 2003), as developed for instance by Sennett in *The Corrosion of Character* (1998). They recall that organizations have never totally determined careers and are doubtful as to whether analyses originating mainly in the US make sense in other countries. Scholars insist upon the lack of systematic investigation in assessing the extension of boundaryless careers and challenge individuals' ability to build their own careers. The rise of uncertainty pushes ordinary people to adopt pragmatic behaviors aimed at protecting themselves against hazards rather than encouraging them to venture out on their own. As can be observed by statistical analysis of interfirm mobility of managers (Capelli 1999), far from disappearing, organizational careers remain prestigious and attractive (Valcourt & Tolbert 2003).

SEE ALSO: Class, Status, and Power; Employment Status Changes; Human Resource Management; Labor Markets; Occupational Mobility; Organization Theory; Postmodern Organizations; Stress, Stress Theories

REFERENCES AND SUGGESTED READINGS

Arthur, M. B. (1994) The Boundaryless Career: A New Perspective for Organizational Inquiry. *Journal of Organizational Behavior* 15: 295–306.

Arthur, M. B., Hall, D. T., & Lawrence, B. S. (Eds.) (1989) *Handbook of Career Theory*. Cambridge University Press, Cambridge.

Capelli, P. (Ed.) (1999) *Change at Work*. Oxford University Press, Oxford.

Cohen, L. & Mallon, M. (1999) The Transition from Organizational Employment to Portfolio Working: Perceptions of Boundarylessness. *Work, Employment, and Society* 13(2): 329–52.

Collin, A. & Young, R. A. (2000) *The Future of Careers*. Cambridge University Press, Cambridge.

Crouter, A. C. (1984) Spillover from Family to Work: The Neglected Side of Work–Family Interface. *Human Relations* 37: 425–42.

Dany, F., Mallon, M., & Arthur, M. B. (2003) Careers Across Nations. *International Journal of Human Resource Management* 14(5): special issue.

Doeringer, P. B. & Piore, M. J. (1971) *Internal Labor Markets and Manpower Analysis*. M. E. Sharpe, Lexington.

Gadrey, J. & Faiz, G. (Eds.) (2002) *Productivity, Innovation, and Knowledge in Services: New Economic and Socioeconomic Approaches*. Edward Elgar, Cheltenham.

Glaser, B. G. (1968) *Organizational Careers: A Source Book for Theory*. Aldine, Chicago.

Granovetter, M. S. (1973) The Strength of Weak Ties. *American Journal of Sociology* 78: 1360–80.

Hall, D. T. (1976) *Careers in Organizations*. Goodyear, Santa Monica.

Hall, D. T. et al. (1996) *The Career is Dead, Long Life to the Career: A Relational Approach*. Jossey-Bass, San Francisco.

Hughes, E. C. (1958) *Men and their Work*. Free Press, Glencoe, IL.

Osterman, P. (1996) *Broken Ladders: Managerial Careers in the New Economy*. Oxford University Press, Oxford.

Peiperl, M., Arthur, M. B., Goffee, R., & Anand, N. (Eds.) (2002) *Career Creativity: Exploration in the Remaking of Work*. Oxford University Press, Oxford.

Roe, A. (1956) *The Psychology of Occupations*. Wiley, New York.

Rousseau, D. (1995) *Psychological Contracts in Organizations: Understanding Written and Unwritten Agreements*. Sage, Thousand Oaks, CA.

Sennett, R. (1998) *The Corrosion of Character: The Personal Consequences of Work in the New Capitalism*. W. W. Norton, New York.

Shein, E. (1978) *Career Dynamics: Matching Individual and Organizational Needs*. Addison Wesley, Reading, MA.

Silberstein, L. R. (1992) *Dual-Career Marriage: A System in Transition*. Lawrence Erlbaum, Hillsdale, NJ.

Super, D. (1957) *The Psychology of Careers*. Harper & Row, New York.

Valcourt, M. & Tolbert, P. S. (2003) Gender, Family and Career in the Era of Boundarylessness: Determinants and Effects of Intra- and Interorganizational Mobility. *International Journal of Human Resource Management* 14(5).

Van Maanen, J. (1977) *Organizational Careers: Some New Perspectives*. Wiley, New York.

Vardi, Y. (1980) Organizational Career Mobility: An Integrative Model. *Academy of Management Review* 5(3): 341–55.

Wilensky, H. (1961) Orderly Careers and Social Participation. *Annual Review of Sociology* 26: 521–39.

organizational communication

Dennis K. Mumby

The term organizational communication denotes both a field of study and a set of empirical phenomena. The former is a largely US-based subdiscipline of the field of communication studies (though programs are being established in New Zealand, Australia, Japan, South Korea, Europe, and China); the latter refers broadly to the various and complex communication practices of humans engaged in collective, coordinated, and goal-oriented behavior. In simple terms, organizational communication scholars study the dynamic relationships between communication processes and human organizing. Communication is conceived as foundational to, and constitutive of, organizations, while organizations are viewed as relatively enduring structures that are both medium and outcome of communication processes. While research has focused traditionally on corporate organizational forms, recently the field has broadened its scope to study nonprofit and alternative organizations.

As a field of study, organizational communication differs in its intellectual origins and current disciplinary matrix from cognate fields such as management, organization studies, and organizational/industrial psychology, though it shares a number of research agendas with these fields. Based in the discipline of communication studies, organizational communication scholars draw on both social scientific and humanistic intellectual traditions, and share academic departments with rhetoricians, media scholars, social psychologists, and discourse analysts, to name a few.

HISTORICAL OVERVIEW

The historical emergence of organizational communication reflects its dual allegiance to both the social sciences and humanities, though it did not emerge as an identifiable field of study until the 1950s. Indeed, the term organizational communication did not become the accepted descriptor of the field until the late 1960s. In his history of the early decades of the field, Redding (1985) identifies its multiple and eclectic precursors, including classical rhetoric (particularly the Aristotelian tradition), business speech instruction, Dale Carnegie courses, early industrial psychology, and traditional management theory. However, Redding suggests that it was the "triple alliance" of the military, industry, and academia during and immediately after World War II that laid the foundation for the development of a coherent and programmatic research agenda. This alliance emerged out of a need for wartime college courses in "basic communication skills" for both military personnel and industrial workers. The task of teaching these courses fell mostly to English and speech (the latter the forerunner of communication programs) instructors, hence generating a network of scholars interested in communication in military and industrial settings. The establishment of a "Training within Industry" program by the Manpower War Commission, part of which focused on training supervisors in human relations skills, further solidified the recognition that "communication in industrial settings" was a legitimate focus of research.

Interestingly, Redding (1985) indicates that, for the most part, communication remained a rather peripheral organizational phenomenon for the already established social science disciplines

such as industrial psychology, management, economics, sociology, and industrial relations. As such, they ceded the study of "industrial communication" to nascent programs affiliated with speech (later, communication) departments. Hence, Redding identifies the 1950s as "the decade of crystallization" during which a number of such dedicated programs were established; the "founding" departments included those at Purdue University, Michigan State University, Ohio State University, Northwestern University, and the University of Southern California. Most of these programs adopted the moniker "business and industrial communication" to describe their domain of study, reflecting both a focus on corporate settings and a strong managerial orientation toward research problems (an orientation also inherent in other organization-related fields, of course). Thus, research agendas typically focused on demonstrating causality between communication processes and corporate efficiency and productivity, and covered topic areas such as diffusion of information, upward and downward communication, communication networks, techniques for improving communication skills, and "human relations" issues.

This research agenda remained fairly stable for more than two decades. Indeed, Goldhaber et al.'s (1978) "state of the art" review of the field – called, simply, "Organizational Communication: 1978" – identifies two broad areas of research: "information flow" and "perceptual/attitudinal factors." The former includes the study of communication networks, communication roles within those networks (liaisons, isolates, bridges, etc.), and channel and message features; the latter examines member perceptions of, for example, organizational climate, information adequacy, and job satisfaction. The review reflects the then-dominance in the field of the "systems" model, with its efforts to understand organizations as systems of interdependent practices engaged in information processing. Such research continued to have a distinctly managerial/corporate orientation, with focus on issues such as efficiency, productivity, employee retention, and human relations.

Goldhaber et al.'s review is an interesting historical document insofar as it presents a snapshot of a field that, just a few short years later, would look very different. In the early

1980s the rather circumscribed research agenda that Goldhaber et al. describe gave way to a more ecumenical approach to organizational communication. This broader agenda is rather neatly summarized by Pacanowsky and O'Donnell-Trujillo's (1982: 116) claim that "more things are going on in organizations than getting the job done ... People in organizations also gossip, joke, knife one another, initiate romantic involvements ... talk sports, arrange picnics." Variously identified as the cultural, interpretive, or meaning-centered approach, this research took seriously the idea that everyday "informal" communication practices are the very stuff of organizing. While earlier research rather assumed "organization" as a given and thus studied communication as a variable that occurred *in* organizations, the interpretive perspective removed the "variable" tag, privileging communication as constitutive of organizing.

Probably the most significant impetus behind this "interpretive shift" was a series of conferences in Alta, Utah, beginning in 1981 and devoted to this nascent research agenda. A number of important publications emerged from the first such conference, including (perhaps most significantly) Putnam and Pacanowsky's edited volume, *Communication and Organizations: An Interpretive Approach* (1983), and a special (1982) issue of the *Western Journal of Speech Communication* devoted to interpretive organizational communication research. While by no means unified in their characterizations of this approach, all of the essays in these two publications took seriously the idea that communication created organizations, conceived as complex systems of meaning.

Examined more closely, this turn toward meaning-centered scholarship reveals the emergence of three distinct yet related approaches to the relationship between communication and organizing. First, interpretive studies drew on both the "linguistic turn" in continental philosophy, including hermeneutics and phenomenology, with its "anti-representational" view of language as the medium of experience rather than expression, and Geertz's development in his classic *Interpretation of Cultures* of an interpretive anthropology that situates meaning as a public, semiotic, communicative – rather than cognitive or structural – phenomenon. In Geertz's view, the study of culture involves the

creation of "thick descriptions" that unpack the relationship between everyday communication practices and collective sense-making and meaning construction. Second, critical studies articulated together three research traditions – hermeneutics and phenomenology, Marxism and critical theory, and Freudian theory – to examine the relationships among communication, power, and organization. This scholarship argued that while interpretive research appropriately focused on how organization members collectively constructed systems of meaning, it overlooked the extent to which such meanings were the product of largely hidden, "deep structure" power relations that systematically distorted meaning construction processes to favor dominant power interests. Third, rhetorical studies brought together developments in continental philosophy with classical rhetoric in the Aristotelian tradition to explore processes of persuasion in organizational settings. Here, the focus was on examination of how organizational rhetoric can produce worker identification with organization values, inculcate decision premises in members through enthymematic corporate discourse, and function as a form of unobtrusive control.

Of course, this "interpretive turn" by no means signaled a complete, overnight paradigm revolution in theory development and research in organizational communication. Indeed, Putnam and Cheney's (1985) overview of the field identifies the four principal "research traditions" in the field as the study of communication channels, communication climate, organizational networks, and superior–subordinate communication. At the same time, they designate information-processing, rhetorical studies, culture studies, and power and politics (i.e., critical studies) as "new directions." In this sense, the 1980s and 1990s represented a period of ferment when the newly emergent approaches competed with the long-established research traditions over what counted as legitimate ways of conceptualizing and studying organizational communication. At the center of these debates were questions not only about appropriate methods, theory development, and so forth, but also about the ontological status of organizations as communication phenomena; that is, do they have real, material features independent of human sense-making and communicative practice, or are organizations reducible to systems of socially constructed meanings?

In the last few years this ferment has given way somewhat to a recognition that the study of organizational communication benefits from an exploration of both the connections and tensions between and among theoretical perspectives. As such, organizational communication as a field of study has developed an interdisciplinary identity that is home to diverse theoretical perspectives and epistemological assumptions, including (post)positivism, realism, interpretivism, rhetoric, critical theory, postmodernism and poststructuralism, feminism, and postcolonialism. In this sense, organizational communication at the beginning of the twenty-first century can be characterized as a multi-perspective field that is ecumenical in its approach to methods, theories, research domains, and philosophical assumptions. The rather fractured, polarized debates of the 1980s and 1990s about "paradigm incommensurability" have developed into, if not paradigm consensus (a condition that no one really considers desirable), a recognition that different epistemologies represent different resources upon which scholars can draw to address the relationship between communication and organization (Corman & Poole 2000).

CURRENT THEORIES, CONSTRUCTS, AND RESEARCH AGENDAS

Taylor et al.'s (2001) overview of organizational communication research provides some sense of the major transformations that the field has undergone in the last 25 years or so. Indeed, in juxtaposing Goldhaber et al. and Taylor et al.'s reviews, it is difficult to believe that the respective authors are – at least ostensibly – addressing the same field of study. Of course, in many respects they are not. If Thomas Kuhn is correct in asserting that, post-paradigm revolution, scholars are not just looking through a new lens but viewing a transformed world, then the field of organizational communication is the product of its own Copernican revolution. A brief enumeration of the theories and topics addressed in Taylor et al.'s review provides some sense of the scope and diversity of the field's current research agenda. Their review includes discussion of interpretivism and its various iterations

(rhetoric, critical theory, feminism, postmodernism), ethnography, structuration theory, activity theory, artificial intelligence, the symbolic–material dialectic, and diversity in organizations. Emergent topics they identify include expanding our notion of what counts as an organizational form to include global, network, virtual, nonprofits, cooperatives, etc.; relationships among technology, organizations, and society; group-based structures (often mediated by communication technology); new forms of leadership; organizational change; new iterations of network research; the relationship between work and non-work domains; organizational ethics; and the connection between local and global organizational forms.

Of course, there are important continuities between organizational communication circa 1978 and 2006. In general, while it no longer enjoys the hegemony it once did, there is still a healthy and vibrant (post)positivist research tradition in organizational communication that both captures the complex dynamics of communication practices and situates that complexity within a concern for the ongoing stability and reproducibility of organizations as social structures. For example, the concern with organizations as social structures is still evidenced in the systems approach to organizing, with its focus on interdependence and collective, goal-oriented behavior; in this regard, network research is still a mainstay of the field. However, the progeny of 1960s and 1970s network research bears only passing resemblance to its forebears, with its current investigation of semantic and relational networks, and employment of chaos theory and principles of self-organizing systems. Furthermore, Monge's (1982) critique of the disjuncture between the process orientation of systems theory and the rather static, reductive empirical methods used to study organizations has led to efforts to develop analytic techniques, including computational analysis, that better capture the dynamic character of these systems features (Monge & Contractor 2003). In addition, leadership research still enjoys considerable currency, though again scholarly focus has shifted from efforts to identify leadership as an individual trait, style, etc., toward more discursively oriented models that see leadership as a communicative, interaction-based phenomenon that is more widely distributed in organizational life.

One interesting measure of both continuity and discontinuity across decades involves a comparison of the first (1987) and second (2001) editions of *The Handbook of Organizational Communication*. In both editions, chapters are allocated to leadership; information technology and information processing; organizational culture; communication networks; organizational structure; organizational entry, assimilation and exit; decision-making; and power and politics. Chapters new to the 2001 edition are discourse analysis; quantitative methods; qualitative methods; globalization; organizational learning; communication competence; organizational identity; new media; and participation. One might claim, then, that there is every bit as much continuity as change over the last 20 years of theory development and research. It is also true, however, that while research domains evince much continuity, approaches to these domains have shifted a good deal, especially given developments in the various meaning-based approaches to organizational communication. Clearly, in a short space it is not possible to provide a complete overview of the current and diverse state of organizational communication research. However, a few key issues, trends, and theoretical developments are worth noting.

First, from a disciplinary perspective, there is a distinct and ongoing effort to constitute the field as simultaneously unique in its approach to organizing and interdisciplinary, with connections to management, organizational sociology, industrial psychology, and so forth. For example, in an effort to develop a distinctly communication-based approach to organizing, Deetz (1996) developed a critique of Burrell and Morgan's classic book *Sociological Paradigms and Organizational Analysis* (1979) and its widely adopted metatheoretical framework. He argued that while Burrell and Morgan provided a useful way of making sense of the field of organizational sociology, they ultimately led organizational communication scholars down a conceptual cul-de-sac. Deetz claimed that their characterization of all sociological paradigms as either subjective or objective in their approach to knowledge generation had the dual – and contradictory – effect of (a) providing a space for critical-interpretive scholars to argue for the legitimacy of their approach, and (b) preserving the "subjective"/"objective" split that ensured the continued hegemony of variable-analytic ("objective") research and the "othering" of critical-interpretive ("subjective") studies. A communication-based approach, Deetz suggested, refuses the subject–object dichotomy inherent in Burrell and Morgan's model, and instead positions communication as the constitutive process through which claims for subjectivity or objectivity even become possible. As such, the study of organizations is less about the relative merits of "subjective" and "objective" epistemologies, methodologies, and so forth, and more about understanding how different perspectives discursively construct the phenomenon being studied. For example, according to Deetz, interpretive studies discursively construct social actors and their own discourse as central to knowledge formation, while normative/social science research views the a priori development and subsequent testing of concepts through study of social actors' behavior as central to the knowledge construction process.

Deetz's efforts to develop a communication-based framework for making sense of organizational communication studies is one among several efforts to frame organizational communication scholarship from within the field itself, rather than relying on concepts, theories, and perspectives developed in cognate disciplines such as psychology, sociology, and management. While Redding (1985) is certainly correct that other fields largely ceded the study of "communication in organizations" to researchers in the field of communication, nevertheless organizational communication researchers have had a hard time developing a body of research that is not derivative of perspectives long established in those other fields. However, current research has shifted significantly toward communication analyses of organizational phenomena, rather than, say, psychologically or sociologically based analyses of "communication in organizations." A number of those efforts are addressed below.

Second, advances in communication technology (CT) in the last 20 years or so have profoundly influenced how organization members engage in information processing and decision-making. Organizational communication scholars have developed a significant body of scholarship that addresses these effects, focusing on how CT has reconfigured the organizing process in important ways. While early research tended to be instrumental in its approach, examining CT as "hardware" that users appropriated as an aid to information processing, more recent scholarship has adopted a more meaning-centered approach, examining the social construction of CT by organization members. Thus, rather than asking, "How is CT used by organization members?" the defining question for organizational communication researchers has been, "What does CT *mean* for organization members?" For example, Poole, DeSanctis, and colleagues have developed adaptive structuration theory (drawing on Anthony Giddens's structuration theory) to study the interaction between group decision-making and CT. Their development and study of group decision support systems – the use of CT to improve participation in collective decision-making – illustrates how, over time, groups adapt CT to their own particular use, constructing it not as determining group decisions, but rather as medium and outcome of the emergent group decision-making dynamic. In this sense, CT is socially constructed as a set of rules and resources that both enables and constrains decision-making processes. Communication scholars therefore resist a determinist view of either the features or social uses of technologies. Studies of CT have also spawned a large body of research on new modes of organizing, including the emergence of online communities, and virtual worlds and identities (through online gaming, role-playing, blogging, etc.). In related fashion, researchers have also examined how advances in CT have challenged basic ideas of organizations as having distinct "internal" and "external" communication processes. For example, research on telecommuting has made problematic traditional conceptions of employee identification with and socialization into organizations. In addition, research on the linkages between "internal" practices of communication and patterns in advertising, public relations, and marketing has played an important role in moving the field beyond the "container" metaphor of organization.

Third, the study of organizations as communicative sites of power and politics has become a ubiquitous feature of the field. While early post-interpretive turn research drew largely on the tradition of Marxism and Frankfurt School critical theory, the last 15 years has witnessed a broadening of perspectives to include feminist, poststructuralist, and postmodern thought. Research motivated by the critical tradition has focused largely on the connections among communication, ideology, and power, exploring how the process of organizing is inflected with deep-structure relations of power that are obscured in the very process of (ideological) meaning construction. In this context, critical organizational communication scholars have explored a variety of discursive phenomena such as stories, metaphors, everyday talk, rituals, and so forth, to examine how particular interests and power relations are ideologically secured, contradictions hidden, and certain social realities reified. A related research agenda takes up philosopher Jürgen Habermas's critical project, addressing the ways that the privileging of technical forms of organizational rationality produce systematically distorted communication and discursive closure ("corporate colonization") that limit possibilities for alternative ways of thinking about, experiencing, and valuing the organizing process. Two related outcomes of this work are an ongoing concern with theorizing models of organizational democracy, and a focus on corporate ethics and social responsibility (a focus that has intensified in the wake of publicity surrounding the exposure of corporate malfeasance).

In recent years critical organization studies has come under increasing criticism and scrutiny for both its rather gender-blind approach to power and politics and for its rather undifferentiated conception of the everyday dynamics of organizational power. Since the early 1990s, then, a number of scholars have actively taken up a variety of feminist perspectives to explore organizational communication as a "gendered" practice. While it is not possible here to differentiate among these feminisms, many share a concern with viewing gender as a constitutive feature of organizing; examining everyday workplace struggles as a gendered process; exploring the mundane production of masculine and feminine workplace identities; examining hegemonic masculinity and patriarchy as endemic features of organizational life; and deconstructing the gendered features of mainstream organizational theory. Postmodern and poststructuralist analytics have provided a similar impetus in providing alternative readings of organizational power. Motivated in particular by the work of Michel Foucault, communication researchers have examined organizations as sites of disciplinary practice that employ various technologies of power to produce identities, docile bodies, and normalized discourses. The shift is thus away from a view of power as repressive, negative, and inimical to emancipation and social transformation, and toward one in which power and knowledge intersect to create the very possibility of particular identities, modes of truth, ways of speaking, and so forth.

More recently, the intersection of feminist and poststructuralist thought has drawn attention to organizations as gendered sites of both disciplinary practice and everyday struggles of resistance. While early critical research tended toward rather non-dialectical accounts of organizational power as monolithic and inescapable, current research has shifted toward exploration of the fissures, gaps, and contradictions of daily organizing that belie the apparent seamlessness of managerial control efforts. Here, discourse and all forms of symbolic action are conceived as latent or actual resources that employees strategically utilize in carving out spaces of resistance, hence limiting the reach of corporate colonization. A key element of this research, then, is the "return of the subject"; that is, an effort to theorize more adequately the role of agency – both individual and collective – in mediating the effects of corporate control processes. Much of this research has adopted a poststructuralist feminist perspective, examining the dialectical relationship between the discursive production of gendered organizational subjects, or identities, and the ways that subjects subversively appropriate these same discourses in order to construct resistant and alternative organizational realities.

Fourth, and related, organizational communication scholars have begun to treat seriously the issue of organizational diversity, particularly as it relates to matters of "voice." For the most part, this effort has moved beyond the question of "managing diversity" – an approach that some scholars have critiqued as a primarily management-defined effort to "deal" with the "problem" of diversity in the workplace. In contrast, organizational communication scholars have examined diversity in terms of the ways in which issues of gender, race, class, and sexuality

are organized into or out of both organizational theory and research and daily organizing processes. For example, scholars have explored the ways that research on organizational socialization implicitly organizes difference out of the socialization process. Researchers have also begun to examine the body and sexuality as both a target of organizational discipline and a locus for transgression and resistance. Extended further, the issue of voice relates also to what "counts" as appropriate organizations to study. Increasingly, organizational communication scholars are expanding their domains of study to address organizing in alternative contexts and structures, including nonprofits, collectives, NGOs, and so forth. In this context, researchers are interested in studying communication as both medium and outcome of issues such as alternative forms of decision-making, organizational ethics, and systems of empowerment. In general, the focus on issues of voice has enabled organizational communication scholars to move beyond rather narrow, managerialist definitions of organizational life.

Fifth, organizational communication scholars have contributed to the ongoing, interdisciplinary debate over the relationship between discourse and organizations. One of the consequences of this scholarship has been to challenge the stability of the very idea of "organization." While for decades scholars have presumed the existence of "the organization," focusing research efforts on communication "within" this stable structure, one current focus lies in exploring the precarious, contingent features of organizing as a moment-to-moment process shot through with ambiguity. In particular, the "Montreal School" of Jim Taylor and his colleagues have articulated together a number of different theoretical perspectives, including ordinary language philosophy (Austin, Searle, Greimas), the actor-network theory of Bruno Latour, and complexity theory, as a means of explaining organizing as a dialectic of conversation and text that implicates social actors in a continuous but never resolvable search for closure and stability. Much of this work intersects with efforts in both management and organization studies to grapple with the discourse–material dialectic; that is, what are the implications of characterizing organizations as purely contingent, discursive constructions on the one hand, or as having stable, material, "extra-discursive" features on the other hand? For example, does the "organization as discourse" perspective underplay the role and impact of economic conditions on organizational life? On the other hand, if we view organizations as "extra-discursive," do we obscure the ways in which even the most apparently "material" features of organizing (e.g., economic conditions) are made sense of and constructed as meaningful through discourse?

Sixth, organizational communication scholars have turned to examinations of the relationship between globalization and organizing. Not only is the very notion of "organization" being brought under scrutiny, but researchers are also challenging the view of the organization as a fixed, physical site that one "enters" and "exits." This rather parochial conception is giving way to a view of organizing as recursively related to processes of globalization. Thus, issues such as the compression of space and time, the fragmentation of identities, increased levels of worker mobility, shifts toward outsourcing and use of temporary employees, the disintegration of local communities, effects of branding, the homogenization of cultures, and so forth, are being studied increasingly in terms of a dialectic between local, micro-level communication processes and global, macro-level movements of information, people, money, etc. This research further redirects our attention to organizations as nodal points of shifting, temporarily stable discursive practices that are increasingly susceptible to the forces of globalization and that, in turn, shape the globalization process. As such, organizational communication scholars increasingly are eschewing treating organizations as if they are self-contained, hermetically sealed entities, and instead contextualizing analyses within larger, macro-level social, political, and economic processes.

The above discussion necessarily paints a picture of the field of organizational communication with a very broad brush. Theoretical nuances are glossed, lines of inquiry are collapsed together, and some research perspectives are overlooked. These limitations notwithstanding, the primary goal of this overview has been to provide a broad sense of the important questions, assumptions, and perspectives that drive research in the field.

FUTURE DIRECTIONS

There is a strong sense in which the future of organizational communication research inheres in the present. Given the shift toward epistemological plurality in the last few years, it seems clear that the seeds of future research agendas are already sown and budding. First, while organizational communication studies has always been strongly interdisciplinary, the reciprocal nature of the ties to other fields – sometimes tenuous – appears to be strengthening. In particular, its connections to both management and organization studies have become particularly dynamic. For example, there is a great deal of cross-pollination between critical scholars in organizational communication and in critical management studies, particularly between those investigating the relations among power, discourse, and organizing. Furthermore, the organizational communication and information systems division of the Academy of Management brings together both communication and management scholars examining CT, communication networks, virtual organizing, and so forth. Such collaborative efforts can only serve to promote interdisciplinary research and the sharing of perspectives, resources, and ideas.

Second, drawing on insights from feminism and poststructuralism, organizational communication researchers will continue to destabilize the notion that organizations are neutral with regard to issues of race, class, gender, and sexuality. Scholars are becoming increasingly sensitized to the idea that organizations are raced, sexed, classed, and gendered institutions that are both medium and outcome of member subjectivities. In this sense, focus will continue on the myriad ways in which difference is organized, normalized, works transgressively, and so forth. From a communication perspective, researchers explore identities as performed and embodied through various symbolic and discursive practices.

Third, research on organizational communication will increasingly turn its efforts to capturing the in situ, moment-to-moment, everyday communication practices of organization members. For much of its history the field of organizational communication has been content to rely on paper and pencil, self-report instruments that, while producing data susceptible to careful measurement, have largely overlooked the complexities, contradictions, and ambiguities of actual organizational behavior. While qualitative research methods are typically associated with the study of real-time human organizing, quantitative researchers are also developing tools that better capture the ongoing, processual features of organizational life.

Fourth, the shift toward viewing organizations as changing, dynamic, permeable sites of discourse will continue apace. This has several implications for future research, in addition to the ones addressed above. For example, it suggests a need to further explore the relationship between work and other domains, such as home and the wider community. As the separation between corporations and these other realms becomes increasingly fragile, it is important to understand the effects of such shifts on individual identities, conceptions of democracy, what counts as private or public, definitions of both work and leisure, and so forth. If organizations are simultaneously *both* more pervasive in their effects on human community *and* less easily identifiable as empirical phenomena with clear boundaries, then it is increasingly important that the field of organizational communication develop perspectives and research agendas that can adequately investigate these effects.

Fifth, and related, the study of alternative forms of organizing will continue apace. This will involve not only the study of non-corporate organizations, but also the exploration of organizing processes where there is no identifiable organizational "site." As mentioned earlier, there is a vibrant and growing body of research that examines virtual organizing; organizational communication scholars are well-placed to study how the development of such organizing structures shapes human identity, enables the development of new discursive practices, and influences participation in public discourse and decision-making.

In sum, organizational communication is, by most standards, a young field that has only just passed its 50th birthday. While it has sometimes struggled to establish an independent identity, it has developed into a vibrant, dynamic research community that has added much to our understanding of the organizational form – a social structure that has, arguably, been the defining institution of modernity over the last 100 years or so.

SEE ALSO: Critical Theory/Frankfurt School; Culture; Foucault, Michel; Hermeneutics; Marxism and Sociology; Organization Theory; Positivism; Postmodernism; System Theories

REFERENCES AND SUGGESTED READINGS

Buzzanell, P. (Ed.) (2000) *Rethinking Organizational and Managerial Communication from Feminist Perspectives*. Sage, Thousand Oaks, CA.

Cheney, G. (1991) *Rhetoric in an Organizational Society: Managing Multiple Identities*. University of South Carolina Press, Columbia.

Corman, S. R. & Poole, M. S. (Eds.) (2000) *Perspectives on Organizational Communication: Finding Common Ground*. Guilford Press, New York.

Deetz, S. (1992) *Democracy in an Age of Corporate Colonization: Developments in Communication and the Politics of Everyday Life*. State University of New York Press, Albany.

Deetz, S. (1996) Describing Differences in Approaches to Organization Science: Rethinking Burrell and Morgan and their Legacy. *Organization Science* 7: 191–207.

Fairhurst, G. & Putnam, L. (2004) Organizations as Discursive Constructions. *Communication Theory* 14: 5–26.

Goldhaber, G. M., Yates, M. P., Porter, D. P., & Lesniak, R. (1978) Organizational Communication: 1978. *Human Communication Research* 5(1): 76–96.

Grant, D., Hardy, C., Oswick, C., Phillips, N., & Putnam, L. (Eds.) (2004) *The Handbook of Organizational Discourse*. Sage, Thousand Oaks, CA.

Jablin, F. & Putnam, L. (2001) *The New Handbook of Organizational Communication: Advances in Theory, Research, and Methods*. Sage, Thousand Oaks, CA.

Jablin, F., Putnam, L., Roberts, K., & Porter, L. (1987) *The Handbook of Organizational Communication: An Interdisciplinary Perspective*. Sage, Newbury Park, CA.

Monge, P. R. (1982) Systems Theory and Research in the Study of Organizational Communication: The Correspondence Problem. *Human Communication Research* 8: 245–61.

Monge, P. R. & Contractor, N. (2003) *Theories of Communication Networks*. Oxford University Press, New York.

Mumby, D. K. & Stohl, C. (1996) Disciplining Organizational Communication Studies. *Management Communication Quarterly* 10: 50–72.

Pacanowsky, M. & O'Donnell-Trujillo, N. (1982) Communication and Organizational Cultures. *Western Journal of Speech Communication* 46: 115–30.

Poole, M. S. & DeSanctis, G. (1991) Understanding the Use of Group Decision Support Systems: The Theory of Adaptive Structuration. In: Fulk, J. & Steinfeld, C. (Eds.), *Oranizations and Communication Technology.* Sage, Newbury Park, CA, pp. 173–93.

Putnam, L. L. & Cheney, G. (1985) Organizational Communication: Historical Development and Future Directions. In: Benson, T. W. (Ed.), *Speech Communication in the 20th Century.* Southern Illinois University Press, Carbondale.

Redding, W. C. (1985) Stumbling Toward Identity: The Emergence of Organizational Communication as a Field of Study. In: McPhee, R. D. & Tompkins, P. K. (Eds.), *Organizational Communication: Traditional Themes and New Directions.* Sage, Beverly Hills, CA, pp. 15–54.

Stohl, C. (2004) Globalization Theory. In: May, S. & Mumby, D. K. (Eds.), *Engaging Organizational Communication Theory and Research: Multiple Perspectives.* Sage, Thousand Oaks, CA, pp. 223–61.

Taylor, J. R., Cooren, F., Giroux, N., & Robichaud, D. (1996) The Communicational Basis of Organization: Between the Conversation and the Text. *Communication Theory* 6: 1–39.

Taylor, J. R., Flanagin, A. J., Cheney, G., & Seibold, D. R. (2001) Organizational Communication Research: Key Moments, Central Concerns, and Future Challenges. In: Gudykunst, W. (Ed.), *Communication Yearbook 24.* Sage, Thousand Oaks, CA, pp. 99–137.

organizational contingencies

Graeme Currie and Olga Suhomlinova

Organizational contingencies are factors that moderate the effect of organizational characteristics on organizational performance. Whether a particular level of organizational characteristic would lead to high performance depends on the level of the contingency factor. If there is a fit between the level of contingency and the level of organizational characteristic, then,

other things being equal, superior performance results; if there is a misfit, performance suffers.

An organizational contingency is thus best understood as one of the variables in a three-variable relationship, the other two variables being an organizational characteristic and organizational performance. Each of these variables has a fairly broad meaning:

1 Organizational contingencies include two general groups of factors: those internal to the organization, such as organizational size, technology, and strategy, and those external to it, covered by the umbrella term "organizational environment."
2 Organizational characteristics most frequently imply dimensions of organizational structure (e.g., formalization, centralization) and an overall structural type (e.g., bureaucratic structure) or structural design alternative (e.g., divisional structure).
3 Organizational performance covers a wide range of measures, including standard financial measures, such as efficiency and profitability, and various indicators of effectiveness, such as rate of innovation and stakeholder satisfaction.

The concept of organizational contingency is the cornerstone of the contingency theory paradigm in organization studies. The contingency theory paradigm covers a plethora of contingency theories that focus on different organizational characteristics and various organizational contingencies. The earliest and arguably most developed stream within this paradigm focuses on those contingencies that influence organizational structure and is therefore usually referred to as *structural contingency theory.* Contingency theories have also spread to other areas of organization studies, including strategy and leadership.

The contingency approach to organizational structure was pioneered by Burns and Stalker (1961), followed closely by Woodward (1965) and Lawrence and Lorsch (1967) amongst others. The main organizational contingencies associated with organizational structure are organizational size, strategy, technology, and environment. Each of these contingencies is linked to a particular typology of organizational structures that highlights a specific set of the salient characteristics of organizational structure.

Organizational size is linked to a typology of organizational structures that distinguishes between simple structure (centralized, low on functional specialization and formalization) and bureaucratic structure (decentralized, high on functional specialization and formalization) (Blau 1970). Small organizations perform better with a simple, non-bureaucratic structure; but, beyond a certain size, a greater degree of bureaucratization is positively correlated with better performance (Child 1988).

Organizational strategy is linked to a typology of organizational structures based on the principle of departmental grouping. This typology distinguishes between functional structure, or U (unitary) form, in which activities are grouped by task (e.g., marketing, finance), and divisional, or M (multidivisional) form, in which activities are grouped by output (e.g., product 1, product 2). Functional structure is said to be better suited to a strategy oriented on the production of a single product line or service, or an undiversified strategy. Divisional structure is said to be better suited to a strategy of diversification. The dictum "Structure follows strategy" refers specifically to the historical shift in the strategy and structure of large firms, first documented in the development of American industry (Chandler 1962). This shift involved the transition in strategy from single to multiple product lines and the concomitant structural innovation, the introduction of divisional structure, which made it possible to overcome the inefficiencies of functional structure (in particular, decision overload at the top of the organizational hierarchy).

Technology is linked to a typology of organizational structures that distinguishes between mechanistic structure and organic structure. In mechanistic structure, tasks are broken down into specialized, separate parts and are rigidly defined; there is a strict hierarchy of authority and control, and there are many rules; knowledge and control of tasks are centralized at the top of the organization; communication is vertical. In organic structure, employees contribute to the common task of the department; tasks are adjusted and redefined through employee teamwork; there is less hierarchy of authority and control, and there are few rules; knowledge and control tasks are located anywhere in the organization; communication is horizontal (Burns & Stalker 1961). Based on the degree of technological complexity, production processes have been subdivided into unit production (production of simple units to order or of small batches), mass production (production of large batches on an assembly line), and process production (continuous flow production of liquids, gases, or solid shapes). Mechanistic structure is said to be better suited for mass production, while organic structure is better suited for unit and process production (Woodward 1965).

Organizational environment is linked to the two sets of typologies: the mechanistic–organic typology and the typology based on the degree of differentiation and integration. Both typologies pertain to one important characteristic of the environment – environmental uncertainty. The first, mechanistic–organic typology, has been already described above. It is sufficient, then, to state here that mechanistic structure is said to be better suited to relatively stable and certain environments, while organic structure is said to be better suited to volatile and uncertain environments (Burns & Stalker 1961). The second typology emphasizes two organizational characteristics: (1) differentiation, i.e., differences in cognitive and emotional orientations among managers in different organizational departments, and the difference in formal structure among these departments, and (2) integration, or the quality of collaboration between departments. It has been noted that organizations that perform well in uncertain environments have high levels of both differentiation and integration; in contrast, organizations that perform well in less uncertain environments have lower levels of differentiation and integration (Lawrence & Lorsch 1967).

Theories focusing on leadership present the most elaborate models of contingency outside structural contingency theory. The essence of a contingency approach to leadership is that leaders are most effective when they make their behavior contingent upon situational factors, such as group member characteristics. For example, a manager who supervises competent employees might be able to practice consensus readily. Fiedler's (1967) theory of leadership is the most widely cited. Its key proposition is that leaders should adopt a more task-oriented style, if the situation is one of high or low control for the leader, but that when a leader has moderate control, a relationship-oriented style works best. In practical terms, the theory suggests that leaders can improve their situational control by modifying leader–member relations, task structure, and position power.

Another example of the contingency approach outside structural contingency theory is Mintzberg's (1990) decision-making framework for dealing with environmental uncertainty. The framework suggests that a rational model of strategy should be followed in a relatively certain environment, while under more complex environmental conditions the decision-maker may need to adopt a more emergent approach to strategy. The practical implication is that the decision-maker should engage other members of the organization, allowing strategy to emerge from existing structures and processes in the context of continuous interaction.

Contingency theory of ownership represents an example of the more recent extensions of the contingency approach to other areas of organization studies. Contingency theory of ownership suggests that in the "opaque" industries – industries which have highly specific capital investments and where the monitoring of managers thus requires special expertise and information, which most shareholders are unlikely to possess (e.g., microprocessors, pharmaceuticals) – large block owner-managers may be more effective. Alternatively, in the more "transparent" industries – industries characterized by less firm-specific capital and thus by relatively simpler monitoring requirements (e.g., textiles, steel) – large block outsider owners may be more effective (Kang & Sorensen 1999).

To return to the general discussion of organizational contingencies, the contingency paradigm belongs to a group of organization theories espousing an adaptationist view of organizations (which also includes, among others, resource dependence theory, transaction cost economics, and neo-institutional organizational sociology). This view holds that organizations are capable of changing their structures, procedures, and practices in such a way as to adapt their characteristics to the requirements and pressures of their environment and to improve thereby their performance and/or survival chances. Contingency approach suggests that organizational

change can be described by the following model of "structural adaptation to regain fit" (SARFIT) (Donaldson 1987): an organization initially in fit changes its contingency and thereby moves into misfit and suffers declining performance. This causes adoption of a new structure so that fit is regained and performance restored. Hence, the cycle of adaptation: "fit → contingency change → misfit → structural adaptation → new fit."

To put research on organizational contingencies into a historical perspective, the contingency theory paradigm emerged in the early 1960s as a counterpoint to classical management theory. The main quest of classical management theory was to find the best organizational structure. In contrast, contingency theory declared that there was no one best structure that would fit any organization under any circumstances and focused instead on specifying what structure would be more appropriate for a particular set of conditions. The emergence of contingency theory can be regarded as the beginning of modern organizational analysis as we know it now.

Research on contingencies, particularly structural contingencies, flourished during the 1970s and 1980s. Since then, its popularity within organization theory has declined. New theories, such as resource dependence (Pfeffer & Salancik 1978), neo-institutionalism (Powell & DiMaggio 1991), and organizational ecology (Hannan & Freeman 1989), have subsumed or superseded contingency theory. The general contingency principle – that different organizational structures, procedures, and practices are suitable to different environmental conditions – has, however, permeated practically all modern organization theories in some shape or form. Contingency theory has also spread to other disciplines such as public administration, information technology, marketing, and accounting, which continue to draw upon and to develop its principles. Contingency theory (unlike many more recent organizational theories) has also found its way into most of the introductory textbooks on organizational behavior, organizational theory, and organizational design. The theory's intuitive appeal, ease of representation, and reasonably unequivocal managerial implications all contributed to this wide acceptance. The concept and the theory, however, are far from being common sense and common knowledge, as research on managers suggests (Priem & Rosenstein 2000).

Despite its favorable status, contingency theory is continually being called into question because of its apparent inability to resolve persistent theoretical and empirical problems. One of the main lines of critique is captured by the concept of "equifinality": even if the contingencies facing the organization are the same, the final state or performance can be achieved through many different organizational structures (all roads may lead to Rome) (Pennings 1987). The possibility of multiple, equally effective designs undermines the predictive value of the contingency approach (Galunic & Eisenhardt 1994). Another line of critique concerns managerial preferences: managers may vary in their response to contingency according to their perceptions, interests, and power. They may prefer to minimize misfit rather than to maximize fit (Drazin & Van de Ven 1985). Thus, there is a degree of "strategic choice" in organizational structuring (Child 1972), particularly apparent in the case of top managers.

Given criticisms of contingency theory, there is a need for more research, particularly in the area of structural contingency theory. One may want to consider, for instance, how classical contingency arguments hold under more dynamic conditions that characterize contemporary organizations. Contingency studies might be designed to permit comparative evaluation of several forms of fit. Relatedly, one might attempt to delineate the boundaries of proactive behaviors possible at the organizational and individual manager level. Other areas of contingency theory, such as those in leadership or strategy, may also benefit from a more explicit examination of fit in their area.

SEE ALSO: Institutional Theory, New; Leadership; Organization Theory; Organizations as Coercive Institutions; Technological Innovation

REFERENCES AND SUGGESTED READINGS

Blau, P. M. (1970) A Formal Theory of Differentiation in Organizations. *American Sociological Review* 35(2): 201–18.

Burns, T. & Stalker, G. M. (1961) *The Management of Innovation*. Tavistock, London.

Chandler, A. D., Jr. (1962) *Strategy and Structure: Chapters in the History of the American Industrial Enterprise*. MIT Press, Cambridge, MA.

Child, J. (1972) Organization Structure and Strategies of Control: A Replication of the Aston Study. *Administrative Science Quarterly* 17: 163–77.

Child, J. (1988) *Organization: A Guide to Problems and Practice*, 2nd edn. Paul Chapman, London.

Donaldson, L. (1987) Strategy and Structural Adjustment to Regain Fit and Performance: In Defense of Contingency Theory. *Journal of Management Studies* 24: 1–24.

Donaldson, L. (2001) *The Contingency Theory of Organizations*. Sage, Thousand Oaks, CA.

Drazin, R. & Van de Ven, A. (1985) Alternative Forms of Fit in Contingency Theory. *Administrative Science Quarterly* 30: 514–39.

Fiedler, F. E. (1967) *A Theory of Leadership Effectiveness*. New York, McGraw-Hill.

Galunic, D. C. & Eisenhardt, K. M. (1994) Renewing the Strategy–Structure–Performance Paradigm. In: Cummings, L. L. & Staw, B. M. (Eds.), *Research in Organizational Behavior*, Vol. 16. JAI Press, Greenwich, CT, pp. 215–55.

Hannan, M. T. & Freeman, J. (1989) *Organization Ecology*. Harvard University Press, Cambridge, MA.

Kang, D. L. & Sorensen, A. B. (1999) Ownership Organization and Firm Performance. *Annual Review of Sociology* 25: 121–44.

Lawrence, P. R. & Lorsch, J. W. (1967) *Organization and Environment: Management Differentiation and Integration*. Harvard Business School Press, Boston.

Mintzberg, H. (1990) The Design School: Reconsidering the Basic Premises of Strategic Management. *Strategic Management Journal* 11: 171–95.

Pennings, J. (1975) The Relevance of Structural-Contingency Model for Organizational Effectiveness. *Administrative Science Quarterly* 20: 393–410.

Pennings, J. M. (1987) Structural Contingency Theory: A Multivariate Test. *Organization Studies* 8(3): 223–40.

Pfeffer, J. & Salancik, G. R. (1978) *The External Control of Organizations: A Resource Dependence Perspective*. Harper & Row, New York.

Powell, W. W. & DiMaggio, P. J. (1991) *The New Institutionalism in Organizational Analysis*. University of Chicago Press, Chicago.

Priem, R. L. & Rosenstein, J. (2000) Is Organization Theory Obvious to Practitioners? A Test of One Established Theory. *Organization Science* 11(5): 509–21.

Woodward, J. (1965) *Industrial Organization: Theory and Practice*. Oxford University Press, Oxford.

organizational deviance

David O. Friedrichs

Deviance has most typically been viewed in individualistic terms. But some of the most significant and consequential deviance and crime is carried out on behalf of organizations, and through the resources that only organizations are able to provide. Accordingly, in the most common invocation of the term organizational deviance, the organization is conceived of as the "actor" that carries out deviant and criminal activities (Bamberger & Sonnenstuhl 1998). Since organizational deviance is inherently social, and collective, it should be of special interest to students of sociology. It has always been a fundamental tenet of sociology that a social entity is more than simply the sum of its individual participants and members.

The concept of organizational deviance or crime has sometimes been used interchangeably or confused with the more familiar concept of organized crime. Organizational deviance is carried out in the context of an organization with a legal and legitimate purpose; organized crime has referred to organizations directly dedicated to the commission of illegal activity. However, corporate crime from the outset has sometimes been characterized as a form of organized crime, and has been compared to more traditional (i.e., Mafioso-type, or syndicated) forms of organized crime. And traditional syndicated crime operations have increasingly infiltrated and merged with legitimate business entities.

The immense growth in the number of organizations and their significance within society has been an especially striking development of the past century or so. In *The Asymmetric Society* (1982), James S. Coleman argued that corporate actors are playing an increasing role in our society while natural actors are playing a decreasing role. Accordingly, the activities of organizations have assumed great importance in the contemporary era. There is a long history of according organizations a legal status parallel to that of natural persons, that is as "juridic subjects," accountable to legal sanctions. In the late nineteenth century, lawyers for American corporations were especially aggressive in demanding that due process rights guaranteed to all American citizens by the 14th Amendment be applied to corporations as well.

Regulatory and administrative agencies play an especially large role in societal efforts to control organizational deviance. These agencies may themselves engage in some forms of deviance or rule breaking. Organizations as organizations have been charged with crimes, have been indicted, tried, and convicted, and have been "punished" *as* organizations. Sentencing guidelines have been developed for organizations as well as for natural persons. Of course, organizations cannot be punished in all the same ways as natural persons can be punished. Corporations cannot be put into prison, or executed. The imposition of fines, which can be applied to both organizations and natural persons, has been the most common form of sanctioning applied to corporations. But corporations have also been put on probation, required to perform services, and "executed" in the sense that their charters have been revoked.

Organizations may deviate from societal norms without necessarily violating the criminal law (Vaughan 1999); they may violate the criminal law without necessarily violating prevailing societal norms; they may deviate from regulatory and administrative agency rules that may or may not be at odds with criminal law and societal norms; they may deviate from the norms subscribed to by peer organizations, but not necessarily those incorporated in the formal law or held by the society as a whole.

With respect to the last of these possibilities, for example, a corporation may produce an inferior quality of goods that are viewed by other corporations producing the same type of goods as harmful to the reputation of their industry, and thus deviant, although these inferior goods do not necessarily violate legal standards. Or a corporation may adopt such progressive labor policies that competing corporations believe they are made to look bad by comparison, and so they treat this corporation as a "deviant" within their industry, stigmatized and shunned. On the other hand, within some industries, a certain level of manipulation of corporate financial reports may be the norm and a widely accepted practice, even if it is technically illegal. Of course, in many cases organizations may engage in conduct that is both deviant and criminal, relative to societies' standards and laws as well as those within the industry in question.

Organizational deviance may be carried out on behalf of governmental organizations, quasi-public entities such as the International Monetary Fund, and private sector entities, or corporations (Ermann & Lundman 2002). Organizational deviance may be carried out by any type of organization, including religious organizations and churches. The monstrous crimes carried out by Nazi Germany – most notably, the extermination of some 6 million people during the Holocaust – required a high level of bureaucratic organization, and could not have been accomplished outside of an organizational framework. Indeed, there is much reason to believe that many of those who participated in the crimes of the Holocaust only did so as part of an organization that promoted and supported these activities, which they would not have engaged in as individuals. Organizations such as the World Bank and the International Monetary Fund carry out policies that seem to disproportionately favor multinational corporations and elite interests in developing countries, but cause various forms of harm to millions of ordinary citizens in such countries. To the extent that high-level officials of the Roman Catholic Church did not adequately address allegations of sexual abuse of children by priests, they engaged in a form of organizational deviance carried out on behalf of the church, to protect the church from scandal and legal liability. And corporations have engaged in a wide range of activities that cause harm to citizens, consumers, workers, and investors.

Organizations foster and promote many forms of harmful and illegal activity, as long as the activity is viewed as advancing the interests or objectives of the organization. The top leadership of an organization may attempt to protect itself from being held liable for forms of organizational deviance that are illegal, by a tactic of "concerted ignorance" or by not becoming directly involved in active engagement in the illegal activity. But insofar as they convey expectations of outcomes from middle managers and employees that they know or certainly should know can only be achieved through the commission of deviant or criminal actions, they are often responsible in a fundamental way for those actions. Organizations generate an organizational culture or ambience that may promote deviant and illegal activities. Some organizations are part of a larger environment – e.g., an industry – that is "criminogenic" in the sense that elements of that environment promote deviant or illegal conduct. Studies of one significant form of organizational deviance – corporate crime – have attempted to identify a range of external and internal factors that seem to be correlated with engagement in such crime (Friedrichs 2004). External factors include the economic climate, political and regulatory environment, level of industry concentration, style and strength of product distribution networks, and norms within industries; internal factors include the size of the corporation, the financial performance of the corporation and the degree of its emphasis on profit, the diffusion of responsibility through different divisions, and a corporate subculture that promotes loyalty and deference to the interests of the corporations.

The effective control of organizational deviance presents special challenges relative to the control of individual deviance. A significant sociological literature has by now explored the regulating, policing, adjudicating, and sanctioning of organizational deviance. Regulatory agencies – such as the Environmental Protection Agency (EPA) and the Occupational Safety and Health Administration (OSHA) – play a key role in the response to organizational deviance. A fundamental dilemma for such agencies has been captured by the title of John Braithwaite's book *To Punish or Persuade?* (1985). An effective response to organizational deviance contends with the fact that organizations typically engage in many productive activities apart from their deviant activities. Given the complexity of much organizational deviance, it is often difficult to prosecute cases of criminal malfeasance against them. Organizations typically have tremendous resources available to them to defend themselves – often far greater than the agencies attempting to sanction them. In addition, when organizations are legally sanctioned, innocent parties may be harmed or threatened; for instance, if a polluting plant is closed down, its workers may be forced onto unemployment lines.

The concept of organizational deviance has also been applied to the deviant or criminal activities of individuals acting within the context of an organizational position (Tittle & Paternoster 2000). Organizations structure opportunities for individuals to engage in deviant or criminal conduct, independent of – and sometimes directly at odds with – the interests of the organization itself. An embezzler must have a formal position with an organization – e.g., a bank – if he or she is to embezzle; a police officer is able to brutalize and infringe on the rights of citizens as a function of being authorized and armed by the state; a priest may have special opportunities to engage in and conceal sexual molestation due to his status within the church.

Organizations are the sites of significant manifestations of deviant or criminal conduct, then, beyond those actions carried out specifically on behalf of the organization. Much corporate crime is carried out primarily to benefit the corporation as a whole, although key executives naturally benefit disproportionally when such crime achieves its objectives. But in the case of high-level executives of corporations who "cook the books" primarily to enrich themselves, or police officers who use impermissible levels of force to achieve social control objectives or extract confessions, or bishops who provide cover for priests who have molested children, the characterization of the activity as organizational deviance is open to different interpretations: is the activity really engaged in on behalf of the organization, or the individual actor, or both? Some crimes – e.g., embezzlement – are carried out by employees against the organization. Some actions – e.g., sexual harassment – may deviate from organizational norms and rules without necessarily being in violation of criminal laws. Some conventional forms of crime – e.g., violent assault on a fellow worker – are carried out in the context of the organizational setting, or workplace, without being linked directly with the organizational role or the basic activities of the organization. Accordingly, one can differentiate between occupational crime (e.g., embezzlement), occupational deviance (e.g., sexual harassment), and workplace crime (e.g., assault), although admittedly such terms have all too often been used quite interchangeably (Friedrichs 2002).

Organizational deviance in its various manifestations is quite certain to achieve even greater significance in the increasingly complex world of the twenty-first century. Within sociology, more dialogue and cooperation will have to be fostered between such specialties as criminology and the sociology of organizations (Tonry & Reiss 1993). The understanding of organizational deviance will also require the expansion of interdisciplinary and transdisciplinary approaches, and the ever more sophisticated development of modes of analysis integrating macro-level and micro-level forms of explanation (Vaughan 2002). A newly emerging science of networks, for example, will play a role in all of this. The formidable methodological challenges involved in the empirical study of powerful organizations – including their frequent resistance to being studied – will have to be overcome.

SEE ALSO: Corruption; Crime, Corporate; Crime, Organized; Crime, White Collar; Culture, Organizations and; Deviance, Crime and; Deviance, Criminalization of; Deviance, Theories of; Organization Theory; Organizations as Social Structures; State Regulation and the Workplace

REFERENCES AND SUGGESTED READINGS

Bamberger, P. A. & Sonnenstuhl, W. J. (Eds.) (1998) *Organizational Deviance*, Vol. 15. JAI Press, Stamford, CT.

Braithwaite, J. (1985) *To Punish or Persuade?* SUNY Press, Albany, NY.

Coleman, J. S. (1982) *The Asymmetric Society*. Syracuse University Press, Syracuse, NY.

Ermann, M. D. & Lundman, R. J. (Eds.) (2002) *Corporate and Governmental Deviance: Problems of Organizational Behavior in Contemporary Society*, 6th edn. Oxford University Press, New York.

Friedrichs, D. O. (2002) Occupational Crime, Occupational Deviance, and Workplace Crime: Sorting Out the Difference. *Criminal Justice* 2: 243–56.

Friedrichs, D. O. (2004) *Trusted Criminals: White Collar Crime in Contemporary Society*, 2nd edn. Thomson/Wadsworth, Belmont, CA.

Jackall, R. (1988) *Moral Mazes: The World of Corporate Managers*. Oxford University Press, New York.

Tittle, C. R. & Paternoster, R. (2000) *Social Deviance and Crime: An Organizational and Theoretical Approach*. Roxbury, Los Angeles.

Tonry, M. & Reiss, A. J., Jr. (Eds.) (1993) *Beyond the Law: Crime in Complex Organizations*. University of Chicago Press, Chicago.

Vaughan, D. (1999) The Dark Side of Organizations: Mistake, Misconduct, and Disaster. In: *Annual Review of Sociology*. Annual Reviews, Palo Alto, CA, pp. 271–305.

Vaughan, D. (2002) Criminology and the Sociology of Organizations. *Crime, Law, and Social Change* 37: 117–36.

organizational failure

Stephen Ackroyd

By organizational failure is usually meant failure against some measure of performance, or failure to achieve a goal that is normally expected. Thus, a company can be identified as failing if it is not profitable, or a school if it does not educate students to a required level, or in sufficient numbers. Clearly, such *measured* organizational failure might be purely nominal (and/or imposed), an artifact of the application of performance criteria, rather than a *substantive* failure of organization as such. Thus, the internal working of an organization might be highly efficient given the resources available; but, nonetheless, because it does not reach a prescribed level of performance, it is deemed to fail. If the price of an indispensable commodity suddenly makes production at a saleable price impossible for a firm, failing profitability is almost inevitable and, for a small or new organization, bankruptcy (the most commonly used indicator of failure) is likely.

Of course, it may be also that an organization that is failing to perform against the customary criteria of success is also failing in some more fundamental way. If there are organizational problems that management has failed to resolve and which detract from measured performance, then there is a correspondence between measured and substantive organizational failure. But failure to perform against particular criteria is a customary or legal definition of failure, and may or may not indicate that there is some more fundamental problem of organization.

Many writers on management have conveniently conflated the distinction between measured and substantive organizational failure. The early or classical theorists of management asserted that an efficient organization, which followed the best practices as they prescribed them, would not fail. Later it was argued that the appropriate modes of organization and management might vary a good deal according to circumstances, but this was merely a more subtle version of the idea that reproducing the features prescribed would lead to the avoidance of failure. Only in the final years of the twentieth century, after considerable development of the sociology of institutions, did awareness emerge that organizations may survive despite judgments that they have failed. In 1989 Meyer and Zucker argued that many "permanently failing organizations" could be identified and their attributes analyzed.

However, even today the features of substantive or actual organizational failures are not seriously analyzed. Today, organizational failures, as indicated by particular measures, are nonetheless thought of as opportunities for learning (Cannon & Edmonson 2005). But when and whether failures are also substantive failures of organization is seldom discussed. It is, obviously, possible to find examples of organizations that have failed in a basic way. A routed army is one. However, instances in which an organization has disintegrated, without some compelling (and usually external) cause, are rare. It is a feature of social organizations that they tend to adapt themselves, despite incipient tendencies to entropy. Because of the evolutionary advantages it confers, a capacity for cooperative activity as well as conflict is deeply rooted in the human psyche. Because this is so, basic organizational failure is unlikely except in extreme or unusual circumstances.

SEE ALSO: Economy (Sociological Approach); Institution; Institutionalism; Management Discourse; Organization Theory; Organizations and the Theory of the Firm; Performance Measurement

REFERENCES AND SUGGESTED
READINGS

Cannon, M. D. & Edmonson, A. (2005) Failing to
Learn and Learning to Fail (Intelligently): How
Great Organizations Put Failure to Work to
Improve and Innovate. *Long Range Planning* 38
(3): 299–319.
Meyer, M. M. & Zucker, L. (1989) *Permanently
Failing Organizations.* Sage, Newbury Park, CA.

organizational learning

Polly S. Rizova

Organizational learning is a construct employed
to depict a set of rational and non-rational processes relevant to the creation, retention, and
transmission of knowledge in organizations.
The concept has been linked to organizational
performance, sustainable competitive advantage, organizational transformation and corporate renewal, organizational and technological
innovation, and entrepreneurship among other
themes. Change, adaptation, and learning have
all been used to denote the process by which
organizations adjust to their environments;
organizational change is often understood as a
manifestation of learning. Various conceptions
of learning have been advanced in the field; for
instance, learning as improving, learning as
recording knowledge, and learning as the evolution of knowledge. Research in the area seeks to
understand how learning in formal organizations takes place, what its sources are, and what
its effect is on the performance and maintenance
of organizational stability. For quite some time
organizational learning and learning organization were used interchangeably; lately, a somewhat tentative agreement has been established
that the two terms are not to be confused.
Whereas in the former the emphasis is on learning, and more specifically on the process of
learning in organizations, the latter stresses the
organization per se. Among the questions
addressed by the scholars of organizational
learning are: what are the essence and the bases
for organizational learning – rational, subconscious, or experiential? Who is the agent of

learning – the individual, the organization, or
both? How does organizational learning manifest itself? How is knowledge in organizations acquired, retained, and transferred? What
affects the ability of organizations to learn?

This field of organization studies developed
in two discrete stages – a theoretical stage,
which began in the 1950s and lasted until the
late 1980s, and an empirical stage. The theoretical implications of organizational learning have
been recognized ever since the notion was introduced in the 1950s with the work of March,
Simon, and Cyert. The idea drew a lot of attention as it was regarded as a needed and viable
alternative to the rational choice assumptions
promoted by economists. It represented an
attempt to explain how knowledge, structures,
beliefs, and actions of an organization could
affect, and in turn be affected by, not necessarily rational and yet critical institutionalization
processes. In light of this, March and Simon
argued in *Organizations* (1958) that the behavior
of organizations is determined by complex and
interconnected processes which introduce a significant degree of unpredictability into the decision-making process. Organizations react to this
challenge by developing highly elaborate, organized sets of responses and operating procedures and they resort to their usage when
recurring decision situations arise. In *A Behavioral Theory of the Firm* (1963), Cyert and
March advanced the understanding of the organizational learning process by depicting it as a
"learning cycle." Organizations, they argued,
respond to environmental upsets by fine-tuning
the probability of relying on specific operating
procedures that have been used successfully in
the past. In this view, organizational adaptation
is attained through the application of a multilevel hierarchy of specific procedures. Organizations use those to respond to externally
imposed uncertainties and calamities and to offset them.

The early notions of organizational learning
regarded the learning process as a by and large
rational response of adaptation to the demands
imposed on the firm by an unstable and unpredictable environment. This viewpoint was challenged by March and Olsen (1975), who argued
that the assumption on which learning models
were built was not viable since ambiguity is both
unavoidable and ubiquitous. They proposed,

instead, that under conditions of ambiguity, non-rational forces – beliefs, interpretations, trust, and perceptions – shape outcomes. Therefore, improved performance, and positive outcomes in general, are not the only plausible consequences of organizational learning. Since then, researchers have acknowledged that learning could have unintended consequences which could be negative. In light of this insight, Levinthal and March (1981) contested the idea of learning as being rationally adaptive and introduced a formalized learning model under conditions of ambiguity.

Therefore, the origins of the field and its first developmental stages were theoretical. Since the late 1980s and early 1990s, however, particularly with a special issue being devoted to organizational learning by *Organization Science* in 1991, interest in the topic surged and attention shifted from theoretical to empirical investigation. Recent approaches to organizational learning tackle the notions of unlearning and emphasize the creation of routines as storage mechanisms of knowledge (Levitt & March 1988). According to this view, organizational learning is a process, in which new organizational routines are created and old ones are modified in response to experiences and environmental changes; thus, knowledge manifests itself in routines. Examples of organizational routines are organizational strategies, rules and procedures, roles, structures, technologies, as well as cultural practices. These mechanisms are used to record and store the knowledge that is gained from various sources: new insights, past experiences, from putting new structures or systems in place, from actions taken by the organization and by other organizations, as well as from experimentation and failure. Most recently, a new direction of empirical investigation has been under development whose concern is the creation of a community of learners.

Despite the widespread acceptance of the concept of organizational learning, no one theory or model has been generally adopted. Some agreement has been reached, though, on several of the early debates that characterized the field. Among those are: organizational learning is a process; there is a distinction between individual and organizational learning; and there is accord that contextual factors affect

the plausibility of organizational learning taking place. For instance, empirical research has found that the following factors affect organizational learning: organizational and corporate culture, an organization's strategy, and the structure and the degree of complexity and unpredictability of both internal and external environments.

Among the unresolved or partly resolved old debates two stand out in particular: (1) how to explain the linkage between the individual and organizational levels of learning and (2) whether organizational learning implies behavioral or cognitive change and how to reconcile the two.

Central to the topic of learning in organizations is the issue of the level of analysis. In other words, who is the learning agent – the individual or the organization? While the old debate between individual and organization levels of analysis has abated, the role of the group level has become more prominent. In addition, research has expanded to examine learning not only within organizations but also between organizations. The scholarship on technological innovation is a case in point. In this venue, the effect of social networks has received great attention in terms of learning both within and between organizations.

Learning in organizations presupposes that individuals gain knowledge and that which they learn is retained, i.e., stored in routines developed not by organizations but by individual organizational members. Thus, the individuals create and carry out the routines, but the latter acquire a life of their own as they endure even when those who have created them leave the organization. Individual learning, therefore, is a necessary but not a sufficient condition for organizational learning. Institutional processes must be put in place to store and transfer what has been learned by individual members to the organization and back to all organizational members. Furthermore, there has been an agreement that organizational learning is not just the cumulative knowledge possessed by individuals (Fiol & Lyles 1985). Thus, the question that any cross-level model needs to provide an answer to is how individual knowledge is shared and how the organizational knowledge, codified in routines and the firm's culture, is transmitted to new and old individual members.

The importance of formal and informal organizational socialization processes through training and mentoring, organizational rituals and ceremonies, and storytelling has been well understood and acknowledged. However, a definitive answer to this question has yet to be found.

A model proposed recently by Crossan et al. (1999) – the 4I framework – addresses several of the above-mentioned cross-level challenges: it is a multilevel model which aims at bridging the individual, group, and organizational levels of analysis throughout the four processes that constitute organizational learning: Intuiting, Interpreting, Integrating, and Institutionalizing; hence the name – 4I. It is dynamic in the sense that it specifies the mechanisms through which learning occurs and knowledge is created, stored, and transferred at each level as well as between levels. Furthermore, it addresses the question of the nature of organizational learning as conscious, experiential, or subconscious. The model also considers what has been known in the literature as the critical challenge to an organization's strategic renewal – the tension between *exploration* (novelty, new learning) and *exploitation* (continuity, using what has been learned).

While the first debate in the field of organizational learning concerns the levels of analysis, the second one looks at the content of organizational learning and adaptation. In this regard, a distinction has been drawn between cognition and behavior. Fiol and Lyles (1985) depict the difference in a sense that *learning* reflects changes in cognition whereas *adaptation* reflects changes in behavior. The cognitive approach emphasizes content at the individual level; it focuses upon the production and sharing of beliefs, as well as on the preservation and dissemination of knowledge. From this perspective, organizational learning is understood as changes in the belief systems. Most of the research in this perspective is based on interpretive methodologies, such as case studies. In contrast, the behavioral approach concentrates on the development of new responses or actions at the organizational level. Examined behaviorally, the focus of learning is on those changes that the organizations create and implement as a response to their own experiences and the

environmental conditions. Researchers study organizations in this perspective by examining the changes in organizational structures, technologies, systems, and routines. The most often used methods of inquiry are those of quantitative studies and simulations.

The tension between these two aspects of learning comes as a result of the fact that cognition and behavior do not necessarily occur in parallel. In other words, it is plausible that changes in behavior may take place without the development of cognitive associations and changes. Vice versa, learning may or may not lead to changes in behavior or organizational performance. For instance, small and incremental behavioral changes do not necessarily result in important learning. At the same time, there is no empirical evidence that suggests that large-scale behavioral changes would lead to proportionally large changes in cognitive associations. Fiol and Lyles (1985) illustrate this point by using the example of the wave of mergers in the 1960s when rapid and profound changes were taking place in the forms of acquisition and yet in the absence of learning. When studying organizational behavior under conditions of immense uncertainty and crisis, Starbuck and colleagues (1978) found that the firms' response was to keep introducing various changes in the hope that one will eventually work. The issue that scholars in the field grapple with is how and in what ways might this tension be resolved and the two perspectives integrated. In recent years the debate about it has subsided as researchers have been more willing to accommodate both aspects under a broader definition of organizational learning.

At present, there are several challenges that are either taking place or beginning to appear in the field and which contain potential for future research. Further exploration and successful reconciliation of the strenuous linkage between behavior and cognition is one. Yet another link remains grossly underexplored – that between organizational learning and power, leadership, and the politics of institutionalization. The question of the nature of organizational learning – whether it is a rational solitary experience or is based on daily social interaction – needs a more definitive answer too. Other unresolved issues are those of methodology – whether quantitative or interpretive studies are more likely to provide answers to the main questions in the field – and where the boundary of organizational learning as a field of organization studies lies. These issues reflect the growing uncertainty of the distinction between organizational learning and knowledge management.

SEE ALSO: Change Management; Knowledge Management; Management Innovation; Organizations; Performance Measurement; Social Movements; Technological Innovation

REFERENCES AND SUGGESTED READINGS

Argote, L. & Ophir, R. (2002) Intraorganizational Learning. In: Baum, J. (Ed.), *Companion to Organizations*. Blackwell, Oxford, pp. 181–207.

Crossan, M., Lane, H., & White, R. (1999) An Organizational Learning Framework: From Intuition to Institution. *Academy of Management Review* 24(3): 522–37.

Easterby-Smith, M., Crossan, M., & Nicolint, D. (2000) Organizational Learning: Debates Past, Present, and Future. *Journal of Management Studies* 37(6): 783–96.

Fiol, C. M. & Lyles, M. (1985) Organizational Learning. *Academy of Management Journal* 10(4): 803–13.

Lawrence, T., Mauws, M., Dyck, B., & Kleysen, R. (2005) The Politics of Organizational Learning: Integrating Power into the 4I Framework. *Academy of Management Review* 30(1): 180–91.

Levinthal, D. & March, J. (1981) A Model of Adaptive Organizational Search. *Journal of Economic Behavior and Organizations* 2: 307–33.

Levitt, B. & March, J. (1988) Organizational Learning. *Annual Review of Sociology* 14: 319–40.

Lundberg, C. (1995) Learning In and By Organizations: Three Conceptual Issues. *International Journal of Organizational Analysis* 3(1): 10–23.

March, J. & Olsen, J. (1975) The Uncertainty of the Past: Organizational Learning Under Ambiguity. *European Journal of Political Research* 3: 147–71.

Schulz, M. (2002) Organizational Learning. In: Baum, J. (Ed.), *Companion to Organizations*. Blackwell, Oxford, pp. 415–41.

Starbuck, W., Greve, A., & Hedberg, B. (1978) Responding to Crisis. *Journal of Business Administration* 9(2): 112–37.

organizations

Stephen Hunt

A broad definition of an organization could be said to be that of any purposeful arrangement of social activity that implies active control over human relations ordered for particular ends. In this sense, organizations involve patterns of relationships beyond primary group associations that are largely spontaneous, unplanned, and informal, and that are typified by kinship relations, peer groups, and localized community networks. There is, however, no generally accepted definition of an organization since its meaning may vary in terms of the different sociological approaches applied to the subject. Moreover, while organizations may be deliberately constructed or reconstructed for specific ends, the problem of definition founders on the specification of "organizational goals," since groups and individuals within organizations may hold a variety of different and competing goals and the level of compliance and cooperation displayed by subordinates may vary, thus leading to the distinction between "formal" and "informal" organizations.

There are numerous existing sociological frameworks of organizational analysis and many have sought to categorize their forms by recourse to various criteria. For example, by using a classification of motivation behind adhering to organizational authority, Amitai Etzioni (1975) identifies three types. Those who work for remuneration are members of a utilitarian organization. Large commercial enterprises, for instance, generate profits for their owners and offer remuneration in the form of salaries and wages for employees. Joining utilitarian organizations is usually a matter of individual choice, although the purpose is that of income. Individuals joining normative organizations do so not for remuneration but to pursue goals they consider morally worthwhile, perhaps typified by voluntary organizations, political parties, and numerous other confederations concerned with specific issues. Finally, in Etzioni's typology, coercive organizations are distinguished by involuntary membership which forces members to join by coercion or for punitive reasons.

Max Weber (1946 [1921]), to whom the first comprehensive sociological treatment of organizations is usually attributed, offered a distinction between modern bureaucracies and other forms of organization (*Verband*). Weber pointed out that patterns of authority in previous forms of organization did not conform to what he regarded as his typology of "legal-rational" authority that infused the modern bureaucracy. Formal organizations, however, as Weber accounts, dated back to antiquity. The elites who ruled early empires, ranging from Babylonian, Egyptian, to Chinese, relied on government officials to extend their domination over large subject populations and vast geographical areas. Formal organizations, and their attendant bureaucratic structures, consequently allowed rulers to administer through the collection of taxes, military campaigns, and construction projects.

Typically, cultural patterns in pre-industrial societies placed greater importance on preserving the past and tradition than on establishing rationally oriented organizational structures. The systems of authority underlying early organization forms were, in Weber's typology, "affectual" or "emotional" loyalties or those solicited from custom or force of habit. In their rationalized bureaucratic form, Weber identified organizations as pervading the structures of modernity and holding increasing sway over human life, including the agencies of the state, business enterprises, education, infirmaries, the military, political parties, penal or rehabilitation institutions, and even religious establishments. This hegemonic hold of such organizations was also exemplified in Etzioni's famous statement that "we are born in organizations, educated by organizations, and most of us spend much of our lives working for organizations" (1975: 1). There were various historical reasons identified by Weber for this expanding mode of bureaucratic existence. These included, in the West at least, the overlapping developments of the calculated pursuit of profit in the emergent capitalization of the marketplace, the diffused Protestant work ethic, an advanced form of geographical communication, the growth of representative democracy, and inscribed formats of legal regulations.

Weber considered the bureaucratic organizational type to be the clearest expression of a rational worldview because its principal elements were intended to achieve specific goals as efficiently as possible. In short, Weber asserted that bureaucracy transformed the nature of western society in the same way that industrialization revolutionized the economy – pointing out that large capitalist enterprises are unequaled models of strict bureaucratic organizations. In his exploration of their proliferation, Weber's "ideal type" bureaucracy displayed a number of overlapping characteristics. Firstly, there is the distinguishing feature of specialization. Throughout most of human history, social activity was dominated by the pursuit of the basic goals of securing food and shelter. Bureaucracy, by contrast, assigns to individuals highly specialized duties. Secondly, bureaucracies arrange personnel in a vertical hierarchy of offices. Each official is thus supervised by superiors in the organization, while in turn supervising others in lower positions. Thirdly, rules and regulations replace cultural traditions through operations guided by rationally enacted rules and regulations. These rules control not only the organization's own functioning but also, as much as possible, its larger environment. Hence, a bureaucracy seeks to operate in a completely predictable fashion. Thirdly, a bureaucratic organization anticipates that officials will have the technical competence to administer their official duties. It follows that bureaucracies regularly monitor the performance of staff members. Such impersonal evaluation based on performance contrasts sharply with the custom or patronage which informed earlier forms of organization. Fourthly, in bureaucratic organizations rules take precedence over personal caprice, encouraging uniform treatment for each client as well as other officials. Finally, rather than casual verbal communication, bureaucracies rest on formal, written reports which subsequently underpin their mode of operation.

While Weber recognized the unparalleled efficiency of bureaucratic organizations, he identified them as simultaneously generating widespread alienation. The stifling regulation and dehumanization of the "iron cage" that came with expanding bureaucracy led to an increasing "disenchantment with the world." Bureaucracies, Weber warned, tended to treat people as objects and a series of "cases" rather than as unique individuals. Moreover, working for large organizations demanded specialized and often tedious routines. Weber therefore envisaged modern society as a vast and growing system of rules seeking to regulate everything and threatening to crush the human spirit. Weber also predicted that the same rationality would overspill into other aspects of social existence and subject individuals to apathetic functionaries. In total, bureaucratic rationality stifled creativity and turned on its creators and enslaved them, reducing the official to "only a small cog in a ceaselessly fixed routine of march."

The alienating nature of organizations was much later to inform such works as that of George Ritzer in his account of "McDonaldization," whereby the rationalizing processes of production in large-scale capitalist enterprises entail "efficiency," the quickest and most effective way of reaching a goal; "calculability," mass-produced uniformity according to a calculated plan; "uniformity" and "predictability," which result from a highly rational system of organization that specifies every course of action and leaves nothing to chance; and technological "control" over people and eventually automation, which replaces even the standardized operations of individual workers. In echoing Weber's fear that rationality may be irrational in its consequences, Ritzer suggests that the "ultimate irrationality" of such processes has a tendency to contaminate other dimensions of social existence and brings the danger that "people could lose control over the system and it would come to control us" (Ritzer 1993: 145).

Weber also added to his fears the observation that the "technical superiority" of bureaucracies was not necessarily superior. Neither, he asserted, was it excluded from personalized interests that were typified by the pursuit of the accumulation of capital. On the latter count, one of the major foci of the extensive literature from the 1970s was on the politico-economic environment which circumscribed organizational dynamics. In this respect, Marxist interest in the nature of organizations offered far-reaching critiques of bureaucracies, particularly in their relations with state and corporate power, alongside an assessment of the embedded interests of professional groupings in organizational life. Such a perspective threw light upon the nature

of domination observable through systems of repression and exploitation.

Weber's fear that bureaucracies were not devoid of personalized interests was taken to its furthest extreme by another classical theorist of organizations, Robert Michels (1958 [1915]). Michels's dictum of the "iron law of oligarchy" supposed that organizational control inevitably gave way to elitist rule that negated democratic participation. This was exemplified by political parties, which tended to have a tendency to replace organization controls with those at the apex of the organizational hierarchy. Hence, a position of dominance invariably led to the pursuit of interest even in opposition to stated organizational goals, alongside the recruitment of underlings involving a system of patronage and deference.

The early critiques of organizational functionality did not, however, curtail the tendency for the discipline of sociology to view the organization as a central hallmark of modernity. This explains the normative appeal of particular schools of organization theory that dominated for so long within the discipline. A yardstick of such an attraction was inherent in the mid-twentieth-century analytical frameworks of the structural functionalist accounts of Talcott Parsons, who established an organizational typology that was underpinned by rational instrumentality (Parsons 1960). In short, functional imperatives and rules established a relationship between the needs of organizations as organic social systems and individual and collective roles and motivations.

The structural functionalist analysis of organization provided a theoretical paradigm that was subsequently subject to attempts to elaborate upon a fairly simplistic model. One challenge was to identify and explain dysfunctional aspects of the organizational structure. A common assumption was that any potential temporary disequilibrium was likely to be generated by one element in the organic system changing more rapidly than others. In contrast, Robert Merton saw the potential for dysfunction built into the very nature of organizational life (Merton 1968). To this end, he coined the term "bureaucratic ritual" to designate a preoccupation with rules and regulations to the point of thwarting an organization's goals. For Merton, ritualism impedes individual and organizational performance since it tends to stifle creativity and innovation. In part, ritualism emerges because organizations, which pay modest fixed salaries, provide officials little or no financial stake in performing efficiently. Merton further argued that if bureaucrats have little motivation to be efficient, their principal incentive derives from endeavors to sustain employment. Hence, officials typically strive to perpetuate their organization even when its purpose has been fulfilled. The result has frequently been termed "bureaucratic inertia" – the tendency of organizations to perpetuate themselves even beyond their former objectives – and this is one of the reasons why, in his account of bureaucracy, Weber wrote that "once fully established, bureaucracy is among the social structures which are hardest to destroy."

A further critique of the structural functionalist framework was developed by theorists such as Crozier (1964) and Simon (1976 [1945]), who suggested that far from exhibiting an underlying principle of rationality, organizations were best identified by fragility, instability, and weakly integrated internal relations. Organizations were thus best appraised as a conglomeration of conflicts, adjustments, and negotiations. Ironically, then, an efficient organization was not necessarily one tending toward an equilibrium and ordered functioning, but one of complexity, compromise, and uncertainty. Such concepts as Simon's "bounded rationality" and Crozier's view of organizational power as being essentially problematic were to become associated with "contingency theory," which pinpointed the dynamics of internal competing forces. Put succinctly, organizations could no longer be conceived as unified organic systems based on rationalizing prerequisites.

In questioning the efficiency of formal rules and regulations, Blau (1963) insisted that unofficial practices are an established and vital part of the structure of all organizations, serving to increase internal efficiency. In particular, it is via informal networks that information and experience are shared and problem solving facilitated. Hence, knowledge of complex regulations is widened, leading to time saving and efficiency, while consultation transforms the organizational staff from a disparate collection of officials into a cohesive working group. Moreover, informality may help to legitimate needs

sometimes overlooked by formal regulation, or may amount to "cutting corners" in the carrying out of duties in order to simplify the means to achieve specified goals. Thus, paradoxically, unofficial practices which are explicitly prohibited by official regulations may further the achievement of organizational objectives.

Other accounts conceptualized environmental effects within the context of the particular goals established by organizations. While different types of environments were surveyed, a popular theme has been the dynamics of entrepreneurial organizations within the market economy. The indications are that they involve a complex web of interdependence and institutional laws that tend to limit organizational dependency in an uncertain economic environment and thus render them dysfunctional: for example, deliberately overproducing or selectively promoting new products. Economists such as Eggertsson (1990) also addressed the nature of organizational practice through what came to be known as the "new institutionalism." Inherent in this developing critique was the insistence that goal-oriented rationality actually provides constraints in the dynamics of bureaucratic structures, especially in terms of the transaction cost endeavors of some forms of organization.

Despite the apparently dysfunctional aspects of a good deal of organizational life, the normative stance that was engrained in structural functionalist perspectives retained its appeal in neorationalist theory. Basic to this school of thought was that functional rationality should remain a desirable and reachable ideal. This view identified organizational managers as the strategic agents in determining roles, goals, and the nature of the organizational structure. Recognizing the actual or potential failures of organizational life, managers were held to be the gatekeepers in identifying goals–means imperatives and ideally responsible for rational order and behavior, while simultaneously accountable for necessary innovation and change. Integral to such an approach was the flexibility demanded by rapidly changing technological systems, the important role of human resource management, and adaptation to environmental conditions.

The postmodern approach to organizations is clearly currently increasingly influential. It has tended to deny the previous sociological preoccupation with organizational analysis. This is because postmodern accounts, which center on the application of literary and cultural theorizing, lead to the neglect or denial of structural theory in any shape or form. The increasing popularity of a postmodern approach, with its central concern of deconstructionism, has in turn added to a further development in organization study and theorizing: its increasing fragmentation and isolation. However, as noted above, organizational analysis, especially in the United States, continues to focus on the intricacies of structure, systems, hierarchy, and technology. Thus there remains an enduring interest in the relationship between organizations and their wider environment, particularly with macroeconomic factors and the dynamics of the contemporary marketplace.

The work of Foucault (1975), to some degree at least, has informed postmodern concerns. Marking a radical departure from the structural analysis of organizational study, Foucault's historical interpretations have attempted to uncover discursive systems that permeate the growth of coercive institutions, including organizational forms which exerted an all-embracing domination over the human subject. Of particular influence has been Foucault's exploration of "surveillance" and discipline in the industrial and institutional fields of the state, and the ways in which new forms of production of information and knowledge led to relations of power in organizational life. Put succinctly, Foucault's concern with the growth of organizational control turned upon a historical appraisal of the role of "mass" organizations in the control, discipline, and surveillance of subject social groups in such settings as the mental hospital, penal institutions, and the large-scale armed forces.

There have proved to be numerous other threads discernible in the postmodern approach to organizations. Overall, however, postmodernists have offered a new wave of critique derived from broader philosophies of culture and language that constitute a thorough undermining of the "project" of modernity. In contradiction to earlier organization theory is the focus on the subjectivity and random nature of "truth" claims and instrumental rationalities at the core of modern organizations. This move away to a postmodern scrutiny of organizations emphasizes the discursive practices of bureaucratic life

and its theorization. Nonetheless, the postmodern analysis of organizations, their agencies and operation, has also taken off in other directions that embrace the problematic areas of management, performance, and productivity. For instance, Clegg (1990) observes that capital-oriented organizations in a post-Fordist economy have often developed as conglomerates with distinct elements dealing with different aspects of the marketplace. The strategy for the company does not therefore originate from a central source coordinating the activities of diverse parts of the conglomerate. Instead, strategy originates from members of the organization with "core competencies," that is, a particular expertise in the area on which the organization concentrates.

In addition to such areas of focus, many other sociological concerns have emerged in organizational studies which would appear to be concomitant with postmodernity: the emergence of micro-level "spontaneous" and temporary forms of organization such as self-help groups and those expressing a variety of mutual interests. Many such forms of organization may be derived from primary association, which subsequently and ironically renders a reworking of those definitions of organizations from which the subdiscipline of sociology initially emerged.

SEE ALSO: Bureaucracy and Public Sector Governmentality; Democracy and Organizations; Institutional Theory, New; Oligarchy and Organization; Organization Theory; Organizational Failure; Organizations as Coercive Institutions; Organizations as Social Structures; Organizations as Total Institutions; Organizations, Voluntary; Political Parties; Postmodern Organizations

REFERENCES AND SUGGESTED READINGS

Blau, P. (1963) *The Dynamics of Bureaucracy*. University of Chicago Press, Chicago.
Clegg, S. (1990) *Modern Organizations: Organizational Studies in the Post-Modern World*. Sage, London.
Crozier, M. (1964) *The Bureaucratic Phenomenon*. University of Chicago Press, Chicago.
Eggertsson, T. (1990) *Economic Behaviour and Institutions*. Cambridge University Press, Cambridge.
Etzioni, A. (1975) *A Comparative Analysis of Complex Organizations: On Power, Involvement, and Their Correlates*. Free Press, New York.

Foucault, M. (1975) *Discipline and Punish: The Birth of the Prison*. Vintage, New York.

Merton, R. (1968) *Social Theory and Social Structure*. Free Press, New York.

Michels, R. (1958 [1915]) *Political Parties*. Free Press, New York.

Parsons, T. (1960) *Structure and Process in Modern Societies*. Free Press, Glencoe, IL.

Ritzer, G. (1993) *The McDonaldization of Society: An Investigation into the Changing Character of Contemporary Social Life*. Pine Forge Press, Thousand Oaks, CA.

Simon, H. (1976 [1945]) *Administrative Behaviour*. Macmillan, New York.

Weber, M. (1946 [1921]) Bureaucracy. In: Gerth, H. & Mills, C. W. (Eds.), *From Max Weber: Essays in Sociology*. Oxford University Press, New York.

organizations as coercive institutions

Joseph Soeters

Coercive organizations are the state's instruments used to ensure safety and public order both of its borders and within its borders. As such, these organizations are authorized to approach the general public in a coercive manner and – in the last resort – they are legitimized to use force and violence against those who intend to harm the interests of the state and its citizens. The military, the gendarmerie (Carabinieri, Guardia Civil, Jandarmerie), and the police as well as fire guards and forest rangers all belong to this specific category of organizations. The police and fire guards traditionally have an internal role, whereas the military has as its primary task protecting the state against threats from abroad. However, these distinctions are not always and everywhere clear. In many countries, including in Western Europe, the military is sometimes called upon to perform internal tasks, whereas police officers increasingly are sent to distant regions outside their own nation-state.

Coercive organizations are peculiar, in particular with respect to the way they treat their personnel. Personnel employed by coercive organizations are highly visible because of their uniforms; they are trained in specific educational institutions such as military, police, and firefighting academies; they are on permanent, 24-hour call with rather idiosyncratic working hours, whereby their leave is subject to cancelation; and the work in coercive organizations may be dangerous and potentially life threatening, for which reason personnel are usually armed or at least equipped with protective materials (Soeters 2000).

As the state's instruments, coercive organizations need to be fundamentally non-discriminatory toward citizens and as a principle they need to comply with decisions taken by elected politicians. If coercive organizations fail to do so, they threaten one of the cornerstones of modern democracy (Caforio 2003). In non-democratic states, coercive organizations may – and indeed sometimes do – take over power if they deem the political situation to be dangerous to their country. The 1981 attack by a few Guardia Civil officers on the Spanish Parliament was the most recent incident in this respect to have occurred in Western Europe, but in many other parts of the world – particularly in Africa – such threats are still present.

ORGANIZATIONAL FEATURES

Coercive organizations are relatively isolated from society, although the level of isolation varies: clearly, the police are more a part of everyday societal life than the military or fire squads. Coercive organizations experience a strong communal life without much privacy, a condition that starts in the training institutes and is continued thoughout the whole working career (Lang 1965). Personnel in coercive organizations know each other very well, their personal and working lives tend to overlap, and their career orientation is traditionally internally directed. For instance, traditional police force members tend to see themselves as cops for the rest of their lives. New personnel are frequently recruited from channels related to personnel already in the organization, such as family or friends. Hence, it helps if one has a father who is a police officer. In the military, female personnel very often marry colleagues from within their own organization, even from within their own unit. As such, coercive organizations' cultures tend to be clearly more collectivistic than organizational cultures in civilian companies (Soeters 2000).

Furthermore, coercive organizations are known for their visible, steep hierarchies and elaborate organizational structures based on a strong, functional division of labor. These structural elements are formalized in documents containing detailed rules and regulations. However, who commands who can even be inferred from the insignia on the uniforms, and there is no discussion about this: rank equals authority. More than in civilian organizations, employees in coercive organizations are used to experiencing relatively high degrees of power asymmetry (Soeters 2000). Relatedly, they know that disobedience can result in overt punishment, and hence discipline is an ingrained characteristic of coercive organizations' cultures. In addition, rules are important to avoid insecurity concerning how to implement the organization's policies, and the use of violence in particular. The organizational output may impact on people's life and death, and for that reason coercive organizations attract considerable political and social attention, through extensive coverage by the mass media.

Coercive organizations do not always maintain an action-ready pose: fire guards even know the distinction between "cold" and "hot" organization, but that distinction applies to the police and the military as well. The "cold" organization obviously does not face the heat of fires and crises, and hence it comprises more white-collar work (although performed in uniform), more planning, more meetings, paperwork, quality and cost control as well as more bureaucratic politics. It is the world of the "management cops" and the "office generals." As such, it conforms to the image of the classical bureaucracy. At the level of the rank and file, the "cold" organization is continuously preparing for the worst case through exercises and simulations in garrison, barracks, or on routine sailing missions. Personnel in the "cold" organization often complain about boredom, stimulus deprivation, perceptions of underutilization, and concerns for privacy. Such matters require specific leadership attention. To compensate for the lack of real action, the "cold" organization attaches high significance to ceremonial practices such as parades and flag-showing, events that – again – are based on discipline and obedience.

The "hot" organization, on the other hand, is built around flexible groups having all the characteristics of either the simple ("one leader") structure or – when explicitly based on self-managing – the adhocracy. For employees in the "hot" organization, local response and flexibility are more important than preplanned and "packaged" solutions to problems. Street police officers as well as the military-in-action have a sense of territoriality ("this place belongs to us"), and they develop their own informal codes of conduct that stress safety, comradeship, but often also cynicism and suspicion (Tonry & Morris 1997). They are often full of "us" and "them" classifications: "them" being the enemy, the criminals, the general public, the media, but also the managers in the "cold" organization. Since personnel in the "hot" organization generally are rather distressed, they need to stick together emotionally, creating outside groups to resist. Sometimes this leads to improper actions and malfeasance, such as corruption, discrimination, and even the beating up or killing of innocent people. Both the police and the military are occasionally accused of committing such crimes.

DEVELOPMENTS

Like most other organizations, coercive organizations experience continuous changes in their task environment and are subject to influences exerted by society at large.

First, coercive organizations are tending to become more active. Probably this is a result of an increasingly critical attitude among the general public that wants "value for money." The police, of course, have always been operational on a day-to-day basis, but fire guards, who used to wait for the next fire, are currently initiating activities to prevent fires and explosions. For instance, they develop educational programs to help the general public take preemptive measures to preclude dangerous situations. The European military has experienced similar developments since the end of the Cold War. Since the 1990s military forces from all around the world have increasingly been engaged in peacekeeping operations, such as in the former Yugoslavia, Afghanistan, and in various African regions. Being active on an everyday basis provides the military and fire guards with continuous "reality checks" from outside the organization; nowadays they receive considerably more feedback than before. The general public, local populations, authorities, NGOs, the media, politicians, and other coercive organizations are all likely to circulate indications of the coercive organizations' performance. According to organization theory (Adler & Borys 1996: 82–3), this particular situation will make the nature of coercive organizations less classically bureaucratic, i.e., less hierarchical and less based on strict compliance with detailed rules and orders from above. This situation, added to the geographical dispersion of the organization's current activities, necessitates the transfer of responsibilities to lower levels in the organization. Hence, the bureaucratic character of the coercive organization is gradually becoming more "enabling." This implies that the rank and file in the organization will need to behave more autonomously and in a self-steering way, albeit in concordance with the organization's general philosophies, standard operating procedures, and frames of references. Such a development is not solely the result of organizational changes. The personnel's increasing educational level is conducive to this development as well. In this way, coercive organizations, such as the military and fire guards, gradually will start to resemble the police and most civilian organizations, which have always been more influenced by reality checks from outside the organization.

A second development relates to the normative orientation of the employees. Coercive organizations' employees have traditionally been motivated by the institution itself. The only thing that traditionally mattered in their working life was the military (or the police, or the fire guard) and the values for which it stood: the nation or constitution, the king or the queen, the safety of society and the general public. In the sociology of the military (Moskos & Wood 1988; Caforio 2003) this is indicated as the institutional orientation. On the other hand – and this seems to be a manifestation of modern times – employees increasingly tend to see working with the military (or the police or the fire guard)

as "just another job." They are progressively becoming more oriented toward continuing their career outside the organization; they are increasingly striving for market wages; and they prefer to acquire educational qualifications that can also be utilized outside the organization. This attitude is labeled as the occupational orientation. It should be noted that this modern work orientation is not the result of changing attitudes among employees only. Increasingly, coercive organizations themselves – the military, in particular – want their personnel (service personnel and officers) to leave the organization after a specific contract period. Such a policy is part of a general organizational ambition to become more flexible and reduce labor costs.

A third development concerns the internationalization of the coercive organizations' activities. When crime crosses borders, the police should deploy actions on a scale that goes beyond national borders. In the post-1990 era, military operations have become inherently international. The international character of an operation contributes to its legitimacy; furthermore, internationalization has become inevitable, because most of today's downsized militaries are no longer capable of carrying out large operations independently. This implies that coercive organizations increasingly need to work together with organizations from other nationalities; such collaborations can also create greater legitimacy than if just one power dispatches its troops alone. The problems that arise correspondingly resemble the issues that civilian companies face when getting involved in a multinational merger or acquisition. It has been demonstrated that coercive organizations display their own national styles of organizing and operating (Soeters et al. 1995; Soeters 2000). The interaction between these various national styles need not necessarily be problematic, but if not well managed it may lead to frictions, misunderstandings, and even severe mutual blame behavior. One way to avoid such problems is to separate the various national organizations, allocating to each its own area of responsibility. This has been a dominant strategy in the former Yugoslavia. But often such a solution is impossible. In that instance, proper cultural awareness and sensitivity among commanding officers are required to prevent the operation ending in failure and fiasco.

Fourth, our world is increasingly becoming multicultural (Kymlicka 2001). Within nation-states indigenous peoples, migrants, and other cultural minorities are strengthening their identities and claiming their citizen rights. These rights may concern language issues, religious affairs, educational policies, and media facilities. For the police and the armed forces this development has important consequences. Often, coercive organizations have not enlisted many representatives of these minority groups and, due to their lack of educational qualifications, those who are recruited generally do not attain the highest ranks. Until World War II, for instance, African Americans were not allowed to become pilots in the US Airforce, because they were not deemed talented enough to master the complex aircraft. Of course, such policies are highly problematic since they are inherently discriminatory, but they also damage the interests of the coercive organization itself because recruiting pools are reduced as a result (Soeters & van der Meulen 1999). It is hardly surprising that this US Airforce policy was banned as soon as the number of suitable candidates no longer met the increasing demand for pilots during the war. Even more questionable is another aspect. If minority groups are barely represented in the police or the armed forces, it is likely that the coercive organizations' personnel are prejudiced toward those particular minority groups. This may lead to serious malfeasance when the coercive organization is called upon to take action with respect to these specific groups. In Bolivia such a situation occurred in 2003 when indigenous people protested against rising prices and unemployment; the army (having a better reputation than the police) was ordered to calm the situation, which they did by killing 100 protesting citizens. Since then, the government resigned and the new government has forced the military to open up its organization for young men and women from indigenous groups. In many other ethnic conflicts similar behavior by police and armed forces (including non-intervention when one ethnic group attacks another) has been reported (e.g., Tambiah 1996).

A comparable but less problematic issue concerns the integration of women. Due to their affinity with violence and physical action, coercive organizations have always had the reputation of being "masculine" (Soeters & van der Meulen 1999; Caforio 2003). Clearly, until some 25 years ago armed forces, fire guards, and the police were largely the "playground" of men only. Even now, the number of women in the armed forces ranges from a negligible 1 percent (Italy, Turkey) to 15 percent (US). But these numbers are likely to increase, and the police currently have considerably higher numbers of women among their rank and file and commanding officers. This does not imply that problems with respect to the integration of women in coercive organizations are absent; sexual harassment still seems to be more prevalent than in civilian organizations, although its occurrence, if proven, is fiercely punished. However, this issue seems to pale in comparison with the integration of minority groups in coercive organizations.

REMAINING ISSUES

Coercive organizations are in a process of permanent development. Issues with respect to effectiveness and efficiency still remain to be solved. The ratio between input of resources and output – preventing and fighting disorder – is usually vague and often perplexing. The Bolivian army, for instance, is twice as large as the Canadian or the Dutch armies, a size which is legitimized by reference to possible threats from neighboring countries which, in the past, have invaded the country, such as Chile in 1879 and Paraguay in 1932. There is another problem as well. The number of deployed military units or policing units on the street compared to personnel in the office (the "cold" organization) is frequently surprisingly low, a general complaint heard among the general public with respect to the police. As regards the western armed forces, it is an opinion often voiced by NATO officials. In general, remonstrations are expressed concerning the lack of coercive organizations' flexibility. If the input–output ratio turns out to be too low, it implies that either the number of actions needs to increase or the resources on the input side could be cut. Hence, the current struggle against decreasing resources is likely to continue for most coercive organizations, not only in the western hemisphere.

Coercive organizations are subject to massive attention from the media, politics, and the general public. It is this fact, combined with an almost worldwide aversion to killing and getting killed (the latter is also known as casualty aversion), which restrains coercive organizations from acting in the way they were free to do in recent historical times. The US armed forces suffered 50,000 casualties during the Vietnam War (1975), a number far from being reached in the Iraq operations at the beginning of the twenty-first century. People, especially mothers, but also unions, nowadays would never accept the loss of lives that they did only 30 years ago. It is a development that can be seen on a worldwide scale, including, for instance, in Russia. If being killed is less acceptable than it used to be, killing is no longer an option either. Every action where not only bystanders but also enemies and criminals die (or are tortured) will be subject to scrutiny. Sometimes this leads to the disbanding of whole units, as happened with a Canadian airborne regiment that saw an innocent boy beaten up and killed during a mission in Somalia.

Permanent downsizing and the cry for more flexibility on the one hand, and an ever increasing critical general public on the other, lead to a situation where privatization of coercive activities tends to become a new solution in both the military and the armed forces (Tonry & Morris 1997; Singer 2004). Private coercive organizations are likely to be more flexible and less scrutinized by the media, politics, and the general public. As far as the military is concerned, private military companies have recently played decisive roles in actions in African and Middle Eastern regions. But those private coercive organizations evade the political and civilian control that democracies have always made a cornerstone of their constitutional arrangements.

SEE ALSO: Bureaucracy and Public Sector Governmentality; Bureaucratic Personality; Change Management; Culture, Organizations and; Military Sociology; Organization Theory; Organizations as Total Institutions; Police

REFERENCES AND SUGGESTED READINGS

Adler, P. S. & Borys, B. (1996) Two Types of Bureaucracy: Enabling and Coercive. *Administrative Science Quarterly* 41, 61–89.

Caforio, G. (Ed.) (2003) *Handbook of the Sociology of the Military*. Kluwer Academic/Plenum, New York.

Kymlicka, W. (2001) *Politics in the Vernacular: Nationalism, Multiculturalism, and Citizenship*, Oxford University Press, Oxford.

Lang, K. (1965) Military Organizations. In: March, J. G. (Ed.), *Handbook of Organizations*. Rand McNally, Chicago, pp. 838–78.

Moskos, C. C. & Wood, F. (1988) *The Military: More Than Just a Job?* Pergamon/Brassey, Washingon, DC.

Singer, P. W. (2004) *Corporate Warriors: The Rise of the Private Military Industry*. Cornell University Press, Ithaca, NY.

Soeters, J. (2000) Culture in Uniformed Organizations. In: Ashkanashy, N. M., Wilderom, C. P. M., & Peterson, M. F. (Eds.), *Handbook of Organizational Culture and Climate*. Sage, London, pp. 465–81.

Soeters, J. & van der Meulen, J. (1999) *Managing Diversity in the Armed Forces: Experiences from Nine Countries*. Tilburg University Press, Tilburg.

Soeters, J., Hofstede, G. H., & van Twuyver, M. (1995) Culture's Consequences and the Police: Cross-Border Cooperation Between Police Forces in Germany, Belgium, and the Netherlands. *Policing and Society* 5: 1–14.

Tambiah, S. J. (1996) *Levelling Crowds: Ethnonationalist Conflicts and Collective Violence in South Asia*. University of California Press, Berkeley.

Tonry, M. & Morris, N. (1997) *Modern Policing*. University of Chicago Press, Chicago.

organizations and sexuality

Jeff Hearn

The recognition of sexuality as a central feature of organization(s) is relatively recent, and prompted by a range of disciplinary and theoretical positions. Foremost of these is second-wave feminism, highlighting concerns with women's control over their bodies and sexuality, and offering critiques of the sexualization of organizations and sexist uses of sexuality, in advertising and other organizational displays. A second force for change has been the modern lesbian and gay movements. Another stimulus has been poststructuralist and postcolonial theory. The most profound impact of such moves has been in problematizing sexuality, especially heterosexuality, and essentialized, naturalized views of sexuality, and, with queer theory, "homosexuality" too.

A strong empirical focus on sexuality and organizations has developed in four main ways. A first aspect was journalistic and political interventions in naming repeated, unwanted sexual behavior as sexual harassment in the mid-1970s. There followed general social analyses, detailed examinations of legal cases, and broad sexual-social surveys (Gutek 1985), establishing the pervasiveness of sexual harassment by men. Second, there have been empirical studies of heterosexual relationships and sexual liaisons in organizations. Third, another empirical strand developed in the 1980s on lesbians' and gay men's experiences in organizations, particularly, though not only, of discrimination and violation. These were often initially part of campaigns or other political interventions. More recent studies have examined the wider experiences of lesbians and gay men throughout organizations, including business, police, military, community, and public service sectors (Humphrey 2000; Lehtonen & Mustola 2004).

Fourth, there have been case studies of specific organizations, including how sexuality may link to appointment processes, reinforcement of gender power relations, managerial controls, and shopfloor dynamics. These build on established case study research on sexuality in total institutions. For example, prisons can be understood as organizations that control sexual relations, as well as creating new possibilities for different sexualities and, indeed, sexual violences. In several workplace case studies, Cockburn (1983, 1991) has examined how men maintain and reproduce power over women in workplaces, including by sexual domination alongside labor market domination. Pringle (1988) has analyzed bureaucracies and boss–secretary relationships and has recorded the pervasiveness of gender and sexual power in organizations. Drawing critically on poststructuralist theory, she has charted how gender/sexual power relations operate in multiple directions and may be understood more fully through psychodynamic, unconscious, and fantasy processes.

These empirical studies have been accompanied by more general reviews of the place of sexuality in organizations. The text *"Sex" at "Work"* (Hearn & Parkin 1995 [1987]) outlined ways in which organizations construct sexuality, sexuality constructs organizations, and organizations and sexuality may occur simultaneously: hence the notion of "organization sexuality." This simultaneous phenomenon may occur in terms of movement and proximity, feelings and emotions, ideology and consciousness, and language and imagery. The concepts of sexual work/labor and sexual labor power are developed, as is perhaps clearest in some retail, advertising, tourism, and leisure industries. Such themes were explored further in *The Sexuality of Organization* (Hearn et al. 1989). The contributors, in different ways, placed sexuality as a very important element in understanding organizational processes, not just something to be added to analysis. Thus, sexual processes and organizational processes are intimately connected, in both the general structuring of organizations and the detail of everyday interaction. Both general and empirical studies emphasize interconnections of sexuality and power in organizations, including the problem of men's power (Gruber & Morgan 2005) and the "male sexual narrative." Some studies recognize the homosexual or homosocial subtext in men's relations with each other, for example, in (homo)sexualized forms of horseplay between men identifying as heterosexual.

Organizations, or at least most organizations, can be understood as *sexualed*, that is, having meaning in relation to sexuality rather than specifically sexualized. This is for several reasons. First, sexual arrangements in private domains provide the base infrastructure, principally through women's unpaid labor in families, for public domain organizations. Second, most organizations continue to exist through dominant heterosexual norms, ideologies, ethics, and practices, for example, in constructions of men top managers' wives. Third, organizational goals and beneficiaries relate to sexuality in many ways, including sexploitation organizations (e.g., sex trade), sexual service organizations (e.g., sex therapy), mutual sexual organizations (e.g., lesbian and gay telephone lines), subordinated sexual organizations (where members' sexual interests appear subordinated to "non-sexual" organizational tasks) (Hearn & Parkin 1995 [1987]). Fourth, gender and sexuality interrelate, intimately and definitionally; it is rather difficult to conceive of gender and sexuality without the other. Fifth, despite links between sexuality and gender, empirical distinctions can be made between sexual and gender dynamics in organizations, for example, in terms of presence/absence of organizational members with different genders and sexualities. Sixth, we live in a period of historical transformation of sexuality, sex trade, and sexual violence, not least with global information and communication technologies (Hearn & Parkin 2001).

Analysis of organizations and sexuality also raises more general theoretical issues: relations of work/labor and sexuality; status of "the economic," specifically capitalism, in constructions of sexuality; relations of material oppressions and discourse; intersectionalities between age, class, disability, ethnicity, gender, generation, "race," religion, and violence in analyzing organizations and sexuality. Critiques of (hetero) sexuality lead onto consideration of relations of surface/appearance and reality/knowledge, in terms of the sexuality of dress or the epistemological significance of looks/appearance for gender analysis. Overall, organizations can be understood as structured, gendered/sexualed, sexually encoded (re)productions, for both organizational members and organizational analysts.

SEE ALSO: Feminism; Feminism, First, Second, and Third Waves; Gender, Work, and Family; Gendered Organizations/Institutions; Queer Theory; Sex and Gender; Sexual Harassment; Sexual Markets, Commodification, and Consumption

REFERENCES AND SUGGESTED READINGS

Cockburn, C. K. (1983) *Brothers: Male Dominance and Technological Change*. Pluto, London.

Cockburn, C. K. (1991) *In the Way of Women: Men's Resistance to Sex Equality in Organizations*. Macmillan, Basingstoke.

Gruber, J. & Morgan, P. (2005) *In the Company of Men: Sexual Harassment and Male Domination*. Northeastern University Press, Boston.

Gutek, B. A. (1985) *Sex and the Workplace: Impact of Sexual Behavior and Harassment on Women, Men, and Organizations*. Jossey-Bass, San Francisco.

Hearn, J. & Parkin, W. (1995 [1987]) *"Sex" at "Work": The Power and Paradox of Organization Sexuality*. Prentice-Hall/Harvester Wheatsheaf, Hemel Hempstead; St. Martin's, New York.

Hearn, J. & Parkin, W. (2001) *Gender, Sexuality, and Violence in Organizations: The Unspoken Forces of Organization Violations*. Sage, London and Thousand Oaks, CA.

Hearn, J., Sheppard, D., Tancred-Sheriff, P., & Burrell, G. (Eds.) (1989) *The Sexuality of Organization*. Sage, London and Newbury Park, CA.

Humphrey, J. (2000) Organizing Sexualities, Organization Inequalities: Lesbians and Gay Men in Public Service Occupations. *Gender, Work, and Organization* 6(3): 134–51.

Lehtonen, J. & Mustola, K. (2004) "Straight People Don't Tell, Do They ...?" Negotiating the Boundaries of Sexuality and Gender at Work. Ministry of Labor, Helsinki. Online. www.esr.fi.

Pringle, R. (1988) *Secretaries Talk: Sexuality, Power, and Work*. Verso, London.

organizations as social structures

Randy Martin

Organizations as social structures is a perspective that focuses on the hardware of human association, the durable factors that govern people's ways of being together as they achieve common goals by coordinated means. As it has been understood in the literature, social structure is what permits the organization's persistence over time; it describes relations among differentiated positions, and references an agency or institutional will that transcends that of individuals. Structure implies wholeness rather than aggregates, predictable patterns of transformation, self-regulation, and closure. Structure itself is a term borrowed from architecture, hence the spatial emphasis on prescribed places that people can inhabit. But if the architect designs the structure before it is inhabited, the organizational cognate can be discerned only after the fact by means of analysis. As the building goes up, its structure is visible to the untrained eye. Only the effects of social structures are visibly manifest in human responses to institutional circumstances – their material is not so much physical as latent. Organizational studies would need to be devised to disclose the plans and patterns of the social edifice.

The possibility of identifying structure rested upon a positive disposition toward the nature of society; namely, that the interconnections among persons were an entity in their own right, but also that these fixtures bore the properties of reason. Society is rational, and structures are the register in which rules can be read. The historical and conceptual novelty and gain of such a sweeping claim needs to be appreciated in relation to its opposite. The rationalistic view confronted the conviction that human action is given by nature, directed from without by omnipotent figures, and that local acts of common people are devoid of logic, insignificant, unworthy of serious attention. The anxieties swirling around the turbulence of market societies derived from the concern that those displaced from traditional beliefs and dispossessed from their ways of life constituted a mass that would devolve into a mob, threatening public order and property. The emerging sociological profile was Janus-faced: modern society was rule giving, but also generated its own forms of unreason; it normalized but engendered abnormality; it imposed association in common but was riven by conflict. As organizational studies coalesced in the twentieth century around the notion of social structure, they undertook the analysis of these societal antinomies in terms that could be either apologetic or critical.

INTELLECTUAL ORIGINS

Early organizational studies, whether prescriptive like those of Taylor (1911) and Fayol (1919) or more predictive like Roethlisberger and Dickson (1939) or Roy (1952), were oriented toward most effective maximization of effort for the reasonableness of profit-taking work. Barnard (1938) and Selznick (1948) launched the turn toward structure by treating the organization as a sui generis entity, an adaptive system in its own right. The concern with labor control that had been so explicit in the first studies seemed masked by the claims that

organization was a universal form that transcended the particularities of the workplace. Yet the seminal studies of the 1950s reflected as much economic changes that increased public sector employment (Selznick 1949), deepened unionization (Gouldner 1954; Lipset et al. 1956), or the rise of professional service fields (Blau 1955).

The consolidation of organizations as a generalizable field of study corresponded less to the passage away from industrialization linked to the first half of the century than to a deepening and extension of the industrial model to domains of activity and association hitherto untouched by it. The resonance of structures across what were presented as functionally distinct domains of polity, culture, and economy made the case that society was becoming increasingly rationalized. At the same time, rationality was itself grounded in problems of labor control and inspired by models of decision-making derived from research and development in the military and the stock market. If the key conceptual turn that gave rise to the field of organizations was the use of structure to treat human association as a system, an architectural metaphor was being used to underwrite the idea that society worked like a machine. But if the system metaphor was to serve the legitimating perquisites of a modernizing society grounded in expanding opportunities for wealth and progressive opportunities for participation in general decision-making, it would need to attend some dynamic of change or morphogenesis in its structure.

The machine is a closed entity, a bounded box, where each part serves the needs of the whole design. Modern society is, by contrast, auto-evolutionary, a machinery that improves itself. To achieve rational evolution (and not simply directionless variation or change), information from the surrounding environment must be taken in to correct the operations of the existing structure. If natural or mechanical systems existed in a state of equilibrium where inputs and outputs were internally recycled, social systems subject to innovation and its uncertain consequences would stray far from equilibrium. Structures would have to change in the face of both internal stresses and external strains. The strategic means to manage these tensions would take the form of systems, operations, informatics, and organizational research. The adaptive structure for the now open system would be the servomechanism (Scott 1975: 3), in actuality a device used in World War II anti-aircraft machine guns to try to get a fix on their moving targets (De Landa 1991). Problems of disequilibrium were also being attacked by students of the stock market, like Henry Markowitz, whose portfolio theory advised internal diversification of positions in stocks to deal with external uncertainty. Internalization of external complexity became a mainstay of organizational theory through the 1970s.

But machines were not simply a metaphor in organizational research and its ideas about structure. The goal of military and portfolio research was to perfect decision-making – or at least mitigate the distorting effects of uncertainty on the capacity to secure predictable outcomes based upon prescribed calculation (a killing on the battlefield or the stock market). The infallible decision-maker, the intelligent machine, the computer first envisaged by Turing was enhanced by the work of computer science pioneer Herbert Simon, who had teamed with Jim March and others in the 1950s and 1960s to model the organization itself on measurably discrete individual decision-making. The notion that structure is the design element of hardware, the architecture of the computer, is as much a literal reference as it is a metaphor. Paradoxically, the work on open and far-from-equilibrium systems initiated in the 1950s had a deferred reception in the field until the 1970s after the reign of structure had its day.

CONCEPTUAL FLORESCENCE AND CHALLENGES

The dialectic between fixity and contingency, continuity and change was expressed in the dualism of structure and process which oriented organizational sociology during its florescence from the 1950s to the mid-1970s. If structure described regularities, process could divine motivation, as decision-makers responded to unintended consequences. Structure could identify variation along three dimensions, complexity, formalization, and centralization. Complexity meant more than that size matters.

It assumed that the sophistication of decision-makers as evident in their specialization, professional experience, and activity spoke to horizontal and vertical differentiation within a given organization as well as to the spatial dispersion of coherent operations at far-flung sites (like a mobile sales force, maintenance and repair staff, or consultants). Formalization measured the rules and procedures used to handle contingencies but also the deformations that could result when rigid bureaucratic personality types were internalized. Finally, centralization referred to the distribution or concentration of power within the organizational hierarchy (Hall 1972).

In their emphasis on professionals within the organization and on decision-making as a function of meritocratic competence, the structural perspective not only displaced labor with norms of participation, but also in so doing reimagined the worker as manager. If people suffered the tyranny of organizations, it was due to "insidious control" that robbed people of their sovereignty, not discretion over how to dispose of associatively created wealth (Blau & Schoenherr 1971). This critical observation returns organizational sociology to its intellectual roots in a tragic Weberian view of rationality that informed critical theory of the Frankfurt School. The technical competency meant to serve fundamental judgments incarcerates social values. The asphyxiating consequence of rule-governed organization was a narrow specialized interest that colonized the general interest in forming associations as an end in itself. The defense of individual iconoclasm against organizational conformity was also part of C. Wright Mills's critique, one which, like the subsequent organizational studies, took the lost autonomy of the professional as its model.

The primacy of structure in organizational sociology was challenged on a number of fronts in the 1970s. The critique of society as a conformity-inducing machine, a staple of sixties movements, was anticipated in the study of organizations. But organizational studies could not sustain the more radical turn that sociology took. The engagement with Marxism, especially the reception of Antonio Gramsci and Harry Braverman, articulated a potent critique of labor, capital, and the state via an interest in the labor process and in cultural studies. The question of structure could no longer be considered formally as a value–neutral mechanism, but pertained to the domination of social life by particular class interests and capacities. Cultural studies unseated the normative conception of culture as shared values, and introduced more nuanced interpretive approaches to questions of agency that the term process had sought to understand.

At the same time, the institutional conditions for organizational studies were undergoing transformation. Professionalization was making itself felt on the liberal arts ideals of education as an end in itself. University enrollments were expanding and much of the growth was concentrated in professional programs like business. Business and management programs, seeking legitimacy as research-based disciplinary endeavors, hired organizational sociologists. The instrumental and prescriptive demands that had characterized the first management studies made themselves felt again. Service to the profession jostled with the claim that organizational structure or theory could be treated as an end in itself. While the 1970s were characterized by labor militancy, a proliferation of social movements politicizing the life world (feminism, environmentalism, civil rights, gay and sexual liberation), and nationalist revolutionary movements for decolonization (from Vietnam to Angola to Nicaragua), managerialism as a way of life was also on the rise. Over the next 20 years, self-help manuals directed toward every conceivable human activity adopted the premise that any problem could be solved or situation improved – be it sex, finances, or personal enlightenment – by application of rational techniques, rules, and formulas. The hubris of organizational studies' confidence in universal structures had been popularized, secularized, commercialized, and profaned. Rationality was specified as providing not just rules, but ruling frameworks for advancing interests attached to historical structures of western colonialism, patriarchy, and capital.

RECENT DIRECTIONS

Over the past 30 years organizational studies have continued within sociology (and perhaps more robustly without). The idea of organizations as bounded entities containing discrete memberships and fixed structures has become untenable, both in concept and in practice. Structure and process have merged and internal and external adaptations have become intertwined (Ahrne 1994). Where once the corporations appeared to have endless capacity for taking the world's complexity into their midst, outsourcing, downsizing, and reengineering have become the order of the day so that now externalization makes suspect the notion of structure as a thing or entity (Scott 2004). On the one hand, organizations have been invited to focus on core competencies, slim down, and become "lean and mean" (Harrison 1994). Yet at the same time, mergers and acquisitions and the ever-enlarging scope and scale of economic activity have continued apace. Corporations over the past 30 years have themselves seen the blurring of inside and outside, and seen structure and process take the form of an amalgamation of the functions of production and circulation, once separated between industrial concerns and banks. Now, General Motors Corporation's largest revenue stream comes from its financial services division, small garment manufacturers trade in currency futures, and, with personal computer-based constant vigilance over one's portfolio, daily life is more finely calibrated than ever before to the discipline of financial management. A plethora of financial instruments has emerged, the value of which has dwarfed the annual global product by a factor of ten.

This trend toward financialization has had significant organizational consequences. Securitization, the bundling together of discrete debts (such as from mortgages, credit cards, or auto loans) into tradeable commodities, achieves a complex spatial dispersion of association via ownership that is no longer localized in a particular institution (like a thrift or savings and loan). Derivatives, financial tools for managing risk that tie a prospective variation in, say, exchange rates to the underlying value of a commodity, are now a $100 trillion market by which relatively small but volatile investments can send ripple effects through global financial markets (as occurred in the Asian financial meltdowns of the late 1990s, the scandals associated with Enron, or the failed high stakes hedge fund Long Term Capital Management) (Li Puma & Lee 2004). Where structure referred to well-bounded closed organizational systems, managerial strategies were oriented toward the externalization of uncertainty. Financialization rewards risk, and suggests a logic where the inside (firm assets, personnel, branding) can be leveraged to forms of association or economic interconnection that are features of organizational environments (Martin 2002). This logic of highly leveraged risk embrace, evident in militaristic foreign policy, approaches to fiscal regulation (tax cuts and anti-inflationary monetary approaches), and the shift from defined benefit to defined contribution notions of social welfare (compassionate conservatism and the ownership society) augur a potential return of organizational structure's interest in patterns and regularities across apparently discrete societal domains. If, contrary to recent sociological formulations, contemporary society is characterized not simply by efforts to externalize risk, but also by risk embrace through structural effects unleashed on the world by a series of organizational initiatives, something like structure, albeit in revised form, may be poised for a return to analytic attentions.

This has certainly been the direction of much recent work in organizational theory, some of which has identified explicitly a "new structuralism" to expand the earlier objectivist concept to embrace external resources and agential meanings and embodiments (Lounsbury & Ventresca 2003). But even this new structuralism has kept its sociological sources and debts closely guarded. Unlike the broad transdisciplinary framework from which it takes its name and to which organizational studies aspired, this trend has tended to stay close to the sociological border. For the idea of social structure to stage a robust comeback, organizational theorists will need to be sufficiently sensitive to nuanced analytic approaches that complicate the basic concept and its attendant metaphors and applications. As historians of the field have noted, organization theorists achieved substantial scholarly recognition by turning inward, engaging a deep and generative conversation and research agenda among themselves (Scott 2004).

What was lost to these endeavors was the benefit of more philosophically endowed interlocutors. Hence sociology's structural functionalism made scant use of the structuralism developed through semiotics and other interpretive approaches from aesthetics, literary studies, psychoanalysis, and anthropology. The cost of this intellectual parochialism was high. Social structure existed in space, but without history. It attained objectivity, but one divorced from subjective intentionality and agency. The result was a highly formalistic separation of structure and process, inside and outside, macro and micro. The two halves of these binaries were always found wanting the other. Adding body to mind, subjective to objective, stasis to change, decision to environment did little to upend the brittle dualistic thinking that had produced these semantic chains to begin with. The more supple cache of approaches – loosely grouped under the rubric of poststructuralism – that were committed to critically rethinking the binary structures of thought that gave rise to the human sciences was, until recently, viewed with suspicion.

During the 1990s, most notably in the pages of the journal *Organizations*, that state of affairs began to change. A much broader disciplinary and philosophical archive has been brought to bear on the study of organizations. New immigrants to business and management and other professional programs that treat organizations as conceptually central to their enterprises have brought with them different customs of reading and research. Appropriate to the times, the architectural metaphor that social structure had rested upon may shift its reference from buildings (the internal skeleton) to computers, where the term applies at once to hardware and software. Structure's future may lie in its ability to transit in between.

SEE ALSO: Organization Theory; Postmodern Organizations; Poststructuralism; Structuralism; Structure and Agency; System Theories

REFERENCES AND SUGGESTED READINGS

Ahrne, G. (1994) *Social Organization: Interaction Inside, Outside, and Between Organizations.* Sage, London.

Barnard, C. (1938) *The Functions of the Executive.* Harvard University Press, Cambridge, MA.

Blau, P. (1955) *The Dynamics of Bureaucracy.* Chicago University Press, Chicago.

Blau, P. & Schoenherr, R. (1971) *The Structure of Organizations*. Basic Books, New York.

De Landa, M. (1991) *War in the Age of Intelligent Machines*. Zone Books, New York.

Fayol, H. (1919) *General and Industrial Management*. Pitman, London.

Gouldner, A. (1954) *Patterns of Industrial Bureaucracy*. Free Press, Glencoe, IL.

Hall, R. (1972) *Organizations: Structure and Process*. Prentice-Hall, Englewood Cliffs, NJ.

Harrison, B. (1994) *Lean and Mean: The Changing Landscape of Corporate Power in an Age of Flexibility*. Basic Books, New York.

Li Puma, E. & Lee, B. (2004) *Financial Derivatives and the Globalization of Risk*. Duke University Press, Durham, NC.

Lipset, S., Coleman, M., & Trow, J. (1956) *Union Democracy*. Free Press, Glencoe, IL.

Lounsbury, M. & Ventresca, M. (2003) The New Structuralism in Organizational Theory. *Organizations* 10: 457–80.

March, J. & Simon, H. (1958) *Organizations*. Wiley, New York.

Martin, R. (2002) *Financialization of Daily Life*. Temple University Press, Philadelphia.

Roethlisberger, F. & Dickson, W. (1939) *Management and the Worker*. Harvard University Press, Cambridge, MA.

Roy, D. (1952) Quota Restriction and Goldbricking in a Machine Shop. *American Journal of Sociology* 57: 427–42.

Scott, W. R. (1975) Organizational Structure. *Annual Review of Sociology* 1: 1–20.

Scott, W. R. (2004) Reflections on a Half-Century of Organizational Sociology. *Annual Review of Sociology* 30: 1–21.

Selznick, P. (1948) Foundations of the Theory of Organizations. *American Sociological Review* 12: 25–35.

Selznick, P. (1949) *TVA and the Grassroots*. University of California Press, Berkeley.

Taylor, F. (1911) *The Principles of Scientific Management*. Harper, New York.

organizations and the theory of the firm

Pursey P. M. A. R. Heugens

When economists speak of a theory of the firm, they mean something very specific. They use the term either to denote a theory that addresses the issue of the existence and boundaries of the multi-person firm, or to explain its internal structure and organization. Examples of the former type may rightly be called *why* theories of the firm, as they seek to explain why firms exist in the face of institutional alternatives like markets and hybrids. Representatives of the latter type are best addressed as *how* theories of the firm, as they set out to provide accounts of how complex organizations succeed in combining the heterogeneous inputs of differentially motivated individuals into meaningful collective outcomes (Heugens 2005).

The distinguishing characteristic of all *why* theories of the firm is that they treat the formal organization as an aberration, which requires explanation because alternative institutions for organizing economic activities exist. In the words of Ronald Coase (1937), theoreticians should "attempt to discover why a firm emerges at all in a specialized exchange economy." Coase's fundamental observation in this respect was that markets are not and can never be without friction, and that there is therefore always a cost attached to using the central coordination system of the market (i.e., the price system). These so-called transaction costs primarily consist of finding prices, negotiating contracts, and bearing the risk of adaptation to changing circumstances. These transaction costs are so fundamental to processes of material exchange that economics Nobel laureate Kenneth Arrow simply refers to them as the "costs of running the economic system."

Coase's observations on the theory of the firm are important because of their unique descriptive qualities, which allow observers of individual firms to determine why some authority (the firm's "entrepreneur") has decided to save certain marketing costs by forming an organization. But what really gave transaction cost economics the predictive power to forecast which transactions would have to be organized within the firm and which could safely be left to the market was Oliver Williamson's specification of the material characteristics and the human behavioral features that drive the transaction cost of each transaction type. The most important material characteristic of economic exchanges is their asset specificity: the extent to which they involve "durable investments that are undertaken in support of particular transactions, the opportunity cost of which investments is much lower in best alternative uses or by alternative users should the original transaction be prematurely terminated" (Williamson 1985: 55). The most important behavioral characteristic of contractual man (*sic*) is that he sometimes (though certainly not always) resorts to subtle or less-subtle forms of deceit to advance his self-interest "with guile" (p. 47). In conjunction, these two characteristics produce market imperfections because no rational producer would invest in non-redeployable assets if there were the likelihood of premature contract termination by an opportunistic buyer. In turn, this explains why firms exist, because these imperfections leave the buyers of goods that require non-redeployable assets for their production no other option than to erect a hierarchy in which professional managers are given the rational-legal authority to safeguard such investments from opportunism.

Alchian and Demsetz (1972) have offered a different but related view on why certain productive activities can better be organized within the firm than across markets. They observe that it is often possible to increase the productivity of a collective of individuals through teamwork. In a team the gains from specialization and cooperative production typically yield a cooperative surplus, which cannot uniquely be attributed to the efforts of any individual member. The problem with team production is that there are costs associated with determining the effort levels and marginal productivity of members. Because of these metering costs, each worker has a greater incentive to shirk when he or she works as part of a team as compared to being self-employed. The metering problem calls for the appointment of a specialist, whose main task is to estimate marginal productivity by observing or specifying input behavior. If this specialist were simply another employee, however, the classical *quis custodiet ipsos custodes* in the background. The only solution to the monitoring-the-monitor problem is to make the specialist the residual claimant of the team, and to endow him or her with the exclusive rights to observe input behavior, to write contracts for the collective, to hire and fire, and to sell all of the aforementioned rights to third parties. This concentration of rights in the hands of a single entrepreneur marks the birth of a classical

capitalist firm, and the tandem of the team productive surplus and the metering problem thus offers a second answer to the question of why firms exist in the face of institutional alternatives.

Agency theorists – representatives of a third *why* theory of the firm – take issue with the Alchian–Demsetz definition of the entrepreneur as "the centralized contractual agent in a team productive process." Fama (1980), for example, suggests that the entrepreneur as manager-risk bearer should be laid to rest because management (i.e., the above functions of observing input behavior and writing contracts) is naturally separated from risk bearing (i.e., the right to economic residuals and the right to sell this right) in the context of the modern corporation. This observation is significant because an acknowledgment of the separation between ownership and control implies a subtle shift of the *why* question. As Jensen and Meckling (1976) have framed it: "How does it happen that millions of individuals are willing to turn over a significant fraction of their wealth to organizations run by managers who have so little interest in their welfare?" The agency theory response to this question hinges on two assumptions. The first of these is that it is not in the best interest of an individual securities owner to participate in the strategic management of any individual company directly, as the optimal portfolio for any investor is likely to be diversified across the securities of many firms. Investors thus need agents. The second assumption is that organizational hierarchies are more efficient instruments for curbing managerial opportunism than market-based contracts (Fama 1980). The logic of this second assumption is completely the opposite of the first. By embedding managers in managerial hierarchies, they are typically prevented from diversifying their most important source of income: the compensation paid for their services. Once the manager is made dependent on the corporation, the agency problem can be solved by making the pay of the manager dependent on the performance of the corporation. In the view of agency theorists, organizations thus exist because they provide the most efficient governance solution for securities holders who cannot or who do not want to participate directly in the securing of their investments.

The marvel of the three types of *why* theories is that they show why the erection of managerial hierarchies is a necessary and efficient response to the opportunism problems faced by investors in non-redeployable assets, loyal team workers, and securities holders, respectively. Arguably, this is the greatest achievement in the field of economic organization of the last six or seven decades. There are nevertheless problems with this combined body of work, the most pressing of which is that the image of the modern business firm that emerges from it is at best an abstract notion like a nexus of contracts and at worst an empty box (Jensen & Meckling 1976). In the words of Fritz Machlup (1967):

> The firm in the model world of economic micro-theory ought not to call forth any irrelevant associations with firms in the real world. We know, of course, that there are firms in reality and that they have boards of directors and senior and junior executives, who do, with reference to hundreds of different products, a great many things – which are entirely irrelevant for the microtheoretical model. The fictitious firm of the model is a 'uni-brain,' an individual decision-unit that has nothing to do but adjust the output and the prices of one or two imaginary products to very simple imagined changes in data.

The *why* theories of the firm thus typically abstract from any notion of organizations as social structures and evade the complex set of questions pertaining to the internal design of the modern firm. Inevitably, a scholarly attempt would come to fill in this lacuna and address the central problem of internal organization: How exactly do firms connect individual actions to collectively productive outcomes?

How theories of the firm typically do not address the question of why firms exist in light of institutional alternatives, but rather take the fact that firms exist as given. In contrast with "why" theoreticians, students of the "how" perspective seek "conceptualizations and models of business enterprises which explain and predict their structure and behaviors" (Grant 1996). The fundamental question these latter alternatives must address therefore is how purposeful collective outcomes can be obtained from the many individuals employed by a given organization. This question is not straightforward to answer because workplace diversity is substantial even for the most homogeneous of organizations. Each individual member has (1) a unique knowledge base, (2) a sheer unlimited set of action alternatives at his or her disposal, and (3) an idiosyncratic interest structure. These three sources of variety (and strategies to manage them constructively) take center stage in the knowledge-based, evolutionary, and behavioral theories of the firm, respectively.

Knowledge-based theory proposes that firms are essentially repositories of individuals whose knowledge bases are irreducibly different (Conner & Prahalad 1996). These differences can be productive. If organization members are allowed to specialize in certain forms of knowledge, significant economies of knowledge acquisition can be realized at the individual level. Collectively, knowledge differences allow for the exploitation of comparative person-to-person advantages within the firm. But the exploitation of knowledge heterogeneity involves a coordination problem because functional specialization breeds internal interdependencies. Knowledge-based theoreticians tend to seek the solution to this problem in organizational design efforts that are highly reminiscent of James Thompson's writings on technology and structure. Thompson has proposed that the key to managing interdependencies lies in the design of work settings: "By delimiting responsibilities, control over resources, and other matters, organizations provide their participating members with boundaries within which efficiency may be a reasonable expectation" (Thompson 1967: 54). The exact shape of the setting has to depend on the type of interdependencies that exist between the tasks required to "get a job done" (see March & Simon 1958). In the situation that each task renders a discrete contribution to the whole, coordination efforts among specialists must take the form of standardization. Where interdependence takes a serial form, such that one specialist's output forms the input for another, coordination by plan is key. When interdependencies are reciprocal, and each specialist simultaneously produces inputs for other specialists and processes their outputs, coordination inevitably takes the form of mutual adjustment. The gist of these arguments is that organizations can foster and accommodate knowledge heterogeneity as long as their work settings are designed in accordance with specialists' coordination needs. The knowledge-based answer to the "how" question is therefore that organizations connect individual actions to collective outcomes by aligning work settings with task interdependencies.

The evolutionary theory of the firm (Nelson & Winter 1982) offers a related perspective on the question of how organizations link individual actions to collective outcomes. Like knowledge-based approaches, evolutionary theories are explicitly microfounded "in the sense that they must involve or at least be consistent with a story of what agents do and why they do it" (Dosi 1997). One of these microfoundations is that agents continuously introduce various forms of novelty in organizations because they continuously discover new organizational set-ups, technologies, and behavioral patterns. Yet the theory simultaneously tries to offer explanations for coherent aggregate phenomena like organizational innovation and learning, economic growth, and industrial change (Nelson & Winter 1982). The central question of the evolutionary perspective is therefore: What is the source of this coherence, or why do firms "hang together" in the face of this continuous variation at the micro level? Nelson and Winter point to the central role organizational routines or decision rules play in this respect: "The basic behavioral premise [of evolutionary theory] is that a firm at any time operates largely according to a set of decision rules that link a domain of environmental stimuli to a range of responses on the part of firms" (Nelson & Winter 1974). The innovative and exploratory behaviors of organization members are thus tamed by decision rules that direct their efforts toward the achievement of organizational goals (Heugens 2005). In contrast with the knowledge-based view of the firm, the basic challenge of the evolutionary perspective is not to explain how firms cope with irreducible knowledge differentials among members, but how they should deal with the a priori limitless array of behavioral options these members have at their disposal. Furthermore, the variety-controlling mechanism that evolutionary theorists propose is not to better design work settings, but to infuse organizational members with decision rules that act upon the menu of behavioral options available to them. The evolutionary-theoretical answer to the *how* question is therefore that organizations connect individual actions to collective outcomes by routinizing the behavior of organizational members.

The behavioral theory of the firm (Cyert & March 1963) offers the third and last perspective on the question of how firms function. The key to understand the behavioral approach is to take into account how it differs from neoclassical theories of the firm. Proponents of the latter theories take the firm to be a homogeneous production unit guided by an undisputed goal (e.g., profit maximization). Behavioralists, in contrast, recognize the fact that a firm consists of a series of component subunits and that idiosyncratic interests and motives typically characterize each of these subunits. This situation potentially leads to conflict within organizations because a given organizational subunit may perceive the goals of other units as plainly unacceptable, as incomparable with its own, or as uncertain factors that may interfere with the realization of its own ambitions in unforeseen ways (March & Simon 1958). The central question of the behavioral perspective therefore is: How can organizations be collectively productive in the face of all this potential internal conflict? Behavioralists propose that this is the case because there are stabilizing factors at work at both the subunit and organizational levels. At the subunit level, managers are compelled to work toward attainable and acceptable outcomes rather than toward maximum outcomes ("satisficing" rather than "maximizing"). This reduces intra-organizational conflict because where maximizing behavior would turn organizations into "winner-take-all" environments tainted by many losers, satisficing behavior offers multiple subunits the opportunity to realize at least some of their objectives. At the organizational level, planning and budgeting cycles act as measures to manage time and reduce organizational conflict (Cyert & March 1963). Not only are these cycles characterized by periodicity – such that they concentrate organizational conflict in certain periods after which business can proceed as usual – they also provide schedules specifying the minimally required actions and outcomes over which haggling is not possible. In sum, the behavioral answer to the "how" question is that organizations connect individual actions to collective outcomes by reducing the potential for intra-organizational conflict.

Measured by the usual strict and forbidding definitional standards that economists tend to employ, organizational sociologists do not have a theory of the firm, only organization theories. What they lack specifically is the ambition to resolve the type of questions that economists typically occupy themselves with ("why do firms exist" and "how do they connect individual inputs to collectively meaningful outputs"). But sociologists do have something that comes pretty close: theories of bureaucracy. Sociologists have long had an interest in bureaucratic life. Most tend to look upon bureaucracies as highly interesting quasi-experimental settings that possess a number of characteristics of due significance to the sociologist's eye: they are large, numerous, permanent, accessible, and purposive (Blau & Meyer 1987). As such, it is hard to imagine a more benign playground in which the empirically inclined sociologist can test his or her theories about authority relations, compliance structures, group coherence, deviance, and a host of other topics the casual reader can find scattered across the pages of the present volume.

But not all sociologists look at bureaucratic organizations as if they were merely convenient laboratories full of briefcase-carrying guinea pigs. Some sociologists have recognized bureaucracies as the socially unique and economically indispensable phenomena they really are, and proceeded by studying them in their own right. Their labors have yielded many fruits that have changed the landscape of organizational sociology forever. Some of these include theories portraying organizations as coercive institutions that manage to lock individual members ever more tightly into the "iron cage" of modernity (Weber 1978). Others have looked upon bureaucracies as powerful instruments that easily spin out of control due to a lack of self-correcting mechanisms, which lead to "trained incapacity" and "overconformity" on behalf of their members (Merton 1968). Still others have demonstrated that even though they possess a number of relatively universal characteristics – impersonal rules, centralization of decisions, isolation of organizational strata – bureaucracies are still institutions that are deeply embedded in and thus unique to the cultures that host them

(Crozier 1964). Finally, others have demonstrated that bureaucracies, due to their propensity to encode new experiences and dilemmas in relatively durable organizational rules, are superior vehicles for organizational learning (Levitt & March 1988).

Such sociological bureaucracy theories have of course attracted a lot of implicit and sometimes rather overt criticism by economists. Much of this criticism can be summed up, in a nutshell, as mistaken imperialism. Many economists simply do not like to acknowledge the fact that it is possible to say sensible things about economic organization by means of sociological methods. But this is unfortunate, since theory-of-the-firm scholars and bureaucracy theoreticians are closer together on many issues than many would be willing to admit. For one, they share an empirical object. Furthermore, it is hard for sociologists to deny that economic factors like efficiency and productivity play a decisive role in the design of private – and increasingly even public – bureaucracies. Alternatively, many economists are slowly warming up to the idea that social factors may have a profound influence on, say, the production functions of firms. More importantly, the profound differences in terms of foci and explanatory strategies that undeniably exist between economists and sociologists could in fact turn out to be beneficial complementarities. With respect to a further, productive integration between theories of the firm on the one hand and theories of bureaucracy on the other, sociologists could certainly benefit from the economic focus on the existence of bureaucratic structures and their ability to generate surplus value. In turn, economic theories of the firm would in many cases be better off with a "thicker" description of economic reality – even if we respect the discipline's almost obsessive fetish for parsimony. A hopeful trend in this respect is the profound increase in the popularity of behavioral boundary conditions to otherwise orthodox economic theories. Seen from that perspective, the chasm that separates theories of the firm and theories of bureaucracy begins to appear less massive and intimidating than it once did.

SEE ALSO: Organization Theory; Organizations as Coercive Institutions; Organizations as

Social Structures; Rational Legal Authority; Strategic Management (Organizations); Teamwork; Time; Workplace Diversity

REFERENCES AND SUGGESTED READINGS

Alchian, A. A. & Demsetz, H. (1972) Production, Information Costs, and Economic Organization. *American Economic Review* 62: 777–95.

Blau, P. M. & Meyer, M. W. (1987) *Bureaucracy in Modern Society*, 3rd edn. Random House, New York.

Coase, R. H. (1937) The Nature of the Firm. *Economica* 4 (November): 386–405.

Conner, K. R. & Prahalad, C. K. (1996) A Resource-Based Theory of the Firm: Knowledge versus Opportunism. *Organization Science* 7(5): 477–501.

Crozier, M. (1964) *The Bureaucratic Phenomenon*. University of Chicago Press, Chicago.

Cyert, R. M. & March, J. G. (1963) *A Behavioral Theory of the Firm*. Prentice-Hall, Englewood Cliffs, NJ.

Dosi, G. (1997) Opportunities, Incentives and the Collective Patterns of Technological Change. *Economic Journal* 107 (September): 1530–47.

Fama, E. F. (1980) Agency Problems and the Theory of the Firm. *Journal of Political Economy* 88: 288–307.

Foss, N. J. (1996) Knowledge-Based Approaches to the Theory of the Firm: Some Critical Comments. *Organization Science* 7: 470–6.

Grant, R. M. (1996) Toward a Knowledge-Based Theory of the Firm. *Strategic Management Journal* 17 (Winter special issue): 109–22.

Heugens, P. P. M. A. R. (2005) A Neo-Weberian Theory of the Firm. *Organization Studies* 26(1).

Jensen, M. C. & Meckling, W. H. (1976) The Theory of the Firm: Managerial Behavior, Agency Costs and Ownership Structure. *Journal of Financial Economics* 3: 305–60.

Levitt, B. & March, J. G. (1988) Organizational Learning. *Annual Review of Sociology* 14: 319–40.

Machlup, F. (1967) Theories of the Firm: Marginalist, Behavioral, Managerial. *American Economic Review* 52: 1–33.

March, J. G. & Simon, H. A. (1958) *Organizations*. Wiley, New York.

Merton, R. K. (1968) *Social Theory and Social Structure*. Free Press, New York.

Nelson, R. R. & Winter, S. G. (1974) Neoclassical versus Evolutionary Theories of Economic Growth: Critique and Prospectus. *Economic Journal* 84: 886–905.

Nelson, R. R. & Winter, S. G. (1982) *An Evolutionary Theory of Economic Change*. Harvard University Press, Cambridge, MA.

Thompson, J. D. (1967) *Organizations in Action: Social Science Bases of Administrative Theory*. McGraw-Hill, New York.

Weber, M. (1978) *Economy and Society: An Outline of Interpretative Sociology*. University of California Press, Berkeley.

Williamson, O. E. (1985) *The Economic Institutions of Capitalism: Firms, Markets, Relational Contracting*. Free Press, New York.

organizations as total institutions

Nick Perry

The analysis of the characteristics of total institutions is the subject of a lengthy essay by Erving Goffman, a Canadian-born sociologist best known for his complex and subtle contributions to the analysis of social interaction. He defined the term as "a place of residence and work where a large number of like-situated individuals cut off from the wider society for an appreciable period of time together lead an enclosed formally administered round of life" (Goffman 1961: xiii). Shorter versions of his argument were first published in 1957. It was, however, through the longer paper's appearance as the lead essay in his second book, *Asylums* (1961: 1–124), that the concept became best known.

The term itself had actually been coined by his graduate school teacher, the Chicago-based sociologist Everett Hughes. Hughes had cited nunneries as an example, but Goffman's development of the idea was based upon his three-year study of psychiatric inmates, including a year-long period of participant observation in a large mental hospital in Washington, DC. Goffman was, however, at pains to emphasize that he understood the concept to have an altogether wider relevance and applicability. Thus in his analysis, examples of total institutions include not only mental hospitals but also prisons, boarding schools, monasteries and convents, ships, army barracks, and isolated work camps. He further argued that all such enterprises are distinguished by the extent to which they share a distinctive cluster of structural characteristics and internal social processes. For as he points out, most members of modern societies tend to sleep, play, and work in different places, with different co-participants, under different authorities and without being subject to some overall design. What distinguishes total institutions, however, is that the barriers between these aspects of life are broken down. Not only are all aspects of life conducted in the same place and subject to the same single authority, those activities are also subject to "batching," that is, they are undertaken alongside others who are treated alike and expected to do the same things together. Moreover, each day's activities are imperatively and tightly scheduled in accordance with a system of rules and the demands of a body of officials. This wide-ranging system for the coordination of daily activities is purportedly in accordance with a single rational plan through which the official aim of the institution may be fulfilled (Goffman 1961: 5–6).

Some commentators have suggested that Goffman's use of the word institution is somewhat misleading, in that the term "social institutions" has a particular cluster of meanings within the sociological literature. It expresses a recognition of the continuity and endurance of social life as it is formed and reformed in and through such phenomena as the law and the family. "Total organization" has therefore been proposed as an altogether more accurate and appropriate category. Against this, Goffman's choice of terminology reflects his conception of a total institution as a "social hybrid, part residential community, part formal organization." What is insinuated by his employment of the term "institution" is that the associated social processes are understood as something more than the impersonal workings of bureaucratic procedures or market forces. For they involve the allocation of identities as well as the distribution of duties and the provision of rewards. Hence what is also conveyed is a diffuse sense of the cultural "embeddedness" of organizational practices. This is a theme that is echoed in the otherwise different approach to organizational analysis of scholars such as

Philip Selznick and subsequently Mark Granovetter – influential practitioners of what Charles Perrow (1972) has identified as the "institutional school" of organizational sociology.

IMPLICATIONS FOR INMATES AND STAFF

What Goffman goes on to explore are the effects of the characteristics of total institutions upon the constituting of selfhood, more specifically the selfhood of mental patients. From the point at which they enter into total institutions, inmates' prior conceptions of their selves are subject to a process of mortification. This occurs directly by way of the institution's degrading admission procedures, and indirectly through the curtailment of the repertoire of roles and opportunities for interaction that are matter-of-factly available to persons in the world outside. In the institution's engagement with the resultant diminished self, its staff strive to establish an alternate, all-embracing notion of inmate identity, one that is consonant with institutional expectations and which is based upon its control of what were hitherto taken-for-granted privileges. The objective is to go beyond eliciting an outward behavioral conformity; the intention is to induce the inmate's active acceptance and internalizing of the institution's conception of what it is to be a "proper" person.

Goffman further suggests that there are clear affinities between the reactions and responses of mental patients and those that are typical of the inmates in other types of total institutions. Faced with a restricted range of opportunities for interaction, inmates seek to preserve and protect a sense of self through various strategies of adaptation and adjustment. These latter include fantasizing and intransigence that, in context, are both meaningful and reasonable. But in what Robert Merton and others might well identify as a self-fulfilling prophecy, such strategies are typically interpreted as warranting the very control procedures that have served to elicit these kinds of responses. For inmates generally, the modal procedure for ensuring the preservation of the self may thus be one of "playing it cool," i.e., being suitably compliant in the presence of staff but supportive of countermores with their peers. What such patterns of interaction suggest with respect to mental patients is thus that it is organizational processes rather than illness which are responsible for the formation of a particular concept of patient identity. As Goffman sardonically notes at one point, "the staff problem here is to find a crime that will fit the punishment" (1961: 85).

As this observation implies, the staff of total institutions face dilemmas of their own. These are a consequence of (1) the difficulties that derive from a conception of people as material to be processed, and (2) the contradiction between what the institution does (functions as a "storage dump for inmates") and what staff are expected to say it does ("reforms inmates in accordance with some ideal standard"). A subsequent sociology of organizations literature would identify this latter contrast as having a wider applicability. Thus for Meyer and Rowan (1977: 340), the formal structures of many organizations are understood to be ceremonial and to "reflect the myths of their institutional environments instead of the demands of their work activities." As a result, such organizations build gaps between the acceptable public face that is enshrined in their formal structures – upon which they depend for funds and legitimation – and those practices through which their real work gets done. The decoupling of these activities and management of the consequent gaps is thus a responsibility of, and dilemma for, the staff of such organizations.

Goffman may have been sardonic about psychiatry, but he was not hostile to its practitioners. This is indicated by his acknowledgment of the intellectual openness and support of psychiatric staff members, and the receptivity that they accorded to his study. Rather, what was distinctive about Goffman's argument was that, in the absence of physical indicators of illness, he saw psychiatrists as adept at generating sociological observations. What they produced were data about rule-following and rule-breaking rather than diagnoses with a material grounding. But as a result of its explicit foregrounding of the social world of the mental patient, Goffman's study was interpreted as congruent with the emerging anti-psychiatry movement associated with the work of Thomas

Szasz, R. D. Laing, and others. His work thus came to be seen as part of a more general critique of the institutionalization of the mentally ill that developed during the 1960s. The associated shift in treatment strategies, with its emphasis on returning inmates to the wider community, linked conservative(s') concerns with costs to radical(s') arguments about personal freedom.

CULTURAL CONTEXT AND CRITICAL RESPONSE

The study's impact was by no means limited to this milieu, however, or to analyses of the mental hospital. Following the initial presentation of his ideas to an audience of psychiatric professionals, the longer version of Goffman's essay had first featured as a contribution to Donald Cressey's (1961) influential volume of papers on the prison. Beyond this, the concept was perceived to be of more general relevance to the sociology of organizations. This is evident from its incorporation in most of the best-known collections of readings and its citation in the standard textbooks of the subdiscipline. For example, in 1965 it was referred to in several of the independently authored chapters of the *Handbook of Organizations* edited by James March. This substantial volume is generally regarded as an authoritative summary statement of the state of play within the field at that time. What total institutions were seen to represent was a categorization of establishments that offered an analytic advance over "commonsense" classifications. Moreover, this was combined with an emphasis upon (inter)actions and meanings rather than what was – at that time – the more conventional focus upon organizational structures. This emphasis facilitated what has come to be recognized as a characteristic oscillation in Goffman's writing – that between the manifest elaboration and nuanced interpretation of subtle differences and the tacit affirmation of an underlying pattern. For what Goffman's study sought to signal is that it was not just total institutions but organizations generally that should be viewed as places for generating assumptions about identity.

The specific social and cultural context in which the total institution concept was developed was that of the US during the 1950s. With hindsight, it can be seen to bear the trace of the Cold War concerns of that time. Thus it is possible to discern both (1) the period's political preoccupation with totalitarianism as a theme and (2) concurrent anxieties about conformity at home, as they were expressed by American cultural commentators and critics such as William Whyte, David Reisman, and C. Wright Mills. Totalitarianism was a notion that both linked together Nazi Germany and Soviet Russia (and, prospectively, Communist China) and clearly contrasted with the pluralism that was understood to be a – if not the – defining attribute of American society and politics. Yet what the total institution concept explicitly pointed out was the presence within plural societies of a distinctive category of social establishments in which the preconditions for pluralism were purposely not met. Goffman's account thus served both to (1) identify affinities between the internal social processes of such local establishments and those of totalitarian regimes and (2) mirror contemporary critical concerns about conformity.

Goffman's elaboration and qualification of the concept is often witty. It also involves something more than a conventional compromise between conceptual clarity and empirical adequacy; between an elegant idea and its altogether more disorderly social expression. It is presented as if empirical but is in part speculative; presented as comparative but with an emphasis on the mental hospital. Goffman is both prolific in his use of footnotes and eclectic with respect to his sources, drawing upon not just academic journals and monographs but also personal memoirs, anecdotes, novels, and popular magazines as well as his own astute observations. The examples he invokes are therefore better understood as designed to illustrate a concept or to elucidate a process rather than to prove an argument. This characteristic mode of presentation has engaged many commentators and enraged some of them. Its import is both textual/aesthetic and methodological. For example, Patricia Clough (1990: 189) offers what is presently the best account of Goffman's distinctive literary style, locating its ambivalent appeal in the way that it "seduces the reader less into the forward movement of a text and more into submission to a detailed behavioral protocol."

METHODOLOGICAL ISSUES AND CONCEPTUAL DEVELOPMENTS

The concept has also prompted a related debate over methodology. First of all, the study had benefited from Goffman having taken up a year-long position as the assistant sports coach in a large mental hospital. This location both placed him outside the main line of authority and allowed him substantial freedom of movement. But the subsequent account does not read like a conventional ethnography, in that the reader is not provided with background material on the research site nor even any quotations from informants. It is instead what Philip Manning (1992: 9) refers to as the ethnography of a concept rather than the ethnography of a place. Second, Goffman acknowledges that the characteristics of total institutions are neither peculiar to total institutions nor shared by every one of them. Rather, they are present to an intense degree, and in later published versions of his analysis he (somewhat misleadingly) invokes the notion of ideal types as a methodological warrant for his emphasis on the similarities between total institutions. Subsequent studies have, by contrast, sought to identify and to explain the differences between them in accordance with a more obviously comparative intent.

Thus Lewis Coser (1974), in noting that that there are overlaps between "total" and his own notion of "greedy" institutions, nonetheless insists on the distinctiveness of the latter. Examples of greedy institutions include traditional domestic servitude, the Bolsheviks, and the Catholic priesthood, and the total loyalty and commitment which they seek from their membership. Although they may in some instances make use of the physical isolation characteristic of total institutions, they are actually defined by, and are concerned to construct, symbolic barriers between insiders and outsiders. They also tend to rely upon voluntary compliance rather than enforced coercion — itself one of the salient distinctions *within* total institutions that is blurred by Goffman's analysis. And in an independently conceived but somewhat similar initiative, Amitai Etzioni (1975: 264–76) put forward the notions of scope and pervasiveness, understood as discrete variables rather than as principles of organizing. Organizations whose participants share many activities are identified as broad in scope, whereas narrow organizations are those which share few. Pervasiveness refers to the normative boundaries of a collectivity whereas scope refers to its action boundaries. That these do not necessarily coincide leads Etzioni to suggest a systematic distinction between two kinds of "total organizations"; both are, by definition, high in scope but one (e.g., the prison) is low and the other (e.g., the nunnery) high in pervasiveness. It is suggested that this distinction is linked, in turn, to other kinds of differences.

Nevertheless, almost 50 years after it was first introduced, what has come to seem most contemporary about the concept of the total institution is what it has to say about the general relationship between any organization and the process of identity formation. "Contemporary" because of the influence of Michel Foucault's writings upon current versions of the sociology of organization and the processes of subject formation. If Goffman's essay is filtered and read through such a framework, then – the differences in their respective idioms notwithstanding – what emerges are some striking parallels. There are clear affinities between total institutions and Foucault's notion of carceral organizations, and between their respective conceptions – Goffman's ethnographic, Foucault's historical – of what Foucault meant by disciplinary practices and normalizing power. Thus when Goffman observes that "Built right into the social arrangements of an organization, then, is a thoroughly embracing conception of the member – and not merely a conception of him *qua* member, but behind this a conception of him as a human being" (1961: 180), what he indicates is that he sees total institutions as the limit cases of a general tendency.

SEE ALSO: Ethnography; Foucault, Michel; Goffman, Erving; Ideal Type; Interaction Order; Mental Disorder; Organizations as Coercive Institutions; Organizations as Social Structures; Prisons; Self; Self-Fulfilling Prophecy; Surveillance; Totalitarianism

REFERENCES AND SUGGESTED READINGS

Burns, T. (1992) *Erving Goffman*. Routledge, London.
Clough, P. (1990) Reading Goffman: Toward the Deconstruction of Sociology. In: Riggins, S. (Ed.), *Beyond Goffman: Studies on Communication, Institution, and Social Interaction*. Mouton de Gruyter, Berlin and New York, pp. 187–202.
Coser, L. (1974) *Greedy Institutions*. Free Press, New York.
Cressey, D. (Ed.) (1961) *The Prison*. Holt, Rinehart, & Winston, New York.
Etzioni, A. (1975) *A Comparative Analysis of Complex Organizations*, rev. and enlarged edn. Free Press, New York.
Goffman, E. (1961) *Asylums: Essays on the Social Situation of Mental Patients and Other Inmates*. Doubleday Anchor, New York.
Manning, P. (1992) *Erving Goffman and Modern Sociology*. Polity Press, Cambridge.
March, J. (Ed.) (1965) *Handbook of Organizations*. Rand McNally, Chicago.
Meyer, J. W. & Rowan, B. (1977) Institutionalized Organizations: Formal Structure as Myth and Ceremony. *American Journal of Sociology* 83: 340–63.
Perrow, C. (1972) *Complex Organizations: A Critical Essay*. Scott, Foresman, Glenview, IL.
Perry, N. (1974) The Two Cultures and the Total Institution. *British Journal of Sociology* 25: 345–55.

organizations, tradition and

Steven P. Feldman

The essence of tradition is sequential pattern, a sequence of related meanings that are received and transmitted over time. The meanings can be related by association to common themes, in the contiguity of presentation and transmission, or in descent from a common origin (Shils 1981). For example, pharmaceutical company Johnson & Johnson has maintained a company "credo" since the 1930s. The credo has been changed multiple times during this period, but similar themes, the style of education and communication, and the connection to its origin have remained. Thus, Johnson & Johnson has a business philosophy tradition. This tradition can be seen in the way managers thought about and reacted to the Tylenol crisis in the early 1980s.

Tradition is anything but unitary or static. Indeed, its form and content are continuously changing. Tradition represents an accumulation of experience that is continuously updated or corrected as new experience challenges accepted beliefs or practices. For example, in 1975 James Burke, then a senior executive at Johnson & Johnson, held a series of "challenge meetings" to reinvigorate the credo and bring it into line with current business and social realities. These meetings brought out the fact that the credo was seen differently by different people. Tradition, in organizations as in societies, is a complex and diversified object, for many reasons. At this point, it is enough to say that a tradition is not one thing, but exists in numerous variations. There are always elements of different ages that are given different weights by different people; and even if given the same weights, the elements are often interpreted differently. Here the sociology of tradition meets political sociology, because dominant powers always try to reduce the manifoldness of tradition to a form that supports and legitimates their base of power. Tradition is always part of political life and conflict in organizations.

RATIONALITY AGAINST TRADITION

Tradition plays a role in organizational life and politics in a second way in addition to being a bone of contention. Traditions are usually tacit. People follow them unthinkingly. Many times organizations follow traditions most unthinkingly just when they think they are most rational and scientific. Actions are not traditions. Traditions are the patterns of thought and belief that surround the field of action where passion and calculation dominate. Traditions define the ends, standards, rules, and even means that are part of the social context of action. Traditions as tacit knowledge can enter into organizational life by stifling learning or creating resistance to organizational change. For example, at DEC Corporation a tacit "engineering culture" developed that made it impossible for managers to

focus fully on the needs of customers who desired "simple" or technologically unsophisticated products (Schein 2003). Tacit assumptions were never part of strategic reviews and perceptions arising from tacit assumptions were defended as unchallengeable. DEC's cultural inflexibility led to its downfall as managers and engineers obsessed with sophisticated technology ignored the huge growth in demand for personal computers.

By and large, people who study organizations have seen tradition as the enemy of organizational health and success. Tradition has been seen as an irrational (unthought) force that undermines organizational rationality and effectiveness. Indeed, much of the study of organizations in the twentieth century has been aimed at ridding organizations of traditional (tacit) forces and replacing them with ever higher levels of rational thought. Early on Barnard wanted to keep the irrational emotions of workers, but to do so under the rational control of rationally superior executives. When it turned out executives could not meet these superior levels of rationality or control the minds of employees even when they did, Dalton (1959) launched a broad-based attack on traditions in organizations – what he called "moral fixity" – in an effort to increase organizational rationality by removing all traditional constraints on action.

This did not increase organizational rationality either. Crozier's and Kanter's data on organizational behavior a decade later is quite consistent with Dalton's. Next came psychological and social psychological attempts to increase the rationality of organizations by addressing the problem on the individual and small group level. A prominent example is Argyris and Schon's double-loop learning model. They draw a distinction between the individual's "espoused theory" of action and the "theory in use," the latter containing all the tacit (traditional) elements of decision and action. By educating the individual to recognize the tacit dimension of behavior, it is hoped that this dimension can be brought under conscious (rational) control. Traditional elements can then be chosen or rejected according to their rational contribution to organizational goals.

The history of the study of organizations in the United States can mostly be characterized by this unending attempt to remove tacit knowledge (traditions) from organizational decision-making and life. Indeed, Schein's (2003) study of DEC Corporation's demise concludes that "innovative cultures" must periodically be dismantled if organizations want to stay innovative, because over time tacit culture will engrain itself and undermine organizational adaptability and change. Interestingly, Schein argues the only way to "dismantle" a culture is to change the people. He appears to have given up on decades of organizational change and development literature purporting to know how to change the organizational culture by *developing* the people.

Culture (tradition) need not be seen as so inflexible. And in any case, tradition cannot be removed from human life. Schein's (2003) suggestion to change the people to rid the organization of the stultifying effects of inflexible traditions would only result in the exchange of one set of traditions for another. One weakness in the literature on "organizations" is its heavy focus on organization-level "cultures" at the expense of the societal culture of which the organization is an example. Some brief comments are sometimes made about profession-level and society-level cultural influences, but the lion's share of attention goes to the relation between organizational "culture" and organizational goals. However, many times changes in leadership and/or organizational mergers and acquisitions fail to achieve the freeing of traditional (cultural) constraints so strongly desired. The reason for this is that "new" leaders often cannot change or even communicate with organizational personnel. In any case, any potential leader not only represents a limited range of cultural knowledge, but also any "new" knowledge he or she has will still need to be adapted and applied. The original organization and its leaders also have this potential for adaptability and change based on their traditional knowledge.

One exception to the lack of attention to supraorganizational cultural forces that influence cultural development on the organizational level is the "new institutionalism." In this tradition, "institutions" are seen as industry, profession, and society-level abstractions that operate on the preconscious, cognitive level, providing routine prescriptions for individual and collective behavior. The new institutionalism can be helpful in the study of tradition in organizations because its focus on supraorganizational ideational influences on behavior brings into view the broader social and historical context from which traditions in organizations originate. But the new institutionalism's commitment to macro structures deemphasizes the centrality of family life and the long socialization human beings go through in the process of becoming socially functional and emotionally integrated. Traditions are first learned and personal identity first established inseparably from the warmth and coldness of family relationships. By focusing on the autonomy of macro structures and the impersonal cognition that results from them, the new institutionalism deemphasizes the centrality of filial relations in the transmission of traditions. This results in an insensitivity to conflict because the complexities of individual development and historical specificity are overshadowed by the generalities of social structure. This can be seen in Vaughan's (1996) study of the *Challenger* disaster where homogenizing, preconscious macro forces override local leadership, power relations, and emotional dynamics at the Marshall Space Center in explaining the decision-making process.

TRADITION AS A PLATFORM FOR RATIONALITY

To exist, an organization must be continually reenacted (Feldman 2002). Its statements about its goals, plans, activities, and identity must be repeatedly resaid. The reenactments and resayings are guided by what individual members remember about what has happened in the past, what roles and responsibilities they had in the past and expect to continue to have in the future, what they remember they share with others about what they and others must do and not do, and what they remember about their rights and duties and the rights and duties of others to act in certain ways (Shils 1981). In addition to memory, some parts of some of this information are recorded in written documents such as job descriptions, strategic plans, formal directives, and informal agreements. Hence, organizations are complex webs of formal and informal knowledge, much of it tacit, that regulate social interaction and make it possible for collective action to take place in a more or less shared and coordinated way. This system of knowledge is maintained to considerable degree in organizational traditions.

The fact that the vast bulk of the organization studies literature sees these systems of knowledge, especially the tacit components, as drags on rational goal-seeking behavior misunderstands the workings of rationality as well as tradition, especially the essential contribution tradition makes to rational action. Without guidelines and constraints organized and maintained in tradition, creativity and goal-seeking would not be more rational but less. Managers would have no way to evaluate their plans and actions and would strike out in many sterile directions, having no organized body of knowledge to give them the benefits of previous experience.

Managers without traditions are akin to novices. Having no platform to orient themselves and from which to start, they would have many more false starts than managers working from established traditions (Shils 1975). The most talented would only discover what others have already discovered. It would take the most powerful and disciplined minds to find their way to essential information in what would be a disorganized and disorderly state of knowledge. The less powerful minds would be lost or misled much of the time. Even geniuses would be constrained in a world without traditions, because they could not possibly rediscover all that traditions, maintained and cultivated by whole communities, past and present, would provide, thus limiting the full utilization of their capacities.

Traditions provide the intellectual and experiential platform by which rational thought and actions can be formulated, critically reflected upon, and advanced. Rationality is an unfolding within traditional knowledge. More to the point at hand, shared understanding is essential for individual and organizational effectiveness. Traditions maintain the knowledge that makes shared understanding possible.

THE UBIQUITY OF TRADITIONS IN ORGANIZATIONS

The survival of traditions in organizations from the attack on traditional authority by forces of rationalism, or what Schumpeter overly optimistically called "creative destruction," can be attributed to several reasons in addition to the necessary role tradition plays in developing knowledge and organizing cooperative effort. First, much of the acceptance of traditional beliefs is due simply to the massiveness of their existence. A newcomer to an organization has her hands full just to try to work effectively in the ongoing processes and systems already in place. The idea that she would create the knowledge she needed for every decision or action just when she needed it is out of the question. She has neither the time, the resources, nor the approval of her superiors to review all organizational procedures and processes. On the contrary, she must find a way to act acceptably and organizational traditions offer her a ready-made and legitimate model. In addition, most people are affected psychologically by the fact that many people around them are working with a common stock of knowledge. The newcomer assumes the legitimacy of this knowledge out of respect for the many and for the ongoing "success" of the organization. The sheer pervasiveness of traditions in organizations is probably the most central reason for their acceptance.

A second reason tradition is so widely accepted is that most people do not have the imagination to create new guidelines for the situations they encounter. In the face of the overwhelming challenges a world with even limited traditions would pose for most people, traditions "permit life to move along lines set and anticipated from past experience and thus subtly converts the anticipated into the inevitable and the inevitable into the acceptable" (Shils 1981: 198). Thus tradition provides answers for the scarcity of information, the limits of intellectual capacity, and the moral and psychological needs of the individual.

The need for collective and individual identity is the third reason people in organizations are powerfully drawn to traditions. It is true individuals vary in regard to how much they internalize an organizational identity, but all individuals do so to some extent if for no other reason than to effectively participate in the life of the organization. For many others, however, a more intensive identification with the organization is sought. At the old

"Ma Bell" telephone system, for example, employees referred to each other as having "Bell heads." Individuals seek organizational traditions to designate themselves as members of the organization. They need to do this to make sense of and give a rationale for their life in the organization. The "Bell heads" understood the organization as a public service organization and this justified the sacrifices that were demanded of them to maintain telephone service in times of natural disasters. Only traditions, generalized and refined over time, provide the integration of diverse experiences around a unifying theme or set of beliefs. It is this integrative process that is able to provide the individual with self-designation in the transindividual organization.

The motivation for seeking organizational identity is complex. Postmodernists and critical theorists have called attention to the "brainwashing" that takes place in organizations through the intimidation of power and the socialization into organizationally self-serving values such as materialism and hierarchical status. But there is another reason: individuals identify with organizations to transcend themselves as individuals in an effort to associate themselves with important and vital things. For the Bell employees this was helping the weak and needy in times of disaster. Important and vital things are not fashions but beliefs or perceptions that have a depth in time. To have a depth in time, these beliefs and perceptions must be encapsulated in traditions. Without this attachment to important and vital things whose existence transcends not just the individual but his contemporaries as well, organizational identity is weak and shallow, making it vulnerable to manipulation and degradation, as was demonstrated, for example, in the moral collapse of Enron's culture.

The need for moral culture is the fourth reason tradition is essential to organizational life. Contemporary organizations such as Enron demonstrate clearly the problem people have in an environment without moral limits. It is not just the interpersonal dishonesty, lying, deception, unbridled aggression, manipulation, and theft. In Enron's case, one high-ranking finance executive at the center of the scandal committed suicide. To say individuals seek to transcend themselves through identification with the organization as a means to order and justify their experience implies the profound moral effect organizations can have on their members. In some organizations – churches and schools, for example – a transcendent realm is sought where sacred values can be reflected upon and cultivated in order to seek help in knowing how to live and even why to live. Hence, organizations maintain and inculcate the most basic and long-standing values that constitute the broader society.

These traditions promulgated by churches and schools are, in a more attenuated form, the same traditions found in most organizations. Non-profit organizations, for example, are "mission-driven" and the mission is the cultivation and practice of moral values. Take for example the Red Cross, which provides assistance to victims of disaster, or the Sierra Club, which seeks to safeguard the natural environment.

In the for-profit area, the record is more mixed. Many businesses merely pursue profits with little regard for anything more than obeying the law to avoid indictments, fines, and jail or the great economic costs of severe stakeholder backlash. But even in the for-profit area, "socially responsible" businesses contribute to the maintenance, cultivation, and practice of some of the most central moral values in our society: Levi Strauss & Company, for example, pulled its business out of China partly because of human rights violations; and the sporting goods maker Patagonia pulled its mountain climbing products off the market because they were damaging the natural environment.

CONCLUSION

As long as we desire to act collectively, we will need organizations; as long as we need organizations, we will utilize structures of authority; as long as we create structures of authority, authority will enmesh itself in tradition to stabilize and prolong itself. This is not, though it often becomes, a mere "power grab" by the possessors of organizational authority. Authority and the traditions that maintain it are a necessary requirement of social organization. For those who seek to correct abuses of power (or to exercise power themselves), the cause of "organizational change" seems right and just. But when changes so undermine the structure of traditional authority, there is little left to oppose the march of power or its total enactment in an Enron-type regression to total exploitation and greed. In these situations, few have the sense or the courage to challenge the powers that be, no matter how corrupt. Indeed, in the Enron case, even the moral leaders and legal experts on the board of directors supported and formally approved management behavior. It is here that traditions in organizations have their most vital role to play: to maintain and cultivate the moral standards by which interpersonal relations and collective action can be limited and regulated. Tradition, because of its partial autonomy from the structure of organizational power through its depth (legitimacy) in time, is most well suited as a force to limit the abuse of power in organizations.

SEE ALSO: Charisma, Routinization of; Collective Memory (Social Change); Culture, Production of; Institution; Institutional Theory, New; Organization Theory; Tradition

REFERENCES AND SUGGESTED READINGS

Dalton, M. (1959) *Men Who Manage*. Wiley, New York.
Feldman, S. P. (2002) *Memory as a Moral Decision*. Transaction, New Brunswick, NJ.
MacIntyre, A. (1981) *After Virtue*. University of Notre Dame Press, Notre Dame, IN.
Schein, E. (2003) *DEC is Dead, Long Live DEC*. Berrett-Koehler, San Francisco.
Shils, E. (1975) *Center and Periphery*. University of Chicago Press, Chicago.
Shils, E. (1981) *Tradition*. University of Chicago Press, Chicago.
Vaughan, D. (1996) *The Challenger Launch Decision*. University of Chicago Press, Chicago.

organizations, voluntary

Jenny Onyx

Voluntary organization is a generic term used to refer to a specific type of organization, sometimes also referred to as nonprofit organizations, NGOs (non-government organizations), third sector organizations, and civil society organizations. Each of these terms reflects a slightly different emphasis. For example, the common definition of a nonprofit is "an organization whose goal is something other than earning a profit for its owners. Usually its goal is to provide services" (Anthony & Young 1990). The definition emphasizes the nonprofit aspect of voluntary organizations but does not distinguish between other organizations that might not be profit-seeking, such as state-run or government organizations. Similarly, NGOs can technically refer to private for-profit organizations as well as voluntary organizations, although the term is usually reserved for large international nonprofit organizations (which nonetheless may earn a profit from some aspects of their operations, such as, for example, the Bangladesh NGO BRAC).

The term voluntary, as the name implies, emphasizes the fact that citizens freely form these organizations, and thus they are autonomous, independent of both government and the market. The term is often taken to refer to the presence of volunteers within nonprofit organizations, although many voluntary organizations are more dominated by professional staff than volunteers. Finally, these organizations are often identified as being independent of both the state and the market, belonging to a third sector or to civil society. As some scholars have argued, the formation of voluntary organizations may occur as a response to the failure either of the market (in providing a low-cost service) or of the state (in providing a service for minority needs) (Hansmann 1987). Indeed, service-oriented nonprofits can be found in fields as diverse as health, education, sport and recreation, social services, and religion.

More recent scholarship has focused on the positive attributes of nonprofits, for example that voluntary organizations provide a "school for democracy," or a form of community mutual support as an expression of social capital (Putnam 2000). Many, though by no means all, voluntary organizations are embedded in social movements that generate new collective social responses to social, economic, or environmental issues (Melucci 1988). International scholarship has also emphasized the variable and complex nature of voluntary organizations, which makes it difficult to identify a set of characteristics that serve as essential criteria for all such organizations.

Voluntary organizations vary greatly in size. The great majority in all countries are small, relying entirely on the voluntary labor of their members. These are grassroots organizations, often with strong traditional roots, but without any formal legal structure, particularly in traditional village societies. Other voluntary organizations are very large indeed, with a national or international reach, with thousands of volunteers and several hundred paid employees (Salamon et al. 1999).

Despite the diversity, there are several characteristics of voluntary organizations that generally set them apart from other organizations. Foremost is the nonprofit distribution principle. Voluntary organizations may make a profit, but that is not their primary purpose. Profits may be used to enhance or expand services; they may not be distributed to individual shareholders. This fundamental principle has implications for internal accounting and external tax and legal considerations. It also means that, unlike business entities, the bottom line cannot be used as a measure of performance. What does count is the mission of the organization. The mission of a nonprofit defines the value of the organization to society and creates the organization's purpose, and so it becomes the measure that must be used to evaluate performance (Moore 2000).

Second, voluntary organizations do not normally create a direct revenue stream, and thus remain dependent on other sectors for financial resources, through corporate sponsorship or government funding, or else on the wider public for donations. Some organizations have attempted to escape the uncertainty that these dependent relationships engender by moving to a user-pays or membership fee basis, or by developing a profit-generating arm of the organization to cross-subsidize the nonprofit arm, thus leading to complaints of unfair tax advantage by for-profit competitors. Volunteer labor is often a major resource for voluntary organizations, but is seldom accounted for as such.

The form of human resources is often quite different in voluntary organizations. Volunteer labor, including the voluntary overtime of paid professional staff, often underwrites the performance of the organization (Salamon et al. 1999).

Professional staff typically accept up to 25 percent lower salary for the privilege of working in a voluntary organization (Preston 1990). Staff are primarily motivated by the mission/value base of the organization rather than by personal rewards (Moore 2000). As such, human resource policies must be designed accordingly.

Given that the organization is voluntary, the forms of governance are likely to be distinctive, being controlled by stakeholders who are citizens rather than shareholders or delegates of government instrumentalities. There are, however, no specific ideal forms of organizational structure or governance. Historically, voluntary organizations have experimented with various forms of dispersed or flat structures designed to maximize the opportunities for participatory democracy. These include variations of the collective model, the cooperative model, and the community management model, all of which apply the subsidiarity principle, in which decisions are made by those most affected by the outcomes of the decision.

Those voluntary organizations seeking government funding or corporate sponsorship are particularly vulnerable to the impact of the isomorphic assumptions of their donors (DiMaggio & Powell 1991). That is, funding bodies tend to be suspicious of organizations that do not look like them. For instance, when organizations are required to incorporate to obtain legal status, or as they increase in size and complexity, thus requiring more formal procedures for decision-making and accountability, they often have to take on the attributes of more formalized, standardized, and centralized organizations to be seen to be acceptable. As a result of these processes, many voluntary organizations acquire large bureaucratic structures and hierarchical systems of accountability, overseen by formal boards of management. Within this corporate model, there is increasing emphasis on the voluntary organization being seen to be run as an effective and efficient business.

A major preoccupation in nonprofit texts and scholarship journals over the past 15 years has been the issue of "governance" and the relationship between the CEO of the voluntary organization and the board of management. Boards comprise voluntary people with responsibility for the governance of the organization.

The functions of boards are variously defined (Harris 1996) as: ensuring accountability; employing staff; formulating policy; securing resources; and acting as "boundary spanner." In fact, there is considerable role ambiguity and potential role conflict between CEO and chair (Otto 2003). There is also enormous variation in the form of governance adopted within the sector. On the one hand, the board carries ultimate legal responsibility under most forms of incorporation, being designed to determine the overall direction of the organization, to represent the interests of the wider constituency or membership, and to monitor staff compliance. On the other hand, board members may well lack the time, detailed knowledge, or expertise to carry out these tasks, and may see themselves rather as a supportive, "rubber stamp" of management. The reality in many organizations is one of interdependence or partnership, in which both staff and board perform a variety of functions in relation to each other, and as negotiated according to the specific skill mix of both.

Balanced against the concern with boards and CEO behavior, there has also been something of a counter-revolution within voluntary organizations over the past five years, leading to a greater demand for participation, reverse accountability, and constituency responsiveness. These countermoves have been driven by several global trends, notably the downsizing of government, the rise in the demand for voice by members of civil society (e.g., with formal representation within United Nations deliberations), and the recognition of the importance of social capital. Social capital as a concept has gained prominence through the work of Putnam (2000); while the concept is still contested, it highlights the importance of social resources (networks, values, and trust) as opposed to economic resources in developing a strong community and a strong organization. As a consequence of neoliberal public policies emerging to steer many late modern capitalist economies, governments have withdrawn from direct welfare provision and transferred increased responsibility for welfare service delivery to voluntary organizations (Nowland-Foreman 1998). At the same time, government-funding bodies have attempted to institute increased surveillance and compliance mechanisms on the ways in which voluntary organizations perform these services. Yet there are also many new advocacy organizations being formed in response to the perceived loss of welfare services and the greater inequalities generated by global economic reform, such as those negotiated by the World Trade Organization and World Bank (examples include CIVICUS and the Social Forum). Right-wing think tanks (often supported by conservative neoliberal governments) object to these advocacy organizations having a voice on the grounds that they have a very limited constituency (though they may claim to speak for the public good) and/or that they have poor forms of representation and accountability. Indeed, these accusations have triggered new debates within the third sector academic community (ISTR conference, 2004) concerning the appropriate forms of democratic action within voluntary organizations and the forms of accountability and transparency required.

After some 15 years of neoliberal economic reform, with its exclusive focus on economic growth at the expense of social justice and the environment, many nations are now identifying serious fallouts in terms of increased social problems (decreased services and populations in rural towns, youth disaffection and unemployment, rising rates of suicide and depression among some demographic categories, and so on). There is also an increased concern about issues of environmental degradation and global warming. There is an emerging recognition that the global preoccupation with economic growth has occurred at the expense of the social infrastructure and the environment. There are many calls for a reconciliation of the social, environmental, and economic imperatives. In this context, the work of Putnam (2000), in particular, has identified the crucial role of civil society organizations in generating social capital and identifying potential solutions to social and environmental problems. Civil society organizations are thus the principle base for active citizenship. They cannot perform that function without high levels of participatory and deliberative democracy, both within and between organizations. The pressure is now felt to find new organizational forms and processes beyond the bureaucratic or corporate model of governance.

SEE ALSO: Collectivism; Community; Decision-Making; NGO/INGO; Organizations; Organizations as Social Structures; Social Capital

REFERENCES AND SUGGESTED READINGS

Anthony, R. & Young, D. (1990) Characteristics of Nonprofit Organizations. In: Gies, D., Ott, S., & Shafritz, J. (Eds.), *The Nonprofit Organizations: Essential Readings*. Brooks/Cole, Pacific Grove, CA.

Di Maggio, P. & Powell, W. (1991) The Iron Cage Revisited: Institutional Isomorphism and Collective Rationality. In: Powell, W. & Di Maggio, P. (Eds.), *The New Institutionalism in Organizational Analysis*. University of Chicago Press, Chicago.

Hansmann, H. (1987) Economic Theories of Nonprofit Organization. In: Powell, W. W. (Ed.), *The Nonprofit Sector: A Research Handbook*. Yale University Press, New Haven.

Harris, M. (1996) Do We Need Governing Bodies? In: Billis, D. & Harris, M. (Eds.), *Voluntary Agencies: Challenges of Organization and Management*. Macmillan, London.

Melucci, A. (1988) Social Movements and the Democratization of Everyday Life. In: Keane, J. (Ed.), *Civil Society and the State: New European Perspectives*. Verso, London, pp. 245–60.

Moore, M. (2000) Managing for Value: Organizational Strategy in For-Profit, Nonprofit, and Governmental Organizations. *Nonprofit and Voluntary Sector Quarterly* 29(2), Supplement. Sage, London, pp. 183–204.

Nowland-Foreman, G. (1998) Purchase-of-Service Contracting, Voluntary Organizations, and Civil Society: Dissecting the Goose that Lays the Golden Eggs? *American Behavioral Scientist* 42: 108–23.

Otto, S. (2003) Not So Very Different: A Comparison of the Roles of Chairs of Governing Bodies and Managers in Different Sectors. In: Cornforth, C. (Ed.), *The Governance of Public and Non-Profit Organizations: What Do Boards Do?* Routledge, London.

Preston, A. (1990) Changing Labor Market Patterns in the Nonprofit and For-Profit Sectors. *Nonprofit Management and Leadership* 1(1): 15–28.

Putnam, R. (2000) *Bowling Alone: The Collapse and Revival of American Community*. Simon & Schuster, New York.

Salamon, L. et al. (1999) *Global Civil Society: Dimensions of the Nonprofit Sector*. Johns Hopkins Center for Civil Society Studies, Baltimore.

Orientalism

Peter Chua

Orientalism is the study of the "Orient" and its "eastern" arts, languages, sciences, histories, faiths, cultures, and peoples by Christian theological experts, humanist scholars, and natural and social scientists since the 1500s. Orientalist writers consider the "Orient" as consisting of societies geographically east of Christian Europe to be explored, acquired, and colonized for their raw materials, abundant labor, and pieces of seemingly opulent civilizations in decline. These colonial explorations resulted in man-made, imaginary geographies and political demarcations such as the Near East, the Middle East, Central Asia, the Far East, the Pacific Isles, the New World, and the "Dark Continent."

Since the 1950s, Orientalist scholarship seriously criticizes the objectionable exoticization, racialization, and cultural embodiment of first world imperialist projects. These critics object to their claims of validity and objectivity and to the authoritative statements and classroom materials on topics such as Islam, Middle Eastern affairs, Indian civilization, and Chinese philosophies. Moreover, they charge that Orientalism assists in the economic and political domination and restructuring of the "Orient" through its denials, distortions, and suppressions of lived experiences under western imperialism with its claims of western and Christian superiority in knowledge, commerce, gender relations, and ways of life.

Cultural theorist Edward Said offers, in his landmark *Orientalism* (1978), a sustained study of Eurocentric discourse representing itself as innocent, objective, and well intentioned (see Clawson 1998). He argues that it is never simply negative racial stereotyping and prejudice by those who never had contact with the orientalized "other." Instead, US, British, French, and other first world scholars often have had and needed direct contacts with their "others" to produce Orientalist knowledge in attempts to explain and justify imperialist projects during their respective periods of conquest and empire.

Said argues that US, British, and French Orientalisms produce racialized discourses in the arts, media, politics, and social science knowledge that are erroneous abstractions, in particular, of people of Islamic faith and from the Middle East. To legitimate and maintain western dominance since the late 1960s, US Orientalism, for instance, represents the Middle East as an Islamic place bursting with villains and terrorists and denies the historical, lived, and racially and religiously diverse realities of dispossessed Palestinians. These varying strategic deployments of Orientalist discourse produce a global politics and civic engagement tinted by a deeply distorted image of the social complexity of millions of people practicing Islam or residing in the third world.

Feminist scholars such as Kum-Kum Bhavnani, Chandra Mohanty, Reina Lewis, and Lila Abu-Lughod document how Orientalist constructions have been significantly sexualized and gendered. Prominent male scholars are not the exclusive producers of these constructions; some feminists and women's studies scholars historically have participated in Orientalism too. Bhavnani, Mohanty, Lewis, Abu-Lughod, and others analyze the ways Orientalist scholars deploy problematic gendered, sexualized, and racialized discourses to further "the [western and liberal] Feminist Project" and to liberate women from seemingly oppressive, traditional third world cultures. The analyses of Bhavnani et al. encourage present research on gender and culture that is sensitive to the complex historical and contextual lives, struggles, and experiences among Muslim, Middle Eastern, and other third world women. These studies overcome defective dichotomies such as "tradition" and "modernity," of "universal sisterhood" and "nationalism," and of "global women's rights" and "local gender empowerment." They consequently examine the dialogue on gender, social, and economic justice, all of which are situated in locally negotiated feminisms and in difficult and dangerous cultural, national, and global contexts.

Sociologists Bryan Turner and Stuart Hall contend that Orientalist discourse exists in the underlying assumptions, fundamental concepts, epistemological models, and methodological procedures of modern sociology. Turner, Hall, and others trace the origins of this discourse in the writings of early influential theorists in Western European sociology and examine their varied legacies, such as Herbert Spencer's social

Darwinism; Karl Marx's materialist analysis of the "Asiatic"-type of societies; Max Weber's comparative historical analysis of religion, culture, economy, domination (particularly its "patrimonial" form), and rational modernities; and Émile Durkheim's and Sigmund Freud's structuralist analysis of indigenous American and Australian totems, taboos, "primitive" classifications, and collective representations. As a consequence, sociology has participated in fostering Orientalism and unduly assists first world imperialist projects through its varied theoretical, research, and policy practices.

Early University of Chicago sociologists such as Albion Small, John Dewey, George Herbert Mead, Robert Park, and Emory Bogardus produced Orientalist formulations as they deliberated on the US empire and one of its own parts of the "Orient" – the Philippines from 1899 to 1946 (Chua 2006). These formulations crucially influenced theoretical and empirical inquiries in the sociology of symbolic interactionism, race relations, and the third world. They demonstrate the racialist epistemologies and Orientalist knowledge of these US sociologists as they deliberated on the Philippine colonial problem. This draws attention to how these Orientalist perspectives assisted in the development of the first hundred years of US sociology and how such Orientalist sociology underlies much of the public ideology and academic edifice justifying the expansion of the US empire from the Philippines to Afghanistan and Iraq.

After half a century of rigorous and multifarious attempts to halt Orientalism and its cooperation with imperialist projects, it persists – yet a bit injured – worldwide within sociology and other arenas of knowledge and power. Often celebratory of neoliberal economics, cultural globalization, and western interventionist politics, defenders and practitioners of Orientalism, as Edward Said had remarked, continue to be provincial. To overcome the provinciality of Orientalism and engage in productive dialogue with its critics, responsible defenders today seek to be less intellectually careless and more ethically accountable to humanity.

SEE ALSO: Culture, Gender and; Empire; Eurocentrism; Globalization, Culture and; Islam; Methods, Postcolonial; Third World and Postcolonial Feminisms/Subaltern

REFERENCES AND SUGGESTED READINGS

Abu-Lughod, L. (2001) Orientalism and Middle East Feminist Studies. *Feminist Studies* 27: 101–13.

Chua, P. (2006) US Empire and Social Thought: Dewey, Mead, and the Philippine Problem. *Philosophy Today*.

Chua, P., Bhavnani, K. K., & Foran, J. (2000) Women, Culture, Development: A New Paradigm For Development Studies? *Ethnic and Racial Studies* 23: 820–41.

Clawson, D. (Ed.) (1998) *Required Reading: Sociology's Most Influential Books*. University of Massachusetts Press, Amherst.

Hall, S. (1996) The West and the Rest. In: Hall, S., Held, D., Hubert, D., & Thomson, K. (Eds.), *Modern Societies: An Introduction*. Blackwell, Malden, MA, pp. 184–227.

Lewis, R. (1996) *Gendering Orientalism: Race, Femininity, and Representation*. Routledge, London.

Mohanty, C. T. (1991) Under Western Eyes: Feminist Scholarship and Colonial Discourses. In: Mohanty, C. T., Russo, A., & Torres, L. (Eds.), *Third World Women and the Politics of Feminism*. Indiana University Press, Indianapolis, pp. 51–91.

Said, E. (1978) *Orientalism*. Vintage, New York.

Turner, B. S. (1974) *Marx and the End of Orientalism*. Allen & Unwin, London.

Turner, B. S. (1978) *Weber and Islam*. Routledge & Kegan Paul, London.

Orthodoxy

Nikos Kokosalakis

Orthodoxy is a major branch of Christianity, represented by the Eastern Orthodox Church, with an unbroken continuity to the apostolic tradition and a claim to be the depositor of the authentic Christian faith and practice. Today, the Orthodox Church consists of the ancient patriarchates (Constantinople, Alexandria, Antiochia, Jerusalem) and various national autocephalous churches. The Patriarchate of Constantinople, also called Ecumenical, enjoys the primacy of honor among all the other patriarchates and the rest of the Orthodox autocephalous churches without having any administrative or other jurisdiction over them whatsoever. The churches of Russia, Serbia, Romania, Bulgaria, and Georgia carry patriarchal status – being led by a patriarch. The churches of Greece, Cyprus, and Albania are led by archbishops. There are also the smaller, autonomous Orthodox churches of Poland, Finland and former Czechoslovakia. The Greek diaspora, with full church organization (dioceses, parishes, etc.) in America, Europe, and Australia, is under the jurisdiction of the Ecumenical Patriarchate. The Russian diaspora is under the Patriarchate of Moscow. In all, the Orthodox populations (practicing in the broad sense) in the world today are estimated between 170–180 million. According to Ware (1963: 15): "The Orthodox Church, thus, is a family of self-governing Churches. It is held together ... by the double bond of unity in the faith and communion in the sacraments."

HISTORICAL PROFILE

The connection of Orthodoxy to the original "undistorted" Christian faith is claimed on the fact that the early Christian communities of the Eastern Church were established by the apostles. The Apostolic synod (49 CE) decided that Christianity should go outside the confines of Judaism and be spread to the Gentiles. This and St. Paul's Hellenic education and the fact that the books of the New Testament (with the exception of the Gospel of St. Matthew) were written in Greek gave the Eastern Church a distinctly Greek cultural character. The early Christian communities around the Mediterranean – including the community of Rome – were mostly Greek speaking and the theology and practice of the Eastern Church gradually developed a different ethos and character to that of the Western Church, which was largely Latin based.

The terms Orthodox and Orthodoxy, however, developed later after Emperor Constantine had transferred the capital of the Empire from Rome to Byzantium (330). The term Orthodoxy (from the Greek *orthe doxa*), meaning both right faith and right worship, developed and came to usage during the fourth and fifth centuries in order to distinguish and protect the faith of the church from a variety of heretical movements, Nestorianism and Arianism in particular. During this period, with the protection of the state, the church acquired the Troeltschian characteristics of the Ecclesia. It thus became an essential institution of the emerging Byzantine Empire.

The early ecumenical councils produced the formal creeds of the church and consolidated the notion of Orthodoxy, but the Nestorians rejected the decisions of the council of Ephesus (431) and the Monophysites those of the council of Chalcedon (451). Out of these quarrels, which produced the first splits in the Eastern Church, derive today's Armenian Orthodox Church and the Coptic Church of Ethiopia.

The Greek Fathers, especially the Cappadocians, wove into Christian theology platonic and neoplatonic ideas. Parsons (1979), in fact, saw in this synthesis the seeds of the subsequent development of religious and economic symbolism in Europe and the western world at large. Along with such basic theological components, the development of hermetic monasticism in Egypt, Asia Minor, and the Middle East during this early period left an indelible mark on Orthodoxy.

The model of church–state relations established by Constantine, who made Christianity not just *religio licita* (permitted religion) but official state religion, persists in modified form in Greece and Cyprus to the present day. The model involved a special fusion of religion and politics, which became the hallmark of Byzantine civilization. In Byzantium there was a total overlap between religion and society and Orthodoxy was synonymous with culture (Nicol 1979). The emperors had power over and direct involvement in ecclesiastical affairs and had the last word in the appointment of the patriarchs. Yet, this model, which has been characterized as Caesaropapism, did not mean arbitrary power of the state over the church. As this was a theocratic empire, the clergy and the monks could exercise essential direct and indirect pressure on the polity. Indeed, many emperors were deposed or killed because of their religious politics.

Evidence of this fusion of religion and politics, based on the fusion of religion and society, is also forthcoming from the quarrels over icons, which shook the empire to its foundations between 726 and 843. Icons in the Orthodox tradition are not just religious symbols or religious art, but material forms of deep spiritual and theological communication (Kokosalakis

1995). Icons are also indicative of the different theological and cultural conception of Christian faith in Orthodoxy compared to the other major branches of Christianity – Roman Catholicism and Protestantism. It was in fact such different appreciation along with major political and cultural differences between the Eastern and the Western Churches which brought about their schism and anathema to each other in 1054. Since then, because of historical and political circumstances (the crusades, etc.), the gulf between the two churches was consolidated and widened. Also, the threat from Islam and the gradual weakening of the empire gave Orthodoxy a more circumscribed and defensive outlook. On the other hand, the claims for supremacy of the pope were not accepted by the Orthodox and led to the failure of attempts for reunification of the two churches in the councils of Lyon (1274) and Florence (1439).

The Byzantine Church was essentially Greek but also ecumenical. Christian elements had existed in the peoples of the Balkans (Illyrians, southern Slavs) and around the Black Sea (Georgia) since apostolic times, but it was the Byzantine mission which transmitted and consolidated Christianity to these people. The missionaries Cyril and Methodios translated the Bible and Orthodox liturgical texts into Slavonic and are considered the founders of the church in the ninth century in contemporary Bulgaria, Romania, and Serbia. In Russia, Orthodoxy was also transmitted from Byzantium and the church was officially established there after the massive baptism of the *Ros*. Queen Olga was baptized in Constantinople (957) and her grandson Vladimir married the Byzantine Princess Anna (988). Orthodoxy in Russia took deep roots and was further strengthened after the collapse of the Byzantine Empire with the conquest of Constantinople by the Ottomans (1453). The marriage of Princess Sophia, niece of the last Emperor of Byzantium, to the Tsar Ivan III was seen as the establishment of Moscow as the Third Rome. The Russian Church, however, became hopelessly entangled with the power and the political whims of the tsars, till its near total elimination by the Bolsheviks after 1917.

For the Patriarchate of Constantinople the end of the empire and its conquest by the Ottomans during the sixteenth, seventeenth, and eighteenth centuries meant, paradoxically, the strengthening of both its ecumenical and ethnic character. It was Islamic practice going back to the Prophet that conquered people be allowed to practice their faith in return for obedience to Islamic authorities and the payment of taxes. The Ecumenical Patriarch was recognized by the Sultan as leader of the Orthodox people (*Milet-Bashi*) on condition of guaranteeing their obedience and collecting taxes. A definite administrative structure thus developed between the High Porte and the Patriarchate. This gave the latter not only special privileges but also a special authority over the Orthodox believers, who now had not only their spiritual but also their civic affairs administered by the church. For the Greeks as for other Orthodox ethnic groups in the Balkans this meant that Orthodoxy was closely interwoven with their national ethnic identities and this at a time when nation-state societies were being formed and consolidated in the rest of Europe. Especially for the Greeks, the church during that period was not just the depositor of the Orthodox faith, but also the main carrier and preserver of the Greek language and identity. Thus, Orthodoxy did not just survive the Ottoman rule, but during the nineteenth century reemerged as a strong ideological and cultural force in the pursuit of independence for Greeks, Romanians, Serbians, and Bulgarians.

The French Revolution deeply affected the revolutionary movements in the Balkans in the nineteenth century. Unlike France and later Russia, however, where religion and the revolution were in conflict, in the Balkans religion became intertwined with nationalism and fostered the revolutionary spirit. One consequence of this was that Orthodoxy acquired a strong ethnic character in the region and the organization of the Orthodox Church was completely transformed with the establishment of national independent churches, severed unilaterally from the Ecumenical Patriarchate, which eventually recognized their autocephalous status as a *fait accompli*. So the church of the new-born Greece was established in 1833 and recognized by the Patriarchate in 1852. The Church of Serbia became autonomous in 1831 and autocephalous in 1879, but the incorporation of Serbia to the Kingdom of Yugoslavia along with Catholic Croatia and Slovenia after World War I created new ethnic conflicts which

became violent after the collapse of the socialist bloc in the early 1990s. The Church of Bulgaria declared its independence in 1870, when the country was still under Turkish rule, but the Patriarchate recognized it only in 1945, after much controversy. The Church of Romania, established in 1862, was recognized by the Ecumenical Patriarchate in 1885.

There were cultural and political anomalies in the establishment and administration of these churches in that the monarchs of Greece, Bulgaria, Serbia, and Romania were initially Catholic, who were heads of church and state in countries with predominantly Orthodox populations. This and the fusion of Orthodoxy and nationalism along with the problems of modernization and secularization in these states created great tensions and politicization in these churches throughout the nineteenth and twentieth centuries.

The Church of Russia after 1917 and the churches in the Balkans after World War II — with the exception of the Church of Greece and Cyprus — were either in severe persecution or mere toleration by the socialist state. The degree of oppression and/or persecution of Orthodoxy, and religion generally, differed from one communist country to another and the church as an institution was forced to compromise variously in each case. It is noteworthy that, especially in Russia, religion in popular form managed to survive over 70 years and even show signs of revival after the collapse of the socialist bloc in 1989–90. This can be partly explained by the cultural anthropological specificity of Orthodoxy and its relation to modernity.

CULTURAL ANTHROPOLOGICAL SPECIFICITY OF ORTHODOXY

Within the Christian religion generally a distinction must be made between the church as an organized institution and the faith and practice of the people. Although this applies to the Orthodox tradition as well, the relation in it between popular and official faith is very vague and blurred. The basic doctrines were formalized by the theologians and the councils of the church during the fourth and fifth centuries and became deeply ingrained in the faith and practice of the Christian communities – above all in the liturgy. Thus, what came to be known as ecclesiastical consciousness expresses the authentic Orthodox ethos, which derives directly from the faith and practice of the community within the church. The bishops are central to the continuity and interpretation of the apostolic faith, but the authority of the church does not rest with the clergy in any legalistic sense but derives from the communion of faith in the *homoousian*, the undivided trinitarian God.

As an ideal this ethos is deeply democratic and is translated in practice into a fusion of official and popular religion. One of the remarkable features of the Orthodox Church, throughout its history everywhere, has been its capacity to absorb in its own lifestyle popular religious culture and even what to outsiders must appear to be the magical and superstitious practices of peasant communities. Basic features of the Orthodox ethos are ambiguity, flexibility, and openness: even Canon Law is subject to popular faith. One reason for this is that early in the life of the church there entered the principle and practice of *oikonomia*. This practice meant that the church compromises in the face of transgression by individual believers. Thus, as a compromise, bishops and priests, who were forced to eat pagan sacrificial meals during the persecutions by the Emperors Decius and Diocletian, were not excommunicated. Also, the second ecumenical council accepted the baptism of heretics as valid, compromising with Apostolic Canon 46 which rejected it. The principle of *oikonomia* continues to be practiced by the Orthodox Church to the present day concerning ethical problems emerging from social change, such as divorce, birth control, bioethical issues, etc.

Another specific cultural feature of Orthodoxy involving official theology and popular faith is the process by which holiness emerges and is recognized. Saints (*Aghioi*) in the Orthodox Church are formally declared as such by the Ecumenical Patriarchate, but only if and long after they are so recognized by the community at the grassroots. Holiness thus enters the liturgical life of the church and becomes publicly recognized from below.

At a deeper and more central theological level the christological, trinitarian, and eschatological doctrines are directly related to a specific anthropological conception of salvation. In Orthodox theology there is a deep phenomenological entanglement of the human and the divine. The sacred permeates nature and human nature as a matter of the divine plan and act of salvation not as a conception of pantheistic fusion, but as a matter of conscious divine and human personal choice. Thus, in the life of the Orthodox believer, salvation and *theosis* become inextricably linked. The prototype to strive toward is the person of Christ, whose image is potentially present in any other human being.

There is a central eschatological vision in Orthodox theology where the past, the present, and the future are intertwined in a projected final dimension of salvation. On the part of the person, this entails struggle and constant *askesis* against the powers of this world (often personified in the devil) and, above all, the outrageous *self*, but the final outcome is victory due to the risen Christ.

These soteriological dimensions are ecumenical, universal in character, and according to St. Paul (Galatians 3: 28) transcend sociocultural boundaries of any kind, but in the actual life of the Orthodox Church they are in tension and often in conflict because of its embodiment in various ethnic groups and local and national societies.

ORTHODOXY AND MODERNITY

Orthodoxy is a premodern culture in the special sense that it was not disrupted directly by the foundational movements of modernity: the Renaissance, the Reformation, and the Enlightenment. Modernity also has been exogenous to societies where Orthodoxy has been the dominant religion because capitalist development and industrialization in these societies came late during the second half of the twentieth century. During the nineteenth century Orthodoxy was in tension with modernity not in the context of possession and transmission of power from clerical to secular hands, but in the context of its connections to ethnic identities and nationalism and the politicization and secularization of the church itself. Secularization thus had a specific and different development in Orthodoxy to that experienced in western Christianity. During the twentieth century, despite the opposition to religion in the communist bloc, Orthodoxy at the popular level survived well and the Orthodox churches in these countries have revived.

During modern and late modern times religion generally has disengaged itself from the social structure and has become a fluid and diffused cultural force and resource. This process seems to be conducive to the revival of the Orthodox cultural ethos, described earlier, at a time when the ideological dimensions of modernity have become attenuated and globalization has further relativized all cultural certainties (Gianoulatos 2001). Although Orthodoxy is undergoing severe tension in late modernity, at the same time it shows renewed vitality and cultural resilience. Both have to do with its salvationist message. In the context of risk society and a world of great uncertainty, a deep Weberian analysis of Orthodoxy would show that its crucial sociological significance lies in its eschatological, optimistic character and its general soteriological message. Weber insisted that the world always was and always will be in need of salvation. Indeed, salvation according to him constitutes the essence of religion. His own severe pessimism about the fate of modernity is well known and the tone of most analyses of global developments in the early twenty-first century seems to share such pessimism. Certainly, the initial optimism characteristic of early modernity at the age of the Enlightenment turned into its polar opposite by the late twentieth century.

In the midst of this general despondency Orthodox theology and the Orthodox culture generally remain optimistic. In Orthodox theological, eschatological terms, the negative forces which militate against salvation, and death itself, are ultimately conquerable through God's plan for the salvation of the world and the power of the risen Christ. Death and renewal as a recurrent historical drama are at the heart of Orthodox theology and culture.

SEE ALSO: Catholicism; Christianity; Church; Civil Religion; Nation-State and Nationalism; Popular Religiosity; Protestantism; Science and Religion; Secularization

REFERENCES AND SUGGESTED READINGS

Gianoulatos, A. (2001) *Globalization and Orthodoxy*. Akritas, Athens.

Kokosalakis, N. (1993) The Historical Continuity and Cultural Specificity of Eastern Orthodox Christianity. In: Cipriani, R. (Ed.), *Religions Sans Frontieres: Atti della Conferenza Internazionalle promossa dall' universita degli Studi di Roma "La Sapienza" 12–16 Juglio 1993*. Presidenza del Consiglio dei Ministri, Dipartmento per l'infromazione e l'editoria, Rome.

Kokosalakis, N. (1995) Icons and non-Verbal Religion in the Orthodox Tradition. *Social Compass* 42(4): 433–49.

Nicol, D. (1979) *Church and State in the Last Centuries of Byzantium*. Cambridge University Press, Cambridge.

Parsons, T. (1979) Religion and Economic Symbolism in the Western World. In: Johnson, M. (Ed.), *Religious Change and Continuity*. Josey Bass, Washington, DC.

Ware, K. (1963) *The Orthodox Curch*. Penguin, London.

outliers

Roger E. Kirk

An outlier is an observation or measurement that is unusually large or small relative to the other values in a data set. Outliers occur for a variety of reasons. They can represent, for example, an error in measurement, data recording, or data entry, or a correct value that just happens to be extreme. Outliers can seriously affect the integrity of data and result in biased or distorted sample statistics, inflated sums of squares, distorted p values and effect sizes, and faulty conclusions. Alternatively, they can be the most interesting finding in the data. History records many scientific breakthroughs that have resulted from following up on extreme observations.

There is no rigorous definition of an outlier; and no mathematical calculation can tell with certainty whether an outlier comes from the population of interest or a different population. Some outliers are obvious: a student's height of

53 feet and their IQ score of 1,200. Not all outliers are so obvious. A number of rules have been suggested for identifying obvious and not so obvious outliers. Most of the rules involve quantifying how far an outlier is from other data values. One rule identifies an outlier as any measurement or observation that falls outside of the interval given by $\overline{Y} \pm 2.5S$, where $\overline{Y}$ and S denote, respectively, the sample mean and standard deviation. Unfortunately, $\overline{Y}$ and S are greatly affected by extreme observations. It is preferable to use rules based on measures of location and variation that are not themselves affected by outliers such as the median, *Mdn*, and interquartile range, $Q_3 - Q_1$. One such rule identifies an outlier as any measurement or observation that falls outside of the interval given by $Mdn \pm 2(Q_3 - Q_1)$. John Tukey (1977) proposed a widely used rule based on a box plot (box-and-whisker plot). A box plot for the scores $Y_i = 7, 9, 10, 12, 13, 15, 32$ is shown in Figure 1. The box plot identified one outlier, $Y_i = 32$. The rule based on the mean and standard deviation failed to detect this outlier. For bivariate data, inspection of a scatterplot is useful for identifying outliers.

Once an outlier has been identified, the next step is to determine whether the outlier is really a correct, extreme value or an error. If the outlier is an error, it should be corrected or deleted. Dealing with a correct, extreme value is more difficult. Including the outlier in an analysis produces summary statistics that describe neither the bulk of the data nor the outlier. One alternative is to transform the data. Square root and logarithmic transformations soften the impact of outliers because they shrink extreme values more than non-extreme values. Another alternative is to use analysis procedures that are robust in the presence of outliers such as nonparametric and distribution-free statistics or Winsorized robust measures. To Winsorize data, the smallest, say, 10 percent of observations are each reset to the smallest value not included in the 10 percent. Similarly, the largest 10 percent of observations are each reset to the largest value not included in the 10 percent. Winsorizing data significantly reduces the variance and the standard error of the mean. If the forgoing procedures are not acceptable, as a last resort, the correct, extreme value can be deleted. If this course is followed, it is desirable to report the results both with and without the outlier.

SEE ALSO: Measures of Centrality

REFERENCES AND SUGGESTED READINGS

Barnett, V. & Lewis, T. (1994) *Outliers in Statistical Data*. Wiley, New York.

Rousseeuw, P. J. & Leroy, A. M. (1987) *Robust Regression and Outlier Detection*. Wiley Interscience, New York.

Tukey, J. W. (1977) *Exploratory Data Analysis*. Addison-Wesley, Reading, MA.

outsider–within

J. Michael Ryan

Patricia Hill Collins's idea of the outsider-within has quickly become a classic in feminist theories. Developed primarily in her book *Fighting Words: Black Women and the Search for Justice* (1998), the term was originally used to describe the location of individuals who find themselves in the border space between groups: that is, who no longer have clear membership in any one group. Dissatisfied with this usage because of its resemblance to early sociology's "marginal man," Collins later modified the term to "describe social locations or border spaces occupied by groups of unequal power"

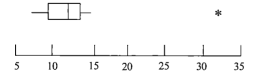

Figure 1   Box plot. The ends of the box represent $Q_1 = 9.25$ and $Q_3 = 13.75$. The vertical line in the middle of the box is the $Mdn = 12$. The two whiskers extend from the ends of the box down to 7 and up to 15. There are the outermost data points that fall within $Q_1 - 1.5(Q_3 - Q_1) = 2.5$ and $Q_3 + 1.5(Q_3 - Q_1) = 20.5$, respectively. One outlier, $Y_i = 32$, is identified by *.

(1998: 5). Rather than static positions, these locations contain a number of contradictions for the individuals who occupy them. While individuals in these unique locations appear to be members of the dominant group based on possession of the necessary qualifications for, and apparent rights of, member standing, they do not necessarily enjoy all of the experiential benefits afforded to formal members. Collins uses the example of blacks in the United States; while they have basic citizenship rights, they are often treated as second-class citizens.

Knowledge production is also central to Collins's work. In a search for social justice, the outsider-within location describes not only a membership position but also a knowledge/power relationship. This unique location is one where members of a subordinated group can access information about the dominant group without being afforded the rights and privileges accorded to group members. It is this unique knowledge of both sides that distinguishes the outsider-within from both elite and oppositional locations.

Collins is particularly interested in the social location of black women as a historically situated group, and the power relations inherent in the construction of knowledge that help influence a notion of critical theory. One of her goals in developing the concept of the outsider-within was to help create a body of knowledge that would be specific to black women and their unique social location in order to insert an identity into the stream of theoretical consciousness that had long been missing. By analyzing social theory in this context, she notes that: "Far from being neutral, the very meaning and use of the term social theory represents a contested terrain" (1998: ix). Collins asserts that social theory is both knowledge *and* lived institutional practices that attempt to answer the questions and concerns facing groups based in specific political, social, and historical situations. Thus it does not derive from elite positions but rather from actual groups of people in specific institutional settings. Since it is these groups of people who legitimate social theory, it is their concerns that should be reflected by it. This ideology demonstrates Collins's commitment to placing outsider groups at the core of her analysis and to create "issues where absence has long been the norm" (1998: 105).

SEE ALSO: Black Feminist Thought; Feminism; Feminist Standpoint Theory

REFERENCES AND SUGGESTED READINGS

Collins, P. H. (1990) *Black Feminist Thought: Knowledge, Consciousness, and the Politics of Empowerment.* Unwin Hyman, London.
Collins, P. H. (1998) *Fighting Words: Black Women and the Search for Justice.* University of Minnesota Press, Minneapolis.

outsourcing

Natalia Nikolova

Outsourcing refers to the fundamental decision to contract out specific activities that previously were undertaken internally. In other words, outsourcing involves the decision to reject the internalization of an activity and can be viewed as vertical disintegration. As it means to obtain by contract from an outside supplier, it is also called contracting out or subcontracting.

Outsourcing is not new. Contractual relationships dominated the economic organization of production prior to and during the Industrial Revolution. However, from the mid-nineteenth century until the last 20 years, the internalization of transactions within organizations became the dominant trend. From the 1880s, there was a shift from a regime of *laissez-faire* production consisting of many small firms to a regime based on large, vertically integrated corporations, or what is called a shift from markets to hierarchies, which culminated in the large-scale public and private sector bureaucracies of the post-war era. Two reinforcing tendencies played an important part in this trend: the growth of direct government involvement in economic activity and the development of production technologies that favored large, vertically integrated organizations. Those same factors forced the retreat from outsourcing in the 1980s and 1990s. In the first years of this outsourcing trend, mainly non-core and less strategically important activities were subcontracted, such as cleaning, catering, and maintenance, also called blue-collar activities. Increasingly, however, organizations began to outsource white-collar, business services, which many might claim are strategic, such as IT and telecommunications. The offshore contracting out of manufacturing and especially of service activities to developing countries is the reason for a growing skepticism toward outsourcing in the developed countries.

There are two main forms of outsourcing. (1) Long-term or embedded outsourcing is characterized by a long-term partnership between the outsourcing organization and the outsourcing provider (e.g., strategic alliance, franchising). It involves an intensive interaction, the development of trust between the involved individuals, better communication, and the sharing of the cooperation of risks and outcomes. Such partnerships are usually called networks. (2) Arm's-length subcontracting is characterized by a loose relationship between the outsourcing organization and the outsourcing provider, which is similar to the traditional market relationship. These two outsourcing forms differ in their economic implications for the outsourcing company and in the associated requirements on the management of the outsourcing process.

The economic effects of long-term outsourcing (networks) and arm's-length subcontracting (arm's-length, market relationships) are discussed in the literature as a part of the broader issue of the boundaries of the firm – what explains why certain transactions are governed in-house (through hierarchy or vertical integration) while others are governed through market relations (arm's-length subcontracting) or through networks (long-term outsourcing)? Two major theoretical streams concentrate on the question of what are the conditions that make one or the other governance form more efficient in governing economic activities: the transaction cost theory and the knowledge-based view of the firm (and its extension, the capabilities approach). These approaches discuss the motives of organizations to undertake outsourcing and the impact of outsourcing on their performance.

Transaction cost theory has its origins in economics. Williamson, one of the leading figures of the transaction cost perspective, developed a model that proposes that the main motive of organizations to outsourcing activities is to reduce transaction costs. The model is based on two underlying assumptions about the individuals involved in the regarded transactions: their bounded rationality and the potential danger that they will behave opportunistically. Furthermore, three exchange conditions – uncertainty, asset specificity, and frequency – determine when long-term outsourcing (called hybrids within the transaction cost approach), arm's-length subcontracting, or vertical integration is more efficient. Asset specificity, which refers to the degree to which an asset can be redeployed to alternative uses without sacrifice of value, is the central category in the argument. Asset specificity creates bilateral dependency and poses contracting hazards to the involved organizations. It is argued that activities that are related to transactions with a mid- to strong degree of asset specificity and a middle frequency should be outsourced and executed in close cooperation with the outsourcing provider because hybrids are the governance form with the lowest transaction costs in such cases. Arm's-length subcontracting is, in contrast, the most efficient governance form in all cases of low degree of asset specificity. Thus, the focus of this approach is on transaction costs – all problems of economic organization (including the motives and effects of outsourcing) are seen as a problem of reducing incentive conflicts. The role of routines, limited knowledge and capabilities, and consequently of production costs, is neglected. Dynamic aspects, such as learning and innovation, are also not discussed. Therefore, this approach delivers only a restricted explanation as to why organizations outsource and what form of outsourcing they choose.

The second approach developed in the late 1980s is still not a coherent theory of the firm but, rather, a collection of ideas and works based on the assumption that firms possess distinct, firm-specific capabilities, which are the reason for differences in their production costs. It is claimed that different capabilities imply differences in terms of the efficiency with which resources are deployed. According to this approach, firms will vertically integrate those activities in which they have greater experience and/or organizational capabilities than potential external providers and will outsource marginal activities. This allows organizations to concentrate on their strengths and to profit from the expertise of specialized outsourcing providers. Furthermore, the approach states that non-core activities that are to some degree strategically important will be executed in a long-term partnership with the outsourcing provider. When the outsourced activities do not have strategic relevance, organizations will choose arm's-length subcontracting. A critical question related to this approach is, therefore, how to identify those activities in which a company believes it has its distinctive advantage. The reality shows that most companies struggle to find the right answer. Furthermore, unlike the transaction cost approach, this approach cannot yet generate empirical predictions but rather ex post explanations only about which activities should be outsourced. In general, the knowledge-based approach cannot explain all reasons why firms outsource (e.g., to achieve specialization effects and, at the same time, to limit the negative effects of opportunistic behavior). Therefore, both views, the transaction cost approach and the knowledge-based approach, contribute to some degree to a better understanding of outsourcing.

Additional to these theoretical approaches, a large number of studies are primarily engaged with the empirical proof of the existence of cost efficiencies from outsourcing (whereas most of them do not clearly differentiate between long-term outsourcing and arm's-length subcontracting). As a leading figure in this research, Domberger undertook several empirical studies of outsourcing in the UK and Australian public and private sector, reporting that, on the average, organizations realized 20 percent increases in efficiency and decreases in cost through outsourcing. These cost efficiencies result, for example, from the reduced capital intensity and lower fixed costs for the outsourcing companies and in the reduced costs of the outsourced activity due to the supplier's economies of scale and scope. Additionally, other positive effects have been proposed, such as higher flexibility through the choice between different suppliers and the easy switch between technologies, quick response to changes in the environment, increased managerial attention and resource allocation to tasks where the organization has its core competences, and increased quality and innovativeness of the purchased products or services due to specialization of the supplier and spreading of risk.

Despite the arguments that outsourcing firms often achieve better performance than vertically integrated firms, there is a lack of consistency as to the extent to which outsourcing improves the performance and the competitive situation of organizations. Several studies show that efficiency gains are often much smaller than claimed, or even that costs increased after services are contracted out. Additionally, it has been argued that using outsourcing merely as a defensive technique can cause long-term negative effects. Because of outsourcing, there is the danger for firms to enter the so-called "spiral of decline" (also called hollowing out of organizations): after contracting out, companies need to shift overhead allocation to those products and services that remain in-house. As a result, the remaining products and services become more expensive and less competitive, which raises their vulnerability to subsequent outsourcing. This process can lead to the loss of important knowledge and capabilities and, as a result, can threaten the long-term survival of organizations. Some other important disadvantages that may result from outsourcing are a negative impact upon employees that remain in the company (e.g., lower employee commitment, drop in promotional opportunities, drop in job satisfaction, and changes in duties), declining innovation by the outsourcer, dependence on the supplier, and the provider's lack of necessary capabilities. Especially the social cost associated with loss of employment in the outsourcing organizations has been strongly criticized by opponents of outsourcing. Partly because of such negative effects, it has been suggested that organizations adopt outsourcing because of the lure of fashionable normalization. From this perspective, efficiency arguments are of less consequence than those that stress institutional factors, especially mimetic isomorphism. It has been claimed that modern societies consist of many institutionalized rules providing a framework for the creation and elaboration of formal organizations. Many of these rules are rationalized myths that are widely believed but rarely, if ever, tested. They originate and are sustained through public opinion, the educational system, laws, or other institutional forms. Thus, many of the factors shaping management and organization are based not on efficiency or effectiveness but on social and cultural pressures to conform to already legitimate practices, especially when influential consultants recommend a course of action such as outsourcing. Thus, the main problem, as these authors see it, is the danger of misapplication of outsourcing simply because it is fashionable.

The problem with the debate between efficiency and fashion is, however, that outsourcing can be sought both because it is a widely institutionalized and legitimized practice and because it delivers cost reductions. Therefore, these approaches are not necessarily competing but can as well be complementary. An organization that primarily adopts outsourcing in order to conform to other organizations can, at the same time, realize some benefits, e.g., cost efficiencies from the outsourcing practice. The crucial questions are, therefore, (1) whether the cost of exchange of goods and services is significantly higher when this transaction occurs between separate organizations than when it takes place within them, and (2) whether these costs are higher when organizations engage in long-term, strategic outsourcing than when they establish arm's-length, market relationships. It has been indicated that the answer to both questions is largely dependent on the management of the relationship with the outsourcing provider. Benefits and costs of outsourcing depend crucially on how outsourcing is designed and implemented.

SEE ALSO: Alliances; Franchise; Institutionalism; Management Fashion; Management Networks; Networks; Social Exchange Theory

REFERENCES AND SUGGESTED READINGS

Bettis, R. A., Bradley, S. P., & Hamel, G. (1992) Outsourcing and Industrial Decline. *Academy of Management Executive* 6(1): 7–22.

DiMaggio, P. J. & Powell, W. W. (1983) The Iron Cage Revisited: Institutional Isomorphism and Collective Rationality in Organizational Fields. *American Sociological Review* 48: 147–60.

Domberger, S. (1998) *The Contracting Organization: A Strategic Guide to Outsourcing.* Oxford University Press, Oxford.

Foss, N. (1999) Research in the Strategic Theory of the Firm: "Isolationism" and "Integrationism." *Journal of Management Studies* 36(6): 725–55.

Uzzi, B. (1997) Social Structure and Competition in Interfirm Networks: The Paradox of Embeddedness. *Administrative Science Quarterly* 42: 35–67.

Walker, R. & Walker, B. (2000) *Privatization: Sell Off or Sell Out. The Australian Experience.* ABC Books, Sydney.

Williamson, O. (1985) *The Economic Institutions of Capitalism.* Free Press, New York.

Williamson, O. (1991) Comparative Economic Organization: The Analysis of Discrete Structural Alternatives. *Administrative Science Quarterly* 36: 269–96.

paradigms

Yvonna S. Lincoln and Egon G. Guba

Paradigms are perhaps one of the most contested terms in qualitative research. While some authors and methodologists use the term to denote a set of methods or methodologies (Tashakkori & Teddlie 2003), others claim that the term has many uses. Some authors point out that Thomas Kuhn, who brought the term into common usage in his *Structure of Scientific Revolutions* (1962), himself used the term in over 25 different ways. Kuhn's general thesis was that paradigms were dominant theories or models by which science proceeded, until they were overtaken and superseded by newer and more encompassing theories or models, or both. Rohmann (1999: 295) defines paradigm as "An ideal or archetypal pattern or example that provides a model to be emulated." A preference here, however, is the definition provided by Reese (1980) and adopted by Lincoln and Guba (1985: 15): "a *set* of basic or metaphysical beliefs ... sometimes constituted into a *system of ideas* that 'either give us some judgment about the nature of reality, or a reason why we must be content with knowing something less than the nature of reality, along with a method for taking hold of whatever can be known' [Reese 1980: 352]."

The distinction between definitions of paradigms as sets of methods or methodologies, and a definition which encompasses an entire set of ideas based on sets of fundamental or metaphysical beliefs, is a crucial one. In general, methods can be utilized in the service of any set of beliefs to a greater or lesser extent. Sets of metaphysical beliefs, however, are rarely transferable (in the same way methods might be deployed and redeployed), nor do they readily mix with other beliefs which are contradictory. That is, sets of beliefs tend to exhibit internal coherence and resonance. For this reason, discussions of paradigms as metaphysics of science tend to involve discussions of ontology (the nature of reality), epistemology (theories of knowing and theories surrounding the nature of the relationship between knower and to-be-known), axiology (theories regarding what is considered *good* and what constitutes an appropriate *aesthetics* for a project or regime), and methodology (or implied best procedures for coming to know). Increasingly, paradigm theorists also discuss teleology, or the explanation of things according to their ends or purposes, or, in ethics, explanations in terms of consequences. Thus, for instance, researchers could speak of the portraits of the poor provided by social scientists of the 1960s and 1970s as having been captured by the political Right, and twisted to its own purposes, including the caricaturing of poverty, welfare recipients, racial and ethnic minorities, and the like (Fine et al. 2000).

Paradigms are important to qualitative research because they perform two critical functions. First, they signal that qualitative methods are being deployed in the service of a paradigm which is an alternative to conventional, experimental, or positivist research. Most often, the alternative paradigm is refered to as phenomenological, interpretive, ethnographic, constructivist, or naturalistic. Unlike conventional research, the goal of such research is neither prediction nor control, but rather explanation, deep understanding of some social phenomenon (*verstehen*), or the creation of a *pattern theory*, or all three. Pattern theories are more likely to emerge from interpretive, phenomenological, or ethnographic inquiry because pattern theories, unlike hypothetico-deductive theories, rarely specify cause–effect chains in variables (factors). Rather, pattern theories theorize motifs, arrangements, or representations of phenomenal elements that appear to be regularized or routinized in their propinquity to each other (Kaplan 1964). For example, less-than-robust health indicators are frequently seen in conjunction with poverty. It is likely that poverty itself does not cause ill health, but rather that other indicators closely aligned with poverty conditions – substandard housing, limited access to adequate health care, the paucity of high-quality nutritional support, and the like – work together to bring about the high incidence of chronic health problems among the desperately poor. Poverty itself is not a causative agent, but rather signals a constellation of factors that often work together to form a pattern of health relative to poverty.

Second, paradigms serve to create "cognitive economy," as Patton (1978) and others have explained. Paradigms are worldviews, entire philosophical systems for guiding how inquirers think about reality and how reality might be broken down, understood, or investigated. Paradigms are simultaneously both evocative (suggesting how one might conceive of some phenomenon or reality) and normative, specifying legitimate and reasonable means of exploring that reality which would be understood and assented to by other inquirers exploring the same reality. Paradigms serve as both metaphysical and methodological frameworks for socializing practitioners into their respective disciplines, and consequently, disciplinary practitioners will understand some portions of their own paradigms well and other portions may remain intuitive. Paradigms are cognitively efficient because, once adopted, they abrogate the necessity of epistemological or methodological debates each time new disciplinary problems present themselves for investigation.

Paradigms have substantial "staying power" and as a result are shifted only when evidence becomes compelling or overwhelming that a new paradigm is more useful. Practitioners of a given paradigm have typically arrived at some cognitive peace with themselves regarding what they believe regarding what is real, and what can be known about what is real, and are able to frame inquiries which conform to those fundamental, basic beliefs. As Patton points out,

this is both the strength and the weakness of paradigms: a strength because it enables action without further metaphysical debate, and a weakness because the paradigm's "version of reality tends to become ingrained, influencing the very choice of questions deemed worthy of study, the methods used to study those questions, and the interpretations of the results" (Rohmann 1999: 296).

Because paradigms represent sets of foundational beliefs, they tend to persist over time in individuals as well as disciplines. They frequently represent both disciplinary commitments and the kinds of questions that adherents believe to be important for social science investigations. A plurality of paradigms is likeliest to provide the richest social science; the question is not which paradigm is best suited to science, but rather which paradigm exhibits the best fit with the kinds of questions being posed.

SEE ALSO: Aesthetics; Constructionism; Epistemology; Kuhn, Thomas and Scientific Paradigms; Positivism

REFERENCES AND SUGGESTED READINGS

Fine, M., Weis, L., Weseen, S., & Wong, L. (2000) For Whom? Qualitative Research, Representations and Social Responsibilities. In: Denzin, N. K. & Lincoln, Y. S. (Eds.), *Handbook of Qualitative Research*, 2nd edn. Sage, Thousand Oaks, CA, pp. 107–31.

Kaplan, A. (1964) *The Conduct of Inquiry: Methodology for Behavioral Science*. Chandler, San Francisco.

Kuhn, T. (1962) *The Structure of Scientific Revolutions*. University of Chicago Press, Chicago.

Lincoln, Y. S. & Guba, E. G. (1985) *Naturalistic Inquiry*. Sage, Thousand Oaks, CA.

Patton, M. Q. (1978) *Utilization-Focused Evaluation*. Sage, Thousand Oaks, CA.

Reese, W. L. (1980) *Dictionary of Philosophy and Religion*. Humanities Press, Atlantic Highlands, NJ.

Rohmann, C. (1999) *A World of Ideas: A Dictionary of Important Theories, Concepts, Beliefs, and Thinkers*. Ballantine Books, New York.

Tashakkori, A. & Teddlie, C. (Eds.) (2003) *Handbook of Mixed Methods in Social and Behavioral Research*. Sage, Thousand Oaks, CA.

parental involvement in education

Sophia Catsambis

Scholarly interest in parental involvement was sparked in the late 1960s, when the seminal Coleman report (Coleman et al. 1966) found family social background to be the most important predictor of children's academic success in the United States. Educational inequalities by social class are found in most countries and such findings prompted researchers' efforts to identify what aspects of family background are responsible for children's educational success (Gonzalez 2004). Some focus on economic resources, family structure, or parental education, while others investigate parental involvement in children's education.

Despite a significant amount of research on parental involvement, there are considerable differences in its conceptualization and measurement. Early researchers conceived of parental involvement as participation in school activities, while contemporary scholars recognize that it consists of a multitude of family activities (Ho 1995; Hoover–Dempsey & Sandler 1997; Epstein 2001). Epstein (2001) developed a widely used classification of parental involvement that defines six distinct types: (1) establishing a positive learning environment at home; (2) communicating with school about educational programs and student progress; (3) participating and volunteering at school; (4) participating in students' learning at home; (5) being involved in school decision-making; and (6) collaborating with the community to increase students' learning.

Many family practices fall within each type of involvement. Findings from a number of countries, such as the US, England, Korea, and Hong Kong, show that the specific practices and the types of involvement that different families adopt may vary across nations and are generally affected by children's age, socioeconomic and race/ethnic background, family relationships and experiences, school policies, or neighborhood living conditions (Ho 1995; Huss-Keeler 1997; Catsambis & Beveridge 2001; Epstein 2001; Gonzalez 2004; Wang 2004).

PARENTAL INVOLVEMENT FROM PRESCHOOL AND BEYOND

Parental involvement in education begins even before children enter school. Parents adopt a number of family practices in order to address children's developmental and educational needs. Parents of preschool children engage in home-based educational practices, such as reading to children, and in activities involving the wider community, such as taking children to museums, zoos, libraries, and daycare centers. Parental involvement reaches its peak when children enter elementary school. At that time, nearly all parents communicate regularly with the school and many engage in school-related activities, such as volunteering at school and participating in PTA. Parental involvement in the elementary grades is often initiated by school personnel and typically consists of notes and memos transmitted by the child. Parents and teachers may also communicate by brief conversations before and after school and on "parent night" or by special appointment and telephone conversations. Less frequently, teachers establish relationships with parents by visiting children's homes (Epstein 2001). While these specific practices are documented in the US, schools in most countries initiate communication with parents and encourage involvement in their children's elementary education (Carvalho & Jeria 1999; Gonzalez 2004).

Monitoring children's homework is the main venue through which parents participate in their children's elementary education. In addition to its academic purpose, homework provides opportunities for communication among parents, children, and their teachers. Teachers often ask parents to help with children's academic and discipline problems, and therefore parents spend more time supervising homework if their children are having trouble at school (Epstein 2001).

Scholars and educators generally believe that parental involvement declines when children enter middle school. At that time parents may lose confidence in their ability to help with more advanced schoolwork and teachers no longer ask for parent participation. However, it is possible that declines in parental involvement are reported because most studies do not investigate developmentally appropriate practices for older students (Hill & Taylor 2004). Parental involvement in secondary education has received little attention and not much is known about its nature and effectiveness for high school students. National longitudinal data tracing changes in parental involvement as children grow have been available only in the US. These data reveal that most parents of middle-grade students continue some of their already established practices of supervising children's lives and education at home (establishing rules for completing homework, TV viewing and curfews, and discussing career aspirations and plans about future education). When children reach high school, parents drop their involvement in learning activities at home and loosen daily supervision. They increase their communication with schools regarding academic programs and student progress, and participate more at school events. Overall, at this stage of schooling, parents are concerned with preparing adolescents for their future lives and careers and they begin to take actions related to college attendance (Catsambis & Garland 1997).

DOES PARENTAL INVOLVEMENT MAKE A DIFFERENCE?

Empirical evidence in the US, Canada, Australia, and many European and Asian countries has established that parental involvement is important for the academic success of students at all stages of schooling (Villas-Boas 1998; Epstein 2001; Gonzalez 2004; Hill et al. 2004). Children whose parents are involved in school have more positive attitudes about school, better attendance and work habits, and higher academic success than do children whose parents are not involved (Epstein 2001; Hill et al. 2004).

Scholars note that not all family practices are effective for children's academic success (Muller 1995, 1998; Lareau 2000). Moreover, given changes in children's developmental needs, children of different ages may respond to different kinds of involvement from their parents (Muller 1998). It is only parental educational aspirations for their children that are strongly associated with academic-related attitudes and success

across all school grades (Astone & McLanahan 1991; Singh et al. 1995; Juang & Vondracek 2001; Wang 2004). In the elementary grades, reading activities at home are most important for students' achievement growth (Epstein 2001). In secondary education, students' achievement is positively related with parent/student discussions regarding school matters and general parental supervision and, to a lesser extent, with parent–school contacts and participation in school activities (Astone & McLanahan 1991; Schneider & Coleman 1993; Ho & Willms 1996). By the last years of high school, effective parental involvement may consist of activities that support adolescents' educational decision-making regarding course selection and plans for postsecondary education (Catsambis 2001). Much more work is needed to identify changes in effective parental practices associated with children's age and to develop a comprehensive theoretical framework of parental involvement.

DOES ONE MODEL FIT ALL?

Factors related to families' social conditions influence the extent and effectiveness of parental involvement practices. Although research indicates that the negative effects of single-parent families and working mothers on parental involvement may be exaggerated (Muller 1995), it has provided consistent cross-national evidence of the importance of socioeconomic status and of parental education (Gonzalez 2004; Hill et al. 2004). Parents from middle and upper classes are more knowledgeable about how to be involved in their children's schooling, and their involvement is more effective than those of less advantaged parents (Lareau 2000).

Race and ethnic variations also exist in the levels and effectiveness of parental involvement, but findings are inconsistent in this regard. Some findings show that in the US, Hispanic and African American parents are more involved in their children's education compared to whites once other factors are controlled (Ho & Willms 1996), while others show no such differences (Hill et al. 2004). These inconsistencies may be explained by limitations in existing theory and research that have not adequately considered national or international variations in family life and parenting (Huss-Keeler 1997; Gonzalez 2004; Hill et al. 2004). Some disadvantaged parents may have had negative experiences with school, which may instill a level of distrust toward schools (Hoover-Dempsey & Sandler 1997). In other cases, ethnic minority parents may participate little in their children's education because they value highly teachers' professional status and delegate authority for their children's education entirely to schools (Hoover-Dempsey & Sandler 1997; Lareau 2000). Others suggest that more study should be devoted to how culturally specific parent–child activities may influence the academic development of children from different ethnic backgrounds (Huss-Keeler 1997).

More study is also needed on how the social environment of communities or neighborhoods may affect parents and their children. Specifically, disadvantaged neighborhoods may pose constraints on parents' ability to adopt effective parental practices (Brooks-Gunn et al. 1997; Catsambis & Beveridge 2001). A recent US study revealed that although disadvantaged neighborhoods suppressed parents' ability to help children succeed in school, parents' frequent communication with children, close monitoring of their activities, and provision of out-of-school learning opportunities offset some of the educational disadvantages associated with living in such neighborhoods (Catsambis & Beveridge 2001).

CAN PARENTS DO IT ALL?

The above findings underscore the importance of institutional interrelationships for children's learning and development. While family is a significant force behind students' academic success, parents alone cannot overcome the educational challenges that many children face. Most parents are interested and make efforts to participate in their children's education, but many of them require assistance in order to engage in educationally supportive activities (Epstein 2001). To be effective, parents need to draw support and resources form the wider social environment, and especially from schools. Both families and schools need to take each other's perspectives, expectations, and actions into account in developing practices that promote

student learning (Huss-Keeler 1997; Epstein 2001). Indeed, the importance of parent–school supportive relationships has gained widespread recognition and many educational reforms and intervention programs throughout the world target parental involvement as a key strategy for improving student achievement (Schleicher 1992; Carvalho & Jeria 1999; Gonzalez 2004). The success of such reforms greatly depends on scholars' continuing efforts to close gaps in existing research and develop a comprehensive theoretical framework of parental involvement.

SEE ALSO: Cultural Capital; Cultural Capital in Schools; Educational Attainment; Educational Inequality; Family, Sociology of; Social Capital; Social Capital and Education

REFERENCES AND SUGGESTED READINGS

Astone, N. M. & McLanahan, S. S. (1991) Family Structure, Parental Practices, and High School Completion. *American Sociological Review* 56: 309–20.

Brooks-Gunn, J., Duncan, G. J., & Aber, J. L. (Eds.) (1997) *Neighborhood Poverty*, Vol. 1: *Context and Consequences for Children*. Russell Sage Foundation, New York.

Carvalho, M. E. P. de & Jeria, J. (1999) Community–School Relations. Current Policies and Community Participation: Cases in Brazil and Chile. Paper presented at the Annual Conference of the Comparative and International Education Society, Toronto, Ontario, Canada, April 14–18.

Catsambis, S. (2001) Expanding Knowledge of Parental Involvement in Children's Secondary Education: Connections with High School Seniors' Academic Success. *Social Psychology of Education* 5(2): 149–77.

Catsambis, S. & Beveridge, A. A. (2001) Does Neighborhood Matter? Family, Neighborhood, and School Influences on Eighth-Grade Mathematics Achievement. *Sociological Focus* 34(4): 435–57.

Catsambis, S. & Garland, J. E. (1997) Parental Involvement in Students' Education: Changes from Middle Grades to High School. Center for the Education of Students Placed at Risk, Johns Hopkins University, Report No. 18.

Coleman, J., Campbell, E., Hobson, C., Mac Partland, J., Mood, A., Weinfield, F., & York, R. (1966) *Equality of Educational Opportunity Report.*

US Government Printing Office, Washington, DC.

Epstein, J. L. (2001) *School, Family, and Community Partnerships: Preparing Educators and Improving Schools.* Westview Press, Boulder, CO.

Gonzalez, M. R. (2004) International Perspectives on Families, Schools, and Communities: Educational Implications for Family–School–Community Partnerships. *International Journal of Educational Research* 41: 3–9.

Hill, N. E. & Taylor, L. C. (2004) Parent–School Involvement and Children's Academic Achievement: Pragmatics and Issues. *Current Directions in Psychological Science* 13: 161–4.

Hill, N. E., Castellino, R. D., Lansford, J. E., Nowlin, P., Dodge, K. A., Bates, J., & Petit, G. (2004) Parent–Academic Involvement as Related to School Behavior, Achievement, and Aspirations: Demographic Variations Across Adolescence. *Child Development* 75(4).

Ho, S.-C. E. (1995). Parent Involvement: A Comparison of Different Definitions and Explanations. *Chinese University Education Journal* 23(1): 39–68.

Ho, S.-C. E. & Willms, J. D. (1996) Effects of Parental Involvement on Eighth Grade Achievement. *Sociology of Education* 69: 126–41.

Hoover-Dempsey, K. V. & Sandler, H. M. (1997) Why Do Parents Become Involved in their Children's Education? *Review of Educational Research* 67(1): 3–42.

Huss-Keeler, R. L. (1997) Teacher Perception of Ethnic and Linguistic Minority Parental Involvement and its Relationship to Children's Language and Literacy Learning: A Case Study. *Teaching and Teacher Education* 13(2): 171–82.

Juang, L. & Vondracek, F. W. (2001) Developmental Patterns of Adolescent Capability Beliefs: A Person Approach. *Journal of Vocational Behavior* 59 (1): 34–52.

Lareau, A. (2000) *Home Advantage: Social Class and Parental Intervention in Elementary Education*, 2nd edn. Rowman & Littlefield, Lanham, MD.

Muller, C. (1995) Maternal Employment, Parent Involvement, and Mathematics Achievement Among Adolescents. *Journal of Marriage and the Family* 57(2): 85–100.

Muller, C. (1998) Gender Differences in Parental Involvement and Adolescents' Mathematics Achievement. *Sociology of Education* 71(4): 336–56.

Schleicher, K. (1992) Cooperation between School and Family: Prerequisites, Implementations, Problems. *European Education* 24(2): 25–49.

Schneider, B. & Coleman, J. S. (Eds.) (1993) *Parents, Their Children, and Schools.* Westview Press, Boulder, CO.

Singh, K., Bickley, P. G., Trivette, P. S., Keith, T. Z., Keith, P. B., & Anderson, E. (1995) The Effects of Four Components of Parental Involvement on Eighth Grade Student Achievement: Structural Analysis of NELS-88 Data. *School Psychology Review* 24: 99–317.

Villas-Boas, A. (1998) The Effects of Parental Involvement in Homework on Student Achievement in Portugal and Luxembourg. *Childhood Education* 74(6): 367–71.

Wang, D. B. (2004) Family Background Factors and Mathematics Success: A Comparison of Chinese and US Students. *International Journal of Educational Research* 41: 40–54.

Pareto, Vilfredo (1848–1923)

Gerald Mozetič

Vilfredo Pareto is famous for his seminal contributions to neoclassical and mathematical economics, his analysis of power, and his inquiry into the psychological and social foundations of human conduct. Born in Paris, where his father, a Genoese *marchese*, supporter of Mazzini and a civil engineer, lived in political exile, Pareto grew up in a bilingual and liberal aristocratic milieu. Upon his family's return to Italy in the 1850s he received a broad humanistic education and studied mathematics, physics, and engineering in Turin. After his graduation in 1870 Pareto moved to Tuscany, where during the next two decades he worked in upper managerial positions for a railway and an iron company. In this period he traveled extensively, frequented the aristocratic salons of Florence, studied the works of Comte, Spencer, Darwin, and J. S. Mill, joined the Italian Adam Smith Society to spread laissez-faire economics, and began to write articles on various economic and policy issues. His political ambitions to be elected to the Chamber of Deputies remained unsuccessful. In 1890 he met the economist and leading Italian proponent of marginalism, Pantaleoni. Pantaleoni introduced Pareto to Walras, whom Pareto succeeded as a professor of political economy at the University of Lausanne in 1893. In the following years Pareto wrote his main works: *Cours d'économie politique* (1896–7), *Les Systèmes socialistes* (1902–3), *Manuale di economia politica* (1906), and *Trattato di sociologia generale* (1916). With age, Pareto grew disillusioned with the workings of the democratic system, especially in Italy and France, and became increasingly conservative. After their rise to power the Fascists conferred honors upon Pareto, using his concept of elites, his critique of parliamentary democracy, and his ideas concerning the function of violence in history for their own purposes. Though Pareto sympathized with the advent of Fascism, it should be noted that he died only a couple of months after the March on Rome, and that his fervent support of laissez-faire economics as well as his conviction that the state should protect the civil liberties of the individual ran counter to totalitarian ideologies.

As one of the great figures of neoclassical economics Pareto built upon Walrasian general equilibrium theory, modifying some of its premises. Trying to go beyond utility maximization in perfect market conditions, he based the analysis of economic equilibrium upon the opposition of tastes and obstacles to satisfying them. In order to avoid the difficulty of comparing interpersonal utilities he used the distinction between cardinal and ordinal utility. Among his many other contributions, it must suffice to point to two ideas that are still discussed in economic theory: the so-called "Pareto's law," which uses a logarithmic formula to describe income distributions, and the concept of "Pareto optimum," or rather "Pareto efficiency," an allocation of resources in which no party can increase its welfare without lowering the welfare of another party.

Realizing that the premises and models of "pure economics" were insufficient for the analysis of human conduct, Pareto argued that economics had to be complemented by a more realistic approach which was able to grasp the complexity of everyday life. This approach, outlined most fully in his sociological masterpiece *Trattato*, is based upon the fundamental distinction between logical and non-logical actions. The former are characterized by the logical linking of means and ends, both from the subjective standpoint of the actor and from the standpoint of the person with objective, scientific knowledge. If there is no logical correspondence between means and ends, an

action is considered non-logical. Despite the fact that people usually try, ex post, to give good reasons for their actions, Pareto argued that the vast majority of human conduct belonged to the non-logical type. Rather than emphasizing the tension between reason and passion, Pareto followed Hume's famous dictum that reason is "the slave of the passions." The main task of sociology, according to Pareto, was to analyze the pervasive influence of non-logical actions in social life. In this context he introduced the categories of "residues" and "derivations," which can be understood as the basic elements of non-logical human conduct. Residues as the more constant part refer to impulses and basic sentiments of human action; derivations as the more variable part comprise the rationalizations people use to explain and justify their behavior. Pareto argued, for example, that within the political sphere the "derivations" *par excellence* of his age were the call for liberty, equality, democracy, etc. After defining and classifying the various residues and derivations, which makes up a large part of the *Trattato*, Pareto sought to combine his analysis of the basic elements of non-logical actions with his idea that the fundamental morphology of all societies was formed, on the one hand, by the opposition between the elites and the masses and, on the other hand, by the incessant circulation of elites. According to Pareto, the ability of an elite to maintain power depended upon a certain mixture of residues of class I ("instinct of combination") and residues of class II ("persistence of aggregates"). When, however, a ruling class remained in power for some time, it tended to become dominated by the residues of class II. This type of elite was only poorly equipped to cope with social transformations. In such a situation a new and innovative elite would emerge in which the residues of class I prevailed and displace the old one. Echoing Marx, Pareto remarked that history was "a graveyard of aristocracies." The assumption of the universal existence of two opposing social strata and the cyclic conception of history are central to the so-called Italian Elitist School, represented, apart from Pareto, by Mosca and Michels.

In economics Pareto's contributions to neoclassical theory have been debated since the 1930s and 1940s, especially within welfare economics. In sociology his ideas – the *Trattato* was translated into English in 1935 – were intensively discussed in the "Pareto circle" at Harvard University in the 1930s, and were the subject of books written by Homans and Curtis in 1934 and Henderson in 1935. In his work *The Structure of Social Action* (1937), Talcott Parsons regarded the Italian sociologist, along with Marshall, Durkheim, and Weber, as one of the eminent figures who had paved the way for a theory of social action. Despite this early appreciation, the reception of Pareto's sociology seems to have been hampered by his anti-democratic bias, his sympathies for Fascism, and by the idiosyncratic nature of the *Trattato*. In contrast to his economic writings, the sociologist Pareto was not a very systematic and analytic author. Some of his key concepts, as critics have repeatedly noted, are poorly defined. Furthermore, his theoretical reflections are interspersed with (not to say buried under) long digressions, containing anecdotes, ingenious and aphoristic remarks, and cynical comments, as well as a mass of data from ancient philosophy, philology, history, jurisprudence, literature, etc. Though the chaotic richness of the *Trattato* makes it difficult to codify his sociology, it also makes it probable that Pareto will be revisited, reinterpreted, and rediscovered by generations to come.

SEE ALSO: Conservatism; Elites; Michels, Robert; Mosca, Gaetano; Political Sociology

REFERENCES AND SUGGESTED READINGS

Aspers, P. (2001) Crossing the Boundary of Economics and Sociology: The Case of Vilfredo Pareto. *American Journal of Economics and Sociology* 60: 519–45.
Bach, M. (2004) *Jenseits des rationalen Handelns: Zur Soziologie Vilfredo Paretos.* Verlag fuer Sozialwissenschaften, Wiesbaden.
Bongiorno, A. (1930) A Study of Pareto's Treatise on General Sociology. *American Journal of Sociology* 36: 349–70.
Pareto, V. (1963 [1935]) *The Mind and Society: A Treatise on General Sociology.* Ed. A. Livingston. Trans. A. Bongiorno & A. Livingston. Dover, New York.
Pareto, V. (1964–2005) *Oeuvres Complètes*, 32 vols. Ed. G. Busino. Librairie Droz, Geneva.
Pietri-Tonelli, A. de & Bousquet, G. H. (1994) *Vilfredo Pareto: Neoclassical Synthesis of Economics and Sociology.* Macmillan, London.
Schumpeter, J. A. (1949) Vilfredo Pareto (1848–1923). *Quarterly Journal of Economics* 63: 147–73.
Tarascio, V. J. (1968) *Pareto's Methodological Approach to Economics: A Study in the History of Some Scientific Aspects of Economic Thought.* University of North Carolina Press, Chapel Hill.
Wood, J. C. & McLure, M. (Eds.) (1999) *Vilfredo Pareto: Critical Assessments of Leading Economists*, 4 vols. Routledge, London.

Park, Robert E. (1864–1944) and Burgess, Ernest W. (1886–1966)

Peter Kivisto

Robert Ezra Park and Ernest Watson Burgess advanced American sociology during its formative period and made lasting contributions to ethnic studies, urban sociology, and the study of collective behavior. Their methodological preference was for ethnography, while they articulated a theoretical perspective shaped in particular by human ecology.

Though the sociology department at the University of Chicago had been successfully established by Albion Small and his successor William Isaac Thomas, Park and Burgess were the two central figures responsible for defining and shaping the Chicago School during its most influential period. Although he was in his fifties before his sociological career began, Park quickly assumed the chairperson's position in the department after the forced departure of Thomas due to a morals charge. His younger colleague Burgess became a valued collaborator and assistant. Although Park was the more original of the two, they formed a creative partnership in which their roles were symbiotic: Park the "idea man," Burgess the "details man"; Park the charismatic leader, Burgess attuned to the needs and concerns of others.

Born in Harveyville, Pennsylvania, Park was raised in Red Wing, Minnesota, where as a child he claims to have encountered Jesse James as the bandit fled a bank robbery. He attended the University of Michigan and Harvard, studying with John Dewey at the former and William James, George Santayana, and Josiah Royce at the latter. As did many of his generation, he spent time studying abroad in Germany, where he attended the lectures of Wilhelm Windelband and Georg Simmel. Simmel's lectures constituted his only education in sociology and had a pronounced impact on his sociological vision.

Upon returning to the US, Park worked as a muckraking journalist for the Congo Reform Association (CRA), an organization committed to challenging Belgian colonial rule. He met Booker T. Washington in the CRA and spent several years thereafter in Tuskegee serving as Washington's personal assistant and ghostwriter. He began his career at Chicago at the invitation of Thomas, who initially employed Park as a part-time summer instructor. Park and Thomas shared an interest in ethnicity and migration, leading to collaborative work on immigration as part of the Carnegie Corporation's project on Americanization. Reflecting his newspaper past, Park was especially interested in the role of the immigrant press. Park chaired the department from 1918 until his retirement in 1933, after which time he taught at Fisk University.

Burgess was born in Tilbury, Ontario, though his family moved to the US early in his life. His formative years were spent in Michigan and Oklahoma. After completing his undergraduate studies at Kingfisher College in Oklahoma, he pursued his PhD at the University of Chicago and was one of the first sociologists to complete his doctorate at a US institution. After one-year appointments at Toledo, Kansas, and Ohio State, Burgess returned to Chicago, where he was to spend the rest of his academic career. Never married, he lived with his father and sister in a home near the campus for many decades. Burgess had warm relations with Jane Addams and her associates at Hull House, though he and Park shared a conviction that for sociology to progress, it needed to separate itself to a large extent from reform activities. Beyond the areas of sociology where he and Park

shared a common interest, Burgess also made contributions to the sociology of the family, aging, and crime and deviance.

The 1921 publication of their co-authored textbook *Introduction to the Science of Sociology* – which became known as the Green Bible – served to codify their particular perspective on the emerging discipline. They identified various substantive concerns that they deemed central to sociology and articulated their commitment to empirical inquiry and to linking research to theory. In terms of theory, Park and Burgess were simultaneously influenced by human ecology and by a perspective that was concerned with meaningful social action as defined by the actors themselves.

Park and Burgess embraced Simmel's conviction that modernity would express itself most tangibly in the city, which increasingly became the locus of the worldwide migration of peoples. This led Park (1950: 160) to comment that the world could "be divided into two classes: those who have reached the city and those who have not yet arrived." Park and Burgess promoted a sociology that focused on the extraordinarily heterogeneous subgroups of urban dwellers. Of special interest were the ethnic and racial minorities migrating to cities, be they immigrants from Europe or Asia, or blacks, who were considered to be internal migrants experiencing dislocations quite similar to those experienced by migrants entering the nation from elsewhere.

The primary focus of much research was on the marginalized and oppressed members of the urban landscape, whom Park and Burgess wanted to see depicted in a dispassionate manner devoid of middle-class disdain or the patronizing attitude of many social reformers. The idea was to produce research that sought to understand, rather than revile or romanticize. Central to their version of sociology was a keen awareness that the modern world brought together, via mass migration, a wide array of racial and ethnic groups as a consequence of a newly emerging economic world system. Immigrants were compelled to adjust to their new social circumstances and to the diverse groups that they encountered. Park in particular was interested in delineating the processes of immigrant adjustment, which he did by developing a version of assimilation theory in 1914.

He would return to this topic in subsequent decades.

Though often viewed as the canonical formulation of assimilation theory, Park's ideas have also been badly misinterpreted. His perspective has been portrayed by some as the theoretical articulation of the melting pot thesis, as a synonym for Americanization, the final outcome of a "race relations cycle," and an expression of a "straight-line" process of incorporation. If any of these was true, Park's understanding of assimilation pits it against theories of cultural pluralism and multiculturalism. However, a close reading of Park's writings on assimilation leads one to conclude that in fact it does not necessarily entail the eradication of ethnic attachments, but instead can be seen as occurring in a multicultural context where ethnic groups maintain their distinctive identities while at the same time being committed to the interests and ideas of the larger societal community.

In their co-authored textbook, Park and Burgess took issue with two perspectives on assimilation common at the time in sociological circles. First, they dispute the idea that identification with the larger society or the nation-state requires a simultaneous decline in ethnic identification. Second, they critique what they refer to as the "magic crucible" view of assimilation. They link this idea to the concept of "like-mindedness," which they associate with the work of Franklin Giddings. They distinguish accommodation – which they describe as a process that reduces levels of conflict and unbridled competition in order to establish social order and stability – from assimilation – which they depict in terms of cultural fusion: "a process of interpenetration and fusion in which persons and groups acquire the memories, sentiments, and attitudes of other persons or groups" with the result being a "common cultural life" (Park & Burgess 1969: 735).

They make three points about assimilation. First, it occurs most rapidly and completely in situations where social contacts between newcomers and native-born occur in the realm of primary group life, while if contact is confined to secondary groups, accommodation is more likely to result. Second, a shared language is a prerequisite for assimilation. Third, rather than being a sign of like-mindedness, assimilation is a reflection of shared experiences and mental frameworks, out of which emerge the possibility of a community with a shared sense of collective purpose.

Park and Burgess's work had a marked impact on American sociology prior to World War II. Among their most prominent students are those who subsequently played significant roles in the discipline, including Herbert Blumer, E. Franklin Frazier, Everett Hughes, and Louis Wirth. However, after that time the center of gravity shifted from Chicago to Harvard with the ascendance of the Parsonian theoretical project, which operated with the assumption that grand system building was essential if a foundational sociology was to be established. The Chicago School brand of sociology was frequently criticized for being atheoretical and unsystematic. Moreover, Park and Burgess were criticized for being inattentive to power and politics. Methodologically, advocates of survey research challenged their emphasis on ethnography. In the area of urban sociology, their ecological approach gave way to approaches more influenced by political economy, while in the area of race relations, the idea of assimilation was widely dismissed.

In recent years there is substantial evidence of a widespread renewal of interest in the work of Park and Burgess, as sociologists and historians alike have sought to reassess their place in the history of the discipline. Since the 1970s, coincident with the demise of Parsonian domination, a spate of books and articles has appeared seeking to revisit and reappropriate the legacy of the Chicago School. The result has been that many earlier misconceptions have been corrected. For example, Park's criticisms of "do-gooders" notwithstanding, he was himself a reformer, from his days as a muckraking journalist to his involvement in the Urban League in Chicago. Their Chicago School was more theoretically sophisticated than has been appreciated, shaped chiefly by the thought of Durkheim and Simmel. Ethnographic research is now far more accepted than it was during the heyday of structural functionalism. At the same time, the ecological approach has largely been abandoned because of its theoretical shortcomings. Critics make a persuasive case when they contend that Park and Burgess were relatively inattentive to power and to many issues related to social class. In short, what has emerged is a clearer portrait of this influential duo that reveals both the weaknesses and the strengths inherent in their work.

SEE ALSO: Blumer, Herbert George; Chicago School; Chicago School: Social Change; Frazier, E. Franklin; Robert E. Park, Ernest W. Burgess, and Urban Social Research; Urban Ecology

REFERENCES AND SUGGESTED READINGS

Faris, R. E. L. (1967) *Chicago Sociology, 1920–1932*. University of Chicago Press, Chicago.

Kivisto, P. (1993) Robert E. Park's Dialectic of Racial Enlightenment. *International Journal of Politics, Culture, and Society* 7(1): 121–31.

Kivisto, P. (2004) What is the Canonical Theory of Assimilation? Robert E. Park and His Predecessors. *Journal of the History of the Behavioral Sciences* 40(2): 1–15.

Lal, B. B. (1990) *The Romance of Culture in an Urban Civilization: Robert E. Park on Race and Ethnic Relations in Cities*. Routledge, London.

Matthews, F. H. (1977) *Robert E. Park and the Chicago School*. McGill-Queen's University Press, Montreal.

Park, R. E. (1950) *Race and Culture: Essays in the Sociology of Contemporary Man*. Free Press, New York.

Park, R. E. & Burgess, E. W. (1969 [1921]) *Introduction to the Science of Sociology*. University of Chicago Press, Chicago.

Persons, S. (1987) *Ethnic Studies at Chicago, 1905–45*. University of Illinois Press, Urbana.

Rauschenbush, W. (1975) *Robert E. Park: Biography of a Sociologist*. Duke University Press, Durham, NC.

Parsons, Talcott (1902–79)

Victor Lidz

Talcott Parsons was the preeminent sociological theorist of his generation. He developed a "general theory of action" that still serves as a comprehensive framework for understanding human social relationships and behavior. First adumbrated in articles published in the late 1920s, the theory was elaborated to a high level of analytic complexity in books and essays published over the next 50 years. Several works, including *The Structure of Social Action* (1937), *The Social System* (1951), *Economy and Society* (with Neil J. Smelser, 1956), and essays collected in *Politics and Social Structure* (1969) remain landmarks in the history of sociology. Parsons was interested in the relations between sociology and other social sciences, including economics, political science, psychology, psychiatry, and anthropology, and he contributed basic ideas to each of these disciplines. At Harvard University, where he served on the faculty from 1927, he became in 1947 the founding chair of the Department of Social Relations, an international center of interdisciplinary teaching and research in sociology, clinical and social psychology, and social anthropology until it split up in 1968.

Parsons was born in Colorado City, Colorado into a family of New England heritage, broad intellectual interests, and progressive political views, characteristics he retained throughout his life. He studied at Amherst College, focusing on institutional economics, Kantian philosophy, and evolutionary biology, the London School of Economics, and the University of Heidelberg, where he encountered the works of Max Weber. Weber's *The Protestant Ethic and the Spirit of Capitalism*, which Parsons later translated, made an immediate and transformative impression, but the comparative studies in religion, the essays on methodology, and the conceptual framework of *Wirtschaft und Gesellschaft* had still greater influence. Under Weber's spell, Parsons completed a DPhil degree at Heidelberg and began his career at Harvard as an Instructor in Economics. He became fully identified as a sociologist only after transferring to Harvard's new Department of Sociology in 1930.

The Structure of Social Action presented Parsons's first attempt at a unified conceptual framework for sociology, a set of categories to apply in all times and places, address all aspects of human social organization, and be open to refinement as the discipline advanced in ability to relate theory to empirical findings. In its elementary formulation, Parsons's conceptual scheme analyzed the "unit act" – the concept of *any* instance of meaningful human conduct – into four essential elements, ends, means, norms, and conditions, and in some statements a fifth, effort, to implement action. Parsons argued that action is not possible unless an instance of each element is entailed in the process and, conversely, all human action can be understood as emerging from combinations of these kinds of elements. This twofold proposition grounded Parsons's argument that his schema, which he called the *action frame of reference*, provided a universal starting point for social science, whatever further development it might require.

Parsons formulated this schema through a probing critique of the theories of Max Weber, Émile Durkheim, Alfred Marshall, and Vilfredo Pareto. He argued that these figures, though working in different intellectual settings, had "converged" on the action frame of reference with its emphasis on normative elements. He concluded that if theories fail to emphasize normative elements, they are in principle flawed. Utilitarian theories, including neoclassical economics, and behaviorist theories are prime examples. Idealist theories are flawed, he claimed, because they overemphasize ends and norms while underemphasizing conditions and means. What we now call structuralism errs by assimilating norms and conditions into its notion of structure, denying their independence, while also underemphasizing ends and means. The action frame of reference was designed to avoid the selectivity among basic concepts that has, in various ways, compromised most social scientific frameworks.

Parsons's focus on frames of reference was based on a methodology, "analytical realism," shaped by his studies of Kant and, more directly, A. N. Whitehead's philosophy of science. Analytical realism views frames of reference as logically prior to other forms of theory, because they guide the abstraction from reality that underlies all empirical observation and, therefore, all propositions, hypotheses, or generalizations pertaining to empirical conditions. Parsons maintained that establishing a sound frame of reference is the logical starting point for a science. His writings contain many examples of other forms of theorizing, but he saw clarifying frames of reference and their theoretical consequences as his distinctive contribution.

In *The Social System*, Parsons replaced the unit act as his central sociological concept. Working in an interdisciplinary department, he had developed interests in sociology's relations to personality psychology and cultural anthropology. His new formulations related social systems to cultural systems, the domain of anthropology, and to personality systems, the domain of psychologists. He defined social systems as involving interaction and relationships among actors; culture as involving symbols and beliefs that orient action; and personality as involving motivational patterns of individuals. He suggested that the three kinds of systems are integrated by normative standards, which derive meaning from contexts of moral culture, are institutionalized in social systems, and are internalized in the superegos of personalities. *The Social System* explored the connections among cultural, social, and personality systems and examined the dynamics by which normative standards are institutionalized in social relationships, notably in chapters on socialization processes and on deviance and social control. A chapter on medical practice analyzed the sick role and the physician–patient relationship as examples of the dynamics of social control. Parsons emphasized that processes of social control are embedded in all relationships and are universals of social life.

The revised frame of reference centering on social relationships raised questions of how social systems sustain themselves over time. Parsons's discussion emphasized two functions: resource allocation and social integration. Resource allocation enables actors in various roles to control means, whether tools, skilled personnel, or financial means, to attain the ends expected of them. Social integration involves mechanisms of social control through which actors, in responding to one another's expectations and use of rewards and punishments, meet obligations associated with their respective roles. Large-scale social systems require formal mechanisms to fulfill these two functions, including economic markets for resource allocation and legal institutions for social integration.

Parsons soon replaced this conception of functions with a more sophisticated "four-function paradigm." The four functions are not, like previous formulations of social functions, an ad hoc list of functional requisites of social systems, but an analysis of the concept of action *system* into four general dimensions or aspects. Parsons's basic insight was that any action system can be analyzed in terms of four universal dimensions. This approach facilitates efficient theorizing as it leads to general knowledge of how operations serving each function are organized across empirical settings. The four functions are:

- *Pattern maintenance* or the processes of developing enduring attachment to basic principles that distinguish a system from its environment, for example, its basic values. In societies, processes of socialization serve this function, as do institutions of religion, family life, and education.
- *Integration* or the processes of reciprocal adjustment among a system's units, promoting their interdependence. In societies, institutions of solidarity and social control, including civil and criminal law, community, and strata formation, serve this function.
- *Goal attainment* or the processes of changing a system's relations with its environments to align them with shared ends. In societies, goal attainment centers on political institutions that set collective ends and mobilize resources for reaching them.
- *Adaptation* or the processes of developing generalized control over the environment. Adaptation involves development and allocation of diverse resources. In societies, it typically involves economic production and exchange through markets.

Parsons's most important application of the four-function paradigm was a theory of four functionally specialized subsystems of society. The outlines of this theory emerged in the mid-1950s, but Parsons elaborated it over the rest of his life. In the later formulations, the four subsystems were identified as (i) the economy for the adaptive function, (ii) the polity for the goal attainment function, (iii) the societal community for the integrative function, and (iv) the fiduciary system for the pattern maintenance function.

In exploiting his idea of four subsystems of society, Parsons first sought to integrate his sociological understanding of economic institutions with Keynesian theory in economics. He then developed his conception of the polity through critique of the scholarship on power and authority as well as electoral, executive, and administrative institutions. These aspects of his work progressed rapidly, producing many applications of the four-function paradigm to the analysis of specific institutional complexes. His writings on the fiduciary system codified previous research on religion, family, socialization processes, and educational institutions, while his writings on the societal community built on scholarship on reference groups, status systems, social classes, ethnicity, and legal institutions. These works faced greater challenges than his writings on the economy and polity, because the extant literatures were less highly developed. The resulting formulations are less tightly integrated and less thoroughly grounded empirically, yet are richly suggestive for future research.

Parsons's work on the societal subsystems led to a general model of action systems. In this model, every subsystem is a complex entity organized in terms of several differentiated sets of structures. The structures are maintained over time by specialized control mechanisms. The system meets functional needs and adjusts to changing conditions through dynamic processes of its own, and it has processes of change and growth for long-term expansion of its capacities. At its boundaries, each subsystem exchanges resources with the other three subsystems, obtaining means essential to its own operations while giving up means essential to the other subsystems. Each subsystem was thus treated as dynamically interdependent with the other three. Parsons proposed that the six pairs of exchanges between subsystems make up a society's general equilibrium, thus giving specific content to Pareto's classic idea.

The idea of exchanges between subsystems was a generalization of economists' treatment of the double exchanges between business firms and households, wages for labor, and consumer spending for goods and services, all of which Parsons located at the boundary between the economy and fiduciary system. Noting that economic processes are mediated and regulated by flows of money, Parsons sought to generalize on money's role by identifying similarly symbolic media for the other subsystems. Essays followed on power as the symbolic medium and regulator of political processes, influence as the medium of the societal community, and value commitments as the fiduciary medium. The concept of generalized symbolic media is among Parsons's most original and potentially fruitful ideas, although critics have identified problems in his particular formulations.

Aside from his contributions to general theory, Parsons wrote over one hundred essays on specific empirical problems. Major topics include the rise of Nazism in Germany, American family and kinship, the professions, social stratification, the McCarthyism of the 1950s, economic and political modernization, the sources of order in international relations, value systems, ethnicity, institutions of higher education, research institutions, and American religious culture and institutions. Many of these essays gained fame for originality and insight, and a number stimulated influential directions of investigation for others. Most applied theoretical ideas that Parsons was exploring when he wrote them, although he often left their conceptual underpinnings implicit.

Parsons was a distinguished teacher who inspired generations of students, including many who became productive social scientists. He was active in the American Sociological Association, the American Association of University Professors, the American Academy of Arts and Sciences, which he served as president, and on faculty committees at Harvard University. In all of these settings he was a steadfast proponent of freedom of thought, investigation, and association.

Parsons was not a Grand Theorist advocating a closed system, as he has often been caricatured. He was a pragmatist who used a keen analytical mind to critique and refine basic concepts of sociological theory step by step and to explore their implications in many empirical fields. He was a persistent critic of his own writings, theoretical and empirical, who was confident of his ability to improve on previous formulations. His main legacy is belief in the value of progressive refinement of general ideas in the social sciences.

SEE ALSO: Culture; Durkheim, Émile; Functionalism/Neofunctionalism; Institution;

Modernization; Professions; Religion, Sociology of; Social Control; Social Integration and Inclusion; Structural Functional Theory; Theory Construction; Values; Weber, Max

REFERENCES AND SUGGESTED READINGS

Bershady, H. J. (1973) *Ideology and Social Knowledge*. Blackwell, Oxford.

Bourricaud, F. (1981) *The Sociology of Talcott Parsons*. University of Chicago Press, Chicago.

Fox, R. C. (1997) Talcott Parsons, My Teacher. *American Scholar* 66(3): 395–410.

Gerhardt, U. (Ed.) (1993) *Talcott Parsons on National Socialism*. Aldine, New York.

Habermas, J. (1987) *The Theory of Communicative Action*. Vol. 2: *Lifeworld and System: A Critique of Functionalist Reason*. Beacon Press, Boston.

Lidz, V. (2000) Talcott Parsons. In: Ritzer, G. (Ed.), *The Blackwell Companion to Major Social Theorists*. Blackwell, Oxford.

Parsons, T. (1951) *The Social System*. Free Press, New York.

Parsons, T. (1968 [1937]) *The Structure of Social Action*, repr. edn. Free Press, New York.

Parsons, T. (1969) *Politics and Social Structure*. Free Press, New York.

Parsons, T. & Platt, G. M. (1973) *The American University*. Harvard University Press, Cambridge, MA.

Parsons, T. & Smelser, N. J. (1956) *Economy and Society*. Free Press, New York.

passing

Nicole Rousseau

Passing is a process by which an individual crosses over from one culture or community into another undetected. The historical connotation of the term, however, is intimately connected with black America, and "passing," "crossing over," or "going over to the other side" typically refers to a black person whose appearance is such that they can *pass* for white. The vivid language of the term itself evokes many images: passing one's self off as white; choosing to pass over into white society; the passing away of a person's black identity, reborn as white. As drastic a choice as this "social death" may seem, for some blacks in segregated America, there was little choice (Gaudin n.d.).

Homer Plessy, an American man, seven-eighths white (and one-eighth black), sued the state of Louisiana in 1892 for being jailed for sitting in a "whites only" railroad car. Plessy's argument was that he should be legally identified as white and thus allowed all the usual civil liberties and privileges of his white peers as stated under the 13th and 14th amendments of the US Constitution (Cozzens 1999). The judge, John Howard Ferguson, ruled against Plessy. Plessy then took his case to the Supreme Court, where the historic 1896 *Plessy* v. *Ferguson* decision upheld Ferguson's ruling, ushering in over 60 years of legally sanctioned segregation, commonly referred to as the Jim Crow Era. This "separate but equal" ideology represented a period of extreme oppression for blacks, socially, economically, and even physically, as many were victims of mob violence. Rather than endure the racist and segregated world that blacks were subjected to at this time, in some instances those who were able opted to pass for white.

In the slave era preceding Jim Crow significant race mixing had occurred. Through rape, forced breeding, and a host of other coercive means, several generations later, the concept of "colored" had developed into a social construction which no longer strictly represented one's phenotype. Though passing and segregation were not new developments of the twentieth century, the dawn of the 1900s saw a definite rise in the number of light-skinned "blacks" passing for white as they particularly felt the sting of segregation.

In order to fully exploit economic, social, and educational opportunities, some blacks, who were able, generally passed into white society on three levels: basic, complex, and fundamental. At the *basic* level of passing, an individual might occasionally accept the mistaken assumption that she or he is in fact white. This allows black citizens certain freedoms that they would otherwise be denied, such as moving about the cities where they live without fear of violence, shopping in any store, and eating at any lunch counter.

The *complex* level of passing is more purposefully planned. Individuals might work on one side of town under the premise of being white, where they could earn money and advancement, or even attend a university as white students. Yet when they return home at night or during holidays, they resume their black lives. This level is quite complicated and dangerous. In order for individuals to navigate this dual reality, they must move seamlessly from one world into another, all the while keeping their two worlds – one black and one white – completely separate.

The *fundamental* level of passing sees the black person actually casting off his or her entire black reality in favor of a white identity. They may choose to move away from family and friends; they might even *pass* them on the street and look the other way in the interest of committing to life as a white person. Oftentimes they marry whites, falsify documents, and never offer any reasonable doubt as to their "race." The changes one makes for this level of commitment are not merely cosmetic. Instead, one must make profound changes to one's thoughts, memories, beliefs, history, culture, language, politics, ethics, etc.

Each level of passing offers its own dangers, as at any time anyone could be discovered. An acquaintance from childhood, a family member who will not be ignored, even a black stranger embittered by the passing person's choices, could be one's downfall. Anything could betray one's black secret. Blacks at the basic and complex levels of passing could be discovered with a little research, while those at the fundamental level may prove to be their own worst threat. Choosing to have children is a 9-month experiment in torture for a person who is passing for white, as very few whites could justify a brown-skinned child to their white spouse.

Living in fear that one's own genes may betray one's entire life leads to two other significant issues inexorably linked to passing: internalized racism and the color complex. In order to survive as a white person in a white-dominated world in an era when the black person is commonly disdained, it stands to reason that the person passing could come to hate blackness. This may include their black family, former black community, and everything reminiscent of that life. Du Bois (1996) asserts that black Americans suffer an internal clash of ideals versus reality that keeps blacks forever at war with themselves. For people passing, this awareness – or double consciousness, as Du Bois references it – may lend itself to bitterness. Black acquiescence coupled with the shame of going over to the other side may result in feelings of disgust towards the struggles of black America, promoting a general feeling of self-loathing as individuals internalize the symptoms of racism. This antipathy for the race often manifests itself as an abhorrence of blackness. When Larsen's (1997) character, Gertrude, states, "nobody wants a dark child," she is not concerned with keeping a secret – she has a white husband, but is not passing, herself. Instead, she is simply verbalizing a commonly held sentiment within black communities: the color complex.

Though the term passing is commonly used as a reference to a long-ago era it is important to note that in the multicultural polyethnic new millennium, color, and now culture, is as ambiguous as ever. Thus, one cannot ignore other populations for whom passing remains a viable option, such as gays and lesbians, Latinos, and people of Middle Eastern descent. In a post-9/11 world, amid a culture of "don't ask, don't tell," many populations other than blacks are employing various elements of passing in order to navigate the rough waters of inequality.

SEE ALSO: Coming Out/Closets; Double Consciousness; Race; Race (Racism); Segregation

REFERENCES AND SUGGESTED READINGS

Cozzens, L. (1999) Plessy vs. Ferguson. *African American History*. Online. www.watson.org/~lisa/black-history/post-civilwar/plessy.html.

Du Bois, W. E. B. (1996 [1903]) *The Souls of Black Folk*. Penguin, New York.

Ellison, R. (1952) *Invisible Man*. Vintage, New York.

Gaudin, W. A. (n.d.) Passing for White in Jim Crow America. *The History of Jim Crow*. Online. www.jimcrowhistory.org/resources/lessonplans/hs_es_passing_for_white.htm.

Golden, M. (2003) *Don't Play in the Sun: One Woman's Journey Through the Color Complex*. Doubleday, New York.

Hall, R. E. (2003) *Discrimination Among Oppressed Populations*. Edwin Mellen Press, Lewiston, NY.

Johnson, J. W. (1989) *The Autobiography of an Ex-Colored Man*. Vintage, New York.

Larsen, N. (1997 [1929]) *Passing*. Penguin, New York.

Russell, K. Y., Wilson, M., & Hall, R. E. (1992) *The Color Complex: The Politics of Skin Color Among African Americans*. Anchor Books, New York.

Washington, B, T. (1995 [1901]) *Up From Slavery*. Dover Publications, Minneola, NY.

Wright, R. (1937) *Black Boy*. Harper & Row, New York.

paternalism

Charles Jarmon

Paternalism is evidenced by a pattern of gift-giving (or sponsorship) from a more powerful or higher-status group or individual to a lower-status group or individual that is consistent with a system designed to maintain privileged positions. It usually occurs in situations where there are sharp differences in power and status between groups or individuals. The "benevolence" associated with the actions of those in the more favorable position is usually reciprocated by acts of dependency or accommodation by those in the less favorable position. It is manifested in the different configurations and levels of race and ethnic identities, such as between national groups and groups and individuals within nations. Fanon (1963) provides an incisive analysis of paternalism in the relations between some of the former European colonial powers and the formerly colonized nations of Africa, Asia, and South America. Much more discussion has focused on paternalism within the nation-state, in countries where slave or apartheid systems developed as in the US and South Africa (DuBois 1903; Frazier 1939, 1957; Myrdal 1944; Thompson 1944; Cox 1948; Stampp 1956; Ruef & Flecther 2003). This discussion illustrates how paternalism has functioned in the US.

In the relationship between African Americans and whites, paternalism was most fully developed under the system of slavery, where the status difference between blacks and whites was most clearly defined. The power and status of the slave owner over the slave was institutionalized by custom and law. But not only did the slave owner have dominion over the slave, the system required him to assume responsibility over his welfare, whether adult or child, man or woman. In this system, paternalism was legitimated by the racial ideology of the time, and it emerged as a way of "normalizing" the associations between the two status groups. It was not a means for changing the inferior status of the slave.

A form of paternalism was perpetuated after slavery and became embedded in the cultural milieu of the late nineteenth and early twentieth century. The most visible occurrences of it were associated with the liberalism of leaders of white Northern philanthropic, religious, and political organizations whose prime consideration was to improve personal and material conditions of blacks under the Southern system of segregation. Many of the educational and religious leaders in the segregated, black communities of the South viewed these organizations as a source of funds to establish and advance their organizations within the context of the black community; their primary goal was not to prepare black folk to go outside their communities to compete directly with whites for non-traditional social, economic, and political positions.

Paternalism continued to be a part of the social conventions of the 1950s and 1960s. For example, Frazier (1957) noted that black churches in big Northern cities were often the beneficiaries of contributions from large corporations, which were made to persuade workers not to join unions. In small towns of the South, a black worker who encountered difficulties with the law could frequently rely on his white employer to extricate him from the legal system simply by providing testimony about his character; the same would have been true if this man had attempted to get a loan from the local bank. A domestic worker, living in the North or South, oftentimes rode the bus home from work across town carrying a large shopping bag filled with old clothing for her family given to her by her white employer, who most often referred to her by her first name, "auntie," or "girl." With respect to this last example, scholars (Clark-Lewis 2003) are beginning to provide in-depth historical analyses of the life and work culture of domestic workers, particularly

on how they negotiated this paternalist system. The vignettes above illustrate the extensiveness of paternalist exchanges marking the decades of racial segregation and that came to structure many of the relations between blacks and whites.

In contemporary America paternalism has become more difficult to identify as the historically entrenched segregated institutions and ideological foundations have weakened. Blacks, who predominantly live in cities or urban metropolitan areas, increasingly work in white-collar occupations in state and federal agencies, industrial enterprises, private corporations, and unions, occupying positions no longer considered along racial lines. Increasingly, other blacks work as newly transformed, high-wage technology workers, bus drivers, policemen, firemen, printers, athletes, actors, etc. In these occupations paternalism may or may not be overtly expressed. But it continues to exist in the hierarchical arrangement of power and authority in the work environment. Whites, who occupy most of the top management and supervisory positions in the organizations and institutions mentioned above, continue to make decisions about hiring practices, salaries, job assignments, and promotions. Most black workers, therefore, continue to be involved in relations with white supervisors, who by virtue of their authority, control the relationship. In this situation many blacks mask their true attitudes and feelings about the relationship, or about values and issues expressed by supervisors, even when they are resentful of what is being expressed; they fear to do otherwise might be interpreted as disrespectful and lead to subsequent loss of sponsorship. Thus, interpersonal contact between white supervisors and black workers can easily develop into paternalistic relationships.

Let us examine briefly two conditions under which paternalism occurs in contemporary society: the glass ceiling and affirmative action. The glass-ceiling phenomenon, a form of institutional discrimination without official sanction that functions to exclude members of certain racial, ethnic, or gender categories from positions in the institution's upper echelons, is another basis for paternalistic relations. Black workers, meeting required credentials, skills, and work habits, begin their jobs with high expectations of moving up the ranks in competition with their white counterparts to gain entry into upper-level positions. However, a large majority run into the glass ceiling, which contributes to low morale among many black government workers, who more frequently receive small annual bonuses than promotions to middle management and senior-level positions. As their white co-workers move up, the build-up of anger, frustration, and disappointment about not moving up the ranks themselves often becomes a morale problem and leads to poor or only average work performance. This then becomes an official reason to deny them promotions. The magnitude of this problem becomes apparent when we note that in some government agencies about 30 percent of the workers are African Americans. While some of these black workers challenge such conditions by joining unions and filing suits in the courts against their agencies, many other workers refuse to engage in such actions, and concentrate on ways to mitigate this situation by cultivating paternalistic relationships with their white supervisors and managers.

Affirmative action policies, the benign race-conscious laws that were enacted to undo and correct past and present discrimination against African Americans and other minority groups, constitute a form of state-sponsored paternalism, despite the fact that it took the struggles of the Civil Rights Movement to pressure the government to introduce these reform measures. But these reform-oriented policies in universities, government agencies, and industry have only partially eliminated racial barriers encountered by blacks, mainly because the enforcement of the laws continues to favor those in power. Affirmative action has created many more opportunities for blacks to participate in organizations of mainstream society (Herring 1997), but not without unfavorable consequences. One baneful side of affirmative action is in the frequent stigma that high-achieving blacks feel when their successes are demeaned by those opposing affirmative action and when recognition is denied for their hard-earned achievements.

Paternalism is one of the complex aspects of the relationship between blacks and whites, and a scientific theory of it is needed to elaborate and connect the elements of gift-giving and sponsorship by whites occupying superior statuses and the patterns of accommodation or non-compliance by blacks. Three questions form the bases for a beginning in this direction. First, for whites, what are the material benefits or psychological consequences associated with paternalism? Second, what is lost or gained when blacks hide behind the mask, conceding dignity, honor, and pride as they act in ways that help to sustain the paternalistic system? Third, what social and political actions from the wider community are likely to diminish the significance of such behavior? Social scientists appear to have left such concerns to novelists, poets, playwrights, and comedians. They interpret and manipulate the associated cultural stereotypes derived from paternalism, but their handling of the subject is usually shallow and insufficient to explain the complex questions that need to be clarified.

SEE ALSO: Affirmative Action (Race and Ethnic Quotas); Occupational Segregation; Race and Ethnic Etiquette; Slavery; Stratification, Race/Ethnicity and

REFERENCES AND SUGGESTED READINGS

Alexander, R. (2003) A Mountain Too High: African Americans and Employment Discrimination. *African American Research Perspectives* 9(1): 33–7.
Bell, D. (1992) *Race, Racism and American Law*. Little, Brown, Boston.
Clark-Lewis, E. (2003) Community Life and Work Culture Among African American Domestic Workers in Washington, DC. In: Norton, M. B. & Alexander, R. (Eds.), *Major Problems in American Women's History*. Houghton Mifflin, Boston.
Cox, O. C. (1948) *Caste, Class, and Race*. Monthly Press, New York.
DuBois, W. E. B. (1903) *The Souls of Black Folk*. A. C. McClurg, Chicago.
Fanon, F. (1963) *The Wretched of the Earth*. Grove Press, New York.
Frazier, E. F. (1939) *The Negro Family in the United States*. University of Chicago Press, Chicago.
Frazier, E. F. (1957) *The Black Bourgeoisie: The Rise of the New Middle Class*. Macmillan, New York.
Herring, C. (1997) *African Americans and the Public Agenda: The Paradoxes of Public Policy*. Sage, Thousand Oaks, CA.
Myrdal, G. (1944) *An American Dilemma: The Negro Problem and Modern Democracy*. Pantheon, New York.

Ruef, M. & Fletcher, B. (2003) Legacies of American Slavery: Status Attainment among Southern Blacks after Emancipation. *Social Forces* 82(2): 445–80.

Stampp, K. (1956) *The Peculiar Institution: Slavery in the Antebellum South.* Knopf, New York.

Thompson, E. T. (1944) Sociology and Sociological Research in the South. *Social Forces* 23(3): 356–65.

path analysis

William H. Swatos, Jr.

Because of the difficulty in sociological research of conducting experiments that will yield valid and meaningful results, sociologists have looked for quasi-experimental designs in which statistical measures can be interrelated in a logical sequence to suggest causality. Path analysis is the most widely used of such approaches. Path analysis combines both a theoretical (or logical) analysis with a statistical analysis, inasmuch as a logical argument must be introduced to suggest appropriate causal sequences. While some of these logical connections are obvious (gender obviously comes before marriage, for example), others are a matter of theoretical argument as part of a larger project (does image of God precede or follow religious affiliation or are

there ongoing interaction effects between the two?). Through multiple and partial regression analysis, and statistical controls that attempt to match test and control populations as closely as possible, a researcher attempts to demonstrate both quantitatively and logically a pattern of causality that would be similar to what might result if an actual experimental design were able to have been put into place by providing estimates of the total direct and indirect effects of one variable on another. In most simple causal modeling, path coefficients are *beta weights*, which represent a measurement of changes in a dependent variable in terms of standard deviation units for each of the other variables (standardized regression coefficients) in series, creating adjusted slopes of the regression line which are comparable from one variable to the next, working backward from the dependent variable.

These results are normally displayed in a *path diagram* (or *path model*), where arrows are drawn to designate the causal sequence connecting the variables and the statistical results are noted as *path coefficients* (see Fig. 1).

On the surface a path analytic model presents the advantage that the analyst must present a logical argument of the interrelationship of variables in a causal sequence that is then tied to both the conduct of the research and the presentation of the results. One does not simply

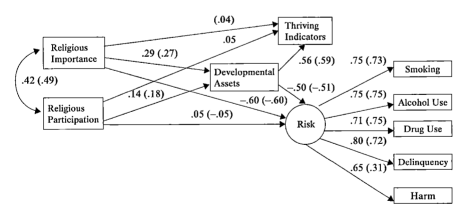

Figure 1 This is a path model showing the standardized estimates for the role of religion as an asset in contributing to junior and senior (in parentheses) high school boys in "thriving" on the one hand, while reducing risk factors on the other. This shows that religious importance and participation contribute both directly in a small degree to thriving and more largely as a developmental asset. Similarly, risk is reduced. Note on the left the strong interaction effect between religious importance and religious participation.
Source: Wagener et al. (2003: 279). © Religious Research Association, Inc. Used by permission.

"control for *a*" without presenting an argument for the relationship between *a* and the posited explanatory sequence. In empirical cases, however, the issue of causal relationships is often unclear. This is most obvious when bidirectional arrows appear in models, suggesting unanalyzed relationships among causal variables. There is also no clear rule or procedure for setting time limits on the posited causal sequence – i.e., how far back in time it is necessary to go to determine a "valid" set of potential causes or cause-and-effect relationships. While it is certainly clear that later events cannot explain prior events, it should not necessarily be assumed that prior events explain later events simply because the prior events are prior, even if there does seem to be some statistical association among them. Those statistical associations may be true statistical associations among variables but not sociologically significant explanations for the variable one is trying to "explain."

In spite of these liabilities, path analysis likely remains the most widely used quasi-experimental analytic tool in the presentation of quantitative sociological research attempting to describe causal sequences.

SEE ALSO: Multivariate Analysis; Regression and Regression Analysis; Statistics

REFERENCES AND SUGGESTED READINGS

Land, K. C. (1969) Principles of Path Analysis. In: Borgatta, E., *Sociological Methodology 1969*. Jossey Bass, San Francisco, ch. 1.
Wagener, L. M., Furrow, J. L., King, P. E., Leffert, N., & Benson, P. (2003) Religious Involvement and Developmental Resources in Youth. *Review of Religious Research* 44, 3 (March): 271–84.

patient–physician relationship

Eugene Gallagher

No topic is more central to a general understanding of medicine in modern society than the patient–physician relationship. Few topics have so actively focused the attention of social scientists, the thinking public, and medical/health practitioners. No other topic is so closely keyed to the emergence in the 1950s of medical sociology as a distinct, important, and very sizable field of research, teaching, and public policy relevance in sociology.

In trying to capture and describe the patient–physician relationship a good starting point is to think of it as generically a helping relationship: one person helping another. The physician as a trained professional possesses resources – knowledge, skills, and experience – from which the patient can benefit. Further, the physician is committed to the well-being of the patient – not unlike the stance of a parent toward their child. Reciprocally, the patient depends upon the expertise and trustworthiness of the physician.

Three stages have marked the sociological study of the patient–physician relationship since the 1950s. Stage 1 predominated from 1950 to 1965. It was guided by the conceptions of Talcott Parsons and the functionalist theory that prevailed in Parsonian thought and in sociological theory more generally. Stage 2 prevailed from 1965 to 1985. It directed a trenchant critique toward the Parsonian model; its theoretical orientation was expressed through conflict theory. It also responded to the ferment and discontent that were expressed in American society during those years. It finds its most cogent expression in the work of Eliot Freidson (1970a, 1970b). As will be seen, it is possible to view Stage 2 less as an attack on the Parsonian model and more as an expansion or enlargement of the model. Stage 3, continuing into the present, is a conceptual response to the rapid growth and complex differentiation of the medical sector in contemporary society. Yet even in the face of staggering changes in the health care enterprise, what goes on within the patient–physician relationship remains as an influential nucleus to guide behavior.

Talcott Parsons was the first sociologist to put forth a broad, logically integrated conception of the patient–physician relationship. Parsons's grand objective in sociology was to build a theory of social action – a conceptual edifice that, though interdisciplinary in its scope, was distinctively sociological in its grasp of human motivation, cognition, and interaction. His formulations of the sick role, the doctor–patient relationship, and health/illness came rather quickly to form the building blocks of medical sociology, whereas his recondite theory of social action had less acceptance in the parent discipline of sociology. For Parsons, medical sociology and the doctor–patient relationship comprised but one chapel in an overarching cathedral of ideas. On several occasions Parsons expressed his satisfaction over the formative influence he had played in medical sociology itself, but also some puzzlement over this impact, which he neither sought nor expected.

We turn now to the Parsonian conception of the patient–physician relationship, as Parsons laid it out in *The Social System* (1951). Pursuing the analogy of the physician with patient, and parent with child, it can be stated that as the parent loves the child so the physician has a positive attachment (often, Parsons used the psychoanalytic term cathexis) to the patient. However, the physician's attachment falls short of parental love in scope and intensity. Further, the parents' stance with their child is "affective," while the physician's stance with the patient is "affectively neutral"; that is, emotionally restrained (but not cold or indifferent). The physician is expected to assess objectively the patient and the latter's illness, clinical needs, and limitations, and not to be swayed by the strong feelings and passions that frequently dominate family life.

In another direction, the parents deal with the child in a "functionally diffuse" manner, while the physician deals with the patient in a "functionally specific" manner. This means that society expects the parent to recognize and cope with any demand, need, or distress expressed by the child, while the physician is expected to deal with only those needs and conditions that can be addressed by his or her medical knowledge and expertise.

Tracing out expectations between physician and patient, and comparing these with the parent–child relationship, lead into the idea of social roles, a key element in Parsonian thinking (and that of many other sociologists). Patient and physician enact social roles. Their role behavior and motivation are subjectively meaningful and voluntary, not forced by biology or instinct, and not rigidly scripted by cultural mandates. Social roles are stereotypically familiar to members of a society or groups within it.

We referred above to patient and doctor as participating in a helping relationship where each enacts a role in mutual response to the other. The physician is the dominant member of the dyad and the bearer of medical responsibility. The patient's role enactment is both generated and circumscribed by the fact that he or she has medical problems – actual or potential. Although the person is free to withdraw from the relationship, within it they have less power than the physician.

It should be noted that several scholars and academic physicians dealt with the patient–physician relationship before Parsons. Among them are the physiologist Lawrence J. Henderson (1935), the medical historian P. Lain Entralgo (1969), and the German social medicine advocate Rudolf Virchow (Ackerknecht 1953). While frequently insightful, their work lacks the systematic rigor and strong sociological orientation that Parsons achieved. In another direction, it is noteworthy that Parsons's work on the patient–physician relationship and other topics in medicine is of necessity highly original because none of the earlier generations of sociologists, whether in Europe or America, touched upon the role of medicine in society. Cockerham (2001: 11) notes this curious lack and accounts for it as follows: "Unlike law, religion, politics, economics, and other social institutions, medicine was ignored by sociology's founders in the late nineteenth century because it did not shape the structure and nature of society."

Parsons's account of the patient–physician relationship depicts it as an ideal-type cultural phenomenon. It can be likened to a thought experiment in physics that assumes impossible things such as a perfect vacuum or a frictionless plane. Parsons attributes various "role-appropriate" attitudes and feelings to the patient such as trust, cooperativeness, and dependency, as well as how the physician feels and acts toward the patient. Such attributions may be reasonable as provisional assumptions. However, unless their empirical accuracy can be ascertained or at least questioned, they chill discussion of vital issues such as patient autonomy and initiative within the relationship.

The Parsonian level of abstraction creates space for other distortions. As noted above, his model portrays the physician as the one in charge in the dyad – in charge not from a tainted drive for dominance or self-aggrandizement, but rather from the argument that by being in charge he or she can more effectively bring therapeutic skills into play. The simplicity of the model fosters an ascription of moral idealism and dedication to the physician. Once again, such ascriptions may be tentatively accepted, but this should not be allowed to inhibit further critical exploration. Even on the premise that the physician is fully competent and dedicated, it should not be taken for granted that, for example, "whatever helps the doctor helps the patient."

Parsons's picture rises from his knowledge of medicine as it was practiced in the 1940s and earlier. Stage 2 accounts, in contrast, rise from a later and much different medicine – a much broader utilization of medicine by a more diverse public, and a greatly expanded medical profession, internally dichotomized into primary care and a rising tide of specialization, and externally assisted by a growing cadre of "health care workers." With these many changes it became inevitable to fill in areas that the Parsonian paradigm ignored. Instead of thinking about "the patient" as an undifferentiated human being, it became necessary to ask about who the patient is and how the patient's pursuit of medical care and responses to the physician vary according to characteristics such as age, gender, ethnicity, religious affiliation, socioeconomic level, and even by health status.

Another phenomenon ignored by Parsons is the very rapid and substantial formation of medical specialties. While the Parsonian account does acknowledge surgery and referral etiquette among physicians, it most comfortably projects the image of an undifferentiated patient under the care of a family doctor in a primary-care environment. It is largely silent about medical hierarchies, technological advances, third-party payment of medical bills, and many other related factors affecting the patient–physician relationship.

While one should not interpret the contrast between the theoretical allegiances of Parsons and Freidson as forming a major clash, there are clear differences in tone and emphasis between them. Cockerham and Ritchey (1997: 44) describe the difference thus: "Parsons's functionalist description of the physician–patient relationship [asserts] that the physician's status

[constitutes] a form of 'medical dominance' that may be detrimental to good patient care and relationships with other health care workers." Neither Parsons's nor Freidson's differences divide them cleanly between the pastel, simple doctrine of functionalism (Parsons) and the more strident, differentiated frame of conflict theory (Freidson).

In Stage 2, medical sociology became unavoidably aware of developments in medical care that resulted in a more complex and contemporaneous picture of the patient–physician relationship. However, old trends and issues have become more acute and new ones have come into view. We see two issues – medical uncertainty and fiduciary trust – as particularly central and inclusive of many other trends in the relationship. Here we will describe each and also indicate why they deserve focused inquiry and research.

Medical uncertainty is certainly not new in medicine. However, new realms and even styles of biomedical knowledge have made the physician simultaneously more knowledgeable and also more tentative about disease and treatment. Consider, for example, two new realms of knowledge: genetics and body imaging. Recent and ongoing research on chromosomes and genes has established a wealth of information about chromosomal defects and rogue proteins that do – or may – underlie clinical pathology, such as cystic fibrosis. While some of this new information provides the basis for fruitful diagnosis and treatment, much of it constitutes a mounting "overhang" of knowledge that is clinically inapplicable, though it may establish bridges to beneficial application in times to come.

This veritable explosion of knowledge can be seen as evidence of the endless advance of biomedical science. It also calls into question a longstanding guardedness by the physician about sharing information with the patient. It tends to move the physician–patient relationship toward greater physician willingness to communicate with patients – even perchance to "impose" information and decision-making responsibility. The choice of treatment (or watchful waiting) in regard to breast and prostate cancer, and in coronary artery disease, affords a current example. The jurisdiction of the physician in the relationship is yielding gradually to a greater share for the patient; this has particular implications for the role of bio-medical and clinical information within the dyad. Also, the relentless pressure on physicians to "keep up" with advances in medical knowledge is now given an additional thrust by the need to involve the patient.

Issues in fiduciary trust confront the relationship with an entirely different set of challenges. They are concerned with the question: Can the physician adhere straightforwardly to his or her professional obligation to serve the patient in the face of conflicting pressures and temptation? The most obvious arena for conflict is the economic, concerning the reimbursement the physician receives for services. In the days when the complete picture of medical care included nothing more than the patient, the physician, and the latter's "small black bag" (containing "tools" and medicines), economic issues were scarcely important. The physician might be forbearing in setting fees, or be greedy and set them high, but at least the issue was clear and relatively open to view and discussion. Economic arrangements are more complicated now and shielded more from view. The physician may very well elicit informed consent from patients, but may not disclose his or her own financial interest in the treatment. Patients do not usually know the extent to which financial interest influences clinical judgment. Consequently, future studies of the patient–physician relationship are likely to be more complex than those in the past because the relationship is changing (Gallagher & Sionean 2004).

SEE ALSO: Health Care Delivery Systems; Health Locus of Control; Health and Medicine; Health Professions and Occupations; Health and Social Class; Illness Narrative; Managed Care; Parsons, Talcott; Professional Dominance in Medicine; Sick Role

REFERENCES AND SUGGESTED READINGS

Ackerknecht, E. H. (1953) *Rudolf Virchow: Doctor, Statesman, Anthropologist*. University of Wisconsin Press, Madison.

Cockerham, W. C. (2001) *Medical Sociology*, 8th edn. Prentice-Hall, Upper Saddle River, NJ.

Cockerham, W. C. & Ritchey, F. J. (1997) *Dictionary of Medical Sociology*. Greenwood Press, Westport.

Entralgo, P. L. (1969) *Doctor and Patient*. World University Library, London.

Freidson, E. (1970a) *The Profession of Medicine*. Dodd & Mead, New York.

Freidson, E. (1970b) *Professional Dominance*. Aldine, Chicago.

Gallagher, E. B. & Sionean, C. K. (2004) Where Medicalization Boulevard Meets Commercialization Alley. *Journal of Policy Studies* 16: 53–62.

Henderson, L. J. (1935) The Physician and Patient as a Social System. *New England Journal of Medicine* 212: 319–23.

Parsons, T. (1951) *The Social System*. Free Press, Glencoe, IL.

patriarchy

Donald P. Levy

Patriarchy is most commonly understood as a form of social organization in which cultural and institutional beliefs and patterns accept, support, and reproduce the domination of women and younger men by older or more powerful men. Literally the "rule of the fathers," today sociologists view as patriarchal any system that contributes to the social, cultural, and economic superiority or hegemony of men. Consequently, sociologists study the manner in which societies have become and continue to be patriarchal by investigating both social institutions and commonly held cultural beliefs. At the same time, scholars investigate the consequences of patriarchy, i.e., differential access to scarce societal resources including power, authority, and opportunity by gender.

Although some scholars simply use the word patriarchy to describe what they consider to be a natural or inevitable form of social organization, more recently scholars, stimulated by the work of early feminist writers (Beauvoir 1972; Bernard 1972), have come to recognize patriarchy as a prevalent system of inequality similar in some ways to racism or classism (Hartsock 1983). Prior to the critical work of feminist scholars, many considered patriarchy to be the natural result of biological difference or rather a truly complementary system based upon differential inclinations that served to address society's need for a division of labor (Durkheim 1933; Parsons 1956). A more critical analysis of the origins of patriarchy, however, looks to its cultural and social genesis as located within both beliefs and specific social institutions.

Scholars today explore the manner in which patriarchy, or male domination, has become institutionalized, that is, built into the major social systems including the family, religion, the economy, government, education, and the media. In so doing, the taken-for-grantedness of patriarchy is exposed and analyzed (Smith 1987). If indeed, as feminist and pro-feminist scholars ask, patriarchy is a socially constructed system of inequality, how is it that despite being exposed patriarchy appears to be natural and continues to reproduce itself?

Many scholars have looked to the institution of the family in order to explain the origins and persistence of patriarchy. Engels (1970) described the patriarchal structure of the family but centered his analysis on its contribution to capitalist rather than primarily gender oppression. Lévi-Strauss (1967) observed and chronicled the cultural roots of patriarchy and highlighted a key implicit component, that of the objectification and devaluation of women by men. More recently, Bernard demonstrated the differential structure of marriage and family by gender that deterministically reproduces patriarchy. The family, including the household division of labor (Hochschild & Machung 1997), divorce, childrearing, as well as power and cultural perception (Smith 1993), have been and are continuing to be specific sites in which patriarchy is seen, analyzed, and in some cases resisted.

As Engels pointed out, the family as an institution is at all times interacting with the economy or public sphere. Despite functionalist assertions of complementarity and balance, the women's movement and feminist scholars have continued to point to the multiple ways in which the economic sphere as well as the interaction between the family and the economy serve to reproduce and enforce patriarchy as a social system. Issues including, initially, access to economic opportunity, and more recently the gendering of occupations, the glass ceiling (Williams 1992), and sexual harassment, have concerned both activists and scholars. A Parsonsian expression of balance between the public (economic) sphere and the private (family) sphere argues in favor of men being primarily active in the public and women in the private. Currently, feminist scholars and most sociologists dismiss this characterization as patriarchal and focus on the manner in which the institutions that perpetuate this unequal system are structured.

Other scholars have demonstrated sociological insight by pointing to the manner in which other significant social institutions interact with both the economy and the family to reproduce patriarchy or to present themselves as sites in which patriarchy can be resisted. Since the beginnings of feminism as a social movement in the nineteenth century, activists have sought equal legal rights for women. Theoretically, this movement demonstrated the irony of a social contract that disenfranchised half of its inferred signers (Pateman 1988). In other words, a democracy that promised equal representation to every citizen only so long as they were men represented a patriarchal system. Needless to say, other marginalized groups were also left unrepresented. Although first-wave feminists succeeded in obtaining women's suffrage, and despite a lull in the social movement subsequent to that victory, the struggle for full and practical legal rights and representation remained a focus of the feminist struggle against patriarchy in the governmental institution. Second-wave feminism rallied around abortion rights and the Equal Rights Amendment (ERA) as core issues in both the exposition of and struggle against patriarchy. Today, activists are once again preparing for a dynamic public debate over abortion, while the ERA is no longer discussed. Still, patriarchy is demonstrated in the continuing disproportionate power of men over women in government, as noted in numbers of men and women in elected positions as well as in legal and judicial debates over issues like family leave, divorce, and sexual harassment. In fact, the interaction of the family, the economy, and the government as that interaction contributes to the persistence of patriarchy is demonstrated in issues or concepts like the "mommy-track" or welfare reform (Hays 2003).

Oftentimes, scholars as well as other social critics look to the educational institution as a potential avenue of either conservative social reproduction or social change. Relative to patriarchy, education is discussed in both ways. Many now cite the successes of women in education in terms of the number of women obtaining college or postgraduate degrees. Today over 50 percent of college graduates are women. This fact supports the lessening of patriarchy as women receive equal education and credentials. Still, critics note the gendering of credentials, i.e., women obtaining degrees in less highly valued fields (Kimmel 2000) as well as the "hidden curriculum" of education (Coleman 1961) in which the structure and beliefs of patriarchy are taught regardless of the gender of the student. Additionally, scholars continue to observe and report the differential treatment of students by gender by teachers (Sadker & Sadker 1994) that begins in some cases in either elementary school (Thorne 1993) or even kindergarten (Jordan & Cowan 2001).

Patriarchy continues to be observed, reproduced, and resisted in other social institutions including the military, religion, and the media. Despite increasing participation in the military by women, the structure and culture of the institution remain patriarchal (Cohn 1993). Religion has long been seen by scholars, of course with extreme variation between traditions, as providing justification for patriarchy. Still, today many traditions are beginning to question and change their theologically mandated patriarchal structure while others remain virtually unchanged. The media, although more inclusive than either the military or religion, remain a domain in which examples of male domination often go unquestioned. One need only consider the centrality of male-dominated sport to see the manner in which the media participate in the perpetuation of patriarchy. Still, recent manifestations of popular culture sponsored by various media sources are beginning to place women in positions of power and centrality, both of which may serve to lessen the seeming naturalness of patriarchy.

Given the ubiquity of patriarchy within individual societal institutions as well as the manner in which these institutions interact, it is no wonder that patriarchy continues to appear natural and necessary, that is, hegemonic (Gramsci 1971). Still, as feminist theory has pointed out, patriarchy is a political issue, for both groups and individuals. The "personal" is indeed "political." As such, patriarchy as a system of social organization, although deeply

ingrained in both social institutions and consequently in the individuals that find themselves living within those institutions, is subject to both contestation and resistance. Gender relations as currently constituted in a patriarchal system are subject to change.

Organizations including the National Organization for Women (NOW), Planned Parenthood, and many others continue to publicize the manner in which patriarchy is built into various social institutions and this serves to perpetuate the social power of men over women. Feminist scholars today continue to struggle against patriarchy but have now broadened their focus to include multiple forms of privilege that serve to oppress not only women, but also other marginalized groups (Collins 1986; Johnson 2001). They are joined today by smaller but active organizations of men as well as scholars of men's studies including the National Organization of Men Against Sexism (NOMAS). At the same time, scholars have begun not only to demonstrate how patriarchy is embedded in social institutions and ingrained in the manner in which we do gender (West & Zimmerman 1987) but also to call for undoing gender, that is, to remove gender and consequently patriarchy as a central organizing principle of social relations (Butler 2004; Lorber 2005).

Patriarchy is a system of social organization that recognizes, encourages, and reproduces the seemingly natural and necessary domination of men over women. Despite the legal and social changes fought for and achieved by activists supported by scholars over the last 150 years, patriarchy is indeed quite persistent. This persistence is due to the manner in which patriarchy has become deeply ingrained in each and every aspect of each and every significant societal institution, and consequently in the manner in which individuals learn to practice gender. The deconstruction of patriarchy is therefore both an individual and an institutional quest dependent on scholarly insight and exposition, as well as individual courage, good will, and commitment to justice.

SEE ALSO: Bernard, Jessie; Doing Gender; Feminism; Feminism, First, Second, and Third Waves; Gender Ideology and Gender Role Ideology; Hegemonic Masculinity; Hidden Curriculum; International Gender Division of

Labor; Matrix of Domination; Personal is Political; Privilege; Sex and Gender; Sexism

REFERENCES AND SUGGESTED READINGS

Beauvoir, S. de (1972) *The Second Sex*. Penguin, Harmondsworth.

Bernard, J. (1972) *The Future of Marriage*. World Publishing, New York.

Butler, J. (2004) *Undoing Gender*. Routledge, London.

Cohn, C. (1993) Wars, Wimps, and Women: Talking Gender and Thinking War. In: Cooke, M. & Woollacott, A. (Eds.), *Gendering War Talk*. Princeton University Press, Princeton.

Coleman, J. (1961) *The Adolescent Society*. Harper & Row, New York.

Collins, P. H. (1986) Learning from the Outsider Within: The Sociological Significance of Black Feminist Thought. *Social Problems* 33(6): 14–32.

Durkheim, É. (1933) *The Division of Labor in Society*. Free Press, Glencoe, IL.

Engels, F. (1970) *The Origin of the Family, Private Property, and the State*. Progress Publishers, Moscow.

Gramsci, A. (1971) *Selections from the Prison Notebooks*. Lawrence & Wishart, London.

Hartsock, N. (1983) *Sex and Power: Toward a Feminist Historical Materialism*. Longman, New York.

Hays, S. (2003) *Flat Broke With Children: Women in the Age of Welfare Reform*. Oxford University Press, New York.

Hochschild, A. R. & Machung, A. (1997) *The Second Shift*. Avon Books, New York.

Johnson, A. G. (2001) *Privilege, Power, and Difference*. McGraw-Hill, Boston.

Jordan, E. & Cowan, A. (2001) Warrior Narratives in the Kindergarten Classroom: Renegotiating the Social Contract? In: Kimmel, M. S. & Messner, M. A. (Eds.), *Men's Lives*. Allyn & Bacon, Needham Heights, MA.

Kimmel, M. (2000) *The Gendered Society*. Oxford University Press, New York.

Lévi-Strauss, C. (1967) *Structural Anthropology*. Basic Books, New York.

Lorber, J. (2005) *Breaking the Bowls: Degendering and Feminist Change*. W. W. Norton, New York.

Parsons, T. (1956) *Family Socialization and Interaction Process*. Routledge, London.

Pateman, C. (1988) *The Sexual Contract*. Stanford University Press, Stanford.

Sadker, M. & Sadker, D. (1994) *Failing at Fairness: How America's Schools Cheat Girls*. Charles Scribner's Sons, New York.

Smith, D. E. (1987) *The Everyday World as Problematic: A Feminist Sociology*. University of Toronto Press, Toronto.

Smith, D. E. (1993) The Standard North American Family: SNAF as an Ideological Code. *Journal of Family Issues* 14(1): 50–65.

Thorne, B. (1993) *Gender Play: Girls and Boys in School*. Rutgers University Press, New Brunswick, NJ.

West, C. & Zimmerman, D. H. (1987) Doing Gender. *Gender and Society* 1(2): 125–51.

Williams, C. L. (1992) The Glass Escalator: Hidden Advantages for Men in the "Female" Professions. *Social Problems* 39(3): 253–67.

peace and reconciliation processes

John Darby

The use of the term peace process may be recent, but the concept is as old as war. Sophisticated conventions on ceasefires and peace negotiations were already well established and accepted when the *Iliad* was composed. The negotiations preceding the Peace of Westphalia in 1648 had some resemblance to contemporary peace processes: they lasted for four years; the principal negotiators never met; and they adopted approaches similar to the "proximity talks" and shuttle diplomacy used at Dayton for Bosnia and in Northern Ireland, with the main parties separately quartered in Münster and Osnabrück. More than three centuries later, these techniques and approaches were formalized and designated as peace processes. Harold Saunders recounts how the term "negotiating process" was used by those working with Henry Kissinger in the Middle East in 1974. Eventually, finding the phrase too narrow, "we coined the phrase peace process' to capture the experience of this series of mediated agreements embedded in a larger political process" (Crocker et al. 2001).

The popularity of the term and the processes themselves increased markedly during the 1990s, reflecting an increase in both internal violence and internal settlements following the end of the Cold War. Fifty-six civil wars came to an end between 1989 and 2000 (Wallensteen & Sollenberg 2001), although not all of these resulted from peace processes. Indeed, the extensive set of variables involved during peace processes greatly complicates the task of defining them. Despite this, peace process has become a convenient term to describe persistent peace initiatives that develop beyond initial statements of intent.

Darby and MacGinty (2003) proposed five essential criteria for a successful peace process: (1) protagonists are willing to negotiate in good faith; (2) key actors are included in the process; (3) negotiations address the central issues in dispute; (4) force is not used to achieve objectives; and (5) negotiators are committed to a sustained process. Outside these general principles, each peace process has its own distinctive dynamic. Nevertheless, most commentators accept that peace processes develop through a four-phase cycle: prenegotiation, the negotiations themselves, the peace agreement, and post-agreement reconstruction and conflict transformation.

If every peace process had to wait for violence to end, few would get off the ground. Conflicting parties rarely want to reach a settlement at the same time. During the 1993–4 war in Bosnia, for example, the willingness of Muslims, Serbs, or Croats to engage in negotiation was determined primarily by their fortunes on the field of war and the resulting territorial gains or losses. By definition, these conditions never coincide for all parties. Windows of opportunity, when all parties are simultaneously prepared to negotiate, are rare, and close down quickly. Yet it is only during such relatively infrequent opportunities that a settlement may be reached. The central metaphor in determining these opportunities is Zartman's (1995) concept of a "ripe moment," when the parties reach a mutually hurting stalemate and "find themselves locked in a conflict from which they cannot escalate to victory and this deadlock is painful to both of them."

Most peace processes begin with secret talks. These are attractive to negotiators because of their low exit costs. Occasionally, the difficult move from secret to open negotiations is managed by the protagonists themselves, but it often benefits substantially from contacts established by intermediaries such as the business community, churches, and academics. In the suspicious climate that accompanies the early stages of prenegotiation, confidence-building measures – concessions by one side to encourage movement from the other – can reassure opponents, but they carry high risks. The symbolic gestures by Mandela to white South Africans greatly eased the first stages of negotiations. The danger is that premature concessions may be banked rather than reciprocated by the recipients, as was the case in 1998 when Andreas Pastrana ceded territory to the Revolutionary Armed Forces of Colombia (FARC). In general, it is more effective to negotiate reciprocal concessions, as when significant demobilization by Guatemala's armed forces and by the FMLN was carried out simultaneously, with UN supervision, by 1993.

Who participates and who manages the process? The fact that negotiations are taking place at all presumes an acceptance that the representatives of militants have been admitted to negotiations in return for giving up violence. Their inclusion, with whatever pressures it imposes on the process, admits militants to the common enterprise and applies some pressure on them to preserve it in the face of violence from dissidents or spoiler groups.

Shuttle diplomacy may be needed to establish the preconditions and ground rules for participants, and proximity talks are often necessary before the participants are willing to meet in plenary sessions. The establishment of agreed ground rules must be acceptable to all parties; these may be negotiated by insiders, as in South Africa, or with the help of outsiders, as in Namibia. In El Salvador and Guatemala the processes were strongly supported by a range of external actors, including the United Nations, the US, and other countries from the region and Europe. Responsibility for preparing discussion papers on procedures for negotiation falls primarily, but never exclusively, to government. The central involvement of both the British and Irish governments in guiding talks in Northern Ireland provided necessary reassurance for both unionists and nationalists.

Peace processes are always played out to a background of violence. Even when political violence is ended by the declaration of a ceasefire, it mutates into other interrelated forms to threaten the evolving peace process. Militant spoilers seeking to continue armed opposition are the most common threat. Elements within the state apparatus may also work through militias or paramilitary organizations to maintain a high security presence, even while their colleagues are engaged in negotiations. Quite apart from these deliberate attempts to foment violence, the declaration of a ceasefire may simply replace conventional war by more volatile face-to-face clashes and a rise in conventional crime. Indeed, the declaration of a ceasefire alters the context of conflict at a stroke. Issues that cannot even be discussed during wars – release of prisoners, amnesties, policing and army reforms – not only become part of the new agenda, but also demand immediate attention. Disarmament of militants and demobilization of security forces are among the most difficult. In retrospect, it seems clear that the decommissioning problems that plagued post-accord reconstruction in Northern Ireland might have been avoided by choreographed demilitarization by both the state and militant organizations.

Christine Bell describes the 1990s as "the decade of the peace agreement" (Darby & Mac-Ginty 2003). Her review of peace accords found "over 300 peace agreements of one description or another" signed in more than 60 situations during the 1990s. Increasingly, peacemakers have tended to borrow the text, frameworks, and approach adopted in earlier peace accords, as demonstrated by the similar language of many Latin American peace agreements.

The fundamental question for most peace negotiations is: Can the central grievances be resolved within the existing national framework, or do they require secession and autonomy? Many contemporary peace processes concentrate on the constitutional options between secession and reform. Most of them demand an element of power sharing, although power-sharing arrangements rarely survive in the long term. It is best to regard them as a transitional process. "Ideally," Sisk argues, "power sharing will work best when it can, over time, wither away" (Darby & MacGinty 2003).

If the peace accord reached through negotiations between elites is to become a settlement accepted by their followers, it must be subjected to democratic validation through referenda or elections. The choice is important – the hurried 1999 referendum in East Timor increased the

level of violence instead of easing it. As a general rule, the need for secrecy must be eased as negotiations proceed, in order to initiate the campaign for public support. An excess of early publicity entrenches differences before an agreement can be reached. An excess of secrecy not only encourages conspiracy interpretations, but also fails to prepare public opinion for the inevitable compromises.

In order to achieve an agreement, it is tempting to assign some sensitive issues for post-accord attention, laying mine fields for the future in the interests of short-term gain. During the Oslo negotiations, for example, five critical issues, including Jerusalem, settlements, and refugee return, were "blackboxed" to enable the two sides to move forward on other less inflexible issues. In Northern Ireland the post-war years were dogged by the deferred issues of policing and decommissioning. The dismantling of war machines is often a dominant theme. The transfer of ex-paramilitary activists into the police and security forces in the Palestinian Territories and South Africa were tangible acknowledgments of past abuses and an effective way of converting a potentially destabilizing armed threat into support for the new structures. It is also a tangible demonstration of commitment to fair employment practices, with the important qualification that the main beneficiaries are militants rather than the general population.

Apart from having to confront these continuing disputes, post-settlement administrations also inherit the problems left by years of violence and confrontation. Truth commissions have become a common but far from universal approach to confront past misdemeanors, with mixed records of success. Latin American truth commissions and the Truth and Reconciliation Commission in South Africa attempted to address the hurts of victims as a basis for reconciliation. The controversy surrounding these bodies demonstrates that it may take as long to repair community dysfunction as it took to create it – decades rather than years.

Reconciliation, if mentioned at all in peace accords, was often "a euphemism for the compromises made during the political negotiations – compromises that papered over the fissures of the past in the interest of national unity but at the expense of the socially marginalized"

(Hamber, in Darby & MacGinty 2003). Recognition that reconciliation should be a central concern in peace agreements is growing, as a consequence of the increasing number of peace processes that have collapsed even after an agreement has been signed. Peace agreements have been typically negotiated by elites and have focused on the minutiae of disputes. They have paid less attention to the need to transform conflicting communities into stable and sustainable societies. The last decade has demonstrated that failure to do this can lead to public disillusionment, and may precipitate the collapse of the agreement itself. The tendency to broaden the nature of peace accords, and to include strategies for reconciliation at every level of society (often called conflict transformation), is already evident. It seems likely to increase.

The success or failure of contemporary peace processes is primarily determined by internal dynamics, but they have also been powerfully shaped by the regional and global environment. Since the 1980s three changes in the global context have significantly affected local approaches to peacemaking and reconciliation. During the Cold War the two superpowers maintained their own forms of order within their respective spheres of control. The Soviet Union stepped in forcibly when it felt its interests were threatened by liberation movements in Hungary, Yugoslavia, and parts of Russia. The US maintained a similar control in the Americas. The collapse of the Soviet Union altered both the nature of ethnic violence and approaches to its resolution. Initially, the United Nations filled some of the vacuum, gradually shifting towards a multidimensional approach (notably in Cambodia and El Salvador). It became involved in peacemaking, peacekeeping, and peacebuilding, sometimes simultaneously. At the same time, the new internal approaches to peacemaking in South Africa and elsewhere began to emerge during the 1990s.

Developments following the al-Qaeda attacks on September 11, 2001 have again shifted the global context within which many traditional conflicts were located. The "War against Terror" has made it increasingly difficult to distinguish between the campaign against al-Qaeda and longstanding guerrilla struggles in Indonesia, Palestine, and Sudan. Some governments, encouraged by growing concern about international terrorism, have introduced or extended tougher security approaches against dissidents. This has angered Muslim groups in many countries, and violent resistance has intensified, especially in parts of Asia and the Middle East. On the other hand, it is clear that the new global temperature has reduced support from diaspora populations for the Tamil Tigers in Sri Lanka and for dissident groups elsewhere. In general, the model of peace processes developed during the 1990s has been increasingly undermined. This model had been characterized by an inclusive approach to peacemaking, one that sought opportunities to negotiate rather than confront; its characteristics were compromise and optimism. The War against Terror encouraged an alternative model, one that sees a greater possibility of victory over dissent; its characteristics are strength and the presentation of stark choices. By 2005 the two models coexisted uneasily, raising two key questions: Are we moving toward a form of peacemaking that is predominantly driven by security interests, rather than by opportunities for a negotiated settlement? Is this a transitory shift or a sea-change?

SEE ALSO: Anti-War and Peace Movements; Peacemaking; Truth and Reconciliation Commissions; War; World Conflict

REFERENCES AND SUGGESTED READINGS

Aall, P. (2001) What Do NGOs Bring to Peacemaking? In: Crocker, C. A., Hampson, F. O., & Aall, P. (Eds.), *Turbulent Peace: Challenges of Managing International Conflict.* USIP, Washington, DC, pp. 365–84.

Crocker, C. A., Hampson, F. O., & Aall, P. (Eds.) (2001) *Turbulent Peace: Challenges of Managing International Conflict.* USIP, Washington, DC.

Darby, J. & MacGinty, R. (Eds.) (2003) *Contemporary Peace Making.* Palgrave-Macmillan, New York.

Lederach, J. P. (1997) *Building Peace: Sustainable Development in Divided Societies.* USIP, Washington, DC.

Lederach, J. P. (2003) Cultivating Peace: A Practitioner's View of Deadly Conflict and Negotiation. In: Darby, J. & MacGinty, R. (Eds.), *Contemporary Peace Making.* Palgrave-Macmillan, New York, pp. 30–7.

Miall, H., Ramsbotham, O., & Woodhouse, T. (1998) *Contemporary Conflict Resolution.* Macmillan, London.

3384 peacemaking

Prendergast, J. & Plum, E. (2002) Building Local Capacity. In: Stedman, S. J., Rothchild, D. & Cousens, E. M. (Eds.), *Ending Civil Wars: The Implementation of Peace Agreements*. Reinner, Boulder.

Rothchild, D. (2002) Settlement Terms and Postagreement Stability. In: Stedman, S. J., Rothchild, D. & Cousens, E. M. (Eds.), *Ending Civil Wars: The Implementation of Peace Agreements*. Reinner, Boulder.

Stedman, S. (2003) Peace Processes and the Challenges of Violence. In: Darby, J. & MacGinty, R. (Eds.), *Contemporary Peace Making*. Palgrave-Macmillan, New York, pp. 103–13.

Stedman, S. J., Rothchild, D. & Cousens, E. M. (Eds.) (2002) *Ending Civil Wars: The Implementation of Peace Agreements*. Reinner, Boulder.

Wallensteen, P. & Sollenberg, M. (2001) Armed Conflict 1989–2000. *Journal of Peace Research* 38 (5). Updated annually.

Zartman, I. W. (Ed.) (1995) *Elusive Peace: Negotiating an End to Civil Wars*. Brookings Institution, Washington, DC.

Zartman, I. W. (2003) The Timing of Peace Initiatives: Hurting Stalemates and Ripe Moments. In: Darby, J. & MacGinty, R. (Eds.), *Contemporary Peace Making*. Palgrave-Macmillan, New York, pp. 19–29.

peacemaking

Wayne Gillespie

Peacemaking is a state of existence or a way of being that is based on love and compassion; in particular, this mode of life calls for an end to human suffering through nonviolent means. It is a philosophy that encourages personal transformation and guides everyday life. Yet the peacemaking perspective also influences broader social changes and informs academic theorizing, research, and public policy. As it applies to criminology, peacemaking takes as its basic assumption that crime is suffering; since the way of peace necessitates an end to suffering, peacemaking criminology envisions an end to crime through the abolition of all suffering. Richard Quinney is the main theorist associated with peacemaking criminology.

The primary goals of peacemaking include an understanding of personal suffering, an end to the many forms of suffering, and the realization of a society that maximizes human development and unites humankind (Quinney 1991, 1995). An awareness of human suffering is an integral element of peacemaking. Quinney (1991) noted that suffering occurs at intrapersonal, interpersonal, societal, and global levels. Intrapersonal suffering involves the physical pains and psychological problems that occur within the human body, whereas interpersonal suffering results from violence inflicted on one person by another. Poverty, hunger, homelessness, pollution, and the destruction of the environment are all examples of suffering at the societal level. Lastly, global suffering includes warfare and the threat of nuclear destruction.

Quinney (1991) also proposed that interpersonal, societal, and global suffering are symptomatic of the intrapersonal suffering within each of us. In order to end social and global suffering, the intrapersonal pain of existence must first be addressed. Quinney believed that the key to ending all suffering lies within cognitive abilities such as mindfulness. An awareness of suffering allows us to understand the true nature of reality as an interconnectedness of all things. Humans are part of the world; we are not separate from it. Care and compassion develop through right understanding or the knowledge that all things are connected. "We cannot end our suffering without ending the suffering of all others" (p. 10). Developing compassion in oneself and loving-kindness toward others is another important step in the peacemaking process. Charity and service then arise from the realizations that everyone suffers and all humans are connected.

Buddhist teachings such as the Dhammapada and Samadhi influenced Quinney's interpretation of peacemaking. In fact, the three essential themes from Quinney's writings are the Buddhist principles of awareness or mindfulness, connectedness, and compassion or caring. Peacemaking also has roots in secular humanism. Klein and Van Ness (2002) discussed the similarities between peacemaking criminology and humanistic sociology. They suggested that humanism and peacemaking both seek to create a better world. As Quinney (1995: 150) remarked, "Peace and the realization of the human project go together; they are one and the same." Both perspectives rely on the development of social justice that emphasizes human rights and just relationships between people. Peacemaking views punishment, particularly incarceration, as a form of state violence that only increases suffering throughout the world. Thus, a model of justice based on social humanism and peacemaking cannot endorse the basic justice model of deterrence. For dealing with individuals who have violated the criminal law, peacemaking favors rehabilitative and restorative programs that emphasize conflict resolution, mediation, reconciliation, abolition, and humanistic action (Quinney 1991).

In addition to religion and secular humanism, feminism and critical theory are traditions closely associated with peacemaking (Pepinski 1991). Harris (1991) outlined three tenets of feminism that are quite complementary to peacemaking: all people have equal value as human beings, harmony and felicity are more important than power and possession, and the personal is the political. Feminist criminology does not objectify criminals as "other"; rather, crime is conceptualized in terms of power. From this realization, a care/response orientation forms where conflicts and injury are dealt with through a process of communication and involvement that treats the needs and interests of all parties.

While critical theory encompasses several perspectives within sociology, the most prominent among them is Marxism. The connection between Marxism and peacemaking criminology is probably best understood in terms of the progression in Quinney's writings from the late 1960s until the present. In *Critique of Legal Order* (1974), Quinney used Marxist theory to interpret the criminal justice system in capitalist society; yet, in later works, he synthesized eastern thought, existentialism, and socialist humanism to form peacemaking criminology (Anderson 2002). There is actually some overlap in the contributions to peacemaking of Marxist theory and feminism. Both see the capitalist social structure as propogating negative values that subjugate the interests of millions to the desires of a few. Through its emphasis on competition and domination, capitalism promotes suffering and violence throughout the world. Thus, capitalism is inadequate in the best possible world offered by peacemaking. However, unlike Marx's Communist Manifesto, peacemaking texts advocate change through nonviolent means that ultimately begin with an intrapersonal awakening to the suffering of oneself and others.

SEE ALSO: Buddhism; Crime, Radical/Marxist Theories of; Criminology; Feminist Criminology; New Left Realism; Peace and Reconciliation Processes; Religion; Truth and Reconciliation Commissions

REFERENCES AND SUGGESTED READINGS

Anderson, K. B. (2002) Richard Quinney's Journey: The Marxist Dimension. *Crime and Delinquency* 48: 232–42.
Harris, M. K. (1991) Moving Into the New Millennium: Toward a Feminist Vision of Justice. In: Pepinsky, H. E. & Quinney, R. (Eds.), *Criminology as Peacemaking*. Indiana University Press, Bloomington, pp. 83–97.
Klein, L. & Van Ness, S. R. (2002) Justice for Whom? Assessing Humanist Criminology as a Catalyst for Change in the Criminal Justice Apparatus. *American Sociologist* 33: 98–110.
Pepinsky, H. E. (1991) Peacemaking in Criminology and Criminal Justice. In: Pepinsky, H. E. & Quinney, R. (Eds.), *Criminology as Peacemaking*. Indiana University Press, Bloomington, pp. 229–327.
Quinney, R. (1991) The Way of Peace: On Crime, Suffering, and Service. In: Pepinsky, H. E. & Quinney, R. (Eds.), *Criminology as Peacemaking*. Indiana University Press, Bloomington, pp. 3–13.
Quinney, R. (1995). Socialist Humanism and the Problem of Crime: Thinking about Erich Fromm in the Development of Critical/Peacemaking Criminology. *Crime, Law, and Social Change* 23: 147–56.

pedophilia

Richard Yuill and David T. Evans

Pedophilia's significance in late modernity rests on its unconventionality, an extreme symbol of sexual decadence threatening "moral" communities and nation-states. Over the past 25 years, pedophilia has mostly been formulated through political campaigns, professional etiologies, and media-led local "moral panics," notably in the campaign for "Megan's Law."

Pedophilia was coined by Krafft-Ebing in *Psychopathia Sexualis* (1892), defining a range of desires and practices associated with adult sexual attraction to children. Contemporary definitions vary from medical psychiatry stressing pathological and behavioral attributes to social policy disciplines emphasizing multifactor personality, familial, and cultural explanations. Subsequent clinical refinements have included Hirschfeld's hebophilia (1906) and Glueck's ephebophilia (1955), specifying adult sexual attraction to pubertal and post-pubertal young people. Historical and cross-cultural studies highlight contrasting non-western cartographies of adult–child sexual practices, including adult male (*erastes*)–youth (*eromenos*) relationships in classical Greece; insemination "rites of passage" in African and Melanesian tribal communities; widespread cultural expressions of pederastic desire in the Near, Middle, and Far East from the Middle Ages through modernity; and finally, revivals of "Pedagogical Eros" in Europe from the Renaissance through the early twentieth century.

Attempts to demarcate child and pedophilic sexualities are compounded by shifting and conflicting cultural notions of childhood, "childhood sexual innocence," and adolescence. This is reflected in significant variations in age of consent statutes, problematic uses of developmental and biological markers to define age categories, and inconsistent approaches to children's agency. Thus, in the UK and US, sexual offenses by children have been increasingly recognized, leading in the UK to legislative regulation (Sex Offenders Act 1993), with 10-year-old males being legally responsible for their actions, as in rape, and having their names placed on the sex offenses register – indications of inherent contradictions in laws demarcating "child sexual innocence."

Efforts to challenge dominant clinical and legal discourses and to promote positive views of pedophilia have met with failure. Following the Gay Liberation Front's (GLF) assault on heteronormativity, the Pedophile Information Exchange (PIE) emerged in the UK. It provided a public forum for pedophiles, whilst seeking political and legal reforms. Following high-profile trials, some members were imprisoned and PIE was effectively wound up in 1984. NAMBLA (the North American Man–Boy Love Association) advocates abolishing age of consent

laws. A number of European countries and Internet sites maintain boylover support groups.

Mainstream contemporary social science research locates pedophilia within wider sociocultural contexts of hegemonic masculinity, patriarchal family, and Enlightenment conceptions of children as powerless. However, previous associations of pedophilia solely with adult male attraction to female children have been questioned due to significant numbers of adult women–boy relationships. Whereas earlier taxonomies drew distinctions between exclusive and infrequent attraction, recent formulations focus on age and gender of victim, recidivism rates, and potential risk factors. Pedophiles have been subsumed within generic approaches to sex offenders, notably causal explanations for seeking child sexual partners including inability to form adult relationships, distorted cognition, and abused/abuser cycles.

Most recent pedophile stories have been recounted by childhood sexual abuse (CSA) survivors. The 1990s and 2000s saw a heightened attention in media and policymaking circles through concerns over Internet chat rooms and sex tourism. Jenkins (1998) identifies such stories as heightened "moral panics," strategically utilized by Christian fundamentalism, mainstream feminism, professional agencies, and national governments for political agendas.

Boylovers criticize the general sex-negative, ageist western cultural scripting for adult–child sexual relationships (including state intervention and professional pastoral monitoring). They adopt two rationales for adult–child sexual relationships: firstly, a child liberationist position which contends that whilst conventionally children are subservient to adults in all areas of social life, their rights in certain contexts (including financial and political) are being institutionally recognized, and that, as future citizens, they are increasingly empowered to make more autonomous choices. Why then should issues of intimacy and sexuality be excluded? By implication, it is argued, unrecognized intergenerational friendship, intimacy, and sexual relationships can also be positive and beneficial. Secondly, they contend that boys especially can benefit from educational guidance and friendship from an adult male.

For opponents, two issues are paramount: firstly, the preexisting power disadvantages and subjectivity discrepancies between adults and children; secondly, omnipresent risks to children in such relationships, including post-traumatic stress disorder (PTSD), sexually transmitted diseases (STDs), and addictions. This "relationship" between CSA and harm was challenged by Rind et al. in 1998, citing considerable neutral and positive outcomes of intergenerational relationships in college and community samples, accounts conventionally silenced in victimological approaches.

The demonization of pedophilia rests on dominant discursive depictions and practical regulations of "innate childhood sexual innocence," but ambiguously such calls for protection contradict escalating empowerment given to children in other areas. Consequently, only adults may speak on intergenerational relationships, where children's voices are silenced alongside certain adults. Furthermore, governments and media demonize the pedophile as the ultimate sexual "folk devil," the shadowy pathological individual "enemy within," effectively distracting attention from a moral crisis in which supposedly "moral" states consistently retreat in the face of amoral market pressures to commodify, exploit, and sexualize childhood, where cases occur within the bastion of "moral" values: the family. Logically, forceful contemporary proscriptions on pedophilia will inevitably be weakened by inherent amoral consumerist capitalism and the political and legal ambiguities that result. Further destabilizing tensions include whether age boundaries remain within Enlightenment paradigms, how far children can be viewed as meaningful social actors, and yet not erotic agents, and the extent to which the legitimacy of CSA discourses may be sustained as they further encroach on idealized notions of the bourgeois family.

SEE ALSO: Child Abuse; Childhood Sexuality; Krafft-Ebing, Richard von; Moral Panics; Sex Tourism; Sexual Citizenship; Sexual Deviance; Sexual Markets, Commodification, and Consumption; Sexual Practices; Sexual Violence and Rape; Sexuality and the Law

REFERENCES AND SUGGESTED READINGS

Evans, D. T. (1993) *Sexual Citizenship: The Material Construction of Sexualities*. Routledge, London.

Foucault, M. (1978) *The History of Sexuality*. Vol. 1: *An Introduction*. Pantheon, New York.

Jenkins, P. (1998) *Moral Panic: Changing Concepts of the Child Molester in Modern America*. Yale University Press, New Haven, CT.

O'Carroll, T. (1980) *Paedophilia: The Radical Case*. Peter Owen, London.

Plummer, K. (1981) The Paedophile's Progress: A View From Below. In: Taylor, B. (Ed.), *Perspectives on Paedophilia*. Batsford, London.

peer debriefing

Valerie J. Janesick

Peer debriefing is a technique used by qualitative researchers for multiple reasons. Good qualitative researchers plan ahead when designing a study to include peer debriefing or a variation of it. Peer debriefing allows a peer to review and assess transcripts, emerging categories from those transcripts, and the final report. In addition, a peer acts as a sort of critical detective or auditor. This peer may detect whether or not a researcher has over-emphasized a point, or missed a rival legitimate hypothesis, under-emphasized a point, and in general does a careful reading of the data and the final report. Many writers have suggested that peer debriefing enhances the trustworthiness and credibility of a qualitative research project (Lincoln & Guba 1985; Creswell 1998; Spall 1998; Spillett 2003; Janesick 2004). Included in the peer review of information might be the full data set such as observations, transcripts, documents, photographs, and videotaped interviews.

The term itself, peer debriefing, is favored in the field of sociology. In other fields, similar terms are used to denote the same process. These terms include the words outside reader, auditor, and peer reviewer. In the history of anthropology, outside reader was the term used to characterize what has evolved into the role of peer debriefing. For example, Margaret Mead and Gregory Bateson used the term outside reader and in fact read each other's field notes. Janesick (2004) uses the term peer reviewer to mean the peer who is involved in the process of peer debriefing. In fact, she advocates that emerging researchers use a statement of verification or peer reviewer form for testifying to the fact that the peer actually read, critiqued, and gave feedback to the researcher throughout the research project. A sample form might use information such as: "I [name] have served as the peer reviewer for the study [title and author]. In this role, I have worked in collaboration with the researcher [name] throughout the study reviewing notes, transcripts, documents, and photographs." Whatever the term selected the notion that a report benefits from a peer review or debriefing is accepted by many qualitative researchers in the social sciences. In fact, in reviewing the latest dissertations over the past ten years using qualitative methods, one can find a regular, sustained use of the peer debriefing technique.

Who might fill the role of peer debriefer? It makes sense to select someone who has the methodological training to understand the purpose and methods of a given study, as well as the analysis and representation of data in the report. Likewise, it makes sense to have a person who is aware of the theoretical framework for the research and who is conversant with the literature on qualitative research in general and someone who knows the particular set of qualitative techniques used in the study. For example, someone doing an oral history project should use a peer reviewer who is knowledgeable about the purposes, theory, and techniques of oral history. Peer debriefing ought to be done with a critical, self-reflective eye, based on content knowledge and willingness to serve as a peer debriefer. It is important that a peer debriefer be articulate in terms of stating personal beliefs and values and trace how the debriefer came to volunteer to act as a reviewer of the project. In other words, the peer is filling roles as a critic, auditor, detective, and expert observer and listener.

In any event, once a peer debriefing is completed, both the researcher and debriefer should be able to describe, explain, and trace throughout the project any changes or confirmations arrived at following the peer review. Just as in any scientific endeavor, there is an elastic-band width for creativity, imagination, and for common sense. Likewise, there is no one way to do peer review or debriefing and quite a bit depends on communication and trust between researchers and peer debriefers.

Many of the questions and even some interest in peer debriefing arises out of some degree of unawareness of the purposes, traditions, theoretical frames, techniques, and conduct of qualitative research in the social sciences. This is unavoidable since as researchers formulate questions best addressed by qualitative research methods, we will only have more emphasis on the checks and balances in the system. One credible, valuable, and dependable technique for checks and balances in qualitative research is peer debriefing.

The enormous amount of written text on qualitative research methods in the social sciences continues to grow as qualitative researchers refine their techniques and methodology. Currently, it is not difficult to find commentary and examples of peer debriefing in projects such as case studies, life histories, narrative inquiry, phenomenological studies, interview studies, biographies, and ethnography. Resources are available in many fields, including nursing, medicine, engineering, education, sociology, anthropology, psychology, and history. Dissertation abstracts contain many resources embedded in dissertations which used a peer debriefing process. Peer debriefing is emerging as a useful technique which provides additional insight into the methods, rationale, and outcomes of a given study. Consequently, emerging and experienced qualitative researchers will find it useful to employ peer debriefing techniques.

SEE ALSO: Ethnography; Interviewing, Structured, Unstructured, and Postmodern; Microsociology; Outsider-Within

REFERENCES AND SUGGESTED READINGS

Creswell, J. W. (1998) *Qualitative Inquiry and Research Design: Choosing Among Five Traditions.* Sage, Thousand Oaks, CA.

Janesick, V. J. (2004) *Stretching Exercises for Qualitative Researchers*, 2nd edn. Sage, Thousand Oaks, CA.

Lincoln, Y. S. & Guba, E. G. (1985) *Naturalistic INQUIRY.* Sage, Newbury Park, CA.

Spall, S. (1998) Peer Debriefing in Qualitative Research: Emerging Operational Models. *Qualitative Inquiry* 4(2): 280–92.

Spillett, M. A. (2003) Peer Debriefing: Who, What, When, Why, How. *Academic Exchange Quarterly* 7(3): 36–40.

peer review and quality control in science

Stephen Turner

Peer review is a practice used in the evaluation of scientific and scholarly papers in order to select papers for publication in scholarly journals. The practice has also been extended to other domains, such as the evaluation of grant proposals, medical practice, book publication, and even to such areas as teaching evaluation. The primary area that has been of interest to sociologists, however, has been publication in scientific journals. The practice is usually understood to have begun in the seventeenth century in the Royal Society in London, but it has also been claimed that there have been precursors to this practice. In the popular mind, peer review in science is a means of "bullet-proofing" research, as a *Wall Street Journal* article once put it, that is to say as a guarantee of quality. But within science it has a very different meaning.

PROBLEM OF LEVELS OF CONSENSUS

The original interest in the sociological study of peer review was in relation to the idea of scientific consensus. It was believed that the physical sciences were high-consensus fields, contrasted to the social sciences and humanities which were low-consensus fields, with the biological sciences falling somewhere in between. An early study by Zuckerman and Merton (1971) compared rejection rates for leading journals in different fields and used this as a measure of consensus. Although the authors recognized that editorial practices (especially the use of numerous referees) differed, they assumed that the rejection rates reflected the fact of scientific consensus.

Subsequently, two of Merton's students, Jonathan and Stephen Cole (1981), did a study of peer review of grant proposals in the National Science Foundation. In this setting, which they characterized as the research frontier, they found that the idea that fields varied according to their supposed degree of consensus did not predict the actual variations

between fields. Indeed, it appeared that fields were strikingly similar in the extent to which disagreements between reviewers occurred, that significant disagreements were quite common, and that funding decisions depended to a significant extent on the luck of the draw of referees. This research used inter-rater reliability as a measure of consensus.

The original Zuckerman/Merton study had not dealt with this kind of peer review process. But the contrast in findings raised the question of which was anomalous, journals or funding decisions. This led to a more careful consideration of differences in editorial practices. One difference was that the review process in physics typically involved one reviewer, with a second review being commissioned only if the first reviewer rejected the paper. Since the acceptance rates for these journals were very high and rejections rare (and often about appropriateness for the journal rather than flaws in the research), it was plausible to think that a rejection by one reviewer indicated a serious error about which there was likely to be less significant differences of opinion. In the social and behavioral sciences, in contrast, there were typically several referees, and acceptance usually required consensus for acceptance.

The standard for acceptance was also different. As an editor of the major physics journal *Physical Review* put it: "The editors consider that their charge is to publish all properly prepared reports of substantial, competently conducted, researches ... And when controversy does arise – as occasionally happens – the editors consider that the argument should be settled in the intellectual agora by the whole community rather than by a few referees and an editor working in camera" (Adair 1980: 12). This was not the ethic of social science journals. The difference was reflected in the divergent paths that science and social science journals took in the 1950s and 1960s. In physics, journals expanded enormously in response to increased research, and charged page charges to authors. In the social and behavioral sciences, however, the typical pattern was for journals to become more selective, rather than expand, and for new journals to be created.

How does this relate to consensus? There is a chicken and egg issue. For the defenders of the idea that rejection rates are an index of consensus, the fact that physics expanded and that it kept its low rejection rates even as it expanded simply reflected its high level of consensus. For those who used inter-rater reliability as a measure, what differed were the editorial practices of the communities.

ISSUE OF QUALITY

Sociologists were not alone in writing on peer review. Practitioners in various fields did their own research, much of which undermined the credibility of peer review. One set of issues, restricted largely to the behavioral sciences and to some extent medicine, concerned journal reviewing. The other major set of issues concerned the reviewing of grant applications for public agencies such as the National Science Foundation and the National Institutes of Health.

A series of studies was performed, primarily on psychology journals, which showed that the peer review process in various journals was (1) biased against authors from less prestigious institutions, (2) prone to significant errors, such as failing to recognize papers that were previously published and resubmitted as part of the experiment, and (3) prone to very high rates of unreliability as a result of randomness that resulted from low rates of inter-rater reliability between reviewers.

The fact that the peer review system, which relied on expert advice, performed so poorly raised fundamental questions about the equitability of the process and the value of relying on the facts of peer review as a guarantee of quality. These studies were generally done by authors. The most compelling studies (e.g., Peters & Ceci 1982) used fake submissions to test the system. They found that previously accepted articles which were resubmitted with fake authorship were typically rejected, usually on methodological grounds, without the supposedly expert authors recognizing them.

This research approach raised ethical questions and was strongly opposed by editors. Editors and persons with access to editorial files granted by editors responded with studies that supported the general equity of journal decision-making processes, though they acknowledged that there was no independent measure of quality and did not address the fact that the grounds for rejection were arbitrary (Bakanic et al. 1987). Yet the fundamental discoveries of exceptional and surprising errors in decision-making and of arbitrariness as shown in the diversity of responses to submissions provided grounds for significant doubt about the peer review system, understood as a means by which decisions about the quality of submissions were accurately made. And the finding of arbitrariness was replicated in many fields by later studies, including journals in science fields where, unlike physics, rejection rates were high.

The second body of research was originally provoked for the opposite reasons. The science community itself, as well as outside critics, had raised questions about the peer review system in major funding agencies, and the criticisms focused particularly on the questions of whether the system was hostile to innovative ideas and whether it promoted group-think. It was also argued that the system allowed a small group of major universities to monopolize research funding. The study by the Coles mentioned above was commissioned by the National Science Foundation to investigate various questions related to its decision procedures and especially to examine peer review. The questions dealt with in peer review of grant applications, however, are different from the question of whether to publish a paper in a journal, and have a zero-sum character. Since this study had access to National Science Foundation files, and access was denied to other researchers, the critics of peer review were forced to use other approaches.

In a study of the National Institutes of Health, researchers gained access through the Freedom of Information Act to rejected proposals, and surveyed the scientists whose proposals were rejected. Surveys of all applicants for grant funding showed a high level of agreement with the idea that reviewers were reluctant to support unorthodox or high-risk research and a substantial body of opinion that viewers were biased against researchers at non-major universities or in certain regions of the US and that ideas were routinely pirated from research proposals by reviewers. The surveys showed no support for the claim that researchers were biased against women or minorities and slight support for the idea that researchers were biased against young researchers (Chubin & Hackett 1990).

ISSUES TODAY

Subsequent research on peer review in science journals has primarily been conducted under the sponsorship of biology journal editors, notably the editors of the *Journal of the American Medical Association* and the *Annals of Internal Medicine*, with an eye towards improving the review process. These journals are influential and have relatively high rejection rates. Some of the research has focused on reviewer quality and indicates that reviewers known to the editor from prestigious institutions are substantially more likely to produce high-quality reviews.

Although peer review is no longer a topic of substantial research interest in either sociology or science studies, the more general phenomena of validation of scientific knowledge and scientific merit have been the subject of theorizing in the area of science studies. From the point of view of this theorizing, scientists face a general problem of providing knowledge to persons who are not in a position to evaluate the grounds for the claim that something is valid knowledge. Consequently, science engages in many elaborate processes of certifying and guaranteeing such things as the quality of a scientist's education and the quality of research contributions through evaluation processes such as peer review, which serve to provide guarantees or assurances to consumers both within science and outside of the work of science. This activity of certification, often relying on peer review, consumes a great deal of the time of scientists and represents a considerable amount of effort. Institutions such as journals compete with one another with respect to their prestige, which represents, according to this theory, their power to certify or assure quality to readers. This approach treats the various forms of peer review as means of adding value to scientific achievements in the competitive market itself and in science understood as a competitive market.

Although there are many criticisms of peer review, the scientists have generally been strong defenders of the peer review as the least bad alternative. In sociology itself, peer review has not been a primary interest of reformers, who have instead concentrated on assuring diversity at the level of journal editors themselves.

SEE ALSO: Matthew Effect; Nobel Prizes and the Scientific Elite; Scientific Norms/Counternorms; Scientific Productivity

REFERENCES AND SUGGESTED READINGS

Adair, R. K. (1980) A Physics Editor Comments on Peters and CEci's Peer Review Study. In: Harnad, S. (Ed.), *Peer Commentary on Peer Review: A Case Study in Scientific Quality Control.* Cambridge University Press, Cambridge, p. 12.

Bakanic, V., McPhail, C., & and Simon, R. (1987) The Manuscript Review and Decision-Making Process. *American Sociological Review* 52: 631–42.

Chubin, D. E. & Hackett, E. J. (1990) *Peerless Science: Peer Review and US Science Policy.* State University of New York Press, Albany.

Cole, J. R. & Cole, S. (1981) *Peer Review in the National Science Foundation.* National Academy Press, Washington, DC.

Cole, S., Simon, G., & Cole, J. R. (1988) Do Journal Rejection Rates Index Consensus? *American Scoiological Review* 53: 152–6.

Peters, D. P. & Ceci, S. J. (1982) Peer-Review Practices of Psychological Journals: The Fate of Published Articles, Submitted Again. In: Harnad, S. (Ed.), *Peer Commentary on Peer Review: A Case Study in Scientific Quality Control.* Cambridge University Press, Cambridge, pp. 3–11.

Zuckerman, H. & Merton, R. K. (1971) Patterns of Evaluation in Science: Institutionalization, Structure and Function of the Referee System. *Minerva* 9 (January): 66–100.

performance ethnography

Ronald J. Pelias

Performance ethnography takes as its working premise that a theatrical representation of what one discovers through participant-observation fieldwork provides a vibrant and textured rendering of cultural others. Performance for the performance ethnographer is typically understood as an aesthetic act within a theatrical tradition. In western cultures this artistic endeavor calls upon actors through their use of presentational skills to evoke others for the consideration of audiences. Not to be confused with the ethnography of performance which examines cultural performances as objects of investigation, performance ethnography relies upon the embodiment of cultural others. As such, it is a method of inquiry that privileges the body as a site of knowing.

This method of inquiry is a close cousin to standard ethnographic practices. In fact, performance ethnographers deploy the same methodological strategies available to all ethnographers in their fieldwork. What marks the performance ethnographer as distinct, however, is their mode of representation. In-print representations of others based upon observation or even full participation in cultural practices is insufficient for the performance ethnographer. Instead, they strive to represent their cultural findings through the enactment of cultural others. By doing so, they believe they add flesh to the dry bones of the traditional ethnographic print account. Furthermore, they argue that by representing others through performance they discover additional, emergent insights born in the performative moment. The actor's body, trained in empathic engagement and nuanced techniques for becoming others, takes on others, not only cognitively, but also affectively. Working at the level of feelings, at the level of embodiment, offers a profound way of coming to understand others. To capture in performance the thinking and feelings of others is quite different than to tell about them in print.

Such thinking was foundational for the two individuals – performance studies scholar Richard Schechner and anthropologist Victor Turner – who are credited with the emergence of performance ethnography in the late 1970s and early 1980s. Schechner was working toward the establishment of the field of performance studies, a field that would move beyond the narrow confines of traditional theater departments to embrace the broad spectrum of human performance practices across western and non-western cultures, from performing arts to rituals, sports, and everyday life entertainments

and actions. Turner had found in performance not only a heuristic metaphor for explaining human behavior, but also a site where cultural logics were most fully displayed. Brought together through a series of conferences on ritual and performance, Schechner and Turner began experimenting with the potential of staging findings from the field and discovered that restoring behavior removed from its place of origin was compelling and enlightening. Based upon their early collaborate efforts, performance ethnography has flourished into a wide range of methodological stances and motives, perhaps best characterized under the labels of ethnographer as reporter, witness, and advocate.

Performance ethnographers who see themselves functioning as reporters strive to foreground cultural others and to minimize or eliminate their own presence in their presentations. Modeled after a scientific sensibility, their performances are offered as reliable, valid, and replicable. While cognizant that no production can be purely objective, these performance ethnographers nevertheless believe that they can offer, within limits, accurate renderings of cultural others – that they can portray what they found in the field. In short, they trust in their ability to bring what is "out there" to the stage and to bury their own role in creating what they present. The audiences for such productions are usually people who live outside the culture that is being staged. When such productions are successful, audience members often feel that they have been invited into another world, perhaps familiar, perhaps not, that captures the culture's complexity in all its sensuousness.

Performance ethnographers who view themselves working as witnesses believe that they are obligated to stage their own role in constructing and, at times, their own interactions with cultural others in order to portray an honest picture of their fieldwork encounters. They take on the role of one who has been there, telling how they made sense of the events they saw, sharing how their presence had an impact on themselves and others, filtering all they want to say through their own experiences. As witnesses, they may confess to what they consider problematic fieldwork behaviors (e.g., betrayal of an informant, sexual encounters). Or they may share how their perceptions changed during their fieldwork; in effect, creating a story that features the ethnographer's coming to awareness. Or they may highlight their own emotional responses to cultural practices different from their own. These and others possibilities place the ethnographer as a central character in the production, one who is fundamental to the unfolding of the plot. Audience members viewing such performances not only sense that they are being invited into another world, but also find themselves responding positively or negatively to the testimony they hear. When such productions work well, audiences feel they met a primary witness who they can trust, one who gave a good account of the events, one whose honesty was disarming and compelling, and one whose company they enjoyed keeping. In such performances the presence of the witness may be so great in fact that audiences feel that what they have before them is an autoethnographic account or a personal narrative.

Performance ethnographers who consider themselves engaged as advocates are convinced that research should make a difference in the world. They work, like critical ethnographers, as social agents on behalf of social justice. They proceed, like all ethnographers, by gaining access and coming to understand another culture, but then, after feeling they know the culture sufficiently well, they call for social change. Their call may be directed at those within or outside the culture. For example, a production might ask cultural members to consider how they are handling sanitation within their village or date rape within their community, or it might ask outside audiences to reflect and act upon discriminatory laws or the economic conditions that affect cultural others. Performance, in this scheme, is used as a tool for intervention. It offers an opportunity to display alternative ways of being, new configurations of social practices, and fresh insights into unproductive behaviors. In this sense, performance ethnography can be linked to critical pedagogy, where actors and audience members are cast as students who are invited to take responsibility for their own and others' education as they move toward a more just world. Audience members of such presentations are urged to drop their typical passive audience role; instead, they are encouraged to take action in the world. Their range of actions may vary, from opening a dialogue to radical political change, but the goal is always to make the world a better place. The best productions make audience members care, and, ultimately, help them act in the name of social justice.

Whether functioning as reporter, witness, or advocate, performance ethnographers face a number of issues as they move from fieldwork to stage work. First, they must decide whether they will cast an ethnographer in the show, and, if so, whether they will cast themselves or someone else to play the role. Productions that do not explicitly have an ethnographer character imply a constructing presence, a backstage person who is offering findings without stepping forward. Most often, however, productions do have an ethnographer on stage who typically serves as a narrator of the events. The narrative role varies – from minor to major, from observational to participatory, from credible to unreliable – with each production. In addition, each production will differ in regard to the degree of showing (replicating the experiences in the field) and telling (featuring the ethnographer's analyses, memories, current feelings, and so on). This jockeying between the "there and then" and the "here and now" is central to how audience members are led through the performance and to how they understand what is before them.

The second issue performance ethnographers meet when moving to the stage is script creation. Performance ethnographers, like all theater practitioners, want their productions to be good theater. In creating their scripts, they write with an eye toward theatrical effectiveness, perhaps structuring their findings into a well-made play or gravitating to moments from the field that display conflict and heightened drama. While doing so, they also keep an eye on what is true to the field, not wanting the desire for good theater to misrepresent what they discovered. Balancing "true to the field" and "effective for the stage" is tricky work. Particularly troublesome is dealing with dialogue. Some performance ethnographers strive only to represent actual conversations from the field; others feel at liberty to alter dialogue for clarity, precision, and focus, or to create altogether new dialogue that is typical of interactions that have occurred. Other considerations, as well, come into play: How best to deal with set design, costuming, and stage properties? How many cast members are needed and what demographic features must the cast members possess in order to stage the show? How to fit findings into the usual length of a theatrical presentation? Such issues may be easily handled or may be irrelevant on the page, but take on considerable weight on the stage.

Some scholars working under the label of performance ethnographer have turned to performative writing as a means for representing field findings on the page instead of the stage. In effect, they create scripts that are never literally performed but imply performances by calling upon the literary and evocative to do the work of the stage. They believe it is the aesthetic, whether in written or staged form, that is key to capturing a feel for the field. A printed script, however, no matter how performatively presented on the page and no matter how well it may signal its readiness for theatrical presentation, does not embody cultural others. Other scholars will employ performative writing when reporting in print about their staged ethnography. In this case, literal performance comes first and performative writing follows to capture the staged experience.

Third, performance ethnographers must make concrete decisions regarding the degree of impersonation. Some performance ethnographers will invite cultural others to portray themselves on stage in the desire to guarantee authentic representations. Having individuals move their everyday behaviors onto the stage, however, is not an easy task. Conspicuously situated, their feelings of self-consciousness may obscure just what the ethnographer wishes to feature. Other performance ethnographers will offer as complete as possible characterizations of the individuals they wish to stage. This typically involves studying video recordings of the vocal and physical details of individuals to such an extent that they may be replicated in performance. Such is the procedure of Anna Deavere Smith. Perhaps the best-known performance ethnographer, Smith puts on display her ability to capture the subtle nuances of each character she portrays in her one-person shows *Fires in the Mirror* and *Twilight: Los Angeles 1992*. The danger here is that audiences may find themselves more focused upon the performer's virtuosity than upon the character being presented. Other performance ethnographers

will present fully developed characters but do not feel the obligation to capture an exact imitation. What individual characteristics get left in and left out, however, may lead to accusations of caricature, stereotyping, and misrepresentation. Still others are content to create a feel for cultural others, including offering composite characters based upon several individuals they have encountered. In this case, performers never imply that they are fully taking on cultural others; instead, they are merely giving a suggestive rendering. They face questions of sufficiency. Each choice described above establishes different accountabilities for the performers and different experiences for audiences. The question of authenticity that emerges across all of these choices is often a critical concern for audience members, even for those who are skeptical about the ability to ever make authenticity claims.

Fourth, performance ethnographers encounter a number of ethical issues when staging their findings. Conquergood (1985) calls upon performance ethnographers to create "dialogical performances," where genuine conversation can occur between self and other. He cautions ethnographers to avoid several morally problematic stances, including "the custodian's rip-off," "the skeptic's cop-out," "the enthusiast's infatuation," and "the curator's exhibitionism." The custodian's rip-off suggests how performances may exploit others, perhaps by performing rituals that only certain members of a culture have the authority to perform, or by making a personal profit by selling replications of cultural artifacts against the objections of cultural members. The skeptic's cop-out points toward ethnographers' hesitancy to perform others on the grounds of difference. Detached and removed, ethnographers within this stance keep themselves enclosed within their own worlds. The enthusiast's infatuation warns against superficiality, against performances that are based upon shallow and naïve understandings and inappropriate identification. The curator's exhibitionism notes the dangers of exoticizing the other, of offering performances that sensationalize or romanticize difference. Conquergood's moral map remains a useful guide for many performance ethnographers, however, as they pursue their desire to produce dialogical performances, and as other ethical risks emerge.

The most important of these is how cultural others process their own enactments by performers. When given the opportunity (and one can argue that it is problematic when not given an opportunity) to view an ethnographic performance based upon their lives, cultural others may meet themselves for the first time, not in manuscript, but presented on stage with all the accuracies and inaccuracies that the embodiment might entail. Regardless of the preparation one has before seeing oneself on stage, even for those with previous theatrical background, the event is often highly charged. It is an event where one sees oneself held up for public display, witnesses the audience's collective and spontaneous response, and sits without the ability to defend or correct. Watching the actors take on their voice and body, cultural others come to realize that reading about themselves is not the same thing as seeing themselves performed. Adding flesh adds consequences, particularly when their portrayal appears to cast them in a negative light. For example, behaviors that typically go unnoticed in everyday interactions may become comic within a theatrical frame. Sometimes, sacred practices and deeply held beliefs may appear mocked when audiences laugh. Other times, performed caricatures may be both recognizable and disheartening. Still other times, seeing oneself performed may reveal aspects of the self never recognized before. The list could continue, but the point seems clear: how an individual processes his or her own enactment is likely to be significant, even profound. Ethical performance ethnographers can help by bringing cultural others into rehearsals, by trying to portray others with respect, and by anticipating possible audience responses, but it is extremely difficult to control for all the contingencies of live performance.

A fifth concern performance ethnographers confront when staging their findings is the question of audience. For whom is the production staged? Is it performed for the members of the culture that is being represented, for a general audience that has limited familiarity with the culture being portrayed, for an academic audience with some expertise on the culture and performance ethnography, or for some combination of the above? Each possibility presents challenges, calling for adaptation in scripting and performance to account for varying motives and knowledge levels. As noted above, some performance ethnographers would maintain that they carry an obligation to stage their work for the culture members that are being studied. Such a demand, however, may encounter insurmountable practical difficulties and may limit the potential of performance ethnography as advocacy. Whatever decision performance ethnographers make, they face the ethical questions surrounding their choice.

The final issue before performance ethnographers is whether they see a production as equivalent to print publication or as a methodological step in the research process. For some, an ethnographic performance, like an article in a journal, offers findings from the field in a polished form that makes its rhetorical case. The difference is only one of venue: stage or page. They may choose to write about their productions, in part because of performance's ephemeral nature, but they do so feeling the inadequacy of print to capture the stage and field experience. For others, all performances offer methodological insights. Each time performers stage others they learn more and more. They write about performances in order to articulate what they have discovered and felt as they used their voices and bodies to become others. This product/process distinction influences how performance ethnographers are likely to proceed and how they narrate their work to various audiences.

Moving findings from the field to the stage, then, is no small matter. Performance ethnographers must not only have the skills and expertise of the ethnographer, but also understand the workings of the theater and its methodological and theoretical commitments. Performance ethnography uses the power of the stage as a tool for representing others. It insists on seeing performance as a method for turning disembodied fieldnotes into a full sense of the cultural other who comes alive when given, once again, voice and body, who appears through the performer's ability to stand in for others, and who is understood, in part, by the portrayal put before an audience. The ultimate challenge for performance ethnographers, whether working as reporter, witness, or advocate, is to embrace their dual role – ethnographer and performer – in the belief that the richest account of cultural others occurs by their combination.

SEE ALSO: Autoethnography; Critical Pedagogy; Ethnography; Narrative

REFERENCES AND SUGGESTED READINGS

Alexander, B. (in press) Performance Ethnography: The Reenacting and Inciting of Culture. In: Denzin, N. & Lincoln, Y. (Eds.), *Handbook of Qualitative Research*. Sage, Thousand Oaks, CA.

Beeman, W. O. (2002) Performance Theory in an Anthropology Program. In: Stucky, N. & Wimmer, C. (Eds.), *Teaching Performance Studies*. Southern Illinois University Press, Carbondale, pp. 85–97.

Conquergood, D. (1985) Performing as a Moral Act: Ethical Dimensions of the Ethnography of Performance. *Literature in Performance* 5: 1–13.

Conquergood, D. (1991) Rethinking Ethnography: Towards a Critical Cultural Politics. *Communication Monographs* 58: 179–94.

Denzin, N. (2004) *Performance Ethnography: Critical Pedagogy and the Politics of Culture*. Sage, Thousand Oaks, CA.

McCall, M. M. & Becker, H. S. (1990) Performance Science. *Social Problems* 32: 117–32.

Schechner, R. (1993) *The Future of Ritual: Writings on Culture and Performance*. Routledge, New York.

Turner, V. (1986) *The Anthropology of Performance*. Performing Arts Journal Publications, New York.

performance measurement

Barbara Townley and Rosemary Doyle

Performance measurement encompasses the role of performance indicators, measures, and targets within a performance management system and is designed to improve organizational functioning. Indicators, or key performance indicators, identify key areas of strategic and operational performance in organizations. Measures seek to give a numerical evaluation of their achievement, while targets are designed as aspirational statements of intended future performance. The purpose of performance measurement is to improve organizational performance by focusing on the key functions or activities that are designed to achieve organizational objectives, and motivate and influence behavior through the setting of targets. Performance measurement is central to strategic management approaches, which utilize core mission statements, strategic objectives, and a focus on outputs to drive organizational performance.

Performance measurement systems are designed to focus all levels of an organization on performance, as reflected in measures and targets. The aim is to integrate the top level of strategic planning with the operational priorities of individual departments and the personal performance of individual employees. A strategic performance management system ensures that achievement at all levels is evaluated against targets, and action is taken in the event of failure to achieve objectives.

Performance measures may play a variety of roles in management: to look back, look ahead, compare, compensate, motivate, cascade down, and roll up an organization. They are designed to improve operational processes and productivity, by providing an incentive for performance improvement and supporting learning. They provide data for strategic planning and assist in the allocation of resources. They may be used as the basis for comparisons between departments or organizations, in order to establish benchmarks of good performance (Meyer 2002).

Within private sector organizations, performance measurement initially focused on financial indicators, such as, for example, market valuation, profit, revenues, or proxies of financial success such as sales, market share, and growth. More recent developments have emphasized the importance of other indicators. For example, the balanced scorecard highlights four categories of performance indicator ("perspectives"), each incorporating a range of specific indicators, for example: revenues, sales, margins (financial); market share, customer satisfaction and retention (customer); product design, production processes (internal business processes); employee retention, productivity or competence (growth and learning). Later forms integrate these perspectives into a strategy map which cascades indicators down through an organization, linking top-level strategic decisions to the actions of individual staff members (Kaplan & Norton 2001).

In the public sector, performance measurement has been associated with the rise of new public management, with its emphasis on an increased reliance on market mechanisms for public service delivery (Osborne & Gaebler 1992). While reflecting private sector concerns of increased productivity and service delivery, performance measures in the public sector are also associated with a democratic imperative, which demands evidence of accountability and transparency in the management of public resources. Performance measures have increasingly replaced the "logic of good faith," which assumed that the provision of public service lay with professional judgment and commitment to the public good.

The experience of working with performance measures varies. They are advocated to increase transparency, learning, incentives for improvement, and as a stimulus to strategic behavior. They may, however, generate perverse consequences. A number of dysfunctions are associated with their operation: tunnel vision (focusing solely on the measure to the exclusion of anything else); goal displacement (trying to affect the measure of performance rather than performance itself); suboptimization (focusing on the unit, rather than organizational performance as a whole); myopia (short-term objectives over long-term needs); ossification (stultifying innovation); gaming (the search for strategic advantage over others); and misrepresentation (Smith 1993).

Generally, measures are less problematic in those organizations where activities are relatively homogeneous, where there are clear and uncontested objectives, where outcomes are tangible and where the relationship between resource input and performance outcomes is relatively direct, and where the organization has a large degree of control over its outcomes. Equally, in the converse situation, i.e., where activities are heterogeneous, objectives contested, outcomes intangible, the relationships between input and outcome lacking clarity, and control less determined, the operation of performance measures is more contested and deemed to be "political" (Carter et al. 1992).

There are two assumptions that sustain the operation of performance measures: basically, that there is something identifiable that may be captured as performance, and that this essence can be reflected by measures. Both assumptions, although seemingly obvious and unproblematic statements, are, in theory and in practice, highly contentious, and lead to different emphases in the understanding and study of performance measurement.

One perspective assumes that performance is an underlying attribute of organizational activity, independent of observers and the process of observation, and accessible through the application of the correct measurement tools. From this perspective, it is possible to define performance adequately and accurately. Sometimes characterized as managerialist, this quasi-realist presentation of performance views performance measures as uncontested, neutral tools of management, designed to reflect an objective position. The reasons for their adoption are technical: to improve organizational performance through the search for better measures that give a more accurate "picture." Dysfunctions associated with their operation are thought to reflect the choice of incorrect measures or managerial and organizational failings in their introduction and implementation. A frequent metaphor associated with this view of performance measurement is that of a "full picture" or "snapshot" that seeks to capture what is before the camera's lens. Measures are a reflection of an objective reality. They seek to represent an activity or series of activities, to those who are not party to them, in a manner that allows knowledge to be gained, decisions to be made, and actions to be taken.

A second perspective emphasizes an interpretivist understanding of performance measure. From this perspective, performance is rather more elusive, fluid, and ambiguous. The interpretivist position emphasizes the plurality of interpretations of performance, dependent on the position of those involved, and does not make such a stark distinction between the observer and the observed. Rather than measures *reflecting* a given performance, measures are a *representation*. Representation is necessarily an abstraction, i.e., it abstracts from, or out of, complex interactions, thus reducing and simplifying a qualitative understanding. Decisions on what to measure, how to measure, how to represent an arena and interpret the results are therefore not seen as technical questions but as political issues. They both represent and constitute how people perceive their interests and what positions they may be able to adopt in political argument. Measures may reflect the agreement, consensual or otherwise, of contested interpretations, or the imposition of a dominant interest. In addition to the issues of accuracy and adequacy that characterize discussions of measures in the former perspective, an interpretivist perspective addresses the added ethical issues of the potential use and abuse of measures: not only whether measures are applicable in this context but also whether or not they *should* be applied, and with what consequences (Paton 2003).

Although the constructivist position has some similarities with the interpretivist position, and shares some of the political understandings of the role of measures, it diverges over its understanding of representation. Both deny the assumption that representation is the neutral reflection of that which is present; however, the constructivist position denies the implicit relativism of an interpretivist position, i.e., that measures solely reflect an intersubjective understanding. For the constructivist, that which is presented is not the "real" but its inscription. Inscription takes the place of that which is present, and "speaks" on its behalf. Measures both represent, i.e., are deemed to authoritatively take the place of, and also re-present the real, i.e., present in a different form. They are thus constitutive of a realm, bringing into being practices, activities, and identities that sustain it (Townley et al. 2003).

This perspective highlights the social processes that are required in making measures routine, taken for granted, and embedded within organizations, and more broadly in society. They require a discourse that sustains them as a legitimate activity in which to be engaged. Embedded within this are theories of behavior, motivation, interests, and identity, not only of those who use and consult them – managers, consumers, citizens, patients, for example – but also those who will operate under them – managers, employees, professionals, and politicians. They require processes of annotation and inscription that allow events to be translated and transferred across time and space, and to be taken to represent that to which they symbolically refer. They require organizational processes and routines that collect, collate, and transfer information as measures, often requiring sophisticated technological resources and

support. They require a degree of numerical familiarity and comfort in those who engage with them, and a learned process of sensemaking that allows measures to be interpreted in a "meaningful" way. Thus performance measures require an elaborate social, technical, and epistemological infrastructure or edifice for them to be able to function (Townley 2002a). These "supports" are required generally, but elements of them are also called into operation every time use is made of performance measures, a failure of any results in the taken-for-granted nature of measures being called into question.

Just as there are different frameworks for understanding performance measures, there are also different explanations as to the apparent emphasis or prominence currently given to performance measures.

Within the private sector, changes in organizational structure, in particular decentralization, downsizing, and outsourcing, reflective of responses to global capital, have introduced a greater role for performance measures as part of the governance mechanism of contracts. Increasing consumerism and competition and intensified production cycles have also placed a growing emphasis on demonstrable performance improvement. Equally, public sector restructuring, with the provision of public services through privatized and devolved agencies, has also seen the increased use of control and contract enforcement through performance measures. Within the public sector, performance measures have gained salience in a climate that has seen the increased questioning of professional judgment, an increased emphasis on consumer choice, and a decline in appeals to the concept of the public good. There has been an increased emphasis on public services providing visible "proof" of performance. Where an organization's "products" are intangible, for example, "education" or "health," and their technologies ambiguous, there is a necessary reliance on wider social legitimation to support an organization's activities and practices. When this broader legitimacy is challenged, an organization may be obliged to adopt certain procedures and practices to demonstrate that they are acting legitimately. Performance measures fulfill this role. Because measures are expressed in numerical form, they also carry some of the connotations that attach to numbers, most specifically their association with hard and objective data, their quasi-scientific status, and their apparent depoliticization of decision-making. In an era that has been characterized by a loss of political ideology, measures are far more conducive to a "what works" public justification and "evidence-based" policy.

A broader interpretation of social change sees the emphasis on performance measurement as reflective of an increased rationalization of social engagement, whereby judgments, decisions, and actions are based on numerical indicators or measures, rather than the reflection of norms, values, or explicit political positions (Townley 2002b). Numbers provide an ease of transportability and a quasi-universal significance that allows them to be transferred through time and space, without the loss of meaning that would accrue to qualitative indicators. In an increasingly globalized environment where cultural and social anchors are less determining, measures of performance take on a greater pertinence. They provide a medium for interaction or coordination between diverse and diversified arenas (Porter 1995).

Measures, and the numbers that attach to them, are integral to the problematizations that shape government and governance: what should be governed and what it is to be governed. From a pluralist perspective, performance measures may provide the basis of contestation to authority, challenge claims to efficiency and effectiveness, and generally contribute to increased accountability and a functioning civil society. Their use reflects a more educated and independent population where traditional bases of authority are increasingly disputed. Or, alternatively, through their functioning as an abstraction, measures may depoliticize politics, i.e., reduce political debate to technical disputes, transforming poverty and hunger into statistical indicators. One question from this perspective is how it is possible to ensure that measures function to increase a democratic agenda. From a perspective of governmentality, measures, such as exam results, fear of crime, unit performance, bring into being entities that are then the foundation of government and management initiatives and interventions, and become incorporated into organizational and individual identities, understandings, and actions (Rose 1999). They are mechanisms that link self-government

with broader programs of government. A question raised by this perspective is, how do domains come into being and acquire their taken-for-grantedness, and with what consequences?

SEE ALSO: Bureaucracy and Public Sector Governmentality; Management Theory; Organization Theory; Organizational Learning; Outsourcing; Strategic Management (Organizations)

REFERENCES AND SUGGESTED READINGS

Carter, N., Klein, R., & Day, P. (1992) *How Organizations Measure Success*. Routledge, London.

Kaplan, R. S. & Norton, D. P. (2001) *The Strategy-Focused Organization*. Harvard Business School Press, Boston.

Meyer, M. (2002) *Rethinking Performance Measurement*. Cambridge University Press, Cambridge.

Osborne, D. & Gaebler, T. (1992) *Reinventing Government: How the Entrepreneurial Spirit is Transforming the Public Sector*. Addison-Wesley, Reading, MA.

Paton, R. (2003) *Managing and Measuring Social Enterprises*. Sage, London.

Porter, T. (1995) *Trust in Numbers: The Pursuit of Objectivity in Science and Public Life*. Princeton University Press, Princeton.

Rose, N. (1999) *Powers of Freedom: Reframing Political Thought*. Cambridge University Press, Cambridge.

Smith, P. (1993) Outcome-Related Performance Indicators and Organizational Control in the Public Sector. *British Journal of Management* 4.

Townley, B. (2002a) Managing with Modernity. *Organization* 9: 549.

Townley, B. (2002b) The Role of Competing Rationalities in Institutional Change. *Academy of Management Journal* 45: 163.

Townley, B., Cooper, D. J., & Oakes, L. S. (2003) Performance Measures and the Rationalization of Organizations. *Organization Studies* 24.

personal is political

Barbara Ryan

The *personal is political* was a term used in the early days of the contemporary women's movement to mean that if something was happening to you, it was happening to other women too.

What appeared to be a personal issue was actually a political one that occurred because of unequal gender relations. Exclusion and exploitation were not individual acts, but were shared under a system of patriarchy.

The branch of the contemporary movement known as the radical or women's liberation sector met in small groups to talk about their lives. The intent and effect was what became known as consciousness raising: becoming aware of things you did not notice or accepted without considering how such assumptions or practices came to be, and especially not questioning who benefited from these practices.

One way to think about the feminist use of the *personal is political* is to put it into a sociological framework. In doing this, a term that comes to mind is the "Sociological Imagination" of C. Wright Mills (1959), who recognized the importance of context and drawing connections between one's experience and social reality. Mills wrote about locating personal troubles in the structural/political realm and the importance of positioning biography within history. Although he never used the term, his ideas are there and predate feminism, but it took the movement to crystallize the meaning and apply it to concrete experiences connected to women's lives.

Another sociological concept tied to the meaning of the *personal is political* is the social construction of reality. This concept can be seen in how we are led to think that what happens to us is our fault rather than a pattern of interactions that places us in a particular sector of society. The idea of "pulling yourself up by your bootstraps" or "any boy [sic] can grow up to be president" are socially constructed ideologies legitimating a system of structured inequality. Also applicable is the "definition of the situation" from W. I. Thomas (closely connected to the Thomas Theorem: "if men [sic] define situations as real, they are real in their consequences"), which calls for us to consider the meaning inherent in our situation and that of others like us. Redefining can be seen in feminist efforts to resist social definitions that lead to internalized oppression. Outside of sociology, socialist feminists, African American feminists, and anarchist feminists (e.g., Emma Goldman) made similar analyses of dominant values and personal troubles for

women, poor people, the working class, and African Americans.

The first reference in print was from Carol Hamish's article "The Personal is Political" in Firestone and Koedt (1970). She is credited with coining the term, which became an early slogan of developing women's consciousness in the late 1960s women's liberation movement (Humm 1995).

Firestone and Koedt (1970) were theorists and activists who defined themselves as radical feminists. Firestone authored *The Dialectic of Sex* (1970), a book advocating the elimination of sex/gender inequalities through the removal of biological differences with artificial reproduction, community childrearing, and abolition of the family (Ryan 1996). Koedt is best known for her article "The Myth of the Vaginal Orgasm" (1973), as well as her writings on lesbian feminism and the radical sector of the women's liberation movement. In the preface to *Radical Feminism*, Koedt, Levine, and Rapone (1973) argue sexism is a political system only understood when women are seen as a political class defined by sexist ideology and institutions; women's experience "reflects this understanding of the political nature of what has always been deemed personal."

The *personal is political* was confronted in the 1970s by lesbians who felt shunned in the larger women's movement and by African American women in the 1980s for the lack of attention to race issues (Ryan 1992). They, and later other racial/ethnic groups, charged the movement with a sisterhood that only represented white middle-class heterosexual women whose concept of the personal extended solely to them, and whose political strategies were forged to address the issues affecting them. By the 1990s, identity politics challenged the concept *women* – as in all women – for the failure to acknowledge the intersections of race, class, ethnicity, sexual orientation, sexuality, disabilities, age, nationality, occupation, and education – in short, all of the differences among women that affect their place in social, economic, and political systems (Ryan 2001).

The discord so rampant in those years actually focused more on the idea of sisterhood than the concept of the personal is political, which could be applied to any group identity, including multiple identities. The concept is germane to seeing how individual lives are delimited and determined by social and political forces that affect not just them, but others like them. No longer were women left to feel that their inability to succeed was a personal failure or a character fault. Indeed, unfulfilling marriages, low-level jobs and incomes, domestic violence, and depression could all be seen as systemic to a social system that purposely denied opportunities to women and that devalued the work that women do. And, importantly, the concept was able to expand and incorporate the recognition that structural inequality impacted women differently based on the other group characteristics they inhabited, including the prejudice and discrimination visited upon men of oppressed social groups.

Other social movements have used this concept, in varying terms, to organize for change in their group's behalf, some before the contemporary women's movement and others after it became part of public discourse. The Civil Rights Movement stressed how being black placed you in a repressed and restricted role, the anti-war movement uncovered common policy patterns from wealthy countries to poor countries, the New Left protested the inherent educational and occupational privilege in class relations, and colonialism and imperialism revealed a dominant–oppressed dynamic on a global scale. Thus, connections could be made with patriarchy and sexism to white supremacy and racism, to imperialism, domination and war.

Since the 1990s the links among structural divisions are more clearly recognized. Not only are activists involved in seeing the personal is political for individual lives, but also that the multiple oppressions in people's lives intersect. Domination of one group over another, whatever the guise, leads to the awareness that the personal is, indeed, political.

SEE ALSO: Consciousness Raising; Feminism, First, Second, and Third Waves; Radical Feminism; Women's Empowerment; Women's Movements

REFERENCES AND SUGGESTED READINGS

Firestone, S. (1970) *The Dialectic of Sex: The Case for Feminist Revolution*. Bantam Books, New York.

Firestone, S. & Allen, P. (1970) *Notes from the Second Year*. New York Radical Women, New York.

Franck, I. & Brownstone, D. (1993) *The Women's Desk Reference*. Penguin, New York.

Humm, M. (1995) *Dictionary of Feminist Theory*, 2nd edn. Ohio State University Press, Columbus.

Koedt, A. (1973) The Myth of the Vaginal Orgasm. In: Koedt, A., Divine, E., & Rapone, A. (Eds.), *Radical Feminism*. Quadrangle Books, New York, pp. 198–207.

Koedt, A., Levine, E., & Rapone, A. (Eds.) (1973) *Radical Feminism*. Quadrangle Books, New York.

Mills, C. Wright (1959) *The Sociological Imagination*. Oxford University Press, New York.

Morgan, R. (Ed.) (1970) *Sisterhood is Powerful: An Anthology of Writings from the Women's Liberation Movement*. Vintage Books, New York.

Redstockings of the Women's Liberation Movement (1975) *Feminist Revolution*. Random House, New York.

Ryan, B. (1992) *Feminism and the Women's Movement: Dynamics of Change in Social Movement Ideology and Activism*. Routledge, New York.

Ryan, B. (1996) *The Women's Movement: References and Resources*. G. K. Hall, New York.

Ryan, B. (2001) *Identity Politics in the Women's Movement*. New York University Press, New York.

phenomenology

Gerhard Schutte

Originally of philosophical origin, phenomenology reasoned that the pure meanings of phenomena were only to be subjectively apprehended and intuitively grasped in their essence. It achieved relevance to the social sciences within the tension between logical positivism and interpretivism or (in nineteenth-century terms) the natural and cultural sciences. At the turn of the twentieth century the neo-Kantians' insistence on a distinctive epistemology and methodology for the "cultural" sciences found a well-considered resonance in German sociological thought (e.g., Weber's). The growth, explanatory force, and extension of natural science's objective perspective and positivistic methodology to the domains of the cultural sciences did not go unchallenged. It was the mathematician-turned-philosopher Edmund Husserl who laid the foundation of the twentieth-century phenomenological movement by taking to task the positivistic approach to psychology.

Turning away from the external objective world as source of knowledge, Husserl reverses the perspective to that of the subject's experience of reality. This experience is always an experience "of" and is directed to the object. Husserl uses the concept of *intentionality* Brentano) to describe this relationship. The subject apprehends the world through passive synthesis by giving meaning to it in an unreflective, spontaneous manner. He or she can share experiences with others in an intersubjective way. Subject or intersubjectivity exists in a world of experience. This is the "lifeworld" experienced in the "natural attitude." To the subjects, this lifeworld is given in an unquestioned way.

Husserl thus grounds his epistemology in the experience of everyday life and moves from there to the next level, which he calls phenomenological reduction. This involves a procedure called bracketing or *epoché*. What is apprehended in the natural attitude as "natural" or naturally given is bracketed and regarded as if it represents only a claim to self-evident existence. It is thus reflected upon and considered to be an "appearance" (i.e., a phenomenon). This level of cognition, though, is insufficient because it leaves the question unanswered as to what something is the appearance of.

In order to address this question Husserl introduces "eidetic reduction," which incorporates the idea of grasping the essence or *eidos* of a phenomenon. The essence has an a priori existence and instead of being grasped through reflection, it is intuitively apprehended. In a somewhat oversimplified example one may look on one level at a red object in a naturalistic way, then bracket and question one's judgment of it as having this hue red and not a different one, and finally proceed to intuit the essence of redness.

Ultimately, it was Husserl's objective to grasp the structure of pure consciousness and the transcendental ego. His thoughts spurred existential philosophers such as Heidegger and Sartre to reflect on the ontological question of "Being" (*Sein*, *Etre*). Alfred Schütz, however, took up the task of making the subject's experience and situatedness in the lifeworld concrete and amenable to empirical investigation. The

intellectual climate he worked in during the early decades of the twentieth century was heavily influenced by the Vienna Circle. It posited an objective world amenable to disclosure and explanation by logical positivist methods. Human realities were part of the objective world. To Schütz, the object of social inquiry was far more complex. He realized that the objects of social inquiry were human *subjects* endowed with freedom of will, and at the same time they and their actions were *objects* of investigation and explanation. He embarked on a rigorous analysis of social action as the point of entry for a phenomenological account of both its subjective and objective dimensions. The perspective of the social actor (instead of the philosopher's "subject") is central and intersubjectively linked to others in a shared lifeworld. His pioneering work *Phenomenology of the Social World* concentrates on the meaningful construction of the social world. He thus reconceptualizes Husserl's lifeworld as the universal dimension of human experience with the more specific "social world." The actor experiences the (social) lifeworld from the "natural attitude," taking it for granted in an unquestioning way. The cognitive style of the lifeworld is that of the "suspension of doubt" and its status is that of "paramount reality" governed by the "fundamental anxiety" of the subject about his or her death. This social world is spatially and temporally structured from the point of view of the actor. Spatially, it slopes away from the actor from social relationships of familiarity to those of greater anonymity. Temporally, it reaches backward to predecessors and forward to successors. It is within this framework that he or she creates or draws on typifications of situations and persons, on typical recipes for action. Schütz calls the actor's typifications in everyday life first-order constructs. These constructs are taken for granted and intersubjectively shared among society's members. With regard to social action it is the task of the social scientist to distinguish the actor's motivation for it from the observational understanding of an outside observer. He thus improves on Max Weber's approach that telescoped the insider and outsider perspectives in an attempt to explain social action through understanding.

Drawing on Husserl's phenomenological reduction and the procedure of bracketing,

Schütz focuses on "second-order constructs," the constructs of science in general and of social science in particular. Scientific constructs go beyond the natural attitude. In transcending the lifeworld of the mundane, phenomenologically oriented scientists utilize a cognitive style that suspends belief rather than doubt. They "detach" themselves as disinterested observers. The typications they produce are not concrete, but more abstract and generic. They are "ideal-types" in Weber's sense and serve heuristic and analytic purposes. Yet, science and social science as "finite provinces of meaning" have to maintain a nexus with the everyday world in order to remain relevant. Schütz produced exemplars of such sociological ideal-types of actors in his essays on the stranger and the homecomer. They ideal-typically reproduce the immigrant and returned soldier, respectively, without sacrificing their relevance to "real" persons.

Science and sociology are not the only domains with cognitive styles and forms of consciousness qualitatively different from that of everyday life and the lifeworld. Schütz distinguishes the world of phantasms and dreams, among others, as different "finite provinces of meaning." The worlds of art and that of religious experience – each with its own cognitive style – are further examples.

Schütz stops short of Husserl's next step of "eidetic reduction," which aims at grasping essential and a priori realities. To him, this was the domain of phenomenological philosophy. However, this dimension of Husserl's phenomenology was taken up by other disciplines such as social philosophy and comparative religion. Rudolf Otto's *The Idea of the Holy* (1917) – in which he intuits the essence of the divine – still stands as an exemplar of eidetic reduction.

In their seminal work, Berger and Luckmann (1972) brought the phenomenological perspective to a much wider audience than their teacher Schütz reached during his lifetime. Their concern was the social construction of *reality* as such and not just that of social reality or that of the social world. They adopt Husserl's bracketing in order to examine the ontological claims of society with regard to the shared vision and beliefs of its members about "reality." In an ambitious integrative project they attempt to account for the intersubjective construction of reality, its institutionalization as structure and internalization in a dialectical fashion that portrays humans as both constructors and constructs. They position their sociology of knowledge between the taken-for-granted "ontology" of the "man in the street" and the reflective ontology of the philosopher.

The relationship between sociology and philosophy is not always clear in phenomenologically inspired sociologies. Some contemporaries and successors to Schütz preferred to present phenomenological sociology in a way as one would define functionalism or the sociology of conflict as paradigms. Phenomenological sociology was thus seen as another paradigm in a Kuhnian sense (Psathas 1973). In this form it found recognition in the American Sociological Association when the first session on phenomenological sociology was organized in 1971. Paradigms, however, tend to be superseded by others.

Luckmann adopts a different perspective by returning to the original Husserlian injunction that installs phenomenology as a fundamental alternative and successor to logical positivism. Phenomenology to Luckmann is a philosophy that pursues knowledge, and thus sociology offers descriptions of universal structures of subjective orientation in the world. It provides the discipline with an *egological* perspective that places human experience at the center and requires a description of that experience by returning to its intentional features. It does not constitute a discipline and is not a paradigm of sociology. Its cognitive style is impersonal rather than the personal reflection of phenomenology; its evidence is public rather than subjective experience. Social realities do however refer to universal structures of subjective orientation and it is here that phenomenology and social theory may articulate with each other.

Schütz's phenomenological approach inspired a further branch of interpretive sociology pioneered by Aaron Cicourel and Harold Garfinkel: ethnomethodology. It focuses on everyday life, but instead of emphasizing the taken-for-grantedness of the world of experience, it problematizes the way in which ordinary members of society achieve that sense of normalcy. It thus breaks away from the idea that lay people share a set of symbolic meanings and replaces it with an exposition of their unending work towards the achievement of a set of shared meanings. What members of a group do share are the methods for making sense of their reality.

Phenomenology has had a lasting impact on the social sciences. More recently a shift of emphasis occurred, moving attention away from reflections on their deeper philosophical and epistemological roots towards studies of mundane realities and the ways people made sense of and acted upon them. Understandably, phenomenology's subjective perspective stimulated a methodological debate on the production of evidence and its analysis. A number of manuals on qualitative research have demonstrated their indebtedness to the phenomenological perspective. Ethnography, though traditionally the preserve of anthropological research, received a new impetus from phenomenology and extended itself to the description and study of mundane realities and lifeworlds within societies. The phenomenological orientation in social science and the humanities today extends well beyond the German and English-language communities of its origin. It spread early to Japan, the Netherlands, France, and Spain, with other European countries, Latin America, and Britain among others to follow.

At the beginning of a new century, phenomenological description and analysis consolidated existing foci on religion, education, art, architecture, and politics (to name but a few) and widened its scope to include such further worlds of experience as medicine, nursing, health care, the environment, ethnicity, gender, embodiment, history, and technology (Crowell et al. 2001).

SEE ALSO: Ethnomethodology; Intersubjectivity; Knowledge, Sociology of; Schütz, Alfred; Weber, Max

REFERENCES AND SUGGESTED READINGS

Berger, P. & Luckmann, T. (1972) *The Social Construction of Reality: A Treatise in the Sociology of Knowledge*. Penguin, London.
Crowell, S., Embree, L., & Julian, S. J. (Eds.) (2001) *The Reach of Reflection: Issues for Phenomenology's Second Century*. Electron Press. Online. www.electronpress.com.
Garfinkel, H. (1967) *Studies in Ethnomethodology*. Prentice-Hall, Englewood Cliffs, NJ.
Husserl, E. (1970) *The Crisis of European Sciences and Transcendental Phenomenology: An Introduction to Phenomenological Philosophy*. Northwestern University Press, Evanston.
Luckmann, T. (Ed.) (1978) *Phenomenology and Sociology*. Penguin, London.
Psathas, G. (Ed.) (1973) *Phenomenological Sociology: Issues and Applications*. John Wiley and Sons, New York.
Schütz, A. (1967) *The Phenomenology of the Social World*. Northwestern University Press, Evanston.

photography

Martin Lister

By chemically fixing the images produced by cameras, photography (literally "light writing") was the first technology in history to automate the production of visual images by freeing them from a reliance on skilled hand–eye coordination. It also enabled the mechanical reproduction of existing visual images. From the mid-nineteenth century onwards, photography radically changed when and where images could be made, their relationship to time and movement, who could make them, and the uses to which images could be put. It placed the visual image at the center of a wide range of social, cultural, and scientific practices. Photography was a key factor in the emergence of modern societies pervaded by throwaway images, seductive spectacles, and surveillance through vision.

Within a decade of their invention photographs were being produced in many parts of the world, and within 20 years the rudiments of commercial, scientific, social, and artistic practices were established. In a remarkably short time, photography was being used for ethnographic, pornographic, surveillance, criminological, medical, and propaganda purposes. From early on, photography was utilized in war reportage, programs of social reform in the new industrial cities, as a means of marketing commodities and celebrity, and in the affirmation and construction of personal identity, biography, memory, and social status.

From the late nineteenth century until the establishment of broadcast television in the

1950s, photography was the socially dominant visual mass medium. Since the early 1990s, photographic technology has been increasingly displaced by digital technology in the form of digital and virtual cameras and computer software for image manipulation and generation. However, images which appear to be photographs, and are received and used as photographs, continue to be produced and circulated on a vast and global scale. Despite the displacement of photographic technology, the aesthetic and signifying properties of the "photographic" continue to be central in contemporary visual culture. "Photographic realism" remains the very benchmark of realism in visual representation. If a fantasy or a physically impossible event is to appear real and credible in a computer-generated image (a tiled floor morphing into the Terminator, in the film of that name, for example), then it needs to look just as it would if it had been photographed (Allen 1998). In this sense, in what is now frequently referred to as a "post-photographic" age, the characteristics of the photographic image and the values invested in it continue to have currency. Two practical systems of fixing images made with cameras were announced in 1839, in France (Daguerre) and in England (Fox Talbot) following a lengthy prehistory of experiment and anticipation in the eighteenth century. Both methods fixed, by chemical means, an image cast by a camera lens upon a light-sensitive surface. Importantly, Fox Talbot's method did more than mechanically produce images. It created a negative image from which multiple positive versions or prints could be made. This was the basis for an eventual industrialization and mass production of visual images. With the invention of the halftone screen in the 1880s, it became possible to print photographs alongside text and other graphic elements and they began to circulate in the mass media of newspapers, magazines, and publicity materials. By the end of the nineteenth century, with continuous technical development in lenses, film speed, and the size of cameras, the limitations posed by the cumbersome nature of earlier photographic apparatus and processes were overcome. Exposures of a fraction of a second became possible, cameras were miniaturized, and the relationship of visual images to time,

movement, and circumstance was effectively changed.

The birth of photography took place broadly within the context of nineteenth-century western industrialization, urbanization, imperial warfare, and colonial exploration and administration. Its development paralleled that of mechanized transport and modern travel and tourism. Via its use in advertising it was a key factor in the emergence of a commodity culture and consumer society. In its popular and domestic forms, photography played a key part in the establishment and celebration of the culture of the nuclear family unit. In relation to an empiricist turn in the natural and social sciences and the demands of complex industrial societies, it rapidly became a tool of social surveillance and ethnic and social class classification. Photography was put to use, developed, and given meaning in each of these contexts.

Given its cultural ubiquity and diversity, it has been widely accepted since the 1970s that the many genres and practices of photography that exist cannot adequately be defined and understood according to essentialist universal characteristics of the medium. Photography is best thought of as many practices (or photographies) arising from the historically specific social and cultural uses of a common technology, some of which are based upon understandings of the medium's nature which are contradictory.

Throughout its history, the nature and ontological status of the photographic image have been a subject of philosophical inquiry and debate. This debate centered upon a kind of paradox, which is reflected in realist and constructivist theories of the photographic image. On the one hand, the photograph has been thought to have a special relationship to the material reality it depicts. In this sense, it has been understood and used as if it were a neutral and objective record, a truthful report, on the appearance of the natural or material world. Such views stem from the perception that photographs are a kind of trace or imprint of the objects and events they depict via the operation of light and chemistry. In this sense, the photograph was (and in many pragmatic ways still is) thought to have a privileged relationship or access to the real; it is conceived as being like a cast that was formed by being physically in touch with an object, and therefore, in this respect at least, unlike other kinds of visual image. In semiotic terms, it is an indexical sign; a sign that is caused by the thing it represents. Temporally, the photograph always refers to something in the past, that did exist or happen. Also contributing to this sense of photography's truth-value was the mechanical nature of the "capture" of images by the photographic process and the lack of evident human (hence subjective) invention or intervention in the process. Importantly in this respect, photography emerged within a period of western culture dominated by empiricism and positivism and was valued from early on as a scientific instrument for the collection, recording, measuring, and classification of appearances that could be treated as reliable facts.

On the other hand, the practice, and indeed the very technology, of photography is part of a longer western tradition of image-making (e.g., photographic lenses embody the optics of linear perspective and cameras are designed to frame and resolve images in traditional "portrait" and "landscape" formats). Photographers also employ a wide range of pictorial conventions. Within the complex photographic process, from exposure to print, a photograph can be subject to many kinds of technical and aesthetic manipulations such as the control of focus, depth of field, contrast, detail, and resolution, and to practices of juxtaposition, combination, and composition. The meanings of photographs also have an important relation to the written texts that usually accompany them and the institutional and discursive contexts in which they appear. In such ways photographs serve a wide range of ideological purposes.

An abiding concern has been the question of photography's status as an art. For many critics, photography was to be excluded from the canon of art because of its unselective and slavish depiction of reality and its inability to penetrate superficial appearances to reveal deeper political and intellectual realities. However, an alternative view, associated particularly with the German critic Walter Benjamin (1970 [1936]), holds that photography brought about a revolution in visual culture with democratic potential. All unique works of art became endlessly reproducible and available to new audiences, while information and knowledge about the world at large became popularly accessible through the mass circulation of photographs. In this process, images lost the aristocratically sanctioned and didactic authority they had held up until the advent of photography. At the same time, photography gave rise to a new way of seeing as it was able to capture aspects, details, and relationships within the visual world which were not perceivable by the naked eye. In the 1920s and 1930s, artists of the Surrealist movement valued photography precisely for its uncanny ability to make the familiar and everyday strange. From the 1930s, particularly in the US, modernist photographers sought to establish photography as an art form in its own right by pursuing and refining what they took to be an essentially photographic vision and language.

Ethnographic and documentary uses of photography arose early in the context of nineteenth-century social anthropology. As colonial subjects, African, Asian, and Australasian peoples were subjected to the surveying and controlling gaze of the camera, framed as exotic "others" and constructed as evidence for social evolutionist and eugenicist theories about racial difference and social class. Within Europe and America, the new social problems arising in the overcrowded and unsanitary industrial cities were documented in photographs. Fears about crime, the spread of disease, and the regulation of the lives of the urban working class became an object of photographic surveillance. Photography came to be viewed as a tool of scientific interrogation and the objective recording of appearances as evidence. Examples of such uses include: the identification of criminals, the representation of mental illness, establishing norms for the "healthy" human body, and providing evidence of the need for social reform.

In the 1930s, social documentary photography and photojournalism became cultural practices of great importance. They were facilitated by the use of lightweight cameras and the expansion of mass circulation photographic magazines and the popular press in Europe and North America. Documentary photography in its mid-twentieth-century form had a social conscience and sought to contribute to social change and reform. It was informed by humanist, social democratic, and sometimes socialist values. The American "Farm Security Administration" project was state funded and designed to provide images for reports on the recovery of the American economy after the Depression of the 1930s, while in England, the "Mass Observation" movement attempted a visual anthropology of "everyday life" in Britain.

Popular photography has been a major factor in the construction of identity and lifestyle choices. It is simultaneously a clear example of the way in which the dynamics of commodity capitalism have shaped a practice of self-representation. Within a decade of its invention, photography had found a place in the high street, where specially built portrait studios with a large middle-class clientele and a high financial turnover were established. Alongside these, disreputable "street photography" establishments run by charlatans sprung up. Both kinds of establishment catered for a growing demand amongst the urban classes for "likenesses." In this way, photography was a new means of production which replaced the expensive, labor-intensive practice of portrait painting which had historically been confined to the aristocracy. The "carte de visite" was an early form of postcard, either a portrait of a middle-class sitter produced in multiples, or a portrait of a celebrity of the day mass produced for sale. This was an early form of the commodification of the photograph and the beginnings of a photographic industry that trades in images of celebrity and glamour.

However, photography remained a difficult craft for much of the nineteenth century and only truly became a form of industrial production for a mass market in the last decades of the century, alongside the continuing development of the popular press, consumer magazines, and advertising. The development of popular photography for private consumption took place firmly within the context of a highly ideological view of the family, a rapidly expanding commodity culture, and tourist, leisure, and lifestyle industries. In 1888 George Eastman introduced the user-friendly Kodak "point and shoot" camera, which used roll film and included processing and printing within its price. This effectively put the means of making photographs into the hands of "ordinary" people and facilitated the possibility of photographing the events and moments of family and everyday life. The extreme simplification of the photographic process which is built into mass market cameras means that "snapshot" photography is severely circumscribed in aesthetic and semiotic terms. It also became evident to the Kodak company that the mere possibility of photographing everyday life that the technology provided was not met by a popular desire to do so. Hence the marketing of popular photography, gendered in its primary address to women, by encouraging images to be made that depicted the family at leisure. In this way, the democratic impulse of popular photography was, to a large extent, channeled into a celebration of the family unit consuming and at leisure, centered upon images such as family festivities, children at play, seaside holidays, suburban life, and the family motorcar. From the 1930s onwards, family photography was reinforced in this direction by popular magazines and advertising offering images of an ideal world of domestic consumption.

Over a history of more than 160 years, vast numbers of photographs have been accumulated in institutional archives, collections, and private albums. Of particular interest is the manner in which these construct a view of history and the politics of the archive as they have been shaped by the purposes and ideologies that originally informed the selection of images for inclusion. Since the early 1990s many large photographic archives (artistic, documentary, journalistic, specialist) have been digitized and become the electronic property of corporate image banks, such as Microsoft's Corbis or Getty Images plc. These online image banks trade globally and now provide a high proportion of all images used in publicity, advertising, and editorial work. Digital cameras are now widely used in personal and snapshot photography and "family albums" are now frequently stored and viewed on computer and television screens and published on websites. The early use of photographs (and now video stills) for surveillance, security, and criminal detection purposes continues and has become truly panoptic in the twenty-first century. The inclusion of digital cameras in mobile (or cell) phones is a recent development which promises, in principle, to turn every man and woman into a photo reporter.

SEE ALSO: Benjamin, Walter; Media; Media and Consumer Culture; Methods, Visual; Semiotics; Surveillance

REFERENCES AND SUGGESTED READINGS

Allen, M. (1998) From Bwana Devil to Batman Forever: Technology in Contemporary Hollywood Cinema. In: Neale, S. & Smith, M. (Eds.), *Contemporary Cinema*. London, Routledge.

Batchen, G. (1997) *Burning with Desire*. MIT Press, Cambridge, MA.

Benjamin, W. (1970 [1936]) The Work of Art in the Age of Mechanical Reproduction. In: Arendt, H. (Ed.), *Illuminations*. Fontana, Glasgow.

Bourdieu, P. (1990 [1965]) *Photography: A Middle-Brow Art*. Polity Press, Cambridge.

Frosh, P. (2003) *The Image Factory: Consumer Culture, Photography, and the Visual Content Industry*. Berg, Oxford and New York.

Ramamurthy, A. (2003) Spectacles and Illusions: Photography and Commodity Culture. In: Wells, L. (Ed.), *Photography: A Critical Introduction*. Routledge, London and New York.

Slater, D. R. (1993) Marketing Domestic Photography. In: Davis, H. & Walton, P. (Eds.), *Language, Image, Media*. Blackwell, Oxford.

Tagg, J. (1998) *The Burden of Representation: Essays on Photographies and Histories*. Macmillan, London.

Wells, L. (Ed.) (2003) *Photography: A Critical Introduction*. Routledge, London and New York.

Pietism

Jean-Paul Willaime

The word Pietism is applied to that religious awareness that developed from within Protestantism, in particular in the seventeenth century. It constituted neither a unified theological tendency nor a structured orientation. This awareness expresses a desire for a more intense and practical expression of piety, which has been articulated throughout the ages and in a number churches. It can be said that Pietism is a reaction to the mundane and intellectualist tendencies of Protestantism, a reaction which stresses the personal religious experience of each believer as well as the mediation of the Bible in everyday Christian behavior. Pietism stems not only from the development and intensification of inner life, but also from the founding of schools, orphanages, and missions. It represents a theology of the heart, which is relatively indifferent to doctrinal matters and for which the fundamental criterion is authenticity. Sociologically, Pietism is a popular and enterprising movement that crosses a range of diverse Protestant denominations. It is particularly manifest in Lutheranism, Methodism, and in the many revivalist religious movements that have punctuated the history of Protestantism.

Historically, Pietism appeared in German Protestantism in the seventeenth century. Philipp Jakob Spener's book published in 1675, *Pia Desideria* (Pious Wishes), is one of the outstanding works of the period. He encouraged the formation of lay conventicles called *collegia pietatis* in order for male and female believers to grow spiritually and to deepen their faith by means of meetings in the official church (*ecclesiola in ecclesia*). For Spener and his followers, Christianity is not primarily a branch of knowledge, but a way of life that has to be expressed through specific behaviors. In the training of pastors, spirituality is more important than theological ability. The aim of the Pietists is to revive, from within the church, Christian faith and the Christian way of life of each believer. But other more radical Pietists go further in thinking that the true Christian church can be found only in small communities of bona fide believers separated from the established churches. Pietism is a kind of protest, developed from the Protestant church, against the fossilization of Christian life in dogmatic orthodoxy and routine liturgy, and for a revival of faith understood as sentiment and action.

Pietism was not only a resurgence of religious sentiments. It operated through many charities and its social and cultural influence was important. The two most important areas where Pietism was active were in Germany, in the faculty of theology at the University of Halle dominated by the work and teachings of A. H. Francke (1663–1727), and the University of Württemberg, where the theologian J. A. Bengel (1687–1752) was known for his notion of biblical sciences (Engels particularly criticized the "Württemberg Pietism"). Francke founded the University of Halle and developed an educational, social, and cultural movement through "foundations" (orphanages, a bookshop, schools, a publishing house, and a Bible society). He also founded a printing house which distributed many millions of Bibles throughout the eighteenth century. He also set up the first Protestant missions in India and supported the first Protestant missions to the Jews. Bengel illustrates the relationship between Pietism and biblical sciences; he established a new Greek edition of the New Testament and its translation.

One other important figure in Pietism is Count Nikolaus Ludwig von Zinzendorf (1700–60), who welcomed religious refugees to his estate in Upper Lusatia, notably the descendants of the pre-Reformation Hussite movement, the Moravian Brethren. He founded religious communities characterized by a number of acts of piety. He wanted to gather Christians into an ecumenical society transcending all confessional divisions. Pietism developed particularly in Prussia under the reign and with the support of King Friedrich I (1713–40). The relationship of *Aufklärung* (Enlightenment) to Pietism was complex – far from being mere opposites, they shared some affinities: the Pietist promotion of a religion centered on the "heart and actions" did not appear strongly opposed to the importance given to individuality and reason.

Pietism had considerable influence because of the charitable work it conducted in missions, the distribution of Bibles, and its educational and charitable institutions. Through such dynamism, Pietism clearly manifested traits that emphasized a practical Christian nature. Nevertheless, it generated moralism and an elitist conception of Christianity based on the good deeds carried out by its followers. Criticized for its anti-intellectualism and the strong sentimental character of its view of the Christian faith, Pietism always had strong opposition; for example, in Württemberg, where it is still present in spite of the vehement and continued resistance from the faculty of theology at the University of Tübingen. The faculties of theology in Wittenberg and Leipzig were anti-Pietist, too, while that of the University of Königsberg was pro-Pietist. That is to say that Pietism created turmoil within religious and secular spheres: not only were theologians and the clergy divided into Pietist and anti-Pietist factions, but parishioners and city councils were as well.

Through its influence and through what it embodies, Pietism has widely surpassed German Protestantism and Lutheranism. It appeared also in the Reformed Church (e.g., in Bremen). Several Pietist tendencies, while condemning infant baptism and promoting adult baptism, resemble Baptist and Puritan concepts. For example, the Brethren churches are a synthesis of Pietism and Anabaptism. With different varieties according to countries and churches (Reformed, Baptist, Methodist, Pentecostal), many elements of Pietism can be found in the different revival movements throughout the history of Protestantism. The same opposition occurred over and over between those who advocated a revival within the established church and those who argued for the need to establish other churches. However, these sensibilities, which advocated a more pious sense of Christianity, subsequently clashed with more liberal and accommodating ones, as well as with orthodox attitudes such as those associated with Lutheranism, Calvinism, Baptism, and so on. All of these were generally alert to religious experience and sensitivity as being the criteria of authentication of the Christian faith. This is true in both doctrinal and moral domains. Today, it can be said that most characteristics of Protestant Pietism are present in Evangelicalism, which emphasizes personal conversion, piety, and a rigorous way of life. Moreover, like Pietism, Evangelicalism is transdenominational. As Martin (2005) wrote, one can trace a genealogy from Pietism to contemporary Pentecostalism.

SEE ALSO: Christianity; Protestantism; Religion

REFERENCES AND SUGGESTED READINGS

Gäbler, U. (Ed.) (2000) *Der Pietismus im neunzehnten und zwanzigsten Jahrhundert. Geschichte des Pietismus* (*Pietism in the Nineteenth and Twentieth Centuries: History of Pietism*), Vol. 3. Vandenhoeck & Ruprecht, Göttingen.

Lehmann, H. (Ed.) (2003) *Glaubenswelt und Lebenswelt des Pietismus* (*Belief-world and Lifeworld of Pietism*), Vol. 4. Vandenhoeck & Ruprecht, Göttingen.

Martin, D. (2005) *On Secularization: Towards a Revised General Theory*. Ashgate, Aldershot.

Strom, J. (2003) Pietism. In: *The Encyclopedia of Protestantism*, Vol. 3. Routledge, New York, pp. 1485–92.

place

Leslie Wasson

The concept of place is used three ways in sociology. First, there is the microsociological concept of place as a material location: a fixed, bounded site which can be identified with a particular set of situated expectations and behaviors. A second use of the term refers to the identification or attachment an individual develops to a particular location, usually geographical, which has an influence on his or her ongoing self-identity. A third use of the term refers to the niche in the social stratification system in which the individual belongs.

It also would be possible to confuse the term place with the very similar term space. However, these are different ideas (Gieryn 2000; Tuan & Hoelscher 2001). Place refers to a specific location in the physical or cultural world and the attributes of that setting or niche. Space refers to the amount of physical or social distance that is maintained among the social actors.

PLACES OF SITUATED INTERACTION OR IDENTITY

In the first use of the term place, much interaction theory rests on the pioneering work of Erving Goffman (1959, 1961, 1963) and his development of dramaturgical theory. Goffman's treatment of social settings as staging areas for the enactment of social scripts demonstrated the importance of places in the social construction of reality. Participant observation or fieldwork studies often contain elements of place or setting as integral framing concepts in their analyses. Place characteristics can have a profound effect on the kind of interaction that will occur. This insight has been influential in architecture and urban planning as well as in sociology (Sommer 1983).

Place can be a predictor variable, but it can also be an outcome variable. People's conception of identities they possess already or aspire to can drive the construction or location of the places they inhabit. Pieces of material culture then become important identity or personal history markers (Csikszentmihalyi & Rochberg-Halton

1981). The desirability of high-status places such as penthouse apartments or the best neighborhoods is another demonstration of the interplay of place and identity.

SENSE OF PLACE OR PLACE ATTACHMENT

In the second sense of place, part of the individual's self-concept may derive from his or her socialization or other experiences in a particular geographical location (Stedman 2002). The individual may express nostalgia or homesickness for the prior location, and link its influence to elements of self or social character in the present (Milligan 1998; Wallwork & Dixon 2004). Oldenburg's *Great Good Place* (1999) might be an example of this pattern, or Milligan's (2003) study of employees in a university coffee shop. Place in this sense is composed of more than just the physical elements of the location. It incorporates also the interpersonal attachments, group identities, or community bonds among those persons routinely interacting in that place.

Place in this second sense can be a key variable in larger studies also. Classical community studies such as Lynd's (1959) study of a medium-sized American city began with a long description of the place and its characteristics before their exposition of human behavior and belief in that location. Likewise, studies such as Rubin's *Worlds of Pain* (1992) or Gans's *The Levittowners* (1992) emphasize the centrality of the physical place and its components for the emergence of certain kinds of community culture within its boundaries.

SOCIAL STATUS AND KNOWING ONE'S PLACE

In its third sense, place is a cultural or social location rather than a physical setting. Having a sense of social place is especially important when a society is highly stratified. Frequently there are elaborate rituals of deference, acknowledgment, and space use associated with the social place of the individual (Creswell 1996). The distribution of access or resources may hinge upon it (Kitchin 1998). Many a comedy or tragedy in fiction and theater has been based on accidents or misunderstandings of social place.

Specific effects of social place on interaction may vary across cultures. Tocqueville reported in *Democracy in America* (2001) his astonishment at the practice of Americans addressing each other boldly as equals, even when the individuals were unknown to one another. He contrasted this brashness with the reserve of the British, whom he described as being reluctant or even unable to converse unless they had been properly introduced, and therefore knew each other's social place and the associated interactive conventions.

SEE ALSO: Dramaturgy; Goffman, Erving; Identity: The Management of Meaning; Levittown; Space

REFERENCES AND SUGGESTED READINGS

Creswell, T. (1996) *In Place/Out of Place: Geography, Ideology, and Transgression.* University of Minnesota Press, Minneapolis.
Csikszentmihalyi, M. & Rochberg-Halton, E. (1981) *The Meaning of Things: Domestic Symbols and the Self.* Cambridge University Press, Cambridge.
Gans, H. (1992) *The Levittowners*, rpt. edn. Columbia University Press, New York.
Gieryn, T. (2000) A Space for Place in Sociology. *Annual Review of Sociology* 26: 463–96.
Goffman, E. (1959) *The Presentation of Self in Everyday Life.* Doubleday, Garden City, NY.
Goffman, E. (1961) *Encounters.* Bobbs-Merrill, Indianapolis.
Goffman, E. (1963) *Behavior in Public Places.* Free Press, New York.
Kitchin, R. (1998) "Out of Place," "Knowing One's Place": Space, Power, and the Exclusion of Disabled People. *Disability and Society* 13(3): 343–56.
Lynd, R. S. (1959) *Middletown: A Study in Modern American Culture.* Harvest/HBJ, New York.
Milligan, M. (1998) Interactional Past and Potential: The Social Construction of Place Attachment. *Symbolic Interaction* 21(1): 1–34.
Milligan, M. (2003) Displacement and Identity Continuity: The Role of Nostalgia in Establishing New Identity Categories. *Symbolic Interaction* 26(3): 381–403.
Nespor, J. (2000) Anonymity and Place in Qualitative Inquiry. *Qualitative Inquiry* 6, 4 (December): 546–69.
Oldenburg, R. (1999) *The Great Good Place: Cafés, Coffee Shops, Bookstores, Bars, Hair Salons, and Other Hangouts at the Heart of a Community*, 3rd edn. Marlowe, New York.
Rubin, L. B. (1992) *Worlds of Pain: Life in the Working-Class Family*, rpt. edn. Basic Books, New York.
Sommer, R. (1983) *Social Design: Creating Buildings with People in Mind.* Prentice-Hall, Englewood Cliffs, NJ.
Stedman, R. C. (2002) Toward a Social Psychology of Place: Predicting Behavior from Place-Based Cognitions, Attitude, and Identity. *Environment and Behavior* 34(5): 561–81.
Tocqueville, A. de (2001) *Democracy in America.* Signet, New York.
Tuan, Y.-F. & Hoelscher, S. (2001) *Space and Place: The Perspective of Experience*, rpt. edn. University of Minnesota Press, Minneapolis.
Wallwork, J. & Dixon, J. A. (2004) Foxes, Green Fields, and Britishness: On the Rhetorical Construction of Place and National Identity. *British Journal of Social Psychology* 43, 1 (March): 21–39.

plastic sexuality

Gail Hawkes

The concept of plastic sexuality is developed theoretically by Anthony Giddens (1993). "Plastic" refers to the malleability of erotic expression, in terms of both individual choice and frameworks of social norms. "Flexible sexuality" is argued to emerge in the context of the social changes in late modernity and postmodernity. It stands in contrast to the features associated with modernist sexuality, conceptualized as fixed, by biology or by social norms. "Fixed sexuality" is associated with the binaries of modernity – either heterosexual or homosexual, either marital (legitimate) or extramarital (illegitimate), either committed or promiscuous, either normal (coital) or perverse (anal, autoerotic, sadomasochistic).

For Giddens, plastic sexuality is the consequence of effective contraception, of the economic and social independence of women that also "liberated" men from the constraints of traditional gender expectations. Plastic sexuality is that which can be shaped according to individual erotic needs and wants. It can also serve as a marker of individual identity and/or as the means by which to make radical sexual demands. Thus, the consequence of disengaging sex from reproduction is to increase the emphasis on pleasure and decrease the emphasis on phallic sexuality.

Giddens's key claim for plastic sexuality is that it is "autonomous" sexuality. It is emancipatory in its positive potential, a potential that is equally representative in the parallel development of a "pure relationship." This is conceptualized as the postmodern prototype of a new form of intimacy. It is "pure" because it is subject primarily to the needs and wants of the individuals involved. It is defined by these needs, and lasts only so long as they are being met by both parties. It may be married and heterosexual but can equally involve same-sex love and intimacy. The correlation between plastic sexuality and the pure relationship is, Giddens argues, partly causal. Through such pure relationships the gender imbalance of power can be neutralized, since the emphasis is on erotic parity and equality of involvement. The place for plastic sexuality in such a relationship is central, since it emphasizes the importance of erotic rights and of the close relationship between erotic expression and individual identity.

Giddens recognizes some limitations to the positive potential of this process. First, that the focus on sexual pleasure does not necessarily defuse the gendered definition of eroticism. He uses pornography, hard and soft, to illustrate how, in this "normalization" of commodified sexual pleasure, the "malleability" of sexual desire and pleasure remains defined through the gaze of the desiring and active man. Second, there may be a tension in the foundation of the pure relationship – equality and parity – and the "rights" implied by the concept of plastic sexuality to adjust one's sexual expression to suit individual needs.

These limitations have been recognized and developed by Lynn Jamieson (1998), who argues that the optimism of Giddens's analysis is overstated. His theory fails to address the persistence of gender and class inequality that militates against the possibility of meaningful engagement with lifestyle choice and individuated self-expression. She cites a range of data gathered in studies of family and intimate relationships in the UK, Australia, and the US that indicate that traditional gendered expectations

persist within the more flexible negotiated forms of intimacy. Jamieson's more pessimistic interpretation of plastic sexuality identifies "rampant self-obsessive individualism" as a destructive rather than a creative dynamic in intimate relationships.

A more optimistic interpretation of plastic sexuality has been developed recently by Bech (1999), Roseneil (2000; Budgeon & Roseneil 2001), and Weeks et al. (2001). These authors ground their optimism in a wider interpretation of the dynamics involved in the concept. Bech (1999) identifies the "normalization" of the homosexual and Roseneil (2000) the destabilizing of the hetero/homosexual binary of modernity. While these works emanate from queer scholarship, their focus is on the fragility of heteronormative categories of sexual and intimate relationships exposed by the positive dynamic involved in the "queering of the social" (Budgeon & Roseneil 2001). Individuals are increasingly making reflexive choices about the role of sexuality and sexual identity that are creating new ways of interacting with or without more traditional notions of "sexuality."

These authors identify the weakening of the "sex/love" bedrock of heteronormative relationships, and instead use research findings to illustrate the replacement of romantic couplings of the heterosexual norm with more flexible and agentic friendship networks that may or may not include sexual intimacy. These new forms of intimacy invest agency and choice that, while empowering individuals, simultaneously create a new social terrain within which to negotiate new forms of intimacy that transcend the former normative distinctions between homosexual and heterosexual relationship priorities and patterns.

SEE ALSO: Bisexuality; Heterosexuality; Homosexuality; Intimacy; Lesbianism; Postmodern Sexualities; Transgender, Transvestism, and Transsexualism

REFERENCES AND SUGGESTED READINGS

Bech, H. (1999) After the Closet. *Sexualities* 2(3): 343–9.

Budgeon, S. & Roseneil, S. (2001) Cultures of Intimacy and Care Beyond "The Family": Friendship and Sexual/Love Relationships in the Twenty-First Century. Online. www.leeds.ac.uk/cava/papers/culturesofintimacy.htm.

Giddens, A. (1993) *The Transformations of Intimacy: Sexuality, Love, and Eroticism in Modern Societies*. Polity Press, Cambridge.

Jamieson, L. (1998) *Intimacy: Personal Relationships in Modern Societies*. Polity Press, Cambridge.

Roseneil, S. (2000) Queer Frameworks and Queer Tendencies: Towards an Understanding of Postmodern Transformations of Sexuality. *Sociological Research Online* 5(3). www.socresonline.org.uk/5/3roseneil.html.

Weeks, J., Heaphy, B., & Donovan, C. (2001) *Same-Sex Intimacies: Families of Choice and Other Life Experiments*. Routledge, London.

play

Thomas Henricks

Within the social sciences, play has been an especially difficult phenomenon to define and study. Some scholars have described play as a pattern of individual behavior or social interaction, which features competition, improvisation, and fantasy. Others have emphasized play as a pattern of experience or awareness. By that standard, some participants in a shared activity may be playing while others are not. Still other researchers have focused on the cultural frameworks or scenes of play, with the understanding that all that happens within those settings should be deemed playful. Such settings frequently include games and sports; gambling; festivals, parties, and masquerades; artistic and musical expression; daydreams; jokes, rhymes, and storytelling; teasing and other forms of disrespect; rough-and-tumble behaviors, dramatic role performances, and adventurous pursuits like caving and skydiving. In that light, many of the daily activities of young children are characterized as play; and playfulness is considered to be an important trait of various species of mammals.

Early theories of play emphasized the unique nature of the activity and posited the functions of play for individual and species survival (see Ellis 1973). Such explanations pointed to play's role in satisfying imitative instincts, training the young, exercising self-restraint, and establishing patterns of dominance and submission. Perhaps the most fully developed portrait of play was offered by the Dutch historian Johan Huizinga in his book *Homo Ludens* (1955). Huizinga characterized play in the following terms. (1) Play is a relatively free or voluntary behavior in which participants set the terms and timing of their involvement. (2) Play differs from routine or ordinary life in that it exhibits few consequences beyond the event itself. (3) Play is secluded or cut off from other activities by the use of curious rules and procedures, equipment, playing spaces, costumes, and definitions of time. (4) Play combines order and disorder in that players frequently create and employ rules to structure their disruptive or creative ventures. (5) Play features the "secret" gathering of people into groups and activities that may be considered outlandish or trivial by others. Although later scholars have challenged aspects of Huizinga's description, his approach remains important because it emphasizes the extent to which play is a general pattern of human expression that can arise in any public or private activity. Moreover, Huizinga argued that play has served significant social functions in the historical development of societies and that it is as important for adults as it is for children.

More recent theories have described the nature of play as a distinctive quality of relationship between individuals and the conditions of their lives (see Sutton-Smith 1997). The developmental psychologist Jean Piaget (1962) argued that play features the conscious effort of people to oppose and manipulate external factors and forces in accordance with their own internal schemes and desires. Through play, children construct and then apply increasingly abstract systems of thought, which they use to comprehend the world and operate within it. In later works, Piaget demonstrated how childhood games are also important contexts for the development of moral reasoning.

This oppositional or assimilative stance of players may be expressed toward cultural objects and patterns (e.g., through inventive processes in science, language, and art), toward aspects of the natural environment (e.g., in forms of physical exploration, assertion, and creativity), and toward social patterns (e.g., through competitions with others, teasing, role play, and status inversion). Play may even focus on the psychological and physical characteristics of the participants themselves (e.g., in tests of endurance, balance, and mental confusion). In such ways, play explores the boundaries of the world and affirms the capabilities of people to comprehend and control that world in their own fashion (see Erikson 1950).

However, play also features significant emotional and relational components. Traditionally, play has been considered to be an activity that people pursue for personal or experiential reasons rather than for external or instrumental purposes. Even when there are clearly defined goals or end-states in play (as in many types of games), these ends are meaningful primarily within the context of the game itself. For such reasons, people at play may feel more deeply focused or engaged – and have stronger feelings of personal control – than they do in other portions of their lives (see Csikszentmihalyi 1990). This search for "optimal" levels of emotional satisfaction or arousal significantly shapes the course of the action. Although play is typically a quite conscious pursuit of sensations and achievements, Freud (1958) emphasized the role of impulsive or even unconscious wishes as determinants of action. These non-rational factors, coupled with the unpredictable resistance and response of the objects that are challenged, tend to give play a dialectical, sometimes mysterious, character (see Sutton-Smith 1997).

Because of the frequently oppositional or even irreverent attitude of its participants, play should be distinguished from more passive forms of diversion and pleasure seeking, such as eating, bathing, and television viewing. Although play often overlaps with leisure and recreation, it is not their equivalent. Unlike other kinds of personal relaxation and rejuvenation, play is typically a search for unusual or even novel challenges that intrigue participants and drive the action forward. In that light, play is sometimes distinguished from more formally controlled activities like ritual and from manipulative, but instrumental, behaviors like work.

Historically, the interdisciplinary study of play has been influenced strongly by researchers in many disciplines. Psychologists and educational researchers have tended to see play in an individualistic and somewhat idealized way. Their studies focus typically on the play of children and emphasize how play contributes to patterns of physical, emotional, and intellectual maturation. Additionally, they have explored the role of adults in guiding the growth and self-awareness of children in school, family, sport, and therapeutic settings.

Folklorists have focused on the play of children alone or in informal groups away from adults (see Sutton-Smith et al. 1995). Through their collections of the stories, songs, jokes, rhymes, and games of children through the centuries, these researchers have emphasized the darker, non-rational side of the experience. In that light, play is a reflection of the persistent tensions of child life and exhibits disruptive, aggressive, and even sexual themes. This emphasis on the special importance of play to young creatures has also been a theme of animal behavior studies.

Anthropologists have focused on the play of adults as well as children in various cultures and subcultures. The close relationship between play and ritual in traditional societies has been well described. In its festive and ceremonial contexts, play activities frequently dramatize prevailing community values and power structures, offer alternative cultural visions, permit the expression of normally forbidden identities and opportunities, and facilitate social bonding among participants in ritual processes (see Handelman 1998).

Sociology has also made important contributions to the study of play by highlighting the dialectical or interactional character of play itself, the social causes and consequences of playful activity, and the ways in which formal organization transforms play. Even more generally, sociologists have emphasized the degree to which social and cultural patterns "frame" playful expression.

George Herbert Mead, one of the founding figures of symbolic interactionism, stressed the concept of role play in explanations of the development of self-concept. In Mead's (1934) analysis of the relationship between thought and action, he argued that people exhibit in their own minds an "internalized conversation of gestures" in which they try to anticipate how certain words and behaviors will be received by others. For Mead then, an important stage of self-development is the "play stage," during which children learn to experience imaginatively and act out dramatically the implications of various roles. This ability to "take the role of the other" is critical to empathetic and informed behavior in the world. A further, more complicated level is the "game stage," in which children examine their standing in social groups involving many persons and roles. In that sense, role-playing games constitute fascinating "social worlds" which players create and explore (see Fine 1983).

Other sociologists pushed forward this view of social life as the interplay of self-interested but culturally aware actors. Erving Goffman created a vision of interaction in general as a kind of information game in which people strategically reveal and conceal clues about their character and intentions to others. Goffman was fascinated by play activities (especially dramas and contests) as metaphors for public behavior; but he was also concerned with the orderliness of play and with the ways in which that activity is framed by cultural devices. In that context, Goffman (1961) analyzed how people create and enforce norms to define the action, protect it from interference, and focus the attention of participants. Among these structures are what he called "transformation rules," devices to help players deal with distractions and interruptions that do arise. In such ways, Goffman argued, play is not so much a spontaneous activity as a clearly understood type of behavior that people anticipate and then perform with assurance. However, the play world is also a delicate "bubble" of social commitments that must be protected and maintained with care.

This view of play as behavioral form was developed most brilliantly by Georg Simmel in an essay on sociability as the "play-form" of association. Simmel (1950) explained that social gatherings like parties or festivals follow their own generally understood logics to which participants submit. For example, guests at a fancy dress party are aware that they should support a collective spirit of generosity, courtesy, and buoyant good will. Matters that are too personal, abstract, or morally urgent should not be central elements of conversations. Moreover, people should appear only as stylized versions of themselves, i.e., in the role of guest

or attendee. For both Simmel and Goffman then, play offered fascinating glimpses of how people construct and maintain social order in settings that are exceedingly fragile and fluid. Furthermore, their shared emphasis on the reserved, fragmentary, and quasi-personal participation of players has been an important correction to psychological approaches.

Other sociologists have emphasized the placement of play within the historically developing context of society itself. For example, Max Weber argued that a hallmark theme of western civilization – the abstract, calculating approach to life he termed "rationalization" – was transforming every aspect of culture including playful and expressive activity. In a book on music, Weber (1958) showed how such cultural inventions as the development of the octave and the movement and fixing of tones within it, systems of written notation, and the standardization of musical instruments led to profound changes in playing. These changes included the development of complicated harmonies, the rise of highly organized "symphonies," and prominent roles for the writers and conductors. In that sense, an older, innovative style of playing became replaced by more precise and merely interpretive styles.

However, Weber was also aware that expressive behavior might develop as a reaction to the wider bureaucratization of culture, as in the case of jazz or other forms of modern music. That view has been developed by other sociologists, including Elias and Dunning (1986), who argued that modern societies are animated by a "quest for excitement" arising from the more socially controlled, purportedly civilized conditions of many people's lives. This issue – whether play activities tend to be reflections of personal and social life or pointed reactions to it – continues to be an important one for the study of play.

By emphasizing the social contexts of play, sociologists have challenged Huizinga's conception of the relative isolation and voluntarism of play. Play activities are frequently sponsored and controlled by social groups pursuing interests different from those of the players. Play in these settings is often colored by external, material incentives. This is especially apparent in the case of games, which represent culturally organized – and often socially competitive – frameworks for playful endeavor. Moreover, access to the playground often is not entirely voluntary or "free" but rather is regulated by a host of economic, social, and political restrictions (see Henricks 1991). Thus, the sociological history of play is as much about processes of exclusion – on the basis of gender, class, race, age, and social affiliation – as it is about the organization and conduct of the participants (see Hargreaves 1994).

Furthermore, sociologists have examined the personal and social consequences of the formal or bureaucratic organization of play. In contrast to most psychologists and educational researchers, sociologists have recognized the negative aspects of highly organized, adult-dominated structures for children's play, especially in the case of youth sport (see Coakley 2004). Under such circumstances, play becomes subordinated to a regime of officials, leagues, record keeping, training procedures, and preoccupations with competitive success. Further complexities are introduced when play becomes display, i.e., when the enjoyment and creative expression of spectators become more important than the event-based satisfactions of the players.

This concern with the role of non-players in managing the expressive life of others has been developed most highly in Marxian sociology and critical theory (see Maguire & Young 2002). That tradition has emphasized that when expressive behavior is reorganized as a commodity, it no longer reflects or rewards the creativity of its producers. In such instances, traditionally playful activities – such as music, art, sport, or sexual expression – reappear as alienated forms of experience. Furthermore, the highly publicized, spectatorial forms of play may promote various social problems – including the encouragement of artificial allegiances and rivalries, misdirection of collective creativity, and the undermining of broader cooperative visions.

Despite these considerable accomplishments, the sociological study of play continues to be hindered by a commonplace view of that activity as trivial, evanescent, and inconsequential – something more for children than adults. This is surprising in light of the now established understanding that many societies have moved into an advanced industrial stage in which personal expression and leisure activity are central

elements. In that context, it should be noted that postmodernist scholars in literature and philosophy have posited play as a central metaphor of contemporary life (see Spariosu 1989). Like players, people in postmodern settings are said to assert themselves provisionally, continually refashion their identities, and savor what satisfactions they can in cultural contexts characterized by fragmentary and transient meanings.

Future studies of play must return to the challenges set forth by Huizinga more than a half century ago. At one level, this means understanding the nature of play within a more general theory of human expression. Like work and ritual, play is one of the fundamental forms of human behavior; and the responsibility of sociology, as a human science, is to comprehend the meaning of such activity for personal and public identity. Furthermore, Huizinga's ambition to understand the different ways in which play has been organized historically as well as its functioning in different types of societies remains uncompleted. Finally, studies of play among various categories of people (distinguished by gender, class, age, etc.) and in different contexts (e.g., sports, casinos, amusement parks, video games, playgrounds) must become the basis of a more comprehensive and differentiated understanding of that phenomenon.

SEE ALSO: Goffman, Erving; Leisure; Mead, George Herbert; Play Stage; Postmodernism; Simmel, Georg; Sport; Weber, Max

REFERENCES AND SUGGESTED READINGS

Coakley, J. (2004) *Sports in Society: Issues and Controversies*. McGraw-Hill, New York.

Csikszentmihalyi, M. (1990) *Flow: The Psychology of Optimal Experience*. Harper & Row, New York.

Elias, N. & Dunning, E. (1986) *The Quest for Excitement in the Civilizing Process*. Blackwell, Oxford.

Ellis, M. J. (1973) *Why People Play*. Prentice-Hall, Englewood Cliffs, NJ.

Erikson, E. (1950) *Childhood and Society*. Norton, New York, ch. 6.

Fine, G. (1983) *Shared Fantasy: Role-Playing Games as Social Worlds*. University of Chicago Press, Chicago.

Freud, S. (1958) *On Creativity and the Unconscious: Papers on the Psychology of Art, Literature, Love, and Religion*. Ed. B. Nelson. Harper & Row, New York.

Goffman, E. (1961) *Encounters: Two Studies in the Sociology of Interaction*. Bobbs-Merrill, Indianapolis.

Handelman, D. (1998) *Models and Mirrors: Toward an Anthropology of Public Events*. Berghahn, New York.

Hargreaves, J. (1994) *Sporting Females: Critical Issues in the History and Sociology of Women's Sports*. Routledge, New York.

Henricks, T. (1991) *Disputed Pleasures: Sport and Society in Preindustrial England*. Greenwood Press, Westport, CT.

Huizinga, J. (1955) *Homo Ludens: A Study of the Play Element in Culture*. Beacon Press, Boston.

Maguire, J. & Young, K. (Eds.) (2002) *Theory, Sport, and Society*. JAI Press, New York.

Mead, G. H. (1934) *Mind, Self, and Society*. University of Chicago Press, Chicago.

Piaget, J. (1962) *On Play, Dreams, and Imitation in Childhood*. Norton, New York.

Simmel, G. (1950) *The Sociology of Georg Simmel*. Trans. and Ed. K. Wolff. Free Press, New York.

Spariosu, M. (1989) *Dionysus Reborn: Play and the Aesthetic Dimension in Modern Philosophical and Literary Discourse*. Cornell University Press, Ithaca, NY.

Sutton-Smith, B. (1997) *The Ambiguity of Play*. Harvard University Press, Cambridge, MA.

Sutton-Smith, B., Mechling, J., Johnson, T., & McMahon, F. (1995) *Children's Folklore: A Source Book*. Garland, New York.

Weber, M. (1958) *The Rational and Social Foundations of Music*. Trans. D. Martindale et al. Scribner, New York.

play stage

D. Angus Vail

The play stage is one of the three central components of George Herbert Mead's seminal discussion of the social foundation and development of the self. According to Mead, the self has a social genesis which becomes evident if one examines the ways that people develop a sense for their own being as something separate from, but also interdependent with, other people. In essence, the self is situated in the individual's capacity to take account of him/herself. By examining children's styles of play, followed by the games they play, one can see how they develop a capacity to take into account not just the role of a singular other person, but also eventually the roles of many people simultaneously. It is only once a person has reached this stage of development that she or he is said to have developed a complete self. Mead (1962 [1934]: 150, 152–4) first addressed the stage of development he called the play stage.

Mead's discussion of the play stage begins with his assertion that children at this stage *play at* specific roles rather than enacting complex relationships. Thus, a child at this stage *plays at* roles of a significant person such as a police officer or nurse or parent. In playing at these roles, children mold their behavior to the set of roles that they tend to associate with the target of their play. Thus, in playing at being a parent, they may send a bad Barbie or GI Joe to her or his room for being naughty. In playing at being another person, they do not have to take account of the varying, divergent, and malleable roles that may become more visible in group settings. According to Mead, this suggests that the child has yet to develop a full sense of his or her effect on social settings. It also suggests that the child is capable of taking the role of the other and is thus coming to realize that she or he is a social animal. It further suggests that the child is developing a capacity to take account of him/herself.

The nature of playing at a particular role also has a temporal character to it. It involves the child's switching alternately between the role of the other and his or her self. Borrowing from Mead, when a child plays "store," she may "pay" for her groceries while playing at being the customer and subsequently "give change" while playing at being a clerk. The temporal structure of these interactions follows a fairly strict sequential order. Thus, a child at this stage of development is not likely to play at the transaction being interrupted by an irate customer returning smashed eggs; nor will she play at the next clerk showing up for a shift change. Such behavior would require too much subtlety and too far advanced skills at taking the roles of several, if not many, people at the same time. Mead suggests that such skills only become apparent in the subsequent game stage of development when the child develops a more sophisticated sense of the rules that govern interactions.

SEE ALSO: Mead, George Herbert; Game Stage; Generalized Other; Play; Preparatory Stage; Role; Self

REFERENCES AND SUGGESTED READINGS

Blumer, H. (2004) *George Herbert Mead and Human Conduct*. Alta Mira Press, Walnut Creek, CA.

Mead, G. H. (1962 [1934]) *Mind, Self, and Society: From the Standpoint of a Social Behaviorist*. University of Chicago Press, Chicago.

Meltzer, B. N. (1959) *The Social Psychology of George Herbert Mead*. Center for Sociological Research, Kalamazoo, MI.

Meltzer, B. N., Petras, J. W., & Reynolds, L. T. (1975) *Symbolic Interactionism: Genesis, Varieties, and Criticism*. Routledge & Kegan Paul, Boston.

Weigert, A. J. & Gecas, V. (2004) Self. In: Reynolds, L. T. & Herman-Kinney, N. J. (Eds.), *Handbook of Symbolic Interactionism*. Alta Mira, New York, pp. 267–88.

Playboy

Kim MacInnis

Playboy is a magazine founded by Hugh Hefner in 1953 when Hefner was 26 years old. The magazine was initially created under the company name HMH Publishing Co., Inc., and then went public under the name Playboy Enterprises, Inc. in 1971. *Playboy*'s original name was to be "Stag Party," but an outdoor magazine called *Stag* contacted Hefner and informed him of their trademark name. Hefner's co-founder and executive vice president Eldon Seller suggested the name *Playboy*, based on a Playboy Automobile Company in Chicago. The first issue of *Playboy* was published in December 1953. The issue sold for $0.50 and was an immediate success, selling out in a few weeks.

Known circulation was 53,991. According to Hefner, *Playboy* was influenced by the Jazz Age, his strict Midwestern Methodist upbringing, and a response to the post-war period, which was described as socially and politically repressive. Additionally, the magazine was inspired by the Kinsey Reports, which focused on the study of sexuality in the United States in 1948. These reports revealed that many Americans were not as conventional as society believed concerning sexual behavior. The Kinsey Reports helped to promote sexual openness. Many scholars such as Kenon Breazeale and Barbara Ehrenreich contend that *Playboy* was inspired by male sociosexual identity crises. Ehrenreich argues that in the 1950s American men revolted against their most prominent role as breadwinner, which largely defined male identity. Men, she contended, needed more than responsibility in their lives, they needed desire. Whether or not Hugh Hefner agreed with this particular assessment, he created the magazine for men.

The *Playboy* logo depicting a profile of a rabbit wearing a bowtie was created by art designer Art Paul for the second issue and is the established trademark. *Playboy* reached its peak in the 1970s with a paid circulation of more than 7 million but has experienced a decline in circulation mainly because of increased competition from *Penthouse* and more current magazines, *Maxim* and *FHM*. The bestselling issue of *Playboy* was the November 1972 issue, which sold 7,161,561 copies. The centerfold was Leno Soderberg and the cover featured the principles of Dharma Art.

Christie Hefner, the daughter of Hugh Hefner, has been the chairperson and chief executive officer for Playboy Enterprises since 1981. She became CEO of *Playboy* in 1988. Playboy Enterprises is located on the 15th and 16th floors of 680 N. Lake Shore Drive, Chicago. Playboy is comprised of many facets or divisions. The company has a publishing group responsible for *Playboy Magazine* and Playboy Newsstand Specials. It has an entertainment group responsible for Playboy TV and Spice Television. Playboy Enterprises is a licensing group handling Playboy trademarks on apparel and accessories as well as an online group responsible for Playboy Online, PlayboyStore.

com, Playboy Cyber Club, Playboy Plus, and Playboy.net. Finally, Playboy Enterprises enjoys a College Division responsible for promoting Playboy on Campus. Interestingly enough, the National Library Service for the Blind and Physically Handicapped has published a braille edition of *Playboy* since 1970. This edition includes all the written words in the non-braille magazines but no image representations.

Playboy is an adult entertainment magazine characterized as "softcore" pornography. *Playboy* is one of the world's best-known magazines published worldwide; however, it is not welcome everywhere. In most parts of Asia (including China, South Korea, India, Malaysia, Thailand, Taiwan, Singapore, and Brunei) *Playboy* is banned. In the United States, the convenience store chain *7-Eleven* removed the magazine from its stores in 1986. The store resumed selling the magazine in 2003. The magazine is published monthly and features articles on sport, fashions, consumer goods, and fiction as well as photographs of nude women. Politically, the magazine generally posits a liberal stance on social issues. More than 50 percent of the women featured in *Playboy* are blondes. The first centerfold for *Playboy* was Marilyn Monroe in 1953. Since then there have been a wide variety of celebrities, including sports figures, movie stars, singers, and television stars. Some include Drew Barrymore (January 1995), Charlize Theron (May 1999), Farrah Fawcett (December 1995 and July 1997), women of *Baywatch* (June 1998), Katarina Witt (December 1998), Gabrielle Reece (January 2001), Nancy Sinatra (May 1995), and Debbie Gibson (March 2005).

Sociologically speaking, theoretical stances on *Playboy* vary. Feminist and legal scholar Catharine MacKinnon characterizes *Playboy* as a form of pornography. To paraphrase, she defines pornography as the graphic, sexually explicit subordination of women, whether in pictures or in words: women are presented as dehumanized sexual objects. MacKinnon would argue that *Playboy* fits the bill as far as dehumanizing women in sexual ways is concerned. Additionally, she contends that all pornography encourages and promotes violence against women. Martha Nussbaum criticizes *Playboy* on the grounds that it dehumanizes and sexually objectifies women. She argues that

women are presented as mere objects for sexual enjoyment and are generally valued for little else. Virginia Sapiro examines this argument in *Women in American Society* (2003). She examines the contention by feminist critics that violence against women is central to dominant male definitions of the erotic and that pornography essentially establishes dominance over women. Sapiro claims that very few studies substantiate these claims that pornographic materials may be a contributing factor to violence against women. Alan Soble in *Pornography, Sex, and Feminism* (2002) argues against these claims, basically stating that many feminists are imposing their own perceptions of sexual enjoyment on *Playboy*. Soble claims there is no definitive evidence that *Playboy* causes harm to women. First Amendment critics would be opposed to feminist claims of sexual objectivity, stating that women are free to express themselves in any form they wish, as are corporations that specialize in portrayals of sexuality and the erotic. First Amendment arguments abound in any discussion of pornography and *Playboy* will likely remain in business as long as it is protected by the First Amendment and supported by the American public.

SEE ALSO: Body and Sexuality; Feminism; Gender, the Body and; Gender Oppression; Kinsey, Alfred; Popular Culture; Pornography and Erotica

REFERENCES AND SUGGESTED READINGS

Andersen, M. L. (2006) *Thinking About Women: Sociological Perspectives on Sex and Gender*, 7th edn. Pearson, Boston.

Breazeale, K. (1994) In Spite of Women: *Esquire* Magazine and the Construction of the Male Consumer. *Journal of Women in Culture and Society* 20 (1): 1–21.

Macionis, J. J. (2002) *Society: The Basics*, 6th edn. Prentice-Hall, Upper Saddle River, NJ.

Renzetti, C. M. & Bergen, R. K. (Eds.) (2005) *Violence Against Women*. Rowman & Littlefield, Lanham, MD.

Sapiro, V. (2003) *Women in American Society*, 5th edn. McGraw-Hill, Boston.

Soble, A. (2002) *Pornography, Sex, and Feminism*. Prometheus, Amherst, NY.

plural society

John Rex

Many of the societies which have problems of multicultural governance are former multiethnic colonies. A theory of such colonial and postcolonial societies draws particularly on the work of J. S. Furnivall and M. G. Smith. According to Furnivall, different ethnic groups in a plural society meet only in the marketplace. This marketplace, however, lacks the characteristics which Durkheim envisaged in his concept of organic solidarity. It lacks the shared values which organic solidarity requires and involves brutal conflict and exploitation. The sense of solidarity on which morality depends is to be found within the different ethnic groups when they go home from the marketplace. Within these groups there is intense solidarity and moral unity. Furnivall worked in Burma but wrote about Java, drawing on the research of Dutch economic theorist Boeke. Boeke wrote that in the economy of Netherlands India "there is a materialism, rationalism and individualism and a concentration on economic ends far more complete and absolute than in homogeneous Western lands" (quoted in Furnivall 1939: 452). As he sees it, this is a capitalism quite different from that which grew slowly over hundreds of years and maintained its moral roots.

M. G. Smith wrote originally about Grenada but his theory of the plural society has been widely used in the analysis of colonial and postcolonial societies in the Caribbean. Smith is aware of the general sociological theory of Talcott Parsons and its assumption of four mutually supportive institutions. In the Caribbean, however, he argues that there are several coexisting ethnic groups, each of which has a nearly complete set of social institutions. Setting his argument within the context of a review of social anthropological theories used in studying the Caribbean, he sees the various ethnic groups as having their own family systems, their own productive economies, their own languages and religion, but not their own political system. In the political sphere they are all controlled by one dominant segment. To put this in more concrete terms, blacks are

descended from slaves, Indians from indentured laborers. The groups have remained distinct and have their own institutions. They exist, however, politically under the domination of an outside power. Thus the defining feature of a plural society is seen as this process of the domination of all ethnic groups by the colonial power. New problems arise when the colonial power withdraws. Whereas Furnivall sees the different ethnic groups as bound together by the economic fact of the marketplace, Smith sees them as bound together by a political institution, the colonial state.

One crucial institution in the Caribbean was the slave plantation. The history of plantations is traced by Max Weber in his *General Economic History* to the manor. But the Caribbean slave plantation comes into existence when capitalism directs horticultural production to the market. Similar developments occur in mining. M. G. Smith's theory has to take account of this. In fact, he sees the plantation as one form of political institution. Smith collaborated with the South African Leo Kuper in producing a series of essays on Africa and also turned his attention to the United States in his book *Corporations and Society*. The case of South Africa is of special interest, calling for an analysis of a society based upon rural labor migrating to the gold mines. The United States has developed as neither homogeneous nor plural but heterogeneous.

Smith has to deal with the question of social class. This is easy enough for he has only to say that each group has its own internal class structure. He does, however, have to compare his own theory to that of Marx. He cannot accept that group formation occurs between those having the same or different relations to the means of production, nor that "in the social production of the means of life men enter into circumstances which are independent of their will." For Smith the culture of ethnic groups in a plural society is not simply determined in this way. The plural segments in colonial society operate according to a different dynamic which it is the purpose of plural society theory to explain.

Rex has attempted to set out a theory of the plural society which does justice to Marxian and other theories as well as those of Smith. This involves first of all recognizing that such societies go through several phases of development, precolonial, colonial, and postcolonial. In the colonial phase relations to the means of production are important, even though they are more varied than Marxist categories suggest, involving such structures as the encomienda in Spanish America. At the same time, however, groups have a relationship to each other reminiscent of the medieval estate system in Europe, different groups having the cultures, rights, and privileges which attach to their function. In the postcolonial phase there would be, according to this theory, a number of developments. One would be the subordination of peasants to the large estates or *latifundia*, a second would be the replacement of the former colonial power by a group able to take over its powers, a third would be a change in which new, primarily economic centers replaced the colonial power. So far as resistance and struggle within the new system are concerned, Fanonism lays emphasis upon the national struggle, which would take precedence over class struggle.

The application of plural society theory to capitalist societies based upon mining produces a different set of problems. There rural agricultural reserves are expected to provide social backup so that males of working age can live in segregated compounds or locations and be intensively exploited. This is a situation very much like that described by Furnivall.

SEE ALSO: Apartheid and Nelson Mandela; Colonialism (Neocolonialism); Conflict (Racial/Ethnic); Decolonization; Indigenous Movements; Multiculturalism; Pluralism, American; Pluralism, British

REFERENCES AND SUGGESTED READINGS

Durkheim, É. (1933) *The Division of Labor in Society.* Free Press, Glencoe, IL.
Furnivall, J. S. (1939) *Netherlands India.* Cambridge University Press, Cambridge.
Rex, J. (1981) A Working Paradigm for Race Relations Research. *Ethnic and Racial Studies* 4(1): 1–25.
Smith, M. G. (1964) *Corporations and Society.* Duckworth, London.
Smith, M. G. (1965) *The Plural Society in the British West Indies.* University of California Press, Berkeley and Los Angeles.
Smith, M. G. & Kuper, L. (1969) *Pluralism in Africa.* University of California Press, Berkeley and Los Angeles.
Weber, M. (1961) *General Economic History.* Collier Books, New York.

pluralism, American

Joseph Gerteis

Pluralism refers to the condition of living amid diversity and also to a positive appreciation for that condition. The many similar metaphors describing America as a "melting pot" of different cultures or a "nation of nations" recognize both the historical fact of diversity and its role in shaping the American national character (see Kohn 1961). "What then is the American, this new man?" asked Jean de Crèvecoeur in an often-quoted passage from *Letters from an American Farmer* (1782): "He is either a European or the descendent of a European, hence that strange mixture of blood, which you will find in no other country ... Here individuals are melted into a new race of men, whose labours and posterity will one day cause great changes in the world" (cited in Gleason 1980: 33).

Crèvecoeur emphasized both ethnic difference and cultural solidarity. From the many come *one*; into the melting pot go many different elements, but out comes a single, homogenized alloy. However clearly this new, emergent solidarity appears in such formulations, it has never been taken for granted. The fact of difference has always been central to the American national self-image, yet there has also been a persistent tension between the recognition and appreciation of difference and a desire for a coherent national culture. By 1915, Horace Kallen painted this tension as one of the central issues for American society in his essay "Democracy Versus the Melting Pot."

Conceptually, pluralism and assimilation have thus been defined against one another, however much they have coincided in practice. Assimilation – or "Americanization" in an older language – deals with difference by insisting that newcomers or outsiders blend into the dominant society. It should be said that this does not necessarily constitute a rejection of those who are different so much as a rejection of the cultural differences that they bring; it insists on a common cultural "core" shared by all members of the society (Alexander 2001; see, e.g., Schlesinger 1991; Huntington 2004). From the pluralist viewpoint, cultural difference is something to appreciate on its own terms. In the past two decades, the term "multiculturalism" has come into vogue as a way to describe the multilayered social differences that are so obvious in modern life as well as the demands for recognition that have surrounded them. At the same time, the modern debate over multiculturalism is simply the latest incarnation of this longstanding tension.

The successive waves of immigration have been at the center of this tension. In a review essay, Gary Gerstle (1997) has pointed out that while an early generation of immigration scholarship emphasized cultural incorporation and assimilation, newer work has accentuated the difficulties that have always gone along with the religious, ethnic, and cultural differences that immigration brings. Whichever way the scholarly literature has blown, this balance between difference and solidarity has always been fragile.

Early on, a figure such as Benjamin Franklin could praise plurality in the abstract as part of the national character, and yet complain privately about German immigrants to Pennsylvania who he thought to be unassimilable. "This will in a few Years become a German Colony: Instead of their Learning our Language, we must learn theirs, or live as in a foreign country," he wrote (cited in Kohn 1961: 143). Later waves of European immigrants were themselves initially seen as problematic, but within a few generations they were often accepted as "white" (Jacobson 1998; Barrett & Roediger 2002). Other groups have posed a more enduring problem for the assimilationist paradigm. Hostility toward Chinese immigrants was manifest in sharp cultural and legal forms of exclusion (see Takaki 2000). Gunnar Myrdal and his co-authors noted the contradiction between the "American creed" of freedom and equality and the blatantly unequal treatment of African Americans as the most obvious challenge; this discrepancy remains a central problem for

modern debates (Myrdal 1996 [1944]; Glazer 1997).

Although pluralism has been broadly defined in opposition to assimilation, it is worth noting that at least three different models of pluralism have been put forward in the scholarly literature (Hartmann & Gerteis 2005). Perhaps the most commonly referenced types are what might be termed "cosmopolitan" and "fragmented" models. Both place much less emphasis than does the assimilationist paradigm on a common cultural "core" that must be shared by all. The difference is that the fragmented version emphasizes instead the different, discrete cultures of the society's component groups (Portes & Rumbaut 2001). The cosmopolitan version does not focus on cultural constraints but instead on the openness and voluntary nature of both group affiliation and personal identity in a "hyphenated" society (Walzer 1990; Hollinger 2000). A third "interactive" model insists on recognition of group differences but also that a new form of solidarity might emerge as such differences are incorporated (Alexander 2001; Taylor 2004). In turn, the nature of the common cultural core is itself transformed.

SEE ALSO: Acculturation; *American Dilemma, An* (Gunnar Myrdal); Assimilation; Ethnicity; Melting Pot; Multiculturalism; Plural Society; Pluralism, British; Race; Race (Racism)

REFERENCES AND SUGGESTED READINGS

Alexander, J. C. (2001) Theorizing the "Modes of Incorporation." *Sociological Theory* 19(3): 237–49.

Barrett, J. & Roediger, D. R. (2002) Inbetween Peoples: Race, Nationality, and the "New Immigrant" Working Class. In: Roediger, D. R., *Colored White: Transcending the Racial Past*. University of California Press, Berkeley, pp. 138–68.

Gerstle, G. (1997) Liberty, Coercion, and the Making of Americans. *Journal of American History*: 524–58.

Glazer, N. (1997) *We Are All Multiculturalists Now*. Harvard University Press, Cambridge, MA.

Gleason, P. (1980) American Identity and Americanization. In: Thernstrom, S., Orlov, A., & Handlin, O. (Eds.), *Harvard Encyclopedia of American Ethnic Groups*. Belknap Press of Harvard University, Cambridge, MA, pp. 31–58.

Hartmann, D. & Gerteis, J. (2005) Dealing With Diversity: Mapping Multiculturalism in Sociological Terms. *Sociological Theory* 23(2): 218–40.

Hollinger, D. A. (2000) *Post-Ethnic America: Beyond Multiculturalism*, rev. edn. Basic Books, New York.

Huntington, S. (2004) *Who Are We? The Challenges to America's National Identity*. Simon & Schuster, New York.

Jacobson, M. F. (1998) *Whiteness of a Different Color: European Immigrants and the Alchemy of Race*. Harvard University Press, Cambridge, MA.

Kallen, H. M. (1915) Democracy Versus the Melting Pot. *Nation* 100(2590): 190–7 (Part 1); 100(2591): 217–20 (Part 2).

Kohn, H. (1961) *American Nationalism: An Interpretive Essay*. Collier Books, New York.

Myrdal, G. (1996 [1944]) *An American Dilemma: The Negro Problem and Modern Democracy*. With the assistance of R. Sterner & A. Rose. New introduction by S. Bok. Transaction, New Brunswick, NJ.

Portes, A. & Rumbaut, R. G. (2001) *Legacies: The Story of the Immigrant Second Generation*. University of California Press, Berkeley.

Schlesinger, A., Jr. (1991) *The Disuniting of America: Reflections on a Multicultural Society*. Norton, New York.

Takaki, R. (2000) *Iron Cages: Race and Culture in 19th-Century America*. Oxford University Press, New York.

Taylor, C. (2004) The Politics of Recognition. In: *Multiculturalism and "The, Politics of Recognition": An, Essay by Charles, Taylor.*, With commentary by A., Guttman (Ed.), S. C. Rockefeller, M. Walzer, & S. Wolf. Princeton University Press, Princeton, pp. 25–73.

Walzer, M. (1990) What Does it Mean to be "American"? *Social Research* 57(3): 591–614.

pluralism, British

Trevor Hogan

The civil societies of most modern nation-states in the world today are "pluralist" if by this we mean the linguistic, ethnic, and subjective dimensions of culture. Cultural definitions of pluralism, however, address neither social factors of hierarchy, status, and power nor the politics of managing cultural difference and diversity in representative democracies. Communal democracies (like Malaysia) are different to the pluralist liberal democracies of the new

world such as Canada and Australia. Arguments about political pluralism as normative goal and practice have largely emanated from liberal democratic societies. British and American pluralism are the two leading examples across the last century.

British pluralism is a critique of the authority and structure of the modern state. American pluralism, in contrast, is a theory of political competition in which organized interest groups seek, but cannot attain, a monopoly of state power. American pluralism as theory and practice is more widely known and debated across the globe, especially during the post-World War II and Cold War period (see especially Robert A. Dahl). British political pluralism, however, in its proposals for the dispersal of the modern state, arguably offers more succor to those committed to the extension of liberal democracy.

British pluralism first emerged as a radical current of thought amongst socialists, Christians, anarchists, and social liberals between 1880 and 1920, partly in response to the rise of the labor and cooperative movements and the challenge of managing an emergent representative democracy that was also the most extensive and largest empire in world history. Key thinkers included the legal theorist and historian F. W. Maitland, the philosopher John Neville Figgis, and the social and political theorists Harold Laski and G. D. H. Cole. Whilst very different thinkers in style and focus, they shared a common interest in law, political institutions, and theory, and in practical forms of social life and democracy. They combined historical arguments (pluralists were important for reviving an understanding of medieval law and forms of civic association in Britain and in continental Europe) and a philosophical defense of civil society vis-à-vis a theory of the state. In particular they were wary of the capacity of states to become tyrannical even in representative democratic societies and were critical of the logic of the will of the majority. The epicurean, Christian socialist monk Figgis, in particular, showed that, in both sociohistorical and analytical terms, the state is derivative of the politics of association, and not vice versa. That is, the state does not grant license to social organizations but rather must codify its laws in such a way as to protect the rights of political association over and against the state's obligation to abstract entities such as "the people" (collective and individual). Group life is intrinsic to individual welfare and precedes it both in practical and in ideal terms. Both Cole and Laski endeavored to show how state power could be dispersed to reflect not only territorial but also functional needs at all levels of the life of society in ways that reflect the specific and diverse interests of citizens.

British pluralism, as a movement and research program, was obliterated in the 1920s and 1930s partly because of its own failed experiments in guild socialism and social credit schemes, but also by the Great Depression and the rise of communist, fascist, and social democratic ideologies and governments. It remained in obscurity until the late twentieth century, when the Oxford political scientist, Anglican priest, and Christian socialist David Nicholls (1994 [1975]) first began to recover its arguments. It was Paul Q. Hirst, the post-Marxist social and political theorist at Birkbeck College, London, however, who most clearly developed political pluralism for contemporary reappraisal in the last two decades of the twentieth century. After putting the first generation of British pluralists back into print in *The Pluralist Theory of the State* (1989), Hirst developed a political pluralist critique of representative democracy in *Representative Democracy and its Limits* (1990), and then constructed a positive set of principles, policies, and programs for developing political pluralism as a viable and workable option in modern complex societies in *Associative Democracy* (1994; see also Cohen & Rogers 1995). In this retrieval and extension of the arguments of the first generation of British pluralists, we have the agenda of a theory and research program that is ripe for development, but – in the absence of a contemporary equivalent of labor and cooperative and mutualist associations – it is still a program without agents and institutions.

SEE ALSO: Civil Society; Democracy; Nation-State; Pluralism; Pluralism, American; State

REFERENCES AND SUGGESTED READINGS

Cohen, J. & Rogers, J. (Eds.) (1995) *Associations and Democracy*. Verso, London.

Hirst, P. Q. (Ed. & Intro.) (1989) *The Pluralist Theory of the State: Selected Writings of G. D. H. Cole, J. N. Figgis, and H. J. Laski*. Routledge, London.

Hirst, P. Q. (1990) *Representative Democracy and its Limits*. Polity Press, Cambridge.

Hirst, P. Q. (1994) *Associative Democracy: New Forms of Economic and Social Governance*. University of Massachusetts Press, Amherst.

Nicholls, D. (1994 [1975]) *The Pluralist State: The Political Ideas of J. N. Figgis and his Contemporaries*, 2nd edn. Macmillan, London.

poetics, social science

Ivan Brady

Poetics in an Aristotelian sense is a system of normative rules for composition. A more practical and theoretically useful definition is to see poetics as a collection of choices concerning style, composition, and thematics made at different levels by an author or a group (Hallyn 1990: 14). These choices help to determine (and are determined by) aesthetic and related representational interests in speech or writing, or both, that is, by *poesis* – the cognitive process of "being" and "doing" in variable contexts, a dynamic and reflexive process of construction, selection, and representation. The composite is an action plan for constructing the work. Putting it into place in the social sciences begs several problems simultaneously, including the place of aesthetic interests in the subject matter traditionally corralled by social scientists, the points of entry into research, and the visibility of the authors in representations.

A careful study of both conventional scientific inquiry (with its distancing methods) and the more immersive and subjective techniques of artisan frameworks, including poetics, shows that nothing we say can be nested in the entirely new; that the field of experience and representation is by definition both culturally cluttered and incomplete for all of us at some level. Scientific inquiry can help us sort this clutter more or less dispassionately, giving us a glimpse of patterned relationships among things and behaviors. But even when that is done to the best advantage, the results are still in the last analysis plural, imperfect, and impermanent. Meanings change with changing perceptions of environmental circumstances, and science does not cover that well. Science does not give us ordinary reality, the world we live in *as* we live it through our senses and our culturally programmed intellects. Self-conscious immersion has a better chance of getting at a realistic account of such experiences primarily because of its devotion to sensuous particulars. Poets are potentially expert *re-presenters* who offer comparative experiences in a commonly held domain, that of the active body itself, and the ultimate aim of poetic expression is to touch the universal through the particular – to evoke and enter into discourse about the sublime, to move the discourse to what defines us all, what we share as human beings. Poetry is necessarily about all of us.

Poetry is also perhaps the most conspicuous or unexpected form for representing aesthetic, social, and ethnographic concerns in the social sciences. It can be verse or prose, of course, and it is not by any means confined to entertainment interests. No subject is beyond its reach, internal or external, in the life of the mind or the quotidian realities of whole societies (e.g., see Brady 2003a; Hartnett 2003; Hartnett & Engels 2005). This argument applies to everything we think and do – to every interpretation (and therefore every representation), from the maskings of rituals to the revelations of things in dreams – from cradle to grave, everything, every waking moment. Bracketed against more scientific modes of inquiry and representation, poetry shows itself as another way to encode and share the foundations of such experiences. It can ground theories of the world that actually involve interactions with it, not just abstractions from it. Instead of writing or talking exclusively about their experiences through abstract concepts, as one might do in applying productive scientific theory, trying to make language as invisible as possible while focusing on the objects of scientific expressions, poets report more concretely, *in* and *with* the facts and frameworks of what they see in themselves *in relation to* Others, in particular landscapes, emotional and social situations. They aim for representation from one self-conscious interiority to another in a manner that flags the language used as proprietary, finds the strange in the everyday, and takes us out of ourselves for a moment to show us something about ourselves in principle if not in precisely reported fact, thereby contributing at one level or another to the whole of our knowledge about any experience.

Because multiple interpretations of the same phenomena are always possible, it follows that any theory that purports to explain or predict everything about particular human behaviors is not actually attainable, at least not by consensus. Methodological pluralism is the key to robust accounts in the social sciences today, especially where an exclusive focus on behavior gives way to the relationship between behavior and meaning as the object of study (Brady 1998). There will always be a plurality or "surplus" of meaning in what we experience, classify, or otherwise try to explain. We can also come to know these things in many ways (Brady 1991, 2003a, 2004, 2005). No single method or genre of thought can conquer it all. The problem is choosing among the alternatives – or worse, having someone choose for you, as a matter of convention, applying political pressure to standardize your work according to the "received" view of social science methods, journals, and funding agencies. That undermines creativity by setting arbitrary limits on both research and reporting modes. Moreover, since every newly established interpretation becomes in its appearance and recognition a source for a new reading, a reopening, the role of the observer (reader, interpreter, writer) in the analytic equation cannot realistically be avoided.

It follows that close interpretations of speech, written texts, or whole societies must be infused at some level with self-conscious accountability for satisfactory results, that is, with *more than* scientific forms of interpretation. Among other considerations, there is a need for cultivating the actor's point of view, ours as observers and participants, and, insofar as it can ever be ascertained, that of the people we study. This is consistent with the need to discover and examine critically all of the ways a subject can be represented. In that diversity the social science poet finds a measure of truth. Unafraid of sensual immersions, subjectivities, mutual constructions of meaningful relationships, political accountability, authorial presence in texts, and sometimes deliberately fictionalized realities that "ring true," poetic rendering is more than another way of telling (writing or speaking). It is another way of interpreting and therefore of knowing the nature of the world and our place in it, some of which is not available to the same extent, in the same form, or at all through other means (Brady 2003a, 2003b, 2004). Privileging one form to the exclusion of the other as Truth for all purposes is to be satisfied not only with one tool for all jobs, but also with the politics of the moment, in and out of the academy. Softening or solving such problems (e.g., by reaching beyond analytic categories whose only reality lies in the minds and agreements of the researchers themselves) matters if we are ever going to get a handle on the realities of the people we study – the universe *they* know, interpret, and act in as sentient beings. These things escape only at great cost to understanding ourselves, how we are articulated socially and semiotically, how we construct our Selves as meaningful entities, in our own minds and in relation to each other, and what that contributes to acting responsibly on a shrinking planet.

For these reasons and others, the entrance point for modern ethnography and related kinds of studies is probably best served by some combination of humanistic and scientific designs – in the realm of "artful science" (Brady 1991, 2000, 2004). At the center of this methodological pool are two prospects put nicely in a plea from cognitive scientist Raymond Gibbs, Jr., namely, learning to recognize the poet in each of us and cultivating the simple fact that *"figuration is not an escape from reality but constitutes the way we ordinarily understand ourselves and the world in which we live"* (1994: 454, emphasis added), no matter what the discipline. Conjectural mentalities and metaphor itself, the raw material for poets everywhere and a tool of and for discovery in what we study, are fundamental to human life, including all of our arts and sciences.

SEE ALSO: Culture; Investigative Poetics; Theory; Theory and Methods

REFERENCES AND SUGGESTED READINGS

Brady, I. (Ed.) (1991) *Anthropological Poetics*. Rowman & Littlefield, Savage, MD.

Brady, I. (1998) Two Thousand and What? Anthropological Moments and Methods for the Next Century. *American Anthropologist* 100(2): 510–16.

Brady, I. (2000) Anthropological Poetics. In: Denzin, N. K. & Lincoln, Y. S. (Eds.), *Handbook of Qualitative Research*, 2nd edn. Sage, Thousand Oaks, CA, pp. 949–79.

Brady, I. (2003a) *The Time at Darwin's Reef: Poetic Explorations in Anthropology and History*. AltaMira, Walnut Creek, CA.

Brady, I. (2003b) Poetics. In: Lewis-Beck, M., Bryman, A. E., & Futing Liao, T. (Eds.), *The Sage Encyclopedia of Social Science Research Methods*. Sage, Thousand Oaks, CA, pp. 825–7.

Brady, I. (2004) In Defense of the Sensual: Meaning Construction in Ethnography and Poetics. *Qualitative Inquiry* 10(4): 622–44.

Brady, I. (2005) Poetics for a Planet: Discourse on Some Problems of Being-in-Place. In: Denzin, N. K. & Lincoln, Y. S. (Eds.), *Handbook of Qualitative Research*, 3rd edn. Sage, Thousand Oaks, CA, pp. 967–1014.

Brady, I. (2006) Greg Dening's *Islands and Beaches*: Or, Why Some Anthropological History is Suspected of Being Literature. In: Lal, B. V. & Munro, D. (Eds.), *Texts and Contexts: Essays on the Foundational Texts of Pacific Islands Historiography*. University of Hawaii Press, Honolulu.

Gibbs, R. W., Jr. (1994) *The Poetics of Mind: Figurative Thought, Language, and Understanding*. Cambridge University Press, Cambridge.

Hallyn, F. (1990) *The Poetic Structure of the World: Copernicus and Kepler*. Zone, New York.

Hartnett, S. J. (2003) *Incarceration Nation: Investigative Prison Poems of Hope and Terror*. AltaMira, Walnut Creek, CA.

Hartnett, S. J. & Engels, J. D. (2005) "Aria in Time of War": Investigative Poetry and the Politics of Witnessing. In: Denzin, N. K. & Lincoln, Y. S. (Eds.), *Handbook of Qualitative Research*, 3rd edn. Sage, Thousand Oaks, CA, pp. 1043–67.

pogroms

Joanna Michlic

The term pogrom came into widespread use in Russia in the late nineteenth century. Originally it defined an organized massacre for the destruction or annihilation of any group of people. Since 1905–6, in the English-speaking world, it evolved into a term chiefly used to describe any riots directed against Jews in the modern era. Both in Russia and the West the term pogrom came to connote "official planning and collusion," and was contrasted with the term riot defined as spontaneous strife or disorder on the part of the populace. It has recently been argued that neither the term riot nor pogrom effectively captures the dynamics of the most violent occurrences involving large crowds, which tend to share the features of both definitions: elements of organization and planning on the one hand, and spontaneity on the other hand (Brass 1996).

The most extensively researched anti-Jewish riots are the pogroms of 1881–2, which swept the southwestern provinces of the Russian Empire. These pogroms are widely regarded as the major turning point in modern Jewish history. Among Jews, the pogroms prompted disillusionment with a solution to the Jewish Question based on civic emancipation and social integration. They resulted in new forms of Jewish politics of a nationalist type, such as Zionism, and the growth of socialist organizations aimed at Jewish proletarians. The Russian state, in turn, moved away from policies designed to promote Jewish acculturation and integration. There were approximately 250 pogroms, varying greatly in length and severity. They produced about 50 fatalities, of whom a half were the perpetrators killed during the suppression of the riots. Both the Russian government and society at the time depicted the pogroms as a popular protest against "Jewish exploitation" in the countryside. This assumption inspired legislative efforts (the so-called "May Laws" of 1882) to segregate peasants and Jews by driving the latter out of the countryside. These measures did not prevent additional pogroms in March 1882, most notably in Balta (Podolia province). There was also a large pogrom in Warsaw on December 25, 1881, and serious but one-off pogroms in Ekaterinoslav (1883) and Nizhnyi Novgorod (1884).

The pogroms of 1881–2 gave rise to a host of assumptions that became firmly established in the historical scholarship on anti-Jewish violence in modern Russia: (1) that the pogroms were instigated, tolerated, or welcomed by Russian officials, on the national, provincial, or local level; (2) that the pogroms were invariably accompanied by atrocities, including rape and murder; (3) that Jews were always passive,

unresisting victims, at least until Jewish socialists organized armed self-defense in the early twentieth century; (4) that, especially in the twentieth century, pogroms were an officially inspired effort to divert popular discontent against the Jews, "to drown the Russian revolution in Jewish blood"; (5) that the great wave of Jewish out-migration from the Russian Empire in the quarter-century before the Great War was prompted by pogroms and restrictive legislation. Since the 1980s, all of these assumptions have been questioned by new scholarship (Aronson 1990; Klier & Lambroza 1992; Rogger 1986).

The anti-Jewish riot of 1903 in Kishinev, then the capital of Bessarabia province, has also been extensively analyzed in the historical literature. It also inspired a classic work of poetry by Chaim Nachman Bialik, "The City of Slaughter," written in Hebrew and Yiddish versions, which led to the creation of the legend of the Kishinev pogrom. The Kishinev pogrom, which broke out during Easter Week, and claimed at least 49 victims, gained greater notoriety than virtually any other anti-Jewish riot in the Russian Empire. It discredited Russia abroad and reenergized all forms of Jewish political activity. As in the case of the anti-Jewish riots of 1881–2, the same major assumptions that the local government was responsible for organizing the pogrom and that the Jews were passive, non-resisting victims were made in the historical analysis in the first half of the twentieth century. These assumptions have been challenged by recent scholarship.

Another wave of anti-Jewish riots discussed in the literature is the violence which accompanied the Revolution of 1905 in Imperial Russia and the attacks on Jews during the Russian Civil War (1919–21). It is recognized that the anti-Jewish violence that erupted during the Civil War was the most brutal case, which exceeded any former riotous events in terms of the number of casualties and savagery. The total number of Jewish fatalities during Civil War pogroms is disputed, but certainly exceeded 500,000. There was also immense damage to Jewish property.

Sharp divisions remain on the issue of the causes of and the responsibility for the pogroms. In the past the general tendency was to put forward a monocausal explanation of violence by looking either to anti-Semitic ideology or the need for plunder. Recent scholarship has tended to recognize that these events are the product of multiple causal tendencies, which may be intertwined, so giving rise to new complex explanations and interpretations of the anti-Jewish violence of 1918–21. The crystallization of similar approaches can be observed in the recent analysis of anti-Jewish violence in Poland between the two World Wars, 1918–39, and during the early post-war period, 1945–6, which erupted on the largest scale in Poland, but also occurred in Slovakia and Hungary.

Other developments in the study of anti-Jewish violence focus on the mass massacres of the summer of 1941 in Eastern Europe in the aftermath of the Nazi invasion of the Soviet Union. The waves of killings carried out by sections of local populations in Lithuania, the Ukraine, Poland, and Romania brought about new questions concerning the nature of the mass murder of the Jews during World War II and about the reactions of segments of local populations to the Nazi anti-Jewish policies. Other questions about the applicability of the word pogrom to these collective massacres and the connection between local anti-Jewish riots and the genocidal project the Nazis brought to Eastern Europe are also being asked.

In recent scholarship one can also observe that most of the main approaches to the study of pogroms have been particular, descriptive, and statistical. There is an urgent need for a comparative approach and the contextualization of the pogroms within broader societal developments.

SEE ALSO: Anti-Semitism (Religion); Anti-Semitism (Social Change); Conflict (Racial/Ethnic); Ethnic Cleansing; Holocaust; Riots; Violence

REFERENCES AND SUGGESTED READINGS

Abramson, H. (1999) *A Prayer for the Government: Ukrainians and Jews in Revolutionary Times, 1917–1920.* Harvard University Press, Cambridge, MA.
Aronson, I. M. (1990) *Troubled Waters: The Origins of the 1881 Anti-Jewish Pogroms in Russia.* University of Pittsburgh Press, Pittsburgh.
Brass, P. R. (Ed.) (1996) *Riots and Pogroms.* New York University Press, New York.
Klier, J. D. & Lambroza, S. (Eds.) (1992) *Pogroms: Anti-Jewish Violence in Modern Russian History.* Cambridge University Press, Cambridge.
Polonsky, A. & Michlic, J. B. (2004) *The Neighbors Respond: The Controversy over the Jedwabne Massacre in Poland.* Princeton University Press, Princeton.
Rogger, H. (1986) *Jewish Policies and Right-Wing Politics in Imperial Russia.* Macmillan, London.

Polanyi, Karl (1886–1964)

James Ronald Stanfield and Jacqueline Bloom Stanfield

Karl Polanyi was born in Vienna on October 21, 1886 and spent his childhood in Budapest. His formal university studies were in law, which he practiced for a very brief time after graduating in 1910. Informally he immersed himself in the rising tide of radical and modern liberal dissent and engaged in political activities, notably on behalf of the short-lived National Citizens' Radical Party, which was formally chartered in June 1914. Polanyi's political and legal career was interrupted by World War I in which he served in the Austro-Hungarian army. Thereafter he began a relationship with the radical activist Ilona Ducyznska, whom he married in 1923.

Polanyi worked as an economic journalist in Vienna from 1924 to 1933, when fascism led him to emigrate with his family, first to England, then to the US. From 1940 to 1943 Polanyi lived in the US, giving guest lectures and holding a visiting scholar's appointment at Bennington College in Vermont. He returned to England for a short period, then returned to the US soon after the end of the war, serving as a visiting professor at Columbia University, where he was co-director (with Conrad Arensberg) of the Interdisciplinary Project on the Institutional Aspects of Economic Growth, which resulted in the very influential *Trade and Market in the Early Empires* (1957). Polanyi's final major project was the founding of *Co-Existence*, an interdisciplinary journal for the comparative study of economics and politics, dedicated to the cause of world peace through knowledge of the realities of cultural differences and the unity of the human condition. After organizing a distinguished editorial board and seeing the first issue to the printer, Polanyi died on April 23, 1964.

Polanyi was influenced by the powerful historic events from his coming of age to his death -- two World Wars, hyperinflation, revolution, global depression, fascism, and Cold War. His idealism was early on evident in his contribution to the socialist economic calculation debate. In sharp contrast to the central focus of the debate on the potential for efficient allocation of resources in a socialist economy, Polanyi's essay in the *Archiv für Sozialwissenschaft* (1922) focused on the moral superiority of socialism. This early concern for the place of economy in society, gleaned from Owen and Marx in his college days, was reinforced by Polanyi's first-hand observation of the cataclysm that a poorly instituted political economy can provoke. Polanyi's central interest became the problem of lives and livelihood: the relation of individual and community life to the manner by which the community makes its living – the place of economy in society. Economic behavior or transacting is structured by political and social conditioning and it has political and social consequences.

Lives and livelihood were the central problem of Polanyi's classic *The Great Transformation* (1944) and his influential essay in *Commentary* (1948), "Our Obsolete Market Mentality." He considered the idea of a self-regulating economy driven by individual economic interest to be utterly unrealistic and profoundly disruptive of the social order. Polanyi's model of market capitalism consists of a "double movement" in which the extension of market exchange to additional areas of social life is met by a spontaneous socially protective response directed at limiting the self-regulating market system to contain its erosion of social and community life. Polanyi referred to the market capitalist economy as disembedded to emphasize that its celebrated impersonal nature means that economic transactions are separated from the traditional moral fabric of interpersonal relationships. The market exchange economy requires social conditioning and legitimation of competitive economic self-interest which is ultimately inconsistent with the social cohesion necessary for orderly social cooperation. The concept of the disembedded economy refers to a tendency for market economic relationships to become superior to the social relationships of kinship and polity.

In his economic anthropology work at Columbia, Polanyi expanded his criticism of the market mentality by developing his criticism of the formalist methodology of economics. He found this approach of taking the economy as a self-contained system to be inadequate in its treatment of the modern economy and incapable of guiding the understanding of premodern economies that were organized on the basis of socially structured reciprocity and redistribution transactions. He saw the market pattern to be ultimately receding in the face of the protective response, and formalist economics, an explicit expression of the market mentality, to be incapable of comprehending the past, and therefore unable to guide the imagination of the future. Polanyi argued that a substantive conception of the economy as an instituted process for provisioning society was necessary in these regards.

Polanyi's emphasis on distinguishing the formalist and substantivist conceptions of the economy and his focus on the place of economy in society, the issue of embeddedness, have been influential in economic sociology, economic anthropology, and institutional economics. Polanyi like Marx before him emphasized the place of economy in society, criticized the ethnocentric interpretation of premodern economies, and wrote of the disembedded, socially dominant character of market exchange transactions in the capitalist social order. However, Polanyi's concept of the protective response is a departure from Marx's expectation that the objective conditions of capitalism would clarify the class struggle and more or less resolve social conflict into capital versus labor. Polanyi's analysis suggests that the protective response interferes with the laws of motion of capitalism, thus preventing the realization of the logical tendencies of capitalism that Marx anticipated. Hence various sectoral interests will persist and class identification will never reach the clear division into the two major classes upon which the Marxist teleology depends.

Polanyi may be considered an early post-Marxian in that he emphasized the Marxian concern with lives and livelihood but presented a different conception of the social economic tendencies of market capitalism. He is a forerunner of today's non-essentialist Marxism. His existential and ethical view of economic relationships has much in common with postmodernism in its deconstruction of the contentious overbearing themes of economic efficiency and progress that permeate the debate between the left and the right. Polanyi's socialism is not so much political economic as ethical and there is running through it a strong conservative respect for cultural tradition.

SEE ALSO: Community and Economy; Economy, Culture and; Institutionalism; Social Embeddedness of Economic Action

REFERENCES AND SUGGESTED READINGS

Levitt, K. P. (Ed.) (1990) *The Life and Work of Karl Polanyi: A Budapest Celebration*. Black Rose Books, Montreal.

McRobbie, K. & Levitt, K. P. (Eds.) (2000) *Karl Polanyi in Vienna: The Contemporary Significance of The Great Transformation*. Black Rose Books, Montreal.

Mendell, M. & Salee, D. (Eds.) (1991) *The Legacy of Karl Polanyi: Market, State, and Society at the End of the Twentieth Century*. St. Martin's Press, New York.

O'Hara, P. A. (2000) *Marx, Veblen, and Contemporary Institutional Political Economy: Principles and Unstable Dynamics of Capitalism*. Edward Elgar, Cheltenham.

Stanfield, J. R. (1986) *The Economic Thought of Karl Polanyi: Lives and Livelihood*. Macmillan, London.

Stanfield, J. R. & Stanfield, J. B. (1997) Where Has Love Gone? Reciprocity, Redistribution, and the Nurturance Gap. *Journal of Socio-Economics* 26 (April): 111–26.

police

Ivan Y. Sun

Police have been traditionally defined as the social agency of a government that is responsible for maintaining public order and preventing and detecting crime. This definition emphasizes the social control function that police are supposed to perform in a society. It has been severely challenged, however, mainly because of the finding of a small number of studies conducted in the 1950s and 1960s. Though police are often portrayed as law enforcers and crime fighters, the large-scale observational study mounted by Reiss and Black showed that they spend a large amount of their time in handling non-crime-related incidents (Reiss 1971; Black 1980).

As a result, scholars propose a "force-centered" definition of police as an alternative to the conventional approach. Bittner (1980) asserted that police are the main, and sometimes the only, mechanism for the state to distribute non-negotiable force in handling emergencies in a society. Similarly, Klockars (1985) argued that it is problematic to define police based on their supposed function. He further explained that the authority of using coercive force given by the state to police entails legal legitimacy and territorial coverage, which distinguish police from other occupations. Klockars (1985) thus defined police as individuals or institutions empowered by the state with the general right to use coercive force within the state's domestic territory.

Why should all modern societies find it necessary to create and maintain such an institution? The necessity for the police lies not only on the distribution of coercive force for disposing of incidents but also on the availability of an agency in handling emergencies *immediately*. Therefore, police are created by the state mainly as a 24-hour available agency to serve public needs.

Major dimensions of police include strategies, discretion, problems, and innovations. Since the establishment of the first modern police department in England in 1829, police have relied heavily on three core strategies in combating crime: preventive patrol by uniformed officers, rapid response to emergency or service calls, and criminal investigation by detectives. Preventive patrol is designed to deter or intercept crime, to increase feelings of public safety, and to make officers available for service (Walker & Katz 2002). Motorized and foot patrol are the most common types of patrol. Other types of patrol include bicycle, motorcycle, marine, and horse patrol. Many departments also adopt a directed-patrol approach, which involves directing officers to spend their uncommitted time in certain areas, utilize certain tactics, and watch for certain types of offenses. Rapid response is thought to have the potential for increasing the probability of an arrest and enhancing citizen satisfaction with the police. Most departments utilize a differential police-response method that involves screening incoming service calls and providing different responses to different kinds of calls. Criminal investigation consists of two stages: the preliminary investigation and the follow-up investigation. The former is carried out mainly by patrol officers who often locate the suspect and make the arrest at the scene, while the latter is normally handled by detectives who may have to spend more time to solve complex and difficult cases (Walker & Katz 2002).

Since its recognition by the American Bar Foundation (ABF) survey in the 1950s (Walker 1993), discretion has been the focal concern of police reform and research. Discretion may be defined as decisions made by a police officer based on his or her own judgment of the best course of action (Walker & Katz 2002). Police discretion is now widely viewed as inevitable and even desirable. Much attention has thus shifted to the control of police discretion. Better control of police discretion can be accomplished through clear written policies and rules. Major improvements have been achieved by American police regarding control of police discretion in the area of use of deadly force and high-speed pursuits (Walker 1993).

Police problems center on two critical issues: use of force and corruption. Although police use of force is relatively rare, it has been the major source of conflict between the police and citizens, especially minorities. Many departments have implemented policies and rules regulating use of force. For example, most departments have a use-of-force continuum in place, ranking force from low coercive (e.g., verbal command and threaten), to medium (e.g., search and seizure and physical restraint), to high coercive (e.g., arrest and deadly force) and specifying levels of force appropriate for particular situations. The general policy for applying deadly force is called the defense-of-life rule, which means that deadly force can be used only if the officer's life, the citizen's life, or another officer's life is in danger. Police use of force remains problematic since perceptions of appropriate levels of force for a particular situation are highly subjective and citizens have little input in the investigation of complaints of excessive force.

Corruption has been a traditional problem for the police. It may be defined as police behavior that involves illegal use or misuse of police authority for personal gain (Sherman 1978). Common forms of corruption include gratuities (e.g., accepting free meals and drinks), bribes (e.g., accepting money for not issuing a speeding ticket), theft and burglary (e.g., stealing drug dealers' money), and internal corruption (e.g., paying for promotions and favored assignments) (Walker & Katz 2002). Police corruption is mainly a result of police working environment and subculture. Corruption may be controlled through internal and external mechanisms, such as writing guidelines, training and education, supervision, early warning systems, federal prosecution, and citizen oversight. It is almost impossible, however, to completely eliminate the problem because of the nature of police work and culture.

Police innovations can be viewed simply as survival tools for police. To survive, police departments need to adjust their philosophy, strategies, and operations in response to external and internal changes and demands. In the United States, for example, since the mid-nineteenth century police have evolved from political-connected control forces to legal-oriented law enforcement organizations to community-centered service institutions. Major police innovations over the past century involved professional movements (e.g., selection and training standards adopted by police), technological advances (two-way radios and mobile digital units mounted in the patrol cars), and legal compliance (search and seizure laws prescribed by the courts).

The most notable recent innovation for police is community policing (CP). The emergence of CP in the 1980s and 1990s promoted fundamental changes in police operational styles and organizational philosophy and structure. Though CP is currently a worldwide movement, there is no generic form of CP. Police agencies have implemented CP with distinctive orientations, such as problem solving, broken windows, and community building (Mastrofski et al. 1995). The problem-solving model focuses on the use of proactive intervention rather than reactive responses to calls for service, the resolution of root causes rather than symptoms, and the mobilization of multiparty, community-based problem-solving resources rather than unilateral police response (Goldstein 1979). The broken windows approach calls for more police attention to minor offenses and disorders since they can grow into larger problems that influence "quality of life" in the neighborhood (Wilson & Kelling 1982). The community-building model stresses building greater rapport with minority neighborhoods, crime prevention, and victim assistance (Mastrofski et al. 1995).

Research on police conducted since the 1960s has been directed toward two general areas. The first body of research examined the impact of various factors on police behavior. Four main approaches have been utilized, including situational, individual, organizational, and community. Situational explanations argue that police behavior is affected by situational characteristics of police–citizen interactions. Several situational variables, such as crime seriousness, evidence strength, and citizen demeanor, have shown consistent influences on police actions. Individual explanations of police behavior assert that police officers' personal characteristics (race, gender, education, and experience), occupational outlooks, and work assignments influence their behavior during police–citizen encounters. Previous studies of the effect of officers' characteristics on police behavior have concentrated on coercive activities (e.g., arrest and use of force) and have generated mixed results. Situational variables are generally found to have greater explanatory power than individual characteristics.

Organizational explanations suggest that police formal and informal socialization, subculture, command and policies, structure, departmental styles, and other organizational factors affect police behavior. Neighborhood explanations posit that the demographic, economic, and political characteristics of communities, such as racial composition, socioeconomic status, and type of local government, influence police behavior. Despite their potential influences over police behavior, organizational and neighborhood factors have received relatively little

empirical attention and the results are far less than conclusive.

A second line of inquiry focuses on the influence of police strategies and activities on crime. Early studies have focused on the effectiveness of the three main strategies (preventive patrol, rapid response, and criminal investigation). Contrary to what people and police expect, the core strategies of contemporary policing showed no or weak impact on crime rates, victimization, and public satisfaction. Though these studies are severely criticized for methodological shortcomings, the effectiveness of traditional police strategies has not been firmly confirmed. More recent research concerns the effectiveness and efficiency of community policing. The results are generally more encouraging. Community policing has been shown to have positive effects on citizen satisfaction with police and police job satisfaction.

Future research should consider the following areas. First, future research should pay more attention to non-coercive police behavior since previous studies have focused predominantly on coercive actions. One may argue that prior research is inadequate in terms of understanding the range and/or effectiveness of police actions in handling incidents since coercive actions are rare events and police routinely utilize non-coercive tactics during their encounters with citizens. If non-coercive behavior can be clearly defined and measured, then the evaluations of these actions may allow us to capture somewhat different aspects of police responses from coercive actions.

Second, more research on the influence of organizational factors on police behavior should be conducted. It will be of interest, for example, to explore how and the extent to which changes in departmental policies and procedures resulting from the 9/11 terrorist attack influence officer behavior in the field. More efforts should also be devoted to further develop and test how variations in neighborhood social, economic, and political dimensions influence police behavior. Finally, more cross-national analysis of police should be considered. Despite the value of comparative studies, systematic investigation of police across countries has been sporadic. Researchers should examine the effects of variations in national-level factors on police operations and effectiveness.

SEE ALSO: Crime, Broken Windows Theory of; Courts; Crime, Hot Spots; Criminal Justice System; Law, Criminal; Organizations as Coercive Institutions; Public Order Crime

REFERENCES AND SUGGESTED READINGS

Bittner, E. (1974) Florence Nightingale in Pursuit of Willie Sutton: A Theory of the Police. In: Jacob, H. (Eds.), *The Political Reform of Criminal Justice.* Sage, Beverly Hills, CA, pp. 17–44.
Bittner, E. (1980) *The Functions of the Police in Modern Society.* Olgeschlager, Gunn, & Hain, Cambridge, MA.
Black, D. (1980) *The Manners and Customs of the Police.* Academic Press, New York.
Goldstein, H. (1979) Improving Policing: A Problem-Oriented Approach. *Crime and Delinquency* 25: 235–58.
Klockars, C. (1985) *The Idea of Police.* Sage, Newbury Park, CA.
Mastrofski, S., Worden, R., Snipes, J., et al. (1995) Law Enforcement in a Time of Community Policing. *Criminology* 33: 539–63.
Reiss, A. (1971) *The Police and the Public.* Yale University Press, New Haven.
Sherman, L. (1978) *Scandal and Reform: Controlling Police Corruption.* University of California Press, Berkeley.
Walker, S. (1993) *Taming the System: The Control of Discretion in Criminal Justice, 1950–1990.* Oxford University Press, New York.
Walker, S. & Katz, M. (2002) *The Police in America: An Introduction.* McGraw Hill, New York.
Wilson, J. Q. & Kelling, G. L. (1982) Broken Windows: The Police and Neighborhood Safety. *Atlantic Monthly* (March): 29–38.

political economy

Francesco Ramella

Political economy refers to a current of study that analyzes the reciprocal influences among economic, social, and political factors and their impact on how activities are regulated in different institutional contexts. Even though historically the origins go back to the birth of economics, over recent decades this subject of study has witnessed a revival in a variety of scientific sectors. Two aspects characterize this recent tendency: on one hand, a new attention – often in a comparative perspective – to the study of institutions and of the interrelations between economic and sociopolitical phenomena, and, on the other, greater interdisciplinary activity.

'That said, the use of the same denomination masks the existence of various analytical perspectives. The term new political economy is used to underline not so much the emergence of a common theoretical framework as renewed interest in a field of inquiry that, because of its very subject, encourages the reopening of dialogue between different disciplinary sectors. The signs of this revival of political economy, limited to some of the more significant developments in the three major disciplines involved – economics, political science, and sociology – are discussed below.

ECONOMICS

An important development in economics is the introduction of the new institutional economics, a theoretical perspective that reintroduces institutions into economic analyses. Unlike the old institutionalism, however, the new version does not place itself as an alternative to mainstream (neoclassical) economics. Nevertheless – thanks to the support of economic history – it widens the analytic perspective toward a comparative reflection on the different modes of organizing economic activities at both a macro and a micro level. This new approach consists of two distinct yet complementary currents. The first concentrates above all on the institutional environment of economies, i.e., on the fundamental political, social, and legal rules that regulate production, exchange, and distribution (Davis & North 1971: 5). The second current – developed by transaction cost economics – studies instead the governance of contractual relations between productive units (through the market, the hierarchy, or hybrid forms). A link exists between these two perspectives because the efficacy of different modes of governance depends not only upon the characteristics of the economic actors, but also upon the institutional context, modeled by history according to the logic of path dependency (Williamson 1994: 95).

Along with the new institutionalism – which has aroused great attention within both economics and the other social sciences – other trends that favor interdisciplinary dialogue are also evident. First is a revival of old economic institutionalism and of evolutionary approaches that underline the role of institutions in economic and technological change and the different trajectories of development of various countries. The same is true for another current of study that, taking up Alfred Marshall's original formulations on industrial districts, concentrates upon the spatial dimension of economic activities, i.e., upon the territorial agglomeration of small and medium-sized firms (Pyke et al. 1990). A tendency to reflect on institutions and new scenarios designed by the crisis of Fordism also characterizes the so-called "French Regulation School" (Boyer 1990), which concentrates upon the economic impact of various coordination mechanisms (market, state, hierarchy, associations, communities). Finally, interesting developments can be seen in the economics of development and in the resurgence of a new comparative economics that analyzes the different forms of capitalism in developing and advanced countries, as well as in economies in transition. These studies tend to emphasize the importance of socio-institutional governance in explaining not only economic performance but also the different results of the transition to capitalism in the former socialist countries (Djankov et al. 2003).

the most well known are: the *theory of committees*, which confronts the theme of the relations between individual preferences and procedures of choice within groups; the *theory of political coalitions*, which studies the formation of political alliances on the basis of a size principle, in which actors tend to construct "minimum winning coalitions"; the *spatial theory of voting*, which deals with the logics of electoral competition between parties; and *public choice theory*, which deals with collective decisions considering public policies as the result of the encounter between the demands of citizens (who aim at maximizing their preferences) and the offer of politicians and bureaucrats (who aim at maximizing their power). A series of studies within this latter current – referring to so-called political business cycles – seeks to explain the inflationist phenomena of the 1970s in advanced economies. Scholars focused upon the increases in public spending decided by governments with the aim of stimulating the economy and in this way obtaining reelection. In the second half of the 1980s, as a result of contamination with the neo-institutionalist current that was affirming itself in political science, there was a partial revision of the economic approach to politics. While still maintaining many of the previous assumptions, the new political economy placed greater emphasis upon institutions, decisional procedures, and the empirical verification of theoretical models (Alt & Alesina 1996).

POLITICAL SCIENCE

Within political science, the spread of political economy – mainly in the United States – has assumed the form of an extension of the economic paradigm to the study of political phenomena. The assumptions of the methodological individualism of the neoclassical matrix, with its corollaries linked to the rational and maximizing behavior of individual actors, have been developed in the formulations of game theory, rational choice, and public choice, giving birth to a variegated "economic approach to politics" (Monroe 1991). Even though its diffusion has taken place especially since the second half of the 1970s, the initiating models were developed in the 1950s and 1960s. Several of

SOCIOLOGY

In sociology, a different orientation of political economy began to spread, especially in economic sociology, starting from the second half of the 1970s. The paradigm of rational choice gained little ground, especially in Europe, while attention was directed toward the sociocultural and political institutional factors influencing instability of advanced economies. In particular, analysis focused upon the changes in class relations and the delegitimization of social inequalities that were at the base of the distributive conflicts that exploded in many industrialized economies. This current, however, underlined the variable intensity of these conflicts, positioning them in relation to the different social and political set-ups of individual countries. A fruitful convergence of sociological and political studies was thus created. The contraposition of neocorporative and pluralist models of representing interests and decision-making assumed particular importance (Schmitter & Lehmbruch 1979).

The neocorporative type (diffused throughout the Scandinavian countries and in continental Europe) is characterized by the presence of a few large associations organizing broad economic-professional sectors and deciding policies together with governments. In the pluralist type (present in countries like the United States, Great Britain, and Italy), on the other hand, there are many organizations that represent more limited and sectorial interests, carrying out policies of pressure on government agencies. Research undertaken has shown that, during the 1970s, neocorporative arrangements were associated with minor social conflict and more contained levels of inflation and unemployment thanks to their capacity to mediate and hierarchize social questions. The debate over neocorporatism was also strictly interwoven with the comparative study of different welfare state models. In this instance too, there was a prevailing attempt to link the characteristics of systems of protection to social political differences present in the various countries, and then to study their fallout upon development and class inequalities (Esping-Andersen 1994). What needs to be underlined is that this first generation of political economy studies in sociology was carried out mainly at the macro (national) level and brought the role of the state and interest groups to the center of analytical reflection.

Starting from the early 1980s, the sociological approach witnessed further developments that dealt with post-Fordism models of production, the varieties of capitalism in advanced societies, and the different paths followed by the less developed countries. The first current started from research that dealt with the question of productive readjustment in the phase of post-Fordism. After the crisis experienced by many large, vertically integrated firms, more flexible and cooperative enterprise forms were introduced. These are based on network forms of organization concerned with the quality and diversification of products. In brief, this research

brought to light the emergence of a new productive paradigm denominated "flexible specialization" or "diversified quality production" (Piore & Sabel 1984; Streeck 1992). Studies on the so-called Third Italy and on industrial districts of small and medium-sized firms underlined the territorial character and the *non-economic* preconditions of these new systems of production that are strongly embedded in local contexts (Bagnasco & Sabel 1995; Trigilia 2002).

The second current analyzed the variety of capitalist systems, connecting micro- and meso-level reflections on industrial readjustment with the tradition of study of the different regulation models at the macro level. In this way, two ideal types of contemporary capitalism were identified: the Rhine model, or the so-called coordinated market economies, and the Anglo-Saxon model of liberal market economies (Soskice 1990; Albert 1991). The Anglo-Saxon model (which includes countries such as the US and Britain) is characterized by the greater space given to the market in socioeconomic regulation. In the coordinated economies (which include, other than Japan, many Central and North European countries), on the other hand, the conjoint action of the political institutions, interest organizations, and banks tends to limit market mechanisms and design more extensive systems of social protection. This literature has analyzed the variable influence of the forms of governance on occupation and economic development during the 1980s and the 1990s. Finally, with regard to the newly industrialized countries, the extraordinary growth in the Asian economies stimulated a strong revival of attention to the complex interrelations between the state and the economy in the processes of development. Thus, in the field of the sociology of modernization, a comparative political economy trend also became established (Evans & Stephens 1988).

To conclude, it is appropriate to mention two present trends in political economy. The first concerns the phenomenon of globalization. In different disciplinary fields, political economic research is spreading, aimed at analyzing the consequences of these processes on international relations, on the regulatory capacity of states, on the varieties of capitalism, and on democratization and the transition of many former socialist economies to capitalism. The second current – connected to the former – examines the processes of economic regionalization with particular reference to the phenomenon of local development, "systems of innovation," and new forms of urban governance.

SEE ALSO: Development: Political Economy; Economic Sociology: Classical Political Economic Perspectives; Economic Sociology: Neoclassical Economic Perspective; Fordism/Post-Fordism; Global Economy; Globalization; Institutionalism; Political Economy of Science; Political Economy and Sport; Rational Choice Theory (and Economic Sociology); Regulation Theory; State and Economy; Transition from Communism; Transition Economies; Welfare State

REFERENCES AND SUGGESTED READINGS

Albert, M. (1991) *Capitalisme contre capitalisme.* Éditions du Seuil, Paris.

Alt, J. E. & Alesina, A. (1996) Political Economy: An Overview. In: Goodin, R. E. & Klingemann, H. D. (Eds.), *A New Handbook of Political Science.* Oxford University Press, Oxford, pp. 645–74.

Bagnasco, A. & Sabel, C. (Eds.) (1995) *Small Firms in Europe.* Pinter, London.

Boyer, R. (1990) *The Regulation School: A Critical Introduction.* Columbia University Press, New York.

Davis, L. E. & North, D. C. (1971) *Institutional Change and American Economic Growth.* Cambridge University Press, Cambridge.

Djankov, S., Glaeser, E. L., La Porta, R., Lopez de Silanes, F., & Shleifer, A. (2003) *The New Comparative Economics.* National Bureau of Economic Research, Working Paper 9608, April.

Esping-Andersen, G. (1994) Welfare State and the Economy. In: Smelser, N. J. & Swedberg, R. (Eds.), *The Handbook of Economic Sociology.* Princeton University Press, Princeton, pp. 711–32.

Evans, P. & Stephens, J. (1988) Development and the World Economy. In: Smelser, N. J. (Ed.), *Handbook of Sociology.* Sage, Newbury Park, CA, pp. 739–73.

Monroe, K. R. (Ed.) (1991) *The Economic Approach to Politics: A Critical Reassessment of the Theory of Rational Action.* HarperCollins, New York.

Piore, M. J. & Sabel, C. F. (1984) *The Second Industrial Divide: Possibilities for Prosperity.* Basic Books, New York.

Pyke, F., Becattini, G., & Sengenberger, W. (Eds.) (1990) *Industrial Districts and Inter-Firm Co-operation in Italy.* ILO, Geneva.

Schmitter, P. & Lehmbruch, G. (Eds.) (1979) *Trends Toward Corporatist Intermediation.* Sage, Beverley Hills, CA.

Soskice, D. (1990) Reinterpreting Corporatism and Explaining Unemployment: Coordinated and Non-Coordinated Market Economies. In: Brunetta, R. & Dell' Aringa, C. (Eds.), *Markets, Institutions, and Corporations: Labour Relations and Economic Performance.* New York University Press, New York, pp. 170–211.

Streeck, W. (1992) *Social Institution and Economic Performance.* Sage, London.

Trigilia, C. (2002) *Economic Sociology: State, Market, and Society in Modern Capitalism.* Blackwell, Oxford.

Williamson, O. E. (1994) Transaction Cost Economics and Organization Theory. In: Smelser, N. J. & Swedberg, R. (Eds.), *The Handbook of Economic Sociology.* Princeton University Press, Princeton, pp. 77–107.

political economy of science

Brian Woods

Science has never been at the forefront of political economy and usually only appears as an "exogenous shock," or is suppressed by an assumption within the theory of the firm of a given stock of scientific and/or technological knowledge from which firms make their choices and then employ them in producing a given volume of output. Nonetheless, some theorists and empiricists have explored (in very broad terms) the role of science and technology in economic growth, the relations between science, technology, the state, and capital, and science and development.

From Adam Smith, Charles Babbage (better known as the pioneer of computers) took the idea that invention was a consequence of the division of labor, but his *Economy of Machinery and Manufactures* went further to explain the implications of the division of labor for science and technology. He saw that the extension of the division of labor and improvements in production technologies would necessarily lead to the establishment of large factories working to economies of scale. Babbage also saw that this progress would come to depend on the deepening relations between science and industry and that, in turn, science itself would become subjected to the law of the division of labor. As science became a full-time activity and the costs associated with the discovery of the "principles of nature" increased, specialization would unavoidably follow.

Babbage's analysis influenced Marx, who in turn considered science a fundamental factor in explaining the exceptional growth in resource productivity and humanity's capacity to manipulate the natural environment for human purposes. Marx's treatment of scientific progress was nonetheless consistent with his broader historical materialism. Just as the economic foundation shapes political, legal, and social institutions, so too did it shape scientific activity. Science did not develop in response to forces internal to science or the scientific community: it is not an autonomous activity, but rather a social one that responded to economic forces. As such, Marx did not see science as a driver of social change. Instead, he thought that specific scientific disciplines developed in response to specific social problems that arose in the sphere of production.

Marx's central point though was that science emerged at a particular point in human history. The marriage of science and industry did not occur with the historical emergence of capitalism, but centuries after when the system of manufacture demanded to be free of human frailty and relied instead on the predictability and impersonality of the machine. It is with the rise of the factory, its organized system of machines, and crucially the point at which machines started to make machines that the application of science became the determining principle everywhere.

Joseph Schumpeter identified with Marx the role played by capitalism in accounting for progress in science and technology. In a direct attack on the rigorously static framework of neoclassical economics, Schumpeter's *Capitalism, Socialism and Democracy* drew upon Kondratiev's hypothesis of long cycles to develop an evolutionary model of economic change within which science (and technology), along with the entrepreneur as innovative agent, plays the most significant role. Like Marx, Schumpeter thought that capitalism was inherently dynamic

and the fundamental drive that kept the system in motion came from new consumer goods, new methods of production or transportation to new markets, and/or new forms of industrial organization. These changes incessantly revolutionized the economic structure from within, destroying old ones and creating new ones. This process, which Schumpeter termed "creative destruction," was for him the "essential fact about capitalism." Innovation leads to the creation of an economic space where swarms of imitators produce other innovations by copying or modifying the new technologies. Thus, in every span of historic time Schumpeter would argue that it is possible to locate the ignition of the process and to associate it with certain industries from which the disturbances then spread over the entire system.

Similar to Marx, Schumpeter also thought that the capitalist system would inevitably self-destruct. Unlike Marx though, this destruction would not come about because of the proletarian revolution, but because first, the rationalizing influence of capitalist institutions (which created the growth of a rational science) would eventually turn back upon the mass of collective ideas and challenge the very institutions of power and property. And second, because scientific and technological progress would increasingly become the business of teams of specialists who would create what is required in a predictable way, so leading to the demise of "the carrier of innovation:" the entrepreneur. The context for this rationalization of innovation was the growth of the large-scale enterprise and, with it, the industrial research laboratory: the site of the systematic harnessing of science and technology to corporate objectives.

The rise of the giant corporation and its role in staving off the crisis of capitalism was the central point of analysis for Paul Baran and Paul Sweezy's seminal work *Monopoly Capital*. For Baran and Sweezy, capitalism had entered a new stage of development -- monopolization -- characterized by the domination of massive corporations sharing rather than competing for production and markets. This domination enabled monopoly firms to extract enormous surplus and then absorb it through imperialism and the permanent arms economy. Increased government spending on evermore sophisticated, evermore destructive weapon systems created the demand required to prevent capitalism from falling into crisis.

While neo-Marxists forwarded the underconsumption argument, another utilitarian argument found strength in Vannevar Bush's *Science – The Endless Frontier* and John Maynard Keynes's *General Theory of Employment, Interest and Money*, both of which changed the political/economic landscape and formalized science policies on the assumption that scientific progress would ultimately improve living standards. Bush's report set the paradigm that influenced both policymakers and academics about the process of science, technology, and economic growth: the so-called linear model as represented by Basic Research–Applied Research–Development–Enhanced Production–Economic Growth.

Keynes proposed that the economic function of government was to correct the follies of the market and stave off crisis through the promotion of full-employment by means of large public works. Different countries adopted various means to achieve the goal of full employment, but Keynes's theorem did stimulate massive state-sponsored scientific/technological projects such as nuclear power, supersonic transport, and space programs. "High technology" and "Big Science" were seen as politically beneficial in that they not only avoided direct competition with private capital, but they also promoted highly skilled employment and contributed to the expansion of the industrial infrastructure.

In *The New Industrial State* John Kenneth Galbraith explored the consequences of these ideas. Following the familiar theme that the dependence of the modern economy on science, technology, and planning necessitated the ever-increasing specialization and division of labor, Galbraith added analytical weight to President Dwight Eisenhower's warning about the inordinate power of the military–industrial complex and the scientific-technological elite. As science and technology become more complex and lead times between design and production become longer (because of the amount of technoscientific knowledge brought to bear on every micro-fraction of the task), the production process becomes inflexible. Increased complexity also leads to increases in capital investment (by orders of magnitude) and increased risk, which

in turn leads to more need for control, for planning, and consequently for large organizations. Power, Galbraith argued, had shifted to those with technical knowledge. The scientific, technical, organizational, and planning needs of the "technostructure" brought into being a large scientific estate, the political consequences of which was that in the modern economy technological compulsions and not political ideology drove industry to seek protection from the state. The technostructure extended its influence deep into the state, it identified itself with the goals of the state (economic growth, full employment, national defense), and designed and developed artifacts and systems to meet those goals. But, ultimately, the goals of the state reflected the needs of the technostructure.

Robert Solow's economic analysis in the late 1950s, however, seemed to confirm and support government involvement in the promotion and production of science and technology when he concluded that capital investment did not determine economic growth, but rather productivity investment did (i.e., investment in research and development – R&D). Since Solow, economists have conducted statistical research to find the scientific/technological determinants of economic growth and while many confirmed the high returns from R&D investment, others laid down three very different propositions about the economics of science. First, the economic value of science is difficult to forecast. Second, the realization of profits or property rights from science is intrinsically difficult to determine because of the organizational norms of "open science." Third, because private returns to investment in science are highly uncertain, there exists a systematic market failure, which in the absence of government action would result in an underinvestment in science. These propositions have over time served as the basis for treating science as a "public good" that requires public funding.

The traditional analysis of the efficient production of public goods was for governments to engage directly in the production of scientific knowledge, allow free use of it, and finance that production from general taxation. This was done either through the university or through government R&D laboratories that publicly disclosed their findings. The rise of a new economic doctrine during the 1980s, however (as epitomized by Milton and Rose Friedman's *Capitalism and Freedom*), called on governments to reduce both taxation and state expenditure, which led not only to large-scale budget cuts, but also to the systematic restructuring and commercialization of public sector R&D laboratories and universities. Accompanying the rise of the new enterprise culture was a range of organizational changes that intended to mimic practice in the commercial sector, in particular a large growth in university companies geared to the commercial exploitation of their staff's expertise.

Notwithstanding, policymakers have long drawn inference from economic studies on the need to focus on R&D investments in the private sector. The argument underlying such a focus is that, through incentives, firms will continue to invest in additional R&D projects that increase the production of scientific knowledge and thus continue to stimulate economic growth and enhance standards of living. The traditional incentive for R&D investment has been the patent system, which grants monopoly rights over a specified period. Research on the economic role of patents has found a strong positive correlation between R&D expenditure and patents, and a positive correlation between patent activity and various measures of economic performance. However, other research has also suggested that the use of counts of patents as an indicator of innovative output can be misleading.

Finally, the role of science and technology in development has long been a matter of investigation for international political economy. Modernization theorists view science as essentially beneficial, in that both knowledge and technology transfer from the North aids developing nations. The idea rests on the linear model of the relationship between science and economic growth, the basic assumption being that science and technology are autonomous from society – that they are able to produce particular effects regardless of the social or cultural context in which they are placed. The Green Revolution is an illustrative case, whereby widespread food shortages, population growth, and predicted famine in India prompted major international foundations to invest in agricultural research. New types of maize, wheat, and rice emerged from this work, which promised higher yields and rapid maturity. But they did not come without other inputs and conditions such as fertilizers, pesticides, herbicides, fungicides, and even irrigation technologies. Moreover, seeds for these new varieties had to be purchased anew each year.

Dependency theorists, on the other hand, argue that relationships with the North, in particular with multinational corporations, are barriers to development, because outside forces controlled economic growth. As such, science is not viewed as a benign force, but rather as one of a group of institutional processes that contribute to underdevelopment. Because scientific research concentrated in the North, dependency theorists claim that the research is also conducted for the benefit of the North and that knowledge and technology transfer are just another means of profit accumulation for Northern corporations.

SEE ALSO: Big Science and Collective Research; Braverman, Harry; Economic Development; Economic Sociology: Classical Political Economic Perspectives; Economic Sociology: Neoclassical Economic Perspective; Marx, Karl; Marxism and Sociology; Mass Production; Military Research and Science and War; Modernization; Political Economy; Schumpeter, Joseph A.; Smith, Adam; Speaking Truth to Power: Science and Policy; State and Economy; Technological Determinism; Technological Innovation

REFERENCES AND SUGGESTED READINGS

Audretsch, D. B. et al. (2002) The Economics of Science. *Journal of Technology Transfer* 27: 155–203.

Clark, N. (1985) *The Political Economy of Science and Technology*. Blackwell, Oxford.

Feldman, M., Link, A., & Siegal, D. (2002) *The Economics of Science and Technology*. Kluwer Academic Publishers, Norwell, MA.

Freeman, C. & Louca, F. (2001) *As Time Goes By*. Oxford University Press, Oxford.

Rosenberg, N. (1994) *Exploring the Black Box: Technology, Economics, and History*. Cambridge University Press, Cambridge.

political economy and sport

George H. Sage

For over 350 years the term political economy has been used to articulate the interdependence of political and economic phenomena. The first published use of the term "political economy" is found in *Treatise on Political Economy* authored by a French writer, Antoyne de Montchrétien, in 1616. The first publication in English using this term was Sir James Steuart's book *Inquiry Into the Principles of Political Economy* in 1767. Political economy is considered to be the original social science because the broad theoretical visions of society articulated by Adam Smith, John Stuart Mill, and Karl Marx in the eighteenth and nineteenth centuries predated the splintering of social science into narrower disciplines of economics, political science, sociology, and anthropology.

Study in the field of political economy has always been a broader field than the conventional study of either economics or political science. Much of political economy scholarship has involved analyzing relational issues of politics and economics because markets are embedded in political and cultural contexts. Therefore, political economic scholarship has also typically addressed basic moral issues of social justice, equity, and the public good (Gondwe 1992; Gilpin 2001).

Scholarship in political economy encompasses three broad perspectives representing fundamentally different visions of the good society. They are classical political economy, neoclassical economics, and radical political economy. Furthermore, three competing ideologies dominate the literature of political economy – liberal, conservative, and radical – as models of social order. Thus, the different political economy perspectives that have persisted over time include pervasive and contested ideological motifs underlying them (Gondwe 1992; Clark 1998).

As one of the most popular forms of cultural practice in the modern world, sport has become a topic of considerable political economic interest. Research on the political economy of mass sports has often involved issues about public

policy on behalf of providing for people's leisure needs. One of the major contested questions has been whether the government should intervene in sporting practices or whether such matters should be left to the private sector.

Studies show that governments throughout the world have taken a larger role in sport and physical recreation at all levels, from local to international. In the United States, for example, support for public high school and college sport was initiated by local and state governments because such sports were believed to foster socialization experiences that would prepare young people, especially young men, to be productive workers. A more common political economy connection is represented by Sport and Recreation New Zealand (SPARC), formed in New Zealand in 2002, as a nationwide government/private partnership committed to ensuring that New Zealand remains a thriving, healthy nation by improving sport and recreation opportunities for all its citizens. Such partnerships, structured in different ways, have been formed in many nations.

Research has also focused on a professional sport industry that has proliferated throughout the world during the past half-century. Young (1986) captures the essence of this trend: "The most significant structural change in modern sports is the gradual and continuing commodification of sports. This means that the social, psychological, physical, and cultural uses of sport are assimilated to the commercial needs of advanced monopoly capital" (p. 12). The professional sport industry, generally privatized and structured to generate profits, is composed of franchise owners, events sponsors, athletes, coaches, and ancillary workers. Although the owners of sports teams have consistently favored a minimum of government interference, they have often lobbied political leaders and received unique and favorable national and local government subsidies, protections, and beneficial legislation. The form of such government support varies from nation to nation, but research shows that government policies have consistently played an important role in how the sport industry operates (Johnson & Frey 1985). In the case of the major men's team spectator sports in the US, owners have benefited from favorable court decisions, enabling them to monopolize their industry. Thus, between their own power of ownership, personal wealth, and legislative and judicial support, the owners' monopoly of professional team sports allows them several means of capital accumulation.

A significant political, economic, and cultural transformation in the world order has been under way during the past half-century as globalization has increased interdependence among the world's nations. One manifestation of globalization is the proliferation of international sporting events, such as the Olympic Games and the World Cup in men's soccer/football. International sports have attracted political economy scholarship because developed nations have the opportunity to demonstrate their power while small nations can obtain recognition for world-class achievements. At the same time, these events are bound up in issues of national identity and ideological rivalries between nations; additionally, they have massive economic significance. The mass media, sporting goods and equipment, travel, lodging, and food industries, to name only a few, are beneficiaries of these events. Economic and political interests become intertwined, and political economy research has often been designed to elucidate the actual functioning and evolution of international sporting events.

One economic aspect of globalization is known as "export-oriented industrialization," which is organized and driven by transnational corporations and their subsidiaries. In this system, product research, development, and design typically take place in developed countries while the labor-intensive, assembly-line phases of product manufacture are relegated to less developed countries (LDCs). The finished product is then exported for distribution in developed countries of the world. Foreign governments provide transnational corporations lavish subsidies, protection against labor organization, and tax relief, while home governments provide relief from tariffs and taxes.

Studies have also shown that the transnational corporations that develop, produce, and sell sporting goods and equipment have moved their manufacturing operations to numerous low-wage export-processing zones across the world (Sage 2005). Moving plants and operations to LDCs boosts profits for corporations such as Nike and Reebok, the world's largest suppliers of sport footwear and apparel, but for workers and their communities in both developed and developing countries the consequences are often dismal.

SEE ALSO: Globalization, Sport and; Political Economy; Politics and Sport; Sport and Capitalism; Sport and the City; Sport and the State

REFERENCES AND SUGGESTED READINGS

Bairner, A. (2001) *Sport, Nationalism, and Globalization: European and North American Perspectives*. State University of New York Press, Albany.
Clark, B. (1998) *Political Economy: A Comparative Approach*, 2nd edn. Praeger, Westport, CT.
Gilpin, R. (2001) *Global Political Economy: Understanding the International Economic Order*. Princeton University Press, Princeton.
Gondwe, D. K. (1992) *Political Economy, Ideology, and the Impact of Economics on the Third World*. Praeger, New York.
Johnson, A. T. & Frey, J. H. (Eds.) (1985) *Government and Sport: The Public Policy Issues*. Rowman & Allanheld, Totowa, NJ.
Sage, G. H. (1998) *Power and Ideology in American Sport*, 2nd edn. Human Kinetics, Champaign, IL.
Sage, G. H. (2005) Sporting Goods Production in the Global Political Economy. In: Nauright, J. & Schimmel, K. S. (Eds.), *The Political Economy of Sport*. Palgrave Macmillan, Houndmills, Basingstoke.
Senn, A. E. (1999) *Power, Politics, and the Olympic Games*. Human Kinetics, Champaign, IL.
Young, T. R. (1986) The Sociology of Sport: Structural Marxist and Cultural Marxist Approaches. *Sociological Perspectives* 29: 3–28.

political leadership

James Walter

Political leadership concerns those who play the decisive roles in institutions that determine "who gets what, when, how" (Lasswell 1977). It is best understood in terms of process (the means by which an individual or group persuades followers to accede to the leadership's purposes) rather than of status (those in specific roles). While power relations, and hence politics, exist in the smallest of groups, and leadership can be studied at every level – from the work group to global forums – political leadership is usually analyzed in a broad societal context in relation to processes of governance.

When the perpetual revolution of capitalism swept away the given authoritative roles and relatively static structures of traditional societies, leadership became an issue: Who should exercise it? In what manner? How was legitimacy to be recognized? Complex modern societies demand high levels of organization and bureaucratic management (promoting the sociological analysis of emergent structures) on the one hand, and the reflexive achievement of individual identity (promoting individualistic theories of psychology) on the other. Both imperatives have influenced the study of leadership. Some social scientists understand leadership as a necessary social function within group and institutions, while others interpret it in terms of individual characteristics that seed the drive for power and facilitate success or failure in its exercise. The first approach drew on the foundational analyses of elite formation and bureaucratic rationalization (Michels 1968; Weber 1961), while the second drew on psychological theory as applied to the question of power (Lasswell 1977). Both were to be tempered by the emergence of social psychology and the best contemporary work bridges institutional structure, historical context, group processes, and psychology (Elcock 2001).

Weber's (1961) exposition of bureaucracy as fundamental to modern society was accompanied by an influential theory of leadership, based on distinctions between traditional authority (deriving from ascribed status, linked to custom and convention), charismatic authority (deriving from subordinates' perceptions of and devotion to extraordinary qualities in a leader), and rational-legal authority (based on the mutual acceptance by those in dominant and subordinate roles of a prescriptive framework defining and supporting leadership roles in relation to specific objectives). Weber's delineation of charismatic authority informed transformational theory and the study of revolutionary leaders, and his view of rational-legal authority decisively shaped organizational analysis (and eventually management studies) while contributing to elite theory.

Leadership as a social function was initially elaborated by elite theorists. Just as Weber was convinced of the inevitability of the "iron cage" of bureaucracy, Gaetano Mosca, Vilfred Pareto, and Robert Michels were persuaded of the inevitability of elite rule. While Mosca provided a historical account of elite dominance, and Pareto sketched the dynamic behind the rise and fall (or "circulation") of elites, Michels's (1968) postulation of the "iron law of oligarchy" was closely linked to a theory of bureaucracy and most influential on later political analysis. He argued that in modern organizations role specialization, differentiated knowledge, and the need for firm direction and adherence to prescribed behaviors mean that leadership inexorably becomes oligarchic; thus, leaders are corrupted, developing vested interests they are driven to defend.

Elite theory became integral to the views of new liberals in the early twentieth century. Walter Lippmann, for instance, sharing the skepticism of Pareto and Michels about democracy, argued that public opinion was formed by elites using modern media to ensure that the "pictures in the heads" of most people were in line with the realities that only an expert few could properly understand and that "the public" itself is a chimera: instead, there are insiders and outsiders, and the course of public affairs is determined by accommodations between insiders who – only at elections, or when a resolution between themselves cannot be achieved – attempt to educate outsiders so as to enlist support for their cause.

At mid-century, C. Wright Mills (1956) was to give this argument a more radical turn, appropriating elite theory to argue that those who enjoyed the corporate, military, and governmental "command posts" in modern society had common backgrounds and used their positions to exploit the masses and to maintain their monopoly of power. Such arguments were to be further developed in the 1960s and 1970s by Marxist theorists such as Ralph Miliband, according to whom the elites of central state institutions act to defend ruling-class interests. Most such studies, however, failed to counter Robert Dahl's critique of Mills: showing that there is potential for those in elite positions to exercise unified power is not equivalent to demonstrating that they act in a concerted fashion. In response, theories have developed of elite pluralism (in which contending elites emerge as representatives of underlying groups and negotiate political settlements) and of fragmented elites (where power is shared and contested between dispersed local, national, and international elites). Studies of elite formation and elite recruitment have remained a staple of political science, and a practical turn especially evident in recent research has been the study of those in executive roles, giving rise to detailed study of the "mandarins."

Elite theorists conceive leadership in terms of social dynamics, but the exploration of leadership psychology has been a more controversial exercise. Individual leaders' actions are not readily amenable to the analytical methods demanded by social science, except when it comes to broad patterns (such as those of elite recruitment). And to the extent that individual political psychology presents problems of empirical verifiability, its application to leadership behavior has been regarded with skepticism. Nonetheless, some scholars saw a need to bridge the gap between popular interest in (and popular writing about) leadership and social scientific method, both in order to understand agency within our institutions and to encourage an informed citizenry. They intended to introduce rigor and methods that would enable productive comparisons and generalizations to be made from single cases.

As with so much else in twentieth-century political science, the initial drive came from North America. Harold Lasswell, at the University of Chicago, was a founding figure in both political psychology and leadership studies. Lasswell's initiatives from the 1930s on (Lasswell 1977) laid the groundwork taken up in the "scientific study of leadership" after the war. Further impetus came from historical studies of the way certain psychological dispositions meshed with contingent circumstances to allow some leaders to speak for "the historical moment" (Erikson 1959). This entailed recognition that leadership success depended on a resonance with followers' needs. Others have since developed more theoretically elaborated insights into this latter point; for instance, Little's (1985) typology of "political ensembles" crystallizing around "strong," "group," or "inspiring" leaders.

One outcome of these approaches was the turn to biographies and psychobiographies of political leaders, a field too capacious to summarize here. We can note in passing the attempts to specify "the tasks of biography" and the argument that theoretically informed biography enables comparative generalization (Edinger 1964), while remarking that the Anglophone tradition of attention to detail still gives substantial insight into leaders at work. Another outcome was the sustained comparative study of presidential leadership, aiming to develop typologies with regard for the qualities that enhanced or diminished performance in particular aspects of the role, and addressing sociological and historical features of the context in which a president acted (Greenstein 2000; Neustadt 1990). Such approaches have since been extended to leaders in non-presidential polities (Elcock 2001). A third outcome has been the emergence of arguments positing particular constellations of characteristics, relating, for example, to trait theory (Stogdill 1974), the investment in power (Winter 1973), contingency (or leadership effectiveness) theory (Fiedler 1967), and political entrepreneurship (Sheingate 2003).

At an intermediate point between the broad study of elites and the close study of individuals, exploration of psychological processes in small groups has generated alternative approaches to leadership. W. R. Bion serves as one example. Bion's (1961) observations led him to distinguish between the tasks a group comes together to achieve ("the work group") and the tacit assumptions that determine interaction within it ("the basic assumption group"). It is the "basic assumption" rather than objective work that governs interaction, and Bion postulated three common types of group behavior: the dependency group (which "gathers to gain security from one individual on whom they depend"); the fight-flight group (which focuses on fighting or fleeing from potential threats and seeks a leader adept in identifying threats and facilitating aggression or evasion); and the pairing group (attuned to unity, to coming together, with symbolic focus on creative "pairing" interactions, but an unrealistic, sometimes messianic vision). Political scientists elaborated on Bion's model to analyze the ties between leaders and followers. Little (1985), for instance, not only illuminated mainstream politics with a sophisticated model of what he called "political ensembles" (based on Bion's basic assumption groups), but also linked these to the "political climates" that favored the success of one type of political ensemble rather than another.

Another approach was to look at group processes as they related to decision-making, in leadership groups themselves. An influential and hotly contested example is Janis's (1972) theory of "groupthink." Seeking to understand the sources of "policy fiasco," Janis came to the conclusion that high cohesiveness and a concurrence-seeking tendency that interferes with critical thinking produce the syndrome he dubbed groupthink. Typical indicators are the group's investment in consensus or compliance with directive leadership, which precludes the open examination of alternative or dissenting views; selective utilization of confirming information; a drive for quick and painless unanimity on issues the group has to confront; the suppression of personal doubts; a belief in the inherent morality of the group; the emergence of "mindguards" who police group orthodoxies; and a view of opponents as evil. While critics routinely condemned Janis's theory (based as it was not on laboratory observation but on case studies of foreign policy decision-making) as incapable of replication or experimental validation, it has recently come to public prominence again as inquiries into intelligence failures in Britain and the US (in connection with the promulgation of the 2002 war in Iraq) each came to the conclusion that "groupthink" had played a role in the acceptance of manifestly inadequate evidence. Despite the contention surrounding groupthink, contemporary attention has shifted to methodical attempts to tie the elements of groupthink more closely to organizational theory and to the nexus between political and bureaucratic decision-making.

Philosophical analyses of leadership stretching back to Plato, Aristotle, and beyond have long been deployed both to scrutinize leaders and as guides to action – Machiavelli remains a staple of political theory. In contrast to the psychological and dynamic typologies above, philosophical theory often relies on archetypes. Attention to values versus pragmatics, to affect and to ethics, encourages consideration of the meanings and moral impact of leadership. An example is John Kane's study of the necessity

for a leader to generate and to maintain moral capital in the eyes of followers if an effective regime is to be maintained.

Despite this history of leadership studies and the enormous popular interest in leadership, it remains a minority interest in political science and sociology. Leadership instead has come to be the preserve of business and management studies, where the attributes of ideal leadership types, or the characteristics that fuel success given particular opportunities, are keenly pursued. In this domain there is frequently an emphasis on behavioral theory as related to organization, and this can also illuminate political behavior. When such studies deploy shared bodies of theory (such as those developed in social psychology, sociology, or group psychology), or give descriptions of the dynamics of recognizable traits, they can be useful and provide analogies for political leadership – see, for instance, the way in which Greenstein (2000) deploys "emotional intelligence," a concept developed by business analyst Daniel Goleman, in explaining the "presidential difference." Too often, however, business studies of leadership are driven by short-term management fads, questionable assumptions about shared norms, or superficial appropriations of psychology to be of much use to the student of politics. More is to be gained by attending to those (e.g., Elcock 2001) who remain attuned to politics as a vocation.

SEE ALSO: Bureaucratic Personality; Charisma; Elites; Groups; Leadership; Mills, C. Wright; Political Parties; Power Elite; Social Movements, Leadership in; Weber, Max

REFERENCES AND SUGGESTED READINGS

Bion. W. R. (1961) *Experiences in Groups.* Tavistock, London.
Edinger, L. J. (1964) Political Science and Political Biography. *Journal of Politics* 26: 423–39, 648–76.
Elcock, H. (2001) *Political Leadership.* Edward Elgar, London.
Erikson, E. H. (1959) *Young Man Luther: A Study in Psychoanalysis and History.* Faber & Faber, London.
Fiedler, F. (1967) *A Theory of Leadership Effectiveness.* McGraw-Hill, New York.

Greenstein, F. (2000) *The Presidential Difference: Leadership Style from FDR to Clinton*. Free Press, New York.

Janis, I. L. (1972) *Victims of Groupthink*. Houghton Mifflin, Boston.

Lasswell, H. D. (1977 [1930]) *Psychopathology and Politics*. University of Chicago Press, Chicago.

Little, G. (1985) *Political Ensembles: A Psychosocial Approach to Politics and Leadership*. Oxford University Press, Melbourne.

Michels, R. (1968 [1911]) *Political Parties: A Sociological Study of the Oligarchical Tendencies of Modern Democracy*. Free Press, New York.

Mills, C. W. (1956) *The Power Elite*. Oxford University Press, New York.

Neustadt, R. E. (1990) *Presidential Power and the Modern Presidents*. Free Press, New York.

Sheingate, A. (2003) Political Entrepreneurship, Institutional Change and American Political Development. *Studies in American Political Development* 17: 185–203.

Stogdill, R. (1974) *Handbook of Leadership*. Free Press, New York.

Weber, M. (1961 [1922]) The Three Types of Legitimate Rule. In: Etzioni, A. (Ed.), *Complex Organizations: A Sociological Reader*. Holt, New York, pp. 4–14.

Winter, D. G. (1973) *The Power Motive*. Free Press, New York.

political machine

Patricia M. Thornton

An urban political machine is a partisan organization that mobilizes its members to vote primarily through the dispersion of material incentives and other forms of preferential treatment, including favoritism based on political criteria in personnel decisions, contracting, and the administration of laws. While the degree and scope of political machines varied, both from city to city as well as over time, they were widely perceived as organizations capable of mobilizing broad swaths of the urban electorate to deliver a vote with mechanical predictability.

The concatenation of historically unique pressures, including industrialization and immigration, presaged the emergence of the political machine during the early nineteenth century.

By the turn of the century, newly arrived immigrants comprised on average nearly a quarter of the total population of America's 50 largest cities; in a few cases, the foreign-born population hovered near the 50 percent mark. Following on the heels of a decade of intense labor conflict and an economic downturn second only to that of the Great Depression of the 1930s, immigrant workers represented a nearly infinite supply of cheap labor, and made their appearance just as many American cities commenced a cycle of intensive growth and expansion. Most historians agree that by the dawn of the twentieth century, the political machine had become the dominant institutional feature of American urban political landscape, and began to wane around the time of the New Deal.

There remains significant scholarly disagreement about how and why political machines emerged, the nature of their long-term impact on American political culture, and whether they persist today. Most scholars agree with Wolfinger (1972), who draws a clear distinction between machine politics – defined as "the manipulation of certain incentives to partisan political participation" – and the political machine as a centralized partisan organization within a jurisdiction that routinely practices machine politics by controlling and distributing patronage. While machine politics remains a common phenomenon, the mature, consolidated political machine is relatively rare today. Scott (1972) argued that the machine represents the product of a particular stage of political development, and noted variations of which could be found in democratizing nations across the globe. Various permutations of the political machine have been described in Japan, Mexico, and post-Soviet Russia.

Many have argued that urban political machines developed in the US as a result of the great waves of mostly European immigrants who arrived in American cities during the latter half of the nineteenth century. Such theorists note that urban political machines were solidly rooted among particular ethnic groups, and that the distribution of material benefits and patronage followed ethnic lines. For example, Glazer and Moynihan (1963) proposed that in New York, "the machine governments resulted from a merger of rural Irish custom with urban American politics." In this view, the operational features of the machine – specifically, its reliance on patronage and the exchange of particularistic benefits – were entirely consistent with the more "private-regarding" cultural backgrounds of the newly arrived immigrant populations. Similarly, some argue that the machine developed as a collective adaptation to the great social dislocation and pressing needs of the swelling immigrant population. Often arriving without either a solid grasp of the English language or the material resources to sustain themselves, new immigrants gravitated toward local leaders rooted in nascent ethnic neighborhoods that provided the services they needed. Neighborhood leaders thus earned their political loyalty in exchange. When such ties hardened into partisan institutional affiliations, such relationships formed the backbone of the urban political machine.

Merton (1968) famously argued that urban political machines evolved and persisted largely because they effectively fulfilled needs left unmet by official political organizations. Merton's functionalist interpretation identified "latent" needs within various strata of urban society that were met by the political machine. For the "deprived classes," the precinct captain provided not only goods and services, but did so in a "humanizing" and "personalizing" manner, effectively transforming impersonal political connections into a dense network of personal ties. Urban businesses, both large and small, turned to the machine boss not only as an economic tsar who organizes and regulates local competition, but also as an ambassador to the more distant realms of government bureaucracy. Thus the machine boss organized, centralized, and effectively managed "the scattered fragments of power" within the political system, an interpretation that echoed Hofstadter's (1960) earlier suggestion that machines developed in order to fill the vacuum created when rapidly growing cities with diverse populations outgrew the managerial capacities of existing government institutions.

Subsequent case studies of individual machines both challenged and extended these early interpretations. Guterbock's 1980 study of machine politics in Chicago found that the correlation between personalistic cultures and machine politics was not supported by empirical evidence. Instead of channeling jobs and services to the mass of economically disadvan-taged voters in the areas under their jurisdiction, Guterbock found that machine bosses tended to funnel resources to wealthy supporters to ensure their continued support, as well as to staff their own party organizations. In his work on New York City's infamous Tammany Hall machine, Shefter (1976) downplayed sociological factors to argue "that the political machine was, in the first instance, a political institution" which, in its time, competed with other urban political institutions for power and resources. Shefter's historical institutional analysis suggested that the cross-class coalitions that served as the backbone of the machine hindered the politicization of the American working class by effectively "organizing out" of urban politics the central cleavage of socioeconomic class. Finally, Erie's 1988 study of Irish-American machines in six cities found that while machine bosses did preferentially distribute jobs, contracts, and services to their Irish-American constituents, the scarcity of resources at their disposal prompted them, on the one hand, to build alliances with state and federal officials in order to expand such supplies, and to offer symbolic recognition to their non-Irish supporters on the other.

While earlier studies of political machines proposed that such political structures, despite their shortcomings, served the larger purpose of assimilating ethnic minorities into mainstream American political culture, case studies have shown that consolidated political machines were more exclusive than inclusive over time. Urban economic restructuring, as well as increased federal oversight during the New Deal era, challenged dominant urban party machines and rendered them vulnerable to internal fragmentation and pressures for reform. One recent trend in studies of political machines is to place them within the broader context of urban regime analysis, comparing machine-based regimes to other types of governing coalitions, in the attempt to elucidate the links between formal and informal structures of political power (DiGaetano 1991a, 1991b).

SEE ALSO: Ethnic Enclaves; Ethnic Groups; Functionalism/Neofunctionalism; Immigration; Institutionalism; Melting Pot; Merton, Robert K.; Political Opportunities; Political Parties; Urban Political Economy

REFERENCES AND SUGGESTED READINGS

DiGaetano, A. (1991a) The Origins of Urban Political Machines in the United States: A Comparative Perspective. *Urban Affairs Quarterly* 26(3): 324–53.

DiGaetano, A. (1991b) Urban Political Reform: Did It Kill the Machine? *Journal of Urban History* 18(1): 37–67.

Erie, S. P. (1988) *Rainbow's End: Irish-Americans and the Dilemmas of Urban Machine Politics, 1840–1985.* University of California Press, Berkeley.

Glazer, N. & Moynihan, D. (1963) *Beyond the Melting Pot: The Negroes, Puerto Ricans, Jews, Italians, and Irish of New York City.* MIT Press, Cambridge, MA.

Hofstadter, R. (1960) *The Age of Reform.* Vintage, New York.

Merton, R. (1968) *Social Theory and Social Structure.* Free Press, New York.

Scott, J. (1972) *Comparative Political Corruption.* Prentice-Hall, Englewood Cliffs, NJ.

Shefter, M. (1976) The Emergence of the Political Machine: An Alternative View. In: Hawley, W. & Lipsky, M. (Eds.), *Theoretical Perspectives on Urban Politics.* Prentice-Hall, Englewood Cliffs, NJ.

Stone, C. (1996) Urban Political Machines: Taking Stock. *PS: Political Science and Politics* (September): 446–9.

Wolfinger, R. (1972) Why Political Machines Have Not Withered Away and Other Revisionist Thoughts. *Journal of Politics* 34(2): 365–98.

political opportunities

David S. Meyer

Political opportunities, sometimes referred to as political opportunity structure or the structure of political opportunities, is a catchall term that refers to the world outside a social movement that affects its mobilization, development, and ultimate impact. The notion that the social and political context matters is well established in the social sciences, but scholars dispute which aspects of the environment influence social movements, and how, and contest the analytic utility of the concept of political opportunities as it has developed. Tarrow's (1998: 19–20) economical definition, "consistent – but not necessarily formal or permanent – dimensions

of the political struggle that encourage people to engage in contentious politics," affords researchers considerable latitude in tailoring the concepts to the case at hand. The challenge for scholars of social movements is to conduct theoretically oriented empirical studies of the interactions of movements with their contexts to test and refine the theory.

Modern use of the term political opportunities is rooted in the scholarly response to the social movements of the 1960s, which challenged the notion that protest was a phenomenon wholly unconnected with more conventional politics. Scholars (e.g., Lipsky 1970) contended that protest could be a rational political strategy for those poorly positioned to exercise influence in other ways.

Establishing the potential rationality of a social protest movement and the individuals who animate it, much research on social protest movements turned to looking at the processes by which organizers mobilized activity, directing their attention to the internal operations of social movement organizations and their relations with sponsors and members. Effectively, they considered the context in which these processes take place as a constant, factoring out much of the stuff that comprises politics.

Political opportunity or political process theory arose as a corrective, explicitly concerned with predicting variance in the periodicity, content, and outcomes of activist efforts over time and across different institutional contexts. The approach emphasized the interaction of activist efforts and more mainstream institutional politics, based on the premise that these phenomena were closely related. The "structure of political opportunities," analogous to the structure of career opportunities individuals face, explicitly refers to the available means for a constituency to lodge claims against authorities.

The primary point of this approach was that activists do not work in a vacuum. Rather, the political context, conceptualized fairly broadly, sets the grievances around which activists mobilize, advantaging some claims and disadvantaging others, encouraging some strategies of influence and forms of organization while discouraging others, and responding through policy reforms more readily at some times than others. The wisdom, creativity, and outcomes of activists' choices, briefly their *agency*, could only be understood by looking at the political context and the rules of the games in which those choices are made, that is, the *structure*.

Peter Eisinger (1973) was the first to use a "political opportunity" framework explicitly, to explain why *some* American cities witnessed extensive riots about race and poverty during the late 1960s. He found that cities with a mix of what he termed "open" and "closed" structures for citizen participation were most likely to experience riots. Cities with extensive institutional openings preempted riots by inviting conventional means of political participation; cities without visible openings for participation repressed or discouraged dissident claimants to foreclose eruptions of protest.

Tilly (1978) built upon this concept to work toward a more comprehensive theory, suggesting national comparisons, recognizing changes in opportunities over time, and arguing that opportunities would explain the more general process of choosing of tactics from a spectrum of possibilities within a "repertoire of contention." For Tilly, activists try to make the most of available openings to pursue a particular set of claims at a particular time. Like Eisinger, he contends that the frequency of protest bears a curvilinear relationship with political openness. When authorities offer a constituency routine and meaningful avenues of access, few will protest, because less costly, more direct routes to influence are available. At the other end of the spectrum of openness, authorities can repress various constituencies such that they are unable to develop the requisite capacity to stage social protest movements altogether. Protest then takes place in a space of toleration, when claimants are not sufficiently advantaged to obviate the need to use dramatic means to express their interests, nor so completely repressed to prevent them from trying to get what they want.

Taken together, Tilly and Eisinger offer models for both cross-sectional comparisons and longitudinal studies, and restrictive and inclusive models. They also set out a spectrum of conceptual possibilities for subsequent scholars. Both broader and more restrictive conceptualizations of political opportunity theory appeared, with findings from one case often generalized to widely disparate cases. Scholars included factors of particular – or exclusive – relevance to the cases they examined. Synthetic theoretical work,

however, was often distant from the particular specifications researchers employed in empirical work. Particularly influential was Doug McAdam's (1982) study of the Civil Rights Movement in the United States. Examining the trajectory of civil rights activism over 40 years, McAdam explicitly offers political process theory as an improvement over previous collective behavior and resource mobilization approaches. African American civil rights activism, McAdam contends, only emerged forcefully when external circumstances provided sufficient openness to allow mobilization. Favorable changes in policy and the political environment, including the collapse of the cotton economy in the South, African American migration to Northern cities, and a decline in the number of lynchings, for example, lowered the costs and dangers of organizing for African Americans, and increased their political value as an electoral constituency. The Supreme Court decision *Brown* v. *Board of Education* legitimated concern with civil rights, and forced political figures to address the issue. In explicitly endorsing integration, it also provided African Americans with a sense of "cognitive liberation" that encouraged action. McAdam's analysis of the Civil Rights Movement, explicitly offered as an exemplar of a political process approach, inspired subsequent analysts looking at other cases.

Tarrow (1989) applied a similar model to explain the broad range of social movement activity over a tumultuous decade, 1965–1975, in Italian politics. He examined a "cycle of protest," including decline, by considering institutional politics along with social protest and disorder. Early on, government openings reduced the cost of collective action, and the initial mobilization of one constituency encouraged others to follow. Workers, students, religious reformers, and leftist factions within parties all took to the streets. Government responses initially encouraged additional mobilization until some turned violent. Violence and disorder legitimated repression, raising the costs of collective action and diminishing protest, while some social movement actors turned their attention to more conventional political activity, reducing their claims and moderating their tactics.

These studies followed the outlines of Tilly's broad theoretical argument, but focused on the emergence and institutionalization of constituencies disadvantaged in institutional politics, emphasizing "expanding opportunities" as a proximate condition for mobilization. In effect, by focusing on emergent mobilization on behalf of excluded constituencies, they emphasized one end of the opportunity curve. Other studies (Meyer 1990; Smith 1996), however, demonstrated that unwelcome policy and government closings could also provoke mobilization. These ostensibly different, but clearly compatible, templates coexist in the scholarly literature.

Most commonly, analysts have written more or less nuanced treatments of particular social movements over time, explaining their trajectory with reference to the broader political field. This approach has been helpful in explaining a wide range of cases, but the diversity of cases has meant that analysts have termed an extraordinarily broad range of factors as elements of political opportunity, depending upon the case at hand. Further, they use a political opportunity approach to explain at least three distinct outcomes: the volume and character of protest; the adoption of organizational forms; and social movement outcomes (Meyer & Minkoff 2004). Often coupled with writing that suggests movements flourish during "favorable" or "expanding opportunities" and fade in times of less favorable or declining opportunities, the collective scholarship has been slow to generate findings that clearly hold across defined categories of cases.

A relatively small number of studies empirically test political opportunity hypotheses against alternative theories. The premises of the political process approach, at least as articulated by the scholars testing it, generally do not perform well. Goodwin (2002) conducted a macroanalysis testing one set of specifications of political opportunity theory, coordinating a large team review of 100 monographs on numerous movements, covering a wide variety of social movements ranging from the Huk rebellion to the Harlem Renaissance. The researchers coded each study along four variables articulated by McAdam (1996): (1) increasing popular access to the political system; (2) divisions within the elite; (3) the availability of elite allies; and (4) diminishing state repression. Despite numerous problems with the survey, acknowledged by Goodwin, the aggregate results raise troubling questions for political opportunity theory: one or more of the political opportunity variables he considers appear in only slightly more than half (59) of the accounts. Excluding explicitly cultural movements such as "hip-hop" from the analysis increases the percentage of cases where political opportunity turns up slightly, but problems remain. Not the least of these is the formulation of "expanding political opportunities" in terms of increased access, which appeared far more frequently in non-democratic contexts (73 percent of cases) than in democratic contexts. Moreover, contracting opportunities, seen in reduced access to the political system, appear important in at least one-third of the cases in which political opportunities matter at all, primarily in democratic contexts.

The mixed record of political opportunity theory in explicit empirical tests highlights important challenges for social movement scholars. First, because competing hypotheses coexist within the literature, virtually any finding can be used to support or refute a preferred version of the theory. Clearly, reconciling these ostensibly conflicting hypotheses theoretically is essential for the continued development of the political opportunity perspective. Second, scholars differ in how broad a range of factors in the political environment they will consider as components of political opportunity. Thus, when grievances, for example, turn up as a significant explanatory variable, this can be used to support or refute political opportunity theory. Third, because there is considerable flexibility in not only the conception of political opportunity but also the specification of opportunity variables, it is rarely clear that scholars have picked the most appropriate specification for the variables in each case. Nonetheless, results from empirical tests demand further theoretical development as well as additional empirical examinations.

Core elements of political opportunity, such as political openness, are likely to operate differently for different outcomes – and for different sorts of movements. Unwelcome changes in policy, for example, may alert citizens of the need to act on their own behalf or may cause elite actors to side with, or try to activate, a largely disengaged public. We can develop a more comprehensive theory of political opportunity by returning to Tilly's (1978) curvilinear conception of openness and mobilization. Well-established constituencies, and the issue-based movements they animate, such as the largely middle-class environmental and peace movements, may need to be forced out of institutional politics in order to stage a social movement. In contrast, more marginal constituencies, such as those based on ethnic identity or sexual orientation, may need to be enabled into mobilization by institutional openings. Whereas the former is pushed out to the social protest part of the curve, the latter is invited into mobilization to reach the same point on the curve. The same differences play out in the question of outcomes. When government openings and favorable policies invite mobilization, a large movement is likely to be accompanied by other political and policy gains. When, in contrast, activism emerges in response to proposed unwelcome changes and political closings, movement influence may be little more than small moderations in proposed policies that veer toward preserving the status quo. In the former case, movement influence is magnified, in the latter, it is obscured, but it can be real.

Sorting out these issues, specifically, assessing the role of threats and openings for different constituencies and different groups within a movement coalition, and separating out different outcomes, is the essential step for building political opportunity theory.

SEE ALSO: Civil Rights Movement; Collective Action; Contention, Tactical Repertoires of; Mobilization; Political Machine; Political Process Theory; Protest, Diffusion of; Resource Mobilization Theory; Revolutions; Social Movement Organizations; Social Movements

REFERENCES AND SUGGESTED READINGS

Boudreau, V. (1996) Northern Theory, Southern Protest: Opportunity Structure Analysis in Cross-National Perspective. *Mobilization* 1: 175–89.
Costain, A. N. (1992) *Inviting Women's Rebellion: A Political Process Interpretation of the Women's Movement*. Johns Hopkins University Press, Baltimore.
Eisinger, P. K. (1973) The Conditions of Protest Behavior in American Cities. *American Political Science Review* 81: 11–28.

Goodwin, J. (2002) Are Protesters Opportunists? Political Opportunities and the Emergence of Political Contention. Working Paper, Department of Sociology, New York University.
Kitschelt, H. P. (1986) Political Opportunity Structures and Political Protest: Anti-Nuclear Movements in Four Countries. *British Journal of Political Science* 16: 57–85.
Kriesi, H., Koopmans, R., Duyvendak, J.-W., & Giugni, M. (1995) *The Politics of New Social Movements in Western Europe: A Comparative Analysis*. University of Minnesota Press, Minneapolis and London.
Lipsky, M. (1970) *Protest in City Politics*. Rand-McNally, Chicago.
McAdam, D. (1982) *Political Process and the Development of Black Insurgency, 1930–1970*. University of Chicago Press, Chicago.
McAdam, D. (1996) Political Opportunities: Conceptual Origins, Current Problems, Future Directions. In: McAdam, D., McCarthy, J. D., & Mayer, N. Z. (Eds.), *Comparative Perspectives on Social Movements*. Cambridge University Press, Cambridge, pp. 23–40.
Meyer, D. S. (1990) *A Winter of Discontent: The Nuclear Freeze and American Politics*. Praeger, New York.
Meyer, D. S. (2004) Protest and Political Opportunities. *Annual Review of Sociology* 30: 125–45.
Meyer, D. S. & Minkoff, D. C. (2004) Conceptualizing Political Opportunity. *Social Forces* 82: 1457–92.
Smith, C. (1996) *Resisting Reagan: The US Central America Peace Movement*. University of Chicago Press, Chicago.
Tarrow, S. (1989) *Democracy and Disorder: Protest and Politics in Italy, 1965–1975*. Clarendon Press, Oxford.
Tarrow, S. (1998) *Power in Movement*, 2nd edn. Cambridge University Press, New York.
Tilly, C. (1978) *From Mobilization to Revolution*. McGraw-Hill, New York.
Tilly, C. (1995) *Popular Contention in Great Britain, 1758–1834*. Harvard University Press, Cambridge, MA.

political parties

Dylan Riley

Political parties are organized currents of opinion that aim to realize a program by controlling a political association. Parties can emerge only where there exists politics defined as a struggle over the leadership or the influence of the leadership of a human group. To the extent that leadership divides among estates, clans, or families according to tradition and is not the object of struggle, neither politics nor parties can exist. Modern party organizations are connected with the rise of the modern state, because modern parties aim at seizing (either through electoral means or violence) state power (Weber 1958 [1946]: 78–81; Sartori 1976: 4; Pombeni 1985: 20; Held 1987: 165). There are three broad schools of thought about parties: Marxism, pluralism, and elitism.

For Marxists, parties emerge as specialized organizational apparatuses of social classes in *capitalist* society. This combines two arguments. The first is a claim about the general conditions of possibility for the "party form" of political organization. The second is a claim about the sociological basis of politics.

The differentiation of economic exploitation and political rule, a structural feature of capitalist society, makes possible the "party form" of political organization. Capitalism is characterized by a split between "bourgeois and citizen," man as a member of civil society and man as a member of political society (Marx 1994: 9). Politics in capitalist society is specifically autonomous from economic production and thus becomes the concern of a specialized class of persons (Gramsci 1971: 144). Parties arise in these conditions to manage the political interests of social classes. Thus it is the basically economic character of classes in capitalist society that explains the need for a specialized apparatus to organize class interests politically. Parties exist neither in non-capitalist class societies (such as feudal or slave societies) nor in socialist societies in which classes have ceased to exist. Thus, the first central claim of the Marxist theory of parties is that the "party form" of political organization is specific to capitalism.

Most Marxist arguments include the further claim that classes, defined as groups that form around the ownership and non-ownership of the means of production, constitute the social basis of parties. Capitalist societies are divided by a fundamental conflict of interest between the owners of the means of production and the direct producers. Parties express and organize the interests of these fundamentally divided social classes (Gramsci 1971: 148; Marx 1994: 119). Parties, in most Marxist accounts, do not however simply express the economic structure and class divisions of capitalist society. They also play an active role in the process of class formation through the mediation of class and intraclass struggles (Gramsci 1971: 180–3; Marx 1994: 166–7).

Both of these theses (the specificity of parties to capitalism and the class basis of parties under capitalism) have been challenged. The first challenge, posed in a particularly acute way by Stalinism, is that party apparatuses have existed in non-capitalist societies. The second problem, posed by the emergence of "catch-all" parties, is that parties may not represent social classes at all, but rather a complex of interests that are not well understood in terms of classes. It is important to distinguish these two types of challenges because they do not logically imply one another. It may be true that party organizations can arise only under conditions of capitalist production, yet not be closely associated with class interests. Alternatively, it may be true that parties are not specific to capitalist production but that in capitalism they are primarily organizations of social classes. Both sets of arguments exist in work on parties.

It is convenient to divide the pluralist position into two subgroups: classical liberalism and modern "interest group" pluralism. Although related, these positions have different views of political parties. Classical liberals distrust political parties. Sovereignty, for them, is located in a chamber that represents (in the double sense of mirroring and constituting) the national interest, understood as an outcome of the deliberative processes of deputies. Classical liberals argue that deputies should represent the material and ideal interests of autonomous, reasonable, and generally propertied *individuals*. This theory is based on the conception of parliament as a "talking shop" or "public sphere" in which interaction among educated men would produce rational political decisions. For most classical liberals, political parties constitute a double threat. First, parties threaten to strip individuals of their means of political expression. By subordinating individuals to a bureaucratic organization, parties undermine the social structural basis of liberal consensus, because they undermine the possibility of reasoned debate in the public sphere. Second, parties, by subordinating deputies to programs elaborated *before* their entry into parliament, undermine the liberal model of deliberation (Schmitt 1985 [1923]: 6–7, 40–1; Weber 1958 [1946]: 102–3).

Interest group pluralism is an attempt to reconstruct classical liberalism in the age of mass democracy. Like their classical liberal forebears, pluralists accept that parliament represents a general interest. But far from seeing party organizations as a threat to the constitution of that interest, they explain how party organizations can function to guarantee it. Pluralists argue that politics in modern societies is the concern of a specialized "political system" (Sartori 1976: 45). Further, they suggest that competing interest groups characterize modern societies, and that these groups are likely to organize for their interests (Sartori 1976: 13).

Unlike classical liberals, however, pluralists argue that the divisions of modern society make possible *consensus*, understood as an "endless process of adjusting many dissenting minds (and interests) into changing 'coalitions' of reciprocal persuasion" (Sartori 1976: 16). Given a plurality of interests, parties, especially in functioning two-party systems, do *not* and indeed *cannot* represent only social classes. Rather, they attempt to both constitute and express common ground among the broadest possible coalition of groups. Thus, parties, even when they represent a "part" of the social whole, propose policies and govern in the "general interest" (Sartori 1976: 26–7).

The pluralist view of parties depends on a specific conception of society. Individuals with preferences constitute society for thinkers in this tradition. Social groups are accidental and temporary coalitions that form around a variety of aims and interests. Parties seek to elaborate and articulate a social consensus by appealing to the interests of voters as individuals. Thus consensus is possible, despite the existence of social conflict, because social structures are fluid. They do not trap individuals into durable groups, such as Marxist classes.

Michels, Pareto, Weber, Mosca, and Schmitt in different ways suggest that the Marxist theory of parties is wrong to assume that political organizations develop as an expression of underlying class interests. For all of these thinkers, party organizations possess distinctive power resources and interests that separate them from their social base. This is particularly true of socialist parties that depended upon large masses of followers with few economic and cultural resources (Michels 1968 [1915]: 70). The elitists, however, do not stop at a critique of Marxism. They generalize their argument to a critique of liberal democracy. While parties are an inevitable development in modern society, party democracy, according to these thinkers, is a contradiction in terms (Held 1987: 143).

A broadly elitist view of party organizations is also common among research influenced by Pierre Bourdieu and the idea of the political field. Bourdieu suggests that parties constitute themselves, and "take positions," primarily in relation to other organizations in the political field. There may exist a homology between position-taking in the political field and social groups outside the political field. Yet, Bourdieu emphasizes, the primary determinant of policies is the interests of those who possess a relative monopoly on political capital (understood as the totality of organizational and cultural resources necessary to represent social interests) (Bourdieu 1991: 172).

One of the most important revisions to the strict elitist traditions is the theory of competitive elitism. The competitive elitists accept much of elitist critique of parties. But instead of drawing the consequence that modern democracy is a sham, they argue that competing party organizations guarantee some responsiveness to the underlying population. This position differs from the pluralist position, because competitive elitists do not argue that parties seek to represent a general interest, or a consensus. Rather, the competitive elitist point is simply that in the face of the overwhelming organizational resources of parties, having competing parties is better than not having competing parties.

Scholars working broadly in the elitist tradition have produced some of the most important work on the internal organization of parties. They identify two organizational dimensions: the structure of membership and the articulation of party organizations. Membership may be structured in three basic ways. In cadre parties most of the party's political supporters are not members. They may vote for the party at election time or support it in other ways, but they do not pay dues and they do not have a party card.

Indirect mass membership parties have a mass membership, but this membership is formed by affiliations with non-party groups such as trade unions. Members of direct mass membership parties in contrast join the party through the voluntary act of purchasing a party card (Duverger 1959: 5–40). Parties may also be articulated in different organizational forms. Caucuses emerged as circles of notables formed to influence opinion in the context of restricted suffrage. Branches are territorial organizations that generally reflect the administrative divisions of the state. Branches, unlike caucuses, aim at increasing their memberships. Cells are based on the workplace. Parties with organized militias first emerged with fascist parties. There were two types. The Nazi Party militia was an affiliate but separate party organization. The Italian Fascist Party was a "party-militia," meaning that the militia organization was initially the basic unit of party organization.

There exist few general works seeking to explain the origins of parties. Most work on parties, however, would agree with the following points. First, at a very broad level, the historical trend, at least up until very recently, has been from cadre parties to mass parties, at least in Western Europe. Most scholars argue that this transition is associated with the emergence of universal suffrage. Second, the emergence of mass parties can occur in one of two ways. They have developed either out of parliamentary groups, which became mass parties in the age of universal suffrage, or from extra-parliamentary social movements, which became parties at a subsequent stage. The first path was typical of parties in England and the United States. The second was typical of the European socialist parties, but is also true of extreme right parties like the fascist parties. Thus in continental Europe and in England a transition occurred from parties of notables or cadre parties, which were loose groupings of local elites, to mass parties that were more ideological and tended to issue membership cards. Socialist parties developed the model of the mass membership party, but socialist organizational techniques were to some extent adopted by other parties, particularly fascist parties. The difference between these two forms of party largely corresponds to a distinction between the Anglo-Saxon world and continental Europe. The transition from cadre to mass parties was most pronounced in countries that had strong socialist parties (particularly Italy and Germany), but also occurred to some extent in England. The United States forms an exception to this rule. In this case, mass parties emerged very early (some scholars date their emergence from the 1820s). Mass party formation in this instance did not occur under pressure from socialism or from other political organizations of the industrial working class.

Work on political parties distinguishes three types of party "systems": single parties, two-party systems, and multiple party systems. Single-party systems are usually considered to differ qualitatively from multiparty and two-party systems. Yet some scholars have pointed out that effective single-party systems at the local level can coexist with multiple or two-party systems at the national level. Further, single parties are compatible with democracy if there is intraparty competition, especially if this competition takes the form of an electoral struggle among organized factions (Epstein 1966: 48).

Many scholars seek to explain the difference between two-party and multiparty systems. Two approaches are common. One focuses on the electoral system. Two-party systems are generally thought to be more compatible with single-member constituencies than proportional representation because in single-member constituencies the "winner takes all." Permanent minorities are not able to gain representation. Therefore, pressure builds to form permanent coalitions of "ins" and "outs." These pressures do not operate in systems with proportional representation.

A second approach explains party systems as the consequence of religious, class, or cultural "cleavages." Overlapping cleavages produce multiparty systems. Unlike the approach focusing on electoral rules, this approach stresses the social basis of party formation. According to this view, multiple party systems may persist even where electoral rules might lead one to expect the emergence of a two-party system.

Perhaps the central question of current debate is: are political parties necessary for the functioning of modern mass democracy? A dominant argument in both political sociology and political science is that parties are functionally necessary to aggregate interests in mass societies. There are two reasons for this. First, the very diversity of modern societies requires some mechanisms to aggregate individual interests. Second, the complexity of modern administration requires that information be summarized in programs that voters can relate to their ideal and material interests. Thus, for purely technical reasons, mass democracy is inconceivable without parties.

There are two possible responses to this argument. The first is that party organizations do not all have the same relationship to their electorate. Indeed, different parts of the electorate are able to subject party organizations to more or less control. Thus the "functions" that parties serve (aggregating interests and summarizing information) are more important for sectors of the population that are culturally and materially deprived. Thus, increases in leisure time (embodied in reductions in the work week) and decreases in cultural and economic inequality should lead to more responsive parties.

A second line of argument suggests that with the advent of mass media, the Internet, and other advanced means of communication, the technical constraints imposed by large states are undermined. According to this argument, direct democracy has now become a technical possibility and, for some thinkers, normatively superior to party democracy.

This raises a key empirical question: are we moving toward a "post-party" democracy under the impact of technological transformation? A strand of literature in the 1990s argued for the increasing irrelevance of parties, especially in the United States. This view, however, now seems decisively refuted by recent historical experience (especially from the elections of 1994), when the rise of a highly disciplined Republican Party and a general increase in partisanship undermined the view that parties were declining. Indeed, parties use the very techniques that the technological argument sees as threatening to them (such as opinion polls and the Internet). The Internet may even have strengthened the "party-ness" of the American Democratic Party. The same is true of political techniques such as referenda. Since referenda place issues directly before voters, they would seem to weaken party organizations. Many scholars, however, point to the limits of referenda. They can work only where issues can be posed

in such a way that a "yes" or "no" vote is appropriate. Further, the role of parties continues to be central in organizing referenda, getting signatures, and mobilizing voters.

Two areas of research on political parties are likely to be particularly fruitful. The first concerns the differential relationships between political parties and the underlying "base" for different social groups. Clearly, parties are in no simple way the "expression" of underlying social forces. Yet parties are also not equally "autonomous" from all social groups. As Bourdieu, Weber, and Gramsci in different ways emphasize, the relationship between parties and wealthy groups with significant leisure time is likely to be very different than the relationship between parties and sectors of the population with little leisure time, cultural capital, and wealth. Thus a crucial area for further research concerns the relations between parties and the more general structures of inequality in society.

The second key area of research concerns the explanation for the rise of political parties. There exist very few such explanations. The consensus view seems to be that two broad historical preconditions must be in place to have political parties: universal suffrage and national states. But these explanations remain overly general. There have been mass democracies without modern political parties, and there have been modern political parties without mass democracy. Further, the relationship between mass parties and nation-states is not as strict as it would seem. Parties often arise as international organizations (particularly socialist parties). While they may primarily be oriented to power at the level of the nation-state, most parties are also committed to a particular international order. Thus researchers would do well to explain the specific relations between parties and social structures, and the broader historical conditions of possibility for the party form of political organization.

SEE ALSO: Capital; Capitalism; Class, Status, and Power; Class and Voting; Democracy; Elites; Habitus/Field; Liberalism; Marx, Karl; Pluralism, British; Political Machine; Political Opportunities; Political Sociology; Politics; Public Sphere; State

REFERENCES AND SUGGESTED
READINGS

Bourdieu, P. (1991) *Language and Symbolic Power*. Harvard University Press, Cambridge, MA.

Duverger, M. (1959) *Political Parties, Their Organization and Activity in the Modern State*. Wiley, New York.

Epstein, L. D. (1966) *Political Parties in Western Democracies*. Pall Mall, London.

Held, D. (1987) *Models of Democracy*. Polity Press, Cambridge.

Gramsci, A. (1971) *Selections from the Prison Notebooks*. International Publishers, New York.

Marx, K. (1994) *Selected Writings*. Ed. L. H. Simon. Hackett, Indianapolis.

Michels, R. (1968 [1915]) *Political Parties: A Sociological Study of the Oligarchical Tendencies of Modern Democracy*. Collier, London.

Pombeni, P. (1985) *Introduzione alla storia dei partiti politici*. Il Mulino, Milan.

Sartori, G. (1976) *Parties and Party Systems: A Framework for Analysis*, Vol. 1. Cambridge University Press, Cambridge.

Schmitt, K. (1985 [1923]) *The Crisis of Parliamentary Democracy*. MIT Press, Cambridge, MA.

Weber, M. (1958 [1946]) *From Max Weber*. Free Press, New York.

political process theory

Neal Caren

The standard explanation for social movement mobilization, known as political process theory (PPT), emphasizes the role of political opportunities, mobilizing structures, and framing processes, along with protest cycles and contentious repertoires. Developed in the US in the 1970s and 1980s and rooted in an analysis of civil rights struggles, PPT focuses on the interaction between movement attributes, such as organizational structure, and the broader economic and political context. Critics argue that the theory is overly structural and invariant. Recent research by core PPT theorists has shifted focus to a more dynamic analysis of the reoccurring mechanisms and processes of contentious politics.

PPT is the culmination of a series of critiques against the then-prevailing social scientific view that protestors and other social movement participants were irrational mobs, overwhelmed by a collective mentality. Movements did not result from alienation or abnormal psychological dispositions, but rather were means to achieve political ends and resolve legitimate grievances. Three precursors to PPT are noteworthy for their contributions to establishing this new analysis. First, Olson's (1965) analysis of collection behavior turned old notions about the irrationality of protestors on its head, exploring the rational and deliberate choices that individuals made before joining a movement. Second, in an influential analysis of the farm workers' movement, McCarthy and Zald (1973, 1977) found that the availability of resources to the movement, as opposed to the degree of oppression, explained much of the variation in the level of mobilization. This resource mobilization perspective counted more than just material goods as resources, including aspects such as organizational strength and the presence of elite allies. Third, Piven and Cloward (1977) brought attention to important aspects of the economic and political system. Only during periods of great system-wide crisis, such as during the Depression, for example, were movements able to extract concessions from elites. Combined, these three developments formed the basis of PPT.

The foundational work in PPT is Charles Tilly's *From Mobilization to Revolution* (1978), which synthesized these insights, along with those of other historical and political sociologists. Tilly asserts that the interaction between three components – interests, organization, and opportunity – explains a contender's level of mobilization and collective action. Interests represent the potential gains from participation; organization represents the level of unified identity and networks; and opportunity represents the amount of political power, the likelihood of repression, and the vulnerability of the target. *From Mobilization to Revolution*'s impact on social movement scholarship is largely indirect, as McAdam's subsequent analysis of the Civil Rights Movement became PPT's central text.

PPT crystallized in McAdam's *Political Process and the Development of Black Insurgency* (1982). Drawing on earlier critiques of classical approaches, and building on resource mobilization and especially the work of Tilly, McAdam analyzed the rise and decline of the US Civil Rights Movement as a direct result of three factors: political opportunities, indigenous organizational strength, and cognitive liberation. Political opportunities resulted from *"any* event or broad social process that serves to undermine the calculations and assumptions on which the political establishment is structured" (p. 41). The definition was broad, and his examples included wars, industrialization, international political realignments, prolonged unemployment, and widespread demographic changes. Political opportunities worked indirectly, by changing the degree of power inequality between the challenging group and the target. Among the opportunities that McAdam found leading up to the Civil Rights Movement was the Southern black population shift from a rural to urban environment, the decline in lynchings, and the potential for international embarrassment during this phase in the Cold War.

A second factor that encouraged mobilization was the strength of indigenous organizations. These are not the organizations that were formed in the heat of the struggle, but rather the preexisting political and potentially political organizations that existed among the aggrieved community. The organizations provide members who can be recruited as a group, respected leaders, a communications network, and individual ties. For the early Civil Rights Movements, these institutions included black churches, black colleges, and the NAACP, all of which saw rapid growth in the decades immediately prior to the movement.

The third element of McAdam's political process model is a sense of cognitive liberation among potential social movement participants. This is a result of a group process, and flows directly from the political opportunities and through local organizations. In order to participate, McAdam argues, drawing on Piven and Cloward (1977), individuals must feel that the current political system lacks legitimacy and their social movement participation could make meaningful change happen. In the case of the Civil Rights Movement, McAdam notes a dramatic shift towards optimism about the future for African Americans in polling data in the 1950s.

In addition to shifts in all three of these factors accounting for the rise of the Civil

Rights Movements, McAdam also argues that PPT accounts for the decline of mobilization as well. He charts a negative shift in all three factors in the late 1960s, which, he argues, accounts for the end of civil rights protesting during that period.

PPT has evolved since McAdam's formulation. Notably, framing has largely replaced cognitive liberation and indigenous organizational strength has been replaced by mobilizing structures. Political opportunities – the element which has received the most attention – have been both narrowed and broadened. Additionally, Tarrow's (1994) notion of protest cycles is sometimes included as a part of PPT, as is Tilly's concept of repertoires of contention.

In place of cognitive liberation, PPTists soon began to speak of a movement's framing process. Drawing heavily on the work of David Snow and colleagues, framing is the "conscious strategic efforts by groups of people to fashion shared understandings of the world and of themselves that legitimate and motivate collective action" (McAdam et al. 1996). While McAdam's cognitive liberation was focused on an individual sense of empowerment prior to involvement, analysis of framing processes emphasizes the more strategic decisions achieved at a higher organizational level as an ongoing, dynamic process. At a minimum, a group needs to describe their grievances persuasively, the diagnostic frame, and present a feasible solution, the prognostic frame. Large movements often provide master frames, such as "civil rights," which subsequent movement and groups can easily refer to. In contrast to the other two primarily structural elements, framing processes are the major place where the cultural is incorporated into the model. As such, framing is sometimes stretched to include all non-structural elements impacting mobilization. This tendency is something that PPT critics fault as a model flaw and that PPT advocates warn against.

In a shift away from the explicit bias in favor of formal preexisting organizations in McAdam's indigenous organizational strength, PPTists moved toward an analysis of mobilizing structures, which are "those collective vehicles, informal as well as formal, through which people mobilize and engage in collective action" (McAdam et al. 1996). This includes not only preexisting groups, but also movement organizations and the informal networks among potential activists.

Similarly, political opportunities were found by scholars in such a variety of places as to make the concept nearly unfalsifiable. As McAdam et al. (1996) noted in their introduction, political opportunities had become an increasingly unwieldy concept, with each author operationalizing the concept in unique ways. They attempt to specify the idea by focusing on four dimensions: (1) the relative openness or closure of the institutionalized political system; (2) the stability of that broad set of elite alignments that typically undergirds a polity; (3) the presence of elite allies; and (4) the state's capacity and propensity for repression. Where McAdam's original definition had grown to fit just about everything external to the movement, this reformulation attempted to narrow the scope by focusing on more specific aspects of the political system. These efforts did not go far enough, however, for critics.

A fourth concept that is often associated with PPT is the protest cycle. This refers to historical periods of heightened contention across the political sphere, such as in 1968 in the US or 1989 in Eastern Europe, when a host of groups was challenging the legitimacy of the state. As a new political opportunity usually affects more than one group and as frames are often transferable across movements, movements that are not obviously linked can share similar life courses.

While the number of ways that a movement can make itself heard is potentially unlimited, in practice the number available to any given movement is actually quite finite. Following Tilly (1995), this limited set of ways that actors can make claims constitutes the repertoire of contention. Tilly finds that the modern repertoire of contention, which includes strikes, demonstrations, and social movements, originated in the second half of the nineteenth century. These modular forms of protest can be transferred across issues, as petitions can be organized to free political prisoners or revive cancelled television shows; in both cases the organizers, signers, and targets all know that a petition is a form of protest.

Combined, these five elements – political opportunities, mobilizing structures, framing processes, protest cycles, and contentious repertoires – constitute the core of contemporary PPT research. In addition to explaining the rise and decline of social movements, they are also used to explain the form that protest takes and the outcomes that result.

In regards to the research by other scholars, the political-opportunities element of PPT has received the most attention. In fact, the terms political opportunities and political process theory are often used interchangeably. Political opportunity has also been the focus of much, but not all, of the critiques. Goodwin and Jasper launched the best-known set of criticisms in a special issue of *Sociological Forum*. Their piece, along with a variety of responses from PPT defenders and agnostics, was published in Goodwin and Jasper (2004).

Goodwin and Jasper, along with other critics from more cultural camps, see PPT as overly structural, centering stable, external factors and analyzing non-structural features as if they were structures. The search for a series of invariant causal variables to explain social movement emergence, which is the hallmark of PPT, is fruitless. The varied historically specific conditions under which movements arise make such causal factors defined either in such a broad way as to be tautological and trivial or so narrow as to be only relevant for the examined case. This is particularly true for political opportunities, they argue, despite some efforts by PPTists to focus the definition. Similarly, they see mobilizing structures, including both formal and informal networks of individuals and institutions, not so much as causal factors for social movement emergence, but rather implicit in the notion of a movement as a collective. As such, it adds little to our understanding of the conditions for movement emergence. Framing process, in contrast, they see as a limited concept, forced to carry all of the non-structural elements, while ignoring such relevant factors as emotions, symbols, and moral principles.

McAdam, Tarrow, and Tilly (2001), the central PPTists, have moved away from general causal arguments to a more dynamic approach to the study of "contentious politics." In place of opportunities, mobilizing structures, and framing processes, they speak of environmental, relational, and cognitive mechanisms. The emphasis is not so much on asserting that all three are causally necessary, but on identifying the specific mechanisms within each that can be found across multiple movements. Examples of such mechanisms that they identify include brokerage, the linking of previously unconnected units; category formation, the creation of identities; and certification, a target recognition of a movement, its tactics or its claims. However, despite this distancing by its founders, PPT remains the dominant paradigm for social movement research.

SEE ALSO: Civil Rights Movement; Framing and Social Movements; Political Opportunities; Social Movement Organizations; Social Movements

REFERENCES AND SUGGESTED READINGS

Goodwin, J. & Jasper, J. M. (2004) *Rethinking Social Movements: Structure, Meaning and Emotions.* Rowman & Littlefield, Lanham, MD.

McAdam, D. (1982) *Political Process and the Development of Black Insurgency, 1930–1970.* University of Chicago Press, Chicago.

McAdam, D., McCarthy, J. D., & Zald, M. N. (1996) *Comparative Perspectives on Social Movements: Political Opportunities, Mobilizing Structures, and Cultural Framing.* Cambridge University Press, Cambridge.

McAdam, D., Tarrow, S., & Tilly, C. (2001) *Dynamics of Contention.* Cambridge University Press, Cambridge.

McCarthy, J. D. & Zald, M. N. (1973) *The Trend of Social Movements in America: Professionalization and Resource Mobilization.* General Learning, Morristown, NJ.

McCarthy, J. D. & Zald, M. N. (1977) Resource Mobilization and Social Movements: A Partial Theory. *American Journal of Sociology* 82: 1212–41.

Olson, M. (1965) *The Logic of Collective Action.* Harvard University Press, Cambridge, MA.

Piven, F. F. & Cloward, R. (1977) *Poor People's Movements: Why they Succeed, How they Fail.* Vintage Books, New York.

Tarrow, S. (1994) *Power in Movement: Social Movements, Collective Action and Mass Politics in the Modern State.* Cambridge University Press, Cambridge.

Tilly, C. (1978) *From Mobilization to Revolution.* Addison-Wesley, Reading, MA.

Tilly, C. (1995) Contentious Repertoires in Great Britain, 1758–1834. In: Traugott, M. (Ed.), *Repertoires and Cycles of Collective Action.* Duke University Press, Durham, NC, pp. 15–42.

political sociology

Ryan Calder and John Lie

Political sociology analyzes the operation of power in social life, examining the distribution and machination of power at all levels: individual, organizational, communal, national, and international. Defined thus, political science becomes a subfield of sociology. Parsons (1951), for example, treated the political as one of the four principal domains of sociological analysis. In practice, however, political sociology has developed as a sociological subfield, with its distinct concerns and fashions.

Aristotle, Ibn Khaldun, or Montesquieu may rightfully claim to be the founder of political sociology insofar as they highlighted the *social* bases of power relations and political institutions. However, most contemporary scholars trace their intellectual lineage to Marx or Weber. Political sociology emerged as a distinct subfield in the 1950s, especially in the debate between pluralists and elite theorists. In the 1980s and 1990s political sociologists focused on social movements, the state, and institutions.

MARX AND WEBER

According to Marx (and Engels), economic structure and class relations are the basis for all political activity (Miliband 1977). The dominant mode of production determines who wields power in society. Under the capitalist mode of production, the capitalist class controls the state, which serves to perpetuate its domination of subordinate classes and manage "its common affairs." There are two principal strands in Marxist political sociology. The instrumentalists portray the state as the tool of a unified capitalist class that controls both the economic and political spheres. In this model, the state is virtually epiphenomenal to the dominance of the ruling class. The structuralists view the state (as well as politics more generally) as a relatively autonomous product of conflict between classes and sometimes within classes.

Whereas Marx viewed social classes as the basic units of competition, Weber (1978) recognized that competition occurs among many different types of entities, including not only social classes but also status groups (defined in terms of consumption, codes of honor, education and credentials, ethnicity, and other criteria), as well as political agencies and agents. Contestation for power occurs both across and within various institutions and organizations: heads of state clash with parliaments and civil-service bureaucracies over legislation; trade unions and professional groups vie to influence legislators; politicians and bosses fight for control of a political party. The political sphere, while linked to events in other spheres, has its own logic of contestation.

Against the Marxian stress on the economy and class struggle, the defining feature of modern western societies for Weber is the ineluctable advance of rationality. Thus, the bases of political authority shift from traditional or charismatic claims toward legal-rational forms of legitimation and administration. For example, the whim of a king or lord who asserts the right to rule based on dynastic precedent (traditional authority) or heroic acts and personal qualities (charismatic authority) is replaced by state control of the populace according to normalized standards and codified laws (legal-rational authority). For Weber, the modern state also extends and entrenches its domination of society by expanding its coercive apparatus, chiefly in the form of bureaucratization. The central function of modern mass citizenship is to legitimize this iron cage; even in a democracy, real power would reside in the hands of a few.

ELITE THEORY, PLURALISM, AND THE THIRD WORLD

That power in society is always concentrated in the hands of a few is the basic assumption of the elite theory of society (Bottomore 1993). The elite theorists drew heavily on Weber, but placed greater emphasis than Weber on *power* rather than *authority* as the key to political dominance. Whereas Weber agreed that the power to make major political decisions always concentrates in a small group, he viewed the authority that stems from popular support as the foundation for all institutions that provide this power. For the elite theorists, it was the reverse: power made authority, law, and political culture possible.

Michels (1966) proposed "the iron law of oligarchy": the thesis that all organizations – whether political parties, trade unions, or any other kind – come to be run by a small group of leaders. He saw the oligarchical tendency as "a matter of technical and practical necessity," citing several causes for this tendency: the impracticality of mass leadership, the organizational need for a small corps of full-time expert leaders, the divergence of leaders' interests from those of the people they claim to represent, and the masses' apathy and thirst for guidance. Schumpeter agreed with elite theorists, including Pareto and Mosca, that mass participation in politics is very limited. Emphasizing the lability and pliability of popular opinion, he stated that "the will of the people is the product and not the motive power of the political process" (Schumpeter 1976).

With *The Power Elite* (1956), C. Wright Mills produced a radical version of elite theory. Mills described a "power elite" of families that dominated three sectors of American society: politics, the military, and business. The power elite was cohesive and durable because of the "coincidence of interests" among organizations in the three sectors, as well as elites' "similarity of origin and outlook" and "social and personal intermingling." Radical elite theory presumed the passivity of mass politics, which was articulated most influentially by Marcuse (1964).

Radical elite theory was largely a response to pluralism, which was particularly influential in US social science in the two decades following World War II. Pluralism has its roots in Montesquieu (1989), an advocate of the separation of powers and of popular participation in lawmaking, and Tocqueville (2004), who famously observed decentralization of power, active political participation by citizens, and a proliferation of associations in the early nineteenth-century US. In addition to these earlier theorists, pluralists also drew inspiration from Weber, particularly in his view of the political sphere as a realm of constant contention.

The basic assumption of pluralism is that in modern democracies power is dispersed among many groups and no single group dominates. Power is dispersed in part because it has many sources, including wealth, political office, social status and connections, and popular legitimacy. Pluralists also note that individuals often subscribe to multiple groups and interests, making pluralist systems more stable in their opinion. In this model, the state is largely an arbiter facilitating compromise between competing interests.

The 1950s and early 1960s were the heyday of pluralist theory, coinciding with the apparent stability of liberal democracy in the US, which most pluralists viewed as an exemplar. David Truman's 1953 book *The Governmental Process* was a defining work of the period, focusing on interest groups as its basic unit of analysis and examining how their interaction gave rise to policy (Truman 1971). In *Who Governs?* (1961), Robert Dahl argued that city policies in education and development were a function of input from many individuals and groups, and that neither individual office-holders nor business leaders wielded overriding influence. Lipset and colleagues (1956) challenged empirically Michel's iron law of oligarchy in their analysis of a trade union.

The Cold War directed attention to democratization in the face of rapid industrialization, transition from colonial rule, and other conditions that prevailed in the third world: the world outside of Europe and North America. Modernization theory posits that societies follow a stage-by-stage process of political, economic, and social development. It typically portrays western democracies as consummately "modernized" societies. Different modernization theorists have highlighted different social conditions as critical to democratization. For example, Lipset (1994) has argued for the importance of "political culture," defined as popular and elite acceptance of civil and political liberties. Allied with pluralism, modernization theory delineated an optimistic, evolutionary account of democratization and development. Moore's *Social Origins of Dictatorship and Democracy* (1966) provided a profound critique – not only stressing the role of power and class struggle, but also the fact of distinct trajectories of political development – and laid the foundations for historically oriented political sociology. Dependency theory emerged in response to the apparent failure of modernization theorists' prescriptions in the developing world. Drawing heavily on Marx, dependency theory argued that the economic and political problems of the developing world were not a function of "backwardness,"

but rather of developing societies' structural positions in the capitalist world-economy (Cardoso & Faletto 1979). Dependency theory inspired much of world-systems theory and would come to engage in dialogue with it (Wallerstein 1984).

SOCIAL MOVEMENTS, THE STATE, AND THE NEW INSTITUTIONALISMS

Crises of authority and production shook the industrialized world in the 1960s and 1970s, including the Civil Rights Movement and protests against the Vietnam War in the US, the social upheaval of May 1968 and radicalization of the Left in France, and the global oil shocks and stalling of growth regimes. These events suggested flaws in pluralist models of democratic society that assumed stable competition among groups and consensus about the rules of the political game. Meanwhile, anti-colonial nationalist movements in Africa and Southeast Asia drew further sociological attention to questions about collective behavior and the conditions for successful mobilization against state structures. In this environment the study of social movements evolved and gained prominence within sociology.

The three major theoretical models of social movements have corresponded with the pluralist, elite, and Marxist models of institutionalized power in society (McAdam 1982). The classical model of social movements portrays them as the result of structural pathologies that led to psychological strain and the desire to pursue nonconventional channels for political participation in an otherwise open system. The "resource-mobilization" model of social movements posits that they arise and grow because rational individuals decide that the benefits of joining outweigh the costs and because the necessary resources are available and worth investing. As such, they do not reflect social pathologies or psychological abnormalities, but are a natural feature of political life (McCarthy & Zald 1977). Finally, the political-process model of social movements blends elite theorists' position that power is highly concentrated in society with the Marxist conviction that the "subjective transformation of consciousness" through popular movements nevertheless has the immanent power to force social change (McAdam 1982). It stresses the interplay between activist strategy, skill, and intensity on the one hand, and the favorability of resources and political opportunity structures to movement tactics and goals, on the other.

One objection raised in the late 1970s to the dominance of post-World War II theoretical models in the pluralist, elite, and Marxist camps was that social scientists had been focusing on social and economic activity and had largely ignored the operations of the state as an autonomous entity. Advocates of "state-centered" approaches sought to remedy what they saw as a "society-centered" bias in scholarship. In the introduction to *Bringing the State Back In*, Theda Skocpol (1985) remarks on the trend toward viewing states as "weighty actors" that shape political and social processes. She notes that "states ... may formulate and pursue goals that are not simply reflective of the demands or interests of social groups, classes, or society" – that is, states are autonomous.

Research on how the modern form of the state arose has been an important part of the movement to refocus attention on the state: how states became centralized, developed functionally differentiated structures, increased their coercive power over their populations, and developed national identities that superseded class and religious differences. The bellicist model of state formation points to the pressure to organize for, prosecute, and pay for war in an environment of interstate competition on the European continent as the driving force behind the evolution of the modern state. As Tilly (1979) put it, "states make war, and war makes states." Other scholars have emphasized different factors. Anderson (1979) stressed the power of class relations and struggles. Gorski (2003) has called attention to the significance of religion and culture. Mann (1986) has traced European state formation and the growth of western civilization in general as a function of interrelations between four types of power networks – ideological, economic, military, and political – with each taking on different levels of importance at different stages and locales in European history.

The initial call to "bring the state back in" was followed by a recognition that as broad a concept as "the state" is best analyzed in terms of the various institutions that compose it. This led to a renewed focus on institutions, both within the state and outside it. The so-called new institutionalisms build on the "old" organizational institutionalism of mid-century. Selznick (1949) had called attention to the importance of informal institutions and extra-organizational interests in shaping policy outcomes.

Each of the new institutionalisms defines and operationalizes institutions differently, largely a function of its origins in a social science discipline. Rational-choice institutionalism, which grew out of the economics literature, defines institutions as the formal rules or "structures of voluntary cooperation that resolve collective action problems" (Moe 2005). Historical institutionalism defines institutions as formal and informal rules and procedures (Thelen & Steinmo 1992). Finally, organizational institutionalism is rooted in the sociology of organizations and embraces a wider definition of institutions than the other two institutionalisms. In addition to formal rules, it considers habits, rituals, and other cognitive frameworks to be institutions, thus situating a large part of the force of institutions within the minds of actors (DiMaggio & Powell 1983).

REDIRECTING POLITICAL SOCIOLOGY

Recent changes in national and international political environments have taken political sociology in new directions. Political sociologists have participated in the proliferation of literature on globalization, including work on postnational citizenship (Soysal 1994) and transnational advocacy networks (Keck & Sikkink 1998). The postmodern turn in the human sciences has found adherents among students of post-industrial politics (Bauman 1999). There is growing interest in the realm of "subpolitics" that analyzes power outside the traditional realm of politics as a contestation for state power (Beck 1992). In this regard, gender remains understudied in the realm of politics (Gal & Kligman 2000). Theorization of the politics of ethnicity and identity has taken on new urgency in the wake of genocide in Rwanda and Bosnia (Lie 2004).

Theoretically, there are serious challenges to the very foundations of political sociology. Rational-choice models are based on game theory, treating individual entities in political contexts as rational actors seeking to maximize their utility (Friedman 1996). In so doing, they deemphasize and at times ignore the social origins or dimensions of politics. From very different perspectives, Unger (1997), who argues for the autonomy of politics, and Foucault (1977), who probes the microphysics of power, bypass traditional sociological concerns with groups and institutions. For Unger and Foucault, political sociology misrecognizes the very nature and operation of power.

The evolution of political sociology has mirrored the great political movements of modern history. Just as class-based models of state and society have drifted upward and downward with the political cachet of socialism and communism, and conservative elite theory linked itself to Italian Fascism in the 1920s, so pluralist models have been fellow-travelers of liberal democracy's credibility and theorists of social movements interrogated the global upheavals of the 1960s and 1970s. Today, as the meaning of national boundaries and identities changes in a global age, political sociology continues to expand its intellectual horizons and investigate new configurations of power.

SEE ALSO: Democracy; Institutional Theory, New; Marx, Karl; Pluralism, American; Pluralism, British; Political Leadership; Political Machine; Political Parties; Politics; Politics and Media; Power Elite; Power, Theories of; Revolutions; Social Movements; State; Weber, Max

REFERENCES AND SUGGESTED READINGS

Anderson, P. (1979) *Lineages of the Absolutist State*. Verso, London.

Bauman, Z. (1999) *In Search of Politics*. Blackwell, Oxford.

Beck, U. (1992) *Risk Society*. Trans. M. Ritter. Sage, Newbury Park, CA.

Bottomore, T. (1993) *Elites and Society*. Routledge, London.

Cardoso, F. H. & Faletto, E. (1979) *Dependency and Development in Latin America*. Trans. M. M. Urquidi. University of California Press, Berkeley.

Dahl, R. (1961) *Who Governs? Democracy and Power in an American City*. Yale University Press, New Haven.

DiMaggio, P. J. & Powell, W. W. (1983) The Iron Cage Revisited: Institutional Isomorphism and Collective Rationality in Organizational Fields. *American Sociological Review* 48: 147–60.

Foucault, M. (1977) *Discipline and Punish*. Vintage, New York.

Friedman, J. (Ed.) (1996) *The Rational Choice Controversy*. Yale University Press, New Haven.

Gal, S. & Kligman, G. (2000) *The Politics of Gender after Socialism*. Princeton University Press, Princeton.

Gorski, P. S. (2003) *The Disciplinary Revolution: Calvinism and the Rise of the State in Early Modern Europe*. University of Chicago Press, Chicago.

Keck, M. E. & Sikkink, K. (1998) *Activists Beyond Borders: Advocacy Networks in International Politics*. Cornell University Press, Ithaca, NY.

Lie, J. (2004) *Modern Peoplehood*. Harvard University Press, Cambridge, MA.

Lipset, S. M. (1994) The Social Requisites of Democracy Revisited. *American Sociological Review* 59: 1–22.

Lipset, S. M., Trow, M., & Coleman, J. (1956) *Union Democracy*. Free Press, Glencoe, IL.

McAdam, D. (1982) *Political Process and the Development of Black Insurgency, 1930–1970*. University of Chicago Press, Chicago.

McCarthy, J. D. & Zald, M. N. (1977) Resource Mobilization and Social Movements: A Partial Theory. *American Journal of Sociology* 82: 1212–41.

Mann, M. (1986) *The Sources of Social Power*, Vol. 1. Cambridge University Press, Cambridge.

Marcuse, H. (1964) *One-Dimensional Man*. Beacon Press, Boston.

Michels, R. (1966) *Political Parties: A Sociological Study of the Oligarchical Tendencies of Modern Democracy*. Free Press, New York.

Miliband, R. (1977) *Marxism and Politics*. Oxford University Press, Oxford.

Mills, C. W. (1956) *The Power Elite*. Oxford University Press, New York.

Moe, T. M. (2005) Power and Political Institutions. *Perspectives on Politics* 3 (June): 215–33.

Montesquieu, C. (1989) *The Spirit of the Laws*. Trans. A. M. Cohler, B. C. Miller, & H. S. Stone. Cambridge University Press, Cambridge.

Moore, B. (1966) *Social Origins of Dictatorship and Democracy*. Beacon Press, Boston.

Parsons, T. (1951) *The Social System*. Free Press, New York.

Schumpeter, J. (1976) *Capitalism, Socialism, and Democracy*. Allen & Unwin, London.

Selznick, P. (1949) *TVA and the Grass Roots: A Study in the Sociology of Formal Organization*. Harper & Row, New York.

Skocpol, T. (1985) Bringing the State Back In: Strategies of Analysis in Current Research. In: Evans, P., Rueschemeyer, D., & Skocpol, T. (Eds.), *Bringing the State Back In*. Cambridge University Press, Cambridge.

Soysal, Y. N. (1994) *The Limits of Citizenship: Migrants and Postnational Membership in Europe*. University of Chicago Press, Chicago.

Thelen, K. & Steinmo, S. (1992) Historical Institutionalism in Comparative Politics. In: Steinmo, S., Thelen, K., & Longstreth, F. (Eds.), *Structuring Politics: Historical Institutionalism in Comparative Analysis*. Cambridge University Press, Cambridge.

Tilly, C. (1979) *Coercion, Capital, and European States, AD 990–1990*. Blackwell, Oxford.

Tocqueville, A. de. (2004) *Democracy in America*. Trans. A. Goldhammer. Library of America, New York.

Truman, D. (1971) *The Governmental Process: Political Interests and Public Opinion*. Knopf, New York.

Unger, R. M. (1997) *Politics*, 3 vols. Cambridge University Press, Cambridge.

Wallerstein, I. (1984) *The Politics of the World-Economy*. Cambridge University Press, Cambridge.

Weber, M. (1978) *Economy and Society*. University of California Press, Berkeley.

politics

Peter Murphy

The discipline of sociology has generated few outright political classics. The most splendid of all of the sociological classics, Weber's *Economy and Society*, contributed a great deal to the understanding of political behavior. Yet it is not a political work in the same sense as Aristotle's *Politics* or Hobbes's *Leviathan*. *Economy and Society* sometimes hints at but never enumerates the "best practical" regime. Aristotle and Hobbes had no doubt that such a regime existed, even if they disagreed about what it was. Weber's comparison of traditional, charismatic, and procedural authority bears a passing resemblance to the comparison of monarchy, aristocracy, and democracy perennially made by the great political thinkers. But the resemblance is limited.

The discipline of politics persistently asks "what is the best type of state?" Answers vary, but the question is constant. The prime object of sociological inquiry is not the state but society. Even Weber, who was politically astute,

preferred terms like "authority" and "domination" to "the state." Sociological categories have a much broader application than expressly political categories like "democracy" or "monarchy." Weber's discussion of legitimate authority was a major and enduring contribution to understanding the consensual foundations of power. But it did not replace the older and equally enduring topic of political regime. The limits of political sociology are exemplified by the following. A democracy can be traditional, charismatic, or procedural, depending on time and circumstance. Even if we can resolve which one of these types of legitimate authority we favor, and which we think would be most feasible for a country in a given period or situation, larger questions still remain. Is democracy preferable to monarchy or military rule? Which regime – stratocracy or democracy, oligarchy or monarchy – is most compatible with tradition, charisma, and procedure?

Lewis (2003) illustrates neatly the difference between political sociology and classic political inquiry. Lewis uses Weber's categories to analyze the pervasiveness of traditional authority – such as clientalism and patrimonialism – in contemporary Arab societies. But the alternative postulated to this – democracy – is originally a Greek term with a very old lineage extending back to antiquity. Its provenance belongs to political thinkers from Plato and Aristotle to Rawls and Strauss.

In short, sociology is not political science reborn. Yet sociology does have a political resonance. It is a kind of deferred politics. This stems from one overwhelming fact. Sociology emerges out of the disintegration of hierarchical societies or, in Weber's terms, out of the fraying of traditional authority. At its core, sociology is an answer to a neo-Kantian question: How is society possible without the binding agent of hierarchy? This is a political question insofar as, until the beginning of the nineteenth century, all states – whether they were city-states, monarchies, or empires – were built around social hierarchies. Political forms turned on the social orders of master and servant, noble and commoner, tribute receiver and giver, citizen and free person, slave owner and slave. Something staggering began to happen in the late eighteenth century. The traditional social authority of hierarchy started to be replaced.

The drive to explain what it was that was replacing hierarchies created sociology. This had a political spin off. Anyone who tried to explain the post-hierarchical social condition also had to hypothesize about the nature of post-hierarchical states.

One of the best hypotheses was Weber's idea that traditional authority was being replaced by legal-rational authority. This, though, applied as much to the business corporation as it did to the state. It was a social not just a political phenomenon. The rise of procedural rationality changed the nature of businesses and associations as much as it did the state. There was also the question of how sociology judged procedural rationality. Political science always operated with the image of the best, or the best practical, state. It might have been a monarchy or a mixed regime, a democracy or a republic. Sociology hedged its bets much more. Weber, for instance, equated the future with legal-rational institutions, seeing their sway as inevitable. Yet he had grave misgivings about procedural bureaucracies dominating decision-making.

Muddying the waters, legal-rational bureaucracy produced its own kind of hierarchy. But this type of hierarchy – organizational hierarchy – was quite unlike traditional social hierarchy. Durkheim introduced the following distinction that helps clarify the situation. The old hierarchical society generated uniformity. Its binding force was "mechanical" or repressive. In contrast, the solidarity of the new society was "organic" or sympathetic. The shift from the old order produced specialized, differentiated, functional hierarchies (i.e., organizations). The qualified labor, professionals, and skilled workers who filled these organizations cooperated out of altruism and imagination rather than because of repressive direction. Yet Durkheim also observed that this "organic" solidarity often failed and was often pathological. The reason for this, Durkheim thought, was the persistence of inequality. The Achilles' heel of the new egalitarian society that emerged out of the old hierarchical order was a lack of equality. This paradox was to perpetually haunt the sociological discipline.

As traditional hierarchies crumbled, organizational ties replaced personal relations, engineers replaced aristocrats, and political parties replaced kings and notables. Legal-rational procedures helped transform social classes into functional classes. Sociology was ambivalent about whether the new world of differentiated, functional organizations was bound together by ethics or by knowledge. It was often unclear whether the cooperation of differentiated organizations was due to the knowledge-seeking of professional and skilled classes – or whether it was due to the moral character of those classes. Notions of professional and vocational ethics (Durkheim, Weber) were a hedge against the need to decide the question definitively. Sociology thus bequeathed two interrelated strands. One said that post-hierarchical societies were knitted together by "constructive knowledge" (Comte). The other attributed social integration to ethical norms like contractual honesty that replaced the loyalty and faith of hierarchical orders.

Often, post-hierarchical society was seen as the product of an epochal transition – from metaphysical to positive knowledge (Comte), militant to industrial society (Comte and Spencer), consumer to producer society (Comte), status to contract, community to society, class to classless society (Marx), uniformity to differentiation, producer to consumer society, ascription to achievement, anarchic local power to pacified territorial power (Elias), and so on.

Each of these stage-like models was obliquely political. Each model assumed that the evolution from martial to industrial society also transformed state, law, and justice. This is evident, for example, in the case of Marx. He observed that the hierarchical state of estates was in decline. The struggle of social classes was both the final gasp of the old order and the first breath of a new world without masters and servants. This was not far from the truth. A different social order was emerging out of the declining world of social hierarchy. Marx was shy when talking about the shape of this new order. His labeling of it as communism was misleading. Yet, like many nineteenth-century thinkers, Marx did think that this new society was being erected on the foundations of science. Knowledge was a bonding agent of societies that were wrenching themselves free from hierarchy. Whether this was creative knowledge or instead more narrowly professional knowledge was less clear. Free time to work at the arts and sciences and the immanent creation of socialism out of capitalist organization were both leitmotifs of the older Marx.

The political thinker most admired by sociologists – Alexis de Tocqueville – spoke repeatedly of the transformation of society from hierarchy to equality. The outgrowth of this shift was democracy. Democracy conceived as the offspring of equality first emerged in the US. The US was a laboratory for inventing the future of the world. This happened because hierarchical ties were weak among the American colonists (Wood 1992). What emerged from this crucible was a new type of society. It had patrimonial political bosses and chattel slavery. But, in many of its fundamental aspects, its social constitution dispensed with traditional hierarchy. American sociologists gave various names to the kind of society that this produced. It was a society of people who were "lonely" or "marginal" and who constantly met other people they were unacquainted with and consequently developed dramaturgical skills to negotiate the expanding public world of strangers. With these stage skills, they learnt to "present" themselves in everyday public situations and manage other people's impressions of them. They also learnt to move adroitly between primary intimate relations, secondary work relationships, and tertiary long-distance anonymous relations.

Underpinning this was the growth of a large-scale pacified political territory in the US. This was akin to what Elias (2000) observed of Europe, but it was on a much more extensive scale. The American polity was integrated by powerful communication networks and was achieved by multiple wars in North America in the eighteenth and nineteenth centuries. Comte had schematized the evolution of society from city-state to nation-state, and had predicted a coming cosmopolitan order of mini-states. America, it seemed, had realized a version of this before Comte had even imagined it. The European transition from hierarchical order was rockier, more fraught, and slower than in the US. Nonetheless, European sociology contributed enormously to understanding the consequences of this epochal development. The pressure on hierarchies in Europe caused sociologists to look closely at social clusters that did not fit into the frame of traditional hierarchies – such as "strangers," "free floating intelligentsia," and "entrepreneurs."

Some sociologists embraced the post-hierarchical world enthusiastically. But most were ambivalent about it. Sometimes the ambivalence grew out of a feeling that equality had not displaced hierarchy sufficiently. It was variously observed that race theorists had invented new pseudo-hierarchies to replace old ones, relations between men and women resisted equality, and that former European colonies embraced the rhetoric of proceduralism but practiced clientalism. Other sociologists wondered whether the loss of hierarchy led to anomie and the "twilight of authority." Some asked whether procedural reason created human beings without character. Many sociologists who pressed for greater equality also regretted the passing of the intimacy and warmth of personalized hierarchies. They were often unfriendly towards procedural social and political forms, and sometimes surprisingly well disposed to collegial patrimonies. Some also wondered whether primitive, heroic, martial, or militant societies made better, more lasting, and more substantial things than the newer egalitarian societies. Democratic societies proclaimed equality but in practice were status-obsessed. This status, though, was not the inheritable kind typical of a hierarchical society. It was rather the status that accrued to the conspicuous consumption of dematerialized signs of display and spectacle that proliferated especially in media-saturated democracies.

This, though, was still politics at a tangent. Sociological anxieties generated a large literature on race, gender, and consumption. Some of it had some impact on legislation. Other times, though, sociology found itself in the contradictory position of arguing for equality but criticizing its outcomes. Such ambivalence neutered it as a political force. Its collective concerns never generated the kind of capital-P politics that we find in Aristotle or Hobbes. A theory of politics invariably rests on a notion of the best way of living. In the classic political tradition there are essentially three answers to the question of "what is the best way of living?" Two were given by Aristotle: (1) citizenship of the city and (2) contemplative or theoretical knowledge. The third answer to the question originated with the Stoics and Epicureans, and was reformulated by Hobbes: freedom from fear, most particularly freedom from the fear of death.

Sociology, for the most part, downplayed these classic axioms. The following examples illustrate some of the ways in which this happened. Weber declared the city to be a "non-legitimate form of domination." Bourdieu held that cultural and symbolic capital frustrated equality. Beck replaced freedom from the fear of death with the incalculable uncertainties of a "risk society."

The skewed distribution of risk was the newest of the new inequalities of the late twentieth century. The risk society was overdetermined by global threats (e.g., viruses) uncontainable by national borders. The analysis of it generated sociology for cosmopolitan bureaucracy. The moral of this is that each new-discovered inequality in post-hierarchical societies leads to the creation of an expert bureaucracy to manage it, which, in turn, creates new unexpected inequalities. The difficulty of sociological politics – as opposed to classical politics – is that its value horizon (equality) is constantly in flux. The polarity between hierarchy and equality generates perpetual dissatisfaction. The forward march of equality is never sufficient while the backward glance to old hierarchies is tinged with regret. The ghosts of the past whisper seductively about the certainty, intimacy, community, and immobility of the old order. The sociological conscience worries that this is antimodern and unprogressive.

Not all sociologists, though, have been indifferent to the classic political ideals of urbanity, intellect, and happiness. Robert Park and the Chicago School, and their legatees like Sennett, eulogized the city. Others, like Daniel Bell, Agnes Heller, and Cornelius Castoriadis, recognized the centrality of creative knowledge in post-hierarchical societies. The analyses of this spirited, inventive knowledge owed as much to Aristotle as to Durkheim. This was more than the sociology of professional or vocational knowledge. It also reached high into the imaginative realms of the arts and sciences and philosophy. Florida applied ideas about creative societies and creative classes to the analysis of cities and workplaces. This urbane sociology drew three basic conclusions. The intensification of creative imagination is the defining trait

of autonomous post-hierarchical societies. Great cities are their incubators. The personality types most at home in these societies are happy, confident, courageous, witty, skeptical Stoic-Epicurean types (Heller 1985).

Such analyses owed something, even if only distantly, to Marx – who, in turn, owed something, again distantly, to Aristotle and Epicurus. Marx's influence on sociological politics, though, overall was ambivalent. For one thing, it confirmed the thinness of sociological theories of the state. This could not be otherwise because Marx's classless society was also a stateless society. The sociological thinkers who resisted this apolitical conclusion tended to have some interest in the classic political tradition from Aristotle to Hobbes. For those sociologists who did not, a tension was created. On the one hand, they carried over tacit assumptions about the coming of the stateless society from nineteenth-century Marxism and classical liberalism. On the other hand, they knew the reality of the twentieth-century state, which had expanded not shrunk, and that delivered roads and hospitals, welfare and social security, defense and education.

Sociology ended up in a double bind. Its mainstream engaged in strenuous polemics with classical liberals or philosophical anarchists who wanted small government as a step toward a stateless society. At the same time, many of its number criticized the bureaucracy, repression, systemic nature, waste, normative discipline, or militarism of the state. Theories touched by anarchism, such as Foucault's, were popular with such critics – as was Habermas's pragmatism that counterposed an idealized public sphere to the institutionalized state.

Alvin Gouldner presents a good example of a sociologist crossing the road from institutionalism to anarchism to pragmatism. Like Selznick and Bendix, Gouldner's political sociology starts with Weber-inspired studies of America's industrial bureaucracies. Yet his work is colored with sympathy for wild-cat strikes against that bureaucracy. The later Gouldner, like C. Wright Mills before him, turns to Dewey's idea of the public in order to resolve the tension between institutional and romantic sociology. In Gouldner's case, he finds his way to the pragmatic public via Habermas. This detour is significant. For while Dewey's notion of the public is much closer in spirit to Comte than to Hegel, the main currents in twentieth-century sociology reinterpret the idea of the public in the spirit of critical negation rather than positive knowledge. For Habermas, in particular, the logic of the public presupposes the defense of the pre-institutional lifeworld against institutional systems. Correspondingly, while systems, based on power and money, are not to be demolished, they are to be constrained.

The difficulty for sociology as an intellectual discipline is that it ends up both defending the state and wanting to be rid of it. The tradition of classic political thought has to bear less of a burden. It supposes that the state is a given. Societies for the most part produce states. The political question is not whether the state exists or not, but what is the endpoint of the state? Does the state serve the *telos* of city life, intellect, and freedom from fear – or not? Classic politics advances a triptych of freedoms: the freedom of the city (citizenship), the freedom of the mind (knowledge), and the freedom from worry (happiness). There is no doubt that the sociological question of whether the state serves hierarchy or equality is important. Yet neither hierarchy nor equality constitutes a substantive end. Without the anchor of such an end, each can turn tyrannical and destructive. Tradition, charisma, and procedure by themselves provide no inherent barrier to this happening.

SEE ALSO: Democracy; Marx, Karl; Political Leadership; Political Opportunities; Political Parties; Political Sociology; Politics and Media; Politics and Sport; State; Weber, Max

REFERENCES AND SUGGESTED READINGS

Aristotle (1998) *Politics*. Oxford University Press, Oxford.

Comte, A. (1988) *Introduction to Positive Philosophy*. Hackett, Indianapolis.

Elias, N. (2000) *The Civilizing Process*. Blackwell, Oxford.

Gouldner, A. (1976) *The Dialectic of Ideology and Technology*. Seabury Press, New York.

Heller, A. (1985) *The Power of Shame: A Rational Perspective*. Routledge, London.

Lewis, B. (2003) *What Went Wrong? The Clash Between Islam and Modernity in the Middle East*. New York, Harper.

Marx, K. (1993) *Grundrisse*. Penguin, London.

Tocqueville, A. de (2003) *Democracy in America*. Penguin, London.

Weber, M. (1978) *Economy and Society*. University of California Press, Berkeley.

Wood, G. S. (1992) *The Radicalism of the American Revolution*. Alfred A. Knopf, New York.

politics and media

Brian McNair

In 1922 the American journalist and social commentator Walter Lippmann wrote that "the significant revolution of modern times is the revolution taking place in the art of creating consent among the governed" (Lippmann 1954). From his vantage point in the early twentieth century, just four years after the end of World War I, Lippmann was drawing attention to the fact that politicians were entering a new era in which the role of the media was going to be central to effective government. Henceforth, they would have to know and understand how the media impacted on public opinion. Such knowledge, he predicted, would "alter every political premise."

And so it has turned out. Politics in the twenty-first century is inconceivable without the part played by media institutions. As reporters, analysts, and interpreters of events to mass electorates the media are integral to the democratic process and no politician, party, or government can afford to ignore or dismiss them. This entry examines how the media came to acquire this role, and its implications for how politics is conducted in modern societies.

POLITICS AND MEDIA: A HISTORY

Since the invention of the printing press by Gutenberg in the late fifteenth century, media have driven politics. Early correspondents were employed by monarchs, bishops, aristocrats, and other elites in feudal societies as sources of information, be it from the far reaches of the kingdom, or from overseas. The first journalists provided a form of surveillance for political elites, making available information on the state of markets and commodity prices, or the progress of wars and court intrigues. The news informed decisions and policymaking, although it was heavily censored to prohibit any criticism of established political power. Feudal monarchies were authoritarian, and like authoritarian regimes then and since, freedom of thought and of media outlets to express it were severely restricted. They were potent political tools, nonetheless. The first books and pamphlets were crucial to Martin Luther's Reformation, spreading revolutionary Protestant ideas and ending the primacy of the Roman Catholic Church in countries where it had previously ruled.

The rise of recognizably free media accompanied the rise of democracy from the ashes of feudalism in the seventeenth century, and was indeed an essential part of that process. The English Civil War saw the relaxation of feudal censorship and the emergence of the first independent newspapers, free to take sides in political disputes. This they did with enthusiasm, promoting and propagandizing the positions of the royalists on the one hand or the roundheads on the other. For the first time journalists became participants in political events rather than merely reporters of them. During the 1640s, as civil war raged in England, leading to the execution of Charles I and the abolition of the monarchy, newspapers and pamphlets were heavily partisan, inflating the atrocities and outrages of the opposing side while downplaying the crimes of their own.

The restoration of Charles II temporarily brought an end to press freedom in England, but as capitalism and constitutional monarchy took root in the late seventeenth and eighteenth centuries the rights of the media to report politics, and themselves participate in political debate as significant actors, came to be viewed as essential elements of an emerging democracy. Philosophers such as John Milton articulated a theory of democracy within which the media would play the role not just of reporting events, but of scrutinizing power. Mindful of the possibility of a return to the censorship practices of feudal times, Britain's rising bourgoisie allotted to journalists the role of Fourth Estate, overseeing the activities of representative government, defending intellectual freedom and diversity, and preventing the restoration of

despotism. A free media and an effective democracy would henceforth be inseparable.

In the late eighteenth century similar ideas also drove the French and American revolutions. In the former's overthrow of a decadent aristocracy the media played a key role, disseminating ideas of liberty, freedom, and equality to a nation ready for revolutionary leadership. In America, fighting for its independence from the colonial master Britain, journalists spearheaded a process within which, as Paul Starr's *Creation of the Media* (2004) puts it, "restrictive information regimes [evolved] into more open ones." With the help of independent media, and with press freedom written into the Constitution, post-revolutionary America developed free of "the legacies of feudalism and absolutism."

Between them, the English, French, and American revolutions defined the modern role of the media in democracy as active, interventionist, and adversarial. The journalist was to be a constraint on the exercise of political power, one of the checks and balances without which democratic government could so easily slip back into authoritarian habits.

The media also became the foundation for what German philosopher Jürgen Habermas called the public sphere, referring to that common communicative space in which events and ideas can be discussed and public opinion formed. If democracy emphasized freedom of political choice exercised through the act of voting, choice could only be meaningful given the availability of reliable and accurate information, and after rational debate. The public sphere was where such debate ideally took place, and the media were the institutions which comprised the public sphere. The early days of democracy saw the rise of "coffee house cultures" in major European capitals such as London, Edinburgh, Paris, and Berlin, where members of the political and intellectual elites would gather to read their newspapers and debate with each other on the meaning of the events reported in them. Journalists helped make sense of political affairs for their readers, who would then use that understanding to make decisions at election time. In America, observes Starr (2004), the media had by the early 1800s become "vehicles of discussion ... immense moral and political engines."

THE MEDIA AND DEMOCRACY

These elites comprised the wealthy, relatively well-educated men who in those days monopolized voting rights. They were often also progressive and reformist, campaigning for the extension of the democratic rights which they enjoyed to broader sections of the population. Under the influence of reformist media and democratic theorists such as John Stuart Mill, suffrage expanded to include more and more of the population, irrespective of social background, property, or educational qualifications. By the early twentieth century in most countries women had the vote, although it took until the 1960s for African Americans to be given full democratic rights in the US. Around the world democracy has expanded from a small minority of countries a century ago, to the great majority today, including Russia and most of the countries of the former Soviet Union after 1989, South Africa in 1994, and Iraq and Afghanistan in recent times.

At the same time as democratic rights were being extended to more and more people, the media were evolving into institutions for the masses. As capitalist societies developed, universal education and mass literacy became a reality and the market for journalism expanded to include the middle and lower classes. In the nineteenth century Britain saw the emergence of a "pauper press" aimed at working people, then a commercial press targeted at a mass readership (Curran & Seaton 1997). At the same time America gave birth to a "penny press," and by the late nineteenth century the number of publications in the US had risen from around 600 to more than 2,000. Newspapers fell in price, and popular journalism as we know it today came into being. Politics remained important in content, but was increasingly presented alongside a journalism of entertainment and recreation.

By the 1920s, and Walter Lippmann's influential study of *Public Opinion*, the combination of mass media and representative democratic institutions had transformed the political environment, making politicians necessarily more responsive to popular feelings than they had ever been required to be before. For the first time in human history, something called public opinion mattered. People had democratic rights, and politicians had to respect them if they wished to be elected. Once elected, the media monitored and scrutinized political performance before a public empowered to remove any government from office. This is what Lippmann meant when observing that every political premise had been altered.

PUBLIC OPINION, PUBLIC RELATIONS, AND PROPAGANDA

The implications of the new political environment became clear during World War I. Although universal suffrage did not yet exist anywhere in the world when war broke out in 1914, democratic rights had by then expanded sufficiently to ensure that the British and American governments could not prosecute war with Germany in the absence of a compliant public. Official efforts began to persuade publics of the merits of war, which included crude propaganda of the type which would have been familiar to the journalistic partisans of the English Civil War, but also more sophisticated efforts at opinion management. World War I saw the US and British governments, among others, establishing the first official information agencies to manage news (and thus public opinion) about conflict. The same tools were used after World War I in the dispute with Bolshevik Russia, and are now standard practice for democratic governments engaged in conflict. Governments can no longer take their countries to war without consideration of the state of public opinion. If they dare to do so they risk electoral defeat and political impotence, as experienced by the government of Jose Maria Aznar in Spain. In that case, Aznar and his party underestimated the popular mood against the country's involvement in the US-led invasion of Iraq. When al-Qaida terrorists killed 200 people in Madrid on March 11, 2004, two days before the general election, they also brought about Aznar's defeat.

The growing importance of public opinion in the twentieth century propelled the growth of a new kind of communication, expressly intended to influence media output and through it public opinion. Lippmann and other pioneers of what we now know as public relations called it "press counseling," meaning the effort to influence what media organizations wrote and said about politics. Practicing this new form of communication were press counselors, skilled in the techniques of making media amenable to the wishes of politicians. There have always been those who played this role, going back to feudal times and beyond. The great English diarist Samuel Pepys was a press counselor for Charles II, and political leaders have always relied on advisers when it comes to managing the opinions of those who matter to them. In those days, such opinion management as was deemed necessary took place largely within and between small groups of courtiers or factions, on whom the king or bishop relied for support for a particular policy.

Public relations in the modern sense is a direct response to the growth of mass democracy on the one hand, and mass media on the other. Both make necessary an intermediate communicative class, a Fifth Estate operating in the space between politics and journalism, whose professional role is to manage, shape, and manipulate public opinion through managing, shaping, and manipulating the output of the media. Today, it is often called spin, a term which carries a negative connotation, but which quite accurately conveys the notion that this form of political communication aims to put a "spin" on the meaning of events as they appear in the public sphere. Events happen, and they are reported. Spin, and spin doctors, strive to ensure that the reportage, as well as the analysis and commentary which make up so much of contemporary political journalism, are advantageous to their political clients.

The importance of this communicative work means that all serious actors in modern politics undertake it. In a world where politics is conducted in public, through the media, competent public relations is an integral element of effective political action. This is true for al-Qaida as much as for the US and British governments; for trade unionists and churches as much as for employers' confederations and consumer lobbies; for all organizations, in short, which aim to influence the political environment in one way or another.

We have seen in the course of the twentieth century, and in recent decades in particular, the growth of military public relations, as governments have sought to persuade publics of the legitimacy of military actions in the Falklands, the Balkans, and the Middle East, among other

places. We have seen the rise of terrorist public relations, as groups such as the IRA and ETA have developed sophisticated media management divisions, capable of capturing the news agenda and influencing public opinion about their respective grievances. An event like the destruction of the Twin Towers on September 11, 2001 can be viewed from this perspective as public relations by al-Qaida insofar as its aim, ruthlessly executed, was to command the news agenda and strike fear into western populations. Al-Qaida's political goals – the destruction of western civilization and democracy – were not made more likely by these spectacularly violent acts of political communication, but they brought forth a change in the political environment which will shape the world for years to come.

We have seen the rise of party political public relations, as parties and their representatives use techniques adapted from advertising and marketing to package and promote themselves. This may involve the "selling" of particular policies and programs, especially during election campaigns, or it may involve image management, making individual politicians more personally attractive to voters. As time passes the sums spent on political public relations increase (as does advertising spend), and the numbers of professional PR advisers expand. Once in government, parties harness official information agencies to promote policy decisions and manage public responses to them. Unelected press secretaries, media spokespersons, and communication advisers proliferate as the government information apparatus expands.

POLITICAL PUBLIC RELATIONS: DANGER TO DEMOCRACY?

The rise of political public relations has been criticized by many observers. For UK scholar Bob Franklin (2004), it amounts to a "packaging" of politics which fundamentally undermines the integrity of the democratic process. Jürgen Habermas, having developed the concept of the public sphere to describe how the media should work in democracy, criticizes the corruption of the ideal by the privately motivated, highly partial communications of the PR professional. If democracy is about rational choice and debate, argue the critics, do not the efforts of professional advisers to manipulate both media and publics represent the antithesis of rationality?

These are powerful arguments, supported by the evidence of the efforts of some spin doctors to intimidate the political media into following their wishes. In Britain, the bullying tactics of Bernard Ingham for Margaret Thatcher in the 1980s, or Alistair Campbell on behalf of Tony Blair, have become emblematic of the excesses of political public relations. After Campbell's resignation from his post as Blair's chief media adviser the Labour government was obliged by hostile journalistic and public opinion to reform its communication apparatus. The names of Ingham and Campbell, of Bill Morris and Karl Rove in America, and their equivalents across the democratic world, have become associated with a perceived erosion of the democratic process, and the contamination of rational political communication with duplicitous propaganda.

The defenders of spin, on the other hand, point to trends in the developing relationship between politics and the media which make managed political communication inevitable and essential, if not necessarily desirable in the best of all possible worlds.

First, there are many more media outlets, providing much more information, circulating at much faster rates than ever before in history. Newspapers and broadcasting and online media have produced a turbulent and chaotic media environment in which it becomes evermore difficult to communicate effectively. Public relations, it is argued, restores order to the chaos of political communication. In a democracy we may choose not to accept the message, but at least we should be aware of what it is.

It has been argued, second, that the traditional adversarialism of the media towards politicians, enshrined in democratic theory since the eighteenth century, has tipped into excessive "hyperadversarialism." American writer James Fallows (1996) has used this term to describe what he sees as the commercially driven tendency for journalism to become confrontational towards politicians, and to turn the legitimate scrutiny of power into gladiatorial spectacle. The commercial pressure to attract readers and viewers has produced a form of political journalism which is all style and no substance,

mistaking argumentation and dispute for debate. Journalists have become celebrities, elevating their own opinions and prejudices over their democratic duty to provide straightforward reportage of politics. British journalist John Lloyd, in a book entitled *What the Media Are Doing To Our Politics* (2004), is one of those who have accused journalists of adopting a stance of "corrosive cynicism" towards politics and politicians, and contributing to declining rates of electoral participation and public apathy.

In this context, public relations and spin become a means of ensuring that political messages are communicated and understood by those for whom they are intended, the public. In an environment where the default position of the journalist towards the politician can be summed up by the phrase "why is that lying bastard lying to me?" the communications adviser is an essential tool in the struggle to be heard.

LOOKING AHEAD

Just as politicians and media professionals have their ethical codes which can be abused, so the profession of public relations can be employed for corrupt ends. To denounce spin in absolute terms is, then, no more rational than denouncing all politicians or all journalists. For better or worse, the spin doctor has become a pivotal element in the politics–media–public relationship. As media channels continue to proliferate and the political environment to grow more volatile as a consequence, that relationship will continue to be a focus of debate about the health of democracy, as it has been since Lippmann's observation of nearly a century ago.

SEE ALSO: Media and the Public Sphere; Political Leadership; Political Sociology; Politics; Public Opinion; Public Sphere

REFERENCES AND SUGGESTED READINGS

Curran, J. & Seaton, J. (1997) *Power Without Responsibility*. Routledge, London.
Fallows, J. (1996) *Breaking the News*. Pantheon, New York.
Franklin, B. (2004) *Packaging Politics*. Arnold, London.

3472 *politics and sport*

Lippmann, W. (1954) *Public Opinion*. Macmillan, New York.

Lloyd, J. (2004) *What the Media Are Doing To Our Politics*. Constable, London.

Starr, P. (2004) *The Creation of the Media*. Basic Books, New York.

politics and sport

Barrie Houlihan

There are many definitions of politics which, while not mutually exclusive, highlight distinct understandings and orientations. The dominant definition limits politics to the study of the institutions of government at national and transnational levels. However, this narrow focus on the public sphere has been strongly challenged by, among others, critical theorists and feminists on the grounds that politics can also be defined more broadly as concerning any social relations which involve the exercise of power and authority. Such a definition expands the focus of the study of politics beyond the institutions of government to include institutions in civil society such as national sports federations, the World Anti-Doping Agency, local sports clubs, and individual teams. A third definition emphasizes processes of decision-making and would, for example, draw attention to the influence of the media and the role of interest groups and individuals in lobbying governments. Finally, there are definitions of politics that emphasize the outcomes of political processes, best summed up by Harold Lasswell as "who gets what, when, and how."

Whether the emphasis is placed on institutions, processes, or outcomes, central to all these definitions of politics is the complex and elusive concept of power. From within a broadly positivist epistemology, power refers to the capacity of one group of interests to impose its will in the face of opposition from other groups. For example, the outlawing of sports considered by some to be dangerous to participants (e.g., professional boxing) has, in many countries, been the regular subject of lobbying and parliamentary debate regarding the need for state regulation.

However, this pluralist conceptualization of power, as an essentially observable phenomenon, was challenged by Bachrach and Baratz (1963) who argued from a neo-elitist position that power may also be exercised covertly to ensure that an issue is kept off the political agenda. The exclusion, at various times and to varying degrees, of women and people from ethnic minorities from participation in sport across a wide range of countries provides ample evidence for the effectiveness of what Schattschneider (1960) referred to as the "mobilization of bias" to steer the agenda so that issues and proposals that challenged established norms and patterns of privilege were not subject to significant public debate.

Working within a broadly Gramscian neo-Marxist ontology, Lukes (1974) further developed the debate by arguing that power could also be conceived of as preference shaping, that is, preventing people from expressing their grievances by shaping their perception of their own interests such that they accept the current social economic arrangements. For example, it could be argued that the underparticipation of certain social groups in sport is due not to the overt or even covert rejection of their claims for access, but to their acceptance that sports participation is inappropriate social behavior. Such groups are considered to be unaware of their true interests or, in Marxist terminology, are victims of false consciousness. This conceptualization of power is central to much Marxist and feminist political theory, which argues that the exercise of power, whether intended to defend capitalism or patriarchy, extends beyond the narrow public political sphere and permeates all social institutions.

A more radical conceptualization of power is provided by Foucault, who emphasized the close interconnection between power and expert knowledge and drew attention to the role of discourse in structuring power in society. For him the capacity to control the discourse used to discuss social issues and relationships was a key reflection of power. According to this view, the medical profession would be considered to fulfill a key role in the complex process of signification and legitimation that shapes the social construction of disability sport and the competitive context within which it takes place.

Political scientists were generally slow to recognize sport as an appropriate topic for analysis, largely because of the dominance of definitions of politics that emphasized the centrality of the role of government and state institutions. Until the mid-1960s few governments took more than an occasional interest in sport. Much of the early systematic political analysis of the relationship between politics and sport came from Marxists, for whom the state was a superstructural phenomenon determined by, and dependent upon, economic power, and for whom concepts such as ideology, false consciousness, class and social control were central to their social analysis. Drawing loosely on Gramscian Marxism, the American Paul Hoch (1972) analyzed the US sports system and concluded that sport fulfilled the same function of ideological control that Marx claimed for religion in the nineteenth century. For Hoch the exploitative capitalist sports system was maintained not through force but through ideological manipulation. A similar analysis was produced by Jean-Marie Brohm (1978) who, writing from within a European context, emphasized not only the ideological importance of contemporary sport, but also the role of the state in constructing and promoting that ideology. For Brohm the state played an important part in the commodification of sport and in facilitating the use of sport as a means for imposing capitalist discipline on the working class.

A related theme in the analysis of sport and politics was provided by those Marxists interested in the colonial experience. James (1963) provided a sophisticated and classic study of the experience of colonialism through an analysis of the role of cricket in Caribbean society and also identified the limitations of western Marxism in dealing with issues of race. The politics of race and sport rapidly became a major theme in sport studies along with other equity issues relating to gender, wealth, and space.

As sport became more firmly established as a normal part of democratic state activity from the late 1960s it began to attract interest from academics who subscribed to the narrower definitions of politics, which focused substantially on the institutions, processes, and impact

of the state. However, it should be remembered that earlier in the 1950s a number of European communist countries, most notably the German Democratic Republic and the Soviet Union, invested heavily in sport, often to support nation building and to use international, especially Olympic, success to demonstrate the superiority of communism over capitalism. For many non-communist industrial countries, the 1960s was the decade when state involvement changed from being substantially reactive, tentative, and episodic to being proactive, extensive, and systematic as governments in many industrialized countries gradually expanded their direct involvement in sport through the establishment of administrative units, the appointment of ministers, the allocation of budgets, and the formulation of strategic plans for sport. By the early twenty-first century, sport had become an established element in the remit of governments of most industrialized countries, both in its own right and, more usually, as an aspect of other policy areas such as foreign affairs, health, and economic development.

As the foregoing discussion suggests, the contemporary scope of the study of politics and sport is broad. With the various definitions of politics and power in mind, it is useful to distinguish between politics *and* sport and politics *in* sport. The study of politics *and* sport directs our attention to the use made by governments, whether democratic or not, of sport and the process by which public policy is made and implemented. A focus on politics *in* sport is derived from the definitions of politics which do not demarcate between the public and the private spheres and which treat politics as a ubiquitous aspect of all social institutions and relations.

A concern with politics *and* sport tends to direct analysis toward the role of the state and particularly the motives for, and modes of, state intervention. In many countries state involvement in sport was initially motivated by a concern to control or outlaw certain activities considered to be cruel (forms of hunting) or dangerous to the participant (sword-fencing/dueling). More recently, governments have been very active in attempting to control the use of drugs in sport. A second common motive is the use of sport to achieve greater social integration and control, whether related to the populations of new states, rapidly urbanized populations, immigrants, or particular groups such as juvenile offenders. Nation building through sport is common even in economically advanced and politically stable countries. Few governments ignore the opportunity to use the symbolism of sporting success to reinforce national identity. However, sport is not always an integrative force as there are many examples of sport being used to emphasize subnational and separatist identity, including in Québec, Catalonia, and among the nationalist community in Northern Ireland. The symbolism of sport is powerful but not always as malleable and stable as governments would like.

A third major motive for government involvement in sport is as a diplomatic tool. The rapid internationalization of sports competition in the last 60 years and the advances in media technology of the last 40 years have combined to make sport an increasingly attractive diplomatic resource. Its attraction to governments lies in its combination of high visibility, low risk, versatility, and low cost. Sport has been·used variously as a device for building a closer relationship between enemies, as was the case when the United States sent a table tennis team to China in 1972 as a first step in improving relations between the two countries. Sports diplomacy is more commonly used as a means of maintaining good relations with allies or neighbors. For example, the importance of the Commonwealth Games has increased as the significance of the Commonwealth in global politics has declined. A further diplomatic use of sport, most common in the 1970s and 1980s, is as a means of registering disapproval of a state's actions through attempts to isolate a state from international sporting contact. Apartheid in South Africa and the Soviet invasion of Afghanistan prompted boycotts of major sports events by disapproving states.

The attempt to isolate South Africa because of its policy of apartheid is a particularly valuable illustration of the use of sport diplomacy as well as of the interaction of domestic sport policy with the actions of international political actors. Much has been made of the powerful symbolism of sport to white South Africans, but an undermining of the opportunity to experience that symbolism through the

application or threat of a boycott was, in itself, an irritation rather than a major threat to apartheid. More important was the way in which the groups opposed to apartheid used international sport as an activity, and international sports organizations as contexts, initially to raise awareness of the issue of apartheid and then to ensure its continued prominence. Lobbying by the South African Non-Racial Olympic Committee through the more easily accessed international sports bodies, such as the International Olympic Commission (IOC), the Commonwealth Games Federation, and the International Amateur Athletics Federation (IAAF), was used as a stepping stone to more powerful organizations such as the Commonwealth Heads of Government Meetings and the United Nations. Sport's value was therefore primarily in providing a point of entry to the agendas of major global political actors (Houlihan & Keech 1999).

A final major motive for government interest in sport is to use it as a tool for economic development and regeneration. At a national strategic level, Japan, South Korea, and Greece used the hosting of the Olympic Games as opportunities to project images of modern sophisticated economies. Other states have selectively developed those sports, such as golf and skiing, that helped to promote tourism. It is also increasingly common for bids to host major sports events to be part of a regional or metropolitan economic strategy. Both Barcelona and Athens, as hosts to the 1992 and 2004 Olympic Games respectively, built major urban regeneration and tourism promotion strategies around their successful bids.

In considering the nature of politics *in* sport, a good starting point is Lasswell's definition of politics as the study of "who gets what, when, and how," which draws attention to the significance of sports organizations and non-sports organizations, especially from the commercial sector, in affecting access to, and the nature of, sports opportunities for individual athletes or of groups which may be defined, for example, geographically or by sport, race, or gender: sports and non-sports organizations are, in effect, part of the private governance of sport.

The growth of commercialism has altered the power relations in sport and has led to changes to the rules of sports to suit major corporate sponsors, the marginalizing of non-western and especially non-Olympic sports, and the undermining of the ethical basis of sport in the interest of more dramatic (aggressive) and more sensational sport to meet the requirements of the media. At a broader level, the increased commercialization of sport raises the prospect of the continued asset-stripping of the sporting talent of poorer countries such as those in Africa and South America and the relegation of these countries to markets for imported televised sports. Increasingly, Africa and South America are becoming sources of sporting talent for the rich countries. Apart from the vulnerability of economically weak countries, the other potential victims of increasing commercialization are the domestic and international governing bodies whose control over sport is undermined by their need to attract sponsors, the increasing pressure from athletes for a greater share of commercial income and a greater say in decision-making, and the growth in profit-oriented clubs and leagues.

A second major issue within sport concerns the relationship between forms of social discrimination such as race and gender, and access to, and take-up of, sports participation opportunities. As many writers (e.g., Lapchick 1976; Hargreaves 1994; Hoberman 1997) have demonstrated, both these dimensions of inequality are intensely political insofar as they can have a profound impact on individual choice and quality of life.

The future direction of research into the relationship between politics and sport will be shaped, first, by the continuing growth in governmental interest in sport at both the national and international levels and, second, by the pattern of prominence of particular issues. At the national level, the place of sport within the range of activities considered to be within the normal remit of the state is acknowledged by governments from across a broad range of the political spectrum. In many countries state interest has broadened to include: a greater willingness of the courts to accept jurisdiction in cases concerning matters previously considered private, for example violence on the field of play; a concern by governments to protect young athletes from abuse; and a willingness by governments to identify sport as a tool in

achieving an increasingly wide range of non-sporting policy objectives such as those related to health, educational attainment, and community development. The concern of many governments has also deepened, as indicated by their willingness to: provide considerable subsidies to host major sports events; invest heavily in the development of elite athletes; and intervene directly to shape the curricular and extracurricular sporting experience of the young. The contemporary motives of governments, the differences between government strategies and the reasons for these differences, the impact of globalization on national sports policies, the techniques of intervention adopted by governments and the impact of their intervention are all seriously underresearched. However, the political scientist whose interest lies in questions relating to public sector management, policy analysis, political party ideology, electoral behavior, and central/federal–provincial/local relations will find that the emergence of sport as an area of sustained government interest not only broadens the range of areas for analysis, but also offers the prospect of providing a distinctive insight into some of the generic concerns in these subfields of political science.

The greater breadth and intensity of interest among national governments has had implications for the sports organizations at the transnational level, not simply because of the growth in international sports events but also because many of the issues which manifest themselves in national contexts, such as doping, sports violence, and the protection of the young, require action at the international level. Consequently, the interaction between international bodies such as the Court for Arbitration in Sport and the World Anti-Doping Agency on the one hand, and domestic sports organizations and national governments on the other, is of increasing significance and interest. A related area for further research concerns the future role of the major international sport bodies such as the international federations and the major event-organizing bodies (e.g., the IOC). The control that they have exercised over the development of sport is coming under increasingly severe challenge, not only from individual governments and from commercial, particularly television, interests, but also more recently from players' unions and agents, and from international organizations such as the European Union, the World Anti-Doping Agency, the Council of Europe, and, to a lesser extent, UNESCO. The capacity of the IOC and the major international federations to plot the course of sports development has always involved a compromise with other interests, but the increasingly interventionist stance of many international governmental organizations and the increasing assertiveness of international athletes and corporate sponsors require international federations and the IOC to operate in a much more complex political environment. The international governance of sport is thus a further area of research that will doubtless attract the interests of an increasing number of political scientists.

SEE ALSO: Nationalism and Sport; Political Economy and Sport; Politics; Sport and Capitalism

REFERENCES AND SUGGESTED READINGS

Bachrach, P. & Baratz, M. (1963) Decisions and Non-Decisions. *American Political Science Review* 57: 632–42.

Brohm, J.-M. (1978) *Sport, a Prison of Measured Time*. Ink Links, London.

Foucault, M. (1981) *Power/Knowledge*. Pantheon, New York.

Hargreaves, J. A. (1994) *Sporting Females: Critical Issues in the History and Sociology of Women's Sport*. Routledge, London.

Hoberman, J. (1997) *Darwin's Athletes: How Sport Has Damaged Black America and Preserved the Myth of Race*. Mariner Books, New York.

Hoch, P. (1972) *Rip Off the Big Games: The Exploitation of Sports by the Power Elite*. Anchor Doubleday, New York.

Houlihan, B. & Keech, M. (1999) Sport and the End of Apartheid. *The Round Table: The Commonwealth Journal of International Affairs* 349 (Spring).

James, C. L. R. (1963) *Beyond a Boundary*. Stanley Paul, London.

Lapchick, R. E. (1976) *The Politics of Race and International Sport*. Greenwood Press, Westport, CT.

Lukes, S. (1974) *Power: A Radical View*. Macmillan, Basingstoke.

Schattschneider, E. (1960) *The Semi-Sovereign People: A Realist View of Democracy in America*. Rinehart & Winston, New York.

pollution zones, linear and planar

Koichi Hasegawa

The concepts of linear and planar pollution zones refer to the geographical figuration of the polluted area caused especially by high-speed transportation pollution. Whereas bullet trains and high-speed expressways create linear pollution zones 20–50 meters wide on each side along their routes, airplanes produce planar pollution zones along their takeoff and landing routes surrounding the airport. In the former case, the number of victims at any given site suffering severe noise pollution may be relatively limited, typically at most several thousands of residents. In the latter case, though, victims may number more than 10,000 residents over several cities and towns.

These differences result in differences of (1) the organizing and mobilizing process of protest movements against noise pollution or the construction of new facilities; (2) the attitude of affected municipalities; and (3) the countermeasures taken.

In general, the planar pollution zone imposes similar sufferings on the residents of whole neighborhoods and their neighborhood associations. The linear pollution zone, however, does not always include whole neighborhoods and their associations, but can run through many of them. In planning the routes of a bullet train line or expressway, the first priority is to make it straight to improve speed. This goal tends to neglect the existing residential area. The degree and type of suffering depend on the noise level, which is reduced by distance.

These different social impacts mean that in the case of the planar pollution zone, organizing and mobilizing based on the neighborhood association and existing local community is relatively easy and quick. Similarity of sufferings makes for common interests and strong solidarity among the residents. Since the Osaka International Airport lawsuit filed in 1969, many similar lawsuits have appealed for reduction in airport noise. For municipalities or local governments, getting involved in the issue is relatively positive and easy.

But in the case of linear pollution zones, organizing and mobilizing based on the neighborhood association and the existing local community is relatively difficult. For victims to respond to this pollution, they have to establish a new specific association. Residents have a variety of interests in the issue, depending on their distance from the route, the noise level they suffer, and their economic backgrounds. For instance, some households prefer to just move to another quieter place. For others, such as self-employed households with small local shops and factories, moving carries the risk of losing customers acquired over many years. The number of lawsuits against bullet train or high-speed expressway noise pollution, such as the Nagoya bullet train lawsuit filed in 1969, is very small and successes are limited. Since the pollution does not affect all the residents of a community, municipalities or local governments have tended to decline getting deeply involved in the issue.

SEE ALSO: Ecological Problems; Environment, Sociology of the; High-Speed Transportation Pollution; Local Residents' Movements

REFERENCES AND SUGGESTED READINGS

Hasegawa, K. & Hatanaka, M. (1985) Jyumin undo to Chiiki Shakai (Local Residents' Movements and Local Community). In: Funabashi, H., Hasegawa, K., Hatanaka, S., & Katsuta, H., *Shinkansen kogai: Kosoku bunmei no shakaimondai (Bullet Train Pollution: Social Problems of a High-Speed Civilization)*. Yuhikaku, Tokyo, pp. 173–203.

polyamory

Christian Klesse

Polyamory is a novel concept. It has surfaced over recent decades in the debates about non-monogamy. Polyamory circumscribes a relationship philosophy, an identity, or a lifestyle that evolves around the belief that it is worthwhile and valid to have more than one partner. Combining word elements derived from Greek (poly) and Latin (amory), the term literally translates into "many loves." The concept of polyamory aims at providing a positive

alternative to the more common term "non-monogamy," which draws its meaning primarily from a negation of the dominant term "monogamy." As a relationship ideology, polyamory encourages multiple or open relationships and challenges the normative ideal of compulsory monogamy.

Polyamory spread in the United States throughout the 1980s and 1990s, where polyamorous communities have formed in many larger cities. Over recent years the term has gained significant popularity. The Internet has been an important tool for the development of an international online community. Today the term provides a point of reference for people interested in alternative lifestyles and sexualities beyond the North American continent and Europe, where the first networks around polyamory originated. There is no essential link between polyamory and any particular sexual identity. However, it seems as if discussions about polyamory have been particularly prominent in bisexual and lesbian contexts (cf. Munson & Stelboum 1999; Anderlini-D'Onofrio 2004).

A range of very diverse cultural and ideological influences has fed into the emerging discourses around polyamory. Compulsory monogamy has been criticized from within a range of social movements around sexuality and gender, including the feminist, lesbian, gay, bisexual, sadomasochist, and queer movements. Experiments in communal living within these movements and the "counterculture" in general have also contributed to the development of new relationship philosophies and family practices. The feminist movement has advocated a range of values that are salient within polyamory, such as caring, intimacy, and honesty. Lesbian and bisexual feminisms have invested in a culture of female friendship that fosters non-exclusive intimate and sexual relationships between women based on relational autonomy and voluntary association. A lot of the contemporary debates about polyamory are strongly influenced by spiritualist ideas and shaped by new age rhetoric (cf. Anapol 1997; Anderlini-D'Onofrio 2004). Thus, polyamory has been merged with paganism, polytheism, and primitivism. Religious references are manifold, but as is common within the new age movements in the West, proponents of polyamory have in particular appropriated ideas from within a range of eastern religious traditions and indulged in an undifferentiated Orientalism (Haritaworn et al. 2006). Polyamory movements have formed at a conjuncture of different social movements and heterogeneous cultural trends and tend to draw on a blend of diverse ideological traditions.

Polyamory covers a vast range of relationship forms: open couple relationships, primary partnerships, open to secondary and tertiary relationships, triads, V-structures, polywebs, open group marriages, closed or polyfidelitous group marriages, and so on (Munson & Stelboum 1999). Polyfidelity is a form of polyamory practiced by a group of people that are intimately and/or sexually related to each other, but promise to be faithful to the group. Polyamory aims at leaving a lot of space to individually work out the shape and boundaries of particular relationships among the people involved. It evolves around the idea that there is no singular valid mold to live relationships and that each relationship should be taken on its own merits. Although polyamory is committed to diversity, certain relationships and sexual practices have been continuously contested within polyamorous movements and communities. Thus, there has been much controversy about whether swinging and casual sex would belong within the realm of polyamory (cf. Lano & Parry 1995; Anapol 1997; Easton & Liszt 1997). Whereas some positions on polyamory take a more sex-radical stance, others are adamant that polyamory would rule out sex-focused approaches to non-monogamy.

Love is a central feature within polyamorous discourse. Even if largely undefined with regard to many aspects, polyamorous partnerships are usually supposed to be "loving" relationships (Anapol 1997). Many texts emphasize that it is not the major point of polyamory to have many sexual partners. Like people who practice serial monogamy (i.e., people who have one monogamous relationship at a time, but have more than one lifetime partner), polyamorists may have either a small or a large number of sexual lifetime partners. The only difference between (serial) monogamists and polyamorists, from this point of view, is that for the former the beginning of a new relationship always marks the end of the existing one.

Other central values within polyamorous relationship ethics are commitment, intimacy, negotiation, mutual respect, and honesty. The expectation is that important emotional issues are communicated and that major decisions about the relationship find consensus among all partners. Against the backdrop of these ideals, polyamory has frequently been defined as "responsible non-monogamy" (Lano & Parry 1995; Anapol 1997).

There has been an absolute lack of research into polyamory. Most of the literature available to date falls either within the genre of popular relationship guides (Anapol 1997; Easton & Liszt 1997) or presents a mix of first-person narratives, activist writing, small studies, and short theoretical contributions (Lano & Parry 1995; Munson & Stelboum 1999). The absence of empirical research is surprising, because polyamorous practice touches on a range of issues that have strongly preoccupied social scientists over recent years.

The spread of the popularity of polyamory testifies to radical changes within intimate and sexual cultures over recent decades. Polyamorous relationships provide a prime example of the social construction of kinship and families through chosen affinities. They illustrate the growth of diversity of relational bonds that has been reflected in a shift from family sociology to a sociology of intimacies. An engagement with polyamory (and other forms of non-monogamy) could further provide novel insights for the study of social and sexual identities, social movements, parenting practices, and the organization of households. Polyamory may also provide an interesting field of study for the growing scholarship that is concerned with the pervasiveness of heteronormativity in hegemonic cultural formations.

SEE ALSO: Compulsory Heterosexuality; Friendship: Interpersonal Aspects; Friendships of Gay, Lesbian, and Bisexual People; Intimacy; Kinship; Lesbian and Gay Families; Love and Commitment; Marriage; New Age

REFERENCES AND SUGGESTED READINGS

Anapol, D. (1997) *Polyamory: The New Love Without Limits.* IntiNet Resource Center, San Rafael, CA.

Anderlini-D'Onofrio, S. (Ed.) (2004) *Plural Loves: Designs for Bi and Poly Living*. Harworth Press, London.

Easton, D. & Liszt, C. A. (1997) *The Ethical Slut: A Guide to Infinite Sexual Possibilities*. Greenery Press, San Francisco.

Haritaworn, J., Lin, C. J., Klesse, C. (Eds.) (2006) *Special Issue on Polyamory of Sexualities* 9(5) (December).

Lano, K. & Parry, C. (Eds.) (1995) *Breaking the Barriers to Desire: New Approaches to Multiple Relationships*. Five Leaves, Nottingham.

Munson, M. & Stelboum, J. P. (1999) *The Lesbian Polyamory Reader: Open Relationships, Non-Monogamy, and Casual Sex*. Harrington Park Press, London.

polyethnicity

Bhavani Arabandi

In a world characterized by massive immigration and high rates of intermarriage, it was inevitable that a new type of ethnicity, polyethnicity, would emerge. Whereas ethnicity is commonly understood to reflect the shared ancestry and history of a people, polyethnicity in this context refers to the ability and willingness of individuals to identify with multiple ethnicities and multiple identities.

Although some scholars have traditionally argued that race and ethnicity are biologically determined, what seems increasingly evident to most scholars today is that race and ethnicity are social constructs, i.e., ideas, assumptions, and classifications that change over time and space (Waters 2000). Thus, ethnic groups are no longer seen as static and unchanging, but as emerging groups whose identities are constantly shifting as groups redefine their boundaries and criteria for membership. Today, for example, there is also the recognition that ethnicity has changed from its initial emphasis on division and exclusion between and among ethnic groups to its increasing importance as an idea and value supporting the intermixing and merger of various ethnicities. This intermixing, through immigration and intermarriage, has not only promoted a sense of interconnectedness and polyethnicity, but has also given rise to new patterns of social organization (Pagnini & Morgan 1990; Spikard & Burroughs 2000) which have served to blur preexisting racial and ethnic lines.

Max Weber (1968 [1922]) anticipated that as the world becomes increasingly modern, traditional attachments such as ethnicity would decline when confronted with advanced rationalization of human action and organization. However, far from eroding, ethnicity and an accompanying heightened sense of ethnic identity have increased in geometric proportion today, with groups fighting over ideology, religion, scarce resources, political spaces, and national identity. Theories of assimilation emphasized by American sociologists (Gordon, Moynihan, and van den Berghe in particular) were based on white European immigrants to the US and argued that, over time, immigrants would be absorbed into the mainstream where they would be indistinguishable from one another and, in the process, adopt an American identity. However, the inadequacy of these theories was revealed when certain groups did not fit the model. For example, they ignored the African Americans for whom economic integration with the mainstream had not been successful. And they did not accommodate the recent immigrants such as Asians and Latinos who have not only kept their ethnicity intact using a pattern of "segmented assimilation," but also used it to achieve economic mobility (Portes & Zhou 1993). Further, these theories failed to recognize immigrants as active agents having a hand in the shaping of their ethnic identity in the host environment (Song 2003; Lee & Bean 2004). And lastly, the increased salience of ethnicity is thought to be "symbolic" (Gans 1979) for the white European immigrants who held onto their ethnicity despite their integration into the mainstream.

Polyethnicity challenges the claim that one has to belong to only one ethnicity, and cannot be both or more. It also challenges the assumption that distinctions amongst individuals are readily identifiable and separable (Cornell 2000). The United States has come a long way from the anti-miscegenation laws that prevented interracial and interethnic marriages prior to 1967 (Spikard 1989), to a growing polyethnic population that could account for one-fifth of the US population by the year 2050 (Lee & Bean 2004). And as interethnic marriages are increasing, both partners and their children are resisting the idea of choosing a singular ethnic identity to define themselves as had once been demanded (Cornell 2000). Further, immigration of various peoples from around the world, especially by the late twentieth century, has also complicated the claim of a single ethnicity, and changed the world's ethnic landscape. Recognizing this change and the increase in polyethnic individuals, the US Census Bureau, for the first time in 2000, offered multiple choices for race/ethnicity.

Despite these changes, the idea of polyethnicity has not been free of ambiguities and contradictions. For example, according to Cornell (2000), "those who carry multiple racial and ethnic identities may struggle not only against the dominant group's insistence on clear boundaries and unitary classifications, but against the similar insistence on the part of the subordinate groups." Thus, the discourse around ethnic identity tends to be binary and exclusive in nature, and even though there is growing inter-ethnic marriage amongst various groups, the experience of the groups is very different. Lee and Bean (2004) posit the view that Asians and Latinos have much higher rates of interethnic marriages than do blacks, and they are more likely to report polyethnicity than blacks who more often than not claim a single ethnicity and racial identity. This is the case, the authors argue, because blacks have a "legacy of slavery," a history of discrimination, and have been victimized by the "one drop rule" (where having any black blood automatically labeled one black) in the US. However, despite this pressure to identify with one ethnicity or another, polyethnic people are asserting their desired identities and affiliations. But one should keep in mind that those characterized as polyethnics in themselves do not constitute an actual group simply because of the diverse experiences of the individuals in that group. Much research needs to be done in order to capture the varied experiences of polyethnic people, and how they conceive of their identity. Future directions in this area might include multiple ethnic memberships in an increasingly transnational context where national borders are less fixed.

SEE ALSO: Accommodation; Acculturation; Assimilation; Ethnicity; Ethnic Groups; Interracial Unions; Melting Pot; One Drop Rule; Passing; Race; Race and Ethnic Consciousness; Race (Racism)

REFERENCES AND SUGGESTED READINGS

Cornell, S. (2000) That's the Story of Our Lives. In: Spikard, P. & Burroughs, W. J. (Eds.), *We Are a People*. Temple University Press, Philadelphia, PA, pp. 41–53.

Gans, H. (1979) Symbolic Ethnicity: The Future of Ethnic Groups and Cultures in America. *Ethnic and Racial Studies* 2: 1–20.

Lee, J. & Bean, F. D. (2004) America's Changing Color Lines: Immigration, Race/Ethnicity, and Multiracial Identification. *American Review of Sociology* 30: 221–42.

Pagnini, D. L. & Morgan, S. P. (1990) Intermarriage and Social Distance among US Immigrants at the Turn of the Century. *American Journal of Sociology* 96: 405–32.

Portes, A. & Zhou, M. (1993) The New Second Generation: Segmented Assimilation and its Variants. *Annals of the American Academy of Political and Social Science* 530 (November): 74–97.

Song, M. (2003) *Choosing Ethnic Identity*. Polity Press, Cambridge.

Spikard, P. (1989) *Mixed Blood*. University of Wisconsin Press, Madison.

Spikard, P. & Burroughs, W. J. (2000) We Are a People. In: Spikard, P. & Burroughs, W. J. (Eds.), *We Are a People*. Temple University Press, Philadelphia, PA, pp. 1–19.

Waters, M. C. (2000) Multiple Ethnicities and Identity in the United States. In: Spikard, P. & Burroughs, W. J. (Eds.), *We Are a People*. Temple University Press, Philadelphia, PA, pp. 23–40.

Weber, M. (1968 [1922]) *Economy and Society*. University of California Press, Berkeley.

popular culture

Toby Miller

The word "popular" denotes "of the people," "by the people," and "for the people." In other words, it is made up of them as *subjects*, whom it textualizes via drama, sport, and information; *workers*, who undertake that textualization through performances and recording; and *audiences*, who receive the ensuing texts.

Three discourses determine the direction sociologists have taken towards this topic. A discourse about art sees it elevating people above ordinary life, transcending body, time, and place. Conversely, a discourse about folklife expects it to settle us into society through the wellsprings of community, as part of daily existence. And a discourse about pop idealizes fun, offering transcendence through joy but doing so by referring to the everyday (Frith 1991). "The popular" circles across these discourses.

For its part, the concept of culture derives from tending and developing agriculture. With the emergence of capitalism, culture came both to embody instrumentalism and to abjure it, via the industrialization of farming, on the one hand, and the cultivation of individual taste, on the other (Benhabib 2002: 2). Culture has usually been understood in two registers, via the social sciences and the humanities – truth versus beauty. This was a heuristic distinction in the sixteenth century (Williams 1983: 38), but it became substantive as time passed. Culture is now a marker of differences and similarities in taste and status within groups, as explored interpretively or methodically. In today's humanities, theater, film, television, radio, art, craft, writing, music, dance, and electronic gaming are judged by criteria of quality, as framed by practices of cultural criticism and history. For their part, the social sciences focus on the languages, religions, customs, times, and spaces of different groups, as explored ethnographically or statistically. So whereas the humanities articulate differences *within* populations, through symbolic norms (e.g., which class has the cultural capital to appreciate high culture, and which does not), the social sciences articulate differences *between* populations, through social norms (e.g., which people play militaristic electronic games and which do not) (Wallerstein 1989; Bourdieu 1984).

What happens when we put "popular" and "culture" back together, with the commercial world binding them? "Popular culture" clearly relates to markets. Neoclassical economics assumes that expressions of the desire and capacity to pay for services stimulate the provision of entertainment and hence – when the result is publicly accepted – determine what is "popular." Value is decided through competition between providers to obtain the favor of consumers, with the conflictual rationality of the parties producing value to society. The connection of market entertainment to new identities leads to a variety of sociological reactions. During the Industrial Revolution, anxieties about a suddenly urbanized and educated population raised the prospect of a long-feared "ochlocracy" of "the worthless mob" (Pufendorf 2000: 144). Theorists from both right and left argued that newly literate publics would be vulnerable to manipulation by demagogues. The subsequent emergence of public schooling in the West took as its project empowering, and hence disciplining, the working class.

This notion of the suddenly enfranchised being bamboozled by the unscrupulously fluent has recurred throughout the modern period. It inevitably leads to a primary emphasis on the number and conduct of audiences to popular culture: where they came from, how many there were, and what they did as a consequence of being present. These audiences are conceived as empirical entities that can be known via research instruments derived from sociology, demography, psychology, and marketing. Such concerns are coupled with a secondary concentration on content: *what* were audiences watching when they … And so texts, too, are conceived as empirical entities that can be known, via research instruments derived from sociology, psychology, and literary criticism. So classical Marxism views the popular as a means to false consciousness that diverts the working class from recognizing its economic oppression; feminist approaches have varied between a condemnation of the popular as a similar diversion from gendered consciousness and its celebration as a distinctive part of women's culture; and cultural studies has regarded the popular as a key location for symbolic resistance of class and gender oppression alike (Smith 1987; Hall & Jefferson 1976).

The foremost theorist of popular culture in the sociological literature is Antonio Gramsci, whose activism against Mussolini in the 1920s and 1930s has become an ethical exemplar for progressive intellectuals. Gramsci maintains that each social group creates "organically, one or more strata of intellectuals which give it homogeneity and an awareness of its own function not only in the economic but also in the social and political fields": the industrial technology, law, economy, and culture of each group. The "'organic' intellectuals which every new class creates alongside itself and elaborates in the course of its development" assist in the emergence of that class, for example via military expertise. Intellectuals operate in "civil society," which denotes "the ensemble of organisms commonly called 'private,' that of 'political society' or 'the State.'" They comprise the "'hegemony' which the dominant group exercises throughout society" as well as the "'direct domination' or command exercised through the State and 'juridical' government." Ordinary people give "'spontaneous' consent" to the "general direction imposed on social life by the dominant fundamental group" (Gramsci 1978: 5–7, 12). In other words, popular culture legitimizes sociopolitical arrangements in the public mind and can be the site of struggle as well as domination.

The counter-idea, that the cultural industries "impress ... the same stamp on everything," derives from Adorno and Horkheimer (1977) of the Frankfurt School, an anti-Nazi group of scholars writing around the same time as Gramsci. After migrating to the US, they found a quietude reminiscent of pre-war Germany. Their explanation for the replication of this attitude in the US lies in the mass production-line organization of entertainment, where businesses use systems of reproduction that ensure identical offerings. Adorno and Horkheimer see consumers as manipulated by those at the economic apex of production. "Domination" masquerades as choice in a "society alienated from itself." Coercion is mistaken for free will, and culture becomes just one more industrial process, subordinated to dominant economic forces within society that insist on standardization.

While much of this dismay is shared by conservatives, for some functionalist sociologists, popular culture represents the apex of modernity. Rather than encouraging alienation, it stands for the expansion of civil society, the moment in history when the state becomes receptive to, and part of, the general community. The population is now part of the social, rather than excluded from the means and politics of political calculation, along with a lessening of authority, the promulgation of individual rights and respect, and the intensely interpersonal, large-scale human interaction necessitated by industrialization and aided by systems of mass communication. The spread of advertising is taken as a model for the breakdown of social barriers, exemplified in the triumph of the popular (Shils 1966).

These approaches have produced a wide array of topics and methods for researching the popular. Cultural studies has perhaps been the most productive. Historical and contemporary analyses of slaves, crowds, pirates, bandits, minorities, women, and the working class have utilized archival, ethnographic, and statistical methods to emphasize day-to-day non-compliance with authority, via practices of consumption that frequently turn into practices of production. For example, UK research on the contemporary has lit upon Teddy Boys, Mods, bikers, skinheads, punks, school students, teen girls, Rastas, truants, dropouts, and magazine readers as its magical agents of history: groups who deviated from the norms of schooling and the transition to work by generating moral panics. Scholar-activists examine the structural underpinnings to collective style, investigating how bricolage subverts the achievement-oriented, materialistic, educationally driven values and appearance of the middle class. The working assumption has often been that subordinate groups adopt and adapt signs and objects of the dominant culture, reorganizing them to manufacture new meanings. Consumption is thought to be the epicenter of such subcultures. Paradoxically, it has also reversed their members' status as consumers. The oppressed become producers of new fashions, inscribing alienation, difference, and powerlessness on their bodies (Hall & Jefferson 1976).

Of course, popular culture leaves its mark on those who create it as well as its audiences. This insight leads us towards a consideration of the popular as itself an industry, whose products encourage agreement with prevailing social relations and whose work practices reflect such agreement. Today, rather than being a series of entirely nation-based industries, either ideologically or productively, popular culture is internationalized, in terms of the export and import of texts, attendant fears of cultural imperialism, and a New International Division of Cultural Labor. That division sees European football teams composed of players from across the globe, and Hollywood films shot wherever talent is cheap, incentives plentiful, and scenery sufficiently malleable to look like the US (Miller et al. 2001a, 2001b).

This relates to other significant changes in popular culture. The canons of aesthetic judgment and social distinction that once flowed from the humanities and social science approaches to culture, keeping aesthetic tropes somewhat distinct from social norms, have collapsed in on each other. Art and custom are now resources for markets and nations (Yúdice 2002) – reactions to the crisis of belonging and economic necessity occasioned by capitalist globalization. As a consequence, popular culture is more than textual signs or everyday practices (Martín-Barbero 2003). It is also crucial to both advanced and developing economies, and provides the legitimizing ground on which particular groups (e.g., African Americans, gays and lesbians, the hearing-impaired, or evangelical Protestants) claim resources and seek inclusion in national and international narratives (Yúdice 1990). This intermingling has implications for both aesthetic and social hierarchies, which "regulate and structure ... individual and collective lives" (Parekh 2000: 143) in competitive ways that harness art and collective meaning for social and commercial purposes. To understand and intervene in this environment, sociologists need to be nimble in their use of textual, economic, ethnographic, and political approaches to popular culture.

SEE ALSO: Birmingham School; Consumption, Mass Consumption, and Consumer Culture; Critical Theory/Frankfurt School; Cultural Studies; Culture Industries; Deviance; Elite Culture; Gramsci, Antonio; Leisure, Popular Culture and; Mass Culture and Mass Society; Media; Media and Consumer Culture; Popular Culture Forms; Popular Culture Icons; Shopping; Shopping Malls; Sport

REFERENCES AND SUGGESTED READINGS

Adorno, T. W. & Horkheimer, M. (1977) The Culture Industry: Enlightenment as Mass Deception. In Curran, J., Gurevitch, M., & Woollacott, J. (Eds.), *Mass Communication and Society*. Edward Arnold, London, pp. 349–83.

Benhabib, S. (2002) *The Claims of Culture: Equality and Diversity in the Global Era*. Princeton University Press, Princeton.

Bourdieu, P. (1984) *Distinction: A Social Critique of the Judgement of Taste*. Trans. R. Nice. Harvard University Press, Cambridge, MA.

Frith, S. (1991) The Good, the Bad, and the Indifferent: Defending Popular Culture from the Populists. *Diacritics* 21 (4): 102–15.

Gramsci, A. (1978) *Selections from the Prison Notebooks of Antonio Gramsci*. Trans. Q. Hoare & G. Nowell-Smith. International Publishers, New York.

Hall, S. & Jefferson, T. (Eds.) (1976) *Resistance Through Rituals: Youth Subcultures in Post-War Britain*. Hutchinson, London.

Martín-Barbero, J. (2003) Proyectos de Modernidad en América Latina. *Metapolítica* 29: 35–51.

Miller, T., Lawrence, G., McKay, J., & Rowe, D. (2001a) *Globalization and Sport: Playing the World*. Sage, London.

Miller, T., Govil, N., McMurria, J., & Maxwell, R. (2001b) *Global Hollywood*. British Film Institute, London.

Parekh, B. (2000) *Rethinking Multiculturalism: Cultural Diversity and Political Theory*. Palgrave, Basingstoke.

Pufendorf, S. (2000) *On the Duty of Man and Citizen According to Natural Law*. Trans. M. Silverthorne. Cambridge University Press, Cambridge.

Shils, E. (1966) Mass Society and its Culture. In: Berelson, B. & Janowitz, M. (Eds.), *Reader in Public Opinion and Communication*, 2nd edn. Free Press, New York, pp. 505–28.

Smith, D. E. (1987) *The Everyday World as Problematic: A Feminist Sociology*. Northeastern University Press, Boston.

Wallerstein, I. (1989) Culture as the Ideological Battleground of the Modern World-System. *Hitotsubashi Journal of Social Studies* 21 (1): 5–22.

Williams, R. (1983) *Keywords: A Vocabulary of Culture and Society*, revd. edn. Oxford University Press, New York.

Yúdice, G. (1990) For a Practical Aesthetics. *Social Text* 25–6: 129–45.

Yúdice, G. (2002) *El Recurso de la Cultura: Usos de la Cultura en la Era Global*. Editorial Gedisa, Barcelona.

popular culture forms

Sociologists have addressed a wide range of topics under the heading of popular culture. In fact, there are far too many to cover adequately in this Encyclopedia. Thus, a decision was made to give at least a sense of this literature by sampling some of the key topics examined by sociologists and offering an indication of the way in which they have been covered. In this entry a variety of forms of popular culture are considered – the beach, hip-hop, jazz, P2P, reality TV, rock 'n' roll, science fiction, soap operas, and zoos. Of course, this is a highly selective and, in most cases (two exceptions are the beach and zoos), time-bound list. Thus, many other topics could have been chosen and, of those that have been included, some (reality TV is a good example) could disappear in a short period of time. However, the point of this entry is not to give the reader a full sense of timeless forms of popular culture, but rather to offer a sampling of work in sociology on this topic. – *GR*

beach

Adrian Franklin

"The beach" is a dominant site and form of recreation and tourism – and not merely on the new pleasure peripheries of Southeast Asia, Mexico, the Caribbean, Bali, or Australia. The seaside towns of the United States and the UK, for example, have been through a turbulent period of change as they faced new competition, but even they are remarkably resilient, morphing into new lives for fashionable nostalgias and kitsches; homes for theme parks; new and desirable locations for weekend villas, condos and spaces of retirement, and as centers for conferences and conventions. At the same time, many have continued to provide a relatively cheap holiday. As an example, the most famous seaside beach of them all, Blackpool Pleasure Beach, is still Britain's most popular tourist attraction. It is visited by over 7 million people annually and has more hotel beds than all of Greece, including its islands (Roodhouse 2001), and its range of clientele has remained very wide. Further, despite British heliotropism (which might be defined as a preference for sunnier beach holidays abroad), according to the UK Day Visits Survey a total of 81 million day trips to the seaside were made in 2000 (www.staruk.org.uk). At the opposite extreme perhaps, in the state of Florida, a recent survey of beach visits revealed that 84 percent of Florida residents visited the beach at least once a week and that these visits might include up to 14 different types of activity. A more extreme example is Australia where an entire nation has been founded on the ideal of proximity to the beach. As Fiske et al. (1987: 54) argued, the ideal beach "contributes to everyday existence"; it

must be "metropolitan and therefore urban," and there are cities "that are planned solely in order to be by the beach thus clearly highlighting the relationship between the beach and the city." The fact that Garland's book *The Beach* (2000) became an international bestseller reveals the continuing relevance of the coast as a tourist destination. Even *water* itself has been a remarkably resilient component of leisure and tourism, as Anderson and Tabb (2002) make clear.

BEACH AS SEASIDE

In its early days as a mass seaside holiday center (as opposed to the earlier "medicinal" seaside that preceded it), the beach was a wonder world, a "dreamland"; a utopian promise of the future brightness and consumerism of a post-depression, post-war world. Seaside was an important ritual of transition into the new world of consumerism, spectacle, and pleasure. However, the more everyday life borrowed or styled itself on the seaside (producing universal all-year-round access to pleasure), the less specific seaside resorts were able to reproduce that rapture, breathlessness, and euphoria. Seaside and the subsequent routinizations of pleasure after the style of seaside produced a second, blasé period of connoisseurship; a more socially stratified, spatially extended, rarefied, and measured set of expectations and ritual. The beach then became just one of very many alternative types of pleasure. However, it remains one of the most important precisely because it retained its basic ritualistic formula: it maintained its liminoid space of the beach, its ritual devotion to the sea, the sun, and the body, and its unhurried basic structure as a ritual of passage. When people say they need to get away, when people conjure an ideal holiday or break, in their imaginations the beach is still a dominant evocation.

BEACH THEORY

The beach was first interpreted in structuralist terms. Placed on the elemental margin between sea and land, much was made of its liminoid, in-between character and comparisons were made with other such spaces and their significance for ritual, freedom, and especially rites of passage. The suspension of everyday social norms at the beach was noted, particularly those related to dress codes, sociability and communitas (especially with fellow travelers), sexuality, time, and social reserve (drinking and spending were more exuberant, for example). The beach at Brighton was one of Shields's (1991) "places on the margin" that opposed the everyday/social center and legitimated transgressive behavior. At various times Brighton embodied such a reputation. It was a place of secret liaisons and planned divorce evidence in the early part of the twentieth century and one of the first nude bathing beaches close to a town later in the century. Fiske et al. (1987: 61), on the other hand, located the beach in Australia between the core structuralist binary of nature and culture/city and made the argument (among others) that the tanned look is an anomalous category between skin (culture) and fur (nature).

Such accounts were criticized for their selective use of evidence. It is quite clear, for example, as Booth (2001) shows, that whether suburban or more remote, the Australian beach has a history of very conservative moral regulation, with beach inspectors employed to make sure bathers complied with relatively prudish rules of beachwear and anti-nude beach campaigns fuming until present times. Urbain (2003: 134) is also opposed to the simplistic application of binaries to understand the beach. Certainly for him (and the French, specifically), it is never nature; rather, the beach has been specifically *denatured* as resorts have made it a place of regulation, selected sites sheltered from the ravages of wild nature (gently shelving beaches, fine undisturbed sands, quiet waters) and with "locals" (especially "savages") chased away, making way for the civilized beach vacationer, those who come to occupy the beach

for set periods. Urbain deploys the "world-making" Robinson Crusoe metaphor to suggest that the beach was part of the ordering or pacification of the world: subjecting nature and "the other" to the norms of his "aesthetic, worldly, therapeutic or technological models" (2003: 127). However, Urbain argues that the Crusoe figure is inconstant and harbors secret desires to transgress the order he creates.

For Urbain, both Crusoes are looking for "a cultic site and a 'prayer rug' for the performance of ritual," and this corresponds closely to Franklin's (2003) reanalysis of the modern beach as a *continuing* site of embodied ritual. Whereas the ritual basis of early seaside forms can be located in emergent consumerism and also, to a degree, nationalism and a new erotic of the healthy body (a body routinely in danger of ill health and disease), later, more contemporary forms relate to a continuing ritual emphasis on the body, albeit deploying new technologies of the "sustainable" body (a body requiring constant and regular attention especially in relation to new dangers of stress, change, and ontological insecurity). It is a body that seeks the "never quite fulfilled" state of "fitness" (Bauman & May 2001). New technologies of the body are also designed to slow down "fast time" and produce yet more liminoid experiences and ritual transformations. From the regimes of healthism to the Goan beach trance parties and the surfer's achievement of "flow," this is a very different beach.

SEE ALSO: Body and Cultural Sociology; Consumption, Tourism and; Leisure; Leisure, Popular Culture and; Ritual

REFERENCES AND SUGGESTED READINGS

Anderson, S. C. & Tabb, B. (Eds.) (2002) *Water, Leisure, and Culture*. Berg, Oxford.

Bauman, Z. & May, T. (2001) *Thinking Sociologically*. Blackwell, Oxford.

Booth, D. (2001) *Australian Beach Cultures*. Frank Cass, London.

Fiske, J., Hodge, B., & Turner, G. (1987) *Myths of Oz*. Allen & Unwin, Sydney.

Franklin, A. S. (2003) *Tourism*. Sage, London.

Garland, A. (2000) *The Beach*. Penguin, Harmondsworth.

Lencek, L. & Boscker, G. (1999) *The Beach*. Pimlico, London.

Roodhouse, S. (2001) Creating Sustainable Cultures. Joint State Conference of Regional Arts. University of Sydney, October 5–6.

Shields, R. (1991) *Places on the Margin*. Routledge, London.

Urbain, J.-D. (2003) *At the Beach*. Trans. C. Porter. Minnesota University Press, Minneapolis.

Walton, J. K. (2000) *The British Seaside: Holidays and Resorts in the 20th Century*. Manchester University Press, Manchester.

hip-hop

Karen Bettez Halnon

Hip-hop originated in 1974 as a local subculture in the South Bronx, New York City with Kingston, Jamaica-born Clive Campbell, the founding "Father of Hip-Hop." In the rented recreation room of the apartment building where he lived, Campbell held house parties, advertised three weeks in advance on index card/flyers simply but provocatively featuring "Kool Herc" (short for Hercules). There Herc played "exclusive" records that were "the bomb," or ones not on the radio. The parties, with admissions under a dollar and often lasting until morning, became so popular that they often grossed $400 or $500 a night. Herc's popularity as DJ was due to an experiment. Using two turntables, double copies of a record, and no headphones, he isolated and repeatedly cued the "breaks," the "get down" percussion sections, or the most danceable part of songs (from his favorites, such as James Brown, Dennis Coffee, or Scorpio). During continued breaks, "freestyle" dancers (later called B-boys and B-girls, or break dancers) would "go off" into a dancing frenzy. Herc's popularity was also due to use of Jamaican "toasts," where he would talk over but to the beat of the music in playful rhymes about people or events in his immediate environment; for example, "Yo this is Kool Herc in the joint-ski saying my mellow-ski Marky D is in the house." As Herc progressed as DJ, he turned over microphone duties to his friends Coke La Rock and Clark Kent, thus constituting the first emcee team, Kool Herc and the Herculoids (Chang & Herc 2005).

The main elements of hip-hop culture, as suggested in part above, include DJing (cutting and scratching with two turntables, and performing with the microphone); B-boying/B-girling (breaking or break dancing); emceeing (rapping, or talking in rhyme to the rhythm of the beat); and tagging and graffiti art. Tagging began in New York City in the early 1970s with Vic 156, a mail courier who wrote his name and courier ID number on every subway and bus he rode. Graffiti was made famous by TAKI 183, a Greek teenager from Washington Heights named Demitrius, and the Ex-Vandals were one of the most revered graffiti crews. The Graffiti Bombing movement began in Philadelphia in the mid- to late 1960s with writers CORNBREAD and COOL EARL. Aided by commercialization, hip-hop is also a style of dress (designer baggy shirts and pants, silver and gold chains, backwards baseball caps, scullies, bright white sneakers, and/or Timberlands). Many would surely add the distinctive urban "street" language and the spirit of "keepin' it real" (or keeping the music reflective of everyday language, happenings, sufferings, perspectives, and/or realities of black urban life, and minimizing the distorting forces of commercialism). However, the "bling, bling" and flashy "cribs" of successful rappers are a central staple of success, and are made explicit to the point of parody in New Orleans rapper band Cash Money Millionaires.

With Herc as first inspiration, house parties, block parties, and club parties soon sprang up all over the New York ghettos for many who did not have the money to go to the expensive mid-town clubs. Emceeing, later known as rapping, also caught on with many urban youth because it was a means of accessible and affordable self-expression. Governed by very few rules, and costing nothing to participate, anyone with the inclination and a bit of verbal skill could rap, hone their rapping skills, convey their personality in rhyme, and (if good enough) elicit affirmation from peers. It should be noted that rapping is continuous with a variety of African American verbal jousting traditions, such as signifying, testifying, Shining of the Titanic, the Dozens, schoolyard rhymes, and/or prison "jailhouse" rhymes.

The rise in hip-hop's popularity can be also attributed to changes in black radio, an important traditional medium of African American self-expression. In the 1970s, disco emerged as a European and generic-sounding, watered-down type of funk music, and soon, to the chagrin of many, found a home on the airwaves of black radio. The loss of a soulful and authentic African American sound thus created a void that hip-hop helped to fill (as did Chicago's house music, Washington, DC's gogo music, and California's reembracement of funk, which all arose at approximately the same time).

Beyond Kool Herc, other co-originators of hip-hop include: Pete DJ Jones, DJ Hollywood, Eddie Cheeba, "Love Bug" Starski, Grand Master Flash, Afrika Bambaataa (founder of the Zulu Nation in New York), and Run DMC. Other best rappers up to the late 1970s include Chief Rocker Busy Bee, Grand Wizard Theodore, the Fantastic Romantic Five, Funky Four Plus One More, Crash Crew, and Master Don Committee. The first rap records were Fat Back Band's "King Tem III" and Sugar Hill Gang's "Rapper's Delight," the latter being the first commercial rap record in 1979, and one that gave wide mainstream exposure to the term "rap."

During the 1980s hip-hop was centered in New York, and gave rise to artists such as Kurtis Blow, LL Cool J, and Slick Rick. Public Enemy gained notoriety and popularity for its political and militant lyrics. By the early 1990s "East Coast" rappers found Los Angeles-centered "West Coast" rivals among Gangsta rap bands such as NWA and Notorious BIG. NWA's gold-status *Straight Outta Compton* (1989) is notable in that the album sold over 2.5 million copies with virtually no radio play and an MTV ban. Most notorious of the LP's tracks was "F*** Tha Police," an angry reactive song accusing police of the racist killing of minorities. NWA's music elicited numerous protests and even FBI intervention. The media fanning the flames between East and West Coast rivalries, the violent tensions culminated in the murders of Tupak Shakur and Notorious BIG in the mid-1990s.

While critics have condemned rap music as sexist, misogynist, homophobic, and violent, the more general influence of hip-hop culture pervades youth culture today in language, styles of dress, cultural and artistic aesthetics, and musical preferences. By the year 2000 hip-hop culture had become a billion dollar industry. Hip-hop has also achieved cultural recognition via the application of much serious scholarly inquiry and being the object of several noted national museum exhibits.

As suggested, the role of women in hip-hop culture is somewhat limited. However, following the first commercially successful female rappers, Salt n Peppa, has been an array of others who turn the objectifying tables on male rappers by demanding that men are at their sexual service. Rapping in this spirit are Foxy Brown, Trina, and Lil Kim.

While hip-hop is an African American subculture, with greatest rappers including Biggie Smalls, Jay Z, Nas, MOP, Ice T, DMX, and Snoop Dog, the most successful rapper of all time (by measures of the music industry) is Eminem, winner of nine Grammy awards and voted number 6 on VH-1's 50 Greatest Hip-Hop Artists of All Time. The debate over hip-hop's racial ownership has included accusations that Marshall Bruce Mathers, a blue-eyed, peroxide-blond kid from a Detroit ghetto, cashed in on black culture. However, Eminem's marketability with fans may be less an issue of race than one of the urgent consumer desire for authenticity and non-conformist individuality amid the alienating pressures of commercialism in a society of the spectacle. For millions of white suburban youth, at least, this desire translates as attraction to what is raw, real, and unmediated, and/or having the "moral daredevil" courage to say "F*** you with the free-est of space this divided state of embarrassment will allow me to have," as the double-M'd rapper explains and inspires with his Slim Shady alter ego in the song "White America" (Halnon 2005).

SEE ALSO: Alienation; Consumption, Youth Culture and; Music; Popular Culture; Subculture; Urban Poverty

REFERENCES AND SUGGESTED READINGS

Chang, J. & DJ Kool, Herc (Introduction) (2005) *Can't Stop Won't Stop: A History of the Hip-Hop Generation*. St. Martin's Press, New York.

George, N. (2005) *Hip Hop America*. Penguin, New York.

Halnon, K. B. (2005) Alienation Incorporated: "F*** the Mainstream Music" in the Mainstream. *Current Sociology* 53(4): 441–64.

Keyes, C. L. (2002) *Rap Music and Street Consciousness*. University of Illinois Press, Urbana.

Kitwana, B. (2003) *The Hip Hop Generation: Young Blacks and the Crisis in African American Culture*. Basic Civitas Books, New York.

Perkins, W. E. (Ed.) (1995) *Droppin' Science: Critical Essays on Rap Music and Hip Hop Culture*. Temple University Press, Philadelphia.

Perry, I. (2005) *Prophets of the Hood: Politics and Poetics in Hip Hop*. Duke University Press, Durham, NC.

Rose, T. (1994) *Black Noise: Rap Music and Black Culture in Contemporary America*. Wesleyan University Press, Hanover, NH.

jazz

Adrian Franklin

Jazz is a musical style that developed from both African and European traditions emerging around the beginning of the twentieth century in African American communities, particularly in New Orleans. While there are now many styles, they all share some or many of the following musical qualities: syncopation, swing, improvisation, "blue notes," call and response, sound innovation such as growls and stretched notes, and polyrhythmic structure. Jazz is one of the most interesting sources of countercultural fusion between black and white cultures in the West and is frequently used as a metaphor for openness, cool, equality, and freedom of expression – often expressed in an embodied way through dance.

The origin of the word jazz is controversial but the most likely genealogy follows *jasm*, an American English word (first seen in print in 1842) for semen that also meant vitality and virility, through *jazz*, a slang term for copulation used among dice players (both black and white) in San Francisco some 70 years later. The word "jazz" first appeared in San Francisco baseball articles in 1913 to describe a player's magical qualities of life, vigor, or effervescence. It was then used to describe the music of a ragtime band who entertained players at a training camp, and from there it spread through musician networks to Chicago and New York by 1916. It was not until 1917 that the term was used in New Orleans, where the music style had its origins (Quinion 2004).

The earliest forms in New Orleans were marching bands where brass instruments and African rhythm and beat fused to form "raggedy" or ragtime music. Ragtime was quickly absorbed into early twentieth-century mainstream white musical cultures (e.g., in Irving Berlin's songs) where black

music and dance had been influential and popular since minstrel shows and public dance hall music. But as the New Orleans ragtime moved north through California and upriver to Chicago and to New York, new variants appeared and with each variation there were both the commercial forms of the major clubs and hotels and the purer musician forms in the bars and speakeasies (Becker 1973). Becker shows how jazz musicians (and jazz itself) were formed into cultural groups and social cliques and how individual musicians negotiated careers between the poles of pure (uncertain and poorly paid) and commercial (secure and affluent) jazz.

As jazz moved through the twentieth century, new forms such as "big band" in the 1930s, "swing" in the 1940s, and "bebop" in the 1940s and 1950s ebbed and flowed. After that there were new styles and fusion styles from the avant-garde sound of Keith Jarrett and Eberhard Weber through jazz funk and acid jazz to jazz house and nu jazz. While there is much talk of the decline of jazz sales, it is also possible to argue that it continues under these and other popular music styles – world music being a genre that continues to deploy many jazz variants.

The sociological interest of jazz is not restricted to its musical styles, its cultural forms, and origins. It is also possible to talk of the social spaces of jazz as a countercultural space or deviant culture. Jazz clubs emerged in the days of alcohol prohibition as sites away from surveillance and the policing of alcohol and drugs. Jazz then become synonymous with a variety of countercultures (black, gangster, immigrant, youth) in which individual freedom and Dionysian values were cultivated. It is for this reason that jazz was often referred to as "the devil's music." Critically, jazz opened up spaces of cultural transition. As a cultural form jazz was socially open, inclusive, and hospitable – anyone and everyone could find a welcome in the spaces of jazz. As Santorno (2001) argued, "Black Americans (and other ethnic outsiders) could use it to enter mainstream society, white Americans could flee to it from mainstream society, and the transactions created a flux and flow that powered American cultural syntheses." In this way, jazz played an important role in breaking down traditional lines of American culture and paving the way for a more permissive, open society. But not just in America.

Meller (1976) showed how jazz jumped the Atlantic to England during and after World War I and the social and cultural impact it had. Up until then, working-class leisure culture was tightly organized around neighborhoods and their chapels. Dancing was strictly supervised and limited and music styles conformed to the stringent moral regime of nonconformist life. The arrival of jazz and watered-down dance variants reconfigured this completely. Coinciding with public transport systems, electrification, and rising youth wages, the new music found expression in new city center dance halls. These were commercial and more permissive, and as the possibility and styles of dancing became more exciting so thousands of dance schools emerged to educate the new generation into jazz-inspired freedoms. Among other things it ushered in more intimate premarital social relations between the sexes, the beginnings of teenage culture, and more freedom for women.

Jazz is also significant in developing a form of individualism commensurate with its counterculture aspirations. It inspired the personal politics of "cool" and "hip," which, as Pountain and Robbins (2000) maintain, now dominate contemporary forms of individualism everywhere. Cool is now a generalized expression of opposition and defiance to a variety of authority figures, especially the state and its agencies and agents. It has become a permanent stance to the world, not necessarily a life stage that one will grow out of. Cool also registers the new significance of individualism and individualized, as opposed to collective, politics. For these reasons, cool is no longer the preserve of the young but is distributed across large sections of society, particularly among those who have lived in the post-1960s countercultures.

SEE ALSO: Cool; Cultural Studies; Music; Music and Social Movements; Popular Culture Icons (Sinatra, Frank)

REFERENCES AND SUGGESTED READINGS

Adorno, T. W. (1967) *Prisms*. MIT Press, Cambridge, MA.
Becker, H. S. (1973) *The Outsiders*. Free Press, New York.
Martin, P. J. (1995) *Sounds and Society*. Manchester University Press, Manchester.
Meller, H. (1976) *Leisure and the Changing City: 1870–1914*. Routledge & Kegan Paul, London.
Pountain, D. & Robbins, D. (2000) *Cool Rules: Anatomy of an Attitude*. Reaktion Books, London.
Quinion, M. (2004) *World Wide Words*. Online. www.worldwidewords.org/qa/qa-jaz1.htm.
Santorno, G. (2001) All That Jazz. *Nation*, January 29.

P2P

Chris Rojek

Peer to peer communication systems enable users to exchange files over the Internet. In the 1990s the spread of file-exchange servers such as Napster, eDonkey, KaZaA, Morpheus, and Grokster became a *cause célèbre* in the recording industry. P2P exchange created a contraction in sales of sound recordings, especially singles. The Recording Industry Association of America (RIAA) engaged in litigation against both consumers and file servers. It alleged copyright violation and demanded heavy penalties to discourage exchange. The RIAA successfully lobbied for the introduction of the Digital Millennium Copyright Act (DMCA 1998), which criminalizes production and dissemination of P2P technology with the capacity to circumvent copyright, and increases penalties of infringement. The act makes provision for exemption for non-profit organizations like archives, libraries, and education institutions, but limits the conditions under which exemption applies. However, the provisions of the act have proved to be very difficult to enforce. The proliferation of the Web and the absence of a commercially viable policing system have impeded detection of copyright violation. In addition, litigation has produced victims and popular reaction against the recording industry. A case in point was the legal action brought against Brianna LaHara, a 12-year-old American Catholic, who was arraigned to face a multi-million dollar lawsuit for downloading sitcom soundtracks and nursery jingles like "If You're Happy and You Know It." The case was eventually settled for $2,000. However, the public perception that the recording industry is greedy and insensitive was reinforced.

The RIAA did achieve a symbolic victory in forcing the P2P pioneer Napster to introduce a fee-paying structure. Launched in 1999, Napster was the most potent symbol of Net banditry. It embodied the spirit of consumer rebellion against multinational super profits and became a legend in campus culture. However, the victory against Napster has not sounded the death knell for P2P systems. Companies like KaZaA effectively transform home computers into mini-servers, so policing copyright detection is problematized. In addition, they divide ownership between many companies as a deliberate strategy designed to evade detection.

The P2P revolution raises thorny questions about the rights of commercial providers of intellectual property and the opportunities produced by globalization and the new technology to widen access. In April 2004, in a set back to the RIAA, the US District Court ruled that file-sharing servers cannot be held responsible for the illegal conduct of their users. Because companies like Morpheus and Grokster are not based in a central index of files, but treat domestic terminals as mini-servers, they support a system of P2P exchange that approximates more faithfully a gift relationship. To the consternation of the recording industry, the ruling was upheld by the US Ninth Circuit Court of Appeals in August 2004.

The pivotal issue here turns on the American Constitution's First Amendment that guarantees freedom of speech and press. By attempting to block P2P exchange, the RIAA was deemed to challenge the First Amendment. Until the US Appeal Court ruling in 2004, the famous 1984 US Supreme Court ruling in respect of the Sony Betamax video recorder set the most significant legal precedent of recent times. This established the principle that the social value of the legal uses of the device outweighed the potential for abuse, and found Sony not guilty of copyright infringement. It is this immunity that is currently being contested by the recording industry. The strategy of the RIAA has now shifted to apply criminal penalties against companies and businesses found to *induce* or actively encourage copyright infringement.

In conflating the issue of illegal exchange with that of the gift relationship, the recording industry opens up a Pandora's Box for consumer culture and copyright law. If copyright holders seek to extend their rights over technologies that induce infringement, they introduce what many would regard as unreasonable restraints on free speech. The future is likely to consist of some

form of differentiated licensing system in which downloads may be purchased or registered for a fixed period. Apple's iTunes Music Store already operates a successful system of fee-based downloading. Other companies have followed suit and the consumer is benefiting from a price war between iTunes, Warner Brothers Online, EMI, Sony Music Entertainment, Universal, and Wallmart. This is likely to change the culture in which popular music is purchased, with record stores needing to diversify in order to stay in business.

SEE ALSO: Globalization, Culture and; Intellectual Property; Internet; Leisure; Music and Media; Popular Culture

REFERENCES AND SUGGESTED READINGS

Goldstein, P. (2003) *Copyright's Highway*. Stanford University Press, Stanford.

Levine, S. (2004) *The Art of Downloading Music*. Sanctuary Press, London.

Pieterse, J. (2004) *Globalization and Culture*. Rowman & Littlefield, Boston.

US Department of Commerce (2000) *Falling Through The Net*. US Department of Commerce, Washington, DC.

Van Horebeek, B. (2003) Napster Clones Turn Their Attention to Academic E-Books. *New World Library* 104(1187/1188): 142–8.

reality TV

Annette Hill

Reality TV is a catchall category that includes a wide range of popular factual programs. Sometimes called factual entertainment, or infotainment, reality TV is located in border territories, between information and entertainment, documentary and drama. Originally used as a category for law and order programming, reality TV has become the success story of television in the 1990s and 2000s.

The rise of reality TV came at a time when networks were looking for a quick fix solution to economic problems within the cultural industries. Increased costs in the production of drama, sitcom, and comedy ensured unscripted, popular factual programming became a viable economic option during the 1990s. The deregulation and marketization of media industries, especially in advanced industrial states such as the United States, Western Europe, and Australasia, also contributed to the rise of reality TV, as it performed well in a competitive, multichannel environment.

There are three main strands to the development of reality TV, and these relate to three distinct, yet overlapping, areas of media production: tabloid journalism, documentary television, and popular entertainment. There are a variety of styles and techniques associated with reality TV, such as non-professional actors, unscripted dialogue, surveillance footage, hand-held cameras, seeing events unfold as they are happening in front of the camera. However, the treatment of "reality" in reality programming has changed as the genre has developed over the past decade. The main formats include infotainment (on-scene footage of emergency services, e.g., *Rescue 911*), docusoap (popular observational documentary, e.g., *Airport*), lifestyle (home and personal makeovers, e.g., *Changing Rooms*), and reality gameshow (experiments that place ordinary people in controlled environments, e.g., *Big Brother*). These formats were successful because they drew on existing popular genres, such as soap opera or gameshows, to create hybrid programs, and focused on telling stories in an entertaining style, usually foregrounding visuals, characterization, and narrative. Reality TV has been the motor of primetime throughout the 1990s and 2000s, drawing at times unprecedented market shares of over 50 percent, and regularly appearing in the Top 20 shows on network TV. With such high ratings, its place in primetime schedules is assured for some time to come. In addition, reality formats are international bestsellers, with local versions appearing all over the world.

Since the early days of reality TV, cultural critics have consistently attacked the genre for being voyeuristic, cheap, sensational television. There have been accusations that reality TV contributes to the "dumbing down," or tabloidization, of society and culture. Such criticism is based on general concerns about quality standards within public service and commercial television, the influence of television on viewers, and the ethics of popular television.

On the topic of quality, the ways in which program makers, or critics, judge the quality of reality TV are different from the ways viewers assess good or bad programs. What makes a reality format "good" according to younger viewers will make it "bad" for older adults. The quality criterion used by different social groups highlights the diverse ways people value popular culture.

The question of influence is a difficult one. There is no doubt television influences viewers, but there is a great deal of doubt about how and to what degree it influences viewers, and whether this influence is prosocial or negative. When it comes to reality TV, there is an argument to be made that it negatively influences viewers, for example encouraging people to manipulate others in order to "win the game," or positively influences viewers, for example in learning about first aid. Until there is more empirical evidence to support either argument, the alleged negative influence of reality TV needs to be treated with some degree of skepticism.

Although some people might argue that ethics are absent from reality programming, in fact ethics are at the heart of reality TV. Ethics inform understanding of the treatment of ordinary people by program makers, and the content of stories about people's private experiences and dilemmas. Rights to privacy, rights to fair treatment, good and bad moral conduct, and taste and decency are just some of the ethical issues that arise when examining reality TV.

Early academic work focused primarily on the definition of the reality genre and its relationship with audiovisual documentation. Work by Bill Nichols (1994), and John Corner (1995) examined the "reality" of reality TV, raising important questions about actuality and the epistemology of factual television that have still not been answered today. Recent work by scholars in documentary studies and cultural studies suggests reality TV is a rich site for analysis and debate. John Dovey (2000) argues that reality TV foregrounds private issues at the expense of wider public debate about social and political matters. Kilborn (2003) examines the economic, aesthetic, and cultural contexts to the genre. Hill (2004) has conducted audience research that suggests viewers are critically engaged with the truth claims of reality formats. Further research has emerged on issues such as surveillance, gender and identity, performance, celebrities, and new media.

Reality TV is an extraordinary success story, an example of television's ability to cannibalize itself in order to survive in a commercially uncertain media environment. However, the costs incurred as a result of its success have been felt most by public service broadcasting, in particular news, current affairs, and documentary. Thus, reality TV has repositioned factual and entertainment programming within popular culture. And this shift between information and entertainment is irreversible, blurring the boundaries of fact and fiction for a new generation of television viewers.

SEE ALSO: Audiences; Genre; Popular Culture; Television

REFERENCES AND SUGGESTED READINGS

Corner, J. (1995) *Television Form and Public Address*. Edward Arnold, London.

Dovey, J. (2000) *Freakshows: First Person Media and Factual TV*. Pluto, London.

Hill, A. (2004) *Reality TV: Audiences and Popular Factual Television*. Routledge, London and New York.

Kilborn, R. (2003) *Staging the Real: Factual TV Programming in the Age of Big Brother*. Manchester University Press, Manchester.

Nichols, B. (1994) *Blurred Boundaries: Questions of Meaning in Contemporary Culture*. Indiana University Press, Bloomington and Indianapolis.

rock 'n' roll

Peter Beilharz

Rock and roll refers to the music generated originally out of the experience of black folks and then whites in the US from the post-war period, which became a global style and key indicator of modern culture. Its semantics refer to sex – rocking and rolling has always had sexual connotations, as in B. B. King's "Rock Me Baby," though its subsequent imaging is also often connected to the guitar and the automobile, both also sexual images in themselves. Images of freedom, movement, release, and romance are all central to the rock and roll legacy, as is alcohol and substance abuse, dance, and noise. The precondition

of rock and roll is not only gasoline, but especially electricity, both actual and metaphorical. Rock and roll is the result of the Electric Age. Rock and roll is Fordism on a Friday night.

Rock and roll is best viewed sociologically as a confluence of influences and origins, which first came together in the US. It has strong connections to white country and hillbilly music, and likely better recognized origins in African American music, gospel, jazz, and blues or plantation field music. Thus the cliché "the blues had a baby and they called it rock and roll" only captures the main line of development, from Memphis to Chicago.

The iconic figures of early rock and roll are indeed black, as exemplified in Little Richard, Fats Domino, and Chuck Berry, Berry even more so for his guitar and licks that ran right through to the Rolling Stones and AC/DC. The central transitional figure, as well as being the icon of rock and roll in his own right, is Elvis Presley. Elvis was the most important messenger between the South and North between black and white audiences. Once black music like rock and roll was no longer cataloged as "race music" its influence extended dramatically, though the critics of this process would also damn it as the dilution of the form via its mainstreaming and commodification. For the critics of this process, whether white musical purists or black pride separatists, mainstreaming rock and roll was tantamount to repackaging it as white bread – white boys, on this account and white music businesses literally took this bread from black tables.

While white boys like Elvis, Johnny Cash, Carl Perkins, and Jerry Lee Lewis were later to record in Memphis at the Sun Studios into the 1950s, African Americans like Jackie Brenston and his Memphis Cats cut the first rock and roll disc, "Rocket 88," there in 1955. The association of this musical form with the automobile was strong, from Robert Johnson's "Terraplane" through to Berry's "No Particular Place to Go," and the Beatles' "Drive My Car." Meantime, in Chicago, the black blues of Chess Records was growing. It reflected the Northern odyssey of black musicians like Muddy Waters, who traveled from the South seeking work after the mechanization of the plantations, and dreaming of freedom and wages we now associate with the era of Fordism. In Detroit, the home of Ford Motors, into the 1960s, soul music was promoted by Tamla Motown, directly associated with Fordism, and then in Atlanta by Stax, where some of the finest mixed-race bands emerged, such as Booker T and the MGs. The Chicago equivalent appeared with mixed-race blues bands like Paul Butterfield's. On the West coast the surf music scene produced at its best bands like the Beach Boys, now thought by some to be the alter egos of the Beatles. Then, later, there was the peculiar genius of the Doors, and the trajectory of cowboy rock which went through to the Eagles, then the Red Hot Chilli Peppers.

But in the beginning, in the big picture, there was Elvis. And then there were the Beatles. How did the Beatles happen? Their influences were also American, via skiffle music, Lonnie Donegan, and lyric harmonies like those of the Everley Brothers, as well as the usual culprits, Little Richard and Chuck Berry. The Beatles offer as clear an example of cultural traffic as might be imagined. They imbibed the local culture of skiffle and American ideas in maritime cities, Liverpool and Hamburg, and then made the momentous decision to write for themselves rather than to copy American rhythm and blues. At the same time the Rolling Stones and the Yardbirds followed a similar path, shifting from mimicry of black music to more evident practices of innovation, the Stones always dirtier. Where the Beatles had "Revolution," the Rolling Stones' equivalent bid for an anthem was "Street Fighting Man," or perhaps it was "Sympathy for the Devil."

Guitar music was central to all this. The Yardbirds alone threw up three signal talents: Eric Clapton, Jeff Beck, and Jimmy Page. Illustrious British guitar players also went through the local blues scene, notably working with John Mayall (Clapton again, Peter Green, and Mick Taylor, the latter replacing Brian Jones in the Stones). For a while the "British invasion" of American rock involved British acts taking American rhythm and blues back to different, new white audiences in the US; the British blues revival had a similar effect. The Stones, indeed, took back to the Northern states music by blacks like Muddy Waters, opening new doors to local listeners whose reception was hitherto obstructed by racial obstacles or absences. British bands like Cream, traveling through the US, did more to legitimate blues music for white audiences than black individuals like B. B. King, Freddie, or Albert King could ever have achieved on their own. But the results of these processes could still be seen as racial

commodification, more white bread. For performers like B. B. King they did, at least, mean bread.

If the British bands took rock and roll back to the US, they also necessarily added something. There was more than a Cockney or Midlands accent to this. In the case of bands like the Animals, the Kinks, and the Who, it included the Carnaby Street fashion sense of swinging London together with mordant wit and romantic love-hate for city and suburb. This was a rock and roll set against the cosy or constricted domesticity of post-war Britain. Rock and roll tongues were now firmly in cheek. Lyrics became critical and ironic, a contrast to the simpler '56 romance of Buddy Holly or the more openly direct sexuality of Little Richard or Muddy Waters. The 1960s were flash, in fashion terms, but the hippie edge of the counterculture also bit. Rock and roll became a vital part of the opposition to the Vietnam War, but it was also the soundtrack for the often-black infantry who had to fight in Vietnam. Certainly, Hendrix was a guitar hero for both sides.

So called psychedelia hit hard. British bands like Pink Floyd were influential here, as were the various permutations of David Bowie, but the hardest hitting drug bands were to be found in the West Coast of the US, as in the Grateful Dead or, more inventively, Frank Zappa and the Mothers of Invention. White American blues took off, exemplified by Southern bands like the Allman Brothers and Lynard Skynard. By 1970 the Beatles were gone as a live presence, and pioneer blues cum heavy metal bands like Led Zeppelin dominated live music. While the Beatles' own version of cultural hybridity included especially influences from the old British Empire, most notably India, Led Zeppelin also took in influences from Africa and the Celts. The Jamaican diaspora in Britain laid a fresh path of reception for reggae and ska. The glam and glitz of seventies pop gave way to punk, and then rap. Punk was extraordinarily influential, both in terms of its in-yer-face attitude and its final step in the direction of democratizing music. By the 1980s garage bands were everywhere, in the metropolis and in the peripheries. The sense that you could do it for yourself, and the availability of the musical technology to facilitate this, then found its ultimate result in the mixing and scratching of electronic music and the DJ scene. Bass and drum, and sometimes guitar and drum setups like the Black Keys, took blues music back, in one sense, to its origins, where bands might skip an instrument like bass simply if there was no one there on the night to play it. More people were producing rock music, more consuming it.

Definitional arguments abound as to how precisely to establish the nature or limits of rock and roll. There are various disputes about exact originary moments, though most of them are dated to the middle 1950s. A more difficult if pertinent question is whether rock and roll is over, or dead. Certainly, video killed the radio star, and the video clip and MTV have dissolved the clear distinction between the music video hit and the advertisement, not least when the sexualized imagery of new female faces and bodies of pop music are added in. Rock and roll, in the stricter sense, say, of 1956–80, was never systematically feminized. Its imagery and practice were much more substantially masculine: the guitar as phallic symbol; women as groupies or fans, consumers or sex-objects rather than producers; automobile imagery dominant as the motif of freedom and male escape. The popularity of girl groups, now ironically called R & B, indicates some change in the gender dynamics of pop music, though via the use of visual imagery that sometimes seems closer to soft porn.

Alongside issues of the gender and race dimensions of rock and roll and the pervasive influence of the visual even at the expense of the aural, the sociological question of periodization also necessarily arises. If rock and roll coincides with Fordism and the cultural traffic characteristic of post-war patterns of migration, then it should reasonably be expected that as the product of its time rock and roll must also pass. Other cultural forms exhaust themselves – why not rock and roll? In this interpretation, rock and roll's last gasp would have been that of Freddie Mercury, or at least Kurt Cobain. An alternative interpretation of this process of change would be to say that rock and roll has disappeared into the mainstream, simply become part of mass or popular culture, and therefore part of the pop or contemporary music scene. Mainstream rock and roll now often seems tediously formulaic, as demonstrated in the seemingly endless tours of the Rolling Stones, or in terms of new variations on basic themes, as in Oasis or more recently Jet. Musical innovation seems more often to occur with the development of the mix, or the more extensive pluralization of musical styles and references and genres by particular bands, such as You Am I and Augie March. Culture remains a massive storehouse of possibilities. In both cases, mainstream and more innovative, the sense of pastiche prevails; it is still, as with the Beatles, the mix that makes it. Alongside the homogenized forms of musical McDonald's, it may also be the case that rock and roll lives on in the garage, and in the club, closer in spirit to where it began.

SEE ALSO: Consumption; Drug Use; Media and Consumer Culture; Music and Social Movements

REFERENCES AND SUGGESTED READINGS

Brunning, B. (2002) *Blues: The British Connection.* Helter Skelter, London.

Hardy, P. & Laing, D. (1990) *Faber Companion to Twentieth Century Popular Music.* Faber, London.

Marwick, A. (1998) *The Sixties: Cultural Revolution in Britain, France, Italy and the United States, 1958–1974.* Oxford University Press, Oxford.

Stephens, J. (1998) *Anti-Disciplinary Protest: Sixties Radicalism and Postmodernism.* Cambridge University Press, Melbourne.

science fiction

Andrew Milner

In science fiction (SF), as in much myth, folktale, and fantasy, the entire narrative is dominated by what Darko Suvin calls the "novum," that is, a fictional novelty or innovation not found in empirical reality. In SF this novum is depicted as compatible with the cognitive logic of science (e.g., rebelliously intelligent robots or time travel), whereas in fantasy it is not (e.g., vampires or werewolves). SF is thus a characteristically modern, post-Enlightenment type of imagining. The term itself first appeared in American interwar "pulp fiction" magazines. Hugo Gernsback coined the word "scientification" in 1926 for the first issue of his *Amazing Stories.* "Science fiction" itself became common after John W. Campbell, Jr. changed the name of a rival pulp from *Astounding Stories* to *Astounding Science-Fiction* in 1938. Gernsback had also traced the genre's origins to an earlier tradition of fictional writing about science represented by Jules Verne in France, H. G. Wells in England, and Edgar Allen Poe in the US (Clute & Nicholls 1993). A common starting point in much recent commentary has, however, been Mary Shelley's *Frankenstein* (Aldiss 1986; Kadrey & McCaffery 1991; Slusser 1992; Clute & Nicholls 1993). Whatever its origins, the genre has spread across the field of popular culture to embrace film, radio, comics, television, computer games, and rock music. Sociological interest in SF tends to focus on four main topics: the kind of SF that might be considered social-science fiction; the application of mainstream social theory to SF texts; the social geography of the genre's production; and the social demography of its audience.

SOCIAL-SCIENCE FICTION

Some SF quite explicitly plays with the notion of hypothetical new social sciences: the best example is probably the science of "psychohistory" depicted in Isaac Asimov's *Foundation Trilogy* (1951–3) and its less interesting sequels. Most social-science fiction is not so much about social science, however, as about society. It thus tends to take the form of either utopia or dystopia. Utopias are much older than SF: the term itself was coined by Thomas More in 1516 and recognizably utopian "ideal states" have been staples of literary and philosophical imagining since classical antiquity. Nonetheless, Suvin (1979) argues that SF retrospectively "englobed" utopia, thereby transforming it into "the sociopolitical subgenre of science fiction." Williams (1980) also treats SF as a distinctly modern form of utopia and dystopia. There are four characteristic types of each, he observes: the paradise or hell, the positively or negatively externally altered world, the positive or negative willed transformation, and the positive or negative technological transformation. The latter two are the more characteristically utopian/dystopian modes, he concludes, especially in SF, because transformation is normally more important than mere otherness.

Neither Suvin nor Williams equates utopia with radical perfection. They understand it comparatively rather than superlatively, as "organized more perfectly" (Suvin 1979: 45) and dealing with "a happier life" (Williams 1980: 196) than that found in empirical reality. Perfect utopias are only a limit case, a subclass of a wider species of merely more perfect worlds. The obverse is also true for dystopias. SF utopias and dystopias have been inspired by much the same hopes and fears that inspire politics and social science in the real world. Late nineteenth-century utopian fictions were thus very often socialistic; for example, Edward Bellamy's scientist and state-socialist *Looking Backward 2000–1887* (1888) or William Morris's neo-Romantic and libertarian-socialist *News from Nowhere* (1890). H. G. Wells's later technocratic utopias were similarly informed by his Fabian socialism. Explicitly Marxist utopias were less common, but there is at least one important Marxist anti-capitalist dystopia, Jack London's *The Iron Heel* (1907). For the most part, however, anti-capitalist dystopias were as likely to be inspired by political liberalism, for example Karel Čapek's *R.U.R. Rossum's Universal Robots* (1920, in English 1923) and Aldous Huxley's *Brave New World* (1932). The middle decades of the twentieth century also witnessed a number of important liberal or libertarian-socialist antitotalitarian dystopias, notably Yevgeny Zamiatin's *My* (1920, in English *We* 1924) and George Orwell's *Nineteen Eighty-Four* (1949).

Late twentieth-century utopias and dystopias were often associated with anti-racism, the movement for gay rights, feminism, environmentalism, and their reconciliation in ecofeminism. At one level, all SF treatments of alien species touch on the politics of race, at least by implication. But Pierre Boulle's *La Planète des singes* (1963, in English *Monkey Planet* 1964) deliberately used the dystopian device of the planet of the apes so as to critique both racism and anthropocentrism. Samuel R. Delany's *Triton* (1976) is perhaps the best-known utopian SF treatment of gay and other alternative sexualities. Important examples of feminist utopias include Ursula K. Le Guin's *The Dispossessed* (1974), Joanna Russ's *The Female Man* (1975), and Marge Piercy's *Woman on the Edge of Time* (1976). The most significant feminist dystopia was almost certainly Margaret Atwood's *The Handmaid's Tale* (1985). Environmentalist themes were central to Kim Stanley Robinson's *Mars Trilogy* (1992–6), albeit in contradictory relation to socialistic notions. Socialist anti-capitalism, with an occasionally Marxist inflection, also reappeared at the very end of the century in China Miéville's dystopian *Perdido Street Station* (2000).

These later utopias often contained significant dystopian motifs, and the dystopia's significant utopian motifs. Indeed, one interesting feature of late twentieth-century SF was precisely its practical resolution of the opposition between utopia and dystopia, in what Tom Moylan and others have termed "critical dystopia." So Moylan observes that much of this writing "burrows" within the dystopian tradition "in order to bring utopian and dystopian tendencies to bear on their exposé of the present moment"; and that, although utopian in intent, it does "not go easily toward that better world," but rather lingers "in the terrors of the present even as they exemplify what is needed to transform it" (Moylan 2000: 198–9). As Williams (1980) recognized, utopias of this kind constitute an inherently more realistic and open-ended form than the earlier variants.

SOCIAL THEORY AND SCIENCE FICTION

Mainstream social theory has inspired a substantial and growing body of SF criticism. Some of this is Marxist: Suvin's *Metamorphoses*, for example, and Moylan's studies in utopianism, but also Carl Freedman's *Critical Theory and Science Fiction* (2000) and Fredric Jameson's many essays on SF, especially his "Progress v. Utopia; or, Can we Imagine the Future?," first published in the journal *Science Fiction Studies* in 1982. Some is feminist: Le Guin's two collections of essays, *The Language of the Night* (1979) and *Dancing at the Edge of the World* (1989), Susan Lefanu's *In the Chinks of the World Machine* (1988), Marleen Barr's *Feminist Fabulation* (1992), Jenny Wolmark's *Aliens and Others* (1994), and Russ's collection *To Write Like a Woman* (1995). Some is postmodernist, notably Scott Bukatman's *Terminal Identity* (1994) and Damian Broderick's *Reading by Starlight* (1995). Some is queer: Eric Garber and Lyn Paleo's *Uranian Worlds* (1990), for example, or Delany's *Silent Interviews* (1994).

In at least two cases –Baudrillard's theory of postmodernism and the debate over posthumanism – SF occupies an unusually central location in relation to the theory itself. For Baudrillard, postmodern culture is above all simulacral and hyperreal. He uses the term *simulacrum* to mean a sign without a referent, "never exchanged for the real, but exchanged for itself"; and *simulation* pects of simulacra, or the non-referential equivalent of representation (Baudrillard 1994: 6).

He argues that there have been three orders of simulacra since the Renaissance, respectively, the natural, the productive, and "the simulacra of simulation." The shift from the second, founded on industrial manufacture, to the third, founded on information, marks the shift to postmodern "hyperreality." Each of the three orders of simulacra has been accompanied by a corresponding "imaginary," he suggests, so that utopia belongs to the first order, science fiction proper to the second, and a new kind of "implosive" fiction, "something else . . . in the process of emerging," to the third (p. 121).

Baudrillard cites the work of Philip K. Dick in the US and J. G. Ballard in Britain as instances of this "science fiction that is no longer one." Commenting on Ballard's *Crash*, he writes: "there is neither fiction nor reality anymore – hyperreality abolishes both . . . science fiction in this sense is no longer anywhere, it is everywhere, in the circulation of models, here and now, in the very principle of the surrounding simulation" (p. 126). This notion that contemporary reality is itself science fictional accords a much more general cultural significance to the genre's wilder speculations. Hence, the judgment that *Crash* "is the first great novel of the universe of simulation" (p. 119). SF cinema famously repaid this compliment in the Wachowski brothers' *The Matrix* (1999), when the character Neo pointedly made use of a simulacral copy of Baudrillard's *Simulacra and Simulation*.

SF has also occupied a central position in recent speculation about the "posthuman." This term seems to have been coined by Ihab Hassan in 1977 to mark the "coming to an end" of "five hundred years of humanism" (Hassan 1977: 212). In itself, this was little more than an elaboration on structuralist and poststructuralist understandings of subjectivity as an effect of discourse. But this theoretical anti-humanism was soon complemented by the practical posthumanism implicit in a whole range of actual or potential new technologies for reembodiment and disembodiment, ranging from genetic engineering to advanced prosthetics, from artifical intelligence to virtual reality. Donna Haraway famously synthesized the claims of the theory, the technology, and feminist politics in her "Cyborg Manifesto," which eagerly anticipated a "cyborg world . . . in which people are not afraid of their joint kinship with animals and machines" (Haraway 1991: 154).

These and similar notions have been widely canvassed in recent philosophy and social and cultural theory, from Elizabeth Grosz's *Volatile Bodies* (1994) and Katherine Hayles's *How We Became Posthuman* (1999), to Chris Gray's *Cyborg Citizen* (2001) and Francis Fukuyama's *Our Posthuman Future* (2002). They are also central to much contemporary SF. In addition to *The Matrix* trilogy, important examples from the cinema would include both versions of Ridley Scott's *Blade Runner* (1982, 1992), the *Terminator* (1984–2002) and *Robocop* (1987–93) trilogies, Steven Spielberg's *AI* (2001), and two of Alex Proyas's films, *Dark City* (1998) and *I, Robot* (2004). From print, one could cite Iain M. Banks's "Culture" novels, Octavia Butler's *Xenogenesis* trilogy (1987–9), Ken Macleod's *The Stone Canal* (1996), Greg Egan's *Diaspora* (1997), Michel Houellebecq's *Les Particules élémentaires* (1998, in English, *Atomized* 2000), Atwood's *Oryx and Crake* (2003), and much of the cyberpunk and post-cyberpunk writing of William Gibson and Bruce Sterling.

SOCIAL GEOGRAPHY OF SF PRODUCTION

The social geography of SF follows a fairly clear pattern. Conceived in England and France at the core of the nineteenth-century world order, it continued in both throughout the twentieth and into the twenty-first century. Its frontiers expanded to include the Weimar Republic, early Soviet Russia, and interwar Czechoslovakia. Exported to Japan in the post-World War II period, it also flourished in communist Poland and more significantly in late-communist Russia. But the US became absolutely central and near-hegemonic, nonetheless, from the interwar period through to the present. Moreover, this American hegemony extended from print to film and television. In the late nineteenth and early twentieth centuries the pattern merely reproduced the general importance of England and France in the commercial production of literature. But more recent trends are less easily explained. Csicsery-Ronay (2003) argues that they are best understood as a correlate of imperialism. A more plausible explanation, however, might be that twentieth-century SF developed in what Moretti (2000), after Wallerstein, would see as the semiperiphery of the world literary system.

This extrinsic pattern is matched by epistemic ruptures within the genre. Verne and Wells had generally written from within a self-confidently optimistic positivism, bordering on the utopian. Science fiction in Germany, Russia, and *Mitteleuropa* abandoned liberal futurology, opting either for an explicitly communist utopianism or, more interestingly, for dystopia, whether communist or capitalist, a theme later reimported into England by Orwell. Positivistic science fiction was resumed in interwar America, but in a different register, as an escapist response to the Great Depression rather than an easy celebration of scientific triumphalism. This second epistemic shift was a distinctly American achievement, though it is worth noting that the US was still then nearer to the periphery than the core of the world literary system. The American variant seems to have become, in turn, the core of a new science-fictional subsystem of the world literary system and the primary source for later mutations into other popular media.

SOCIAL DEMOGRAPHY OF SF AUDIENCES

As to the social demography of SF audiences, there is evidence to suggest that they are disproportionately male and concentrated among supervisors and technicians rather than either higher professionals or manual workers (Bennett et al. 1999). It is also clear that SF, like sport and popular music, tends to acquire "fan" audiences (literally, fanatics). The most famous example are the *Star Trek* fans, or "Trekkers." For structuralist semiology, fans often seem the most readerly of readers, subjected to the most closed of closed texts (Eco 1981). But recent quasi-ethnographic research has tended to suggest otherwise. Fan reading seems not only *not* passive, but also positively creative, to the point of stimulating cultural production, in the full sense of the active making of new artworks. Jenkins (1992) uses the term textual poaching (borrowed from Michel de Certeau) to describe how SF fans appropriate materials from the dominant media and rework them in their own interests (de Certeau 1984; Tulloch & Jenkins 1995). The analogy is with poaching from a gamekeeper, rather than poaching eggs.

An extreme example of textual poaching is in the so-called "slash fiction" devoted to the theme of a gay relationship between Captain Kirk and

Mr. Spock, two leading characters in the first *Star Trek* TV series. The "slash" in slash fiction refers to that in "K/S," a code indicating that the stories, artwork, etc. appearing in the fanzine will be concerned with same-sex relationships. There are other slashed couples, but K/S pornography/erotica is still by far the most extensive and prolific. Perhaps the most striking finding to emerge from research on the subject is that K/S fiction is overwhelmingly written not by gay men but by women, many of them quite conventionally heterosexual (Jenkins 1992). As Penley (1997) concludes, these "amateur women writers" are writing their own "sexual and social utopias" through the materials to hand; in short, they are poaching – actively, creatively, and subversively.

SEE ALSO: Fans and Fan Culture; Popular Culture; Popular Culture Icons (*Star Trek*); Post-humanism; Postmodernism

REFERENCES AND SUGGESTED READINGS

Aldiss, B. (1986) *Trillion Year Spree: The History of Science Fiction*. Victor Gollancz, London.

Baudrillard, J. (1994) *Simulacra and Simulation*. Trans. S. F. Glaser. University of Michigan Press, Ann Arbor.

Bennett, T., Emmison. M., & Frow, J. (1999) *Accounting for Tastes: Australian Everyday Culture*. Cambridge University Press, Cambridge.

Certeau, M. de (1984) *The Practice of Everyday Life*. Trans. S. Rendall. University of California Press, Berkeley.

Clute, J. & Nicholls, P. (Eds.) (1993) *The Encyclopedia of Science Fiction*. Orbit, London.

Csicsery-Ronay, Jr., I. (2003) Science Fiction and Empire. *Science Fiction Studies* 30(2): 238–45.

Eco, U. (1981) *The Role of the Reader: Explorations in the Semiotics of Texts*. Hutchinson, London.

Haraway, D. J. (1991) *Simians, Cyborgs and Women: The Reinvention of Nature*. Routledge, London.

Hassan, I. (1977) Prometheus as Performer: Toward a Posthumanist Culture? A University Masque in Five Scenes. In: Benamou, M. & Caramello, C. (Eds.), *Performance in Postmodern Culture*. Coda, Madison, WI.

Jenkins, H. (1992) *Textual Poachers: Television Fans and Participant Culture*. Routledge, New York.

Kadrey, R. & McCaffery, L. (1991) Cyberpunk 101: A Schematic Guide to Storming the Reality Studio. In: McCaffery, L. (Ed.), *Storming the Reality Studio: A Casebook of Cyberpunk and Postmodern Science Fiction*. Duke University Press, Durham, NC.

Moretti, F. (2000) Conjectures on World Literature. *New Left Review* 2(1): 54–68.

Moylan, T. (2000) *Scraps of the Untainted Sky: Science Fiction, Utopia, Dystopia*. Westview Press, Boulder.

Penley, C. (1997) *NASA/TREK: Popular Science and Sex in America*. Verso, London.

Slusser, G. (1992) The Frankenstein Barrier. In: Slusser, G. & Shippey, T. (Eds.), *Fiction 2000: Cyberpunk and the Future of Narrative*. University of Georgia Press, Athens.

Suvin, D. (1979) *Metamorphoses of Science Fiction: On the Poetics and History of a Literary Genre*. Yale University Press, New Haven.

Tulloch, J. & Jenkins, H. (1995) *Science Fiction Audiences: Watching "Dr Who" and "Star Trek."* Routledge, London.

Williams, R. (1980) Utopia and Science Fiction. In: *Problems in Materialism and Culture*. New Left Books, London.

soap operas

Adrian Franklin

Soap operas originated in 1930s American radio and are so named because they were programs sponsored by soap companies such as Proctor and Gamble who were seeking a means of advertising their domestic products to housewives (or, more precisely, women in the 18–49 demographic who combined bought a lion's share of the market). The format they chose (and many of the companies were owned by them) was similar to opera in that it was melodramatic, larger than life, and about the universal human condition. Allen (2005: 1) also argues that the American press who coined the phrase suggested "an ironic incongruity between the domestic narrative concerns of the daytime serial and the most elevated of dramatic forms." Their radio format was highly restricted: they were only of 15 minutes duration, their casts were very small, and the themes were largely those surrounding domestic life and romance.

The structure of soap operas is based on seriality, and here the link between maintaining a continuous narrative and brand loyalty is made: the audience is hooked into a storyline that has no obvious end in sight and so inadvertently exposes them to the sponsor's continuous advertising message. Various devices emerged in the history of soaps to make this arrangement more secure. Over time and especially as they made the leap from radio to television in the mid-1950s, they created more elaborate and numerous plot lines between the more finely crafted characters, they left multiple loose ends between episodes, and they left cliffhangers at the end of the week to entice audiences back at the beginning of the next. Soap operas were also long-lived, so in addition to the fact that characters changed over time and could come and go, the audience developed a knowledge of and intimacy with them. In the time between episodes, soaps engendered the practice of imagining possible configurations and futures, guessing the resolution of cliffhangers, and being drawn into moral and ethical debates. Soaps not only developed an audience, therefore, they also developed an interacting community of viewers and their plots provided the content for a considerable amount of discussion at workplaces, mealtimes, and pubs (Brown 1984; Allen 1995).

Soap operas have been a very significant element of popular culture since the 1930s onwards. By World War II there were 64 daytime soap operas in the United States and in recent years there have been approximately 50 hours of soap operas on the main US TV networks (NBC, ABC, and CBS). In the UK there were fewer but the intensity of interest was no less. Whereas advertising and ratings were the key driving force among the main US networks, a fact that produced a bland, spatially and culturally Middle American feel, in the UK locality and culture were key. The radio audience was dominated by *The Archers*, in its archetypal rural setting and themed around the vicissitudes of country life. However, much of UK commercial television was regionally and popularly based and so each regional station produced its own culturally specific version. These were largely working-class, gritty, realist, and culturally authentic formats that echoed the successful genre of working-class films from the 1950s. Thus, the Manchester-based Granada TV made the most successful of them all, *Coronation Street*, while *Crossroads* hailed from the Midlands, *Brookside* from Liverpool, and *EastEnders* from the BBC's base in London.

Coronation Street is a nationally significant program, however, mostly topping the ratings during its very long life, and it was mirrored in the US by *Dallas*, *Hill Street Blues*, and *St. Elsewhere*. These formats were very different from the earliest soaps in that they had expanded their demographics to include the very widest range of people possible to their new slots in primetime. By the 1970s women were no longer at home to provide an easy advertising target, nor were they the mainly responsible agents of retail spending.

Although soaps had their critics in the past, who argued that they were artless and exploitative, in recent years sociologists and cultural scholars have noticed their cultural significance and value. Fiske (1987) argues that as key, if not exclusive, viewers, women draw some benefit from the strong female characters, particularly in affirming the sexual power of middle-aged women and questioning "traditional family values" in relation to bad relationships and marriages.

This relates to another finding, that in using *social* themes to drive interest and appeal and in being set in everyday space and culture, soaps provide a moral discussion forum that might otherwise not exist. It is now an everyday occurrence to see reported in the British tabloid press the latest scandals and incidents screened by the soaps. The articles report these events as news, and, just as with all news, they add comment and solicit collective responses from readers.

This is not as bizarre as it sounds. British and American society does not properly correspond to the contrived communities that the soaps construct; rather, it is the opposite. Most people live relatively isolated, individualized lifestyles where the continuity and solidarity of the soap communities have all but vanished. We do not, in fact, have the opportunity to discuss at great length in a number of community settings the various issues that come our way, nor are we taken care of by a maternal, caring state. We have to make the most of the many lifestyle choices alone, but we have come to rely increasingly on advice and information from the media and the soap is, arguably, one of the more important ways in which individuals share in a collective conscience.

When *The Archers* first began, it was explicitly a tool of state government designed to feed valuable information to rural communities about new agricultural technologies. The contemporary soaps are now commercial affairs, but their place in educating individuals in the techniques of lifestyle is not dissimilar.

SEE ALSO: Celebrity and Celetoid; Celebrity Culture; Mass Media and Socialization; Media; Popular Culture; Television

REFERENCES AND SUGGESTED READINGS

Allen, R. C. (1985) *Speaking of Soap Operas*. University of North Carolina Press, Chapel Hill.
Allen, R. C. (1995) *To Be Continued...: Soap Operas Around the World*. Routledge, London.
Allen, R. C. (2005) *Soap Opera*. Museum of Broadcast Communications, Chicago. Online. www.museum.tv/archives/etv/S/htmlS/soapopera/soapopera.htm.
Ang, I. (1985) *Watching Dallas: Soap Opera and the Melodramatic Imagination*. Methuen, London.
Brown, M. E. (1994) *Soap Opera and Women's Talk*. Sage, London.
Buckingham, D. (1987) *Public Secrets: EastEnders and Its Audience*. British Film Institute, London.
Dyer, R. (1981) *Coronation Street*. British Film Institute, London.
Fiske, J. (1987) *Television Culture*. Routledge, London.
Geraghty, C. (1991) *Women and Soap Operas*. Polity Press, Cambridge.
Hobson, D. (1982) *Crossroads: The Drama of a Soap Opera*. Methuen, London.
Intintoli, M. (1984) *Taking Soaps Seriously: The World of Guiding Light*. Praeger, New York.
Silj, A. (1988) *East of Dallas: The European Challenge to American Television*. British Film Institute, London.
Williams, C. T. (1992). *"It's Time for My Story": Soap Opera Sources, Structure, and Response*. Praeger, Westport, CT.

ZOOS

Adrian Franklin

The number of zoos ("zoological gardens") around the world grew dramatically during the twentieth century from 120 in 1920, to 309 by 1959, to 883 by 1978 (Mullan & Marvin 1987: 113), though according to recent work by Nils Lindahl-Elliot their visitor numbers peaked in the 1960s. By the 1980s, however, zoos still rivaled most other leisure attractions. San Diego and Washington Zoos are both visited by over 3 million people annually, London Zoo by over 1.3 million, Berlin Zoo by 2.5 million, Ueno Zoological Gardens in Tokyo by 7.2 million, and Beijing Zoo by 8 million.

ANIMALS AND THE CARNIVALESQUE

From the sixteenth century onwards, Europe expanded in all directions after having been more or less confined to its old borders. New explorations and discoveries encouraged interest in all manner of natural and cultural phenomena. A market for exotic animals emerged by the seventeenth century and although some were bought for private collections, others were bought for public display. Up until the mid-nineteenth century, the pattern of leisure in Europe was quite different. The most significant feature or highlight of the leisure calendar was local festivals, or revels — survivals or remainders from the medieval carnivals. The various activities that comprised such events were carnivalesque, a series of inversions of normal day-to-day life. While much of the content was specifically local, professional traveling entertainers introduced exotic novelties. Many of these traveling entertainments were based on the brief gaze: customers paid for a fleeting glimpse of such exhibits as human freak shows, historical or religious artifacts, and exotic animals. Only in London were menageries open to the public for most of the year.

It was a characteristic of these menageries that a large number of animals were crammed into a very small space. This was partly to do with the logistics of a traveling show, but the concentrated nature of the exhibit was related to its purpose as spectacle. The public could get quite close to the animals and were guaranteed a good view. Cages were made of iron bars, they were very small and of uniform rectangular shape, and they gave the animal no respite from the public gaze. The public were to be roused into a pleasurable delight based on strangeness, grotesqueness, dangerousness, and otherworldliness. The gaze was frightful, exciting, hideous. Because the animals were little more than monsters, the idea that they should have restricted movement and that their accommodation was prison-like was perfectly consistent and sensible.

In any case, the audience had no idea whatsoever about the animals' natural habitat, other than that perhaps this too was dangerous and probably unpleasant. Animal menageries were typical of the carnivalesque: they created a liminal zone or space where, upon entering, people stepped outside their normative day-to-day world and were suspended in a halfway space. Crudely speaking, this space might be described as between culture and nature, or this-worldly and otherworldly, Britain and darkest Africa, or "home" and the "frontier." Nothing distracted the gazer from this dark, sensory pleasure. The brevity of the glimpse prevented, perhaps, the opposite (possible) realization of familiarity, sameness. The structure of the menageries as buildings or frames for the gaze was plain, purely functional, and non-distracting. There were no extraneous, decorative embellishments to detract from the full impact of otherness, or to domesticate it, to render it more acceptable and normative. Indeed, it is characteristic of the carnivalesque, rooted as it was in the social permanency of the feudal regime, that social inversions and the return from liminal experiences were functional to the reproduction of social order.

The experience of the menagerie reinforced, through a look into the terrible specter of the other side, a sense of belonging to a superior, civilized, and ordered society. It positively confirmed the civilizing force and European ordering of the New World. It maintained a sense of superiority which was based on an inflexible, ordered social hierarchy. This was the zoological gaze before social progress and egalitarianism became a powerful driving force of modernity. Up until the late eighteenth century and into the nineteenth, this was how the majority of people experienced exotic wild animals (see Anderson 1998 for a "colonial zoo" perspective).

During the French Revolution the revolutionaries took liberation itself seriously: they liberated all of the animals, dangerous and otherwise, from the king's magnificent menagerie. The transformation from menageries to recognizably modern zoos did involve major changes in the zoological gaze. The royal menageries in France, for example, had been opened up to the scientific as well as the public gaze before the Revolution, and clearly, from then on, the zoological gaze could be not merely spectacular but also educational. Moreover, the world was smaller and the colonial discoveries became less the object of wonder and spectacle as

they became more routinized in the content of education and scientific investigation. Widespread familiarization was achieved in the French royal menageries, and the inclusion of exotic animals in highly stylized, extensive, decorative gardens, complete with picturesque oriental architecture, highlights how they also became ornate and domesticated. These spacious, decorative, domesticated, and familiar spaces in which to view animals encouraged a leisurely, relaxed form of gaze, with an emphasis on recreation. Although the building of private parklands and gardens and an interest in the educational benefits of zoology were more or less confined to the social elite in the eighteenth and nineteenth centuries, both were to feature in the approved leisure pursuits recommended to the working class in the nineteenth-century city. Modern zoos were going to be different because they were oriented to a *popular* market.

MODERN ZOOS

The scientific foundation of modern zoos such as the first one in London emphasized zoological science and exploring "useful purposes" to which animals may be put, but this was only part of the project. Apart from training zoologists, a general knowledge of animals was to be encouraged in the general public. The object of the popular zoological gaze, then, was instruction or improvement, an activity entirely consistent with rational recreation. The model or medium for this instruction was clearly the museum.

Zoos were about social progress; they were safe diversions, rational recreation, approved leisure. Being amused by the "antics" of animals was harmless, clean fun. The educational gloss was not completely bogus, people could become aware of zoological diversity and minimal other data about exhibits. But zoos were more like gardens than museums, more artifice than nature, and the information about animals was scarcely more than the labels on plants or trees. Indeed, they soon got back into entertainment to pay their way.

Zoo animals were *set up* to be infantile, amusing, and entertaining. There was certainly nothing inevitable about the chimpanzees' tea party, which was the main attraction at London Zoo from the 1920s to the 1970s. The tea party was a set piece of comic theater. As the former curator of mammals at London Zoo explained, the chimps had to learn this role: "they had to learn to misbehave" (cited in Bostock 1993: 34). This was not a one-off: zoos in this period gave plenty of cues as to the appropriate manner in which humans, especially children, their main clientele, were to relate to their animals. They were there to provide fun and games; elephants and camels were made to give rides; cheetahs were made to go on walks; llamas were made to pull carts. According to Bostock (1993: 34), "the 'wolf man' in London zoo ... used to take wolves for walks and wrestle with them."

For the most part, zoological gardens of the nineteenth century used cages with iron bars or wire, and some animals, such as the big cats, were no better off than they had been in the traveling menageries – according to Bostock (1993: 29), their average life expectancy in the early years of London Zoo was two years. There was also an emphasis on having a large collection rather than a healthy, happy collection. Short-lived, single, sulking specimens in small cages were the norm in the nineteenth century.

From their inception, modern zoos differed from the earlier commercial menageries in their middle-class institutional approval and educational and scientific gloss. The object of the gaze was also different. Zoos were less about spectacle and more about entertainment. There was nothing particularly liminal in the setting and archeology of the zoo; it recreated an ideal (affluent) domestic setting and animals were in various ways either ornamental or domesticated. No attempt was made, for example, to simulate natural habitat gardens in zoos, despite the considerable knowledge and ability of the Victorian gardener. Instead, the lavish, eye-catching gardens were formal and concentrated on shows of blooms, merely superior versions of most people's house gardens.

Under Hagenback's influence, zoos of the first half of the twentieth century drifted away from lofty ideals about instruction and improvement. Zoos were in the children's entertainment business and as the century progressed they faced stiffer competition from new sources, particularly the cinema. The new "sets" and the theatrical routines performed by the animals made zoos closer to circuses than museums. Like theaters and circuses, zoos had to generate new attractions, new acts. Under the secretaryship of Chalmers-Mitchell in the 1930s, London Zoo introduced a long sequence of new attractions. First, in 1931, it introduced the concept of larger-scale enclosures and wider, open spaces on a par with deer parks in stately homes, or parkland farms. Whipsnade in Bedfordshire was set in 500 acres in an attractive rolling landscape, with buildings designed by Berthold Lubetkin. Second, in 1938, it introduced the penguin pool into the main zoological gardens. The pool, another Lubetkin design, has been vaunted as a twentieth-century design classic, even significant in "widening the acceptability of modern design." This project had a strong sense of humanism, which was evident in its brief and choice of architect.

From the 1970s onwards the entertainment spaces of zoos began to be influenced by the postmaterialism of the times. Animals as well as environments became the subject of the new biopolitics. At first zoos suffered from being labeled as unedifying prisons for oppressed species and their mid-century visitor numbers crashed. However, zoos were able to use this decentered, rights-oriented, and environmentalist attitude to animals and turn it to good advantage. Several innovations took place, earning them the title of new zoos.

NEW ZOOS

New zoos emphasized conservation and animal rights. New private zoos such as Howletts Zoo in England were expressly set up to breed a few endangered species, and their specialist knowledge of these led to spectacular successes. When Howletts finally opened to the public, it was on the animals' terms. The visitor's gaze was not privileged over the needs of the animals and many went unseen.

The new zoos made life more interesting for the animals, with things to do such as *finding* their food, more life-like habitats, and more interaction with their human keepers (prior to that it was felt that such interaction would denature the animals, whereas in fact mostly they became isolated and depressed).

At Sea World several accounts (e.g., Mullan & Marvin 1987; Desmond 1999; Franklin 1999) tell how the three manifestations of the killer whale *Shamu* exhibit demonstrate shifting relations to animals. In the first, *Shamu Take a Bow* of the early 1980s, the whale is pure spectacle and its athletic body and power is on display for a sports-like audience. By *Celebration Shamu* of 1986, the whale is admired by an audience not as a spectacle but as an animal that needs our understanding and care. Then, by 1996, with the new *Shamu Backstage*, the *distance and distinction* between audience and animal are canceled. The audience are now "guests" and Shamu plays "host" in a theatricalized space clearly modeled on ethnic tourism. The three manifestations chart the progress of animals from distant, exotic others to more proximate fellow travelers in the world, a significant reduction in the distinctions hitherto made between humans and animals.

SEE ALSO: Anthrozoology; Childhood; Human–Non-Human Interaction; Leisure; Leisure, Popular Culture and; Nature; Popular Culture

REFERENCES AND SUGGESTED READINGS

Anderson, K. (1998) Animals, Science, and Spectacle in the City. In: Wolch, J. & Emel, J. (Eds.), *Animal Geographies*. Verso, London.

Bostock, S. (1993) *Zoos and Animal Rights*. Routledge, London.

Desmond, J. C. (1999) *Staging Tourism: Bodies on Display from Waikiki to Sea World*. University of Chicago Press, Chicago.

Franklin, A. S. (1999) *Animals and Modern Cultures: A Sociology of Human–Animal Relations in Modernity*. Sage, London.

Gruffudd, P. (2000) Biological Cultivation: Lubetkin's Modernism at London Zoo in the 1930s. In: Philo, C. & Wilbert, C. (Eds.), *Animal Spaces, Beastly Places: New Geographies of Human–Animal Relations*. Routledge, London.

Mullan, B. & Marvin, G. (1987) *Zoo Culture*. Weidenfeld & Nicolson, London.

popular culture icons

All of the points made in the introduction to the entry on popular culture forms apply here, as well, to popular culture icons. However, the focus in this entry is on people (Bob Dylan, Jimi Hendrix, Michael Jackson, Bob Marley, Frank Sinatra, the Grateful Dead and Deadheads), ideas (Myth of the American Frontier), and programming (*The Simpsons, Star Trek*) that have achieved iconic status in popular culture; that is, they have become important symbols to large numbers of people around the world. – GR

Dylan, Bob (b. 1941)

Peter Beilharz

Robert Zimmerman was born in Hibbing, Minnesota. Unlike Jimi Hendrix, who peaked and died young, Dylan has become a kind of weathervane as well as leader of musical taste since the 1960s. Influences on Dylan included Woody Guthrie, Ramblin Jack Elliott, John Koerner and Tony Glover, Dave Van Ronk, and the whole folk-blues scene in Greenwich Village in that period. His earliest persona was that of the folk player, the pioneer singer-songwriter then poet and protestor, protesting as much against the absurdity of life as anything else, and helping to transform lyrics in popular music in the process. In the earlier period his persona was that of a singer with a harmonica in a rack and a guitar. Dylan revolutionized this image in 1965 when he appeared with an electric band at the Newport Jazz Festival. Heckling ensued from purists who could not abide electricity, but Dylan's creative phase opened into hallmark albums such as *Highway 61 Revisited* (1965) and *Blonde on Blonde* (1966). If Dylan helped to lead a revolution in lyrics, he also paved the way indirectly for punk by legitimating the practice of singing off-key, chanting, almost, with a kind of infectious drone, hitting the listener so hard with dense lyrics that many with the patience would endeavor to transcribe and decode them, a practice often aided by the ingestion of hallucinatory substances.

Dylan's life subsequently includes moments of mystery, including his 1965 motorcycle crash and much later conversion to Christianity. His musical tastes shifted through to country and western, as in *John Wesley Harding* (1968) and *Nashville*

Skyline (1969), and this was later continued in a rediscovery of Nashville and the tradition of the Grand Old Opry. Dylan became a journeyman, always willing to surprise by changes in style, but nevertheless reclusive, even playing with his back to the audience. His personal silence was broken by the publication in 2003 of *Chronicles*, widely applauded for its prose as well as its rumination. At this point, the remaining image is of Dylan as a family man, a Nashville cowboy, fancy shirt, snakeskin boots, guitar, no rack.

The extent of Dylan's influence is difficult to imagine. Its material results included major contributions to electric music, including the work of the Byrds, Manfred Mann and The Band, later the Weathermen and the Zimmermen. Its broader results included the confirmation of the sense of sea change in popular music from its more innocent and sweet inflexion to realms of social critique, sarcasm, and irony. After Dylan, rock and roll had bite, but fewer illusions.

SEE ALSO: Popular Culture Forms (Rock 'n' Roll); Popular Culture Icons (Grateful Dead and Deadheads; Hendrix, Jimi)

REFERENCES AND SUGGESTED READINGS

Dylan, B. (2004) *Chronicles: Volume One*. Simon & Schuster, New York.

Heylin, C. (2000) *Bob Dylan: Behind the Shades*. Viking, London.

Scaduto, A. (1971) *Bob Dylan: An Intimate Biography*. Castle, Seacausus.

Williams, P. (1990) *Bob Dylan Performing Artist*. Xanadu, London.

Grateful Dead and Deadheads

Rebecca G. Adams

The Grateful Dead is usually described as a psychedelic rock band, but its improvisational music cannot be neatly categorized as rock or, for that matter, as folk, blues, jazz, or country, though each of these types influenced it, as did classical and other genres as well. Deadheads, as the fans of the Grateful Dead call themselves, followed the band from venue to venue from 1965 through 1995, when Jerry Garcia, the band's lead guitarist, died and the members of the band stopped playing together as the Grateful Dead. Many of these fans remain committed to this community and continue to gather at performances of cover bands and of bands featuring one or more of the Grateful Dead, including the recently reconstituted band, The Dead. The Grateful Dead were almost always on tour and played different songs, in a different order, in different ways, each night, which encouraged Deadheads to attend many shows in a given tour and to travel large distances to hear the band play. The Deadhead community is not only remarkable because of how long it has survived and for how intensely committed its members are, but also because of how large and geographically dispersed it is. At least a half million Deadheads live in every state and province in North America, as well as in more than 20 countries elsewhere.

The roots of this migrating community are in the hippie culture which grew up in the Western US during the 1960s. Known as the Warlocks for a spring, summer, and autumn, the band became the Grateful Dead in December of 1965. They were the "house band" for the Acid Tests, public psychedelic celebrations held in 1965 and 1966 before LSD became illegal in the US. By late 1966 the Grateful Dead were headquartered in San Francisco at 710 Ashbury, near its intersection with Haight Street, the symbolic heart of the hippie community. From this address it was a short walk to Golden Gate Park, where they often gave free concerts for their increasing crowd of fans.

The Deadhead community continued to grow in size after its inception in the 1960s, but the band did not become a commercial success until "Touch of Grey," a single on their 1987 album, *In the Dark*, hit the charts. By the 1990s the Grateful Dead was considered the most successful touring band in concert history. It was the top-grossing touring act in 1991 and 1993 and finished in third place in 1995, despite having completed only two of a typical three tours. The Grateful Dead played 2,314 shows during their career, often to sell-out crowds of more than 50,000 people.

Deadheads did not attend shows merely for entertainment or to socialize with like-minded people; many of them reported having spiritual experiences. Although the spiritual experiences of

Deadheads varied widely and included feelings of déjà vu, out-of-body sensations, connections with a higher power, and living through the cycle of death and rebirth, the most commonly mentioned ones were self-revelations and feelings of unity with others. Although dancing and psychedelic drugs contributed to these experiences for some Deadheads, others attributed their occurrence, at least in part, to the power and trajectory of the music. "Getting it" is an expression Deadheads use to describe the process of learning to perceive shows as spiritual experiences and to understand these experiences as inseparable from the music, the scene, and a cooperative mode of everyday existence.

The scholarship on the Grateful Dead and Deadheads is interdisciplinary and has largely been produced by Deadheads themselves, sometimes while they were college or graduate students, but often after they had established themselves as scholarly experts in a relevant field. Each year since 1998, Deadhead scholars have gathered at the Annual Meetings of the Southwest/Texas Popular Culture Association, which provides a home to this vibrant intellectual community. Although many Deadhead undergraduate papers, master's theses, and dissertations remain unpublished, two collections of such scholarly works are in print (Weiner 1999; Adams & Sardiello 2000). Other papers on the topic have appeared in various disciplinary journals and edited volumes, as well as in *Deadletters*, a scholarly magazine developed by Deadheads as an intellectual outlet for their work. Deadhead scholars and journalists have also produced a great deal of source material, including magazines (e.g., *Golden Road, Relix, Dupree's Diamond News, Unbroken Chain, Spiral Light*), a bibliography (e.g., Dodd & Weiner's *The Grateful Dead and Deadheads: An Annotated Bibliography*, 1997), a dictionary (Shenk and Silberman's *Skeleton Key: A Dictionary for Deadheads*, 1994), documentation of set lists (Scott et al.'s *DeadBase XI: The Complete Guide to Grateful Dead Song Lists*, 1999), interviews with key members of the band and community (e.g., Gans's *Conversations with the Dead: The Grateful Dead Interview Book*, 1991), an insider's history (McNally's *A Long Strange Trip*, 2003), an annotated historical timeline (Jackson et al.'s *The Illustrated Trip*, 2003), and a collection of annotated lyrics (Dodd's *The Complete Annotated Grateful Dead Lyrics*, 2005).

The sociological scholarship on Deadheads focuses mainly on three interrelated themes: the trajectory and functions of the show ritual, the development and management of Deadhead identity, and the complexity and diversity of the Deadhead community. Perhaps because the music and show experience are so central to the Deadhead phenomenon, the most commonly studied topic in this literature is the ritual in which Deadheads participate while they listen to the music play. Drawing and building on the theoretical insights of such scholars as Joseph Campbell, Mircea Eliade, William James, and especially Victor Turner, Deadhead scholars such as Pearson (1987), Sardiello (1994), and Sutton (in Adams & Sardiello 2000) have described Dead shows as rituals, agreeing that they have profound spiritual meaning and transformational consequences for the participants and disagreeing only over whether they should be considered secular or religious. Freeman (in Adams & Sardiello 2000), in his case study of a Dead cover band, describes how both the musicians and the audience contribute to the feelings of community that result from the show experience. Other scholars such as Carr and Goodenough (each in Weiner 1999) have emphasized the interconnections between these ritual occasions, the myths that unite Deadheads, and Deadhead identity.

Alternative approaches to the subject of Deadhead identity are illustrated by Jennings's discussion of "becoming a Deadhead," which is guided by and contributes to Howard Becker's social learning theory; David's discussion of the development of Deadhead identity over the life course, which is written in the tradition of Erik Erickson; and Lehman's application of Morris Rosenberg's discussion of self-concept and ego-extension to Deadheads (all in Adams & Sardiello 2000). In addition, Adams and Rosen-Grandon (2002), Dollar (2003), and (Jeremy) Ritzer (in Adams & Sardiello 2000) discuss the identity challenges facing Deadheads. Using Erving Goffman's notion of tribal stigma, Adams and Rosen-Grandon discuss the issues that Deadheads have when they marry non-Deadheads and argue that the stigma associated with being a Deadhead is stronger because the identity is a voluntary one. Similarly, Dollar describes how Deadheads must decide whether to identify themselves as such in public and in the presence of strangers. Their choices are to blend into the mainstream or to abide by community norms requiring that they communicate their Deadhead identity by the way they talk and act. Using John Fiske's perspective on popular culture to frame his discussion, Jeremy Ritzer (in Adams & Sardiello 2000) chronicles the way in which Deadheads choose between the characteristics of the dominant society and those of their community in constructing lives that suit their needs. Furthermore, he discusses the diversity of Deadhead culture, noting that there are "preferred" ways Deadheads interpret their culture, but also a range of possible other interpretations as well.

In addition to Ritzer's descriptions of Netheads (one of many online Deadhead communities) and tourheads (those who followed the band from venue to venue), scholars have described some of the many other groups of Deadheads as well. For example, Hartley (in Adams & Sardiello 2000) provides an insider's portrayal of the lifeworld of a group variously known as "The Family," "The Spinners," and the "Church of Unlimited Devotion," a religious group that developed out of the show experience whose theology combined elements of Catholicism and Krishna Consciousness. Spinners, as Deadheads commonly called them, whirled like Dervishes at shows, using their dance to help them focus on the music. They viewed the members of the band as channels for God's energy. Similarly, Sheptoski (in Adams & Sardiello 2000) describes the contingencies facing the parking lot vendors who comprised the underground economy on tour, including challenges posed by life on the road and by security guards and police. He also described the vendors' business philosophy, which eschewed many of the mainstream values of competitiveness and profit in favor of Deadhead values of cooperation and satisfaction of community needs. Elsewhere, Epstein and Sardiello (1990) discuss the Wharf Rats, the Deadhead community's version of a 12-step program, and Gertner (in Weiner 1999) addresses the question of why there are so many Jews who are also Deadheads. The existence of these two latter groups often mystifies tourists who visit the Deadhead community. They are surprised that people who are trying to stay straight and sober choose to affiliate with Deadheads, let alone to attend shows where illegal substances are frequently imbibed. They are equally intrigued to notice Jews celebrating their Sabbath or even Rosh HaShanah.

Studying the Deadhead community always presented a methodological challenge, mainly because not all Deadheads identify themselves as such, Deadheads are not always forthcoming about their experiences, and no complete sampling frame is available (Adams 1998). Despite the continuation and survival of the Deadhead community since Jerry Garcia died (Pattacini 2000), its fragmentation and the retirement of many Deadheads from "the scene" (Irwin 1977) have posed further challenges to Deadhead researchers seeking new data. Fortunately, however, Deadheads were conscientious about documenting the community's experience and so many sources of primary data are available in addition to media coverage and other documents (see Paterline's analysis of newspaper coverage in conjunction with US Census data in Adams & Sardiello 2000). Furthermore, the proliferation of so-called "jam bands," most of which were influenced by the Grateful Dead at least to some degree, provides an opportunity for Deadhead scholars to compare and contrast their community to other similar ones.

SEE ALSO: Community and Media; Fans and Fan Culture; Identity, Deviant; Identity: Social Psychological Aspects; Music; Popular Culture Forms (Rock 'n' Roll); Ritual

REFERENCES AND SUGGESTED READINGS

Adams, R. G. (1998) Inciting Sociological Thought by Studying the Deadhead Community: Engaging Publics in Dialogue. *Social Forces* 77(1): 1–25.

Adams, R. G. & Rosen-Grandon, J. (2002) Mixed Marriages: Music Community Membership as a Source of Marital Strain. In: Goodwin, R. & Cramer, D. (Eds.), *Inappropriate Relationships: The Unconventional, the Disapproved, and the Forbidden*. Lawrence Erlbaum, Mahwah, NJ, pp. 78–100.

Adams, R. G. & Sardiello, R. (Eds.) (2000) *Deadhead Social Science: "You Ain't Gonna Learn What You Don't Want To Know."* Altamira Press, Walnut Creek, CA.

Dollar, N. (2003) Communicating Deadhead Identity: Exploring Identity from a Cultural Communication Perspective. In: Fong, M. & Chuang (Eds.), *Communicating Ethnic and Cultural Identity*. Rowman & Littlefield, Lanham, MD, pp. 247–59.

Epstein, J. S. & Sardiello, R. (1990) The Wharf Rats: A Preliminary Examination of Alcoholics Anonymous and the Grateful Dead Head Phenomenon. *Deviant Behavior* 11: 245–57.

Irwin, J. (1977) *Scenes*. Sage, Thousand Oaks, CA.

Pattacini, M. M. (2000) Deadheads Yesterday and Today: An Audience Study. *Popular Music and Society*: 1–14.

Pearson, A. (1987) The Grateful Dead Phenomenon: An Ethnomethodological Approach. *Youth and Society* 18(4): 418–32.

Sardiello, R. (1994) Secular Rituals in Popular Culture: A Case for Grateful Dead Concerts and Dead Head Identity. In: Epstein, J. (Ed.), *Adolescents and Their Music: If It's Too Loud, You're Too Old.* Garland, New York, pp. 115–39.

Weiner, R. G. (1999) *Perspectives on the Grateful Dead: Critical Writings.* Greenwood Press, Boston.

Hendrix, Jimi (1947–70)

Peter Beilharz

James Marshall Hendrix was born in Seattle, Washington and died in London. He became the guitar icon of the modern period and helped to make electric guitar itself iconic of modern popular culture. Hendrix began playing in soul and rhythm and blues bands, including Curtis Knight, B. B. King, and Little Richard's band. His many influences included blues showman T-Bone Walker, Muddy Waters, and Bob Dylan. Hendrix's rise to fame began in the backwash of the British rock and roll invasion. Chas Chandler, lapsed bass player in the Animals, saw Hendrix play in New York in 1966 and persuaded him to come to London. There Hendrix joined with bass player Noel Redding and jazz-influenced drummer Mitch Mitchell to form the Jimi Hendrix Experience. The Experience released three epoch-making albums – *Are You Experienced?* (1967), *Axis: Bold as Love* (1968), and *Electric Ladyland* (1968) – and left period visual classics on film at concerts from Monterey to Woodstock. Into the edge of this period, Hendrix formed the Band of Gypsys, with a more conventional rhythm section. The Experience was the peak of his musical innovation.

The extraordinary achievement of Hendrix was to encounter existing guitar technology and revolutionize its creative scope. Hendrix became identified with the image of the Fender Stratocaster, often white and played upside down (he was a lefthander) and the Marshall stack of amplifiers mediated by technological transfer devices like the wah-wah pedal. Hendrix made the electric guitar sound like nobody had heard it before: weird, electronic, experimental, but also stunning in the steely beauty of songs such as *The Wind Cries Mary* or later, *Little Wing*. His sound was unmistakable, his writing or song construction memorable, as in *Purple Haze* or *Foxy Lady* (Hendrix could not read music, but he certainly could create it). His influence is extraordinary, and ubiquitous, but perhaps is best witnessed in the period case of his friend, Eric Clapton, whose parallel work in Cream represents, together with that of The Experience, the height of blues-rock innovation in the 1960s. Hendrix's sociological significance may be even more powerful than that of Clapton, however, for Hendrix was perhaps the first black rock star and the greatest 1960s African American crossover. Unlike the great black blues players associated, say, with Chess Records in Chicago, Hendrix broke through into a majority white audience and market, anticipating later figures such as Prince. Where a figure like Elvis took black music to a white American audience, Hendrix invented, went avantgarde and in a sense mainstream, for better and for worse.

SEE ALSO: Popular Culture Forms (Rock 'n' Roll); Popular Culture Icons (Dylan, Bob; Grateful Dead and Deadheads)

REFERENCES AND SUGGESTED READINGS

Lawrence, S. (2004) *Betrayed: The True Story of Jimi Hendrix.* Sidgwick & Jackson, London.

Murray, C. S. (1989) *Crosstown Traffic: Jimi Hendrix and Postwar Pop.* Faber, London.

Schapiro, H. & Glebbeek, C. (1995) *Jimi Hendrix – Electric Gypsy.* Random House, New York.

Tate, G. (2003) *Midnight Lighting: Jimi Hendrix and the Black Experience.* Lawrence Hill, Chicago.

Jackson, Michael (b. 1958)

Ellis Cashmore

During the last 20 years of the twentieth century, Michael Jackson was one of the supreme icons of popular culture. Few performers and certainly no

African American performer have ever commanded a following like Jackson's: in one remarkable decade, Jackson sold 110 million records (over 75 million as a solo artist). *Bad*, his follow-up to *Thriller*, was considered a virtual failure, selling 20 million copies. The tour to promote it in 1987 was watched by a total of 4.5 million people. The video of his single "Black or White" was simultaneously shown to an estimated 500 million television viewers in 27 countries in 1991. A six-album deal with Sony was worth up to $1 billion. Jackson's rare public appearances, though fleeting and uneventful, were accorded a status akin to a royal visit. The word enigmatic is overused when describing taciturn pop and movie stars, but, in Jackson's case, it fits. He was truly an enigma and this played no small part in deepening the public's interest in him. Of all the questions asked of Jackson, the most perplexing concerns his physical transformation: was he a black man trying determinedly to become white?

Seven years separated the ages of the Jackson 5, Michael being the youngest. By the time he was 10, he had featured on two singles released on a small independent label, Steeltown Records. The band consisted of five brothers, managed, often dictatorially, by father Joe. In 1969, Berry Gordy, the head of Motown Records, spotted the potential of the band. Influenced by the success of the assembled-for-TV band the Monkees, Gordy initially wanted to create a black version, complete with cartoon series and a range of merchandise. He launched the Jackson 5, using established stars such as Diana Ross and Sammy Davis, Jr. as endorsers. In fact, the band's first Motown album was *Diana Ross Presents the Jackson 5*.

A white compeer of the band, the Osmonds, flickered briefly, but the Jackson brothers went from strength to strength with Motown in the early 1970s, Gordy cleverly issuing single releases by Michael independently of the band, while keeping the unit together. Like all artists in the Motown fold, the Jackson 5 was given the full grooming treatment: no detail was ignored. As such, Michael was a seasoned showbusiness professional by the time he was a teenager.

Father Joe, however, was dissatisfied with Gordy's handling of his son's career and, in 1976, negotiated a deal with CBS's subsidiary label, Epic. For contractual reasons, the band became known as the Jacksons, its first album being released in 1977. While both the band and Michael

continued to sell records, progress was unspectacular until 1979 when a collaboration with producer Quincy Jones yielded Michael's *Off the Wall*, which sold 6 million copies – and continues to sell. The album spawned four hit singles. Around this time, the facial changes that were to become the stuff of myth began: two rhinoplasty operations followed an accident in which Jackson broke his nose.

Despite his commercial success, MTV was impervious to Jackson for a long while. In 1983, the 24-hour all-music cable TV channel rejected Jackson's "Billie Jean," giving rise to the suspicion that the station wanted only "safe" acts that appealed to white youth; and, for this reason, concluded that black artists were not good for business. CBS threatened MTV with a boycott by all its artists, forcing a change of heart. In a way, MTV's decision may have been a historic one, providing a black artist with a genuine mainstream showcase. The track was taken from Jackson's album *Thriller*, which turned him into the bestselling recording artist of his time. It became the top-selling album in history. The title track's video was made into an extravagant TV event, receiving a premiere in December 1983 and going on to sell 48 million copies independently of the album.

As the world's leading artist, Jackson had to contend with the attendant publicity. This was intensified by the fact that consumers' fascination with celebrities, the gossip about them, the stories surrounding them, and the minutiae of their personal lives, had begun in earnest. Jackson's response was to become a virtual recluse, giving interviews sparingly and making infrequent public appearances. Perversely, this promoted even greater interest in him; and hearsay proliferated.

Throughout his career, the questions that contributed so fulsomely to his enigma were rarely answered. Did he really sleep in an oxygen tent? Why did he want to buy the bones of the Elephant Man? Was he so obsessed with Diana Ross that he actually tried to look like her? Did he seriously believe, as suggested in an *Ebony* interview, that he was a messenger from God? And, how come he always seemed to be in the company of young boys? This last question was asked time and again and eventually turned into one scandal too many.

In 1993, Jackson was accused of child molestation by a 13-year-old boy. Jackson agreed to talk about the charges on a "live" satellite hookup from his Neverland ranch in California. He complained that the police had subjected him to a humiliating inspection and taken photographs of his genitalia. In 1994, Jackson agreed to pay Jordy Chandler, then 14, an undisclosed sum, thought to be more than $25 million, to stop a sex abuse lawsuit ever reaching court. Jackson was never put under oath for a civil deposition, which could be used in a criminal trial. The deal was negotiated on Jackson's behalf by his lawyer, Johnnie Cochrane, Jr., later to represent O. J. Simpson, and Larry Feldman, who was retained by Chandler's parents. Part of the agreement reached was that the payment did not constitute an admission of guilt by Jackson. After the charges, Jackson was forced out into the open and made to defend himself, whether he liked it or not. In the process, the qualities that were once integral to his appeal became implements of immolation. Was he weird-unusual, or weird-sicko?

The answers were forthcoming. Further legal action ensured that Jackson stayed in the public consciousness, though less for his music, more for his apparent sexual proclivities. In 2003, he was charged in California for child molestation. His acquittal in June 2005 brought to a close the first genuinely global *cause célèbre* of the twenty-first century.

Meanwhile, a business drama unfolded. In the early 1990s, Jackson had bought the rights to the Beatles music and added them to his own vast catalogue of more than 3,000 songs, valued (in 2004) at $650 million. In 1995, he merged his ATV company with Sony to create a joint venture, which, by 1999, capitalized at $900 million, yielding an income for Jackson and Sony of about $80 million per year. Yet, by the end of the 1990s, Jackson's profligacy had led him to seek a series of loans totalling over $200 million from the Bank of America. Disappointing record sales and legal bills combined to exacerbate Jackson's financial position.

Jackson epitomized a perfect confluence of personality and history. A black male, precociously talented as an entertainer, he emerged as a child star in the 1970s, a time when America's dilemma had become a glaring paradox. The land of opportunity had finally granted civil rights to all citizens, yet continued to deny whole portions of the population access to the kinds of jobs, goods, and other resources germane to an egalitarian society. As the rioting of the 1960s subsided and African Americans poured their fury into more cultural

expressions, Jackson came to the fore, sporting an Afro hairdo and a clenched fist salute. He was a young man who looked like he had all the trappings of black power.

In reality, he was an innocent, a child who could be admired paternalistically, living proof that black people had gifts that were uniquely their own. For some, he was testimony to the continued self-hatred that beset African Americans. For all his success, Jackson seemed ill at ease with his blackness and his transformation might be seen as proof of this. In a 1991 interview with Oprah Winfrey, Jackson said that he suffered from a skin disorder called vitiligo, which causes discoloration, but few accepted that Jackson had not undergone some sort of treatment. His face seemed to be in a state of perpetual alteration, giving rise to the suggestion that he was actually trying to rid himself of his blackness. Certainly, his blanched complexion, small pointed nose, and thin lips lent substance to this theory, though Jackson himself remained silent on the subject and was famously prickly about unflattering descriptions. Speculation about his motives fueled the abundant mysteries surrounding Jackson.

It is not necessary to impute motives: no one will ever know whether Jackson actually wanted to rid himself of his blackness. But, he certainly gave many precisely that impression. He was a black man so successful that he could have almost anything in the world. In one stroke, he convinced America that it was truly the land of opportunity, while emphasizing that whiteness was still the most valued commodity in that land. Don King, who promoted a world tour for Jackson and his brothers, once said of Michael: "He's one of the megastars in the world, but he's still going to be a nigger megastar" (Taraborelli 1991).

SEE ALSO: Celebrity and Celetoid; Celebrity Culture; Charisma; Consumption of Music; Fans and Fan Culture; Popular Culture; Whiteness

REFERENCES AND SUGGESTED READINGS

Andersen, C. (1994) *Michael Jackson: Unauthorized.* Simon & Schuster, New York.

Bishop, N. (2003) *Freak: Inside the Twisted World of Michael Jackson.* AMI Books, Boca Raton, FL.

Cashmore, E. (1997) *The Black Culture Industry.* Routledge, London.

Cashmore, E. (2004) Jackson, Michael (1958–). In: Cashmore, E. (Ed.), *Encyclopedia of Race and Ethnic Studies*. Routledge, London, pp. 221–3.

Jackson, M. (1992) *Dancing the Dream*. Doubleday, New York.

Jones, B. & Brown, S. (2005) *Michael Jackson: The Man Behind the Mask*. Select Books, New York.

Taraborelli, R. (1991) *Michael Jackson: The Magic and the Madness*. Birch Lane, New York.

Marley, Bob (1945–81)

Ellis Cashmore

While his putative remit was to produce music, Marley's status extended far beyond, embracing that of a prophet, sage, and emissary for Ras Tafari, a cultural movement that attracted acolytes wherever there were black people. In common with other charismatic leaders who have been attributed by their followers with divine qualities, Marley never explicitly denied that he was some sort of holy messenger. He was sincere: the credo of Ras Tafari included the assurance that God's presence was a uniting force within all believers – a principle captured in the expression "I and I." (In Rastafarian grammar, "I" is often substituted for "you" to affirm the oneness of people.)

Marley was not exactly chosen to represent Ras Tafari: his emergence as a prominent and globally popular singer/songwriter in the 1970s allowed him to disseminate the messages of the hitherto cultic religious group of the Caribbean to an international audience. He popularized the tenets, theological directives, and political values of Ras Tafari not by proselytizing but by performing his music. By the late 1970s his influence was pervasive and, though he never expressly proclaimed his role as a *de facto* leader of Ras Tafari, he seemed at ease with the ascription.

Born Robert Nesta Marley on February 6, 1945 in Nine Miles, Jamaica, he was brought up by his mother in the ghetto area of Trenchtown in Kingston. Like many prospective Jamaican musicians, Marley began writing and playing reggae and in 1961 recorded one of his own compositions, "Judge Not." He later formed a band called the Wailers for whom he wrote most of the material.

In 1971 the Wailers signed a record deal with Island Records and produced two albums, *Catch a Fire* and *Burnin'*, both of which alluded to the combustible nature of a world where black people were habitually oppressed and subjugated. The albums contained frequent references to "Babylon," which described the post-imperial condition. The commercial success of both albums prompted a name change, Marley becoming a more prominent figure in the line-up. As Bob Marley and the Wailers the band had more success with the next album, *Natty Dread*, which included the iconic "No Woman, No Cry."

Marley's reputation was enhanced by his image: his hair was a wild Medusa-type shock of dreadlocks; he dressed in the red, black, green, and gold favored by Rastas (as devotees of Ras Tafari are known), and he would often carry a spliff of ganja. The ambiguity of his lyrics, many of which were couched in Old Testament imagery, added mystery. But the more Marley mystified, the more he seemed to reveal. His followers were fascinated enough to explore his songs and interpret their logic and meaning rather than simply listen to them. By 1977, when he released the album *Exodus*, Marley's reputation had become global. His songs about captivity, oppression, and redemption seemed to have resonance almost everywhere in the world.

Marley's death was untimely. He injured a toe while playing soccer and the toe became cancerous. Rastafarian beliefs prevented his having surgery to remove the affected areas and Marley died from cancer on May 11, 1981, aged 36.

Many singers have fans; Marley had disciples. His death did little to dampen their zeal and, for a while, many refused to accept that he had died, suspecting he had gone into hiding or been captured by the repressive forces of Babylon.

SEE ALSO: Celebrity and Celetoid; Charisma; Counterculture; Diaspora; Ethnicity; Millenarianism; Popular Culture Icons (Dylan, Bob); Social Movements

REFERENCES AND SUGGESTED READINGS

White, T. (1998) *Catch a Fire: The Life of Bob Marley*. Owl Books, New York.

Myth of the American Frontier

Richard Slotkin

The Myth of the Frontier is the oldest and most durable of American national myths. Like all nation-state mythologies, its function is to provide a historical account and an ideological justification of national development, and a repertoire of exemplary fables – based on historical events – which offer plausible precedents for dealing with contemporary crises. The myth recognizes that the US developed as a settler state, which grew geographically and increased in political and economic power by advancing European settlements into the territory of Native Americans and the "wilderness." It builds upon that historical basis a set of historical fables which explain and justify the development of American nationality as the product of this perennial advance into the wilderness, or the "virgin land."

The Frontier Myth addresses simultaneously two central and persistent problems of American development: the problem of nationality (which subsumes the concepts of race and culture), and the problem of capitalist development. The Myth answers the perennial question, "What is an American?" by creating a virtual genealogy – Americans are the descendents (by blood or acculturation) of those heroes who discovered, conquered, and settled the virgin land of the wild frontier. Only a small minority of Americans ever had actual experience of frontier life; but through history texts and the media of mass culture, generations of Americans who had no ancestral tie to the West nonetheless came to see the frontier as the symbol of their collective past, the source of such "American" characteristics as individualism, informality, pragmatism, and egalitarianism. The Myth also asserts that American capitalist development has been exceptional (part of a unique nationality), especially in its successful combination of economic growth with liberal democracy; and finds the material basis of that unique developmental history in America's continual expansion to new "natural" or "wilderness" frontiers.

The Myth combines two ideological themes into a single powerful fable: the themes of "bonanza economics" and "savage war." The first is an economic mythology, implicitly a theory of economic development; the second is a political and social myth, which defines the rights, powers, and roles of different classes and races in the making of American society.

"Bonanza economics" holds that the key to American development is the continual discovery and exploitation of cheap and abundant resources *outside* the metropolitan center of society. It is critical to the myth that the New World, the virgin lands of the West and their wealth, come to Americans *as if out of nowhere*: unlooked-for, a windfall. Nature, not labor, gives such resources their value, and hence they come to Americans free of the social costs that burden development in metropolitan Europe. In the Old World (so the story goes), persons or classes could only better their conditions by undergoing the deprivations of primitive accumulation, by exploiting scarcity and need, or by engaging in social warfare against more established classes. In the New World, on the Frontier, resources are so superabundant that prosperity can be enjoyed by all, without prejudice to the interests of any – except the natives who, as savages, are outside the limits of civil society and public concern.

It is important to note that although illusion and falsification figured prominently in the economic myth of the frontier, the myth remained credible because it had some basis in reality. For most of US colonial and national history, geographical expansion went hand in hand with economic development. In the century following the Revolution, the 13 coastal colonies expanded across the continent and beyond to Alaska and the Pacific basin, while at the same time the country grew from an agrarian adjunct of the European economic system to a leading industrial and financial world power. It was perhaps inevitable that these two dramatic expansions be linked in American historical mythology. But it took mythopoetic imagination to see the westward movement of population as a *cause* – rather than a *consequence* – of American economic development.

Over the course of 300 years, from 1600 to 1900, through the myth-making labor of preachers, novelists, publicists, and promoters, westering became a metaphor – or rather, the objective correlative – of the motives that drive economic behavior in capitalist societies. Pioneering presents the profit motive in its most appealing form, as the basis for heroic action and the creation of a unique new nation that somehow manages to be both arcadia and imperium. As the national economy developed, and American territory incorporated new regions, the specific form of the frontier bonanza changed. Agriculture and land speculation gave way to "bonanzas" based on agricultural commodities (cotton, wheat, cattle-ranching), mining (gold, silver, iron, coal), and railroad-building (especially after 1865).

But according to the Myth, the American bonanza can only be achieved through "savage war": the violent conquest, displacement, or subjugation of non-white races or peoples of "primitive" cultural development. Like the virgin land and bonanza myth, the myth of savage war is also rooted in historical fact. Every stage of westward expansion, from Jamestown on, was marked by Indian wars. Moreover, to exploit the cheap land frontier to the West, Americans exploited cheap labor frontiers to the East and South: at least half of the land seized from the Indians before 1850 was exploited by means of African slave labor; and the railroad frontier of the Gilded Age was built on cheap immigrant labor from Europe and Asia.

Crucial to the creation of a national myth is the conception of an Enemy. Because the US developed as a settler state, it has always defined itself against two kinds of enemy: the Native American to the West, who is seen as savage, close to nature, non-Christian, non-white, anarchically free in lifestyle; and the European to the East, excessively civilized, rigidly hierarchical, bound by custom and ideological creed – the triumph of the letter over the spirit. The American hero, the frontiersman or "The Man Who Knows Indians," holds a moral balance between these ideological extremes, defining and defending an American nation which blends the best of both extremes. However, according to the myth, that balance can only be achieved through the violence of warfare.

The "savage war" theme mystifies politics in a way that complements the mystification of economics in the virgin land/bonanza myth. In the Old World (so the story goes), social violence is directed inward, deployed by one class to subjugate or overthrow another in the struggle for scarce resources, with the result that Europe is both unstable and resistant to genuine democracy. But in America, the social costs of development are externalized – in effect, symbolically exorcized. Social violence is projected outward against "them that are not a People" (as the Puritans liked to say) – against tribes of alien race and culture, living beyond the geographical borders of civilization (in the case of Indians and Africans) or beyond the margins of civil society (in the case of domestic slaves and other, non-naturalized immigrants).

As the virgin land/bonanza myth sanctifies the territorial boundaries of national society, the savage war myth defines and sanctifies a concept of national identity and character. In each stage of its development, the Myth of the Frontier represents progress as achieved through a scenario of *regeneration through violence*: a heroic departure from the limits of existing society; purification through a regression to a more primitive or "natural" state; and redemption, through triumph over the wilderness and its native people, which makes the West safe for civilization (symbolized by white women). The hero of the myth is a figure, "The Man Who Knows Indians," modeled on historical figures like Washington (who began as an Indian-fighter), Boone, Crockett, Buffalo Bill, and Custer and fictional heroes like Hawkeye and The Virginian. The hero embodies, and so is able to deal with, the central conflict of values that marks the frontier. He knows both savagery and civilization, is at home in both; and what he knows is that (with noble exceptions) "Indians" as a race cannot be trusted or lived with. The savage enemy kills and terrorizes without limit or discrimination, in order to exterminate or drive out the civilized race. To achieve victory in such a war, Americans are entitled and indeed required to use any and all means, including massacre, terrorism, and torture. This logic has found explicit expression in certain characteristic forms of American social violence, including vigilantism and lynching. Any class which can be likened to the mythic savage as an enemy to civilization and progress becomes eligible for treatment according to the savage war scenario: becomes a candidate for subjugation, segregation, or even extermination; becomes the legitimate object of violent, perhaps military, coercion, rather than a fellow subject and citizen of the democratic polity.

At the end of the nineteenth century, as the US was making the transition to a modern industrialized nation-state, two versions of the Myth were formally codified as major interpretations of national history. Frederick Jackson Turner's "Frontier Hypothesis" held that America's democratic culture and politics had been shaped by the existence of a cheap land frontier, which provided a social safety valve for class conflict and a reservoir of unappropriated wealth available for the fulfillment of the American Dream. Turner thought that the closing of the Frontier deprived American democracy of its material basis, and threatened the US with Europe's fate of concentrated wealth and class conflict. Theodore Roosevelt offered a contrary hypothesis: that the Frontier had been a Darwinian laboratory in which a new class or "race" of masterful executives and entrepreneurs had emerged triumphant; and that a corporate America could now undertake the conquest of an imperial frontier in Asia and Latin America. Both versions of the Myth still influence both popular culture and political thinking in the US: the Turnerian (or "Populist") strain speaks in our nostalgia for the free, innocent, and abundant past that we have "lost"; the Rooseveltian (or "Progressive") strain, for our determination to find or fabricate "new frontiers" (new natural resources, new technologies, outer space, etc.) to replace the ones that have closed.

SEE ALSO: Myth; Mythogenesis

REFERENCES AND SUGGESTED READINGS

Billington, R. A. (1966) *America's Frontier Heritage.* Holt, Rinehart, & Winston, New York.

Billington, R. A. (1981) *Land of Savagery, Land of Promise: The European Image of the American Frontier.* Norton, New York.

Kolodny, A. (1975) *The Lay of the Land: Metaphor as Experience and History in American Life and Letters.* University of North Carolina Press, Chapel Hill.

Slotkin, R. (1998 [1985]) *The Fatal Environment: The Myth of the Frontier in the Age of Industrialization, 1800–1890,* 3rd edn, corrected. University of Oklahoma Press, Norman.

Slotkin, R. (1998 [1992]) *Gunfighter Nation: The Myth of the Frontier in Twentieth-Century America,* 2nd edn, corrected. University of Oklahoma Press, Norman.

Slotkin, R. (2000 [1973]) *Regeneration Through Violence: The Mythology of the American Frontier, 1600–1860,* 3rd edn, corrected. University of Oklahoma Press, Norman.

Smith, H. N. (1950) *Virgin Land: The American West as Symbol and Myth.* Vintage, New York.

Simpsons, The

Jeremy Ritzer

The Simpsons, an American animated television show, has transcended the position of a mere popular cultural artifact to the status of a bona fide sociological phenomenon. Instead of just entertaining the masses, the show devotes a significant amount of time to addressing social issues.

The Simpsons first appeared as very brief (30 seconds–2 minutes) animated segments as part of the *Tracey Ullman Show,* a variety show that aired on Fox from 1987 to 1989. The popularity of these shorts led to a Christmas special in the fall of 1989 (a Christmas special entitled *The Simpsons Roasting Over an Open Fire,* which first aired December 17, 1989), and then the official introduction of the Simpsons family to the American public as the stars of their own weekly series beginning in 1990 (with the airing of *Bart the Genius,* on January 14).

The Simpsons family consists of Homer, the boorish father, Marge, the moralistic and worrying mother, Bart, the oldest child, a modern version of Dennis the Menace, Lisa, the family nerd and the moral compass of the family and of the show, and little Maggie, the baby of the family, with only one word expressed over the course of 15+ seasons ("daddy," in *Lisa's First Word,* which first aired on December 3, 1992, a word that went unheard by everyone except for the viewers).

In addition, the Springfield community is populated by an assortment of caricatures and larger than life figures such as Ned Flanders, the Simpsons' hyper-religious neighbor, Reverend Lovejoy of the First Church of Springfield (whose marquee has read "Every Sunday is Super Sunday" and "We Welcome Other Faiths (Just Kidding)"), Barney Gumble, Homer's drunken friend, Moe Czyslak, the proprietor of Moe's Tavern, Principal Seymour Skinner, of Springfield Elementary, and C. Montgomery Burns, the evil owner of the Springfield Nuclear Power Plant, among many others. Each comes and goes throughout the episodes, and often each plays a key role in highlighting the moral of the episode.

This one television show manages each week to address serious contemporary social issues, from religion, to the role of the family, to child abuse and endangerment, to gay marriage. *The Simpsons* has always been very responsive to, and willing to remark, social change. In some cases, this has caused some controversy. A couple of examples can highlight the sociological perspective found in *The Simpsons.*

First, the show has always had a significant religious component. The Simpsons family attends church regularly as a family. Some have argued that *The Simpsons* is virtually alone in primetime television in its representation of a family that is truly dedicated to attending church. However, in one classic episode (*Homer the Heretic*, which first aired on October 8, 1992), Homer chooses to forego church. While his family is stuck in church because of a snowstorm, Homer has the best day of his life. When God confronts him for forsaking religion, Homer responds, "I'm not a bad guy! I work hard, and I love my kids. So why should I spend half my Sunday hearing about how I'm going to Hell?" God's response is, "Hmm … You've got a point there," agrees that the sermons are really tiring, and promises to give the reverend a canker sore.

The episode concludes when Homer almost perishes in a fire. He is saved by his dedicated churchgoing neighbor, Ned Flanders, and other volunteer firefighters of faith. In a conversation between Homer and God, God accepts Homer back into the flock with the statement, "Don't worry Homer. Nine out of ten religions fail in their first year" (*Homer the Heretic*).

This episode highlights the complicated relationship that *The Simpsons* has with religion, as well as with other social institutions. While the show contains much more religious content that most of the rest of what appears on American television, it is content that is willing to test the boundaries of what is acceptable. Further, the criticisms found in *The Simpsons* are often criticisms of blind obedience or dogma, not of religion or religious belief.

In a more recent example, *The Simpsons* waded into the gay marriage controversy with an episode entitled *There's Something About Marrying*, which first aired on February 20, 2005. In this episode, which was preceded by a parental advisory message, Lisa encourages Springfield to legalize gay marriage in order to attract tourists. Homer starts his own church to cater to same-sex couples who come to Springfield to get married, but are turned away by Reverend Lovejoy. Patty, Homer's sister-in-law, asks Homer to officiate at her marriage to a professional golfer, who is exposed as a man posing as a woman. However, Patty is a lesbian, and refuses to marry her fiancé, now male.

Despite the widespread use of stereotypes, this episode of *The Simpsons* can be seen as a very tolerant approach to an area of social change. The moral of this episode is more about love and tolerance, not a judgment as to whether gay marriage is appropriate in the United States. However, the fact that the show chose this topic as its focus, and was slapped with a parental advisory, indicates how *The Simpsons* is still willing to comment on issues that affect society.

Each week *The Simpsons* can be counted upon to wrestle with timely social issues. And a careful analysis of the range of episodes and topics would likely show that no single ideology is expressed. Instead, *The Simpsons* actively works to bring humor to America's sacred cows, often hiding a pointed social commentary within ludicrous situations and characters. This combination of humor and relevance is what has made *The Simpsons* the longest running animated series, the longest running sitcom of any kind and, when its current contract ends in 2009, after its nineteenth season, perhaps the longest-running prime time series of any kind.

SEE ALSO: Culture; Media; Popular Culture; Religion

REFERENCES AND SUGGESTED READINGS

Alberti, J. (Ed.) (2004) *Leaving Springfield: The Simpsons and the Possibility of Oppositional Culture.* Wayne State University Press, Detroit.

Episode Guide (2004) *The Simpsons Archive*, September 7. Online. www.snpp.com/episodeguide.html.

Irwin, W., Conrad, M., & Skoble, A. (Eds.) (2001) *The Simpsons and Philosophy: The D'oh! of Homer.* Open Court, Chicago.

Keslowitz, S. (2004) *The Simpsons and Society: An Analysis of Our Favorite Family and Its Influence in Contemporary Society.* Hats Off Books, Tucson.

Pinsky, M. (2001) *The Gospel According to The Simpsons: The Spiritual Life of the World's Most Animated Family.* Westminster John Knox Press, Louisville.

The Simpsons (2005) Wikipedia.org, March 5. Online. www.en.wikipedia.org/wiki/The_Simpsons.

The Simpsons Episode Guide (*The Simpsons* Official Site). Online. www.thesimpsons.com/episode_ guide/index.htm.

Turner, C. (2004) *Planet Simpson: How a Cartoon Masterpiece Defined a Generation*. Da Capo Press, New York.

Sinatra, Frank (1917–98)

Chris Rojek

Frank Sinatra was a popular singer, actor, and night-club entertainer who dominated American popular culture for nearly six decades. Born in Hoboken, Sinatra was the son of Italian immigrants who first gained attention on a popular talent radio show as part of a singing ensemble called the *Hoboken Four*. After the group folded Sinatra worked as a singing waiter in New Jersey, where he was discovered by Harry James and invited to become lead vocalist with the *Harry James Orchestra*. Sinatra's success led to him being poached by the *Tommy Dorsey Band*.

A dedicated technician rather than a naturally gifted vocalist, he developed his trademark *bel canto* legato singing style, which enabled him to enunciate more words than other singers, by building up lung capacity through swimming and track work. He also copied Tommy Dorsey's method of breath control. During the war years, Sinatra became the greatest popular performer since the days of Charlie Chaplin, Rudolf Valentino, Al Jolson, and Bing Crosby. His boyish appearance and slight figure made him a surrogate for American troops fighting in Europe and Asia.

Sinatra went solo in 1942 and played a series of concerts at the Paramount Theater in New York that became legendary for the unprecedented mass female hysteria that they generated. Sinatra became the prototypical pop idol, with a string of hit records, popular films, and successful concert appearances. He also became a figure of controversy and even notoriety for gossip columnists. His involvement with the Left and Civil Rights Movement led to insinuations that Sinatra had sympathies with communism. At this time, too, unsavoury allegations were published about Sinatra's violence and connections with the Mafia.

Sinatra began to acquire a reputation for perversity which, combined with some uninspired film and music choices, the divorce from his wife Nancy, the highly public courtship of the film star Ava Gardner, and the antagonism of some returning American troops who resented Sinatra for avoiding the draft, sent his career into a tailspin. He referred to the period between 1947 and 1953 as the Dark Ages. It was a 6-year slump marked by declining record sales and box office catastrophes. Capitol cancelled its record contract with him and MGM followed suit by terminating his film contract.

The tailspin in his career was reversed by his performance as the victimized infantry man, Angelo Maggio, in the film *From Here To Eternity* ed an Oscar for the role. The renewal of public interest in his career prompted Columbia Records to offer him a recording contract. The punitive terms would be a source of tension between Sinatra and the record company for a decade and a half. However, the inspired teaming of Sinatra with a series of brilliant music arrangers, notably Billy May, Gordon Jenkins and, above all, Nelson Riddle, resulted in a series of classic popular recordings. Albums like *Songs for Swingin' Lovers*, *In the Wee Small Hours*, *Only the Lonely*, and *Where Are You?* provided the soundtrack for the affluent society of the 1950s and early 1960s. In contemplative recordings like *Only the Lonely* and *The Wee Small Hours* Sinatra has some claim to have invented the concept album. This material can be read as providing consumer culture with a poetic vernacular in which popular romance and the collapse of relationships were addressed.

Sinatra combined a resurgent recording career with a revitalized movie career. He starred in a string of successful light comedies : *The Tender Trap* (1955), *Guys and Dolls* (1955), *High Society* (1956), and *Pal Joey* (1957). But he also tackled more challenging roles in *Suddenly* (1954), in which he is a would-be assassin; *The Man With the Golden Arm* (1955), which deals with drug addiction; *The Joker Is Wild* (1957), which explores victimization in the entertainment industry and mob violence; and, above all, in *The Manchurian Candidate* (1962), which focused on political corruption and Cold War intrigue.

During the 1950s Sinatra refined the image of a priapic, whisky-marinated, free-wheeling playboy, especially through his association with the Rat Pack (Dean Martin, Sammy Davis Jr., Peter Lawford, and Joey Bishop). The Rat Pack provided an antidote to Cold War anxieties. However, the image of masculinity which they cultivated was deplored by many sections of the media and popular opinion. Rat Pack hedonism and cool became an object of censure as protest artists became prominent after the 1960s.

In 1961 Sinatra founded Reprise Records as a venture designed to give recording artists maximum artistic control. He sold the company to Warner Brothers in 1963, but retained a significant share-holding. The venture into successful business, and the release of the successful Rat Pack films in the 1960s, reinforced Sinatra's popular image as the king of cool.

Sinatra was a powerful male symbol of *parvenu* success. His best film and recording work captured a romantic fatalism and the tendency of modern life to provide a strain of psychological and social isolation. In the 1950s and 1960s he was omnipresent in American popular culture, dominating popular music, film, stage shows, and even politics. He was closely involved with John F. Kennedy's successful presidential campaign and even aspired to hold public office. But he was rejected by the Kennedys after they judged that his Mafia connections would be an electoral liability. Sinatra turned to the Right in the 1970s and became publicly associated with Ronald and Nancy Reagan. The Reagans were instrumental in helping him regain his casino gambling licence, which had been stripped from him in 1963 following allegations that he had entertained the notorious Chicago Mafia boss Sam Giancana at his gambling casino. He retired in the early 1970s, but was coaxed back to recording, concert tours, and some limited film roles. In his declining years he bestrode the stage with poignant Lear-like intensity, a living legend from the free-wheeling heyday of post-war Hollywood.

SEE ALSO: Cool; Popular Culture

REFERNCES AND SUGGESTED READINGS

Granta, C. (2003) *Sessions With Sinatra*. Chicago Review Process, Chicago.

Rojek, C. (2004) *Frank Sinatra*. Polity Press, Cambridge.

Smith, M. (2005) *When Ole Blue Eyes Was A Red*. Redwords, New York.

Star Trek

Andrew Milner

Star Trek is the most successful "brand" in the history of American television science fiction. The first version ran from 1966 to 1969; an animated children's series followed in 1973 and 1974; *The Next Generation* ran from 1987 to 1994; *Deep Space Nine* from 1993 to 1999; *Voyager* from 1995 to 2001; and *Enterprise*, launched in 2001, reached its fourth season during 2004–5. A movie spin-off, *Star Trek: The Motion Picture*, was released in 1979, with nine further movie sequels following between 1982 and 2002. Both TV series and films acquired a worldwide fan base. Sociological interest has concentrated on three main topics: the ideological meanings at work in *Star Trek*; the more specific interplay between the program's fictional Starfleet and the real National Aeronautics and Space Administration (NASA); and the sociology of its fan base.

Commentary on ideology tends to situate *Star Trek* in relation to 1960s American liberalism. So its quasi-utopian optimism about technological and social progress is reminiscent of the official enthusiasm for the space race and social reform under the Democratic administrations of Presidents Kennedy and Johnson. *Star Trek* is set in the twenty-third and twenty-fourth centuries, at a time when technological innovation has effectively solved the practical problems that confound humanity. People travel the galaxy in starships, their food and drink supplied by replicators, their fantasies enacted out and fulfilled in holodecks. Their collective social life appears similarly unproblematic. On Earth, poverty, inequality, and social conflict have been eliminated, so that both genders, all races, and (in the later versions) various sexualities are all equal. In the wider universe, humanity lives at peace with neighboring alien species in a United Federation of Planets.

Early commentary tended to stress the positive significance of the show's optimism and its liberalism. The original series featured the first "interracial" kiss – between Kirk and Uhuru – to appear on American television. Its non-American officers included the half-alien Spock, the Russian Chekov, and the Chinese Sulu, as well as the African Uhuru. But the limitations were also apparent: there were more humans than aliens on the bridge of the starship *Enterprise*, more Americans than non-Americans, more whites than blacks, more men than women. Uhuru might have been a black woman officer, but she did little more than answer the interplanetary phone. Later versions included more non-Americans (a French captain, Picard, in *The Next Generation*), more non-whites (a black station commander, Sisko, in *Deep Space Nine*), and more women (a female captain, Janeway, in *Voyager*). But Starfleet and the United Federation of Planets remained as subordinate to white American men as the real-world international organizations of the late twentieth and early twenty-first century.

Such limitations prompted critics to question the show's liberalism. Worland (1988) stressed its cold war militarism, Blair (1983) and Cranny-Francis (1985) its sexism, Bernardi (1997) its racism. But these criticisms could easily be leveled at Kennedy liberalism itself. Indeed, the program replicated the strengths and weaknesses of its home culture with precision. And it responded, more or less creatively, to such criticism and to the increasingly postmodern character of American culture. So later commentators would see *The Next Generation* as seriously questioning existing gender stereotypes (Roberts 1999) or even as placing "the project of humanity ... center-stage" (Barrett & Barrett 2001: 204).

Star Trek's initial successes and those of the NASA space program were roughly contemporaneous. NASA's funding had been dramatically increased in 1961, when Kennedy approved the Apollo mission to send astronauts to the moon within a decade. As the decade proceeded, the Agency's status was enhanced by the show, the show's by the Agency. Eventually, what began as temporal overlap evolved into institutional symbiosis: the first NASA space shuttle was named after the *Enterprise*; and the fourth *Star Trek* movie was dedicated to the astronauts killed in the shuttle *Challenger*. Penley describes how the Agency and the TV show merged symbolically to "form a powerful cultural icon ... 'NASA/ TREK'," which "shapes our popular and institutional imaginings about space" (Penley 1997: 16).

Star Trek's fan base is exceptionally active. When the NBC network threatened to cancel the series in 1967, a "Save Star Trek" campaign produced over 114,667 letters of protest and finally secured its renewal (Tulloch & Jenkins 1995: 9). This mass "movement" of "Trekkers" has since become a semi-permanent accompaniment to the

franchise. For *Star Trek*, as for SF more generally, the convention, where fans meet with each other and with actors, directors, and writers, has become a crucial fan institution. But the Trekker conventions are both more numerous and typically much larger. The 4th official Las Vegas Star Trek Convention, scheduled for August 2005, catered for thousands of fans, at prices ranging from $35 to $239 for a weekend package, and featured no fewer than 35 *Star Trek* actors as "guests." Much commentary has seen the "Trekkie" phenomenon in quasi-Adornian terms as manipulation by the culture industry. But Jenkins casts Trekkers and other fans in a much more positive light as "consumers who also produce, readers who also write, spectators who also participate." "In each case," he concludes, "fans are drawing on materials from the dominant media and employing them in ways that serve their own interests and facilitate their own pleasures" (Jenkins 1992: 214).

SEE ALSO: Fans and Fan Culture; Popular Culture; Popular Culture Forms (Science Fiction); Postmodernism

REFERENCES AND SUGGESTED READINGS

Barrett, M. & Barrett, D. (2001) *Star Trek: The Human Frontier*. Polity Press, Cambridge.

Bernardi, D. (1997) *Star Trek* in the 1960s: Liberal-Humanism and the Production of Race. *Science Fiction Studies* 24(2): 209–25.

Blair, K. (1983) Sex and *Star Trek*. *Science Fiction Studies* 10(2): 292–7.

Cranny-Francis, A. (1985) Sexuality and Sex-Role Stereotyping in *Star Trek*. *Science Fiction Studies* 12(3): 274–84.

Jenkins, H. (1992) Strangers No More, We Sing: Filking and the Social Construction of the Science Fiction Fan Community. In: Lewis, L. (Ed.), *The Adoring Audience: Fan Culture and Popular Media*. Routledge, London.

Penley, C. (1997) *NASA/ TREK: Popular Science and Sex in America*. Verso, London.

Roberts, R. (1999) *Sexual Generations: "Star Trek: The Next Generation" and Gender*. University of Illinois Press, Urbana.

Tulloch, J. & Jenkins, H. (1995) *Science Fiction Audiences: Watching "Dr Who" and "Star Trek."* Routledge, London.

Worland, R. (1988) Captain Kirk, Cold Warrior. *Journal of Popular Film and Television* 16(3): 109–17.

popular religiosity

Manuel M. Marzal

Religion refers to a system of beliefs, rites, forms of organization, ethical norms, and feelings about the divine which help human beings to transcend and make sense of life. Popular religiosity is the equivalent of the religion of the common people, or popular piety, the way common people live their religion. It contrasts with official religiosity, which characterizes the specialists and the elites. There are several differences between these two kinds of religiosity (see Dupront 1987).

The first difference is that official religiosity considers the foundational hierophany, or manifestation of the sacred, to be very important. The more complex religious systems have specialists who analyze the contents of the original sacred mysteries and consider them as something to be preserved and protected. On the other hand, popular religiosity pays attention to ritual practices and how to obtain help from divine beings. For example, in Buddhism, specialists discuss Buddha's thoughts on nirvana and the value of religious silence to assure transcendence, while the common people take part in rites honoring Buddha in order to obtain favors in day-to-day life.

The second difference is that official religiosity is transmitted by the mechanisms of socialization within each religious institution, such as formal instruction or catechesis. Popular religiosity, on the other hand, is transmitted by cultural forms that are received in the process of socialization. The third difference is that while official religiosity contains the five elements mentioned above – beliefs, rites, forms of organization, ethical norms, and feelings about the divine – it does not give each the same value. Popular religiosity, especially in syncretic religions, adapts the inherited religious system to its own interests and cultural reality. It preserves some elements of the system and eliminates others. It reinterprets certain elements, adding new meanings or changing the original meaning. This process is different in different contexts, although there are some similarities. Thus there is no popular religiosity strictly speaking in denominations that practice some

form of excommunication for members who do not observe the established norms. Such is the case for Adventists, Mormons, and many confessions of North American evangelism. Finally, the relation between official and popular religion is marked by the complex history of a religious tradition.

Social sciences analyze popular religiosity in Buddhism, Islam, Catholicism, and other Christian denominations. The focus here, however, will be on Catholic popular religiosity, which has been studied extensively in recent decades and is very widespread. It is the religion of the majority in Latin America and of large sectors of Catholic Europe and its former colonies in Africa and Asia. It also exists in the United States with the increasing Hispanic immigration. Much of what is said about Catholic popular religiosity can be applied to the popular religiosity of other traditions.

Catholic popular religiosity is a complex social and religious fact which has been described rather more easily than it has been interpreted. Social scientists, depending on their different disciplines (anthropology, sociology, psychology, history, philosophy of religion), analyze this religiosity as "people speaking to God," in other words, as people communicating with a divine mystery that is beyond them. Theologians, however, analyze it as "God speaking to people," in other words, they consider popular religiosity to be an expression of Christian revelation. In attempting a definition, six key questions will be considered here. How should Catholic popular religiosity be defined? How do human societies function? What is the founding experience and what are the key concepts in the vocabulary of popular religiosity? What are the common traits? How is popular religiosity different from magical behavior? How does popular religiosity influence social and political change?

DEFINING CATHOLIC POPULAR RELIGIOSITY

The concept is not easy to define because, despite its apparent uniformity, there is a great diversity of popular religious forms, and also because a definition frequently involves a value judgment. Indeed, some consider popular religiosity to be an expression of true faith and proof of the strong roots of the Catholic Church in two regions that formed medieval Christendom and modern American Christendom, respectively (Brading 1991). Others see it as a refuge of ancient syncretism and modern religious alienation. However, many students of Catholic popular religiosity consider it to be the way that the great majority of people express themselves in order to give a sense of transcendence to their lives. This is the case in Latin America and the other areas mentioned above where the people define themselves as Catholics despite their very limited institutional formation. This results from the limited attention given by the church because of a shortage of clergy, while in other sectors of society it is due to the growing secularization of public life. It is a case of the great majority not seeking more religious attention and being content with "being religious in their own way."

There are three other characteristics in defining Catholic popular religiosity. Firstly, popular religiosity is a culture in the anthropological sense of the term. This means that it is a way of seeing life and constructing the world. Like any other culture, it is transmitted from generation to generation, but in this case transmission takes place not so much by catechesis as by a socialization process full of popular devotions.

Secondly, popular Catholicism forms different subcultures according to the social, economic, and historical framework of the human group experiencing it. These human groups include indigenous and African peoples, who retain characteristics of their ancestral cultures. Other such groups are small rural farmers and fringe populations of cities that resulted from recent rural-to-urban migration. There are also middle-class sectors and the bourgeoisie. From this it is obvious that such religiosity is not the prerogative of the poor, but of poorly catechized majorities. If the majority of these people are poor, it is because the majority of Latin Americans are poor; and the poor find in popular religiosity their own way to live their faith and to express their social solidarity.

Finally, popular Catholic religiosity, like any other religious system, is formed by a group of beliefs, rites, organizational forms, ethical norms, and feelings about the divine. Indeed,

popular Catholics believe in God, the saints, and demons. They go to church for baptism, first communion, funeral rites, and marriage. Matrimony is a cultural ideal even though many do not get married in church. People participate in the feasts of patron saints, the most common celebrations in the whole of Latin America. There are also massive pilgrimages to sanctuaries of Christ, the Virgin Mary, and the saints. Popular Catholics, as censuses reveal, are conscious of belonging to the church. They participate in associations and other traditional forms of religious organization. They usually respect priests and religious. In the majority of Latin American countries there is no anticlericalism, despite the church's importance in public life. Finally, popular Catholics have deeply religious feelings and accept Christian values in spite of the absence of doctrinal instruction.

POPULAR RELIGIOSITY AS A CULTURE

Anthropology has always asked three big questions about religion. How is religion born and how does it develop? What does religion do for society? What does religion mean for the believer? Anthropologists of religion have usually asked the first two questions because of their obsession with origins and because of the functional interest that developed after the failure of the study of origins. However, the third question is the most important and the one that has produced the most studies. Evans-Pritchard (1956) was the first to pose the question, later restated and answered by Geertz (1973) in a systematic form. For him religion works as a "perspective," i.e., as a way to see life and construct the world. There are different perspectives (commonsense, scientific, aesthetic, and religious), which are complementary and can be used simultaneously to study a single event. Each one studies a different aspect of reality.

Popular religiosity acts like a culture, not only because it transmits socialization and communicates subjective certainty about the majority religion in Latin America, but also because it generates in the popular Catholic states of mind and peculiar motivations, and because it offers an answer to the problem of the meaning of life. Indeed, such religiosity provides its followers with psychological strength to accompany them and motivation to guide them in what they do. These dispositions are deep, penetrating, and lasting. They give stability to popular experience and form what is usually called the religious feeling of the people. This feeling seems to be based on faith in a just, provident, and nearby God, and also in the saints who manifest themselves in difficult moments, in dreams or otherwise, to save the situation.

The religious feeling also seems to be based on the concept of the world as cosmos, where everything is wisely ordered by God, and on the necessity to worship with prayer, feasting, and so on. This religiosity provides its followers with an appropriate worldview. Such religiosity may seem to have little value because it gives an important place to certain rites, like the sacramentals or secondary religious symbols such as crosses, crucifixes, holy cards, statues, rosaries, holy water, and blessings, and to religious symbols which are marginal for the church, and also because it preserves residues of indigenous and African traditions that are somewhat incoherent. Its real importance lies not in its beliefs or rites but in the role that these play in helping to solve the problem of the meaning of life. With this popular Catholic worldview, many Latin Americans convert the daily threat of chaos – the unexplainable, the unendurable, and evil in general – into cosmos – the whole universe which is beautiful, ordered, predictable, friendly, understandable, God's masterpiece. Thus they develop a basic social personality that is more secure than that of higher social classes or of more developed countries that have lost the religious meaning of life.

FOUNDING EXPERIENCE AND KEY CONCEPTS

One of the principal elements of popular religiosity is the experience that founds it and that in some way orders all its beliefs, rites, organization, feelings, and ethical norms. Every religion and every spirituality within a religion starts from a manifestation of the sacred (hierophany),

which conditions it. Although popular Catholics, like other Catholics, admit the Bible, the sacraments, the healing of the Holy Spirit, and so on, they consider the saint, such as the visible image of Jesus, the Virgin Mary, or a saint from the Catholic calendar, to be their founding hierophany, and this image explains all their popular religious behavior. All over Latin America and especially in the lower economic sectors, people learn from their earliest childhood that the saints venerated in the local church, in their own houses, and in strategic places in the city or in the countryside are somehow alive. They listen to prayers directed to them, and are pleased by feasts and promises. They give blessings, perform miracles, and send punishments. Such early socialization usually has its concrete manifestation for each person in one particular saint to which that person is devoted. It might be the local patron saint or some other image of Christ or the Virgin Mary in the region he or she visits on a pilgrimage. Thus eight concepts – devotion, saint, miracle, blessing, punishment, promise, feast, and pilgrimage – make up the "generating words" of popular religious experience.

Devotion to the saint is a form of faith, not intellectual but trusting. It establishes a deep relationship between the saint and the person devoted to the saint. The person devoted to the saint is confident that the saint will always be there to help when needed. This relationship starts almost always for cultural reasons; for example, the saint has been venerated for many years in the family or the saint is the patron saint of the town. The relationship becomes more personal as the saint blesses or performs miracles for the devoted person. This devotion leads to familiar expressions such as "Mi Negrito" (Saint Martin de Porres) or "Mi Santa Rosita" (Saint Rose of Lima). This familiarity is made possible because the image is visible and the devoted person can and frequently does touch the image. But there is also an aura of respect because the saint belongs to the realm of the sacred and can punish.

How the devoted person sees the *saint* is a reinterpretation of what a saint is for in Catholic theology. In Catholic theology, saints are Christians who have died and have been canonized by the church because of their heroic virtues. Canonization is a long process, after which the saint can be honored publicly in the Catholic liturgy and considered to be an intercessor. He or she is also a model of good conduct. However, for the popular Catholic, the saints are visible representations (statues or paintings) of canonized saints, people who are not canonized, and people who probably never will be canonized. The saints also include representations of the Virgin Mary, Jesus Christ, and the cross of Jesus in their different avocations. Many popular Catholics venerate the saints, choosing them from the calendar to be intercessors with God, but they do not take them as models to imitate because they are unaware of their history. A survey conducted in different towns revealed that people were ignorant of the biographies of the saints represented in baroque panels before whom they prayed or placed flowers and candles. But that does not detract from the importance of the saint. Even though the saint does not provide a role model for conduct, he or she still acts as a myth and represents Christian virtues (help for the needy, goodness, closeness to God, kindness and compassion for those who are suffering). Thus the saint is an inspiration and motivation to live a good Christian life.

Many popular Catholics live in a world of *miracles* narrated in pious literature. The miracle is visibly represented in votive offerings in churches and shrines. The people devoted to the saint claim that the saint continues to perform miracles today. However, they are not referring to miracles in the strict theological sense of a wonder that can be explained not by science but only by the direct intervention of God. Miracles in the popular sense do not go beyond the laws of nature, only beyond the people's limited possibilities. The people are limited by their low level of formal education, poor medical and sanitary conditions, structural poverty, and lack of savings for emergencies. In such cases people approach the saint and ask for a miracle. For a person devoted to the saint, it is not so important to know the cause that produced the event considered miraculous. The people know that God governs through created things and through the free actions of other people. People give a religious interpretation to the events that occur, and that is where they find the action of the saint. This religious interpretation denies neither the commonsense

interpretation nor the scientific interpretation. It is an interpretation on another level of reality where God acts and uses natural forces and the free actions of others to obtain the desired results. Each miracle strengthens the faith of the devoted person and multiplies the possibility of further miracles.

Saints do not always perform miracles. Sometimes they give simple *blessings* which give security and peace to the devoted. In this there is another reinterpretation of Catholic theology. In Catholic theology a blessing is a sacramental, a sacred sign established by the church, somewhat like the sacraments established by Christ. To ask for a blessing is to implore divine help in different moments of life. Holy water is a sacramental that is very common in Latin America. For the secularized world, holy water borders on superstition. For popular Catholics, holy water is an easy way to get close to God and to be free from life's dangers. A blessing is a frequent religious resource which, when used, charges the religious images and other religious symbols with sacred energy. Although the blessing usually expresses faith in the providence of God and in the intercession of the saints, it is quite possible for it to degenerate into a manipulation of the sacred independently of personal faith.

Paradoxical as it may seem, *punishments* attributed to the saint increase the devotion of the people just as much as miracles and blessings. Through these punishments, the saint ceases to be a simple benefactor and becomes a demanding and jealous friend who does not like to be forgotten. These punishments are the reverse of miracles. If they are considered to be fair, a religious interpretation is given to the misfortune. Some social scientists think that punishments have their roots in pre-Hispanic religions whose gods demanded human sacrifices in some extreme cases, and also in colonial preaching that insisted on the punishments of God as described in the pages of the Old Testament (e.g., Genesis 19, Isaiah 26 and 40). Even though some popular Catholics have this Old Testament vision of misfortune, many say that they deserve it for their sins. Thus punishments reinforce the relationship between the saint and the people devoted to the saint, more than the "silence of God" in the secular world. In spite of the masochistic interpretation of punishments by scholars who reduce religion to its psychological aspects, the popular devoted person seems to prefer punishments because they prove that the saint is watching over them. They show the saint's concern just as much as miracles and messages in dreams.

A counterpart of devotion to the saints is found in *promises*. They may seem interesting because they are often associated with requesting favors. Thus many popular Catholics promise to wear a habit, make a pilgrimage to a shrine, fast, or make some other sacrifice if the saint grants them some favor. They may seem to be transferring to a religious world the social relationships of human societies. But such interpretations forget that the promises of devoted people do not always have a utilitarian motive. Many studies and surveys among different groups of popular Catholics attest to this. Promises express the sacred character of the commitment, something like religious vows in institutes of consecrated life. They are one of the most consistent forms of expressing devotion to the saint.

The most frequent form of expressing devotion to the saint is celebrating the saint's *feast* day. The patron saint's feast is an opportunity to venerate the saint, ask for the saint's intercession, and give thanks. But functional anthropology discovers other functions. The first is integration. The feast brings everybody together: the inhabitants of the town and the rural farmers who are relatively scattered outside the town. It also brings back those who were forced to leave the area to seek their fortune elsewhere. Dead ancestors, who are more alive in the popular mind than in more modern circles, are also part of the feast. They started the feast and kept it going during their lifetime. The second function is that of social prestige accorded to those who take care of the different tasks related to the feast. This prestige is present in the more traditional communities which maintain the "system of jobs" (a progression in which people ascend to jobs that are more costly and have more responsibility) in a way that redistributes power and riches. The jobs tend to impoverish the richest members of the community, because they pay the expenses out of their own pocket (the food is free for the people). This tends to create a more egalitarian society. In any case, if the jobs are assumed by

very rich people who spend a lot of money for the benefit of everyone, it legitimates economic differences in the town in the eyes of the poorest. The third function is that of collective relief from the harsh life of the town, an imaginary return to "the beginning of time" when everything was festive. All this happens in a world that seems to have preserved the genuine sense of what a feast is.

Quite similar to the feast is the *pilgrimage*. According to Eliade (1959), for a religious people time and space are not homogeneous. There are hierophantic moments and places. Feasts are based on sacred time, holy moments, the liturgical cycle that recalls the events of the history of salvation, or the cycle of the feasts of the saints that recalls the triumph of the saints over death. In a similar way, the pilgrimage is based on sacred space, holy places. All over Latin America there are sacred places where Jesus Christ, the Virgin Mary, and the saints have manifested themselves in different ways. This manifestation is then narrated in a legend or myth which becomes part of the oral tradition of the place. The structure of these myths is very similar: a critical situation, especially of a very poor person, then the miraculous intervention of the saint who comes to the rescue. Then the word gets around and people start coming to see the miraculous saint. Pilgrimages in Latin America have elements that are pre-Hispanic and others that are Spanish. Pre-Hispanic elements are taken from the developed cultures of Mexico and Peru and from other cultures in search of "the land without evil." Spanish elements include "the road to Saint James" to visit the tomb of the apostle who is said to have evangelized Spain and to be buried in Galicia, despite dying in Jerusalem. This pilgrimage is a sign of collective identity. In general, a pilgrimage is full of religious symbols, beginning with the long walk to a place that is difficult to access. This is a kind of exodus to get to a promised land. Then there are the other religious symbols such as springs to purify the soul and body, the multiplication of miracles, the wearing of habits, the promises that are being kept by making the pilgrimage, making the pilgrimage in the form of a procession, religious songs and dances, tears, and deep emotions. In addition to all this, like the feast, the pilgrimage is a focal point of social, political, and economic relations in the region where the shrine is located.

COMMON TRAITS IN CATHOLIC POPULAR RELIGIOSITY

Despite its great diversity of beliefs, rites, and organization, popular religiosity is fairly similar throughout Latin America. Hispanic immigrants to other places have brought their saints with them and have common traits that can be summarized as follows.

Sociological. Catholic popular religion is transmitted by the process of socialization more than by catechesis. It is part of Latin American culture. There are highly visible examples of such Catholicism, such as the devotion to Our Lady of Guadalupe in Mexico. This sociological character is a strong point of Latin American Catholicism and proof of the success of the first evangelization in an era when religion was a public rather than a private affair. Such Catholicism influences many Latin American cultural patterns in transition rites, feasts, and even in mentality, which can be observed in the way people talk.

Sacral. Popular Catholicism, especially in the lower classes, involves a vision of reality that is sacral, not secular like modern technical civilization. According to this sacral vision, the saints and other sacred beings are felt directly in the life and history of human beings. As a result of this way of seeing reality, many popular Catholics occasionally adopt a somewhat fatalistic attitude toward certain social problems and seem more interested in preserving a world they see as "cosmos" than in making "history."

Syncretic. Popular Catholicism often reinterprets official Catholicism, adding to or changing its meaning according to the experience of the people in its different subcultures. Adding to its meaning implies that popular Catholicism, besides its religious functions, has other functions in the sociological, psychological, economic, or political orders. This is observable in the patron saint's feast with its systems of jobs. Changing its meaning implies, especially for indigenous people, attributing to certain Catholic rites the meaning of their ancient beliefs. An example would be the way some rural farmers in the Andes and in Central America offer mass for the dead, not to "free" the dead from punishment for their sins but to "free themselves" from the return of the dead to bother the living ("leave us in peace" instead of "rest in peace"). Another way of changing the meaning of official Catholicism is to make it magic.

Emotive. Many popular Catholics have a deep religious lived experience even though they know little about the dogmas, rites, and norms of the church. Such experience is related to the religious practice of calling on God and the saints in extremely difficult situations. Its principal moments are the feast, the pilgrimage, and the life cycle of one's own family (birth, marriage, and death). In addition, the harsh economic conditions of many popular Catholics in Latin America often make religious beliefs and practices an emotional "sedative," instead of being a moment to question and adjust one's own attitudes.

Ritualist. Popular Catholicism gives much importance to rites, because religious socialization is carried out mainly through rites. This explains why the religious lived experience of popular Catholics is so rich in emotions and activities, and so poor in theological formulas; so rich in mythical content, and so poor in historical content. This ritualism in popular Catholicism can lead the less educated to see the rites as absolutes. This requires an effort to remove their magic element and ensure that the rites are seen as means and not ends. But this should not involve eliminating rites, as has been done in certain sectors of the church following secularist lines. No religion can exist without rites.

Mythic. Popular Catholicism contains myths about the origin and end of humanity and about different hierophanies, especially the apparition of patron saints and historical events that are rationalized in a religious way. In addition, there are certain popular Catholic rites, such as the "payment to the Pachamama" performed in August in the Andes of Southern Peru, Bolivia, Chile, and Argentina, which is a rite to thank Mother Earth for her harvests (*pacha* means "earth," *mama*, "mother," in the Quechua language). This ceremony is based on mythical knowledge and expresses a view of reality that is not so much scientific or historical as symbolic of the personal and cultural experience of the Andean farmers. However, when the true meaning of myth is lost, certain rites and beliefs can assume a false historical or scientific dimension.

POPULAR RELIGIOSITY AND MAGICAL BEHAVIOR

One characteristic of certain forms of popular Catholicism is its ability to change into magic or superstition. So far anthropology has not found definite criteria to distinguish magic from religion. But there have been some efforts in that direction, such as manipulation versus petition (Frazer 1959 [1922]), utilitarianism versus celebration (Malinowski 1954 [1948]), the individual context versus the communitarian context (Durkheim 1961 [1912]), and environmental control versus social control (Aberle 1966). These theories provide indicators that do not completely explain the magical or religious character of an event. But they line up on a continuum between a magic pole and a religious pole, and thus help to analyze the practices of popular Catholicism. According to these indicators, magic involves the following: practices to manipulate the sacred, practices that have only utilitarian objectives, practices that are conducted by a specialist who is marginal to the group, and practices that try to control certain moral or cosmic forces without any reference to personal behavior. On the other hand, religion involves the following: practices that express a petition to sacred powers, practices that are an end in themselves and are celebratory instead of being utilitarian, practices that are performed in union with the community, and practices that demand ethical behavior on the part of the people. But in analyzing a concrete phenomenon using these indicators, one cannot forget the symbolism of the events nor the analogy of their languages.

POPULAR RELIGIOSITY AND SOCIAL CHANGE

The social sciences have established several correlations between religious conduct and the socioeconomic category of social groups and have formulated some macro theories about the influence of religion in social change. For example, for Marx and Weber, religion could be a trap or a springboard for change. However, the relation between religion and social change so far has not been studied sufficiently. It is a question that has come into vogue since the fall of the regimes of Eastern Europe and the role that religion may have played in it.

As for popular religion, it seems to contain a certain political ambiguity. On the one hand, it appears apolitical because of its disincarnated spiritualism and because it maintains the status quo in its rites and beliefs, and without doubt the dominant groups have influenced its assimilation. Geertz (1973) observed that the religious perspective, which serves to resolve the problem of the meaning of life, can infiltrate and "color" other fields of human conduct. This is a result of religion being called to mind frequently. This seems to be the case for minority groups that offer a religious explanation for the socioeconomic differences in Latin America. But, on the other hand, popular Catholic religion has a real political dimension. This is because it helps people maintain their identity in transition rites and in the feasts of the patron saints. It also helps them preserve their own forms of organization, religious associations, brotherhoods, sisterhoods, and so on, as well as labor unions and spontaneous organizations founded by external and internal emigrants. They find strength in the election of a patron saint, without forgetting that the associations and brotherhoods and sisterhoods usually stand in opposition to the vertical structure of the church. Popular Catholicism cultivates in the people values of fraternal solidarity and equality of opportunities for all before God, in spite of the existence of structures of domination and marginalization in the Latin American world. Popular Catholicism has often been a source of mobilization and even of armed rebellion, as happened in the Cristero war in Mexico and other incidents in Latin America.

SEE ALSO: Buddhism; Catholicism; Christianity; Church; Denomination; Folk Hinduism; Islam; Magic; Myth; Primitive Religion; Religion; Religion, Sociology of; Religions, African; Rite/Ritual; Sacred; Secularization

REFERENCES AND SUGGESTED READINGS

Aberle, D. F. (1966) Religious-Magical Phenomena and Power, Prediction and Control. *Southwestern Journal of Anthropology* 22: 221–30.

Brading, D. A. (1991) *Orbe indiano: de la monarquía católica a la república criolla, 1492–1867.* Fondo de Cultura Económica, Mexico City.

Dupront, A. (1987) Religión popular. In: Poupard, P. (Ed.), *Diccionario de las religiones.* Herder, Barcelona.

Durkheim, É. (1961 [1912]) *The Elementary Forms of the Religious Life.* Collier, New York.

Eliade, M. (1959) *The Sacred and the Profane: The Nature of Religions.* Harcourt, New York.

Evans-Pritchard, E. E. (1956) *Nuer Religion.* Oxford University Press, Oxford.

Frazer, J. (1959 [1922]) *The New Golden Bough.* Ed. T. H. Gaster. Criterion, New York.

Geertz, C. (1973) *The Interpretation of Cultures.* Basic Books, New York.

Malinowski, B. (1954 [1948]) *Magic, Science, and Religion and Other Essays.* Doubleday Anchor, Garden City, NY.

Marzal, M. M. (2002) *Tierra encantada. Tratado de antropología religiosa de América Latina.* Trotta, Madrid, and Pontificia Universidad Católica del Perú, Lima.

Otto, R. (1958 [1917]) *The Idea of the Holy.* Trans. J. W. Harvey. Galaxy, New York.

population and development

Peter McDonald

While development can include a wide range of meanings, here development is taken to mean economic development defined to refer narrowly to economic growth, and then more broadly to the economic transformations leading to the emergence of modern economic institutions and practices and the disappearance of traditional forms. The processes of development are associated, both as cause and consequence, with population processes.

The relationship between population and economic development is highly contested and has been so for centuries. Adam Smith saw population growth as a stimulus to economic growth because it enlarged the size of the market and provided opportunities for economies of scale, and hence more efficient production. This was contested by Thomas Malthus and David Ricardo, who argued that there was a law of diminishing returns to scale. Their view was that population growth would eventually lead to natural resource constraints, especially a shortage of cultivable land. This would lead to inflation, unemployment, and absolute scarcity. The Malthusian conclusion was that population growth should be reduced through "moral restraint," a postponement of marriage that leads to a decrease in the birth rate. For a time, the preponderance of poverty-stricken landless agricultural laborers in Malthus's England in the 1830s and the Irish famine in the 1840s provided strength to the Malthusian argument, and the Irish married at much later ages following the famine. Subsequently, however, the advance of technology and the associated rise in human capital through education evidently changed the equation. On a global scale, according to Angus Maddison, gross production rose considerably faster than population and has continued to do so until today.

Concern about the negative effects of rapid population growth on economic development arose again in the postcolonial era. In 1958, Coale and Hoover argued that a reduction in fertility would reduce the number of children that a country needed to support while, at the same time, having little or no impact on the size of the labor force for the following two decades. This reduction in dependency would reduce consumption and increase savings and investment, and hence stimulate economic growth. In addition, greater emphasis could be placed on the education and development of each child so that the country's pool of human capital would be enhanced. An implicit assumption in the argument was that this country-level argument could also be applied at the level of the individual household. Fewer children in a family would mean a higher standard of living for the family – fewer mouths to feed. Families would come to have higher aspirations for each child and have greater opportunity to educate each child. This relatively simple argument took on great force because it was accepted by persons and organizations of considerable influence in both developed and developing countries. In 1967, 30 heads of government signed a *Statement on Population* that included the following assertions:

- Too rapid population growth seriously hampers efforts to raise living standards, to further education, to improve health and sanitation, to provide better housing and transportation, to forward cultural and recreational opportunities – and even in some countries to assure sufficient food.
- The population problem must be recognized as a principal element in long-range national planning if governments are to achieve their economic goals and fulfill the aspirations of their people.

The result was the funding and implementation of government family planning programs in many developing countries from the 1960s onwards. The economic rationale for this approach was challenged later in academic and policy circles, but these challenges did little to change the policy direction already established. Government family planning programs have contributed to dramatic decline in fertility rates in most developing countries: the projected population of the world in 2050 has fallen from around 16 billion as projected in 1960 to around 9 billion as projected in 2003.

At the beginning of the 1970s, in the writings of Paul Ehrlich and the Club of Rome, a more sophisticated Malthusian argument arose around the theme of "limits to growth." Population and economic growth were projected to lead to the depletion of the global supply of non-renewable resources, particularly oil and various minerals. This resources argument was associated with the argument that population and economic growth led to environmental degradation. Zero population growth (ZPG) was advocated as a solution along with a slowdown in economic growth. This was a message directed mainly at developed countries that, ironically, were beginning to experience declines in fertility to rates that were *below* zero growth of population in the longer term. Developing countries in the 1970s reacted to both the family planning approach and the

limits to growth approach by reemphasizing the importance of development and economic growth to their populations. Their view was encapsulated in the catch-cry from the 1974 World Population Conference: "development is the best contraceptive." This was an assertion that the causal direction was from development to fertility control, not the reverse.

Largely in reaction to the new Malthusian argument, several economists in the 1970s and 1980s, including Simon Kuznets and Julian Simon, reasserted the eighteenth-century view of Adam Smith that population growth stimulated economic growth. They argued that a growing population leads to increases in the supply of labor, preventing wage inflation and promoting mobility, productivity, and innovation. Notably, Ester Boserup argued that population growth provided a stimulus to technological progress through the innovative character of a young labor force, through increased competition in the labor force, and through economies of scale in technological research and development.

The pendulum swung again in the 1990s with the revitalization of the 1960s argument that a fall in fertility reduced dependency while having no impact on the size of the labor force. The ensuing fall in the "burden of dependency" was labeled as a demographic dividend or demographic bonus to the economy. Countries that still have relatively high fertility rates are invited to take advantage of the demographic dividend that awaits them if they reduce their fertility. Of course, countries are only able to take advantage of this dividend if their economies are able to expand to absorb the large cohorts of young workers who were born in the past period of high fertility. If this is not the case, the result is not a demographic dividend but high unemployment among young people and frustration of aspirations that can be politically explosive. Frustration of aspirations can also result in emigration of the country's best and brightest young people.

The environmental argument for reducing population growth has also reemerged in recent times. Of principal concern at the local level is land degradation. While the root cause may be poor regulation and planning policies, in the absence of environmental protections, rapid population growth is associated with deforestation, overcropping, use of marginal lands and watersheds for farming, and excessive fertilization and irrigation. These result in erosion, floods, subsidence, salinity, and desertification, leading potentially to deterioration of economic development in rural areas. Another major concern is the growth of megacities induced by migration from overpopulated rural areas. Where the growth of cities outpaces city planning, the ensuing congestion, poverty, and poor health consequences arising from inadequate sanitation and air pollution may slow the rate of economic development and channel funds into housing and away from other more productive capital investments.

As more empirical evidence has been examined on the relationship between population and economic development, conclusions have become increasingly indefinite. This is evidenced by the progression across three nationally commissioned reports from 1971 to 1995. The US National Academy of Sciences Report of 1971 concluded, in keeping with the conventional wisdom of the time, that, in general, rapid population growth had a negative impact on economic development. By the time of the 1986 Report of the US National Academy of Sciences, the conclusion was consistent with the 1971 Report but was couched in caveats that left the conclusion in heavy doubt. A report commissioned by the Australian government in 1994 was almost totally agnostic, concluding that population growth is likely to produce both positive and negative impacts on economic development and the size of the net effect cannot be determined from existing evidence.

As academic researchers have debated the population–development relationship, fertility rates have fallen almost everywhere and a major new debate has emerged. Many countries today, including all economically advanced countries, have fertility rates that are below the long-term level that replaces the population, many well below this level. The combination of longer life expectancy with very low fertility produces very rapid population aging. There is a concern about the future capacity of countries to support an aging population when labor supplies are projected to fall. For example, Peter McDonald and Rebecca Kippen have shown that, given current trends, Japan is facing a fall in the size of its labor force of around 20 million

workers over the next 40 years, while, at the same time, its population ages rapidly. Very low fertility increases old-age dependency, the reverse of the 1950s increase in child dependency. As old-age dependents are generally more expensive to the public purse than children, the current problem may be more serious.

Very low fertility also leads to a reversal of the notion of a demographic dividend arising from shifts in the age distribution of the population. If fertility has been higher in the recent past, the size and organization of the economy will have become contingent upon a growing labor supply of young workers in the period of the demographic dividend. If there is a sudden fall in the availability of young workers, as will be the case in many countries in the immediate future, considerable economic adjustment is required. It is possible that labor shortages will provide a stimulus to technological development and to higher productivity resulting from increases in capital per worker, as argued by Yutaka Kosai et al. However, it is also possible that the high wages of young people in labor-scarce economies will induce capital to move to lower-wage economies. This is feasible given that today's technology is owned by firms rather than by countries, and is highly transportable. At the same time, emerging economies today have an abundant supply of highly skilled young workers. In a future world in which financial capital, human capital, and technology are all highly mobile and skilled human capital is the vital resource, the outcomes for specific countries are unpredictable. Nevertheless, it can be concluded that the extent of economic adjustment required is reduced where there are smooth transitions in age structure. From this perspective, the boom–bust effects of very low fertility on age structure are an undesirable population feature. This opinion is widely shared; every country in the world with a fertility rate lower than 1.5 births per woman reported to the United Nations in both 1997 and 2003 that it considered its fertility rate to be "too low."

SEE ALSO: Demographic Techniques; Economic Development; Fertility: Low; Fertility and Public Policy; Malthus, Thomas Robert; Population and Economy; Population and the Environment; Population Projections and Estimates

REFERENCES AND SUGGESTED READINGS

Ahlburg, D., Kelley, A., & Mason, K. (Eds.) (1996) *The Impact of Population Growth and Well-Being in Developing Countries*. Springer-Verlag, Berlin (based on a report to the Australian government in 1994).

Boserup, E. (1981) *Population and Technological Change: A Study of Long-Term Trends*. University of Chicago Press, Chicago.

Coale, A. & Hoover, E. (1958) *Population Growth and Economic Development in Low-Income Countries*. Princeton University Press, Princeton.

Kuznets, S. (1979) *Growth, Population, and Income Distribution*. Norton, New York.

McDonald, P. & Kippen, R. (2001) Labor Supply Prospects in 16 Developed Countries, 2000–2050. *Population and Development Review* 27(1): 1–32.

Maddison, A. (2001) *The World Economy: A Millennium Perspective*. OECD, Paris.

Population Council (1967) *Statement on Population from World Leaders*. Population Council, New York.

Simon, J. (1990) *Population Matters: People, Resources, Environment, and Immigration*. Transaction, New Brunswick, NJ.

population and economy

Edward M. Crenshaw

From the inception of the social sciences, population variables have been recognized as crucial determinants of economic development and organization. From the start, two competing schools of thought vied for predominance, one a pessimistic view of population's role in economic change derived from Thomas Malthus, the other a far more optimistic view of population as the wellspring of prosperity.

Neo-Malthusianism came to dominate the social sciences after World War II. Derived from Malthus's dictum that increases in agricultural surplus are outstripped by geometric population growth, many social scientists became convinced that demographic growth and economic growth are antithetical processes. Coale and Hoover (1958), for instance, theorized that rapid population increase forces the consumption of savings, adversely affecting both capital formation and investment rates. High youth dependency ratios force nations to divert scarce capital to activities with few *immediate* economic multipliers (e.g., education), thereby underinvesting in the existing labor force. Such theorizing led quite naturally to the view that rapid population growth and dense habitation cause habitual poverty.

Ironically, this pessimism stood in sharp contrast to the pronatalism of western philosophy (e.g., Cicero, Machiavelli), an optimism reflected in the theories of several founders of the social sciences (e.g., Smith, Spencer, Durkheim). In classical models, increasing population size and density encourage economic complexity, a dynamic Smith and Spencer attributed to market opportunities and Durkheim to competition. As individuals and groups vie for resources in crowded environments, they innovate and specialize to realize new markets, thereby reducing competition. These processes lead to a more complex division of labor – the sine qua non of economic change. For these population optimists, organizational specialization and technological innovation are emergent properties springing from population pressures.

Since the mid-1980s, this optimism has made gradual inroads into neo-Malthusian intellectual terrain. Owing to the ambiguity of empirical research on the relationship between population growth and economic growth, as well as to a few contemporary (lone-wolf) optimists (e.g., Julian Simon), the pessimism of the "population bomb" era (i.e., the 1960s through 1980s) has gradually been replaced with a more balanced view of population's role in economic change.

This new demography of development has focused primarily on the influence of age structure on economic development. In a nutshell, population growth does affect economic growth, but this effect differs depending on the age segment that is growing. As dominant economic actors, working adults compete for jobs, specialize to avoid competition, start enterprises, and consume the lion's share of products and services. Growth in the adult working population therefore boosts economic growth. Conversely, rapid growth in the population of children or the elderly has far fewer immediate multipliers and some substantial costs (e.g., education, medical care) (Bloom & Freeman 1988). Put bluntly, working-age adults are an immediate economic asset, whereas children are necessary investments in the future and older people constitute (inevitable) overhead.

These countervailing effects of age structure create demographic windfalls and ratchets (Crenshaw et al. 1997). Demographic transitions are characterized by rapid adult population growth unmatched by growth in the child and elderly populations. Demographic transition is therefore a unique situation, providing a society with a demographic windfall – a generation-long increase in economic activity driven by labor force expansion that is unhindered by population growth in other age segments. In time, of course, and all else constant (e.g., immigration), these relatively childless cohorts retire and place heavy demands on the greatly diminished labor force left in their wake. Yet, as Easterlin (1968) notes, undermanned labor markets boost wages and provide opportunities that could translate into earlier marriage and increased fertility. If so, a demographic ratchet results – rapid economic growth during baby busts followed by slower growth during subsequent periods of higher fertility. On the other hand, should a shrinking domestic labor force not translate into higher fertility (via the overabundance of immigrant labor or the burden of a rapidly aging population), population contraction and social decline are likely.

Health has also been linked to economic growth. As Bloom and Canning (2000) note, longevity is related to lower rates of morbidity and thus higher economic productivity. Moreover, longevity promotes higher investment in human capital, greater savings for retirement, and the demographic windfall described above (i.e., lower mortality encourages lower fertility). While the link between health and economic growth is plausible, more empirical work is required to differentiate this effect, typically represented by life expectancy, from the overall effect of falling fertility (given that the two are strongly correlated via infant mortality).

Population density also affects economic development. Urbanization has garnered by far the most attention in this area. Although disagreements continue about the appropriate balance between urbanization and economic activity (Henderson 2003), there is broad agreement that the level of urbanization and economic development are positively correlated because the concentration of labor, firms, and consumers allows efficiencies of scale and distance (Kasarda & Crenshaw 1991). Nonetheless, negative externalities associated with rapid urbanization such as pollution, crime, and poverty are also well represented in the literature (Brockerhoff & Brennan 1998). Whether we view urbanization as boon or bane may depend on our theoretical assumptions. For instance, the common view that urban economies are strained by unprecedented immigration encourages a negative evaluation of rapid urbanization. On the other hand, if density is *required* for economic growth, we might conclude that rapid urbanization (with attendant social problems) is just the necessary first phase in building the type of agglomerations required by the global economy, and this phase will be particularly painful for poor, sparsely populated countries experiencing rapid rural population growth (Crenshaw & Oakey 1998).

Following classical theorists, the broader population density of countries may be viewed as a telltale indicator of historic differences in social and physical environments (i.e., climates, disease regimes), differences that influence a nation's struggle to modernization (Crenshaw & Oakey 1998; Burkett et al. 1999). Protomodern societies, for instance, are countries where historical population pressures forced advanced agrarianism and institution building (e.g., political development), thereby easing today's transit into "developed" status. That is, population-induced multicrop plow agriculture produced sufficient economic surplus for urbanization, written language, monied economies, complex divisions of labor in the economy and government, and many other hallmarks of "advanced" societies (Lenski & Nolan 1984). Because of this institutional homophily with already developed societies, historically dense societies are thought to transit into modernity more rapidly.

Ascribed status (e.g., ethnicity, race) is also an integral (if controversial) part of the new demography of development. Recent research emphasizes the economic benefits of ethnicity-based social capital. Ascribed statuses provide axes of organization such as phenotypic markers, tight social interdependencies, and common cultural understandings which create effective social order and control (Hechter 1987: 176). Nonetheless, economic miracles dependent on such "bounded solidarity" have a darker side that involves "outgrouping," delayed diffusion of information and technology, and even interethnic violence, none of which optimizes economic activity. In theoretical terms, sociocultural diversity may truncate social interactions and stymie economic interdependence, impeding cross-cultural social ties and complicating the development of property law and public policy in general (Easterly & Levine 1997).

This brief overview of population's influence on economic change highlights the need for more precise theory. The influences of population age structure, health, density, and composition on economic behavior, organization, and change are possibly non-linear, conjunctural, and sometimes path dependent, but understanding them holds out the hope for a more complete understanding of demography's role in social change. The principal contribution of the current literature is to remind us that *people* create and distribute wealth, and so the macro- and microstructures of population will always be pertinent for economic sociology.

SEE ALSO: Age, Period, and Cohort Effects; Demographic Transition Theory; Development: Political Economy; Durkheim, Émile and Social Change; Economic Development; Income Inequality, Global; Industrial Revolution; Malthus, Thomas Robert; Population and Development; Spencer, Herbert

REFERENCES AND SUGGESTED READINGS

Bloom, D. E. & Canning, D. (2000) The Health and Wealth of Nations. *Science* 287: 1207–9.

Bloom, D. E. & Freeman, R. B. (1988) Economic Development and the Timing and Components of Population Growth. *Journal of Policy Modeling* 10: 57–81.

Brockerhoff, M. & Brennan, E. (1998) The Poverty of Cities in Developing Regions. *Population and Development Review* 24: 75–114.

Burkett, J. P., Humblet, C., & Putterman, L. (1999) Preindustrial and Postwar Economic Development: Is There a Link? *Economic Development and Cultural Change* 47: 471–95.

Coale, A. J. & Hoover, E. M. (1958) *Population Growth and Economic Development in Low-Income Countries.* Princeton University Press, Princeton.

Crenshaw, E. M. & Oakey, D. R. (1998) Jump-Starting Development: Hyper-Urbanization as a Long-Term Economic Investment. *Sociological Focus* 31: 321–40.

Crenshaw, E. M., Ameen, A., & Christenson, M. (1997) Population Dynamics and Economic Development: The Differential Effects of Age-Specific Population Growth Rates on Per Capita Economic Growth in Developing Countries, 1965 to 1990. *American Sociological Review* 62: 974–84.

Easterlin, R. A. (1968) *Population, Labor Force, and Long Swings in Economic Growth: The American Experience.* National Bureau of Economic Research, New York.

Easterly, W. & Levine, R. (1997) Africa's Growth Tragedy: Policies and Ethnic Divisions. *Quarterly Journal of Economics* 112: 1203–50.

Hechter, M. (1987) *Principles of Social Solidarity.* University of California Press, Berkeley.

Henderson, V. (2003) The Urbanization Process and Economic Growth: The So-What Question. *Journal of Economic Growth* 8: 47–71.

Kasarda, J. D. & Crenshaw, E. M. (1991) Third World Urbanization: Dimensions, Theories, and Determinants. *Annual Review of Sociology* 17: 467–501.

Lenski, G. & Nolan, P. (1984) Trajectories of Development: A Test of Ecological Evolutionary Theory. *Social Forces* 63: 1–23.

population and the environment

Sara R. Curran

The relationship between population and environment is a topic that has garnered attention from many disciplines, including sociology, economics, ecology, history, anthropology, demography, and geography. An early and important essay, which continues to serve as an intellectual starting point for characterizing the population and environment relationship, is T. R. Malthus's "First Essay on Population" (1798). In it, Malthus draws a direct link between population and environment, stressing that the growth of human population tends to outstrip the productive capabilities of land resources. However,

Malthus also argues that growth rates will change in response to reduced natural resource quality and quantity. *Malthusian theory* predicts that changes in population growth occur because famine increases mortality or decreases fecundity or social behavior shifts to decrease family sizes, through delayed marriage, non-marriage, or reduced fertility. Although this framework has undergone significant challenges, it remains one of the central paradigms within the field.

For most scholars, the population and environment relationship is a dynamic one with assumed reciprocity, which is affected by the quality, amount, and regenerative or resilient capacity of the environmental resource at stake. Environmental change can induce population change and population change can also induce environmental change, but some environmental resources, once depleted, may be irreparably transformed and unable to return to their original character, quality, or quantity. Empirically disentangling results to account for reciprocal causation is one of the key methodological dilemmas in the field.

Within sociology, population and environment research has focused upon the social institutions (e.g., families or households, social movements, governance structures, markets) and social processes (industrialization, development, innovation, or globalization) which mediate population and environment relationships (e.g., famine, deforestation, land use and land cover change, environmental values, environmental refugees, environmental racism, air pollution, and climate change). Research sites have varied from micro-level analyses of individual and household behavior in both developed and less developed settings to macro-level, longitudinal, and cross-national comparisons.

Population as a concept and variable is understood and measured in different ways, depending on the level of analysis and the research question. For cross-national studies (as well as cross-community-level studies), measures have included population size, population density, population growth rates, fertility rates, dependency ratios, and rates of immigration or emigration. For household-level or individual-level studies of population and environment, measures of population have included household size, number of children, dependency ratios,

contraceptive prevalence, and migration experience. In fairly equal measure, there have been studies that examine how these population characteristics are predictors of environmental outcomes and studies that have used environmental conditions to predict population outcomes.

Environment as a concept and variable has also been measured and understood in many different ways by population and environment scholars. Environmental resource quality and quantity measures include forest area, rates of deforestation, air quality, water quality and quantity, emission rates of air and water pollutants, biodiversity, the quality and quantity of agricultural land, productivity of agricultural, fisheries, and forestry resources, and landfill or toxic waste sites. Other proxy measures include observing the amount and rate of consumption of resources, such as energy, hydrocarbons, fresh water, and land for human activity (e.g., industrial, urban, and suburban sprawl). The focus on the consumption of these particular resources derives from the concern that some natural resources are renewable and others non-renewable. Non-renewable resources such as coal and oil reserves, land, water, or species are not easily replenished. Thus, patterns of consumption of non-renewable resources are viewed as particularly troubling for the future well-being of humans or the earth's resources.

One of the main challenges for scholars and policymakers is that environmental resources are frequently characterized as *common pool resources*. Common pool resources are bundles of goods that are defined by the following characteristics: (1) exclusion of beneficiaries through physical and institutional means is especially costly and (2) exploitation by one user reduces resource availability for others. These two characterizations are typically summarized as the problems of exclusion and subtractability, respectively. Population and environment relationships that pertain to common pool resources challenge scientists and policy because it is difficult to precisely pinpoint the linkage between human activity and environmental outcomes. Theoretical predictions about the relationship between human behavior and environmental resources in a common pool resource context present methodological challenges for study design, sampling, and measurement. One of the most productive areas of research on population and environment has focused upon land use and land cover change because of the easily bounded character of land resources, allowing scholars to overcome some of the methodological challenges presented by other types of common pool resources.

Along with Malthus's relatively pessimistic account of humans' relationship to food resources, Garrett Hardin (1968), in his classic essay on the tragedy of the commons, also identifies the inability of human nature, at the individual level, to restrain consumption of common pool resources at the expense of the common good. Hardin's essay followed upon Rachel Carson's profoundly galvanizing book, *Silent Spring* (2002 [1962]), capturing the mood of the time to fuel a scientific and social movement that would argue for limiting population growth, provide greater understanding of the intricacies and delicacies of the biotic world (including human interactions), and lobby for substantial government regulation of social and economic behavior in the interests of the environment.

Approaches that continue to derive significantly from the Malthusian paradigm have invested in the concept of *carrying capacity*, which has spawned research modeling and projecting how many people can be supported on a given amount and quality of ecological resource (e.g., agricultural land or fresh water). This research has incorporated a variety of conditions (or mediating variables) within its models (e.g., governance, distribution, population age structure, wealth, consumption) to simulate a variety of scenarios (see Cohen 1995; Lutz et al. 2002 for recent examples). A related line of research proposes that understanding the impact of population on the environment requires a multiplicative perspective that identifies an interaction between population, affluence, and technology. Frequently referred to as the I = PAT or *IPAT model*, it has been extensively evaluated (see Dietz & Rosa 1997 for an early attempt to estimate this model; York & Rosa 2003; York et al. 2003, 2004). The underlying assumption of these models is that the impact of population size or growth upon the environment is dependent on how many resources per person are consumed or used, which is a function of wealth and technology.

Alternative approaches emphasize mediating conditions and the reciprocal and dynamic character of the relationship between population and environment. Importantly, some argue that innovation, whether behavioral, institutional, or technological, mediates the population and environment relationship, sometimes reversing the negative impact of population size on environmental resources. Kingsley Davis's (1963) *multiphasic response theory* proposes that a population can respond in a number of ways to reduce the resource pressures induced by population size and resource constraints (e.g., by migrating out of resource-limited regions to resource-rich destinations or by reducing fertility). Empirical evidence supporting this claim has been found in a variety of agrarian settings, including Africa and Latin America. Other, alternative approaches employ political economy, dependency theory, or systems theory to propose institutional factors that either mediate the relationship between population and environment or structure both population and environment outcomes. These institutional factors might include modes of migrant incorporation, laws regulating the movement of people, international relations, trade imbalances, internal governance, and the formation of values and preferences, for example.

The wealth of competing and complementary theoretical models in the field of population and environment has spawned significant empirical work that has examined micro-level patterns, as well as macro-level, cross-national comparisons. Technological innovations, especially the application of geographical information systems to link social and physical data, have yielded intense, information-rich investigations of a number of sites from around the world. Because much of these data include historical or longitudinal information, scientists are now able to simultaneously elaborate the more nuanced aspects of both population dynamics and ecological systems. For population scientists this means going beyond simple measures of population size and growth.

Recent research that draws upon evidence derived from long-term studies or geo-referenced data using sophisticated analytic techniques in the field of population and environment has yielded particularly fruitful endeavors that have begun to uncover the relationship between population and climate change, particularly CO_2 emissions, population and energy consumption, and population, environment, and health. Findings from much of this research suggest that it is not so much population size that affects the environment as the growth in the number of households. The physical size of households and the location of residences relative to workplaces appear to have a greater impact on the environment than the number of people. In addition, several research initiatives have yielded insights on distributive concerns that emphasize the reverse relationship, such as environmental refugees (migrants fleeing environmental deterioration) and environmental racism (the siting of toxic or hazardous sites near minority residences). Studies of famine have also produced insights on the population and environment relationship, frequently revealing the political, economic, and social institutions that mediate the relationship. Land use and land cover change studies have also been a productive source of research in the field. Since 1994, this field of research has received significant investment from a number of national funding sources and is likely to lead to improvements in our knowledge base during the first two decades of the twenty-first century.

Future research in the field of population and environment will begin to tackle other elements of the environmental equation, including biodiversity, air pollution, and water quantity and quality. Also, increasing interest is being paid to how health and epidemiology link population and environment, from food security concerns to disease vectors. In addition, urban environments have recently received some scrutiny with regards to how they can concentrate ill effects on people and the environment and how they can ameliorate a negative relationship between population and environment. Finally, recent work in ecology has begun to elaborate upon the resilience of ecosystems and the valuation and maintenance of ecosystem services, foci that draw closer connections to the human interface and the population and environment research of social scientists.

SEE ALSO: Consumption, Green/Sustainable; Davis, Kingsley; Demographic Techniques: Population Projections and Estimates; Demographic Techniques: Population Pyramids and Age/Sex Structure; Demographic Transition Theory; Ecology and Economy; Households; Hyperconsumption/Overconsumption; Lifestyle Consumption; Malthus, Thomas Robert; Migration: Internal; Migration: International; Nature; Population and Development

REFERENCES AND SUGGESTED READINGS

Carson, R. (2002 [1962]) *Silent Spring.* Houghton Mifflin, New York.

Cohen, J. (1995) *How Many People Can the Earth Support?* Norton, New York.

Davis, K. (1963) The Theory of Change and Response in Modern Demographic History. *Population Index* 29(4): 345–56.

Dietz, T. & Rosa, E. A. (1997) Effects of Population and Affluence on CO_2 Emissions. *Proceedings of the National Academy of Science* 94: 175–9.

Hardin, G. (1968) Tragedy of the Commons. *Science* 162: 1243.

Lutz, W., Prezkawetz, A., & Sanderson, W. (Eds.) (2002) *Population and Environment: Methods of Analysis.* Supplement to *Population and Development Review* 28 (2002). Population Council, New York.

Malthus, T. R. (1960) *On Population (First Essay on Population, 1798, and Second Essay on Population, 1803).* Modern Library and Random House, New York.

Meadows, D., Randers, J., & Meadows, D. (2004) *Limits to Growth: The 30-Year Update.* Chelsea Green Publishing, White River Junction, VT.

York, R. & Rosa, E. A. (2003) Key Challenges to Ecological Modernization Theory: Institutional Efficacy, Case Study Evidence, Units of Analysis, and the Pace of Eco-Efficiency. *Organization and Environment* 16(3): 273–88.

York, R., Rosa, E. A., & Dietz, T. (2003) A Rift in Modernity? Assessing the Anthropogenic Sources of Global Climate Change with the STIRPAT Model. *International Journal of Sociology and Social Policy* 23(10): 31–51.

York, R., Rosa, E. A., & Dietz, T. (2004) STIRPAT, IPAT, and ImPACT: Analytic Tools for Unpacking the Driving Forces of Environmental Impacts. *Ecological Economics.*

population and gender

Sunita Kishor

Gender represents the different roles, rights, and obligations that culture and society attach to individuals according to whether they are born with male or female sex characteristics. Gender is often described as being socially constructed since gender-specific roles, rights, and obligations, with the exception of giving birth and breastfeeding, are ascribed, not biological, correlates of the sex of an individual. Gender is not just a characteristic of individuals, however; it is fundamental to the organization of societal institutions, including families, communities, laws, religion, and labor markets. While the specific manifestations of gender vary by culture, class, and, for individuals, life cycle stage, the common dimensions of gender critical for understanding the why and how of the gender–population link include the following:

• Gender is not "value" neutral. Although the roles that males and females are assigned are both valued, male roles and rights are valued more highly than female roles and rights socially, culturally, economically, and often, legally. In some societies this translates into a greater value being placed on the health and survival of males than of females. Examples of population indicators that are affected by gender-driven differences in the perceived worth of males and females include population sex ratios and sex ratios at birth, infant and child mortality by sex, maternal mortality, sex preferences for children, age at marriage, and contraceptive choice.
• Gender involves differences in power, both *"power to"* and *"power over."* "Power to" encompasses legal and informal rights and the ability to access household and societal resources and act in ways that help in the pursuit of knowledge and personal goals. "Power over" speaks to issues of control, including control of household and societal resources and decisions, cultural and religious ideology, and one's own and others' bodies. In general, men have greater power than women in most domains, and in some domains even have power over *women*. In recognition of this dimension of gender, demographers use indicators of women's relative empowerment or disempowerment to study the relationship between gender and demographic outcomes at household and societal levels. Gender-driven

differences in power have consequences for the basic building blocks of any population, namely fertility, mortality, and migration, as well as for the quality of life of the population, including its health, ability to meet its aspirations, and freedom from all forms of violence.
• Gender is not static or immutable; being socially constructed, gender roles, rights, and expectations change as societal needs, opportunities, and mores change. Changing gender norms affect and are affected by changes in population – its mobility, growth rate, and composition.

Together and individually, these dimensions of gender dynamically affect and are affected by the overall size, composition, distribution, and quality of life of populations.

Two fundamental determinants of a population are its fertility and mortality rates. Fertility is affected by age at marriage of women, since, in most societies, this marks the initiation of sexual activity for women, family size and composition desires, and knowledge of, access to, and use of contraception. Gender norms that value women mainly in the role of mothers and men in the role of providers, value sons more than daughters, and emphasize women's dependence on men encourage high fertility. Under such gender regimes, parents have little to gain from educating daughters and delaying their marriage, and both women and men, though for different reasons, have few incentives to limit their number of children. For men, the non-substitutability of gender roles ensures that most of the non-economic costs of rearing and not just of bearing children are largely borne by women; for women, children are a major source of status and sons, additionally, are a form of insurance. Moreover, with limited education and exposure, women are unlikely to have the knowledge, the means, or the authority to control their own fertility. Many institutions also reinforce such gender regimes and provide an indirect support to high fertility. These include polygamy, marriage payments such as dowry (which reflects and perpetuates the devaluation of women), and bride-price (which perpetuates the commodification of women's productive and reproductive capacities), laws that require a husband's permission for fertility-related medical decisions, and the social and legal condoning of gender-based violence against women, particularly by husbands. Women's limited economic and social power implies that even the potential for violence or polygamy can act as implicit controls on women's sexuality and behavior.

Alternative gender regimes that permit greater flexibility in gender roles, provide support to women for non-maternal roles, and allow men to share in childrearing are often associated with low fertility. Since changes in gender norms can precede, result from, or accompany other economic and societal changes, the direction of causality for the fertility–gender association need not be the same across time or country.

Gender affects mortality by modifying biologically determined sex differences in mortality in many different ways. A vast literature attests to the importance of gender preferences for the sex-specific survival rates of children. For example, strong son preference underlies the higher rates of female than male child mortality in India. In addition, the advent and easy availability of low-cost technologies that can distinguish the sex of a fetus early in pregnancy permit couples to meet their family size and sex composition goals through sex-selective abortions. The use of sex-selective abortion to eliminate female fetuses is reflected in sex ratios at birth that are much higher than the expected 103 to 106 males per 100 females observed in most populations. Gender also plays a role at other times in the life cycle. Gender regimes that encourage very early ages at marriage contribute to higher mortality rates, since both maternal and infant mortality rates bear a U-shaped relationship with maternal age. Maternal mortality is also higher where women's access to proper nutrition, effective means to space births, and timely and appropriate antenatal, delivery, and postnatal care are limited. While poverty severely curtails the overall availability of resources, the amount that societies and households invest in keeping women and girls alive is reflective of the roles, rights, and perceived worth of women.

Gender roles and expectations also affect men's health and mortality, particularly because the social construction of "manhood" is often consistent with male risk-taking and violence.

For example, fighting in wars, going down into mine shafts, or engaging in other high-risk occupations has traditionally been the role of men. In fact, the gendered expectation of much greater risk-taking by males than females, particularly when young, is codified in the higher auto insurance rates for young men than for women of the same age in the United States.

Epidemics of different diseases can also have longlasting effects on the size and composition of a population. Whether men or women are more likely to survive a given epidemic depends not just on the availability of appropriate health care and the sex-specific susceptibility to the disease, but also on gender: gender can affect both who gets sick and who can access available health care. A case in point is the Human Immunovirus/Acquired Immune Deficiency Syndrome (HIV/AIDS) epidemic that has sharply increased mortality rates in affected countries. Gender plays a central role in both the heterosexual spread and the containment of HIV infection. Physiologically, women are more vulnerable to HIV than men, and the disease transfers more easily from men to women than the other way around. Women's greater vulnerability is further enhanced by the expectation that women, particularly wives, should be subservient to the sexual needs of their husband; that men will and can have multiple sexual partners; and the widespread acceptance of very young women being married to much older, sexually experienced men, including men with multiple wives. Gender-based violence, including physical and sexual abuse, and practices such as female genital cutting contribute to and reinforce the control of female sexuality by males, while also directly increasing women's risk of acquiring the infection. Further, women's limited access to knowledge and resources, the understanding that women's social status stems largely from their roles as wives and mothers, their economic dependence on men, and the acceptance of norms that support the use of violence by men against women all combine to reduce the likelihood that women will seek counseling or testing for HIV infection, leave a partner who is infected, insist on condom use, or be in a position to protect themselves effectively against infection in other ways. The much higher rate of HIV infection among women than men in high epidemic countries, particularly at younger ages, attests to the cogency of both sex and gender in the epidemiology of HIV/AIDS.

Gender affects migration as it does fertility and mortality. At the household level, the need to migrate as well as migration decisions, including who should leave and what the destination should be, are all gendered. The gender context of the living conditions, as well as the availability of jobs and occupational sex segregation, in both the sending and the receiving areas also affect who migrates. In keeping with their traditional gender roles, women can be the ones less likely to migrate (since they are seen as better able to care for children and the elderly) or more likely to migrate (if the demand for receiving areas is for jobs seen as more suited to women, such as domestic help or nursing). Similarly, men more often than women are the ones who migrate for purposes such as professional jobs, the military, or education. More recently export-oriented industries in several developing countries have created a demand for female labor. This has led to women's migration and entry into what might appear at first glance to be non-traditional female jobs. However, this sex-specific demand is itself driven by a gendered understanding of female labor as being more docile and undemanding, patient with work that can be very repetitive and tedious, and generally cheaper than male labor. The sex composition of voluntary migratory streams has been changing with changing gender roles, the increasing importance of education, delays in marriage and childbearing, the gradual whittling down of occupational barriers, equal-pay-for-equal-work movements, and the raising of the glass ceiling for women. The sex composition of involuntary migration has traditionally tended to include more women than men. For example, the gendered traditions of female exogamy and patrilocal residence give women little choice but to move at the time of marriage from their paternal homes to those of their husbands, and trafficking of women for the sex trade appears to be increasing over time.

With the 1994 landmark United Nations International Conference on Population and Development (ICPD), gender gained explicit recognition as an essential ingredient of national-level population and development policies. In particular, the conference brought reproductive rights to the forefront of population policy and emphasized that the elimination of gender inequities in education and employment and all forms of violence against women would contribute to, not detract from, the twin goals of sustainable population growth and development, while also improving human rights. Despite the fact that most of the world's countries were signatories to this and related agreements, progress toward the agreed-upon goals of enhancing reproductive rights and gender equity has remained slow and inconsistent.

SEE ALSO: Differential Treatment of Children by Sex; Family, Men's Involvement in; Gender, Development and; Gender, Health, and Mortality; Gender Ideology and Gender Role Ideology; Gender, Work, and Family; Infant, Child, and Maternal Health and Mortality

REFERENCES AND SUGGESTED READINGS

Chant, S. (1992) *Gender and Migration in Developing Countries*. Belhaven Press, London.

Dixon-Mueller, R. (1993) *Population Policy and Women's Rights: Transforming Reproductive Choice*. Praeger, Westport, CT.

Jejeebhoy, S. J. (1995) *Women's Education, Autonomy, and Reproductive Behavior: Experience for Developing Countries*. Clarendon Press, Oxford and East-West Center, Honolulu.

Kabeer, N. (1994) *Reversed Realities: Gender Hierarchies in Development Thought*. Verso, London.

McDonald, P. (2000) Gender Equity in Theories of Fertility Transition. *Population and Development Review* 26(3): 427–39.

Mason, K. O. (1997) Gender and Demographic Change: What Do We Know? In: Jones, G. W., Douglas, R. M., Caldwell, J. C., & D'Sousa, R. M. (Eds.), *The Continuing Demographic Transition*. Clarendon Press, Oxford.

Presser, H. B. & Sen, G. (Eds.) (2000) *Women's Empowerment and Demographic Processes*. Oxford University Press, New York.

Riley, N. E. (1997) Gender, Power, and Population Change. *Population Bulletin* 52(1). Population Reference Bureau, Washington, DC.

Sen, G., Germaine, A., & Chen, L. (Eds.) (1994) *Population Policies Reconsidered: Health, Empowerment, and Rights*. Harvard University Press, Cambridge, MA.

World Bank (2001) *Engendering Development Through Gender Equality in Rights, Resources, and Voice.* World Bank and Oxford University Press, Washington, DC.

populism

Myriam Brito

In general terms, the concept of populism aims to describe sociopolitical movements, forms of government, political regimes, and/or ideological formulae that focus around the idea of the *people*, understood as a "virtuous" social ensemble that carries values that are considered to be "superior." Populism is also characterized by the action of charismatic leaders, the use of a rhetoric discourse, a particular relationship between the leaders and the social groups that give them support, and different types of social mobilizations. Populism is nevertheless a problematic concept for both political science and political sociology since this notion has been used and is still used to describe a multiplicity of phenomena that have important differences.

The word populism was initially used to refer to the movement of intellectuals organized in Russia toward the end of the nineteenth century. This movement proposed the establishment of a new society based on the model of Russian peasant communities (the *mir*). It was an anti-tsarist and anti-capitalist movement that idealized the values and traditions of the *people* projected onto the peasants of those days. On the other hand, this notion of populism was also applied to the movement of farmers and small independent producers organized in the Central West of the United States at the beginning of the twentieth century. Those participating in this movement demanded the intervention of the state in order to control the trusts, monopolies, and economic organizations that affected their interests as producers and consumers. As Worsley (1969) explained, both movements took place in rural areas where the vast majority of the population lived in those days. *Russian populism* by the end of the

nineteenth century was nonetheless a movement of intellectuals where peasants were not involved, whereas *North American populism* at the beginning of the twentieth century was a movement where different sectors of the rural population participated without an important intellectual point of reference.

The notion of populism has also been used to characterize different political regimes and social movements that developed in Latin America from the 1920s to approximately the 1970s. In the case of Latin America, this concept makes reference to a broad spectrum of widely different social phenomena. De la Torre (1994) sets forth that the notion of populism has been used to characterize: forms of mobilization where the "masses" are manipulated by charismatic leaders; multi-class social movements with a middle-class leadership or a workers and/or peasant basis; a historical phase in the development of the Latin American region or a stage of transition toward modernity; redistributive or nationalistic public policies; a political party with a middle-class leadership, a strong popular basis, a nationalistic rhetoric, a charismatic leader, and an undefined ideology; and an ideological discourse that divides society into two antagonistic fields.

It is important to note that social sciences in Latin America have conducted important studies on populism since some of the most representative cases have appeared in this region. Populism, however, has been studied from different approaches and forms of analysis coming from different traditions of thought. The most representative studies can be classified into three groups: those that explain populism from the perspective of "modernization," those that link populism to the "development" question, and those that analyze populism from a Marxist perspective.

Germani (1977), Di Tella (1977), and Ianni (1977) represent the modernizing perspective. For these authors, populism in Latin America emerged under the form of mobilizations of broad social sectors that are explained as resulting from the transition from a traditional to a modern society. In this transition, the processes of industrialization, urbanization, formation of a predominantly capitalistic economy, consolidation of nation-states and their institutions, and the impact these processes have had on the traditional values and customs have all generated important changes in the social structures and the sociopolitical forms of action and participation. From this perspective, all these elements make broad sectors of the population incorporate en masse into different fields of a nation's life, thus saturating the institutional channels of absorption, control, and participation. On the other hand, these authors give great importance to the role the elites play in heading and leading these mobilizations. According to the theorists of modernization, populism would thus be but a specific way in which the popular masses express themselves politically in situations where they have not been able to develop an autonomous ideology and organization (Bobbio & Matteucci 1985). For this reason, the charismatic leaders or political elites in turn have the conditions to lead and control popular mobilizations. For the theorists of modernization, populism is an undesirable phenomenon resulting from social, economic, and political maladjustments in societies that have a low level of development in comparison to other more advanced societies.

Cardoso (1992) and Faletto (Cardoso & Faletto 1979) are among the authors who have linked the emergence of populism in Latin America to *development*. For Cardoso and Faletto, populism also emerged in a moment of transition intimately related to economic processes and the alliance between different social classes. The events and the international economic changes that took place between the 1930s and the 1940s affected the economic development of Latin American countries to such an extent that they triggered the development of a form of industrialization based on the substitution of imports and the strengthening of domestic markets. This process in turn caused a redistribution of income that favored the social groups that had generally been marginalized from national development and generated the conditions for the different social classes to establish alliances between each other and produce social mobilizations. Populism was thus explained as the result of a coalition of classes that had traditionally been excluded from social and political participation. Cardoso and Faletto see populism as a positive phase in Latin American history since it encouraged economic growth, industrial development, income

redistribution, and the participation of broad social groups.

Based on Althusser's main theses on ideology and taking up some of the proposals of Gramsci's thought, Laclau (1977) studied populism from a Marxist perspective. Laclau criticized both the authors of the modernization school and the categories that they use to explain the phenomenon of populism, such as "traditional and modern industrial society," and considers that populism can be explained neither as part of a transition process in a society nor as an expression of a specific elite or social group. According to Laclau, rather than being a sociopolitical movement, a particular type of organization, a political party or state regime, populism is an ideological phenomenon that can be present in different types of movements, organizations, or regimes. Laclau thus considers populism an ideological phenomenon that not only calls on the *people*, but also specifically places itself as antagonistic to the ruling ideology. This does not imply that all forms of populism are revolutionary, since any social group or class fraction can become hegemonic and thus consolidate a populist experience. In this sense, Sala de Touron (1983) explains that there is a populism of the ruling classes that develops when a fraction that attempts to impose its hegemony is unable to do so and calls upon the masses to develop its antagonism vis-à-vis the state. This form of populism will always be more repressive than parliamentarian. The main critiques to Laclau's theoretical proposal point to the fact that he considers populism only as an ideological issue, which implies a serious oversimplification of a more complex phenomenon that does not consider other elements and dimensions that a more complete explanation would demand.

On the other hand, the notion of populism has also been used to conceptualize certain political movements in Europe, particularly those movements considered to be "right wing." This notion fell out of use shortly after the 1970s, only to reemerge in the 1990s with the appearance of certain *populist* phenomena. This also renewed the interest in studying and analyzing populism. In a different historical context of worldwide processes of change, such as globalization, under a different economic scheme and with democratic regimes that were either consolidated or in the process of consolidation, some authors started to use the notion of *neo-populism* to describe certain events in which the political actors had once again begun to use a discourse addressing the people, strategies based on a direct relationship between leaders and groups, and popular mobilizations, but with a new element: the notion of neo-populism as opposite to neoliberalism. It should be noted that in the implementation of neoliberal policies that were claimed to aim to correct the excesses committed by preceding populist governments, populist strategies were used in the application of certain policies geared to specific social groups. Instead of applying the technical criteria the neoliberal theory indicated, strategies considered to be populist were resorted to, such as clientelist manipulations and the use of a rhetorical and anti-political discourse.

According to Hermet (2001), there are important differences between earlier populisms and the populisms that have appeared since the 1990s, which is why – paraphrasing Benjamin Constant, the illustrious French philosopher – Hermet marks a distinction between "old" and "modern" populism. In an attempt not to fall into generalizations, it can be said that "old populism" is characterized by challenging the established order or the political regime in turn, showing hostility toward those who exercised power, mobilizing marginalized groups, and denying politics as an art of governing. On the other hand, "modern populism" is characterized above all by not opposing the whole logic of politics and is multi-class, including the participation of social groups that are well off. Furthermore, what is observed is not a mere repetition of this phenomenon but the appearance of a new populist logic that coexists with earlier populism at the same time as it contradicts it. Modern populism is a sui generis variety that in the end could well be given another name.

SEE ALSO: *Caudillismo*; Democracy; Faletto, Enzo; Germani, Gino; Nation-State and Nationalism; Political Leadership; Popular Culture

REFERENCES AND SUGGESTED READINGS

Álvarez, J. (1994) El populismo como problema. In: Álvarez, J. & González, A. (Eds.), *El populismo en España y América*. Catriel, Madrid, pp. 11–38.

Bobbio, N. & Matteuci, N. (1985) Populismo latinoamericano. In: Bobbio, N. & Matteuci, N. (Eds.), *Diccionario de política*. Siglo XXI, Mexico, pp. 1288–94.

Cardoso, F. H. (1992) Desafíos de la democracia en América Latina. *Leviatán* 48: 63–82.

Cardoso, F. H. & Faletto, E. (1979) *Dependency and Development in Latin America*. University of California Press, Berkeley.

De la Torre, C. (1994) Los significados ambiguos de los populismos latinoamericanos. In: Álvarez, J. & González, A. (Eds.), *El populismo en España y América*. Catriel, Madrid, pp. 39–60.

Di Tella, T. S. (1977) Populismo y reformismo. In: *Populismo y contradicciones de clase en América Latina*. Era, Mexico, pp. 38–82.

Germani, G. (1977) Democracia representativa y clases populares. In: *Populismo y contradicciones de clase en América Latina*. Era, Mexico, pp. 12–37.

Hermet, G. (2001) Del populismo de los antiguos al populismo de los modernos. In: Hermet, G., Loaeza, S., & Prud'homme, J. F. (Eds.), *Del populismo de los antiguos al populismo de los modernos*. Colegio de México, Mexico, pp. 13–23.

Ianni, O. (1977) Populismo y relaciones de clase. In: *Populismo y contradicciones de clase en América Latina*. Era, Mexico, pp. 83–150.

Incisa, L. (1985) Populismo. In: Bobbio, N. & Matteuci, N. (Eds.), *Diccionario de política*. Siglo XXI, Mexico, pp. 1280–7.

Ionescu, G. & Gellner, E. (Eds.) (1969) *Populism: Its Meanings and National Characteristics*. Weidenfeld & Nicolson, London.

Laclau, E. (1977) *Politics and Ideology in Marxist Theory*. Verso, London and New York.

Prud'homme, J. F. (2001) Un concepto evasivo: el populismo en la ciencia política. In: Hermet, G., Loaeza, S., & Prud'homme, J. F. (Eds.), *Del populismo de los antiguos al populismo de los modernos*. Colegio de México, Mexico, pp. 35–63.

Sala de Touron, L. (1983) Algunas reflexiones sobre el populismo en América Latina. In: *El populismo en América Latina*. Universidad Autónoma de México, Mexico, pp. 7–29.

Torres, S. (1987) El populismo, un concepto escurridizo. In: Álvarez, J. (Ed.), *Populismo, caudillaje y discurso demagógico*. Centro de Investigaciones Sociológicas, Siglo XXI, Madrid, pp. 159–80.

Wiles, P. (1969) Un síndrome, no una doctrina: algunas tesis elementales sobre el populismo. In: Ionescu, G. & Gellner, E. (Eds.), *Populismo. Sus significados y características nacionales*. Amorrortu, Buenos Aires, pp. 203–20.

Worsley, P. (1969) El concepto de populismo. In: Ionescu, G. & Gellner, E. (Eds.), *Populismo. Sus significados y características nacionales*. Amorrortu, Buenos Aires, pp. 258–304.

pornography and erotica

Simon Hardy

The terms "pornography" and "erotica" are often defined in opposition to each other and are best treated together. As a minimal descriptive definition we may say that both refer to mediated communication that depicts sexually explicit subject matter. But beyond this the two terms part company in a variety of ways. "Erotica" was coined in the 1950s to designate something more elevated and exclusive than pornography. Social scientists have drawn up typologies for categorizing sexually explicit material. These usually oppose the "ideal" character of erotica, in which no power relations are discerned, with the degrading and sexist nature of "standard" or "violent" pornography. Today the term erotica is often used in reference to material produced by and for women and gays as opposed to (male) pornography. There is also a range of distinctions made in terms of intentions and outcomes; pornography is designed to sexually arouse the producer and/or audience, whereas erotica is whatever a given individual finds arousing; pornography induces a purely sexual response, whereas erotica combines sexual with emotional and aesthetic responses; pornography stimulates solitary male masturbation whereas erotica provides an aphrodisiac for interpersonal sex.

Another approach is to see the category of pornography as a function of censorship: that to which the social elite bars popular access by means of administrative or legal exclusion. Here we must introduce another important distinction: that between "hard-core" and "soft-core." What must be excluded is the pornographic hard-core: namely, whatever is left once erotic material with any artistic or scientific value has been redeemed. Another way of drawing the distinction between soft-core or erotica and hard-core is to class the former as the creative *representation* of sexual subject matter, using literary, graphic, photographic, and filmic techniques, and the latter as the direct *documentation* of sexual acts, which by definition is confined to photography and especially to the moving image (via film, video, and digital technology). There is, in short, no universally accepted way of defining either term.

Although the words "pornography" and "erotica" hark back to classical antiquity, it is safest to assume that in Greco-Roman culture the sexual was not separated from other themes of representation as it is now. The segregated categories of pornography and erotica are therefore modern constructions. Sexually explicit images and writing intended to be arousing appeared during the Renaissance, most notably the work of Pietro Arentino. From then until the end of the eighteenth century the shock of the sexual was usually harnessed to satirical attacks on religious or political authority, a tradition that culminated with the French Revolution and the writings of the Marquis de Sade. During the nineteenth century pornography became an increasingly popular item of consumption for its sexual content alone. Devoid of satirical ramifications, pornography was now subject to regulation solely for its *obscenity*: its offense against what were held to be universal values. Yet even by the 1850s the application of the word "pornography" was still largely confined to specialized scientific discourses, designating either a category of antiquarian classification or a genre of medical writing concerned with prostitution and social hygiene. It was not until the late nineteenth century that "pornography" came to be widely applied to, and synonymous with, obscenity.

For a hundred years from the 1860s the concern of political and moral authorities with pornography/obscenity was that it was likely to deprave and corrupt what they regarded as the more susceptible parts of the population, such as the young or the uneducated. Yet an important consequence of the cultural exclusion of pornography was that the old association with political radicalism was revived in new ways. By the 1960s left-wing political theory had absorbed enough psychoanalysis to conclude that sexual de-repression would be an integral part of any future revolution. Pornographic obscenity came to be seen by some as an expression of the "collective unconscious." In the context of what Michel Foucault, in *The History of Sexuality* (1976), called the "incitement to discourse" about sexuality, pornography, which was about nothing else, acquired a certain intrinsic value. At this time many western societies began to ease restrictions on pornography. The liberal trend culminated in the *Report of the United States Commission on Pornography and Obscenity* (1970), which contained a major series of empirical studies and drew the majority conclusion that the social effect of pornography was benign. Although the report was rejected by President Nixon, it marks the end of the effort to control pornography on the grounds that it "depraves and corrupts." The liberal view was broadly reproduced in Britain by Bernard Williams's *Report of the Committee on Obscenity and Film Censorship* (1979).

Yet during the 1970s a new concern about the effect of pornography began to be expressed with increasing stridency by members of the women's liberation movement. Feminist thinkers, such as Andrea Dworkin in *Pornography: Men Possessing Women* (1981) and Susan Griffin in *Pornography and Silence* (1981), saw the genre as dedicated to the objectification and dehumanization of women, so as to make them seem legitimate targets of sexual violence. In 1983 Dworkin and Catherine MacKinnon began to introduce city ordinances in the United States, which sought to control pornography by providing legal remedy to women who could prove that they had been harmed as a direct result of its production or consumption. Eventually the ordinances were ruled unconstitutional by the Supreme Court on the grounds that they infringed the First Amendment right of free speech. By this time the analysis of anti-porn feminism had been assimilated into the anti-permissive rhetoric of Pope John Paul II and Christian fundamentalists in Reagan's America. These ideas also underpinned a new Commission on Pornography overseen by US Attorney General Edwin Meese, whose *Final Report* (1986) disavowed any moral agenda, while condemning pornographic imagery as the cause of harm to women. Its conclusions, however, were generally disregarded, accept by those who vigorously disputed their evidential basis.

In response to these developments other feminists, such as those contributing to the celebrated volume *Pleasure and Danger*, edited by Carole Vance (1984), began to organize anti-censorship campaigns in defense of free sexual expression. Many of these feminists agreed that

much existing pornography was sexist but argued that the best way to bring about change was through a diversification of erotic representation. This would involve the production of new forms of erotic material by lesbians, gay men, and straight women. Lesbian erotica, in particular, is often self-consciously designed to subvert conventional gender roles and identities. While gay male products have been accused of imitating the worst excesses of "objectification" found in heterosexual pornography, the very fact that the female object is replaced by a male one is a radical change in itself. Linda Williams, in *Hardcore* (1989), analyzes the development of heterosexual pornographic film from its early history as a highly exclusive male genre to one that begins to acknowledge a female audience in the couples' films of the 1980s, especially those directed by women. Yet it is this very process of diversification that many saw as being most threatened by extensions to the definition and control of pornography advocated by Dworkin–MacKinnon and the Meese Commission.

The intervention of anti-porn feminism has meant that since 1970 most social science research has been framed in terms of the harmful effects of pornography upon men's conduct toward women. The large body of research data generated during this period can be divided fairly neatly into three categories: survey, experimental, and testimonial. Survey research has used quantitative statistics to find correlations between the availability of pornography and levels of sex crime at given social locations. The results have been mixed, and even where correlations appear we cannot safely infer a *causal* relation. Experimental research carried out by social psychologists has sought to measure the behavioral or attitudinal effect of various degrees of exposure to pornography on men of various predispositions. This type of research is open to the charge of behaviorism, because it seeks a direct causal relation between stimulus and response, and thus ignores the fact that in real life the relation between the consumption of pornography and subsequent conduct is mediated by meaning and the subjectivity of the social actor. Testimonial evidence linking pornography to sex crime has been provided by both victims and convicted offenders. This is the type of evidence most valued by feminists and which has carried most weight in legal deliberations. However, even though pornography may be found at the scene of the crime, we should not rush to conclude that *it*, rather than the offender, is the causal agent in the commission of the offense. In short, in spite of a huge effort over many years, no hard evidence that pornography causes sexual violence has been produced.

During the 1990s both the political debate and the research effort concerning the effects of pornography petered out, while existing restrictions were further relaxed and the Internet extended access to unregulated material. At present the only serious concern of either the police or the public is with the abuse of minors in the production of child pornography. The porn industry has continued to grow and now operates on a massive scale (the American industry alone is variously estimated at between $5 billion and $10 billion a year). Yet this huge part of modern mass culture, which must have a significant impact on contemporary social life, now goes virtually unnoticed by the social sciences.

The current scope for research can be divided into two broad and often overlapping areas: questions about the industry and production, and questions about audiences and cultural impact. As far as the porn industry is concerned, there are issues about the health and exploitation of performers. HIV and other sexually transmitted diseases (STDs) are perennial problems. There is anecdotal evidence that female performers are routinely pressured to indulge the gonzo porn obsession with anal penetration. While particular types of pornographic text are highly formulaic, it is also true that the genre as a whole caters to a wide range of tastes and preferences, so we must ask: to what extent does porn reflect the full gamut of human sexual diversity or simply the commercial homogenization of desire? How far is the content of porn changing? Has the development of porn/erotica produced by and for women disrupted the old pattern of male ownership and female objectification?

As regards audiences and cultural impact, in light of the costly failure of the "effects" research, a more interpretive approach might be fruitful. Qualitative data can greatly enhance our understanding of the diverse experiences and subjective responses of those who view pornography. In this way we can begin to evaluate neglected questions about the impact of pornography. For example, what influence does it have on contemporary sexual mores? What role does it play in the development of young people's sexuality and erotic imaginations? Finally, there are questions about the impact of pornography as a medium in late modern society. To what extent have new media technologies of visual reproduction and distribution broken down the old division between producer and consumer, viewer and performer? What contribution are these developments making to the growth of radical new pornographies, which challenge the conventions of the genre? What is the significance of so-called "virtual communities" of shared sexual preference in the context of recent social trends toward the isolation of the individual and the breakdown of traditional forms of association and identity?

SEE ALSO: Audiences; Masturbation; Psychoanalysis; Sexual Markets, Commodification, and Consumption

REFERENCES AND SUGGESTED READINGS

Hunt, L. (Ed.) (1993) *The Invention of Pornography: Obscenity and the Origins of Modernity, 1500–1800.* Zone Books, New York.
Kappeler, S. (1986) *The Pornography of Representation.* Polity Press, Cambridge.
Kendrick, W. (1996) *The Secret Museum: Pornography and Modern Culture.* University of California Press, Los Angeles.
MacKinnon, C. (1987) *Feminism Unmodified: Discourses on Life and Law.* Harvard University Press, Cambridge, MA.
Soble, A. (1986) *Pornography.* Yale University Press, New Haven.

positive deviance

Druann Maria Heckert and Daniel Alex Heckert

Positive deviance remains an intriguing concept with potential to foster new areas of research inquiry (Ben-Yehuda 1990). The roots for the idea are not new; in fact, West (2003) maintains that the theoretical roots of positive deviance are contained in the seminal works of Durkheim, Simmel, and Weber. He contends, moreover, that these theorists recognized the synergies in deviance in that both positive and negative deviance occupy a "shared symbolic form." For example, Weber analyzed charisma and argued that this type of legitimate authority can produce positive and negative deviants.

The contested quality of positive deviance reflects the controversial nature of the sociology of deviance itself. Many deviance theorists claim that positive deviance is oxymoronic or a concept that is not viable or possible (Goode 1991; Sagarin 1985). Even among its defenders, positive deviance has been variously conceptualized, although most definitions have been developed within the two major perspectives in deviance: normative and reactivist. Guided by a normative perspective, positive deviance has been defined as behaviors or characteristics that exceed normative expectations. Negative deviance, on the other hand, describes that which under-conforms or fails to meet normative expectations. For example, Wilkins (1965) was an early proponent of the normative perspective, advocating the idea of a continuous distribution ranging from good to bad. Normal acts constitute most of the continuum. At the negative end of the normal curve are bad acts, such as serious crimes. At the other end, are good acts, such as saintly acts. He concluded that geniuses, reformers, and religious leaders are also deviant. Influenced by the labeling perspective, positive deviance has also been identified as behavior or characteristics that are positively evaluated or labeled. Dodge (1985) has synthesized these two definitions as that which is positively valued that both violates norms and generates positive reactions in others. Finally, some researchers have developed their own unique ways to explain positive deviance; for example, Palmer and Humphrey (1990) propose specifically that innovators, in realms of culture such as science and art, are positive deviants.

Various actions or characteristics have been specifically cited as examples of positive deviance. The diversity of that list is impressive. A few examples include Congressional Medal of Honor winners, Gandhi, Darwin, altruists, Nobel Prize winners, and movie stars. To categorize these divergent examples and to suggest potential types of positive deviance, Heckert (1998) has created a non-exhaustive typology to include the following: altruism, charisma, innovation, supraconformity, innate characteristics, and the ex-deviant. Altruism describes behavior that seeks to help another or others and that is not based on a need for reciprocity. Examples would include saints and heroes who sacrifice themselves. Charisma – a type of legitimate authority – refers to individuals believed to possess an extraordinary gift by a group of followers. Religious leaders and Gandhi constitute examples. Innovators create innovations, or new cultural elements, by combining previously existing cultural elements. These changes can occur in various areas of culture ranging from science to literature to religion. Examples would include reformers and creative individuals like Darwin. Supraconformity includes individuals who achieve at the idealized level, or what people believe is better but few can achieve, rather than the realistic level, which is believed to be what normally can be realized by most people. Examples include zealous weightlifters and runners. Innate characteristics suggest individuals that possess beauty, intelligence, or talent. While culturally defined, movie stars and superstar athletes possess characteristics that are partially innate and partially the product of environmental factors. The ex-deviant is another potential type that describes how previously stigmatized individuals overcome their negative deviance to become conformers, through purification or transcendence. Ex-alcoholics and rehabilitated criminals are examples. The typology has since been extended. In her study of elite tattoo collectors and tattooists, Irwin (2003) adds two categories to this typology. High culture icons refer to the creators of phenomena such as ballet and opera and other cultural elements, sponsored by the economically powerful in society. Those creators – such as artists – are positively evaluated. She also suggests popular culture celebrities are elevated based on their status of popularity in mass culture. Examples include actors, athletes, and popular musicians.

Recently, to further clarify the concept of positive deviance and embed it more fully in the context of deviance, Heckert and Heckert (2002) have proposed a typology that cross-classifies the normative and reactivist perspectives. Thus, negative deviance denotes under-conformity that is negatively labeled, deviance admiration refers to under-conformity that is positively evaluated, rate-busting describes over-conformity that is negatively labeled, and positive deviance refers to over-conformity that is positively evaluated. This typology accommodates the complexity of deviance, acknowledging that there are both norms and social reactions and that there is not always consistency between them.

A fascinating possibility is the potential of utilizing – or modifying – existing deviance theories to illuminate positive deviance. For example, anomie fosters the creative as well as negative deviation. Differential association theory and social learning theory should be capable of providing insight into positive deviants, as well as negative deviants. Furthermore, new theories to foster explanation of positive deviance may need to be developed to account for the unique acquisition of positive deviance. While this would benefit social scientists as they attempt to explain positive deviance, it would also potentially augment social scientific understanding of negative deviance and, perhaps, conformity as well. Sorokin (1950) argued that social science concentrates on negative behaviors; by examining positive deviations, negative deviations would be more fully understood. In support of Sorokin's contention, the concept of positive deviance has taken root in various disciplines, including nutrition, health, and business. Researchers in the area of nutrition, for example, find that examining "positive-deviance" children (and their mothers' behaviors) who thrive in situations of nutritional inadequacy facilitates understanding of children who do not fare so well. According to Dodge (1985), the field of medicine has advanced from examining the positive, as preventive medicine emerged in the context of focusing on the healthy and not just the ill. He recognized similar potential for sociology when he contended the discipline would thrive from examining positive deviance, as well as negative deviance. Sociology, and the substantive area of deviant behavior, will benefit from positive deviance becoming a core, rather than marginalized, concept.

SEE ALSO: Deviance, Constructionist Perspectives; Deviance, Normative Definitions of; Deviance, Reactivist Definitions of

REFERENCES AND SUGGESTED READINGS

Ben-Yehuda, N. (1990) Positive and Negative Deviance: More Fuel for a Controversy. *Deviant Behavior* 11: 221–43.

Dodge, D. L. (1985) The Over-Negativized Conceptualization of Deviance: A Programmatic Exploration. *Deviant Behavior* 6: 17–37.

Goode, E. (1991) Positive Deviance: A Viable Concept? *Deviant Behavior* 12: 289–309.

Heckert, A. & Heckert, D. M. (2002) A New Typology of Deviance: Integrating Normative and Reactivist Definitions of Deviance. *Deviant Behavior* 23: 449–79.

Heckert, D. M. (1998) Positive Deviance: A Classificatory Model. *Free Inquiry in Creative Sociology* 26: 23–30.

Irwin, K. (2003) Saints and Sinners: Elite Tattoo Collectors and Tattooists as Positive and Negative Deviants. *Sociological Spectrum* 23: 27–57.

Palmer, S. & Humphrey, J. A. (1990) *Deviant Behavior*. Plenum Press, New York.

Sagarin, E. (1985) Positive Deviance: An Oxymoron. *Deviant Behavior* 6: 169–81.

Sorokin, P. A. (1950) *Altruistic Love*. Beacon Press, Boston.

West, B. (2003) Synergies in Deviance: Revisiting the Positive Deviance Debate. Online. *Electronic Journal of Sociology*.

Wilkins, L. T. (1965) *Social Deviance*. Prentice-Hall, Englewood Cliffs, NJ.

positivism

Steve Fuller

Positivism is the name of a social and intellectual movement that tried to learn from the mistakes of the Enlightenment project that eventuated, first, in the Reign of Terror following the French Revolution of 1789, and second, in the irrationalism of the Weimar Republic following Germany's defeat in World War I. While it has been customary to distinguish between the quasi-political movement called "positivism" originated by Auguste Comte in the 1830s and the more strictly philosophical movement called "logical positivism" associated with the Vienna Circle of the 1930s, both shared a common sensibility, namely, that the unchecked exercise of reason can have disastrous practical consequences. Thus, both held that reason needs "foundations" to structure its subsequent development so as not to fall prey to a self-destructive skepticism.

The history of positivism can be neatly captured as a Hegelian dialectic, the three moments of which are epitomized by the work of Auguste Comte (thesis), Ernst Mach (antithesis), and the Vienna Circle (synthesis). However, these moments have historically overlapped, occasionally coming together in figures such as Otto Neurath, more about whom below. The career trajectories of positivism's standard bearers help explain the direction taken by their thought.

Comte was an early graduate of the École Polytechnique who believed that its Napoleonic mission of rendering research a vehicle for societal transformation had been betrayed, once he himself failed to achieve a permanent academic post. Mach was a politically active physicist on the losing side of so many of the leading scientific debates of his day that his famous chair in Vienna, from which the logical positivists sprang, was awarded on the strength of his critical-historical studies, *not* his experimental work. Finally, the intellectual leader of the Vienna Circle, Rudolf Carnap, had to abandon physics for philosophy because his doctoral dissertation topic was seen as too "metatheoretical" for a properly empirical discipline. For Carnap and others who came of age in World War I, physics had devolved into another specialized field of study, rather than − as it had still been for Einstein − natural philosophy pursued by more exact means.

Taking the long view of western intellectual history, positivism incorporates a heretofore absent empiricist dimension to the risk-averse orientation to the world historically associated with Platonism. More specifically, positivism inflects Plato's original philosophical motivation through a secularized version of the Christian salvation story, in which Newton functions as the Christ figure. This captures both the spirit of Auguste Comte's original project and its residual effects in twentieth-century logical

positivism, which dropped the overt historicism of Comte's project while retaining the fixation on Newton as the model for what it means to express oneself scientifically and a vague belief that greater scientific knowledge will deliver salvation. Indeed, positivism's core conceptual problem has been to define a scientific vanguard capable of both offering guidance to the unenlightened and itself changing in light of further evidence and reflection.

Positivism's relationship to democracy has been checkered. Where Plato had hoped to produce implacable philosopher-kings who would rule as absolute monarchs, positivists have typically envisaged a more differentiated but no less authoritative (authoritarian?) rule by experts, each an oligarch over his or her domain of knowledge. In this respect, positivism is bureaucracy's philosophical fellow-traveler. Like Plato, positivists have feared protracted public disagreement most of all and hence have tended to demonize it as "irrational" and "non-cognitive." Their image of "plural" authority presumes non-overlapping competences, such that legislative questions are reduced to judicial ones concerning the expertise to which one should defer.

Thus, there is a fundamental ambiguity in positivism's appeal to organized reason, or "science," in the public sphere. Sometimes this ambiguity is finessed by saying that positivists regard science as the main source of political unity. At the very least, this implies that it is in the interest of all members of society to pursue their ends by scientific means, as that may enable them to economize on effort and hence allow more time for the fruits of their labor to be enjoyed. Ernst Mach comes closest to defending this position in its pure form. He is normally credited (or demonized, in the case of Marxists) with having removed positivism's politically subversive implications, reducing the movement to a purely "instrumentalist" approach to scientific theories. But in its day, Machian positivism fitted comfortably with the libertarian idea that democratic regimes should enable maximum self-empowerment.

However, many positivists have drawn a further conclusion that can thwart this libertarian impulse. From Comte onward, it has been common to argue that science can unify the polity by resolving, containing, or circumventing

social conflict. Here a well-established procedure or a decisive set of facts is supposed to
replace more "primitive" and volatile forms of
conflict resolution such as warfare and sometimes even open debate – all of which supposedly compromise the integrity of opposing
viewpoints in the spirit of expedience. Accordingly, a scientific politics should not merely
satisfy the parties concerned: it should arrive
at the "correct" solution.

To be sure, even this mentality admits of a
democratic interpretation, as positivist social
researchers have been in the forefront of presenting "data" from parties whose voices are
unlikely to be heard in an open assembly. Typically, this has occurred in surveys designed to
represent the full empirical range of a target
population. Nevertheless, the question remains
of exactly who reaps the political benefits of
these newly articulated voices: the people under
investigation; the investigators themselves; or
the investigators' clients? Moreover, once a target population has been empirically registered,
do its members remain "objects of inquiry" or
are they promoted to full-fledged inquirers
capable of challenging the original investigators' findings and methods? Probably the most
sophisticated treatment of these questions in
the context of positivistically inspired US social
policy research is to be found in Campbell
(1988).

These delicate questions arise because ultimately positivism turns Plato on his side by
converting a static hierarchy into a temporal
order. Where Plato imagined that authority
flowed downward from the philosopher-king
in a caste-based social structure, positivists
have envisaged that all of humanity may pass
(at a variable rate) through a sequence of stages
that retrace the socio-epistemic journey from
captivity to autonomy. In the positivist utopia,
it is possible for everyone to be an expert over
his or her own domain. Moreover, there is a
recipe for the conversion of Platonism to positivism. It proceeds by isolating a domain of
inquiry from the contingencies surrounding
its manifestations so that its essential nature
may be fathomed. Whereas Plato reserved such
inquiry to philosopher-kings, positivists have
more often turned to state-licensed professional
bodies. And instead of Plato's intellectual intuition (*nous*), positivists attempt to gain epistemic

access by comparative historical and experimental methods.

This recipe can be illustrated in the work
of Otto Neurath, an organizer of the Vienna
Circle. He wanted to isolate the essence of the
"war economy" so that its efficient central planning mechanism could be transferred to environments where it would have more socially
salutary consequences. Here Neurath anticipated what Alvin Gouldner would call the
Janus-faced character of the "welfare-warfare
state," whereby the same organizational structure (in this case, a concentration of resources in
the nation-state) can have radically different
consequences, depending on the supporting
political environment. Nevertheless, as Neurath's many critics pointed out, positivism seems
to have inherited Platonism's political naïveté,
which confuses the fact that, say, the "war economy" can be identified analytically as a feature
of many societies and the analyst's ability to
transfer it to new social environments – barring
the imposition of sufficient force to hold all
other environmental factors constant. If anything deserves the name of the "positivist fal-
lacy," it is this too easy assimilation of the forum
to the laboratory.

After the leading members of the Vienna Circle migrated to the US in the 1930s, logical
positivism seeded that country's analytic philosophy establishment for the second half of the
twentieth century. However, this is the only
context in which positivism possibly dominated
an established discipline. For the most part,
positivism has been embraced by disciplines that
have yet to achieve academic respectability, even
in the natural sciences, where Mach found his
strongest support among chemists, biomedical
scientists, and psychologists – not physicists.
(It is often overlooked that positivism's reliance
on Newtonian mechanics as the model for all
science was not generally appreciated by a physics community jealous of guarding its guild
privileges.) Unsurprisingly, positivism's most
ardent supporters have been social scientists,
not for the Comtean reason that sociology is the
pinnacle of all science but for the more mundane
reason that positivism seemed to offer a strategy
for rendering one's activities "scientific."

These matters came to a head with the publication of Thomas Kuhn's *The Structure of
Scientific Revolutions* in 1962, which Carnap

enthusiastically endorsed as the final install-ment of the logical positivists' International Encyclopedia of Unified Science. It provided an account of scientific change based largely on the history of physics that was quickly embraced by social scientists, as Kuhn stressed science's self-organization over its larger socie-tal impact. However, unlike previous positivist accounts, Kuhn's was explicitly a model of knowledge production within particular scienti-fic disciplines (or "paradigms") that did not presume that science as a whole is heading toward a unified understanding of reality. By implication, then, all scientific standards are discipline-relative. Kuhn's approach suited what is now called the "postmodern condition." Indeed, in retrospect, the popularity of Kuhn's book is better understood as signifying positi-vism's decadent phase than, as it was originally seen, a fundamental challenge to positivism.

If positivism has a future, it lies in rekind-ling a sense of "Science" that transcends the boundaries of particular scientific disci-plines. This is how Comte originally thought about the discipline he called "sociology." He claimed that it was the last to develop, not simply because of the complexity of its human subject matter, but more importantly, because sociology had to reconstitute the (natural) sciences that historically preceded it. Too often the history of positivism's quest for unified science has been interpreted as exclusively a matter of applying the methods of physics to the less developed sciences. The reciprocal movement is actually more important, namely, the application of sociological findings to the future direction of science as a whole. Such interdisciplinary projects as "social epistemol-ogy" and the "science of science" have tried to fulfill this side of the Comtean promise, which, unless the present intellectual climate changes, is unlikely to be redeemed.

SEE ALSO: Comte, Auguste; Kuhn, Thomas and Scientific Paradigms; Postpositivism; Science; Social Epistemology

REFERENCES AND SUGGESTED READINGS

Adorno, T. (Ed.) (1976) *The Positivist Dispute in German Sociology*. Heinemann, London.

Campbell, D. (1988) *Methodology and Epistemology for Social Science*. University of Chicago Press, Chicago.

Fuller, S. (1993) *Philosophy of Science and Its Dis-contents*, 2nd edn. Guilford Press, New York.

Fuller, S. (2000) *Thomas Kuhn: A Philosophical His-tory for Our Times*. University of Chicago Press, Chicago.

Hayek, F. (1952) *The Counter-Revolution in Science*. University of Chicago Press, Chicago.

Kolakowski, L. (1972) *Positivist Philosophy*. Penguin, Harmondsworth.

Proctor, R. (1991) *Value-Free Science? Purity and Power in Modern Knowledge*. Harvard University Press, Cambridge, MA.

postcolonialism and sport

C. Richard King

Although subject to much conceptual and political debate, postcolonialism simultaneously refers to a range of sociohistorical conditions associated with empire, its aftermath, and reconfiguration, and a set of theories designed to question the naturalness of the categories and practices central to such contexts. Signifi-cantly, both have implications for the sociology of sport, because athletics almost invariably has animated colonial cultures.

Increasingly, the study of sport and society interrogates colonialism and its consequences. Bale and Cronin (2003: 4) identify seven spe-cific relationships of note: (1) the introduction of sports that were adopted without change, like soccer and cricket; (2) colonial sports mod-ified in settler states, such as Australian foot-ball; (3) local and regional adaptations, for example, Kenyan running; (4) hybrid cultural forms incorporating western games, including Trobriand cricket; (5) indigenous pastimes that were institutionalized as modern sports, most notably, lacrosse; (6) precolonial sporting activ-ities that have remained relatively unaltered, like Rwandan high jumping; and (7) novel sports created in settler states, such as baseball. In addition, an eighth and final relationship deserves attention, namely, neocolonialism, or the intersections of media, commercialization, and globalization in the dissemination of sports, particularly basketball.

Postcolonialism also has introduced novel concepts and questions to the sociology of sport. Closely related to postmodernism and post-structuralism, and deeply associated with thinkers like Edward Said, Gayatri Spivak, Homi Bhabha, and Franz Fanon, it took root first in literary studies before impacting work in history, anthropology, and sociology. Postcolonialism encourages the study of representation, power relations, alternative readings of texts written by, for, and about the colonized, and the social construction of cultural difference, social meanings, and ethnic identities. In the sociology of sport, postcolonialism has prompted scholars to investigate the eight connections between sport and empire previously outlined. Specifically, they have posed novel questions about the cultural work of play: the relationships between the colonized and the colonizers, imperial accounts of sport and sporting, uses of sports to further and unsettle imperial ends, colonial representations, revivals and survivals of sport.

The rapidly expanding and increasingly sophisticated literature on sport, society, and (post)colonialism directs attention to the entanglements of power, the body, identity formation, processes of social change, racial stratification, and representation. On the one hand, it underscores the centrality of sport to imperial projects designed to transform non-western societies. Playing civilized games was thought to offer a unique opportunity to teach colonized societies the values, rules, and discipline prized by the colonizers. On the other hand, sport has proven to be of fundamental importance in efforts to challenge imperialism as well. It has facilitated resistance to empire. The Black Power salute at the 1968 Summer Olympics and the more recent refusal of amateur athletes to rise for the American national anthem in the wake of the war in Iraq offer clear examples of anti-colonial defiance in the sport arena. At the same time, sport has afforded indigenous peoples an occasion to reclaim traditional practices, glimpsed in the formation of the Iroquois National Lacrosse team and the staging of the World Indigenous Games. And sport allows the (formerly) colonized (like West Indian cricketers) a space in which to make powerful statements of equality, humanity, and changing global order.

SEE ALSO: Colonialism (Neocolonialism); Globalization, Sport and; Identity, Sport and; Nationalism and Sport

REFERENCES AND SUGGESTED READINGS

Bale, J. & Cronin, M. (Eds.) (2003) *Sport and Postcolonialism*. Berg, Oxford.

posthumanism

Adrian Franklin

Posthumanism is a fast-growing area of ontological debate and research that has emerged from broad currents of poststructuralist thought. In particular it gathers together the work of important scholars such as Donna Haraway (her "Cyborg Manifesto," for example, and her more recent work on companion species), Bruno Latour (his development of actor-network theory and its aftermath and his work on the "pasteurization" of France, for example), John Law (his work on relational materialism, orderings, and complexity), Andrew Pickering (his book *The Mangle of Practice* is a methodological masterpiece of post-humanist studies), and Nigel Thrift (his non-representational geography project has opened up "human" geography to a much wider range of agency and forms of being in the world). Posthumanism is characterized by its opposition to humanism, as well as moving beyond it. It rejects the notion of the separability of humanity from the non-human world, as is suggested by the very idea of sociology, and the division of knowledge into separate domains. Rather, it seeks to recover the complex ways in which humans are entangled with non-humans. Latour and Law promote the idea of a symmetrical approach to all objects, human and otherwise, without giving humans the central organizing position and the only source of agency. Instead they advocate the idea of distributed cognition and a radical extension of semiotics. As Latour says:

> But a semiotics of things is easy, once one simply has to drop the meaning bit from semiotics. ... If one now translates semiotics as path breaking, or order making or creation of directions, one does not have to specify whether it is language or objects one is analyzing. Such a move gives a new continuity to practices that were deemed different when one dealt with language and "symbols" or with skills, work and matter. This move can be said either to elevate things to the dignity of texts or to elevate texts to the ontological status of things. (Latour 1997)

For these reasons they dismiss the idea that truth and explanation are hidden in human-made structures or semiotic fields and instead seek to build explanation from material connectivity. Those who follow their approach look less for what things mean (to humans) than what things *do*. Law captures it well when he says he wants "a sociology of verbs not nouns" (Law 1994: 15).

Hayles defines posthumanism in a suggestive rather than a prescriptive way, as a view that makes the following assumptions. First, consciousness and cognition have been a wrongly elevated or privileged aspect of human identity and human constructions of agency in the world. Second, posthumanism privileges "informational pattern" over "material instantiation" and considers the latter accidents of history rather than naturally given. Third, because posthumanism considers the body to be like a prosthesis that we all learn to manipulate and control in relation to the world around us (Haraway 2003 talks of "graspings" and "prehensions" in this regard), adding further prostheses or replacing body parts with prostheses is only adding to human experience, not replacing it with something else (this is an important element in Haraway's "cyborg manifesto"). Finally, and related to the last point, Hayles argues that "in the posthuman there are no essential differences or absolute demarcations between bodily existence and computer simulation, cybernetic mechanism and biological organism, robot teleology and human goals" (Hayles 1999: 2–3).

Scholars have been trying to grasp at posthumanism, unsuccessfully, for a very long time. Pickering suggests that C. P. Snow's "two cultures" of the humanities and sciences in the 1950s and the "Great Divide" they described demanded reconciliation in a world where it had become imperative to understand both, simultaneously: "[T]he world was changing more rapidly than ever, but no one could see the picture whole; no one could grasp the social and the scientific at once; events had escaped traditional democratic forms of control" (Pickering 2001: 3).

Pickering argues that over the past 30 years or so, his subfield, science and technology studies (STS) (and this includes all of the key scholars noted above), has been the only movement to bridge the divide that focuses on humanism and anti-humanism. For him, the humanities are humanist because they pose the possibility of studying and knowing a world of humans among themselves. By contrast, the sciences are "anti-humanist" in that they pose the possibility of studying and knowing a material world from which humans are largely absent. In contrast to these two impossible ontologies, STS poses a world in which the border between humans and the material world is unstable and where "much of the interesting action in the world occurs at or across the interface – that the human, say, needs to be studied in relation to the nonhuman, and vice versa" (Pickering 2001: 4).

However, their efforts have not extinguished the Great Divide; instead there is a new one, with established humanities and science on one side and STS/posthumanism and its growing band of converts on the other. For Pickering, "posthumanist" denotes a decentered perspective in which humanity and the material world appear as symmetrically intertwined, with neither constituting a controlling center.

New empirical studies inspired by posthumanism are coming in thick and fast and have been applied, for example, to the city (Gandy 2005); agriculture/postcolonialism (Gill & Anderson 2005); human relations with trees (Cloke & Jones 2001; Franklin 2006); and domesticity and water (Kaika 2004). Rather than extinguish sociology, posthumanism probably represents a rare opportunity for major expansion and development.

SEE ALSO: Actor-Network Theory; Actor-Network Theory, Actants; Cyberculture;

Humanism; Poststructuralism; Technology, Science, and Culture

REFERENCES AND SUGGESTED READINGS

Cloke, P. & Jones, O. (2001) Dwelling, Place, and Landscape: An Orchard in Somerset. *Environment and Planning A* 33: 649–66.

Franklin, A. S. (2006) Burning Cities: A Posthumanist Account of Australians and Eucalypts. *Environment and Planning D: Society and Space*, forthcoming.

Gandy, M. (2005) Cyborg Urbanization: Complexity and Monstrosity in the Contemporary City. *International Journal of Urban and Regional Research* 29(1): 26–49.

Gill, N. & Anderson, K. (2005) Improvement in the Inland: Culture and Nature in the Australian Rangelands. *Australian Humanities Review* 34 (January/February).

Haraway, D. (1991) *Simians, Cyborgs, and Women: The Reinvention of Nature*. Routledge, New York.

Haraway, D. (2003) *The Companion Species Manifesto*. Prickly Paradigm Press, Chicago.

Hayles, N. K. (1999) *How We Became Posthuman*. University of Chicago Press, Chicago.

Jones, O. & Cloke, P. (2002) *Tree Cultures*. Berg, Oxford.

Kaika, M. I. (2004) Interrogating the Geographies of the Familiar: Domesticating Nature and Constructing the Autonomy of the Modern Home. *International Journal of Urban and Regional Research* 28(2): 265–86.

Latour, B. (1997) On Actor-Network Theory: A Few Clarifications. *Soziale Welt* 47: 369–81.

Law, J. (1994) *Organizing Modernity*. London, Sage.

Pickering, A. (2001) In the Thick of Things. Keynote paper given to the conference "Taking Nature Seriously." University of Oregon, February.

post-industrial society

Michael R. Smith

From its beginnings sociology has used evolutionary typologies. The industrial capitalism of the nineteenth century provided the background and preoccupations for the writings of the principal early theorists. Consequently, much of the writing of Comte, Marx, Durkheim, and Weber was concerned to distinguish industrial capitalism from what preceded it. Key *dramatis personae* in their accounts, couched at varying levels of generality, were capitalists controlling ever larger enterprises, male manual workers and their trade unions, and the political instruments through which these competing groups expressed their interests. In one way or another, class conflict was present in the analyses of each. It was the core in Marx's analysis.

As it progressed, the twentieth century posed problems for these analyses – especially for the Marxist version. If not disappearing altogether, class conflict seemed to settle into a distinctly muted form. Small business proved resilient. Union membership stopped growing, settling in at 50 percent or less of employees in most countries. In the US it withered. The political space taken by the old male-dominated union–management issues that seemed to set industrial capitalism's political agenda was increasingly encroached upon by apparently new issues: feminism, environmentalism, nationalisms expressed within nation-states, and sexual liberation, including gay rights. The idea of post-industrialism was developed to make sense of this apparent shift away from the dominant forms of industrial capitalism, while retaining the interpretive structure provided by an evolutionary typology.

The changes described above have provoked three sorts of response:

1 Marshal evidence that suggests that the working class and trade unions remain important forces shaping societies. This is the "class power" approach (e.g., Korpi & Palme 2003).

2 Assert the continuing centrality of class conflict but argue that the protagonists are different. In Touraine's (1971) version, interlocking government agencies and large corporations (the technocracy) confront the more educated: technicians in the private sector, employees in research agencies, and students and faculty in universities.

3 See conflict as dispersed over a wide range of arenas. In Bell's (1973) seminal statement the central political problem of post-industrial societies is the aggregation of widely disparate preferences.

These positions are not necessarily mutually exclusive. What is at issue is *emphasis*.

The "class power" approach mainly rests on cross-national evidence. The Scandinavian countries, in particular, have large, relatively traditional, labor movements. Despite substantial service sectors they have less inequality and more employment security than the US. It is possible to maintain a strong union movement. Doing so makes a difference. Nonetheless, the proportionately enormous union movement in Scandinavia and its smaller counterpart in the US are certainly different from their predecessors. Women now make up a significant part of the membership and influence union policies. The conciliation of family and work is higher on union agendas than it would otherwise have been. Even in Scandinavia, non-standard issues emerge. A good example is the Swedish 1980 referendum that banned nuclear power plants – against the preferences of much of the political establishment. Classes may still matter, as they did 50 and a 100 years ago. Still, some things have changed.

Living standards have increased spectacularly. There is evidence that this has caused a shift in preoccupations from issues of survival to broader quality of life concerns, a tendency that has perhaps been reinforced by the *form* taken by economic growth. The mass market often involves strip malls and mass advertising. Growth is associated with waste and pollution. Rich people can afford to worry about the environment and some aspects of growth provide them with reasons to do so. At the same time, over the long haul, educational standards have risen. Most jobs now require some degree of literacy. There is a large set of jobs that requires very high educational levels indeed (Brint 2001). The same *generalized* requirement for education was absent in the nineteenth and early twentieth centuries. There is, then, a population that might be expected to want to go beyond bread and butter issues, and that may be equipped to participate in political debate in an informed way.

Jobs in manufacturing and extractive industries – the traditional recruitment bases for unions – have been replaced with service sector jobs. This has been a problem for many union movements. And, it is often argued, many service sector jobs are inferior, providing less security and lower wages than the jobs they replaced. This, it is said, produces increasing income inequality (Sassen 2003). The distributional outcomes of the process of economic restructuring add to the problems that set the political agenda in post-industrial societies.

Has protest been transformed by the changes listed above? "New social movements" are said to display novel features: a concern with quality of life and lifestyle; a preference for participative organizational forms; the use of non-standard political channels; an over-representation of middle-class participants. These characterizations distance new social movements from the bureaucratic, trade union mastodons thought to have represented the manual working class at the high point of industrial capitalism. These contrasting models of protest are, however, overdrawn. There are new social movements that pursue their objectives using participative structures and that act outside standard political institutions. Others may be about as bureaucratic as the Teamsters, and are drawn into standard politics – lobbying, getting out the vote, court cases, etc. (Pichardo 1997). By the same token, it turns out that there was considerable variety in nineteenth-century social movement fauna (Tilly 1988).

None of this is to suggest that conflict and protest were the same in the second halves of each of the last two centuries. Technology makes a difference. It took the development of nuclear weapons to make anti-nuclear demonstrations possible. Using a demonstration to attract media attention required content-hungry mass media. It is hard to imagine nineteenth-century feminist groups displaying the same vigor, ambition, and size as their late twentieth-century equivalents, in their recent incarnations addressing issues ranging from terms of employment to access to abortion. There are, then, differences between nineteenth and late twentieth-century protest.

Even if the organization of employers and labor may suggest the continuing relevance of class conflict in Scandinavia (modified in response to the more active participation of women), that sort of organization of employers and employees is much less present in other rich countries. Is what happens in those countries best understood as class conflict along different (from the nineteenth and early twentieth) axes?

Or is class conflict being replaced by struggles between many different interest groupings, pursuing a wide range of objectives, as Bell suggested? The answer to this question tends to hinge on rather sterile issues of definition. With enough ingenuity some common characteristics can be found that allow the assignment of large numbers of people to the same class. It is not clear that the exercise is worthwhile, though a strong prior theoretical commitment to class analysis may require it.

The literature on post-industrialism has served to identify some important characteristics of protest that have been more prevalent in the last part of the twentieth century than they were before. It also points in the direction of factors (higher living standards, some of the problems of growth, the expansion of the service sector) that provide at least some explanation for the shifts that are observable in the character of protest. What may well be a problem with the literature is that it rests on the premise that it is useful to construct large, aggregate, typologies of societies. It was probably not useful to construct the monolithic concept, "industrial society." In fact, during the nineteenth and early twentieth centuries there was very considerable variation across countries and over time in living standards, industrial structure, and in the pattern and magnitude of protests. A concept of "post-industrial society" that is equally monolithic is at least as implausible.

SEE ALSO: Deindustrialization; Fordism/Post-Fordism; New Social Movement Theory; Social Movements, Participatory Democracy in

REFERENCES AND SUGGESTED READINGS

Bell, D. (1973) *The Coming of Post-Industrial Society: A Venture in Social Forecasting*. Basic Books, New York.
Brint, S. (2001) Professionals and the "Knowledge Economy": Rethinking the Theory of Postindustrial Society. *Current Sociology* 49: 101–32.
Korpi, W. & Palme, J. (2003) New Politics and Class Politics in the Context of Austerity and Globalization: Welfare State Regress in 18 Countries, 1975–95. *American Political Science Review* 97: 425–46.
Pichardo, N. A. (1997) New Social Movements: A Critical Review. *Annual Review of Sociology* 23: 411–30.
Sassen, S. (2003) Epilogue. In: Roulleau-Berger, L. (Ed.), *Youth and Work in the Post-Industrial City of North America and Europe*. Brill, Leiden.
Tilly, C. (1988) Social Movements, Old and New. *Research in Social Movements, Conflicts and Change* 10: 1–18.
Touraine, A. (1971) *The Post-Industrial Society; Tomorrow's Social History: Classes, Conflicts and Culture in the Programmed Society*. Random House, New York.

postmodern consumption

Alladi Venkatesh

The origins of postmodernism cannot be traced to a single source or set of circumstances. At first glance, the different trails may appear diffused, disparate, and disconnected. A closer look might reveal a common pattern woven by those different threads. Postmodernism is generally viewed as a reaction against or rejection of modernist tendencies in philosophy, social and cultural theory, literature, and politics (Featherstone 1991). Postmodernism is closely related to poststructuralism, whose origins are slightly different but whose arguments are very similar – so much so that in the eyes of many, postmodernism subsumes poststructuralism and therefore they are treated interchangeably. The last quarter of the twentieth century witnessed the most intense excursions into postmodern ideas. Among the many key figures are Derrida (deconstruction and the decentered subject), Foucault (regimes of truth), Jameson (cultural logic of late capitalism), Kristeva (language and construction of identity), Deleuze and Guattari (desiring machines), Cixous (*l'écriture féminine*), Butler (queer theory), Rorty (questions of representation), Gehry (postmodern architecture), Baudrillard (the economy of signs and simulacrum), Lyotard (the problematic of science and legitimation), Greenblatt (new historicism), Said (Orientalism), Harraway (cyborgs and posthumanism), and Featherstone and Bauman (consumer culture).

In architecture, where postmodernist tendencies were first noticed, there was a reaction against modernist definitions of form and style, questioning the emphases on universalism, functionalism, and rationalism. Postmodern architecture considered the modernist approach to be too rigid and argued for greater fluidity of design, the mixing of styles, and local variability. In literature, postmodernism was a reaction against the entrenched notions of the "western" canon. It has given rise to the poststructuralist movement away from the signifier to the signified, and toward displacement, difference, and dispersal instead of rigid origins and representations of human nature. In politics, postmodernism rejected neoclassical liberalism and triggered intense debates on gender and ethnic issues. At the global level, it has induced the postcolonial discourse.

Postmodernism can be considered a rejection of what Lyotard (1984) terms metanarratives of modernism and (equally importantly) products of the Enlightenment. These grand themes of modernism include rationalism in philosophy; the pursuit of science as the only path to ultimate truth and human advancement; and the individual subject as the most powerful and universal self, whose destiny is to conquer and establish decisive superiority over nature. Postmodernism argues that for all its claims of enlightened humanism and progress, the results of modernism are hardly salutary. The realm of science has become a hegemonic regime of dogma and is dismissive of alternative sources of knowledge; human progress has been equated with oppressive industrialism; individualism has become basically a phallocentric ideology; and western/European narratives have become the master discourse. Once postmodernism gained the necessary momentum and provided the umbrella under which marginal(ized) discourses could take refuge, other submovements followed in its footsteps. These groups consisted mainly of feminists, (multi)cultural anti-essentialists, and postcolonial critics. Postmodernism pointed out that there is a world beyond science and instrumental rationality and that human experiences are embedded in culture, language, aesthetics, art, symbols, and visual forms.

During the 1990s postmodernism came under attack from various quarters. The criticism can be summarized as follows: (1) it promotes a spurious relativism and an anything goes philosophy; (2) it is anarchic and self-indulgent; (3) it incites anti-science thinking and throws the baby out with the bath water; (4) it is intentionally blind to scientific contributions to human health and happiness; and (5) its claims are false and unsustainable within any reasonable discourse. Such criticism reached extraordinary levels of intellectual insecurity when a (panic-stricken) physical scientist under the name of Alan Sokal (1996), unable to face legitimate criticisms of science, published a parody in *Social Text* that was dubbed by his admirers as a successful hoax, but in actuality vindicated the postmodern critique.

There is no question that there has been a slowing down of postmodernist writings in the last five or six years. Does it mean that postmodernism has become less relevant or is it the case that postmodern ideas have met with success and is being slowly absorbed into the mainstream? It is probably a bit of both. In cultural studies and derivatively in the study of consumer culture, postmodernist ideas may have had the greatest impact.

Modernist thought tended to privilege production as the handmaiden of the capitalist industrial machine, for production meant the creation of value within the social order. Correspondingly, consumption was viewed as a value-destructive function serving no useful purpose in the industrial economy. Postmodernism exposed the absurdity of this position (Firat & Venkatesh 1995) by simply pointing out that production and consumption are two sides of the same economic coin and by asking what was the value of production if what is produced is not consumed. Postmodernism elevated the discourse on consumption critically and analytically as an inevitable and highly significant condition of modern societies. Postmodernism views consumption as a complex social phenomenon and the postmodern vocabulary includes such wide-ranging topics as aesthetics, sign value, cultures of consumption, fragmentation, hyperreality, everyday life experiences, consumer identities, liberatory consumption, and the like – terms that were either non-existent before or remained at the margins of social science discourse. In the face of these developments, traditional theories of consumption based on positivist psychology and economic utility theories were found to be quaint and inadequate. Even the Frankfurt School – with its scathing attack on culture industries – seems to have misdirected its analysis, for it failed to recognize the critical and essential role of consumption in the formation of modern societies. Postmodernism was the first to recognize that consumption is a positive social activity despite the fact that marketers exploit consumers to gain economic advantage, while Marxist economists and feel-good-patronizing sociological critics consider consumption as wasteful. For postmodernists, consumption could be a liberatory force if consumers were allowed to pursue their consumptive goals as part of their everyday life experiences.

Postmodernism affects consumerism in two ways: first, by creating a sense of pastiche which involves an "ironic mixing of existing categories and styles," and second by rendering the "consumer lifestyle itself as a kind of work of art" (Solomon et al. 2002: 561, 563). Recent works on postmodernism suggest that modernistic and mechanistic notions of aesthetics have given way to paradoxical sensibilities in aesthetic experiences, including the juxtaposition of opposites, a lack of quest for unity, and a search for hybridity, theatricality, and a mixing of aesthetic objects. While modernity does allow for mixing and blending, the aim of such activities is unification or convergence to a central idea. The postmodernistic ideal would look for mingling without unification, or as Jameson (1983) calls it, pastiche. The ultimate goal of art (and therefore aesthetic experience) in modernism is to attain some sort of (Kantian) sublime, while under postmodernism it is closer to what Bourdieu (1984) calls "both transgression and an element of personal/social distinction." Thus "high art" and "low culture" can comingle in popular consumer imagination and reach their substance in consumption objects. One of the driving ideas of postmodernism is that instead of (or in addition to) looking for universal and objective standards of aesthetic taste, consumers look for personal perspectives that may run counter to such standards.

Our notions of everyday life rely on the seminal ideas of Lefebvre (1971) and Certeau (1984). These authors, in their own way, distinguish "the space of experience and its everyday life with its embodied interactions" from more abstract and impersonal notions of economy and culture. They are mainly concerned that life in modern industrial cultures can become very structured and devoid of human content. In such a culture, the rational order is represented by the industrial structure and the non-rational order is oriented toward the private non-work life (Habermas 1984). The structures of work environments are such that they are stripped of humanistic appeals, while individual workers or consumers need to escape from such an oppressive environment. Perhaps the individual can find relief by directly participating in such endeavors and by seeking experiences in everyday consumption practices. To meet consumers' needs, the marketing enterprise provides opportunities for sensory consumption through everyday products. Sometimes, as the critics of market culture argue, this is done with excessive zeal rather than appropriate sensitivity. The question is, do consumers buy into the marketing system to meet their aesthetic and emotional needs?

Kozinets (2002) suggests that consumers resort to some sort of Bakhtinian carnivalesque-type escapism, as depicted in his work on "burning man." On the other hand, Mackay (1997) takes a more inclusive view, arguing, for instance, that consumption activities can be studied as part of everyday life, as being integral to consumers' identity construction and creative pursuits. "Rather than a passive, secondary, determined activity, consumption is increasingly seen as an activity with its own practices, tempo, significance, and determination" (p. 4). While everyday life refers to "routine activities and control of ordinary people as they go about their day-to-day lives," he also sees consumers as being "endlessly creative in the appropriation and manipulation of consumer goods" (p. 5).

Numerous writers on the postmodern have advanced the idea that everyday life in western consumer culture has become aestheticized, as boundaries between high art and popular culture and between different styles (of art, architecture, etc.) have been effaced (Debord 1983; Featherstone 1991; Baudrillard 1995). Research on aestheticization processes occurring in consumer culture has focused largely upon aesthetic principles integral to the design of products and corporate images (Schmitt & Simonson 1997) and has not paid sufficient attention to the aesthetic nature of the consumption experience itself. Nevertheless, some exceptions can be found: (1) Holt's (1995) classification of consumption practices into experience (i.e., an aesthetic or emotional reaction to a consumption object), integration, classification, and play, using the game of baseball as exemplar; (2) Peñaloza's (1999) work on the experiential and spatial dimensions of consumption in a particular retail setting (Nike Town); (3) Schroeder's (2002) perspective on visual consumption as a means of sensory communication and experiential system; and (4) Brown et al.'s (2001) exposition of contemporary aesthetics as a postmodern condition.

Although the marketing and consumer literature on aesthetics is somewhat limited, it is not insignificant. On the firm side, Schmitt and Simonson (1997) focus on brand images and identity issues through the management of product and/or corporate aesthetics. Their main arguments are related to how strategic branding can be employed to interact with product attributes and what impacts they have on customer sensory experiences, and how this system of interaction creates brand appeals and ultimately brand differentiation in the marketplace. Thus, the emphasis is on the aesthetic appeal of ad presentation; that is, its creative execution.

From the consumer side, as everyday objects become commodified through mass production and lose their aura, a natural tendency appears to be to elevate them from ordinary to extraordinary status, or to (re)aestheticize objects. This point has been made compellingly by Heilbrun (2002). According to Heilbrun, aestheticization becomes a defense against the "impoverishment of sensory experience."

In the 1980s consumer research began to move away from a cognitive paradigm to an interpretive one. People started to introduce such terms as consumer experiences, meanings, symbols, images and cultural categories, and a host of other similarly evocative terms which stood in stark contrast to product attributes, brand loyalty, lifestyle marketing, and other analytical categories that are measurable and quantifiable. A major move in this direction

came in the mid-1980s when authors began to examine how postmodern culture influences consumption patterns. In fact, consumption systems were themselves viewed as culturally coded systems. Research has begun to address how consumers' understanding of products and brands derives from the meanings that consumers attach to them. A question that is asked is where do the meanings come from and how are they attached to consumable objects and consumer environments. The fact that any given culture forms the basis of relevant symbolic systems and aesthetic representations means that these symbolic systems transcend into sensory experiences – which is the basis of postmodern consumption.

SEE ALSO: Commodities, Commodity Fetishism, and Commodification; Consumption, Mass Consumption, and Consumer Culture; Disneyization; Hyperconsumption/Overconsumption; Media and Consumer Culture; Postmodern Culture; Postmodern Social Theory; Postmodernism

REFERENCES AND SUGGESTED READINGS

Baudrillard, J. (1995) Transaesthetics. In: *The Transparency of Evil: Essays on Extreme Phenomena.* Trans. J. Benedict. Verso, New York.

Bourdieu, P. (1984) *Distinction: A Social Critique of the Judgment of Taste.* Harvard University Press, Cambridge, MA.

Brown, S., Hirschman, E. C., & Maclaran, P. (2001) Presenting the Past: On Marketing's Re-production Orientation. In: Brown, S. & Patterson, A. (Eds.), *Imagining Marketing: Art, Aesthetics and the Avant-Garde.* Routledge, New York, pp. 145–91.

Certeau, M. de (1984) *The Practice of Everyday Life.* Trans. S. Rendall. University of California Press, Berkeley.

Debord, G. (1983 [1967]) *Society of the Spectacle.* Black & Red, Detroit.

Featherstone, M. (1991) *Consumer Culture and Postmodernism.* Sage, Newbury Park, CA.

Firat, A. F. & Venkatesh, A. (1995) Liberatory Postmodernism and the Reenchantment of Consumption. *Journal of Consumer Research* 22 (December): 239–67.

Habermas, J. (1984) *The Theory of Communicative Action*, Vol. 1. Beacon Press, Boston.

Heilbrun, B. (2002) Alessi: Italian Design and the Re-Enchantment of Everyday Objects. In: Solomon,

M., Bamossy, G., & Askegaard, S. (Eds.), *Consumer Behavior: A European Perspective*. Prentice-Hall Colchester, pp. 569–673.

Holt, D. B. (1995) How Consumers Consume: A Typology of Consumption Practices. *Journal of Consumer Research* 22 (June): 1–16.

Jameson, F. (1983) Postmodernism and Consumer Society. In: Foster, H. (Ed.), *The Anti-Aesthetic: Essays on Postmodern Culture*. Bay Press, Seattle, WA, pp. 111–26.

Kozinets, R. V. (2002) Can Consumers Escape the Market? Emancipatory Illusions from Burning Man. *Journal of Consumer Research* 29 (June): 20–38.

Lefebvre, H. (1971) *Everyday Life in the Modern World*. Trans. S. Rabinovitch. Allen Lane, London.

Lyotard, J.-F. (1984) *The Postmodern Condition: A Report on Knowledge*. University of Minnesota Press, Minneapolis.

Mackay, H. (1997) Introduction. In: Mackay, H. (Ed.), *Consumption and Everyday Life*. Sage, London, pp. 1–12.

Peñaloza, L. (1999) Just Doing It: A Visual Ethnographic Study of Spectacular Consumption Behavior at Nike Town. *Consumption, Markets and Culture* 2(4): 337–400.

Schmitt, B. & Simonson, A. (1997) Aesthetics: The New Marketing Paradigm. In: *Marketing Aesthetics: The Strategic Management of Brands, Identity, and Image*. Free Press, New York, pp. 3–49.

Schroeder, J. E. (2002) *Visual Consumption*. Routledge, New York.

Sokal, A. (1996) Transgressing the Boundaries: Toward a Transformative Hermeneutics of Quantum Gravity. *Social Text* 46/47 (spring/summer): 217–52.

Solomon, M. R., Bamossy, G., & Askegaard, S. (2002) *Consumer Behavior: A European Perspective*. Prentice-Hall Europe, Colchester.

postmodern culture

Victor E. Taylor

Postmodern culture is a far-reaching term describing a range of activities, events, and perspectives relating to art, architecture, the humanities, and the social sciences beginning in the second half of the twentieth century. In contrast to modern culture, with its emphasis on social progress, coherence, and universality, postmodern culture represents instances of dramatic historical and ideological change in which modernist narratives of progress and social holism are viewed as incomplete, elastic, and contradictory. In conjunction with the end of modernist progress narratives, an insistence on coherence gives way to diversity and the dominance of universality is subverted by difference within a postmodern condition. Additionally, postmodern culture stands for more than the current state of society. Postmodern culture is characterized by the valuing of activities, events, and perspectives that emphasize the particular over the global or the fragment over the whole. This reversal of a modernist ideology necessitates a valuation of variation and flexibility in the cultural sphere. Primarily through the writings of Jean-François Lyotard, whose seminal book *The Postmodern Condition: A Report on Knowledge* (1984) remains the definitive exposition of the term and its significance to society, postmodern culture has come to be identified with a radical critique of the relationship between the particular and the universal in art, culture, and politics.

The most visible signs of postmodern culture appear in art, architecture, film, music, and literature after the 1950s. The most prominent stylistic features that unite these diverse forums are pastiche, non-representationalism, and non-linearity. In the art and architecture of postmodern culture, collage and historical eclecticism are emphasized. The American painter Mark Tansey depicts historical scenes and figures in anachronistic situations. His 1982 painting *Purity Test* positions a group of "traditional" Native Americans on horseback overlooking Smithson's 1970 *Sprial Jetty*, a temporal impossibility. In architecture, Robert Venturi combines classical and modern architectural features, juxtaposing distinct historical styles. Art and architecture within postmodern culture celebrate collage and do not symbolize historical, thematic, or organic unity. Their postmodern quality can be found in the artist's or architect's desire to abandon the constraints of temporal, stylistic, and historical continuity.

In film, literature, and music representative of postmodern culture there is an emphasis on non-linearity, parody, and pastiche. Postmodern film, such as the Coen brothers' *Blood Simple* or *Fargo*, disrupt narrative timelines and emphasize the work of parody. Quentin

Tarantino's *Pulp Fiction*, for instance, "begins" at the end and continually recycles crime scene clichés throughout the plot. Similar aesthetic principles are at play in postmodern literature in which the "realist mode" is thwarted in favor of the seemingly nonsensical. The Canadian writer Douglas Coupland epitomizes this departure from realism. *All Families Are Psychotic* (2001) depicts the surreal life of the Drummond family – a disparate familial group brought together by the daughter's impending launch into space and the financial woes of the father. In film and fiction the everydayness of life is shown to be complex, parodic, and undetermined. The division between the so-called "real" and "unreal" is collapsed and vast excesses of postmodern society are allowed to spiral out of control. Postmodern culture "adopts a dedifferentiating approach that willfully subverts boundaries between high and low art, artist and spectator and among different artistic forms and genres" (Best & Kellner 1997: 132).

Music in postmodern culture shares a great deal with the previous artistic forms. The discontinuity that one associates with John Cage's atonal compositions is taken to another level. Contemporary postmodern musicians mix and match different musical styles and traditions, adding a cultural pastiche to Cage's theory of improvisation. Bubba Sparxxx's (a.k.a. Warren Anderson Mathis) "Dirty South," "Southern Hip Hop," or "Hip-Hop Country" style mixes the sound and theme of traditional hip-hop music with a Country nuance. His lyrics, especially in his 2001 song "Ugly," address issues of identity and the hybridity and similarity that one finds among urban and rural youth as they attempt to attain stardom within the entertainment industry. Along the same lines, Rapper Kanye West combines hip-hop music with Caribbean styles, including the reggae sound and motifs one would associate with Ziggy Marley. West, in addition to his political and cultural messages, offers a "Christian-Rap" testimony in his music. His 2004 "Jesus Walks" integrates a heavy, military urban sound with gospel themes drawn from direct references to biblical passages. In popular music, figures such as Paul Simon and Sting utilize non-Western (primarily African and Middle Eastern) sounds and style in their recent albums.

Music in postmodern culture is heterogeneous, stylistically mixed, and international in influence.

While postmodern culture can be illuminated by reference to specific cultural products, it is important to keep in mind the underlying philosophical logic driving the phenomenon. Postmodernity as a reaction against a modernity, as Lyotard observes, is grounded in the Enlightenment, with its confidence in the faculty of reason to ascertain philosophical "truths" and its dedication to the progress of science and technology to enhance and improve the human situation. Taken together, this confidence and dedication to a particular intellectual framework produces monolithic accounts of the nature of reality and humankind's place within it. The "postmodern condition," therefore, is a disruption in the claim of totality found in these Enlightenment-generated accounts. According to postmodernists, the western worldview, with its commitment to universality in all things related to being human, gives way under the weight of its own contradictions and repressions. The comprehensive grand theories or grand narratives, as Lyotard describes them, subsequently fail in a postmodern era insofar as the plurality of human existence emerges within a wider cultural space. Postmodern knowledge of the world, as Lyotard explains, must take into account the multiplicity of experience or "phrasings" and the possibility of new, unanticipated experiences or phrasings that will assist in making sense of reality in ways either not permitted or not imagined by a modernist ideology. The content of knowledge we presently possess is continually being transformed by technology and "the nature of knowledge cannot survive unchanged within this context of general transformation" (Lyotard 1984: 4). Culture, as it pertains to postmodernism, is more than a repository of data; it is the activity that shapes and gives meaning to the world, constructing reality rather than presenting it.

Postmodern culture, as a valorization of the multiplicity found in "little narratives," exhibits anti-modernist tendencies, with art and politics rejecting calls to narrative totalization. Jameson (1984), referring to the social theorist Jürgen Habermas, states that "postmodernism involves the explicit repudiation of the modernist

tradition – the return of the middle-class philistine or *Spießbürger* (bourgeois) rejection of modernist forms and values – and as such the
expression of a new social conservatism." While
an emphasis on the particular over the universal
captures the revolutionary impulse found in the
political and aesthetic sentiments of Lyotardian
postmodernism, it runs counter to a lengthy
critique of postmodernism by social theorists,
mainly Marxists, who view this turn to the particularity of "little narratives" as a symptom
of late capitalism, with its valuation on proliferating commodities and flexible corporate
organizational models. The characteristics of
multiplicity, pastiche, and non-linearity, while
viewed as offering new aesthetic, epistemological, and political possibilities by postmodern
artists, architects, writers, filmmakers, and theorists, are understood by those who reject
postmodernism as examples of the "logic of
late capitalism" (Jameson 1984) in which commodities and consumers enter into rapid, undifferentiated exchange in ever-increasing and
diversified markets.

Harvey (1989) argues that postmodernism is
the ideological ally of global capitalism, which is
characterized in part by decentered organizational modes, intersecting markets, and hyper-
consumerism. While social theorists such as
Daniel Bell, Philip Cooke, Edward Soja, and
Scott Lash see postmodern culture as a symptom of global capitalist ideology, others view it
as an extension or completion of the modernist
project. Bauman (1992) notes that "the postmodern condition can be therefore described
… as modernity emancipated from false consciousness [and] as a new type of social condition marked by the overt institutionalization of
characteristics which modernity – in its designs
and managerial practices – set about to eliminate and, failing that, tried to conceal." In this
account, postmodern culture is viewed as having a continuity with modernism and not necessarily an affiliation with a late capitalist mode
of production. Although the features of postmodern culture are similarly described and
agreed upon by social and literary theorists from
across the ideological spectrum, the meaning of
postmodern culture remains largely in dispute,
with its advocates seeing it as a new condition
and its detractors seeing it as an accomplice to
late capitalism and conservative ideology.

In the few decades since its inception as a
critical concept in the arts, architecture, humanities, and social sciences, postmodern culture
remains controversial. Artists, architects, writers, philosophers, social theorists, and filmmakers continue to explore its vast possibilities,
however. Whether it is a new condition, an
emancipation from modernist false consciousness, a subsidiary of late capitalism, or a indefinable *Zeitgeist*, the debate over postmodern
culture will be a central feature of intellectual
life for years to come.

SEE ALSO: Art Worlds; Barthes, Roland;
Capitalism; Cultural Critique; Culture; Culture: Conceptual Clarifications; Globalization,
Consumption and; Postmodern Consumption; Postmodern Social Theory; Postmodernism; Poststructuralism

REFERENCES AND SUGGESTED
READINGS

Bauman, Z. (1992) *Intimations of Postmodernity*. Rou-
tledge, London.
Best, S. & Kellner, D. (1991) *Postmodern Theory:
Critical Interrogations*. Guilford Press, New York.
Best, S. & Kellner, D. (1997) *The Postmodern Turn*.
Guilford Press, New York.
Debeljak, A. (1998) *Reluctant Modernity: The Institu-
tion of Art and Its Historical Forms*. Rowman &
Littlefield, New York.
Harvey, D. (1989) *The Condition of Postmodernity:
An Enquiry into the Origins of Cultural Change*.
Blackwell, Oxford.
Jameson, F. (1984) Forward. In: Lyotard, J.-F., *The
Postmodern Condition: A Report on Knowledge*. Uni-
versity of Minnesota Press, Minneapolis, pp. vii–xxi.
Lyotard, J.-F. (1984) *The Postmodern Condition: A
Report on Knowledge*. University of Minnesota
Press, Minneapolis.
Taylor, V. (2000) *Para/Inquiry: Postmodern Religion
and Culture*. Routledge, London.

postmodern feminism

Kristina Wolff

Postmodern feminism is a body of scholarship
that questions and rejects traditional essentialist
practices, as established in and by modernity.

The general premise of postmodern social theory is a rejection of the western ideal of establishing universal grand narratives as a means of understanding and explaining society. Postmodern theory directly challenges claims of a unified subject, which is then presented as representing an objective point of view, in essence, a "view from nowhere." Postmodern theory and practices recognize differences, making room for all to contribute and thus having a "view from everywhere" and eliminating the practice of positing one way or one understanding as representing or being "truth." The combination of postmodernist theory and feminism allows for a questioning of essentialist approaches within and outside of feminism, an expansion of feminist scholarship as well as contributing the lens of "gender" and other issues inherent to feminism to the body of postmodern scholarship.

Postmodern thought follows early feminist challenges to dualistic concepts, such as modernist practices of objectivity being favored over subjectivity, belief in rational over irrational thought, and the strength of nature over cultural constructions. Generally, this body of scholarship can be divided into three areas, *postmodernity*, *postmodernism*, and *postmodern social theory*. Postmodernity represents a specific political or social time period that follows the modern era. Some theorists believe that modernity has ended and that we are currently in a postmodern era. Postmodernity stresses the importance of recognizing specific cultural, political, and historical moments connected to "who" or "what" is being studied. Postmodernism represents the cultural products that differ from modern products. These consist of a variety of things including architecture, movies, art, poetry, music, and literature. Lastly, postmodern social theory is a distinct way of thinking which is open to a range of possibilities, consisting of different approaches that move away from the constraints of modern thinking.

Early postmodern studies focus on language and discourse as sites of analysis. This practice emerges out of *poststructuralism*. While there is debate as to whether or not poststructuralism is a postmodernist project, it is recognized as the precursor of postmodernism. Poststructuralism seeks to uncover and understand general structures guiding all forms of social life. Early

scholarship primarily emerged out of France with the work of Derrida, Foucault, Irigaray, and Kristeva. It focused in the areas of language, particularly linguistics and semiotics. Similar to postmodernism, it posits that subjectivity is not something that is fixed or variable; simply, it is socially constructed, therefore creating social reality. This field quickly expanded to include literary studies, philosophy, history, and the social sciences. Both poststructuralism and postmodernist approaches work to bring the margins into the mainstream as well as to deconstruct and decenter society, as a means to discover where and how power operates. *Deconstruction* posits that language is itself a social construction, therefore to understand its meaning we need to examine language in relationship to culture and society, in relationship to language itself. This process provides a means to uncover and understand the power connected to language, the ways in which language is used as a means of oppression. The concept and practice of deconstruction has been expanded beyond language, to understanding various complexities of human society as a means to uncover inequality. Postmodern feminism also examines the same academic areas and "traditional" feminist subjects including gender and sexuality, as well as the development of science and our conceptions of knowledge.

Gender is the core foundational piece of feminism. Recognizing the various roles of gender within society is also one of many strong contributions and accomplishments of feminism. Postmodern feminist theory challenges the very notion of gender, recognizing that it is socially constructed, fluid, and conceptualized within a specific historical, political, and cultural context. One of the critiques of feminism and feminist thought is the reliance upon essentialist beliefs of gender, the assumption that all "women" are the same based on biological as well as cultural understandings of what is defined as "female." Women of color, women from non-industrialized nations as well as lesbian and socialist feminists often challenge the assumption that "woman" alone is a unifying category, and its usage often excludes the complexities and differences of race, ethnicity, nation status, social class, and sexuality. Theorists such as Susan Bordo, Judith Butler, and

Jane Flax criticize the traditionally fixed binary structure of gender. Their early work within postmodern feminism called for new narrative approaches to gender, ones that recognize the multiplicity of gender. Using postmodernist approaches, constructions of "woman" (as well as "men") were now viewed through a variety of lenses at the same time, thus widening the scope to include issues of race, ethnicity, class, sexual orientation, and other differences that women face (Nicholson 1990; Butler 1999). Included within this analytical shift is the acknowledgment that the category of gender is simultaneously used as a means of oppression as well as a source of liberation.

Entangled with conceptions of gender is an assumption of heterosexuality. The combination of gender and sex is also intertwined with personal and public identities. Butler theorizes the interplay of these things as *performativity*, that gender and sexuality exist as a performance. Gender and sexual identities are layered, emerging in manifest and latent ways based on the individual as well as the cultural moment that she or he is in. For example, the manner in which a woman presents herself in public as well as the ways in which "she" is conceptualized in society is reliant upon cultural assumptions as well as her actual gender performance. There are layers of illusion in and on her exterior as well as interior levels of her body and soul. The repercussion of this is that societal norms are reified while other parts of us, our gender and sexual identities, remain hidden. The aspects that remain out of view as well as what is performed illustrates what is "right" or "true," thus reinforcing essentialist ideologies of gender and sexuality (Nicholson 1990; Butler 1999).

Therefore reality is a fabrication, what is seen on the exterior satisfies societal expectations, what resides on the inside remains hidden. Yet, our understandings and conceptions of sex, gender, and identity are social constructions. This then raises the question of what is real, demonstrating that the boundaries between what "is" and what is expected become blurred. Our concepts of what gender and sexuality are, are based on these constructions, therefore, there is no true meaning. Critics argue that this results in fragmentation between one's consciousness and idea of self. If people keep changing from moment to moment and our understandings of components of our identity continually are in flux, then how do we determine a sense of self? This split challenges not only understandings of male and female but also the distinction between public and private lives and identities. The combination of postmodernist theory with feminism expands the investigation and analysis of gender, looking at the relationships with other characteristics, differences, and identities, and thus the scholarship is reflective of the complexities of identity.

The shift from dualistic approaches to multifaceted examinations directly challenges the subject/object split existing in essentialism. The postmodern project of deconstructing and decentering understandings of "subject," in essence, creates the "death of man" as "man" ceases to be the center subject and therefore "woman" is no longer the object. Some feminists are opposed to this, fearful that women will lose their sense of agency in the process and that the foundation of "woman" will be erased. However, women have rarely been recognized or held in the subject position. One of the overarching tasks for postmodern feminists is to reconstruct conceptualizations of the subject/object split, recognizing it as a recreation of self, as a constituted self that has endless revolutionary potential. This shift is representative of one of the core purposes of feminism, to combine theory with practice.

One result of the challenge to and change in defining the relationship of subject and object is the reconception of understandings and practices of science. Certainly, the structures of western science consist of dualistic approaches, theories that are used to explore and explain the complexities of human life, our physical and social worlds. The emergence of postmodernist thought pushes science to move beyond a singular, individual focus to an all-inclusive one, recognizing and containing multiple voices and viewpoints. Feminist theory recognizes the foundations of science as inherently masculine in structure, and while it includes essentialist, dualistic approaches to understanding the complexities of gender, feminism also inherently contains postmodernist practices as well. Feminist scholars such as Sandra Harding, Seyla Benhabib, Nancy Fraser, and Linda Nicholson explore philosophy, science, and western understandings of knowledge. While some scholars argue that science cannot exist without its grounding in essentialism, without "objectivity," these feminist theorists directly challenge this belief. They call for feminist approaches that remove women and other marginalized groups from the position of subject, that which is being studied, to more central positions, where they are advancing knowledge in a variety of ways.

Sandra Harding's argument for the establishment of feminist epistemologies is one example of postmodernist feminist thought. Early approaches to questioning western science and scholarship focused on bringing women to the center of analysis and calling for the establishment of feminist science. This is grounded in cultural feminist approaches, which focus on the differences between women and men. Therefore, by shifting the lens of inquiry away from a male viewpoint and instead stemming from and onto a female viewpoint, we can gain new insights, develop new bodies of knowledge, and use this as a means of eliminating gender inequality. Postmodern feminists directly challenge this approach due to its singular focus on understanding gender from a biological essentialist position. Simply changing the center does little to challenge the masculine, patriarchal structures used in western scholarship. Harding argues for feminist science through the development of new feminist theories, methods, and epistemologies. She continues to utilize *feminist standpoint* as the cornerstone of developing new scholarship. Feminist standpoint recognizes that women's understanding of the world is different from that of men due to their experiences and knowledge (Smith 1987; Hartsock 1997). Postmodernist, postcolonial, and feminist scholars expand this concept to an inclusive standpoint, one recognizing the multiplicity of difference. This change becomes the foundation of developing feminist epistemologies, bodies of knowledge that do not reinforce existing hierarchical structures, that seek to expand scholarship, moving away from essentialist approaches.

Harding conceptualizes feminist epistemologies as justificatory strategies, challenging dominant understandings of knowledge, science, and scholarship, providing an alternative to traditional procedures grounded in hollow claims of objective, value-free research. These various "ways of knowing" add a richness, an opportunity to expand and enhance bodies of knowledge rather than focusing on the "self" of a particular powerful group or speaker. Feminist scholarship brings a diversity of women's work, which recognizes the complexities of difference and the ways in which these differences contribute to the quest for knowledge without privileging one type, approach, understanding, or interest (s) over another. The development of these strategies also provides methods, specific procedures that guide feminist research, theories, practices, and policies that advance knowledge and work to eliminate oppression and domination.

Inherent to feminism is the analysis of and challenges to existing power structures as well as how power and resistance operate. Postmodernist thought and practice ushers in new understandings of the ways in which social structures, boundaries, and power itself have changed. Donna Haraway's work illustrates these shifts in viewpoints. Utilizing the metaphor of a cyborg, she explores the complexities between modern and postmodern worlds, noting that women are no longer dominated by traditional means such as through the control of male expectations of mothering to beliefs of the purity and submission of all women. Haraway also uses discursive examples of the emergence of a postmodern world, noting that the term "women of color" represents an identity constructed out of difference and otherness (Nicholson 1990).

The focus on the role(s) and impact of discourse, particularly as a site of power, is another common theme in postmodernist feminist scholarship (Nicholson 1990; Fraser 1995; Hartsock 1997; Butler 1999). The idea of a "female subject" is constituted in and by discourse. Resistance to this concept also exists within discourse; as Foucault theorizes, where there is power there is also resistance. Postmodern approaches disrupt discourse, particularly in relation to what the state produces and transmits to the whole of society. Traditionally, marginalized groups have created counterdiscourses as a means of resisting power and as an attempt to enter into mainstream discourse, but these directly fought against dominance in modernist ways that kept them on the outer boundaries. With the shift and widening of focus that postmodernism brings, boundaries are blurred between public and private spaces, discourse and critiques of dominant discourses stemming from marginalized groups become part of the larger public debate. Therefore the complexities of gender, the inclusion of difference across race, ethnicity, nation, sexuality, age, and so on, become part of the conversations. Discourse is a site of power as well as a tool for social change. The creation of postmodern feminist methodologies allows for a deconstruction of texts, of discourse, which provides means to follow and understand the ways in which power flows through discourse and also creates vehicles for revolutionary change through the use of discourse.

There are critiques of postmodern feminism, which include the lack of the development of a critical political agenda, of a realistic means of social change beyond theorizing. Concerns center on the issue of social location, identity, and difference. Postmodernist approaches need to be mindful of recognizing and celebrating difference simply because it exists. Social location, particularly based on difference, is a site of negotiation and conflict. Some theorists define differences merely as illusion, disregarding real-life experiences due to difference. By universalizing all differences as inherent to all women, in turn women become marginal and united due to the status of "difference." This concentration on difference reproduces the "all or nothing" situation that is being critiqued with essentialist approaches. Cultural feminism unites women due to sameness of gender, whereas postmodern feminism unites women due to their differences. Both are viewed as extreme positions.

Scholars such as Paula M. L. Moya explain that categories such as race and nation status invoke specific experiences and identities that are often deconstructed or displaced within postmodernist scholarship. The result of this is a dismissal of women's identity and experiences as well as an erasure of characteristics inherent to their sense of identity, of self, and of commonalities that bind people together. Theorizing changes in identity is important, but there must be some integration with the realities of the real world, with actual experiences. Connections need to be made between

conceptualization and feelings. The concern over the outright rejection of essentialist understandings of gender also results in the concern felt by many feminists about the erasure of woman as well as conceptions about gender overall. Can there be feminism, feminist thought, without the concept(s) of "woman," without a feminist standpoint? This also brings in concerns about the elite nature of postmodernist thought, particularly in relation to rejecting modern understandings of race, gender, class, and so on, as it has a different impact on white women with privilege than on women of color, women from non-western nations, women who do not fall into the same categories as the elites.

One answer to the apparent limits of postmodernist feminism is the need to clearly situate it within specific historical, cultural, and political frameworks. This helps to avoid false generalizations and the development of similar situations that are being critiqued in essentialism. As Harding noted through defining feminist epistemologies as strategies, postmodernist practices can be strategically used. Linda Alcoff points out that women's position in society is continually changing, it is not static. Postmodern feminism can be successful through shifting approaches to combating oppression and domination, as women's statuses change. This includes working on collaborations and building coalitions across differences while also recognizing these differences.

SEE ALSO: Cultural Feminism; Deconstruction; Derrida, Jacques; Feminism; Feminist Standpoint Theory; Foucault, Michel; Postmodern Sexualities; Postmodern Social Theory; Postmodernism

REFERENCES AND SUGGESTED READINGS

Alcoff, L. (1988) Cultural Feminism Versus Post-Structuralism: The Identity Crisis in Feminist Theory. *Signs: A Journal of Women in Culture and Society* 13: 405–36.

Benhabib, S., Butler, J., Cornell, D., & Fraser, N. (1995) *Feminist Contentions: A Philosophical Exchange*. Routledge, New York.

Bordo, S. (1990) Feminism, Postmodernism, and Gender-Skepticism. In: Nicholson, L. (Ed.), *Feminism/Postmodernism*. Routledge, New York.

Butler, J. (1999) *Gender Trouble: Feminism and the Subversion of Identity*. Routledge, New York.

Cixous, H. (1981) The Laugh of the Medusa. In: Marks, E. & Courtivron, I. de (Eds.), *New French Feminisms*. Trans. K. Cohen & P. Cohen. Schocken Books, New York, pp. 245–61.

Flax, J. (1990) *Thinking Fragments: Psychoanalysis, Feminism, and Postmodernism in the Contemporary West*. University of California Press, Berkeley.

Foucault, M. (1980) *Power/Knowledge: Selected Interviews and Other Writings, 1972–1997*. Ed. C. Gordeon. Pantheon, New York.

Fraser, N. (1995) Politics, Culture, and the Public Sphere: Toward a Postmodern Conception. In: Nicholson, L. & Seidman, S. (Eds.), *Social Postmodernism: Beyond Identity Politics*. Cambridge University Press, New York, pp. 287–312.

Haraway, D. (1991) *Simians, Cyborgs, and Women: The Reinvention of Nature*. Routledge, New York.

Hartsock, N. (1997) The Feminist Standpoint: Developing the Ground for Specifically Feminist Historical Materialism. In: Nicholson, L. (Ed.), *The Second Wave: A Reader in Feminist Theory*. Routledge, New York, pp. 216–40.

Heckman, S. (1990) *Gender and Knowledge: Elements of a Postmodern Feminism*. Northeastern University Press, Boston.

Kipnis, L. (1989) Feminism: The Political Conscience of Postmodernism? *Social Text* 21: 149–66.

Longino, H. (1993) Feminist Standpoint Theory and the Problems of Knowledge. *Signs* 19(1): 201.

Nicholson, L. (Ed.) (1990) *Feminism/Postmodernism*. Routledge, New York.

Smith, D. (1987) *The Everyday World as Problematic: A Feminist Sociology*. Northeastern University Press, Boston.

Yeatman, A. (1994) *Postmodern Revisionings of the Political*. Routledge, New York.

postmodern organizations

Stephen Linstead

Postmodern organizations are organizations that have broken with the traditional principles of organization as defined by modernist theory dominated by rationalism; they are also characterized by having developed new and original forms and practices in response to the changing environmental conditions of postmodern society. Such organizations can be identified both by the extent to which they are not epistemologically modern and by the extent to which they adopt and create new and different patterns of operation and regulation. Nevertheless, the continued persistence of modern methods of organizing is not to be doubted. Postmodern organizations, then, may themselves be hybrids of modern and postmodern modes of organizing, and coexist in mixed populations that include organizations that still run on predominantly modern lines. Furthermore, just as there was a variety of versions of modernism, there are different responses to the challenges of postmodernity, which display radicalism on both the right and the left. Boje and Dennehey (1999) follow Pauline Rosenau in distinguishing between *skeptical* and *affirmative* versions loosely based on Nietzsche's passive and active nihilisms, and there is also a fertile and heterogeneous middle ground. This said, we can attempt a broad and cautious typology of the familiar features of each, as shown in Table 1.

The break between modernism and postmodernism in organizational forms is not a clean one. Table 1 provides an indicative inventory of possibilities, not all of which can be found together empirically, nor should they be considered to be either necessary or sufficient for an organization to be considered postmodern. Early contributions to the question of postmodern organizations were divided (Parker 1992) into those that reflected on postmodern organization as a process (Hassard & Parker 1993; Cooper & Burrell 1988) and those that reflected on postmodern organizations as a phenomenon (Clegg 1990; Boje et al. 1996; Boje & Dennehey 1999). Hardt and Negri (2000) offer an illuminating account of postmodernization as a process and its effect on both economic organization and individual subjectivity. They identify three historical economic paradigms: tradition, modernization, and postmodernization or informatization. It is significant that rather than focus on defining an epoch (e.g., premodern, modern, postmodern (as Boje and Dennehey and others do), Hardt and Negri concentrate on its characteristic animating process. Tradition was dominated by processes of primary production, such as agriculture and the extraction of raw materials (e.g., mining). Modernization saw a shift to secondary production, with industrialization and the manufacture of

Table 1   Modern and postmodern forms of organization

	Modern organizations	*Postmodern organizations*
Mission, strategy, and goals	Producer-led specialization	Customer-led diffusion
Structures	Hierarchy Bureaucracy Functions Product management	Flat, lean, internal market Heterarchy Networks, meshworks Matrix, project teams Brand management
Orientation to size	Growth-driven, mergers	Downsizing, glocalization, alliances
Decision-making	Centralized, determinist	Devolved, collaborative
Planning orientation	Short-term calculability	Long-term sustainability
Relation to market	Unresponsive	Responsive/flexible
Relation to state	Externally regulated	Deregulated or internally regulated
Relation to stakeholders	Financial, economic, profit maximization	Ethical, socially conscious
Mode of competition	Resources/competencies/economies of scale	Speed/information/managing knowledge
Means of production	Differentiated/dedicated	Dedifferentiated/dededicated
Means of delivery/ consumption	Dedifferentiated/standardized	Differentiated/customized
Mode of operation	Mass production Fordism	Mass customization Toyotism
Mode of communication	Vertical	Horizontal, network
Means of control	Supervisory micro-management	IT-led and peer-led surveillance
	Panoptic control	Chimerical control
Cultural orientation	Exchange, social, material	Symbolic, virtual
Leader archetype	Heroic	Post-heroic
Worker archetype	Mass production worker	Knowledge worker
Employee relations	Collective, dialectical, mistrust	Polyphonic, dialogical, trust
Reward systems	Individually based, collectively negotiated	Collectively based, individually negotiated
Skill formation	Deskilling, inflexible	Multiskilling, flexible
Jobs	Simple	Complex
Roles and accountability	Rule governed	Empowered
Managers	Supervisors	Coaches
Performance achievement	Measured activities	Negotiated key results
Careers	Planned, internal capital	Portfolio, social capital

durable goods. Yet agriculture did not disappear – it remained an important part of even the most advanced manufacturing economies; indeed, it remained the dominant sector well into the nineteenth century. But it did change its nature – it became industrialized agriculture, dominated by the demands of industry, financial and social pressures, automated and focused on the development of agricultural products. Yet not only agriculture was transformed along with industrialization, for as Hardt and Negri (2000: 284–5) argue, society itself was industrialized in the transformation of human relationships. The nature of being human and what it meant to be human were changed utterly as the machine metaphor came to dominate how human subjects began to think of themselves – as human machines.

Hardt and Negri argue that modernism has not ended and its elements will be with us for some time to come, but modernization as a process has ended. They argue that in the advanced economies there has been a shift to those areas where higher value can be more easily extracted, which means a move to the provision of services: finance, health care, education, transportation, entertainment, advertising, and tourism all being growth industries. These industries require highly mobile flexible skills emphasizing knowledge, information, affect (emotionality), and communication. Just as modernization transformed agriculture, Hardt and Negri argue that these processes transform industry, as manufacturing becomes more like a service. Manufacturing does not in these circumstances die; rather, it is rejuvenated in a different form. The dominant metaphor of the industrial age gives way to information metaphors, as we think of ourselves not as machines, but as computers – and learn to act accordingly. We might consider the difference as being represented by the contrasting predicaments of the characters played by Charlie Chaplin in *Modern Times* and Keanu Reeves in *The Matrix*.

The shift in manufacturing processes has moved away from the dominance of mass production familiar in Fordism, which was characterized by a high degree of differentiation at the point of production (specialized technologies dedicated to one particular product) and dedifferentiation at the point of consumption (limited product choice or provision for customer-individual or market-niche requirements – Henry Ford's famous dictum "any color as long as it's black"). Postmodern production arrangements, sometimes labeled Toyotism, provide faster communication and response between production arrangements and consumer requirements. There is increasing dedifferentiation at the point of production (with dededicated and flexible technologies that can produce a variety of products with minimal set-up times) and higher differentiation at the

point of consumption (a wide range of options and choices available to the consumer, sometimes called mass customization). This proliferation of choice is not without its down side and can lead to confusion marketing, where consumers are inundated with such a variety of apparent choices that they are unable effectively to sift through the information and make their choice based on recidivistic characteristics such as aesthetics or availability rather than performance or content. In an information-rich environment competitive advantage may be achieved by communicating to customers and clients in ways that help them to discriminate effectively between products, via the service and support given to them, rather than by the technical features of the product or service itself. Such service-led manufacturing Hardt and Negri term the immaterialization of labor.

Immaterial labor occurs where information and communication combine in producing a service, cultural product, knowledge, or communication. There are three types of immaterial labor. *Informated* labor occurs when the production process is enabled by information technology to allow humans simply to push buttons rather than operate machines or work directly on the product. *Analytic* or *symbolic* labor is of two subtypes: the creative and intelligent labor done by analysts, problem-solvers, consultants, programmers, artists, copywriters, and other knowledge producers; and the routine tasks performed by data entry workers, call center operatives, and similar. *Emotional* labor involves the production and manipulation of affect or feelings and in contrast to the other types requires the full involvement of human bodies.

The processes of modernization resulted in the geographical centralization of production into industrial centers such as Manchester in the UK, Detroit in the US, and Osaka in Japan. Postmodernization allows manufacturing to be globally networked – as long as the required information can be transferred, products can be designed in one country, their components manufactured in several countries depending on skill availability and the cost of labor, assembled in another country, and sold in a variety of markets. Models of collaboration and cooperation in both modern and traditional systems are transformed as a result – in the context of global communication, industrial and social relations are no longer grounded in local conditions. It also allows manufacturers to collaborate on one product or service while competing on others, simultaneously sharing and protecting vital knowledge. Networks of organizations replace the tiers of hierarchy with the flatness of heterarchy, yet the equitarian appearance of such arrangements may be only illusory. Organizations now simulate team meetings in virtual team meeting rooms using the Internet, and project teams may be formed, carry out their duties successfully, and disband without ever meeting face to face; organizations themselves may be simulated in the "virtual organization," that usually involves a core of a few full-time people enjoying high levels of benefits (the netocrats), coordinating, controlling, and exercising power over contractors, part-timers, and net-slaves (telecommuters) who often receive no benefits at all (Boje and Dennehey 1999).

Gilles Deleuze and Felix Guattari throughout both volumes of *Capitalism and Schizophrenia* use the concept of deterritorialization to understand the way that capital, in particular, can have an abstract quality that allows it to move freely around the world. Capital itself has to be territorialized – that is, attached to a concrete value such as a pound of gold – in order to be realized. The value of a commodity that may be attached to a currency varies from place to place. Currencies that are transferable such as the dollar or sterling can be realized or territorialized in a variety of settings and can be deterritorialized – that is, hoarded – played on the money markets, or moved around from one country to another as investment in order to maximize returns. Other weaker currencies, such as the Brazilian *real* or the Chinese *renminbi*, cannot be transferred out of their home and have no value outside it, thus being completely territorialized. The removal of regulations that limit currency movements into local financial and commercial markets has enabled the rapid deterritorialization of capital. Indeed, the international financial markets are built on capital that may move in a virtual space on a stock exchange monitor without much prospect of being territorialized, which enables catastrophes of the magnitude of Barings Bank and Enron to escalate. Coupled with the

removal of other limiting legislation such as labor law and corporate regulations and the dedifferentiation of technology, the rapid transfer of jobs from one country to another, such as the relocation of financial industry call centers from the UK to India in the first decade of the twenty-first century, becomes possible. Paul Virilio in *The Lost Dimension* calls this *hypermodernity* rather than postmodernity, as there has been little evidence of an epistemological break with modernity – the society hooked on speed has replaced bureaucracy with dromocracy, the organizational form of rapid circulation whose model is the velodrome. Yet as both Castells (1996–8) and Bauman (1998) have pointed out, labor is not similarly deterritorialized – only a very small and privileged section of the managerial population is empowered to follow capital around the globe, and where labor seeks to move to follow demand (although labor generally is more mobile across state borders now than it has been since World War II) it poses problems of social order for the host states, which has led to the black market in human beings becoming more valuable globally than that for drugs.

Along with the shift in processes, the nature of necessary control has changed. Traditional control was direct and personal, based on close supervision and actual or perceived presence. Modern control shifted to a more impersonal basis, to rules, regulations, and requirements that were inspected more periodically rather than constantly supervised. Movements toward organizational structures and processes of greater complexity, often requiring greater skill and judgment in informated systems, require organizational subjects to be self-governing and self-policing at the same time as they are empowered. The work of Michel Foucault documents these shifts at societal levels and also at the level of institutions, including medicine, mental health, and prisons. Foucault's ideas on the development of governmentality have been taken up widely in organization studies. Sewell (1998) looks at the ways in which team working has been developed to create teams that police themselves through peer control, which combined with late modern methods of electronic surveillance produces a hybrid or chimerical control in which active supervision is not required. Additionally, interventions into the development of corporate culture are attempted by organizations to ensure that employees espouse and enact common organizational value sets, and use these as a template to self-regulate their behavior against that of the archetypical committed organizational member.

Baudrillard (1983) regards this emphasis on the creation of corporate culture as more evidence of the society of simulation obvious to any observation of consumer behavior – what Scott Lash and John Urry call an "economy of signs and space" in their eponymous book. A simulacrum is a copy of an imagined original that does not exist. For example, in Las Vegas, simulated New York, simulated Paris, simulated Egypt, and simulated Venice are on offer to entice consumers and gamblers to part with their money while enjoying a special simulation of authentic experience. Such is the extent of belief engendered in these simulacra that Ritzer (2005) terms them "cathedrals of consumption." Not only are these simulations conveniently located whereas the originals are several hours' flight apart, they are also safer, cleaner, easier to get around, and more user-friendly than the real places – which are full of natives going about their everyday lives, laid out with the random hand of history, dirty, untidy, rude, crude, and with plumbing problems. People are often disappointed with the real thing after visiting the simulacrum. In Disneyworld, the simulacrum clearly does not have an original to copy, yet the millions of visitors annually are happy to pretend that it does – while the management of the company itself is conducted on highly modernist disciplinary lines. Here Baudrillard identifies the difference between the society of the spectacle of Guy Debord, where the alienated spectator, like Marx's alienated worker, watches the world go by, and the society of the simulation, which requires the spectator reflexively to take up a role within it and actively reproduce it. Jean-François Lyotard has commented that McDonald's is a postmodern organization, while Ritzer's *The McDonaldization of Society* (2004) considers it to epitomize the unfolding of Weber's modernist principle of bureaucracy – and they are both right. Ritzer emphasizes the material elaboration of rationalization and efficiency in the production-line fast-food model of McDonaldization, where Lyotard appreciates that the key to McDonald's' success over its competitors lies in its immateriality – the simulated world of characters, events, toys, and films that seduces its customers into participation in an experience that involves purchasing, rather than the simple purchase of a product.

The greatest source of debate regarding postmodern organizations is whether they could be said to exist at all, given the emphasis in postmodernism on process and multiplicity and the continued persistence of modernist organizational forms and practices. There is an increasing amount of empirical evidence for emerging organizational forms, but it remains possible to analyze these with either a modern or a postmodern lens. Current research tends to emphasize the significance of image and signification less, and concentrates on three areas in particular: new patterns of relationships and network forms; new non-deontological ethical approaches; and the possibilities of new forms of power and resistance. There is also a trend towards the exploration of postmodern alternatives to the Protestant work ethic, centered on play (Kane 2004). In a more expansive vein the recent work of Hardt and Negri (2005) looks at possibilities of counter-organization by the multitude to resist the global spread of empire, which entails new forms of political, social, and even anti-capitalist organization.

SEE ALSO: Deindustrialization; Disneyization; Empire; Fordism/Post-Fordism; Foucault, Michel; McDonaldization; Management Networks; Post-Industrial Society; Postmodern Culture; Postmodern Social Theory; Postmodernism; Simulacra and Simulation

REFERENCES AND SUGGESTED READINGS

Baudrillard, J. (1983) *Simulacra and Simulation.* University of Michigan Press, Ann Arbor.

Bauman, Z. (1998) *Globalization: The Human Consequences.* Polity Press, Cambridge.

Boje, D. & Dennehey, R. (1999) *Managing in the Postmodern World: America's Revolution Against Exploitation.* Kendall/Hunt, Dubuque, IO.

Boje, D., Gephart, R., Jr., & Thatchenkery, T. J. (Eds.) (1996) *Postmodern Management and Organization Theory.* Sage, Thousand Oaks, CA.

Castells, M. (1996–8) *The Information Age: Economy, Society, Culture*, 3 vols. Blackwell, Oxford.

Clegg, S. (1990) *Modern Organizations: Organization Studies in the Postmodern World*. Sage, London.

Cooper, R. & Burrell, G. (1988) Modernism, Post-modernism and Organization Studies: An Introduction. *Organization Studies* 9(1): 91–112.

Hardt, M. & Negri, A. (2000) *Empire*. Harvard University Press, Cambridge, MA.

Hardt, M. & Negri, A. (2005) *Multitude: War and Democracy in the Age of Empire*. Hamish Hamilton, London.

Hassard, J. & Parker, M. (Eds.) (1993) *Postmodernism and Organization*. Sage, London.

Kane, P. (2004) *The Play Ethic*. Macmillan, London.

Parker, M. (1992) Postmodern Organizations or Postmodern Organization Theory. *Organization Studies* 13(1): 1–17.

Ritzer, G. (2004) *The McDonaldization of Society: Revised New Century Edition*. Pine Forge Press, Thousand Oaks, CA.

Ritzer, G. (2005) *Enchanting a Disenchanted World: Revolutionizing the Means of Consumption*, 2nd edn. Pine Forge Press, Thousand Oaks, CA.

Sewell, G. (1998) The Discipline of Teams: The Control of Team-Based Industrial Work Through Electronic and Peer Surveillance. *Administrative Science Quarterly* 43: 397–428.

postmodern sexualities

Ken Plummer

Sexuality is often located within various epochs – classic, premodern, modern, and the like – and the most recent stage has been controversially identified as "postmodern." Here human sexualities are not seen as well-fashioned patterns, solid identities, grand truths, or essential natures. In contrast, new social accounts of sexualities usually offer up more modest, constructed, and fragmented narratives of sexualities. For example, those found in the modern sexological world – from Freud to sexology – try to develop scientifically a knowledge of sexuality. Such views have haunted much of the modern world's analysis of sexuality, seeing it as an autonomous sphere of reality. For postmoderns this is a deeply flawed idea: "sex" is no longer the source of a truth, as it was for the moderns with their strong belief in science. Instead, according to William Simon in *Postmodern Sexualities* (1996), human sexualities have become "destabilized, decentred and de-essentialized." Sexual life is no longer seen as harboring an essential unitary core locatable within a clear framework with an essential truth waiting to be discovered; instead it is partial and fragmented, with little grand design or form. Indeed, it is "accompanied by the problematic at every stage" (Simon 1996: 20). As he argues: "all discourses of sexuality are inherently discourses about something else; sexuality, rather than serving as a constant thread that unifies the totality of human experience, is the ultimate dependent variable, requiring explanation more often than it provides explanation."

Human sexualities, then, are always more than "*just* human sexualities." They overlap with, and are omnipresent in, all of social life. At the simplest level, the proliferation of fragmented and diversifying sexualities is marked by rapid changes and fluidity. It is also marked by a high level of openness, or as Anthony Giddens, in *The Transformation of Society* (1992), calls it, a "plastic sexuality" in which it is no longer tied so strongly to biology. Sexualities are fluid; in the words of Zygmunt Bauman (2003), there is "liquid love."

In a fairly straightforward fashion, Ken Plummer's *Telling Sexual Stories* (1995) looks at the narratives of postmodern sexualities and suggests a number of ways of identifying such stories. First, there are no unitary cores with an essential truth waiting to be discovered; they focus more on fragments and slices of competing realities. No one story can be found. Secondly, the stories are often borrowings, reassembled into pastiche; they can even be old stories told in new and ironic ways. Third, they are indeterminate: there are many more choices available – classic ways of telling sexual lives (for example, as linear) break down and sexual actions become much more open-ended. Fourth, sexual identities become more blurred and changing. Thus whilst being "homosexual" or "gay" became relatively clear and stable identities in the modern world, they become much more fluid and ambiguous in the postmodern world. Fifth, there is a loss of belief in one Grand Story of sexuality (such as that of biology, religion, or psychotherapy). There is an incredulity toward major stories, and an openness to a plurality of (often rival) stories. Sixth, a language of excess and hyperbole develops around the sexual – as discussed in the Krokers'

(1987) ideas of panic sex, excremental sex, and indeed "unproductive sex." Seventh, many of the stories become high-tech and consumerist. At their most inventive, sexualities now become fluid through new technologies – as worlds of cyborgs, cyborg sex, and virtual sex. "Pomosexual" is sometimes seen as both noun and adjective in describing this new field. Yet although these changes are in the air, the modern still dominates.

For some, postmodern sexuality is used in a relatively straightforward fashion. But others take the position potentially to more extremes, sometimes harking back to the work of de Sade in the eighteenth century, and to others like Georges Bataille (1897–1962) (and *The Story of the Eye*) in the twentieth. In the work of writers like Jean Baudrillard, the sexual comes to live in a world of simulacra and signs: it is everywhere – in media, fashion, advertising, and engulfing bodies – making it more visible and more perverse compared to the local and limited ways sexuality was lived in the past. "Everything," he says in *Forget Foucault* (1987), "is sexuality." For Judith Butler, any idea of stable, essentially inner gendered identity is fragmented and indeed lacks any foundation. In her words, "there is no gender identity behind the expressions of gender ... identity is performatively constituted by the very expressions that are said to be its results" (1999: 33). Arthur and Marilouise Kroker see sexualities as hyperreal and fictional, as if sexuality no longer exists outside "an endless labyrinth of media images." Indeed, the rise of cyberworlds has brought complex new patterns of sexualities – cybersex – which are also closely allied to the postmodern. Likewise, Michel Maffesoli, in his *Contribution to the Sociology of the Orgy* (1993), sees the orgiastic and Dionysiac as a ubiquitous challenge to the banal. Further, some theorists (queer theorists amongst them) attempt to seriously untie and weaken any binaries or polarities that link to gender (male and female) and sexuality (homosexual and heterosexual).

The rapidity of these changes around sexualities has also brought a backlash, where countermovements (especially the family and the religious movement) have reasserted traditional, tribal, and fundamentalist views and critiques of postmodern sexualities.

SEE ALSO: Cybersexualities and Virtual Sexuality; Foucault, Michel; Plastic Sexuality; Queer Theory; Sexual Identities

REFERENCES AND SUGGESTED READINGS

Bauman, Z. (2003) *Liquid Love: On the Facility of Human Bonds*. Polity Press, Cambridge.

Butler, J. (1999) *Gender Trouble: Feminism and the Subversion of Identity*. Routledge, New York.

Eadie, J. (Ed.) (2004) *The Essential Glossary: Sexuality*. Hodder, London.

Kroker, A. & Kroker, M. (Eds.) (1987) *Body Invaders: Panic Sex in America*. New World Perspectives, Montreal.

Queen, C. & Schimel, L. (1997) *Pomosexuals: Challenging Assumptions about Gender and Sexuality*. Cleis Press, San Francisco.

Simon, W. (1996) *Postmodern Sexualities*. Routledge, London.

Stone, A. R. (1995) *The War of Desire and Technology at the Close of the Mechanical Age*. MIT Press, Cambridge, MA.

postmodern social theory

J. Michael Ryan

Postmodern social theory is a field which is both difficult to define and rejects being defined. It is, in fact, a field that struggles against definitions, against norms, against protocols. Instead, it seeks to deconstruct, decenter, and delegitimize scientific claims to universal truths. With these characteristics in mind, it is easy to understand why defining such a field would be a difficult, if not counterproductive, task. Various authors have sought to overcome this difficulty by relying on common characteristics of various postmodern theories, others have defined the field by those who work in it, and still others – particularly those who work in the field itself – have avoided any attempts to define it at all. Regardless of which of these approaches one takes, however, there is no denying that something called postmodern social theory was at one time a flourishing presence in sociology (and elsewhere). There is also little denying that that time has passed and that now postmodern social theory is little more than a memory of a past epoch in social thought. Despite this "death" of postmodern theory, however, its short life has had profound effects on the way social theorists do theory, and will, no doubt, continue to have such an effect for a long time to come.

It should be noted that this entry does not deal with the postmodern as a broad-reaching academic and/or cultural phenomenon, but instead considers its effects on social thought and theory. While the effects of the postmodern have touched most, if not all, subjects in the academy, they have done so in different ways and to varying degrees. So while some fields – notably art, architecture, and literature – are still being heavily influenced by the postmodern, other fields – notably many of the hard sciences – have remained largely unaffected by it. This analysis, therefore, will remain limited in scope to the field of social thought and theory.

Postmodernism grew out of many strands of thought, including poststructuralism. During the 1950s and 1960s, the linguistic turn occurred in many fields in the academy. Set off in large part by the revolutionary work of linguist Noam Chomsky, the linguistic turn prioritized language and helped spark the cognitive revolution that prioritized mental structures over the previously dominant behaviorist ideologies. The work of Saussure, Bourdieu, Foucault, and Barthes was key in establishing this fledgling field. Postmodernism also shifted attention from language and communication to a broader concern with theory, culture, and society. Thus, particularly during the 1970s and 1980s, postmodern thought and thinkers began to occupy a more prominent place within academia.

Postmodern social thought shifts thinking from the center to the margins. It seeks to decenter, deconstruct, and delegitimize the center. Rather than seeking answers and the Truth, it seeks to keep the conversation going and denies the possibility of Truth. Above all, it represents the death of the grand narrative. It opposes theory (thus to speak of postmodern social theory is a bit paradoxical), is irrational, anti-science, and anti-essentialist. It directs attention toward consumption, the body, and signs. There is a loss of history, a disorienting sense of geography, and a breakdown between nature, culture, and society. Postmodernism emphasizes pastiche, the ephemeral, and play. Although not completely antithetical to modern social theory, postmodern social theory does present a radically different way of looking at the world.

In many ways the methodological ideas of the postmodern theorists were more important than their substantive contributions. Many of these methodological ideas were posed in critical terms. That is, the postmodernists were critical of the modernists' propensity to think in terms of truth, of "grand (or meta-) narratives," to offer totalizations, to search for origins, to try to find the center, to be foundational, to focus on the author, to be essentialistic, to be overly scientistic and rationalistic, and so on. Many of these things went to the heart of modern theorizing and, after reading the critiques, it became very difficult to theorize in that way, at least unself-consciously. But the postmodernists went beyond critiquing modern theory: they developed a variety of more positive ideas about how to theorize, including keeping the conversation going (instead of ending it with the "truth"), archeology, genealogy, decentering, deconstructing, pastiche, *différance*, and so on. Involved here were new ways to theorize, and these had a more positive impact on social theory. Thus, in both positive and negative ways, postmodern thinking affected and continues to affect social theorists.

Then there are thinkers associated, sometimes loosely, with postmodern social theory. The list reads like a Who's Who of major contemporary (especially French) theorists and includes Jacques Derrida, Jean-François Lyotard, Jacques Lacan, Michel Foucault, Jean Baudrillard, Fredrick Jameson, Judith Butler, and Paul Virilio. Beyond that, every major contemporary modern social theorist has had to confront postmodern social theory, either directly (most notably Jürgen Habermas) or indirectly, including developing alternatives to the idea that we live in a postmodern world. Included in the latter category are Anthony Giddens, Ulrich Beck, and Zygmunt Bauman.

A good way to get at the impact of postmodern social theory more concretely is through the work of Bauman. Bauman is sometimes thought of as a postmodern theorist, and some of his works have postmodern in the title and focus on issues relating to postmodernity. Yet Bauman is better thought of as a modern social theorist who has been profoundly affected by postmodern thinkers and the postmodern era in which we live. He developed a well-known distinction between postmodern sociology and a sociology of postmodernity, the former being a new type of sociology and the latter being sociology as usual but with postmodernity as the topic. While Bauman has been more affected by postmodern ideas than most modern theorists, and while he is far more sensitized to the realities of the postmodern world, he is still a modernist. In that sense, he epitomizes the point that while in one way postmodern social theory might be dead, in another it lives on in the work of contemporary modern (or "late modern") theorists. Those who fail to understand the critiques of the postmodernists, and who fail to at least think through some of the alternatives they offer, are doomed to repeat the mistakes of the modern theorists.

The analogy here is to the Holocaust and to Bauman's (1989) analysis of it, not as a failure of modernity but as an expression of it, especially Weberian rationality. To avoid repeating such egregious crimes against humanity, we need to understand the negative lessons of modernity. While few, if any, were killed in its name, the same point applies to modern social theory. To pursue theoretical alternatives, we need to understand that the failures of modern social theory are traceable to its modern roots and orientation. Postmodern social theory points us in the direction of such an understanding and provides us with ideas and orientations for theorizing differently.

Postmodernism has given rise, or at least has significantly helped to pave the way for, a number of other theoretical orientations. The newly privileged periphery that found itself center stage with postmodern considerations allowed for the meaningful development and academic institutionalization of feminist studies, queer studies, multicultural studies, and postcolonial studies, among others. It did this by decentering the traditional academic focus and privileging those things traditionally thought of as feminine or irrelevant under traditional modern guises. Concerns with the body, leisure, consumption, and space and place were closely aligned with the considerations of many long left out in the cold of academic discourse. Thus, the growing power and privilege of postmodern social theory and its associated ideals gave corollary power and privilege to other theoretical engagements that took off from similar standpoints. The issue of standpoint itself became a central concern for many.

Postmodernism quickly came under several attacks. It was argued that the theory itself represented the kind of grand narrative that it sought to oppose. It was argued that its methods failed to live up to scientific standards and that it offered critiques without a normative basis for judgment. Its lack of alternative visions for the future made it highly pessimistic, and a sense of agency is difficult to uncover. Perhaps most troubling for modern thinkers were the unresolved questions and ambiguities postmodernism left in its path.

Few theories have had as meteoric a rise and fall in sociology as postmodern social theory. While it had various antecedents, it burst on the scene in sociology in the 1960s and within two or three decades observers were writing its obituary. In a sense it *is* dead because there have been few, if any, major contributions to it in the last few decades. The statement that postmodern social theory is dead is simultaneously controversial, clichéd, and meaningless. It is controversial because there are still a few who believe themselves to be doing work in this area. It is clichéd because it has been a taken-for-granted assumption by many for years, even among those who never realized it was born or what its life was like. It is also meaningless because many of those associated with postmodern thinking – Foucault, Baudrillard – would argue that such a theory has never existed to die.

In other ways postmodern social theory is alive and well. For one thing, many of the basic ideas and concepts (consumer society, simulation, implosion, hyperreality, hyperspace, governmentality, panopticon, schizoanalysis, dromology, etc.) associated with postmodern social theory have made their way into the heart of contemporary social theory. Many theorists, and some empiricists, work with, and on, these ideas. For another, the practice of sociology in general, and social theory in particular, was greatly affected, or at least should have been, by the methodological ideas associated with postmodern theory. It is certainly the case that theorists who familiarized themselves with postmodern ideas found it difficult, if not impossible, to theorize as usual. This should also have been true of empiricists, but the fact is that few of them had the time or interest to work their way through the often arcane work of postmodern thinkers. Had they done so, they too would have found it nearly impossible to work in anything like the same way that they had before.

SEE ALSO: Foucault, Michel; Modernity; Postmodern Consumption; Postmodern Culture; Postmodern Feminism; Postmodern Organizations; Postmodern Sexualities; Post-modernism; Poststructuralism; Reflexive Modernization

REFERENCES AND SUGGESTED READINGS

Barthes, R. (1972) *Mythologies*. Trans. A. Lavers. Cape, London.

Baudrillard, J. (1975) *The Mirror of Production*. Telos Press, Saint Louis, MI.

Baudrillard, J. (1983) *Simulations*. Trans. P. F. P. Patton & P. Beitchman. Semiotext(e), New York.

Baudrillard, J. (1998 [1970]) *The Consumer Society*. Sage, London.

Bauman, Z. (1989) *Modernity and the Holocaust*. Polity Press, Cambridge.

Bauman, Z. (1993) *Postmodern Ethics*. Blackwell, Oxford.

Bauman, Z. (2000) *Liquid Modernity*. Polity Press, Cambridge.

Bourdieu, P. (1977) *Outline of a Theory of Practice*. Cambridge University Press, Cambridge.

Bourdieu, P. & Wacquant, L. J. D. (1992) *An Invitation to Reflexive Sociology*. University of Chicago Press, Chicago.

Chomsky, N. (1957) *Syntactic Structures*. Mouton, The Hague.

Derrida, J. (1974) *Of Grammatology*. Trans. G. Spivak. Johns Hopkins University Press, Baltimore.

Derrida, J. (1978) *Writing and Difference*. Trans. A. Bass. University of Chicago Press, Chicago.

Featherstone, M. (1991) *Consumer Culture and Postmodernism*. Sage, London.

Foucault, M. (1977) *Discipline and Punish: The Birth of the Prison*. Trans. A. M. S. Smith. Pantheon, New York.

Foucault, M. (1978) *The History of Sexuality*. Vol. 1: An Introduction. Trans. R. Hurley. Pantheon, New York.

Hage, J. & Powers, C. H. (1992) *Post-Industrial Lives: Roles and Relationships in the 21st Century*. Sage, Newbury Park, CA.

Lyotard, J.-F. (1984) *The Postmodern Condition: A Report on Knowledge*. Trans. R. Durand. University of Minnesota Press, Minneapolis.

Virilio, P. (1986) *Speed and Politics: An Essay on Dromology*. Semiotext(e), New York.

postmodernism

Julie M. Albright

Postmodernism is an orientation toward knowledge that encompasses a wide range of theories and theorists, drawing from the fields of philosophy, sociology, linguistics, and others. The word "postmodernism" may suggest an important historical shift ("after modernism"), but this is a misnomer, since the precepts of modernism are still alive and well.

To contextualize the development of postmodern theory, one can view the history of the western world as comprising three major eras: the premodern, the modern, and the postmodern. The premodern era took place before the Renaissance in Europe (pre-fifteenth century) during the period including the Dark Ages. During this time, religion played a key influence in terms of providing a cohesive epistemology or worldview. The Catholic Church was the main source of "Truth" at this time, with the authority for that truth being God and God's laws. Later, religion began to lose ground in providing a coherent worldview, as scientific discoveries challenged the Church's version of Truth. Technical discoveries such as the compass made world travel possible. Copernicus challenged the Church's contention that the sun revolves around the Earth, and thus that man is the center of the universe. His ideas were so heretical that he kept them to himself until on his deathbed at the end of the 1500s.

Galileo Galilei in 1609 heard about the Dutch invention of a telescope and subsequently built one himself, which he later demonstrated in Venice. The telescope allowed him to "prove" that the Copernican idea of the sun being the center of the universe was correct. He went to Rome to try to convince Church leaders of his findings, but his ideas were labeled heretical and he was ordered to keep them quiet. He was later placed under house arrest by the pope after continuing to disseminate this idea. The printing press allowed Galileo's book and other such scientific discoveries to be disseminated and discussed more widely, loosening the Church's hold on the production of Truth in Europe.

Modernism thus challenged the worldview provided by the Church, moving an understanding of Truth to a more rational, scientific explanation of reality, beginning in the seventeenth century. A key progenitor of this shift was Francis Bacon, who promoted a systematic approach to understanding the world through observing reality, not just by reasoning, thereby rejecting the legacy he inherited from such thinkers as Plato. René Descartes was another key figure in the development of modernism. He possessed a deep Catholic faith, yet was fascinated by "scientific" rational ways of understanding the world. His main contribution was the idea to "doubt everything." He believed that through doubting, one could arrive at certainty. He said: "Cogito, ergo sum" – I think, therefore I am. Descartes viewed the world as a machine and believed that by applying the principles of mathematics, one could solve the puzzles and mysteries of the world. He is credited with the creation of the Cartesian split – the gap between knower and known – which serves as a cornerstone of scientific objectivity. After Descartes, science, with its reliance on neutrality and objectivity, became the dominant worldview, ushering in the modern era.

Social and scientific/technological developments continued through the 1700s into the early twentieth century, ushering in the modern capitalist-industrial state and bringing about great social change in its wake, such as industrialization and the rise of the factory system, urbanization, and the development of weapons of war. Weber, Tönnes, and Simmel theorized the impact of increasing economic and bureaucratic rationalization on the social world. With the development of nuclear physics as a scientific endeavor came Heisenberg, whose Uncertainty Principle stated that the act of observing changes that which is observed. This principle shook the foundation of certainty and objectivity upon which the scientific method and the Cartesian split are based.

Scientific progress continued through the twentieth century, with the social penetration of radio, television, and the Internet creating new marketing vehicles and mass culture. Weapons of war continued to develop through the nuclear age, culminating in World War II. The devastation left in its wake in Europe led to an era of great change as rebuilding began, alongside increasing urbanization. As a result, much postmodern social theory came out of post-World War II Europe, particularly France, as philosophers and social theorists there tried to grapple with the rapid social change occurring around them.

Postmodernism as a theoretical school encompasses many disparate ideas. It embodies a shift in sensibility, particularly evidenced in the arts, music, and architecture. Changes included a shift from concern with form to a concern with artifice, from structure to surface, from purity to pastiche, and from substance to image or simulation. The shift from modernism to postmodernism is best exemplified by two quotes. The first is from Mies Van der Rohe, the definitive modernist architect: "Less is more." This encompasses the modernist sensibility of form following function, stripping to essences, simplification and lack of ornamentation in architecture. The second quote, from postmodern architect Robert Venturi, is "Less is a bore." It captures the spirit of postmodern architecture and, indeed, postmodernism itself, which revels in playfulness, irony, ornamentation, and a pastiche of styles.

Postmodern social theory includes a wide variety of views lumped together under the rubric of postmodern theory. Postmodern theorists include the poststructuralist Michel Foucault, as well as philosophers François Lyotard and Gilles Deleuze, sociologist Jean Baudrillard, the neo-Marxist Fredrick Jameson, and the deconstructionist Jacques Derrida. Many of these theorists have never claimed to be postmodern, yet each has been labeled as such. Though each is very different in his approach, they share a perspective that theorizes a break in social development, calling into question notions of knowledge, Truth, and reality.

Baudrillard, born in 1929, completed a doctorate in sociology at Sorbonne University in Paris, where he worked under Henry Lefebvre. From 1966 to 1972 he worked as a graduate assistant and later an assistant professor. In 1972 he became a professor of sociology at the Université de Paris-X Nanterre. Currently, he is a professor of philosophy of culture and media criticism at the European Graduate School in Saas-Fee, Switzerland. Baudrillard was influenced by Marx and his work on commodity fetishism, and wrote about how value has moved from "use-value" to a "fractal point of value" where there is no connection to any use or exchange-value at all. We have come to a point in time where things are purely simulated – a simulacra of pure fantasy.

Baudrillard is considered among the extreme avant-garde in terms of postmodern theorists. His work sometimes is playful, ironic, and fanciful. He became fascinated by American culture, particularly consumer culture and the media, opinion polling, and environmental design as embodied by Disneyland and Las Vegas. Baudrillard was interested in simulation and simulacra, as in Disneyland's Main Street. He also coined the term hyperreality to describe a condition that he describes as "more real than real," and for which there is no natural referent. It is, as he puts it "always already reproduced." Examples include videotaped workout routines and suburban tract housing. In each case there exists no original, only endless reproduction. Baudrillard's theorizing was concerned with the end of postmodernism, the rise in simulation and simulacra, and the erosion of boundaries between high and pop culture, between appearance and reality, and between other such oppositions.

Gilles Deleuze (1925–5) was born in Paris and lived most of his life there. He received his doctorate in philosophy in 1948 from the Sorbonne, where he later taught beginning in 1957. In 1969 he took a teaching position at the University of Paris VII. There he met Félix Guattari, with whom he co-authored a number of influential texts, including *Capitalism and Schizophrenia*, *Anti-Oedipus*, and *A Thousand Plateaus*. Deleuze suffered health problems in his later years, and took his own life in 1995. Pierre Félix Guattari (1930–92) was born in Villeneuve-les-Sablons, France, and pursued studies in psychiatry, influenced by Jaques Lacan among others. He took up practice at the psychiatric clinic La Borde. In their collaborative work, Deleuze and Guattari were concerned with medical discourses as part of a system of domination and social control. Their main contributions to postmodern theory include an analysis of desire in society. As outlined in *Anti-Oedipus* it was essentially a poststructuralist Foucaldian critique of modernity via a scathing critique of Marxism and Lacanian psychoanalysis, as well as an attack on representation, the modern subject, and "the tyranny of the signifier." In *Anti-Oedipus* Deleuze and Guattari attempt to reconstitute the modern subject as "schizo-subjects" who become "desiring machines." A suggested alternative to psychoanalysis – "schizo-analysis" – centers on a deconstruction of binaries and an emphasis on the postmodern concepts of multiplicity, plurality, and decenteredness. Both Deleuze and Guattari were very interested in politics and saw their theorizing as a way of creating new forms of political thought and action. They viewed desire as revolutionary and as a productive force; as such, desire becomes the centerpiece of control in modern societies. The process of repressing desire they term "territorialization" and the process of freeing desire from these repressive social forces is "deterritorialization" or "decoding." These ideas were developed further in their book *A Thousand Plateaus*, where they elaborate the concept of the rhizome, by which they mean deterritorialized movement. Rhizomatics attempts to uproot traditional modes of thought in order to pluralize and disseminate new ideas, to make new connections, and to produce difference and multiplicities. Rhizomes are lines which connect with others in a decentered way, and rhizomatics is meant to provide an alternative to traditional Marxist structural analysis.

Born 1926 in Poitiers, Michel Foucault attended the prestigious lycée Henri-IV in Paris, followed by the École Normale Supérieure, where he studied philosophy under Merleau-Ponty. He received his license in philosophy in 1948, in psychology in 1950, and in 1952 earned his psychopathology degree. He went on to teach French in the universities of Sweden, Warsaw, and Hamburg, finally returning to France to chair the department of philosophy at the University of Clermont-Ferrand. Foucault later headed the philosophy department at the University of Paris-VIII at Vincennes during the time of the student uprisings of May 1968, an event which affected him deeply. His influential books *An Archeology of Knowledge* and *Discipline and Punish: The Birth of the Prison* came out after that time. He died of AIDS in 1984.

Foucault's contributions began with the notion of an "archeology of knowledge" from his book by the same name. Through such an archeology, Foucault hoped to uncover the underlying rules which constituted an epistemology of various discourses which were particular to specific cultural and historical contexts. For example, he looked at the history of confinement related to madness, including notions of sane and insane, normal and abnormal, and traces the changes in these discourses from the premodern to the rational-scientific modern era. Later, in *Discipline and Punish*, Foucault turned his attention to the connection between discourse and power, which he called "power/knowledge." He traced how the technologies of surveillance and information gathering are used to make "normalizing judgments" used to shape and discipline identity, desire, and the body. Later, in *The History of Sexuality*, he continued to explore how discourses are used to inscribe the body and produce normal versus abnormal sexualities. Foucault implicated the fields of psychiatry, sociology, and criminology in the refinement and proliferation of new techniques of power.

Fredrick Jameson (1930–) trained in the tradition of Marxism and developed his own neo-Marxist analysis of the postmodern era. Like Foucault and others working in Europe in the 1960s, Jameson was very influenced by the anti-war and New Left political movements. He integrates many disparate theories into his work, from Marxism to psychoanalysis, and from structuralism to poststructuralism. In his key text *Postmodernism, or the Cultural Logic of Late Capitalism*, Jameson outlines the development of postmodernism in a vein similar to Marx's model of the stages of capitalist development.

François Lyotard was born in 1924 in Versailles and enjoyed a long and illustrious career. At the time of his death in 1998 he was University Professor Emeritus of the University of Paris-VIII, and Professor at Emory University, Atlanta. Like Jameson, although Lyotard had his theoretical beginnings based in Marxism, he later moved away from the Marxist approach to develop his theories of the postmodern. Unlike some social theorists, Lyotard clearly connected himself to postmodern theory, as evidenced by the title of his well-known text *The Postmodern Condition: A Report on Knowledge*. In it, Lyotard examines the connection between knowledge, technology, and science in societies. He theorized that the postmodern era as a time in which what counts as knowledge will be that which can be translated into binary code and stored in computerized databases. He postulated that society is losing its faith in science and grand metanarratives such as Marxism, and that society now finds itself in a state of incredulity toward legitimating metanarratives. Rather than creating more metanarratives, we need knowledge which he terms *petit récit* – those which are small, local, and specific.

New developments coming after postmodernism include Gilles Lipovetsky's argument that we have entered a new phase he terms hypermodernity, characterized by hyper-consumption and the hypermodern individual, who is characterized by movement, pleasure, and hedonism, yet who is also filled with tension and anxiety, since belief systems which previously brought comfort have been eroded.

SEE ALSO: Foucauldian Archeological Analyses; Foucault, Michel; Hyperreality; Implosion; Postmodern Culture; Postmodern Feminism; Postmodern Organizations; Postmodern Sexualities; Postmodern Social Theory; Poststructuralism; Simulacra and Simulation

REFERENCES AND SUGGESTED READINGS

Baudrillard, J. (1983) *Simulations*. Semiotext(e), New York.

Best, S. & Kellner, D. (1991) Deleuze and Guattari: Schizos, Nomads and Rhizomes. In: *Postmodern Theory: A Critical Interrogation*. Guilford Press, New York, pp. 76–110.

Best, S. & Kellner, D. (1991) Foucault and the Critique of Modernity. In: *Postmodern Theory: A*

Critical Interrogation. Guilford Press, New York, pp. 34–68.

Best, S. & Kellner, D. (1991) Fredric Jameson. In: *Postmodern Theory: A Critical Interrogation*. Guilford Press, New York, pp. 257–8.

Cashmore, E. & Rojek, C. (1999) Jean-François Lyotard. In: *Dictionary of Cultural Theorists*. Arnold, London, pp. 327–9.

Foucault, M. (1995). *Discipline and Punish: The Birth of the Prison*. Vintage, New York.

Jameson, F. (1999) *Postmodernism, or, the Cultural Logic of Late Capitalism*. Duke University Press, Durham, NC.

Kellner, D. (1988) Postmodernism as Social Theory: Some Challenges and Problems. In: *Theory, Culture and Society*, Vol. 5. Sage, London, pp. 239–69.

Lipovestsky, G. (2005) *Hypermodern Times*. Polity Press, Cambridge.

Lyotard, J. (1993) *The Postmodern Condition: A Report on Knowledge*. University of Minnesota Press, Minneapolis.

Poster, M. (1998) *Jean Baudrillard: Selected Writings*. Stanford University Press, Stanford.

Sarup, M. (1989) Foucault and the Social Sciences. In: *Poststructuralism and Postmodernism*. University of Georgia Press, Athens, pp. 63–96.

postnationalism

Mabel Berezin

Postnationalism as an analytic frame articulates with a hypothesized decline of the nation-state in the face of globalization and reterritorialization (Berezin 2003; Ansell 2004). The increasing presence of immigrants on the territories of established nation-states, particularly but not exclusively in Europe, has pushed the discussion of postnationalism to the forefront of social science research. Soysal (1994) describes immigrant organizations in six European nation-states. Soysal identifies four types of "incorporation regimes" and argues that a new form of postnational citizenship has emerged that decouples territory from legal membership. Trans-territorial membership is based upon human rights – the rights of persons as persons, rather than persons as citizens of nation-states.

Scholars have contested the postnational argument – Soysal's variant as well as other

articulations of it (e.g., Jacobson 1996; Tambini 2001). Postnationalism as theory is based on a paradox that squares poorly with political reality (Eder & Giesen 2001). Postnationalism upholds the autonomy of national cultural difference at the expense of political membership. By privileging culture and nature, nationality and humanity over territorially based institutional ties, postnationalism as concept leaves itself open to criticism that it is utopian and, that in practice, it may actually threaten the legal rights of migrants.

Empirical research based on Europe underscores the point that a European is only European, as defined by the European Union, if he or she is a citizen of one of the member states. Koopman and Statham (1999) tested the postnational hypothesis by examining immigrant claims in Britain and Germany. They found that minorities structure their claims in the language of citizenship and rights prevailing in the national territory in which they find themselves and not in terms of the national identities and cultural practices of their homeland. Bhabha (1999) demonstrates, using data from cases before the European Court of Justice, that residents of a territory who are not legally incorporated members of the territory (i.e., citizens) have little recourse to the full array of constitutionally protected rights. Many of her examples focus on marriage. Citizens of non-member states, even if married to naturalized citizens, face the threat of deportation.

Legally, transnationality within Europe is a tightly bounded concept. Indeed, the juridical evidence makes postnationalism appear moot. The continuing hegemony of the nation-state, even in the presence of an expanding European Union, suggests why "transnational" is a better descriptor of the contemporary European political culture than "postnational." "Transnational" captures the hybrid potential implicit in the "postnational" without attenuating the difficulties of a rapidly diversifying Europe (Kastoryano 2002).

Despite the scholarly discourse on postnationalism, compelling counter-arguments exist from a purely structuralist and normative perspective that suggest that the territorially defined nation-state is hardly withering away (e.g., Evans 1997; Mann 1997; Paul et al. 2004; Waldinger & Fitzgerald 2004). The continued legal and cultural importance of the national state coupled with a resurgence of ethnic nationalism throughout the world suggest that we are a long way from a postnational political or cultural universe.

SEE ALSO: Citizenship; Culture; Migration: International; Nation-State and Nationalism; Nationalism

REFERENCES AND SUGGESTED READINGS

Ansell, C. K. (2004) Restructuring Authority and Territoriality: Europe and the United States Compared. In: Ansell, C. K. & DiPalma, G. (Eds.), *Restructuring Territoriality: Europe and the United States Compared.* Cambridge University Press, Cambridge, pp. 3–16.

Berezin, M. (2003) Territory, Emotion and Identity: Spatial Recalibration in a New Europe. In: Berezin, M. & Schain, M. (Eds.), *Europe Without Borders: Remapping Territory, Citizenship and Identity in a Transnational Age.* Johns Hopkins University Press, Baltimore, pp. 1–30.

Bhabha, J. (1999) Belonging in Europe: Citizenship and Post-National Rights. *International Social Science Journal* 159 (March): 11–23.

Eder, K. & Giesen, B. (Eds.) (2001) *European Citizenship between National Legacies and Postnational Projects.* Oxford University Press, New York.

Evans, P. (1997) The Eclipse of the State? Reflections on Stateness in an Era of Globalization. *World Politics* 50(1): 62–87.

Jacobson, D. (1996) *Rights Across Borders: Immigration and the Decline of Citizenship.* Johns Hopkins University Press, Baltimore.

Kastoryano, R. (2002) *Negotiating Identities: States and Immigrants in France and Germany.* Princeton University Press, Princeton.

Koopmans, R. & Statham, P. (1999) Challenging the Liberal Nation-State? Postnationalism, Multiculturalism, and the Collective Claims Making of Migrants and Ethnic Minorities in Britain and Germany. *American Journal of Sociology* 105(3): 652–96.

Mann, M. (1997) Has Globalization Ended the Rise and Rise of the Nation-State? *Review of International Political Economy* 4 (Autumn): 472–96.

Paul, T. V., Ikenberry, G. J., & Hall, J. A. (Eds.) (2004) *The Nation-State in Question.* Princeton University Press, Princeton; Oxford University Press, Oxford.

Soysal, Y. N. (1994) *Limits of Citizenship.* University of Chicago Press, Chicago.

Tambini, D. (2001) Post-National Citizenship. *Ethnic and Racial Studies* 24(2): 195–217.

Waldinger, R. & Fitzgerald, D. (2004) Transnationalism in Question. *American Journal of Sociology* 109(5): 1177–95.

postpositivism

Thomas J. Fararo

In the twentieth century the heritage of positivism as a philosophy of science underwent major changes. Earlier intellectual developments in the century led to logical positivism (and, with some variation in ideas, logical empiricism). The continuity with classical positivism was maintained in terms of opposition to metaphysics, but other and more specific doctrines were elaborated. A scientific theory, for instance, was said to be a formal deductive system with an empirical interpretation that enabled verification by appeal to observations.

However, Popper (1959), while not disputing the deductive system formulation, argued that the universality of theoretical statements made them impossible to verify. Rather, a theory was credible to the extent that it "proved its mettle" by surviving falsification efforts. But Kuhn (1970) noted that scientists usually worked within a paradigm and resisted efforts to revise it until anomalies that could not be resolved led to a revolutionary change of paradigm. By the late 1970s there was consensus that a postpositivist era had emerged in the philosophy of science, in which the "received view" was replaced by a variety of critical reformulations concerning the nature of scientific knowledge and, in particular, the structure of scientific theories (Suppe 1977).

These developments have had ramifications for sociology. Sociological theory, in the view of theorists who favor a scientific approach, has been and largely remains deficient both in its structure and in its empirical testability. Earlier, logical empiricism was looked to for guidance about science, but more recently such theorists have favored postpositivist ideas that emphasize models and mechanisms in scientific explanation.

Other theorists have made quite different postpositivist proposals in support of general theory or metatheory in contrast to empirically testable theoretical model building. For example, Alexander (1982) formulates an explicit contrast between postpositivism and positivism in the history and philosophy of science. Contrary to the positivist standpoint, for instance, postpositivism denies any radical break between empirical and non-empirical statements: all scientific data are theory-laden. Also contrary to positivism, postpositivism accepts the legitimacy of general intellectual or metaphysical issues in science.

Based on these and related ideas, Alexander argues that social science has institutionalized what is an aberration in natural science, namely, presuppositional debates about the most general conceptual problems in the field. The function of theoretical logic in sociology, he maintains, is to make explicit the fundamental choices or issues around which such enduring debates will continue, such as rational versus non-rational action principles. One example that supports this view is the continuing debate between advocates and critics about the use of rational choice theory in sociology. Although Alexander's approach leads him to a useful critique of theorizing in sociology, it also may lean too far in a non-empirical direction. One can accept a good part of Alexander's argument while also favoring the construction and empirical testing of theoretical models that embody generative rules or mechanisms (Fararo 1989).

SEE ALSO: Metatheory; Positivism; Theory Construction

REFERENCES AND SUGGESTED READINGS

Alexander, J. C. (1982) *Positivism, Presuppositions, and Current Controversies.* University of California Press, Berkeley.

Fararo, T. J. (1989) *The Meaning of General Theoretical Sociology: Tradition and Formalization.* Cambridge University Press, New York.

Kuhn, T. S. (1970 [1962]) *The Structure of Scientific Revolutions.* University of Chicago Press, Chicago.

Popper, K. (1959) *The Logic of Scientific Discovery.* Hutchinson, London.

Suppe, F. (Ed.) (1977) *The Structure of Scientific Theories,* 2nd edn. University of Illinois Press, Urbana.

postsocial

Karin Knorr Cetina

Postsocial theory attempts to develop an understanding of current changes of sociality and social forms. Human beings may by nature be social animals, but forms of sociality are nonetheless changing; the term postsocial refers to contemporary challenges to core concepts of human interaction and solidarity that point beyond a period of high social formation to one of more limited sociality and alternative forms of binding self and other. Postsocial analysis assumes that social principles and structures as we have known them in the past are emptying out in western societies and other elements and relationships are taking their place. It assumes that new forms of binding self and other arise from the increasing role nonhuman objects play in a knowledge-based society and consumer culture and from changes in the nature of objects and the structure of the self.

One of the great legacies of classical social thought is the idea that the development of modern society involved the collapse of community and the loss of social tradition. Yet what followed was not an asocial or non-social environment but a period of high social formation – a period when the welfare state was established, societies became societies of complex organizations and structures, and social thinking took off in ways captured by the idea of a social imagination. Central to our experience today is that these expansions of social principles come to a halt. In western societies we experience a "second break" with earlier forms of sociality and solidarity manifest in the retraction of the welfare state, a shift in the collective imagination from social and political concerns to topics fueled by the life sciences, and changes in patterns of relationships, etc. (Lasch 1978). What sociologists have posited, accordingly, is a further boost to individualization (Beck 1992). This interpretation is not wrong, but it is nonetheless one-sided in looking at current transitions only from the perspective of a loss of human relationships and received forms of the social. What postsocial theory offers instead of the scenario of "desocialization" is the analysis of alternative forms of binding self and other, changes in the structure of the self that accommodates these forms, and forms of social imagination that subordinate sociality to new concerns.

One focus of postsocial theory is the role non-human objects play in the contemporary remaking of societies. The argument starts from the massive expansion of object environments in the social world: we live in environments full of technological objects, consumer goods, and objects of knowledge. Postsocial arguments point out that object environments can situate and stabilize selves, define individual identity just as much as communities or families used to do, and they promote forms of sociality (of binding self and other) that feed on and supplement the human forms of sociality studied by social scientists. Objects may also become the risk winners of the relationship risks that many authors find inherent in contemporary human relations. A condition for understanding this role of objects is that we break with the tradition of seeing objects as abstract technologies that promote the alienation of the worker (Berger et al. 1974), as fetishized commodities as in the Marxian tradition, or simply as instruments that serve particular ends. Postsocial theory conceptualizes objects as they are understood in science, where their "hooking power" and relational potential lie with their indefiniteness of being (Rheinberger 1992).

A second condition for understanding object relationships as part of how we live and understand sociality is that we also reconsider our models of the self, a further focus of postsocial theory. The dominant model of the self in the social sciences dates back to the beginning of the twentieth century and captures the social self of a bourgeois society. Mead, Freud, and others saw the self as composed of an ego and an inner censor that represents society as an "internalized other" (Wiley 1994). This model can be contrasted with a second based on Lacan that understands the self not as a relation between the individual and society but as a structure of wantings in relation to continually renewed lacks stimulated by images of the perfected self and the apparent wholeness of others (Knorr Cetina 2001). This second model fits with a consumer society in which ever-tempting new images lure persons into continued searches for new objects (Ritzer 1999). The liberalization of partnership and family life (Lasch 1978), the detraditionalization of education, and the individualization of choice also conspire to prevent a strong social self founded on the internalization of a censor. A media, image, and knowledge culture that continually reactivates a lack-wanting dynamic may describe contemporary selves better than the Meadian system and may be in the process of reshaping it. In this sense, a media, image, and knowledge culture is also a postsocial culture that stimulates and sustains postsocial selves.

The expansion of a social imagination had involved, since the Enlightenment, hopes for the perfectibility of human society in terms of equality, peace, justice, and social welfare, with the high point being Marxist visions of a socialist revolution. These ideas have not disappeared with the retraction of social principles and the collapse of Marxism. But the excess imagination that went into visions of social salvation is now extended to other areas where it finds progressive inspiration – and this is a third focus of postsocial analysis. What has become thinkable today is the perfectibility of life – through life enhancement on the individual level, but also through the biopolitics of populations, through the protection and reflexive manipulation of nature, through the idea of intergenerational (rather than distributional) justice. The notion of life can serve as a metaphor and anchoring concept that illustrates a cultural turn to nature and how it replaces the culture of the social. One massive source of life-centered thinking is the life sciences themselves. They produce a stream of research that inspires imaginative elaborations of the human individual as enriched by genetic, biological, and technological supplements and upgrades. The ideas suggest the perfectibility of individual life, but they also strongly implicate unrelated populations, those sharing particular genes, exposures, or histories of adaptation to environmental conditions, and benefiting in the aggregate from genetic measures and drugs. The "biosociality" (Rabinow 1996) that arises from collective structures forming around biological concepts further illustrates a postsocial culture.

Postsocial systems include sociality, but in reconfigured, specialized, more mediated and limited ways, as liminal forms of sociality. Post-social relations are human ties triangulated with object relations and forming only with respect to these relations. A postsocial system may be one where information structures have replaced previous forms of social coordination, as when sophisticated hardware and software systems substitute for social networks and enable expanded, accelerated, and intensified global financial markets. Postsocial is what one might call a level of intersubjectivity that is no longer based on face-to-face interaction and may in fact not involve interaction at all, but rather "communities of time" formed by the joint observation of common, electronically transmitted content. Postsocial systems may arise around the sort of relatedness enabled by the Internet, for which the characteristics that have traditionally defined human relationships (feelings of obligation and trust, etc.) are not constitutive or even relevant. Postsocial forms are not rich in sociality in the old sense – but they may be rich in other ways, and the challenge is to analyze and theorize these constellations.

SEE ALSO: Actor-Network Theory; Individualism; Posthumanism; Post-Industrial Society; Postmodern Culture; Scientific Knowledge, Sociology of; Social Identity Theory; Theory

REFERENCES AND SUGGESTED
READINGS

Beck, U. (1992) *Risk Society: Towards a New Modernity*. Sage, London.

Berger, P. L., Berger, B., & Kellner, H. (1974) *The Homeless Mind: Modernization and Consciousness*. Vintage Books, New York.

Knorr Cetina, K. (1997) Sociality with Objects: Social Relations in Postsocial Knowledge Societies. *Theory, Culture and Society* 14: 1–30.

Knorr Cetina, K. (2001) Postsocial Relations: Theorizing Sociality in a Postsocial Environment. In: Ritzer, G. and Smart, B. (Eds.), *Handbook of Social Theory*. Sage, London.

Lasch, C. (1978) *The Culture of Narcissism: American Life in an Age of Diminishing Expectations*. Norton, New York.

Rabinow, P. (1996) Artificiality and Enlightenment: From Sociobiology to Biosociality. In: *Essays on the Anthropology of Reason*. Princeton University Press, Princeton, pp. 91–111.

Rheinberger, H.-J. (1992). Experiment, Difference, and Writing: I. Tracing Protein Synthesis. *Studies in History and Philosophy of Science* 23: 305–31.

Ritzer, G. (1999) *Enchanting a Disenchanted World: Revolutionizing the Means of Consumption*. Pine Forge Press, Thousand Oaks, CA.

Wiley, N. (1994) *The Semiotic Self*. University of Chicago Press, Chicago.

poststructuralism

Charles McCormick

Like postmodernism, this relatively recent coinage encompasses a wide range of intellectual schools and levels of analysis. These approaches tend to cluster around two somewhat overlapping camps: the "literary" theorists interested in describing the structure of language and culture, and the "sociological" camp consisting of sociologists and anthropologists interested in describing the structure of society and human agency.

MICROSYSTEMS OF MEANING

Linguistic and cultural uses of poststructuralism draw from linguistic and philosophical debates regarding whether the essential nature of language, and by extension human consciousness, is rooted in constantly shifting systems of meaning. The founder of linguistic structuralism, Ferdinand de Saussure (1857–1913), deviated from linguistic thinkers of the time who generally were interested in tracing universal systems of meaning within diverse languages, for example through the study of historical philology. Saussure founded the school of semiotics when he argued that language only has meaning in relation to a specific cultural framework. He argued that the system of meaning that underlies language or *signifiers* is always shifting and can only be studied synchronically (at a given moment in time). Signifiers only make sense in relation to other signifiers and have no fixed relationship to the real world they represent at a given time. To illustrate, consider how the terms "gay" and "queer" have shifted from their conventional meanings, to pejorative terms for people with alternate sexual orientations and, more recently, to a more contested positive connotation for identifying the same group.

While Saussure was primarily interested in studying the system of meaning that underlies language itself, the literary strain of poststructuralist thought argues that other human creations such as film, advertisements, and other cultural forms can be studied as systems of meaning that only make sense within a specific cultural framework and time period. Members of this camp agree with Saussure's assertion that language, and by extension culture, exists as a system of signifiers with no relation to the signs they represent, while rejecting his belief that this system of signs forms a well-defined and cohesive system of meanings that can be mapped through semiotics.

The first step towards literary poststructuralism was taken by Roland Barthes in his analysis of French popular culture. Barthes is notable for developing Saussure's link between the signified and signifier into the study of culture. In *Mythologies* (1972) he explored the meaning underlying many forms of popular culture, including the characters and performances that made professional wrestling meaningful to spectators of the time who, he argued, were more interested in the way that culturally meaningful dramas and characters such as "the clown" and "the traitor" interacted than they were in the athleticism involved. Barthes explained that myths acted to naturalize a society's values while cloaking this form of socialization behind entertainment or objectivity. His science of semiotics involves looking at various forms of literature and popular culture to uncover the social values they communicate and the practices they encourage.

Barthes was also interested in *intertextuality*, the idea that a work of art, such as a novel or performance, has a meaning that shifts according to the audience experiencing it and its relationship to other works of art. This meaning shift can be seen in, for example, the "rereading" of Shakespeare's *The Tempest* and Samuel Richardson's *Pamela* as feminist texts. The search for the myths that underlie texts and other forms of culture has been expanded into feminism by Julia Kristeva and Judith Butler, among others, and into the studies of race and ethnicity, and into lesbian, gay, and queer theory. While Barthes is generally identified as a member of both the structuralist and poststructuralist schools of thought, more recent theorists have built upon his ideas to develop the literary camp of poststructuralism.

Barthes's ideas were further expanded by thinkers such as Derrida and Baudrillard who emphasize the constantly shifting nature of any system of signifiers. Signifiers only make sense as they are interpreted by a reader, viewer, or participant, and since the experience and interpretations of cultural systems vary widely between individuals and across time, there is a constant shifting of cultural meanings. Baudrillard and Derrida, among others, examine the effect that this uncertain mapping between signifiers and the signified has for systems of meaning.

Through his concept of *différance*, Derrida explains that any given signifier only makes sense in relation to its opposition to other signifiers. Because these relationships are not linked to any specific real-world referent and shift across different works and the interpretation, the true meaning of a text is always "deferred." By extension, Derrida argues that attempts to close systems of meaning within literary or philosophical texts under the guise of accurately described real-world experiences, or providing a system of "ultimate truths," are power games masked as objectivity. Derrida's attempt to seek inconsistencies within these texts, to *deconstruct* the contingency of an author's belief system, parallels postmodernism's rejection of metanarratives which describe the world as a whole.

THE "MICROPOWERS" OF SOCIETY

The sociological usage of the term poststructuralism refers to a shift from structuralist models of agency, society, and power to a more general understanding of the way that social structures influence our behavior and identity. Like Derrida and other poststructuralists in the literary camp, these poststructuralists borrowed many of the methods of structuralism while reaching very different conclusions. Durkheim and Parsons were two prominent structuralists whose ideas and methods were appropriated by the social poststructuralists.

Structural-functionalist anthropologists and sociologists such as Durkheim, Parsons, and Lévi-Strauss labored to understand the underlying utility or "function" of social institutions, practices, and beliefs. While these ideas provided an important foundation for the disciplines of sociology and anthropology, they also provided a limited view of human agency, which was viewed as a function of the internalization of social values.

Durkheim did much to articulate and popularize social structuralism. He argued that despite the fact that the machinations of society are invisible, they can be studied as objectively as any other realm of the natural world by examining the effects that social forces have on human beliefs and actions. For example, his empirical study *Suicide* (1997) explained that an individual's decision to commit suicide is best explained by their level of internalization of social values, with suicides occurring both when people were over and under-socialized. Similarly, sociologist Talcott Parsons argued that social institutions primarily exist to condition individuals to internalized social roles and to adapt psychological and biological needs to fit within a larger social order.

Social poststructuralists extended these ideas, arguing that human agency is shaped but not determined by a wide variety of social structures and cultural forces, including systems of belief and knowledge, disciplines of the body, and other systems of thought and action. This camp of poststructuralists is primarily interested in the way that culture and other "ideologies" shape human identities and act as unconscious systems of power over individuals. This group of thinkers also developed a more nuanced approach towards explaining human agency. Several social postmodernists, including Bourdieu and Foucault, attempt to describe the "microstructures" internal to every socialized person, which mediate any decision we choose to make, that (like Freud's concepts of the Id and Superego) remain invisible without extensive sociological analysis. Bourdieu's concept of *habitus* provides a notable example of an approach that builds upon the structuralist approach to explaining society and human behavior. Like Parsons, Bourdieu argued that social control is implanted upon individuals through mutually

reinforcing interaction between individual psyche and social institutions.

While Bourdieu accepts many of the structuralist assumptions of this view of human agency and social structure, he provides two major additions that place him within the poststructuralist camp. First, he argues that any society-wide conception of the social forces or structures that shape our lives ignores the diversity of practices and beliefs that exist within a society across different occupations and other social groupings. He explains that as a person enters any one of these *social fields* she is immersed within a different cultural and value system that affects her behavior. Bourdieu's second deviation from the structuralist approach toward human agency occurred with his development of the concept of *habitus* – the collection of tastes (e.g., in hobbies, occupations, and music) and proclivities towards behavior and beliefs that we develop as a result of the social sphere we grow up in, and which act as forms of *symbolic capital* which are valued or denigrated within various social fields.

Bourdieu argues we are not simply socialized or not socialized into society, as structuralists argue. Instead, we are brought into a specific *habitus* that leads us to see and interact with others in a way that feels natural and correct. At the same time, our *habitus* unconsciously encourages us toward activities and individuals that, in the long run, return us to a similar level of social status as our parents and lead us to act in scripted ways towards others. In short, *habitus* provides an explanation for a reproduction of power differences within society while providing individuals with the belief that they are making free decisions and interacting "naturally" with the world.

Similarly, Foucault provides detailed expositions of how *discourses* or ethical systems and ways of describing the world (including academic disciplines) became prominent within modern societies primarily because they provide more effective applications of social power while at the same time appearing to solve newly identified social problems. In *Discipline and Punish* (1995) Foucault explores the paradox of how punishment has become more human as we shifted our focus from punishing the body of a criminal to reforming their soul and then psyche, while at the same time these new powers became more difficult to rebel against.

Foucault uses the term *discourses* to emphasize that in modern society, power most often takes a moral form. New systems of moral control develop as a result of a compulsion to discuss and scientifically study issues that have been problematized. As a result, the academic disciplines, classifications, and practices that emerge from these discourses become systems of power. In *The History of Sexuality* (1990) Foucault explains how a compulsion to discuss and classify sexuality is not a sign of liberation from the sexually repressive Victorian era, but rather a foundation for developing more pervasive systems of control over sexuality. Although the practice of confession has become less popular in modern societies, Foucault explains that psychology and other forms of public discourse such as talk shows have risen to fill this need for us to discuss and internalize new ethical systems. In turn, we internalize new "disciplines" because they also provide us with new pleasures and advantages.

IMPLICATIONS FOR SOCIAL RESEARCH AND PRAXIS

Critics of both camps of poststructuralism provide two objections to these ideas: (1) a scientific study of culture or society is nearly impossible if these forces are viewed as situational and constantly shifting, and (2) there is little or no opportunity for resistance against social forces if they are internalized and invisible to individuals.

In response to the first objection, literary and social poststructuralists have developed research methods that they argue provide them with an indirect approach to understanding the invisible and ever-shifting forces of culture and society. Barthes's method of semiology provided a foundation for the methods of content analysis, which attempts to use scientific methods to measure the systems of meanings or "myths" that underlie texts and other cultural creations. Similar methods have been adopted within the school of cultural studies. For example, content analysis of the presentation and description of women in advertising provides an indication of cultural expectations around

gender and how these expectations have changed over time.

Foucault's method of *genealogy* (also known as *discourse analysis*), a second research method based on the ideas of poststructuralism, is in effect a widening of the methods of semiology. Foucault studied the history of academic disciplines and "discourses" to uncover the genesis of systems of knowledge such as psychiatry that are taken for granted as descriptions of reality but were in fact contested systems for defining and controlling human experience, with implications for which people and behaviors are rewarded or problematized. Similarly, Bourdieu explains that the microstructures that drive human decisions can be studied scientifically by observers who work to fully understand the ways that specific social fields interact with the *habitus* of individuals who enter a field. For example, in *Homo Academicus* (1988), his study of the French academic system, Bourdieu uses extensive interview and survey methods to understand the interaction between the cultural capital of academics and their resulting level of status within a given department and the academic system as a whole.

The second objection to the poststructuralist approach is that it does not allow for an individual's resistance to micropowers and ideologies that they have internalized. As a result, it is argued that poststructuralist research and theory have no value for improving society because they cannot tell individuals how to escape from the yoke of social power. This criticism of poststructuralism has led many reform-minded readers of Foucault and other poststructuralists to conclude that their theories have little use in improving the lot of those living within oppressive systems because the systems of power they describe are internalized and all-pervasive.

Poststructuralists conceive of power as the interaction between systems of meaning and action, such as Foucault's discourses and disciplines, Bourdieu's social spaces, or Barthes's mythologies. They contend that we accept these descriptions of the world due to previous conditioning in the form of *habitus* or other microstructures and the pleasures and advantages that these new yokes of power provide. As Foucault (1980: 98) explains, power is "never in anybody's hands [and individuals] are always in the position of simultaneously undergoing and exercising this power."

While social poststructuralists generally provide no direct challenge to these systems of power because there is no direct way to rebel against the micropowers, several theorists believe that understanding the workings of social power can provide a limited degree of resistance and reform. For example, Certeau (2002) explores how mundane practices such as the use of language and cooking can provide temporary forms of resistance to the internalized systems of cultural power described by poststructuralists.

SEE ALSO: Barthes, Roland; Bourdieu, Pierre; Certeau, Michel de; Cultural Studies; Deconstruction; Derrida, Jacques; Discourse; Foucault, Michel; Foucauldian Archeological Analysis; Habitus/Field; Postmodern Social Theory; Postmodernism; Saussure, Ferdinard de; Semiotics; Structuralism

REFERENCES AND SUGGESTED READINGS

Barthes, R. (1972 [1957]) *Mythologies*. Hill & Wang, New York.
Baudrillard, J. (1995) *Simulacra and Simulation*. University of Michigan Press, Ann Arbor.
Belsey, C. (2002) *Poststructuralism: A Very Short Introduction*. Oxford University Press, Oxford.
Bourdieu, P. (1984) *Distinction: A Social Critique of the Judgment of Taste*. Harvard University Press, Cambridge, MA.
Bourdieu, P. (1988) *Homo Academicus*. Stanford University Press, Stanford.
Bourdieu, P. (1998) *Practical Reason: On the Theory of Action*. Stanford University Press, Stanford.
Butler, J. (1990) *Gender Trouble*. Routledge, New York.
Certeau, M. de (2002) *The Practice of Everyday Life*. University of California Press, Los Angeles.
Derrida, J. (1980) *Writing and Difference*. University of Chicago Press, Chicago.
Derrida, J. (1998) *Of Grammatology*. Johns Hopkins University Press, Baltimore.
Durkheim, É. (1982) *The Rules of Sociological Method*. Free Press, New York.
Durkheim, É. (1997) *Suicide: A Study in Sociology*. Free Press, New York.
Foucault, M. (1980) *Power/Knowledge: Select Interviews and Other Writings 1972–1977*. Pantheon Books, New York.
Foucault, M. (1990) *The History of Sexuality: An Introduction*. Vintage Press, New York.
Foucault, M. (1995 [1977]) *Discipline and Punish: The Birth of the Prison*. Random House, New York.
Kristeva, J. (1980) *Desire in Language: A Semiotic Approach to Literature and Art*. Columbia University Press, New York.
Lévi-Strauss, C. (1971 [1949]) *The Elementary Structures of Kinship*. Beacon Press, Boston, MA.
Parsons, T. (1967) *The Structure of Social Action*, Vol. 1. Free Press, New York.
Saussure, F. de (1977 [1916]) *Course in General Linguistics*. McGraw Hill, New York.

Poulantzas, Nicos (1936–79)

Wendy A. Wiedenhoft

Nicos Poulantzas was born in Athens, Greece. He was active in the Greek student movement of the 1950s and participated in various communist and leftist organizations throughout his career. After completing a degree in law in Greece, Poulantzas moved to France, where he received a doctorate in the philosophy of law in 1965. His first major work, *Political Power and Social Classes*, was published in 1968. Poulantzas held a number of academic appointments in France, and at the time of his suicide was professor of sociology at the University of Vincennes.

Poulantzas was a structural Marxist who attempted to advance Marxist theory by emphasizing the role of the state in constituting and reproducing class struggle. Poulantzas argues that the state mediates all class relations, specifically economic, political, and ideological relations. Class relations are determined at the economic level by whether or not one produces material goods that create surplus value. Thus, wages or ownership of the means of production do not define class. Poulantzas's emphasis on the production of material goods excludes many workers from the proletariat, including state employees and service workers. Workers engaged in "non-productive" labor constitute a class that Poulantzas calls the new petty bourgeoisie, which may or may not form a class alliance with the capitalist class. At the political level class is determined by relations of authority, while relations of knowledge determine class at the ideological level. Poulantzas differentiates between manual and mental laborers at the ideological level, positing that those with technical expertise should also be excluded from the proletariat.

According to Poulantzas, the state does not dominate through repression, but by consent of both the dominant and subordinate classes. Critical of instrumental Marxists who view the state as a mere tool of the dominant capitalist class, Poulantzas suggests that the capitalist state is relatively autonomous from the economy, even if it does function to benefit the interests of the dominant class much of the time. The notion of a unified dominant class or working class may itself be a misnomer, as Poulantzas argues both classes are often divided. The capitalist state, however, functions as a unifying force to provide cohesion. This cohesion may appear contradictory, as it is a consequence of what Poulantzas calls the isolation effect. Instead of recognizing capitalist relations in terms of class struggle, individuals experience competition as isolated citizens or factions of a particular power bloc. Thus, the hegemonic power of the state rests upon a "false" notion of unity and the fact that, while the state itself constitutes class struggle, it appears to exclude class struggle from its center.

The rise of fascism and military dictatorships in Southern Europe and South America influenced Poulantzas's theory on state power, especially his advocacy of democratic socialism. He was concerned with how the hegemonic power of authoritarian statism grew as the state apparatus was able to incorporate resistance into its dominant ideology and use technocratic discourse to espouse liberalism. Poulantzas came to view all forms of statism as suspect, including Leninism. He feared that a party that followed a Leninist path, obliterating the capitalist state and the political liberties it provided, could hijack the long road to democratic socialism. According to Poulantzas, the Leninist transition to socialism rested upon the fallacies that the capitalist state functioned solely in the interests of the bourgeoisie, that the capitalist state was repressive, and that the working class

was unified. Poulantzas did not view the working class as unified, therefore it could not claim to represent the interests of the masses, especially the interests of the new social movements that were beginning to emerge. Poulantzas saw no point in replacing one dominant discourse with another, and argued that "socialism will be democratic or it will not be at all."

SEE ALSO: Class Conflict; Marx, Karl; Marxism and Sociology; State

REFERENCES AND SUGGESTED READINGS

Jessop, B. (1985) *Nicos Poulantzas: Marxist Theory and Political Strategy*. St. Martin's Press, New York.

Poulantzas, N. (1973) *Political Power and Social Classes*. New Left Books, London.

Poulantzas, N. (1974) *Fascism and Dictatorship*. New Left Books, London.

Poulantzas, N. (1975) *Classes in Contemporary Capitalism*. New Left Books, London.

Poulantzas, N. (1976) *The Crisis of the Dictatorships*. New Left Books, London.

Poulantzas, N. (1978) *State, Power, Socialism*. New Left Books, London.

Pound, Roscoe (1870–1964)

Michael R. Hill

Roscoe Pound, sociologist, ecologist, and noted jurist, originated and promulgated the legal movement known as the American school of sociological jurisprudence. This revolutionary perspective remains the single most consequential application of sociological thinking in American society. Pound's sociological theories and empirical methodologies fundamentally transformed the prosecution and administration of US law for a full half-century.

Widely remembered as the dynamic and authoritative Dean of Harvard's Law School (1916–36), Pound was also a creative and insightful plant ecologist as well as a pioneering and innovative sociologist. Albion W. Small, writing privately in 1916, observed that Pound is central to our understanding of the development of American sociology after 1906, concluding – with regard to sociology and law – that Pound was "not merely *magna pars* but practically the whole thing." Pound's integration of sociology and law began after 1901 at the University of Nebraska where Edward A. Ross's groundbreaking theoretical work in *Social Control* (1901), *Foundations of Sociology* (1905), and *Social Psychology* (1908) set Pound "in the path" that became the American school of sociological jurisprudence. Later, as Dean of Harvard's prestigious Law School, Pound inculcated sociological ideas into cadres of legal students destined to positions of power and influence, resulting in a widespread, sociologically infused legal perspective that dominated decision-making in the US Supreme Court for 50 years during the mid-twentieth century. A prodigious scholar, Pound wrote hundreds of legal, sociological, and botanical articles and published several well-received books, including *The Spirit of the Common Law* (1921), *Law and Morals* (1924), and *Social Control Through Law* (1942). Frequently cajoled by E. A. Ross to write a short monograph on sociological jurisprudence per se, Pound's five-volume *Jurisprudence* finally appeared in 1959.

Conceptually, Pound's sociological perspective holds that law is a social creation – an astonishing and deeply heretical idea for most lawyers at the beginning of the twentieth century. In 1906, Pound fired his first major salvo on behalf of sociological jurisprudence in an address to the American Bar Association, baldly painting American lawyers and judges as harmful conservatives (*Report of the 29th Annual Meeting of the American Bar Association*, 1906, Vol. 29, I: 395–417). Rejecting concepts of absolute legal "rights" (*Journal of Ethics*, 1915, Vol. 26: 92–116), Pound's sociological "theory of interests" defines law as an institutional mechanism for balancing the complex and often competing claims of individual, public, and social interests (*Publications of the American Sociological Society*, 1920, Vol. 15: 16–45). In the modern world of rapid technological and social change, sociological jurisprudence mandated the "reshaping of our institutions of public justice to the requirements of the times." When established legal

precedents fail to illuminate the intricacies of current situations, according to Pound, up-to-date sociological data become fundamentally important to jurists who must adjudicate conflicting claims lodged by divergent interests. Pound's theory thus made empirical sociological research "a presupposition of the work of the lawmaker, judge and jurist."

Leading by example, after co-founding the American Institute of Criminal Law and Criminology (1909), Pound – together with Felix Frankfurter – organized and directed the first full-scale interdisciplinary empirical survey of crime in America (*Criminal Justice in Cleveland*, 1922), a project immediately cited as a methodological exemplar by Robert E. Park and Ernest W. Burgess in the second edition of their influential *Introduction to the Science of Society* (1924). Pound's subsequent sociological synthesis appeared as *Criminal Justice in America* (1930). At Harvard, Pound championed the Survey of Crime and Criminal Justice in Boston (1934–6) and sponsored Sheldon Glueck's *One Thousand Juvenile Delinquents* (1934). As a commissioner working largely behind the scenes on Herbert Hoover's National Commission on Law Observance and Enforcement (popularly known as the Wickersham Commission, 1929–31), Pound framed much of the massive final *Report* (1931), lauded the meticulous work of Chicago's Edith Abbott, his former Nebraska student, in her *Crime and the Foreign Born* (1931), and successfully blocked the persistent tendency of Chicago's Clifford Shaw and Henry McKay to overreach their ecological data in *The Causes of Crime* (1931). Pound undertook his last empirical study at age 75: the Survey of Criminal Justice in China (1946–8), personally conducting site visits and interviews on mainland China. The results remain today embedded in Taiwan's legal code. Within the social sciences, Pound's welding of sociology and law is most often compared to and contrasted with the decidedly anthropological interpretation of law adopted by Karl Llewellyn.

Pound died in Cambridge, Massachusetts, still an active scholar, on July 1, 1964.

SEE ALSO: American Sociological Association; Law, Criminal; Law, Sociology of; Park, Robert E. and Burgess, Ernest W.; Small, Albion W.

REFERENCES AND SUGGESTED READINGS

Glueck, S. (Ed.) (1964) *Roscoe Pound and Criminal Justice*. Intro. S. Glueck. Foreword by E. Warren, Chief Justice of the United States. National Council on Crime and Delinquency, Dobbs Ferry.

Hill, M. R. (1989) Roscoe Pound and American Sociology. PhD dissertation. Department of Sociology, University of Nebraska-Lincoln.

Hull, N. E. H. (1997) *Roscoe Pound and Karl Llewellyn: Searching for an American Jurisprudence*. University of Chicago Press, Chicago.

Pound, R. (1907) The Need of a Sociological Jurisprudence. *Green Bag* 19 (October): 607–15.

Pound, R. (1945) Sociology of Law. In: Gurvitch, G. & Moore, W. E. (Eds.), *Twentieth-Century Sociology*. Philosophical Library, New York, pp. 297–341.

Setaro, F. C. (1942) *A Bibliography of the Writings of Roscoe Pound*. Harvard University Press, Cambridge, MA.

Strait, G. A. (1960) *A Bibliography of the Writings of Roscoe Pound, 1940–1960*. Harvard University Law School, Cambridge, MA.

Tobey, R. C. (1981) *Saving the Prairies: The Life-Cycle of the Founding School of American Plant Ecology, 1895–1955*. University of California Press, Berkeley.

Wigdor, D. (1974) *Roscoe Pound*. Greenwood Press, Westport, CT.

poverty

John Iceland

While poverty generally refers to material deprivation, it is a multifaceted experience for those who are struggling to get by. It can certainly involve economic hardship, such as difficulty in paying food bills or living in housing in severe disrepair. For some, poverty means lacking some of the basic consumer items that their neighbors have, such as telephones and cars. The term poverty can be used to describe a lack of other types of goods, such as education or human rights. The focus here, however, is more narrowly on the economic dimensions of poverty.

There are several reasons why poverty is considered a critical social issue. First, the hardship that often accompanies poverty can have adverse effects on individuals' physical and psychological well-being. A number of studies have shown that children raised in poor families are worse off in terms of their cognitive development, school achievement, and emotional well-being. Poor individuals are also more likely to have health problems and shorter life expectancies. Many people would also agree that it is morally troubling to have poverty amidst relative affluence.

Second, poverty has broader economic consequences. Economies thrive in societies with vibrant working and middle classes. For example, much of the strong economic growth in the United States in the twentieth century was fueled by the expansion of consumer markets. As the demand for new products increased, so did technological innovation, productivity, and wages and benefits. Thus, declining levels of poverty contribute to a healthy economy by increasing the number of people who can produce and purchase goods and services; that increase, in turn, stimulates economic growth and raises average standards of living.

Third, high levels of poverty can have serious social and political consequences. Poor people often feel alienated from mainstream society. Poverty can provoke social disorder and crime and reduce public confidence in democratic institutions if people do not feel their needs are being addressed by the prevailing system. The unequal distribution of resources can contribute to a fragmentation of society, both nationally and globally.

There are a number of measures one could use to estimate the prevalence of poverty in society. *Income* poverty measures are perhaps the most common. They usually involve comparing a household's income to a poverty threshold to determine whether that household is poor. Two basic types of income poverty measures are *absolute* and *relative* measures. Absolute measures, such as the current US official measure, are ones that typically attempt to define a truly basic – absolute – needs standard that remains constant over time and perhaps updated only for inflation. Relative measures, which are more commonly used by researchers in Europe, explicitly define poverty as a condition of comparative disadvantage, to be assessed against some evolving standard of living.

The most common poverty thresholds used in developing countries are absolute ones. The

World Bank, for example, uses a poverty standard of $1 to $2 per person per day, or $1,095 to $2,190 per year, for a family of three in developing countries in Africa or Latin America. The World Bank measures are actually *consumption* rather than *income* poverty measures, as families are considered poor if they consume goods with monetary values below the thresholds, rather than whether they have incomes below those thresholds.

The main theoretical criticism of absolute poverty measures is that what people judge to be poor varies across both time and place. Applying the World Bank measures, for example, to developed countries would be fairly meaningless. Even within the US, as standards of living have changed, so have people's perceptions of what poverty means (Fisher 1997). Economists describe this phenomenon as the income elasticity of the poverty line – the tendency of successive poverty lines to rise in real terms as the real income of the general population rises.

Poverty remains pervasive in all societies for several reasons, including the way we understand and define poverty, the features of the global market system, social stratification across "status" groups (such as racial and ethnic groups), and policy responses to these issues. Because views of what it takes to avoid poverty increase as standards of living rise, as described above, achieving inroads against poverty over the long run is difficult. Poverty is also a common, if not endemic, feature of most economic systems, and the market system, whose principal goal is the individual accumulation of capital, is not one of the exceptions. On the one hand, as the engine of economic growth and technological change, the market system contributes to increases in wages and overall standards of living. On the other hand, the market economy often exerts a contrary effect; to maximize profits, businesses usually seek to pay low wages to workers, and this can serve to increase inequality and poverty.

While economic forces determine overall levels of economic growth and inequality, social stratification across social groups determines who becomes poor. Status groups in today's society are commonly defined by the intersection of ethnic, gender, and class affiliations. Social stratification across status groups occurs when social groups seek to maximize their rewards by restricting others' access to resources and opportunities. The process of stratification is usually a cumulative one. A person may begin life at a disadvantage, and disadvantages accrue through the stages of people's lives, such as during schooling, then in the labor market, and so on.

Policy could reduce (or increase) the harmful effects of inequality. The rise of the welfare state in the US in the 1930s, for example, was a response to the hardship of the Great Depression. Policy, however, has limits within the context of the market system. It is not always used as an instrument for promoting equality because it is thought that pushes for broad-based economic equality of outcomes may serve to reduce, if even by a modest amount, incentives to work. Supplying a guaranteed income runs contrary to the central ethos of the market system. Thus, policies devised to address poverty often differ according to how societies prioritize competing values and goals.

SEE ALSO: Family Poverty; Family Structure and Poverty; Feminization of Poverty; Great Depression; Poverty and Disrepute; Poverty and Free Trade; Urban Poverty

REFERENCES AND SUGGESTED READINGS

Danizer, S. & Haveman, R. (2001) *Understanding Poverty*. Harvard University Press, Cambridge, MA.

Fisher, G. M. (1997) From Hunter to Orshansky: An Overview of (Unofficial) Poverty Lines in the United States from 1904 to 1965. US Census Bureau, Poverty Measurement Working Paper.

Iceland, J. (2003) *Poverty in America*. University of California Press, Berkeley.

National Research Council (1995) *Measuring Poverty: A New Approach*. Ed. C. F. Citro & R. T. Michael. National Academy Press, Washington, DC.

O'Connor, A. (2001) *Poverty Knowledge: Social Science, Social Policy, and the Poor in Twentieth-Century US History*. Princeton University Press, Princeton.

Patterson, J. T. (2000) *America's Struggle Against Poverty in the Twentieth Century*. Harvard University Press, Cambridge, MA.

Rainwater, L. & Smeeding, T. M. (2003) *Poor Kids in a Rich Country*. Russell Sage Foundation, New York.

Sen, A. (1999) *Development as Freedom*. Alfred A. Knopf, New York.

Townsend, P. (1993) *The International Analysis of Poverty*. Harvester-Wheatsheaf, Hemel Hempstead.

World Bank (2001) *World Development Report 2000/2001: Attacking Poverty*. Oxford University Press, Oxford.

poverty and disrepute

David L. Harvey

On the face of it, the association of poverty and disrepute seems obvious. Poverty's material misery is to be avoided, just as is the diffuse sense of shame that attaches to those who "never had what it took," or "should have made it, but didn't." Indeed, the commandment to succeed is central to Merton's (1968: 185–214) theory of deviance. His "Anomie and Social Structure" posits an endorsement of success among all classes and an equal aversion to failure. Hence, his "anomic adaptations" Conformity, Innovation, Ritualism, and Retreatism (Rebellion is another matter) revolve around achieving success or in finding an alternative route to success.

Modern poverty, then, carries with it a *moral stain* as vexing as material uncertainty itself. Our understanding of poverty's disrepute is further complicated by the fact that poor persons are labeled disreputable even as disrepute has become increasingly associated with today's ruling elites (Lasch 1995: 25–49). Moreover, nostrums describing the poor as "good and hard-working" merely confuse the issue. Too often, these shibboleths shield contempt for the poor and our own fear of falling.

David Matza has cut through this casuistry by defining the disreputable poor as being those who for extra-economic reasons remain unemployed even during periods of high labor demand and who, by dint of that fact, become objects of moral censure (Matza 1966). Guided by this definition, he identifies several "disreputable fractions" of the poor: the *Dregs* whose occupational careers deviate from the normal

trajectories of their cohort; the *Newcomers*, strangers in a strange land, segregated and victimized by nativist prejudice; the downwardly mobile *Skidders*; and, finally, the *Infirm*. These categories echo Marx's (1979) *Lumpenproletariat* and Jack London's "people of the abyss."

POVERTY AND DISREPUTE AS PROCESS

Like all sociological entities, poverty's disrepute is ontologically stratified. It is structured by the complex interaction of six elements. First, modern poverty originates in the objective contradictions of capitalism: in the dictum that industrial efficiency requires the continuous generation of *superfluous populations*. The production of these surplus populations is a *systemic requirement* of capital's political economy. That is, the structure of commodity production requires some portion of the workforce to be held in reserve in order to accommodate sudden increases in market demand. Failure to maintain this standing army of unemployed or sub-employed workers risks a breakdown of both market equilibrium and its integrative pricing function. And, to the extent that markets are free (i.e., their pricing mechanisms operate independently of moral imperatives), this economic superfluity generates perduring poverty amid material plenty.

Second, viewed *sociologically*, modern poverty's disrepute manifests itself as a social exclusion of the poor from full civic participation (Townsend 1962, 1970; Byrne, 1999). While the degree of exclusion varies, its legitimation requires the moral marginalization of the poor. This second element – the moral exclusion of the poor – lies at the symbolic core of modern poverty's disrepute. Indeed, it sets modern poverty off from historically prior poverties. As Polanyi (2001) reminds us, because pre-capitalist markets were embedded in analgesic social institutions, poverty, no matter how grinding, provided a social nexus that guaranteed the poor a legitimate claim to social inclusion (Block 2001). Unabrogated access to these embedded rights formed a "social contract" protecting the poor. That social contract came to an end, though, with the triumph of self-regulating markets. The commodification of life's necessities stripped the poor of those cultural buffers that had insured them their social personage. No longer shielded by traditional ties of kinship, communal fealty, or Christian charity, the utilitarian cast of bourgeois culture and self-regulating markets paved the way for socially excluding the economically superfluous.

Third, modern poverty has an ideological component: a set of indispensable accounts that either justify or deny the legitimacy of excluding the poor. Exclusionary accounts are invariably class-based. They center upon naturalistic accounts of poverty that justify existing inequalities. They are situated within a reified penumbra of pejorative judgments hierarchically ranking classes and their subcultures. Standing over and against such stigmatic labeling are those subterranean ideologies that debunk the accuracy and fairness of such labeling.

Taken together, these opposed constructions form the core of "ideological space." This space is composed of rhetorics of exclusion fabricated from above and communicated downward through the class system, and subaltern arguments for inclusion manufactured from below and communicated upward. This double flow is integral to the class struggle. It morally partitions the superfluous into "deserving" and "undeserving" factions and, thereby, morally anchors the class system.

The fourth aspect of this process underscores the historically conditioned nature of disrepute's social construction. Both hegemonic justification and subaltern pleadings of defeasibility draw their rationales from the immediate historical situation as they morally anchor the class system. Fifth, how an excluded group acts out its moral stain is "ecologically and locally conditioned." That is, the shifting terms of moral exclusion depend upon the *community's concrete situation and past experiences*. Sixth, the "wild card" of *human agency* allows individuals and collectives to negotiate "special terms" by which their ritual segregation from the community's moral paragons is played out.

These six factors form a plausible starting point for grasping the dynamic link between poverty and disrepute. This link can best be seen by comparing the exclusionist ideology promulgated by Thomas Robert Malthus (1766–1834) and the inclusionist alternative Karl Marx (1818–83) offered, especially as they relate to

(1) the origins of economic superfluity and (2) the assigning of moral responsibility for that superfluity.

THE IDEOLOGICAL CONSTRUCTION OF DISREPUTE

The opposed paradigms of Malthus and Marx have remained paradigmatic of the modern poverty debate for more than 150 years. The ideological power of Malthus's *An Essay on the Principle of Population* (1960) lies in its contention that poverty is rooted in the natural order of things and is, moreover, part of the Divine design. Superfluous populations are generated by two demographic tendencies characteristic of all life forms. Animal populations, inclusive of humans, naturally reproduce at an ascending geometric rate while their means of subsistence increase at a slower, "arithmetic" rate. In a specific ecological setting, the incommensurate increase of the two ratios eventually precipitates a demographic catastrophe. During such catastrophes "excess populations" outstrip their resource base and are subsequently winnowed until their numbers once more conform to environmental capacity.

Malthus goes on to note that these "winter kills" occur less frequently than one might expect. This is because the "positive checks" of war, famine, plague, and misery (poverty) continually keep human populations below the catastrophic breakpoint. His religious training allows him, moreover, to move effortlessly from science to moral philosophy and theology by suggesting these positive checks have their final cause in Divine intention. Poverty, famine, etc. are, in the last analysis, trials for testing moral fiber and faith. As part of God's grand design, positive checks should not be eliminated by Enlightenment reform, but endured as annealing devices of Christian virtue.

In a revision of his original essay – sometimes called *The Second Essay* – Malthus provides an exit from this dire scenario by giving "negative checks" – reason, foresight, and free will – a countervailing role. Together, they form the basis of disciplined self-constraint and the cultivation of moral habits that limit family size. He argues that if the poor are schooled in moral self-discipline, most will willingly diminish their numbers and thereby command wages capable of lifting themselves from poverty. Moreover, the costs of church or state-based poor relief, once reduced, can lead to increased capital investment and new job creation. Hence, in his *Second Essay*, Malthus shifts the liberation of the poor from their squalor squarely on the shoulders of the poor, while simultaneously making their refusal to rationally limit family size a moral failure. That is, if bourgeois society magnanimously underwrites the education of all classes, the lower orders must reciprocate. Failure to do so would be tantamount to an act of free choice and, hence, of moral perversity.

Malthus's line of reasoning not only blames the poor for their poverty, but in good conscience relieves society and Christian conscience of any further concern with these incorrigibles. Malthus can only make this argument, however, by reifying poverty on three levels: (1) by locating the origins of surplus populations in two natural ratios; (2) by defining poverty as part of God's benevolent plan; and (3) by locating the continued causes of economic malaise outside the political economy of capital. Indeed, this triad of reifications is the prototype of all ideologies designed to "blame the victim."

Marx's approach is diametrically opposed to Malthus's. While granting the validity of the latter's "laws of population" in pre-capitalist formations, Marx argues they no longer apply in modern industrial societies. These latter have technologically superseded Malthus's demographics of wealth and poverty. Indeed, the mechanized, mass production of commodity wealth has produced a new crisis: "overproduction," not over-population, now threatened the new industrial order.

In the early stages of industrialization, the production of commodity wealth hinged on the number of workers employed and on how effectively they could be sweated. Mechanization, however, largely resolved this problem. Labor's productive powers were so effectively enhanced that workers now risked being replaced by their machines. This substitution of machines for men created a new economic entity: industrial reserve armies of unemployed and sub-employed workers. Indeed, superfluous populations existed, as Malthus claimed, but not because of undisciplined natural increase. Instead, superfluous populations were a product of capital's rational pursuit of ever-increasing rates of capital accumulation. Competing for an ever-diminishing number of occupational slots, Marx's industrial reserves formed the *demographic core* of the new poverty. Only a thoroughgoing reform of capitalist relations could eliminate poverty.

Malthus's and Marx's accounts still ideologically bracket debates over poverty's enduring enigma. The former's naturalistic doctrine, while cognizant of the contradictions of capital, nonetheless defends entrepreneurial capitalism by holding the poor accountable for their own misery. By contrast, Marx avoids victim blaming by locating modern poverty's roots in the structural contradictions of industrial capitalism itself.

THE HISTORICAL EVOLUTION OF IDEOLOGICAL SPACE

Despite its evolution from entrepreneurial capitalism to monopoly capitalism, and from monopoly capitalism to globalization, today's capitalism still requires industrial reserve armies to sustain itself. It is little wonder, then, that debates over the disreputable poor have added but little to Malthus and Marx's original parameters – accounts that "blame the victim" and proposals for reforming capital's anti-social tendencies.

Following Phillips (2004), we can go a step further in suggesting that at any given moment the plausibility of these opposed accounts is a function of capital's ability to maintain its hegemony over the warring class subcultures composing capital's *Lifeworld*. In surveying the recent history of the US, Phillips identifies three periods of "capitalist blow-outs" – eras in which the equilibria of class power so necessary for democracy have been shattered by a rampant "plutography." These eras of America's anti-democratic excesses occurred during the Gilded Age, the Roaring Twenties, and in our own era. During each blow-out, the differences defining capital's class hierarchies intensified and victim bashing of the poor flourished.

These asymmetrical blow-outs were punctuated by periods of economic crisis in which an egalitarian "contraction" of the class hierarchy and a relative restoration of political balance between classes ensued. These periods of contraction witnessed the agrarian revolts and Populist movements of the 1880s and 1890s; the Midwestern Progressivism of the last century; and, finally, what Phillips calls the Great Contraction of the New Deal. With each contraction, the personal stain of poverty diminished, the working class and the poor were celebrated, reforms were implemented, and, in several instances, social banditry in the name of the poor was given folkloric treatment in the arts.

The history of the social sciences in America shows parallel cyclic variations. Hence, the antithetical sociologies of William Graham Sumner (1840–1910) and Lester Ward (1841–1913) continued the debate between social Darwinians and socialist reformers while remaining within the boundaries first set by Malthus and Marx. Baltzel (1987: 87–142) demonstrates that Malthusian-inspired social Darwinism scientifically buttressed the xenophobic sentiments and racist doctrines that legitimated the WASP establishment's stigmatizing of foreign workers and agrarian populists alike. Opposing this misappropriation of science, the "New Social Science Movement" used a nature/nurture paradigm to explain the alleged racial differences dividing rich and poor. For them, these differences resided neither in biology nor in temperament. They were seen, instead, as originating in the caste-like monopolies in the education and economic systems that perpetuated the hegemony of the WASP establishment. Developing this line of thought, social science scholarship celebrated the self-redemptive powers of the poor and effectively refuted the Malthusian reifications of the upper-class establishment. In time, the New Social Science became an intellectual linchpin of the social reform programs of the New Deal.

In the 1960s the War on Poverty extended New Deal entitlements to previously by-passed populations. When that movement foundered on the fiscal shoals of the Vietnam War, conservative counterattacks freely marshaled Malthusian-inspired "victim bashing." Edward Banfield's *The Unheavenly City* (1968), for example, argued that anti-poverty reforms had hit a point of diminishing returns beyond which uplift and reform could not move. Striking a

Malthusian stance, he argued that the impoverished residue remaining in America's cities were moral incorrigibles. Their "present-oriented" culture and their preference for the excitement of "street life" placed them beyond redemption. Indeed, the growing number of poor suggested reformers themselves had become part of the problem. Advances in public health and poor support programs were now blunting the beneficial power of Malthus's positive checks that in times past had limited the reproductive life spans of the incorrigibles.

Some 15 years later, Charles Murray's *Losing Ground* (1984) appropriated these same Malthusian motifs, taking Banfield's work several steps further. Murray now contended poverty was caused by the welfare system itself: by the dependencies transfer payments induced among the poor. In the grand fashion of Malthus's *Second Essay*, Murray suggested poverty could be ended not only by eliminating government welfare programs, but also by ending all federal transfer payments *tout court*. Rhetorically parodying the closing pages of the *Second Essay*, Murray leads the reader through a "thought experiment," asking what would happen if all such programs suddenly ended. He concludes little would change: legitimate programs would be continued by local agencies or private welfare groups; the remainder would deservedly die on the vine.

It would now appear that as capital's global reach expanded into the twenty-first century, poverty and its disrepute have also become globalized. Not surprisingly, the debate over poverty's global origins and its amelioration has developed along the lines discussed here. In *Globalization and Its Discontents* (2002), Nobel Laureate Joseph Stiglitz suggests that anti-poverty policies at the World Bank and the Import-Export Bank have divided in accordance with the paradigms discussed here: neoliberal "market fundamentalism" and "neo-Keynesian" interventionism. The former has cloaked itself in a Smithian adulation of the free market, arguing that if free markets are allowed to operate without societal interference, they will "naturally" eliminate both poverty and unemployment. For many neoliberals, unemployment is created largely by the individual "deciding" not to work (i.e., to engage in activities more pleasurable than disciplined wage labor). Beginning with this assumption, neoliberal anti-poverty strategies move away from Adam Smith and assume a distinctly Malthusian cast. When a given national economy falters due to lack of fiscal restraint on the part of those managing a nation's economy, neoliberal cures move directly to "restructuring" that economy: restricting as much as possible the latitudes of those traditional institutions impairing the impersonal mechanisms of the free market. In short, "market fundamentalists" seek to enhance the power of self-regulating markets by negating the buffering effects of the institutions that embed the economy.

Neo-Keynesians do not share this faith in untrammeled markets. They assume markets processes are, a priori, imperfect and hence periodically invite temporary intervention if poverty is to be eliminated. Hence, efforts to ameliorate poverty often begin with strengthening those institutions embedding markets and protecting the social personage of the poor. Once these embedding agencies are stabilized, enforcing market discipline can follow. This approach is, of course, anathema to the neoliberals. And just as neoliberalism is ideologically isomorphic to Malthusianism and Neo-Darwinism, so the Neo-Keynesian paradigm remains isomorphic to a Marxist critique of capital. The former moves directly to place "disreputable traditions" on the Procrustean bed of market fundamentals, while the latter pragmatically repairs the embedding institutions themselves before proceeding.

THE STRANGER AND THE VANQUISHED

If modern poverty lies at the very heart of the capitalist mode of production and its exploitive social relations, then the stigma of its disrepute resides in the vastness of the differential distribution of wealth and power marking class society. This axiom holds for the burgeoning system of global capital and its by-passed Fordist-Keynesian constellation, just as much as it held for nineteenth-century entrepreneurial capitalism. In each sociohistorical formation class differences must be technically reproduced each generation, just as they must be morally vindicated. Because class warfare has

been, historically, a pandemic possibility, rendering the poor morally suspect stabilizes capitalist society in two ways. First, the stigma of poverty sustains the morale of ruling groups by legitimating their belief that they are naturally endowed with the moral capacity to rule. Second, the disreputable label has a *preemptive* function. It communicates to the "dangerous classes" both their social incompetence and the inferiority of their class subculture. This preemptive degradation thus becomes a powerful mechanism of social control, educating the poor and the near-poor into a grudging acceptance of the moral correctness of their social exclusion.

Given these functions, there is still the issue of who among the poor get labeled "disreputable." In addressing this question, one turns from the *systemic* issues of superfluity to the concrete communal processes regulating the assignment of disrepute. Matza (1966: 291–292) bundles these processes under the rubric of "pauperization." Pauperization can occur at two sociohistorical junctures. First, a community or a society can be momentarily swamped by waves of unassimilated "newcomers." This produces an institutional anomie that requires the social order to defend against social disorganization. Pauperization is one such defense. It allows the community to distance itself from the recent arrivals by treating them as anathema – as morally disreputable.

However, the label of disrepute can also be applied to already assimilated members of a community. This second type of pauperization usually occurs when traditional modes of production and their occupational cultures are suddenly displaced by new technologies and new productive protocols of efficiency. Under these conditions, traditionally validated norms of care and craftsmanship are suddenly defined as dilatory, undisciplined, and indolent.

Hence, depending on pauperization's sociohistorical nexus, disrepute can assume one of two social forms: the "Stranger" or the "Vanquished." Following Simmel (1965; Hvinden 1995), the Stranger role emerges when migrants possessing a viable way of life resist immediate assimilation. Like Simmel's Stranger, they walk *among* a people, but are not *of* them. In time, most Strangers will either move on or accommodate to the host order. There will be a residue, however, that does not adapt occupationally and that continues to resist acculturation. They are soon relegated to the ranks of the disreputable poor.

The Vanquished, by contrast, belong to families that were assimilated long ago. They are descendants of those who earlier challenged the reigning hegemony and failed. These families or kin groups are subsequently folded into the life of the community, often as a distinct caste. In accepting their subaltern status such groups are asymptotically assimilated, even as certain differences are tolerated and even nurtured by the reigning orthodoxy. As occupants of a circumscribed social niche, the Vanquished learn how to play to the vanity of their betters and, in time, wrest from them special dispensations. In time, such exemptions can mature into long-term indulgences so that the Vanquished are paternalistically exempted from living up to the standards of social and moral competence expected of the rest of the citizenry. As part of a longstanding system of patronage, the Vanquished are seldom "dangerous," only disreputable. Indeed, their periodic failures at self-improvement are tolerated since their failures testify to the metaphysical rightness of the existing hegemony. Moreover, having "learned their place," they can often form cross-class coalitions with communal elites by forming united fronts against the latest wave of Strangers. Indeed, in particularly stable communities disrepute can pass from one generation to the next as part of a symbolic family estate. In America, poor white Southerners and various persons of color have played the role of the Vanquished. When enlisted in reactionary alliances, they are labeled by self-described progressives as "Red Necks" and "Uncle Toms," or worse.

SEE ALSO: Economic Sociology: Classical Political Economic Perspectives; Global Economy; Gramsci, Antonio; Labeling Theory; Malthus, Thomas Robert; Marx, Karl; Merton, Robert K.; Neoliberalism; Polanyi, Karl; Poverty; Simmel, Georg; Social Exclusion; Spencer, Herbert

REFERENCES AND SUGGESTED READINGS

Baltzell, E. D. (1987 [1964]) *The Protestant Establishment: Aristocracy and Caste in America*. Yale University Press, New Haven.

Banfield, E. C. (1968) *The Unheavenly City: The Nature and the Future of Our Urban Crisis*. Little, Brown, Boston.

Banfield, E. C. (1974) *The Unheavenly City Revisited: A Revision of the Unheavenly City*. Little, Brown, Boston.

Block, F. (2001 [1944]) Introduction. In: Polanyi, K., *The Great Transformation: The Political and Economic Origins of Our Time*. Beacon Press, Boston, pp. xviii–xxxviii.

Byrne, D. (1999) *Social Exclusion*. Open University Press, Buckingham.

Desmond, A. & Morris, J. (1991) *Darwin*. Warner Books, New York.

Hvinden, B. (1995) Poverty, Exclusion, and Agency. *Research in Community Sociology* 5: 15–33.

Lasch, C. (1995) *The Revolt of the Elites and the Betrayal of Democracy*. W. W. Norton, New York.

Malthus, T. R. (1960 [1798]) *An Essay on the Principle of Population, as it Affects the Future Improvement of Society. With remarks on the speculations of Mr. Godwin, M. Condorcet, and other writers*. In: Himmelfarb, G. (Ed.), *On Population*. Modern Library, New York, pp. 3–143.

Marx, K. (1979 [1852]) *The 18th Brumaire of Louis Bonaparte*. In: *Collected Works of Karl Marx and Frederick Engels*, Vol. 11. International Publishers, New York, pp. 99–197.

Matza, D. (1966) The Disreputable Poor. In: Bendix, R. & Lipset, S. M. (Eds.), *Class, Status and Power: Social Stratification in Comparative Perspective*, 2nd edn. Free Press, New York, pp. 289–302.

Merton, R. K. (1968 [1949]) *Social Theory and Social Structure*. Free Press, New York.

Murray, C. (1984) *Losing Ground: American Social Policy, 1950–1980*. Basic Books, New York.

Phillips, K. (2004) *American Dynasty: Aristocracy, Fortune, and the Politics of Deceit in the House of Bush*. Viking, New York.

Polanyi, K. (2001 [1944]) *The Great Transformation: The Political and Economic Origins of Our Time*. Beacon Press, Boston.

Simmel, G. (1965 [1908]) The Poor. *Social Problems* 13: 118–39.

Stiglitz, J. (2002) *Globalization and Its Discontents*. W. W. Norton, New York.

Townsend, P. (1962) The Meaning of Poverty. *British Journal of Sociology* 13: 210–27.

Townsend, P. (1970) Measures and Explanations of Poverty in High Income and Low Income Countries: The Problems of Operationalizing the Concepts of Development, Class, and Poverty. In: Townsend, P. (Ed.), *The Concept of Poverty: Working Papers on Methods of Investigation and Lifestyles of the Poor in Different Countries*. American Elsevier, New York, pp. 1–45.

poverty and free trade

Christoph Henning

The relation of poverty and free trade is not obvious. Exactly for this reason it needs scientific clarification in order to be able to come to terms with it. From a sociological point of view, free trade is one of the cures of the poverty of nations, yet at the same time it must be named as one of the main sources of global poverty.

Among the reasons for poverty *within* a society are economic inequalities with regard to initial endowments. Though modern society is normatively based on equal opportunities, the unequal endowments that can be found in real life may worsen in trade. Both parties might benefit through trade, yet the richer party in many cases benefits more than the poorer party (even though that is not pictured in the "perfect" world of economic models), so inequality can and in many cases will grow. This is one of the reasons why trade is regulated from time to time. Yet poverty is measured in relative terms here: as the total wealth in industrialized countries is growing, so is the average standard of living within those countries, even for the disadvantaged groups. So in spite of increasing inequality, the standard of living of the poor can be lifted in absolute terms. Standard political philosophy, following John Rawls, considers this as just.

This theoretical win-win scenario (though in detail some gain a little, others gain a lot) looks different from the global perspective. The amount of global poverty is growing not only relatively, but absolutely. There are whole countries that are becoming poorer and poorer. According to the United Nations Development Report 2003 this is true for more than 50 nations in the last few decades. Hunger is the number one global problem, followed by diseases that are equally widespread. Technically, the means to avoid these diseases have in many cases long been established. However, some nations cannot afford to buy such medical remedies on the global market. Usually, they are not even allowed to produce generic drugs themselves, although there are exceptions, such as in the case of AIDS in South Africa. There are other problems intrinsically related to poverty. Worldwide migration, for example, is most often caused by poverty. Disasters caused by global climate change, as another example, usually hit the poorest regions the hardest, as poor regions cannot afford to protect the environment. Finally, civil wars often break out where people are hopeless due to their poverty. In other words, poverty is an urgent global problem itself, and indirectly it is the source of many other global problems. Global poverty calls for an explanation.

Worldwide poverty goes along with growing wealth in some regions. This obviously is a paradox. In search of explanations, pre-sociological theories sometimes turned to morality: those that are well off *deserve* to be well off because they are virtuous and diligent. Likewise, the poor *deserve* to be poor because they are corrupted, not able to work, or not willing to work. Sociology cannot take such value judgments at face value. The science of society instead has to find social forces and structural reasons for this paradox. Among such explanations are political and economic approaches. Both deviate form the orthodox textbook image of free trade.

The standard economic explanation from undergraduate textbooks, following Ricardo's theorem of comparative advantage, is that all partners automatically benefit from free trade. If one country has disadvantages in the production costs of every good, it will still benefit from free trade if it finds another country that agrees not to produce the goods where the first country has a comparative advantage in production costs. Comparative advantage means that the opportunity costs for producing a certain good are expressed in the cost of production for another good: it may take Canada 4 units of beer to produce one unit of wine, whereas in Mexico the relation may be 2 to 1. This does not mean that it is actually cheaper to produce beer in Mexico. A comparative advantage can go along with an absolute disadvantage. If we follow this theory, Canada is expected to focus on beer and Mexico on wine, even when absolute costs for *both* products are lower in Canada. This is a strong assumption and resembles a planned economy more than a market. Another assumption is that the richer country will in the end exchange the goods produced in the poorer country for their own products. Parties benefit from trade only if these strong assumptions are met. Let us say, instead of Canada producing 100 units of wine and 400 units of beer and Mexico producing 50 units of wine and 100 units of beer with half of their productive powers for each good and for their own use, we now have Canada producing beer only and Mexico producing wine only, which they exchange afterwards. Instead of 500 units of beer, we now have 800 units of beer in total, and instead of 150 units of wine we have 100 units of wine. The total wealth has increased from 650 to 900 units, even though the cost of wine goes up (but this will only benefit Mexico). Because it would cost Canada 4 units of beer to produce 1 unit of wine, Canada is assumed to exchange 50 units of Mexican wine for 200 units of Canadian beer (or even more). After this "international trade," Canada ends up with 600 units of beer and 50 units of wine; that is, 50 units of wine less, but 200 units of beer more. Mexico ends up with 50 units of wine and 200 units of beer; that is, the same amount of wine, but double the quantity of beer. In this example, both parties benefit in total. Yet it is very clear that there are many theoretical flaws in this harmonious picture.

The first one is that there are often political barriers to trade, and this is what recent theories of international trade have stressed. Every time a party starts to lose its gains from trade, it will try to introduce tariffs in order to protect its industry. Yet only strong countries will have the power to do so. A weaker party will often not have the means to introduce such measures, even where economic reasons would recommend them. Secondly, there are various economic arguments that cast doubt on this perfect picture, as for example dependency theory or the theory of unequal exchange. Many of these schools have a Marxist background, yet one can read in Adam Smith that countries with an absolute disadvantage can hardly gain from trade. Why should a country that has an absolute advantage in one good abstain from producing it? Besides, this story only works under the assumption of the quantity theory of money, which says that momentary gains from trade will lead to inflation (more money imported and more goods exported result in higher prices, and these in turn level the advantage from trade). As soon as another, more realistic theory of money is used, the theory of comparative advantage is no longer convincing. Money can not only be used to purchase goods, it can also be used to invest in better production technologies or in order to lend it to other countries. If these other countries do not gain from international trade but experience a worsening of their "absolute disadvantage," this can result in a crisis of international debt. And this is what can be perceived during the last few decades.

SEE ALSO: Capitalism; Colonialism (Neocolonialism); Dependency and World-Systems Theories; Globalization; Inequality, Wealth; Neoliberalism; Poverty

REFERENCES AND SUGGESTED READINGS

Briggs, T. (1875) *Poverty, Taxation, and the Remedy: Free Trade, free Labour, or direct Taxation the true principle of Political Economy*. W. Reeves, London.

Landes, D. (1998) *The Wealth and Poverty of Nations: Why Some Are So Rich and Some Are So Poor*. Little, Brown, London.

Ricardo, D. (1992 [1817]) *The Principles of Political Economy and Taxation*. Dent, London.

Sachs, J. (2004) *The End of Poverty: Economic Possibilities for our Time*. Penguin, New York.

Shaikh, A. (1979–80) Foreign Trade and the Law of Value. *Science and Society* (fall 1979): 281–302; (spring 1980): 27–5.

Shaikh, A. (1980) On the Laws of International Exchange. In: Nell, E. J. (Ed.), *Growth, Profits, and Property: Essays in the Revival of Political Economy*. Cambridge University Press, Cambridge, pp. 204–35.

Shaikh, A. (1996) Free Trade, Unemployment, and Economic Policy. In: Eatwell, J. (Ed.), *Global Unemployment: Loss of Jobs in the 90s*. M. E. Sharpe, New York.

Shaikh, A. (2003) Globalization and the Myth of Free Trade. Paper for the Conference on Globalization and the Myth of Free Trade, New School University, New York, April. Online. www.homepage.newschool.edu/~AShaikh/globalization-myths.pdf.

United Nations, Development Programme (UNDP) (2003) *Human Development Report 2003*. United Nations, New York. Online. www.undp.org/hdr2003/.

power

Jason L. Powell

Power is an "essentially contested and complex term" (Lukes 1974: 7) that cuts right across social science disciplines. The literature on power is marked by a deep disagreement over the basic definition of power. Some theorists define power as getting someone else to do what you want them to do (power over), whereas others define it more broadly as an ability or a capacity to act (power to). Thomas Hobbes's (1985 [1641]: 150) definition of power as a person's "present means ... to obtain some future apparent Good" is a classic example of this understanding of power, as is Hannah Arendt's definition of power as "the human ability not just to act but to act in concert" (1970: 44). Feminist theorists of power Stacey and Price (1983) define power as the more or less one-sided patriarchal ability to position women's lives through the actions of men over them. Conversely, Michel Foucault (1977) suggests that power itself is "relational" in that whilst one social actor may exercise power with other individuals, we also need to be aware that all other individuals have "power" in their social relationship that can be expressed through "resistance."

The historical emergence of sociological discussions of power has been crystallized in the work of Max Weber. In Max Weber's famous work, *Economy and Society: An Outline of Interpretive Sociology*, he clarifies his typology of power. Weber highlights the distinction between coercive power and power based on various types of authority: charismatic, traditional, and legal rational. People obey charismatic leaders because of the personal qualities of the person doing the telling. Well-known charismatic figures include Jesus Christ and Hitler. However, charismatic figures may arise in any social grouping and such people assume positions of authority over others on the basis of personal qualities of leadership perceived in that individual by other group members. Traditional authority involves acceptance of rules that symbolize ritual or ancient practice such as religion. By contrast, Weber also focused on the power of modern bureaucracies, such as civil service, whose formal rules of procedure are legitimized by legal rational authority.

Pluralist theories see power being held by a variety of groups in society (some of which are more powerful than others) that compete with each other. Since no one group or class is able to dominate all other groups (because of checks and balances built into a democratic system of government), a "plurality" of competing interest groups, political parties, and so forth is seen to characterize democratic societies.

Elite theory involves the idea that rather than there being a simple plurality of competing groups in society, there are instead a series of competing elites – powerful groups who are able to impose their will upon the rest of society. The theory of "circulating elites" is a conservative form of theorizing associated with writers such as Mosca and Pareto (Lukes 1974). C. Wright Mills's analysis has been termed as elite theory as well, but stems from the idea that certain elite groups arose to control various institutions in society. Since some institutions were more powerful than others (an economic elite, for example, is likely to be more powerful than an educational or religious elite), it followed that the elite groups who controlled such institutions would hold the balance of power in society as a whole – they would dominate politically on the structural level of power and involve the creation of a "power elite."

The Marxist tradition elaborated the role of cultural hegemony in ideology as a means of bolstering the power of capitalism and the nation-state. This is a Marxist form of theorizing that argues that power is fundamentally lodged with the owners and controllers of economic production (the bourgeoisie). Political power is seen to derive from economic ownership and, in this respect, we can identify a ruling class which not only controls the means of production, distribution, and exchange in capitalist society, but also dominates and controls the institutions of political power. There are two variations of Marxist views on power. Instrumental Marxism, associated with the work of Ralph Milliband and especially *The State in Capitalist Society* (1969), attempts to demonstrate empirically the nature of ruling class domination in society. Structuralist Marxism, associated with the work of writers such as Nicos Poulantzas, especially his *Classes in*

Contemporary Capitalism (1975), and Louis Althusser, concentrates more upon the structural arrangements of capitalist society. It attempts to show how a ruling class is able to dominate the rest of society economically, politically, and ideologically without the need for its members to personally oversee the workings of the state.

Finally, Michel Foucault's analysis of power has arguably been the most influential discussion of the topic over the last 30 years. Foucault's (1977) work analyzes the link between power and knowledge. He outlines a form of covert power that works through people rather than only on them. As he puts it, "power is everywhere, not because it embraces everything, but because it comes from everywhere" (1978: 93). Foucault endeavors to offer a "microphysics" of modern power (1977: 26), an analysis that focuses not on the concentration of power in the hands of the sovereign or the state but instead on how power flows through the capillaries of the social body. For Foucault, "experts" such as medical doctors are key interventionists in societal relations and, in the management of social arrangements, pursue a daunting power to classify, with consequences for the reproduction of medical knowledge. At the same time, Foucault also recognized that power itself lacks any concrete form, occurring as a locus of struggle. Resistance through defiance defines power and hence becomes possible *through* power. Without resistance, power is absent.

SEE ALSO: Feminism; Foucault, Michel; Ideology; Marxism and Sociology; Mills, C. Wright; Power Elite; Power, Theories of; Weber, Max

REFERENCES AND SUGGESTED READINGS

Arendt, H. (1970) *On Violence*. Harcourt Brace, New York.
Foucault, M. (1977) *Discipline and Punish*. Penguin, London.
Foucault, M. (1978) *The History of Sexuality*. Vol. 1: *An Introduction*. Trans. R. Hurley. Vintage, New York.
Hobbes, T. (1985 [1641]) *Leviathan*. Penguin, New York.
Lukes, S. (1974) *Power: A Radical View*. Macmillan, London.
Milliband, R. (1969) *The State in Capitalist Society*. Quartet Books, London.
Poulantzas, N. (1975) *Classes in Contemporary Capitalism*. Verso, London.
Stacey, M. & Price, M. (1983) *Women, Power, and Politics*. Tavistock, London.
Weber, M. (1978) *Economy and Society: An Outline of Interpretive Sociology*. Trans. E. Fischoff et al. University of California Press, Berkeley, CA.

power–dependence theory

Linda D. Molm

Power-dependence theory is the name commonly given to the social exchange theory originally formulated by Richard Emerson (1962, 1972a, 1972b). As the name suggests, the dynamics of the theory revolve around power, power use, and power-balancing operations, and rest on the central concept of *dependence*. Mutual dependence brings people together; that is, to the extent that people are mutually dependent, they are more likely to form exchange relations and groups and to continue in them. Inequalities in dependence create power imbalances that can lead to conflict and social change.

The publication of Emerson's theory in 1972 marked a turning point in the development of the social exchange framework in sociology. Power-dependence theory departed from earlier exchange formulations by Peter Blau, George Homans, and John Thibaut and Harold Kelley in three important ways. First, Emerson replaced the relatively loose logic of his predecessors with a rigorously derived system of propositions that were more amenable to empirical test and the development of a strong research tradition. Second, Emerson established power and its use as the major topics of exchange theory – topics that would dominate theory development and research for the next 30 years. Third, by integrating principles of behavioral psychology with social network analysis, Emerson developed an exchange theory in which the structure of relations, rather than the actors themselves, became the central focus.

These distinctions influenced not only the character of power-dependence theory, but also the continued development of the social exchange tradition.

The theoretical program of research conducted by Emerson, his colleague Karen Cook, and their students further developed the theory's character and logic while testing its basic tenets. After Emerson's untimely death in 1982, Cook's work with Toshio Yamagishi continued to modify and expand the theory. In addition, other established scholars who were not students of Cook or Emerson used the theory as a framework for developing related theories of power and power processes.

BASIC CONCEPTS AND PRINCIPLES

Power-dependence theory shares with other exchange theories the basic concepts of actors, resources, rewards, and costs, but places greater emphasis on the form, rather than the content, of exchange relations. The participants in social exchange, called *actors*, can be either individual persons or collective actors such as groups or organizations, and either specific entities or interchangeable occupants of structural positions. This insight, along with the use of network concepts, allowed the theory to span different levels of analysis more successfully than earlier exchange theories. Resources are tied to relations rather than actors. That is, possessions or behavioral capabilities that are valued by other actors are *resources* in an actor's relations with those others, but not necessarily in other relations.

Power-dependence theory also shares with other exchange theories the basic assumption of self-interested actors. Emerson's original formulation deliberately eschewed cognitive assumptions of rationality or conscious calculation of benefits, however, in favor of a theory based on operant psychology. Emerson avoided the problems of tautology and reductionism that plagued earlier behavioral approaches by recognizing that the core concepts of operant behavior, reinforcer, and discriminative stimulus form a single conceptual unit. Furthermore, their relation to each other is defined only across repeated occurrences of behavior and stimuli. By maintaining the integrity of this conceptual unit, Emerson established the *social relation*, rather than the individual actor, as the basic unit of power-dependence theory.

Although Emerson and others would later bring more cognitive concepts into the theory, the initial absence of assumptions about cognitions or motives helped build a theory that emphasized structure rather than individuals' thoughts or needs. This emphasis on structure is evident in the theory's analysis of both power–dependence relations – its theoretical heart – and exchange networks and groups.

Social exchange relations develop within structures of mutual dependence, in which actors control resources valued by each other. An actor's dependence on another is defined by the extent to which outcomes valued by the actor are contingent on exchange with the other. B's dependence on A increases with the *value* to B of the resources A controls, and decreases with B's *alternative* sources of those resources. The theory's title derives from the basic insight that actors' mutual dependence provides the structural basis for their *power* over each other. A's power over B derives from, and is equal to, B's dependence on A, and vice versa. Thus, power is a structural attribute of an exchange relation, not a property of an actor. *Power use* is the behavioral exercise of that structural potential.

Power in dyadic relations is described by two dimensions: *cohesion*, actors' absolute power over each other, and *balance*, actors' relative power over each other. Cohesion is equal to the average dependence of two actors on each other. If actors are equally dependent on each other, power in the relation is balanced; if B is more dependent on A, power is imbalanced, and A has a *power advantage* in the relation equal to the degree of imbalance.

Over time, the structure of power has predictable effects on the frequency and distribution of exchange as actors use power to maintain exchange or gain advantage. A's initiations of exchange with B increase with A's dependence on B. Also, the frequency of exchange in a relation increases with cohesion and, in imbalanced relations, the ratio of exchange changes in favor of the more powerful, less dependent actor. One of the theory's most important tenets is that these effects are produced even in the absence of intent to use power. That is, they are determined by the structure of relations, not the cognitions of actors.

Emerson also argued that imbalanced relations are unstable and lead to *power-balancing* processes. These processes reduce imbalance by decreasing the value of exchange to the less powerful actor ("withdrawal"), increasing value to the more powerful actor ("status-giving"), increasing alternatives available to the less powerful actor ("network extension"), or decreasing alternatives available to the more powerful actor ("coalition formation").

Emerson was the first to link exchange theory with the growing field of social network analysis, a move that fundamentally changed the nature of exchange research. He began by distinguishing between groups and networks as different structural forms. *Groups* are collective actors, such as teams or organizations, that function as a single unit in exchange with other actors. *Exchange networks* are sets of *connected* exchange relations among actors. Two relations are connected if the frequency or value of exchange in one relation (e.g., A–B) affects the frequency or value of exchange in another (e.g., B–C). Network connections are *positive* to the extent that exchange in one relation increases exchange in the other, and *negative* to the extent that exchange in one decreases exchange in the other. Mixed networks consist of both. Emerson linked these processes to his conception of an *exchange domain*, a class of functionally equivalent outcomes.

The concepts of exchange networks and corporate actors allowed power-dependence theory to bridge the gap between micro and macro levels of analysis. With these tools the theory could explain the emergence and change of social structures, including network expansion and contraction, coalition formation, and norm formation.

CONTEMPORARY DEVELOPMENTS

To test power-dependence theory, Emerson, Cook, and their students constructed a laboratory setting that was to become the prototype for studying power in exchange networks. In contrast to the reciprocal exchanges envisioned by Homans and Blau and implicitly assumed in Emerson's original formulation, subjects in Cook and Emerson's setting *negotiated* the terms of exchange, through a series of offers and counteroffers, to reach binding agreements. In conjunction with the negotiated exchange setting, the theory itself came to take on more of an economic flavor, with more emphasis on rational actors and comparison of alternatives. At the same time, however, Cook introduced concerns with commitment and equity that were not part of the theory's original formulation and that increased the motivational complexity of actors.

Cook and Emerson's (1978) work supported key tenets of the theory, showing that networks imbalanced on structural dependence produce unequal distributions of benefits, in favor of the less dependent actor, and that these effects occur even in the absence of actors' awareness of power. Later studies showed that disadvantaged actors can improve their bargaining position by forming coalitions – one of Emerson's power-balancing processes – and demonstrated the critical importance of the distinction between negatively and positively connected networks (Cook et al. 1983). In positively connected networks, centrality yields power because central actors can serve as "brokers" in cooperative relations. But in negatively connected networks, centrality is less important than access to highly dependent actors with few or no alternatives.

Early tests of power-dependence theory also displayed its inadequacies for analyzing complex networks. Although the theory takes account of the larger network in which actors are embedded, it predicts the distribution of power within dyadic relations, not the network as a whole. The need for new algorithms for measuring power in exchange networks stimulated a flurry of new, competing theories. In response, Cook and Yamagishi introduced a new algorithm in 1992, the equi-dependence exchange ratio, for predicting the distribution of power in negatively connected networks. This algorithm determines the exchange ratios that will produce "equal dependence" of actors on each other in all relations throughout a network, based on iterative calculations of the value of actors' exchanges relative to the value of their best alternatives.

At the same time that Cook and Emerson were developing their research program, other scholars, particularly Edward Lawler and Linda Molm, were drawing on concepts from power-dependence theory to develop their own theories of power and related processes. Their work introduced ideas and concepts that were not part of Emerson's original formulation: greater attention to cognition and affect in exchange, consideration of punitive as well as rewarding actions in exchange, and analysis of different forms of exchange.

In the late 1970s and early 1980s, Bacharach and Lawler (1981) integrated power-dependence theory's analysis of structural power with bargaining theories' analyses of tactical power. Traditional work on bargaining neglected the power structure within which parties negotiate; Lawler and Bacharach used ideas from power-dependence theory to fill that gap. Their approach differed from Cook and Emerson's in important ways, however. They were concerned not only with the terms of agreements (the measure of power use), but also with whether and how actors reach agreement and the tactics they use. In contrast to Emerson's strongly structural approach, they argued that actors' perceptions of power affect their choices of tactics, and they envisioned the use of power as a more conscious choice.

Molm's (1997) work on coercion in exchange also focused more attention on strategic power use and expanded the theory to include punishment and coercion. While power-dependence theory originally addressed only reward-based power, Molm argued that both reward power and coercive power are derived from dependence on others, either for obtaining rewards or avoiding punishment, and potentially can be explained by the same principles. Unlike reward power, however, the use of coercive power is not structurally induced by power advantage (as Emerson argued), but strategically enacted as a means of increasing an exchange partner's rewards. To explain strategic power use, Molm introduced concepts of decision-making under risk and uncertainty.

In contrast to the focus on negotiated exchanges in the experimental work of Emerson, Cook, Lawler, and others, Molm's work on coercion examined *reciprocal* exchanges, in which actors individually provide benefits for another without negotiating the terms of an exchange and without knowing whether or when

the other will reciprocate. Her later work showed that the form of exchange affects how structural dimensions of alternatives affect power use (Molm et al. 1999).

The most recent development among power-dependence researchers is the shift from the study of power and inequality to the study of integrative outcomes: commitment, trust, emotions, and solidarity. Cook, Yamagishi, Lawler, and Molm have all turned their attention in this direction. Most recently, Lawler (2001) has proposed a new affect theory of exchange that – in sharp contrast to Emerson – makes affect and emotion the driving force underlying commitments in exchange relations. The theory still incorporates a number of concepts from power-dependence theory, but focuses on the emotions produced by social exchange and their attribution to social units.

SEE ALSO: Blau, Peter; Emerson, Richard M.; Exchange Network Theory; Homans, George; Power, Theories of; Social Exchange Theory

REFERENCES AND SUGGESTED READINGS

Bacharach, S. B. & Lawler, E. J. (1981) *Bargaining: Power, Tactics, and Outcomes.* Jossey-Bass, San Francisco.

Cook, K. S. & Emerson, R. M. (1978) Power, Equity and Commitment in Exchange Networks. *American Sociological Review* 43: 721–39.

Cook, K. S., Emerson, R. M., Gillmore, M. R., & Yamagishi, T. (1983) The Distribution of Power in Exchange Networks: Theory and Experimental Results. *American Journal of Sociology* 89: 275–305.

Emerson, R. M. (1962) Power–Dependence Relations. *American Sociological Review* 27: 31–41.

Emerson, R. M. (1972a) Exchange Theory, Part I: A Psychological Basis for Social Exchange. In: Berger, J., Zelditch, M., Jr., & Anderson, B. (Eds.), *Sociological Theories in Progress*, Vol. 2. Houghton Mifflin, Boston, pp. 38–57.

Emerson, R. M. (1972b) Exchange Theory, Part II: Exchange Relations and Network Structures. In: Berger, J., Zelditch, M., Jr., & Anderson, B. (Eds.), *Sociological Theories in Progress*, Vol. 2. Houghton Mifflin, Boston, pp. 58–87.

Lawler, E. J. (2001) An Affect Theory of Social Exchange. *American Journal of Sociology* 107: 321–52.

Molm, L. D. (1997) *Coercive Power in Social Exchange.* Cambridge University Press, Cambridge.

Molm, L. D., Peterson, G., & Takahashi, N. (1999) Power in Negotiated and Reciprocal Exchange. *American Sociological Review* 64: 876–90.

power elite

Jason L. Powell

As a concept, "power elite" can be defined as a small group of people who control a disproportionate amount of power, wealth, and privilege and access to decision-makers in a political system. In a pathbreaking book, Mills (1956) claims that the US power elite consists of elite members of society characterized by consensus building and the homogenization of viewpoints. This power elite has historically dominated the three major sectors of US society: economy, government, and military. Elites circulate from one sector to another, consolidating their power as they go. Mills rejects pluralist assertions that various centers of power serve as checks and balances on one another – the power-elite model suggests that those at the top encounter no real opposition and it implies a concentration of power, wealth, and prestige in the hands of the wealthy and powerful in American society. Mills wrote that the power elite refers to "those political, economic, and military circles, which as an intricate set of overlapping small but dominant groups share decisions having at least national consequences. Insofar as national events are decided, the power elite are those who decide them" (Mills 1956: 18).

According to Mills, the governing elite in the US draws its members from three areas: (1) the highest political leaders (including the president) and a handful of key cabinet members and close advisers; (2) major corporate owners and directors; and (3) high-ranking military officers. First, the elite occupies what Mills terms the top command posts of society. These positions give their holders enormous authority over not just governmental, but also financial, educational, social, civic, and cultural institutions. A small group is able to take fundamental actions that touch everyone. Decisions made in the boardrooms of large corporations and banks affect the rates of inflation and employment, for example. Secondly, the influence of the chief executive officers of large corporations often rivals that of the secretary of commerce. Thirdly, the military play a key role in positioning themselves to address "threats" that require resources to be mobilized, as in the case of war.

Having seen how the governing elite derives its strength, it is important to consider how this power is exercised in the political arena. What roles are played by the three parts of what Mills called the "pyramid" – the elite, the middle level, and the masses – in politics? Mills suggests that the power elite establishes the basic policy agenda in such areas as national security and economics. Of course, since it only sets the general guidelines, the middle level has plenty to do implementing them, but the public has been virtually locked out. Its main activities – writing campaign posters, expressing opinions to pollsters, voting every two or four years – are mostly symbolic. The people do not directly affect the direction of fundamental policies. Power-elite theory, in short, claims that a single elite, not a multiplicity of competing groups, decides the life-and-death issues for the nation as a whole, leaving relatively minor matters for the middle level and almost nothing for the common person. It thus paints a dark picture. Whereas pluralists (e.g., Dahl 1961) are somewhat content with what they believe is a fair, if admittedly imperfect, system, the power-elite school decries the unequal and unjust distribution of power it finds everywhere (Lukes 1974). These "top positions" encompass the posts with the authority to run programs and activities of major political, economic, legal, educational, cultural, scientific, and civic institutions.

The presence of the power elite in the political, economic, and military bureaucracies is obvious in America's recent "War on Terror" and the Middle East crisis. The oil interests (economic) are involved with President G. W. Bush and Vice-President Cheney (political) through their past connections in that field. These interconnections make the triangle complete in interconnecting war, business, and politicians.

One criticism of Mills is that there are many wealthy people in the US, but they are not all members of the power elite. Advantageous positions for power, prestige, and wealth include the uppermost administrative positions in the three top bureaucratic organizations: the Pentagon, corporate America, and the executive branch of the US government. President Clinton had a lot of power when he was the president of the US, but as a retired president his power has been diminished. Similarly, the power of Richard Nixon eroded when he resigned as president after the Watergate affair in 1974. Indeed, the position or office holds the privilege of power, not the person. Holding these positions or offices enables the elite to gain administrative control of the main bureaucratic organizations, so they are able to maintain their own wealth, power, and privilege.

For Mills, the power elite has ensured the demise of the public as an independent force in civic affairs. Mills suggests that instead of initiating policy, or even controlling those who govern them, men and women in America have become passive spectators, cheering the heroes and booing the villains, but taking little or no direct part in the action. Citizens have become increasingly alienated and estranged from politics, as can be seen in the sharp decline in electoral participation over the last several decades. As a result, the control of their destinies has fallen into the hands of the power elite.

SEE ALSO: Elites; Marxism and Sociology; Mills, C. Wright; Pluralism, American; Pluralism, British; Politics; Power, Theories of

REFERENCES AND SUGGESTED READINGS

Dahl, R. A. (1961) *Who Governs*. Yale University Press, New Haven.
Lukes, S. (1974) *Power: A Radical View*. Macmillan, London.
Mills, C. W. (1956) *The Power Elite*. Oxford University Press, New York.

power, theories of

Shane Thye

In contemporary sociology, the term power is used in two distinct but interrelated ways. In the broadest usage, power refers to a *structural capacity* for an actor A to cause any change in the behavior of another actor B (Weber 1968). This meaning of power captures the potential for power to be exercised or not in social interaction. The second meaning refers to a *concrete event* in which one individual benefits at the expense of another. Modern theorists refer to such events as *power use* or *power exercise*. Importantly, both meanings imply that power is a relational phenomenon. Thus, theories of power take as their focus the relationship between two or more actors, and not the characteristics of actors themselves. Although the terms are sometimes conflated, power is theoretically distinct from other relational concepts such as *influence* (which is voluntarily accepted), *force* (wherein the target has no choice but to comply), and *authority* (which involves a request from a legitimate social position). French and Raven (1968) recognized these distinctions over four decades ago, and they remain useful today.

Theories of power cross many ideological and epistemological lines. As a result, this literature has seen many debates. Theorists have contemplated whether power is best conceptualized as (1) a potential or something that must be used; (2) "forward looking" calculated actions or "backward looking" responses to reward and punishment; (3) intentional or unintentional behavior; (4) benefit or control, and so on. These early debates generated much heat, but very little light. They did, however, stimulate efforts to develop more formal theory. The majority of this work occurred within behavioral psychology and the exchange tradition of sociology.

Perhaps the first formal theory of power was proposed by Thibaut and Kelley (1959). They asserted that individuals evaluate their current relationship against some standard, or comparison level (CL). The theory also claims that actors assess the attractiveness of a relationship by comparing their focal relationship to benefits expected from others (CL_{ALT}). The power of actor A over B is defined as "A's ability to affect the quality of outcomes attained by B." There are two ways that this can occur. *Fate control* exists when actor A affects actor B's outcome by changing her or his own behavior, independent of B's action. For example, if regardless of what B does, B receives $1 when

A chooses behavior 1 and $10 when A chooses behavior 2, then A has fate control over B. *Behavior control* exists when the rewards obtained by B are a function of both A and B's behavior. To illustrate, when A can make rewards obtained by B contingent on B's actions (A dictates that behavior 1 yields $2 for B, while behavior 2 yields $4 for B), then A can control the behavior of B. In either case, whether A has fate control or behavior control, B is dependent on A for rewards and thus A has a source of power over B. Other power theories that emerged during that same timeframe echoed the importance of dependence.

A major theoretical shift occurred in the early 1970s with the development of Richard Emerson's power-dependence theory (Emerson 1972a, 1972b). Unlike previous theorists, Emerson cast power processes in broader terms. He put forth the notion that relations between actors are part of a larger set of potential exchange relations (i.e., an exchange network). Thus, in analyzing a dyad, he asserted it is important to consider its broader connection to other dyads – the larger network in which it is embedded. Emerson considered two kinds of connection. A *negative connection* exists when interaction in one dyad reduces interaction in another. A *positive connection* exists when interaction in one dyad promotes interaction in another. The attention to dyadic connectedness gave Emerson's theorizing a decidedly structural theme: his were network-embedded dyads.

Power-dependence theory is anchored in operant psychology and relies heavily on the principle of satiation. The theory claims that power emerges because individuals in different network locations are satiated at different rates. The implication, as with previous theories, is that some individuals are more dependent than others for the exchange of valued goods. Dependence is the centerpiece of the theory. The theory asserts that the power of actor A over actor B is equal to the dependence of B on A, summarized by the equation $P_{AB} = D_{BA}$. In turn, dependence is a function of two key factors: the availability of alternative exchange relations and the extent to which the actors value those relations. To illustrate, imagine an auto builder (A) who must purchase specialized parts from a supply dealer (B). When auto parts are not widely available from other suppliers,

but auto builders are in high supply, then A is more dependent on B than B is on A, ($D_{AB} > D_{BA}$), due to availability. When the auto maker values parts more than the supplier values customers, then A is more dependent on B: ($D_{AB} > D_{BA}$). As such, the theory predicts B has power over A.

Since the original formulation, power-dependence theory has given rise to numerous other branches of theory. For instance, Molm (1990) has expanded the power-dependence framework to include both reward-based power and punishment-based power. She finds punishment-based power is used less often than reward-based power, due to the potential cost it entails. Lawler (1992) has developed a theory of power that includes both dependence-based power and punitive-based power. This work shows how structures of interdependence can promote either punitive or conciliatory bargaining tactics. Bargaining tactics, in turn, are theorized to mediate power exercise in negotiations. Both lines of work extend the basic power-dependence framework, and affirm the importance of dependence in generating power.

An alternative approach to power is found in David Willer's *elementary theory*, which is based on classical understandings of power from Marx and Weber. Elementary theory opposes the notion of satiation as the basis for power, and instead anchors power in the ability of some actors to *exclude* others from valued goods. The theory identifies three kinds of social relations, defined by the kinds of sanctions found in each. A *sanction* is any action transmitted from one individual and received by another. *Exchange* occurs when A and B mutually transmit positive sanctions (e.g., I mow the yard, you do the dishes). *Coercion* occurs when a negative sanction is transmitted for a positive sanction (e.g., as when a mugger threatens "your money or your life"). *Conflict* exists when A and B each transmit negative sanctions (e.g., when two countries engage in bombing). The majority of research has centered on power in exchange.

Within exchange, the theory identifies three kinds of power structures. *Strong power* structures are those that only contain two kinds of positions: high-power positions that can never be excluded and two or more low-power positions, one of which must always be excluded.

The classic example is the 3-person dating network, in which B can date A or C but not both on any given night (A—B—C). B is powerful because B is always guaranteed a partner, while either A or C must be excluded. Strong power networks promote extreme power exercise. *Equal power* networks contain only one set of structurally identical positions, such as dyads or triangles. In *weak power* networks no position is necessarily excluded, but some may be. The simplest weak power structure is the 4-actor line (A—B—C—D). Note that when B and C exchange, A and D are excluded. Studies find that this produces a slight power advantage for the positions who need not be excluded.

At the heart of the theory is a resistance model that relates the distribution of profit when two actors exchange to the benefits lost when they do not. An actor *i*'s resistance to exchange is defined using the following equation:

$$R_i = \frac{P_i \max - P_A}{P_A - P_A \text{con}}$$

P_i max represents *i*'s best hope from the exchange, P_A represents the payoff if the exchange is complete, and $P_A$con represents the payoff when exchange is not complete. The numerator captures how far away the current offer is from one's best hope. The denominator represents the benefit of consummating exchange relative to no exchange at all. The model assumes that actors balance these motives when negotiating exchange. The theory predicts that when two actors *i* and *j* exchange, they do so at the point of equi-resistance. That is, exchange is predicted when the resistance is mutually balanced for *i* and *j*. Tests find that the resistance model predicts power exercise in a range of settings.

The ability to predict powerful positions in exchange networks was an important methodological issue that occupied the attention of theorists during the late 1980s and early 1990s. Competing solutions were offered from power dependence theory (i.e., vulnerability), game theory (i.e., the core), utility theory (i.e., an expected value model), and network exchange theory (i.e., a graph theoretic power index). Each index offered unique predictions for power, and in 1992 an entire issue of *Social Networks* was devoted to comparing and contrasting these approaches. In retrospect, the significance of this competition was to promote rapid theory growth, increased formalization, and the discovery of new phenomena.

Perhaps spurred by these advancements, modern theorists have identified numerous links between power and emotion, cohesion, and status. For instance, Lovaglia finds that power exercise often produces negative emotional reactions. In contrast, Lawler and associates have identified conditions under which equal power networks promote high exchange frequency, positive emotion, and a sense of relational cohesion. Thye (2000) offers a *status value theory of power* that anchors power, not in the structural conditions of networks, but in the culturally valued status characteristics that individuals possess. The theory claims that when exchangeable goods are relevant to the status (high or low) of actors, those goods acquire the same status value. That is, goods relevant to high-status actors become more valued than they otherwise would be; goods relevant to low-status actors become less valued. As with virtually all theories of power, the theory predicts that actors who possess less-valued goods (i.e., the low-status individuals) are at a power disadvantage. Tests find that high-status actors have a power advantage over lower-status actors, and that status value plays a crucial role.

SEE ALSO: Class, Status, and Power; Elementary Theory; Emerson Richard M.; Exchange Network Theory; Power-Dependence Theory; Social Influence

REFERENCES AND SUGGESTED READINGS

Emerson, R. (1972a) Exchange Theory, Part I: A Psychological Basis for Social Exchange. In: Berger, J., Zelditch, M., & Anderson, B. (Eds.), *Sociological Theories in Progress*, Vol. 2. Houghton-Mifflin, Boston, pp. 38–57.

Emerson, R. (1972b) Exchange Theory, Part II: Exchange Relations and Networks. In: Berger, J., Zelditch, M., & Anderson, B. (Eds.), *Sociological Theories in Progress*, Vol. 2. Houghton-Mifflin, Boston, pp. 58–87.

French, J. R. P. & Raven, B. R. (1968) The Bases of Social Power. In: Cartwright, D. & Zander, A. (Eds.), *Group Dynamics: Research and Theory*. Harper & Row, New York, pp. 259–69.

Lawler, E. J. (1992) Power Processes in Bargaining. *Sociological Quarterly* 33: 17–34.

Molm, L. (1990) Structure, Action, and Outcomes: The Dynamics of Power in Social Exchange. *American Sociological Review* 55: 427–47.

Thibaut, J. W. & Kelley, H. H. (1959) *The Social Psychology of Groups*. Wiley, New York.

Thye, S. (2000) A Status Value Theory of Power in Exchange Relations. *American Sociological Review* 65: 407–32.

Weber, M. (1968 [1918]) *Economy and Society*. University of California Press, Berkeley.

Willer, D. (Ed.) (1999) *Network Exchange Theory*. Praeger, London.

Zelditch, M. (1992) Interpersonal Power. In: Borgatta, E. F. & Borgatta, M. L. (Eds.), *Encyclopedia of Sociology*. Macmillan, New York, pp. 994–1001.

practical knowledge

Nico Stehr

The assertion about the unique "complexity" or the peculiarly intricate character of social phenomena has, at least within sociology, a long, venerable, and virtually uncontested tradition. The classical theorists make prominent and repeated reference to this attribute of the subject matter of sociology and the degree to which it complicates the development of sociological knowledge. More specifically, the complexity of social reality has, it is widely argued, a most inhibiting effect on the production of powerful *practical* social science knowledge.

The assertion that social phenomena happen to be complex phenomena is designed to sensitize social scientists, from an epistemological perspective or in a more mundane sense, for the purposes of practicing their craft, to the kind of explanatory and methodological devices that are equal to the task of adequately capturing social reality. Thus, complexity means that a particular social process (e.g., exchange rates, unemployment, deviant behavior, etc.) are set in motion, reproduced, or changed by a multiplicity of interdependent factors and that it is most difficult to make a detailed and precise forecast about price changes, employment trajectories, or crime rates.

Any empirically valid representation, and therefore any effective and manageable *control*

of such a complex process, requires, according to this conception, a faithful and *complete* understanding of all the intricate factors involved and their interconnections. The alternative is to reconsider the notion of complexity, as an obstacle to practical knowledge, in quite a radical fashion.

Weber and Popper are among a few philosophers of (social) science who appear to be quite unimpressed with the familiar assertion about the intricate complexity of social phenomena. Popper is convinced that the thesis actually constitutes a subtle form of prejudice which has two origins. First, the judgment is a result of a meaningless and inaccurate comparison of circumstances; for example, of a comparison of limited and controlled conditions found in a laboratory and real social situations. Second, the thesis is the result of the orthodox methodological conception which demands that any adequate description of social phenomena requires a complete account of the psychological and material circumstances of all actors. Since humans behave in most situations in a rational fashion, Popper maintains, it is possible to reconstruct social interaction with the aid of relatively simple models which assume such rational conduct among the participants.

Weber, in his essay "Objektivität sozialwissenschaftlicher und sozialpolitischer Erkenntnisse" (1922), emphasizes that social science can only portray a fraction of the complexity of social reality and therefore cannot grasp it fully: "Every knowledge of infinite reality achieved by the finite human spirit is therefore based on the tacit assumption that only a finite *part* of it should be object of scientific inquiry and 'essential' in the sense of 'worth knowing.'"

In addition, there are two further questionable premises of the orthodox position about the significance of capturing the full complexity of a specific social context in order to generate powerful practical knowledge. First, "mastery" and change of social conditions are not under all circumstances identical with and possibly based on the *complete* intellectual control of the complex origins and processes of social situations. Whatever control may be possible under given circumstances, such control likely is restricted to a few attributes of the context. Second, efforts to raise the theoretical complexity of social science knowledge may therefore have the unanticipated effect of propelling such knowledge to an even greater distance to social action and its possibilities. Put bluntly, it is not the "scientificity" of social science knowledge (i.e., knowledge that captures the full complexity of social reality, conforms to specific methodological rules, or is expressed in a quantitative language) that ensures that such knowledge is practical.

Reflections about the conditions or constituents of practical knowledge have to start from the assumption that the adequacy (usefulness) of knowledge, produced in one context (*of production*), but employed in another context (*of application*), pertains to the *relation* between knowledge and the local conditions of action. Within the context of application constraints, conditions of action are apprehended as either *open* or *beyond the control* of relevant actors. Given such a differentiation, practical knowledge pertains to open conditions of action which means that theoretical knowledge, if it is to be effective in practice, has to be reattached to the social context in general and to those elements of the situation that are actionable in particular.

A brief example may serve as a first illustration. A rather common knowledge claim (at least, it appears to be central to a number of theoretical traditions within sociology) states that the degree of urbanization is closely related to the birth rate or the divorce rate. But such a knowledge claim clearly does not pertain, in all likelihood, to conditions that are open to action. Even very powerful politicians in a centralized state, concerned about a decline in the birth rate or an increase in the divorce rate and ways of affecting either rate in the opposite direction, would consider such a claim as highly irrelevant knowledge, since the degree of urbanization cannot be effected within their context of action. But that is not to say that the same context of action is void of attributes and conditions which are, in some sense, open and may in fact influence the rates under discussion.

Yet there is another way in which social science knowledge becomes practical, namely as knowledge that represents the becoming of social worlds. That is, a powerful but largely invisible effect of social science (as Michel Foucault and Helmut Schelsky among others remind us) is the impact it has on *interpretations of reality* in everyday life and therefore the extent to which the self-understanding of actors and the media in terms of which such convictions are expressed are shaped by social scientific conceptions.

Whether one is prepared to describe this process as a "social scientification" of collective and individual patterns of meaning may be left open. However, one might suggest that many of the current problems the social sciences face in practice are related to the fact that the self-understanding of many groups and actors is affected, often in ways difficult to trace, by elements of social science knowledge. The empirical analysis of social problems by social science research then evolves into a form of self-reflection or doubling of social scientific conceptions.

SEE ALSO: Knowledge; Knowledge, Sociology of; Knowledge Societies; Literacy/Illiteracy; Scientific Knowledge, Sociology of; Speaking Truth to Power: Science and Policy; Weber, Max

REFERENCES AND SUGGESTED READINGS

Sowell, T. (1980) *Knowledge and Decisions*. Basic Books, New York.
Stehr, N. (1992) *Practical Knowledge: Applying the Social Sciences*. Sage, London.
Stehr, N. & Meja, V. (Eds.) (2005) *Society and Knowledge: Contemporary Perspectives in the Sociology of Knowledge and Science*. Transaction Books, New Brunswick, NJ.
Wildavsky, A. (1987) *Speaking Truth to Power: The Art and Craft of Policy Analysis*. Transaction Books, New Brunswick, NJ.

practice

Richard Biernacki

Practice is a rich if contested term on which sociologists converge when they endeavor to portray human action in its cultural and institutional settings. Concepts of practice highlight the influence of taken-for-granted, pre-theoretical assumptions on human conduct.

Such covert assumptions embrace everything that is left out of economists' standard portrayals of intellectual calculations based on personal goals and known facts. For example, theorists of practice highlight the influence of bodily experience, practical know-how, and institutionalized understandings of self and agency. Among the diverse theorists whose research has sustained this turn to practice are Garfinkel, Bourdieu, Foucault, Swidler, and Giddens. Their practice-centered views of social life share three major themes.

First, thinking as situated activity. Thinking and feeling are not preparations for action, they *are* action – just as public, material, and situationally conditioned as other goings-on. Classical social and economic theory once viewed thinking and feeling as mental processes separable from observable action. An invisible mind inside the person orchestrated in advance the actions to be observed from the outside. But as sociologists from the 1960s onward plumbed the life of science labs, hospitals, and other theaters of coordinated action, they concluded that individuals' thoughts are indefinable apart from the public protocols in which they come to expression. For example, the psychologist can scarcely define or reflect upon deviants without recourse to the routines for classifying and controlling them. Action is bound to the observable tools and tactics of a cultural setting.

Second, know-how as the glue of actions. From the perspective of practice theory, it is not transcendent goals and values that link an individual's discrete acts together in a coherent life trajectory. As we know, a dancer cannot carry out the steps of a ballet by choosing each step as a means to an end. Instead, ingrained know-how and routines for getting things done merge the steps from the very start into a coherent flow. Analogously, theorists of practice emphasize how know-how anchors coherent lines of action across the career of an individual, or, for a group, across whole civilizations – even when the ends of action change for the individual or group. For example, after the religious ends of Protestant discipline faded in eighteenth-century Europe, the ingrained know-how of self-asceticism continued to steer a whole style of life, from accounting to science and art. Practices define "truth." The implicit assumptions by which we execute practices set up a ground for ideology that is difficult to bring to awareness or to critique rationally. Practice theorists therefore emphasize how that implicit ground of knowledge comes to define the natural and real, including forms of selfhood. For instance, the practices of free market exchange in capitalist society seem to make the individual the ultimate unit of intercourse and consecrate the free will of the individual self as a reality of its own kind.

Third, what makes the operative assumptions of practice implicit and what keeps them that way? For practice theorists such as Bourdieu, who underscore our physical emplacement in the world, the answer is in part the nonverbal but a priori quality of corporeal experience. For practice theorists who highlight the uncertainties of any setting, such as Garfinkel, the answer is the inability to articulate fully how one puts general rules of the game to work in a particular setting. For practice theorists who emphasize the routinized qualities of much of our everyday life, such as Giddens, the answer is unreflective habit. Of these answers, that based on habit is perhaps least adequate, since it does not explain why custom remains implicit. With help from those outside sociology, practice theorists are reaching beyond study of the habitual. Historians such as Michael Baxandall have shown how unpredictable revolutions in the arts emerge from artists adapting old routines for new settings of action.

SEE ALSO: Agency (and Intention); Bourdieu, Pierre; Ethnomethodology; Foucault, Michel

REFERENCES AND SUGGESTED READINGS

Baxandall, M. (1985) *Patterns of Intention*. Yale University Press, New Haven.

Bourdieu, P. (1977) *Outline of a Theory of Practice*. Cambridge University Press, Cambridge.

Foucault, M. (pseudonym Maurice Florence) (1994) Foucault, Michel, 1926–. In: Gutting, G. (Ed.), *The Cambridge Companion to Foucault*. Cambridge University Press, Cambridge.

Garfinkel, H. (1967) *Studies in Ethnomethodology*. Prentice-Hall, Englewood Cliffs, NJ.

Giddens, A. (1984) *The Constitution of Society*. University of California Press, Berkeley.

Reckwitz, A. (2002) Toward a Theory of Social Practices: A Development in Culturalist Theorizing. *European Journal of Social Theory* 5(2): 243–63.

Schatzki, T. (1996) *Social Practices: A Wittgensteinian Approach to Human Activity and the Social.* Cambridge University Press, Cambridge.

Swidler, A. (2001) *Talk of Love: How Culture Matters.* University of Chicago Press, Chicago.

pragmatism

David L. Elliott

Pragmatism began in the United States of the 1870s, in the wake of the intellectual revolution touched off by Darwin, as a term for a method designed to clarify disputed, abstract intellectual concepts by defining them with reference to their concrete behavioral consequences. It later took on a broader meaning as the name for a comprehensive philosophical perspective which became widely known and influential from 1898 to its waning during the period of the Cold War. Nevertheless, the perspective continued to influence sociology throughout the twentieth century and into the twenty-first, especially in the tradition of symbolic interaction.

A resurgence of research and interest in pragmatism, beginning in the 1980s and accelerating since 1990, has been seen in general sociology in the work of such authors as Hans Joas, Mustafa Emirbayer, Dmitri Shalin, and David Maines. The perspective's assumption of the social phylogenesis and ontogenesis of humans, together with its antifoundationalism, fallibilism, meliorism, its view of nature as processual and relational, and its dissolution of the need for dualistic thinking, fit well with contemporary sociological concerns. Nevertheless, Eugene Halton's observation that symbolic interactionism (not to mention sociology in general) has not yet fully tapped the riches of pragmatist thought describes equally well the situation today.

A group of six Harvard graduates and scholars, having common intellectual interests in British philosophy and in the recent evolutionary work of Charles Darwin, organized themselves in 1871 into a discussion group that met regularly for about two years and came to be known as the Metaphysical Club. Three had experience in experimental science (Chauncey Wright, Charles Peirce, and William James), and the other three were lawyers (Nicholas St. John Green, Oliver Wendell Holmes, Jr., and Joseph Warner, of whom Holmes and Warner were less active). Pragmatism was born out of the thoughts developed and shared by this group (Fisch 1986).

Peirce and Holmes, who would be the first to publish pragmatism-inspired papers, were agreed that they learned the most from their senior associates Wright and Green. Wright taught them to think of the universe as contingent and indeterminate (later expressed by Peirce's concept of tychism), and Peirce referred to Green as the grandfather of pragmatism (with himself as the father) because of Green's persistence in arguing for the importance of applying Scottish psychologist Alexander Bain's theory of belief to their own work.

Bain had defined a belief as that for which a person is willing and committed to act, even in the face of considerable risk. For Bain, the opposite of belief was doubt, a state of confusion, uncertainty, anxiety, or frustration about how to act next. Peirce expanded on this theory of belief in his doubt–belief theory of inquiry. Peirce maintained that belief breaks down and doubt ensues when the requirements of human organisms and those of their environment fall out of step with each other. Human doubt triggers inquiry, the goal of which is the "fixation of belief." In Peirce's hands, belief became defined as habit, or a disposition to act in a certain way under certain circumstances.

According to Peirce's pragmatic maxim, as expressed in its 1906 revision, the best definition of a concept is "a description of the habit it will produce" (quoted in Short 1981: 218). Concepts defined in this way are empirically testable, and a concept can be tentatively considered true so long as it passes all such testing. Hence, Peirce's pragmatic maxim is a part of his theory of inquiry. The maxim is also part of his semeiotic or general theory of signs, which was Peirce's crowning achievement and which became the linchpin of his entire philosophy.

Although Peirce was justified in calling himself the father of pragmatism, William James was the first to use the term publicly, in an 1898 lecture (published the same year) at the University of California. It would also be James whose lectures and publications would popularize pragmatism and cause its wide dissemination throughout the world (Fisch 1986). However, James had already made his greatest contribution to the perspective in his 1890 *Principles of Psychology* because of the major influence this work would have on John Dewey and George Herbert Mead. In his *Principles*, James replaced traditional introspective, faculty, and associationist psychologies with a functional and processual psychology, in which the self and consciousness are seen not as entities but as functions that are actively engaged with the world (Sleeper 2001 [1986]).

John Dewey combined James's theory of the process by which logical forms emerge and change as products of concrete experience with Peirce's doubt-belief theory in developing his own theory of inquiry. Henceforth for Dewey an empirical and critical method of inquiry (also referred to as the experiential method, the experimental method, the method of intelligent behavior, or the logic of experience) would provide the general model for philosophy and science. The foundation provided by traditional metaphysics, whether a priori, transcendental, or supernatural, is replaced by the test of experience in contexts of concrete problem solving. With Dewey and Mead, pragmatism as a procedure for clarifying the meaning of intellectual concepts expands into a general theory of inquiry that is applicable to all specialized areas of inquiry (including ethical inquiry and artistic work) and that explains how meaning in the broadest sense emerges (Sleeper 2001 [1986]).

Dewey undertook a special inquiry to discover the most general and irreducible traits of the natural world experienced by living organisms in and of that world. The resulting theory could serve as background assumptions and guiding principles for inquiry. Dewey identified five generic traits: the stable, the precarious, qualities (or the qualitative), ends, and histories. These traits and their interrelations are combined in the concept of the situation (or context), which always involves a transaction between an organism and its environment (Gouinlock 1972).

The use of the general term organism highlights the continuity of human behavior with that of other living forms and the continuity of the systematically reflective intelligence of

human science with human common sense as well as with the trial and error intelligence of the behavioral responses plants and animals make to their environments. Nevertheless, pragmatism focuses mainly on situations of the human organism and its cultures.

Dewey did not claim that the generic traits he identified make an exhaustive list. Instead, Dewey said that they are ones the neglect of which resulted in the principal dualisms of western thought, such as mind/body, fact/value, theory/practice, analytic/synthetic, a priori/a posteriori, art/science, affective/cognitive, individual/social, etc. Since the specified traits are drawn from an analysis of experience and are subject to experiential or empirical testing, social scientists as well as philosophers and all systematically reflective persons are called upon to test, critique, refine, and add to the list as the results of inquiry warrant.

The members of the trio Dewey, Mead, and Jane Addams (sometimes called the Chicago pragmatists) influenced each of the others significantly, and they shared a mostly common perspective. To date, Mead has received much more attention from sociologists.

RACE, GENDER, AND CLASS

Nancy Fraser (in Harris 1999) argues that Alain Locke, a student of James most widely known for his theories of multiculturalism and of the Harlem Renaissance, made a significant contribution to critical race theory in 1916 lectures published in 1992 as *Race Contacts and Interracial Relations*. According to Fraser, Locke offers "another pragmatism" through the greater role he gives to power, domination, and political economy in a sociological race theory that is pragmatist through and through.

Locke's analysis of race proceeds through three connected steps. The first step concerns so-called scientific theories of race, usually biological or anthropological. These theories posit fixed, static, and "pure" races. They overstate variation between races while understating variation within races.

Locke's principal refutation of scientific racialism occurs in the second step of his analysis on the practical and political conceptions of race. Locke argues that the political and economic domination resulting from such imperialist practices as colonialism and slavery led to notions of racial superiority for which pseudo-scientific explanations were formulated.

After having refuted the inherited race concept and having shown the invidious results of white supremacist practices, Locke argues in the third step of his analysis that the race concept should be reconstructed rather than being discarded. Locke's reconstruction of race consisted of two aspects. The first aspect was a civilization type with the characteristics necessary for a group solidarity that is not based on blood or ethnicity along with the characteristics required by modern institutions. The second aspect was a secondary race consciousness as a strategy for African Americans to promote racial pride and to use cultural means as part of the struggle to overcome racism.

In a more recent argument that Cornel West considered the finest defense for maintaining the concept of race, Paul Taylor (in Lawson & Koch 2004) laid out what he calls a pragmatic racialism. According to Taylor, pragmatism's practicalism, contextualism, pluralism, experimentalism, and social ontology allow us to think more productively about race.

Like Locke, Taylor describes race as a sociohistorical construction arising from the practices of white supremacy. Without the race concept, Taylor says, we would likely miss populations for which a common bloodline, identified through socially defined racial markers, is connected with a common social location and opportunity structure. The suggested conceptual substitutes for race, such as ethnicity, culture, and national origin, cannot be relied upon alone to identify such patterns of common outcomes. Despite the general, widespread character of racial markers and outcomes, Taylor insists that race is the outcome of a particular history and that solutions to race problems must be tied to the conditions of individual situations.

While Dewey and Mead supported the work of their women students and freely acknowledged their intellectual debts to women, the acknowledgments were mostly made in prefaces, footnotes, popular journals, or privately. In the text of their major publications, they followed the professional convention of recognizing and discussing only male philosophers

and scientists. This was one type of sexist practice that led to the marginalization of women's contributions to pragmatism, a marginalization that Charlene Haddock Seigfried (1996) has worked to correct.

The very limited opportunities for women professors in early twentieth-century American universities contributed to a gendered division of labor between theory and practice in early pragmatism. Most of the early women pragmatists wrote theory, most notably Hull House founder Jane Addams, but their major contribution was to put the theories of Dewey and the other male pragmatists to the test of practice and, through their practice, to influence male theory construction. For example, the women's practice in Dewey's Laboratory School had influenced and inspired Dewey's early theory of education as well as other areas of his thought. In turn, some of these women later founded and ran progressive, experimental schools designed around Dewey's theory. The women pragmatists exemplified the ideal expressed by male pragmatists of a unity of theory and practice, an ideal also widely shared by sociologists.

Addams, perhaps because of the high value she placed on inclusiveness, multiculturalism, pluralism, and what Mead called international-mindedness, did not often theorize in explicitly feminist terms. Yet, she anticipated the thesis of Friedan's *The Feminine Mystique* (1963) in a more socially conscious way, and she also anticipated aspects of feminist standpoint theory (Seigfried 1999). Recently, Sullivan (in Seigfried 2002) argued for a pragmatist-feminist standpoint theory that seeks to use Dewey's conception of objectivity to improve upon Sandra Harding's. In a related discussion, Gatens-Robinson (in Seigfried 2002) drew similarities and differences between the respective ecological conceptions of objectivity of Donna Haraway and John Dewey.

The central and frequent use in classical pragmatist texts of such terms as scientific method, experimentalism, and instrumentalism has often led to interpretations of pragmatism as scientistic and instrumental in the narrow sense. However, the early women pragmatists, recognizing the emancipatory potential of experimentalism, embraced it. For them, pragmatist experimentalism offered a justification to trust their own experience and their own judgment as well as a means to evaluate problems and possible solutions without relying on the prescriptions of oppressive traditions and authorities.

Pragmatist experimentalism is democratic, including the values, ideas, and experiences of all parties affected by the problem prompting inquiry. The working methods of the women of Hull House exemplified the notion of experimentalism as community problem solving. These methods contrasted sharply with the growing detachment of social scientific methods and the top-down, paternalistic practices of other burgeoning institutions of expertise. By living together in Hull House, amidst a mainly poor and immigrant neighborhood, the settlement workers were participant experimenters. Besides solving the particular problem at hand, a more general goal of the community engagement of the mostly upper-middle-class Hull House residents with the mostly lower-class neighbors was to enlarge the selves of all parties through an enlargement of their experience. This goal reflected the core of the social ethical theories of Addams and of Mead.

Meera Nanda (2001) argued for the emancipatory potential of science in its broader pragmatist sense as a tool for improving the lot of India's untouchables by helping to overcome the cultural hold of India's caste system. She discusses in particular B. R. Ambedkar, a student of Dewey and a critic of Ghandi and the Congress Party for their paternalism and tacit Hindu acceptance of the caste system as natural. Ambedkar wrote on the parallels between pragmatism and the original Buddhist texts in terms of their naturalistic ontologies and their method of submitting knowledge to the test of experience. Toward the end of his life, Ambedkar led close to a million untouchables in renouncing their Hinduism and converting to Buddhism.

SEE ALSO: Addams, Jane; Dewey, John; Game Stage; Generalized Other; James, William; Mead, George Herbert; Play Stage; Role-Taking; Semiotics; Symbolic Interaction

REFERENCES AND SUGGESTED READINGS

Fisch, M. H. (1986) *Peirce, Semeiotic, and Pragmatism: Essays by Max H. Fisch*. Indiana University Press, Bloomington.

Gouinlock, J. (1972) *John Dewey's Philosophy of Value*. Humanities Press, New York.

Harris, L. (Ed.) (1999) *The Critical Pragmatism of Alain Locke*. Rowman & Littlefield, Lanham, MD.

Lawson, B. E. & Koch, D. F. (Eds.) (2004) *Pragmatism and the Problem of Race*. Indiana University Press, Bloomington.

Nanda, M. (2001) A "Broken People" Defend Science: Reconstructing the Deweyan Buddha of India's Dalits. *Social Epistemology* 15: 335–65.

Seigfried, C. H. (1996) *Pragmatism and Feminism: Reweaving the Social Fabric*. University of Chicago Press, Chicago.

Seigfried, C. H. (1999) Socializing Democracy: Jane Addams and John Dewey. *Philosophy of the Social Sciences* 29: 207–30.

Seigfried, C. H. (Ed.) (2002) *Feminist Interpretations of John Dewey*. Pennsylvania State University Press, University Park.

Short, T. L. (1981) Semeiosis and Intentionality. *Transactions of the Charles S. Peirce Society* 17: 197–223.

Sleeper, R. W. (2001 [1986]) *The Necessity of Pragmatism: John Dewey's Conception of Philosophy*. University of Illinois Press, Urbana.

praxis

Susan Wortmann

Praxis is a term most commonly associated with the ability of oppressed groups to change their economic, political, and social worlds through rationally informed reflection and deliberate social action. As advocated and critiqued by contemporary theorists, the term itself is often loosely associated with the melding of theory to liberatory human action.

In classical sociological theory, praxis is connected with Karl Marx and his emphasis on the revolutionary potential of the proletariat. Interpretations of Marx's usage of praxis vary (see, for instance, Gouldner 1980, who discusses Marx's dual treatment of the term), but most associate a Marxist-based praxis with societal transformation that involves a concomitant change in the proletariat's material activity, consciousness, and social relations. Hence, Marx is frequently quoted: "The philosophers have only *interpreted* the world, in various ways; the point, however, is to *change* it" (1978

[1844]: 145). Moreover, Marx and Friedrich Engel's *Communist Manifesto* lays out this theory and plan of praxis: the dual abolition of class and class exploitation in the forms of private property, the patriarchal nuclear family, traditional religion, and country and nation. At issue for Marx is holistic human and social transformation.

Contemporary theorists advocate praxis-based solutions to end the subaltern status of many oppressed groups, including, but not limited to, the colonized, the poor, women, people of color, and gays and lesbians. For many, the institution of education is fundamentally linked to praxis. For instance, Paulo Freire's (1972) theory of praxis specifically offers Brazilian *campesinos* as a mechanism that combines reflection and action to transform a psychological, social, political, and economic legacy of imperialism and colonialism. For Freire, praxis is the act of creativity and social change achieved through the oppressed's own experience and the creative process of education: that is, acquiring and developing literacy and reactive responses to the ruling social and political structures. Freire's model of educational praxis is not realized in a "banking model," wherein students merely memorize and repeat "expert" knowledge. Instead, it is accomplished through a dialogic problem-posing process in which the oppressed use their experiences and education to create new understandings. Hence, praxis and its ends are not preordained, but are, instead, a creative process of becoming. Like Freire, feminist bell hooks identifies the potential for active and transformative processes of education. It is hooks's declared oeuvre to interrogate and to critique systems of what she calls "Imperialist White Supremacist Capitalist Patriarchy," and to change them.

The above-described renditions of praxis have their critics. For some postmodernists, for instance, praxis is solidly tied to a flawed Enlightenment project that erroneously connects liberation with rationality, thereby suggesting that a transcendent critic's body of knowledge should be privileged. Such critics question how enlightening happens, who facilitates it, and what actually changes as a result.

Contemporary sociologists continue to debate what role sociology and sociologists play in praxis. For instance, in 2005, both *Critical Sociology* and the *British Journal of Sociology* devoted issues to international scholarly responses to American Sociological Association President Michael Burawoy's 2004 call for sociology as a critical public endeavor.

SEE ALSO: Feminist Activism in Latin America; Marx, Karl; Social Change; Social Movements

REFERENCES AND SUGGESTED READINGS

Albert, M. (1974) *What Is To Be Undone? A Modern Revolutionary Discussion of Classical Left Ideologies.* Porter Sargent, Boston.

Bailey, G. & Noga, G. (2003) *Ideology: Structuring Identities in Contemporary Life.* Broadview, Peterborough, Ontario.

British Journal of Sociology (2005) Continuing the Public Sociologies Debate: Replies to Michael Burawoy. 56(3): 333–524.

Critical Sociology (2005) 31(3): 311–90.

Freire, P. (1972) *Pedagogy of the Oppressed.* Harmondsworth, Penguin.

Gouldner, A. (1980) *The Two Marxisms.* Macmillan, London.

hooks, b. (1984) *From Margin to Center.* South End Press, Boston.

hooks, b. (1994) *Teaching to Transgress: Education as the Practice of Freedom.* Routledge, New York.

McLellan, D. (1998) *Marxism After Marx.* Macmillan, Basingstoke.

Margonis, F. (2003) Paulo Freire and Post-Colonial Dilemmas. *Studies in Philosophy and Education* 22: 145–56.

Marx, K. (1978 [1844]) *Theses on Feuerbach.* In: Tucker, R. (Ed.), *The Marx Engels Reader.* Norton, New York.

Vrankicki, P. (1965) On the Problem of Practice. *Praxis* 1: 41–8.

prejudice

Laura Jennings

Prejudice is the judging of a person or idea, without prior knowledge of the person or idea, on the basis of some perceived group membership. Prejudice can be negative, as in the case of racist or sexist ideology, or positive, as in the case of a preference for a particular ethnic food, and can thus either help or harm a person so judged. Some writers, in defining prejudice, stress an incorrect or irrational component; others maintain that it is incorrect to do so because prejudice is often rooted in a quite rational self- or group interest. Prejudice is often used synonymously with such terms as discrimination and racism.

Social scientists began to show great interest in prejudice in the early to mid-twentieth century when anti-immigrant sentiment was widespread and often erupted in violence. Later concerns over fascism and the Holocaust fed scientific interest in prejudice. Psychologist Gordon Allport, in his seminal work *The Nature of Prejudice* (1954), described prejudice as the result of a normal – albeit emotion-laden and faulty – psychological process of categorizing people into in-groups and out-groups. In-groups are considered desirable and in possession of positive attributes, while out-groups are seen as possessing negative or undesirable attributes and, thus, as appropriate targets for abuse. Allport noted the role of stereotyping in prejudice and discussed the acquisition of prejudice, its dynamics, personality types thought to be prone to prejudiced thinking, and possible ways to reduce prejudice, including legislation, education, and therapy.

Other works investigated further the idea of a prejudiced personality type, commonly known as the authoritarian personality, linking it with a tendency toward overly rigid thinking, acceptance of stereotypes, excessive conformity and submission to authority, discomfort with ambiguity, and highly conservative and/or fundamentalist beliefs. Uncomfortable with the linkage of prejudice and authoritarianism with right-wing beliefs, other researchers attempted to show that those on the political left, too, could possess overly rigid thought patterns that might predispose them to prejudiced thinking.

STEREOTYPING

Stereotyping is thought to play an important role in the formation and maintenance of prejudice. Like prejudice, stereotyping involves the attribution of certain characteristics to a person based on her or his membership in a particular group. Experimental and survey-based studies have shown variously that prejudice and stereotypes are both remarkably resilient and subject to change over time in response to changes in social norms, that stereotypes can be based in either illusion or reality, and that stereotypes and prejudice can either overrule or be overruled by evidence to the contrary. Some research suggests not only that people seek with their behavior to confirm the prejudices to which they subscribe, but also that this behavior can actually elicit responses consistent with the prejudiced belief. For example, students believed by their teachers to be gifted begin to display greater ability in their subject than their fellow students, even if the students identified as gifted are so identified randomly by researchers. Similarly, people who believe that they are talking via telephone with attractive, outgoing members of the opposite sex speak with greater warmth and humor to their phone partners than do people who believe their fellow conversant to be unattractive and socially backward. The phone partners, in turn, respond accordingly, with those perceived to be attractive, humorous, and confident actually displaying those traits, and those perceived to be unattractive and introverted responding coolly and with reservation.

Prejudice and stereotyping have been shown to influence not only current behavior but also memory of past events; holders of stereotypes are prone to selectively remembering information consistent with the prejudices they hold. Furthermore, people are more likely to view negative behaviors as internally caused (i.e., through some personal or cultural flaw) if performed by those against whom they are prejudiced and externally caused if performed by members of their own group. Conversely, people credit positive behaviors by members of their own group to inner positive qualities, and positive actions by those against whom they are prejudiced as rare exceptions to the rule.

FORMATION OF PREJUDICE

Early theories on formation of prejudice in children stressed the importance of personality characteristics of parents, hypothesizing that prejudice is the result of being reared in an overly strict and harsh home environment. Research, however, has shown that this is not necessarily true. Children from a very early age show an ability to categorize people into groups; they also show marked preference for some groups – especially the groups to which they themselves belong – over others. Moreover, children's attitudes do not appear to be entirely determined by the attitudes of their parents, which suggests that children are far from being passive receptacles for their parents' prejudiced views.

Herbert Blumer advanced the notion of racial prejudice as "a sense of group position" in which the words and actions of influential public figures establish a public perception not only of social group hierarchy but also of the positioning of one's own group relative to that of others. Blumer emphasized that feelings of superiority and identification of intergroup difference alone cannot account for prejudice; these must be accompanied by a sense of entitlement to certain resources or privileges and also by a sense that this entitlement is threatened by other groups. Attempts by oppressed groups to improve their social conditions are thus seen as threatening by the dominant group, which views these attempts as a rejection of the proper social order. Dominant groups are acutely aware of – and protective of – their superior social status, and prejudice flares when this status is questioned. Prejudice is thus not merely an individual ideology but a social phenomenon rooted in intergroup relations and arising from specific historical contexts. Blumer stressed that the formation of group identity, and thus of prejudice, does not take place in individual interactions but at an abstract level in the public sphere and is articulated most forcefully by widely respected figures in the public eye.

Blumer points out, as do other scholars, that prejudice is not only a way of identifying and denigrating out-groups but also a powerful means of self-definition of the in-group in opposition to these out-groups. Important qualities thought to be lacking in out-groups are thus by definition thought to be possessed in abundance by in-groups. Negative qualities attributed to members of out-groups are overlooked or viewed as rare exceptions when exhibited by in-group members.

As social scientists began to uncover the structural foundations of racism and sexism, interest in prejudice as a research topic began to wane. Focusing attention on the individual ideological aspects of prejudice was thought to divert attention from its even more harmful structural counterpart: institutionalized racial and sexual discrimination and violence. The uncovering of the racist and sexist practices of the state, of business, of the legal justice system, of commerce and real estate and employers, of science and systems of higher education, seemed to render the beliefs and behavior of individual racists and sexists trivial and insignificant. More recently, however, scholars are reemphasizing the importance of prejudice and the severity of its consequences; several prominent sociologists have urged that cumulative daily encounters with prejudice not be discounted in the rush to study structural factors. These writers encourage scholars to consider the impact of repeated experiences with prejudice at an individual level in conjunction with experiences of institutional racism and sexism. Both, they argue, are crucial in the formation of group and individual identity and in determination of the response – or lack of response – of victims of prejudice.

SUBJECTS OF PREJUDICE

Another current debate within sociology concerns new versus old forms of prejudice. Since the civil rights and women's movements of the 1960s, levels of racial and sexual prejudice have shown a decline by traditional measures. Some theorists maintain that this is evidence signaling that society is becoming less prejudiced. Others argue that the overt behaviors and vocabularies of racism and sexism have simply been driven underground by social pressures to be politically correct and that prejudiced ideology still flourishes in a more publicly acceptable new form. In terms of racism, this new form is sometimes described as aversive prejudice, in which people who score low on traditional measures of prejudice and antipathy toward out-groups nevertheless display fear or discomfort at contact with members of out-groups and so seek to avoid this contact. Another theory of a new form of prejudice is colorblind racism; colorblind racists are those who view racism as a thing of the past and not something with which society ought to concern itself now. Proponents of a colorblind approach insist that those who wish to succeed can do so on their own merits and that to acknowledge race at all is to be racist. In this way of thinking, attempts to redress historical wrongs against non-whites and females amount to current "reverse" discrimination against white males. Yet another theory, that of *laissez-faire* racism, suggests that the new racists of today are characterized by protectiveness of their own group interest, their antipathy toward any kind of race-targeted social programs, and their willingness to publicly condemn those who fail to achieve the American Dream. The *laissez-faire* theory grew out of an earlier theory of symbolic racism; symbolic racism involved the substitution of ostensibly non-racial vocabulary and symbols for the overtly racist rhetoric no longer considered acceptable.

All of these new theories are presented in contrast to old-fashioned prejudice (often called Jim Crow racism), which had its roots in beliefs of the biological inferiority of non-whites. The new forms, in contrast, are grounded in beliefs and rhetoric about the cultural inferiority of non-white groups. Holders of the newer version of prejudice maintain that the unfortunate situation of the non-white poor is their own fault. In these forms of prejudice, poverty and misfortune are viewed as pathology and the natural result of a failure to accept and conform to mainstream values. Those who do not succeed fail because they have simply not tried hard enough. The implication of such a view is that the dominant group has no responsibility to do anything to try to help members of less fortunate groups because the less fortunate are refusing to help themselves.

Because of the research linking prejudice to stereotyping and to various other traits such as conformity and lower levels of education, some social scientists have suggested education as a cure for prejudice. Others have suggested that prejudice arises from ignorance about the group(s) in question and hence that the remedy lies in increased contact between members of various groups. The theory in both cases is that access to new and better information can replace a flawed and harmful prejudiced thought process.

This contact theory, with its hypothesis that intergroup prejudice can be reduced by increasing the levels of contact between members of different groups, has been tested repeatedly, with mixed results. One such test was Sherif's 1966 summer camp study in which researchers first stimulated intergroup antagonism and then attempted, with some success, to reduce it. Other studies monitored the effects of school or neighborhood desegregation on levels of prejudice. In some cases, increasing contact between groups actually results in higher levels of prejudice, especially when the quality of contact is negative or when the contact situation is competitive in nature. Those situations in which contact does seem to result in lower levels of prejudice are those in which members of different groups have ample opportunity to interact in positive ways and to work together on cooperative tasks. Another essential element of successful contacts is that the participants are of equal status in the social situation(s) under study. The mixed success of this theory has left researchers seeking new and better ways to reduce levels of prejudice.

There is some evidence that, because stereotypes often have widespread social support, people's attitudes and prejudices are not likely to change unless positive individual interactions occur in a climate which encourages prejudice reduction. A vital component of such a climate is leadership support for change, and the willingness of authority figures to impose rewards and sanctions to further change. This suggests that leaders who adopt a color- or gender-blind approach, insisting that prejudice and discrimination are no longer problems, may actually help to preserve prejudice.

SEE ALSO: Adorno, Theodor W.; Authoritarian Personality; Blumer, Herbert George; Discrimination; Homophobia and Heterosexism; In-Groups and Out-Groups; Race; Race (Racism); Sexism; Stereotyping and Stereotypes

REFERENCES AND SUGGESTED READINGS

Adorno, T. W., Frenkel-Brunswick, E., Levinson, D. J., & Sanford, R. N. (1950) *The Authoritarian Personality*. Harper, New York.

Allport, G. W. (1954) *The Nature of Prejudice*. Addison-Wesley, Reading, MA.

Blumer, H. (2000) *Selected Works of Herbert Blumer: A Public Philosophy for Mass Society*. University of Illinois Press, Urbana.

Brown, R. (1995) *Prejudice: Its Social Psychology*. Blackwell, Oxford.

Stangor, C. (2000) *Stereotypes and Prejudice: Essential Readings*. Psychology Press of Taylor & Francis, Philadelphia, PA.

preparatory stage

D. Angus Vail

While George Herbert Mead never explicitly mentions this stage of development, many contend that he implies it in several of his seminal writings on the social, not biological, root of the self. According to Mead, the self arises from a process of interaction among one's consociates. As an individual develops a facility for language, he or she begins to understand the symbolic meanings of social objects and eventually develops the capacity to make him/herself into a social object. In Mead's model, children begin to show signs of developing a self when they learn how to play at the roles of important people in their lives. At this *play stage* they show elementary understanding of role-taking, but their understanding of complex rules and subtle differences of individual positions in social settings is limited. As they develop more sophisticated understandings of social settings, they enter a *game stage* where they learn to take account not only of individual roles, but also of the abstract rules that make those divergent roles make sense in a given situation. Mead calls this set of rules the *generalized other*. The *preparatory stage* precedes these phases in the social genesis of the self, representing a stage of mimicry where a child, in essence, is preparing him/herself for the more complex, subtle, and sophisticated social tasks that are starting to become a part of his or her routine.

Children in the preparatory stage develop a capacity for mimicking the behavior of those with whom they come in contact on a regular basis. Thus, in this stage a child may "read" the Sunday newspaper with her parents even though she knows neither how to read nor why the activity is important to her parents. Since the child has yet to develop the linguistic and social capacities for assigning meanings to social objects and/or activities, most would claim that this mimicry is not meaningful. It does, however, suggest a growing capacity to take account of social objects. While the child may not understand what a newspaper is, let alone why reading a Sunday newspaper is so ritualistically complex, she is showing that she understands that the activity is somehow important.

While preparatory stage behavior is not considered meaningful, it does lay the foundation for understanding role-taking and the development of meaning. Children at this stage begin to learn that their activities generate responses from other people. While they are a long way off from being able to predict those responses, their behavior – and the reactions it generates – soon will lead to their developing a sense of their own independence and eventually to their own ability to make a social object of themselves.

In spite of the fact that Mead never explicitly discussed the preparatory stage in his essays on the sociogenesis of the self, the concept has become a staple in introductory texts and sociological social psychology texts as the first of the three stages of self-development.

SEE ALSO: Game Stage; Generalized Other; Mead, George Herbert; Play Stage; Role; Self

REFERENCES AND SUGGESTED READINGS

Blumer, H. (1969) *Symbolic Interactionism: Perspective and Method*. University of California Press, Berkeley.

Mead, G. H. (1962 [1934]) *Mind, Self, and Society: From the Standpoint of a Social Behaviorist*. University of Chicago Press, Chicago.

Meltzer, B. N. (1959) *The Social Psychology of George Herbert Mead*. Center for Sociological Research, Kalamazoo, MI.

Meltzer, B. N., Petras, J. W., & Reynolds, L. T. (1975) *Symbolic Interactionism: Genesis, Varieties, and Criticism*. Routledge & Kegan Paul, Boston.

Weigert, A. J. & Gecas, V. (2004) Self. In: Reynolds, L. T. & Herman-Kinney, N. J. (Eds.), *Handbook of Symbolic Interactionism*. Alta Mira, New York, pp. 267–88.

prevention, intervention

Franz-Xaver Kaufmann

The terms "prevention" and "intervention" are used in many social sciences, from international politics to social work. They concern certain classes of intentional behavior by collective actors which are considered as interfering with given situations. Prevention means measures or actions to reduce potential risks, i.e., to hinder the future happening of certain kinds of damage, e.g., accidents at work, deviant behavior, or the spreading of contagious infections. Intervention, by contrast, means the interference with some actual situation or process in order to change the course of an ongoing problematic event "to its best." From an analytical perspective, both terms are rather equivalent: prevention in the ordinary sense means an interference in earlier stages of an assumed causal process than intervention.

Given the pervasive character of both kinds of actions, it is impossible to discuss here their implications with respect to specific fields of action. This is rather an attempt to specify their sociological character as a tool for reflecting on the operation of applied social sciences. Therefore, both terms are used here as concepts of a sociological observer interpreting actions of an actor pursuing defined goals in social situations defined by herself as problematic. The task of social science consists first in working out the implications of that very widespread form of social action. It has then to demonstrate the utility of such an inquiry.

There are three main fields of sociological inquiry related to the subject, namely, research and discourse about social problems, evaluation research, and political governance. For a long time, applied social science took for granted the definitions of social problems by certain ("focal") actors themselves and discussed only the means to influence or solve the problem. Meanwhile, the sociology of social problems has worked out the implications and contingencies of processes of the definition of social problems. In order to contribute valid knowledge for action, applied social science has to reflect the multiple perspectives of actors involved in a process of intervention and to reconstruct itself the problem at stake and its issues.

Evaluation research began as the measurement of outputs and moved then to program evaluation. This paradigm supposed a technological understanding of intervention: the program was considered as a causal process introduced by an external authority pursuing certain goals. Evaluation then had to measure program effects, i.e., the changes observed in consequence of the introduction of a program were attributed to the program alone. This causal model of intervention makes sense in a laboratory, where the researcher has control over the whole situation and possesses standardized knowledge about the operation of intervening factors.

This model is not applicable to intervention in real-life social situations, as the development of evaluation research has shown (Guba & Lincoln 1989). Compared to, for example, biochemical interventions, the bulk of social interventions are poorly standardized, and their "technological kernel" remains weak. The operator of the intervention cannot be left outside the conceptualization of the intervention process. Social intervention implies focal actors, their aims, resources, and relationships to the field of intervention, not only their action. Social intervention is directly or indirectly a process of interaction between the intervening actor and selective, reacting persons, whose perceptions and interests are mostly unknown to the former. Moreover, the target persons of an intervention live in circumstances and opportunity structures which can never be wholly controlled or kept constant by the intervening actor. The measurable changes of, for example, the behavior of target persons may be attributed to the intervention or to other changes in their situation.

Research on social intervention becomes therefore a more complicated task than the measurement of program inputs and outputs, the operation of the program remaining a "black box." The research design has to include:

1   *Relevant properties of the intervening (focal) actors*: What is their authority? Their problem? How do they define the situation? What are the resources and instruments at

their disposal? In short, what are their programs or models of problem solution? Moreover, focal actors are usually not individuals but collective, especially corporate, actors. In the case of corporate actors, a division of labor takes place so that intervention becomes a multistep process coordinating diverse operations, i.e., a process of governance.

2 *Relevant properties of the target persons or addressees*: How do they perceive the intentions of the program? Does it meet *their* problems? Have they competencies to resist the intervention or to use the operations of the program for other purposes than those intended by the focal actor?

3 *Relevant properties of the field of intervention*: What other factors contribute to the situation deemed problematic by the intervening actor? To what extent does the focal actor depend on third parties for affecting her program? Are the target persons isolated or may they interact? Are there in the field institutions shaping opportunity structures which may divert the operation from the aims of the program? To what extent is a program in accordance with value orientations shared by institutions and actors in the field?

Though not every one of these and related questions may find clear-cut answers in a research situation, the different approach to an experimental design is evident. Especially in the case of complex multistep interventions (such as the introduction or modification of a policy), this kind of inquiry sensitizes researchers to the pitfalls of naïve quasi-technological programming. The aim of intervention research is then not only the evaluation of outputs but also the inquiry into the processes of governance operating a program, as well as into the conditions for its implementation.

Such a program of research is not very promising for generalized knowledge. If each problematic situation and the operation of social intervention is unique, how can professional knowledge emerge? In fact, the results of evaluation research and of implementation research have not thus far proved to be particularly suitable for establishing generalized knowledge.

Professional knowledge is related not to the concept of intervention but to the institutionalized fields of action. For economists, the tools of economic policy are rather well known, and they may even be able to distinguish among the conditions under which such tools are promising. Nevertheless, even the practice of economic policy is not a science but an art in the Aristotelian sense. Its success depends on a capacity of diagnosis and a feeling for the peculiarities of a situation. This is even more true for fields of action where the impact of institutional structures and the functions of utility are less clear and where there is less "technological" knowledge available than in the economic field.

"Prevention" and "intervention" are useful as sensitizing concepts. They reconstruct political or social action so as to make us aware of their intricacies. To be sure this may not be helpful for quick decisions, but this has never been the task of social science. Applied social science may become useful in this context insofar as the sociologist is involved in the processes of planning and implementing an intervention as a kind of participant observer using tools of sociological observation and continuously providing evidence about the operation of a program. Social interventions are seldom effective without continuous processes of learning.

Though intervention may be openly hostile (e.g., in foreign affairs or in a criminal situation), discourse about social or sociopolitical intervention normally presumes it to be in the primary interest not of the intervening actor but of the "beneficiaries" of the intervention. From a humanistic point of view, this "reformist" cultural orientation merits being taken seriously. The "goods" which may be provided through sociopolitical intervention are of four kinds, and it is possible to organize "technological" knowledge about intervention following these four dimensions of social participation or inclusion:

- *Status, especially rights*: The basic condition of social inequality consists in the inequality of rights or of the opportunities to claim one's title. Legal intervention aims at securing the rights of the weaker actors. This may happen on different levels of social action, from governmental initiatives to the legal aid by social work.

- *Resources, especially money*: In capitalist societies, self-sufficiency has become marginal; everyone depends on income. Economic intervention aims at securing the means of life for those excluded from sufficient market income. Again this form of intervention begins with governmental institution building and ends with cash in the hands of the needy.
- *Opportunities, especially infrastructure*: Social inequality has not only a socioeconomic and cultural but also a spatial aspect of access. Opportunities (e.g., for work and leisure, for health and education, for mobility and administrative access) are distributed unevenly in space, usually favoring those who are better off in the other three dimensions. Interventions to improve local settings follow their own rules and depend particularly on local organizations and the given circumstances in place.
- *Competencies, especially personal services*: It is well known that competent persons tend to succeed in adverse circumstances. The enabling of persons is therefore the most promising way out of problematic situations. "People processing" operates mainly on the level of interaction and depends on both professional knowledge and empathy.

To be sure, improvements of the situation of socially disadvantaged people need interventions in several or all of the dimensions just mentioned.

Prevention intends to ban risks before they become actual. From an action point of view, one may distinguish two kinds of preventive measures: those influencing conditions and opportunity structures in order to minimize the frequency of risk, and those influencing persons, their resources and competencies, to cope with risky situations. From the actor's point of view, preventive seems preferable to corrective intervention. From the perspective of a sociological observer, the situation is more complicated, however.

Preventive action presupposes the idea of a coherent chain of events which can be interrupted at various points. One can prevent a risk or damage only if one can control its causes. In the physical world, appropriate knowledge is often available and follows the laws of simple

or probable causality. In the social world, such knowledge is – if available at all – incoherent and fuzzy. Normally, several factors, not just one, may influence the emergence of risk with unknown probabilities. The contingency is higher as potential risk is more remote from actual damage. The preventive control of specific factors therefore remains uncertain and may have additional undesirable side-effects. Preventive measures thus have to be assessed for alternative consequences. A somewhat general improvement of the situation may often be preferable to targeted measures.

SEE ALSO: Actor-Network Theory; Evaluation; Intervention Studies; Knowledge; Political Process Theory; Political Sociology; Risk, Risk Society, Risk Behavior, and Social Problems; Social Integration and Inclusion; Social Policy, Welfare State; Social Problems, Concept and Perspectives; Social Problems, Politics of; Social Work: Theory and Methods

REFERENCES AND SUGGESTED READINGS

Albrecht, G. (1991) Methodological Dilemmas in Research on Prevention and Intervention. In: Albrecht, G. & Otto, H.-U. (Eds.), *Social Prevention and the Social Sciences*. Aldine de Gruyter, Berlin, pp. 397–428.
Guba, E. G. & Lincoln, Y. S. (1989) *Fourth-Generation Evaluation*. Sage, Newbury Park, CA.
Hurrelmann, K., Kaufmann, F.-X., & Lösel, F. (Eds.) (1987) *Social Intervention: Potential and Constraints*. Aldine de Gruyter, Berlin and New York.
Kaufmann, F.-X. (1999) Konzept und Formen sozialer Intervention (Concept and Forms of Social Intervention). In: Albrecht, G., Groenemeyer, A., & Stallberg, F. W. (Eds.), *Handbuch soziale Probleme (Handbook of Social Problems)*. Westdeutscher Verlag, Opladen/Wiesbaden.

primary groups

David L. Elliott

Cooley (1909) coined the term primary group to denote intimate, comparatively permanent, and solidary associations of mutually identifying persons, and a century of sociological research has increased our understanding of primary groups in their variety of forms and multi-faceted, contingent functions. According to Cooley, primary groups are primary in the sense of providing the first and (because of the greater openness and pliability of children) the most important socialization. The most important examples he cited in this sense are the family, children's play-groups, and the neighborhood or village community.

Primary groups are also primary in the sense of being the source out of which emerge both individuals and social institutions. Cooley agreed with George Herbert Mead that the self and its ideals emerge out of such primary relations. As examples of social institutions, Cooley cites democracy as an outgrowth of the village community and Christianity as an outgrowth of the family.

These groups are primary in the additional sense of providing primary human needs such as attachment, security, support, and recognition. Since these needs persist in some forms and to some degree throughout the life cycle, primary relations never cease to be important. In Cooley's conceptualization, a primary group instills feelings in its members of sympathy and identification with the group, its goals, values, and members. All that is distinctively human is a product of this feeling of a "we," which constrains but does not eliminate people's animal passions of greed, conflict, and so forth.

Classical sociologists (in the period roughly from 1890 to 1920) focused most of their attention on the rise and consequences of modernity, which they theorized as a general historical trajectory moving from the predominantly primary relations of primitive and feudal communities to the predominantly formal, rational, secondary relations of modern, urban, industrial societies. For example, Tönnies contrasted *Gemeinschaft* (or village community) relations with *Gesellchaft* (or societal) relations, Durkheim contrasted mechanical with organic solidarity, and Weber saw modern western history as a process of ever increasing rationalization.

The problem that engrossed the classical sociologists was how to maintain or recreate the recognition, solidarity, and support provided by primary relations and required for the health and flourishing of individuals within the increasingly impersonal, formal, and rationalized environment of modern societies, while at the same time preserving the instrumental advantages of modern institutions. Some of these concerns have been resolved by subsequent research (e.g., Granovetter 1983; Freudenberg 1986).

In a number of organizational, political, and community studies of the 1940s and 1950s, primary groups were not the intended object of study, but were found to provide the intervening variable required for an adequate explanation of the phenomena behind the data. In their "Yankee City" studies, Lloyd Warner and colleagues expected income, neighborhood, and family variables to explain social mobility in the town. They found that the process of social mobility was largely mediated through membership in face-to-face primary groups they called cliques. The cliques were second only to family (another primary group) in explaining social mobility in the town.

Stouffer and colleagues' 1949 study of American soldiers and Shils and Janowitz's 1948 study of German soldiers in World War II found that soldiers' morale and motivation to fight were explained more by the loyalty, solidarity, and mutual protection and identification they felt for their fighting unit than by personal loyalty to national symbols or national war goals.

Lazarsfeld and colleagues in 1948 found individuals were influenced in their voting decisions by members of their primary groups that the researchers called "opinion leaders." Katz and Lazarsfeld (1955) found that the mass media influenced individuals through the mediation of opinion leaders belonging to one of an individual's primary circles. These mid-century studies led to the widely shared proposition that a formal organization's effectiveness depended on the integration of its informal (primary group) structure with its formal structure.

Eugene Litwak was the primary user in sociology of the traditional primary group concept from the 1960s to the 1990s. According to Litwak, technological changes such as in communications and transportation lead to structural changes in existing primary groups and to new, more differentiated forms of primary groups. Litwak and colleagues expanded upon organizational contingency theory in their task-specific model of social support, in which the task requirements of the whole variety of primary human needs are matched to the specific primary group structure or formal organizational structure able to satisfy a particular need most effectively and efficiently. Litwak's research and analysis illustrates when and how tasks traditionally performed by primary groups can be performed by formal organizations and vice versa.

From the 1970s to the present, social network theorists such as Mark Granovetter and Barry Wellman have contributed significantly to the sociological understanding of the interrelations and functioning of primary and secondary relations. Granovetter (1983) conceived of a social tie (within one or more social networks) as varying in strength as measured by the tie's duration, its emotional intensity, its degree of intimacy, and its type and intensity of reciprocal services. Strong ties are characteristic of primary groups or primary relations, and weak ties are characteristic of formal organizations and work relations in less formal settings. Granovetter asserted that weak ties are important for social integration. Strong ties alone lead to societal fragmentation.

SEE ALSO: Cooley, Charles Horton; Intimacy; Secondary Groups; Significant Others; Social Influence; Social Network Theory; Social Support; Socialization, Primary; Weak Ties (Strength of)

REFERENCES AND SUGGESTED READINGS

Beggs, J. J., Haines, V. A., & Hurlbert, J. S. (1996) Situational Contingencies Surrounding the Receipt of Informal Support. *Social Forces* 75: 201–22.

Cooley, C. H. (1909) *Social Organization: A Study of the Larger Mind*. Charles Scribner's Sons, New York.

Freudenburg, W. R. (1986) The Density of Acquaintanceship: An Overlooked Variable in Community Research? *American Journal of Sociology* 92: 27–63.

Granovetter, M. S. (1983) The Strength of Weak Ties: A Network Theory Revisited. *Sociological Theory* 1: 201–33.

Katz, E. & Lazarsfeld, P. F. (1955) *Personal Influence: The Part Played by People in the Flow of Mass Communications*. Free Press, New York.

Messeri, P., Silverstein, M., & Litwak, E. (1993) Choosing Optimal Support Groups: A Review

and Reformulation. *Journal of Health and Social Behavior* 34: 133–7.

Shils, E. A. (1951) The Study of the Primary Group. In: Lerner, D. & Lasswell, H. D. (Eds.), *The Policy Sciences*. Stanford University Press, Stanford, pp. 44–69.

primate cities

Michael Timberlake

A primate city usually refers to a city that is disproportionately large in terms of population size relative to other cities contained within a given geographically bounded area, such as a region, a nation, or even the globe. Occasionally, other qualities of cities than relative population size are used to identify primacy, for example, indicators of the relative concentration of important organizations, such as headquarters for leading corporations. While the term is often applied to cities considered excessively (and pathologically) large, this is not technically appropriate. In fact Jefferson (1939), who first used the term, argued that primate cities play an important generative role with respect to national development.

The closely related concepts of primate city and urban primacy are rooted in theoretical approaches to urbanization in geography and sociology's human ecology that are about "central places" and "city systems." From these perspectives, a system of cities emerges historically when economic relationships among locales are first established and then elaborated. For example, once isolated locales may become interlinked through trade. Over time, such exchange relations lead to increasing interdependence among the locales as economic competition induces specialization. Locales specialize by providing a home for producers of the goods and services that are in demand and that they can produce and deliver more efficiently than those in other locales within the system. Cities that host the most efficient producers of the most desired goods and services become relatively dominant economically and politically, and this should be reflected in the relative population sizes of cities in a given system of cities. Hawley (e.g., 1981) argued that cities in which were located the "key functions" of the particular territorially circumscribed economic system become the dominant cities in that system.

Urban primacy is operationally defined variously by comparing the population size of the largest city to the population in one or more other cities in the same system. Often it is measured in terms of the shape of the size distribution of cities which are included in a purported system of cities, with an understanding of what constitutes a normal distribution. The notion of normalcy in a city size distribution is based on the same theoretical approaches to systems of cities. These assume that in an economically "healthy" system of cities, exchanges among cities will be relatively free, and this will lead to a lognormal distribution of the cities' population sizes. Clearly underlying this understanding, but almost always remaining unstated, is the assumption that capitalist markets, including labor markets, operate relatively unfettered, and, therefore, the benefits of development will "trickle down" the urban hierarchy from the primate city to the other, subdominant cities that are spread across the region in question.

In a lognormal city size distribution, the second-largest city will be half the size of the primate city, the third-largest city will be one-third the size of the primate city, and so on. (Though at some point down the hierarchy, there may be many cities of about the same population size.) This definition of normalcy is known as the "rank size rule," and was put forward by Zipf (1941). Scholars have proposed different measures of the degree of urban primacy. One, proposed by Davis (1976), uses the ratio of the size of the largest city's population to the total of the sum of the population sizes of the four most populous cities. Walters (1985) uses the assumption of lognormalcy to propose a measure of urban primacy that is tied to deviations from lognormalcy, where increasingly positive numbers indicate increasingly high levels of urban primacy, i.e., the primate city is increasingly more primate relative to the standard of a lognormal city size distribution. Increasingly larger negative numbers indicate flatter city size distributions; these are city systems in which the leading cities are more similar to one another in terms of population size (or whatever other

attribute is being used as a standard of urban primacy) than would be predicted on the basis of the rank size rule. Yet most empirical studies use cruder measures. A rare recent study of the causes of urban primacy uses the proportion of the urban population living in the most populous city of a country as a measure of the degree of urban primacy (Ades & Glaeser 1995).

Most research on urban primacy has defined the city system at the national level. Studies have shown that, in general, higher-income countries tend to have city size distributions that are closer to the rank size rule than lower-income countries, and in many of the latter, abnormally large primate cities are not unusual. For example Bangkok, Thailand is many times larger than the second-largest city in the country, and Mexico City is nearly nine times more populous than Guadalajara. However, London and Paris are also significantly larger than the rank size rule would predict, while the city size distribution in the United States is less primate than the lognormal standard. Nevertheless, most cases of extreme urban primacy are in the low- and moderate-income countries of the periphery and semiperiphery, most prevalently in South American countries, rather than in wealthy, core countries. Thus, in the context of development studies, high levels of primacy are thought to be indicative of poorly integrated systems of cities, which means poorly integrated national economies – a form of socioeconomic "dualism," or disarticulation, that not only signifies developmental problems for the national or regional economy, but also serves as an impediment to successful socioeconomic development. Abnormally large primate cities – cities far more populous than would be expected on the basis of the lognormal distribution – are said by scholars to indicate a poorly integrated national or regional economy, one in which developmental advances in the primate city lack mechanisms to "trickle down" the urban size hierarchy and across the country or region. In fact some scholars have argued that such primate cities are "parasitic" with respect to the national economy, sucking resources from the rest of the country and providing little in return. It is this apparent correlation between excessive urban primacy and underdevelopment that is responsible for the preponderant pejorative view of the primate city.

Geographers and sociologists have suggested several possible contributing factors underlying the emergence and persistence of such primate cities at the national level. These include political, economic, geographical, technical, historical, and global factors. For example, some have argued that in many low-income countries state policies are biased in favor of urban areas in general, and the leading city in particular. Thus the largest city in the country, often the capital city, receives a disproportionate share of central government expenditures for social and economic infrastructure. This results in greater opportunities for employment, housing, education, and health care, creating a "city lights" effect and making these cities more attractive destinations for migrants from rural areas as well as from other, smaller cities than they would otherwise be. This understanding emphasizes the role of demographic factors in sustaining the primate city, and relates urban primacy to the broader phenomenon of "hyperurbanization" or "overurbanization." In some cases the primate city represents a relatively modern enclave in an otherwise "backward" economy, isolated from the rest of the country by poor transportation and communication linkages with the rest of the country, which, in turn, keeps it from developing the kinds of healthy economic exchanges that would occur in an integrated economy. Thus, in the extreme, the primate city is seen as a hallmark of the disarticulated national economy. Along these lines, some have suggested that the primate city is often a concomitant of internal social and political inequality, particularly in countries in which geographically distinct ethnic groups are the winners and losers in struggles for political power, with the winners implementing policies that favor "their" region and the leading city therein. This may exacerbate these cities' levels of primacy by making them more attractive destinations for migrants from rural areas and from relatively disadvantaged secondary cities.

On the other hand, some scholars have identified the primate city as an outcome of colonial and neocolonial economic and political relations. This seems evident when the primate city was the administrative headquarters of a former colonial power, maintaining, after independence, stronger ties with the former imperial country than with its own national hinterland.

Dependency theorists argued that such cities served as siphoning points in the asymmetrical flows of wealth out of former colonies or neocolonies back to the "metropole," thus contributing to the "development of underdevelopment" (Frank 1967). This approach to the primate city led to framing other aspects of urbanization in terms of theoretical perspectives sensitive to international or global relations of power, such as the world-system perspective on social change. Since the mid-1980s there has been considerable research relating various aspects of urbanization, including primate cities, over-urbanization, and world cities, to what is sometimes called world-system theory.

The bulk of the research and theorizing on the effects of urban primacy has focused on excessive urban primacy relative to "normal" urban primacy (e.g., the rank size rule). Few have discussed the implications of unusually "flat" city size distributions in which the leading cities are similar to each other in terms of population size. An exception is Chase-Dunn's (1985) very long-term study of the global city size distribution, which shows that it has become alternately flatter and more hierarchical (i.e., more lognormal) in response to historically conditioned changes in the world system. For example, when the capitalist world system emerged in the seventeenth century, the city size distribution became more hierarchical with consolidation, integration, and the emergence of a hegemonic core power. But during periods of declining hegemony and corresponding increased rivalry among core powers, the world city size distribution became flatter.

In spite of considerable theoretical conjecture about the causes and consequences of excessive urban primacy, systematic research has provided little in the way of conclusive evidence in support of a particular approach. A fair conclusion from the research seems to be that excessively primate cities emerge from a variety of conditions associated with disarticulated or uneven development in nations (or regions), and that cases of extreme primacy serve as obstacles to achieving balanced regional economic development. Policy solutions have focused on creating alternative "growth poles," where investments in social and economic infrastructure are to be redirected in an effort to boost development in locales other than the primate city but at the same time providing integration (e.g., by improving transportation and communication linkages) with each other and with the primate city. Such policies can be seen as efforts to create balanced development by attempting to build a healthy system of cities.

There has also been a tradition of scholarship on primate cities emphasizing their problematic qualities as places to live, particularly with respect to low-income countries. Rapid population growth, overcrowding, strained infrastructure (including health, education, housing), and even political instability have been themes in the literature on the primate city. However, in recent years, with the remarkable growth in the population sizes of many of the world's largest cities, some within the same country, this line of scholarship has been subsumed under the rubric of "megacities." The megacity literature considers the livability and sustainability of the world's largest cities quite apart from the consideration of systems of cities in which the study of the primate city is embedded theoretically.

Also in recent years, the study of systems of cities has gone global. Scholarship on urbanization has produced a spate of work on "world cities" and "global cities" that theoretically frames the study of the world's great cities as an interrelated system of cities. Some of this research has involved ranking cities in terms of attributes that are theoretically related to their relative importance in the world system of cities. These attributes include indicators of the extent to which each city is an important site for operations of globally powerful firms, such as the top firms in finance and insurance. Similar studies, using formal network analysis, have identified global city hierarchies over time on the basis of each city's role as destination or point of origin in air passenger travel.

The recent research on the primate city per se seems to be primarily about managing urban growth so as to achieve balance across a region or nation, with the goal of implementing policies that promote growth in relatively lagging areas of a nation or region, whereas many of the other concerns that originally gave rise to interest in primate cities are addressed under new rubrics, including megacities, world cities or global cities, and world city systems.

SEE ALSO: Development: Political Economy; Economic Development; Global Economy; Global/World Cities; Megalopolis; Migration and the Labor Force; Modernization; Population and Development; Uneven Development; Urbanization

REFERENCES AND SUGGESTED READINGS

Ades, A. & Glaeser, E. (1995) Trade and Circuses: Explaining Urban Giants. *Quarterly Journal of Economics* 110 (February): 195–227.

Chase-Dunn, C. (1985) The System of World Cities, AD 800–1975. In: Timberlake, M. (Ed.), *Urbanization in the World-Economy*. Academic Press, Orlando, pp. 269–92.

Davis, K. (1976) *World Urbanization, 1950–1970*. Vol. 1: *Basic Data for Cities, Countries, and Regions*, edn. Institute of International Studies, University of California, Berkeley.

Frank, A. G. (1967) *Capitalism and Underdevelopment in Latin America*. Monthly Review Press, New York.

Hawley, A. (1981) *Urban Society: An Ecological Approach*, 2nd edn. Ronald, New York.

Jefferson, M. (1939) The Law of the Primate City. *Geographical Review* 29 (April): 226–32.

Walters, P. B. (1985) Systems of Cities and Urban Primacy: Problems of Definition and Measurement. In: Timberlake, M. (Ed.), *Urbanization in the World-Economy*. Academic Press, Orlando, pp. 63–86.

Zipf, G. (1941) *National Unity and Disunity*. Principia, Bloomington, IN.

primates and cyborgs

Amanda Rees

Where the figures of the primate and the cyborg appear together, they are ineradicably associated with the work of the American historian of consciousness Donna Haraway. Representing utterly different clusters of form, meanings, and demonstrations, the two images share at least one distinct function: they are literally littoral figures, to be found on the category edges, both enacting and transgressing the boundary between nature and culture, body and machine, human and animal. But their significance is not merely to be found in their presentation as a persistent reproach to the philosophical dualisms that have characterized western culture. Both figures invoke politics as well as philosophy, exhibiting and intimating the ways in which politics is implicit in one's philosophical position, and one's political philosophy represents the active choice and creation of a sense of social and cultural identity. In some ways, the primate and the cyborg represent opposite ends of the range of Haraway's understanding of the thematic and practical possibilities for humanity's imagined future, and as such, a consideration of layered meanings that underlie these iconic emblems can be used as a means of accessing and interrogating her wider theoretical project.

The figure of the cyborg came to wider public notice in the "Manifesto for Cyborgs," which appeared in the *Socialist Review* in 1985. This piece was produced and published during the early Reagan years, a period in which American political attitudes toughened both internationally, with the intensification of the Cold War, and internally, with the introduction of hardline neoconservative social and economic policies. The "Manifesto" was an attempt by Haraway to tell a number of different stories, a series of fables or legends, that could allow for an escape from the politics of dualism and would enable socialist feminists to develop new ways of thinking about society, politics, science, and war. At the heart of this ironic parable was the figure of the cyborg. Haraway did not invent the term: according to her account, the neologism originated with the work of Manfred Clynes and Nathan Kline, who used it to refer to the "*cyber*-ernetic *organism*" that would have to be created if humanity was to explore and to colonize extraterrestrial environments. At the moment of the word's inception, then, it was profoundly implicated not just in the nature of the boundary between "man" and "machine," but in the wider politics of the Cold War era and the persistent and profoundly non-prescient presumption that the coming decades would see the unproblematic adoption of technoscientific strategies as the key elements in the pursuit of human happiness and security. For Haraway, the cyborg was the figure that could stand as a symbol of her critique of contemporary politics.

A being that was both animal and machine, but neither bisexual nor gendered, neither innocent nor guilty, would enable one to demonstrate the nature of the breakdown of identity and identity politics and the realignment of both globalized and domestic social relations as a result of technoscience revolutions – and in particular, to demonstrate the consequences of these developments for women. Having shown the extent to which situated identities had shifted as high technology made it harder to maintain the old dichotomies of hierarchical domination, replacing them with the authoritative informatics of the command–control–communication intelligence characteristic of the developed military-industrial society, she further developed her account of the meanings and significances of the cyborg in a 1992 article, "The Promise of Monsters."

Far more than the "Manifesto," this article represented a sustained attempt to show how the figure of the cyborg could be used to illuminate different networks of social, political, and technological relationships. "Promise of Monsters" is presented as a mapping exercise and as a series of demonstrations that the power to speak, or to speak out, is not restricted to particular positions or roles, but can depend on the destabilization of such positions. In this article, Haraway uses the notion of the cyborg as a means of moving through art and literature, science and advertising, protest and practice, to show how presumed analytical border lines can become front lines in the struggle to understand and so to avoid the structures and technologies of domination that underlie much that is taken for granted in the cultures that surround us. Much of this work turns on the idea that contradiction and confusion are in fact the only safe places from which to begin the reconstructions of identity that would enable the escape from the dialectics of dichotomy. Only by attending to the chaotic, enculturated circumstances of each border crossing – each encounter between the individual and the Other, nature with culture, body with machine – can one hope to move beyond dualisms and approach an understanding of a much messier, context-laden, contradictory version of biopolitics, where the nature of authority and the authority to speak of nature are simultaneously intertwined and in opposition.

Similar themes within a different series of perspectives are illuminated by the figure of the primate, which appeared within Haraway's work at much the same time, and sometimes in similar places, as did the cyborg. Unlike the cyborg, however, the primate was much more evidently situated within particular examples of scientific practice – specifically, the history of primatology, or of human encounters with the non-human primates. Haraway cast her explorations of primate convergences firmly within the context of the interrogation of the relationships and boundaries that could be shown to exist between nature and culture in the late twentieth century, using primate investigations as a means of illuminating the ways in which the broader themes of western culture – race, gender, ethnicity, class, nationality, and sexuality – had been and were being written into and onto nature. Primates, known to be the closest living relations of humanity, could be shown to occupy the trading zones, the transit zones between nature and culture, and depending on the location of the observer, could reveal either the naturalness of culture, or the enculturation of nature. It all depended on which standpoint one looked from, in which direction, and where one chose to focus one's gaze.

When the scientific investigations of the lives, the societies, and the psychology of the non-human primates began in the early twentieth century, they were explicitly presented as a means by which humans could come more closely to apprehend the nature of their own biological history and the capacities and limitations of human nature itself. That is, the non-human primates were not necessarily being studied for their own sake, but in order to advance our understanding of humanity itself. Some elements of human behavior that appeared central to the definition of humanity itself were difficult, if not impossible, to study in humans. The origin of language or of social life could not be directly observed in the laboratory, and to attempt to produce them in the laboratory using human subjects was clearly impossible – both the ethical and the practical problems were formidable. Additionally, since human relationships simply did not exist in the absence of a shared culture, it was deemed difficult to

investigate human nature in a way that would not be confounded by such cultural expectations. Initially, some scientists had turned to what were considered to be more primitive versions of human cultures – those societies that had come under progressively greater European imperial control during the nineteenth century – but decolonization and a more historicized understanding of the development of, for example, hunter-gatherer society made this approach difficult, if not impossible, to sustain. However, the close relationship between humans and non-human primates, which had been recognized long before it was possible to measure the amount of DNA shared between species, meant that the behavioral strategies and mental capacities of the other primates would probably be similar to our own – but would be expressed in a much simpler way, since the biological signal would be free of the cultural noise.

Since this was the intention, it is ironic in the extreme that the work of Haraway and other writers such as Pamela Asquith, Shirley Strum, and Linda Fedigan should so effectively have demonstrated the extent to which the study of primatology and the image of the primate are hopelessly impacted with encultured expectations of the human, the non-human, the natural, and the social. Asquith's work was based on a comparison of the Japanese and the western styles of studying primates, and she was able to show that the accounts of primate social life emerging from these distinct traditions bore a close resemblance to the cultural expectations of appropriately socialized behavior in the different national contexts. Strum and Fedigan, primatologists themselves, successfully illustrated the ways in which the concerns of westernized primatology shifted over the decades following World War II in accordance with wider cultural shifts concerning the role of women, the practices of politics, and the shifting line being drawn between human and animal intelligences over the course of that half-century. Haraway's impressive survey of the field (*Primate Visions*, 1989) allusively and elusively indicated the ways in which the study of primates over the course of the twentieth century was thoroughly embroiled and implicated in attempts to define and to demarcate something that was shaped by so many dimensions as to refuse distinction: nature both produces and is itself produced by culture, and the attempt to resist the imposition of this fundamental natural/cultural duality is what lies at the heart of Haraway's wider project.

Like the cyborg, the primate is used by Haraway to demonstrate the extent to which the dichotomies, the demarcations, and the distinctions that have been at the heart of the western apprehension of the world have either become, or are becoming, unsustainable. Whether the perspective is philosophical, political, or personal, if one is to reach a fuller understanding of the range of relationships that can potentially exist within the world, then nature cannot be opposed to culture, female cannot be opposed to male, society cannot be opposed to science. Primates in particular are used to illustrate the ways in which science and society are categories artificially imposed on an incoherent cultural landscape: understanding primatology requires attention and sensitivity to the role of gender, the specificities of the animal–human relationship, the politics of science, of art, culture, practice, and institution. It can be understood as trading zone, a hybrid zone, an implosive zone, especially perhaps a transitory zone – but simultaneously as a place where real events occur, where practice becomes theory as theory is enacted.

The primate and the cyborg are not the only creatures (real and chimeric) to play these roles on Haraway's analytic stage. She has alternatively adopted such figures as the coyote, the modest witness, the vampire, the white rabbit, the trickster keyboard, and the metaphorical mirror – but in the recent past, the concept of the companion animal has come to loom large in her work, and to bear comparison with the earlier boundary figures. Like the primate and the cyborg, the companion animal represents a blending of nature and culture, lying on and therefore crossing the boundary that is so elemental to the socialized westerner's understanding of the world. In a sense, dogs have replaced cyborgs in Haraway's work, since where cyborgs represented individual beings, the idea of a companion animal requires that beings must by definition be in a relationship. Rather than humans domesticating dogs for protection, for hunting, and for herding, it is possible to regard the relationship as co-constitutive: dogs and humans evolved together, and each had a role to play in the creation of each other. We specify breeds of dog in the same way that humans used to specify race, with a similar lack of genetic support for the idea of purity or separation – dog breeds, like human races, represent both morphological reality and historical contingency and consequences. Although Haraway's account remains fragmentary, like the earlier primates and cyborgs, companion animals – or companion species, which is an even wider acknowledgment of potential moral community – demonstrate the analytical fluidity of categories thought to be concrete.

SEE ALSO: Anthrozoology; Body and Society; Feminism and Science, Feminist Epistemology; Feminist Methodology; Science and Culture

REFERENCES AND SUGGESTED READINGS

Asquith, P. (1996) Japanese Science and Western Hegemonies: Primatology and the Limits Set to Questions. In: Nadler, L. (Ed.), *Naked Science: Anthropological Inquiry into Boundaries, Power, and Knowledge.* Routledge, New York.

Haraway, D. (1985) A Manifesto for Cyborgs: Science, Technology, and Socialist Feminism in the 1980s. *Socialist Review* 80: 65–108.

Haraway, D. (1991) *Simians, Cyborgs, and Women: The Reinvention of Nature.* Routledge, New York.

Haraway, D. (1992) The Promise of Monsters: A Regenerated Politics for Inappropriate/d Others. In: Grossberg, L., Newlson, C., & Treichler, P. (Eds.), *Cultural Studies.* Routledge, New York.

Haraway, D. (2004) *The Haraway Reader.* Routledge, London.

Harding, S. (1998) *Is Science Multicultural? Postcolonialism, Feminism, and Epistemologies.* Indiana University Press, Indiana.

Keller, E. F. (1992) *Secrets of Life, Secrets of Death.* Routledge, New York.

Rees, A. (2000) Anthropomorphism, Anthropocentrism, and Anecdote: Primatologists on Primatology. *Science, Technology, and Human Values.*

Strum, S. & Fedigan, L. (Eds.) (2000) *Primate Encounters.* University of Chicago Press, Chicago.

primitive religion

Peter B. Clarke

The evolutionary character of theories of primitive religion is present in the sociological literature from the beginning. It is evident, for example, in the writings of the so-called founding father of sociology, Auguste Comte (1798–1857), who believed that religion originated in fetishism or the worship of inanimate things, then developed into polytheism which in turn developed into monotheism (Comte 1853). The view that religion evolved from polytheism to monotheism is, of course, much older than the formal beginnings of sociology and anthropology as academic disciplines. It is present in the Scottish philosopher David Hume's *The Natural History of Religion* (1759). The nineteenth-century theorists – they would today be classified as armchair anthropologists and sociologists – most closely associated with the construction of the concept of primitive religion were less concerned about religion per se and its nature and more about finding proof with which to discredit the so-called higher religions and in particular Christianity. Their intention was to discover the origins of primitive religion or religion in its most basic or elementary form in order to show that it was profoundly mistaken and arose from ignorance or some emotional need and that the so-called higher religions which derived from such erroneous ideas and behavior did not therefore merit the assent and commitment of rational and emotionally mature and balanced people. In fact, religion held society back.

Among the better-known of the nineteenth-century theorists of primitive religion was the Orientalist and authority on mythology Max Müller (1823–1900) who claimed (1893) that religion was grounded in an intuitive sense of the divine which everyone possessed and which was awakened by the wonder and power of nature. Religion began in this way as metaphor and symbol and eventually the natural objects that evoked thoughts and feelings of the infinite were personified as gods in their own right. Others like the sociologist Herbert Spencer (1820–1903), who defined progress and the development of the heterogeneous out of the homogeneous, maintained that religion began with ancestor worship, or more precisely with belief in the continued existence of the souls or ghosts of remote ancestors which in time were deified (Spencer 1901–7). The process of deifying ancestors exists in many societies, including the Yoruba society of southwestern Nigeria, but there is no evidence that the religion of these people began in this way. Spencer then asserts that the notion of soul or ghost developed into that of god or divinity. Thus, it is assumed without any supporting evidence that the notion of ghost is the first ever notion of divinity devised by humans.

The anthropologist Edward Tylor (1832–1917), whose main interest was in the evolution of society and its institutions, opposed theories of religion that reduced the phenomenon to the psychological immaturity of early human beings, and sought to base his own theory on reason, hence the description of his approach as intellectualist. Like Spencer, Tylor also traces the origins of religion to the development of the idea of the soul, which he contended originated in dreams. So-called primitive people were alleged to believe that the soul left the body during sleep and actually experienced what they had been dreaming about while asleep, and inferred that this behavior would continue after death. Hence also the idea of immortality. Tylor went further, however, claiming that such people not only personified all other beings like themselves, but also natural phenomena, and endowed the latter also with souls. Tylor's use of the term soul in preference to ghost or spirit led to his being regarded as the founder of the animist theory of the origins of religion. As for his approach to the question of religion's origins, this is described as intellectualist principally for the reason that it insists on offering a rational basis for the belief in the soul, which it argues did not derive from fear or superstition or psychological immaturity on the part of the primitive, but resulted instead from a deductive and logical process, even if the reasoning was mistaken. While, as Evans-Prichard (1965: 25) has pointed out, it is possible that the notion of the soul developed in this way, there is no evidence to say it did.

Tylor's successor at Oxford, the barrister and anthropologist Robert Marett (1866–1943), is credited with being the father of the pre-animist theory of religion (Marett 2001). He argued that in terms of its beginnings, a rudimentary religion, a form of supernaturalism consisting of awe of the mysterious, existed prior to ideas of soul, ghost, and spirit. It was this attitude of mind that provided religion with its raw material and could exist apart from animism and indeed might well have been the basis for animistic beliefs. This theory was based on Marett's interpretation of studies on Melanesian religious life and in particular its concept of *mana*. Religion, he insisted, was something that was lived or acted out: it helped the primitive to live, it provided the necessary assurance of being in touch with a higher power, and it offered hope and induced fear. Marett reduces both magic and religion to psychological states and suggests that they function most effectively in situations of emotional stress.

Sir James Frazer (1854–1941), author of the monumental and widely known work on primitive superstitions *The Golden Bough* (1920), also differed from Tylor in propounding a developmental theory of religion in which he introduced a pre-religious stage in the form of a magical phase. His theory bears a striking resemblance (in the way it describes religion's evolution from magic to religion and religion to science) to Auguste Comte's three phases of intellectual development: the theological, metaphysical, and positive. Relying on ethnographical data of poor quality, Frazer, the last of the great armchair evolutionists, was to claim that magic characterized simple societies, and as they became more complex they also became less superstitious and more scientific and rational, a line of argument for which there is no proof worthy of the name. Moreover, like Lucien Lévy-Bruhl, he wrongly viewed magic as an elementary form of modern science, but differed from the latter by mistaking ideal for real connections between things.

Intellectualist theories of the kind advanced by Tylor and Frazer were in turn opposed by thinkers concerned to locate the origins of "primitive" religion in social structure rather than logic and emotion. The best known and most influential theorists to adopt this approach were Robertson Smith (1846–94) and Émile Durkheim (1858–1917). According to Smith, the clan cult or totemism was the earliest and most elementary form of religion

and was best accounted for and understood by reference to its social character, an idea for which he was indebted to Fustel de Coulange (1830–99) and in particular to his major work *The Ancient City* (1980), a work that also influenced Durkheim.

Durkheim was unimpressed by the kind of animist, intellectualist, emotionalist, and action-based theories of primitive religion advanced by Spencer, Tylor, Frazer, Marett, and others, and indeed by any theory that suggested religion was false or an illusion. Primitive religion was the earliest in the sense of simplest form of religion. It was the form that was practiced when human society was passing through its simplest form. Moreover, far from being an illusion, it was as much a thing or social fact, in the sense that it was a reality external to the individual, as any other thing or social fact. It enjoyed the same degree of reality as any material thing. It rested on a permanent underlying reality that could be uncovered if studied objectively: that is, society. Religion belonged, Durkheim argued, to the class of social facts that includes established beliefs and practices that were the product of the collectivity and/or a group within society. By treating religion in this way Durkheim believed he had given it a foothold in reality and made it accessible to scientific analysis. As to its earliest, most elementary or primitive form, Durkheim maintained that this was to be found in totemism, an idea he borrowed from Robertson Smith. He used the available ethnographic material on the Australian aboriginals and in particular the Arunta to demonstrate his thesis, published as the *The Elementary Forms of the Religious Life* (1915). What bound clan members together, he argued in this study, was that each and every one of the members had the same totem, which in several senses was regarded as sacred, including the sense that it symbolized the totemic principle in the form of an impersonal religious force which he referred to as *mana*.

In Durkheim's evolutionist understanding of it, religion would regress – regression was also a notion used by Spencer in respect to civilizations and their institutions – as social institutions developed. As an example he pointed to religion's loss of control in modern society over men's (*sic*) minds compared with primitive society (where he contended religion dominated everything) and went on to argue that to become intensely religious again it would be necessary for society to return to the beginning. In his own words religion could not regain its domination over people's minds as in primitive society "unless the great societies crumble and we return to small social groups of long ago, that is unless humanity returns to its starting point, religion will never be able to exert deep or wide sway over consciousness" (Durkheim 1952: 430).

Although Durkheim's highly speculative account of the origins of religion has been heavily criticized on methodological, logical, ethnographic, and other grounds, it nevertheless contains many valuable insights and remains one of the most thought provoking and influential studies of the sociological character of religion, particularly that part of it that treats the purposes and functions of ritual.

An almost exact contemporary of Durkheim, the German sociologist Max Weber (1864–1920), regarded as one of the founders of modern sociology and most widely known for his thesis linking Protestantism to the rise of modern capitalism and his comparative sociology based on the principle of *verstehen* or empathic understanding, also began his analysis of religion from an evolutionist perspective by looking at its most elementary forms. These, he believed, were to be found in the religions of tribal societies in which, he contended, questionably, people were so preoccupied with meeting their everyday needs that they had little alternative but to practice magic rather than religion. Such people were largely concerned with attempting to manipulate and coerce the gods, whom they conceived as being part of this world and immanent, rather than as in religion, which has a more transcendental conception of their status, with worshipping them. Thus, according to Weber (1965), elementary or primitive religion tends toward the magical and out of this emerges religious conceptions, as human society evolves. Magic begins to develop into religion when the extraordinary qualities or mystical powers (referred to as *mana* by Durkheim, Marett, and others, and as *charisma* by Weber) that are believed to inhere in objects are attributed less to the objects themselves and increasingly to a reality behind them, as it were, such as a soul, spirit, or demon. Thus, once the source of this

power came to be perceived as being outside the material world, and the spirits behind it came to be regarded as being more and more removed from this world, the way was open, Weber maintained, for ethical rationalization to begin to dominate religious attitudes. At this stage of religious evolution the gods become increasingly bound up with ethical considerations, and values and principles replace self-interest as the core concerns of religion. Thus, Weber suggests, religion only truly begins with the appearance of ethical rationalization, and coterminous with this development is the demise of the central role of the magician and the rise of a priesthood that concerns itself with intellectual matters such as the formulation of doctrinal and ethical systems.

PRIMITIVE RELIGION AS MONOTHEISTIC

Andrew Lang (1844–1912) and the Catholic priest Wilhelm Schmidt (1868–1954) challenged the traditional understanding of the content of primitive religious belief. The latter contended that primitive monotheism predated the technological advances some believe led to it. Schmidt, founder of the journal *Anthropos* (1906), sought to establish a chronology of primitive cultures from circumstantial evidence. Like Lang, he maintained that people who were on the lowest rung of the ladder of social and cultural development were monotheists. Schmidt, though he was concerned to discredit the evolutionary kind of ethnography and ethnology prevalent in his day, did not escape their influence. He also believed he had been able to identify the ethnologically oldest people whom he claimed belonged to the most primitive culture. However, this was a culture in which totemism, fetishism, magic, and belief in ghosts or spirits were absent. Instead, these were a people who, by observation and inference, had come to believe in one, eternal, all-knowing, all-powerful, beneficent God who satisfied all their desires and wants. Once again, no strong evidence is supplied in support of this thesis on the origins of religion and primitive thinking about God and the supernatural order. As a theory, however, it was not without influence, shaping as it did the thinking of some missionaries working in various part of the world about the beliefs of so called primitive people.

LÉVY-BRUHL AND THE PRELOGICAL PRIMITIVES

The notion of primitive religion is closely linked not only to that of primitive society but also to the concept of primitive mentality, especially as it was developed by the French philosopher Lucien Lévy-Bruhl (1857–1939), who in his *La Mentalité primitive* (1922) set about describing its attributes. He was not convinced by the theories of Tylor and Frazer, which assumed that the only difference between primitive and more advanced people was not one of intellect but of ignorance, the former being more ignorant than the latter. In terms of intellect, both were the same.

Lévy-Bruhl saw things differently. Starting from the assumption that each type of society has its own distinctive mentality he contended that, broadly speaking, there were two types of society: primitive and civilized. He then proceeded to argue that there existed two types of mentality: primitive and civilized. These modes of thought, Lévy-Bruhl maintained, were collective in the sense of being all-pervasive, taken-for-granted ways of thinking to which there were no exceptions. The primitive mode he characterized as essentially prelogical and/or mystical, and the civilized as logical. The primitive mentality is prelogical and/or mystical in the sense that primitive people do not make the distinctions between the natural and the supernatural order that so-called modern, civilized people make. The latter are capable thus of seeking the causes of things in natural processes and explaining them scientifically. Primitive thought is guided by what he termed the law of participation and does not concern itself with contradiction or the rule of logic, but is rather held together by links or connections that do not conform to the logical thought patterns of more advanced peoples.

Lévy-Bruhl is not suggesting by this that primitives are innately incapable of reasoning or thinking logically or that they are a-logical, illogical, or anti-logical. He is describing the categories in which they reason, their collective representations and the mystical realities in which they move and which shape their thought. It is for this reason that primitives reason incorrectly and not because, as Tylor and Frazer suggest, their logical processes were mistaken. However, like the rest of the above-mentioned theorizing about primitive religion, there is no evidence to support Lévy-Bruhl's argument that "primitive thought" differs in quality from "civilized thought." Neither is there any basis for classifying en bloc whole peoples who differ so much from each other socially, culturally, and economically as either primitives or civilized, nor can it be automatically assumed that there is a contradiction between a scientific, causal explanation and a mystical one, or that because something is thought of in mystical terms it cannot also be understood scientifically (and the converse).

MODERN USAGE

While realizing its limitations and controversial character, some scholars have nevertheless offered a robust defense of their use of the term primitive religion. Douglas (1966: 81–2) considers her use of the term in the more general context of a discussion of the distinguishing features of the notion of primitive worldview, which she suggests be characterized by non-differentiation. She also describes this worldview as subjective and personal, one in which different modes of existence are confused, and one in which the limitations of man's (*sic*) being are not known. It is anthropomorphic and resembles, Douglas maintains, a pre-Copernican worldview. The belief of the !Kung Bushmen of the Kalahari Desert in N!ow provides a good example in her view of belief in anthropocentric powers.

Regarding the question of the use of the term primitive and whether it should be abandoned, Douglas expresses the hope that its use will not be discontinued, on the grounds that if this concept can be given a valid meaning in art and technology, and possibly economics also, then presumably it can also be given a similar sense when used of a certain kind of culture. While accepting that it can have a pejorative sense when used of religious beliefs, she is not convinced that because of this the label should be abandoned and suggests that to do so could well amount to an inverted form of superiority.

Evans-Pritchard (1965) defends his use of the term primitive on the following grounds: that he uses it in a value-free sense, is obliged to use the language of those he is critiquing, that it is too firmly established to be dropped, and that etymologically it is unobjectionable. He also points out that the term primitive can be used in both a chronological sense (as it is used by him) and a logical sense, both of which should be kept distinct.

Others do not go to such lengths to defend their use of the term. Bellah (1964) in his treatise on religious evolution – in which one of the categories used is that of primitive religion – is more anxious to make clear what he means by evolution in this case. Evolving religion as he understands it is a symbol system that develops from a compact or primitive form or state to a more differentiated or modern one, the latter not necessarily being better or truer or more beautiful than the former. Thus, religious evolution involves a process of increasing differentiation and complexity of organization. The outcome of this process is to endow the particular system in question, in this case religion, with the greater capacity to adapt to its environment, thus becoming more autonomous in relation to that environment than was the case in its less complex stage. This is the underlying assumption on which Bellah constructs his evolutionary scheme of religion, which begins with primitive religion and evolves into archaic religion, followed by historic religion, early modern religion, and modern religion. These types are not seen as completely distinct, nor does Bellah suggest that this kind of evolution is either inevitable or irreversible.

Confining comment to Bellah's primitive religion, this owes much to Lévy-Bruhl's (1922) notions of the mythical world and to research on the mythical world of Australian religion – in particular, anthropological interpretations of the core concept of Dreaming. Bellah's world of primitive religion is a world in which the actual and mythical worlds are closely related to each other, and one which – in terms of its organization – is extremely fluid. He characterizes primitive religion itself in language reminiscent of Marett: it is given over not to worship or sacrifice, but is characterized by identification, participation, or acting out. It is ritual based. As to primitive religion's social implications, Bellah suggests in line with Durkheim that they consist in reinforcing social solidarity and in socializing the young into the norms of tribal society. These goals and the fluidity and flexibility of primitive religion militate against any kind of radical change.

Stark and Bainbridge (1987) construct a general theory of religion that is also evolutionist after a fashion. Again, it suggests that religion develops from more compact to more differentiated forms. It is argued that when societies reach a certain size and level of complexity specific social organizations emerge, including religious organizations. While in its early stages religion was closely related to magic, Stark and Bainbridge suggest that as society becomes more complex they become increasingly differentiated in terms of specialists and organizations. With increasing complexity the idea of gods emerged, who, though considered to be supernatural beings, were believed to share with humans the attributes of consciousness and desire and come to be seen as supernatural exchange partners who bestow upon humans rewards in return for the fulfillment of certain obligations. As society became even more complex the number of gods decreased – in other words polytheism has tended to give way to monotheism – and religious specialists have emerged to provide explanations of how rewards can be obtained, or if not the actual rewards themselves then how general "compensators" of a supernatural kind can be guaranteed and the costs involved assessed.

Prior to all of this in a simpler, less differentiated world people had resort to magic, which in the opinion of Stark and Bainbridge differs from religion in that it offers very specific compensators that are easily disconfirmed. Therefore, unlike religion, it does not have the capacity to foster long-term exchange relationships and as a consequence does not develop into an organization such as a church.

CONCLUSION

The reasons behind the largely pointless search for the origins of religion in the nineteenth

century and first part of the twentieth century
have been outlined above. We have also seen that
well into the late twentieth century some scholars – in their attempt to construct a refined
evolutionist theory of the development of religion – have continued to apply the term primitive to what they consider to be its earliest form.
Despite the caveats and qualifications offered for
the continuing use of this term, the question
whether it should be retained remains. It is such
a highly controversial term as to suggest that
there is a strong need for a replacement, such
as *traditional* or *early forms* of religion, although
these two terms also have their limitations.
While the label *early forms* is virtually free of
any pejorative meanings, the limitations associated with the term primitive are especially
evident in relation to the term traditional, which
can convey the sense of stagnation and imply
that a society where this type of religion is the
norm is a society that is unchanging and lacking in dynamism and creativity. Although the
term traditional is hardly value-free either and
raises serious methodological problems, it is less
pejorative than the concept of primitive and of
greater value analytically. As Evans-Pritchard
(1965) pointed out, the term primitive as used of
religion creates only confusion and is likely most
of the time to generate in the mind of the reader
a negative stereotype about the religious beliefs,
worldview, and practices to which it is applied
and by implication about those who adhere to
them.

SEE ALSO: Belief; Durkheim, Émile; Magic;
Myth; Positivism; Religion; Religion, Sociology
of; Sacred

REFERENCES AND SUGGESTED READINGS

Bellah, R. (1964) Religious Evolution. *American Sociological Review* 29: 358–74.
Clarke, P. B. & Byrne, P. A. (1993) *Religion Defined and Explained*. Macmillan, Basingstoke.
Comte, A. (1853) *The Positive Philosophy*, 2 vols. Trans. H. Martineau. Trübner, London.
Douglas, M. (1966) *Purity and Danger*. Routledge & Kegan Paul, London.
Douglas, M. (1973) *Natural Symbols*. Penguin, London.
Durkheim, É. (1915) *The Elementary Forms of the Religious Life*. George Allen & Unwin, London.
Durkheim, É. (1952 [1897]) *Suicide: A Study in Sociology*. Routledge & Kegan Paul, London.
Evans-Pritchard, E. E. (1965) *Theories of Primitive Religion*. Clarendon Press, Oxford.
Frazer, J. (1920) *The Golden Bough*. Macmillan, London.
Fustel de Coulange, N.-D. (1980) *The Ancient City*. Johns Hopkins University Press, Baltimore.
Hume, D. (1977) *The Natural History of Religion and Dialogues Concerning Natural Religion*. Ed. A. W. Culver & J. V. Price. Clarendon Press, Oxford.
Lévy-Bruhl, L. (1922) *La Mentalité primitive*. Alcan, Paris.
Lévy-Bruhl, L. (1926) *How Natives Think*. George Allen & Unwin, London.
Marett, R. (2001 [1909]) *The Threshold of Religion*. Elibron, London.
Müller, M. F. (1893) *Introduction to the Science of Religion*. Longman, London.
Runciman, W. G. (Ed.) (1978) *Weber: Selections in Translation*. Cambridge University Press, Cambridge.
Schmidt, W. (1931) *The Origin and Growth of Religion*. Cooper Square Publishers, New York.
Spencer, H. (1901–7) *Principles of Sociology*. D. Appleton, New York.
Stark, R. & Bainbridge, W. S. (1987) *A Theory of Religion*. Lang, New York.
Weber, M. (1965) *The Sociology of Religion*. Methuen, London.

print media

Dan E. Miller

Print refers to the production of text and images
by applying inked types or plates with direct
pressure onto paper. The process of printing,
reproducing a manuscript in printed pages,
allows the rapid production of multiple copies
of books, pamphlets, periodicals, and newspapers that can be distributed to a reading public.
A *medium* (pl. media) refers to the materials and
format through which significant symbols are
arranged, formatted, presented, and delivered
from one person to others. The printed page
is a medium of mass communication. Words,
visual images, and other symbols are arranged
on printed pages as discrete units, most often
in linear sequences that cumulatively construct
observations, ideas, arguments, and stories.

Produced in large numbers, printed pages are bound together and dispersed to people who, if literate, read the same text. In this way, the medium of print binds people together into a larger community.

Print media include books, pamphlets, periodicals, newspapers, and typewritten or photocopied manuscripts. A book is any printed publication of substantial length. Books are distinguished from pamphlets by their length, with pamphlets having fewer than 96 (or 64) pages. Books are distinguished from periodicals and newspapers not only by their length, but also because they are issued as a single unit whereas periodicals and newspapers are available with new content on a regular basis. Also, books are considered more important, requiring preservation, whereas periodicals are most often discarded after a short period of time. Books preserve information, knowledge, and narratives of enduring relevance, while newspapers and magazines are more constrained by events of the moment. Books preserve timeless information; newspapers present timely information.

Print media meet several needs for a complex society. These include the following functions.

1 *Information function*: the public learns about significant events and government actions.
2 *Surveillance function*: the public learns about dangers and opportunities.
3 *Solidarity function*: community identity and cultural continuity are developed.
4 *Agenda-setting function*: social, political, and economic priorities are set by leaders.
5 *Community forum function*: through print important issues are discussed.
6 *Entertainment function*.

In addition to these positive functions, Merton and Lazarsfeld (1948) have identified a troubling process – the *narcotizing dysfunction* – wherein the inundation of information about an issue or event tends to make the reader complacent, comfortably numbed by the overcoverage. Aware but tired of the issue, people fail to act even if the issue is highly compelling.

Reading the history of print leads to the conclusion that the printing press was a key agent of social change (Eisenstein 1979), but only in those places in which the printing press developed in a marketplace context (Couch 1996).

The general principle concerning the development of print and subsequent social change was first articulated by H. A. Innis and Marshall McLuhan. Both offered a soft technological determinist argument that new forms of information technology undermine established media and traditional authority, ultimately establishing a new dominant medium and a new form of authority. The development of the printing press, the mass production of books and pamphlets, and the subsequent development of mass literacy undermined the authority of prior written texts and their interpretation by church officials. The Protestant Reformation and the emerging rational logic of the Enlightenment led to massive social, political, and intellectual change in Europe.

Developed in China in the first century CE, papermaking techniques were introduced into Europe via Spain by Arabs in the thirteenth century. Manuscripts became far less expensive to produce, and paper allowed writing on both sides. Collected sheets of paper were then bound into books. Most early books were reproduced by scribes affiliated with the Catholic Church. The majority of books written and reproduced were ecclesiastical. Ownership of books and literacy were restricted to a small, elite minority. Collections of books often were stored in monasteries. Readers of books, writers, and those who copied them settled near the collections, forming communities of scholars.

In Europe, the first mechanical printing press was invented around 1450 by Johannes Gutenberg (ca. 1397–1468), a goldsmith and merchant, in Mainz, Germany. Gutenberg was not the first to reproduce manuscripts onto paper via moveable type. This process was first accomplished in eleventh-century China. Gutenberg's method of printing with moveable type was developed without knowledge of printing being done in Asia. To make the printing process more efficient, Gutenberg converted a winepress into a mechanical printing press, and using cast metal moveable type he was able to reproduce books quickly and inexpensively. Gutenberg's masterpiece, the 42-line Mazarin Bible, was published in 1455. Gutenberg's printing press was the first mass production technology. The publication of an increasing number of books created the potential for mass literacy, particularly in societies where written language was composed using a phonetic alphabet – the visual representation of sounds (phonemes) which could be sounded out in sequence to form words (morphemes), sentences, and so on.

The European printing industry grew slowly at first, with only ten cities having printing presses in 1471. By 1481 over 100 printing presses were spread throughout Europe. By the end of the fifteenth century nearly every city in Europe had commercial printing presses. While printing presses proliferated, the number of books published grew slowly. Only 219 books were published in 1580 in England. That number grew to 600 books in 1800 and nearly 14,000 books in 1990. Some of the earliest population centers to adopt a printing press were university cities, where a symbiotic relationship was established between scholars and printers. The scholars both wrote and purchased books, while the printers reproduced and sold them.

In the early decades of the printing press neither state nor religious authorities attempted to control the growing print industry. Those authorities did not feel threatened. Before 1500 most books were printed in Latin and were much the same as those reproduced by scribes. However, within a few decades most books were published in the vernacular, the language spoken by the people. In the 1520s Martin Luther published the German Bible, believing there should be no mediation between the common man and the Bible, proclaiming that every Christian was a priest and every citizen was able to read the word of God. By 1550, over 30 vernacular translations of the Bible were in circulation.

Church authorities took little note of the printing industry until criticisms of the church began to be published and distributed in the early sixteenth century. Papal edicts did little to stem the flow of criticism. That criticism grew to major proportions when Martin Luther nailed his 95 theses to the door of Wittenberg church in 1517. With printing presses as commercial enterprises and printed materials increasingly oriented to public concerns, the Catholic Church could not contain the spread of alternative definitions of reality offered by Protestants and other reformers. As more people became literate, nearly every home became a school where the Bible and other books were

studied without the interference of a priest or other authority.

McLuhan's famous aphorism, "the medium is the message," suggests that each new medium of communication creates new symbolic and perceptual environments, making possible new forms of consciousness, thought, and knowledge as we adapt to the new environments. For example, the print medium and the act of reading formed the foundation of critical and reflexive thought. Access to books without direct surveillance and accountability allowed people to read, interpret, stop, think, write, and begin reading again. Inherent in the social form of reading is an absence of immediate reciprocity. Rather, the reader is alone with the text and his thoughts. Consequently, individual identities developed. A culture of individual thinking in a world of ideas was born. Readers tend to have an active life of the mind, full of knowledge, imagination, and a heightened awareness of the world and the possibilities it holds – a form of consciousness that was threatening to the traditional ecclesiastical authority of the church and to the uncritical obeisance demanded by the state.

In those societies where the printing press was controlled by state or ecclesiastical authorities, large-scale social change did not occur. For example, shortly after manuscripts were first printed in China, the state took control of the printing and distribution of those manuscripts. Print technology spread from China to other Asian nations, but always as a state-controlled activity. While a great many books were published, only a few of each were printed and very few were circulated. The printing process, libraries, and literacy were tightly controlled. Standing authorities were not threatened. Similarly, a printing press was not established in a Muslim country until 1727 and then for only a few years. The first permanent printing press was established in Egypt after Napoleon's conquest in 1798. Nearly all printing presses were and continue to be controlled by Islamic authorities.

As printing developed, an interest in accuracy and correct interpretations emerged. Scholars began to note inconsistencies between traditional writings and their own observations. Removing or correcting inconsistencies in texts grew increasingly common. For example, Roger

Bacon called for the correction of the calendar because Easter was no longer being observed after the vernal equinox. By the sixteenth century, secular books began to outsell religious books. At the same time, secular intellectuals began to replace the clergy as sources of knowledge. Both secular scientific and pragmatic knowledge received greater attention and was increasingly accepted as valid knowledge. As the Enlightenment expanded in the eighteenth century, reason and science trumped faith as rationalizations for action. The printed page had undermined religious authority and teachings. Print media had altered society and the minds of those who read.

As printing continued to grow as a commercial enterprise, an increasing number of people began reading for pleasure – *ludenic reading* – which requires solitude and an expansive period of time. Ludenic reading is not always a trivial pursuit. It, too, can lead to significant social change by fostering a sense of injustice and desire to correct that injustice. Published in 1776, Thomas Paine's *Common Sense* sold 100,000 copies in two months and went through 25 editions. It is estimated that half the adult population in the American colonies read Paine's incendiary pamphlet and, in doing so, redefined the colonies' relationship to Great Britain and the British monarchy. Another example of this process involves the success of Harriet Beecher Stowe's *Uncle Tom's Cabin*, published in 1850. Several million people read this book, and within a year of its publication strong public sentiment in opposition to slavery had arisen in the Northern states, culminating in the abolitionist movement. These books provided an awareness of injustice, of alternative arrangements, and they provided a vocabulary for change. By the end of the nineteenth century, books had become the dominant sources of entertainment, valid information, and knowledge. Citizens consulted books and not people when they were searching for information. Knowledge became significant in and of itself – worthy of being preserved.

The spread of information through a community predates newspapers. Town criers, visitors with information from elsewhere, and rumors all reported information about current issues and events. However, "the news" as the regular reporting of significant daily events emerged along with the establishment of the printing press, particularly in cities. In order to capture a large share of the reading public, the news as a regular forum of information was dependent on the gathering, rapid production, and dissemination of desired information and ideas. For this a printing press was required.

The first news sheet, the *Notizie Scritta*, was published in 1556 in Venice. This irregular paper reported on the arrival of ships, items for sale, and happenings from abroad. It was called a *gazetta* for the coin it cost to purchase it. By 1605, newspapers appeared in Germany, France, and Belgium. These newspapers typically carried stories about the happenings in a community, including economic and political activities, and hijinks involving the ruling elite. Governmental authorities, who had been slow to react to books, responded quickly to newspapers, particularly those critical of the government and the aristocratic elite. In 1632 the monarchy banned all "news books" in England. However, nearly all newspapers were profitable commercial enterprises and governmental acts to suppress or destroy them proved to be ineffective. Some editors and publishers were jailed and their presses destroyed, but as soon as one was suppressed another newspaper appeared. In 1644 John Milton advocated the concept of "the marketplace of ideas" and opposed the practice of censorship. His position was based on the notion that from the free flow of ideas came truth which would free us.

Most early newspapers were fiercely partisan, competing to establish a consensual definition of reality. The term "public opinion" emerged early in the eighteenth century as newspaper reading increased and those who regularly read the news began to develop a reflective standpoint toward authorities and the issues of the day. Those who regularly read the same newspaper tended to form a shared standpoint toward political and religious authorities. Regular reporting on and criticism of the actions of government authorities rendered those authorities mundane and profane, their actions often a source of ridicule, their authority compromised.

Newspapers and pamphlets not only can solidify public opinion, but also can move people to action. In the American colonies many newspapers were critical of the British control. Unjust actions were criticized – particularly the Stamp Act of 1765. As the governmental authorities increased their controlling actions, a great increase in newspaper and pamphlet publishing ensued. Well-read newspapers and pamphlets, such as Tom Paine's *Common Sense*, justifications for rebellion not only against particular acts and officials, but also against monarchy itself as a valid form of government. Phrases like "freedom of the press" and "no taxation without representation," first introduced in newspapers and pamphlets, along with the positions articulated by Milton and Paine, became the rationale behind the freedom of the press provision in the first amendment to the United States Constitution adopted in 1791.

The emotional response to reading newspaper accounts differs from that of reading books. Newspaper readers often show anger or pride as they read. Also, they are inclined to enter into agitated discussions about the stories they have read. On the other hand, book readers express far less emotional response. Cooler and more analytical, book readers more often enter into detached, intellectual discussions about the ideas they have read in books.

Beginning in the early twentieth century newspapers transformed. Prior to this time they had been highly partisan, representing the interests of labor unions, political parties, and ethnic groups, making money largely from newspaper sales. Increasingly, newspaper profits were realized through the sale of advertisements. In order to maintain a steady flow of advertising revenue, a style of reporting and editorial policies developed that did not alienate the business community. The principle of "objective reporting" most likely was derived from the nonpartisan approach to reporting the news that became the norm after newspapers grew increasingly dependent on advertising revenue. The values of advertising and business became intertwined with news. Newspapers changed, offering fewer news accounts while adopting more sports, fashion, entertainment, and family stories, which often corresponded to the ads. Newspapers became advocates for businesses.

Early in the nineteenth century, public schools were established in the United States with the democratic intention that all children should learn to read and compute mathematics. Textbooks began to be written and published in a format that began with simple ideas and progressed to increasingly complex ideas and operations. Prior to the printing press school instruction was conducted by a teacher reading from a solitary text, often with students repeating what had been spoken in order to memorize the material. With the advent of printed texts distributed to each student, public reading was replaced by silent reading. Similarly, with the increasing availability of printed material in general, people began to read silently. In North America reading was not an elitist activity. Instead, because print media had developed as a commercial enterprise, the content of print tended to serve the diverse interests of the reading public. A classless, democratic reading culture evolved.

Periodicals (journals and magazines) are published regularly at greater intervals than newspapers – weekly, monthly, or quarterly instead of daily. The content of periodicals ranges from technical and scholarly journals whose content has some longevity to mass-circulated, highly illustrated magazines focusing on celebrities and entertainment whose reading life is very short. The first periodical, the *Journal des savants*, was published in France from 1665 to 1792. A literary, scientific, and art weekly, it has been widely imitated. Even today, many contemporary magazines are similar in appearance and content. By the end of the eighteenth century periodicals targeted to special identity groups appeared. Journals for lawyers and scholars were introduced, as were magazines targeted to women. In the nineteenth century, novels began to be serialized in magazines. For example, many of Charles Dickens's novels first appeared in popular magazines. A common theme of popular magazines was comedy, particularly political and cultural satire. In the United States, *Mad* magazine survived for decades. Today, the *Onion*, an Internet "publication," is a popular source of political and cultural satire, as are the stories and cartoons found in periodicals such as the *New Yorker*.

Magazines intended for women have been in existence for 200 years. However, since the development of modern advertising in the early twentieth century, women's magazines have changed. Increasingly, women's magazines are filled with advertisements – often much more than text. The ads are intended to promote consumerism. Stories, advice columns, and reports of current trends illustrate how beauty, sexuality, health, happiness, career success, cooking skills, and social status are available, if not quite affordable. A superficial reading of these magazines may lead a reader to believe that such magazines equate status with consumerism. Ironically, women's magazines set the foundation for the women's movement by illustrating how women can gain control of their lives and find happiness through education and by entering into the professional and business worlds formerly dominated by men.

Increasingly, social scientists and historians are concerned over recent trends in the print media. While books continue to be published in record numbers – about 75,000 new titles in 2004 – book sales have stagnated and even decreased slightly in recent years. Similarly, newspapers continue to be published and continue to be profitable, but with less competition due to the fact that most cities have only one major daily newspaper. The number of daily newspapers has dropped only slightly since mid-century – 1,763 in 1946 and 1,534 in 1994. As with books, newspapers in the United States are losing readers. It is rare to find a regular reader of a newspaper under the age of 40. The culture of print has ceased growing and is showing signs of significant decline.

Another concern is an increasing concentration of ownership of the print media by large corporations. About 75 percent of all newspapers are owned by corporate chains. Fewer corporations own and control an increasing number of newspapers, magazines, and book publishing houses. Many of these corporate entities are media conglomerates with print media constituting only a part of larger business empires that include radio, television, movies, and music industries. With conglomeration, a synergy develops wherein the different components of a corporate conglomerate work together to produce benefits for each other in a way that would not be possible without the interlocking connections that define this form of social organization. Thus, book publishers may favor the publication of books that can be made into movies, which subsequently are made in the conglomerate's movie studios and distributed by the conglomerate to the public. Magazines owned by the conglomerate featuring stories and photographs of celebrities who have just made a movie are distributed to coordinate with the release of the movie in the theater chain owned by the conglomerate. The movie's stars and director appear on the conglomerate's television network talk shows to discuss the movie between commercials advertising the conglomerate's material products. The fear is that with this process fewer "good" books will be published.

Conglomeration, the concentrated ownership of the media, and the increasing reliance on advertising revenue strongly suggest a significant decrease in investigating and reporting corrupt business and governmental practices, a paucity of valid information, and the demise of competing views of reality. Social scientists and historians fear that these trends may lead to a single, dominant, uncritical, business-friendly worldview – a condition of *ideological hegemony*, of ideas and values and little awareness of alternatives. Certainly, this condition does not yet exist in the United States, although the trend does fall in that direction. Recent research indicates that the content of print media has not yet become homogenized, that vast amounts of information and multiple perspectives on reality are readily available, and that the readers of print media continue to determine the types of articles and books that are written.

SEE ALSO: Ideological Hegemony; McLuhan, Marshall; Media; Media and Globalization; Media Literacy; Media Monopoly; Media, Network(s) and; Media and the Public Sphere; Media, Regulation of; Social Change

REFERENCES AND SUGGESTED READINGS

Bagdikian, B. H. (2000) *The Media Monopoly*, 6th edn. Beacon Press, Boston.
Couch, C. J. (1996) *Information Technologies and Social Orders*. Aldine de Gruyter, Hawthorne, NY.
Eisenstein, E. (1979) *The Printing Press as an Agent of Social Change*, Vols. 1 and 2. Cambridge University Press, Cambridge.
Entman, R. (1989) *Democracy Without Citizens*. Oxford University Press, New York.
Febvre, L. & Martin, H.-J. (1976) *The Coming of the Book*. Lowe & Brydone, Norfolk.
Gramsci, A. (1971) *Selections from the Prison Notebooks*. International Publishers, New York.

Innis, H. A. (1951) *The Bias of Communication*. University of Toronto Press, Toronto.

McLuhan, M. (1962) *The Gutenberg Galaxy*. University of Toronto Press, Toronto.

Merton, R. K. & Lazarsfeld, P. (1948) Mass Communication, Popular Taste, and Organized Social Action. In: Bryson, L. (Ed.), *Communication of Ideas*. Harper & Brothers, New York, pp. 95–118.

Meyrowitz, J. (1994) Medium Theory. In: Crowley, D. & Mitchell, D. (Eds.), *Communication Theory Today*. Stanford University Press, Stanford, pp. 50–77.

Postman, N. (1985) *Amusing Ourselves to Death*. Penguin, New York.

prisons

Melvina Sumter

Prisons are secure institutions which house juvenile and adult felons with sentences that range from one year to life who are remanded to the custody of a state or federal correctional agency for incarceration. These facilities have the task of carrying out the sentence imposed by the courts as well as protecting the public by preventing escapes through maintaining custody and safe and secure institutions. As well, these facilities are charged with the responsibility of providing all of the programs and services necessary to care for the inmate population remanded to their custody.

Prisons are operated by all 50 states and the District of Columbia, the federal government, and the military. Each of the 50 states and the District of Columbia operates its own correctional system; as such, there is considerable variation in terms of the organization, administration, operation, and management of these facilities as well as the programs and services offered. However, in the majority of state systems the administration of the prison is the function of the executive branch of state government in which the governor appoints a state director (also known as commissioner or secretary) to oversee the administration and operations of the state prison system (Clear & Cole 2003).

The Federal Bureau of Prisons is responsible both for juvenile and adult offenders who have been convicted of federal crimes and for managing and operating federal facilities in the United States. Although the first federal prison was opened in 1790, it was not until 1930 that Congress created the Federal Bureau of Prisons to served as a centralized administration to manage and regulate the 11 federal prisons in operation at that time (Bartollas 2002; Champion 2005). Today, the Federal Bureau of Prisons is headed by a director who oversees eight centralized divisions, an Office of the General Counsel, an Office of Inspections, six US regions in which federal prisons are located, and the National Institute of Corrections.

The US Army, Navy, Air Force, and Marine Corps manage prisons for military personnel who have been turned over to the military for trial, sentencing, and imprisonment after committing crimes in military or civilian jurisdictions (Stinchcomb & Fox 1999). Military prisons are also responsible for individuals who have been convicted of violations of the Uniform Code of Military Conduct or being Absent Without Leave. As well, military prisons house prisoners of war whose freedom is deemed a national security risk by military or civilian authorities (Stinchcomb & Fox 1999).

The Walnut Street Jail is considered to be the first penitentiary used exclusively for the correction of convicted offenders in the United States (Stinchcomb & Fox 1999). Moreover, in 1790, a portion of the Walnut Street Jail was converted to a wing called the penitentiary house to use imprisonment as an alternative sanction to the widespread use of corporal and capital punishment. As such, solitary confinement with labor inside the cell was viewed as a mechanism to provide inmates time for contemplation, repentance, and reformation in hopes that the introspection process would allow them the opportunity to reflect on, and thereby atone for, their crimes, and place themselves on the right path (Friedman 1993; Stinchcomb & Fox 1999; Clear & Cole 2003). The Walnut Street Jail served as the model for what became known as the Pennsylvania and Auburn Penitentiary Systems. While both systems included solitary confinement in separate cells and enforced silence at all times to prevent inmates from communicating, there were distinct differences in the operation of the two models. The Pennsylvania system was designed to isolate each inmate for the duration of confinement; therefore, inmates remained in their cells during the entire period of incarceration. Conversely, the Auburn system developed a congregate system of prison discipline whereby inmates were held in isolation at night but congregated in workshops during the day with enforced silence at all times (Clear & Cole 2003). Because the inmates did not need large cell space to work and were able to generate productive labor, since they worked in a factory during the day, the Auburn system proved to be more financially practical than the Pennsylvania system. As a result, the Auburn system eventually prevailed in becoming the dominant penal model for maximum security prisons in the United States (Champion 2005).

TYPES OF PRISONS

After being sentenced to prison, inmates are transferred to a reception and evaluation center where they are assessed in order to determine the appropriate level of physical barriers and degree of staff supervision needed inside the prison to prevent escapes and maintain safe and secure correctional facilities. During the diagnostic phase, a classification instrument is used to evaluate the risk and dangerousness of the inmate and to match the inmate's programming needs and need to protect the community with a facility commensurate with the appropriate custody and security level (Champion 2005). As such, prisons are classified and designated by security levels that identify the type of institution required to house inmates based on their final classification score. This score is determined by factors such as the severity of the current offense, history of escapes or violence, sentence length, and number of prior convictions or commitments. Although there is administrative and operational variation among the three jurisdictions, inmates are generally assigned to a minimum, medium, or maximum security prison from the reception and evaluation center.

Minimum security prisons, also called open camp correctional institutions, or camps, house the least restrictive, low-risk, non-violent first-time inmate. Inmates with violent offenses or long sentences who have clean disciplinary records and good behavior, and who have thus advanced through the classification system from

a more restrictive facility, may also be housed in minimum security prisons. These facilities have a minimal amount of external control, therefore generally possess only a single fence, with grounds and physical plant features resembling a university campus rather than a prison. There is a relatively low staff to inmate ratio and housing is often of dormitory style. Since a primary focus of these institutions is reintegration of the inmate back into the community, a significant portion of the department of correction's educational, vocational, and treatment programs are allocated to these facilities.

Medium security prisons, also called correctional facilities or institutions, house a wide variety of inmates who are less dangerous and escape prone than inmates housed in maximum security, but not of a sufficiently low enough risk to be entrusted a minimum level of security. These facilities are generally surrounded by a double chain-link fence, topped with barbed or razor wire and electronic devices, and often use congregate housing or dormitory-style living arrangements, which contain a group toilet and shower. These facilities also have a higher staff to inmate ratio than minimum security facilities, inmates live in cell-type housing, and a wide variety of work, educational, vocational, and treatment programs are provided.

Maximum security prisons, also called penitentiaries, house inmates who have long sentences and pose a severe threat to society. There facilities were traditionally surrounded by tall thick walls, usually 30 to 50 feet high and several feet thick, topped with barbed or razor wire, with gun towers that are strategically placed in corners with armed correctional officers. As a result of cost, however, modern structures are more likely to be surrounded by chain-link fences bounded by electrified wire than by thick walls (Clear & Cole 2003). The inmates generally live in small cells that contain their own sanitary facility. These prisons have a significantly higher staff to inmate ratio than medium security prisons, inmates live in multiple and single occupant cell housing, and there are fewer work and treatment opportunities offered than at medium security prisons.

Super-maximum prisons are independent correctional facilities or a distinct unit within an existing prison that provide for the management and secure control of inmates who are generally reassigned from a maximum, medium, or minimum security prison because of disruptive behavior. Moreover, super-maximum prisons house inmates who have been officially designated as exhibiting aggressive or violent behavior, and therefore are unmanageable when housed with the general inmate population or placed in administrative segregation. The inmates placed in super-maximum facilities often have assaulted other inmates or staff, are believed to be members of a security threat group, or have incited riots or other disturbances. These inmates eat and exercise alone and are not allowed contact visits.

Since the 1980s, some correctional facilities have been run by private corporations. Here the total operation and management of a correctional facility is transferred to a private corporation that operates the facility for a profit. Although the concept of private prisons emerged during the 1980s, correctional agencies have long contracted with private corporations for a variety of services to include providing medical and dental care, school programs, counseling, nursing homes, halfway houses, juvenile facilities, and alcohol and drug treatment services (Bartollas 2002). In addition to contracting with state and federal government for the total operation and management of a correctional facility, private corporations also finance, site, and build prisons.

PRISONS TODAY

Prison populations have more than tripled during the past several decades as a result of "get-tough" policies such as the war on drugs, mandatory minimum sentences, habitual offender statutes, truth in sentencing and three strikes you're out legislation, and the abolition of parole. All of these were designed to provide inmates longer sentences as well as keep them in prison for longer periods of time. As a result of the escalation in the prison population, current inmate populations exceed cell capacity in almost all state and federal prisons; therefore, many prisons are overcrowded. Prison crowding presents several challenges for correctional personnel. Overcrowding makes it difficult to manage safe and secure correctional facilities by placing more stress on correctional staff, who

are expected to maintain order within a facility holding more inmates than it was designed for (Mays & Winfree 2002). Likewise, prison overcrowding increases the propensity for violence among offenders, results in more serious injuries and assaults of inmates and staff by inmates, facilitates more disciplinary infractions, leads to more inmate lawsuits challenging conditions of confinement, and decreases access to programs and services (Clear & Cole 2003).

In addition to an influx of inmates, the composition of the prison population has also changed. More specifically, today there is an increase in the number of African Americans, females, juveniles, and geriatric offenders. Similarly, there is a substantial growth in the number of special needs offenders to include mentally ill and retarded offenders, offenders with AIDS, and alcohol- and substance-abusing offenders. As such, correctional administrators are tasked with the responsibility of supervising an increasing influx of diverse inmates without corresponding increases in funds, facilities, and/or other resources (Mays & Winfree 2002). Consequently, funds barely cover the programming and treatment needs of inmates or the increasing health costs because of the rise in the special needs population and offenders with AIDS. Hence, although correctional budgets have increased substantially, these funds are used primarily to build more prisons and for operational expenses. As such, prison administrators are limited to providing minimal treatment programs, educational and vocational programs, and health and medical services to the inmate population.

SEE ALSO: Corrections; Courts; Crime; Criminal Justice System; Criminology; Law, Criminal

REFERENCES AND SUGGESTED READINGS

Bartollas, C. (2002) *Invitation to Corrections*. Allyn & Bacon, Boston.
Champion, D. J. (2005) *Corrections in the United States*, 4th edn. Prentice-Hall, Upper Saddle River, NJ.
Clear, T. R. & Cole, G. F. (2003) *American Corrections*, 5th edn. Wadsworth, Belmont, CA.

Friedman, L. M. (1993) *Crime and Punishment in American History*. Basic Books, New York.

Mays, G. L. & Winfree, L. T. (2002) *Contemporary Corrections*. Wadsworth, Belmont, CA.

Stinchcomb, J. B. & Fox, V. B. (1999) *Introduction to Corrections*, 5th edn. Prentice-Hall, Upper Saddle River, NJ.

privacy

Gary T. Marx

Privacy, like the weather, is much discussed, little understood, and difficult to control. It is a multidimensional concept with fluid and often ill-defined, contested, and negotiated borders, depending on the context and the culture. Along with its opposite *publicity*, it is nonetheless a cornerstone of modern society's ideas of the person and of democracy.

As the impacts of computerization on society (and the reverse) become ever more apparent, issues of privacy and publicity are vital for understanding society and for the creation of the good society.

Privacy and *publicity* are nouns. For purposes of explanation, they can be seen as polar ends of a continuum. This perspective draws attention to the moral or normative aspects of withholding and disclosing of information and asking or not asking for information. Depending on the context, social roles, and culture, individuals or groups may be required, find it optional, or be prohibited from engaging in these activities.

These in turn involve a broader area called the sociology of information. Governing rules here vary from situations where information must be kept private to those where it must be made public (or perhaps better, must be revealed – whether as part of a confidential relationship or to the public at large). There is considerable subjectivity with respect to expectations about how information is to be treated.

In contrast, *private* and *public* are adjectives that can tell us about the status of information. They describe whether or not the information is known. This has an objective quality and can be relatively easily measured. For example, the gender of persons we pass on the street is generally visible and known. The information is "public." In contrast, the political and religious beliefs of pedestrians are generally invisible and unknown.

Of course, normative expectations of privacy and publicity do not always correspond to how the adjectives public and private are applied to empirical facts. Thus the cell phone conversations of politicians and celebrities that have privacy protections may become public. Information subjected to publicity requirements such as government and corporate reports and disclosure statements may be withheld, destroyed, or falsified. Information not entitled to privacy protections, such as child or spouse abuse, may be unknown because of the inaccessibility of the home to broader visibility. Confidential or classified information may be leaked, hacked, or mistakenly released.

Privacy and publicity can also be thought of in literal and metaphorical spatial terms involving invisibility–visibility and inaccessibility–accessibility. The physical privacy offered by a closed door and walls and an encrypted email communication share information restriction, even as they differ in other ways. Internet forums are not geographically localized, but in their accessibility can be usefully thought of as public places, not unlike the traditional public square.

Privacy needs to be separated from related terms. *Surveillance* simply involves scrutiny (often using technical means that extend the senses) for a variety of goals such as control, protection, management, documentation, and entertainment. It is a way of discovering information. It may involve obvious invasions of privacy, as with selling the results of DNA and other testing to insurance companies, or illegal wiretapping or spyware placed on a computer. Yet surveillance can also be the means of protecting privacy. Consider biometric identification and audit trails required to access some databases or defensive measures such as a home security video camera.

Privacy is inherently social. The term was irrelevant to Robinson Crusoe when he thought he was alone on the island. It is social in the sense that it implies an "other" from whom information is withheld, or to whom it is supplied and who may, or may not, be under equivalent expectations to reveal and conceal.

Social roles structure the treatment of information and this often involves issues of power.

Thus, close friends in an equal relationship are expected to reveal parts of themselves that they would not reveal at the mall or at work. Sharing one's inner thoughts and feelings is expected to be reciprocal. A relationship of intimacy is partly defined by the mutuality of revelation. This contrasts with the more impersonal roles of doctor and patient. Thus the revelations of a patient to a doctor are not likely to be reciprocated.

Rules regarding who can collect personal information, what is collected, the conditions under which it is gathered, and how it is used (and by whom) are very much connected to social stratification. Rose Coser (1961) uses the felicitous phrase "insulation from observability" to describe the norms and resources that protect the actions of higher-status roles in bureaucratic organizations.

Many contemporary concerns over privacy invasion involve large organizations and their employees and customers or police and suspects, professionals and clients, as well as interpersonal relations such as parents and children. In these contexts the rules are relatively clear about who can ask or observe and who is expected to reveal (or is entitled to conceal). Situations involving power differences with respect to gender and ethnicity may also reflect information inequality. On the other hand, maids, valets, butlers, chauffeurs, and personal assistants often know a great deal about the private lives of those they work for and this tends to be unreciprocated.

Confidentiality often accompanies expectations of privacy. It reminds us that information issues are fundamentally social. It refers not to the initial revelation or creation of information but to an expectation that personal information, once legitimately known by others, will be treated appropriately. This may involve sharing it according to established rules (e.g., as in medical treatment involving several specialists who discuss a patient), but otherwise keeping the information *secret* (as with social security numbers that must be given to an employer).

Secret is an adjective like private which can be used to describe the status of information. In restricting information, *secrecy* overlaps privacy. But it goes beyond it to characterize the information-protecting activities of organizations as well as individuals. It generally has a culturally and morally more ambiguous status than privacy.

When personal privacy is viewed as a *right*, it calls attention to the individual's ability to control the release of information. This does not mean that it cannot be shared, but that the individual has a choice. The 5th Amendment, for example, does not prohibit individuals from offering information, it simply prohibits this information from being coercively obtained.

In contrast, the rules applying to secrecy are more likely to involve an *obligation* that prohibits the release of information. This is often accompanied by sanctions for violation. In principle, individuals and organizations don't have a choice about divulging information appropriately deemed to be secret. Such protective rules, along with the fact that the very existence of the secret may be unknown to outsiders, can protect untoward behavior. As Georg Simmel (1950) suggested, the secret, whether legitimate or illegitimate, can also be a factor contributing to group solidarity.

SOME TYPES OF PRIVACY

In the age of new surveillance, we increasingly see techniques that break through borders that previously protected personal and organizational data, whether involving computer databases, Internet monitoring, videocams, drug testing, RFID chips, or DNA analysis. As a result, questions of *informational privacy*, or the ability of individuals to choose what information about themselves will be offered to others and how this will be treated, are important social issues. Rights to freedom of religion and thought, association, and speech are fundamental here.

Another form of privacy which calls more explicit attention to behavior itself (rather than information about it) involves *decisional privacy*. Consider, for example, personal choices involving reproduction and the refusal of medical services, as well as lifestyle issues such as sexual preference. The right to liberty is fundamental to this.

A concept encompassing both of the above involves privacy as *access* to the person. The metaphor of a border or wall surrounding the person can be applied. Is it (and when should it be) impenetrable or porous? To what extent can the individual, in principle and in actuality, control information flowing *outward* involving telephone or computer communication, credit card and other transactions, beliefs and feelings, location, facial appearance, or biometric data such as DNA, voice print, heat, and scent?

Conversely, to what extent can the individual control information and stimuli going *inward* sent from others? This goes in the other direction – entering rather than leaving the person. The desire for solitude, often viewed as an aspect of privacy, may be seen here. Individuals seek to screen out undesirable sounds, smells, and sights, whether these involve propaganda and advertisements, or unwanted music and cooking smells from an adjacent apartment. This is part of an expectation to be left alone.

The telescreen in George Orwell's novel *1984* illustrates both forms. It transmitted the person's image and communication to Big Brother, while simultaneously broadcasting propaganda to the individual. There was only one channel and it couldn't be turned off.

A more descriptive definitional approach simply looks at the institutional setting. Thus we can speak of privacy as it involves consumption, finances, employment, medical, religious, political, and national security arenas. We can also consider a particular means used or activity (e.g., locational privacy, communication privacy – whether involving computers, telephones, or television). Distinct types of data may be involved – e.g., financial, genetic, or beliefs – and these can be expressed in different forms – e.g., as numbers, narratives, images, or sound. While there are commonalities, expectations and practices vary depending on the setting, means, activity, content, and data form. Social science and philosophy have only begun to disentangle these.

SOME CROSS-CULTURAL ASPECTS

While information control is a factor in all societies and some activities such as procreation and elimination are generally shielded from others, there is enormous historical and cultural variability (Moore 1984). The Greeks, for example, placed the highest value on public life. One's sense of identity was found there. Privacy, being the realm of slaves, women, and children who

were restricted to the home, was not valued. To be private meant de*privation*. In traditional communal societies where life is lived in close proximity to others, the distinction between privacy and publicity has little meaning.

We also see differences in how contemporary societies protect privacy. With respect to personal information issues, in the United States there is greater emphasis, relative to Europe, on the liberty to choose behavior and less government regulation, whether of monitoring in the workplace or of organizations that buy and sell personal information. Large organizations warehouse and sell vast amounts of personal data on the most intimate of subjects, generally without the consent of, and with no direct benefit to, the subject.

In contrast, the secondary use of information in Europe generally requires the informed consent of the subject. In much of Europe, citizens are offered general protection from new, potentially privacy-invasive technologies through constitutional guarantees involving (a rather unspecific) right to personhood or personal dignity. Europe, Canada, and many Asian societies also have privacy commissions charged with protecting privacy and anticipating future problems.

The approach in the US is to regulate technologies on a case by case basis as they appear, rather than on the basis of a broad inclusive principle. This is particularly the case for new forms that are dependent on judicial review or legislation specifically crafted for the technique. This in turn is often dependent on some indignation-raising misuse becoming public and a drawn-out political process. Individuals also have greater responsibility for protecting their own privacy, whether through using protective technologies or suing privacy invaders (assuming the invasion can be discovered).

Conceptions of privacy (and publicity as well) are relatively new and are related to the emergence of the modern nation-state and the economic and political rights associated with capitalism and democracy. Rules requiring privacy and publicity are very much a part of the modern state and, while going in opposite directions, developed in tandem.

Private property, particularly the home, suggested a location to be protected from outsiders. A laissez-faire marketplace where participants pursued their self-interest required strategic control over information and the idea of information as property. The metropolis, with its social and geographical mobility and larger scale, offered a kind of anonymity unknown to the small village and new means for validating the claims of strangers. Larger living quarters meant more physical privacy as societies became richer. Most homes now have more than one bedroom and individuals have the possibility of their own bed.

Political democracy required both openness in government as a means of accountability and public discussion of issues. The latter required citizens with the liberty to form associations that were free to express their views in the public forums of civil society and that needed protection from government interference. Yet government was also given limited powers to cross personal borders to gather information relevant to health and safety, criminal justice, and national security in an increasingly complex and interdependent world.

Privacy is usually thought of as something belonging to individuals. The ability to control information about the self is central to the personhood and dignity implied in the notion of the modern citizen. However, the ability to control information is also significant to group and organizational borders. Privacy is a social as well as an individual value (Regan 1995). For example, a legal oppositional political group (or indeed any group) needs to be able to control information about members, resources, and plans and to feel that freedom of expression within the group is respected. To the extent that a group's borders are porous – punctured by informers and intensive surveillance – its ability to act strategically is weakened and, of course, democratic ideals are undermined.

Privacy can be seen either as a commodity or as a right to which individuals are entitled. The social implications of the view taken are quite different. As a commodity, individuals may sell, trade, or be coerced into giving away their private information (e.g., for frequent flyer miles or the convenience of using a credit card). They may pay for privacy protection, as well as purchase personal information on others – note the large number of Internet sites offering this service.

The US Constitution is seen by many scholars to imply a right to privacy, although this is not explicit. Justice William Douglas in *Griswold* v. *Connecticut* (1965) used the term "penumbra" in identifying various places where "zones of privacy" were guaranteed (e.g., the 1st, 3rd, 4th, and 5th Amendments to the Constitution). Some state constitutions (particularly in the western states) guarantee a right to privacy, as do the constitutions of most European countries. Privacy is also protected by organizational policies and privacy-protecting technologies (e.g., encryption, shredders, and devices to discover bugs).

The notion of unrestrained, all-powerful privacy invaders with ravenous and insatiable information appetites waiting to pounce on the unsuspecting individual is too one-sided. Most organizations are inhibited by values and by concern over negative publicity should they go too far in crossing personal information borders. Furthermore, as the work of Erving Goffman (1956) suggests, through manners and rituals we also cooperate to varying degrees with each other to maintain individual privacy and self-respect.

SEE ALSO: Bureaucracy and Public Sector Governmentality; Celebrity and Celetoid; Censorship; Civil Society; Goffman, Erving; Information Society; Media; Public and Private; Public Sphere; Surveillance

REFERENCES AND SUGGESTED READINGS

Alderman, E. & Kennedy, C. (1995) *The Right to Privacy*. Knopf, New York.
Allen, A. (2003) *Accountability for Private Life*. Rowman & Littlefield, Lanham, MD.
Bennett, C. & Grant, R. (Eds.) (1999) *Visions of Privacy*. University of Toronto Press, Toronto.
Brinn, D. (1999) *The Transparent Society*. Perseus, New York.
Coser, R. (1961) Insulation from Observability and Types of Social Conformity. *American Sociological Review* 26: 28–39.
Flaherty, D. (1972) *Privacy in Colonial New England*. University Press of Virginia, Charlottesville.
Gandy, O. (1993) *The Panoptic Sort: A Political Economy of Personal Information*. Westview Press, Boulder, CO.

Goffman, E. (1956) *The Presentation of Self in Everyday Life*. Doubleday, New York.

Lyon, D. (Ed.) (2003) *Surveillance as Social Sorting*. Routledge, London.

Marguilis, S. T. (Ed.) (2003) Contemporary Perspectives on Privacy: Social, Psychological, Political. *Journal of Social Issues* 59: 243–61.

Marx, G. (2001) Murky Conceptual Waters: The Public and the Private. *Ethics and Information Technology* 3(3).

Marx, G. (2006) *Windows Into the Soul: Surveillance and Society in an Age of High Technology*. University of Chicago Press, Chicago.

Moore, B. (1984) *Privacy: Studies in Social and Cultural History*. M. E. Sharpe, New York.

Regan, P. (1995) *Legislating Privacy: Technology, Social Values, and Public Policy*. University of North Carolina Press, Chapel Hill.

Rule, J. (1974) *Private Lives and Public Surveillance: Social Control in the Computer Age*. Schocken Books, New York.

Shils, E. (1956) *The Torment of Secrecy: The Background and Consequences of American Security Problems*. Free Press, Glencoe, IL.

Simmel, G. (1950) The Secret and the Secret Society. In: Wolff, K. W. (Ed.), *The Sociology of Georg Simmel*. Free Press, New York.

Solove, D. (2004) *The Digital Person*. New York University Press, New York.

Westin, A. (1967) *Privacy and Freedom*. Atheneum, New York.

Whitman, J. (2004) The Two Western Cultures of Privacy: Dignity Versus Liberty. *Yale Law Review* 113: 1151–222.

Zureik, E. & Salter, M. (2005) *Global Surveillance and Policing*. Wilan, Devon.

privatization

Burkart Holzner

Privatization is a transfer of public services provided by various levels of governments in national states to the private sector of business. It is a relatively recent transformation of governance and markets in countries worldwide. In fact, it is an extraordinary, rapidly expanding phenomenon that is rising in global waves, transferring ownership from governments to private enterprises.

Rendering public services via private businesses creates important political, economic, and cultural changes. The actual methods for privatization are manifold; they can be outright purchases, leases, subsidies or other cooperative partnerships, or yet other approaches. However, they put the privatized public service into the hands of private managers. The concept of privacy is not identical with privatization, but it is a part of the cluster of values linked to other changing values for governance and for markets. Privacy of enterprises emphasizes autonomy, independence, secrecy, and profit for the owners; both governance and markets demand transparency, accountability, and benefits for the public good. Democracy can be benefited by the efficiencies of privatization if the provided service responds to public needs and sensitivities, but it may be harmed where the private owners of a function are alien to the public.

The history of privatization begins relatively late in the western industrial nations. Monarchical nations were less differentiated than modern democratic institutions. Much of common (rather than public) property was that of the monarch, encompassing the functioning of government. The differentiation of modern societies includes now multiple institutions in government, such as foreign affairs, the military, health, education, justice, and markets. This growth of institutions gave room for the distinction of private versus public ownerships.

The Great Depression in the 1930s raised doubt about the viability of capitalism. Citizens were inclined to trust national states rather than risky markets. At the end of World War II the major industrial nations turned to the task of state rebuilding and reconstruction. This effort focused on the importance of state-owned enterprises (SOEs) and on strategic sectors of the national economy. The reliance on the state was predominant, especially in "statist" Europe. The US, however, was and remained more flexible in encouraging enterprises as well as government. The role of the federal government was also strengthened, for example, by establishing social security and regulations. Yet private and public partnerships occurred well before strong efforts at privatization in the US.

Early efforts to reduce the economic role of the state included Churchill's "denationalization" of the British steel industry and Adenauer's withdrawal of the West German government's major investment in Volkswagen in 1961. However, denationalization at the time was not very popular. The major movement toward privatization was energized much later by Margaret Thatcher. She also coined the concept of privatization. At that time (the early 1980s) a number of privatization goals were pursued by the British government: (1) provide new revenue through privatization of pubic enterprises; (2) improve economic efficiency; (3) limit the government's role in the economy; (4) encourage broader share ownership; (5) encourage competition; (6) require SOEs to aspire to market discipline. In the US Ronald Reagan won a landslide victory in 1980 and easily won his second term in 1984. His policies were to reduce taxes, cut government programs, and finance an astounding defense buildup, resulting in a large budget deficit. Privatization in various forms was encouraged by Reagan. Reducing the role of government (except the military) was a high priority.

The collapse of the Soviet Union was completed in December 1991, but the breakdown had begun with the dismantling of the Berlin Wall in November 1989. The 1980s and 1990s saw a revitalization of capitalism and the rapid expansion of democracy, especially among the East European countries as well as in many other parts of the world. During this period a great sense of urgency arose to transform communist centrally planned economies to free markets. There was also a demand to reduce the powers of governments and make the building of democratic institutions possible, resulting in experiments in privatization, lawmaking, and institution building. In many ways the transition included an enormous wave of corruption in governments, but also in the rising private sector.

The ideology of freeing the citizenry from the constraints of government grew in the US, Britain, and to a much lesser degree in Europe. Some politicians in these countries believed privatization might eliminate government altogether in significant ways. However, the experience of "shock privatization" in the Russian Federation and difficulties in many of the transforming East European countries led to recognition of the necessity of the rule of law, the creation of democratic institutions, and effective regulations for a functioning market.

After the expansionist enthusiasm for privatization in the 1990s, a more balanced approach is now emerging, increasingly based on the empirical experiences of successes and failures. Privatization of certain public services has actually proven to be efficient and workable, but this cannot be assumed to be generally true. However, great differences exist in cultural values, legal frameworks, regulations, and commitment to transparency and social responsibility. Some countries may be without workable institutional frameworks to support effective and ethical privatization. Where these conditions allow mismanaged or secretive measures, serious harm can occur. Unfortunately, such conditions prevail in several privatized military functions, certain privatized prisons, and in many other fields.

Public services have to be assessed for their mission, efficiency, ethics, and freedom from corruption. The idea that privatization can always reduce government effectively has to be questioned – it is likely to be very limited. There are other risks: privatization can reduce citizens' participation in democracy and may indeed be harmful to democracy (e.g., in the case of a public service carried out by a global corporation at a great distance). The emerging research literature will make it possible to reduce the ideology of "freedom from government by privatization" and provide the needed empirical knowledge to use privatization positively for the public.

SEE ALSO: Capital: Economic, Cultural, and Social; Capitalism; Change Management; Development: Political Economy; Labor Movement; Neoliberalism; Outsourcing; Political Economy; Public and Private; Public Sphere; Unions; Welfare State, Retrenchment of

REFERENCES AND SUGGESTED READINGS

Fitzgerald, R. (1988) *When Government Goes Private: Successful Alternatives to Public Services*. Pacific Research Institute for Public Policy Book, Universe Books, New York.

Gupta, A. (2000) *Beyond Privatization*. St. Martin's Press, New York.

Mac Avoy, P. W., Stanbury, W. T., Yarrow, G., & Zeckhauser, R. J. (1989) *Privatization and State-Owned Enterprises: Lessons from the United States, Great Britain and Canada*. Kluwer Academic Publishers, Boston.

Parker, D. & Saal, D. (Eds.) (2003) *International Handbook on Privatization*. Edward Egar, Cheltenham.

Sclar, E. D. (2000) *You Don't Always Get What You Pay For: The Economics of Privatization*. Century Foundation Book, Cornell University Press, Ithaca, NY.

Weizsäcker, E. U. von, Young, O. R., Finger, M., & Beisheim, M. (Eds.) (2005) *Limits to Privatization: How to Avoid Too Much of a Good Thing*. Earthscan, London.

Yarrow, G. & Jasiski, P. (Eds.) (1996) *Privatization: Critical Perspectives on the World Economy*, 4 vols. Routledge, New York.

privilege

Deana A. Rohlinger

There is a historical and cultural tendency for dominant groups to institutionalize discrimination against subdominant groups. Discrimination is justified by arguing that members of the subdominant group are deficient in some way when compared to members of the dominant group. The idealized characteristics of the dominant group are intertwined in social, cultural, and legal institutions and ultimately work to advantage, or privilege, members of the dominant group and disadvantage those of the subdominant group. Sociologists most often discuss privilege in terms of gender (how women are subordinated to men), race/ethnicity (how people of color are subordinated to those with white skin), and sexuality (how homosexuals, bisexuals, and transsexuals are subordinated to heterosexuals).

In the United States, gender roles and expectations have been governed by the doctrine of the separate spheres. This ideology holds that women are virtuous, nurturing, and frail and therefore unable to contend with the demands of politics and commerce. Men, in contrast, are aggressive, competitive, and strong and, thus,

better suited for public life. Even as these beliefs were challenged throughout the twentieth century, the inequities between men and women persisted. Sociologists identify male privilege as being both embedded in the structure of complex organizations and reproduced in social relations.

Sociologists analyze the ways in which male dominance in the public sphere affects complex structures such as the workplace and school. Scholars argue that gender stratification in the workplace (with women largely confined to low-level jobs at the bottom of the organizational hierarchy) and the use of male characteristics to define the ideal worker diminishes the career mobility of women by shaping hiring and promotion practices, employee performance assessment, and the distribution of work tasks. Moreover, when women break through unacknowledged barriers to their advancement, or the "glass ceiling," they are treated like "tokens" rather than capable employees who possess the skills and wherewithal to do the job. Gendered expectations about the kinds of skills women and men possess and the kinds of jobs they are best suited for are learned in school. Textbooks and the courses targeted to girls (home economics) and boys (woodworking) reinforce stereotypes about the fields in which boys and girls are likely to excel.

Sociologists note that male privilege also is reproduced through interactions in these structures. At work, women's jobs often require deference to and caregiving for a male authority. For example, secretaries, paralegals, and nurse assistants tend to the schedules and well-being of their (male) bosses. In school, teacher interactions with students often reinforce gender stereotypes about the fields in which boys and girls excel by giving boys more attention than girls in science and math classes and by differently praising their work (commending boys for content while commending girls for being neat).

Race and ethnicity, like gender, are social concepts. While race and ethnicity have different sociological meanings, they are often used interchangeably. Race and ethnic categories are given meaning through the social relations and within the historical context in which they are embedded. For example, in colonial America, class and whether one was native born were more important than skin tone in determining status. The American Revolution, which was based on the premises of equality and freedom, threw the institution of slavery into question, and an ideology that justified slavery and kept African Americans out of the increasingly competitive labor market for unskilled labor formed. The obvious characteristic was skin color, and the idea that non-white groups, particularly African Americans, required supervision, education, and guidance quickly took hold.

While much of the early research on race and ethnicity tried to justify the subordination of people of color by citing biological and cultural differences, sociologists argue that white privilege, like male privilege, is embedded in institutional structures and interactions. Scholars specifically examine how institutional racism, or the system of beliefs and behavior by which a racial or ethnic group is defined and oppressed, affects the opportunities and realities of people of color. For example, many scholars have shown that the lack of access to decent jobs, adequate housing, high-quality education, and adequate health care in the US has resulted in higher rates of poverty among African Americans.

Sociologists discuss two additional dimensions of institutional racism. First, scholars make distinctions between intentional and unintentional racism. After World War II, the federal government intentionally supported white privilege by refusing to combat racial segregation in social institutions that are instrumental for upward mobility (education, housing, and employment). For example, the Federal Housing Administration supported segregation and only underwrote loans in white neighborhoods, which prevented African American veterans from taking advantage of the suburban boom and locked them into urban areas. Racism may also be unintentional. White privilege becomes invisible to those who benefit from it. In the above example, the white veterans that took advantage of the suburban boom probably did not think about how the color of their skin enabled them to do so. Just as today, those with white skin think little of the fact that a "flesh-colored" bandaid most closely resembles their skin tone.

The second dimension scholars analyze is the hierarchical organization of race and ethnicity.

Because the white ideal is the standard by which race and ethnic groups are evaluated, this creates a hierarchy both within and among racial groups. Within a racial or ethnic group, those with lighter skin and Caucasian features are considered closer to the white ideal, better positioned to succeed in a white world, and are at the top of the hierarchy. Race and ethnic groups are also hierarchically organized and evaluated against a white ideal. Asian Americans fall just below whites in the racial hierarchy and often are labeled a "model minority" because of their ability to immigrate and achieve relative financial and social success in a white world. This becomes a source of racial division as politicians and pundits compare groups to one another and offer insight into the relative success and failure of different groups, while ignoring the invisible white ideal and the differing historically embedded experiences of racism.

Sexuality too is rooted in privilege. Sociologists have followed two different analytical threads in the study of sexuality. Some scholars linked research on race, ethnicity, gender, class, and sexuality together. These scholars conceptualize race, gender, class, and sexuality as interlocking systems and argue that an individual's location in the system determines the kinds of privilege and oppression he or she will face. For example, beliefs about African American sexuality are important to maintaining institutional racism. The stereotype of the "welfare queen" ignores white privilege and attributes the inability of African Americans to pull themselves out of poverty to promiscuity and laziness.

The second analytical thread conceptualizes sexuality as a system of oppression comparable to race, class, and gender. These sociologists argue that heterosexism, or the institutionalized structures and beliefs that define heterosexual behavior as normative, privileges heterosexuality and subordinates alternative definitions of sexuality and sexual expression. Thus, like gender and race, sexuality is a historically rooted social concept that privileges one set of social relations between the sexes. The presumed inborn sexual instinct for a member of the opposite sex is a relatively recent phenomenon. The increased prominence of doctors as a professional group in the 1880s positioned them to scientifically contribute to discussions of gender differences and to define and medicalize the ideal male–female relationship.

Research on heterosexism has been fairly limited. While the movements of the 1960s served as a catalyst for talking about sexuality and sexual oppression, meaningful discourse in research was stymied by the focus on AIDS in the 1980s. This "epidemic," which was framed as a problem in the gay community, caused the remedicalization of homosexuality and reinforced traditional notions of heterosexuality as natural and ideal. To date, sociological research has examined three aspects of heterosexism. First, scholars analyze how gay and straight identities are performed, maintained, and managed in different arenas (Connell 1995). Second, scholars examine how gender and sexuality categories are reproduced in cultural productions such as mass media texts (Sender 1999; Hart 2000). This line of work "deconstructs" cultural products and illuminates how privilege is embedded in texts. Finally, scholars have examined how heterosexism and homophobia work together to reproduce and buttress economic privilege and patriarchy (Pharr 1997). The literature on the repercussions of heterosexism is growing and sociologists are increasingly exploring how heterosexism is embedded in institutions, such as the workplace, and reinforced through practices (such as intentional and unintentional discrimination) and legal institutions.

In sum, beliefs about gender, race, and sexuality are embedded in social, cultural, and legal institutions and affect the realities and opportunities of dominant and subdominant members of these groups. Those in the dominant group (male, white, and heterosexual) are privileged and reap the benefits from their membership, while those in the subdominant group (female, non-white, and homosexual, bisexual, or transsexual) are disadvantaged and are intentionally and unintentionally discriminated against. That said, it is important to recognize that gender, race, ethnicity, and sexuality are interlocking systems, and that one's privilege varies according to one's status within these systems.

SEE ALSO: Discrimination; Gender, Development and; Gender Ideology and Gender Role Ideology; Homophobia and Heterosexism; Homosexuality; Race (Racism); Racism, Structural and Institutional; Sex and Gender

REFERENCES AND SUGGESTED READINGS

Acker, J. (1990) Hierarchies, Jobs, Bodies: A Theory of Gendered Organizations. *Gender and Society* 4: 139–58.

Boorstein, K. (1994) *Gender Outlaw: On Men, Women, and the Rest of Us.* Vintage, New York.

Collins, P. H. (1990) *Black Feminist Thought: Knowledge, Consciousness, and the Politics of Empowerment.* Unwin Hyman, Boston.

Connell, R. W. (1995) *Masculinities.* University of California Press, Los Angeles.

England, P. (1992) *Comparable Worth: Theories and Evidence.* Aldine de Gruyter, New York.

Greenberg, D. (1988) *The Construction of Homosexuality.* University of Chicago Press, Chicago.

Hart, K.-P. (2000) Representing Gay Men on American Television. *Journal of Men's Studies* 9: 59–79.

Hochschild, A. (1989) *The Second Shift: Working Parents and the Revolution at Home.* Viking, New York.

Hubbard, R. (1990) *The Politics of Women's Biology.* Rutgers University Press, New Brunswick, NJ.

Kanter, R. M. (1977) *Men and Women of the Corporation.* Basic Books, New York.

Kinsey, A., Pomeroy, W., & Martin, C. (1948) *Sexual Behavior in the Human Male.* W. B. Saunders, Philadelphia.

Pharr, S. (1997) *Homophobia: A Weapon of Sexism.* Chardon Press, Berkeley, CA.

Sadker, M. & Sadker, D. (1994) *How America's Schools Cheat Girls.* Scribner, New York.

Sender, K. (1999) Selling Sexual Subjectivities: Audiences Respond to Gay Window Advertising. *Critical Studies in Mass Communication* 16: 172–96.

Wilson, W. J. (1996) *When Work Disappears: The World of the New Urban Poor.* Knopf, New York.

Pro-choice and Pro-life Movements

Tracy A. Weitz and Carole Joffe

Abortion is one of the most contested social issues in the US. Despite its recognized status as a polarizing force in politics, a relatively small number of sociologists have studied the social movements that sustain the abortion debate.

As a result, the topic of abortion social movements, while widely written about by journalists, is often under-theorized. The following review summarizes the study of movements supporting and opposing abortion rights as studied by sociologists and other social scientists, predominantly in the US, with some attention to the changing international dimensions of this debate.

Social movements that take up the issue of abortion are often thought of as resulting from the 1973 Supreme Court decision *Roe* v. *Wade* (410 U.S. 113) recognizing a constitutional right to abortion. However, social contestation over abortion predates this decision with two periods of high social movement activity: the physician anti-abortion movement of the mid-1800s and the abortion rights reform/repeal movement of the 1960s.

A number of scholars, most notably Mohr (1978) and Luker (1984), argue that the early physician anti-abortion movement was part of a larger professionalizing project within organized medicine. Formally trained physicians sought to rid the profession of practitioners without such training, as well as lay-midwives who were the main providers of abortion to women. In opposition to abortion regular physicians could distinguish themselves from other unregulated practitioners. Because of its capacity to both control and distinguish the profession, abortion became a high priority for the American Medical Association (AMA), formed in 1847. In many ways the AMA can be thought of as the first abortion-related social movement organization in the US. In large part due to the anti-abortion campaign of the AMA, abortion became illegal in every state by 1900. (For a Foucaultian analysis of the early physician opposition to abortion, see Stormer 2002.)

Smith-Rosenberg (1985) examines the cultural context in which the medical profession's crusade against abortion occurred. In the mid-1800s the transition to smaller family size evident among society's most affluent and influential groups contrasted with the more prolific childbearing of recent immigrants. That white, married, Protestant, middle and upper-class women used abortion to space and limit their number of children concerned the elite class that comprised the medical profession. The need for social and ideological control over reproduction helped justify a medical crusade against abortion.

There was no organized counter-movement to the first anti-abortion social movement. Although the dates of the anti-abortion movement coincide with those of "first wave feminism," the early women's movement sought to articulate disparate male–female relationships in alternative language and sexual imagery rather than support for abortion rights (Smith-Rosenberg 1985). They endorsed "voluntary motherhood," not through abortion but through abstinence and control of men's sexual activity.

Abortion did not reappear on the larger public agenda until the 1960s, when both the medical community and the general public became increasingly frustrated with the inability of most American women to obtain a legal abortion. The works of historians Garrow (1998) and Hull and Hoffer (2001) provide details of the development and tactics of the reform/repeal abortion rights movement. Initially, efforts sought to reform laws by allowing more conditions under which a physician could perform an abortion (e.g., when the pregnancy was the result of a rape or when the developing pregnancy suffered from a genetic anomaly). Although these claims had widespread public appeal, they comprised only a small number of reasons why women sought abortions and thus few women qualified for abortions under these reform conditions. Eventually the limitations of the reform agenda would give way to a demand for the full repeal of abortion laws.

Two medical crises appeared in the 1960s that reengaged physicians in the debate over abortion: The use of the drug thalidomide by pregnant women (as in the Sherri Finkbine story) and the exposure of pregnant women to German measles (rubella) (Hull & Hoffer 2001). Thalidomide was never approved for use in the US, but it was used by many American women as a tranquilizer. When used in early pregnancy thalidomide causes gross fetal deformities. Similarly, women exposed to German measles in early pregnancy were also at higher risk of genetic abnormalities. An epidemic of German measles in the mid-1960s resulted in many physicians being asked to perform abortions. Joffe's (1995) work on physicians who practiced prior to and at the time of *Roe* illuminates the reasons for physicians' additional engagement in the efforts to fully repeal abortion laws rather than simply reform them. Both the witnessing in hospital emergency rooms of the disastrous results of illegal abortion and the lack of clarity regarding the legal status of the few in-hospital abortions that physicians were providing served as motivation for social movement action.

In addition to the role of physicians in the reform/repeal efforts, feminist scholars highlight the role of the 1960s "second wave" women's movement in the pressure for full abortion law repeal. The claim was that women deserved the right to have an abortion for the reasons of their choice. Women engaged in both political action geared at changing the laws as well as in directing women to safe illegal abortion providers and in some cases performing safe illegal abortions themselves. The history of both the Society for Humane Abortion and the Jane Collective contribute to an understanding of the efforts of feminist activists at this time.

The efforts to repeal abortion laws through the states' legislative processes experienced increased resistance, in part due to rising opposition from the Catholic Church. As such, the leaders of the reform/repeal movement began to prefer a judicial strategy challenging the constitutionality of abortion laws. The path of the case that would become associated with the right to legal abortion, *Roe* v. *Wade*, is discussed in several books, most usefully by Garrow (1998) and Luker (1984).

The *Roe* decision served as a catalyst for two new umbrella social movements: supporters and opponents of the right to legal abortion as articulated in *Roe*. The titles for these movements are contested between the movements, but they are commonly referred to as the Pro-life Movement and the Pro-choice Movement.

Within social movement literature, the Pro-life Movement can be understood as a countermovement developing in response to success of the abortion law reform/repeal movement culminating in *Roe*. In the 1970s changes to the tax code facilitated the formation of political action committees (PACs) and thus the opportunity for the Pro-life Movement to actively engage in the political arena. Pro-life PACs were formed to target vulnerable abortion rights-supporting politicians using single-issue voting, thereby aligning the growing Pro-life Movement with the newly developing Christian Right. The

merger of the Pro-life Movement and the New Right resulted in the adoption of a pro-life platform by the Republican Party and the election of Ronald Reagan as a pro-life candidate for president in 1980.

In addition to seeking to affect national politics the Pro-life Movement maintained a state-based strategy to limit access to abortions through the passage of laws in state legislatures. The first regulations to be upheld by the Supreme Court (1977) were state-based restrictions on the use of Medicaid funding to pay for abortions for poor women; the court would eventually uphold the federal prohibition on Medicaid funds known as the Hyde Amendment in 1980. Until 1989 further restrictions were struck down at both the state and the district court level, based on the *Roe* decision. In 1989 the Supreme Court heard *Webster* v. *Reproductive Health Services* (109 US 3040) challenging the constitutionality of Missouri's restrictions on abortion. When *Webster* was announced, the court fell short of overturning *Roe*, but a slim majority upheld every restriction of the law.

With the green light from the court that some state-based restrictions might be acceptable, the Pro-life Movement increased its efforts to pass more restrictive state legislation. In 1992 the Supreme Court heard a challenge to the Pennsylvania law which included compulsory antiabortion lectures by doctors, a 24-hour waiting period, a reporting requirement, spousal notification, and parental consent in *Planned Parenthood of Southern Pennsylvania* v. *Casey* (505 US 833). In *Casey* the majority opinion upheld most of the abortion restrictions, articulating a new standard whereby state-based restrictions on abortion would be found constitutional if they did not represent an "undue burden" on women. No definition of undue burden was provided.

In the mid-1980s some opponents of abortion began to take direct action against abortion providers. The most written about group of the direct action wing of the Pro-life Movement is Operation Rescue. Breaking with the focus on simply limiting the legality of abortion, Operation Rescue sought to stop the actual provision of services. Initial tactics included blockading entrances to abortion clinics. These sit-ins were billed as "non-violent" and often referenced the work of civil rights activists. Operation Rescue's most successful action occurred in 1991 with what would be called the Summer of Mercy, in which Wichita Kansas was under siege for 42 days as thousands of pro-life protesters converged on the city to blockade its clinics. A federal judge eventually issued an injunction ordering Operation Rescue to call off its demonstrations.

Although Operation Rescue claimed to be non-violent, harassment, bombings, arson, vandalism, invasions, and picketing became routine tactics of direct action activists. Blanchard (1994) argues that the adoption of violence as a tactic was fueled by feelings of alienation from the agenda of the more mainstream Pro-life Movement which had begun to focus its efforts to restrict abortion at the state level rather than to seek a full ban. The perceived failure of traditional lobbying tactics and executive regulation to bring about the level of change required to stop abortion led many in the movement to adopt a more aggressive and violent stance. The apex of violence was the actual killing of abortion providers.

In comparison to the Pro-life Movement, the Pro-choice Movement receives less scholastic attention. Staggenborg (1991), who studied the social movement organizations that comprise the Pro-choice Movement, provides the most comprehensive sociological discussion to date. According to Staggenborg, no demobilization of the abortion repeal movement occurred after the passage of *Roe*. Rather, the growing strength of the counter-movement required the institutionalization of the Pro-choice Movement and the use of tactics geared at maintaining abortion legality through legislative and judicial processes.

Although the Pro-life Movement had successfully elected Reagan as president there remained insufficient support for the pro-life agenda in Congress. Despite numerous attempts, the Pro-life Movement failed to pass a constitutional amendment banning abortion. These attempts, however, raised concern about the right to abortion among the pro-choice public. The Pro-choice Movement was additionally concerned with the ability of the counter-movement to forward its agenda by changing the composition of the courts. In 1987 open warfare broke out over the nomination of Robert Bork for the Supreme Court. The Pro-choice Movement galvanized opposition, eventually defeating Bork,

resulting in the appointment of an abortion-rights moderate who, while not willing to overturn *Roe*, accepted new restrictions on abortion in the *Webster* decision.

The Pro-choice Movement experienced its greatest successes in the early 1990s. As the court heard *Casey* in 1991, the Pro-choice Movement sponsored the March for Women's Lives, drawing between 500,000 and 700,000 marchers to Washington, DC. The momentum of the Pro-choice Movement culminated with the election of President Bill Clinton in 1992. Just two days after his inauguration, President Clinton issued several executive orders overturning five abortion restrictions put in place by the prior Reagan/Bush administrations. During his term he appointed two pro-choice judges to the Supreme Court. In March 1993 Dr. David Gunn was shot and killed, shocking the nation and prompting a call for federal legislation to protect women from clinic violence. As the Freedom of Access to Clinic Entrances Act (FACE) was being debated in Congress, two additional physicians were shot (one wounded and one killed). These killings prompted the quick approval of the federal FACE legislation.

Like the Pro-life Movement, however, the Pro-Choice movement lacked the votes to pass national legislation to codify in law their position on legal abortion. Efforts instead focused on challenging state laws to restrict access to abortion. No large national efforts of the Pro-Choice movement were undertaken until the legal right to abortion was again threatened by the election of a pro-life president, George W. Bush. In 2004 a repeat of the March for Women's Lives drew over 1,000,000 abortion rights supporters to Washington, DC. Despite this showing, a majority pro-life Senate was elected along with the reelection of President Bush. Although the Pro-choice Movement has sought to galvanize grassroots support for its cause, two new Pro-life Supreme Court justices received confirmation in 2005 and 2006.

Saletan (2003) examines the overall successes and failures of the Pro-choice Movement strategy in his work on how conservatives allegedly "won the abortion war." His particular interest is the adoption by the Pro-choice Movement of the "who decides" frame – a frame in which support is sought not for abortion rights but for keeping the government out of the decision.

(For a more detailed discussion of how discursive formations are used to forward a particularized understanding of abortion, see Condit 1990; for a discussion of how the fetus has been used, see Petchesky 1987.) Saletan argues that while the "who decides" frame is successful in maintaining abortion as legal, it fails to gain actual support for abortion rights as women's rights. With a few exceptions, most observers of social movement activity and abortion have failed to deal with issues of race. In her work on the subject, Nelson (2003) helps connect the reproductive rights movement with resistance to the eugenics movement and efforts to address sterilization abuse.

In addition to studying the political histories of the movements, sociology is interested in the people that actively join the two movements and in particular the meaning of abortion to those activists. The first major study in this arena was Luker's (1984) landmark work on activists in California. Luker found that differing views of motherhood explained women's engagement in abortion social movements. For those on the pro-life side, legal abortion was a referendum on the value of "stay at home" motherhood. Ginsburg's (1989) study of the battle over the opening of an abortion clinic in Fargo, North Dakota reached a similar conclusion – that those engaged in oppositional movements saw the meaning of abortion differently. Her work concludes that abortion is a symbolic focus for the assertion of mutually exclusive understandings about the place of women in society.

In her work on pro-life activists, Maxwell (2002) uses social movement theory to focus on the individualized meaning of abortion for pro-life activists; she argues that many activists view their efforts as fulfilling a personal obligation to God. Other women use activism as a means to resolve personal conflict with their own abortion experiences. Mason's (2002) work on the apocalyptic narrative of pro-life politics seeks to locate the extremist position which justifies "killing in the name of life" within the Pro-life Movement as part of a larger effort to reestablish the US as a Christian nation.

The rapid decline in the number of abortion providers in the US requires a renewed attention to the role of abortion within US medicine. In addition to driving some physicians away from providing abortion care, the rise in violence is understood to have prompted the activation of a new pro-choice physician countercounter movement. The creation of the organization Medical Students for Choice is seen as a turning point in the reengagement of physicians as a social movement player in the current fight over abortion. The uneasy alliance between physician-led activism and feminist-led activism, which historically was critical of physician power and dominance, is discussed by Joffe et al. (2004). Another development within medicine that receives some attention is the 12-year political battle over the approval by the US FDA of mifepristone, known as RU486 in France and most commonly as the "abortion pill." Although widely adopted by the health care providers already offering abortion services, medication abortion is not routinely offered by regular physicians as originally projected when RU486 was thought to be a solution to the "abortion war."

While the debate regarding abortion in the US is not mirrored throughout the world, a growing globalization of the Pro-life/Pro-choice struggle is underway. This tension was played out at both the International Conference on Population and Development in Cairo in 1994, and the Fourth World Conference on Women held in Beijing in 1995, where disagreements regarding abortion dominated many efforts to build an international agenda. Opposition to international recognition of abortion rights was initially raised by a small group of countries (some Muslim, some Catholic, including the Vatican delegation), but is now led by the US. In 2000 newly elected President George W. Bush reimposed the "global gag rule," a measure which stipulates that no US foreign aid funds for family planning services could go to organizations which use their own funds for abortion services or referrals. This ban also precludes organizations that wish to receive US funds from engaging in advocacy related to abortion, thereby silencing many pro-choice voices within developing nations. Delegations from the US to recent international convenings have mandated that opposition to abortion be a central component of any agreement to which the US would take part. Within many developing nations as well as former republics of the Soviet Union, anti-abortion efforts are receiving substantial financial support from US-based Pro-life Movement organizations (for case examples, see Kulczycki 1999).

Within other developed nations little attention has been paid to the existence or non-existence of abortion social movements, in part due to the lack of extreme polarization within electorates and the absence of violence. Francome (2004) briefly discusses the existence of abortion social movements within the UK, while Ferree et al. (2002) expose those groups working within Germany.

SEE ALSO: Abortion as a Social Problem; Family Planning, Abortion, and Reproductive Health; Feminism, First, Second, and Third Waves; Gender, Social Movements and; Marriage, Sex, and Childbirth; New Reproductive Technologies; Women's Health; Women's Movements

REFERENCES AND SUGGESTED READINGS

Blanchard, D. A. (1994) *The Anti-Abortion Movement and the Rise of the Religious Right: From Polite to Fiery Protest.* Twayne, New York; Maxwell Macmillan, Toronto.

Condit, C. M. (1990) *Decoding Abortion Rhetoric: Communicating Social Change.* University of Illinois Press, Urbana.

Ferree, M. M., Gamson, W. A., Gerhards, J., & Rucht, D. (2002) *Shaping Abortion Discourse: Democracy and the Public Sphere in Germany and the United States.* Cambridge University Press, Cambridge.

Francome, C. (2004) *Abortion in the USA and the UK.* Ashgate, Burlington, VT.

Garrow, D. J. (1998) *Liberty and Sexuality: The Right to Privacy and the Making of Roe v. Wade.* University of California Press, Berkeley.

Ginsburg, F. (1989) *Contested Lives: The Abortion Debate in an American Community.* University of California Press, Berkeley.

Hull, N. E. H. & Hoffer, P. C. (2001) *Roe v. Wade: The Abortion Rights Controversy in American History.* University Press of Kansas, Lawrence.

Joffe, C. (1995) *Doctors of Conscience: The Struggle to Provide Abortion Before and After Roe v. Wade.* Beacon Press, Boston.

Joffe, C., Weitz, T. A., & Stacey, C. L. (2004) Uneasy Allies: Pro-Choice Physicians, Feminist Health Activists and the Struggle for Abortion Rights. *Sociology of Health and Illness* 26: 775–96.

Kulczycki, A. (1999) *The Abortion Debate in the World Arena.* Routledge, New York.

Luker, K. (1984) *Abortion and the Politics of Motherhood.* University of California Press, Berkeley.

Mason, C. (2002) *Killing for Life: The Apocalyptic Narrative of Pro-Life Politics.* Cornell University Press, Ithaca, NY.

Maxwell, C. J. C. (2002) *Pro-Life Activists in America: Meaning, Motivation, and Direct Action.* Cambridge University Press, Cambridge.

Mohr, J. C. (1978) *Abortion in America: The Origins and Evolution of National Policy, 1800–1900.* Oxford University Press, New York.

Nelson, J. (2003) *Women of Color and the Reproductive Rights Movement.* New York University Press, New York.

Petchesky, R. P. (1987) Fetal Images: The Power of Visual Culture in the Politics of Reproduction. *Feminist Studies* 13: 263–92.

Saletan, W. (2003) *Bearing Right: How Conservatives Won the Abortion War.* University of California Press, Berkeley.

Smith-Rosenberg, C. (1985) *Disorderly Conduct: Visions of Gender in Victorian America.* Oxford University Press, New York.

Staggenborg, S. (1991) *The Pro-Choice Movement: Organization and Activism in the Abortion Conflict.* Oxford University Press, New York.

Stormer, N. (2002) *Articulating Life's Memory: US Medical Rhetoric about Abortion in the Nineteenth Century.* Lexington Books, Lanham, MD.

professional dominance in medicine

Donald W. Light

Professional dominance is a theory about professionalization and a profession's relation to society that implies that this relationship is out of balance. It thus opens up issues of trust, exploitation of patients and society, suppression of competing groups, subordination of allied professions, and escalation of costs. The term is inherently less neutral than "professionalism" or the study of professions in society. It is largely used in literature on the medical profession in modern times.

ORIGINS AND HISTORY

Eliot Freidson developed the concept and theory of professional dominance in 1970 in a book of that title. He also detailed its dynamics and pathologies in a second 1970 book, *Profession of Medicine*. His overall argument is that an occupation with valued and complex esoteric knowledge and skills strives to get special legal and institutional privileges from the state and society more generally, so that it can become a profession. This gives it critical powers, such as exclusive rights of licensure and control over its domain of work, which it tries to define as broadly as possible.

Other exclusive rights and powers include prescribing controlled substances, admitting patients to hospitals, ordering tests and procedures, putting patients into a death-like state, cutting into their bodies, excusing people from work, enabling people to receive service and financial benefits, and exempting people from criminal prosecution in the case of insanity. In the twentieth century, professions typically were granted control over the content and execution of training, certification and licensure, defining whether other providers were practicing medicine without licensure, defining the standards of care, assuring good quality of care and ethical standards, and disciplining members who violated professional standards.

These powers reflect a tacit social contract between society and the profession: Because you have highly valued skills and address critical social needs (to heal, to cure, to stave off death), we will grant you autonomy over these powers with the understanding that you will serve patients' needs first and behave in an altruistic manner.

In his early seminal work, Freidson emphasized the ways in which the medical profession had parlayed autonomy into dominance by exploiting this kind of social contract. The American health care system in the 1950s and 1960s offered considerable evidence, as hospitalization, subspecialization, surgery, tests, other procedures, and charges rapidly escalated. Complaints of unnecessary tests, procedures, hospitalization, and overcharging proliferated in the 1960s. Without the constraints of a national health care system that most other countries had in some form, these pathologies

of professionalism flourished. Many other studies and books on the pathologies of professionalism soon followed. One of Freidson's observations was that the organized profession cannot police or discipline its members very strongly without alienating them.

Subsequent to Freidson, Larson (1977) wrote an influential history of the rise of professionalism as a form of monopoly, where a profession charges rents (fees) on its capital (exclusive expertise), which it can expand through specialization and control over health care institutions. Ivan Illich, a Jesuit priest with a worldwide audience for his wide range of incisive critiques of modern society, wrote *Medical Nemesis* in 1975. Just by extrapolating from clinical studies, Illich documented the ways in which the medical profession was poisoning patients with toxic drugs, mutilating them with bad surgery, making patients increasingly dependent on them, and medicalizing more and more of human life. *Medical Nemesis* was professional dominance gone mad. Wherever Illich spoke in the western hemisphere, there was standing room only.

Paul Starr's landmark history, *The Social Transformation of American Medicine* (1982), built on a body of historical work to detail how the American medical profession parlayed its professional powers into institutional, legal, and financial dominance. Of particular note are the ways in which physicians incorporated their practices, started corporations for hospitals, clinics, and other services, formed strong alliances with medical supply and pharmaceutical corporations, and started hospital chains in the 1970s. A short, more analytic update has been written by Donald Light (2004). In other countries, professional dominance was evident in different forms. Light and Alexander Schuller (1986) led a team that documented a similar rise from autonomy to dominance that occurred in Weimar Germany and led to private physicians strongly supporting Hitler's rise to power. He quickly gave them new legal powers to destroy early models of community-based, inexpensive, patient-run clinics; strip the licenses of doctors who worked in them; and institute a professionally dominated model of medical services that formed the basis of the West German health care system after World War II. Most of its problems of escalating costs and fragmented services can be traced to this history. This is one of many examples of how the medical profession came to control the central regulatory, financial, and institutional bodies in countries with universal health insurance or services.

CHALLENGES TO PROFESSIONAL DOMINANCE

Soon after the relentless ascent of professional dominance was declared, it started to face challenges. One challenge came from the logical extension of professional dominance itself – the development of hospital and other corporate chains by investors who saw that the profession's economic and legal autonomy meant that it could make a lot of money with almost no downside risk. Even mistakes were billable. This led a great spokesman of the profession, Arnold Relman (1980), to write about "the new medical-industrial complex." Relman and thousands of other physicians were appalled at the corporate takeover of American medicine. What he ignored was 30 years of increasingly commercialized practice by the physicians themselves. Also overlooked were the ways in which dedication to good practice and altruism were easy because they paid. The more thorough and careful one was, the more money one made. The health care corporations simply dropped the altruism and said they wanted to make money. Their size and power, however, constituted a new dominant force.

Meantime, Congress and employers became increasingly restive about the escalating medical bills they had to pay, and studies kept coming from top clinical researchers that showed much care was unnecessary. Other studies documented large variations in how physicians treated patients with the same medical conditions. These constituted deep pathologies of professional dominance and even autonomy. A stream of studies up to this day shows unmonitored autonomy results in continued use of outmoded or discredited tests and procedures; under- and over-diagnosis of conditions; careless mistakes with dangerous consequences; incomplete work-ups and treatment plans; and unnecessary exposure of patients to risks. Was professional dominance based on a false pretense at its core?

In response to such evidence, institutional payers began to behave like buyers, what Light (2004) calls "the buyers' revolt." A new constellation of corporate middlemen arose in the later 1970s to help them contain costs and buy better value. Institutional buyers started to hire corporations to review costly tests, procedures, and hospitalizations. They hired other teams to identify which physicians and hospitals practiced more cost-effective medicine and rewarded employees or beneficiaries to use them. Congress funded long-range programs to assess different ways to treat common problems in order to identify which were more cost-effective. Still other corporations specialized in managing the small percent of costly, chronic cases. These and other elements came together in the late 1980s to be called "managed care."

Physicians began to feel like the proletariat (the exploited workers of capitalists) and proletarianization arose as a competing theory to professional dominance. The benchmark article (McKinlay & Arches 1985) regarded all infringements on autonomy as forms of proletarianization, even government prohibitions against practices that discriminated by race and gender. A few years later the Marxist framework was dropped and the same analysis was called corporatization.

On another front, as early as 1973, Marie Haug identified several ways in which deprofessionalization was developing. Alternate and paraprofessionals were proliferating; lay people increasingly challenged professional authority; and computers were enabling people to become expert patients. Haug and Bebe Levin summarized their work in *Consumerism in Medicine* (1983).

FROM DOMINANCE TO COUNTERVAILING POWERS

In a review of these competing theories, Light and Sol Levine (1988) faulted each as identifying one trend and one part of the whole. Each lacked a sense of historical development and could not explain change. In particular, professional dominance as a theory was unable to explain decline, because dominance begets further dominance. The authors called for a new framework. Some years later, Light developed a theory of countervailing powers that allows one to analyze historical changes in professional dominance or decline within or between countries. The theory, depicted in Figure 1, looks at the medical profession as one of several countervailing powers that pursue their agendas with varying intensity from era to era (Light 2000).

Particularly notable is the historical, comparative study by Elliott Krause (1996).

Future developments seem to center on two issues. First, the medical profession is still reeling from the revolt of the buyers and the

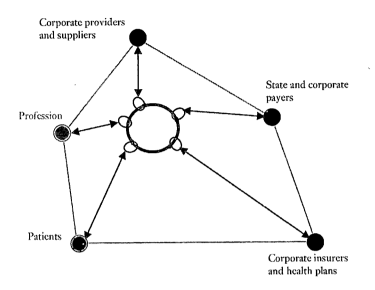

Figure 1 Countervailing powers in health care.

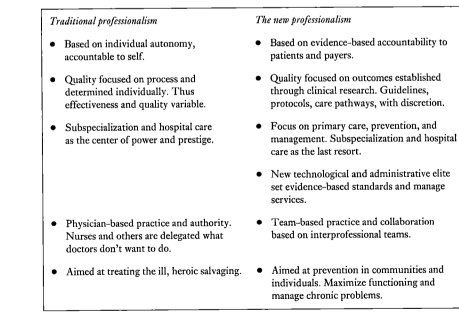

Traditional professionalism	The new professionalism
● Based on individual autonomy, accountable to self.	● Based on evidence-based accountability to patients and payers.
● Quality focused on process and determined individually. Thus effectiveness and quality variable.	● Quality focused on outcomes established through clinical research. Guidelines, protocols, care pathways, with discretion.
● Subspecialization and hospital care as the center of power and prestige.	● Focus on primary care, prevention, and management. Subspecialization and hospital care as the last resort.
	● New technological and administrative elite set evidence-based standards and manage services.
● Physician-based practice and authority. Nurses and others are delegated what doctors don't want to do.	● Team-based practice and collaboration based on interprofessional teams.
● Aimed at treating the ill, heroic salvaging.	● Aimed at prevention in communities and individuals. Maximize functioning and manage chronic problems.

Figure 2 The new professionalism.
Source: Light (2000).

challenges to its core, autonomy and control over its work. Yet the uneven quality of professional services when left to autonomous providers is well documented, and autonomy at the individual level leads to fragmentation at the organizational level. In the journal *Academic Medicine* and reports of the Association of American Medical Colleges, one can follow the struggles by the American medical profession to reaffirm altruism, dutifulness, and autonomy as core values of a renewed professionalism. A basic problem, however, is that one cannot expect a profession to behave much differently than the institutional and cultural framework in which it works. If the health care system is based on the corporate practice of medicine, if selection of more profitable patients and procedures is rewarded, if elaborated care and "defensive medicine" pay well, how much differently can one expect professionals to behave? More promising is a reconceptualization of professionalism centered on accountability, as illustrated in Figure 2. Second, Stefen Timmermans and Emily Kolker (2004) point out that clinical guidelines and protocols have not affected professional behavior much and argue that it would be more useful to stop focusing on professional dominance or decline and study the specific forms of professional power and knowledge. That focus, in turn, opens up the question of whether there are, in practice, not a profession but multiple professions, and even made-up forms of professionalism to carry out the dominant interests of governments or corporations like the pharmaceutical industry.

SEE ALSO: Deviance, Constructionist Perspectives; Deviance, Medicalization of; Deviance Processing Agencies; Health Professions and Occupations; Patient–Physician Relationship; Ideology; Illness Behavior; Managed Care; Medical School Socialization; Professions, Organized; Schools, Professional; Science and Culture

REFERENCES AND SUGGESTED READINGS

Freidson, E. (1970a) *Profession of Medicine*. Dodd, Mead, New York.

Freidson, E. (1970b) *Professional Dominance*. Atherton, New York.
Haug, M. (1973) Deprofessionalization: An Alternative Hypothesis for the Future. *Sociological Review Monographs* 20: 195–211.
Haug, M. & Levin, B. (1983) *Consumerism in Medicine*. Sage, Beverly Hills, CA.
Illich, I. (1975) *Medical Nemesis: The Expropriation of Health*. Calder & Boyers, London.
Krause, E. (1996) *Death of the Guilds*. Yale University Press, New Haven.
Larson, M. (1977) *The Rise of Professionalism*. University of California Press, Berkeley.
Light, D. W. (2000) The Medical Profession and Organizational Change: From Professional Dominance to Countervailing Power. In: Bird, C., Conrad, P., & Fremont, A. (Eds.), *Handbook of Medical Sociology*, 5th edn. Prentice-Hall, Englewood Cliffs, NJ, pp. 201–16.
Light, D. W. (2004) Introduction. Ironies of Success: A New History of the American Health Care "System." *Journal of Health and Social Behavior* 45 (Special issue): 1–24.
Light, D. W. & Bourgeault, I. (Eds.) (2004) Health and Health Care in the United States: Origins and Dynamics. *Journal of Health and Social Behavior* 45 (Special issue).
Light, D. W. & Levine, S. (1988) Changing Character of the Medical Profession: A Theoretical Overview. *Milbank Quarterly* 66 (Suppl. 2): 1–23.
Light, D. W. & Schuller, A. S. (Eds.) (1986) *Political Values and Health Care: The German Experience*. MIT Press, Cambridge, MA.
McKinlay, J. B. & Arches, J. (1985) Toward the Proletarianization of Physicians. *International Journal of Health Services* 15: 161–95.
Relman, A. (1980) The New Medical-Industrial Complex. *New England Journal of Medicine* 303: 963–70.
Starr, P. (1982) *The Social Transformation of American Medicine*. Basic Books, New York.
Timmermans, S. & Kolker, E. (2004) Clinical Practice Guidelines and the Reconfiguration of Medical Knowledge. *Journal of Health and Social Behavior* 45 (Special issue): 177–93.

professions

Keith Macdonald

Professions have been of interest to all the main schools of sociology, both in their own right and in relation to such topics as capitalism, the state, social stratification, patriarchy, power, and knowledge.

Contemporary studies broadly agree that the professions are those occupations based on "advanced, or complex, or esoteric, or arcane knowledge"; or on "formally rational abstract utilitarian knowledge" (Murphy 1988), whose associations, in order to protect their knowledge and the market in services based on it, have entered into a regulative bargain with the state. These features usually enable an occupation to achieve good economic rewards and relatively high social status; this leads other occupations to try to emulate them.

The regulative bargain typically includes the means of controlling members of the occupation, and the obligation to adhere to ethical standards and to act with probity in relation to their clients and to the public. These features drew the attention of functionalist sociologists, from Émile Durkheim in the late nineteenth century to Talcott Parsons in the 1950s and 1960s, and led them to see professions as the bearers and defenders of important social values in modern society. This emphasis on the eufunctional value of the professions led some sociologists to adopt the "trait approach," whereby they devised ways of deciding which occupations were professions or semi-professions and which were not.

This rather sterile exercise provoked Everett C. Hughes (1963) to write that he "passed from the false question 'Is this occupation a profession?' to the more fundamental one, 'What are the circumstances in which people in an occupation attempt to turn it into a profession and themselves into professional people?'" This symbolic interactionist stance stimulated much fruitful work on the professions. Eliot Freidson's notable work on the medical profession in the 1970s provided the stimulus for what became known as the "power approach" to the study of the professions. Freidson himself considered that to examine power alone was not the way forward and in his own work took a broader and more nuanced position. This was developed further by M. S. Larson's seminal work, *The Rise of Professionalism* (1977), which extended the interactionist analysis by drawing on Marxian ideas of production, market, and social class, and Weber's concepts of social closure and qualifications as a basis for both economic advantage and social status. Larson sees professionalization as an attempt to translate one order of scarce resources – special knowledge and skills – into another – economic and social rewards. Maintaining scarcity helps to achieve a monopoly of expertise in the market, and to enhance status in a system of stratification. Larson's work emphasizes that social mobility and market control are not merely straightforward reflections of skill, expertise, or ethical standards, but that they are the outcome of the collective efforts of members in pursuit of the "professional project."

The concept of "professional project" is seen as much less important by Andrew Abbott in another important analysis, *The System of the Professions* (1988). Instead he emphasizes the importance of studying the actual work that an occupation does, the extent of its "jurisdiction," and its competition with other occupations. One may draw many distinctions between the work of Larson and of Abbott but there is an affinity between the two approaches in the sense that they both have added structural elements to an interactionist theme, to provide an eclectic but coherent theorizing of professions. An important element was added by Anna Witz's study, *Professions and Patriarchy* (1992), which elucidates the practices of those occupations, one of whose original defining features was that they were fit for gentle*men*. Macdonald, on the other hand, in *The Sociology of the Professions* (1995), takes the professional project as his starting point, and elaborates and contextualizes it in an effort to show its applicability to a number of aspects of the professions in a variety of cultural contexts.

Marxian sociology of the professions, in contrast to the interactionist theme, is one of structure and system, whose "processes," such as state formation, polarization of social classes, and monopolization of the means of production, are the consequences of the capitalist mode of production. The professions are seen as integral to these processes, which are depicted not as the consequences of the actions of individuals and collectivities but as part and parcel of the exploitative relations of capitalist production. Any control that a profession has of its knowledge, any gain it might achieve in its class position, would be regarded as merely contingent on the advantage that global capital derived from such circumstances. There is also a Marxian flavor to one version of the power approach, that of Terry Johnson, which, in contrast to Freidson, is more concerned with the relative advantages that an occupation could derive from its market position and relationship with the state.

Michel Foucault has also studied the power of professions and their relation to the state, focusing on the connection between knowledge and power. He sees the modern state as developing the science of the right disposition of all things leading to the welfare of all. Professionals (as the experts in these new scientific disciplines) are crucial to modern government, and their professional associations, in which expertise is institutionalized, are integral to the governance of the modern state. Foucault's originality has stimulated many studies of the professions but some writers fail to find a connection between that originality and the sociological tradition, while others regard his work as opaque and devoid of flesh and blood actors.

The study of the professions has the virtue not only of providing an insight into one particular segment of society, but also, as Freidson demonstrates in *Professionalism: The Third Logic* (2001), of linking up with the wider sociological themes referred to above.

SEE ALSO: Knowledge; Occupations; Power, Theories of; Professions, Organized; Stratification and Inequality, Theories of

REFERENCES AND SUGGESTED READINGS

Durkheim, É. (1957) *Professional Ethics and Civic Morals*. Free Press, New York.

Foucault, M. (1980) *Power–Knowledge*. Harvester Press, Brighton.

Freidson, E. (1970) *The Profession of Medicine*. Dodd, Mead, New York. (Afterword added 1988.)

Hughes, E. C. (1963) Professions. *Daedalus* 92: 655–68.

Johnson, T. (1972) *Professions and Power*. Macmillan, London.

Murphy, R. (1988) *Social Closure*. Clarendon Press, Oxford.

professions, organized

Chris Carter

Professions are one of the main forms of institutionalizing expertise in western societies (Giddens 1991). The term "profession" is a curious one. It immediately conjures up images drawn from television shows featuring lawyers or medical doctors. Such representations point to the hold that certain professions have on our imagination. In *Bleak House*, Charles Dickens's celebrated novel, Richard Carstone considers which profession he wants to take up. The realm of possibilities – according to the definitional criteria of the age – is the military, the clergy, the law, and medicine. Professions such as law and medicine have successfully maintained both their power and status across several centuries and are seen as quintessential exemplars of what constitutes a profession. In the late nineteenth century and throughout the twentieth, a raft of new professions emerged. Some, like accountancy, have accrued considerable power.

While the dazzling array of different professions renders a definition of a profession difficult (Friedson 1986), the legacy of structural functional research suggests that features of a profession include: a body of abstract and specialized knowledge; a professional's autonomy over the labor process; self-regulation by the profession; legal rights restricting those who can practice; control of the supply and licensing of practitioners by the professional body; altruism; and the enjoyment of high status within society. Such characteristics form an "ideal type" of professional labor – one which is rarely observed in professions themselves.

The professional associations of many so-called "new" professions, such as marketers and human resource specialists, have expended considerable effort in trying to emulate the traits of the more established professions. Professions are complex and variegated and there are crucial distinctions in their relative status, the length of their history, and power (Friedson 2001).

THE SOCIOLOGY OF THE PROFESSIONS

The early influential thinkers on the professions included Durkheim (1957), Parsons (1951), and Tawney (1921). Their views held sway for much of the twentieth century and saw professions in a benign way, representing them as the bearers of a neutral and technocratic logic. Being experts in a specific area, professions came into being because there was a functional need for them and they used their skills and knowledge toward the betterment of society. This was particularly so in their role in mediating between individuals and society. Parsons did not regard professionals as selfless; rather, he saw their interests as being non-pecuniary and directed toward enjoying high status and reputation in society, which in turn ensured the provision of the best possible services to society. Structural functionalist research was generally directed to ascertaining the characteristics of a profession in contrast to a non-profession (Etzioni 1969). This research did much to establish the trait approach to understanding professions – something that has been influential to many occupational figurations seeking to establish themselves as professions.

Resonant with structural functionalism was the developmental approach to studying professions over time. Wilensky (1964) argued that increasing numbers of occupational groups were laying claim to professional status. This had the effect of stretching the definition of professions to the point where it was meaningless. In his seminal study of the professions, Wilensky analyzed 18 different occupations. He developed a sequential model of the development of professions, which highlighted the stages in the development of a profession. Wilensky concluded that many of the aspirant occupations would fail in their quest to achieve professional status as many of the stages took considerable time.

The Parsonsian orthodoxy was subject to radical critique from the 1960s onwards. A generation of writers theorized professions through looking at the prevailing relations of power. Many writers, coming out of the Chicago School tradition, sought to debunk the notion of professionals as disinterested and altruistic. Instead they sought to understand the means through which professions organized themselves, how they were able to uphold their privileges and status, how they managed their relations with the state, and the effects they had on other groups (Friedson 1970). British sociologist Terry Johnson (1972) analyzed professions from a neo-Marxist perspective, seeing them as mechanisms of control where a profession is able to control its own members. For Johnson, the state had an important role to play in upholding the power of professions. In the late 1970s, Margali Larson's *The Rise of Professionalism* (1977) integrated both Marxist and Weberian perspectives and argued that professions are interest groups whose objective was a "collective mobility project" aligned to the class system of capitalist societies. Achieving professional status allowed occupations to ameliorate both their economic and their social standing. Similarly, MacDonald and Ritzer (1988) argued that professional groups seek to establish monopoly control over a particular jurisdictional area. They then seek to control the related activities, while keeping a distance from subordinate groups.

The critique of functionalism shifted attention to the means through which professions achieve and retain power. Andrew Abbott (1988) developed this work further by outlining a dynamic theory of professions. According to Abbott, competition ensues between aspirant groups, thereby creating stratified professions which vary markedly in their levels of jurisdiction. He argued that expertise became institutionalized through this jurisdictional competition, which established who controlled which domain, which in turn determined relative status and prestige. Abbott's analysis emphasizes that there is an ongoing process of competition among different groups, which means that over time the relative power of a profession might change dramatically.

PROFESSIONS, ORGANIZATIONS, AND MANAGEMENT

Many professions have changed dramatically over the last 20 years with the economic restructuring that had its genesis in the election of Margaret Thatcher in the UK and Ronald Reagan in the US. Welsh sociologist Mike Reed (1996) argued that the experience of professions differs markedly. According to Reed, it is useful to draw a distinction between three distinct forms of profession. They are the "liberal," "organizational," and "entrepreneurial" professions, respectively. Liberal professions are those such as law and medicine. Their characteristics are that they are independent, work for fees, and enjoy autonomy over their work organization. Organizational professions owe their status and professional warrant to the organization in which they work. Many organizational professions are employees of the state. They are typically a product of the great expansion of the state experienced during the twentieth century. Schoolteachers, social workers, government scientists, and the utility engineers would count among the ranks of the organizational professionals. "Entrepreneurial" professions exploit opportunities offered by markets, such as IT and management consultants.

Liberal professions such as law, chartered accountancy, and medicine have encountered many changes. Research carried out at the University of Alberta in Canada identified two archetypes within professional service work, which were titled "professional partnership" and "managed professional business." The former emphasizes collegiality, serving the client and the public interest, while being dismissive of managerialism. In contrast, the managed professional business (MPB) embraces the market and is resolutely corporate in its approach to the conduct of the profession. MPB professional service firms have developed corporate brands in their own right and their interpretive schemes owe as much to the discourse of strategic management as to law or accounting. Hanlon (1994) has characterized this broad shift as the commercialization of the service class, which involves large law and accounting firms being engaged in capital accumulation strategies. In a fascinating study of the socialization of trainee accountants, Grey et al. demonstrate that commercialization has redefined what constitutes professional conduct. Broader civic concerns have been displaced by "pleasing the client," which in the case of accounting firms is the

company that pays for the audit. The wave of accounting scandals – such as Enron, Parmalat, and WorldCom – are for many the consequence of the commercialization of the accounting profession.

In contrast to the expansionary climate experienced by many liberal professions, the last 20 years have witnessed organizational professions encountering hostility from new right governments and attacks in the media. State-sponsored professions such as teachers, social workers, and utility professionals have seen their status and autonomy eroded. This has led to speculation as to whether we are seeing the twilight of some professions – mainly those that expanded through state support in the twentieth century. In some cases the decline is for material reasons. In the United States, the high cost of higher education combined with the relatively low economic rewards make many professions unattractive to newcomers. Throughout the western world, industries have been privatized. In some cases this has led to a managerialist assault on established organizational professions. Carter and Mueller (2002) report the removal of a previously dominant cadre of professional engineers from a British electricity utility in the years following privatization. More generally, new public management or managerialism has challenged the autonomy and self-governance of professions throughout the public sector. Professions such as nursing have been much changed in an attempt by western health authorities to respond to the challenges of the increasing demand and costs of health care. Nurses' responsibilities have been expanded greatly. The needs of western health care systems cast a long shadow over developing world countries as nursing staff are lured to the West by the promise of relatively good wages and conditions.

Entrepreneurial professions are those that have gained the most over the last 20 years. For purists, they do not constitute professions at all, yet occupational figurations such as management consultants and IT consultants have experienced unprecedented growth in both their turnover and their influence in civil society. The commercialization processes discussed above led many of the large accounting firms away from core accounting activities. For instance, Arthur

Andersen billed Enron for $25 million for consulting services and $27 million for the audit in their final year of trading. Of course, consulting does not fall into any neat categories of professional work. Many have characterized the activity as knowledge work or immaterial labor, whereby "symbolic analysts" manipulate signs, symbols, and images. Lacking an obvious "right answer," knowledge work is inherently ambiguous. Consequently, Mats Alvesson has suggested that technical expertise – whilst important – is becoming increasingly secondary to image and rhetoric intensity, which help persuade a client of the efficacy of a knowledge worker's proposed course of action. In short, it is not so much a case of being an expert as *appearing* to be an expert. Entrepreneurial professions do not typically possess the institutional pillar of a strong professional body and it will be interesting to see how such groups develop. In time will they emulate the traditional liberal professions, or do they represent a new form of professional organization centered on brand, image, and reputation?

It is a fascinating time for analysts of the professions, especially those with a management focus. Managerialism, commercialization, and privatization have radically changed the context in which professions operate. Professions are likely to remain important means of institutionalizing expertise, although how professions organize and what it is to be a professional are likely to be fruitful areas for research.

SEE ALSO: Labor Process; Management Consultants; Professions

REFERENCES AND SUGGESTED READINGS

Abbott, A. (1988) *The System of Professions*. University of Chicago Press, Chicago.

Carter, C. & Mueller, F. (2002) The Long March of the Management Modernizers. *Human Relations*.

Cooper, D. J., Hinings, C. R., Greenwood, R., & Brown, J. L. (1996) Sedimentation and Transformation in Organizational Change: The Case of Canadian Law Firms. *Organization Studies* 17: 623–48.

Durkheim, É. (1957) *Professional Ethics and Civic Morals*. Free Press, New York.

Etzioni, A. (1969) *The Semi-Professions and their Organization: Teachers, Nurses, and Social Workers*. Free Press, New York.

Friedson, E. (1970) *Medical Dominance*. Aldine-Atherton, Chicago.

Friedson, E. (1986) *Professional Powers*. University of Chikago Press, Chicago.

Friedson, E. (2001) *Professionalism: The Third Logic*. Polity Press, Cambridge.

Giddens, A. (1991) *Modernity and Self-Identity: Self and Society in the Late Modern Age*. Polity Press, Cambridge.

Hanlon, G. (1994) *The Commercialization of Accountancy: Flexible Accumulation and the Transformation of the Service Class*. Macmillan, Basingstoke.

Johnson, T. (1972) *Professions and Power*. Macmillan, London.

Larson, M. S. (1977) *The Rise of Professionalism: A Sociological Analysis*. University of California Press, Berkeley, CA.

MacDonald, K. & Ritzer, G. (1988) The Sociology of the Professions: Dead or Alive? *Work and Occupations* (August): 251–72.

Parsons, T. (1951) *The Social System*. Free Press, Glencoe, IL.

Reed, M. (1996) Expert Power and Control in Late Modernity. *Organization Studies* 17(4): 573–98.

Tawney, R. H. (1921) *The Acquisitive Society*. Harvester Press, Brighton.

Wilensky, H. L. (1964) The Professionalization of Everyone? *American Journal of Sociology* 70: 137–58.

professors

Joseph C. Hermanowicz

Professors are people with academic appointments at institutions of higher education. Compared to just a half-century ago, higher education is differentiated on many counts, including the professorial role. While definitions delimit boundaries, they are sometimes ambiguously drawn. Professors in the American context typically hold advanced terminal degrees in the specialty in which they hold rank as assistant, associate, or full professor, those ranks composing an ascent in an institutional career. Yet vast numbers of people with academic appointments occupy roles, often without advanced terminal degrees, as lecturer, instructor, or, increasingly, as a temporary or part-time adjunct or affiliate of a unit within colleges and universities. Thus one can be more liberal or restrictive in the application of the term, but this complexity raises core theoretic questions about the very topic of professors in contemporary society: Who are they? What roles do they perform? What is the academic profession to which these individuals purportedly belong? How has the profession changed over time in its form and function? Answers to these questions become even more complex when extending them across national boundaries, perhaps explaining why little systematic comparative work on higher education faculties has been attempted. A total of 138 national systems of higher education, involving most countries of the world and employing nearly all professors across the globe, are described over the four volumes of *The Encyclopedia of Higher Education* (Clark & Neave 1992).

There are over 560,000 professors (i.e., full-time instructional faculty and staff) employed in over 4,000 accredited institutions in the US. The size alone of such a population speaks of variety, but when dimensions of institutional type, field, individual age, and career stage are added it is little wonder that scholars of higher education have alternatively referred to the landscape of small worlds or different worlds, each of which exhibits its own characteristic form of variety and constraint.

Professors – normatively performing roles of disciplined free inquiry through teaching, research, and other professional activities – have been studied as an object of inquiry unto their own. At root, the reasons for treating professors as an object of study are twofold. First, professors extend culture and civilization. As teacher, researcher, and scholar, professors transmit to their audiences knowledge that has, in principle, been socially certified by their professional-disciplinary community. In this sense, they extend culture by both transmitting and building upon knowledge. In another sense, they extend culture by passing along a set of generalized values, attitudes, and beliefs to new generations who learn institutional patterns of life through the process of education.

Second, professors guard culture and civilization. Their profession writ large is uniquely situated in society as the profession that trains people for all other professions and numerous other lines of work requiring certified education. In this sense, they guard culture by upholding cognitive and behavioral standards that have been created by their professional-disciplinary communities to ensure competent role performance. In another sense, they guard culture by upholding a set of generalized ideals: as masters in their various roles, they seek precision and excellence, cogent and articulable thought – and seek to inculcate these characteristics in their student clientele – so as to produce a higher learning and more advanced civilization.

For these reasons, professors assume a privileged place in the social organization of modern societies. But while professors may be viewed as central to society, the development of the study of them has been erratic, and less central to the core disciplines that can arguably yield major insights into the social organization of professors, sociology chief among them. One can find a sociology of higher education within which professors are a subject of study, but it is a nascent and thus small specialty area within sociology proper, and an area of inquiry that emerged and developed apart from what some take to be a kind of specialty cousin, the sociology of education, which customarily takes schools and schooling in grades K–12 as its province. While it would seemingly make sense for sociologists of education and sociologists of higher education to be nearly one of a kind, in regular contact and exchange with one another, attending the same professional meetings, and reading and publishing in the same journals, they are not, and instead inhabit different universes that rarely coincide. This has occurred much to the loss of higher education specialists. It is conceivable that a sociology of higher education would have developed sooner and with greater theoretic grounding had a boundary between it and the sociology of education – where concept and theory development has proceeded more swiftly – not been drawn so heavily. But the divide developed and has become institutionalized, more so for intellectual than political reasons. Sociological theorists turned their attention in the early twentieth century – to the extent they turned to education – to early schooling, since this was where, in Durkheim's terms, "real life began." Higher education involving and affecting the masses, and thereby inspiring interest in its systematic study, would not reach that stage until roughly a half-century later.

The bulk of work on professors has been completed by higher education specialists working outside the discipline of sociology. This body of work tends to be more descriptive than theoretic, and thus less focused on such core sociological concerns as the organization of the academic profession and professionalization, or selection, recruitment, and socialization. Nevertheless, this body of work has yielded significant findings pertaining to professors. Topics of inquiry run a gamut, from the educational background of professors, their demographic profile, their attitudes and values about faculty roles and rewards, to their teaching strategies and goals and their allocation of time among work roles.

If, though, one is interested in a bona fide sociology of professors, rooted thereby in key sociological concepts and theory, one has to turn to the sociology of science. Save for a small handful of sociological classics on the professoriate – all of which now bear a heavy patina – beginning with Logan Wilson's *Academic Man* (1942) and including such works as Lazarsfeld and Thielens's *Academic Mind* (1958), Caplow and McGee's *Academic Marketplace* (1960), and Jencks and Riesman's *Academic Revolution* (1968), a sociology of professors proceeded under the rubric of the sociology of science, concerned as it is with the production and organization of socially certified knowledge. Because many of the studies on the sociology of scientists are based on the functioning of the academic reward system and its consequences, they often have general applicability – in theme, substance, and significance – to professors outside of the natural and social sciences. Evocative discussion by Braxton and Hargens (1996) suggests frameworks for the study of academics within and across various fields.

Robert K. Merton, often taken to be the "father of the sociology of science," is typically credited with having inspired this tradition of research through his own vastly productive work in the field. Among his more central contributions to the sociology of science – and to a social organization of the roles of scientists

in particular – is his articulation of four norms said to undergird an "ethos" of science (and academe more generally). The norm of *universalism* stipulates that when scientists contribute to knowledge, the science community's assessment of the merits of the contribution should not be influenced by personal or social attributes of the contributor; and scientists should be rewarded in ways that are commensurate with their contributions. The norm of *communism* (later called *communalism*) stipulates that knowledge must be shared, not kept secret, for it is only by placing knowledge in the public domain that others can build upon it. The norm of *disinterestedness* stipulates that scientists should engage in scientific work with the motive of extending knowledge, free of any biases or other motives that compromise the integrity of the scientific role. The norm of *organized skepticism* stipulates that scientists must suspend judgment about conclusions to be drawn from research until all available evidence is on hand to render qualified assertions about the contributions of a piece of scientific work.

While these four norms are understood to carry equal weight in the performance of scientific/academic roles, one of them – the norm of universalism – has been the object of disproportionate inquiry, perhaps because it is the norm that most centrally governs scientific output, an avenue by which to assess productivity and, ultimately, a stratification system of scientists. Thus, researchers have investigated how the reward system in science operates and what consequences its functioning has on matters such as the job placement of PhD graduates, promotion, tenure, productivity, recognition, and other foci of participation and attainment in a systematically stratified system of science.

The norm of universalism, however, emphasizes research productivity. Other research finds that clear majorities of professors across many institutional types are inactive in research. Consequently, assessing role performance – and the organization of scientific roles more broadly – on the basis of this norm becomes problematic.

Hermanowicz (1998) proposed an alternative to conceptualizing the academic profession. Instead of focusing on compliance with the norm of universalism in the operation of the scientific reward and stratification system, the focus shifted to accounts scientists (and, in principle, other academics) provide of their careers. Here the "subjective career" becomes the object of study. Professors – and the profession that socially organizes them and their work – are understood through narrative: how people account for what they do, how and why they do it, and the ways in which they envision their roles and the evolution of such understandings over the time spent in an academic career.

Hermanowicz advanced a view of the academic profession as consisting of three social worlds, each organized by specific patterns in the way academics account for their careers. The *elite* world consists of professors who place the highest premium on research. "Elite" uniformly describes the members who work in this world and the external definition of them and their academic departments. It also expresses the aspiration of its members – "to be among the best" – and the key collective goal that brings them together and establishes their membership in universities that are also elite.

The *pluralist* world answers to considerably more varied demands, those of mass teaching as well as research and service to the wider community and state. A pluralist department includes some members as eminent as those found in elite departments, but the pursuit of still more eminence is not what holds members together, nor does it provide a standard that all members unhesitatingly adopt. This type of department answers to considerably more varied demands, those of mass teaching as well as research and service to the wider community and state. Often, this results in a blend of people who exhibit radically different affinities, talents, and motivations: plurality thus conveys the essence of this type of world. As a division of labor, departments of this type mirror something of a "multiuniversity" of which they are a part.

The *communitarian* world, like that of pluralists, answers to many demands, but the fundamental basis of comparative worth is within the institution itself. "Good citizenship" is demanded of all and is a primary basis on which individuals are accorded honor and esteem. Commitment to and identification with science is varied and uneven. Scientists in these departments are heterogeneous in their beliefs and practices about what defines a legitimate career. Those who lead essentially teaching careers, or careers in which research has been sporadic over the course of time, are most likely found here. In accounting for the way in which individuals establish legitimacy here, this is a world in which scientists believe that the person comes before the work: individuals are respected on the basis of their human virtues.

While each of the three prototypical academic worlds possesses central tendencies, they each also contain variety and partially overlap with each other. Consequently, one may speak of and find empirically professors who individually represent hybrids: elite professors employed in pluralist or communitarian departments; communitarian professors employed in elite or pluralist departments. This work makes an explicit attempt to reveal and conceptualize the profession's internal differentiation, attending to the ways in which its diverse membership construes the professorial role and its unfolding in an academic career. If research on professors is to advance, it must more firmly locate itself within disciplinary traditions, so that it may break new ground by building upon foundational concepts and theory.

SEE ALSO: Colleges and Universities; Deviance, Academic; Education; Scientific Productivity; Teachers; Teaching and Gender

REFERENCES AND SUGGESTED READINGS

Ben-David, J. (1991) *Scientific Growth: Essays on the Social Organization and Ethos of Science*. University of California Press, Berkeley.

Braxton, J. M. & Hargens, L. L. (1996) Variation Among Academic Disciplines: Analytical Frameworks and Research. In: Smart, J. C. (Ed.), *Higher Education: Handbook of Theory and Research*, Vol. 11. Agathon, New York, pp. 1–46.

Clark, B. R. (1987) *The Academic Life: Small Worlds, Different Worlds*. Carnegie Foundation for the Advancement of Teaching, Princeton.

Clark, B. R. & Neave, G. (Eds.) (1992) *The Encyclopedia of Higher Education*, Vols. 1–4. Pergamon, New York.

Hermanowicz, J. C. (1998) *The Stars Are Not Enough: Scientists – Their Passions and Professions*. University of Chicago Press, Chicago.

Merton, R. K. (1973) *The Sociology of Science: Theoretical and Empirical Investigations.* University of Chicago Press, Chicago.

Zuckerman, H. (1988) *The Sociology of Science.* In: Smelser, N. J. (Ed.), *Handbook of Sociology.* Sage, Newbury Park, CA, pp. 511–74.

progress, idea of

Bernd Weiler

The idea of progress, commonly considered one of the most influential and multifaceted ideas in the philosophy of history, states that material, political, social, intellectual, and moral conditions have continually and by necessity improved throughout human history and that such an improvement will continue in the foreseeable future (Nisbet 1980: 4–5). Since the Enlightenment the idea of progress and the controversies concerning its validity and ideological connotations have played a crucial role in modern social science discourse. The idea has not only been employed as a powerful conceptual framework to explain social change and the emergence of a new type of society, but also as a means to legitimate the entire endeavor of social science itself. By discovering the mechanism of societal progress and by identifying possible obstacles to progress, social scientists have claimed an authoritative role for themselves in the management of society's affairs. This sociocratic promise, encapsulated in the Comtean positivistic formula *savoir pour prévoir, prévoir pour pouvoir*, has drawn and continues to draw its strength from the fact that knowledge of nature's laws has been accompanied by an increased control over nature.

Regarding the question of the intellectual origins of the progressivist idea, four ideal-typical positions can be distinguished. According to one line of thought the idea of progress is rooted in human nature and presents the ever-present chasm between the real and the ideal. As a societal force the idea is seen to ebb and flow, gaining momentum in specific social and historical contexts. A second school traces the origins of the idea of progress back to the anti-metaphysical disenchantment and to the scientific worldview of a group of classical Greek and Roman thinkers, often citing the words of the Ionian philosopher Xenophanes from the late Archaic period that "not from the beginning did the gods reveal everything to mortals, but in course of time they discover improvements" as the birth certificate and Lucretius' poem *De Rerum Natura* as the fullest embodiment of the idea of progress. A third position holds that the idea of progress is religious in origin and that it represents a special variant of the Judeo-Christian eschatological tradition. The last school, following Walter Bagehot's dictum that "the ancients had no conception of progress," emphasizes a rather recent origin of the idea and its intimate linkage to the project of modernity (Bury 1955). In this context it is argued that by seeing the future as intrinsically dynamic, open, and indefinite the idea of progress, in fact, marked a sharp break with the belief in a timeless and unchanging heaven which formed a crucial element of the Judeo-Christian notions of millenarianism and redemption. As in Pascal's argument about increases in knowledge being proportional to the awareness of one's ignorance, expectations of future progress are seen to rise in accordance with the perception of past and present progress. The idea of progress, according to this interpretation, accompanied the rise of modern science and technology in the seventeenth century, gained force throughout the Enlightenment, and peaked in the second half of the nineteenth century. Despite disagreement concerning origins, the last three views concur in the opinion that the idea of progress originated in the West and that it has been one of its driving forces.

Within the modern social sciences the progressivist doctrine that all societies are bound to follow the same path of development and that the differences between societies merely reflect different temporal stages of development was firmly established by the middle of the eighteenth century and figured prominently in the works of French and Scottish theorists such as Turgot and Smith (Meek 1976). Condorcet's unfinished and posthumously published *Sketch for a Historical Picture of the Progress of the Human Mind* (1795), in which he even pondered the possibility of scientific progress abolishing illness and death, is often regarded as the epitome of the Enlightenment's belief in societal progress. The progressivist idea of the eighteenth century rested on the widely held belief that contemporary society was on the brink of far-reaching changes in terms of its political, economic, technological, and cultural structure, on the trust in the human potential to emerge from one's "self-incurred immaturity," and the emphasis on the "psychic unity of mankind," as well as on the rich ethnographic accounts of "savage nations" which came to represent the starting line of the triumphant march of civilization. *Cum grano salis* one might generalize by saying that the French tradition viewed progress primarily as the result of the conscious and rational workings of the mind that is increasingly freed from tradition and religion, whereas the Scottish social theorists tended to see progress as the unintended result of intentional action. In the first case progress was often equated with the moral betterment and enlightenment of individual actors, in the second with the evolution of an institutional framework that enhanced the chances that individuals who pursued their self-interest also contributed to the commonweal.

With the increasing dominance of western civilization, the rise of technology (especially the spread of railways, steamships, and telegraphs), and the concomitant transformation of everyday life, the progressivist doctrine flourished throughout the nineteenth century and became part and parcel of the social scientific worldview. The idea of progress can be seen as the missing link between such diverse concepts and theories as Hegel's idealistic philosophy of history, Comte's law of the three stages, Marx's materialist conception of history, Buckle's conjectural history of civilization, Spencer's law of social differentiation, Bachofen's evolutionary scheme of the family, Durkheim's distinction between two forms of solidarity, and Ward's doctrine of social telesis. The two world wars in the "age of extremes" weakened, but could not stop, the idea of progress from exerting a strong impact on social thought throughout the twentieth century. In this context it might suffice to point to the various modernization theories, popular in the 1950s and 1960s, that argued for the existence of a unilineal, lawful pattern of development for all countries, to the contemporary "liberal-minded" discourse

on globalization, with its focus on the convergence of traditions and the emergence of "one world," and to recent military attacks against "backward" regimes justified in the name of democracy's and the free market's inevitable success in the near future.

Like all great ideas the idea of progress has had its great enemies ever since. Critics of progressivism are commonly of a conservative, pessimistic, or skeptical bent, arguing either that there is nothing new under the sun or that what is new is worse than what was there before. In the eighteenth century the main ethical and intellectual arguments that have made up the anti-progressivist tradition until today were deeply entrenched in social theory. By emphasizing the unchanging nature and the indomitable passions of humans, as well as the irrational and a-rational side of social interactions, the idea of human and societal perfectibility is discarded as naïve. At the same time the technological optimism that nature could be controlled and harnessed by science and human ingenuity is rejected. When technological progress is admitted, it is either seen as insignificant or as harmful to the true values of human existence. Throughout the centuries the question regarding the relationship between knowledge and moral conduct has remained the essential element of the debate on progress. In modern anti-progressivist social discourse the loss of tradition, family life, and religion is usually lamented, the past glorified, and the future feared. Since the Enlightenment anti-progressivist thinkers have criticized the idea that all societies develop along the same path and that all non-western societies necessarily follow the footsteps of the West as repugnantly Eurocentric, falsely teleological, and as resting upon an erroneous dichotomy of tradition versus modernity. Severe criticism of the various aspects of the idea of progress can be found, for example, in the social thought of Herder, Burke, and Malthus in the eighteenth century, the sociological writings of Weber and the Italian elitist theorists Pareto and Mosca in the late nineteenth century, the cultural anthropology of Boas and his school in the early twentieth century, and the German tradition of *Kultursoziologie* and *Kulturphilosophie* in the inter-war period. After World War II the Popperian epistemological critique of historicism, the emphasis on "multiple modernities" by Eisenstadt, the ideology of the environmental and the anti-globalization movement, and recent postmodernist crusades against "grand narratives" can be seen as continuing the different strands of the anti-progressivist tradition. If the power of a doctrine is to be judged also by the vehemence of opposition, the idea of progress has certainly been one of the most stimulating ideas in intellectual history.

SEE ALSO: Comte, Auguste; Cultural Relativism; Eurocentrism; Malthus, Thomas Robert; Spencer, Herbert

REFERENCES AND SUGGESTED READINGS

Bury, J. B. (1955 [1932]) *The Idea of Progress: An Inquiry Into Its Origin and Growth*. Dover, New York.

Dodds, E. R. (2001 [1973]) *The Ancient Concept of Progress and Other Essays on Greek Literature and Belief*. Clarendon Press, Oxford.

Eisenstadt, S. N. (2000) Multiple Modernities. *Dædalus: Journal of the American Arts and Sciences* 129(1): 1–29.

Granovetter, M. (1979) The Idea of "Advancement" in Theories of Social Evolution and Development. *American Journal of Sociology* 85(3): 489–515.

Kosselleck, R. & Meier, C. (1975) Fortschritt. In: Brunner, O., Conze, W., & Kosselleck, R. (Eds.), *Geschichtliche Grundbegriffe: Historisches Lexikon zur politisch-sozialen Sprache in Deutschland*, Vol. 2. E.-G. Ernst Klett Verlag, Stuttgart, pp. 351–423.

Latham, M. E. (2000) *Modernization as Ideology: American Social Science and "Nation Building" in the Kennedy Era*. University of North Carolina Press, Chapel Hill.

Marx, L. & Mazlish, B. (Ed.) (1999) *Progress: Fact or Illusion*. University of Michigan Press, Ann Arbor.

Meek, R. L. (1976) *Social Science and the Ignoble Savage*. Cambridge University Press, Cambridge.

Meinecke, F. (1972) *Historism: The Rise of a New Historical Outlook*. Routledge and Kegan Paul, London.

Nisbet, R. (1980) *The History of the Idea of Progress*. Basic Books, New York.

Popper, K. R. (1960) *The Poverty of Historicism*. Basic Books, New York.

Sztompka, P. (1994) *The Sociology of Social Change*. Blackwell, Oxford.

Weber, M. (1949) The Meaning of "Ethical Neutrality" in Sociology and Economics. In: *The Methodology of the Social Sciences*. Free Press, New York, pp. 1–47.

Zilsel, E. (1945) The Genesis of the Concept of Scientific Progress. *Journal of the History of Ideas* 6(3): 325–49.

propaganda

Randal Marlin

The term propaganda arouses considerable interest and apprehension in modern society, conjuring up in the minds of many Orwellian images of totalitarian control. Any survey of contemporary popular usage is likely to find it used in a pejorative sense, as for example when labor and management call each other's information packages "propaganda." But there also exists a more neutral sense of the term, tied to its derivation from the Latin word *propagare*, meaning "to propagate."

In this neutral sense propaganda means spreading messages, conveying information, getting the word out through some means of communication. The means may or may not be devious, deceptive, and underhanded. The message itself, and any goals sought in spreading the message, may also be good or bad, but in this usage, no moral evaluation is conveyed by the word propaganda.

Many attempts have been made to define propaganda in a way that brings out the negative connotation. Propaganda in this sense essentially involves communicating in artful and manipulative ways with the aim of getting one's audience to think, feel, and eventually act in a way desired by the propagandist. The motivation may be self-interested or it may be to promote a specific cause, such as universal free medical care, or a more abstract ideology. Typically, truth is valued only insofar as it contributes to the end sought. Where it does not, then lies, deceptions, appeal to emotions, or other tactics may be employed. A defining feature is the bypassing or suppression of a recipient's ability to evaluate properly the message that is imparted. One important way of doing this is by disguising the true source of a given message, for example by funding seemingly disinterested bodies to do one's advocacy. Another is by selectively presenting factual material. G. K. Chesterton once drew attention to the hugely mendacious possibilities available to those who report only truths, but select them so as to present a false picture, as when one reports only misery, corruption, and hardship from a country that is no worse than others overall. Discourse as dialogue, open-ended, and with respect for the freedom and autonomy of the other is the opposite of propaganda so defined.

Recent efforts have been made to rehabilitate the term by distinguishing between "old" and "new" versions. "Old" propaganda would be deceptive and constraining, whereas "new" propaganda would be enlightening, empowering, and respectful of its audience's autonomy. One difficulty with this proposal is that supposedly new propaganda is not all that new, and supposedly old propaganda is still very much alive today. An alternative to talking about new and old propaganda would be to speak of good and bad propaganda. Here it is important to bear in mind two components in the moral assessment of propaganda. One relates to the ends promoted by the messages, which can be good or bad; the second relates to the means chosen, which can be good or bad independently of the ends sought. It is possible to use morally disreputable means to promote a worthy cause, for example.

The impetus to study propaganda comes from many sources and sometimes for opposing reasons. Propaganda has proven highly successful as a route to totalitarian power, for Nazis, communists, and liberal democrats alike. It is understandable that a new generation of power seekers wants to know how to use it. But there are others who object to propagandistic (in the negative sense) methods for attaining power. These others would like to expose bureaucratic, political, and commercial propaganda techniques whereby a powerful few dominate the large majority The aim of such exposure is to enable people to resist their influence. The effect of exposing propaganda is to negate its influence.

LANDMARKS OF MODERN PROPAGANDA

The French Revolution led to a mass-oriented culture, which Napoleon exploited through tight control over opinion, seeing this as the foundation of political power. Carl von Clausewitz in the nineteenth century knew about the need in wartime to maintain morale on one's own side, undermine the morale of the enemy, and seek the good opinion of neutrals. Theorists such as Vilfredo Pareto, Georg Simmel, Albert Venn Dicey, and Gustav Le Bon have pioneered, from diverse standpoints, the study of opinion and mass behavior. British propaganda in World War I set a new benchmark for the extent and thoroughness of its worldwide reach. As the war progressed British propaganda became more hard-nosed, and demonized Germans by concocting and widely disseminating a story about corpse factories in which the Germans supposedly boiled their own dead soldiers down to make glycerine, fertilizer, and suchlike. The aim of atrocity propaganda was to fuel hatred and enhance recruitment, but when the war ended it made peacemaking more difficult.

Woodrow Wilson brought the US into World War I with the help of government-sponsored propaganda, and the experience provided some lessons for business. But much of the pioneering public relations work of Ivy Lee in the US actually predated the war.

Harold Lasswell's sustained review of British World War I propaganda was an early milestone of propaganda analysis. Walter Lippmann paid close attention to those biases in communication that derived from wishful thinking rather than deliberate intent. The success of both Nazi and Leninist propaganda seems to suggest the vindication of V. I. Bekhterev's ideas about how crowds can be manipulated through developing reflex responses. But as regards media influence such a "hypodermic needle" concept has been much criticized by subsequent research. Studies, notably by Carl Hovland and others, revealed that people's beliefs and attitudes are shaped in more complex ways than the Pavlovian, including reliance on others whose opinions they trust. Noam Chomsky exposed dubious assumptions underlying analysis of verbal behavior in terms of stimulus and response mechanisms. Nevertheless new methods of catching message recipients off guard are continuously being devised. Product placement in film and television gained support from the reported marketing success of the candy Reese's Pieces in the widely viewed film *E.T.*

Jacques Derrida and Michel Foucault revealed much about the framing of discourse and how this framing can shape opinion in the interests of an existing dominant group. Martin Buber, Karl Jaspers, Gabriel Marcel, and Emmanuel Levinas have sought to make discourse more open to the personhood of the other, in contrast to treating others as means to one's own ends. George Orwell, who engaged in propaganda for the British in India during World War II, was well versed in the deceptive use of language, and exposed not only Soviet and fascist but also Tory imperialistic propaganda.

In the US alarm bells have sounded, from both right and left, at the way governments and corporations have manipulated opinion, concealing conflicts of interest, using shoddy accountancy practices and the like. During the Vietnam War, Senator Fulbright exposed some of the Pentagon techniques for getting the public to acquiesce to its plans, including installation of ballistic missiles. George H. W. Bush got support for his war against Iraq in 1991 through use of the atrocity story about Iraqi soldiers supposedly dumping babies out of incubators in Kuwait hospitals. Later, the story was discredited. Despite this revelation, misleading information aimed at gaining support for the US-led coalition in the build-up to the war against Iraq in 2003 still found wide acceptance among the US public.

SCOPE OF RESEARCH

The scope of propaganda research today is very broad. The kind of study undertaken by the Institute of Propaganda Analysis in the late 1930s has continued, as new techniques of deception, intimidation, and co-optation are discovered and exposed. Researchers in linguistics, informal logic, cognitive science, and media studies continue to shed new light in these areas. More recently, philosophers have taken up the challenge of ethical examination of propaganda, and Stanley Cunningham (2002) has begun the task of reconstructing the idea of propaganda for useful academic service, linking the concept to its epistemic deficiencies. A different challenge relates to the conundrum of controlling hate propaganda while trying to preserve freedom of expression. The massacre of Tutsis in Rwanda in 1994 was preceded by intense feelings of hatred and fear generated by radio broadcasts in which Tutsis were dehumanized by referring to them with words such as "cockroaches."

French theorist Jacques Ellul's seminal and provocative work in the early 1960s continues to inspire researchers today. While his form of expression is often dogmatic and seemingly exaggerated and contradictory at times, there is no doubt about his profound understanding of the modern-day propaganda phenomenon, reflecting his exposure to it in France under Nazi occupation. Ellul's central theme is that human technique in industrial society has turned into a leveling process that always seeks the most cost-effective results, oblivious to artistic expression and humanistic values. He sees propaganda as an essential component of this new technological world, as advertising and public relations contribute to the self-augmentation of technology to a point where means take precedence over ends and control over human destiny is lost. From Ellul's point of view the differences between Soviet, Nazi, and US propaganda conceal a basic similarity, which is acceptance in each case of a world in which the needs of technological society take precedence over all else. Propaganda has to be all encompassing, he writes, or it is not propaganda. To be effective, propaganda must not be contradicted and all different sources of information and perception need to be controlled. A propagandist builds on existing myths and presuppositions of a given audience, and may spend time preparing these background beliefs so that on an appropriate occasion they may be harnessed. Hitler made obvious use of racial myths in this way, but Ellul characterizes beliefs in the hero, in work, in democracy, in the nation, etc. as sometimes having the character of myth, in the sense that they are capable of motivating action and at the same time are treated as above questioning. When democracy is invoked to justify installing a subservient and repressive government in another country, the word democracy has passed into that mythical realm.

Ellul's categories of propaganda reach beyond the political, top-down, agitative and irrational model, to include propaganda which is *sociological*, meaning diffuse as to source; *horizontal*, meaning spread among people of the same socio-economic level; *integrative*, meaning binding people together as a nation or other group; and *rational*, meaning the use of polls, figures, and statistics in ways and contexts where there is no opportunity for scrutiny of their methods and premises, so that the scientific appearance is illusory.

Finally, Ellul's enduring contribution to propaganda study includes his important focus on individuals actually needing and wanting to be propagandized. Wanting to seem knowledgeable and responsible, citizens in a democratic society will not wish to reveal the many conflicts and gaps in knowledge that result from confusing news accounts. They are inclined therefore to latch onto a simplified, moralized view of current affairs when it is available to them (which may partly explain Fox News's success). For most people, the simplified account is also more likely to be entertaining. The lesson Ellul would have us draw is that our freedom and autonomy come at a price; namely, a struggle against the passivity and laziness that make us easy targets for propaganda.

A strong counter-culture opposing domination by corporate-controlled media has developed through alternate media and the Internet. Noam Chomsky, Jeff Cohen (of FAIR: Fairness and Accuracy in Reporting), Sheldon Rampton, and John Stauber (of PR Watch), along with many other academics such as Robert W. McChesney, have worked for many years to alert people to the often subtle ways in which their minds are influenced by selective presentation of news and opinion in the mainstream media, particularly with convergence of the media under fewer owners, and owners with other commercial interests. Under US President Ronald Reagan, and again under President George W. Bush, there has been a deliberate and concerted attempt to gain more control over public opinion at home and abroad, and to prevent a reoccurrence of the kind of groundswell of opposition over the Vietnam War. Conservative think tanks have flourished, supported by private corporations, supplying "expert" facts and arguments to the mass media. Public funding has existed for public interest groups that favor a liberal and left of center stance, but since the Reagan era the mainstream media have paid

more attention to conservative voices than previously. Chomsky and Edward Herman introduced a "propaganda model" detailing filters that operate on the mass media, skewing the process of news reporting that would be determined by journalistic values alone. When well-financed think tanks produce elaborate content analyses claiming to show that "liberal" newspapers are biased, it may be hard to refute such studies even when they are off the mark. They put pressure on the media to tilt more towards a conservative vision of what is fair and balanced. Other filters that Chomsky and Herman describe are the ownership and profit orientation of the mainstream media; the need to satisfy advertisers' interests; the need to rely on information provided by government and business and their approved "experts"; and lastly, the use of anti-communism as a means of control. By depicting communism as an absolute evil, an effect is to scare commentators from supporting measures that benefit labor, for fear of being labeled "pinko." Since the events of September 11, 2001 anti-terrorism has been similarly exploited, as those who protest infringements on civil liberties and the rule of law are treated as "soft on terror."

FUTURE PROSPECTS

Future analysis of persuasion and propaganda can always benefit from a study of Aristotle's *Rhetoric*, the principles of which still apply even when the means of communication differ. Source credibility continues to be a paramount consideration, and it can be confidently predicted that the ingenuity of propagandists at disguising their (and their paymasters') hands in manipulative communications will constantly be seeking outlets, and the propaganda detectors will have no shortage of work to detect them. Watchdogs are proliferating on both ends of the political spectrum. For example, while FAIR's perspective tends to be left-oriented, that of AIM (Accuracy in Media) monitors the media from a rightist standpoint.

While the Internet has provided previously undreamt of opportunities for pooling the information resources of scattered counter-culture practitioners, the problem of reaching the wider public still remains, and activist groups have recently been exploring the possibilities of communicating through short-range radio.

Orderly society presupposes a minimum of shared beliefs among the general population, at least regarding procedures to resolve conflicts in interests and ideologies. Some believe that resolution of conflicts will require a measure of "bamboozling" the public into accepting measures in their own interest, in other words, making use of propaganda. Others, having more faith in the public's ability to think through the merits even of complicated policy matters, put their energies into exposing deceitful communications and making complex matters more intelligible to wider audiences. It will be an interesting job for sociologists and philosophers to trace the impact of these conflicting approaches, and to argue for a suitable communication ethics in the light of contemporary and historical experience.

SEE ALSO: Hegemony and the Media; Ideological Hegemony; Media Monopoly; Media and the Public Sphere; Politics and Media; Public Opinion

REFERENCES AND SUGGESTED READINGS

AIM (Accuracy in Media) Online. www.aim. org.
AlterNet Online. www.alternet.org.
Altheide, D. L. & Johnson, J. M. (1980) *Bureaucratic Propaganda*. Allyn & Bacon, Boston.
Cull, J. C., Culbert, D., & Welch, D. (2003) *Propaganda and Mass Persuasion: A Historical Encyclopedia, 1500 to the Present*. ABC-CLIO, Santa Barbara.
Cunningham, S. B. (2002) *The Idea of Propaganda: A Reconstruction*. Praeger, Westport, CT.
Ellul, J. (1973) *Propaganda, The Formation of Men's Attitudes*. Vintage, New York.
FAIR (Fairness and Accuracy in Reporting) Online. www.fair.org.
Herman, E. & Chomsky, N. (1988) *Manufacturing Consent: The Political Economy of the Mass Media*. Pantheon, New York.
Lasswell, H. (1927) *Propaganda Technique in the World War*. Alfred Knopf, New York.
Marlin, R. (2002) *Propaganda and the Ethics of Persuasion*. Broadview, Peterborough, Ontario.
PR Watch Online. www.prwatch.org.
Truthout Online. www.truthout.org.

property crime

Heith Copes and Crystal Null

Property crimes are defined as those offenses where offenders take money or property from victims without the use or threat of force. They include a long list of offenses such as burglary, larceny-theft, motor vehicle theft, arson, shoplifting, fraud, embezzlement, and forgery. The Federal Bureau of Investigation (FBI) defines the first four of these offenses as Part I property crimes. These crimes make up the property crime index published yearly in the Uniform Crime Report (UCR). The majority of data collected by the FBI on property crime is concentrated around Part I offenses. The remaining offenses are classified as Part II property crimes in the UCR (FBI 2003).

By far the largest number of crimes committed in the United States in any given year are crimes against property, which make up about three-quarters of all crime in the United States. Trends from the UCR and the National Crime Victimization Survey (NCVS) indicate that property crime rates have varied considerably over the past few decades. However, since 1992, property crime rates have begun to steadily decline to their current level. The estimated rate of property crime offenses known to the police in 2001 was 3,656 per 100,000 inhabitants, which is the lowest the rate has been since 1972. According to the NCVS, the rate of households victimized by property offenders has been steadily dropping from 544 in 1977 to 159 in 2002.

With such high numbers of property crime it is not surprising that the financial loss from these crimes is enormous. In 2002, the estimated loss attributed to property crimes (excluding arson) was $16.6 billion. Although excluded from estimated property crime tabulations, arson had an average dollar loss of $11,253 for the offenses in which monetary values were reported. Crimes against businesses and institutions are excluded from the NCVS, so losses from property crime are much higher than reported. For example, it is estimated that shoplifting alone costs retailers an estimated $10 billion each year.

Despite the prevalence and cost of property crime, clearance rates for property crime are considerably lower than those of violent crimes. A crime is considered cleared when at least one person is arrested, charged with the commission of an offense, and turned over to courts for prosecution. Property crime clearance rates have been relatively stable since 1971, fluctuating from 16.1 percent to 18.5 percent with an average clearance rate of 17.5 percent.

The majority of property crimes are committed by occasional or amateur offenders who engage in a variety of offenses to supplement their incomes. Typically, these offenders do little in the way of planning, have few technical skills, and rely on found opportunities when choosing targets. Although the low clearance rate of property crimes makes profiles of offenders suspect, researchers have compiled a general view of property crime offenders that suggests they are disproportionately male, young, and non-white. Historically, males commit twice as many property crimes as females. In 2002, for example, males accounted for 69.6 percent of property crimes and females accounted for 30.4 percent. However, property crime accounts for a larger percentage of the total crime committed by females.

Property crime offenders are disproportionately young. Almost one-third of property crime offenders are under the age of 18 (30.4 percent). The peak age of property crime offenders is between 16 and 18. After this age, offending rates by age steadily decrease until around age 60, when property crime offenses level off at 0.4 percent.

The majority of property offenders are white (66 percent), followed by blacks (31.4 percent), Asian and Pacific Islanders (1.5 percent), and American Indian and Alaskan Native (1.3 percent). While the majority of property offenders are white, victims of property crime are disproportionately non-white.

Although property crime has dropped in the previous decade, this drop has not affected all citizens equally as some groups continue to be at a higher risk than others. Both race and ethnicity of the head of the household are important factors when determining risk factors for victimization. The rate of victimization in households headed by a white person is 157.6, by a black person is 173.7, and by a Hispanic person is 210.1. These patterns of victimization have been relatively consistent for the past decade.

Household income, location of residence, and homeownership are also important predictors of the likelihood of property crime victimization. It appears that property offenders are more likely to victimize households with annual incomes below $7,500. Offenders are also more likely to victimize households that are located in an urban area. Target households are usually rented, not owned.

Victims of property crime are often hesitant to report their victimization to police. Less than half of all victims of property crime report their victimization to law enforcement agencies. There is tremendous variation in reporting rates by types of property crime, however. For instance, 86.1 percent of victims of motor vehicle theft reported the theft, whereas only 32.8 percent of victims of larceny-theft reported it. Not surprisingly, the main reason that victims reported the offense to police was to recover their lost property. The most common reasons for not reporting the offense were because the objects were recovered, the offender was unsuccessful, or there was a lack of proof.

SEE ALSO: Crime; Crime, Hot Spots; Criminology; Index Crime; Law, Criminal; Robbery; Violent Crime

REFERENCES AND SUGGESTED READINGS

Federal Bureau of Investigation (FBI) (2003) *Uniform Crime Report, 2002*. US Government Printing Office, Washington, DC.

US Department of Justice, Bureau of Justice Statistics (2003) *Criminal Victimization in the United States, 2002 Statistical Tables*. Online. www.ojp.usdoj.gov/bjs/pub/pdf/cvus02.pdf. Accessed March 3, 2004.

property, private

Jack Barbalet

Property implies ownership, to which rights attach. These rights may take usurpatory, moral, or legal form. The types of things that can be owned as property, and therefore subject to property rights, are enormously varied. Depending on the particular circumstances, they might include, for instance, a human person, a person's capacities (especially for labor), the products of another's labor, any material of use or exchange, land, options, patents, ideas, and so on. The structure of ownership is also variable. In ancient societies, classically described as the "indian village community" in Maine's *Ancient Law* (1861), co-ownership or communal property prevailed. In peasant societies, on the other hand, the household rather than the community is typically the unit which exercises controlling rights over productive possessions. From early capitalist societies private property arose as the dominant form of ownership in which individual persons exercise rights over their objects of possession. In late capitalist societies corporate and public property forms emerge, combining elements of both communal and private property. Corporate property is communal insofar as ownership rights are shared by a number of proprietors, each of whom can exercise or dispose of their rights as they choose as individuals without collective constraint, and similarly use the benefits of their ownership as they individually see fit. Public property excludes private ownership and only nominally involves co-ownership, as various forms of statutory authorities exercise such property rights, putatively on behalf of the public, subject to legal and political controls.

The concept of private property, at least since the seventeenth century in Europe, is central in political and social theory. This is because the issue of private property is fundamental to moral, political, psychological, and social principles and outcomes. Private property is closely associated with the concept of individual freedom, for instance, where other forms of property may curtail such freedom. Economic and industrial efficiency is also frequently regarded as optimized under conditions of private property and compromised – if not undermined – by communal or public property. Psychologically, however, private property is more than other forms of property held to promote an unhealthy regard for material possession and corrode ethical orientations, as well as undermine respect for the natural and social environment

experienced in common. Similarly, private property is regarded as the source and consolidator of inequitable and unjust distributions of earnings and wealth.

In liberal theory property rights have a distinctive role insofar as they attach not just to possession of land and movable objects but also to a human being's own person and the capacities of that person, especially the capacity to labor. In the chapter on property in his *Treatise of Government* (1690) John Locke famously declared "every Man has a Property in his own Person." The notion of a person's proprietorship of their own capacities has become foundational in liberal theory to other rights of the person, including civil and political rights. In this sense private property is the institutional basis of the entire edifice of liberal thought. The vexed question of ownership of the products of the exercise of a person's own capacities in the context of capitalistic labor is classically dealt with by John Stuart Mill. Factory operatives produce an object that they are legally prevented from claiming as their own property. This is no contradiction, says Mill, because "the labour of manufacture is only one of the conditions which must combine for the production of the commodity" and all the other conditions are the private property of the employer (*Principles of Political Economy*, 1848).

Marxism, on the other hand, focuses not on rights but on the productive relationships constitutive of private property. In this sense private property is understood in terms of power relations rather than rights. Marx holds that ownership or possession of property is the principle of organization within relations of production and distribution. Those who possess private property have direct access to means of consumption; those who do not must offer their labor services to owners, who pay wages in exchange for activating their property productively. In this exchange the reciprocity between property owners and property-less workers is asymmetrical, with the material benefits being greater for owners and the opportunity costs being greater for non-owners. This relationship Marx characterizes as exploitation. In this manner Marx holds that there is a characteristic endogenous dynamic within each form of property, corresponding to historical stages of societal development, including primitive communism, Asiatic society, feudalism, and capitalism.

Sociological treatments of private property adopt elements of liberal or Marxist accounts. Private property, for Weber, results from appropriation and closed social relationships or closure (*Economy and Society*, 1921). The appropriation of economic opportunities, from which others are excluded, is the basis of an advantage, according to Weber, which may take the form of a right. If this right is enduring and can be transferred between individuals, then the appropriated advantage is property. Weber goes on to discuss how appropriation and property have taken different forms under different historical conditions and in different economic settings. Durkheim argues that inheritance of private property is responsible for a forced division of labor, resulting in anomie, through distortion of a natural distribution of talents (*The Division of Labor in Society*, 1893). He provides a historically insightful descriptive account of property rights in *Professional Ethics and Civic Morals* (1950), but without developing a theory of private property.

Frank Parkin (*Marxism and Class Theory: A Bourgeois Critique*, 1979), following Marx, distinguishes between two forms of private property: personal property and property as capital. Property as capital, he argues, following Weber, is exclusionary closure. Out of these relations arises class exploitation. The difficulty here is Parkin's exclusive focus on distributional relations and competition for resources; while addressing the production of life-chances this account fails to treat the production of the means of production of life-chances. Marx achieves this by understanding property as a productive relation. For Parkin, property is an essentially political facility. But practically all accounts of private property acknowledge in different ways its connection with power. It is also recognized, from Adam Smith (*Theory of Moral Sentiments*, 1759) to Thorstein Veblen (*Theory of the Leisure Class*, 1899), that private property as personal possession confers status or social standing on its owner.

SEE ALSO: Capitalism; Capitalism, Social Institutions of; Communism; Enterprise; Exploitation; Money; Political Economy; Property Crime; Robbery; Socialism

REFERENCES AND SUGGESTED READINGS

Macpherson, C. B. (Ed.) (1978) *Property: Mainstream and Critical Positions.* Toronto University Press, Toronto.
Munzer, S. (1990) *A Theory of Property.* Cambridge University Press, Cambridge.
Ryan, A. (1984) *Property and Political Theory.* Oxford University Press, Oxford.
Waldron, J. (1988) *The Right to Private Property.* Oxford University Press, Oxford.

prosocial behavior

Nancy Wisely

Social psychologists invented the concept of prosocial behavior to characterize a range of voluntary actions that benefit the welfare of others. Because prosocial behavior is socially defined, its specific nature may differ across societies or by situations. For example, the widespread norm, "Thou shall not kill," does not apply on the battlefield where killing may be rewarded with praise and medals. Prosocial behavior is consistent with social norms and provides a convenient antonym for antisocial behavior, or non-normative behaviors such as crime and most forms of aggression. *Helping* is a prosocial subtype and refers to any behavior that has positive consequences for another. The helper's motivation may be altruistic or egoistic. Altruism is a special form of helping. The altruist is motivated by the ultimate goal of improving another's well-being regardless of possible personal costs. Although the altruist may garner rewards in the act of helping, this does not preclude the altruistic intent. In contrast, egoistic responses are self-serving and motivated by the desire to improve one's own welfare. The connection between altruism and prosocial behavior varies. Prosocial behavior will not always be altruistically motivated, and altruistic motivation will not always generate prosocial behavior (Batson 1991).

Prosocial activity includes emergency intervention, charity, donation, cooperation, volunteering, comforting, sacrifice, and sharing.

These behaviors require investment of time, energy, or material goods and often feature a single helper. Cooperation, or coordinating activities for mutual benefit, is a cornerstone of every society but is not considered helping because it implies intent to benefit the actors. Because all of these behaviors involve positive consequences, they can be classified as prosocial, but to determine whether they meet the criteria for altruism requires knowledge of helpers' motives.

Interest in prosocial behavior dates from the Greeks and is embodied in the Judeo-Christian directive to "love thy neighbor." In the eighteenth century, Scottish pragmatists David Hume and Adam Smith separately advanced the radical notion that human nature includes a capacity for benevolence and compassion for others. This possibility continues to challenge the conventional model of egoistic human actors.

Within early social science, Comte is credited with coining the term altruism to describe the motivation to help others. By the early 1900s, McDougall recognized an altruistic instinct, but the idea faded as academic interest shifted from internal factors to the behaviorist focus on observable phenomena. In the 1930s and 1940s, Kurt Lewin set the guidelines for contemporary social psychology by proposing that behavior is the result of both the person and the environment (situation). Lewin summarized this then revolutionary idea in social psychology's most famous formula: $B = f(P, E)$, signifying that behavior is a function of the person and the environment. Lewin's conception of the person includes individual hereditary attributes, skills, and personality. The environment refers mainly to the situation and others who are present. Later researchers have debated which of Lewin's variables best explains prosocial behavior – personality traits or social situations.

It fell to George Herbert Mead, a modern pragmatist, to perhaps unwittingly rekindle interest in altruism. In developing symbolic interactionism, Mead proposed that role-taking (taking the other's perspective) is integral to the development of the self as empathy enables the child to act reflexively. Current theories linking cognitive development and altruism are indebted to the observations of Piaget, while Kohlberg identified stages of moral development. Within the social problem-centered discipline of sociology, Sorokin risked his reputation by dedicating part of his later career to the examination of altruism and love. He conducted an empirical study of "good neighbors" and headed the Harvard Research Center in Creative Altruism. Prosocial study again received attention when Gouldner (1960) concluded that the neglected norm of reciprocity is a universal component of moral codes. This norm of social obligation makes two simple demands: people should help (and not harm) those who have helped them.

Until the 1960s, scientific study of helping was sporadic and only loosely connected. But in 1964, 39 witnesses failed to help Kitty Genovese, a murder victim, in Queens, New York. The brutal incident and the onlookers' apparent callousness captured national attention and generated concern about urban apathy and alienation. The public outcry awakened social psychologists and legitimated the relevancy of prosocial research. The puzzle of why so many bystanders had the same unexpected reaction to this crime spurred an investigation by Bibb Latané and John Darley. Their book, *The Unresponsive Bystander: Why Doesn't He Help?* (1970), is considered a classic in the field. Since then, prosocial behavior and altruism have been studied continuously and comprise a routinely recognized subfield of social psychology. Although the bulk of empirical work has investigated helping by strangers in emergencies, researchers have recently extended their studies to include the more mundane activities of volunteering, donation, and everyday helpfulness.

Philosophers, theologians, economists, and biologists have analyzed altruism and prosocial behavior for centuries. Current debate within social psychology and beyond is moving away from the established belief that behavior is ultimately and universally egoistic. A related issue is whether altruism is genetically transmitted and manifests itself as a personality trait.

THEORIES: ALTRUISM AND HELPING BEHAVIOR

Helping theories address internal motives and personality characteristics as well as external situations and social contexts.

Evolutionary theories apply the Darwinian principle of natural selection to explain helping motives. Thus, any trait that helps an organism survive will be genetically transmitted to the next generation. Under this rule, a gene for altruism seems contradictory because altruistic responses can require self-sacrifice over self-interest. Evolutionists emphasize that group survival depends on survival of the gene pool, not the individual organism. The major mechanisms for genetic transmission of altruism are group selection, kin selection, and reciprocal altruism. Kin selection implies that altruistic parents will save their children. This process, along with a reciprocity gene for mutual help, would enhance group fitness over time. Research confirms that people tend to help others who are genetically similar. Generally, successful groups should have a higher proportion of altruists than groups who die off. Applied to humans, this perspective is controversial. While it does show how self-sacrifice can be consistent with natural selection, the theory reveals nothing about human goals. However, evolutionists have added fuel to the possibility of an altruistic personality.

Social learning theory posits that socialization, not heredity, is why people help. Learning to be altruistic occurs through instruction, reinforcement, and imitation. For individuals who internalize the altruistic tendency, self-reward (self-approval) and self-cost (guilt, shame) can serve as reinforcements or punishments for helping or inaction. Exchange theory extends the reinforcement principle by viewing humans as rational actors who assess the ratio of costs to benefits in helping situations. Helping is less likely if costs predominate. Equity theory emphasizes fairness and distributive justice – helping should be reciprocated.

Developmental theorists observe that cognitive skills and capacities increase in complexity and sophistication in sequential stages as humans mature. Older children develop cognitive empathy and then learn to make internal self-attributions. Eventually, they see their own helping as personality driven. Internalizing the belief that they are helpful persons sets a standard for self-judgment of future behavior. Kohlberg's (1985) model shows how moral reasoning evolves. Martin Luther King, Jr. is often given as an example of one of few who reach the highest level where moral decisions are based on concern for universal justice and personal ethics even if they contradict social norms.

The most sociological theories of helping, or normative theories, stem from symbolic interactionism and its dramaturgical metaphor. A theatrical analogy compares the social world to a stage where actors give scripted role performances for an audience. Thus, individuals are regulated by norms that prescribe the appropriate behavior in a situation. Conformity to three norms encourages helping: the norm of giving; the norm of social responsibility, or helping dependent others; and the norm of reciprocity or mutual help. "Mind your own business" is one of several norms that inhibit helping.

RESEARCH AND DEBATES

Bystander Intervention Studies

Early research studied intervention in emergency situations and produced several decision-making models to understand when people will help. Latané and Darley identified steps that lead to action. Failure at any point cancels the possibility of helping. Researchers repeatedly find a counterintuitive bystander effect – as the number of bystanders increases, helping tends to decrease. Three explanations have been tendered. First, pluralistic ignorance occurs when bystanders seem to be unconcerned. Also, multiple bystanders diffuse responsibility whereas lone individuals carry full responsibility. Finally, bystanders may be unsure of their competence in a situation and find inaction preferable to failure or criticism.

By the 1980s, prosocial research had revealed that most people's behavior varies by situations, and evidence of behavioral consistency across situations was scant. This climate of preference for situational variables spurred personality theorists to demonstrate the impact of individual differences. Thus, empirical support for Lewin's original formula holds; the environment and person together explain behavior. Recently, Penner et al. (2005) suggested a multilevel approach (meso, micro, and macro) to understand helping.

Altruism

For centuries the image of egoistically motivated humans prevailed. Self-interest was thought to be the ultimate goal of all behavior, and altruism was rarely mentioned. In this intellectual milieu, Daniel Batson (1991) initiated a 25-year crusade to demonstrate that empathy-motivated altruism is an ultimate goal for some people some of the time. His research program is a classic example of scientific revolution. Batson systematically tested his empathy–altruism hypothesis against three alternatives. In two of the models, empathy motivates helping, but the goals differ: in one case, social and self-rewards are the ultimate goal (Cialdini et al. 1987); in the second, avoiding punishment is the ultimate goal. In the third and most popular model (aversive-arousal reduction), helping is the best way to relieve empathic distress (Dovidio et al. 1991). Dozens of empirical challenges have failed to refute the empathy–altruism hypothesis.

Demographic Variables

Generally, small-town residents are more helpful than urbanites. Milgram identified information overload as the underlying cause of supposed urban apathy. City dwellers use several strategies to cope with the bombardment of urban stimuli: they identify high-priority information, selectively attend to it, and limit some interactions to superficial involvement, all of which would reduce helping. But not all cities are the same. Experiments in 36 US cities show population density (not size) to be the strongest predictor of helping. Internationally, Hispanic cultures, where simpatico is the norm, rank highest in helping.

In the 1980s, researchers focused on gender differences. They found the kinds of help given to be consistent with gender role expectations. Men are more likely to help strangers in emergencies, or in situations of danger or requiring physical strength. Women are more likely to provide routine help and ongoing commitment to care for children and the elderly or support a friend. Gender differences peak when an audience is present, there is potential danger, and the recipient of help is female. Overall, men are more likely to give help, and women are more likely to ask for it.

Planned Helping

Recently, researchers have studied long-term helping as in giving blood, charitable donation, and volunteering. Social factors (norms) combine with psychological factors (empathic feelings) to produce altruism in volunteers. Conceptualizing helping behavior as role behavior reveals how repeat blood donors experience role-person mergers (blood donation becomes a core part of their identities) (Callero et al. 1987). Others view volunteering as productive work and analyze the capital inputs required (Wilson & Musick 1997). A third approach identifies six functions of helping. Volunteers can express humanitarian values, increase their understanding of the world, enjoy personal growth, acquire career experience, enhance social relationships, and address personal problems. Generativity or commitment to the welfare of future generations is another possible motive. This research has yielded practical results for volunteer recruitment.

SEE ALSO: Aggression; Comte, Auguste; Crime; Evolution; Gender Ideology and Gender Role Ideology; Lewin, Kurt; Mead, George Herbert; Norm of Reciprocity; Role-Taking; Social Learning Theory; Social Psychology; Society and Biology; Symbolic Interaction

REFERENCES AND SUGGESTED READINGS

Batson, C. D. (1991) *The Altruism Question: Toward a Social Psychological Answer.* Lawrence Erlbaum, Hillsdale, NJ.

Callero, P. L., Howard, J. A., & Piliavin, J. A. (1987) Helping Behavior as Role Behavior: Disclosing Social Structure and History in the Analysis of Prosocial Action. *Social Psychology Quarterly* 30: 247–56.

Cialdini, R. B., Schaller, M., Houlihan, D., Arps, K., Fultz, J., & Beaman, A. L. (1987) Empathy-Based Helping: Is it Selflessly or Selfishly Motivated? *Journal of Personality and Social Psychology* 52: 749–58.

Dovidio, J. F., Gaertner, S. L., Schroeder, D. A., & Clark, Russell D., III (1991) The Arousal-Cost-Reward Model and the Process of Intervention: A Review of the Evidence. In Clark, M. S. (Ed.), *Review of Personality and Social Psychology:*

Prosocial Behavior. Sage, Newbury Park, CA, pp. 86–118.

Gouldner, A. W. (1960) The Norm of Reciprocity: A Preliminary Statement. *American Sociological Review* 25: 161–78.

Kohlberg, L. (1985) *The Psychology of Moral Development*. Harper & Row, San Francisco.

Penner, L. A, Dovidio, J. F., Schroeder, D. A., & Piliavin, J. A. (2005) Prosocial Behavior: A Multi-level Perspective. *Annual Review of Psychology* 56: 365–92.

Wilson, J. & Musick, M. (1997) Who Cares? Toward an Integrated Theory of Volunteer Work. *American Sociological Review* 62: 694–713.

prostitution

Julia O'Connell Davidson

The term prostitution is popularly used to refer to the trade of sexual services for payment in cash or kind, and so to a form of social interaction that is simultaneously sexual and economic. This makes prostitution a difficult cultural category, for in most societies sexual and economic relations are imagined and regulated in very different ways. Prostitution therefore straddles two quite different symbolic domains. Since these domains are highly gendered, the female prostitute has long represented a troubling figure, disrupting what are traditionally deemed to be natural gender binaries (active/passive, public/private, etc.), and stigmatized as unnatural, immoral, and polluting. Yet prostitution is often simultaneously viewed as an inevitable feature of all human societies, for it is held to meet the supposedly powerful and biologically given sexual impulses of men. Thus it is sometimes described as a "necessary evil" and considered to protect the virtue of "good" girls and women by "soaking up" excess male sexual urges which would otherwise lead to rape and marital breakdown.

This traditional view of prostitution found sociological expression in a classic article by Kingsley Davis (1937), which explained the institution of prostitution as a necessary counterbalance to the reproductive institutions of society (such as the family) that placed a check upon men's sexual liberty. Furthermore, Davis argued, because prostitution enables "a small number of women to take care of the needs of a large number of men, it is the most convenient sexual outlet for an army, and for the legions of strangers, perverts, and physically repulsive in our midst" (1937: 754). This line of analysis was widely accepted by sociologists until Mary McIntosh subjected it to devastating critique in a seminal essay titled "Who Needs Prostitutes? The Ideology of Male Sexual Needs" (1978). Prostitution had been an important focus of feminist thought in the nineteenth and early twentieth centuries, and McIntosh's essay, alongside Kate Millett's *The Prostitution Papers* tz's *Prostitution and Victorian Society* (1980), marked a renewal of feminist interest in the topic.

This interest has subsequently grown, not least because prostitution is part of a wider market for commercial sex that has expanded and diversified rapidly in both affluent and developing nations over the past two decades. Old forms of sex commerce, including prostitution, are taking place in more and different settings; new technologies have generated possibilities for entirely new forms of commercial sexual experience; women are now amongst consumers of commercial sex; the boundaries between commercial sex and other sectors, such as tourism, leisure, and entertainment, have shifted. But there are also continuities with the past. Female prostitution in particular remains a hugely stigmatized and often criminalized activity. Even where certain forms of prostitution are either legal or tolerated, female prostitutes are still frequently subject to forms of surveillance and social and legal control that are not applied to non-prostitute citizens (or, very often, to male prostitutes).

There are also continuities as regards the strong relationship between colonialism, imperialism, nationalism, militarism, and war on the one hand, and prostitution on the other. The presence of international peacekeepers and police, civilian contractors and aid workers in post-conflict settings has acted as a stimulus for the rapid growth of a prostitution market in many regions. Very often, working conditions and employment practices in these newly emerged markets are abysmal. Historically, links between prostitution and migration, and children's presence in prostitution have both attracted intense public and policy concern. Such concerns recently resurfaced, for there are still children present in the sex trade, and in many places the majority of prostitutes are now undocumented migrants from poorer countries or regions.

Prostitution has commanded much attention from feminists in recent years, but has also highlighted deep theoretical and political divisions within feminism. On one side of the divide stand "radical feminists" or "feminist abolitionists" who foreground the sexual domination of women by men in their analyses of gender inequality, and view prostitution as the unambiguous embodiment of patriarchal oppression. All prostitution is a form of sexual violence and slavery that violates women's human right to dignity and bodily integrity, and buying sex is equivalent to the act of rape. This account rests on the assumption that no woman freely chooses or genuinely consents to prostitute. It leaves little room for women as agents within prostitution, and provides what critics deem to be a gender essentialist, totalizing, and reductive analysis of prostitution. Although grounded in a critique of patriarchy, the feminist abolitionist account emphasizes sexual experience as a source of individual and collective moral harm, and privileges sexual acts that take place in the context of intimate, emotional relationships. It thus shares a certain amount of ground with moral conservatism. For this reason, critics point to uncomfortable parallels between contemporary feminist campaigns for the abolition of prostitution (and especially those against "sex trafficking") and the moral purity and race hygiene movements that flourished in the early twentieth century.

On the other side of the divide stand those who might loosely be described as "sex work feminists." They reject the assumption that prostitution is intrinsically degrading and, treating prostitution as a form of service work, make a strong distinction between "free choice" prostitution by adults and all forms of forced and child prostitution. Whilst the latter should be outlawed, the former can be an economic activity like any other, and should be legally and socially treated as such. This perspective emphasizes women's capacity (and right) to act as moral agents within prostitution. Within this, there are sex radical theorists who celebrate sex

commerce as a practice that potentially subverts the legal and social binaries of normal/abnormal, healthy/unhealthy, pleasurable/dangerous sex, as well as of gender itself. Though some sex work feminists pay attention to the impact of global economic and political structures and processes on sex commerce, others have been criticized for their failure to engage seriously with questions about the sex industry as a site of labor exploitation.

Because the term "prostitution" embraces a diverse range of experience, and because "prostitutes" are not a homogeneous group, diametrically opposed positions on prostitution can each be partially supported by empirical research. Thus, feminist abolitionists refer to studies showing, for example, that entry into prostitution can be precipitated by the experience of rape and/or incest, and that prostitution can be associated with drug abuse, various forms of sexual and physical violence, and suicide. Yet sex work feminists can also back their claims by citing studies in which women describe themselves as having actively chosen prostitution, either for positive reasons or as preferable to other employment opportunities open to them.

Male sex workers rarely feature in such debates on the rights and wrongs of prostitution, and this may partly reflect an (untested) assumption that sexual transactions between men are inherently less exploitative than those involving a female seller and a male buyer (Altman in Aggleton 1999: xiv). Research on male prostitutes' experience has largely been driven by concerns about sexual health and HIV/AIDS prevention, and to a lesser extent by interest in the relationship between male sex work and gay identities. However, this research also reveals that male prostitution, like female prostitution, varies enormously in terms of social organization, working conditions, and earnings, and that men's and boys' motivations for trading sex are as diverse as women's and girls'. Questions about agency, choice, labor exploitation, and violence are thus just as relevant to the analysis of male prostitution as they are to that of female prostitution, even if they have to date been largely overlooked.

As sellers of sex, men may often have been ignored in research and debate on prostitution, but they have received attention as buyers of sex. So, for example, radical feminists have argued that buying sex is an act of aggression, equivalent to rape, but this has been challenged by a number of researchers who have demonstrated the highly differentiated nature of demand for commercial sex and the diversity of male clients in terms of their social identities, motivations, and practices, as well as by researchers who have examined the phenomenon of female demand for the services of male sex workers (for instance, Sánchez Taylor 2001).

As the sex industry has expanded and diversified in recent years, so the literature (popular and policy as well as academic) that variously describes, criticizes, or celebrates it has also proliferated. This literature is increasingly an object of analysis in its own right, and a growing number of works are devoted to deconstructing historical and contemporary discourse on prostitution, revealing its basis in deeper anxieties about – or desires for – social change, especially as regards sexuality; relations of gender, class, and race; imperial decline, national identity, and migration patterns; the nature and boundaries of childhood; and/or public health. Yet prostitution continues to serve as a symbolic battleground for broader disputes about such issues, and there is still no consensus on how best to define, theorize, or respond to the phenomenon.

Although debates on prostitution are intractable in the sense that they are disputes about the moral and normative values that *should* inform sexual and economic life, they also hinge on claims about the empirical reality of prostitution in the contemporary world. For this reason, the existing body of research evidence on prostitution is important. However, the existing body of research evidence is patchy, incomplete, and unreliable, for the study of prostitution presents many methodological difficulties. First, there are definitional problems. "Prostitution" does not always involve a simple, anonymous, and instantaneous commodity exchange. It can also be organized in less explicitly contractual and more open-ended ways, and so shades off into more diffuse, longer-term relationships that are not always easily distinguished from conventional and legally sanctioned relations between spouses or partners. By the same token, the exchange of sex for some economic benefit is not legally defined as prostitution where it takes place within a marriage, or, in many countries, between people who are dating each other.

Sexual and economic life are not easily disentangled, for in most societies "sex is a resource with both symbolic and material value" and so also an exchange-value (Zalduondo & Bernard 1995: 157).

Even when research focuses on sexual-economic exchanges that are organized as commodity exchanges, methodological problems persist. Much prostitution takes place in an illegal and/ or hidden economy, so that official statistics on the size and earnings of the sex trade in any given country are not available and it is extremely difficult to gather accurate unofficial data. Female prostitution has received much more research attention than has male prostitution. Within this, female street prostitution has been studied more extensively than other forms of prostitution, and it is sex workers rather than their clients who have received the lion's share of research attention. Few studies of prostitution use control samples, so that claims about its unique properties remain difficult to substantiate empirically. More generally, the existing body of evidence on prostitution is unsatisfactory because it is an amalgam of information from different sources, collected in different ways, at different times, using different definitions of the phenomenon, by different agencies for very different reasons. Different political concerns about prostitution lead to very different research agendas – the questions that preoccupy policymakers, feminist abolitionists, HIV/AIDS prevention activists, and sociologists, for example, are not identical.

Though some commentators remain embroiled in the debate on whether prostitution should be viewed as a form of work or a form of male sexual violence, most sociologists now recognize the need to develop analyses of prostitution that can embrace its diversity and its particularity as both a sexual and an economic institution. This will require dialogue with scholars working on broader theoretical and substantive topics, for example with sociologists who study work, migration, and globalization, such that theoretical insights into the diversity and complexity of the power relations that surround human labor in the contemporary world can be applied to prostitution. And since the metaphor of slavery is frequently invoked in relation to prostitution and "trafficking," there is room for much closer engagement with historical and theoretical analyses of slavery, and more particularly the work of theorists who address questions about gender, property, and slavery (e.g., Brace 2004). Such scholarship highlights the fact that the lines between tyranny and consent, domination and freedom, and objectification and moral agency are not and never have been clearcut, and thus may help prostitution theorists to move beyond simple forced/free dichotomies. The social and political construction of the market for commercial sexual services is another area requiring development. Here, it will be important to draw on theories of consumption to explore the consumer market for commercial sex as a site in which status relations and hierarchies along lines of class, race, nation, age, and gender are expressed and reproduced. Finally, with some notable exceptions (e.g., Kulick 1998; Aggleton 1999), little research attention has been paid to questions about male and transsexual/transvestite prostitution, and it is to be hoped that work in this area will contribute significantly to theorizing on commercial sex.

SEE ALSO: Globalization, Sexuality and; Sex and Gender; Sex Tourism; Sexual Markets, Commodification, and Consumption; Sexuality, Masculinity and; Sexuality Research: Methods; Traffic in Women

REFERENCES AND SUGGESTED READINGS

Aggleton, P. (Ed.) (1999) *Men Who Sell Sex*. UCL Press, London.
Barry, K. (1995) *The Prostitution of Sexuality*. New York University Press, New York.
Brace, L. (2004) *The Politics of Property: Labour, Freedom, and Belonging*. Edinburgh University Press, Edinburgh.
Davis, K. (1937) The Sociology of Prostitution. *American Sociological Review* 2 (October): 746–55.
Kempadoo, K. & Doezema, J. (Eds.) (1998) *Global Sex Workers*. Routledge, London.
Kulick, D. (1998) *Travesti: Sex, Gender, and Culture Among Brazilian Transgendered Prostitutes*. University of Chicago Press, Chicago.
O'Connell Davidson, J. (2005) *Children in the Global Sex Trade*. Polity Press, Cambridge.
Sánchez Taylor, J. (2001) Dollars Are a Girl's Best Friend? Female Tourists' Sexual Behaviour in the Caribbean. *Sociology* 35(3).
Weitzer, R. (Ed.) (2000) *Sex for Sale*. Routledge, London.
Zalduondo, B. de & Bernard, J. (1995) Meanings and Consequences of Sexual-Economic Exchange. In: Parker, R. & Gagnon, J. (Eds.), *Conceiving Sexuality*. Routledge, London.

protest, diffusion of

Sarah A. Soule

The term diffusion as it is used by social scientists refers to the spread or flow of some innovation, through direct or indirect channels, across actors in a social system (Rogers 1995). Diffusion of protest, then, implies that social protest (or some element thereof) is spreading across (or flowing between) some set of actors in a social system.

There are several components of this core definition of diffusion that are worth highlighting (Rogers 1995). First, implicit in this definition are four different types of actors. First, there are *innovators*, who are the very first actors to adopt an innovation. Innovators are said to be adventurous, willing to take risks (and incur losses at times), and connected to actors outside of the social system. Second, there are the *early adopters* of the innovation who, by adopting it, help to legitimize the innovation in the eyes of other actors who have yet to adopt. Third, there are the *later adopters* who come slowly to the process of adoption, but who nonetheless choose to adopt the innovation after careful deliberation. Finally, there are the *non-adopters*, or those who have not, and presumably will not, adopt the innovation.

Thinking about the different types of actors relevant to the diffusion process has been of central importance to scholars of protest cycles (Tarrow 1998). A cycle of protest is a period of increased conflict, across many sectors of a social system, characterized by the diffusion of new tactical forms, identities, frames, and so on. Work on protest cycles distinguishes between "early riser" movements (which help to set a protest cycle in motion) and movements that are sparked by these earlier movements via processes of diffusion within the protest cycle.

In addition to the importance of the different actors in the diffusion process, this core definition also emphasizes that there is some *innovation* or object that is perceived as new and that spreads across these actors (Rogers 1995). Research in social movements has found that innovative protest tactics, frames, and ideology may all diffuse between actors and organizations.

Finally, this core definition emphasizes the channel or conduit along which the innovation spreads. As such, work in the area of social movements has emphasized the importance of both direct (or network) ties and indirect (or socially constructed) ties (Soule 1997).

Early work in the social movement literature was a product of the intellectual and social climate of the 1950s and 1960s. Early treatments of diffusion, like much of the social science in this era, were framed by an interest in psychology and micro-level processes. As such, these tended to view diffusion as motivated by contagion between individuals in groups or crowds, for example when individuals react to stimuli from others. Maladaptive and aggressive impulses were to be feared, since they were thought to spread from person to person and drive collective action. Observers of race riots, lynching, Nazism, fascism, McCarthyism, and Stalinism viewed individuals as non-rational and susceptible to the diffusion of these movements.

With the development of the resource mobilization tradition in the 1970s, and its focus on social movement organizations, it became possible to consider diffusion as a function of connections between different organizations. Thus, more recent treatments of diffusion recognize that the boundaries between movements and movement organizations often overlap, leading to a web of connections (both real and imagined) between actors and social movement organizations.

Most recent work on the diffusion of protest has gone beyond merely noting the existence of diffusion and has instead tried to better specify the mechanisms by which an innovation diffuses. As such, there are two broad categories of diffusion studies: those which focus on how *direct network ties* facilitate diffusion and those which focus on how *indirect ties* facilitate diffusion.

One of the earliest examples of the role of direct network ties in the diffusion of protest is Rude's (1964) examination of the diffusion of information about rebellions along transportation routes in England and France between 1730 and 1848. Similarly, Bohstedt and Williams (1988) show that dense community networks formed through market transactions facilitated the imitation of food riots across communities in Devonshire in the late eighteenth century. Finally, and more recently, Hedstrom et al. (2000) found that the diffusion of the ideas of the Swedish Social Democratic Party between 1894 and 1911 followed the travel routes of political agitators at that time.

In addition to examining trade and travel routes, other studies have focused on additional types of direct ties. Petras and Zeitlin (1967), for example, found that the propensity of an agricultural municipality to vote for Salvadore Allende in the Chilean elections of 1958 and 1964 was directly related to the number of mining municipalities to which the agricultural municipality was connected. In their study, the mining industry spawned high levels of Marxist ideology and activism, which spread to agricultural municipalities via direct ties.

In another historical account, Gould (1991) argued that overlapping enlistment in the National Guard (i.e., people belonging to battalions outside their own districts) produced interdependencies across districts in the commitment to resistance of the Versailles army in Paris in 1871. More specifically, insurrection against the impeding Versailles army in one district depended on the levels of resistance in other districts to which the district was directly linked.

Direct network ties have also been found to facilitate the diffusion of rioting behavior. Singer (1970), who interviewed 500 African American men about their sources of information on the Detroit riot of 1967, found that the chief source of information, according to his informants, was personal communication. This finding is similar to those reported in other studies of riots.

Finally, direct network ties can facilitate the diffusion of innovative protest tactics. Morris (1981) shows that the sit-ins associated with the Civil Rights Movement were not spontaneous and uncoordinated activities, but rather that preexisting organizational and personal ties facilitated communication necessary for the emergence and development of this then innovative protest tactic.

In addition to direct connections between individuals and/or organizations, indirect ties can also facilitate the diffusion of protest. One type of indirect tie is the shared cultural understanding of similar activists or organizations in different locales. While not directly connected, activists who define themselves as similar to other activists may imitate the actions of others. An example of this process is the imitation by activists at Seabrook in 1976 of a mass demonstration at a nuclear site in Germany in 1974 (McAdam & Rucht 1993). In related work, Soule (1997) shows that innovative student protest tactics diffused among educational institutions which were similar along certain dimensions. The construction of categories of similarity served as indirect channels between colleges and universities in the mid-1980s, leading to the diffusion of the shantytown protest tactic during the student anti-apartheid movement.

The mass media is another important type of indirect channel of diffusion. Noting that the urban riots of the late 1960s appeared to cluster in time, Spilerman (1976) hypothesized that riots diffused throughout urban black areas and were facilitated by television coverage of civil rights activism, which helped to create solidarity that went beyond direct ties of community. To Spilerman, then, the media served as an indirect channel of diffusion by creating a cultural linkage between African Americans in different metropolitan areas. Television, he argues, familiarized individuals all over the country with both the details of riots and the reasons why individuals participated in riots. Singer's (1970) aforementioned work on the Detroit riot of 1967 points to the media (as well as interpersonal or direct communication) as a leading source of information on the riot in that city. In more recent treatments, Myers (2000) finds evidence for the claim that riots that received national media attention increased the subsequent national level of riots, while smaller riots that received only local media attention increased riot propensities only in their local area.

In the literature on the diffusion of protest, there are at least three unanswered questions worthy of consideration. First, most of the empirical work on diffusion of protest has not adequately conceptualized which actors are truly at risk for adopting an innovation. When we consider the previously discussed types of actors essential to the definition of diffusion, it is clear that some of these actors (in particular, the non-adopters) are likely not really at risk of adopting the innovation to begin with. In Soule's (1997) work on the student divestment movement in the United States, she defines campuses as "at risk" of experiencing a shantytown event if the college/university had investments in companies doing business in South Africa. At one level, this is perfectly adequate and logical, especially from a methodological point of view. However, in thinking about the set of colleges and universities which at that time had investments in South African-related companies, it is quite plausible that some of them would not *truly* be at risk for a shantytown event because, for example, they had no history of student activism. The difference may be a minor one: *technically* a university may be at risk for experiencing this type of protest because it is guilty of investing in South African-related companies; however, in *actuality*, a university may not really be at risk simply because a good predictor of student activism is a history of activism. Diffusion scholars should carefully consider the "risk set" of potential adopters of an innovation so as to adequately discern between non-adopters who were at risk of adoption and non-adopters who were never really at risk to begin with.

A second consideration relates to the concept of *theorization* as advanced by diffusion scholars (Strang & Meyer 1993). Theorization is the development of abstract categories and hypotheses about patterns of, and relationships between, these categories. It is a way for individuals to make sense of the world around them. In many ways, the concept of theorization is similar to the way in which *collective action frames* are used by scholars of social movements. For example, consider the way in which an innovation (e.g., tactic, ideology) is framed strategically to improve its chances for adoption. In many ways, this is similar to the diffusion literature's focus on the role of theorization in helping to document the virtues of a particular innovation. Drawing connections between theorization and framing would be an interesting area in which social movements and diffusion processes might be advanced.

Finally, thus far scholarship on the diffusion of protest has not compared the relative *effectiveness* of indirect and direct channels of diffusion for spreading elements of social movements. In the literature, there is an often overlooked distinction between *communication* and *influence* (Soule 2004). Both processes convey information, thus both have the potential to impact the actions of others. However, communication is less likely to change opinions than is influence. The former of these is exemplified by the mass media and may be parallel to indirect ties, while the latter is exemplified by direct, interpersonal ties. Thus, we might expect that, at least in certain contexts, direct ties may be better or more effective channels than are indirect ties. Most studies of diffusion in social movements have tended to focus on either direct or indirect ties and their role in the diffusion process; however, there is a need to carefully examine the differences between these two conduits of diffusion.

SEE ALSO: Contention, Tactical Repertoires of; Crowd Behavior; Framing and Social Movements; Resource Mobilization Theory; Social Movements, Networks and

REFERENCES AND SUGGESTED READINGS

Bohstedt, J. & Williams, D. (1988) The Diffusion of Riots: The Patterns of 1766, 1795, and 1801 in Devonshire. *Journal of Interdisciplinary History* 19: 1–24.

Gould, R. (1991) Multiple Networks and Mobilization in the Paris Commune, 1871. *American Sociological Review* 56: 716–29.

Hedstrom, P., Sandell, R., & Stern, C. (2000) Meso-level Networks and the Diffusion of Social Movements: The Case of the Swedish Social Democratic Party. *American Journal of Sociology* 106: 145–72.

McAdam, D. & Rucht, D. (1993). The Cross-National Diffusion of Movement Ideas. *Annals of the American Academy of Political and Social Science*. 528: 36–59.

Morris, A. (1981) Black Southern Sit-In Movement: An Analysis of Internal Organization. *American Sociological Review* 46: 744–67.

Myers, D. J. (2000) The Diffusion of Collective Violence: Infectiousness, Susceptibility, and Mass Media Networks. *American Journal of Sociology* 106: 173–208.

Petras, J. & Zeitlin, M. (1967) Miners and Agrarian Radicalism. *American Sociological Review* 32: 578–86.

Rogers, E. M. (1995) *Diffusion of Innovations*, 4th edn. New York, Free Press.

Rude, G. (1964) *The Crowd in History, 1730–1848*. Wiley, New York.

Singer, B. D. (1970) Mass Media and Communication Processes in the Detroit Riot of 1967. *Public Opinion Quarterly* 34: 236–45.

Snow, D. A. & Benford, R. D. (1999) Alternative Types of Cross-National Diffusion in the Social Movement Arena. In: Della Porta, D., Kriesi, H., & Rucht, D. (Eds.), *Social Movements in a Globalizing World*. Macmillan, London, pp. 23–9.

Soule, S. A. (1997) The Student Divestment Movement in the United States and Tactical Diffusion: The Shantytown Protest. *Social Forces* 75: 855–83.

Soule, S. A. (1999) The Diffusion of an Unsuccessful Innovation. *Annals of the American Academy of Political and Social Sciences* 566: 120–31.

Soule, S. A. (2004) Diffusion Processes Within and Across Movements. In: Snow, D. A., Soule, S. A., & Kriesi, H. (Eds.), *The Blackwell Companion to Social Movements*. Blackwell, Oxford, pp. 294–311.

Spilerman, S. (1976) Structural Characteristics of Cities and the Severity of Racial Disorders. *American Sociological Review* 41: 771–93.

Strang, D. & Meyer, J. W. (1993) Institutional Conditions for Diffusion. *Theory and Society* 22: 487–511.

Strang, D. & Soule, S. A. (1998) Diffusion in Organizations and Social Movements: From Hybrid Corn to Poison Pills. *Annual Review of Sociology* 24: 265–90.

Tarde, G. (1903) *The Laws of Imitation*. Holt, New York.

Tarrow, S. (1998) *Power in Movement*, 2nd edn. Cambridge University Press, Cambridge.

Wejnert, B. (2002) Integrating Models of Diffusion of Innovations: A Conceptual Framework. *Annual Review of Sociology* 28: 297–326.

Protestantism

Jean-Paul Willaime

Of the 2 billion Christians in the world today, Protestants make up about a quarter, while Roman Catholics represent a little over a half. If Protestant Christendom appeared in the sixteenth century within European Latin

Christianity and represented a number of fractures within it, then it would be wrong to associate modern Protestantism with western society (especially with North America). Protestantism has become a world phenomenon, present in Asia (more than 25 percent of South Korea's population is Protestant), Latin America (at least 10 percent of its population), and Africa (17 percent of the population). In the year 2000, out of every 100 Protestants, 31 were in Africa, 25 in Europe, 17 in North America, 12 in Asia, 12 in Latin America, and 3 in Oceania (where they represent 42 percent of the population, the highest proportion in any continent) (Hillerbrand 2004).

Protestantism has its origins in a number of key reformations within European Christianity in the sixteenth century: the Lutheran Reformation in the Germanic world, the Calvinist Reformations in France, Switzerland, and Scotland, the Anglican Reformation in England, and the Radical Reformation of the Anabaptists and Spiritualists. Even if the Protestant world includes branches which appeared later (Baptism in the seventeenth century, Methodism in the eighteenth, and Pentecostalism in the twentieth), it was these reforms which laid the doctrinal foundations for Protestantism and gave it shape. The Protestant world constitutes an extremely diversified and complex religious situation. It is polycentric – Geneva is not Rome – pluriconfessional, and multifaceted. A Lutheran church service in Sweden is quite different from a Pentecostal assembly in Brazil, or from a Baptist service in the Southern US. It is, in each case, one of the number of different faces of Protestantism. Although the Protestant world is uniform neither in its doctrine nor its organization (it is characterized by its theological and ecclesiastical pluralities), three fundamental principles give it a certain unity: (1) reference to the Bible, (2) religious individualism, and (3) a sense of Christian duty in the world.

Whatever the Protestant confession – whether it be Reformed/Presbyterian, Lutheran, Baptist, Methodist, or any other – great importance is given to the Bible within individual and collective piety, and reference to the holy scriptures is considered a fundamental source of religious truth and Christian behavior. From there, the ecclesiastic institution and its authorities have been relativized. They are fallible and their faithfulness is measured according to the given scriptures (*sola scriptura*, "only scripture"). Luther's heirs felt freer to found other ecclesiastic organizations when they realized their church had become disloyal: there has been, throughout the course of history, a number of reforms among the heirs of the Reform itself. In certain respects, it can be stated that the desacralization of ecclesiastic institutions favored the development of free enterprise in religious spheres, as was the case of denominalizationism in North America. This stance is thought to be the cause for the strong division between clergy and laity, which has contributed to "the universal ministry of the faithful" and the calling for each believer.

The second point which the Protestant world has in common is the concept of religious individualism (not to be confused with being isolated within religion; such individualism, on the contrary, nurtures all facets of sociability, including a sense of community-centered sociability). Durkheim (1951) found that the highest incidences of suicide in Protestant populations were linked to such individualism and to a low level of collective integration. This depended on the community, whether Lutheran, Baptist, or Methodist, although it is primarily the concept of personal suitability of religion which is of primary importance in the Protestant interpretation of Christian living; whether this suitability be intellectual or emotional, whether it subscribes to the psychosocially "liberal" branches of the church (those which are pluralist and care little for monitoring the beliefs and practices of their faithful), or whether it subscribes to the psychosocially "orthodox" branches of the church (aimed at a society of believers sharing a common model and having the necessary means for control).

The third major characteristic deals with fulfilling one's Christian duty. The reformers, while criticizing monasticism, valued worldly saintliness rather than non-worldly saintliness; that is, an inner rather than external monasticism being the source of an intramundane asceticism within the puritan posterity of Protestantism. The Protestant world is active in contributing to education (through schools and youth organizations), society (a variety of activities, the "social gospel"), and culture (philosophy, literature, music, etc.).

These three principles – reference to the Bible, religious individualism, and religious vocation, practiced in the secular world – have generated a particular religious culture and have shaped certain modes of behavior. From a sociohistorical point of view, Protestantism represents the beginning of a new way of living Christianity individually and collectively and which has not only endured but also grown. Far from being a historical digression, the Protestant Reforms of the sixteenth century were able to accomplish a lasting institutionalization of new religious societies as well as new individual attitudes. The result is a sociology of Protestantism which must not only research all branches of Protestantism and their inner dynamics, but also analyze the relationships within its environment and see where such relationships stand in the modern world.

STRICT IDEOLOGICAL CONTROL OF RELIGIOUS GROUPINGS

The domains of ritual, ideology, and charisma are present within every religious group, but in differing ways. Above all, they are hierarchically different according to religious tradition. One can immediately notice the importance of ritual in an Orthodox church service (the main role being the liturgy), the importance of charisma in Pentecostalism (the main role is played by the preacher-prophet), and the importance of ideology in a Reformed service (the main role is played by the preacher-theologian). In Protestantism, ideology is important owing to the strong emphasis on the Bible and its interpretation. The question of faith in the Protestant perspective is no longer an institutional one, but rather a question of hermeneutics. The objective is the interpretation of the Bible, and the debate about the truth of Christianity becomes a debate for exegetes and academics. The claim that religious truth is a question of interpretation leads straight to the heart of religious organization – a permanent debate on religious truth. The world of Protestantism is one of debates and controversies, divisions and unifications, based on disagreements and agreements of doctrine. Ritual is by no means absent, as it is emphasized quite heavily in certain spheres of Lutheranism and Anglicanism,

but within the symbolic economy of this religious world, in general, it takes second place. Charisma is equally important, but it is only in certain Pentecostal assemblies that it tends completely to relativize its ideology. Protestantism is a religion of the senses, of sound more than vision, expressed particularly through music and song (from Huguenot psalms and Lutheran choirs to Afro-American spirituals and Gospel music). Protestantism is overall a religion centered on the senses just as much as the intellect.

Protestantism is beset by a tension between church and sect, so it is unsurprising that the sociology of Protestantism still accords attention to the classic Weberian/Troeltschian distinction between church and sect. Within this religion, the notion of church is also interpreted as being that body which administers what is required for salvation and whose function it is to exercise authority. It embraces everyone irrespective of their religious qualification, whereas the concept of sect is seen as a grouping unifying only people who are religiously qualified on the basis of their voluntary approach to religion. Within Protestantism there is constant tension between the religious group perceived as coextensive with society and delivering its requirements for salvation to all, and the religious group perceived as an association of militants making up a particular subculture within society. This tension is constitutive of Protestantism and is also constituted by established and liberal churches whose criteria are more flexible with regard to religious inclusion and religious practice (such as the Lutheran church) and those churches regarded as local voluntary assemblies where the faithful are qualified believers (as is the case for the Federations of Baptist Churches).

The Reforms of the sixteenth century are linked with the emergence of a new type of clergy (in the sense of religious profession): a clergyman/theologian allowed to marry, yet enjoying the state of being a lay person. The emergence of the pastorate represents a certain secularization of the clergy, a secularization marked by the passing of sacred power to intellectual and moral power (Willaime 1986). With the Protestant pastor, in effect, the clergyman is no longer considered to be a holy figure who enjoys a peculiar ontological position. On the contrary, he is a man like any other. Protestant ministers are ordained, but their ordination is not a sacrament; they are not intermediaries bound to the religious lives of the faithful. This first secularization contributed to the reintegration of the clergy into society and everyday life. But the important intellectual and moral magisterium practiced by the pastor, added to the fact that all sacred authority had not disappeared – notably by means of the monopoly to administer the sacraments of baptism and communion –was limited to the effects of this first secularization. The priest-dispenser-of-rites was substituted with the Protestant-pastor-doctor and preacher of holy scripture, thereby placing great importance on theological knowledge within access to religious legitimacy.

The concept of the ordered ministry was not very ecclesiastic and facilitated the admission of female pastors, who are nowadays accepted by the majority of Protestant and Anglican churches. Consequently, with the Protestant figure of the clergy, women having access to theological knowledge constituted a decisive step for Protestantism. If in effect it considered theological qualifications fundamental to exercising religious authority, then the fact of women holding qualifications in theology would only seriously weaken the argument of those opposed to female pastors. The admission of women into the pastorate can be seen as a second secularization of the role of the clergy, a second secularization marked by the loss of power by the clergy and the dissolution of its status. The acceptance of women into the pastorate serves to reinforce a functional concept of the ministry (women pastors placing on hold their pastorate when on maternity leave). The feminization of the pastorate is party to a broader transformation of pastoral practice and moves quickly in the direction of secularization, and toward a type of declericalization distinguished even more than the pastoral ministry.

PROTESTANTISM, ECONOMICS, AND POLITICS

From a sociohistorical point of view, religions could not be confined to the religious sphere, but must be considered as sociocultural facts that have exerted some influence in the various spheres of social life. Whether dealing with work, economics, family life, education, or politics, people's behavior in these fields is linked to the way they represent the world and humanity. These representations, arranging social activities in a hierarchy and giving them meaning, influence people's attitude towards them, positively or negatively. Religious cultures played a role in shaping thought and people because of a system of representations that determines a certain kind of behavior in one sphere of activity or another. From this perspective, social sciences study the influence of Protestantism on economic and political domains.

Weber (1998), in his famous thesis on the Protestant ethic and capitalism, established a relationship between some Protestant concepts and the spirit of enterprise. Disclosing some affinities between the behavior of the Protestant Puritans and the spirit of capitalism, he wanted only to show that some forms of Protestant religious thinking encouraged the rationalization of business and its development: it is a matter of considering, says Weber, "how the contents of the religious beliefs biased the emergence of an 'economic mentality' or 'ethos' of economics." A more precise title for Weber's study could have been "The Contribution of Puritan Work Ethics in Shaping the Ethos of Western Capitalism." As Weber's friend Ernst Troeltsch, theologian and sociologist, quite rightly wrote in a 1923 text, "religions are not economic ideals, no more than economic structures and financial interests are religious laws. Their relationship is thus only indirect" (Troeltsch 1991: 138).

It is undeniable that the Calvinist perspective and its Puritan posterity developed a strong religious legitimization of work. From the Calvinist point of view, not to work means not to honor God. Since people do not own their possessions but only "administer" them, they should act as good administrators of worldly goods. Money is not evil in itself – it is how it is used that makes the difference. Such a view of work answered the needs of the petit bourgeois – craftsmen and farmers – who totally devoted themselves to production and who were about to become entrepreneurs. As Hill (1962: 223) points out, they needed a conceptual system which "would attribute full dignity to their work and bring into question at the same time the wealthy, the negligent and the squandering, and the poor, the lazy and the irresponsible. They found both these things in Puritanism."

According to Weber, the importance given to work and economic success by religion does not explain all. In order to devote themselves to business completely, people needed a psychological drive. It is at this level that Puritan Protestantism, acting like a "spiritual motive power," positively influenced economic development. There are various examples supporting this point of view: Baptists, Congregationalists, Quakers, and Methodists have all excelled in business. John Wesley himself, who deplored the rise to the bourgeoisie of his flock, remarked: "The Methodists become industrious and frugal everywhere they are, and as a consequence their wealth increases."

Weber's thesis was very controversial and led to a great number of studies and critiques. Troeltsch, whose line of thinking followed the direction of Weber's, insisted very much on the difference between "old Protestantism" (sixteenth and seventeenth centuries) – especially characterized by the ecclesiastic culture of the Middle Ages – and "modern Protestantism" (eighteenth and nineteenth centuries), which fully accepted the emancipation of the secular world from religious protection: "In so far as Calvinism applied to the capitalistic production, that it had tolerated, its methodical and permanent zeal, contributed notably to the emergence of the capitalistic mentality which rewarded work for work. As was the case for both sects and Pietism" (Toeltsch 1991: 163). As long as the religious factor is considered as just one among many others that played a role in the development of western economic rationality; as long as it is kept in mind that influence on economic activity was exerted in an indirect and temporary way through certain individuals; and as long as there is an awareness of its shortcomings (as Weber was aware), then it is justifiable to give Weber credit for his thesis. It is undeniable that a kind of work-based religion is present in the Puritan consciousness, a work-based religion where work is conceived as regular and dutiful practice of an activity. This practice has a link partly with a worldly ascesis and partly with the growing importance of efficiency (and thus with the development of the activity and its results).

Protestantism, in some respects and through some of its components (especially Calvinist and Baptist ones), made a contribution to democracy. By provoking a new division within Christianity, and being divided in itself, Protestantism first of all promoted the secularization of politics. In the political sphere, this is the consequence of the secularizing effects of pluralism: "The fragmentation of Protestantism represented an important element in the development of religious tolerance" (Bruce 1990: 48). In desecrating religious authority, Protestantism contributed to desecrated political authority and asserted the willingness that it should be controlled by people (although Lutheranism increased the princes' power over the church). The ecclesiastical organization of Protestantism had some political elements which were in line with the process of democratization: synodal assemblies and the importance of the local church (Congregationalism). In France, during the reign of Louis XIV, Protestantism had "republican" features that threatened absolute monarchy. In the US, although some Puritans were theocratically oriented, others, such as the Baptist Roger Williams (1603–84) and the Quaker William Penn (1644–1718), experienced some elements of democracy before their time. The US was founded by immigrants who brought a "democratic and republican" Christianity, remarked Tocqueville, who was impressed by the relation in the US between the "spirit of freedom" and the "spirit of religion."

Although Protestantism influenced democracy through some of its principles, it does not mean that its relationship with politics was just one-way. Three main attitudes characterized the connection between Protestantism and politics: conformist passiveness, radical conviction, and an ethic of responsibility. Thus, there were two extreme attitudes – withdrawal due to indifference and radicalism due to an ethic of conviction – in which one can distinguish a third: that one which, originating in the ethic of responsibility, induces a kind of mistrust of power and commitment in public matters. From a historical point of view, conformist passiveness was fostered inside Lutheran Protestantism and inside Evangelical and Pentecostal Protestantism. Since, in contrast to indifference, it is religious approval of sociopolitical commitment that is rewarding, the politician will often be inspired by an ethic of conviction, inciting radicalism in any given domain (e.g., abortion laws, military installations, the environment, education, and civil rights). Whether it deals with fundamentalist theologies or theologies of freedom, political commitment is thus a categorical imperative and a religious duty. This radicalism can be either "conservative" or "progressive." The third attitude, inspired by an ethic of responsibility, consists in being a "good administrator" of the worldly issues promoting both individual and collective responsibility and never trusting power and its appeal.

PROTESTANTISM WITHIN CONTEMPORARY ULTRAMODERNITY

Since Protestantism embodies a process of deinstitutionalization, declericalization, and deconfessionalization of Christianity, it represents a secularization of Christianity from within. Making tradition relative, Protestantism also introduced a permanent principle of transformation that enabled it to go with modernity and adapt to changes, notably in the area of the family ethic. The Reformed Churches have since been quite permeable to social and cultural change. And because of this permeability, they evolved together with global society, despite the strong opposition of fundamentalist groups to change. But the social paradox is that Protestant churches did not take advantage of their comparatively positive adaptation to modernity. As shown in various studies (Kelley 1972; Bruce 1990; Willaime 1992), those liberal churches that were more open to their secular environment often declined before the more conservative churches with a strong identity. If, as Gauchet (1985) put it, Christianity is the "religion of the *sortie*/end of religion," is Protestantism the denomination of the end of Christianity? Its comparatively good adaptation to modern societies carries with it the risk of dissolution into the secular environment and a lack of visibility.

At the same time, in secularized and pluralist societies, the Protestant way of living Christianity is in accordance with developments pointing to identity reassertion and religious revitalization in the shape of groups of militant converts. Protestant sensibilities that insisted on personal conversion are in line with this context, where religion is no longer inherited but made by conversion. In secularized societies where religion is no longer an objective dimension of society but a subjective dimension of the individual, Protestant religious individualism is a sign of the exhaustion not only of Christianity (Christianity with respect to political structures) but also of Christianness (Christianity with respect to global culture). Underlining the fact that the church is not a geographical space, nor something coming from tradition, but a regularly called local meeting of converts, the Protestant movement, especially in its Evangelical and Pentecostal expressions, witnesses in particular the dissolution of Christianity as an all-inclusive culture in synchrony and as an inherited culture over time. Evangelical Protestantism, in its social expression of religion, is an example of the recomposition of religion within ultramodernity. Evangelical churches formed reference groups with a social importance for their members. In these groups, individuals, strongly symbolically structured and supported by a worshipping milieu, learned how to operate in a complex and uncertain secular universe. In societies where Christianity does not have the same cultural strength and capacity to organize society, it finds a way to reassert itself through some minor and militant forms, which – in Protestantism as in Catholicism – question and can sometimes destabilize ecclesiastic institutions accustomed to the quieter mass Christianity.

SEE ALSO: Catholicism; Christianity; Church; Pietism; Religion; Religion, Sociology of; Secularization

REFERENCES AND SUGGESTED READINGS

Bruce, S. (1990) *A House Divided: Protestantism, Schism and Secularization.* Routledge, New York.

Durkheim, É. (1951) *Suicide: A Study in Sociology.* Free Press, New York.

Fath, S. (Ed.) (2004) *Le Protestantisme évangélique. Un christianisme de conversion. Entre ruptures et filiations* (Evangelical Protestantism. A Conversion Christianity. Between Ruptures and Filiations). Brepols, Turnhout.

Gauchet, M. (1985) *Le Désenchantement du monde. Une histoire politique de la religion* (World Disenchantment: A Political History of Religion). Gallimard, Paris.

Hill, C. (1962) *Puritanism and Revolution: Studies in Interpretation of the English Revolution of the 17th Century*. Secker & Warburg, London.

Hillerbrand, H. J. (Ed.) (2004) *The Encyclopedia of Protestantism*, 4 vols. Routledge, New York.

Kelley, D. (1972) *Why Conservative Churches Are Growing*. Harper & Row, New York.

Troeltsch, E. (1991) *Die Soziallehren der christlichen Kirchen und Gruppen* (The Social Thought of Christian Churches and Groups). Mohr, Tübingen.

Troeltsch, E. (1991) *Protestantisme et modernité* (Prostestantism and Modernity). Gallimard, Paris.

Weber, M. (1998) *The Protestant Ethic and the Spirit of Capitalism*. Roxbury Publishing, Los Angeles.

Willaime, J.-P. (1986) *Profession: Pasteur* (Profession: Preacher). Labor et Fides, Geneva.

Willaime, J.-P. (1992) *La Précarité protestante. Sociologie du protestantisme contemporain* (Protestant Precariousness: Sociology of Contemporary Protestantism). Labor et Fides, Geneva.

Willaime, J.-P. (2005) *Sociologie du protestantisme* (Sociology of Protestantism). PUF, Paris.

psychoanalysis

Siamak Movahedi

Freud defined psychoanalysis as a form of therapy, a mode of observation and inquiry, and a theoretical system. However, his passion lay primarily in psychoanalysis as a mode of scientific investigation. Psychoanalytic theory is based on Freud's image of the individual and his notion of psychic reality. The individual is presented as profane, irrational, self-deceptive, narcissistic, power hungry, and the slave of the most primitive desires. This is the image of the decentered man, and is perhaps one reason for Freud's popularity among postmodernists.

According to psychoanalytic theory, the ground on which the individual stands is paved with uncertainty, and the reality to which he or she appeals is highly suspect. The past is a reconstruction, the memory is a perception, and the perception is a fantasy. The person's conviction of the validity of recall is much more important than its factual authenticity. The patient's beliefs or fantasy about the experience of a sexual seduction have greater impact than the seduction itself. If one defines a seduction fantasy as real, it will become real in its

consequences. As with symbolic interaction theory, Freud was concerned not with the situation but with the individual's interpretations of it. Deconstructing such interpretations is the goal of psychoanalysis. Although psychoanalysis has gone through profound changes since Freud, it continues to remain an elegant mode of listening to a patient or reading a text. Contrary to other psychotherapeutic techniques, the analyst does not ask the patient to change, to give up his symptoms, to be normal, to adapt or behave in a particular way. The analyst is not to have any desire or plan for the patient but to help him discover his own desires rather than being the slave to others' demands.

Psychoanalysis is concerned primarily with the patient's mind rather than the patient's life. Reports of life activities in the analytic situation are understood as symptomatic of the patient's state of mind, or of her experience of the analytic relationship. Inference about the mind is to be made through the narrative activities in the psychoanalytic situation. The analyst focuses attention not so much on the content of life narratives as on their communicative functions and on what is omitted, disowned, avoided, and inattended. Although mind is not clearly defined in operational terms, it is assumed to reflect the joint analytic activities in the session. The patient comes to analysis with a conscious expectation that the analyst will help her search for the sources of her trouble. The analysand's sources of trouble are presumed to be unconscious. Their manifestation through symptoms is part of the individual's defensive system of keeping sources of trouble out of conscious mind. Thus a sharp distinction is made between the manifest (explicit) and the latent (implicit) meanings of the individual's communications.

Psychoanalysis unfolds through three critical processes: *transference, countertransference,* and *resistance*. Transference is what the patient brings to the analytic situation. It is the patient's characteristic mode of conflict, perception, expectation, object relation, or definitions of situations. These internalized patterns of conflict, object relation, and expectation tend to constrain the individual's external relations and to create problems that must be worked through. Transference also entails an emotional involvement with the analyst, not as a real object but as a projected figure from the past. Transference is highly ambiguous and paradoxical. On one hand, almost everything that the patient reports in the analysis is addressed by the analyst. On the other hand, the patient's reports of positive or negative feelings *toward* the analyst are presumed to be in reference to the analyst as a fantasy figure of some sort.

Countertransference is what the analyst brings to the psychoanalytic situation. It consists of all of the analyst's subjective states, blind spots, and attitudes toward the analysand. Here a rough distinction is made between two kinds of countertransference feelings: (1) feelings that are evoked or elicited by the analysand and as such are grounds for valid inference about the analysand's state of mind and (2) feelings that are evoked by the analyst's own unresolved conflicts and that have to be kept in check.

Resistance is any defensive interpsychic activity that interferes with the analytic process. Working through resistance is critical, as its resolution entails new paths to memories. When Freud found hypnosis ineffective in ridding the patient's resistance to talk or recall, he created the psychoanalytic situation. The analytic situation is intended to be an inherently ambiguous situation, an intermediate state of experience between reality and illusion, where ideally there are no clear boundaries between fantasy and reality, past and present, and self and others. The goal is to bring about a partial suspension of the analysand's sense of reality in a safe mode where his unexamined assumptions, delusions, expectations, and self-deceptions may be explored.

To be analyzed is a contract into which the patient enters by showing up for the first appointment and lying on the couch. Although many patients, as part of their pathology, unwittingly try to defeat the analyst, they also try to put their best foot forward and help the process get started. It is in this sense that, for an analysis to unfold meaningfully, the patient has to come of her own will and has to incur the cost personally rather than through a third party.

The methodological debates in psychoanalysis today are reminiscent of those in psychology and sociology almost a half century ago. A lively debate is in progress in psychoanalysis between those who call themselves "natural" scientists and those who maintain that psychoanalysis is inherently interpretive and hermeneutic and should be studied with that fact in mind. Those adopting the natural science position are hopeful that, by reducing meaning to some form of brain functioning, they can become the biologists of the *mind* rather than the analysts of the *soul*. In turn, members of the hermeneutic circle reduce psychoanalysis to textual analysis, subject only to the requirement of internal coherence. There are also those who agree with the interpretive tradition, but maintain that psychoanalysis goes beyond the hermeneutic method in that interpretation of the text in psychoanalysis changes the text itself. Since psychoanalytic data consist of emotional exchanges in the analytic situation, the primary method of investigation in psychoanalysis remains participant observation and case study. The analytic situation is considered to be both a laboratory and an operation room for scientific and clinical work. The emotional climate of the analytic situation is of critical importance in interpreting any exchange in the analytic hour. Yet, for the analysis of emotional communication in a session, some researchers are increasingly experimenting with more standardized methods that may lend themselves to replication by other researchers.

SEE ALSO: Definition of the Situation; Frame; Freud, Sigmund; Intersubjectivity; Lacan, Jacques; Mind; Patient–Physician Relationship; Postmodernism; Psychoanalytic Feminism; Symbolic Interaction; Text/Hypertext

REFERENCES AND SUGGESTED READINGS

Freud, S. (1957 [1904]) Psychoanalytic Procedure. In: Strachey, J. (Ed. and Trans.), *Standard Edition of the Complete Psychological Works of Sigmund Freud*, Vol. 7. Hogarth Press, London, pp. 249–56.

Gill, M. (1994) *Psychoanalysis in Transition*. Analytic Press, Hillsdale, NJ.

Levenson, E. A. (1991) *The Purloined Self*. Contemporary Psychoanalysis Books, New York.

Malcolm, J. (1981) *Psychoanalysis, the Impossible Profession*. Vintage Books, New York.

Movahedi, S. (1996) Metalinguistic Analysis of Therapeutic Discourse. *Journal of the American Psychoanalytic Association* 44(3): 837–62.

Ricoeur, P. (1977) The Question of Proofs in Freud's Psychoanalytic Writings. *Journal of the American Psychoanalytic Association* 25: 835–71.

Schafer, R. (1992) *The Analytic Attitude*. Basic Books, New York.

Spence, D. S. (1982) *Narrative Truth and Historical Truth*. Norton, New York.

psychoanalytic feminism

Kristina Wolff

Psychoanalytic feminism is a theory of oppression, which asserts that men have an inherent psychological need to subjugate women. The root of men's compulsion to dominate women and women's minimal resistance to subjugation lies deep within the human psyche. This branch of feminism seeks to gain insight into how our psychic lives develop in order to better understand and change women's oppression. The pattern of oppression is also integrated into society, thus creating and sustaining patriarchy. Through the application of psychoanalytic techniques to studying differences between women and men as well as the ways in which gender is constructed, it is possible to reorganize socialization patterns at the early stages of human life. Societal change, or a "cure," can be developed through discovering the source of domination in men's psyche and subordination in women's, which largely resides unrecognized in individuals' unconscious.

This type of feminism emerged out of *cultural feminism*, which investigates the differences between women and men to understand women's positions in society. Psychoanalytic feminists concentrate on early childhood development, primarily before the age of 3, examining how gender is constructed and practiced on societal, familial, and individual levels. Through understanding how the conscious aspects of personality evolve at the infant stages of life, we better comprehend identity formation and gender roles including expectations surrounding what is deemed "feminine" and "masculine." Freud's theories of the human psyche, including psychosexual development, as well as Lacan's reworking of Freud's theories provide a foundational framework for this body of feminism.

Psychoanalytic feminism addresses a variety of issues related to gender in society, concentrating on explanations as to why men continue to repress women. There are two main sections. One branch focuses on examining differences between women and men, on a micro level, particularly on women's psychology as well as the environment in which the personality of a child develops. This includes childhood learning and formation, relationships with parents, and early sexuality traits. It also explores the establishment of femininity and masculinity and the relationship with identity and personality.

The other branch concentrates on investigating the construction of gender. This encompasses examinations of masculinity, femininity, the emergence of adult sexuality including recognition of the female libido, and the continual reinforcement of patriarchy (Mitchell 1974; Irigaray 1985; Kristeva 1987; Benjamin 1988). While continuing the use of psychoanalytic techniques on the micro level, this section also utilizes macro-level analysis through studying societal institutions such as the economy and employment, science and knowledge, arts and language. From a psychoanalytic viewpoint, the first branch represents man's need for an heir, to create something that outlasts him, largely due to fear of mortality, while also providing a means of domination over women and his children. The second section also fulfills this need to create permanency such as through the establishment of business, wealth, science, art, and architecture. These larger structures and social systems organize society, creating a patriarchal system that serves to oppress and dominate women.

The exploration of women's roles as mother and daughter is a central topic in both branches of psychoanalytic feminism. Early theorists such as Jessica Benjamin, Jane Flax, Dorothy Dinnerstein, and Nancy Chodorow view mothering as a means for understanding the continual reproduction and production of the status quo, and therefore a place where social change can occur. Utilizing Freud's techniques as starting points of analysis, many psychoanalytic feminists examine people's pre-Oedipal and Oedipal experiences in relation to gender and identity formation. It is at these stages, from birth until their third year, that children learn gender roles. Freud theorized that children develop their understanding of their gender due to their natural tendency to identify with the same-sex parent. Some psychoanalytic feminists align with this theory, examining gender formation at the Oedipal stage for boys and pre-Oedipal stage for girls. Others, such as Chodorow, begin the analysis of gender acquisition at the pre-Oedipal stage. Utilizing Freud's object relation theory, Chodorow examines the relationships of mothers and their children.

During infancy children are symbolically attached to their mothers. For women, the role of mother represents a dual identity, one of mother and the other as a child who was raised by a mother. Therefore her relationship with her daughter differs from that with her son. When raising a daughter, the mother imagines her life as a child and her own experiences being raised by her mother. This results in a deep bond with her daughter. This is also where the baby learns her identity as well as gender, through her mother, through representations of sameness. Theoretically, this creates less individuality in girls and as a result they develop more flexible egos and only feel a sense of completeness when closely connected to another person.

For sons, their identity becomes formed in a similar manner, yet it is through representations of difference. He signifies the "other" to the mother, defined by her expectations of him. This creates more individuality in boys and a sense of completeness through achievement and competition. In order for boys to develop their masculinity, they must separate from their mothers, just as girls need to be connected to their mothers in order to develop their femininity. This split from the mother creates a dualistic relationship between the two, making femaleness the polar opposite of maleness, distancing sons from mothers and giving rise to "abstract masculinity." As the children grow into adulthood, their gender identities can become threatened by challenges to these early practices. For men, they develop feelings of vulnerability when dealing with intimacy and women feel threatened by separation.

These varying levels of intimacy, of "relatedness" between children and their mother, create a different sense of self for girls and boys, solidifying femininity and masculinity as distinct, opposite categories, which maintain close relationship with one another. Femininity is representative of a strong tie to the mother; masculinity manifests itself as distance from both mother and father. Another theory posits

that the relationship between parents and children is a symbolic process. Masculinity and femininity are constructed on the basis of castration, which consists of a splitting that occurs with the desire for unity between genders, but this desire is repressed. Therefore, masculinity represents the possibility of gratification and femininity signifies the impossibility of union.

Gender roles are based on the household practices of the parents as well as how the children are socialized on conscious and subconscious levels. Children witness power imbalances between mother and father due to their roles within and outside of the household. This reinforces boys' desire to dominate girls and girls' willingness to cooperate and compromise their agency. The key to changing gender construction and, therefore, the practice of men dominating women can be achieved through altering parenting practices within each family. Men need to take a more active, personal role in caregiving and raising the children. This shift would significantly transform the structures of masculinity and femininity that provide the foundation for the sexual division of labor. This then leads to changes in gender construction, diminishing men's domination over women and women's subordination and increasing women's independence and men's relatedness to others.

The development of a person's sexuality and romantic desires also begins at an early age. Many theorists recognize that children have the potential for bisexuality during the pre-Oedipal stage of their lives. Through the combination of parenting and the development of boys' masculinity and girls' femininity, they are socialized to be heterosexual. A young girl's relationship to her father is an essential element in her heterosexual development. In essence, she is competing with her mother for her father's attention. Due to her father's emotional and often physical absence, she remains emotionally attached to her mother, never completely leaving her. As boys move from the pre-Oedipal to the Oedipal stage, they develop a sense of sexual or romantic love for their mothers, partially due to her physical otherness. As they enter the Oedipal stage, there is a realization that they cannot compete with their father for their mother's attention, therefore they begin to emotionally separate from their mothers. This draws them closer to males, thus making the separation less painful and important to their male identity. This process reinforces the sexual and familial divisions that the children witness from birth. Boys and girls adopt their father's and mother's roles. Thus, boys join a larger collective group of males, who in turn dominate women, whereas girls remain close to their mothers, remaining on the margins of society, being ruled by men.

When entering into romantic and/or sexual relationships, men and women seek different things, often due to the separateness created from the construction of masculinity and femininity. Women desire completeness, intimacy, an end to emptiness, and therefore they seek men for completeness; men remain uncomfortable with intimacy, often criticizing women for their emotions, thus reinforcing their position as dominant and separate from women. Both Freud and Lacan provide a valuable framework for understanding the mechanics of sexual desire. Freud focused his analysis on the biological foundations of sexuality and placed the phallus as central to sexual desire and sexual difference, rather than constructions of masculinity and femininity. Therefore men and women place the phallus at the symbolic center of sexual behavior and leave their own personal understandings and desires for themselves to a level of internal fantasy. Lacan concentrates on sexual behavior as the desire for unity between men and women, moving beyond biological understandings of sexuality. Men and women are sexual together in order to fulfill fantasies that are culturally produced but not a result of being "male" or "female" due to essentialist definitions. This concept is then extended to understanding society as constructed as a phallocentric patriarchy which represses female sexuality, particularly female desire, thus reinforcing women's position as "other," remaining defined in opposition to men's desire. Irigaray challenges Lacan's theory and his central focus on the penis and definition of the clitoris as a "little penis." Instead, she notes that women experience pleasure everywhere, forcing a shift in the analysis and placing women in an equal position to men, rather than remaining defined in relationship to men (Irigaray 1985; Kristeva 1987).

The centrality of the phallus extends to the organization of society. Psychoanalytic feminism describes society as representative of men's egos, their sense of self-importance and desire for immortality. Therefore structures such as buildings, machines, bridges, and towers are made to outlast them while also replicating shapes that are most pleasing to them. Social systems are patriarchal, maintaining maleness and masculinity as central to their structures and operations. Some areas of examination by psychoanalytic feminists include the division of labor and economic systems, science and philosophy, as well as symbols and language. They seek to understand these systems while also using psychoanalytic techniques as a method for examining the reproduction of the status quo and as a means for social change.

The division of labor begins in the home, with women operating as the primary caretakers in society. Men are propelled into the work world due to their sense of independence, competitiveness, and desire to achieve, which developed during early childhood. This process produces the ideology and psychology of male dominance and denial of their dependence on women to help maintain the home, raise the children, and provide support for their needs. Male behavior is the norm of success, therefore if women have a desire to be successful in the paid work world, they are expected to act and often dress like a man. Often there is some deviation from this, but usually with unfavorable circumstances. Utilizing Marxist theory with psychoanalysis, the reproduction of mothering is viewed as the basis for the reinforcement of women's responsibilities in the domestic, largely unpaid work, sphere of society. As wives and mothers, women contribute to the continual production of people. Girls are socialized as caretakers, responsible for supporting their husbands and families. Boys are socialized as workers who are responsible for activities outside of the domestic arena and therefore for continual support of capitalistic production.

Experiences from the pre-Oedipal and Oedipal stages of life shape our conceptions of science and philosophy. Western approaches to knowledge are founded on a male worldview, a male understanding of the world where there is a desire for separation and individuation. Early psychoanalytic feminist studies sought to reveal the male bias in academics, art, philosophy, and science (Gilligan 1982; Irigaray 1985; Kristeva 1987; Flax 1989; Elliot 1991). For example,

Carol Gilligan studied the work of Lawrence Kohlberg and his theory of moral development in which he concluded that girls were morally inferior. Gilligan exposed the bias in his work. Kohlberg used only boys' stories in his model. She argues that both cognitive and developmental psychology are biased due to their use of male subjects to establish a standard of normality. Gilligan reformulated the theory, concluding that morality is a negotiated path where people balance self needs and interests while caring for the "other" (Gilligan 1982; Dimen 1995). Within this body of research, of uncovering the male biases inherent within the practices and structures of science, philosophy, and the overall quest for knowledge, these scholars offer a solution through the reformulation of epistemology and metaphysics in our society. Dualistic thinking, the split between subject/object and mind/body, must be replaced by thinking that accepts differences without creating a hierarchy of superiority. This can be achieved by studying and reshaping early childhood experiences which create and reinforce the existing system of patriarchy and dominance.

Certainly, there are critiques about psychoanalytic feminism and the approaches used by its scholars. Due to the focus on early human development, the few strategies offered for creating change primarily concentrate on this period and are reliant upon parents raising their children in different ways. The theories that provide the foundation for a large portion of this body of feminism rely on scholarship by Freud and Lacan. While this classical body of work is valuable in that it illustrates that masculinity and femininity are achieved and that women have sexual desires and needs, many of these theories are also misogynistic and place men in positions of superiority over women. Some question the use of basing psychoanalytic feminism on theories created by men, particularly since they are often presented as "truth claims" and "cures" for those who are subject to psychoanalysis. Additionally, psychological theory interpreted the feminine experience largely in relation to masculinity, which is one of the critiques of science and knowledge offered by psychoanalytic feminism.

While there is an acknowledgment of the need to change dualistic thinking, by framing the examination of women's subordination on the differences between genders, the either/or split that is being challenged by psychoanalytic feminism is actually being reified. Women are assumed to naturally want to have and raise children and men are assumed to be satisfied being away from their families, both physically and emotionally. There is no accounting for ambiguity in gender or that sexuality and sexual differences are not necessarily related to gender. Within this type of feminism, there is no space for sexuality other than heterosexuality. Other assumptions including those of race/ethnicity, class, nation status, ability, and other issues that affect family structure, childhood, and parenting also largely remain unacknowledged and unexamined. Also, by primarily placing the focus of change on individuals, either in the realm of parenting or in that of creating knowledge, larger societal institutions and systems that create, produce, and reproduce oppression continue without question. There are scholars within psychoanalytic feminism who are actively working to answer these critiques and therefore expand this body of feminism. This includes integrating concepts of gender that are more fluid, ambiguous, and expansive. Through the incorporation of postmodernist perspectives, understandings of gender, particularly "female," are no longer defined in relationship to and from what is "male" (Weedon 1987; Dimen 1995). By widening the approach beyond dualistic definitions and assumptions of gender and sexuality, this work seeks to encompass the influence of history, politics, and cultural influences shaping understandings and experiences of gender and women's multiple locations in society.

SEE ALSO: Cultural Feminism; Feminism; Freud, Sigmund; Lacan, Jacques; Patriarchy; Postmodern Feminism; Psychoanalysis

REFERENCES AND SUGGESTED READINGS

Benjamin, J. (1988) *The Bonds of Love: Psychoanalysis, Feminism, and the Problem of Domination.* Pantheon, New York.

Chodorow, N. (1978) *Reproduction of Mothering.* University of California Press, Berkeley.

Dimen, M. (1995) The Third Step: Freud, the Feminists, and the Postmodern. *American Journal of Psychoanalysis* 55(4): 303.

Dinnerstein, D. (1976) *The Mermaid and the Minotaur: Sexual Arrangements and Human Malaise.* University of California Press, Berkeley.

Elliot, P. (1991) *From Mastery to Analysis: Theories of Gender in Psychoanalytical Feminism.* Cornell University Press, Ithaca, NY.

Flax, J. (1989) *Thinking Fragments: Psychoanalysis, Feminism, and Postmodernism in the Contemporary West.* University of California Press, Berkeley.

Flax, J. (1993) *Disputed Subjects: Essays on Psychoanalysis, Politics, and Philosophy.* Routledge, New York.

Gilligan, C. (1982) *In a Different Voice.* Harvard University Press, Cambridge, MA.

Irigaray, L. (1985) *Speculum of the Other Woman.* Trans. G. Gill. Cornell University Press, Ithaca, NY.

Kristeva, J. (1987) *Tales of Love.* Trans. L. Roudiez. Columbia University Press, New York.

Mitchell, J. (1974) *Psychoanalysis and Feminism.* Vintage, New York.

Weedon, C. (1987) *Feminist Practice and Poststructuralist Theory.* Blackwell, Cambridge, MA.

psychological social psychology

Joel Powell

Psychological social psychology is concerned with social influences on individual behavior. In its century of modern history, psychological social psychology has addressed issues of attitude, perception, memory, prejudice, personality, emotion, conformity, learning, socialization, persuasion, and cognition. In topics, methods, and theory there has been minimal overlap with sociological social psychology primarily because of psychology's persistent emphasis on the individual as the most important unit of analysis.

Social scientists made no significant proprietary claims on early modern social psychology. Anthropologists and sociologists were investigating small groups and large populations. Psychologists had already staked out productive areas of research and debate in learning, memory, motivation, and animal behavior. Before the twentieth century, psychological experiments in human social influence had been conducted, notably Norman Triplett's 1897 study of the effects of competition upon performance. But social context was seen as a given feature of the environment and psychologists seemed content to share the study of social life with other disciplines.

The first systematic attempt in psychology to account for human group life was William McDougall's *Introduction to Social Psychology* in 1908. McDougall argued that group behavior was innate, instinctive, and modified in experience. A popular text primarily for its unique subject matter, McDougall's *Social Psychology* was influential for a short time until it fell from favor along with most instinct theories. The more foundational work was accomplished by Floyd Allport in his 1924 *Social Psychology*. Allport identified social psychology as an exclusive subfield of psychology, and as an experimental science of the individual, dismissing what he saw as sociology's reliance on imaginary social forces to explain human behavior. In casting social psychology as an experimental science, Allport invited the control and predictability of the laboratory. His desire for clear, scientific results precluded the study of face-to-face transactions in favor of scenarios involving individuals behaving in the presence of others. By insisting on a social psychology of the individual, Allport liberated the new science from merely speculative social mechanisms like LeBon's crowd contagion or Durkheim's collective conscience. Instead, social psychology would observe and explain the influences that individuals exert upon one another.

These central features of early social psychology created a divide between psychological and sociological social psychologies that has lasted to the present. The division becomes sharper in consideration of how Allport set the direction of causal analysis. Phenomena for sociology – contexts, conditions, or structures – in psychological study became relevant only insofar as they influenced individual behavior. Moreover, features of the individual could be formulated as dependent variables. So while sociologists were struggling with the self as dependent upon and determined by social relations, psychologists were able to investigate the impact of social variables on stable entities like personalities. Comte's description of the individual as both cause and consequence of society was inapplicable to the elegant and controlled psychology that made independent variables of sociology's subject matter.

It is widely acknowledged that social psychology surged forward shortly after Allport's bold initiatives. To some extent this is because Allport's construction of social psychology as a science of the individual conformed the discipline to conventional topics and methods, making social psychology more competitive with differential (individual) psychology. Survey research and psychological testing found places in social psychology as new, sophisticated tools were invented. Thurstone proposed attitude scaling measures by 1929 (the first publication year of the *Journal of Social Psychology*), and by 1932 Likert had perfected the simple 1 to 7 continuum of agreement and disagreement. The most memorable stagecraft in experimental social psychology was also a product of this era. A classic example of laboratory experiments in social influence is Sherif's study of group convergence in judging the movement of a light. Although the light in his laboratory was stationary, autokinetic effects produced the illusion of movement, and Sherif found that individuals tailored their reports about the distance a light moves to fit a group norm. This study was modeled by many researchers over the next 40 years, and the famous conformity studies of the 1940s and 1950s by Solomon Asch and the obedience studies of the 1960s by Stanley Milgram are often mentioned in tandem with Sherif's work.

Increasingly complex instances of social influence were managed in laboratories throughout the middle decades of the twentieth century. The acclaimed creative champion was the gestalt psychologist Kurt Lewin, whose influential field theories and group dynamics characterized psychology as a social science. Lewin felt that psychology should consider the total situation of an individual's "life spaces" by attending to environmental and social variables. Although Lewin produced elaborate, geometrical descriptions of individuals moving through systems, these were upstaged by his provocative laboratory simulations of leadership groups. Lewin and his associates created different leadership conditions for small groups of boys who were assigned to produce crafts. In an authoritarian leadership condition, adults made decisions, concealed the

ultimate goals of projects, acted aloof, and freely rewarded and punished individual group members. Democratic leaders encouraged group decision-making and the free discussion of alternatives, and stated goals clearly. Boys in the democratic leadership condition were more productive and cohesive. They were also more adaptable than their authoritarian counterparts, as was evidenced by their superior ability to adjust when placed in the opposing condition.

These and similar experiments inspired by Lewin led many to credit him with moving social psychology away from a purely individualistic effort toward more transactional studies of group phenomena. However, the balance of Lewin's work (and subsequent investigations built upon his systems) consistently privileged individual responses to social stimuli. Lewin's legacy is pervasive in virtually all areas of psychological social psychology, not because he moved psychology away from its study of the individual, but because he encouraged the integration of creative experimentation and holistic gestalt principles of perception and form.

The energizing work of Lewin and the influence of gestalt principles fostered a new family of cognitive social psychologies. These perspectives are linked by the observation of a basic urge to see consistency in and between thoughts and feelings. Fritz Heider's balance theories were the first in this generation of contemporary influences. Heider asserted that individuals confronted with incomplete information about others will pattern beliefs, attitudes, or motives of others in consistent and sensible ways. These can be familiar processes such as friends assuming they share attitudes, beliefs, or tastes about things they have not discussed. They can also be complex, as when an individual attributes motives to a stranger. Regardless of the relative accuracy of assumptions and attributions, people will try to balance their elements. It completes a pattern in a balanced way, for example, when friends assume that they share interests and attitudes. Ideas about consistency in attributions continue to be refined and elaborated, and have grown to include research on how people associate positive traits, motives, actions, and other qualities of people they encounter. Topics such as personal attractiveness have generated an immense number of studies revealing that people tend to associate many positive traits with physical beauty. More important than these intriguing studies is the channeling of social psychology toward the study of individuals making mental representations of social reality. The social cognition theories that dominate psychological social psychology are still developing from these basic ideas.

The touchstone for cognitive social psychologies is cognitive dissonance theory. As interest in the processing of conflicting information grew, Leon Festinger's observations of the consequences of holding contradictory thoughts and feelings were among the most discussed, cited, and developed findings in all of modern psychology. Festinger's initial assumptions were simple: two cognitive elements in relation to each other will produce consonance or dissonance. Opposing thoughts or feelings produce uncomfortable dissonance in individuals. They will try to reduce it. The areas of interest for experiment and observation are in the strategies for reducing dissonance, and studies have yielded surprising cognitive and emotional responses. Festinger's own real-world study in 1956, *When Prophecy Fails*, details the behaviors of members of a UFO Doomsday cult whose predicted day of apocalypse came and went without incident. Rather than abandon their beliefs and activities, believers intensified group activities including efforts to recruit new members. In laboratory experiments Festinger found that participants asked to describe a dull task as exciting rated their own enjoyment of the task differently according to how much they were paid. Festinger confirmed the presence of dissonance reduction when lower-paid (high dissonance) participants expressed more enjoyment than higher-paid (low dissonance) participants. There are supportive findings from studies of behaviors that spring from the production of consonant thoughts and feelings. Eliot Aronson (Aronson & Mettee 1968) produced a typical instance of this work. Aronson lowered the self-esteem of laboratory participants by telling them they had tested as immature, uninteresting, and shallow on a personality inventory. Given opportunities to cheat later in a card game, participants whose self-esteem had been manipulated cheated significantly more than participants in a control group.

Experiments, theoretical refinements, formalizations, and debates about cognitive dissonance

continue into the twenty-first century. By the middle 1980s, much of this work had explicitly acknowledged that consistency theory and research had pulled together many threads of mental representations of social reality into a greater understanding of social cognition. As a theory of how social and individual realities are represented in thought, contemporary social cognition is perfectly situated to address key conceptual and theoretical areas in social psychology, including attitude formation and change, attribution, judgment, personality, and self. Its level of abstraction and its status as the most cumulative and integrated of psychological social psychologics has allowed social cognition to infiltrate and influence virtually all topical areas of modern psychology.

In its present incarnation, psychological social psychology is mostly in the business of formalizing and mathematizing theories, and making incremental refinements in perspectives through controlled experimentation. Along with long-term adherence to the study of individuals and to strict scientific protocols, this provides a contrast to sociological social psychology – seen as absent controls, struggling with methods, and grappling with many versions of its basic unit of analysis. It is therefore not surprising that cross-fertilization is minimal between the two social psychologies and that the majority of contributions flow from psychology to sociology. At present, social psychological research in the traditions of analyzing individual behavior has had the most impact on exchange, rational choice, and expectation states perspectives – the most psychological of the sociological social psychologies.

SEE ALSO: Cognitive Balance Theory (Heider); Cognitive Dissonance Theory (Festinger); Exchange Network Theory; Expectation States Theory; Social Psychology; Symbolic Interaction

REFERENCES AND SUGGESTED READINGS

Aronson, E. & Mettee, D. (1968) Dishonest Behavior as a Function of Different Levels of Self-Esteem. *Journal of Personality and Social Psychology* 9: 121–7.

Berscheid, E. (1992) A Glance Back at a Quarter Century of Social Psychology. *Journal of Personality and Social Psychology* 63: 525–33.

Boutilier, R. G., Roed, J. C., & Svendsen, A. C. (1980) Crises in the Two Social Psychologies: A Critical Comparison. *Social Psychology Quarterly* 43(1): 5–17.

Cartwright, D. (1979) Contemporary Social Psychology in Historical Perspective. *Social Psychology Quarterly* 42(1): 82–93.

Charon, J. M. (2004) *Symbolic Interactionism: An Introduction, an Interpretation, an Integration*, 8th edn. Prentice-Hall, Upper Saddle River, NJ.

House, J. S. (1977) The Three Faces of Social Psychology. *Sociometry* 40(2): 161–77.

Lewin, K., Lippitt, R., & White, R. (1939) Patterns of Aggressive Behavior in Experimentally Created "Social Climates." *Journal of Social Psychology* 10: 271–99.

Machado, A., Orlando, L., & Silva, F. J. (2000) Facts, Concepts, and Theories: The Shape of Psychology's Epistemic Triangle. *Behavior and Philosophy* 28: 1–40.

Schwartz, N. (1998) Warmer and More Social: Recent Developments in Cognitive Social Psychology. *Annual Review of Sociology* 24: 239–64.

public broadcasting

Stuart Allan

Precisely what counts as public broadcasting varies from one national media system to the next across the globe. Common to most definitions, however, is the understanding that it revolves around a public service ethos that may be contrasted with the economic (profit-oriented) priorities of private or commercial broadcasting. A continuum of sorts exists between the model of public broadcasting introduced in the US, on one end, and that developed in countries such as the UK, Germany, Japan, and Australia, on the other. In the US this type of programming constitutes a small proportion of audience share in television and radio, and is perceived to be of marginal significance in public life. The reverse is the case in the UK, for example, where public service broadcasting – led by the British Broadcasting Corporation (BBC) – is the predominant institutional

arrangement wielding considerable influence. Public broadcasting systems around the world can be situated within the parameters of this continuum.

Several contentious issues – and conflicting philosophies – have informed the historical evolution of public broadcasting, all of which remain pertinent today. In the US, broadcasting was defined from the outset as a business enterprise, raising concerns about the quality and diversity of its provision – especially in public service terms – as well as its relationship to government regulation. Most of the emergent radio stations in the 1920s were commercial, with a small number of public stations appearing in association with educational institutions on an ad hoc basis. By 1925 the Association of College and University Broadcasting Stations (ACUBS) was campaigning to ensure frequencies remained open for educational purposes (it would evolve into the National Association of Educational Broadcasters (NAEB) in 1934). The Radio Act of 1927 created the Federal Radio Commission (FRC) as the body responsible for regulating the radio spectrum as a public resource, although critics – such as the Broadcast Reform Movement – challenged its commercial orientation. No provision was made available by the state to establish a national network, which meant that noncommercial stations struggled to endure financial hardship, many of them succumbing to the dictates of the marketplace. Fewer than 50 such stations were broadcasting by the early 1930s.

The Roosevelt administration's Communications Act of 1934 replaced the FRC with the Federal Communications Commission (FCC), the remit of which included coordinating the use of radio (as well as the telegraph and telephone). It possessed the powers to revoke, or refuse to renew, a license where it determined that a station's policies and programs were inconsistent with "the public interest, convenience and necessity" (fines could also be imposed). Such action was extremely rare, however, leading to charges that the FCC was little more than a "paper tiger." In the eyes of broadcast reformers fearful about the growing network control of radio in commercial terms, the FCC was failing to meet its public responsibility to ensure access to the airwaves for those groups who felt that their right to free speech was being denied (they included educators, agricultural interests, the labor movement, civil libertarians, and religious groups). Any notion of public service broadcasting, they maintained, was incompatible with the conformity of opinion represented by an advertising-dominated commercial system.

Such claims were countered by organizations such as the National Association of Broadcasters (NAB), a powerful lobbying group capable of bringing formidable pressures to bear on the FCC in order to protect the interests of commercial radio. NAB sought to discourage the airing of "controversial" viewpoints by imposing on its membership what it considered to be a new ethical code of practice. This code prohibited the discussion of issues deemed to be divisive outside of those news and related programs specifically devoted to the expression of opinions. In this way, NAB argued, it was ensuring that radio stations would be self-regulating so as to reduce the likelihood of the federal government intervening to monitor the content of programming. Although the code was legally unenforceable, it succeeded in severely restricting the diversity of voices being heard. Most broadcasters were content to interpret the code in such a manner as to virtually rule out the exploration of any subject which even had the potential to upset program sponsors.

Critics of NAB argued the values endorsed by the code affixed broadcasting's proclaimed commitment to public service within strictly commercial imperatives. Members of radio's audience were being defined, they argued, not as citizens in need of a public forum for argument and debate, but rather as consumers in search of entertaining diversions from everyday life. Under pressure, the FCC began to set aside high-frequency band radio channels for educational broadcasting prior to the start of World War II. While the number of non-commercial radio stations slowly increased in the years following the war, few were broadcasting beyond a narrowly defined target listenership. It would take the arrival of television to propel these developments forward.

The impetus to establish an educational television network in the US was made feasible by a grant from the Ford Foundation in 1952. The first station went on the air in 1953, slowly

joined by 43 others over the course of the decade (many of which broadcast for only a few hours a day). National Educational Television (NET) facilitated the exchange and distribution of programs – criticized by some for their "highbrow" content – between local television stations. By 1954 it was airing 5 hours of programming per day, frequently covering topics otherwise marginalized or ignored altogether by commercial stations. News and current affairs programming on the main television networks – ABC, CBS, and NBC – were becoming increasingly ratings-driven due to the high sponsorship revenues they could demand. In general, network newscasts did their best to avoid controversy for fear of offending either advertisers or government officials. Such apprehensions routinely led to self-censorship, thereby calling into question the networks' provision of impartial journalism consistent with the public interest.

Meanwhile, the FCC sought to ensure that the networks observed the tenets of what would eventually evolve into a fully fledged "Fairness Doctrine" as part of their license obligations. Attempts had been made by the FCC even before a statutory basis for the doctrine was established in 1959 to enforce a principle whereby the right of stations to "editorialize" on the air would be strictly limited. These attempts at regulating fairness, promoted under the FCC's 1949 report "In the Matter of Editorializing by Broadcast Licensees," revolved around a declaration: "Only insofar as it is exercised in conformity with the paramount right of the public to hear a reasonably balanced presentation of all responsible viewpoints on particular issues can such editorialization be considered to be consistent with the licensee's duty to operate in the public interest."

In general, the FCC's efforts met with little success throughout the 1950s, partly due to its inability to adequately police agreed requirements. A further contributory factor was the Commission's internal confusion over how best to delimit a balance between advocacy on the part of the broadcaster, on the one hand, and the rights of those expressing opposing views, on the other (these issues were clarified to some extent in the Communications Act (1960), although not to the satisfaction of any of the parties involved). The net effect of the fairness requirements was to encourage the makers of news and current affairs programs to avoid items likely to attract the attention of the FCC even if, as was likely the case, its strictures would lack sufficient bite to be meaningful.

By the early 1960s public opinion surveys were routinely indicating that television was beginning to displace both radio and the newspaper press as the principal source of news for audiences in the US (and likewise in countries such as Britain). Many commentators were asserting that the capacity of broadcast news and current affairs programming to shape the "public agenda" signified that the electronic media were providing a progressive, even democratizing function with regard to public enlightenment about social issues and problems. Other commentators were far more pessimistic, arguing that the lack of democratic accountability over broadcasting institutions was ensuring that public service would always be rendered subordinate to their financial interests.

Against this backdrop, President Kennedy signed the Educational Television Facilities Act in 1962, which provided the first substantive federal aid package (some $32 million) to build new stations. Three years later the Carnegie Commission on Educational Television was formed to provide a blueprint for public broadcasting as a national service. Following its report, President Johnson signed into law the landmark Public Broadcasting Act on November 7, 1967. The Act established the Corporation for Public Broadcasting (CPB) to coordinate a national system in support of both radio and television. However, the Commission's recommendation that a tax be affixed to the sale of television sets to generate revenue for the CPB was not implemented, nor was its commitment to establishing a relationship of relative autonomy to government upheld. Nevertheless, the Act required a "strict adherence to objectivity and balance in all programs or series of programs of a controversial nature."

In 1969 the CPB oversaw the founding of the Public Broadcasting Service (PBS), the first national network of non-profit television stations. Launched in October of the following year, PBS initially pulled together some 128 television stations into a centralized organization. PBS is effectively operated by its individual member stations, many of which are associated with local educational institutions and community organizations. Programming is provided from these stations in the main – ranging from news and current affairs to the fine arts, science, entertainment, and children's genres – although material from independent producers and international sources (such as the BBC) rounds out the provision. This emphasis on distribution (a role set down by its predecessor, NET) means, in turn, that PBS does not produce its programs centrally. The Service's income is derived from private donations made by viewers (the principal source), as well as from fees paid by member stations and funding from the CPB. Some member stations are also able to draw on other sources – government and corporate – to help underwrite their costs. Today, PBS is owned and operated by 346 public television stations and reaches some 99 percent of US homes with televisions.

Also in 1970, National Public Radio (NPR) was created by the CPB as a non-profit coordinator for national program distribution. Its remit, in contrast with PBS, included program production, making it the center for news, information, and cultural programming for the service. At the time of its launch with 90 stations as charter members, NPR's role as a producer and distributor of programming was funded primarily from government. However, the relative share of such support was sharply reduced over the 1980s, to the extent that funding today is derived mainly from fees member stations pay for programming (funds from listeners via on-air pledge drives, charitable foundations, and corporations are also important sources of finance). In 2003 NPR received $200 million from Joan B. Kroc, philanthropist widow of McDonald's founder Ray Kroc – reportedly the largest single donation bequeathed to a US cultural institution (the amount was almost twice NPR's annual operating budget at the time). NPR is widely respected for high-quality news and information and the diversity of viewpoints it brings to bear on issues of public concern. Its programming is currently heard on over 750 independent stations by an audience of some 22 million listeners each week (stations can be members of NPR and also affiliates of either American Public Media or Public Radio International, both competing public radio networks, selecting content from each).

Highlighted in this historical overview is a range of longstanding questions which continue to be the subject of considerable debate. In its appraisal a decade after the launch of PBS and NPR, the Carnegie Commission on the Future of Public Broadcasting concluded that "public broadcasting's financial, organizational, and creative structure [is] fundamentally flawed." In the course of investigating why the system is "out of kilter and badly in need of repair," the Commission argued that the "power of the communications media must be marshaled in the interest of human development, not merely for advertising revenue. The outcome of the institution of public broadcasting can best be understood as a social dividend of technology, a benefit fulfilling needs that cannot be met by commercial means." In this way the Commission neatly pinpointed the key source of tension between the values of business and the ideals of public service before outlining, in turn, a detailed strategy for introducing a system free of commercial constraints. Its vision of public broadcasting as "a forum for debate and controversy," providing a "voice for groups in the community that may otherwise go unheard" so as to "help us see America whole, in all its diversity" was all but ignored in Washington.

Little has changed over recent decades. Most appraisals concur that the future for public broadcasting is far from assured. For some critics, the privatization of public broadcasting is overdue. They have long maintained that government involvement in broadcasting is an inappropriate use of taxpayers' monies and, moreover, poses a threat to freedom of expression that only a market-based system can adequately preserve. Some claim to detect a "liberal bias" in its programming, which they insist is out of step with popular opinion. Still others contend that the relatively small audience figures for public broadcasting – there is an average audience rating of about 2 percent of households for PBS in primetime, for example – constitutes evidence that commercial television more than satisfies public demand.

Advocates of public broadcasting, in sharp contrast, highlight what they perceive to be the shortcomings of ratings-driven commercial media. Many believe that it caters to a wider spectrum of interests than those which

advertisers are inclined to support, thereby addressing important gaps in programming – news and documentary being regularly cited in this regard, as well as children's programming (the award-winning *Sesame Street* being one example). While conceding that audience figures are small, they nevertheless point out that a high percentage of viewers and listeners are decision-makers in corporate, political, scientific, and educational realms whose perceptions of program quality contrast with the "lowest common denominator" orientation of the commercial networks. Hence the calls made for new types of support to be introduced so as to offset both political pressures and the influence of corporate financing, and thereby better reflect the values, tastes, and preferences of diverse communities.

Looking beyond the US model, the term public service broadcasting is typically employed to describe those systems which share its educative aims as a means to redress market failure. From its origins in the 1920s the BBC has pioneered a conception of public service broadcasting that is free of commercial advertising and, in principle, political influence. Its mission statement, as expressed by John Reith, the Corporation's first director-general, is to "inform, educate, and entertain." Funded primarily through a license fee system, the BBC is currently the largest public broadcaster in the world. Its annual budget (£3.8 billion in 2005) enables it to offer a comprehensive provision of programming – news, current affairs, arts, and entertainment – across radio, television, and the Internet. Facing intensifying pressures from commercial rivals (both nationally and globally), it strives to balance its public service remit with a commitment to attracting wide audiences to its services. In addressing these audiences as citizens, as opposed to prospective consumers, the BBC's preferred definition of the public interest is privileged over and above what interests the public.

The BBC model has proven to be considerably influential, with several of its main tenets closely emulated in a variety of national contexts. The social and moral ideals of the Reithian conception of public service, thrown into sharp relief by profit-led alternatives, informed broadcasting's development throughout the Commonwealth from the 1930s onward (examples include the Australian Broadcasting Corporation and the Canadian Broadcasting Corporation). The BBC model has similarly served as an exemplar for some countries in Europe, Scandinavia, and Asia, and more recently in the former Soviet bloc. It is recurrently the case, however, that these systems have evolved to the point where they have come to rely, to varying degrees, on commercial revenue to meet operating costs. This trend appears to be accelerating, with powerful business interests acting in concert with "market-friendly" regulatory authorities.

New challenges are emerging for public broadcasting across its varied inflections in different national contexts. The era of interactive digital and high-definition technologies poses important questions about its continued viability. The growing competition for viewers, together with contending demands on governmental support, raises concerns about how best to sustain a public service ethos for a type of broadcasting increasingly being fragmented into narrowcasting. While some insist that public broadcasting is no longer relevant or necessary in a multi-channel universe, others believe that its daily reaffirmation of common values and traditions underscores the vital contribution it makes to enhancing mutual understanding and dialogue among a citizenry in accordance with the public trust.

SEE ALSO: Community and Media; Media; Media and Globalization; Media Literacy; Media Monopoly; Media and the Public Sphere; Media, Regulation of; Public Sphere; Radio; Television

REFERENCES AND SUGGESTED READINGS

Barnouw, E. (1990) *Tube of Plenty*, 2nd edn. Oxford University Press, New York.
Day, J. (1995) *The Vanishing Vision: The Inside Story of Public Television*. University of California Press, Berkeley.
Price, M. E. (1995) *Television, the Public Sphere, and National Identity*. Clarendon Press, Oxford.
Smith, A. (1995) *Television: An International History*. Oxford University Press, Oxford.
Tracey, M. (1998) *The Decline and Fall of Public Service Broadcasting*. Oxford University Press, Oxford.

public housing

D. Forbes-Edelen and J. Wright

Public housing policy in the United States did not emerge in response to the social needs of citizens but more out of economic necessity. Its development has been shaped by ideological, economic, sociopolitical, and demographic forces that emerged from the Great Depression. Some of these forces and their associated controversies include: ideological differences about whether it is the business of government to provide housing for needy citizens or whether this is better left to the private business sector; discriminatory practices among real estate, mortgage, and banking interests whose actions created concentrations of poor, segregated, African American ghettos; demographic changes that led to the suburbanization of America; an increasingly conservative fiscal and political climate, which has contributed to chronic underfunding of public housing initiatives, depletion of the public housing stock, and deterioration of existing units; and the unintentional effects of housing policies intended to help the poor but that functioned as disincentives for escaping poverty.

The first Housing Act of 1934 established the Federal Housing Administration (FHA) and was designed to resuscitate the real estate and finance markets during the Great Depression. The FHA and later the Veterans Administration (VA) accomplished this by restructuring housing market practices and financing, including introducing homebuilding and homeownership subsidies. These federal interventions put homeownership within the reach of middle-income families and within a few years transformed America from a nation of renters into a nation of homeowners. These early successes encouraged further governmental interventions in the housing market. One important new intervention was the effort to provide temporary housing for working families (the working poor) who aspired to middle-class status and homeownership but who required short-term housing subsidies in order to accumulate sufficient capital. This was the animating vision of the nation's first true public housing law, the Housing Act of 1937.

This 1937 Act signaled the beginning of efforts to address the housing needs of the working poor. Local public housing authorities were established and given power of eminent domain to condemn and redevelop privately owned land for use as rental housing for working low-income families. The Housing Act of 1949 introduced urban renewal to the overall effort, that is, the removal of old, decaying housing and its replacement with improved new homes. Urban renewal was founded on the principle of "a decent home and suitable living environment for every American family." This principle reflected the post-war thinking that good housing (like other essential services regulated by government such as drinking water, highway development, and public safety) was in the national interest and so was the government's responsibility, especially for those Polton (1996) describes as the "deserving poor," the "suppressed middle class," and the nation's veterans.

Between 1949 and 1968, however, numerous factors combined to create a public housing system that was far from the temporary refuge for the working poor that was originally envisioned. Among the more important were discriminatory practices by local housing authorities who steered African Americans into inner-city housing units far from affluent white neighborhoods; opposition of business and real estate interests to any government intervention in housing markets, which was seen as a threat to the free market system; and the unintended consequences of legislation like the Brooke Amendments which put caps on earnings of public housing residents, resulting in eviction of many upwardly mobile poor. Instead of temporary housing for the working poor, public housing rapidly evolved (certainly by the 1960s) into the housing of last resort for the poorest, neediest, and most dependent sectors of the urban population.

Today, public housing is populated almost exclusively by young, African American women with children, typically two or more. This population is characterized by high rates of welfare dependency, low skills, limited or nonexistent labor force experience, and limited educational credentials and literacy skills. In short, the public housing population has become the chronically impoverished, welfare-dependent, female-headed household that is the principal object of welfare reform.

Recent research presented by Sams-Abiodun and Sanchez at the National Poverty Center Conference (2003) has refined our sense of the female-headed household in impoverished public housing communities. They found that although women are usually the leaseholders of record and are not formally married, they often cohabit with men "in relationships of greater and lesser reciprocity and dependency." Many of these men, it was found, are attached to multiple households, to each of which they contribute either financially or in other ways (e.g., by caring for children, stepchildren, elderly mothers, nieces and nephews). These officially invisible cohabitating black males were also found to be "persistently unemployed or underemployed and the victims, and perpetrators, of violence"; and they often had drug and alcohol issues as well. So while the pecuniary value of their contributions to the households with which they are attached may be limited, they are, nonetheless, present in a surprisingly large fraction of public housing families.

Many citizens and elected officials tend to blame (or perhaps want to blame) the deplorable conditions in many public housing developments on the undesirable characteristics of the people who live there. At best, this is simplistic. The problems of public housing are the combined result of failed policies, social and spatial isolation of residents in these racially and economically segregated communities, and the discriminatory practices of powerful business and real estate interests. For example, the isolated locations of many public housing dwellings limit access to job opportunities, restrict social networks, and lead to civil disengagement. This creates a climate where many residents view dealing drugs as an economic necessity, appeasing drug dealers as the only way to ensure personal safety, and taking drugs as medicine to numb the feelings of inadequacy and indignity they experience daily.

By the end of the 1970s, reform programs such as Section 235 and 236 were developed by the Department of Housing and Urban Development (HUD) to address some of the problems of public housing through public–private partnerships aimed at urban renewal and revitalization. These programs provided subsidized loans, market insurance, and low interest rates to encourage private sector partnership in achieving the urban renewal goals of increasing public housing stock and redeveloping deteriorated units. These programs generally failed to accomplish their goals largely due to mismanagement and fraud. Another factor contributing to failure was the economic pressures exerted by the stagnant wartime economy of the mid-1970s. These ushered in a fiscally conservative political climate, which continues today, and in the 1970s led to a moratorium being placed on public housing spending. This moratorium brought urban renewal to a standstill. Housing that had been demolished to make room for urban renewal was never replaced, other housing slated for redevelopment fell into disrepair, and without the promised capital expense subsidies and tax abatement incentives provided by Section 235 and 236, private homebuilding and mortgage-lending partners retreated from the now unprofitable public housing market.

These fiscal and economic pressures of the 1970s coincided with growing ideological shifts in national values in which any government involvement in public housing came to be viewed as problematic (housing and everything else is better left to private market forces, according to this view). These shifting values reflected the emerging belief that the poor were no longer *deserving* people who had fallen on hard times, but were to be blamed for their own conditions largely because they were lazy, undisciplined, drug addicted, and welfare dependent. This view continues to prevail today and has led to a zero-tolerance climate: basically a one strike and you're out standard that has proven a very useful public housing policy tool for evicting public housing tenants judged to be undesirables. These ideological biases drive the public housing debate and shape national housing policy to this very day.

Interestingly, many people on the left have also concluded that government must disengage from managing public housing and cede management, administration, and ownership to the private sector, a process known as privatization, not because they are ideologically opposed to governmental intervention in the housing market, but because the records of the past three decades can be taken as evidence that

government lacks the ability, commitment, or vision to satisfactorily address the problems of public housing. The commitment to privatization has recently become the cornerstone of federal and local housing policy, although the origins of the policy can be traced to Jack Kemp's tenure as HUD secretary during the first Bush administration.

Privatization of public housing has also become the trend in European countries since the 1970s, primarily out of economic necessity. For example, the increasing cost of fully subsidizing new public housing construction has resulted in a shift from solely federal government financing of public housing in the Netherlands, Germany, and the United Kingdom. Each of these countries has devised various partnership and funding strategies for sharing the financial burdens of providing housing for their poor with the private and non-profit sectors and local municipalities represented in each country.

Germany uses private landlords or institutions willing to adhere to certain conditions, including rent controls and minimum building standards established by the government, to provide housing for its lowest- and just below middle-income populations. These investors receive incentives in the form of low interest loans, operating cost subsidies, and interest-adjusted loans, and are allowed to make a profit as long as they accept tenants who meet the income qualifications for public housing need. Although the federal government largely withdrew from direct financing of these public housing subsidies in the early to mid-1980s, leaving it solely to the states and local authorities, reunification and other social changes have dramatically increased the need for public housing and the federal government has responded by tripling its public housing budget allocations throughout the 1990s. The result is that the rate of public housing construction in Germany rebounded to only about 7 percent lower in the early 1990s than its peak 1970s rates.

By contrast, the rate of public housing construction in the UK has dropped sharply, about 34 percent, since the 1970s, largely due to strict government controls over local authorities' borrowing of public money for public housing construction and cuts in federal subsidies. The UK also uses what Smith and Oxley call a *rebate element* and *housing element* system to award local authorities their subsidies based on market values of public housing property. Because the UK system does not use rent controls, rent increases are set each year according to assumed increases in property values. From these estimates, local public housing authorities are provided with increases or decreases in their subsidies (the housing element) to make up for any deficits due to anticipated increases in housing costs or to control for any overages expected due to lower anticipated costs. As for the rebates, these are provided to lower-income tenants who cannot afford any rent increases; in essence, as Smith and Oxley (1997) point out, the tenants who are financially better off subsidize their less well-off peers.

Hence the move toward privatization is not unique to the United States, although the political, fiscal, and social forces that drive the trend, and how it is implemented, are unique to each country. In the US, the move toward privatization has been strongly influenced by shifts in perceptions of the poor; it has been fueled by the persistent tendency to disfavor the poor, which has shifted the focus of public housing reform away from social structural causes and toward holding public housing residents accountable. HUD has freed local housing authorities from the mandate to function as the housing of last resort and has encouraged zero-tolerance policies. At the same time, HUD has shown its renewed commitment to market interventions by expanding the Section 8 voucher program and the newer HOPE VI housing reform program, staples of public housing policy since the 1990s.

The Section 8 program is meant to promote privatization by allowing low-income families to rent apartments from private sector landlords at market rates. Local housing authorities in essence provide vouchers that pay the difference between the market rent and what these families can afford to pay for housing (stipulated in the Brooke Amendments as no more than 30 percent of gross monthly income). HOPE VI in turn intends to deconcentrate poverty by demolishing densely populated public housing complexes and replacing them with mixed-income, low-rise apartments and townhomes.

The evidence so far suggests that Section 8 programs have achieved mixed results, and that the HOPE VI program, while doing a fairly good job of meeting its deconcentration goals, still falls short of fully achieving the goal of eliminating the concentration of poverty in public housing. For example, a 2003 study by Kingsley, Johnson, and Pettit of 73 housing developments in 48 cities, published in the *Journal of Urban Affairs*, found that Section 8 recipients who were relocated from HOPE VI developments did indeed show lower poverty rates than their public housing peers who remained behind, but there was still "significant clustering" of the poor in some neighborhoods in most of the 48 cities in this study.

In an earlier Housing Policy survey study prepared for the American Sociological Association's annual meeting in 1998, Wright and Devine examined the potential impact of welfare reform on public housing tenants of a New Orleans public housing development. Interestingly, more than half of the respondents felt that welfare reform would not impact their personal lives substantially. A majority also felt it would have no effect or a positive effect on welfare recipients in particular, and on African Americans in general, as well as on New Orleans and American society as a whole. It is, of course, too early to tell whether the optimism of these public housing tenants is well founded because solid, broad-based empirical evidence of the consequences of welfare reform and other recent devolutionary federal policy changes on public housing residents remains quite scarce.

Similarly, an innovative trend, one being used in developing countries like Bangladesh, Egypt, Ghana, and Zimbabwe to increase public housing supplies and reduce the public costs of maintaining them, is to transform public housing occupants into owners of their housing units. With the help of government subsidies that are shifted from private investors and non-profit housing authorities, public housing tenants are allowed to purchase their public housing units and to add extensions on them for a variety of personal uses. These uses can include providing rent-free housing for poorer family members; earning income as landlords, by renting the extra rooms to other low-income tenants; or engaging in other business ventures that can range from operating nursery schools to night clubs and food stores. These ventures are seen as a way to encourage employment and income-generating opportunities in economically deprived areas, and to allow these residents to earn self-employment income providing services in their own communities that are usually not readily available, to other residents in these areas, at costs that are affordable to their low-income peers. While hopes are high, it remains to be seen whether the goals of this innovative approach will lead to decreases in poverty, economic revitalization of public housing communities, and a reduction in the burdens of providing housing for low-income and poor residents in these countries. The results of several studies, now underway, will soon tell us more about the impact of this emerging public housing policy.

Other key areas for future research include studies of the impact of HUD's abandoning its role as the provider of last resort for the most vulnerable members of society. Where will homeless people, the mentally ill, disabled veterans, women who have exhausted their welfare eligibility, and other vulnerable groups find housing if not in the public housing developments? Will these policies create even more homelessness? Or will the new emphasis in HUD and elsewhere on self-sufficiency make it possible for the excluded and dispossessed to obtain their own housing? Only time will tell.

As this body of research grows, it will allow social scientists to assess the true impact of welfare reform, zero tolerance, devolution, privatization, and deconcentration interventions on public housing residents and the nation. It will also provide insights into the long-term effects of Section 8, HOPE VI, and other tax credit and block grant programs passed during the 1990s to facilitate these shifts in public housing policy. Research of the next decade will tell us whether it was a good idea or not to abandon a principle expressed in the 1987 Stuart B. McKinney Homeless Assistance Act: that it is the fundamental duty of good government to provide decent housing for its most vulnerable citizens.

SEE ALSO: Class, Status, and Power; Family, Men's Involvement in; Family Poverty; Family Structure and Poverty; Ghetto; Homelessness; Hypersegregation; Marginality; Poverty and Disrepute; Residential Segregation; Steering, Racial Real Estate; Welfare Dependency and Welfare Underuse

REFERENCES AND SUGGESTED READINGS

Biles, R. (1998) New Towns for the Great Society: A Case Study in Politics and Planning. *Planning Perspectives* 13(2): 113–32.

Carter, W. H., Schill, M. H., & Wachter, S. M. (1998) Polarization, Public Housing, and Racial Minorities in US Cities. *Urban Studies* 35(10): 1889–1912.

Gotham, K. F. (2000) Separate and Unequal: The Housing Act of 1968 and the Section 235 Program. *Sociological Forum* 15(1): 12–37.

Gotham, K. F. & Wright, J. D. (2000) Housing Policy. In: Midgley, J., Tracy, M. B., & Livermore, M. (Eds.), *The Handbook of Social Policy*. Sage, Newbury Park, CA, pp. 237–55.

Polton, R. E. (1996) Assessment Issues in the Valuation of Subsidized Housing. *Assessment Journal* 3(6): 40–50.

Reingold, D. A. (1997) Does Inner City Public Housing Exacerbate the Employment Problems of its Tenants? *Journal of Urban Affairs* 19(4): 469–87.

Smith, J. & Oxley, M. (1997) Housing Investment and Social Housing: European Comparisons. *Housing Studies* 12(4): 489–508.

Stegman, M. A. (1995) Recent US Urban Change and Policy Initiatives. *Urban Studies* 32(10): 1601–9.

Tipple, G. A. (1999) Transforming Government-Built Housing: Lessons from Developing Countries. *Journal of Housing Technology* 6(3): 17–23.

Van Ryzin, G. (2001) Factors Related to Self-Sufficiency in a Distressed Public Housing Community. *Journal of Urban Affairs* 23(1): 57–70.

Varady, D. P. (1994) Middle-Income Housing Programmes in American Cities. *Urban Studies* 31(8): 1345–67.

Von Hoffman, A. (1998) The Curse of Durability: Why Housing for the Poor Was Built to Last. *Journal of Housing and Community Development* 55(5): 34–9.

public opinion

Connie de Boer

The concept of public opinion is widely used in the social sciences: psychology, sociology, political, and communication science. Three distinct perspectives emerge from the many different definitions of the concept: individual, collective, and process.

The most general and inclusive approach is that which conceives of public opinion at the individual level as an aggregation of the preferences of a group of individuals. Scholars with a more holistic view describe public opinion at the collective level as an emergent product of debate and discussion that cannot be reduced to individuals. Within this perspective, the public is not just a group of individuals but a dynamic collectivity. Public opinion refers to a group of people who are confronted by an issue, are divided in their ideas as to how to meet the issue, and engage in discussion over the issue (Blumer 1946). Public opinion is also defined as a communication process that allows people to organize into publics within which opinions are formed and which enable them to exercise their influence. In this perspective, the individual and collective aspects of public opinion are more integrated (Price 1992).

There is a tendency for social scientists to emphasize in their definitions those dimensions of the concept that are related to their own academic discipline. Thus, psychologists are mainly interested in the process of opinion formation and focus on the factors that influence individual opinions. Political scientists draw attention to the role of public opinion in the political system by limiting their definitions to opinions, which governments find it prudent to heed, or to opinions about public affairs. By observing public debates or opinion polls, politicians and other government officials come to know what the public thinks and in that way public opinion can have a political impact. Moreover, politicians may be influenced by their expectations of the opinions of the public. Such latent or unvoiced opinions do not have to be expressed to be deemed to have an effect.

Public opinion is structured, which means that not all opinions have the same value: the opinions of those in powerful positions will always matter more than those of common citizens. And, because not everybody in the public is equally informed or equally active in the public debate, the extent of information and deliberation on which opinions are based varies among members of the general public.

Sociologists have a preference for definitions of public opinion at the collective level, and they emphasize the role of public opinion in a social system as a form of social control. Communication scientists emphasize that public opinion is confined to opinions that are made public, and hence they limit their accounts of public opinion to opinions that are expressed. Given the linkage with the public debate and discussions about issues, they see public opinion as a communication concept.

Social scientists from all disciplines thus acknowledge that public opinion is closely related to the notion of public debate. In the rational model of public opinion, people are understood to develop their opinions during a public debate by listening to and presenting arguments in which their opinions are rationally sound judgments based on thoughtful consideration. Public opinion is also conceived, however, as a form of social control, where its role is to promote social integration and to ensure that there is a sufficient level of consensus on which actions and decisions may be based. These two models differ from each other as to the mode of opinion expression, the effort required for opinion expression, and the conceptualization of the public. The rational model emphasizes the verbal expression of rational arguments and opinions. Opinions are formed as a result of a process of deliberation. For participation in rational discussions, the ability and motivation to acquire information and to discuss the issues are prerequisites. When public opinion is viewed as social control, various forms of opinion expression are possible, ranging from rational debates and casual talks to facial expressions, gestures, and publicly visible symbols. In the latter forms, participation in the process of opinion formation is interpreted as requiring much less deliberate effort than in a rational debate. In the rational model, the term public refers to a group of politically interested and knowledgeable citizens, as, for example, they are described in Blumer's classic account, whereas in the model of social control the notion of public involves everybody (Scheufele & Moy 2000).

Public opinion emerges in and through the mass media, where people play the role of actors and spectators in the public debate. The media are interpreted as carrying out a surveillance function when they alert publics to problems, and they provide the principal mechanism for allowing the public to monitor the social and political environment. The mass media are also the carriers of public opinion by reporting the views and arguments on an issue. Exposure to the media and participation in discussions allow people to assess the extent of consensus and controversy. It is this mutual awareness of the extent of consensus and controversy which ensures that public opinion can act as a social force, whereas the aggregation of individual opinions that are not expressed does not have such power. The media provide the means by which members of a public communicate. Elites use the media to influence public opinion, and at the same time those media provide elites with an impression of the views of the public on the issue at stake. Perceptions of public opinion matter not only because individuals attend to their social environment, but also because these perceptions potentially influence the behavior and attitudes of individuals and officials in political, social, and commercial organizations.

Ideas about public opinion can be found in eighteenth-century philosophy, in Renaissance literature, and even in the works of Plato and Aristotle. Up to the mid-nineteenth century, the bulk of writings dealing with public opinion were normative and philosophical in nature, being studies in political theory rather than studies of public opinion itself. Toward the close of the nineteenth century, public opinion came under increasingly systematic analysis in the empirical manner, characteristic of the developing social sciences. In tandem with the growth of the social sciences within the academy, twentieth-century works on public opinion more clearly reflected sociological and psychological rather than political and philosophical concerns. Analysts increasingly turned their attention to the problem of understanding the social and behavioral aspects of public opinion, but considerations of the underlying normative questions concerning public opinion have continued throughout the twentieth century.

Over the course of the late seventeenth and early eighteenth centuries, a variety of novel social institutions came to prominence: the coffeehouses of England, the salons of Paris, and the table societies of Germany. In these gatherings public opinion emerged as a result of a free exchange of information and arguments about political issues. This emerging public opinion,

which was closely followed by those in power, became a new form of political authority. In contemporary politics, legislators, interest group leaders, politicians, and journalists have multiple means for gauging the public mood. They attend to the mass media, communicate (in many different ways) with colleagues and citizens, conduct focus groups, and monitor the behavior of voters. Yet the opinion poll is the most ubiquitous and authoritative measurement instrument.

Earlier analysts were far more likely to frame public opinion as an inherently collective, supra-individual phenomenon. As survey research and opinion polling got underway in the 1930s, the daunting task of empirically observing the public as a fluid and complexly structured group, consistent with the sociological model of public opinion, led to its replacement with a far more tractable approach – essentially, an aggregate "one person, one vote" conception. The advent of opinion polling redirected attention toward social psychological as opposed to broadly sociological concerns, and it placed problems of individual-level opinion measurement at the top of the research agenda. The combination of advances in measurement and sampling techniques placed researchers in a position to study opinions and attitudes in large populations and also to gather what were increasingly believed to be very accurate readings of public opinion on matters of political and social significance. Opinion polling has changed the essential nature of public opinion itself. The assumption implicit in all polls that everyone might have an opinion and that all opinions are equally important creates an impression of public opinion as the aggregate of opinions of individuals who are also uniformly informed. In some situations one might even say that opinion polls have replaced public opinion. When heeding public opinion, politicians increasingly turn to opinion polls in order to validate and defend their positions on the issues of the day.

Since the inception of public opinion research, great emphasis is placed on questions concerning how to conceptualize individual opinions and how to measure them accurately. Studies of public opinion attempt to describe and account for the preferences and beliefs of citizens, and to assess the (political and social) impact of these preferences and beliefs.

Researchers have tried to explain individual opinions using concepts such as values, attitudes, and ideologies. Converse (1964) showed that survey respondents rarely make use of systematic ideological concepts. The opinions expressed by respondents are often inconsistent and unstable (non-attitudes). After the abandonment of the role of ideologies as a central variable in the 1960s, this topic has reappeared on the research agenda, but the focus of the research has shifted from how many citizens think ideologically to what impact ideology has on the political beliefs, opinions, and actions of citizens.

Theories about schematic information processing have improved our understanding of the process of opinion formation. Schemas, understood as cognitive structures that represent one's general knowledge about a concept or stimulus domain, provide shortcuts in thinking about an issue. Schemas are used as heuristics, simplifying the task of evaluating objects. Another such heuristic is the elite cue, which refers to the practice of individuals making decisions by considering not the details of the issue but rather the positions taken by trusted elites.

Subjective estimates of the climate of opinion, or perceptions of public opinion, are also recognized as having an impact on the process of opinion formation. Such perceptions of public opinion do not necessarily reflect the objective reality of aggregated opinion, but may be distorted by pluralistic ignorance, false consensus effects, and by overestimating the impact of events or media messages on the opinion of others ("the third person effect").

The process of opinion formation is heavily influenced by the context in which the opinion is expressed, in that it depends upon the situation and on which attitudes, values, schemas, group identifications, or perceptions of public opinion come to mind. Thus, the same person may well express different views about an issue in different situations. This also explains why slight changes in the way opinion questions and response choices are formulated in a survey produce different results.

There are recurring concerns in the writings about public opinion. First of all, it is suggested that the public at large lacks the competence to be active and involved in all the pertinent issues of the day. Although in simpler societies rule by public opinion might be a possibility, the modern world has become too large and too complicated. Second, attention is drawn to the lack of resources available to the public. The necessary information to form rational opinions is not adequately disseminated by the public communication system. Despite a lack of detailed information about ideologies, policies, and candidates, people nevertheless make sense of the political world, but they do so using information shortcuts and gut-reasoning.

A third enduring concern is the danger that a kind of mediocrity in opinion will prevail created and maintained by the pressure of the majority. The notion of conformity to majority opinion has been a persistent theme, both in social criticism and in social science. A fourth theme centers on the public's susceptibility to persuasion and to highly emotional and non-rational appeals, nourished by the growth of and developments within the mass communication system. Fifth, it is also suggested that, as a correlate of the domination of government and corporate elites, sections of the public are increasingly passive.

Normative concerns about the quality of public opinion have led to the development of "deliberative polling," designed to combine the efficiency and representativeness of conventional opinion polls with the informative and deliberative aspects of a town meeting. Respondents are brought together with policy experts, public officials, moderators, and one another to consider political issues in depth. With deliberative polling the aim is to find out what the public would think if it was fully informed and if it had time and opportunity to think and talk about the issue. There is a considerable difference between the opinion which people produce in an artificial situation such as a survey and the opinion they produce in a situation closer to the daily-life situations in which opinions are challenged and/or confirmed.

Analysts of public opinion continue to face the challenge of trying to understand large-scale social and political processes: the constitution of publics around shared problems, the negotiation of competing policy proposals, the emergence of issues, and the formation of coalitions among political elites, shadowed by broader coalitions among their supporters or detractors in the spectator public. In studying these processes the researcher is confronted by the need to understand individual phenomena: the attention given to particular issues, the determination of which issues are personally or socially relevant, the acquisition of information, the formation of opinions in people's minds, and the translation of those opinions into political action.

There has been a growing interest in the deliberative aspects of democratic politics. The theory of deliberative democracy, in which public opinion is interpreted within the rational model, assumes that egalitarian, reciprocal, reasonable, and open exchanges among citizens about public issues will lead to a number of individual and collective benefits. Mendelberg (2002) argues that existing research shows that while deliberative processes in and of themselves are no guarantee of a more participatory, communal, and rational democracy, there is enough evidence in support of these ideals to make further research worthwhile. Research focusing on the communicative processes within the model of public opinion as social control is still scarce (de Boer & Velthuijsen 2001).

SEE ALSO: Mass Media and Socialization; Media and the Public Sphere; Politics and Media; Propaganda; Ratings

REFERENCES AND SUGGESTED READINGS

Blumer, H. (1946) Collective Behavior. In: Lee, A. M. (Ed.), *New Outlines of the Principles of Sociology*. Barnes & Noble, New York, pp. 167–222.

Converse, P. E. (1964) The Nature of Belief Systems in Mass Publics. In: Apter, D. E. (Ed.), *Ideology and Discontent*. Free Press, New York, pp. 206–61.

De Boer, C. & Velthuijsen, A. S. (2001) Participation in Conversations about the News. *International Journal of Public Opinion Research* 13(2): 140–58.

Mendelberg, T. (2002) The Deliberative Citizen: Theory and Evidence. In: Delli Carpini, M. X., Huddy, L., & Shapiro, R. Y. (Eds.), *Political Decision-Making, Deliberation, and Participation*. Elsevier, Amsterdam, pp. 151–93.

Price, V. (1992) *Public Opinion*. Sage, Newbury Park, CA.

Scheufele, D. A. & Moy, P. (2000) Twenty-Five Years of the Spiral of Silence: A Conceptual Review and Empirical Outlook. *International Journal of Public Opinion Research* 12(1): 3–28.

public order crime

David Huffer

Complex, collective actions, people adjusting, cooperating, accommodating, and compromising in social intercourse, are the constituent elements of civil societies. Binding societies are social meanings and expectations of acceptable behavior, a social fabric. This tacit understanding, shared by residents and users of public spaces, reflects a pervasive sense of civility, mutual responsibility, and morality as well as desires for a pleasurable life and a safe environment. Public order crimes threaten, prevent, or otherwise interfere with these pursuits.

Laws maintaining public order focus on physical acts and their residual effects. Physical acts span a menagerie of petty crimes and inappropriate behavior. These include soliciting alms; aggressive panhandling; loitering; obstruction of streets and public spaces; vandalism; unlicensed or unsolicited vending, peddling, or services; public drinking; public intoxication; public urination and defecation; street prostitution; and illegal drug sales. Residual effects of these acts include the presence of graffiti; abandoned cars, homes, and buildings; sustained disrepair; unsupervised, rowdy teens; open prostitution and drug sales; and vacant, trash-filled lots. Though clearly among the least extreme of crimes, such collective victimization has consequences for both real and perceived quality of life that, left unchecked, can spiral communities into a sequence of decline.

Disorder and order maintenance are not new concepts. Disorder has plagued communities since their inception and, from their beginnings, policing agencies were charged with its prevention. This model was, by most accounts, effective through the 1950s when crime rates were consistently low. Rocketing crime rates in the 1960s spurred national concern, reshaped political thought, and diverted policing focus from its roots. Attention drifted as police instead began to favor making arrests, solving crimes, and gathering evidence to quell serious crime. This shift from an order maintenance into a crime-fighting model was essentially pandemic by the early 1970s when, in reflecting contemporary social and political emphases, policing agencies increasingly responded to escalating crime rates by gradually narrowing the scope of their work. Order maintenance gave way to the sole pursuit of fighting serious crime.

Research in the 1970s renewed interest in disorder. Seemingly inconsistent findings began emerging mid-decade both from analyses of the National Crime Victimization Surveys (NCVS) and from independent policing studies. Research indicated fear of victimization greatly exceeded what would be expected given local crime patterns. In grappling with this disjunction, theorists attempted to identify causes and sources of fear perceptions and began exploring its effects once it became pervasive. Aside from actual crime levels, they noted community characteristics such as disorder influenced resident fear of crime. Early work focusing exclusively on the psychological effects of disorder reasoned that higher than expected victimization fear was an experiential consequence of exposure to widely occurring disorder. Conceptual elaborations to this purely micro-level process were introduced beginning in the late 1970s that both increasingly recognized the significance of human agency and broadened the theoretical scope. Theorists incorporated a greater respect for cognition, conceptually freeing residents to perceive, reason, and judge disorder, and they introduced broader, contextual effects into a system linking disorder, fear, and neighborhood decline.

While early models held that fear of crime was simply an evaluative reaction to disorder, elaborations asserted instead that residents observed disorder, ascribed it meaning, and subsequently reacted to these ascriptions. The ascriptions rather than the observations shaped fear and, further, residents attributed concentrated, unregulated disorder to a community-wide inability to protect the social fabric, which thus engendered a general sense of uncertainty and left residents questioning whether order could be maintained, and, if not, how then crime could be controlled. Individual responses to this uncertainty theoretically ushered in gradual, practically inescapable community decline.

Wilson and Kelling (1982) likened this declining process to that unfolding given persistent, unkempt community physical features.

The metaphorical broken window signals to observers there may be little social investment in improvement, and for some, like delinquent groups and petty offenders, this provides opportunity. More windows are broken and if these too remain unattended, it further substantiates perceptions of disinvestment, and thus observers reason there is little regulating the area. It neither is the window alone, the building, nor the street; rather, observers ascribe meaning to the sign inferring that, as a whole, there is little community interest in mobilizing resources – particularly those responsible for public safety. This concern sparks dissatisfaction, selective migration, and inhibits effective informal social control.

Minor, disorderly behaviors needle at, potentially unraveling, the social fabric. Satisfaction sinks, solidarity collapses, and mutual responsibility vanishes while fear of victimization grows larger. This stimulates withdrawal among all but opportunists and those unable to flee, leaving informal social controls otherwise curtailing minor breaches of order virtually disabled. Able law abiders take flight and, over time, serious offenders, capitalizing on available opportunities, take their place. Further, area avoidance and compositional shifts negatively affect the local housing market and economy, increasing inequality and instability. Those able avoid commercial and residential areas perceived as unsafe. They move, market elsewhere. Businesses close, housing prices plummet, neighborhoods fall into ruin, and entire communities decline. This impairment is dynamic, developmental, and creates a context favorable for persistent, serious crimes.

SEE ALSO: Crime; Crime, Broken Windows Theory of; Property Crime; Social Control; Social Disorganization Theory; Violent Crime

REFERENCES AND SUGGESTED READINGS

Kelling, G. L. & Coles, C. M. (1996) *Fixing Broken Windows: Restoring Order and Reducing Crime in Our Communities.* Simon & Schuster, New York.

Reiss, A. J., Jr. (1986) Why Are Communities Important in Understanding Crime? In: Reiss, A. J., Jr. & Tonry, M. (Eds.), *Communities and Crime.* University of Chicago Press, Chicago, pp. 1–33.

Skogan, W. G. (1992) *Disorder and Decline: Crime and the Spiral of Decay in American Neighborhoods.* University of California Press, Berkeley.

Taylor, R. B. (1999) Incivilities Thesis: Theory, Measurement, and Policy. In: Langworthy, R. (Ed.), *Measuring What Matters: Proceedings from the Policing Research Institute Meetings.* National Institute of Justice, Washington, DC, pp. 65–88.

Wilson, J. Q. & Kelling, G. L. (1982) Broken Windows: The Police and Neighborhood Safety. *Atlantic Monthly* 211: 29–38.

public and private

Charles Turner

The analytical distinction between public and private life has proved to be a useful tool for charting long-term social change and in particular for understanding modern society. In classical Greece the equivalent distinction would be one between participation in the (public) life of the polis and the management of one's (private) household, within an ethical framework which saw the political life as higher and more self-sufficient (Aristotle) than the life devoted to meeting mere material needs. In this world, privacy implies privation, the lack of something required for a full human life. This ideal of the polis, of politics as the highest form of human activity, has hovered over modern social and political thought since Machiavelli. But it has appeared ever more ethereal with the emergence of modern industrial society. For if in feudal society political power is the source of wealth, mature industrial society (or what Tocqueville calls "democracy") makes possible the pursuit of wealth without recourse to politics, and the putting of self-interest before the public good. The modern state becomes either the minimum framework necessary for the pursuit of individual self-interest (liberalism) or a mechanism for the maximization of collective wealth (a possibility utilized by modern welfare states and by state socialism). In either case politics loses its status as the most self-sufficient activity and becomes a means with which something else can be achieved. The most sustained intellectual assault on this

development – in which, for instance, liberalism and Marxism are seen as two sides of the same coin – is found in the writings of Arendt, Oakeshott, and Wolin. Against this judgment stands the claim, popular with eighteenth-century political economy, that it is precisely the pursuit of private gain in commercial society which opens individuals to the variousness and nuance of human affairs and which indirectly fosters the moral sentiments consistent with public virtues (Pocock 1985).

If classicist political theory equates public/private with politics/economics and laments the triumph of privacy, sociology, social history, and philosophy introduce new distributions. For instance, for sociology, the release of the energies required for the pursuit of individual self-interest brings with it a more complex division of labor, the growth of new forms of refinement, and a greater variety of marks of social distinction. Privacy begins to be equated not with the household economy but with the family as a source of individual labor. This process of visible individualization is accompanied by a new organization of domestic space. The growth of the city, too, gives rise to new possibilities of distance, reserve, and inwardness (Simmel's blasé attitude), which fuse with already-existing ideas about the inwardness of the self borne by (especially) Protestant Christianity. Public/private is equated with external/internal to the self.

The tradition of philosophy which begins with Kant provides another sense of public and private. The fusion of eighteenth-century rationalism with German pietism led Kant to what is now called the "deontological" view of the self, in which individuals have the capacity to abstract from all of their determinate social and political relations. The fruit of such abstraction is not melancholy introspection or personal brooding, but the discovery of the individual's capacity for reason and judgment; at their most inward and private, individuals discover not their own uniqueness, but the moral law, a principle of duty which is the same for all. Individuals are also equipped with the capacity to make use of their unaided, autonomous reason in public. Indeed, the public use of reason is Kant's definition of enlightenment. "Public" here cannot be equated with politics in the classical sense, but exists as a republic of letters between the private (both economic and intimate!) sphere and that of government and administration. For Habermas, the story of the twentieth century is that of the loss of the public sphere's distinctiveness as a result of the inter-penetration of state and society under modern welfare regimes and political democracy. A series of partial publics emerges instead, pervaded by large organizations representing sectional inter-ests, overlain with a thin veneer of publicity in the form of "public opinion," to be mobilized for demagogic as well as democratic purposes.

The idea of a loss of the public-as-polis, and of the public-as-republic-of-letters, lies at the heart of theories of European modernity. Alongside them, a third theme emerges in the-ories of American modernity: the loss of civi-lity. Whether it be a culture of narcissism, the triumph of the therapeutic (Rieff 1966) or the fall of public man (Sennett 1977), American individualism is held to have developed to such a degree that individuals now view public ques-tions in private terms, see the world as a mirror for the self, and fail to display the requisite distance-from-self which makes possible civil behavior between strangers. New forms of col-lectivity can arise out of this imbalance, but they are forms of community based upon the private principle of resemblance-to-self rather than forms of sociality based upon the public principle of commonality of purpose.

Curiously enough, in the 1960s this plea for civility, self-distance, and a clear distinction between private and public matters was coun-terbalanced by the feminist slogan "the perso-nal is political." This has been interpreted in two ways. According to the first, the neglect of the operation of power mechanisms in the sphere of personal relations is a major lacuna in modern social and political thought, to be filled both by consciousness raising and by new forms of empirical research; according to the second, the very tradition at the heart of which is a concern for the fate of the polis, or the public sphere, or civility, is itself pervaded by a masculinist reason. Both have had far-reaching consequences for public and private life and for scholarship.

SEE ALSO: Aron, Raymond; Households; Politics; Public Realm; Public Sphere; Welfare Fraud

REFERENCES AND SUGGESTED READINGS

Arendt, H. (1958) *The Human Condition*. Free Press, New York.

Habermas, J. (1982 [1962]) *The Structural Transfor-mation of the Public Sphere*. Polity Press, Cam-bridge.

Oakeshott, M. (1975) *On Human Conduct*. Clarendon Press, Oxford.

Pocock, J. G. A. (1985) *Virtue, Commerce and His-tory*. Cambridge University Press, Cambridge.

Rieff, P. (1966) The Triumph of the Therapeutic. Chatto & Windus, London.

Sennett, R. (1977) *The Fall of Public Man*. Faber, London.

Wolin, S. (2004) *Politics and Vision*. Princeton Uni-versity Press, Princeton.

public realm

Lyn H. Lofland

While widely used in the contemporary dis-course of such diverse fields as philosophy, political theory, sociology, art, media studies, architecture and urban planning, and gender studies, as well as in everyday speech, the con-cept of public realm has no consensual defini-tion and definitions that are proffered are often both imprecise and enigmatic. What all the diverse usages do agree upon is that their refer-ent is some sort of non-private arena of social life and most judge that arena to be both criti-cally beneficial and unappreciated; what they disagree about is its exact character. To add to the confusion, the non-private arena may also be discussed under other names such as public sphere, public order, public domain, public world, and civic space.

Arendt's (1958) usage is at once among the most enigmatic, evocative, and, perhaps, influ-ential. She traces the term back to the Aristote-lian and Roman distinctions between the private world of the household and the public world of the *bios politikos* (for the Greeks) or the *polis* (for the Romans). And although the meanings attached to each realm shift somewhat through time, the dyadic distinction remains and is, for her, of considerable philosophic import.

The public realm is that arena where "everything that appears . . . can be seen and heard by everybody and has the widest possible publicity . . . [and] appearance – something that is being seen and heard by others as well as by ourselves – [is what] constitutes reality" (p. 50). The public realm is also the world common to all of us and is "distinguished from our privately owned place in it. This world, however, is not identical with the earth or with nature, . . . it is related, rather to the human artifact, the fabrication of human hands, as well as to affairs that go on among those who inhabit the man-made world together" (p. 52). In contrast, "To live an entirely private life means above all to be deprived of things essential to a truly human life: to be deprived of the reality that comes from being seen and heard by others" (p. 58). Interpreters seem to agree that what Arendt is talking about here, despite what her words may seem to imply, is not all publicly visible human social life outside of the household, but political activity – especially political speech – the goal of which is to exchange views about and to formulate shared purposes and to take action on them. Other areas of non-household social life like government, administration, and economic activity seemingly are excluded.

Habermas's (1964) discussion of what he calls the public sphere is somewhat similar and may rival Arendt's in its influence, and it too has an elusive quality. In his conceptualization, the public sphere is a "realm of our social life in which something approaching public opinion can be formed[, a]ccess is guaranteed to all citizens[, and a portion of it] comes into being in every conversation in which private individuals assemble to form a public body . . . Today newspapers and magazines, radio and television are the media of the public sphere" (p. 49). He also differentiated among the political public sphere and other arenas of discourse, such as the literary, his own interest being primarily in the former. Unlike Arendt, Habermas saw the political public sphere as not emerging until the eighteenth century, when the distinction between opinion and public opinion developed, but similar to Arendt he viewed this arena as centrally important, not just to a fully human life, but especially to democratic governance. Some readers of Habermas have equated the political public

sphere with government and with electoral politics, but his interpreters insist that this is a misreading, that the state and the public sphere are in opposition to one another, the latter being "the sphere of non-governmental opinion making" (Hohendahl 1964: 49). Because he insisted that the requisite discourse in the sphere be reasoned and critical, Habermas was not sanguine about its post-World War II character or future. He argued that it was being undermined by such forces as advanced industrial capitalism, the social welfare state, and a mass media which tended to translate public communication into public relations.

Movement toward a more limited, technical, and precise definition can be seen in the work of four sociologists: Richard Sennett, Claude Fischer, Albert Hunter, and Lyn Lofland, although three of the four (Fischer excepted) also carry on the larger tradition of attempting to remedy what they see as an unfortunate disattention. Sennett (1977) equates the "public domain" with "the world of strangers, the cosmopolitan city" and he contrasts it with the private arena of intimate relationships. Though still retaining the historic private–public dichotomy, the word "public" here shifts somewhat from the difficult-to-locate realm of political talk and action to the more ordinary and mundane intercourse between urban people who do not know one another personally. This public domain, Sennett argued, is tragically undervalued in the contemporary West, primarily as a result of the rise of privatism and its overvaluation of intimacy. And this is dangerous because "the notion of a civilized existence [is one] in which people are comfortable with a diversity of experience and indeed find nourishment in it . . . In this sense, the absorption in intimate affairs is the mark of an uncivilized society" (p. 340).

Fischer (1981) explored the longstanding assertion that urban life is necessarily alienating and is the locus for interpersonal estrangement. In doing so, he distinguished between the "public world" (or sphere) and the private world (or sphere) of city life, and like Sennett he defined the public world as the "world of strangers," a "world of people who are personally unfamiliar to one another" (p. 307). He concluded (using survey data) that in the public world, alienation and estrangement from others could be discerned, but that in the private world of city life composed of close associates and other familiar people such as neighbors, it could not.

Hunter (1985), pursuing his interest in the issue of social control, also grounded his definitions in everyday interactions, but made a break from the traditional divide of public and private to suggest the utility of understanding these everyday interactions in terms of the specific normative "orders" in which they are embedded. He identified three of these: the *private order* is "found in both informal and more formal primary groups where the values of sentiment, social support, and esteem are the essential resource"; the *parochial order* is "based on the local interpersonal networks and interlocking of local institutions that serve the diurnal and sustenance needs of the residential community"; and the *public order* is "located preeminently in the formal, bureaucratic agencies of the state" (pp. 233–4). And like Sennett, Hunter's concerns are also moral ones: "The private, the parochial and the public social orders cannot maintain social order throughout a society without a mutual interdependence ... A civil society, that provides both for safety *from* strangers and safety *for* strangers, requires an acknowledgment of the intrinsic limits [of each order] and a recognition of the need for better articulation among [them]" (p. 240).

Borrowing freely from prior work, especially that of Sennett and Hunter, but also extending and altering them, Lofland (1998) contrasted both the private realm (the world of the household and friend and kin networks) and the parochial realm (the world of neighborhood, workplace, or acquaintance networks) with the public realm (the world of strangers and "the street"). Specifically, she defined the *private realm* as "characterized by ties of intimacy among primary group members who are located within households and personal networks"; the *parochial realm* as "characterized by a sense of commonality among acquaintances and neighbors who are involved in interpersonal networks that are located within 'communities'"; and the *public realm* as "the non-private sectors of urban areas in which individuals in co-presence tend to be personally unknown or only categorically known to one another" (pp. 9–10). Despite the hint of geographical concreteness

in the last definition, Lofland conceived of the three realms as social psychological rather than territorial spaces. They come into existence when one or another of the three relational types reaches a proportion and density in some territorial space such that it dominates that space. And while each realm may be most "at home" in its associated territorial space, each may also exist in "alien" space (e.g., a wedding in a public park, an "open" house in a private residence, a neighborhood bar in a "downtown" location). Like Sennett, Lofland's special focus is on the public realm and for a similar reason: she argues that it is a realm of immense social value which offers, among other benefits, a rich environment for learning, a site for needed respites and refreshments, a locus of communication, an opportunity for the practice of politics, a stage for the enactment of social arrangmements and social conflict, and assistance in the creation of cosmopolitans (pp. 231–46).

These more extended discussions of "public realm" and related concepts probably represent only a fraction of contemporary usages. More frequently, the term is employed loosely, with little attempt at definition, although the author's meaning is usually implied by the context and bears some resemblance to one or another of the meanings developed in the longer treatments. In discussions of architecture and urban planning, for example, public realm seems primarily to mean legally public space – specifically, outdoor public space, as in parks, plazas, and promenades. Among those interested in the Internet, the public realm translates as cyberspace, where non-corporeal interactions blossom. For some artists, it is identified with sites of public art, and for some media scholars and/or defenders of the public ownership of media, it refers to government-sponsored enterprises like the BBC in Britain or the ABC in Australia. To some students of higher education, the public realm finds embodiment in the institution of the university, and in gender studies treatments it often refers to that social arena where laws, contracts, and other civic agreements are reached and which has traditionally been considered "off limits" to women.

SEE ALSO: Goffman, Erving; Interaction; Primary Groups; Public Sphere; Secondary Groups; Simmel, Georg; Spatial Relationships

REFERENCES AND SUGGESTED
READINGS

Anderson, E. (1990) *Street Wise: Race, Class and Change in an Urban Community*. University of Chicago Press, Chicago.

Arendt, H. (1958) *The Human Condition*. University of Chicago Press, Chicago.

Fischer, C. S. (1981) The Public and Private Worlds of City Life. *American Sociological Review* 46: 303–16.

Goffman, E. (1963) *Behavior in Public Places*. Free Press, New York.

Habermas, J. (1974) The Public Sphere: An Encyclopedia Article. *New German Critique* 3: 49–55.

Hohendahl, P. (1964) Jürgen Habermas: "The Public Sphere." *New German Critique* 3: 45–8.

Hunter, A. (1985) Private, Parochial and Public Social Orders: The Problem of Crime and Incivility in Urban Communities. In: Suttles, G. D. & Zald, M. N. (Eds.), *The Challenge of Social Control*. Ablex, Norwood, NJ, pp. 230–42.

Lofland, L. H. (1998) *The Public Realm: Exploring the City's Quintessential Social Territory*. Aldine de Gruyter, New York.

Milligan, M. (1998) Interactional Past and Potential: The Social Construction of Place Attachment. *Symbolic Interaction* 21: 1–33.

Morrill, C., Snow, D., & White, C. (2005) *Together Alone: Personal Relationships in Public Places*. University of California Press, Berkeley.

Sennett, R. (1977) *The Fall of Public Man*. Knopf, New York.

public sphere

Gerard Delanty

The concept of the public sphere has become a key term in sociology since it was introduced by Jürgen Habermas as a sociologically pertinent concept. The public sphere refers to the space that exists in modern societies between the state and society. It concerns a domain that is generally related to civil society, but goes beyond it to refer to the wider category of the public. The public sphere comes into existence with the formation of civil society and the forms of associational politics to which it led. But it refers essentially to the communicative content of political modernity. Although the English term public sphere suggests a spatial notion of the public, the German term *Öffenlichkeit* conveys a stronger notion of a realm of communication, suggesting a discursive condition of "publicness."

The public sphere can be seen as a modern approach to the older question of "public man" or the public realm that Hannah Arendt believed came into existence with the Athenian polis and political relations based on citizenship. The turn to the public was originally a development within political theory, as reflected in the writing of de Tocqueville and Arendt. Although Arendt saw a decline in the public realm in modernity, de Tocqueville believed it was one of the key features of modernity. Habermas's major work *The Structural Transformation of the Public Sphere*, originally published in German in 1962, has generally provided the main point of reference for recent debates on the public sphere (Habermas 1989). The work can be seen as a combination of de Tocquevillian and the Arendtian stance.

According to Habermas, modern society from the seventeenth century to the early nineteenth century saw the emergence of a social domain distinct from court society, on the one side, and the absolute state, on the other. This was the space of the public, which was formed in new spaces such as the coffee house, public libraries, a free press, and wherever public debate took place outside formal institutions. One of its main features was public opinion. Initially, the public sphere was defined by opposition to the court society, but it also increasingly became defined by opposition to the private domain of domestic life. In Habermas's early theory of the public sphere, it was characteristically associated with the political and cultural world of the European Enlightenment. So the structural transformation occurred when the culture of the Enlightenment declined and the public sphere was absorbed by capitalism. The decisive event in this was the commercialization of the press, which was originally an organ of public debate, but with the rise of commercial newspapers that came with the consolidation of bourgeois society and intrusion of the market into civil society the public sphere went into decline. In an approach that reflected Arendt's pessimistic view of modernity and one that was influenced by the cultural critique of modernity by the Frankfurt

School, Habermas saw only the decline of the public sphere with modernity. The rise of modern mass society in the twentieth century with the manufacture and control of public opinion by political parties completed the structural transformation of the public sphere that had begun in the previous century.

By the time of the translation of Habermas's book into English in 1989 he had moved on to a new theory of the public sphere which no longer concentrated on the decline of the Enlightenment model. However, the English translation opened up a huge debate on the public sphere (Calhoun 1992). The point of departure for many of these new approaches was a critique of Habermas's earlier model. The new theory of the public sphere that emerged in the 1980s can be summed up under four points.

The first was a rejection of the idealization of the historical model adopted by Habermas. Many critics argued that there was not a single historical model, but several, and the notion of a pure domain of public space opposing power was a romanticization of historical reality. Indeed, much of what Habermas called the public sphere occurred within the broader category of the state and cannot so easily be accounted for in terms of a domain of free communication.

Second, any account of the public sphere must consider the existence of alternative or counter-public spheres. In this regard, what many critics drew attention to were alternatives to the bourgeois public sphere. Negt and Kluge (1993) wrote about the "proletarian public sphere," which did not figure in Habermas's model. In addition to this there is the feminist charge that the early conceptualization of the public sphere assumes a too-strict separation of the public and the private, whereby the latter is reduced to a non-political condition (Landes 1988).

Third, more recent debates on the public sphere concern the existence of the public sphere in non-western societies (Hoexter et al. 2002). In contrast to the Eurocentric bias of Habermas's early theory, the public sphere was not a condition peculiar to eighteenth-century Europe and North America and does not consequently require an "Enlightenment."

Fourth, a question that has been at the forefront of much of the recent debate on the public sphere is whether there is a cosmopolitan public sphere (Kögler 2005). Where Habermas largely assumed the existence of discrete national public spheres, the idea of a global or cosmopolitan public sphere has contemporary relevance as a result of globalization. One important application of this is in the idea of a European public sphere (Eriksen 2005).

In sum, the notion of the public sphere is today generally seen as a plural condition: there is not one single or ideal public sphere, but many. The public sphere is the space of debates and the ongoing contestation of power.

SEE ALSO: Modernity; Privatization; Public and Private; Public Realm

REFERENCES AND SUGGESTED READINGS

Calhoun, C. (Ed.) (1992) *Habermas and the Public Sphere*. Blackwell, Oxford.
Eder, K. (2005) Making Sense of the Public Sphere. In: Delanty, G. (Ed.), *Handbook of Contemporary European Social Theory*. Routledge, London.
Eriksen, E. O. (2005) An Emerging European Public Sphere. *European Journal of Social Theory* 8(3): 341–63.
Habermas, J. (1989) *The Structural Transformation of the Public Sphere*. Polity Press, Cambridge.
Hoexter, M. S., Eisenstadt, N., & Levtzion, N. (Eds.) (2002) *The Public Sphere in Muslim Societies*. State University of New York Press, New York.
Kögler, H.-H. (2005) Constructing a Cosmopolitan Public Sphere. *European Journal of Social Theory* 8 (3): 207–20.
Landes, J. B. (1988) *Women and the Public Sphere in the Age of the French Revolution*. Cornell University Press, Ithaca, NY.
Negt, O. & Kluge, O. (1993) *Public Sphere and Experience*. University of Minnesota Press, Minneapolis.

purdah

Hasmita Ramji

Purdah literally translated from its Persian origins means veil or curtain. It is a concept that is used as a synonym for social practices that isolate or separate different groups in society. Although purdah can refer to many different social practices of isolation, the term is most immediately associated with a practice of gender segregation in mostly although not exclusively Muslim societies.

There are various forms and degrees of purdah that may be observed in Islamic societies. Purdah, for instance, can refer to the use of high walls, curtains, and screens erected within the home as well as public places to keep women separate from men or strangers. However, the most widespread practice of purdah refers to the seclusion of women from public observation by wearing concealing clothing. This form of purdah is also seen in other religions such as Christianity and Judaism – it is not unknown for certain Christian and Jewish denominations to require women to be "covered" whilst worshipping (if only by a hat or similar symbolic object). The practice in Islam is traced to both the Qur'an and the Hadith. The usual garment worn to accomplish this form of purdah in Islamic societies is termed a *chador* (all-enveloping black mantle), which may or may not include a veil to conceal the face, a *yashmak* (De Souza 2004).

The limits imposed by this practice vary according to different countries. Purdah, for example, was rigorously observed under regimes such as that of the Taliban in Afghanistan, where women had to observe complete purdah at any time they were in public. Only their husbands, fathers, siblings, children, and other women were allowed to see them out of purdah. In other societies, purdah is often only practiced during certain times of religious significance.

The practice of purdah has become increasingly controversial in recent times. Feminists, for instance, have perceived the practice of purdah to be an extension of men's control over women in patriarchal society (El Guindi 1999). Purdah suffocates the rights of women and is used as an instrument that enables men to dominate the family structure, resulting in a gendered division of labor that leaves women extremely dependent upon them.

Others, mostly believers in Islam, see purdah as a practice that liberates women, by enabling them to be judged not by their physical beauty but by their intellect, faith, and personality (Ahmed 1992). By covering themselves, women are prevented from being viewed as sex objects that can be dominated, enabling them to enjoy equal rights with men.

Purdah, however controversial, still remains an integral part of everyday life for many people as it is practiced to greater and lesser degrees in most contemporary Islamic cultures.

SEE ALSO: Feminism; Feminism, First, Second, and Third Waves; Fundamentalism; Gender Oppression; Islam; Patriarchy; Racialized Gender; Religion; Women, Religion and

REFERENCES AND SUGGESTED READINGS

Ahmed, L. (1992) *Women and Gender in Islam: Historical Roots of a Modern Discourse*. Yale University Press, New Haven.

De Souza, E. (Ed.) (2004) *Purdah: An Anthology*. Oxford University Press, Oxford.

El Guindi, F. (1999) *Veil: Modesty, Privacy, and Resistance*. Berg, Oxford.